HANDBOOK OF CLINICAL DIETETICS, SECOND EDITION

SECOND
EDITION

HANDBOOK OF CLINICAL DIETETICS

THE AMERICAN DIETETIC ASSOCIATION

YALE
UNIVERSITY
PRESS
NEW HAVEN
& LONDON

THE AMERICAN
DIETETIC
ASSOCIATION

Published with assistance from the foundation established in memory of Calvin Chapin of the Class of 1788, Yale College.

Designed by Nancy Ovedovitz and set in Times Roman type with Helvetica Condensed by Keystone Typesetting, Inc., Orwigsburg, Pennsylvania. Printed in the United States of America by Arcata Graphics Book Group, West Hanover, Massachusetts.

A catalogue record for this book is available from the British Library.

Library of Congress Cataloging-in-Publication Data

Handbook of clinical dietetics / American Dietetic Association — 2nd ed.
    p. cm.
  Includes bibliographical references and index.
  ISBN 0-300-05218-9 (alk. paper)
  1. Diet therapy.   I. American Dietetic Association. [DNLM: 1. Diet Therapy. 2. Dietetics.   WB 400 H236]
RM216.H267   1992
615.8′54—dc20
DNLM/DLC
for Library of Congress   91-35610

The paper in this book meets the guidelines for permanence and durability of the Committee on Production Guidelines for Book Longevity of the Council on Library Resources.

10   9   8   7   6   5   4   3   2   1

CONTENTS

PREFACE

The second edition of the *American Dietetic Association's Handbook of Clinical Dietetics* is an update of the first edition, which was developed in response to the need for a manual as expressed in a resolution to the House of Delegates of the American Dietetic Association in 1971. The resolution stated in part, "Whereas, there is a great national and regional diversity in defining dietetic diet content and terminology; be it therefore resolved, that the American Dietetic Association develop definitions of dietetic diet contents and terminology and accompanying scientific documentation" (1).

A committee of the Diet Therapy Section was appointed with Doris Johnson, Ph.D., R.D., as chairman of the project. Juliette Signore, M.A., R.D., was the principal researcher and writer for both editions. The material has been reviewed by a great number of people with expertise in particular areas. We are grateful to all the individuals who have contributed to the book.

The handbook deals mainly with therapeutic nutrition and nutritional interventions in disease states. It is intended to guide the current practice of nutritional therapy. It is also intended to foster some degree of uniformity in the composition of diets by providing a comprehensively researched basis for the definitions, purposes, effects, physiology, indications, possible adverse reactions, contraindications, nutritional assessments, and quality assurance priorities as well as strategies for implementation and education.

The reader should be aware that several areas are beyond the scope of this text. Specifically, the book is not intended to provide comprehensive information on normal nutrition or on nutrition as it relates to various stages of the life cycle. Furthermore, although some basic educational tools are included in many of the diets, the book is not intended to provide comprehensive information on the psychology of nutritional counseling or dietary compliance.

REFERENCES

1. Annual Report and Proceedings, 1971. Chicago: American Dietetic Association, 1971.

ACKNOWLEDGMENTS

The American Dietetic Association wishes to thank the following persons for their contributions in authorship, editing, and review of the *Handbook of Clinical Dietetics,* Second Edition.

Principal Researcher and Writer
Juliette Signore, M.S., R.D.
West Haven, Connecticut

Contributing Authors
Christine A. Beebe, M.S., R.D., C.D.E.
Director, Diabetes Program
St. James Hospital and Health Centers
Chicago Heights, Illinois

Sheila M. Campbell, M.S., R.D.
Clinical Research Associate, Medical Department
Ross Laboratories
Columbus, Ohio

Joanne Faust Friedman, M.A., R.D.
PKU Nutritionist, Children's Hospital of New Jersey,
and Assistant Professor, University of Medicine and Dentistry
School of Health Related Professions
Newark, New Jersey

Editorial Coordinator
Gill Robertson, M.S., R.D.
Acquisitions Editor
The American Dietetic Association
Chicago, Illinois

Editorial and Technical Assistance
Betsy Hornick, M.S., R.D.
Acquisitions Editor
The American Dietetic Association
Chicago, Illinois

Review Coordinator
Margaret D. Simko, Ph.D., R.D.
Clinical Professor
Department of Family Medicine
University of Medicine and Dentistry of New Jersey
Robert Wood Johnson Medical School
New Brunswick, New Jersey

Reviewers
Elizabeth D. Munves, Ph.D., R.D.
Clinical Professor, Department of Medicine
University of Medicine and Dentistry of New Jersey, New Jersey Medical School
Newark, New Jersey

Susan Bradford, M.S., R.D., C.N.S.D.
Assistant Director, Clinical Nutrition
Long Island College Hospital
Brooklyn, New York

Sharron Dalton, Ph.D., R.D.
Department of Nutrition, Food, and Hotel Management
New York University
New York, New York

Lynn D. Dugan, M.S., R.D.
Chicago Center for Clinical Research
Rush-Presbyterian-St. Luke's Medical Center
Chicago, Illinois

Johanna Dwyer, D.Sc., R.D.
Professor of Medicine, Tufts Medical School
Director, Frances Stern Nutrition Center
New England Medical Center Hospitals
Boston, Massachusetts

Joanne Faust Friedman, M.A., R.D.
PKU Nutritionist, Children's Hospital of New Jersey,
and Assistant Professor, University of Medicine and Dentistry
School of Health Related Professions
Newark, New Jersey

Cecilia P. Fileti, R.D.
President
C. P. Fileti Associates, Inc.
Ann Arbor, Michigan

Teri Gargano-Barabash, M.B.A., L.D.
Coordinator, Policy Administration
The American Dietetic Association
Chicago, Illinois

Judith A. Gilbride, Ph.D., R.D.
Department of Nutrition, Food, and
    Hotel Management
New York University
New York, New York

Kathy Gumbel, M.S., R.D.
Rush-Presbyterian-St. Luke's Medical
    Center
Chicago, Illinois

Mindy G. Hermann, M.B.A., R.D.
The Hermann Group, Inc.
Mt Kisco, New York

Joanne Kouba, R.D., M.S., L.D.
Holy Cross Hospital
Silver Spring, Maryland

Elisabeth Luder, Ph.D., R.D.
Assistant Professor of Pediatrics
Mount Sinai School of Medicine
New York, New York

Lucinda Katherine Lysen, R.D., L.D.,
    R.N., B.S.N.
Center for Nutritional Research—South
Port St. Lucie, Florida

Julie O'Sullivan Maillet, Ph.D., R.D.
University of Medicine and Dentistry of
    New Jersey
Dietetic Internship Program
Newark, New Jersey

Ellen Metzger, M.S., R.D.
Clinical Dietitian
Northwestern Memorial Hospital
Chicago, Illinois

Kimberlee Michals, Ph.D., R.D.
Associate Professor and Senior Scientist
Research Institute, Miami Children's
    Hospital
Miami, Florida

Kathleen Mrock, R.D.
Co-op Medical/Nutrition Systems
Burr Ridge, Illinois

Charles Mueller, M.S., R.D.
New York University
New York, New York

Tony M. Pipkin, M.S., R.D., L.D.
VA Medical Center
Little Rock, Arkansas

Meenakshi Rammohan, M.S., R.D.
Northwestern Memorial Hospital
Chicago, Illinois

Daphne A. Roe, M.D., F.R.C.P.
Division of Nutritional Sciences
Cornell University
Ithaca, New York

Joanne L. Slavin, Ph.D., R.D.
Department of Food Science and Nutri-
    tion
University of Minnesota
St. Paul, Minnesota

Mary Sullivan, R.D., M.P.H.
Nutrition Support Specialist
University of Chicago Medical Center
Chicago, Illinois

Riva Touger-Decker, M.S., R.D.
Bronx VA Medical Center
Dietetic Internship
Bronx, New York

Rita T. Vermeulen, R.D., M.Ed.
Community Hospital of Roanoke Valley
Roanoke, Virginia

Judith Wylie-Rosett, Ed.D., R.D.
Associate Professor of Epidemiology
    and Social Medicine
Albert Einstein College of Medicine
Bronx, New York

Steven Yannicelli, M.M.Sc., R.D.
Metabolic Nutritionist, Inherited Meta-
    bolic Diseases Clinic
The Children's Hospital in affiliation
    with the University of Colorado
    Health Sciences Center
Denver, Colorado

Mary K. Young, M.S., R.D.
Nutrition Specialist
University of Chicago Hospitals
Chicago, Illinois

HANDBOOK OF CLINICAL DIETETICS, SECOND EDITION

INTRODUCTION

PURPOSE AND SCOPE OF THE HANDBOOK

As the charge to the committee to develop a handbook of dietetic diet content and terminology was carried out, the scope of the project was broadened in order to establish as precise terminology as possible, based on sound, well-documented principles that govern the modification of each diet being defined. It has been stated that "when the rationale for a diet is not firmly established, the terminology is likely to be less exact" (1). Thus the second edition of the handbook has evolved to provide not only definitions for each diet and documentation for the formulation of the diet prescriptions, as in the first edition, but also an expansion of the original format.

The new format includes brief notes on key issues in quality assurance for each diet prescription as well as data on the nutritional assessment of individuals for whom the diet may be indicated. Specific priorities for nutritional assessment include clinical determinations, biochemical determinations, and potential drug interactions. The material is intended to serve as a reference for prescribing and implementing appropriate diets for a projected audience of dietitians, dietetic technicians, nutritionists, physicians, physician's assistants, nurse practitioners, and nurses. Sample menus for each diet have been evaluated and compared with the 1989 Recommended Dietary Allowances (2) for a male aged 25 to 50 (unless otherwise specified), using a computerized nutrient analysis program (3).

FORMAT OF THE HANDBOOK

As in the first edition, this edition of the handbook is based on the concept of the therapeutic diet as a modification of the normal diet, in which altered nutritional components should be prescribed in the same manner that governs the prescription of any other mode of therapy. The book has a basic format that is utilized in each section to describe in detail the rationale for the diet. In sections in which a diet prescription is not provided in detail, where validity of the diet is questioned, or where the format is inappropriate to the topic, the format is not followed. Therefore, the complete format is not used in Chapters 1, 10, 12, 18, 30, 31, 34, and 35 and in parts of Chapter 15. In all other sections the following basic topics are included.

DEFINITION(S)

Standardized nomenclature used in describing qualitative and quantitative aspects of the diet. Definition of the diet itself, as well as definitions of certain terms related to the diet.

PURPOSE OF THE DIET

The aims and specific goals of the diet.

EFFECTS OF THE DIET

The nature and extent of clinical, biochemical, physiological, nutritional, and psychological effects of the diet.

PHYSIOLOGY, FOODS, AND NUTRIENTS

Related physiology and disease etiology, as applicable. Nutritional implications of the diet in terms of food sources, foods

emphasized or de-emphasized, and nutritional adequacy.

INDICATIONS FOR USE

Clinical applications of the diet, either in the area of preventive nutrition or in the treatment of a preexisting disorder. Diagnostic criteria helpful in prescription of the appropriate diet, if known. Duration and scope of the diet where appropriate.

POSSIBLE ADVERSE REACTIONS

Undesirable side effects that may result from the use of the diet and suggested mechanisms for minimizing these effects. Severe nutritional deficits, excesses, or imbalances caused by the diet.

CONTRAINDICATIONS

Specific instances of accompanying conditions in which the consequences of possible adverse reactions would outweigh the beneficial effects of the diet.

CLINICAL ASSESSMENT

Specific clinical or physical parameters that are applicable to the condition or diet prescription and should be included in nutritional assessment.

BIOCHEMICAL ASSESSMENT

Biochemical parameters germane to the diet prescription or disorder that have implications for assessment of nutritional status.

ASSESSMENT OF POTENTIAL DRUG INTERACTIONS

Nutritional effects of drugs commonly used in treatment of the disorder and potential effects of the diet prescription on drug therapies.

IMPLEMENTATION AND EDUCATION

Techniques of administration or introduction of the diet. Educational priorities or strategies and compliance issues.

PRIORITIES FOR QUALITY ASSURANCE

Specific areas where quality assurance problems may occur or suggestions for the development of a quality assurance monitor and its implementation.

MENU PLANNING

Food lists and meal plans as appropriate. Example of a one-day menu that meets the 1989 Recommended Dietary Allowances (2). Nutrient analysis of menus using Food Analyst Plus is provided (3).

REFERENCES

Sources of statements on the basis for the diet or lack of such basis from the medical literature.

LIMITATIONS OF THE HANDBOOK

A sound scientific basis for diet therapy principles cannot be documented where well-controlled, well-designed clinical trials are absent or where controversy exists over the efficacy of a particular form of nutritional management. Library research for the book often uncovered more questions that need to be addressed in clinical trials than it supplied answers.

Another problem has been the increased media coverage of medical reports in recent years. Journalistic interpretation of reports has at times presented inaccurate data. A case in point was the media blitz over an article indicating that oat bran had no effect on blood cholesterol. Television reporters neglected to tell the public that the study design did not lend itself to answering the question, Does oat bran lower serum cholesterol levels in individuals with hypercholesterolemia? The study was undertaken in a

group of dietitians, none of whom had elevated levels of serum cholesterol (4).

Limitations in currently available tables of food composition continued to be a handicap in the development of the second edition of the *Handbook,* as they were in the first edition. For example, in the first edition a lack of data on the dietary fiber content of foods presented a problem. Ten years later, we are still lacking comprehensive tables that outline the specific amounts of each of the components of dietary fiber in specific foods, particularly the amounts of soluble and insoluble fiber.

As with the first edition, the second edition is intended to stimulate interest, discussion, and research to clarify gaps in clinical diet therapy. We hope it will focus attention on the facts that subjective clinical impressions cannot be used as the basis for the formulation of therapeutic diet prescriptions and that careful consideration of any possible adverse consequences from alterations in the nutritional components of the normal diet should be a prerequisite to the prescription of any modified diet.

TERMS USED TO DESCRIBE DIETS

Diets should be prescribed, whenever possible, in qualitative and quantitative terms that leave no room for misinterpretation. When a limitation must be set on the amount of any particular nutrient, the diet contents should be defined in terms of the specific amount to be provided, e.g., 40 g protein and 1 g sodium. Additional terminology may also be used to define further the relationship of a specific diet prescription to the normal diet.

Modified Diet   A diet based on the normal diet but designed to meet the requirements of a given situation. It may be modified in individual nutrients, caloric value, consistency, flavor, techniques of service or preparation, content of specific foods, or a combination of these factors.

Levels of specific nutrients provided by any modified diet may be described as being any of the following:

Increased   Providing more of any nutrient than is usually present in the normal diet.

Decreased   Providing less of any nutrient than is usually present in the normal diet.

Restricted   Limiting the amount and/or type of one or more nutrients provided to a prescribed level.

High   Providing an amount of a specific nutrient that is substantially increased above the amount present in the normal diet.

Low   Providing an amount of a specific nutrient that is substantially decreased below the amount present in the normal diet.

Controlled   Implying careful regulation or adjustment of levels of one or more nutrients from day to day as needed according to biochemical changes; referring to a diet in which both the amount and type of one or more nutrients are regulated.

Free   Eliminating, as far as possible, all sources of a particular nutrient, food, or food component from the diet.

REFERENCES

1. Robinson, C. H.: Updating clinical dietetics terminology. J Am Diet Assoc 62:645, 1973.
2. Food and Nutrition Board, National Research Council: Recommended Dietary Allowances. 10th ed. Washington, D.C.: National Academy Press, 1989.
3. Hopkins Technology: Food Analyst Plus. 421 Hazel Lane, Hopkins, MN 55343-7117, March 1990.
4. Swain, J. F., Rouse, I. L., et al.: Comparison of the effects of oat bran and low-fiber wheat on serum lipoprotein levels and blood pressure. N Engl J Med 322:147, 1990.

PART I
NORMAL DIET

1.

NUTRITIONAL ASSESSMENT

DEFINITIONS

1. NUTRITIONAL ASSESSMENT

Nutritional assessment is a process in which the status of nutritional health of an individual is evaluated, specific nutrition needs are estimated, and plans for nutrition intervention are determined. It is a systematic method of drawing together and appraising nutritionally related data that permits early intervention in both the treatment of established malnutrition and the prevention of malnutrition in individuals at high risk. A thorough assessment of nutritional status includes examination of clinical, anthropometric, biochemical, and dietary information.

2. NUTRITION SCREENING

Nutritional assessment begins with screening that involves comparison of individual data with predetermined risk levels. This systematic method of collecting data allows for the identification of individuals with current or potential nutrition problems that might affect the incidence of complications or disease outcome.

3. NUTRITION INTERVENTION

After individuals identified by screening are assessed, a nutrition care plan is developed. This plan may include evaluation of diet practices, nutrition counseling, calculation of nutritional requirements, and recommendations for meeting those requirements. It concludes with evaluation and documentation of the intervention, and follow-up plans as needed.

4. NUTRITION SUPPORT

The term *nutrition support* is most often used in reference to enteral (tube feeding) or parenteral nutrition, although it can be used in a more general sense to describe any intervention that includes supplementation with oral supplements or specially formulated food products.

5. MALNUTRITION

Malnutrition is poor nutritional status resulting primarily from dietary intakes either above or below the required range. Secondary malnutrition may be caused by increased or decreased needs that are due to an underlying disease. Although both undernutrition and overnutrition are forms of malnutrition, the term is most often used to depict undernutrition, which is also referred to as protein-energy malnutrition.

6. PROTEIN-ENERGY MALNUTRITION (PEM)

Protein-energy malnutrition (PEM) results from an acute or chronic protein deficiency associated with severe underconsumption of energy-producing foods. PEM can be primary when it results from the inadequate intake of nutrients or secondary when it results from a disease state that impairs food ingestion, interferes with nutrient absorption or utilization, or increases nutritional requirements.

7. KWASHIORKOR

The clinical syndrome called kwashiorkor is a form of PEM resulting mainly from acute caloric and protein deficiency. Protein is utilized as an energy source so that visceral proteins are decreased, resulting in edema and a swollen appearance. Kwashiorkor is common in individuals with a combination of catabolic stress and low protein intake.

8. MARASMUS

Also a form of PEM, marasmus is characterized by a progressive loss of fat and muscle tissue due to a chronic deficiency of calories or energy. As a result, the individual appears extremely thin and is weak and listless. Visceral proteins are maintained at the expense of somatic protein, and resistance to infection is often impaired.

9. MARASMIC KWASHIORKOR

Marasmic kwashiorkor is a life-threatening condition that results from a combination of chronic energy deficiency and severe protein deficits, such that visceral proteins can no longer be maintained. The main characteristics are edema, muscle wasting, and decreased subcutaneous fat stores.

PURPOSE

Nutritional assessment is a prerequisite to the initiation of nutrition support. It provides an objective data base upon which to make cost-effective nutrition intervention judgments. Goals of nutrition assessment include the following:

- Identifying the type and severity of any preexisting or potential malnutrition
- Estimating the nutrition needs of the patient

- Correcting nutritional imbalances
- Minimizing complications of mal-nutrition
- Promoting normal growth and de-velopment in children and adolescents

The ultimate goal of nutritional as-sessment is to provide early intervention for high-risk patients. This process cannot be implemented, however, nor can the efficacy of nutrition services be evaluated, unless nutrition screening is completed first (1). Nutrition screening accomplishes 2 essential objectives: identification of patient acuity level, and prioritization of patients into risk catego-ries or levels. This information is then used to determine which patients will re-quire a more comprehensive assessment of nutritional status.

In the interest of cost control, the sig-nificance of malnutrition, the cost-bene-fit ratio of nutrition support, and the value of the nutritional assessment must be documented (2). Outcomes of nutri-tion screening and assessment may in-clude reduction of nutrition-related com-plications and morbidity, and decreased length of hospital stay, which results in decreased costs (3–6). Cost-benefit anal-ysis requires that all benefits and costs be determined and converted into monetary terms in order to be compared. In the clinical setting, demonstrating cost-effectiveness is often more realistic. Cost-effectiveness analysis continues to express costs as dollars, but bene-fits are expressed as measurable out-comes such as biochemical values, an-thropometric measurements, or dietary changes. By recording baseline (screen-ing) and follow-up (after nutrition in-tervention) values, the effectiveness of nutrition services can be demonstrated (7, 8).

Nutritional assessment and screening systems are not limited to individuals and may encompass selected populations and population subgroups in the form of nutrition survey or surveillance methods.

FIG. 1.1. MAXIMIZING THE TIME FOR PATIENT NUTRITIONAL CARE PLANNING.

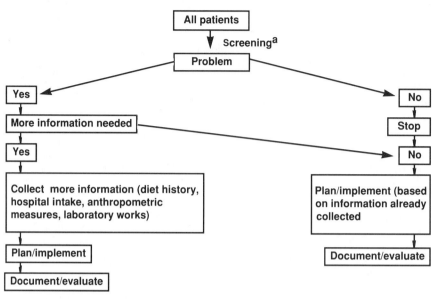

Source: Adapted from Hopkins, C. (11).
aSee table 1.1.

Data from survey methods can be used to define the extent of existing nutrition problems in order to allocate resources and formulate policies. Surveillance methods are useful in formulating and initiating intervention measures at the population or subgroup level. Various sources are available for assessing and interpreting nutrition data from a popula-tion or subgroup (9, 10). The scope of this handbook limits further discussion of assessment for populations to allow a more comprehensive review of nutri-tional assessment for the individual.

PROGRAM DEVELOPMENT

One approach to the development of a nutritional assessment program begins with the formulation of an algorithm that enables the dietitian to decide which pa-tients need additional care and the depth of the required care. It involves a screen-ing procedure for identifying nutrition problems as well as a methodical way of allocating time and resources to individ-uals at greatest nutritional risk. A sample algorithm is given in figure 1.1.

To identify individuals who are at nu-tritional risk, screening criteria should be developed that are consistent with the re-sources of the dietitian and clinically rel-evant to the population being assessed. Medical and dietetic records should be reviewed for specific problems, and the initial patient interview should be struc-tured in order to obtain the required in-formation (11, 12).

The design of nutrition screening and assessment tools should be evaluated for validity, precision, accuracy, sensitivity, and specificity prior to implementation (8). Effective utilization of equipment and personnel is also important.

1. SCREENING TOOLS

Nutrition screening functions to differen-tiate patients who require a comprehen-sive assessment from those who do not. An effective screening tool should be

- Inexpensive
- Easily administered with minimal nu-tritional expertise
- Site- and population-specific
- Designed to incorporate only routine tests and data done on admission

TABLE 1.1. INITIAL SCREENING OF PATIENTS FOR NUTRITIONAL PROBLEMS

Look for the following in medical record or nursing Kardex:
- Needs for patient education
- Patients on modified diets causing deficiencies in recommended allowances for more than 3 days (i.e., clear liquid diet) without nutrient supplementation or with inappropriate nutrient supplementation
- IV or NPO for more than 3 days without supplementation
- Low intakes of formula or tube feedings
- Weight 20% above ideal body weight or 10% below (taking into account any edema)
- Children—inconsistent growth or weight for stature above or below normal limits
- Pregnancy—weight gain deviating from normal pattern
- Conditions causing increased needs or decreased intake of nutrient—cancer, malabsorption, diarrhea, hyperthyroidism, excessive inflammation, postoperative states, hemorrhage, wounds, burns
- Chronic use of any drugs that affect nutritional status
- Alterations in chewing, swallowing, appetite, taste, smell
- Fever consistently above 37° C for more than 2 days
- Hematocrit less than 43% (males), 37% (females); hemoglobin less than 14 g/dL (males), 12 g/dL (females), with mean cell volume less than 82 cµ or greater than 100 cµ
- Absolute decrease in lymphocyte count (below 1,500 cells/mm³)
- Elevated or decreased cholesterol (above 250 mg/dL or below 130 mg/dL)
- Serum albumin less than 3 g/dL (in patients without nephrosis, hepatic insufficiency, generalized dermatitis, overhydration)

Source: Hopkins, C. (11).

Preliminary screening criteria such as those in table 1.1 will vary from institution to institution. Among the biochemical screening tests routinely performed in most hospitals are a complete blood count and SMA-12. The latter includes nutrition-related laboratory tests such as levels of cholesterol, total protein, albumin, alkaline phosphatase, blood urea nitrogen, creatinine, serum sodium, serum potassium, and serum chloride (11–15). Serum albumin and other selected biochemical data should be recorded as part of the nutrition screening process. Baseline screening data should also include data such as age, sex, height, weight, usual weight, primary diagnosis, diet order, usual diet, allergies or intolerances, and all medications.

Developing a screening tool that can be administered by a dietetic technician and interpreted by a dietitian is a cost-effective and efficient method for prioritizing and identifying patients at risk

(16, 17). The tool may provide only the objective data outlined above or may also include assignment of a risk category and plans for intervention. A more comprehensive screening tool may be used as an initial assessment note. Risk categories can be determined by comparing screening data with established criteria such as those in table 1.2 or by the use of a point system that can determine nutrition risk at the time of admission (19, 20). In a setting in which the dietitian functions as the clinical nutrition specialist, a disease-specific screening tool aimed at the particular type of patient will help to focus on more-relevant assessment parameters (15, 21).

2. CLIENT INTERVIEW

The patient interview is an integral part of the screening process and should include questions about weight change, patterns of eating, changes in appetite or taste, food intolerances, digestive disorders, knowledge of the diet, and use of supplements, in addition to clinical ob-

TABLE 1.2. RISK CATEGORIES

High Risk	Moderate Risk

1. Weight
  a. 5% weight loss in less than 1 month
  b. 10% weight loss in less than 6 months
	1. Weight: loss needs to be evaluated, e.g., is it self-induced or disease related?

2. Laboratory
  a. Albumin 3.0 gm/dL or less
  b. TLC (total lymphocyte count)— 1,200/mm³ or less
  c. Prealbumin 10 mg or less
	2. Laboratory: albumin 3.5 g/dL or less

3. Disease state or systems:ᵃ kidney, liver, pancreas, GI tract, oncology	3. Disease state or systems:ᵃ cardiology, neurology, obstetrics

4. Feeding modalities
  a. Parenteral nutrition
  b. Tube feeding
  c. NPO or liquids more than 5 days
	4. Feeding modalities
	  a. Stable transitional feeding for parenteral and tube feeding
	  b. Selected modified diets

Source: DeHoog, S. (18). Copyright © 1985 by the American Dietetic Association.
ᵃSelection of disease state or systems is dependent upon individual populations determined to be at nutritional risk.

servations indicative of malnutrition or high nutritional risk. Although the initial interview need not accomplish all these things, observational and interviewing skills need to be perfected if the dietary interview is to serve as an effective instrument for nutritional assessment (11).

3. USE OF SCREENING DATA

If a nutritional problem requiring intervention is not identified during preliminary assessment, the data collection process should stop here with a brief note in the patient's medical record. Intervals at which the process is to be repeated should be built into the assessment program in order to avoid missing any nutritional problems that occur after admission. Specific indications or criteria for referring those individuals requiring further evaluation should be well established prior to implementing a screening procedure.

If more information is needed, or if a nutritional problem has been identified in preliminary screening, a more detailed and comprehensive nutritional assessment is indicated. Complete assessments include a dietary history and extensive clinical, anthropometric, and biochemical data.

TOOLS AND TECHNIQUES

1. CLINICAL DATA

Clinical assessment includes review of the medical and social history and a physical examination. An alternative to these methods is the subjective global assessment technique, which is also described below.

A. Medical and Social History This component involves a review of the medical record, an interview with the patient, or both. Data obtained from this portion of the assessment should include medical history with emphasis on conditions that influence nutrient utilization, as well as relevant environmental, social, and family factors that influence nutrient intake. Information should provide a description of the patient and current and past medical problems that may influence nutritional status.

TABLE 1.3. PHYSICAL AND LABORATORY FINDINGS ASSOCIATED WITH MICRONUTRIENT DEFICIENCIES

Physical or laboratory finding	Associated deficiency
Mucocutaneous organs and hair	
Angular stomatitis, cheilosis, magenta tongue	Riboflavin
Glossitis, pellagrous dermatitis, atrophic papillae	Niacin
Xerosis, follicular hyperkeratosis	Linoleic acid
Acneiform forehead rash, nasolabial seborrhea, stomatitis	Vitamin B-6
Conjunctival and corneal xerosis, follicular hyperkeratosis, Bitot's spots, keratomalacia	Vitamin A
Petechiae, ecchymoses, swollen and hemorrhagic gums, prominent hair follicles, corkscrew hair	Vitamin C
Petechiae, ecchymoses	Vitamin K
Parakeratosis, alopecia	Zinc
Dystrophic nails (koilonychia), pale conjunctiva	Iron
Neurologic system	
Peripheral neuropathy, Wernicke's encephalopathy	Thiamine
Peripheral neuropathy, convulsive seizures, depression	Vitamin B-6
"Burning feet" syndrome	Pantothenic acid
Peripheral paresthesias, spinal cord symptoms	Vitamin B-12
Peripheral neuropathy, myelopathy, encephalopathy (pellagra)	Niacin
"Night blindness"	Vitamin A
Hematologic system	
Hemolytic anemia	Vitamin E
Macrocytic anemia	Vitamin B-12, folic acid
Microcytic and hypochromic anemia	Iron, copper
Microcytic anemia	Vitamin B-6
Coagulopathy	Vitamin K
Sideroblastic anemia, neutropenia (infants)	Copper
Thrombocytopenia	Linoleic acid
Musculoskeletal system	
Osteomalacia, tetany, rickets	Vitamin D
Tender, atrophic muscles	Thiamine
Joint pain, muscle weakness	Vitamin C
Osteopenia (infants)	Copper
Visceral organs	
Congestive heart failure	Thiamine
Diarrhea	Folic acid, zinc, niacin
Goiter	Iodine
Hypogonadism, hepatosplenomegaly	Zinc
Other	
Anorexia, hypogeusesthesia	Zinc

Source: Buzby, G. P., and Mullen, J. L. (22).

B. Physical Signs Examining the patient for physical signs and symptoms associated with malnutrition is an integral part of the assessment. Physical signs of malnutrition are manifested by al-

TABLE 1.4. DISEASE STATES AND HISTORICAL FEATURES ASSOCIATED WITH MICRONUTRIENT DEFICIENCIES

Disease state or historical feature	Associated deficiency
Gastrointestinal disorders	
Pancreatic insufficiency	Vitamins A, D, E, K
Gastrectomy	Vitamins A, D, E, B-12, folic acid, iron, calcium
Liver disease, alcoholism	Vitamins A, D, C, riboflavin, niacin, thiamine, folic acid, magnesium, zinc
Short-bowel syndrome, ileal resection	Vitamins B-12, folic acid, calcium, magnesium
Blind-loop syndrome	Vitamin B-12
Sprue, gluten enteropathy	Vitamin A, folic acid
Bile salt depletion, cholestyramine ingestion	Vitamins A, K
Obstructive jaundice	Vitamins A, K
Prolonged antacid therapy, peptic ulcer disease	Thiamine, vitamin C
Endocrine disorders	
Thyrotoxicosis	Vitamins A, B-6, B-12, C, thiamine, folic acid
Diabetes mellitus	Magnesium, chromium
Cardiorespiratory disorders	
Chronic obstructive pulmonary disease	Vitamin A
Congestive heart failure	Vitamins A, C, thiamine
Cystic fibrosis	Vitamin A
Hematopoietic disorders	
Sickle-cell anemia	Folic acid
Leukemia	Folic acid
Renal disorders	
Chronic renal failure	Magnesium, calcium, vitamin D[a]
Miscellaneous disorders	
Prolonged antibiotic therapy	Vitamin K
Fever	Vitamins A, C, thiamine, riboflavin, folic acid

Source: Buzby, G. P., and Mullen, J. L. (22).
[a]Inability of renal tissue to synthesize the metabolically active form of vitamin D.

terations in the hair, face, eyes, lips, tongue, gums, skin, nails, and musculoskeletal system. Performing a physical examination involves observation of any physical finding that suggests a nutritional abnormality or deficiency. Care must be taken in interpretation because most signs or symptoms reflect 2 or more nutrient deficiencies, although some deficiencies of single nutrients result in a unique or specific physical finding. Tables 1.3 and 1.4 outline physical findings and diseases associated with nutrient deficiencies.

C. Subjective Global Assessment Subjective global assessment (SGA) is an alternative to nutritional assessment methods that rely on anthropometric and biochemical data (23). Studies comparing SGA data with objective measurements of nutritional status have demonstrated a good correlation between the subjective and objective measurements, a high degree of interrater reproducibility, and a predictive validity equal to or better than objective measurements (24–26).

The method involves collection of data from the history and physical exam. The medical history emphasizes 5 features: weight changes, dietary intake, gastrointestinal system symptoms, functional capacity or energy level, and metabolic demands of the patient's underlying disease state. The physical exam features a rating system based on degree of abnormality for subcutaneous tissue loss, muscle wasting, edema, and ascites. An SGA rank is assigned by using a weighting system that allows clinicians to make a subjective judgment for classifying degree of malnutrition. Emphasis is placed on the variables of weight loss, poor dietary intake, loss of subcutaneous tissue, and muscle wasting. This technique has been described in detail elsewhere (23).

2. ANTHROPOMETRIC MEASUREMENTS

Anthropometric indices are the measurements of gross composition and physical dimensions of the body. These measurements may include height, weight, body circumferences, knee height, and skinfold thicknesses and may be used for measuring growth or assessing body composition.

Anthropometric measurements are taken with simple, safe, and noninvasive techniques requiring mostly inexpensive, portable, and durable equipment. Relatively unskilled personnel can perform the measurements, provided that standardized techniques are used. The results are often readily available and thus are valuable in screening for nutrition risk. The usefulness of single anthropometric measurements is limited, but serial measurements may be more valuable in assessment of body composition changes or growth over a period of time. Anthropometric measurements are nonspecific and cannot distinguish between changes in growth or composition induced by imbalances in intakes of protein, energy, or other nutrients (9). Evaluating anthropometric data involves comparison of the data with predetermined reference limits or cutoff points that allow classification into 1 or more risk categories and, in some cases, identification of the type and severity of malnutrition. The various measurements are discussed below.

A. Height An individual's stature can be properly measured at the observed point of maximum inspiration of a breath and while the individual is shoeless. Under certain conditions, however, measurements of upright stature are either inappropriate or unfeasible. Aging, for example, is accompanied by a progressive decrease in height (27–31). For children a stadiometer or flat wall-mounted metal tape with a headboard should be used, with the child's heels, buttocks, shoulders, and head contacting the wall (32, 33).

B. Recumbent Length For individuals who are unable to stand upright or who have spinal curvature or contracture, recumbent height measures have been shown to be as reliable as standing height measures (28, 29).

A length-measuring board is used for children who are less than three years of age or are unable to stand. Two people are often needed to take an accurate measurement by ensuring that the child is correctly positioned with the knees straight (33).

C. Sitting Height and Crown-Rump Length Sitting height and crown-rump length may be used for children who are unable to stand or who have severe contractures. The stadiometer can be used for measuring sitting height, with a sitting surface in front. For crown-rump length, the length board can be used, with the legs raised at 90° to the body (33).

D. Body Segment Lengths Another method for measuring height is the use of a total arm span measurement, which correlates well with height at maturity. Because the bones involved in the arm span are primarily long bones, this measurement is affected little by the aging process. Arm span measurements are useful for adults who are bedridden or wheelchair-bound (27, 33–37). Care must be taken when extrapolating arm span measurements to the height of elderly clients, because height generally decreases with age.

For children with joint contractures, the upper arm length or lower leg length can be used to assess linear growth (33, 35–37). Growth charts using these alternative measurements are included in the Appendix (figures A.6a–d).

In the elderly, knee height can be measured to estimate stature by using the following formulas (29):

Stature in men (cm) = 64.19 − (0.04 × age) + [2.02 × knee height (cm)]

Stature in women (cm) = 84.88 − (0.24 × age) + [1.83 × knee height (cm)]

These formulas have been incorporated into a nomogram in figure 1.2. Special broad-based calipers for estimating stature from knee height are available from Ross Laboratories in Columbus, Ohio.

E. Head Circumference Head circumference for age can be used during the first 2 years of life as an index of chronic protein energy malnutrition. An abnormally low head circumference may reflect chronic malnutrition during the first few months of life, intrauterine growth retardation, or microcephaly of non-nutritional origin. This measurement is not useful after 2 years of age, because head circumference growth slows significantly. It is also less sensitive to mild malnutrition and may add little to the assessment of nutritional status in the normal or mildly malnourished child.

Head circumference is measured with the infant sitting on the lap of the parent or an attendant. A flexible cloth or plastic measuring tape is used to measure the largest occipital-frontal circumference of the infant's head. Hair ornaments or hats should be removed, and the hair flattened.

F. Body Weight When accurately measured, body weight is a simple, gross estimate of body composition. Detailed descriptions of the proper techniques using different types of scales have been published (30, 38). A beam scale with nondetachable weights or an electronic scale is recommended for obtaining an accurate result. Infants are weighed nude, lying on a pan-type pediatric scale accurate to within 10 g. A platform scale should be used for older children and adults who can stand still without assistance. For patients who are unable to stand, chair and bed scales are available. Frequent calibration of the equipment is important (33).

When used to identify changes, weight measurement can be an effective nutritional screening tool (39, 40). Percent weight loss is a useful nutritional index and may be computed as follows:

% weight change from usual weight = $\frac{\text{(usual weight − actual weight)}}{\text{usual weight}} \times 100$

% weight change from admission weight = $\frac{\text{(admission weight − actual weight)}}{\text{admission weight}} \times 100$

% weight change since nutrition intervention = $\frac{\text{(pre-intervention weight − actual weight)}}{\text{pre-intervention weight}} \times 100$

In individuals with edema, ascites, or severe dehydration, weight changes may reflect fluid shifts rather than changes in body composition. A rapid weight gain of more than 1 lb. per day suggests excess fluid. A modified weighing method

FIG. 1.2. NOMOGRAM FOR ESTIMATING STATURE FROM KNEE HEIGHT.

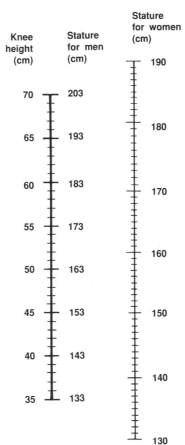

Directions

1. Locate the person's age on the column farthest to the left.
2. Locate the person's knee height on the next column.
3. Lay a ruler or straightedge so that it touches these 2 points—age and knee height.
4. Note where the straightedge crosses the stature column for the appropriate sex. The stature column for women is the farthest right column. The stature column for men is between that column and the knee-height column. The point where the ruler crosses the appropriate column is the person's estimated stature.
5. Enter the estimated stature in the person's record.

Source: Chumlea, W. C., Roche, A., and Mukherjee, D. (29). Copyright © 1987 by Ross Laboratories.

for the evaluation of fluid balance has been published (44). In instances of massive tumor growth, where losses of fat and lean body mass such as skeletal muscle are masked, body weight is a poor guide to energy and nitrogen reserves (39, 41–43).

The concept of desirable weight may vary for different populations and for the same population in relation to different causes of mortality. Similarly, an ideal weight cannot be identified at a point in time for a person or persons differing from the group upon which the desirable weight was based (40–44).

G. Body Weight in Amputees For patients with amputations, figure 1.3 can be used to estimate the body weight contributed by individual body parts so that desirable body weights can be calculated. Adjusted weight ranges based on type of amputation and on figures from the Metropolitan Life Insurance Company are provided in table 1.5. Either method may be used to estimate a desirable body weight (45).

H. Body Frame Size The measurement of body frame size allows the weight to be adjusted for height to reflect a more accurate desirable weight range. One of the easiest and most reliable indicators of frame size is the elbow breadth measurement (48). It is not affected by obesity or greatly affected by age, making it useful for all adults. Table 1.6 includes the method for measuring elbow breadth and values based on height for medium-frame men and women. Measurements lower than those listed indicate a small frame, whereas higher values indicate a large frame.

FIG. 1.3. PERCENTAGES OF TOTAL BODY WEIGHT CONTRIBUTED BY INDIVIDUAL BODY PARTS.

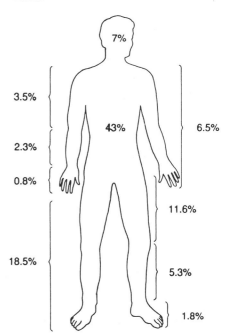

Source: Brunnstrom, M.A. (45).

TABLE 1.5. WEIGHT ACCORDING TO TYPE OF AMPUTATION

Sex and height	Reference weight range[a]	Type of amputation and percent loss							
		Single below knee, 6%	Single at knee, 9%	Single above knee, 15%	Double below knee, 12%	Double at knee, 18%	Double above knee, 30%	Single arm, 6.5%	Single arm below elbow, 3.6%
Males									
5'2"	128–150	120–141	116–137	109–128	113–132	105–123	90–105	120–140	123–145
5'3"	130–153	122–144	118–139	111–130	114–135	107–125	91–107	122–143	125–146
5'4"	132–156	124–147	120–142	112–133	116–137	108–128	92–109	124–146	127–151
5'5"	134–160	126–150	122–146	114–136	118–141	110–131	94–112	125–150	129–154
5'6"	136–164	128–154	124–149	116–139	120–144	112–134	95–115	127–154	131–158
5'7"	138–168	130–158	126–153	117–143	121–148	113–138	97–118	129–157	133–162
5'8"	140–172	132–162	127–157	119–146	123–151	115–141	98–120	131–161	135–166
5'9"	142–176	133–165	129–160	121–150	125–155	116–144	99–123	133–165	137–170
5'10"	144–180	135–169	131–164	122–153	127–158	118–148	101–126	135–169	139–174
5'11"	146–184	137–173	133–167	124–156	128–162	120–151	102–129	137–172	141–177
6'0"	149–188	140–177	136–171	127–160	131–165	122–154	104–132	140–176	144–181
6'1"	152–192	143–180	138–175	129–163	134–169	125–157	106–134	143–180	147–185
6'2"	155–197	146–185	141–179	132–167	136–173	127–162	109–138	145–184	150–190
6'3"	158–202	149–190	144–184	134–172	139–178	130–166	111–141	148–189	153–195
6'4"	162–207	152–195	147–188	138–176	142–182	133–170	113–145	152–194	157–200
Females									
4'10"	102–131	96–123	93–119	87–111	90–115	84–107	71–92	95–123	98–127
4'11"	103–134	97–126	94–122	88–114	91–118	84–110	72–94	96–125	99–130
5'0"	104–137	98–129	95–125	88–116	92–121	85–112	73–96	97–127	100–133
5'1"	106–140	100–132	96–127	90–119	93–123	87–115	74–98	99–130	102–136
5'2"	108–142	102–134	98–130	92–122	95–126	89–117	76–100	101–133	104–138
5'3"	111–147	104–138	101–134	94–125	98–129	91–121	78–103	104–137	107–142
5'4"	114–151	107–142	104–137	97–128	100–133	93–124	80–106	107–142	110–146
5'5"	117–155	110–146	106–141	99–132	103–136	96–127	82–109	110–146	113–150
5'6"	120–159	113–149	109–144	102–135	106–140	98–130	84–111	113–150	116–154
5'7"	123–163	116–153	112–148	105–139	108–143	101–134	86–114	116–154	119–158
5'8"	126–167	118–157	115–152	107–142	111–147	103–137	88–117	119–156	122–162
5'9"	129–170	121–160	117–155	110–145	114–150	106–139	90–119	121–160	125–165
5'10"	132–173	124–163	120–157	112–147	116–152	108–142	92–121	124–163	128–168
5'11"	135–176	127–165	123–160	115–150	119–155	111–144	95–123	127–166	130–170
6'0"	138–179	130–168	126–163	117–152	121–158	113–147	97–125	130–169	133–173

Sources: Chatterjee, S. (46, 47).

[a]Reference weight ranges are from Metropolitan Life Insurance Company, 1983. The figures represent weights for ages 25–29, based on lowest mortality. Weights are in pounds, according to frame, and include indoor clothing weighing 5 lbs. for men and 3 lbs. for women. Height includes 1" for shoes.

I. Weight for Height   The height and weight tables of the Metropolitan Life Insurance Company have long been accepted as norms for ideal or desirable weights and are based on mortality data from healthy subjects collected over a 20-year period. The weights presented are those associated with the lowest mortality rate but may not be representative of the population as a whole because subjects with heart disease, cancer, diabetes, and other diseases were screened out to determine the effect of weight alone on mortality. Three weight ranges were determined for each sex based on frame sizes, although frame size was not actually measured in the study. The 1983 weights are generally higher than those

TABLE 1.6. DETERMINATION OF BODY FRAME SIZE

Men		Women	
Height[a]	Elbow breadth	Height[a]	Elbow breadth
5′2″ to 5′3″	2½″ to 2⅞″	4′10″ to 4′11″	2¼″ to 2½″
5′4″ to 5′7″	2⅝″ to 2⅞″	5′0″ to 5′3″	2¼″ to 2½″
5′8″ to 5′11″	2¾″ to 3″	5′4″ to 5′7″	2⅜″ to 2⅝″
6′0″ to 6′3″	2¾″ to 3⅛″	5′8″ to 5′11″	2⅜″ to 2⅝″
6′4″	2⅞″ to 3¼″	6′0″	2½″ to 2¾″

The method for determining elbow breadth is as follows:

1. Extend one arm and bend the forearm upward at a 90° angle. Keep the fingers straight, and turn the inside of the wrist toward the body.
2. Place the calipers on the 2 prominent bones on either side of the elbow.
3. Measure the space between the 2 bones.
4. Compare the measurement with those listed above.
5. Measurements lower than those listed indicate a small frame, whereas larger values indicate a large frame.

Sources: Metropolitan Life Insurance Company, 1983; Frisancho, A. R. (48). Copyright © 1983, *American Journal of Clinical Nutrition,* American Society for Clinical Nutrition.
[a]Height includes 1″ for shoes.

in the 1959 tables, although the increases are not evenly distributed throughout the table. Both the 1959 and 1983 tables can be found in the Appendix (tables A.6a–d).

The Metropolitan weight tables may not be the best method for determining weight goals for malnourished or seriously ill individuals and may be more appropriate for determining weight goals for healthy individuals. An alternative to this method for estimating desirable or optimal weight can be found in table 1.7. This alternative method can only be used for adults taller than 5 ft. and can be adjusted for frame size.

J. Body Mass Index Proposed as an alternative to the traditional use of height-weight tables in the assessment of obesity, body mass index (BMI) measures body weight corrected for height. This index is calculated by dividing weight in kilograms by height in square meters (kg/m²) or by using the nomogram provided in figure 1.4. The number obtained from this calculation allows for classification of body weight into categories

of obesity-related risk independent of height. A discussion of the uses and limitations of this index can be found in Part VI.

K. Pediatric Heights and Weights In growing children, serial measurements of height, weight, and head circumference plotted on growth charts provide a simple monitoring system. Growth charts may be found in the Appendix (figures A.2a–A.5d). Accurate serial anthropometric records and growth charts are

essential components of the assessment process in children. Trends can be used to detect growth abnormalities, to monitor nutritional status, and to evaluate the effects of nutritional intervention or disease treatment. A weight-for-height measurement below the 5th percentile is an indicator of acute depletion while a height for age below the 5th percentile is an indication of chronic depletion. Tables 1.8 and 1.9 give some reasons for a child's being above the 95th or below the 5th percentile. Much more complete presentations of anthropometric techniques used with children have been published elsewhere (32, 38, 51–58).

L. Skinfold Thickness Skinfold measurements can be used to estimate subcutaneous fat stores, which in turn can provide an estimation of total body fat. Assessing the amount and rate of change in body fat can aid in establishing the presence and severity of protein-energy malnutrition (PEM). Although a small amount of fat reserves may imply limited energy stores, massive losses over a period of time suggest severe energy depletion, whereas very rapid loss of fat reserves indicates a potentially life-threatening condition. Body fat alone, however, is not an index of the severity of PEM. As with other anthropometric measurements, skinfold data should be used in conjunction with other indices and followed over time to provide accu-

TABLE 1.7. CALCULATION OF DESIRABLE BODY WEIGHT

Build	Women	Men	Children
Medium frame	Allow 100 lb. for first 5 ft. of height, plus 5 lb. for each additional inch	Allow 106 lb. for first 5 ft. of height, plus 6 lb. for each additional inch	Chart growth pattern on Wetzel, Iowa, or Stuart graph, preferably every 3–6 months
Small frame	Subtract 10%	Subtract 10%	
Large frame	Add 10%	Add 10%	

Source: Davidson, J. K. (49).

FIG. 1.4. NOMOGRAM FOR BODY MASS INDEX (KG/M²).

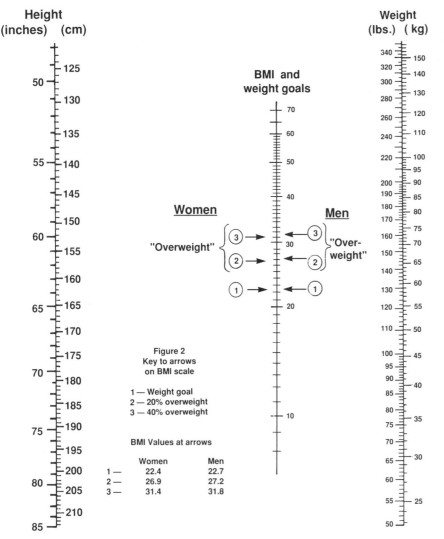

The ratio weight/height² (metric units) is read from the central scale after a straightedge is placed between the scales for height and body weight.

Source: Burton, B. T., and Foster, W. R. (50).

Note: Figures are based on 1983 Metropolitan Life Insurance Company tables. Weights and heights are without clothing. With clothes, add 5 lbs. (2.3 kg) for men or 3 lbs. (1.4 kg) for women, and add 1 inch (2.5 cm) in height for shoes.

rate and thorough assessments of nutritional status.

Measuring skinfolds requires only a tape measure and calipers of acceptable quality. Detailed instructions for measuring various body-site skinfolds have been published and should be reviewed carefully (59–61). The practitioner's skill in performing the measurements is extremely important to minimize intraobserver error. Subsequent measurements should also be made by the same practitioner.

Approximately 50% of total body fat is located as subcutaneous fat in well-nourished individuals. Because skinfold measurements indicate only the amount of subcutaneous fat, this method assumes that subcutaneous and internal fat will respond similarly to changes in energy balance. Although available data are limited, studies indicate that skinfold thickness and total body fat do not change in proportion to each other, making the interpretation of skinfold measurements somewhat ambiguous.

Single skinfold measurements may produce inaccurate estimations of total body fat because the distribution of subcutaneous fat is not uniform. For this reason, it is suggested that the measurements be compared with percentages of standards, be taken from multiple body sites, or be collected as serial measurements to assess changes in fat stores over time. Reference values for triceps and subscapular skinfold measurements based on height, age, and body frame are available for classifying the values as percentiles (62). The most commonly used skinfold measurements are triceps, biceps, subscapular, and suprailiac. Measurement techniques are described in detail elsewhere (59–61). Table 1.10 provides the fat content as a percentage of body weight for the sum of four skinfold measurements. The result may be compared with normal levels in table 1.11.

M. Midarm Muscle Circumference Midarm muscle circumference (MAMC) provides an index of skeletal muscle mass or somatic protein stores. The value is derived from measurements of both the triceps skinfold and the midarm circumference (MAC). It provides a quick approximation of muscle mass and has the advantage of being minimally affected by edema of malnutrition. MAMC

TABLE 1.8. SOME REASONS FOR A CHILD'S BEING ABOVE THE 95TH PERCENTILE

Measurement	Reason
Weight	Tallness
	Obesity
	Edema
Length or stature	Tall parents
	Accelerated maturation
	Marfan syndrome
	Pituitary gigantism
Weight-for-length or weight-for-stature	Obesity
	Edema
	Achondroplasia
Head circumference	Hydrocephaly
Triceps skinfold thickness	Obesity

Source: Moore, W. R., and Roche, A. F. (32). Copyright © 1987 by Ross Laboratories.

TABLE 1.9. SOME REASONS FOR A CHILD'S BEING BELOW THE 5TH PERCENTILE

Measurement	Reason
Weight	Shortness
	Malnutrition
	Chronic renal disease
	Psychosocial deprivation
	Infectious disease
	Iron-deficiency anemia
Length or stature	Short parents
	Malnutrition
	Psychosocial deprivation
	Delayed maturation
	Endocrinopathies, especially hypothyroidism and hypopituitarism
	Chromosomal and genetic abnormalities, e.g., Turner's syndrome
	Chronic renal disease
Weight-for-length or weight-for-stature	Dehydration
	Recent febrile illness
	Recent malnutrition
	Marfan syndrome
Head circumference	Microcephaly, e.g., fetal alcohol syndrome
	Craniostenosis
	Genetic disorders
Triceps skinfold thickness	Malnutrition
	Chronic illness, e.g., cystic fibrosis

Source: Moore, W. R., and Roche, A. F. (32). Copyright © 1987 by Ross Laboratories.

is estimated using the following equation:

$$\text{Midarm muscle circumference (cm)} = \text{midarm circumference (cm)} - [0.314 \times \text{triceps skinfold (mm)}]$$

Nomograms for estimating arm muscle circumferences are provided in figures 1.5 and 1.6.

If the patient is unable to assume an upright position, triceps skinfold measurements and midarm circumference estimations can be accurately measured with the patient in the supine position. Left and right arm measurements have not been found to be significantly different (66).

MAMC is not a good index of tissue repletion and is insensitive to small changes in muscle mass resulting from illness or repletion therapy (67). The validity of applying a percentage analysis method to skinfold and arm muscle circumference estimates to define depletion as moderate or severe has been questioned. A more reliable interpretation can be made using a percentile rank system, in which measurements falling below the 5th percentile are considered to indicate depletion and those between the 15th and 25th percentiles are considered to represent marginal reserves (68).

N. Underwater Weighing   The percentage of body fat may be calculated from body density, which is determined by weighing the subject in water and in air. Corrections are made for water temperature and for residual air in the lungs and gastrointestinal tract.

Results can be very reproducible with well-trained examiners and subjects. The theoretical error of body fat predictions from underwater weighing is 3% to 4%, attributed to variable water content of the fat-free mass and variable bone mineral density. This method is not suitable for children below 8 years of age or for elderly, obese, or unhealthy individuals. It

TABLE 1.10. EQUIVALENT FAT CONTENT, AS A PERCENTAGE OF BODY WEIGHT, FOR THE SUM OF 4 SKINFOLDS (BICEPS, TRICEPS, SUBSCAPULAR, AND SUPRAILIAC)

Skinfolds	Males (age in years)				Females (age in years)			
(mm)	17–29	30–39	40–49	50+	16–29	30–39	40–49	50+
15	4.8				10.5			
20	8.1	12.2	12.2	12.6	14.1	17.0	19.8	21.4
25	10.5	14.2	15.0	15.6	16.8	19.4	22.2	24.0
30	12.9	16.2	17.7	18.6	19.5	21.8	24.5	26.6
35	14.7	17.7	19.6	20.8	21.5	23.7	26.4	28.5
40	16.4	19.2	21.4	22.9	23.4	25.5	28.2	30.3
45	17.7	20.4	23.0	24.7	25.0	26.9	29.6	31.9
50	19.0	21.5	24.6	26.5	26.5	28.2	31.0	33.4
55	20.1	22.5	25.9	27.9	27.8	29.4	32.1	34.6
60	21.2	23.5	27.1	29.2	29.1	30.6	33.2	35.7
65	22.2	24.3	28.2	30.4	30.2	31.6	34.1	36.7
70	23.1	25.1	29.3	31.6	31.2	32.5	35.0	37.7
75	24.0	25.9	30.3	32.7	32.2	33.4	35.9	38.7
80	24.8	26.6	31.2	33.8	33.1	34.3	36.7	39.6
85	25.5	27.2	32.1	34.8	34.0	35.1	37.5	40.4
90	26.2	27.8	33.0	35.8	34.8	35.8	38.3	41.2
95	26.9	28.4	33.7	36.6	35.6	36.5	39.0	41.9
100	27.6	29.0	34.4	37.4	36.4	37.2	39.7	42.6
105	28.2	29.6	35.1	38.2	37.1	37.9	40.4	43.3
110	28.8	30.1	35.8	39.0	37.8	38.6	41.0	43.9
115	29.4	30.6	36.4	39.7	38.4	39.1	41.5	44.5
120	30.0	31.1	37.0	40.4	39.0	39.6	42.0	45.1
125	30.5	31.5	37.6	41.1	39.6	40.1	42.5	45.7
130	31.0	31.9	38.2	41.8	40.2	40.6	43.0	46.2
135	31.5	32.3	38.7	42.4	40.8	41.1	43.5	46.7
140	32.0	32.7	39.2	43.0	41.3	41.6	44.0	47.2
145	32.5	33.1	39.7	43.6	41.8	42.1	44.5	47.7
150	32.9	33.5	40.2	44.1	42.3	42.6	45.0	48.2
155	33.3	33.9	40.7	44.6	42.8	43.1	45.4	48.7
160	33.7	34.3	41.2	45.1	43.3	43.6	45.8	49.2
165	34.1	34.6	41.6	45.6	43.7	44.0	46.2	49.6
170	34.5	34.8	42.0	46.1	44.1	44.4	46.6	50.0
175	34.9					44.8	47.0	50.4
180	35.3					45.2	47.4	50.8
185	35.6					45.6	47.8	51.2
190	35.9					45.9	48.2	51.6
195						46.2	48.5	52.0
200						46.5	48.8	52.4
205							49.1	52.7
210							49.4	53.0

Source: Murray, R. L. (60); *adapted from* Durnin, J. V. G. A., and Womersley, J. (63).

TABLE 1.11. NORMAL RANGES OF PERCENTAGE OF BODY FAT

	Age (years)				
	0–30	31–40	41–50	51–60	61–100
Males	12–18	13–19	14–20	16–20	17–21
Females	20–26	21–27	22–28	22–30	22–31

Source: Staff of R.J.L. Systems, Inc. (64).

Note: These ranges were developed by Victor Katch at the University of Michigan Physiology Department. From BIA-101 software users manual for IBM-PC RJL Systems, Version 1.2. 9930 Whittier, Detroit, MI 48224, 1986.

is not a simple procedure and is certainly impractical in the clinical setting (9).

O. Bioelectric Impedance This technique for estimating body fat involves attaching electrocardiogram (ECG) electrodes to the wrist and ankle, along with an instrument that introduces a tiny electrical current into the body and measures the resistance to the current across the electrodes. Because lean tissue contains most of the water and electrolytes in the body, the more lean tissue a person has, the less will be the electrical resistance. The electrical resistance data are then used in an equation to estimate the percentage of body fat (69–72).

This method may underestimate fat-free mass in surgical patients and overestimate it in obese individuals or following weight reduction, compared with underwater weighing (69, 73, 74). With the elderly, equations that predict bioelectric impedance overestimate fat-free mass by about 6 kg. A specific equation has been developed for use with the elderly that provides more-accurate results (75).

The menstrual cycle has an effect on the reliability of bio-impedance assessments of body composition, probably related to changes in weight caused by water retention. For women with large menses-associated weight fluctuations, an average of several measurements is better than reliance on 1 measurement alone (76).

3. BIOCHEMICAL DATA

For a laboratory measurement to be useful as a nutritional assessment tool, it must have a high degree of sensitivity and specificity. The sensitivity of a biochemical index refers to the extent to which it predicts changes in nutritional status and to its ability to detect small changes in nutritional status. The specificity of an index refers to its ability to measure only the substance of interest. Thus an ideal biochemical index should be sensitive to short-term nutritional

FIG. 1.5. NOMOGRAM FOR ESTIMATING MIDARM MUSCLE AREA, AN INDEX OF TOTAL MUSCLE MASS.

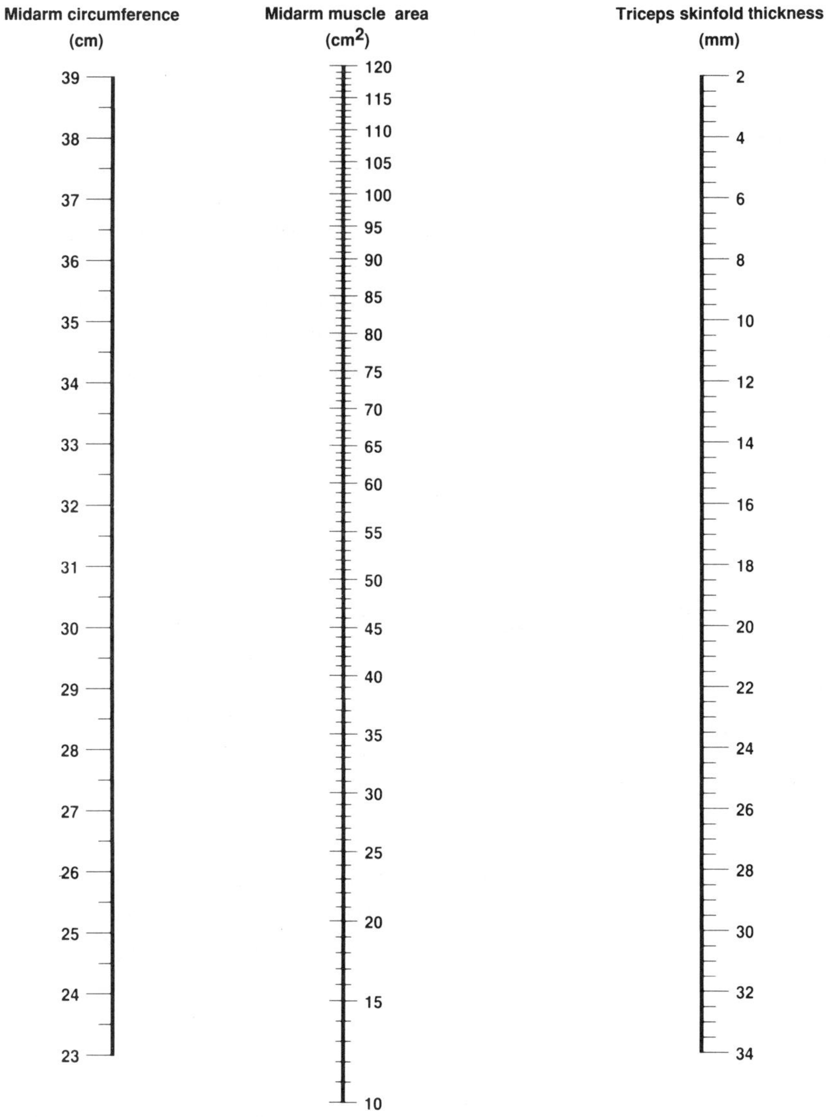

Directions

1. Locate the person's midarm circumference on the left column. Numbers in this column *decrease* going down the scale.
2. Locate the person's triceps skinfold thickness on the right column. Numbers in this column *increase* going down the scale.
3. Lay a ruler or straightedge so that it touches these 2 points—midarm circumference and triceps skinfold thickness.
4. Note where the straightedge crosses the center column. This is the person's midarm muscle area.
5. Record the midarm muscle area measurement in the person's chart.

Source: Chumlea, W. C., Roche, A., and Mukherjee, D. (29), copyright © 1987 by Ross Laboratories; *adapted from:* Gurney, J. M., and Jelliffe, D. B. (65).

changes and be minimally influenced by other factors that can result in false-positive or false-negative findings.

Differences in the assay methods for measuring laboratory values should also be taken into account in interpretation. Standards from the laboratory conducting the analysis should be used in interpreting results (77).

Guidelines for interpreting biochemical laboratory findings are provided in table 1.12, and the biochemical differentiation of anemias are outlined in table 1.13. More-comprehensive assessment criteria as well as algorithms for the evaluation of normocytic and macrocytic anemia have been published elsewhere (11, 12, 80).

A. Visceral Protein Status Although most of the body's protein is found in the skeletal muscle, a smaller but significant amount is found in the visceral protein pool. Visceral proteins are made up of circulating serum proteins and proteins found in organs, including the liver, kidneys, pancreas, and heart. Measurement of visceral protein status is used as an index of protein-energy malnutrition because the liver is the main site of serum protein synthesis and also is the first organ to be affected by a limited supply of protein substrate. Care should be taken in interpreting serum protein levels, because many non-nutritional factors can influence the concentrations of these proteins, including stress, sepsis, hydration status, pregnancy, drug therapy, and reduced protein synthesis due to disease state (9).

Concentrations of 1 or more serum proteins can be measured to assess visceral protein status. In determining which protein is most appropriate, it is important to consider the protein's usefulness in measuring short-term versus long-term changes, the size of the body pool, the protein's synthesis rate and half-life, and the cost of measuring the concentration.

FIG. 1.6. NOMOGRAM FOR ARM ANTHROPOMETRY FOR CHILDREN.

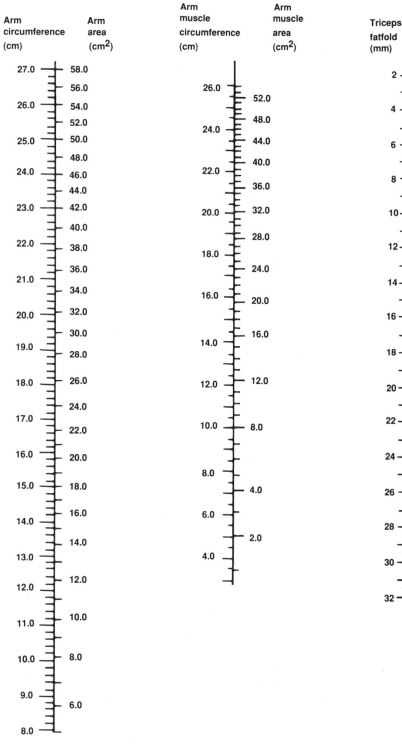

i. Serum Albumin The measurement of serum albumin is relatively simple and is included in most routine admission protocols. For this reason, it is often used as a standard tool for monitoring baseline visceral protein status as well as changes induced by nutrition intervention or support therapy. The measurement of serum albumin reflects changes occurring only within the intravascular space and cannot control for the redistribution of albumin from the extravascular to the intravascular space that occurs during decreased hepatic synthesis. In addition, albumin's half-life is relatively long (14–20 days), making it insensitive to short-term changes in protein status. As a result, this measurement is more usefully applied to monitoring long-term changes during convalescence.

Low serum albumin concentrations, or hypoalbuminemia, may result from zinc deficiency (because zinc is bound to albumin), pregnancy, congestive heart failure, liver disease, certain gastrointestinal and renal diseases, or infection. Serum albumin concentrations are also affected by changes in the amount and distribution of body fluids and capillary permeability. A shift in albumin concentration from the extravascular space to the intravascular space may occur as a result of traumatic injury, ongoing stress, removal of the thyroid or pituitary glands, and corticosteroid therapy. Age differences in serum albumin levels are controversial (39, 81–83).

A serum albumin concentration of less than 3.4 g per 100 mL warrants further nutritional investigation. Serum albumin concentrations below 3.0 g per 100 mL are often associated with edema, and concentrations of less than 2.5 g per 100 mL are extreme and indicate severe depletion. Preoperative serum albumin levels have been shown to be effective predictors of outcome in surgical patients with colorectal cancer. When the measure is considered singly, however, the

To obtain muscle circumference:
1. Lay ruler between values of arm circumference and fatfold.
2. Read off muscle circumference on middle line.
To obtain tissue areas:
1. The arm areas and muscle areas are alongside their respective circumferences.
2. Fat area = arm area − muscle area.

Source: Gurney, J. M., and Jelliffe, D. B. (65). Copyright © *American Journal of Clinical Nutrition*, American Society for Clinical Nutrition.

TABLE 1.12. GUIDELINES FOR CRITERIA OF NUTRITIONAL STATUS FOR LABORATORY EVALUATION

Nutrient and units	Age of subject (years)[a]	Criteria of status		
		Deficient	*Marginal*	*Acceptable*
Hemoglobin (g/100 mL)[b]	6–23 months	Up to 9.0	9.0–9.9	10.0+
	2–5	Up to 10.0	10.0–10.9	11.0+
	6–12	Up to 10.0	10.0–11.4	11.5+
	13–16 M	Up to 12.0	12.0–12.9	13.0+
	13–16 F	Up to 10.0	10.0–11.4	11.5+
	16+ M	Up to 12.0	12.0–13.9	14.0+
	16+ F	Up to 10.0	10.0–11.9	12.0+
	Pregnant (after 6+ months)	Up to 9.5	9.5–10.9	11.0+
Hematocrit (packed cell volume in percent)[b]	Up to 2	Up to 28	28–30	31+
	2–5	Up to 30	30–33	34+
	6–12	Up to 30	30–35	36+
	13–16 M	Up to 37	37–39	40+
	13–16 F	Up to 31	31–35	36+
	16+ M	Up to 37	37–43	44+
	16+ F	Up to 31	31–37	33+
	Pregnant	Up to 30	30–32	33+
Serum albumin (g/100 mL)[b]	Up to 1	—	Up to 2.5	2.5+
	1–5	—	Up to 3.0	3.0+
	6–16	—	Up to 3.5	3.5+
	16+	Up to 2.8	2.8–3.4	3.5+
	Pregnant	Up to 3.0	3.0–3.4	3.5+
Serum protein (g/100 mL)[b]	Up to 1	—	Up to 5.0	6.0+
	1–5	—	Up to 5.5	5.5+
	6–16	—	Up to 6.0	6.0+
	16+	Up to 6.0	6.0–6.4	6.5+
	Pregnant	Up to 5.5	5.5–5.9	6.0+
Serum ascorbic acid (mg/100 mL)[b]	All ages	Up to 0.1	0.1–0.19	0.2+
Plasma vitamin A (μg/100 mL)[b]	All ages	Up to 10	10–19	20+
Plasma carotene (μg/100 mL)[b]	All ages	Up to 20	20–39	40+
	Pregnant	—	40–79	80+
Serum iron (μg/100 mL)[b]	Up to 2	Up to 30	—	30+
	2–5	Up to 40	—	40+
	8–12	Up to 50	—	50+
	12+ M	Up to 60	—	60+
	12+ F	Up to 40	—	40+
Transferrin saturation (percent)[b]	Up to 2	Up to 15.0	—	15.0+
	2–12	Up to 20.0	—	20.0+
	12+ M	Up to 20.0	—	20.0+
	12+ F	Up to 15.0	—	15.0+
Serum folacin (ng/mL)[c]	All ages	Up to 2.0	2.1–5.9	6.0+
Serum vitamin B-12 (pg/mL)[c]	All ages	Up to 100	—	100+

(continued)

TABLE 1.12. *CONTINUED*

Nutrient and units	Age of subject (years)[a]	Criteria of status		
		Deficient	Marginal	Acceptable
Thiamine in urine (μg/g creatinine)[b]	1–3	Up to 120	120–175	175+
	4–5	Up to 85	85–120	120+
	6–9	Up to 70	70–180	180+
	10–15	Up to 55	55–150	150+
	16+	Up to 27	27–65	65+
	Pregnant	Up to 21	21–49	50+
Riboflavin in urine (μg/g creatinine)[b]	1–3	Up to 150	150–499	500+
	4–5	Up to 100	100–299	300+
	6–9	Up to 85	85–269	270+
	10–16	Up to 70	70–199	200+
	16+	Up to 27	27–79	80+
	Pregnant	Up to 30	30–89	90+
RBC transketolase-TPP-effect (ratio)[c]	All ages	25+	15–25	Up to 15
RBC glutathione reductase-FAD-effect (ratio)[c]	All ages	1.2+	—	Up to 1.2
Tryptophan load (mg xanthuronic acid excreted)[c]	Adults	25+ (6 hr)	—	Up to 25
	(dose: 100 mg/kg body weight)	75+ (24 hr)	—	Up to 75
Urinary pyridoxine (μg/g creatinine)[c]	1–3	Up to 90	—	90+
	4–6	Up to 80	—	80+
	7–9	Up to 60	—	60+
	10–12	Up to 40	—	40+
	13–15	Up to 30	—	30+
	16+	Up to 20	—	20+
Urinary N-methylnicotinamide (mg/g creatinine)[b]	All ages	Up to 0.2	0.2–5.59	0.6+
	Pregnant	Up to 0.8	0.8–2.49	2.5+
Urinary pantothenic acid (μg)[b]	All ages	Up to 200	—	200+
Plasma vitamin E (mg/100 mL)[b]	All ages	Up to 0.2	0.2–0.6	0.6+
Transaminase index (ratio)[c]				
EGOT[d]	Adult	2.0+	—	Up to 2.0
EGPT[e]	Adult	1.25+	—	Up to 1.25

Source: Christakis, G. (78).

[a]M, male; F, female.

[b]*Adapted from* the Ten State Nutrition Survey.

[c]Criteria may vary with different methodology. RBC, red blood cell; TPP, thiamine pyrophosphate; FAD, flavin-adenine dinucleotide.

[d]Erythrocyte glutamic oxalacetic transaminase.

[e]Erythrocyte glutamic pyruvic transaminase.

TABLE 1.13. ANEMIAS

	Hemoglobin	Hematocrit	Mean corpuscular volume	Serum iron	Total iron-binding capacity	Transferrin	Reticulocytes
Iron deficiency	↓	↓	↓	↓	↑	↑	↔
B-12, folate deficiency	↓	↓	↑	↑	↓	↓	↔
Iron, plus megaloblastic	↓	↓	↔	↔	↑	↑	↔
Dehydration	↑	↑			↑	↑	↔
Malnutrition	↓ [a]	↓ [a]	↔	↓	↓ ↔	↓	↔
Malabsorption	↓	↓	↑	↔			↔
Liver disease	↓ [a]	↓ [a]	↑	↑	↑	↓ ↔	↔
Kidney disease	↓ [a]	↓ [a]	↔	↓	↓	↓ ↔	↓
Gastrectomy	↓	↓	↑ ↔	↔	↑	↑	↔
Small-bowel surgery	↓	↓	↑	↑	↓ ↔	↓ ↔	↔
Blood loss	↓↓	↓↓	↓↓	↓	↑	↑	↑
Sepsis	↓ [a]	↓ [a]	↔	↓	↓ ↔	↓	↔

Source: Quality Assurance Committee, Dietitians in Critical Care Dietetic Practice Group (79).
[a]Mild decrease.

sensitivity of serum albumin for the prediction of postoperative complications is 10% (39, 84–86).

ii. Serum Transferrin Transferrin is synthesized by the liver and is located almost totally intravascularly. It serves as the iron transport protein and is frequently used as an indicator of visceral protein status. Because of its shorter half-life (8 days), smaller body pool, and more rapid response to short-term changes in protein status, transferrin is a more sensitive indicator of protein depletion than albumin is. But transferrin is also affected by a variety of factors, making its interpretation difficult. The average serum concentration is 295 mg per 100 mL. Concentrations between 100 and 200 mg per 100 mL are marginal, whereas those below 100 mg per 100 mL indicate severe depletion.

Serum transferrin concentrations are decreased with liver disease, iron overload, fluid overload, or vitamin A deficiency. Increased serum transferrin concentrations occur with iron-deficiency anemia, hypoxia, chronic blood loss, pregnancy, and the use of oral contracep-

tives or estrogen (87). In cases in which both iron deficiency and chronic protein-energy malnutrition are identified or suspected, serum transferrin is not an appropriate index of protein status. In such situations, a decreased transferrin concentration may be masked, with transferrin concentration appearing to be increased because of iron deficiency.

Although serum transferrin concentrations can be measured directly, this method is expensive and time-consuming and is seldom done in most laboratories. Instead, transferrin can be estimated indirectly by using one of a number of prediction equations based on total iron binding capacity (88–90). The following formulas depict three different methods for calculating transferrin (TFN) levels from measured total iron-binding capacity (TIBC):

$$\text{TFN} = (\text{TIBC} \times 0.83) - 5.6$$

$$\text{TFN} = (\text{TIBC} \times 0.8) - 43$$

$$\text{TFN} = (\text{TIBC} \times 0.76) + 18$$

The mathematical relationships expressed in these formulas vary with the

assay methods, and it has been recommended that any laboratory deriving serum transferrin concentrations from measured total iron-binding capacity must first determine the specific mathematical relationship that applies to its own laboratory procedures (89, 90).

iii. Serum Thyroxine-Binding Prealbumin Serum thyroxine-binding prealbumin (TBPA) serves as a carrier protein for retinol-binding protein and a transport protein for thyroxine. Its half-life of 2 days and its high specificity make it useful for monitoring short-term changes in visceral protein status. Normal serum levels range from 20 to 50 mg per 100 mL and are determined by overall energy and nitrogen balance (91, 92).

TBPA concentration is influenced by surgical trauma, stress, inflammation, and infection and by liver, gastrointestinal, and renal disease, reducing its specificity as an index of protein status (81). It is not a useful index for critically ill patients, because of its high sensitivity to even minor stress and inflammation. Age and sex, as well as ethnicity and geographical location, may also influence TBPA levels (93). Therefore, it may be necessary to compare TBPA values with control values matched for age, sex, geographical area, and ethnic group.

iv. Retinol-Binding Protein   Retinol-binding protein (RBP) is the carrier protein for retinol and is the smallest of the circulating proteins. Because of its short half-life of 12 hours and its small body pool, it responds rapidly to protein deprivation and to subsequent nutrition therapy.

Like other serum transport proteins, it is affected by various clinical conditions. Serum concentrations are reduced with liver disease, vitamin A deficiency, zinc deficiency, catabolic stress, and hyperthyroidism (81).

v. Fibronectin   The need for specific nutritional markers has resulted in the investigation of other body proteins for their potential use in nutritional assessment. A large-molecular-weight glycoprotein found in plasma, lymph, and tissue fluid, fibronectin has been investigated as a potential early indicator of protein depletion. Malnourished patients with burns, sepsis, and trauma have significantly decreased levels of fibronectin. It has a half-life of less than 20 hours and may be essential for recovery from infection (94, 95).

Increased fibronectin concentrations without similar changes in serum prealbumin levels, or decreases in both, are not specific. Changes may be due to worsening malnutrition, another concurrent illness, or inflammatory conditions. When both prealbumin and fibronectin are increased, however, they serve as a reliable short-term indicator of the efficacy of nutritional therapy. During the first week of enteral or parenteral feeding, plasma fibronectin rises to near-normal levels, but in subsequent weeks, there are no additional increases to correlate either with the clinical evidence of nutritional rehabilitation or with changes

in other serum proteins. Therefore, the usefulness of this measure in the assessment process is limited to short-term follow-up (95–97).

vi. Ribonuclease C   A preliminary report indicates an association between concentrations of circulatory ribonuclease C and the degree of malnutrition in cancer patients. Further evaluation of the potential use of ribonuclease C as a nutritional marker is indicated (98).

vii. Insulin-like Growth Factor I   The insulin-like growth factors are a family of peptides that may mediate the growth-promoting effects of growth hormone (GH). Insulin-like growth factor I (IGF-I), also called somatomedin C, parallels changes in urinary urea nitrogen that occur after fasting and refeeding (99). This protein may be a useful indicator of the nutritional results of refeeding malnourished individuals.

B. Immune Function   Although immunological parameters cannot identify specific nutrient deficiencies, immunocompetence can be used as a functional index of nutritional status. Because the immune system is impaired by nutrient deficiencies, several immunological tests can be utilized to identify or verify a malnourished state.

i. Total Lymphocyte Count   Lymphocyte cells are a type of white blood cell involved in the production of antibodies. The measurement of total lymphocyte cells (TLC) can be used as a screening tool to identify malnutrition and evaluate immune function. TLC is derived from the percentage of lymphocytes and the white blood cell (WBC) count, both readily available from a routine complete blood count.

$$\text{Total lymphocyte count} = \frac{\text{percentage of lymphocytes} \times \text{WBC count}}{100}$$

A TLC above 2,750 cells/mm^3 is considered normal, levels between 900 and

1,500 indicate moderate depletion, and levels below 900 represent severe depletion (100).

The total lymphocyte count should not be used as an absolute indicator of nutritional status, because numerous conditions can affect its results. The white cell count can be decreased by a viral infection, for example, and increased by tissue necrosis or other types of infection. It is also decreased by the administration of immunosuppressive medications such as steroids and chemotherapeutic agents, by radiotherapy, and by drugs such as Temaril, Tagamet, penicillin, Dalmane, Lasix, phenothiazines, sulfonamides, phenylbutazone, chloramphenicol, and topical silver sulfadiazine (39).

ii. Delayed-Hypersensitivity Skin Testing   Delayed-hypersensitivity skin testing measures the response to an intradermal injection of an antigen to which an individual has been exposed. Failure to elicit a swelling response around the injection site reflects the inability to mount an immune response, also referred to as anergy. Anergy is common in malnourished individuals with protein or energy deprivation and in cases of nutrient deficiency, including deficiencies of vitamin A, zinc, iron, and vitamin B-6. Although malnutrition is one of many factors affecting immunocompetence, it may not be the sole cause of anergy. If malnutrition or a nutrient deficiency is the primary cause of anergy, the skin response is restored after nutritional rehabilitation.

The usefulness of delayed-hypersensitivity skin testing in the clinical setting is limited by various drugs, diseases, and treatments, as well as the variability in administering and interpreting results (101).

A modification of the skin-testing method has been proposed as an assessment tool for zinc status. Zinc deficiency affects the T cell system and produces lymphocytopenia and a delayed hyper-

TABLE 1.14. IDEAL URINARY CREATININE VALUES

Men		Women	
Height (cm)	Ideal creatinine (mg)	Height (cm)	Ideal creatinine (mg)
157.5	1,288	147.3	830
160.0	1,325	149.9	851
162.6	1,359	152.4	875
165.1	1,386	154.9	900
167.6	1,426	157.5	925
170.2	1,467	160.0	949
172.7	1,513	162.6	977
175.3	1,555	165.1	1,006
177.8	1,596	167.6	1,044
180.3	1,642	170.2	1,076
182.9	1,691	172.7	1,109
185.4	1,739	175.3	1,141
188.0	1,785	177.8	1,174
190.5	1,831	180.3	1,206
193.0	1,891	182.9	1,240

Source: Blackburn, G. L., Bristian, B. R., et al. (100).

Note: Creatinine coefficient for men = 23 mg/kg of ideal body weight; creatinine coefficient for women = 18 mg/kg of ideal body weight.

sensitivity reaction (DHR) (102). The ability of the addition of topical zinc to enhance the DHR response to skin antigens may be a simple method of evaluation of functional zinc status. Further testing is needed, however, to determine the specificity and the sensitivity of this technique.

C. Somatic Protein

i. Creatinine Height Index The 24-hour excretion of urinary creatinine is used to assess the degree of muscle mass depletion (103). Creatinine is derived from the catabolism of creatine phosphate, a metabolite present in skeletal muscle. In the presence of normal renal function, urinary creatinine excretion can be used as an index of skeletal muscle mass (104). The actual daily urinary

creatinine excretion may be compared with an ideal value from table 1.14 to compute the creatinine height index and a percent deficit, as follows:

Creatinine height index (CHI) =
$$\frac{\text{measured 24-hour urinary creatinine} \times 100\%}{\text{ideal 24-hour urinary creatinine}}$$
Percent deficit = 100% − CHI

A percent deficit of 5% to 15% represents a mild deficit; 15% to 30%, a moderate deficit; and greater than 30%, a severe deficit. Blackburn et al. suggest that a CHI index of 60% to 80% indicates a moderate deficit in muscle mass, whereas an index less than 60% represents a severe deficit (100); these interpretive values should be used with caution, however, because they have not been validated.

Despite its apparent usefulness as an index of somatic protein reserves, the CHI is limited by a number of factors. Ideal urinary creatinine values are calculated on the basis of a medium frame size, making it difficult to extrapolate the values to individuals with small or large frames. Accurate measurement of the CHI requires the collection of a complete 24-hour urine sample, which can be difficult to obtain in the acute-care hospital setting. In addition, the use of the CHI may not be valid in the elderly, because of decreases in the glomerular filtration rate and reduced creatine production from the loss of muscle mass associated with aging, both of which result in decreased creatinine excretion. Thus, if norms based upon standards developed for young adults are being used to calculate the CHI for the elderly, the severity of the losses of lean body mass may be overestimated. Ingestion of creatine and creatinine found in meat can influence urinary creatinine values. Also, when kidney function is impaired, creatinine clearance may be decreased. Steroids, tobramycin sulfate, and Mandol may decrease creatinine clearance (39, 104–106).

ii. 3-Methylhistidine Another index of muscle mass and turnover rate is the urinary excretion of 3-methylhistidine. Present almost exclusively in myofibrillar protein, it is formed by the methylation of histidine residues after synthesis of actin and myosin peptide chains and is excreted in the urine during protein breakdown. Because dietary meat yields 3-methylhistidine during digestion, a diet free of meat and meat stock is required for 3 days prior to the urine collections (107). The test may be useful for the nutritional assessment of relatively healthy populations. The metabolic changes following injury and infection cause variations in the urinary excretion of 3-methylhistidine that limit its usefulness in the acute-care setting.

D. Nitrogen Balance A nitrogen balance study can be performed to compare nitrogen intake with nitrogen losses for assessment of net protein catabolism or anabolism. This method of evaluating the net changes in total body protein mass aids the clinician in determining the effectiveness of nutritional therapies and in calculating actual protein requirements.

The method for calculating nitrogen balance is based on the assumption that almost all of the body's nitrogen is incorporated into protein and that visceral and somatic proteins are degraded and synthesized at a fairly constant rate. Thus, comparing measured actual nitrogen loss with actual intake provides an index whereby energy and protein needs can be evaluated. In healthy adults with adequate protein intakes, no net change in total body protein mass is observed—a state referred to as nitrogen equilibrium. Anabolic states such as pregnancy, growth, and nutritional repletion are associated with positive nitrogen balance, or a net increase in body protein mass. Catabolic states are associated with a net decrease in protein mass, or a negative nitrogen balance; these conditions may include trauma, stress, and inadequate protein intake. If negative nitrogen balance persists, all body organ systems will eventually be adversely affected.

Nitrogen intake is calculated from actual protein intake over the same 24-hour period in which the urine is collected for measurement of the urinary urea nitrogen. Because protein is about 16% nitrogen, nitrogen intake is calculated as protein intake (g) divided by 6.25. Considerable error can be introduced if protein intake from parenteral formulas, commercial enteral formulas, or an oral diet is not recorded or is not calculated accurately. Accuracy and completeness of the 24-hour urine sample are also imperative for a valid estimate of nitrogen balance. The use of 4-aminobenzoic acid tablets given with meals has been proposed as a method of checking the completeness of 24-hour urine collections (108, 109).

Numerous limitations to nitrogen balance studies have been identified, as have conditions for which this method of assessing protein adequacy is appropriate (110). These limitations should be carefully studied prior to initiating a nitrogen balance study. An easy-to-use nomogram has been published for estimating nitrogen balance (111). Nitrogen balance can also be calculated by the following formula (39):

Estimated nitrogen balance (g) =
$$\frac{\text{protein intake (g)}}{6.25} -$$
[urinary urea nitrogen (g) + 4]

In patients with unstable renal function, nitrogen balance can be more accurately determined by the use of urea kinetics, which takes into consideration changes in blood urea nitrogen. Formulas for the estimation of nitrogen balance using urea kinetics are included in the Appendix (see "Using Urea Nitrogen Appearance in Nutritional Assessment").

Nitrogen excretion may vary with periods of activity, rest, feeding, and fast-ing. Nitrogen balance data obtained over a 24-hour period are reliable under the conditions of clinical, nutritional, and environmental steady state. For clinical investigations, however, shorter balance periods may lack precision because of diurnal variations in urea excretion (108).

E. Vitamin and Mineral Status   It may be desirable to monitor vitamin and mineral status, especially in cases in which poor absorption or increased need are suspected. Serum levels may be measured, or functional indices, such as enzyme activities, may be used. Table 1.12 gives criteria for evaluation of test results. Detailed discussions of assessment of vitamin and mineral status have been published (112).

F. Composite Nutrition Risk Indices   A composite of several nutrition indexes may be combined to permit a quantitative biometric estimate of nutrition-related risks that attempts to relate nutritional status to operative outcome. Developed at the University of Pennsylvania, the prognostic nutritional index (PNI) quantitatively estimates the risk of operative complications for an individual patient, using the following equation:

$$\text{PNI}(\%) = 158 - 16.6(\text{ALB}) - 0.78(\text{TSF}) - 0.2(\text{TFN}) - 5.8(\text{DH})$$

where PNI = risk of complications, ALB = serum albumin (g/100 mL), TFN = serum transferrin (mg/100 mL), TSF = triceps skinfold measurement (mm), and DH = delayed hypersensitivity or maximal skin reactivity to any one of three recall antigens (0 = nonreactive, and 1 = less than 5 mm induration reactivity, and 2 = 5 mm or more reactivity). The predictive ability and interpretation of the index have been discussed elsewhere (113, 114).

G. Hair Analysis   When chronic or long-term exposure to heavy metals such as cadmium, arsenic, mercury, and, in particular, lead is suspected, hair analysis is an appropriate tool. As a nutritional assessment tool, however, it has many pitfalls, including contamination by sweat, results that may differ depending upon the rate of hair growth, lack of clear definition of a normal range, critical dependence upon location of the hair sample, and use of hair treatments (115, 116).

4. DIETARY INTAKE DATA

There are several methods of assessing nutrient intake, each of which has advantages and limitations. It is important to choose the method best suited to the type of data required. Also, the limitations must be understood in order to minimize their effects and interpret data appropriately. A brief overview of methods of collection, analysis, and interpretation of data follows.

A. Data Collection   Data may be collected through recall or records. Recall, or retrospective reports, has the advantage that clients are not alerted in advance and thus do not alter their usual eating habits. Recall does depend upon the memory, motivation, and awareness of the client, however, as well as on the client's ability to estimate portion sizes. Record keeping, on the other hand, tends to increase consciousness of eating behavior. Clients may be tempted to change their usual pattern of intake for ease of recording or to create a favorable impression (117).

i. 24-Hour Diet Recall   The client, parent, or caregiver is asked to report all foods consumed during the last 24 hours or on the previous day, including detailed descriptions of all foods, beverages, cooking methods, brand names, condiments, and supplements, with portion sizes in household measurements. A sample form for a 24-hour recall is given in figure 1.7. This method has the advantage that it takes only 15 to 20 minutes and can be used for patients of any age.

FIG. 1.7. SAMPLE 24-HOUR RECALL FORM.

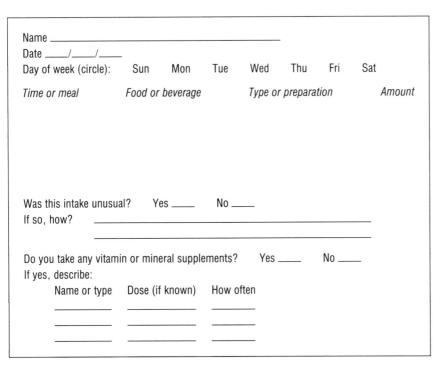

It can be self-administered but can also be obtained by interview or even by telephone (118), so literacy is not required. Food models, measuring cups, life-size pictures, or abstract shapes may be used to assist in estimation of portion size. Such recalls can be valuable as a screening tool and as a basis for counseling, especially if combined with questions about usual intake. They can also be used during follow-up to evaluate adaptation to dietary recommendations. It is important, however, not to draw unwarranted conclusions about usual eating habits or dietary status from a single recall. Intakes fluctuate daily, so one day may not be representative of the actual diet (9, 119).

ii. Food Frequencies A checklist is completed indicating whether specified foods (usually 40 to 80) are eaten and how often. If portion sizes are not included, the questionnaire provides qualitative data. The frequency questionnaire may be made quantitative by including portion sizes on the form. A typical de-

sign for a simple frequency checklist is given in figure 1.8, and a more quantitative questionnaire in figure 1.9. Extensive food lists become tedious to complete, a situation that tends to decrease the quality of the data obtained. Limited lists, however, tend to be less representative of total intake. It is important to use a food frequency checklist that reflects cultural and ethnic food practices of the individual client. Food frequencies can

provide valuable information on usual intakes and may be used as a basis for counseling or as a measure of change in dietary habits over time. Computerized checklists are now available. They save time but suggest an unwarranted degree of precision, especially if the computer is programmed to make dietary recommendations without professional input and judgment (9, 118).

iii. Food Records All foods, beverages, snacks, and supplements are recorded, usually over a period of 1 to 7 days. In the clinical setting, household measures are used. For research purposes, actual weights may be recorded to provide a greater degree of precision, but doing that increases the burden on the client. Devices that link a digital scale to a computer with interactive software have been shown to be helpful in obtaining accurate food records and reducing time spent in analysis (119). When using household measurements, training with food models, measuring cups, life-size pictures, or abstract shapes has been found to be helpful in increasing the accuracy of portion sizes. Cooking methods, recipe ingredients, and descriptions should be as complete and detailed as possible. Record keeping may influence customary food choices to varying degrees, but in some cases this effect may be desirable if records form part of be-

FIG. 1.8. SAMPLE DESIGN FOR A SIMPLE FOOD FREQUENCY CHECKLIST.

Indicate how often you eat each of the following foods by checking one box for each.

Food	Daily	Weekly	Monthly	Yearly	Never
Ground beef	☐	☐	☐	☐	☐
Other beef	☐	☐	☐	☐	☐
Pork	☐	☐	☐	☐	☐
Ham	☐	☐	☐	☐	☐
Bacon	☐	☐	☐	☐	☐
Lamb	☐	☐	☐	☐	☐
Poultry	☐	☐	☐	☐	☐
Fish	☐	☐	☐	☐	☐
Eggs	☐	☐	☐	☐	☐
Legumes	☐	☐	☐	☐	☐
Nuts	☐	☐	☐	☐	☐
[etc.]					

FIG. 1.9. SAMPLE DESIGN FOR A QUANTITATIVE FOOD FREQUENCY QUESTIONNAIRE.

For each food, indicate the number of given servings you would eat and how often you would eat it. For example, if you drink a 12-oz. glass of orange juice 5 times each week, enter "2" under "Number of servings" and "5" under "Week?" as shown.

Food	Serving size	Number of servings	How many times per day?	week?	month?
Example:					
Orange juice	6 oz.	☑ 2	☐	☑ 5	☐
Apple or pear	1 medium	☐	☐	☐	☐
Applesauce	½ cup	☐	☐	☐	☐
Apple juice	6 oz.	☐	☐	☐	☐
Apricot or peach	1 medium	☐	☐	☐	☐
Cantaloupe	¼ medium	☐	☐	☐	☐
Grapefruit	½ medium	☐	☐	☐	☐
Grapefruit juice	6 oz.	☐	☐	☐	☐
Orange	1 medium	☐	☐	☐	☐
Orange juice	6 oz.	☐	☐	☐	☐
Strawberries	1 cup	☐	☐	☐	☐
Watermelon	1 slice	☐	☐	☐	☐
[etc.]					

havioral change strategies. In such situations the record may include locations, times, events, and feelings in addition to the foods eaten, in order to identify behavioral as well as strictly nutritional patterns. A 7-day record is considered optimal to account for weekly variations in intake, especially if results are to be compared with biochemical parameters. A longer period may become tedious, depending on the commitment and motivation of the individual. Shorter periods are less representative of usual intake but can be improved by including proportional numbers of weekend days (for example, 2 weekdays and 1 weekend day for a 3-day record). The need for literate, numerate, well-motivated clients may limit collection of food records (9, 118).

iv. Calorie Counts In the hospital or institutional setting, the most common form of food record is a calorie count. In practice, both caloric and protein intakes are usually quantified. Additional nutrients can be computed if computer analysis is available. Data from calorie counts are used to document the need for nutritional support or the adequacy of oral intake. Such important issues warrant development and implementation of well-defined procedures to ensure collection of accurate data. The patient, family, and nursing staff must all be aware of the need to record all foods, beverages, and supplements taken, whether provided by the hospital or brought from outside. The staff member responsible for recording intake, whether the nurse, nursing aide, or food service aide, should be appropriately trained. The amount of each item actually eaten may be recorded on the tray menu or on separate forms and placed in the chart or in an envelope on the door or the patient's bed. The period most commonly used to account for daily variation is 3 days.

v. Dietary History A 24-hour dietary recall is combined with questions about usual intake, likes, dislikes, and food habits. Nutrition questionnaires for use with different age groups have been published elsewhere (120). A food frequency checklist or food record may also be included as a cross-check. If a wide variety of foods are eaten, a food record may be more useful than a frequency questionnaire (121). The combination of methods is intended to overcome the limitations of each method and to identify inconsistencies. Data collection can be time-consuming for the dietitian, however, and it requires an observant client. Also, the interpretation of combined data has not been standardized (9, 117).

vi. Interviewing Skills It is important to establish rapport with the client in order to increase cooperation, motivation, and accurate reports. A nonjudgmental attitude of respect and understanding is especially important for meaningful communication. An explanation of the reason for data collection should always be communicated. Tactful probing may minimize omissions, especially if the interviewer understands the client's cultural food heritage (117).

B. Data Analysis The method for analysis of nutrient intake should be appropriate to the method of data collection. Nutrient analysis software should be reviewed for its appropriateness. Although it is tempting to obtain detailed analysis of several nutrients, this strategy may not be justified, depending on the accuracy and completeness of the recall or record. For less precise data, either a simpler method of analysis should be used or the lack of precision should be considered in interpretation of the data.

i. Food Scoring Food scoring is simple and fast and may therefore be useful for immediate analysis as a basis for counseling. Foods may be scored according to food groups or specific foods. The method may be superficial and insensitive and is not applicable to unconventional or hospital liquid diets. It can be used to monitor changes in intakes over time, however. One form of scoring involves the use of exchange values. These values may be used to quantify data from calorie counts, especially if computer analysis is not available. Exchanges may also be used to evaluate compliance to meal plans for weight reduction, diabetes, or renal disease (117).

ii. Food Composition Tables and Data Bases Tables provide values for the nutrient content of foods. Most tables are based on U.S. Department of Agriculture data, incorporating recipes and manufacturer information. The most commonly used table in clinical practice is Bowes and Church's "Food Values of Portions Commonly Used" (122). Various ethnic tables are also available.

Food composition tables are limited by the inherent variability in nutrient content of foods according to season, variety, growing conditions, processing, and treatment. Chemical analysis is time-consuming and expensive. Methods may vary, giving different results with different degrees of precision. Terminology for certain nutrients is inconsistent. Also, tables list the total amount of a nutrient present without taking into account its availability to the body, a factor that will affect the amount absorbed. Hand calculations from food tables are tedious, and dietary analysis has been made much more readily available by use of computer software programs.

Computerized nutrient data bases vary according to their sources, comprehensiveness, currentness, and size. It is important to research the completeness of the data base and to be aware of the method used by the various programs to compute missing values. Some data bases leave blanks that are calculated as zero. This procedure may result in a diet analysis that looks deficient but is merely based on incomplete data. Other data bases use an estimated value. The appropriateness of a data base will depend on the use of the data (9, 117).

C. Data Interpretation It is important not to infer too much from impressive analysis of imperfect data. The method of collection and analysis must be considered at the time of interpretation.

i. Recommended Dietary Allowances Recommended Dietary Allowances (RDAS) are often used as an index of dietary adequacy. RDAS, however, are "the levels of intake of essential nutrients that, on the basis of scientific knowledge, are judged by the Food and Nutrition Board to be adequate to meet the known nutrient needs of practically all healthy persons" (123). The 10th edition of the RDAS emphasizes that they do not cover individuals with special nutrient needs, so they may not be appropriate as a standard for many individuals in the clinical setting. The RDAS are neither minimal requirements nor optimal levels of intake. They represent safe and adequate intake levels, incorporating margins of safety intended to encompass the presumed variability in requirement among people. Therefore a lesser intake does not necessarily mean deficiency. RDAS are also intended to reflect average intake over time and thus should not be used to evaluate intake on a single day. A standard often used is that if intake is consistently below two-thirds of the RDA, the individual may be at risk of deficiency, although biochemical or other confirmation would be necessary

ii. Food Group Plans Results of dietary analysis may be compared with various food group plans to determine dietary adequacy, such as the Dietary Guidelines for Americans, the Basic Four, or other plans appropriate to the ethnic or cultural group or prescribed for a specific disease. Such an evaluation can be made rapidly, allowing for immediate feedback as a basis for counseling or for determining dietary compliance. A food group guide with suggested numbers and sizes of portions assumes that a variety of foods are chosen within each

group to ensure dietary adequacy. Professional interpretation is therefore important with this method (120).

iii. Calculated Needs In the clinical setting, intake may be compared with calculated needs for energy, protein, fluid, and other nutrients. This comparison allows for an individual determination of adequacy, according to the disease state. Calculation of nutritional needs will be discussed in detail below, in the section "Needs Assessment."

5. DRUG-NUTRIENT INTERACTIONS

The amount and rate of drug absorption can be affected by composition and timing of the diet. Conversely, food intake, body weight, and nutritional laboratory parameters can be altered by medications. The Joint Commission on Accreditation of Healthcare Organizations (JCAHO) strongly recommends evaluation of drug and diet combinations as part of nutritional screening, with subsequent counseling when appropriate.

In clinical practice, actual occurrence and significance of drug-nutrient adverse reactions may vary, depending upon the patient's physical and metabolic status and accompanying conditions. Drug-nutrient reactions have the potential to reduce drug efficacy, to interfere with disease control, to promote nutritional deficiencies, to influence food intake, or to induce a toxic reaction (124). The risk of adverse outcomes due to drug-nutrient interactions depends on the clinical condition, which influences the prescribed drug and diet therapy. Practitioners should be familiar with the nutritional effects of new drugs and should counsel patients on the potential effects of documented drug-nutrient reactions to reduce incidence of adverse reactions. An excellent and complete resource is available for evaluating drug-nutrient interactions, based on disease state (124). Documentation of counseling on drug-nutrient interactions is an essential component of complying with JCAHO standards.

6. PSYCHOSOCIAL DATA

For a complete assessment of nutritional risk, the client or caregiver should be interviewed to determine economic, physical, or emotional barriers to adequate food intake. These barriers may include visual impairment, loss of manual dexterity, fatigue or weakness, lack of transportation, inadequate financial resources, poor cooking or food storage facilities, depression, or loneliness. Tact and assurance of confidentiality are necessary to obtain accurate information without embarrassment.

In children, obesity or eating disorders may often reflect psychosocial patterns in the home. In such cases, nutritional intervention will be ineffective without input from a social worker or psychologist.

NEEDS ASSESSMENT

1. ENERGY

A. Calculated Estimates In the clinical setting, it is not usually possible to measure metabolic rate by indirect calorimetry. Therefore energy expenditure is estimated from formulas.

i. The Harris-Benedict Equation The Harris-Benedict equation (HBE) is a formula that uses age, height, and weight to estimate basal energy expenditure (BEE). BEE is the minimum amount of energy needed by the body at rest in the fasting state. The mathematical relationships in the formula were developed by Harris and Benedict from oxygen consumption measurements using a gas analyzer and are represented as follows (125):

In men:
BEE (kcal/day) = 66.5 + (13.8 × W) + (5.0 × H) − (6.8 × A)

In women:
BEE (kcal/day) = 655.1 + (9.6 × W) + (1.8 × H) − (4.7 × A)

where W = weight (kg), H = height (cm), and A = age (years).

Because it is difficult to achieve conditions for measurement of BEE, resting energy expenditure (REE) is often used

instead. REE is the energy expenditure under conditions similar to those for BEE except after eating (taking into account the specific dynamic action or thermal effect of food) or exercise. When ver-

FIG. 1.10. RESTING ENERGY EXPENDITURE FOR MALES.

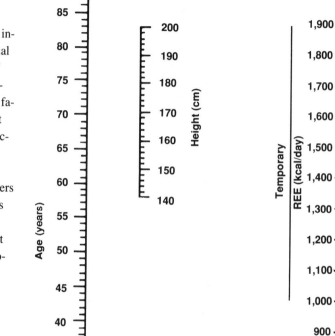

Directions

1. Locate the height and weight on their respective scales, placing a straightedge (ruler) between these points, intersecting the temporary variable time.
2. Holding a pencil at the point of intersection (on temporary variable line), locate the age and pivot the straightedge to this point on the age scale. The point of intersection on the REE scale is the predicted REE.

Source: Rainey-MacDonald, C. G., Holliday, R. L., and Wells, G. A. (128).

FIG. 1.11. RESTING ENERGY EXPENDITURE FOR FEMALES.

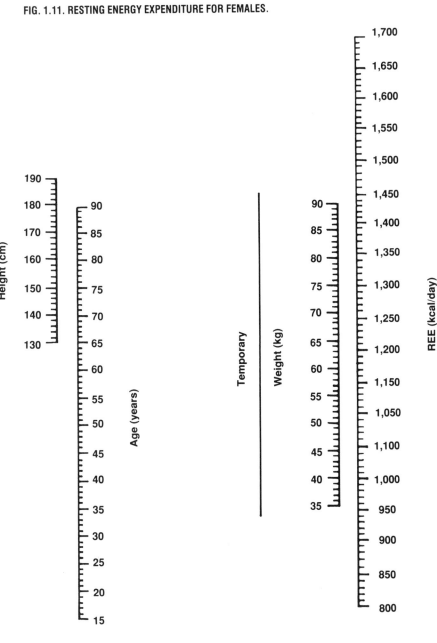

Height (cm)

Age (years)

Temporary

Weight (kg)

REE (kcal/day)

Directions
See figure 1.10.

Source: Rainey-MacDonald, C. G., Holliday, R. L., and Wells, G. A. (128).

penditure were therefore derived from data from 480 healthy subjects (129).

In men:
REE (kcal/day) = (9.99 × W) + (6.25 × H) − (4.92 × A) + 5

In women:
REE (kcal/day) = (9.99 × W) + (6.25 × H) − (4.92 × A) − 161

ii. Total Daily Energy Expenditure or Total Metabolic Energy Expenditure The BEE as derived from the Harris-Benedict equation is multiplied by an activity and an injury factor to predict the total daily energy expenditure (TDE) or the total metabolic energy expenditure (TME), as follows (130):

TDE (kcal/day) = BEE (HBE) × activity factor × injury factor

Activity factor

Confined to bed = 1.2
Out of bed = 1.3

Injury factor

Surgery:
  Minor = 1.0–1.1
  Major = 1.1–1.2
Infection:
  Mild = 1.0–1.2
  Moderate = 1.2–1.4
  Severe = 1.4–1.8
Trauma:
  Skeletal = 1.20–1.35
  Blunt = 1.15–1.35
  Head trauma treated with steroids = 1.6
Burns (BSA = body surface area):
  Up to 20% BSA = 1.0–1.5
  20–40% BSA = 1.5–1.85
  More than 40% BSA = 1.85–1.95

Source: Long, C. L. (130), by permission of Blackwell Scientific Publications, Inc.

ified by direct calorimetry and 2 different indirect calorimeters, the Harris-Benedict equation has recently been shown to overestimate BEE by 10% to 15%, giving a figure closer to REE (126). On this basis, Long has proposed that the Harris-Benedict equation be used to measure REE instead of BEE (127). Nomograms

for measuring REE (as opposed to BEE) have been developed based upon the Harris-Benedict equation and are included as figures 1.10 and 1.11.

Several authors have stated that the Harris-Benedict equation overestimates energy expenditure. The following alternative equations for resting energy ex-

iii. Energy Expenditure per Square Meter of Body Surface Area To calculate energy needs, one first determines body surface area (BSA) in square meters from height and weight using either figure 1.12, the Mayo Clinic nomogram for calculating BSA, or a similar tool (131, 132).

To calculate BEE in calories per hour

for a specific age, the surface area is multiplied by the estimated calories used per square meter per hour (cal/m²/hr; kilocalories per square meter per 24 hours are given in table 1.15). This basal value can be multiplied by 24 hours to give calories/day and by activity and injury factors as above for TDE.

Instead of the table, either of two sets of equations may be used to estimate basal energy expenditure (also referred to as basal metabolic rate, or BMR) based on body surface area and age (134). The first set of equations is from Wilmore and Fleisch (133, 134):

Up to and including age 19:
$$\text{BMR (kcal)} = (55 - \text{age}) \times \text{BSA (m}^2) \times 24$$

More than 20 years of age:
$$\text{BMR (kcal)} = (37 - \frac{\text{age} - 20}{10}) \times \text{BSA (m}^2) \times 24$$

The second set of equations is from Boothby (135):

TABLE 1.15. METABOLIC RATES IN MALES AND FEMALES, BASED ON BODY SURFACE AREA

Age (years)	kcal/m²/24 hr	
	Males	Females
1	1,272	1,272
2	1,258	1,258
3	1,231	1,229
4	1,207	1,195
5	1,183	1,162
6	1,159	1,128
7	1,135	1,090
8	1,111	1,051
9	1,085	1,027
10	1,056	1,020
11	1,032	1,008
12	1,020	991
13	1,015	967
14	1,010	941
15	1,003	910
16	994	886
17	979	871
18	960	862
19	941	852
20	926	847
25	900	845
30	883	842
35	876	840
40	871	838
45	869	828
50	859	814
55	850	799
60	838	785
65	826	773
70	811	761
75 and over	797	751

Source: Murray, R. L. (133).

For men 20 through 74 years of age:
$$\text{BMR (kcal)} = [43.66 - (0.1329 \times \text{age in years})] \times \text{BSA (m}^2) \times 24$$

For women 20 through 74 years of age:
$$\text{BMR (kcal)} = [38.65 - (0.0909 \times \text{age in years})] \times \text{BSA (m}^2) \times 24$$

iv. Energy Needs Based on Weight and Activity Level A prediction of energy needs may be based on weight in kilograms and adjusted for activity level as follows (136):

FIG. 1.12. MAYO CLINIC NOMOGRAM FOR CALCULATING BODY SURFACE AREA.

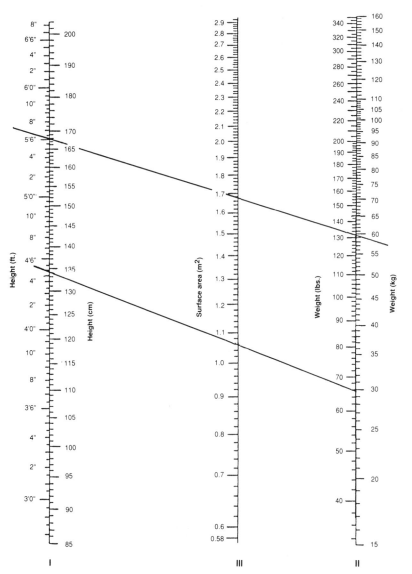

Source: Walker, W. A., and Hendricks, K. M. (131); reprinted by permission of Macmillan Publishing Company from Pike, R. L., and Brown, M. L. (132). Copyright © 1975 by Macmillan Publishing Company.

TABLE 1.16. BASAL METABOLIC RATES FOR INFANTS AND CHILDREN

Age 1 week to 10 months		Age 11 to 36 months			Age 3 to 16 years		
Weight (kg)	Metabolic rate[a] (kcal/hr) Male or female	Weight (kg)	Metabolic rate (kcal/hr) Male	Female	Weight (kg)	Metabolic rate (kcal/hr) Male	Female
3.5	8.4	9.0	22.0	21.2	15	35.8	33.3
4.0	9.5	9.5	22.8	22.0	20	39.7	37.4
4.5	10.5	10.0	23.6	22.8	25	43.6	41.5
5.0	11.6	10.5	24.4	23.6	30	47.5	45.5
5.5	12.7	11.0	25.2	24.4	35	51.3	49.6
6.0	13.8	11.5	26.0	25.2	40	55.2	53.7
6.5	14.9	12.0	26.8	26.0	45	59.1	57.8
7.0	16.0	12.5	27.6	26.9	50	63.0	61.9
7.5	17.1	13.0	28.4	27.7	55	66.9	66.0
8.0	18.2	13.5	29.2	28.5	60	70.8	70.0
8.5	19.3	14.0	30.0	29.3	65	74.7	74.0
9.0	20.4	14.5	30.8	30.1	70	78.6	78.1
9.5	21.4	15.0	31.6	30.9	75	82.5	82.2
10.0	22.5	15.5	32.4	31.7			
10.5	23.6	16.0	33.2	32.6			
11.0	24.7	16.5	34.0	33.4			

Source: Walker, W. A., and Hendricks, K. M. (131); *from* Altman, P. L., and Dittmer, D. S. (157).

Note: To calculate basic metabolic rate (BMR): (1) Determine age of patient, and locate appropriate column on table; (2) find weight of child (in kilograms), and read across to appropriate sex; (3) read kcal/hr, and multiply by 24 to determine daily BMR.

[a]There is only one BMR for children of either sex at ages 1 week to 10 months.

	Energy needs (kcal/kg)		
	Sedentary	Moderate	Active
Overweight	20–25	30	35
Normal	30	35	40
Underweight	30	40	45–50

v. Energy Needs by Weight for Children Less than 6 Years of Age Calculation of surface area is difficult in infants and small children. Their BEE can be measured by using table 1.16, which gives kcal/hr by weight for children who are close to their ideal weight.

Example: A 23-month-old male infant weighs 12 kg and is 82 cm long. For a male infant at 12 kg, the hourly BMR is 26.8 cal/hr.
26.8 kcal/hr × 24 hours = 643 kcal

The infant's basal caloric needs are 643 kcal/day.

Extra calories will be needed, depending upon the level of activity:

- 10% for bed rest and nursing procedures
- 30% for light activity such as sitting or working with hands
- 50% for moderate activity such as standing
- 75% for heavy activity such as vigorous play

vi. Energy Needs in Thermal Injuries Patients with burns are often hypermetabolic. Several formulas have been proposed to calculate caloric requirements in order to avoid wasting, taking into account burn surface area, body size, and a stress factor. Many of the formulas have been found to overestimate actual energy needs. More recently the Toronto formula (TF) has been found to be a closer estimate. The only factor not built into the formula is activity, which the authors suggest warrants further research. The formula is as follows (137):

$$TF = -4,343 + (10.5 \times \%TBSA) + (0.23 \times CI) + (0.84 \times BEE) + (114 \times Temp) - (4.5 \times PBD)$$

where %TBSA = percentage of total burn surface area, estimated on admission and corrected where amputation is performed; CI = patient's caloric intake (in calories) in the previous 24 hours, including all dextrose infusions and parenteral and enteral feedings; Temp = average hourly rectal temperature of the previous 24 hours in degrees centigrade; and PBD = number of postburn days as of the day prior to the study (that is, not counting the day of the study).

The Curreri formula was widely used but has been criticized for overestimation of caloric needs. The following modified Curreri formula is easier to use than the Toronto formula but may still estimate a higher value than the actual requirement:

$$Mod\ Curreri = (20 \times weight) + (40 \times \%TBSA)$$

where %TBSA reaches a maximum value of 50 (137).

vii. REE from 24-Hour Urinary Creatinine Researchers have proposed the use of a formula to calculate REE from 24-hour urinary creatinine excretion, as follows (138):

$$REE = (0.488 \times X) + 964$$

where X is 24-hour urinary creatinine expressed in mg. Investigators state that this equation is applicable to both healthy and hospitalized individuals. They assert that it will be a more accurate estimate of energy expenditure than conventional methods based upon height, sex, weight, and age (138, 139).

B. Indirect Calorimetry The technique of measuring REE through indirect calorimetry is used most often in research settings. The use of mobile metabolic carts (MMCS) to assess REE has become more common in the clinical setting, however. Metabolic carts provide information on the volume of oxygen consumed ($\dot{V}O_2$), the volume of carbon dioxide produced ($\dot{V}CO_2$), and the respiratory quotient (RQ) (140).

The respiratory quotient is the ratio of the volume of carbon dioxide produced to the volume of oxygen consumed during the same time interval. A useful indicator of substrate utilization, the RQ normally ranges from 0.7 to 1.0. Fat utilization, as during resting starvation, is reflected by an RQ close to 0.7, whereas an RQ approaching 1.0 suggests carbohydrate utilization. A high carbohydrate intake that exceeds energy expenditure causes the RQ to exceed 1.0, reflecting conversion of carbohydrate to fat (134).

2. PROTEIN

In considering protein needs of hospitalized patients, the increase in catabolic rate of protein that is a characteristic response to injury should be considered. The extent of nitrogen loss following severe injury depends in part on the nutritional status of the individual prior to trauma. Nitrogen loss after injury and infection is less than expected in the elderly and in already depleted individuals (130). In hypermetabolic states a common approach is to determine energy needs and then calculate protein needs using a given kcal:N ratio (usually 100 to 200 kcal per g of nitrogen), depending on stress level and disease state (141). A more precise approach is to use the measures already discussed, such as nitrogen balance studies, to determine actual losses.

Protein requirements may also be

FIG. 1.13. COMPUTATION OF FLUID REQUIREMENTS, BASED ON PATIENT'S SURFACE AREA.

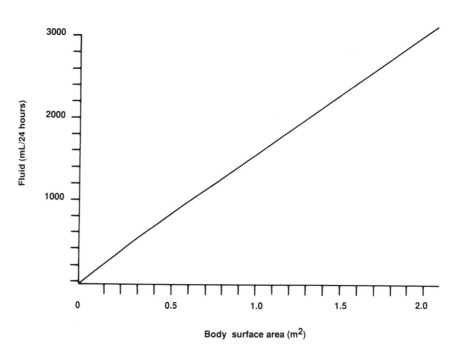

1. Determine the patient's body surface area using height, weight, and figure 1.12. A straightedge connecting the height and the weight will provide surface area.
2. Calculate the patient's 24-hour fluid needs based on surface area by using the chart above.
   Example: Patient: John Doe
   Height: 5′11″
   Weight: 160 lbs.

Body surface area based on height, weight, and figure 1.12 is 1.9 m². The 24-hour fluid requirement, based on body surface area, is approximately 2,800 mL.

An acceptable weight gain for a patient on total parenteral nutrition is 0.23–0.34 kg/day. Any higher amount of weight gain is most likely caused by excessive fluid retention.

Source: Rhode, C. L., and Braun, T. M. (158); *adapted from* Dubois et al. (159). Copyright © 1916, American Medical Association.

based on body weight in kilograms, as follows (142).

	g protein/kg body weight
Normal requirement	0.8
Fever, fracture, infection, wound healing	1.5–2.0
Protein repletion	1.5–2.0
Burns	1.5–3.0

3. FLUID

Normal fluid needs can be calculated by a number of different techniques. One technique suggests that for every calorie fed, 1 mL of water should be provided (143). Another recommends that 1,500 mL water be provided per square meter of body surface area or that an average of 32 mL per kilogram of body weight for adults and 100 to 150 mL per kilogram of body weight for infants be provided

TABLE 1.17. BASELINE DAILY FLUID REQUIREMENTS IN ADULT AND PEDIATRIC PATIENTS

Patient group	Fluid requirement
Children (<16 years)[a]	
0.5–3 kg	120 mL/kg
3–10 kg	100 mL/kg
10–20 kg	1,000 mL plus 50 mL/kg each kg over 10 kg
>20 kg	1,500 mL plus 20 mL/kg each kg over 20 kg
Adults[b]	
Young active (16–30 years)	40 mL/kg
Average adult (25–55 years)	35 mL/kg
Older patients (56–65 years)	30 mL/kg
Elderly (>65 years)	25 mL/kg

Source: Blackburn, G. L., Bell, S. J., and Mullen J. L. (139).

[a]*From* Campbell, S. M.: Practical guide to nutritional care for dietitians and other health care professionals. Birmingham: University of Alabama, 1986; *data from* Robbins, S., Thorp, J. W., and Wadsworth, C.: Tube feedings of infants and children. ASPEN monograph, 1982.

[b]*From* Randall, H. T.: Fluid, electrolyte, and fluid base balance. Surg Clin N Am 56:1019, 1976.

TABLE 1.18. BASELINE FLUID REQUIREMENTS

Method 1

Based on standard body weight for height, sex, and age for obese patients and on actual body weight for others, except infants weighing less than 5 kg:
- First 10 kg of body weight: 100 cc/kg/day
- Second 10 kg of body weight: 50 cc/kg/day
- All weight above 20 kg: 20 cc/kg/day if <50 years; 15 cc/kg/day if >50 years

Example: For a 30-year-old person weighing 50 kg, the calculation is as follows.

$$10 \text{ kg} \times 100 \text{ cc/kg/day} = 1,000 \text{ cc}$$
$$10 \text{ kg} \times 50 \text{ cc/kg/day} = 500 \text{ cc}$$
$$30 \text{ kg} \times 20 \text{ cc/kg/day} = 600 \text{ cc}$$
$$\text{Total fluid requirement} = 2,100 \text{ cc}$$

Method 2

Based on standard body weight for height, sex, and age for obese patients and on actual body weight for others:
- Children over 20 kg: 1,500 cc + 30 cc/kg each kg over 20 kg
- Previously vigorous young adults with large muscle mass: 40 cc/kg/day
- Adults aged 18–55 years: 35 cc/kg/day
- Older patients with no major cardiac or renal disease: 30 cc/kg/day

Source: Quality Assurance Committee, Dietitians in Critical Care Dietetic Practice Group (79).

(144–146). Additional fluid requirements are created by oxygen masks or respirators without humidifiers. Also, fever increases fluid needs by 13% for each degree centigrade above normal.

Baseline fluid requirements are given in tables 1.17 and 1.18 and figure 1.13. Electrolytes present in lost extraneous fluids (table 1.19) may need to be replaced.

Signs of decreased total body water or dehydration include loss of sweat in the axillary area, loss of tissue turgor, increased pulse rate, decreased urinary output, rapid weight loss reflecting loss of extra cellular fluid, elevated blood urea nitrogen levels, a blood urea nitrogen-creatinine ratio of greater than 10:1, hypernatremia, and elevated hematocrit.

4. VITAMINS AND MINERALS

Most computerized nutrient analysis programs in existence today permit the dietitian to analyze individual diets and to estimate the percentage of the Recommended Dietary Allowance for each nutrient provided by the diet. Although this estimate is a good starting point, disease-specific needs of individuals or populations being assessed should always be considered. Examples of published data for specific conditions have already been given. Other sources for clinical dietitians in specialty areas are guidelines published by American Dietetic Association practice groups, such as for renal nutrition therapy (148).

To permit a greater degree of accuracy in recommendations made for specific nutrient levels, a new approach to defining nutrient needs in the next edition of *Recommended Dietary Allowances* has been proposed that would also include vitamin and mineral needs in specific disease states. One proposal is a conceptual framework for the estimation of nutrient needs for different levels of nutriture. Three or more levels are proposed, ranging from a state that represents the presence of ample tissue stores and a state that might represent the presence of nutritional disease. Whether or not the level of intake of a nutrient is considered adequate would thus depend on whether the state of nutriture referred to means a state that borders on overt deficiency or one that includes an ample supply of tissue reserves (149).

TABLE 1.19. ELECTROLYTE CONTENT OF EXTRANEOUS FLUID LOSS

Source	Electrolyte lost (mEq/L)				
	Sodium	Hydrogen	Potassium	Chloride	Bicarbonate
Gastric	40–65	90	10	100–140	
Pancreatic	135–150		5–10	60–75	70–90
Bile	128–160		4–12	90–120	30
Intestinal (jejunum)	95–120		5–15	80–130	10–20
Intestinal (ileum)	110–130		10–20	90–110	20–30
Diarrhea	90–120		5–10	75–120	5–40

Source: Lang, C. E. (147). Copyright © 1987 by Aspen Publishers, Inc.

EVALUATION

1. PATIENT FOLLOW-UP

An integral part of the overall nutritional assessment program is a reevaluation of the patient to determine the effectiveness of nutrition intervention and to provide a basis for any changes. Included in the program should be a plan for patient reassessment at regular intervals. Not every test or measurement performed at the time of the original patient assessment needs to be repeated during follow-up. In fact, the cost-effectiveness of each measurement for the particular population being assessed should be substantiated. Adjustments should be made regularly if it is found that tests are being done too often or that the amount of information received does not justify their frequency. For suggested reevaluation intervals for selected indices of nutritional status, see table 1.20.

2. PROGRAM EVALUATION

Excellent guidelines for the evaluation of nutritional assessment programs have been published elsewhere. Evaluation measures the extent and effects of nutritional assessment services rendered and determines whether the actual results of the program met the stated goals and objectives. Program evaluation addresses the issue of quality assurance by comparing measurements of the results achieved with established criteria. It should focus on the appropriateness, adequacy, effectiveness, efficiency, and side effects of nutritional assessment and interventions (150). It should demonstrate the real value of what has been accomplished and what changes in the program, if any, are needed to improve it.

Nutritional assessment of specific groups of individuals with special needs has not been fully explored here. Guidelines for the nutritional assessment of pediatric patients, pregnant women, patients with spinal cord injuries, and quadriplegic patients, as well as a procedure for determining nitrogen balance for burned patients have been published elsewhere (151–156). Dietitians with such patients should review these materials before starting a nutritional assessment program.

TABLE 1.20. REEVALUATION INTERVALS FOR SELECTED INDICES OF NUTRITIONAL STATUS

Test	Reevaluation intervals
Body weight	Daily
Nutritional analysis of intake	Once a week; daily if computer is available
Skin tests	Every 3 weeks; every 7–10 days in anergic patients
Serum albumin	Every 3 weeks
Serum transferrin	Every 7 days; baseline levels should increase by 10% with effective repletion

REFERENCES

1. Kamath, S. K., Lawler, M., et al.: Hospital malnutrition: A 33-hospital screening study. J Am Diet Assoc 86:203, 1986.
2. Disbrow, D. D.: Costs and benefits of nutrition services: A literature review. J Am Diet Assoc 89 (Supp), 1989.
3. Dionigi, R., Dominioni, L., Diagnosing malnutrition. Gut 27 (Supp 1):5, 1986.
4. Robinson, G., Goldstein, M., and Levine, G. M.: Impact of nutritional status on DRG length of stay. JPEN 11:49, 1987.
5. Brown, R. O., Carlson, S. D., et al.: Enteral nutritional support management in a university teaching hospital: Team vs. non team. JPEN 11:52, 1987.
6. Mughal, M. M., and Meguid, M. M.: The effect of nutritional status on morbidity after elective surgery for benign gastrointestinal disease. JPEN 11:140, 1987.
7. Simko, M. D., and Conklin, M. T.: Focusing on the effectiveness side of the cost-effectiveness equation. J Am Diet Assoc 89 (4):185, 1989.
8. Splett, P. L.: Assessing effectiveness of nutrition care: Prerequisite for cost-effectiveness analysis. Top Clin Nutr 5 (2):26, 1990.
9. Gibson, R. S.: Principles of nutritional assessment. New York: Oxford University Press, 1990.
10. Jelliffe, D. B., and Jelliffe, E. F. P.: Community nutritional assessment. New York: Oxford University Press, 1989.
11. Hopkins, C.: Developing an approach to nutritional assessment. Unpublished paper presented April 28, 1978, Portland, Oreg.
12. Powers, C. A.: A system for nutrition screening of hospitalized children. Top Clin Nutr 2 (4):11, 1987.
13. Beissner, R. S., and Trowbridge, A. A.: Clinical assessment of anemia. Postgrad Med J 80 (Nov. 1):83, 1986.
14. Grant, A., and DeHoog, S.: Nutritional assessment and support. 3d ed. Seattle: 1985 (self-published).
15. Hunt, D. R., Maslovitz, A., et al.: A simple nutrition screening procedure for hospital patients. J Am Diet Assoc 85:332, 1985.
16. Hedberg, A. M., Garcia, N., et al.: Nutritional risk screening: Development of a standardized protocol using a dietetic technician. J Am Diet Assoc 88:1553, 1988.
17. Christensen, K. S., and Gstundtner, K. M.: Hospital-wide screening improves basis for nutritional intervention. J Am Diet Assoc 85:704, 1985.
18. DeHoog, S.: Identifying patients at nutritional risk and determining clinical productivity: Essentials for an effective nutrition care program. J Am Diet Assoc 85:1620, 1985.
19. Kwong, C., Wirth, J., and Avera, E.: Improved quality assurance through admission nutritional screening. Nutr Supp Ser 4:48, 1984.
20. Ford, D. A., and Fairchild, M. M.: Managing inpatient clinical nutrition services: A comprehensive program assures accountability and success. J Am Diet Assoc 90:695, 1990.
21. Lundvick, J.: Nutritional screening of the oncology patient. Nutr Supp Ser 3 (Sept.):21, 1983.
22. Buzby, G. P., and Mullen, J. L.: Nutritional assessment. In Rombeau, J. L., and Caldwell, M. D.: Enteral and tube feeding. Philadelphia: W. B. Saunders, 1990.
23. Detsky, A. S., McLaughlin, J. R., et al.: What is subjective global assessment of nutritional status? JPEN 11:8, 1987.
24. Baker, J. P., Detsky, A. S., et al.: Nutritional assessment: A comparison of clinical judgment and objective measurements. N Engl J Med 306:969, 1982.
25. Detsky, A. S., Baker, J. P., et al.: Evaluating the accuracy of nutritional assessment techniques applied to hospital patients: Methodology and comparisons. JPEN 8:153, 1984.
26. Baker, J. P., Detsky, A. S., et al.: A comparison of the predictive value of nutritional assessment techniques. Hum Nutr Clin Nutr 36c:233, 1982.
27. Lipschitz, D. A., and Mitchell, C. O.: Nutritional assessment of the elderly—special considerations. In Wright, R. A., Heymsfield, S., and McManus, C. B.: Nutritional assessment. Boston: Blackwell Scientific Publications, 1984.
28. Gray, D. S., Crider, J. H., et al.: Accuracy of recumbent height measurement. JPEN 9:712, 1984.
29. Chumlea, W. C., Roche, A., and Mukherjee, D.: Nutritional assessment of the elderly through anthropometry. Columbus, Ohio: Ross Laboratories, 1984.
30. Cockram, D. B., and Baumgartner, R. N.: Evaluation of accuracy and reliability of calipers for measuring recumbent knee height in elderly. Am J Clin Nutr 52:397, 1990.
31. Bastow, M. D.: Anthropometrics revisited. Proc Nutr Soc 41:381, 1982.
32. Moore, W. R., and Roche, A. F.: Pediatric anthropometry. 3d ed. Yellow Springs, Ohio: Ross Laboratories, 1987.
33. Feucht, S.: Assessment of growth. Nutr Focus Child Spec Health Care Needs 4 (6):1, 1989.
34. Mitchell, C. O., and Lipschitz, D. A.: Arm length measurement as an alternative to height in nutritional assessment of the elderly. JPEN 6:226, 1982.
35. Lohman, T. G., Roche, A. F., and Martorell, R., eds.: Anthropometric standardization reference manual. Champaign, Ill.: Human Kinetics Publishers, 1988.
36. Belt-Niedbala, B. J., Ekvall, S., et al.: Linear growth measurement: A comparison of single arm-lengths and arm-span. Dev Med Child Neurol 28:319, 1986.
37. Spender, Q. W., Cronk, C. E., et al.: Assessment of linear growth of children with cerebral palsy: Use of alternative measures to height or length. Dev Med Child Neurol 31:206, 1989.
38. Moore, W. M., and Roche, A. F.: Pediatric anthropometry. 2d ed. Columbus, Ohio: Ross Laboratories, 1983.
39. Jensen, T. G., Englert, D. M., and Dudrick, S. J.: Nutritional assessment: A manual for practitioners.

East Norwalk, Conn.: Appleton-Century-Crofts, 1983.

40. Harrison, G. G.: Height-weight tables. Ann Intern Med 103 (6 [pt. 2]):989, Dec. 1985.

41. Russell, R. M., McGandy, R. B., and Jelliffe, D.: Reference weights: Practical considerations. Am J Med 76:767, 1984.

42. Heymsfield, S. B., McManus, C. B., III, et al.: Anthropometric assessment of adult protein-energy malnutrition. In Wright, R. A., Heymsfield, S. B., and McManus, C. B., III: Nutritional assessment. Boston: Blackwell Scientific Publications, 1984.

43. Heymsfield, S. B., and McManus, C. B., III: Tissue components of weight loss in cancer patients. Cancer 55:238, 1985.

44. Indraprasit, S.: Modified method of weighing for accurate fluid balance. Nephron 37:140, 1983.

45. Brunnstrom, M. A.: Clinical kinesiology. 3d ed. Philadelphia: F. A. Davis, 1981.

46. Chatterjee, S.: Weight according to type of amputation. Network: DPMR 6 (2):2, 1987.

47. Chatterjee, S.: Weight according to type of amputation: Network: DPMR 6 (3):9, 1987.

48. Frisancho, A. R., and Flegel, P. N.: Elbow breadth as a measure of frame size for U.S. males and females. Am J Clin Nutr 37:311, 1983.

49. Davidson, J. K.: Symposium: Controlling diabetes mellitus with diet therapy. Postgrad Med 59:114, 1976.

50. Burton, B. T., and Foster, W. R.: Health implications of obesity: An NIH Consensus Development Conference. J Am Diet Assoc 85:1117, 1985.

51. Tulchinsky, T. H., Acker, C., et al.: Use of growth charts as a simple epidemiological monitoring system of nutritional status of children. Bull World Health Org 43:1137, 1985.

52. Lieberman, L. S., and Kurtz, C. S.: Anthropometrics: An update on techniques. Dir Appl Nutr 1:6, 1987.

53. Leleiko, M. S., Luder, E., et al.: Nutritional assessment of pediatric patients admitted to an acute pediatric service utilizing anthropometric measurements. JPEN 10:166, 1986.

54. Georgieff, M. K., and Sasanow, S. R.: Nutritional assessment of the neonate. Clin Perinatol 13:73, 1986.

55. Sorva, R., Tolppanen, E. M., and Perheentupa, J.: Variation of growth in length and weight of children. 1. Years 1 and 2. Acta Paediatr Scand 79:490, 1990.

56. Sorva, R., Lankinen, S., et al.: Variation of growth in height and weight of children. 2. After infancy. Acta Paediatr Scand 79:498, 1990.

57. Sorva, R., Tolppanen, E. M., et al.: Growth evaluation: Parent and child specific height standards. Arch Dis Child 64:1483, 1989.

58. Sokol, R. J., and Stall, C.: Anthropometric evaluation of children with chronic liver disease. Am J Clin Nutr 52:203, 1990.

59. Grant, A., and DeHoog, S.: Nutritional assessment and support for dietitians. 3d ed. Box 75057, Northgate Station, Seattle, WA 98125, 1985.

60. Murray, R. L.: Clinical methods in anthropometry. In Krey, S. H., and Murray, R. L.: Dynamics of nutritional support: Assessment, implementation, evaluation. East Norwalk, Conn.: Appleton-Century-Crofts, 1986.

61. Behnke, A. R., and Wilmore, J. H., eds.: Field methods. In Evaluation and regulation of body build and composition. Englewood Cliffs, N.J.: Prentice-Hall, 1974.

62. Frisancho, A. R.: New standards of weight and body composition by frame size and height for assessment of nutritional status of adults and the elderly. Am J Clin Nutr 40:808, 1984.

63. Durnin, J. V., and Womersley, J.: Body fat assessed from total body density and its estimation from skinfold thickness: Measurements on 481 men and women aged from 16 to 72 years. Br J Nutr 32:77, 1974.

64. Staff of R.J.L. Systems, Inc.: Appendix A: Nutritional assessment. In Staff of R.J.L. Systems, Inc.: Nutritional medicine: A case management approach. Detroit: R.J.L. Systems, Inc., 1986.

65. Gurney, J.M., and Jelliffe, D. B.: Arm anthropometry in nutritional assessment: Nomograms for rapid calculation of muscle circumference and cross sectional muscle and fat areas. Am J Clin Nutr 25:912, 1973.

66. Jensen, T. G., Dudrick, S. J., and Johnston, D. A.: A comparison of triceps skinfold and upper arm circumference measurements taken in standard and supine positions. JPEN 5:519, 1981.

67. Jeejeebhoy, K. N., Baker, J. P., et al.: Critical evaluation of the role of clinical assessment and body composition studies in patients with malnutrition and after total parenteral nutrition. Am J Clin Nutr 35:1117, 1982.

68. Gray, G. E., and Gray, L. K.: Validity of anthropometric norms used in the assessment of hospitalized patients. JPEN 3:366, 1979.

69. Deurenberg, P., Weststrate, J. A., and van der Kooij, K.: Body composition changes assessed by bioelectric impedance measurements. Am J Clin Nutr 49:401, 1989.

70. Luklaski, H. C., Johnson, P. E., et al.: Assessment of fat free mass using bioelectric impedance measurement of the human body. Am J Clin Nutr 41:810, 1985.

71. Segal, K. R., Gutin, B., et al.: Estimation of fat free mass using the bio-impedance method: A comparative study. J Appl Physiol 60:1327, 1986.

72. Fox, E. A., Boylan, L. M., and Johnson, L.: Clinically applicable methods for body fat determination. Top Clin Nutr 2 (4):1, 1987.

73. Schroeder, D., Christie, P. M., and Hill, G. L.: Bioelectric impedance analysis for body composition: Clinical evaluation in general surgical patients. JPEN 14:129, 1990.

74. Gray, D. S., Bray, G. A., et al.: Effect of obesity on bioelectric impedance. Am J Clin Nutr 50:255, 1989.

75. Deurenberg, P., van der Kooij, K., et

al.: Assessment of body composition by bioelectric impedance in a population aged >60 y. Am J Clin Nutr 51:3, 1990.

76. Gleichauf, O. P. N., and Roe, D. E.: The menstrual cycle's effect on the reliability of bioimpedance measurements for assessing body composition. Am J Clin Nutr 50:903, 1989.

77. Schoeller, D. A.: Changes in total body water with age. Am J Clin Nutr 50:1176, 1989.

78. Christakis, G.: Nutritional assessment in health programs. Am J Public Health 63:1, 1973.

79. Quality Assurance Committee, Dietitians in Critical Care Dietetic Practice Group: Suggested guidelines for the nutrition management of the critically ill patient. Chicago: American Dietetic Association, 1984.

80. Isaacs, B. L.: Understanding the pathway for the diagnosis of nutritional anemias. Dietitians Nutr Supp 8 (5):8, 1987.

81. Golden, M. H.: Transport proteins as indices of protein status. Am J Clin Nutr 35:1159, 1982.

82. Carpentier, Y. A., Barthel, J., and Bruyns, J.: Plasma protein concentration in nutritional assessment. Proc Nutr Soc 41:405, 1982.

83. Mitchell, C. O., and Lipschitz, D. A.: Detection of protein-calorie malnutrition in the elderly. Am J Clin Nutr 35:398, 1982.

84. Shukla, V. K., Roy, S. K., et al.: Correlation of immune and nutritional status with wound complications in patients undergoing abdominal surgery. Am Surg 51:442, 1985.

85. Hickman, D. M., Miller, R. A., et al.: Serum albumin and body weight as predictors of postoperative course in colorectal cancer. JPEN 4:314, 1980.

86. Jeejeebhoy, K. N., and Meguid, M. M.: Assessment of nutritional status in the oncologic patient. Nutr Canc 2:1077, 1986.

87. Editor: Vitamin A deficiency and iron nutriture. Nutr Rev 42:167, 1984.

88. Stromberg, B. V., Davis, R. J., and Danziger, L. H.: Relationship of serum transferrin to total iron binding capacity for nutritional assessment. JPEN 6:392, 1982.

89. Crosby, L., Giandomenico, A., et al.: Relationships between serum total iron binding capacity and transferrin. JPEN 8:274, 1984.

90. Blackburn, G. L., Bistrian, B. R., et al.: Nutritional and metabolic assessment of the hospitalized patient. JPEN 1:11, 1977.

91. Vanlandingham, S., Spiekerman, M., and Newmark, S. R.: Prealbumin: A parameter of visceral protein levels during albumin infusion. JPEN 6:230, 1982.

92. Tuten, M. B., Wogt, S., et al.: Utilization of prealbumin as a nutritional parameter. JPEN 9:709, 1985.

93. Carpentier, Y. A., and Ingenbleek, Y.: Serum thyroxine-binding prealbumin: An unreliable index of nutritional status. Nutr Res 3:617, 1983.

94. Howard, L., Dillon, B., et al.: Decreased plasma fibronectin during starvation in man. JPEN 8:237, 1984.

95. Linden, C. J., Burman, W. A., et al.: Fibronectin levels in stressed and septic patients fed with total parenteral nutrition. JPEN 10:360, 1986.

96. Yoder, M. C., Anderson, D. C., et al.: Comparison of serum fibronectin, prealbumin and albumin concentrations during nutritional repletion in protein-calorie malnutrition. J Pediatr Gastroenterol Nutr 6:84, 1987.

97. Kirby, D. F., Marder, R. J., et al.: The clinical evaluation of plasma fibronectin as a marker for nutritional depletion and repletion and as a measure of nitrogen balance. JPEN 9:705, 1985.

98. Ohlebowski, B. T., Abramson, S. B., et al.: Influence of nutritional status on circulatory ribonuclease C levels in patients with cancer. Cancer 55:427, 1985.

99. Minuto, F., Barreca, A., et al.: Insulin-like growth factor-I in human malnutrition: Relationship with some body composition and nutritional parameters. JPEN 13:392, 1989.

100. Blackburn, G. L., Bristrian, B. R., et al.: Nutritional and metabolic assess-

ment of the hospitalized patient. JPEN 1:11, 1977.

101. Twomey, P., Ziegler, D., and Rombeau, J.: Utility of skin testing in nutritional assessment: A critical review. JPEN 6:50, 1982.

102. Smith, D. K.: Topical zinc and delayed hypersensitivity responsiveness. Nutr Clin Prac 4:206, 1989.

103. Rudman, D., Feller, A. G., et al.: Relation of serum albumin concentration to death rate in nursing home men. JPEN 11:360, 1987.

104. Long, C. L.: Nutritional assessment of the critically ill patient. In Wright, R. A., Heymsfield, S. B., and McManus, C. B., III: Nutritional assessment. Boston: Blackwell Scientific Publications, 1984.

105. Shizgal, H. M.: Nutritional assessment. In Winters, R. W., and Greene, H. L.: Nutritional support of the seriously ill patient. New York: Academic Press, 1983.

106. Heymsfield, S. B., McManus, C. B., et al.: Measurement of muscle mass in man: Validity of the 24-hour urinary creatinine method. Am J Clin Nutr 36:131, 1982.

107. Huszar, G., Golenwsky, G., et al.: Urinary 3-methylhistidine excretion in man: The role of protein-bound and soluble 3-methylhistidine. Br J Nutr 49:287, 1983.

108. Bingham, S. A., and Cummings, J. H.: Urine nitrogen as an independent validatory measure of dietary intake: A study of nitrogen balance in individuals consuming their normal diet. Am J Clin Nutr 42:1276, 1985.

109. Bingham, S. A., and Cummings, J. H.: The use of 4-aminobenzoic acid as a marker to validate the completeness of 24h urine collections in man. Clin Sci 64:629, 1983.

110. Kopple, J. D.: Uses and limitations of the nitrogen balance technique. JPEN 11:795, 1987.

111. Wilmore, D. W.: The metabolic management of the critically ill. New York: Plenum Medical Book Co., 1977.

112. Olson, J. A., ed.: Nutrition monitor-

ing and nutrition status assessment. J Nutr 120 (11S):1459, 1990.

113. Buzby, G. P., Mullen, J. L., et al.: Prognostic nutritional index in gastrointestinal surgery. Am J Surg 139:160, 1980.

114. Mullen, J. L., Buzby, G. P., et al.: Reduction of operative morbidity and mortality by combined preoperative and postoperative nutritional support. Ann Surg 192:604, 1980.

115. Rivlin, R. S.: Misuse of hair analysis for nutritional assessment. Am J Med 75:489, 1983.

116. Laker, M.: On determining trace element levels in man: The use of blood and hair. Lancet 1:260, 1982.

117. Smiciklas-Wright, H., and Guthrie, H. A.: Dietary methodologies: Their uses, analyses, interpretations, and implications. In Simko, M. D., Cowell, C., and Gilbride, J. A.: Nutrition assessment: A comprehensive guide for planning intervention. Rockville, Md.: Aspen, 1984.

118. Dubois, S., and Boivin, J. F.: Accuracy of telephone dietary recalls in elderly subjects. J Am Diet Assoc 90:1680, 1990.

119. Fong, A. K. H., and Kretsch, M. J.: Nutrition evaluation scale system reduces time and labor in recording quantitative dietary intake. J Am Diet Assoc 90:664, 1990.

120. Simko, M. D., Cowell, C., and Hreha, M. S., eds.: Practical nutrition: A quick reference for the health care practitioner. Rockville, Md.: Aspen, 1989.

121. Bergman, E. A., Boyungs, J. C., and Erickson, M. L.: Comparison of a food frequency questionnaire and a 3-day diet record. J Am Diet Assoc 90:1431, 1990.

122. Pennington, J. A. T.: Bowes and Church's food values of portions commonly used. 15th ed. Philadelphia: J. B. Lippincott, 1989.

123. National Research Council: Recommended dietary allowances. 10th ed. Washington, D.C.: National Academy Press, 1989.

124. Roe, D. A.: Handbook on drug and nutrient interactions. 4th ed. Chicago: American Dietetic Association, 1989.

125. McManus, C., Newhouse, H., et al.: Human gradient-layer calorimeter: Development of an accurate and practical instrument for clinical studies. JPEN 8:317, 1984.

126. Daly, J. M., Heymsfield, S. B., et al.: Human energy requirements: Overestimation by widely used prediction equation. Am J Clin Nutr 42:1170, 1985.

127. Long, C. L., Schaffel, N., et al.: Metabolic response to injury and illness: Estimation of energy and protein needs from indirect calorimetry and nitrogen balance. JPEN 3:452, 1979.

128. Rainey-MacDonald, C. G., Holliday, R. L., and Wells, G. A.: Nomograms for predicting resting energy expenditure of hospitalized patients. JPEN 6:59, 1981.

129. Mifflin, M. D., St. Jeor, S. T., et al.: A new predictive equation for resting energy expenditure in healthy individuals. Am J Clin Nutr 51:241, 1990.

130. Long, C. L.: The energy and protein requirements of the critically ill patient. In Wright, R. A., Heymsfield, S. B., and McManus, C. B., III: Nutritional assessment. Boston: Blackwell Scientific Publications, 1984.

131. Walker, W. A., and Hendricks, K. M.: Manual of pediatric nutrition. Philadelphia: W. B. Saunders, 1985.

132. Pike, R. L., and Brown, M. L.: Nutrition: An integrated approach. 2d ed. New York: John Wiley and Sons, 1975.

133. Murray, R. L.: Protein and energy requirements. In Krey, S. H., and Murray, R. L.: Dynamics of nutrition support. East Norwalk, Conn.: Appleton-Century-Crofts, 1986.

134. Chernoff, R., Forlaw, L., and Long III, J.: Enteral feeding of the critically ill patient. Chicago: American Dietetic Association, 1985.

135. Staats, B. A., Gastineau, C. F., and Offord, K. P.: Predictive equations for basal caloric requirement derived from the data of Boothby, Berkson, and Duncan. Mayo Clin Proc 63:409, 1988.

136. Goodhart, R. S., and Shils, M. E.: Modern nutrition in health and disease. 6th ed. Philadelphia: Lea & Febiger, 1980.

137. Allard, J. P., Pichard, C., et al.: Validation of a new formula for calculating the energy requirements of burn patients. JPEN 14:115, 1990.

138. Shanbhogue, R. L. K., Bristrian, B. R., et al.: Twenty-four hour urinary creatinine: A simple technique for estimating resting energy expenditure in normal populations and hospitalized patients. Clin Nutr 6:221, 1987.

139. Blackburn, G. L., Bell, S. J., and Mullen, J. L.: Appendix B: Macronutrient requirements. In Blackburn, G. L., Bell, S. J., and Mullen, J. L.: Nutritional medicine: A case management approach. Philadelphia: W. B. Saunders, 1989.

140. Weissman, C., Sardar, A., and Kemper, M.: In vitro evaluation of a compact metabolic measurement instrument. JPEN 14:216, 1990.

141. Krause, M. V., and Mahan, L. K.: The nutritional care process. In Krause, M. V., and Mahan, L. K.: Food, nutrition, and diet therapy. 7th ed. Philadelphia: W. B. Saunders, 1984.

142. Dikovics, A.: Nutritional assessment. Philadelphia: George F. Stickley, 1987.

143. Food and Nutrition Board, National Research Council: Recommended Dietary Allowances. 10th ed. Washington, D.C.: National Academy of Sciences, 1989.

144. Talbot, N., Crawford, J., and Butler, M.: Homeostatic limits to safe parenteral fluid therapy. N Engl J Med 248:1100, 1953.

145. Talbot, N., Kerrigan, G., and Crawford, J.: Applications of homeostatic principles to the practice of parenteral fluid therapy: Fluid therapy. N Engl J Med 252:856, 1955.

146. Vaughn, V. D., McKay, R. J., Jr., and Behrman, R. E., eds.: Nelson textbook of pediatrics. 11th ed. Philadelphia: W. B. Saunders, 1979.

147. Lang, C. E.: Nutrition support in critical care. Rockville, Md.: Aspen, 1987.

148. Wilkens, K.: Suggested guidelines for nutrition care of renal patients. Chicago: Renal Dietitians Practice Group, American Dietetic Association, 1986.

149. Beaton, G. H.: Toward harmonization of dietary, biochemical and clinical assessments: The meanings of nutritional status and requirements. Nutr Rev 44:349, 1986.

150. Owen, A. L.: Planning and evaluating nutrition services to ensure quality. In Simko, M. D., Cowell, C., and Gilbride, J. A.: Nutrition assessment: A comprehensive guide for planning intervention. Rockville, Md.: Aspen, 1984.

151. Hassager, C., Gotfersen, A., et al.: Prediction of body composition by age, height, weight, and skinfold thickness in normal adults. Metabolism 35:1081, 1986.

152. Cooper, A., and Heird, W. C.: Nutritional assessment of the pediatric patient, including the low birth weight infant. Am J Clin Nutr 35:1132, 1982.

153. Gueri, M., Jutsum, P., and Sorhaindo, B.: Anthropometric assessment of nutritional status in pregnant women: A reference table of weight-for-height by week of pregnancy. Am J Clin Nutr 35:609, 1982.

154. Peiffer, S. C., Blust, P., and Leyson, J. F. J.: Nutritional assessment of the spinal cord injured patient. J Am Diet Assoc 78:501, 1981.

155. Shizgal, H. M., Roza, A., et al.: Body composition in quadriplegic patients. JPEN 10:364, 1986.

156. Bell, S., Molnar, J. A., and Burke, J. F.: Prediction of total urinary nitrogen from urea nitrogen for burned patients. J Am Diet Assoc 85:1100, 1985.

157. Altman, P. L., and Dittmer, D. S.: Metabolism. Bethesda, Md.: Federation of American Societies for Experimental Biology, 1968.

158. Rhode, C. L., and Braun, T. M.: Home enteral/parenteral nutrition therapy. Chicago: American Dietetic Association, 1986.

159. Dubois et al.: Arch Intern Med 17:863, 1916.

2.

NORMAL DIET

DEFINITION

A diet that provides amounts of energy, protein, vitamins, minerals, and other nutrients sufficient to meet the needs of the individual in his or her particular stage of the life cycle, consistent with the 1990 Dietary Guidelines for Americans.

PURPOSE OF THE DIET

The aim of the diet is to maintain a healthy person in a state of nutritive sufficiency, while avoiding excesses and minimizing risk of diet-related chronic diseases, such as coronary heart disease and certain cancers (1, 2).

EFFECTS OF THE DIET

The effect of a nutritionally adequate normal diet is to permit a state of health and normal bodily functions.

PHYSIOLOGY, FOODS, AND NUTRIENTS

All foods are permitted, and a variety of different foods is encouraged. Adjustments to the normal diet should be based on the stage of the life cycle of the individual. Such adjustments are beyond the scope of this book but have been covered in other publications (3).

INDICATIONS FOR USE

The diet is indicated for normal healthy individuals who do not require adjustments in nutrient intake for any preexisting disorder.

POSSIBLE ADVERSE REACTIONS

There are no possible adverse reactions when the diet is used by healthy individuals without excessive intakes.

CONTRAINDICATIONS

The diet is not intended for individuals who have abnormal nutrient needs or who need special dietary modifications.

CLINICAL ASSESSMENT

1. PERIODIC ASSESSMENT OF NUTRIENT INTAKE

In the institutionalized setting, individuals on regular diets should have their actual intakes periodically evaluated so that any irregularities can be monitored before they develop into serious nutritional problems. Intake may be assessed informally by examining trays during meal rounds or may be more precisely documented by plate waste studies. Calorie counts are indicated for individuals whose intake appears to be inadequate.

2. PERIODIC ASSESSMENT OF HEALTH STATUS

Periodic health assessments should include height, weight, blood pressure, and observations of any clinical signs of malnutrition.

3. PATIENT COMPLAINTS

Food is an important component of emotional as well as physical health. Patient comments and complaints should be addressed quickly by the food and nutrition staff. Individual preferences and cultural and ethnic food practices should be accommodated whenever possible. Allergies should be noted.

BIOCHEMICAL ASSESSMENT

Total serum cholesterol (nonfasting) should be screened every 5 years in asymptomatic individuals and more frequently in persons with previous evidence of elevated cholesterol (4). If the clinical evaluation indicates the presence of a nutritional problem, more in-depth laboratory testing may be called for, such as measurement of serum protein levels or other indices.

ASSESSMENT OF POTENTIAL DRUG INTERACTIONS

Over-the-counter (nonprescription) drugs may have nutritional implications. No drug should be ingested without the individual's knowledge of how to use it— i.e., whether it should be taken on an empty stomach or with food, as well as the potential consequences of abuse or overuse such as can occur with laxatives.

IMPLEMENTATION AND EDUCATION

1. RECOMMENDED DIETARY ALLOWANCES

The Recommended Dietary Allowances (RDAS) are levels of intake of essential nutrients considered by the Food and Nutrition Board of the National Academy of Sciences, on the basis of available scientific knowledge, to be adequate to meet the known nutritional needs of practically all healthy persons (5). These allowances do not take into account special needs arising from infection, metabolic disorders, chronic disease, injuries, drug therapies, or other abnormal conditions that necessitate therapeutic modifications of the diet. They should not be confused with either the minimum requirements or the U.S. Recommended Daily Allowances (USRDAS). The USRDAS are a standard for nutritional labeling derived by the U.S. Food and Drug Administration, using the highest recommendation for any age group in the 1968 RDAS (5).

Except for kilocalories, the Recommended Dietary Allowances are designed to afford a margin of safety that reflects the state of knowledge concerning each nutrient, its bioavailability, and variations among individuals in the U.S. population. The 10th edition of *Recommended Dietary Allowances,* released in October 1989, adds RDAS for 2 nutrients: vitamin K and selenium (5).

In using the RDAS to assess the diet of an individual, it is preferable to consider an average of several day's intakes as opposed to a single 24-hour dietary recall before making judgments about the adequacy or inadequacy of the diet. The terms *per day* and *daily* should be interpreted as an average intake over time (6). The length of time necessary for averaging depends upon the nutrient, the size of the body pool, and the rate of turnover of that nutrient. Some nutrients, such as vitamins A and B-12, can be stored in relatively large quantities and degrade slowly. Others, such as thiamine, are turned over rapidly, and total deprivation in a person can lead to relatively rapid development of symptoms over a period of days or weeks. If the allowance for a nutrient is not met on a particular day, body stores or a surplus consumed shortly thereafter will compensate for the inadequacy. For most nutrients the RDAS are intended to be averaged over at least 3 days; for others, such as vitamins A

and B-12, they may be averaged over several months. If individual intakes can be averaged over a sufficiently long period and compared with the RDAS, the probable risk of deficiency for that individual can be estimated (5).

2. DIETARY GUIDELINES

Data on the role of diet as a causal or contributing factor in chronic and degenerative diseases have led to the use of approaches different from the approach used in formulating the RDAS. During the past few years, other guidelines with special emphasis on nutritive adequacy, dietary variety, weight control, and in particular the intakes of fat, sugar, sodium, and fiber have been published. *Dietary Goals for the United States* was published in 1977 by the U.S. Senate Select Committee on Nutrition and Human Needs (7). Those goals were revised in 1980 (8), 1985 (9), and 1990 (10, 11) by the U.S. Department of Agriculture (USDA) and the U.S. Department of Health and Human Services (DHHS), resulting in the following Dietary Guidelines for Americans (10):

- Eat a variety of foods.
- Maintain a healthy weight.
- Choose a diet low in fat, saturated fat, and cholesterol.
- Choose a diet with plenty of vegetables, fruits, and grain products.
- Use sugars only in moderation.
- Use salt and sodium only in moderation.
- If you drink alcoholic beverages, do so in moderation.

In 1989, *Diet and Health* was published by the Food and Nutrition Board of the National Academy of Sciences, outlining recommendations for reducing chronic disease risk (2). The Surgeon General published a report on nutrition and health in 1988 (12). It is significant that in *Promoting Health/Preventing Disease: Year 2000 Objectives for the*

Nation, released in 1989, nutrition is the first health-promotion priority discussed (13).

The dietary recommendations of the Food and Nutrition Board's Committee on Diet and Health for normal healthy North American adults and children, published in 1989, are as follows (2).

A. Fat   Reduce total fat intake to 30% or less of calories. Reduce saturated fatty acid intake to less than 10% of calories, and the intake of cholesterol to less than 300 mg daily. The intake of fat and cholesterol can be reduced by substituting fish, poultry without skin, lean meats, and low or nonfat dairy products for fatty meats and whole-milk dairy products; by choosing more vegetables, fruits, cereals, and legumes; and by limiting oils, fats, egg yolks, and fried and other fatty foods.

B. Complex Carbohydrates   Increase the intake of complex carbohydrates to 55% of calories. Every day eat 5 or more servings of a combination of vegetables and fruits, especially green and yellow vegetables and citrus fruits. Also, increase intake of starches and other complex carbohydrates by eating 6 or more daily servings of a combination of breads, cereals, and legumes.

C. Protein   Maintain protein intake at moderate levels.

D. Body Weight   Balance food intake and exercise to maintain appropriate body weight.

E. Salt Intake   Limit daily intake of salt (sodium chloride) to 6 g or less. Limit the use of salt in cooking, and avoid adding it to food at the table. Salty, highly processed, salt-preserved, and salt-pickled foods should be consumed sparingly.

F. Calcium Intake   Maintain adequate calcium intake.

FIG. 2.1. DAILY FOOD GUIDE.

When shopping, planning, and preparing meals for yourself and others, use this guide for a varied and nutritious diet.

• Choose foods daily from each of the first 5 major groups shown below. The following table lists some foods in each group.

• Include different foods from within the groups. As a guide, you can use the subgroups listed below the major food group heading.

• Have at least the smaller number of servings suggested from each group. Limit total amount of food eaten to maintain desirable body weight.

• Most people should choose foods that are low in fat and sugars more often.

• Go easy on fats, sweets, and alcoholic beverages.

Food group	Suggested daily servings
Breads, cereals, and other grain products • Whole-grain • Enriched	6 to 11 (Include several servings a day of whole-grain products.)
Fruits • Citrus, melon, berries • Other fruits	2 to 4
Vegetables • Dark-green leafy • Deep-yellow • Dry beans and peas (legumes) • Starchy • Other vegetables	3 to 5 servings (Include all types regularly: use dark-green leafy vegetables and dry beans and peas several times a week.)
Meat, poultry, fish, and alternates (Alternates include eggs, dry beans and peas, nuts and seeds.)	2 to 3 servings—total 5 to 7 oz. lean
Milk, cheese, and yogurt	2 servings; 3 servings for teens and for women who are pregnant or breast-feeding; 4 servings for teens who are pregnant or breast-feeding
Fats, sweets, and alcoholic beverages	Avoid too many fats and sweets. If you drink alcoholic beverages, do so in moderation.

Note: The pattern for daily food choices described here was developed for Americans who regularly eat foods from all the major food groups listed. Some people such as vegetarians and others may not eat one or more of these types of foods. These people may wish to contact a registered dietitian in their community for help in planning food choices.

WHAT COUNTS AS A SERVING?

The examples listed below will give you an idea of the amounts of food to count as 1 serving when you use the guide shown here.

• *Breads, cereals, and other grain products:* 1 slice bread; ½ hamburger bun or english muffin; a small roll, biscuit, or muffin; 3 to 4 small or 2 large crackers; ½ cup cooked cereal, rice, or pasta; or 1 oz. ready-to-eat breakfast cereal.

• *Fruits:* whole fruit such as an apple, a banana, or an orange; a grapefruit half; a melon wedge; ¾ cup of juice; ½ cup berries; ½ cup cooked or canned fruit; or ¼ cup dried fruit.

• *Vegetables:* ½ cup cooked or chopped raw vegetables; or 1 cup leafy raw vegetables, such as lettuce or spinach.

• *Meat, poultry, fish, and alternates:* Serving sizes will differ. Amounts should total 5 to 7 oz. lean meat, fish, or poultry a day. A serving of meat the size and thickness of the palm of a woman's hand is about 3 to 5 oz., and of a man's, 5 to 7 oz. Count 1 egg, ½ cup cooked dry beans, or 2 tbsp. peanut butter as 1 oz. of lean meat.

• *Milk, cheese, and yogurt:* 1 cup milk, 8 oz. yogurt, 1½ oz. natural cheese, or 2 oz. process cheese.

WHAT ABOUT THE NUMBER OF SERVINGS?

The amount of food you need depends on your age, sex, physical condition, and how active you are. Almost everyone should have at least the minimum number of servings from each food group daily. Many women, older children, and most teenagers and men need more. The top of the range is about right for an active man or teenage boy. Young children may not need as much food. They can have smaller servings from all groups except milk, which should total 2 servings per day. You can use the guide shown here to help plan for the variety and amounts of foods your family needs each day.

FOOD GROUPS: SOME FOODS THEY CONTAIN

BREADS, CEREALS, AND OTHER GRAIN PRODUCTS

Whole-grain

Brown rice	Oatmeal	Whole wheat bread
Buckwheat groats	Popcorn	and rolls
Bulgur	Pumpernickel bread	Whole wheat
Corn tortillas	Ready-to-eat cereals	crackers
Graham crackers	Rye crackers	Whole wheat pasta
Granola		Whole wheat cereals

Enriched

Bagels	Farina	Muffins
Biscuits	French bread	Noodles
Corn muffins	Grits	Pancakes
Cornbread	Hamburger rolls	Pasta
Cornmeal	Hot dog buns	Ready-to-eat cereals
Crackers	Italian bread	Rice
English muffins	Macaroni	White bread and rolls

FRUITS

Citrus, melons, berries

Blueberries	Honeydew melon	Raspberries
Cantaloupe	Kiwifruit	Strawberries
Citrus juices	Lemon	Tangerine
Cranberries	Orange	Watermelon
Grapefruit		

Other fruits

Apple	Grapes	Pineapple
Apricot	Guava	Plantain
Banana	Mango	Plum
Cherries	Nectarine	Pomegranate
Dates	Papaya	Prune
Figs	Peach	Raisins
Fruit juices	Pear	

VEGETABLES

Dark-green

Beet greens	Dandelion greens	Romaine lettuce
Broccoli	Endive	Spinach
Chard	Escarole	Turnip greens
Chicory	Kale	Watercress
Collard greens	Mustard greens	

Deep-yellow

Carrots
Pumpkin
Sweet potatoes
Winter squash

Starchy

Breadfruit	Lima beans
Corn	Potatoes
Green peas	Rutabaga
Hominy	Taro

Dry beans and peas (legumes)

Black beans	Lima beans (mature)
Black-eyed peas	Mung beans
Chickpeas (garbanzos)	Navy beans
Kidney beans	Pinto beans
Lentils	Split peas

Other vegetables

Artichokes	Cabbage	Green beans	Radishes
Asparagus	Cauliflower	Green peppers	Summer squash
Bean and alfalfa	Celery	Lettuce	Tomatoes
sprouts	Chinese cabbage	Mushrooms	Turnips
Beets	Cucumbers	Okra	Vegetable juices
Brussels sprouts	Eggplant	Onions (mature and green)	Zucchini

MEAT, POULTRY, FISH, AND ALTERNATES

Meat, poultry, and fish

Beef	Ham	Pork	Veal
Chicken	Lamb	Shellfish	Luncheon meats,
Fish	Organ meats	Turkey	sausage

Alternates

Eggs	Nuts and seeds
Dry beans and peas	Peanut butter
(legumes)	Tofu

MILK, CHEESE, AND YOGURT

Low-fat milk products

Buttermilk	Low-fat plain yogurt
Low-fat milk (1%, 2%)	Skim milk

Other milk products with more fat or sugar

American cheese	Chocolate milk	Fruit yogurt	Swiss cheese
Cheddar cheese	Flavored yogurt	Process cheeses	Whole milk

FATS, SWEETS, AND ALCOHOLIC BEVERAGES

Fats

Bacon, salt pork	Mayonnaise
Butter	Mayonnaise-type
Cream (dairy,	salad dressing
nondairy)	Salad dressing
Cream cheese	Shortening
Lard	Sour cream
Margarine	Vegetable oil

Sweets

Candy	Jam	Popsicles and ices
Corn syrup	Jelly	Sherbets
Frosting	Maple syrup	Soft drinks and colas
Fruit drinks, ades	Marmalade	Sugar (white and
Gelatin desserts	Molasses	brown)
Honey		

Alcohol

Beer
Liquor
Wine

Source: Dietary Guidelines for Americans (15).

G. Supplements   Avoid taking dietary supplements in excess of the RDA in any one day.

H. Fluoride   Maintain an optimal intake of fluoride, particularly during the years of primary and secondary tooth formation and growth.

3. FOOD GUIDES

The best way to utilize the RDAS is to plan a diet derived from diverse food groups rather than achieve proposed levels by either supplementation or fortification of foods. In order to be practical and meaningful, a standard such as the Recommended Dietary Allowances must be translated into guidelines for the proper selection of foods. The Human Nutrition Information Service of the USDA has assumed the role of developing such guidelines, starting with the Basic Seven (1943), the Basic Four (1956, and modified in 1980), and the 1984 Food Wheel, promoted by the USDA in collaboration with the American Red Cross. The Food Wheel provides guidance for a total diet rather than for a foundation diet (6, 14). The daily food guide in figure 2.1 is adapted from the Dietary Guidelines for Americans (15).

PRIORITIES FOR QUALITY ASSURANCE

A monitoring system is necessary to assure that individuals actually consume the diet as planned. In the hospital setting, this system may take the form of meal rounds and calorie counts.

On a national scale the Nationwide Food Consumption Survey (NFCS), conducted by the USDA, and the National Health and Nutrition Examination Survey (NHANES), conducted by the DHHS, provide ongoing assessments of food intake and health parameters. In the future, National Nutrition Monitoring (NNM) will ensure more timely, complete, and accurate information to guide

MENU PLANNING

SAMPLE MEAL PLAN AND MENU FOR THE NORMAL DIET (FOR A MALE, AGE 25–50)

Food	Serving size	Food group
BREAKFAST		
Orange juice	½ cup	1 fruit
Dried prunes	½ cup	1 fruit
All-bran cereal	1 cup	3 grains, breads, cereals
Milk, 2% fat	1 cup	1 milk, yogurt, cheese
Whole wheat bread	2 slices	2 grains, breads, cereals
Margarine	2 tsp.	2 fats, sweets, alcohol
Jam preserves	1 tbsp.	1 fats, sweets, alcohol
Brewed coffee	6 oz.	
LUNCH		
Minestrone soup	1 cup	1 vegetable
Sandwich:		
Swiss cheese	2 oz.	1 meat, poultry, fish, and alternates
Lettuce and tomato	1 leaf, ½ tomato	1 vegetable
Rye bread	2 slices	2 grains, breads, cereals
Mayonnaise	1 tbsp.	3 fats, sweets, alcohol
Apple, raw	1 apple	1 fruit
Milk, 2% fat	1 cup	1 milk, yogurt, cheese
AFTERNOON SNACK		
Granola bar	1 bar	1 grains, breads, cereals; 1 fats, sweets, alcohol
DINNER		
Chicken breast	3 oz.	1 meat, poultry, fish, and alternates
With corn oil	2 tsp.	2 fats, sweets, alcohol
Baked potato	1 large	2 vegetables
Spinach, cooked	½ cup	1 vegetable
Pumpernickel bread	3 slices	3 grains, breads, cereals
Margarine safflower	4 tsp.	4 fats, sweets, alcohol
Angel food cake	1 slice	1 grains, breads, cereals; 2 fats, sweets, alcohol
With sliced strawberries	½ cup	1 fruit
EVENING SNACK		
Oatmeal cookies	2	2 fats, sweets, alcohol
Herbal tea	8 oz.	
Honey	1 tsp.	1 fats, sweets, alcohol

Approximate Nutrient Analysis

Energy	2,863 kcal
Protein	114.5 g (16% of kcal)
Fat	92.4 g (29% of kcal)
Polyunsaturated fat	23.0 g
Monounsaturated fat	26.4 g
Saturated fat	28.2 g
Cholesterol	185 mg
Carbohydrate	437.7 g (61% of kcal)

(continued)

Vitamin A	16,907 IU
	2,912 RE
Thiamine	2.77 mg
Riboflavin	3.58 mg
Niacin	40.2 mg
Folate	611 mcg
Vitamin B-12	3.29 mcg
Vitamin B-6	3.91 mg
Vitamin C	203.1 mg
Calcium	1,758 mg
Phosphorus	2,753 mg
Iron	33.6 mg
Copper	2.57 mg
Zinc	19.8 mg
Magnesium	680 mg
Sodium	4,132 mg
Potassium	5,814 mg

health, nutrition, and dietary policy (2). Such policy would aim to ensure adequate intake for high-risk population groups via national programs and services such as the Food Stamp Program; the Supplemental Food Program for Women, Infants, and Children (WIC); the National School Lunch Program; the Child Care Food Program; and the National Nutrition Program for the Elderly. NNM data would also steer policy to reduce nutritional risk factors implicated in the development of chronic disease. *The Surgeon General's Report on Nutrition and Health* includes suggestions for future research and surveillance that are priorities for the quality assurance of the nutrition and health of our nation (12).

REFERENCES

1. Turner, D.: Handbook of diet therapy. 5th ed. Chicago: University of Chicago Press, 1970.
2. Food and Nutrition Board, National Research Council—National Academy of Sciences: Diet and health: Implications for reducing chronic disease risk. Report of the Committee on Diet and Health. Washington, D.C.: National Academy Press, 1989.
3. American Dietetic Association: Manual of clinical dietetics. Chicago: American Dietetic Association, 1988.
4. Report of the U.S. Preventive Services Task Force: Guide to Clinical Preventive Services. Washington, D.C.: U.S. Department of Health and Human Services, 1989.
5. Food and Nutrition Board, National Research Council: Recommended Dietary Allowances. 10th ed. Washington, D.C.: National Academy of Sciences, 1989.
6. Guthrie, H. A.: The 1985 Recommended Dietary Allowance Committee: An overview. J Am Diet Assoc 85:1646, 1985.
7. U.S. Senate Select Committee on Nutrition and Human Needs: Dietary goals for the United States. Washington, D.C.: U.S. Government Printing Office, 1977.
8. Nutrition and your health: Dietary Guidelines for Americans. Washington, D.C.: U.S. Department of Agriculture and U.S. Department of Health and Human Services, 1980.
9. Nutrition and your health: Dietary Guidelines for Americans. Washington, D.C.: U.S. Department of Agriculture and U.S. Department of Health and Human Services, 1985.
10. Nutrition and your health: Dietary Guidelines for Americans. Home and Garden Bulletin no. 232. Washington, D.C.: U.S. Department of Agriculture and U.S. Department of Health and Human Services, 1990.
11. Dietary Guidelines Advisory Committee: Report of the Dietary Guidelines Advisory Committee on the Dietary Guidelines for Americans, 1990. Hyattsville, Md.: Human Nutrition Information Service, June 1990.
12. U.S. Department of Health and Human Services: The Surgeon General's Report on Nutrition and Health—Summary and Recommendations. DHHS Publication no. (PHS) 88-50211. Washington, D.C.: U.S. Government Printing Office, 1988.
13. U.S. Department of Health and Human Services: Promoting Health/Preventing Disease: Year 2000 objectives for the nation. Washington, D.C.: Public Health Service, 1989.
14. Better eating for better health. Washington, D.C.: American Red Cross, 1984.
15. Dietary Guidelines for Americans: Eat a variety of foods. Home and Garden Bulletin, no. 232-1. Washington, D.C.: Nutrition Information Service, U.S. Department of Agriculture, April 1986.

3.

VEGETARIAN DIETS

DEFINITIONS

1. VEGAN DIET OR STRICT VEGETARIAN DIET

A diet that includes some or all of the following foods: vegetables; fruits; enriched or whole-grain breads and cereals; dry peas, beans, and lentils; nuts; and seeds. The diet specifically excludes all foods of animal origin: meat, poultry, fish, eggs, and dairy products, such as milk, cheese, and ice cream (1, 2).

2. LACTOVEGETARIAN DIET

A diet that adds dairy products to the foods included in the vegan diet. It excludes meat, poultry, fish, and eggs (1).

3. OVO-LACTO-VEGETARIAN DIET

A diet that adds eggs and dairy products to the foods included in a vegan diet. It excludes meat, poultry, and fish (1, 3).

4. SEMIVEGETARIAN OR PARTIAL VEGETARIAN DIET

A diet that includes some but not all groups of animal-derived foods. It usually excludes red meat but may include poultry, fish, or seafood.

5. OMNIVOROUS DIET

A diet that includes foods of both animal and vegetable origin.

6. ZEN MACROBIOTIC DIET

A dietary regimen of vegan or very limited vegetarian type followed by adherents of a sect founded by Georges Ohsawa. Specific practices vary, but animal foods are eaten only as condiments, and milk is usually avoided. Natural and organic foods are used, and fluid restric-

tion may be practiced. Vitamin and mineral supplements are rarely taken (4).

PURPOSE OF THE DIET

The aim of the diet is to exclude some or all foods of animal origin and to utilize foods of vegetable origin for religious, ethical, philosophical, ecological, economic, or health reasons. The variety of individual variations in foods included or excluded and the range of philosophies and motivations make individual evaluation essential to ensure nutrient adequacy of the regime.

EFFECTS OF THE DIET

1. LOWER BODY WEIGHT

Vegetarians and especially vegans have lower body weights than nonvegetarians, closer to desirable levels. Some vegetarians may actually be emaciated, and growth may be compromised in children. Pregnancy weights and weight gains in vegan women may be low, with increased risk of low birth weight (5–7); reasons may include more-spartan and more-controlled eating styles and greater physical activity. A high-fiber, high-carbohydrate, low-fat diet may also contribute to earlier satiety (7). Lower incidence of obesity probably contributes to reduced rates of obesity-related disorders among vegetarians, such as non-insulin-dependent diabetes mellitus, gallstones, hypertension, and coronary artery disease (7).

2. REDUCED BLOOD PRESSURE

Vegetarians tend to have lower blood pressures, and less of a rise in blood pres-

sure with aging, than do meat eaters and nonvegetarians. Blood pressure appears to be negatively correlated with the extent of avoidance of animal food. Blood pressures of nonvegetarians fed vegetarian diets do not fall as much as expected, however. It appears that vegetarians' relative leanness and other lifestyle factors—such as nonsmoking, abstinence from alcohol, greater physical activity, and perhaps responses to stress—may also affect blood pressure. The effect of dietary sodium intake seems to be smaller than previously suspected, because some groups of vegetarians, especially those using meat analogs (soy or tofu-based "burgers" or "hot dogs"), do not have lower sodium intakes than nonvegetarians (7–11).

3. REDUCED CORONARY ARTERY DISEASE

Mortality and morbidity from coronary artery disease are lower in vegetarians than in nonvegetarians. Other lifestyle factors may be involved in lowering health risks, such as smoking, exercise habits, and weight status. However, total serum cholesterol, low-density lipoprotein (LDL) cholesterol, and, to a lesser extent, high-density lipoprotein (HDL) cholesterols are lower in vegetarians and especially vegans than in lactovegetarians or omnivores. Vegetarian diets usually produce a selective lowering of LDL-cholesterol levels, with lowered ratios of total cholesterol to HDL-cholesterol or of LDL to HDL-cholesterol. Vegans or very restrictive vegetarians whose diets are low in fat, high in dietary fiber, and low in cholesterol, with high polyunsaturated : saturated fatty acid ratios, have lower total cholesterol and LDL-cholesterol levels than do omnivores. Vegetarians' LDL-cholesterol levels are usually decreased, but HDL-cholesterol levels vary, some being higher than those of nonvegetarians, and some lower. Studies generally indicate that serum lipids depend upon the amount and type of dietary fat and therefore vary according to the kind of vegetarian diet, making generalizations difficult (7, 12).

4. CHANGES IN PLATELETS

Platelet composition and platelet functions may vary and plasma viscosity may be decreased in individuals on a vegetarian diet (13).

5. DECREASED RISK OF RENAL STONES

Vegetarians excrete less calcium, oxalate, and uric acid (3 of the 6 urinary risk factors for calcium oxalate stones) than do nonvegetarians. One study has shown incidence of kidney stones to be lower among vegetarians than among nonvegetarians; however, the evidence is weak (7, 11).

6. DECREASED CANCER RISK

Vegetarians have a lower death rate from certain cancers than do nonvegetarians. A low-fiber diet has been associated with lower fecal bulk, which increases the concentration of the bile acids in the aqueous phase of feces (fecal water). This condition has been linked to an increased risk of colon cancer. A shift from a normal to a vegetarian diet results in a decrease in the total concentration of soluble fecal fatty acids, which may decrease cancer risk (14, 15).

PHYSIOLOGY, FOODS, AND NUTRIENTS

Most vegetarian diets in the United States are high in fiber and low in total fat, saturated fat, and cholesterol (16). The ovo-lacto-vegetarian diet resembles the average Western diet in many ways. The main difference is that it replaces

meat with a variety of legumes, meat analogs, cereals, nuts, milk and milk products, and eggs. In contrast, the pure or strict vegetarian diet is devoid of any animal foods and must be skillfully implemented. Because many plant foods are low in kilocalories, greater quantities of many different varieties must be chosen in order to ensure nutritional adequacy. Even given such wise choices, the diet must be supplemented with vitamin B-12, because plant foods contain no known source of this vitamin, unless they are contaminated by microbes that produce it (7, 16, 17). Ovo-lacto-vegetarian diets may be low in iron and zinc. Vegan diets may be low in energy, vitamins B-12 and D, and calcium (18).

In a recent comparison of the biotin nutritional status of vegans, ovo-lacto-vegetarians, and nonvegetarians, no significant difference was noted (19). A comparison of omnivore and vegetarian postmenopausal women demonstrated that when care was taken to provide adequate calcium intakes, there was no significant difference in bone mineral content (20).

Vegetarians consume more carbohydrates, thiamine, and ascorbic acid than nonvegetarians do (21). One author has reported that vegetarian women have lower dietary intakes of energy, riboflavin, calcium, and iron; the author suggested that women increase ascorbic acid in their diets in order to increase the amount of nonheme iron absorbed (22).

INDICATIONS FOR USE

The diet may be indicated for religious, ethical, philosophical, ecological, or economic reasons as well as for health reasons, such as hypercholesterolemia and high blood pressure.

POSSIBLE ADVERSE REACTIONS

Strict vegans are more likely to experience dietary inadequacies than are more-

liberal vegetarians. The more restricted the diet, the more difficult it becomes to provide adequate nutrients for age, sex, and physiological and disease states. During times of increased need, such as infancy, childhood, pregnancy, lactation, and convalescence, careful planning is necessary to prevent malnutrition (7).

1. VITAMIN B-12 DEFICIENCY

Megaloblastic anemia has been reported in a large percentage of a mainly lactovegetarian London Hindu community, many of whom were also iron deficient (23). The availability of iron was low in their diets and was most likely hindered further by the use of tea, which contains inhibitors to iron absorption, at meals. For most Western vegetarians, nonheme iron absorption is enhanced by relatively high intakes of ascorbic acid from fruits and vegetables (7).

The urinary excretion of methylmalonyl-CoA is increased with vitamin B-12 deficiency. The increase of this substance, a growth medium for the tuberculosis bacillus, is one possible reason for the high rate of tuberculosis in these individuals (23). The speed with which vitamin B-12 deficiency develops in the vegan infant emphasizes the vitamin's important role and rapid use in growth. Vitamin B-12 deficiency can also affect breast-fed infants of women on vegan diets (18).

Total abstinence from foods of animal origin is known to be associated with low serum vitamin B-12 levels, megaloblastic anemia, and subacute degeneration of the spinal cord (24). To a much lesser degree than vegans, some lactovegetarians and ovo-lacto-vegetarians may be at risk of developing vitamin B-12 deficiencies during periods of increased need. Repeated blood loss, repeated blood donations, and pregnancy increase this risk. In these instances and for vegetarians with a dietary vitamin B-12 intake of less than 0.5 mcg per day, supplementation with additional vitamin B-12 is recommended (25, 26).

2. CALCIUM DEFICIENCY

Unless milk in some form is included in the diet, particularly in the diet of children, it may be difficult to consume enough calcium (1, 17, 27). Vegans who do not compensate for the loss of milk in the diet by use of a vitamin-and-mineral-fortified milk substitute and by increased use of calcium-containing foods run the risk of provoking a calcium deficiency as well as a riboflavin or vitamin B-12 deficiency. Low calcium intakes may be compounded by high dietary fiber and phytic and oxalic acids, which inhibit calcium absorption (7).

3. VITAMIN D DEFICIENCY

Children of strict vegetarians who are not significantly exposed to sunlight at regular intervals, especially dark-skinned individuals and infants whose only source of vitamin D is breast milk after 4 to 6 months of age, are prone to develop vitamin D deficiency and rickets unless a source of vitamin D is included in their diets (18, 28). Plasma 25-hydroxy-vitamin-D levels have been reported to be lower in pregnant vegetarians than in pregnant nonvegetarians (29).

4. ZINC DEFICIENCY

Plant foods are less abundant in zinc than are animal foods. Also, fiber, phytate, and oxalate may reduce the bioavailability of zinc. High calcium intakes in lactovegetarians may also reduce the availability of zinc. Taste detection thresholds have been found to be higher in vegetarians. It has been suggested that taste acuity may be a functional index of zinc nutriture and that these results may indicate compromised zinc status in vegetarians (30).

5. CHILDREN'S FAILURE TO THRIVE

High-fiber, low-fat vegan diets tend to have low energy density. Limited stomach capacity and higher needs for nutrients per unit weight may lead to inadequate weight gain and poor growth in children. Clinical signs of wasting, poor growth rates, and delayed psychomotor development have been reported in children of macrobiotics. Some vegan infants and children may have inadequate intakes of protein or some amino acids, and their bioavailability may be reduced by inadequate energy intakes (4, 28, 31, 32).

CONTRAINDICATIONS

Some forms of the Zen macrobiotic diet are grossly inadequate in many nutrients and have produced disastrous nutritional consequences in some of its younger adherents (4).

CLINICAL ASSESSMENT

Nutrients that affect growth and development and that may be deficient in the diets of vegetarian infants and children are energy, protein, calcium, zinc, iron, riboflavin, and vitamins D and B-12 (6, 18, 33). During the assessment interview, the dietitian should determine the daily intake of foods that are good sources of these nutrients. Mineral analyses of vegetarian foods such as wheat-protein hamburger, vegetarian egg substitutes, soy protein milk, and soy-isolate frankfurters indicate that they are low in zinc. Unrefined grains were found to be high in zinc but were also high in fiber and phytate, both of which are zinc-binding components. Manganese content, on the other hand, was increased in most vegetarian foods (30, 34). Findings of one study indicate that the copper and selenium status of long-term vegetarian women is comparable to that of nonvegetarian women, but the manganese intake of the vegetarian women is higher, despite their high intake of dietary fiber (35).

Because young children have small stomach reservoirs and may have difficulty consuming the total amounts of many bulky vegetarian foods that they need, the composition of snacks should be a point of focus. The specific ingredients, times, and amounts of foods used for snacks should be determined. Energy intake can be increased through the use of nut and legume butters for snacks (12, 28, 35).

BIOCHEMICAL ASSESSMENT

Vitamin B-12 status should be evaluated regularly, particularly in vegans. Serum protein levels should also be a part of regular health assessments, especially in children.

ASSESSMENT OF POTENTIAL DRUG INTERACTIONS

Potential drug interactions are the same as for a normal diet.

IMPLEMENTATION AND EDUCATION

1. MEAL PLANNING

Several approaches have been taken to meal planning based on the Basic Four (2), diabetic exchange lists (36), and other guides designed to ensure adequacy of key nutrients (37). Variety, nutrient density, and sufficient quantity should be stressed more than with nonvegetarians, to ensure adequacy (38). The normal food guide may be used by substituting fortified soy milk formula if milk is omitted and by using eggs (if eaten), meat analogs, legumes, nuts and seeds, peanut butter, and tofu to meet the requirements of the meat or alternate group.

When indicated, the vegetarian diet can be modified successfully to fit the confines of a number of therapeutic diets (39). An excellent diet manual has been published that includes many therapeutic vegetarian diets that should prove helpful to the dietitian (40).

2. COMPLEMENTARY PROTEINS

Plant foods contain less of the essential amino acids than do equivalent quantities of animal food, but a plant-based diet provides adequate amounts of amino acids when a varied diet is consumed on a daily basis. A mixture of proteins from unrefined grains, legumes, seeds, nuts, and vegetables will complement one another in their amino acid profiles so that deficits in one are made up by another (16). The amino acid content of various vegetarian protein sources and how they can be combined to provide more-complete proteins are given in table 3.1 (41).

Intakes of different types of protein that complement one another should be eaten over the course of the day. After absorption, however, amino acids from exogenous and endogenous sources combine in the body's protein pool. It is therefore not necessary to combine complementary protein sources within each meal as commonly suggested by the "combined proteins theory" (16).

3. ENSURING DIETARY ADEQUACY

In modifying the diet of an individual from a nonvegetarian diet to a vegetarian pattern, the intake of low-nutrient-density foods should be reduced. High-nutrient-density foods should be used in their place. Also, choices of grains, legumes, nuts, seeds, fruits, and vegetables should be as varied as possible, to provide a range of nutrients.

Vigilance in the consumption of sufficient amounts of food is necessary to meet caloric needs for weight maintenance and protein sparing. Closer nutritional surveillance is needed for adequate implementation of vegan diets than for more-liberal vegetarian diets. Many plant foods are very low in kilocalories; consequently, the sheer bulk of food required to meet energy needs may constitute a problem for certain individuals.

Milk and milk products are excellent sources of protein, riboflavin, calcium, and vitamins D and B-12. In the absence

TABLE 3.1. AMINO ACID CONTENT OF VARIOUS VEGETARIAN PROTEIN SOURCES

Food group	Limiting essential amino acid(s)	High levels of essential amino acid(s)	Protein complementation
Eggs	None	Cystine, lysine, methionine, tryptophan	Complete protein
Grains	Lysine, isoleucine	Cystine, methionine, threonine, tryptophan (except for cornmeal and rye flour, which are low in tryptophan)	Grains and legumes Grains and milk or eggs
Legumes	Methionine, cystine, tryptophan (except soybeans, which are high in tryptophan)	Lysine, threonine	Legumes and grains Legumes and seeds/ nuts
Milk products	None	Lysine, isoleucine, methionine	Complete protein
Nuts and seeds	Lysine, isoleucine (except cashews and pumpkin seeds)	Cystine, methionine, tryptophan (except peanuts, which are low in methionine and tryptophan)	Nuts/seeds and legumes
Other vegetables	Cystine, methionine, isoleucine (except spinach)	Lysine, tryptophan	Vegetables and nuts/ seeds and legumes Vegetables and grains and legumes Vegetables and eggs or milk/milk products

Source: American Dietetic Association (41).

of dairy products, it becomes difficult to obtain adequate amounts of these nutrients. Fermented foods may contain vitamin B-12 but cannot be considered a reliable source (28). Compensatory measures to offset the lack of vitamin B-12 in the diet and the large nutritional gap left by the omission of dairy products include the following:

- Including fortified meat analogs, if acceptable
- Increasing the use of legumes, nuts, and dried fruits
- Increasing the use of green leafy vegetables
- Obtaining regular significant exposure to sunshine to synthesize vitamin D
- Including a fortified soybean-based milk, such as an infant formula (This measure is essential for the young child.)
- Adding inactivated yeast occasionally, although not necessarily daily

If possible, older people, children, and pregnant women should include dairy products to ensure adequate intake of riboflavin, vitamin B-12, calcium, and magnesium as well as essential amino acids (37).

4. VEGETARIAN DIETS IN INFANCY

The importance of breast-feeding should be stressed. Breast-feeding should be continued until the infant is at least 6 months of age, and special attention should be given to the diet of the vegetarian lactating mother. Mothers of vegan infants should be encouraged to give them commercial formulas made of soy protein isolate with added methionine, calcium, zinc, riboflavin, vitamin B-12, and other vitamins and minerals. Breast-fed infants should be given vitamin D supplements beyond 6 months of age, either in fortified formula or as cod-liver oil. The importance of vitamin D to the health and safety of the vegan child should be conveyed to parents (7, 42, 43).

Homemade soy milk, heat-treated to destroy the antitrypsin factor, may be a suitable source of vitamin B-12 and calcium if it is supplemented with calcium and *Saccharomyces cerevisiae* (brewer's yeast) that has been grown on media enriched with vitamin B-12. A recipe for a homemade version of soy milk fortified with calcium has been published (37). Calcium fortification may be unsuccessful, however, because of the tendency of calcium to coagulate the protein in the beverage. This tendency may explain why many of the soybean beverages available in food cooperatives and vegetarian food markets are not fortified (33).

Parents should be cautioned against the use of honey, now associated with botulism in infancy, and of other foods that are not safe for a young baby to ingest (37). More-complete data on nutrient priorities and techniques for maximizing the nutritional adequacy of vegetarian infant diets have been published elsewhere (33).

Recommended eating patterns for

vegan infants and children are presented in table 3.2.

5. COUNSELING THE VEGETARIAN

Care must be taken to respect the beliefs and value systems of the client and to ensure that recommended substitutions are acceptable. Several steps have been suggested to elicit a positive behavioral outcome: establishing rapport, reinforcing positive nutrition practices, assessing dietary practices accurately, assuring both quality and quantity of nutrient sources, prioritizing nutritional concerns, investigating attitudes, identifying appropriate changes, individualizing counseling, and simplifying information (4, 44).

PRIORITIES FOR QUALITY ASSURANCE

In the planning of a vegetarian diet, nutritional assessment and counseling must give priority to high-risk population groups—i.e., infants, pregnant women, and new vegetarians, who are more at risk of developing problems on the diet. Infants of new vegetarian families who were not raised as vegetarians may not be aware of the right combination of foods necessary to supply all nutrients. Consequently, new vegetarian children have been reported to have lower growth rates than nonvegetarians or than Seventh-Day Adventist vegetarians who were raised as vegetarians. Pregnant adolescents less than 14 years of age are particularly at risk; for them, dietary consultation with recommendations for increasing calories and protein are of paramount importance (18, 33, 35, 45–47).

TABLE 3.2. EATING PATTERNS FOR VEGAN INFANTS AND CHILDREN

Food group	Servings per day	Average size of serving		
		6 months to 1 year	1 to 4 years	4 to 6 years
Soy milk (fortified)[a]	3	1 cup	1 cup	1 cup
Protein foods	2–3	1–2 oz.	1–2 oz.	2–3 oz.
Fruits				
Citrus[b]	2	—	¼–½ cup	¼–½ cup
Other	2 or more	1–3 oz.	1–3 oz.	
Vegetables				
Green leafy or deep yellow	1	¼ cup	¼–½ cup	½ cup
Other	1	¼ cup	¼–½ cup	½ cup
Breads and cereals (whole grain or enriched)	2–4	1 slice or 2 oz.	1 slice or 2 oz.	1 slice or 3 oz.
Miscellaneous				
Brewer's yeast[c]	0–1	—	1 tbsp.	1 tbsp.
Molasses	0–1	—	1 tbsp.	1 tbsp.

Source: Debruyne, L. K. (18); *data adapted from* D. D. Truesdell and P. B. Acosta (48).
[a]Fortified soy milks include soy-based infant formulas.
[b]Citrus fruits and juices are not recommended for infants younger than 9 months of age.
[c]Nutritional yeast is an inappropriate food for infants. Yeast does not naturally contain vitamin B-12. Specially grown yeast or fortified products are available; the amounts of vitamin B-12 vary.

MENU PLANNING

SAMPLE MENU FOR THE OVO-LACTO-VEGETARIAN (FOR A MALE, AGE 25–50)

BREAKFAST

Granola	½ cup
Skim milk	1 cup
Poached egg	1 large
Whole wheat toast	2 slices
Margarine	2 tsp.
Grapefruit	½ medium

LUNCH

Lentil soup	1 cup
Whole wheat bread	1 slice
Margarine	1 tsp.
Low-fat cottage cheese	¼ cup
Raw spinach	½ cup
Low-fat fruit yogurt	1 cup
Fresh blueberries	½ cup
Canned pineapple chunks	½ cup
Cantaloupe	½ medium

AFTERNOON SNACK

Sunflower seeds	2 tbsp.
Raisins	2 tbsp.
Roasted peanuts	2 tbsp.

DINNER

Orange juice	½ cup
Cheese pizza	3 slices (each ¹⁄₁₂ of a 12-inch pizza)
Steamed green beans	½ cup
Steamed broccoli	½ cup
Mayonnaise	1 tbsp.
Banana	1 medium
Skim milk	1 cup

EVENING SNACK

Whole wheat bread	2 slices
Peanut butter	2 tbsp.
Fresh pear	1 medium
Skim milk	1 cup

Approximate Nutrient Analysis

Energy	2,822 kcal
Protein	117.4 g (17% of kcal)
Fat	86.3 g (28% of kcal)
Polyunsaturated fat	20.4 g
Monounsaturated fat	24.8 g
Saturated fat	23.9 g
Cholesterol	275 mg
Carbohydrate	424.7 g (60% of kcal)
Vitamin A	16,280 IU
	2,031 RE
Thiamine	2.11 mg

(continued)

Riboflavin	3.14 mg
Niacin	20.8 mg
Folate	428 mcg
Vitamin B-12	4.64 mcg
Vitamin B-6	2.28 mg
Vitamin C	313.7 mg
Calcium	1,981 mg
Phosphorus	2,467 mg
Iron	17.0 mg
Copper	1.92 mg
Zinc	10.9 mg
Magnesium	450 mg
Sodium	4,082 mg
Potassium	5,512 mg

SAMPLE MENU FOR THE LACTOVEGETARIAN (FOR A MALE, AGE 25–50)

BREAKFAST

Granola	½ cup
Skim milk	1 cup
Whole wheat toast	2 slices
Margarine	2 tsp.
Cantaloupe	½ medium
Grapefruit	½ medium

LUNCH

Lentil soup	1 cup
Garbanzo bean spread:	
Garbanzo beans	½ cup
Ground sesame seeds	1 tbsp.
Whole wheat pita bread	1 (6-inch)
Sliced cucumbers	½ cup
Raw spinach	½ cup
Tomato	½ medium
Fresh pineapple chunks	1 cup
Low-fat fruit yogurt	1 cup
Skim milk	1 cup

AFTERNOON SNACK

Sunflower seeds	2 tbsp.
Raisins	2 tbsp.
Roasted peanuts	2 tbsp.

DINNER

Orange juice	½ cup
Stir-fry:	
Tofu	½ cup
Slivered almonds	1 tbsp.
Broccoli	½ cup
Safflower oil	1 tsp.
Steamed green beans	½ cup
Whole wheat bread	2 slices
Margarine	2 tsp.
Fresh pear	1 medium
Skim milk	1 cup

(continued)

EVENING SNACK

Whole wheat bread	1 slice
Peanut butter	2 tsp.
Banana	1 medium
Skim milk	1 cup

Approximate Nutrient Analysis

Energy	2,837 kcal
Protein	124.0 g (17% of kcal)
Fat	92.3 g (29% of kcal)
Polyunsaturated fat	33.8 g
Monounsaturated fat	27.8 g
Saturated fat	20.2 g
Cholesterol	32 mg
Carbohydrate	416.2 g (59% of kcal)
Vitamin A	15,685 IU
	2,132 RE
Thiamine	2.15 mg
Riboflavin	2.99 mg
Niacin	17.1 mg
Folate	589 mcg
Vitamin B-12	4.79 mcg
Vitamin B-6	3.07 mg
Vitamin C	350.9 mg
Calcium	3,068 mg
Phosphorus	2,812 mg
Iron	32.0 mg
Copper	3.26 mg
Zinc	14.8 mg
Magnesium	636 mg
Sodium	2,787 mg
Potassium	6,604 mg

SAMPLE MENU FOR THE VEGAN (FOR A MALE, AGE 25–50)

BREAKFAST

Grape Nuts	1 cup
Soy milk[a]	1 cup
Whole wheat bread	2 slices
Peanut butter	2 tbsp.
Grapefruit	½ medium

MORNING SNACK

Whole wheat bread	2 slices
Dried peach spread	¼ cup

LUNCH

Lentil soup	1 cup
Garbanzo bean spread:	
Garbanzo beans	½ cup
Ground sesame seeds	1 tbsp.
Safflower oil	1 tsp.
Whole wheat pita bread	1 (6-inch)
Sliced cucumbers	½ cup

(continued)

Tomato	½ medium
Fresh pineapple chunks	½ cup

AFTERNOON SNACK

Sunflower seeds	2 tbsp.
Raisins	2 tbsp.
Roasted peanuts	2 tbsp.
Soy milk[a]	1 cup

DINNER

Orange juice	½ cup
Stir-fry:	
Tofu	5 oz.
Miso	2 tbsp.
Slivered almonds	1 tbsp.
Broccoli	½ cup
Safflower oil	2 tsp.
Steamed green beans	½ cup
Bulgur-wheat salad	½ cup
Whole wheat bread	1 slice
Baked apple	1 medium
Soy milk[a]	1 cup

Approximate Nutrient Analysis

Energy	2,771 kcal
Protein	123.3 g (18% of kcal)
Fat	98.0 g (32% of kcal)
Polyunsaturated fat	44.2 g
Monounsaturated fat	27.2 g
Saturated fat	13.2 g
Cholesterol	6 mg
Carbohydrate	396.1 g (57% of kcal)
Vitamin A	8,620 IU
	1,864 RE
Thiamine	4.22 mg
Riboflavin	3.26 mg
Niacin	41.6 mg
Folate	878 mcg
Vitamin B-12	6.02 mcg
Vitamin B-6	3.68 mg
Vitamin C	188.1 mg
Calcium	1,582 mg
Phosphorus	2,363 mg
Iron	43.8 mg
Copper	4.35 mg
Zinc	14.8 mg
Magnesium	666 mg
Sodium	3,933 mg
Potassium	4,931 mg

[a]For adults and older children who do not drink soy milk, try to substitute it for regular milk in baking and use miso, a soybean paste fortified with vitamin B-12.

REFERENCES

1. Raper, N. R., and Hill, M. M.: Vegetarian diets. Nutr Prog News, July–Aug., 1973.

2. Register, U. D., and Sonnenberg, L. M.: The vegetarian diet. J Am Diet Assoc 62:253, 1973.

3. Zolber, K.: Producing meals without meat. Hospitals 49 (June 1):81, 1975.

4. Inadequate vegan diets at weaning. Nutr Rev 48:323, 1990.

5. Levin, M., Rattan, J., and Gilat, T.: Energy intake and body weight in ovo-lacto vegetarians. J Clin Gastroenterol 8:451, 1986.

6. Food and Nutrition Board, National Academy of Sciences: Alternative dietary practices and nutritional abuse in pregnancy. Washington, D.C.: National Academy of Sciences, 1982.

7. Dwyer, J. T.: Health aspects of vegetarian diets. Am J Clin Nutr 48:712, 1988.

8. Rouse, I. L., Beilin, L. J., et al.: Blood-pressure-lowering effect of a vegetarian diet: Controlled trial in normotensive subjects. Lancet 1:5, 1983.

9. Beilin, L. J.: Vegetarian approach to hypertension. Can J Physiol Pharmacol 64:852, 1986.

10. Rouse, I. L., Beilin, L. J., et al.: Nutrient intake, blood pressure, serum and urinary prostaglandins and serum thromboxane B-2 in a controlled trial with a lactoovovegetarian diet. J Hypertens 4:241, 1986.

11. Margetts, B. M., Beilin, J. J., et al.: Vegetarian diet in mild hypertension: A randomized controlled trial. Br Med J 293:1468, 1986.

12. Kestin, M., Rouse, I. L., et al.: Cardiovascular disease risk factors in free-living men: Comparison of two prudent diets, one based on lactoovovegetarianism and the other allowing lean meat. Am J Clin Nutr 50:280, 1989.

13. Fisher, M., Levine, P. H., et al.: The effect of vegetarian diets on plasma lipid and platelet levels. Arch Intern Med 146:1193, 1986.

14. Vyhmeister, I. B.: Advantages of vegetarian diets. Nutr & M.D. 10 (6):1, 1984.

15. Allinger, V. G., Johansson, G. K., et al.: Shift from a mixed to a lactovegetarian diet: Influence on acidic lipids in fecal water—a potential risk factor for colon cancer. Am J Clin Nutr 50:992, 1989.

16. American Dietetic Association: Position of the American Dietetic Association—vegetarian diets. J Am Diet Assoc 88:352, 1988.

17. Vyhmeister, I. B., Register, U. D., and Sonnenberg, L. M.: Safe vegetarian diets for children. Pediatr Clin N Am 24:203, 1977.

18. Debruyne, L. K.: Vegetarian diets during vulnerable times. Nutr Clin 4 (6):1, 1989.

19. Lombard, K. A., and Mock, D. M.: Biotin nutritional status of vegans, lactovegetarians, and nonvegetarians. Am J Clin Nutr 50:486, 1988.

20. Hunt, I. F., Murphy, N. J., et al.: Bone mineral content in postmenopausal women: Comparison of omnivores and vegetarians. Am J Clin Nutr 50:517, 1989.

21. Taber, L. A. L., and Cook, R. A.: Dietary and anthropometric assessment of adult omnivores, fish-eaters and lacto-ovo-vegetarians. J Am Diet Assoc 76:21, 1980.

22. Shultz, T. D., and Leklem, J. E.: Dietary status of Seventh-Day Adventists and nonvegetarians. J Am Diet Assoc 83:27, 1983.

23. Chanarin, I., Malkowska, V., et al.: Megaloblastic anemia in a vegetarian Hindu community. Lancet 2:1168, 1985.

24. Smith, A. D. M.: Veganism: A clinical survey with observations on vitamin B-12 metabolism. Br Med J 1:1655, 1962.

25. Ledbetter, R. B., and Del Pozo, E.: Severe megaloblastic anaemia due to nutritional vitamin B-12 deficiency. Acta Haematol 42:247, 1969.

26. Armstrong, B. K., Davis, R. E., et al.: Hematological, vitamin B-12 and folate studies on Seventh-Day Adventist vegetarians. Am J Clin Nutr 27:712, 1974.

27. Zmorea, E., Gorodischer, R., and Bar-Ziv, J.: Multiple nutritional deficiencies in infants from a strict vegetarian community. AJDC 133:141, 1979.

28. Jacobs, C., and Dwyer, J. T.: Vegetarian children: Appropriate and inappropriate diets. Am J Clin Nutr 48:811, 1988.

29. Dent, C. E., and Gupta, M. M.: Plasma 25-hydroxy-vitamin D levels during pregnancy in Caucasians and in vegetarian and non-vegetarian Asians. Lancet 2:1057, 1975.

30. Freeland-Graves, J.: Mineral adequacy of vegetarian diets. Am J Clin Nutr 48:859, 1988.

31. Sanders, T. A. B.: Growth and development of British vegan children. Am J Clin Nutr 48:822, 1988.

32. Acosta, P. B.: Availability of essential amino acids and nitrogen in vegan diets. Am J Clin Nutr 48:868, 1988.

33. Truesdell, D. D., and Acosta, P. B.: Feeding the vegan infant and child. J Am Diet Assoc 85:837, 1985.

34. McNeill, D. A., Ali, P. S., and Song, Y. S.: Mineral analyses of vegetarian, health, and conventional foods: Magnesium, zinc, copper, and manganese content. J Am Diet Assoc 85:569, 1985.

35. Gibson, R., Anderson, B. M., and Sabry, J. H.: The trace metal status of a group of post-menopausal vegetarians. J Am Diet Assoc 82:246, 1986.

36. Franz, M. J.: Exchanges for all occasions: Meeting the challenge of diabetes. Wayzata, Minn.: International Diabetes Center, 1987.

37. Robertson, L., Flinders, C. and Godfrey, B.: Laurel's kitchen: A handbook for vegetarian cookery and nutrition. Petaluma, Calif.: Nilgiri Press, 1976.

38. Mutch, P. B.: Food guides for the vegetarian. Am J Clin Nutr 48:913, 1988.

39. Velkers Smith, M.: Development of a quick reference guide to accommodate vegetarianism in diet therapy for multiple disease conditions. Am J Clin Nutr 48:906, 1988.

40. Beckner, A., Hayasaka, R., et al.: Diet manual utilizing a vegetarian diet plan. 7th ed. Loma Linda, Calif.: Seventh-Day Adventist Dietetic Association, 1990.

41. American Dietetic Association: Man-

ual of clinical dietetics. Chicago: American Dietetic Association, 1988.

42. MacLean, Jr., W. C., and Graham, G. G.: Vegetarianism in children. AJDC 134:517, 1980.

43. Alfin-Slater, R. B., Aftergood L., et al.: Planning a vegetarian meal. Nutr & M.D. 10 (5):3, 1984.

44. Johnston, P. K.: Counseling the pregnant vegetarian. Am J Clin Nutr 48:901, 1988.

45. Erhard, D.: The new vegetarians: Part 1. Nutr Today 8 (6):4, 1973.

46. Erhard, D.: The new vegetarians: Part 2. Nutr Today 9 (1):20, 1974.

47. Dwyer, J. T., Andrew, E. M., et al.: Growth in "new" vegetarian preschool children using the Jenss-Bayley curve fitting technique. Am J Clin Nutr 37:815, 1983.

48. Truesdell, D. D., and Acosta, P. B.: Feeding the vegan infant and child. J Am Diet Assoc 85:837, 1985.

PART II

MODIFICATIONS IN CONSISTENCY AND TEXTURE

4.

CLEAR LIQUID DIET

DEFINITION

A diet that includes only foods that are clear and liquid at body temperature, such as fat-free broth, bouillon, coffee, tea, decaffeinated coffee, strained fruit juices, flavored gelatin, carbonated beverages (1), Popsicles, fruit ices, and hard candies.

PURPOSE OF THE DIET

The diet is intended to provide an oral source of fluids and a small amount of energy and electrolytes. It is used to prevent dehydration and to reduce colonic residue to a minimum.

Maintenance of the body's fluid balance becomes a matter of prime concern whenever an acute illness produces a marked intolerance of food. The most common fluid disorder in the surgical patient is extracellular fluid volume deficit involving the loss of both water and electrolytes. Fluid and electrolyte losses may be caused by vomiting, nasogastric suction, diarrhea, fistula drainage, infections and burns, sequestration or accumulation of fluid in injury sites, or poor intake (2).

EFFECTS OF THE DIET

The diet will provide the daily requirement for water while minimally stimulating the gastrointestinal tract (3). This effect is achieved at the expense of adequate fat and protein intake; fat and amino acids are potent stimuli of gastric and pancreatic secretions and gastrointestinal motility. The minimal dietary fiber intake and colonic residue result in a reduction in fecal weight and bacterial mass (3). The use of glucose as a source of kilocalories promotes sodium reabsorption in the small intestine, where there is coupled transport of sodium and glucose (4).

PHYSIOLOGY, FOODS, AND NUTRIENTS

A clear liquid diet is nutritionally inadequate for almost all required nutrients, except water. It is highly restrictive, providing only small amounts of some electrolytes, mainly sodium chloride and potassium, and kilocalories, mainly in the form of carbohydrate.

INDICATIONS FOR USE

1. VEHICLE FOR ORAL FLUID

The clear liquid diet may be used as a transitional step from intravenous feedings or glucose and electrolyte solutions to oral feedings as tolerated.

Although this diet can by no means serve as a complete replacement for lost fluids and electrolytes in diarrheal and prolonged gastric diseases, it may serve as a short-term adjunct to other therapies. In patients who are mildly volume-depleted or hypovolemic, an increase in dietary sodium and water intake may be sufficient (4). In patients who have more severe hypovolemia, are unable to take oral fluids, or have drainage losses exceeding 500 mL per day, volume repletion requires the administration of intravenous fluids (4, 5).

For infants and children, for whom unchecked diarrheal fluid losses can have disastrous consequences, oral solutions with sodium contents of 50 to 90 mEq per liter have been recommended for rehydration (6). Specific oral solutions containing glucose or electrolytes have been described (7). Although no ideal product fits all circumstances, such solutions can control osmolality, composition, and rate of administration better than the clear liquid diet can. Bottled preparations such as Lytren (Mead Johnson) or Pedialyte (Ross Laboratories) are widely available. In developing countries where childhood and diarrheal diseases are common and where commercial products may not be readily available, the oral rehydration formula

TABLE 4.1. COMPOSITION OF ORAL REHYDRATION FORMULA RECOMMENDED BY THE WORLD HEALTH ORGANIZATION

Nutrient	Per liter
Glucose	20 g
Sodium	2,070 mg (90 mEq)[a]
Potassium	780 mg (20 mEq)
Bicarbonate	1,830 mg (30 mEq)
Osmolality	330 mOsm

Source: Krause, M. V., and Mahan, L. K. (6); *adapted from* (21) and reprinted by courtesy of Marcel Dekker, Inc.
[a]One author has suggested that for infants and children with immature renal function, an intake of 50–60 mEq sodium is safer because it eliminates the need for the additional free water recommended by the WHO for maintenance therapy (2).

TABLE 4.2. MOLECULAR WEIGHTS AND NUTRIENT COMPOSITION OF PHYSIOLOGICAL SALTS

Salt	Atomic weight	Molecular weight	% Na^+	% Cl^-	% K^+	% Ca^{2+}	% CO_3^{2-}	% HCO_3^-	mg Na^+/g	mg K^+/g	mg Cl^-/g	mg Ca^{2+}/g
NaCl	23+35.5	58.5	39.3	60.7					393		607	
CaCl$_2$	40+(35.5×2)	111.0		64.0		36.0					640	360
CaCO$_3$	40+12+(16×3)	100.0				40.0	60.0					400
KCl	39+35.5	74.5		47.7	52.3					523	477	
NaHCO$_3$	23+1+12+(16×3)	84.0	27.4					72.6	274			

recommended by the World Health Organization (WHO) and described in table 4.1 may be useful (6). Tables 4.2 and 4.3 may be used to develop such a formula.

2. PREPARATION FOR BOWEL PROCEDURES

It has been reported that commercial low-residue-formula diets used over a 48-hour period preceding bowel surgery, colonoscopic examination, or barium enema may provide at least as good-quality preparation for the test as a clear liquid diet (3, 8, 9).

3. RECOVERY FROM PARTIAL PARALYTIC ILEUS

The clear liquid diet may be used as a short-term measure in the recovery phase of conditions in which partial paralytic ileus has occurred, such as abdominal surgery or severe burns (3). One newly proposed alternative to this approach is the insertion of a needle-catheter jejunostomy in certain patients at the time of abdominal surgery (10).

4. TEMPORARY REDUCTION IN BOWEL RESIDUE

The clear liquid diet may represent a transitional step in oral alimentation following colonic surgery or conditions in which there has been a disturbance in colonic function or when it is desirable to reduce residue in the bowel temporarily (3).

POSSIBLE ADVERSE REACTIONS

1. NUTRITIONAL DEFICIENCIES

The diet should not be used for more than 24 hours, as it is inadequate in kilocalories and most nutrients even when supplemented with low-residue, liquid-protein products. Its continued use leads to weight loss, tissue wasting, and multiple nutritional deficiencies, particularly if instituted in individuals with increased caloric needs or those whose nutritional status is marginal.

Excessive reliance on soft drinks, tea, and beverages such as Gatorade, which contain little sodium chloride, may make it difficult for the clear liquid diet to provide the recommended 50 to 90 mEq of sodium per liter. On the other hand, a liquid diet that provides excessive amounts of highly salted foods such as bouillon may actually worsen diarrhea by exceeding the absorptive capacity of the gut (10–12).

2. GASTROINTESTINAL INTOLERANCE

The relationship of osmolality to gastrointestinal tolerance and absorption is a function of the following variables: substance concentration, fluid balance, volume, and time. The major determinants of gastrointestinal side effects are the osmolality of a liquid and the rate at which it is given. Individuals with hyperthyroidism, dumping syndrome, or a nonfunctioning pyloric sphincter are particularly sensitive to hyperosmolar solutions (11). In a normal individual, the higher the osmolality of a meal, the slower the rate of gastric emptying (13). Because intestinal absorption occurs only when intestinal contents are isoosmolar, their osmolality determines the amount of fluid that must diffuse into the stomach and small bowel before absorption begins (14, 15).

The importance of the initial osmolality of a substance can be outweighed by the amount and rate of administration (11). Although hyperosmolar solutions, particularly those with large amounts of simple sugars, distend the bowel and cause nausea and diarrhea, so does the rapid feeding of excessive amounts of

TABLE 4.3. SAMPLE FORMULATION OF GLUCOSE-SALT SOLUTION FOR REHYDRATION

	Na^+(mg)	Cl^-(mg)	K^+(mg)	HCO_3^-
To 1 L of water add:				
NaCl: 3.5 g	1,371	2,124		
NaHCO$_3$: 2.5 g	685			1,816
KCl: 1.5 g		716	785	
Glucose: 20.0 g				

Source: Krause, M. V., and Mahan, L. K. (6); *adapted from* Wolman, I. J. (21), by courtesy of Marcel Dekker, Inc.

isotonic solutions. For example, drinking an isotonic sodium chloride solution rapidly, at the rate of 1 qt. per hour, will result in an osmotic diarrhea in 3 to 4 hours (11). Even a healthy person with an intact pyloric sphincter may experience dumping if an unusually large meal is hastily consumed, and especially so if a carbohydrate-laden dessert is also eaten. The diarrhea is due mainly to feeding too much too fast to permit the gut to absorb it.

No well-controlled comparative research studies have been done on the effect of a clear liquid diet or on its use as an oral feeding. Because some of the foods served on the diet are hyperosmolar liquids, however, certain assumptions can be made related to known adverse consequences of hyperosmolar solutions. If such solutions are fed very rapidly in large amounts, the capacity of the intestine to adapt may be overcome. If, however, they are fed under normal conditions at a rate slow enough to permit the intestine to adapt, hyperosmolar diarrhea is highly unlikely (11). In addition, some clear liquid commercial formulas also contain nutrients, such as whole proteins, that slow down the rate of hydrolysis and protect against hyperosmolar effects (11).

3. CAFFEINE

Excessive amounts of strong coffee or tea should be avoided, because they increase hydrochloric acid production in the stomach. Although low doses of caffeine (less than 50 mg) have little effect on intestinal function, large amounts (greater than 200 mg) decrease transit time (3).

CONTRAINDICATIONS

The diet is contraindicated in any condition when used for more than 24 hours as the sole means of nutritional support, especially for nutritionally depleted patients or for patients with extraordinary

needs. In such cases, the use of semi-synthetic diets may be indicated. The diet is also contraindicated in the absence of adequate gastrointestinal function, including paralytic ileus and suspected small bowel trauma, perforation, or obstruction. Clear liquids are also inappropriate whenever parenteral rather than enteral feeding is indicated (16).

CLINICAL ASSESSMENT

The patient requiring clear-liquid-diet therapy, whether alone or with adjunctive intravenous therapy, may exhibit clinical signs of either insufficient fluids and subsequent hypovolemia or, conversely, fluid overload and hypervolemia. Extracellular fluid volume deficits affect the central nervous system with sleepiness and apathy; the gastrointestinal system with decreased food intake; the cardiovascular system with orthostatic hypotension, tachycardia, collapsed veins, and collapsing pulse; the skin with decreased skin turgor (17); and the metabolism with a mild decrease in body temperature (2). The elderly and patients who cannot identify or respond appropriately to a sensation of thirst are particularly prone to dehydration (18). Fluid overload on the other hand is manifested by elevated venous pressure, distension of peripheral veins, and edema (2).

BIOCHEMICAL ASSESSMENT

Fluid deficits may be manifested by a blood urea nitrogen level that is elevated out of proportion to the serum creatinine. The specific gravity of the urine is high, the urine sodium concentration is low except in renal disease or adrenal salt wasting, and the urine volume is decreased. The hematocrit and serum protein concentrations are elevated. Although serum sodium level reflects the relationship between total amounts of extracellular sodium and water, it is not a guide to volume depletion (17). Table 4.4 is a capsule of abnormal laboratory values that may be useful in the assessment of the candidate for a clear liquid diet (4).

ASSESSMENT OF POTENTIAL DRUG INTERACTIONS

See Chapters 8, 11, and 12.

IMPLEMENTATION AND EDUCATION

Following gastric surgery or myocardial infarction, it may be desirable to eliminate caffeine-containing beverages such

---

TABLE 4.4. SELECTED ABNORMAL LABORATORY FINDINGS IN HYPOVOLEMIA

- Ratio of blood urea nitrogen to plasma creatinine greater than 20 : 1 with a normal urinalysis
- Occasional elevations in the hematocrit and plasma albumin concentration
- Urine osmolality greater than 450 mOsm/kg
- Variable effects on plasma Na^+, K^+, and HCO_3^- concentrations
- Urine Na^+ concentration less than 10–15 mEq/L

Changes in urinary Na^+ concentrations

Less than 10–15 mEq/L	*Greater than 20 mEq/L*
Gastrointestinal losses	Renal disease
Skin losses	Diuretics (while drug is acting)
Third-space losses	Osmotic diuresis
Diuretics (late)	Adrenal insufficiency
	Certain instances of metabolic acidosis

Source: Adapted by permission of McGraw-Hill, Inc., from Rose, B. D. (4). Copyright © 1984, McGraw-Hill, Inc.

as tea, coffee, and colas. Caffeine stimulates hydrochloric acid secretion and increases heart rate (19). It may also be advisable to avoid citrus juice in postoperative patients who are nauseous, at least at the first feeding (20).

If the diet is to be used for more than two meals, it should be supplemented with foods such as prepackaged, clear liquid surgical diet, high-protein broth, and high-protein gelatin, which at least increase the intake of protein and total kilocalories.

Patients should be informed as to the foods allowed and excluded on the clear liquid diet. They should be advised against eating excluded items that may be brought to them by well-meaning visitors.

PRIORITIES FOR QUALITY ASSURANCE

Controversy surrounds the use of the clear liquid diet (15). The controversy is fueled by a void in research data on the effects of the diet versus other types of oral feedings in postoperative and post-diarrheal states. The unsupplemented clear liquid diet has been implicated as one of the causative factors in the high incidence of hospital malnutrition (15). Particularly in the depleted patient, measures should be taken to ensure only short-term use.

The efficacy and status of the clear liquid diet in hospital diet manuals has been questioned. Of 299 hospitals responding to a survey, 100% included some form of clear liquid diet in their diet manual (15), perhaps because diet manuals often follow the prescribing practices of physicians. If doctors persist in ordering clear liquid diets, dietitians who must implement those orders will continue to describe the diets.

The Joint Commission on Accreditation of Healthcare Organizations (JCAHO) has mandated quality assurance monitoring for both food service and clinical nutritional systems. The inclu-

MENU PLANNING

FOOD LIST FOR THE SUPPLEMENTED CLEAR LIQUID DIET[a]

Food group	Foods allowed	Foods excluded
Beverages	Clear fruit juices, such as apple, cranberry, or grape, or strained juices	All others, including nectars, milk, cream, juices with pulp
Desserts	Clear flavored gelatin, Popsicles, clear flavored fruit-juice ices, sugar, honey, sugar substitutes, hard candy	All others
Soups and miscellaneous	Clear broth or bouillon; high-protein gelatin; other low-residue, high-protein, high-calorie oral supplements; iodized salt	All others

[a]For an unsupplemented clear liquid diet, the same lists are used but commercial supplements are omitted.

SAMPLE MENU FOR THE UNSUPPLEMENTED CLEAR LIQUID DIET (FOR A MALE, AGE 25–50)[a]

BREAKFAST
Apple juice	½ cup
Cherry-flavored gelatin	1 cup
Ginger ale	1 cup
Coffee or tea	1 cup
Sugar	2 tsp.

MORNING SNACK
Lemon-flavored gelatin	½ cup

LUNCH
Bouillon	1 cup
Strained orange juice	½ cup
Grape-flavored gelatin	½ cup
Coffee or tea	1 cup
Sugar	2 tsp.

AFTERNOON SNACK
Ginger ale	1 cup

DINNER
Bouillon	1 cup
Sweetened cranberry juice	½ cup
Lime-flavored gelatin	½ cup
Coffee or tea	1 cup
Sugar	2 tsp.

EVENING SNACK
Pineapple-flavored gelatin	½ cup

Approximate Nutrient Analysis
Energy	916 kcal
Protein	14.7 g (6% of kcal)

(continued)

Fat	2.4 g (2% of kcal)
Polyunsaturated fat	0.5 g
Monounsaturated fat	0.8 g
Saturated fat	0.7 g
Cholesterol	1 mg
Carbohydrate	218.2 g (95% of kcal)
Vitamin A	146 IU
	23 RE
Thiamine	0.19 mg
Riboflavin	0.16 mg
Niacin	1.5 mg
Folate	47 mcg
Vitamin B-12	0.10 mcg
Vitamin B-6	0.14 mg
Vitamin C	86.8 mg
Calcium	63 mg
Phosphorus	68 mg
Iron	2.1 mg
Copper	0.24 mg
Zinc	0.5 mg
Magnesium	53 mg
Sodium	3,265 mg
Potassium	700 mg

[a]This menu supplies only 32% of energy needs and 23% RDA for protein (none of high biological value). It is adequate only in vitamin C content and provides less than 20% RDA for all other nutrients.

SAMPLE MENU FOR THE SUPPLEMENTED CLEAR LIQUID DIET (FOR A MALE, AGE 25–50)[a]

BREAKFAST
Apple juice	½ cup
High-protein gelatin	4 oz.
Ginger ale	1 cup
Coffee or tea	1 cup
Sugar	2 tsp.

MORNING SNACK
| High-protein, clear-liquid commercial supplement[b] | ½ serving or 100 mL |

LUNCH
High-protein broth	6 fluid oz.
Strained orange juice	½ cup
High-protein gelatin	4 oz.
Coffee or tea	1 cup
Sugar	2 tsp.

AFTERNOON SNACK
| High-protein, clear-liquid commercial supplement[b] | ½ serving or 100 mL |

DINNER
High-protein broth	6 fluid oz.
Sweetened cranberry juice	½ cup
High-protein, clear-liquid commercial supplement[b]	½ serving or 100 mL
Coffee or tea	1 cup
Sugar	2 tsp.

(continued)

sion of a monitor of clear liquid diets would be an appropriate way to identify misuse and any individual nutritional problems that result. One approach in an acute-care setting might be to use existing record-keeping systems, such as completed nutritional assessments, to evaluate the frequency of nutritional deficiencies due to inadequate intakes from clear liquid diets.

If the clear liquid diet is implicated, one potential action plan is to set up a system via the institution's nutritional support committee in which the initial order for the clear liquid diet is valid only for 24 hours. This order would be similar to a 10-day order for antibiotics that is automatically discontinued when the 10 days are up. The physician must then reevaluate the patient and either reorder the diet for another day with documented justification or choose a more appropriate method of feeding. There should also be a mechanism to identify patients who have had more than 3 repeat orders for clear liquid diets.

EVENING SNACK

High-protein gelatin	4 oz.
Ginger ale	1 cup

Approximate Nutrient Analysis

Energy	1,334 kcal
Protein	120.9 g (36% of kcal)
Fat	0.8 g (1% of kcal)
Polyunsaturated fat	0.1 g
Monounsaturated fat	0.1 g
Saturated fat	0.1 g
Cholesterol	0 mg
Carbohydrate	272.6 g (82% of kcal)
Vitamin A	1,354 IU
	10 RE
Thiamine	0.76 mg
Riboflavin	0.70 mg
Niacin	9.2 mg
Folate	173 mcg
Vitamin B-12	2.25 mcg
Vitamin B-6	0.88 mg
Vitamin C	109.3 mg
Calcium	301 mg
Phosphorus	281 mg
Iron	6.5 mg
Copper	0.72 mg
Zinc	6.23 mg
Magnesium	152 mg
Sodium	1,478 mg
Potassium	1,800 mg

[a]This menu supplies only 46% of energy needs. It provides greater than the RDA for protein, vitamin C, and vitamin B-12, only 86% RDA for folate, 65% RDA for iron, and less then 50% RDA for all other nutrients.

[b]Examples: Ross SLD, Nutrex CLD, Nutrex Drink.

REFERENCES

1. Turner, D.: Handbook of diet therapy. 5th ed. Chicago: University of Chicago Press, 1970.
2. Shires, G. I., and Canizaro, P. C.: Fluid, electrolyte and nutritional management of the surgical patient. In Schwartz, S. I.: Principles of surgery. 3d ed. New York: McGraw-Hill, 1979.
3. Alpers, D. H., Clouse, R. E., and Stenson, W. F.: Manual of nutritional therapeutics. Boston: Little, Brown, 1983.
4. Rose, B. D.: Clinical physiology of acid-base and electrolyte disorders. 2d ed. New York: McGraw-Hill, 1984.
5. Mirtallo, J. M.: Parenteral therapy. In Lang, C. E.: Nutritional support in critical care. Rockville, Md.: Aspen, 1987.
6. Krause, M. V., and Mahan, L. K., eds.: Food, nutrition and diet therapy. Philadelphia: W. B. Saunders, 1984.
7. Santosham, M., Daum, R. S., et al.: Oral rehydration therapy of infantile diarrhea. N Engl J Med 306:1070, 1982.
8. Scheurich, J. W., Wierman, M. E., et al.: Preparation for barium enema: Comparison of a commercial formula diet and low-residue, clear-liquid diets in inpatients. South Med J 78:838, 1985.
9. Kruss, D. M., DeBartolo, M., et al.: Explosion-safe, enema-free, nutritious colonoscopy preparation using a pre-packaged formula diet. Gastrointest Endosc 31:18, 1985.
10. Hoover, H. C.: Enteral elemental nutrition in major abdominal surgery. Contemp Surg 28:3, 1986.
11. Randall, H. T.: Osmolality and its relationship to GI tolerance. In Current concepts in nutritional support. New York: Biomedical Information Corp., Norwich Eaton Pharmaceuticals, 1983.
12. Fordtran, J. S.: Diarrhea. In Wyngarrden, J. B., and Smith, L. I.: Cecil textbook of medicine. 16th ed. Philadelphia: W. B. Saunders, 1983.
13. Schiller, L. R.: Motor function of the stomach. In Sleisinger, M. H., and Fordtran, J. S.: Gastrointestinal disease. Philadelphia: W. B. Saunders, 1983.
14. Binder, H. J.: Absorption and secretion of water and electrolytes for small and large intestine. In Sleisinger, M. H., and Fordtran, J. S.: Gastrointestinal disease. Philadelphia: W. B. Saunders, 1983.
15. Murray, D. P., Welsh, J. D., et al. Survey: Use of clear and full liquid diets with or without commercially produced formulas. JPEN 9:732, 1985.
16. Philips, S.: Water and electrolytes in gastrointestinal disease. In Maxwell, M. H., and Klienman, C. R.: Clinical disorders of fluid and electrolyte metabolism. New York: McGraw-Hill, 1979.
17. Campbell, J. W., and Frisee, M.: Manual of medical therapeutics. 24th ed. Boston: Little, Brown, 1983.
18. Austin, C.: Water: Guidelines for nutritional support. Nutr Supp Serv 6 (Sept.):27, 1986.
19. Goodman, L. S., and Gilman, C. A.: The pharmacological basis of therapeutics. 3d ed. New York: Macmillan, 1980.
20. Pemberton, C. M., and Gastineau, C. F.: Mayo Clinic diet manual. Philadelphia: W. B. Saunders, 1981.
21. Wolman, I. J., ed.: The rehydration treatment of acute diarrhea with inexpensive oral fluids. Clin Pediatr 15:1095, 1976.

5.

SUPPLEMENTED FULL LIQUID DIET

DEFINITION

A diet consisting of foods that are liquid at body temperature (1), supplemented with commercial liquid supplements.

PURPOSE OF THE DIET

- To provide a source of oral nourishment and fluid that is well tolerated by individuals with alterations in pharyngeal function who are unable to chew or swallow solid foods
- After esophageal surgery in individuals with anastomotic edema (2)
- As a more nutritious postoperative alternative to clear liquids for patients still too weak to chew

EFFECTS OF THE DIET

With proper planning and the inclusion of commercial nutritional supplements, normal caloric and nutrient requirements can be met. Because the diet is low in fiber and residue, the number and volume of stools may be decreased.

PHYSIOLOGY, FOODS, AND NUTRIENTS

If properly planned, the diet can be nutritionally adequate. A variety of foods may be included, such as fruit and vegetable juices, strained hot cereals, broths, milk, eggs, egg substitutes, commercial liquid formulas, high-protein broths, high-protein cereals, puddings, and gelatins.

INDICATIONS FOR USE

A full liquid diet is indicated following oral or plastic surgery of the face and neck or in other postoperative states such as in esophageal surgery (3). It may also be used as a transition between a clear liquid diet and a fiber-restricted or regular diet. It is used in conjunction with dilatation procedures in the management of esophageal stricture, following mandibular fractures, or with any patient who cannot chew properly or who has an esophageal or pharyngeal disorder that interferes with the normal handling of solid foods.

POSSIBLE ADVERSE REACTIONS

1. LACTOSE INTOLERANCE

Full liquid diets with increased amounts of lactose-containing foods such as milk may precipitate an exacerbation of symptoms in individuals with a lactose intolerance who were previously asymptomatic. Other individuals may be temporarily lactose intolerant after surgery (4) and demonstrate nausea, vomiting, distention, or diarrhea when given a high-lactose full liquid diet. Milk should be given in small amounts at first if lactose intolerance is suspected.

2. HYPERCHOLESTEROLEMIA

Excessive use of whole milk products, ice cream, milk shakes, and eggs as protein sources in the diet may result in increased intakes of saturated fats and cholesterol.

CONTRAINDICATIONS

The full liquid diet is contraindicated in any individual with dysphagia who cannot swallow thin liquids.

CLINICAL ASSESSMENT

The effect of the diet on body weight, as well as the clinical status of the disorder that necessitated the diet, should be regularly assessed. Stool patterns should be monitored for any sign of lactose intolerance. Clinical parameters of fluid and hydration status should be utilized.

BIOCHEMICAL ASSESSMENT

Just as important as monitoring total amounts of food ingested is an evaluation of serum proteins both before and during this diet to be sure that protein needs are being met. Biochemical parameters of fluid and electrolyte status discussed in Chapters 4 and 11 should be applied in the assessment of the patient on a full liquid diet.

ASSESSMENT OF POTENTIAL DRUG INTERACTIONS

No potential drug interactions are specific to the full liquid diet.

IMPLEMENTATION AND EDUCATION

1. HIGH-CALORIE, HIGH-PROTEIN SUPPLEMENTS

Careful planning is needed to ensure nutritional adequacy, because of the large volume of liquid. Individuals on a full liquid diet should receive high-calorie, high-protein soups, cereals, desserts, and drinks. The reader should refer to Chapter 11 for more-specific information on the types of feedings available. For additional calories, powdered glucose or glucose polymers may be dissolved in fruit juices. The use of a sugar such as glucose, which is not as sweet as sucrose, will permit larger amounts to be added. For additional protein, there are several high-protein-efficiency whey powders now on the market. These powders far surpass their casein predecessors in taste and can be incorporated into such foods as milk, puddings, hot cereals, and milk shakes. For lactose-intolerant patients, a plethora of lactose-free supplements is now available. For the patient with chronic obstructive pulmonary disease or the diabetic, for whom it is not desirable to provide large amounts of simple sugars, fortified margarine may be added to hot liquids.

2. LOW-SODIUM DIETS

If a low-sodium diet is indicated, low-sodium soups, eggnogs, drinks, and custards should be used.

3. INFECTION CONTROL

To prevent the danger of salmonella infection, raw eggs should not be used. In addition, raw egg white contains a heat-labile protein called avidin, which interferes with the body's absorption of biotin (5). Liquid nutritional formula supplements should be refrigerated after opening and consumed within 24 hours. When unrefrigerated—i.e., at the bedside—they should be consumed within 4 hours or discarded. In any institution where full liquid diets are still used for tube feedings, the protocol should include written educational guidelines for the sanitary handling of the liquids as well as a strict infection-control policy to monitor compliance.

4. DIET FOLLOWING TONSILLECTOMY

Soft, smooth, cold, or lukewarm foods may be given in a semiliquid form following a tonsillectomy or throat surgery. Some physicians prefer to eliminate milk and milk products in the immediate period following a tonsillectomy to avoid

MENU PLANNING

FOOD LIST FOR THE SUPPLEMENTED FULL LIQUID DIET

Food group	Foods allowed	Foods excluded
Beverages	Milk, milk drinks, milk substitutes, carbonated beverages, cocoa, coffee, tea, decaffeinated coffee, eggnogs, milk shakes, instant breakfast, cereal beverages, liquid dietary high-protein or high-calorie supplements, complete liquid diets, yogurt drinks, fruit-flavored beverages	Any containing raw eggs or egg white; fruits; other prohibited foods
Breads	None	All
Cereals	Refined cooked cereals, strained whole-grain cereals, high-protein cereals	All others
Desserts	Cornstarch puddings, high-protein puddings, custard, regular and high-protein gelatin desserts, plain ice cream, frozen yogurt, sherbet, fruit ices, Popsicles, Bavarian cream, yogurt (plain, coffee, vanilla, or lemon)	Any dessert containing solid foods such as nuts, fruits, and seeds
Eggs	Clean fresh eggs cooked to a liquid consistency or in custards; egg substitutes; puddings; plain ice cream; pasteurized eggs used in eggnogs or cooking; salmonella-free frozen eggs	Raw eggs and egg whites, pasteurized eggs, any egg cooked in a manner that renders it to a hard consistency
Miscellaneous	Honey, sugar, syrup, glucose, lactose, sucrose, salt, flavorings, chocolate syrup, cinnamon, nutmeg, brewer's yeast	All others
Soups	Bouillon; regular or high-protein consommé; broth; strained vegetable, meat, or cream soups containing finely homogenized meat	All others
Vegetables	Vegetable juice and vegetable purees that are strained and diluted in cream soups; mashed white potato diluted in cream soups	All others
Fruits	Fruit juices, nectars	Fresh, cooked, frozen, canned, or dried fruit

DAILY MEAL PLAN FOR THE SUPPLEMENTED FULL LIQUID DIET

Food and serving size	Number of servings
Milk, yogurt, or pudding (1 cup)	2
Eggs—in custards or puddings or pasteurized in eggnogs	1
Strained cooked regular or high-protein cereal (1 cup)	1
Citrus juice (½ cup)	1
Vegetable juice (½ cup)	1
High-protein broth or soup (¾ cup)	2
Fortified corn-oil margarine (1 tsp.)	2
Sugar (1 tsp.)	2
High-protein dessert (½ cup)	2
High-calorie liquid commercial supplements (8 fluid oz.)	3
Tea, coffee, carbonated beverages	As desired

SAMPLE MENU FOR THE SUPPLEMENTED FULL LIQUID DIET (FOR A MALE, AGE 25–50)

BREAKFAST
Orange juice	½ cup
Cream of Wheat	1 cup
Margarine	2 tsp.
Sugar	1 tsp.
Low-fat milk	1 cup
Poached egg	1 large
Coffee or tea	1 cup
Sugar	1 tsp.

MORNING SNACK
High-protein, clear liquid commercial supplement[a]	½ serving or 100 mL

LUNCH
High-protein broth	¾ cup
Tomato juice	½ cup
Cranberry juice	½ cup
Fortified pudding[b]	½ cup
High-calorie liquid commercial supplement[c]	1 cup

AFTERNOON SNACK
High-protein gelatin	½ cup

DINNER
High-protein broth	¾ cup
Pineapple-orange juice	½ cup
High-protein gelatin	½ cup
High-calorie liquid commercial supplement[c]	1 cup

EVENING SNACK
High-calorie liquid commercial supplement[c]	1 cup

Approximate Nutrient Analysis
Energy	2,893 kcal
Protein	178.2 g (25% of kcal)

(continued)

excessive mucus production. Chocolate products, as well as foods and beverages that contain red or orange coloring, may mask hemoptysis and are therefore usually excluded. The use of straws is usually also prohibited (6).

PRIORITIES FOR QUALITY ASSURANCE

1. NUTRITIONAL ADEQUACY

Precautions designed to ensure nutritional completeness of the diet should be instituted whenever the diet is used for more than a few days. A written cycle menu that includes between-meal nourishments of commercial liquid supplements may be helpful to ensure the variety needed. In addition, the actual total amounts consumed by individual patients should be monitored by daily nutrient-intake analyses, which are then compared with the Recommended Dietary Allowances.

2. POTENTIAL FOR MISUSE

Although full liquid diets can be given through gastrostomy tubes, the practice is not recommended, because of potential infection-control hazards (5). See Chapter 11 for more details.

Fat	70.3 g (22% of kcal)
Polyunsaturated fat	27.8 g
Monounsaturated fat	8.3 g
Saturated fat	15.9 g
Cholesterol	268 mg
Carbohydrate	439.0 g (61% of kcal)
Vitamin A	9,728 IU
	868 RE
Thiamine	2.77 mg
Riboflavin	3.50 mg
Niacin	31.4 mg
Folate	655 mcg
Vitamin B-12	10.59 mcg
Vitamin B-6	3.28 mg
Vitamin C	294.1 mg
Calcium	1,609 mg
Phosphorus	1,515 mg
Iron	29.1 mg
Copper	1.98 mg
Zinc	20.5 mg
Magnesium	452 mg
Sodium	2,723 mg
Potassium	4,073 mg

[a]Examples: Ross SLD, Nutrex CLD, Nutrex Drink.
[b]Examples: Forta pudding, Sustacal pudding.
[c]Examples: Ensure Plus, Sustacal HC.

REFERENCES

1. Turner, D.: Handbook of diet therapy. 5th ed. Chicago: University of Chicago Press, 1970.
2. Palombo, R. D., and Carey, M.: Massachusetts General Hospital Department of Dietetics—diet reference manual. 2d ed. Boston: Little, Brown, 1984.
3. Randall, H. T.: Enteric feeding. In Bollinger, W. F., Collins, J. A., et al.: Manual of surgical nutrition. Philadelphia: W. B. Saunders, 1975.
4. Appel, J. A., and Briggs, G. M.: Biotin. In Goodhart, R. S., and Shils, M. E.: Modern nutrition in health and disease. 6th ed. Philadelphia: Lea & Febiger, 1980.
5. American Dietetic Association: Manual of clinical dietetics. Chicago: American Dietetic Association, 1988.
6. Alpers, D. H., Clouse, R. E., and Stenson, W. G.: Manual of nutritional therapeutics. Boston: Little, Brown, 1983.

6.

CONTROLLED-CONSISTENCY, MODIFIED-FLUID (DYSPHAGIA) DIET

DEFINITIONS

1. CONTROLLED-CONSISTENCY, MODIFIED-FLUID DIET

A diet formulated for patients with chewing and swallowing disorders in order to maximize individual ability to meet nutritional needs and to prevent aspiration. The diet is controlled and periodically adjusted as changes occur in consistency tolerance. Diets may be ordered to include thickening agents to provide varying levels of consistency according to individual needs.

2. DYSPHAGIA

The inability to swallow normally or freely or to transfer liquid or solid foods from the oral cavity to the stomach (1). The inability may be due to an underlying central neurologic or isolated mechanical dysfunction (2).

PURPOSE OF THE DIET

The purposes of dietary management of dysphagia are to provide nutrition in a form that fits the specific anatomical and functional needs of the patient, to maintain or improve nutritional status, to avoid or limit possible adverse reactions such as aspiration that result from attempts to feed the dysphagic patient, to provide adequate hydration in the patient who cannot handle thin liquids, and to help the patient achieve the highest level of consistency tolerance possible. Thin liquids are usually the most difficult texture to control, especially in the oral stage of the swallow. Patients who cannot have thin liquids may need intra-

venous fluids or, in some cases, tube feedings if fluid, energy, or protein needs cannot be met orally (1).

EFFECTS OF THE DIET

1. BOLUS ATTRIBUTES

Certain bolus attributes such as volume (3), viscosity (4), temperature (5), and consistency (6) are known to affect esophageal peristalsis and therefore to affect the success of a swallow. Two studies have shown that the osmolality of the bolus has no effect on esophageal motility (7, 8).

2. INDIVIDUALIZATION OF THE DIET

Each individual displays unique manifestations of the disorder that require individualized dietary intervention. Specific conditions or aspects of dysphagia, their dietary interventions, and their effects or rationale are listed in tables 6.1, 6.2, and 6.3.

3. ADEQUACY

The diet is adequate if carefully planned. Care must be taken to ensure adequate fluid intake.

PHYSIOLOGY, FOODS, AND NUTRIENTS

1. ANATOMY AND PHYSIOLOGY OF SWALLOWING

A normal swallow has 4 stages (table 6.4): anticipatory, oral, pharyngeal, and esophageal. Swallowing is controlled by 5 cranial nerves. Each nerve has a different role, so the nature and severity

of dysphagia depend on which nerve or nerves are damaged. The trigeminal (5th) nerve controls chewing, sensations of texture and temperature in the mouth, salivation, and swallowing. The facial (7th) nerve controls taste (anterior tongue) and facial expression and movement. The glossopharyngeal (9th) nerve controls taste (posterior tongue), sensations to the soft palate and pharynx, the sensory component to the pharyngeal (gag) reflex, and salivation. The vagus (10th) nerve controls movement of the soft palate, pharynx, and larynx, as well as salivation, the gag reflex, peristalsis, and speech. And the hypoglossal (12th) nerve controls tongue movement, chewing, and speaking (10, 11).

2. ORAL MANAGEMENT OF DYSPHAGIA

In oral dietary management of dysphagia, consideration must be given to bolus consistencies, positioning of the patient, rate of feeding, and specific swallowing techniques.

A. Bolus Consistencies The level of bolus consistency tolerated by the patient is determined by videofluoroscopy examination, or cookie swallow. In the elderly stroke population, a delayed or absent pharyngeal swallow is the most frequent swallowing disorder. Delayed pharyngeal swallow indicates the need for a pureed diet, because the consistency of pureed food provides stimulation to trigger the reflex swallow. In individuals with a reduced pharyngeal swallow, liquids tend to be the most difficult consistency to handle. Thickening agents are often necessary to achieve the

TABLE 6.1. DIETARY CONSIDERATIONS FOR DYSPHAGIA: NEUROLOGIC DISORDERS

Condition	Dietary consideration	Rationale
Slow, weak, or uncoordinated swallow	Include highly seasoned, flavorful, aromatic foods; add sugar, spices	Maximize stimulus for swallow
	Serve food at either very warm or very cold temperatures	Maximize stimulus for swallow
	Include highly textured foods such as diced cooked vegetables, finely chopped raw vegetables in gelatin base, diced canned fruit	Maximize stimulus for swallow
	Maintain semisolid consistencies that form a cohesive bolus	Need to avoid consistencies that will tend to fall apart in the pharynx
	Avoid sticky or bulky foods	Reduce risk of airway obstruction
	Be cautious with thin liquids (water, juices, milk); try: • Carbonated beverages (carbonation may stimulate reflex) • Iced tart juices or crushed Popsicles—banana and vanilla melt slowest (flavor and temperature may stimulate reflex) • Medium- or spoon-thick liquids may be substituted • Thickening thin liquids with nonfat dry milk powder, fruit flakes, or commercial thickeners	Thin liquids are difficult to control, are unpredictable, and may spill into pharynx prior to swallow reflex
	Small frequent meals	Minimize fatigue; optimize food temperature and total nutrient intake

Source: Megan S. Veldee, R.D., and Robert M. Miller, Ph.D., Seattle Department of Veterans Affairs Medical Center, Seattle.

viscosity required to minimize the risk of aspiration (11–14).

For individuals with cricopharyngeal dysfunction (incoordination of the upper esophageal sphincter), thin liquids are often appropriate (12).

B. Positioning It is essential to have the patient upright at a 90° angle and to stabilize the head, neck, and trunk with wedges or pillows. Head positioning can aid a successful swallow. For patients with delayed pharyngeal swallow, bringing the chin to the chest reduces the risk of aspiration prior to the swallow. A swallow reflex can often be elicited by pressure to the Adam's apple (12).

Patients with oral difficulties such as pocketing of food in the lateral sulci are requested to tilt the head away from the affected side, thus directing the bolus to the intact side (12). Patients should be encouraged to check the affected side for pocketing.

C. Rate of Feeding Some patients eat too quickly, potentially stuffing food into their mouths. They require close supervision by trained staff to monitor feeding amounts and rate. Careful cueing may help to reduce intake to 1 teaspoon, to complete the swallow sequence, and to pace the intake of the next bolus adequately.

D. Swallowing Techniques The speech therapist may be able to teach patients to compensate for swallowing problems, using various techniques. The supraglottic swallow allows voluntary airway protection and is appropriate for patients with reduced laryngeal function. The technique involves taking a breath prior to swallowing, consciously holding the breath during the swallow, exhaling forcefully or coughing gently after the swallow, and finally reswallowing to clear (12).

The Mendelson maneuver is appropriate for individuals with cricopharyngeal dysfunction. It involves teaching the patient to elevate the larynx voluntarily to the maximal level during a swallow to allow for the safe passage of the bolus (12).

3. NONORAL MANAGEMENT OF DYSPHAGIA

A. Alternate Feeding Methods In cases when nonoral management is indicated, transpyloric tube feeding has been recommended (15). In a recent study of 90 patients with dysphagia in which both enteral and parenteral nutrition support were used, patients receiving upper gastrointestinal feeding (oral supplements, nasoenteric intubation, or gastrostomy) had a significantly higher complication incidence (aspiration pneumonia, tracheal perforation, massive diarrhea, or persistently high residuals). Mortality was significantly higher in patients receiving nasoenteric feeding than other

TABLE 6.2. DIETARY CONSIDERATIONS FOR DYSPHAGIA: MECHANICAL DISORDERS

Condition	Dietary consideration	Rationale
Stricture or partial obstruction of the pharynx or esophagus	Semisolids or liquids	Solids may stick or lodge in throat or esophagus
Partial glossectomy	Maintain semisolid consistencies that form a cohesive bolus	Reduce oral manipulation necessary
	Assure very moist, well-lubricated foods; add gravies, extra margarine, sauces	Aid oral manipulation
Base-of-tongue resection	Caution with thin liquids; maintain consistencies that form a cohesive bolus	Quick, easy laryngeal penetration before the swallow
Total glossectomy	Very individual; may persistently aspirate all textures and thus require nonoral feedings	
Floor-of-mouth resection	May require soft or semisolid textures; maintain consistencies that form a cohesive bolus	Difficulty chewing
Palate resection	Very individual; mastication problems and nasal regurgitation dependent on degree of resection and adequacy of obturation	
Pharyngectomy	Assure moist, well-lubricated foods; caution with thin liquids	
Supraglottic laryngectomy	Caution with thin liquids; maintain consistencies that form a cohesive bolus; try supraglottic swallow technique[a]	Quick, easy laryngeal penetration
Hemilaryngectomy, frontolateral laryngectomy	Generally can resume normal diet, assuming precautions are taken to protect airway	Airway protection usually intact if a vertical half of the larynx remains
Weakened or poor oral-muscular control	Maintain semisolid consistencies that form a cohesive bolus; avoid slippery, sticky foods	Requires less oral manipulation; purees are difficult to control
	Avoid thin liquids (see table 6.1 for description of thin liquids and for recommendations)	See table 6.1 for rationale
	Small frequent meals	Minimize fatigue; optimize total nutrient intake
Reduced oral sensation	Position food in most sensitive area; do not mix textures (e.g., vegetable soup); use colder temperatures; use highly seasoned, flavorful foods	Maximize sensation possible
Cricopharyngeal dysfunction	Maintain diet of liquids and purees if no other contraindications present	Liquids and purees will pass into the esophagus more easily
Decreased laryngeal elevation	Limit diet to medium- and spoon-thick liquids and soft solids	Thin liquids easily penetrate larynx
	Avoid sticky or bulky foods or food that will fall apart	Reduce risk of airway obstruction
Decreased vocal cord closure	Avoid thin liquids	Easy, quick laryngeal penetration
	Avoid foods that will fall apart	Reduce risk of small pieces entering larynx after the swallow

Source: American Dietetic Association (1).
[a]Technique involves inhaling before swallow, consciously holding breath during swallow, forcefully exhaling or gently coughing after swallow, and finally reswallowing to clear.

modalities, such as gastrostomy, jejunostomy, or total parenteral nutrition (TPN). The authors suggested the use of jejunal feeding or TPN (2). For further discussion, see Chapters 11 and 12.

B. Oral Motor Exercises   Speech therapists and occupational therapists may also use oral motor exercises to increase labial and lingual range of motion, coordination, and strength. Bolus control exercises are also useful to develop oral coordination. Thermal stimulation has been successfully utilized in individuals with delayed or absent pharyngeal swallow. It may be used to heighten the patient's sensation and to stimulate swallowing, just before presentation of the bolus when an oral feeding program is begun (12).

4. USE OF THICKENERS

Particularly in the early stages of dysphagia, patients may be unable to toler-

TABLE 6.3. SIDE EFFECTS OF ANTICANCER THERAPY

Condition	Dietary consideration
Xerostomia	Try very moist, well-lubricated foods; add gravies, extra margarine, sauces, salad dressings Dunk dry foods in a soup or beverage Use artificial salivas, sugarless lemon drops Optimize hydration status Maintain good oral hygiene
Mucositis esophagitis	Try soft, bland foods like soups, eggs, flaked fish, pastas, quiches, souffles, cheese dishes, dairy products, and liquids Avoid rough, raw, salty, and spicy foods Avoid acidic foods such as citrus and pineapple juices and tomato products Avoid extreme temperatures
Thick saliva	Maintain good oral hygiene Optimize hydration status Try to thin secretions with papain, meat tenderizers, carbonated soda, or hot tea with lemon Avoid milk and chocolate products Avoid dry bread products and foods requiring chewing

Source: American Dietetic Association (1).

TABLE 6.4. STAGES OF SWALLOWING

Stage	Purpose	Control	Action
1. Anticipatory	Makes decisions about what, when, and how much to eat	Voluntary	Stage occurs before food reaches mouth.
2. Oral	Manipulates and breaks down food into a manageable size and consistency (bolus)	Voluntary	Lips are sealed, and tongue manipulates food as teeth grind and reduce the material. Cheek muscles are tensed. Particles are collected into a bolus with the help of salivary secretions. Tongue moves the food posteriorly. When the bolus passes the anterior faucial arches, the swallow reflex is triggered.
3. Pharyngeal	Propels the bolus through the pharynx and protects the airway	Involuntary, reflexive action	Tongue prevents reentry of food into the mouth. Elevation and contraction of the soft palate closes the velopharyngeal port and prevents food from entering the nasal cavity. Pharyngeal peristalsis, i.e., the downward squeezing action of the muscles, carries bolus through the pharynx to the cricopharyngeal sphincter. Elevation, anterior displacement, and closure of the larynx prevents food from entering the airway. The cricopharynx relaxes, and food passes from pharynx into esophagus.
4. Esophageal	Guards against reflux of food particles, and transports the bolus through the esophagus into the stomach	Involuntary	The cricopharyngeal muscle contracts to prevent reflux. Peristaltic waves move the bolus.

Source: Glickstein, J. K. (9).

ate thin liquids. Foods may need to be thickened by adding baby cereal, potato flakes, soft bread crumbs, dry milk powder, unflavored gelatin, instant gel products, fruit or vegetable purees, or an artificial thickener. Some of these additions will also contribute important calories and nutrients (14).

The most effective artificial thickeners have a base of modified cornstarch. Cornstarch-based thickeners enable the user to achieve any of the 3 levels of fluid consistency. Table 6.5 is a recently published comparative evaluation of several commercial thickening products (16).

Cornstarch-based thickeners have several useful characteristics. Water or fluid is not bound, so cornstarch-thickened fluids still help to hydrate patients. (Gum-based thickeners may bind water, making it unavailable for absorption.) Cornstarch-based products are low in sodium and contribute calories for undernourished patients. They dissolve easily without cooking, have neutral taste, and are less expensive than gum-based thickeners. Thickened foods can be attractively reassembled using a piping bag and made to resemble closely the original food. This factor can be important in patient acceptance of the food and in improvement of quality of life (17).

5. FOOD CONSISTENCIES

Semisolid foods that form a cohesive bolus, spoon-thick liquids, and medium-thick liquids are most likely to be tolerated. The best consistency will depend on the individual patient. Thin liquids, foods that fall apart, and sticky or bulky foods are poorly tolerated (14). Specific foods are classified according to their consistency in table 6.6.

6. FIBER CONTENT

The diet tends to be low in dietary fiber and shows many of the characteristics of the fiber-restricted diet, described in Chapter 8.

TABLE 6.5. COMPARATIVE EVALUATION OF THICKENING AGENTS FOR DYSPHAGIA

Product name	Characteristics	Available from
NutraThik	Grainy Starch taste Requires less than other thickeners to thicken Fortified with vitamins and minerals Packaged in resealable plastic tubs	Menu Magic Food Division of North American Laboratory Co. 1717 W. 10th St. Indianapolis, IN 45222 (800) 732-5805
Thick-It	Smoothest Most acceptable consistency and least change in flavor Packaged in resealable 12-oz. cans and individual packets of 2 tbsp.	Milani Foods, Inc. 2525 Armitage Ave. Melrose Park, IL 60160 (800) 333-0003 (312) 450-3189
Thick 'N Easy	Not tested	American Institutional Products Co. P.O. Box 5387 Lancaster, PA 17601 (717) 569-1866
Thick-Set	Lumpy Changes flavor More concentrated than most Packaged in resealable 8-oz. containers	Bernard Fine Foods Inc. P.O. Box 610490 San Jose, CA 95161-0490 (800) 538-7941
Thixx	Grainy Continues to thicken as it stands Packaged in 12-oz. cans (not resealable)	Bernard Food Industries, Inc. P.O. Box 1497 Evanston, IL 60204 (800) 323-3663 (708) 869-5222

Source: Houck, H. (16).

Note: Samples were tested by stirring equal amounts of product into orange juice and milk.

INDICATIONS FOR USE

1. PREDISPOSING DISORDERS

Dysphagia may occur with achalasia, stroke or cerebral vascular accident, closed head trauma, cerebral palsy, poliomyelitis, diagnoses that indicate stricture or inflammation of the pharynx or esophagus, tumor or obstruction of the throat, head or neck cancer or surgery, degenerative diseases, Parkinson's disease, amyotrophic lateral sclerosis (ALS), multiple sclerosis, muscular dystrophy, myotonic dystrophy, myasthenia gravis, Huntington's chorea, reflux esophagitis, or complications of AIDS, such as oral or esophageal thrush (18–20).

All team members should be watchful for warning signs of possible dysphagia, including collection of food under the tongue, pocketing of food in cheek, collection of food on the hard palate of the mouth, spitting food out of the mouth or tongue thrusting, poor tongue control, excessive tongue movement, slow oral transit time (more than 1 second), delay or absence of elevation of Adam's apple (thyroid cartilage), coughing or choking, excessive secretions, drooling from the corner of the mouth, gargled voice after

TABLE 6.6. EXAMPLES OF FOOD CONSISTENCIES

Consistency	Food examples
Semisolids that form a cohesive bolus	Hot cereals; souffles, quiches, poached or scrambled eggs; egg, tuna, or meat salad; ground meats with gravy; moist, soft meat or fish loaf; soft cheeses; macaroni or rice casseroles; macaroni salad; aspic; vegetables in sauces; canned fruit; custard; pudding; mousse; finger gelatin; whipped gelatin; cheesecake with sauce
Spoon-thick liquids	Frozen juices, frozen sodas, Popsicles, frozen shakes, ice cream, sherbet, gelatin desserts, pudding, yogurt, pureed fruit
Medium-thick liquids	Vegetable juice, blenderized or cream soups, eggnog, nectar, milk shakes or malts, high-protein or high-calorie commercial supplemental formulas
Thin liquids	Water, broth, milk, chocolate milk, coffee, tea, hot chocolate, fruit juices, soda, alcoholic beverages, standard commercial supplemental formulas
Foods that fall apart	Plain ground meats, dry crumbly breads, crackers, plain rice, thin hot cereals, cooked peas or corn, plain chopped raw vegetables and fruits, thin pureed foods (such as applesauce)
Sticky or bulky foods	Peanut butter, fresh white bread, plain mashed potatoes, bran cereals, refried beans, raw vegetables and fruits, bananas, chunks of plain meats

Source: Adapted from American Dietetic Association (1).

eating or drinking, inadequate intake of food or fluid, unexplained weight loss, prolonged feeding time, or regurgitation of material through the nose, mouth, or tracheostomy tube.

2. PATIENT EXAMINATION

The successful evaluation of the patient with dysphagia requires a comprehensive team approach that effectively utilizes key team members to assess and follow high-risk patients. Patients may be comatose or may require tube feeding prior to an oral diet. All team members—physician, nurse, dietitian, speech therapist, and physical therapist—should be aware of the high risk of aspiration and be watchful for warning signs (21).

The speech therapist should then be requested to conduct a thorough evaluation both at the bedside and with vid-

eofluoroscopy. The bedside examination should assess attention span, positioning, oral motor function, and laryngeal function (12, 22). Videofluoroscopy is a critical diagnostic tool for detection of aspiration. Patients with dysphagia secondary to pharyngeal disorders often aspirate, and this form of aspiration often cannot be identified at the bedside evaluation. The procedure is a modified barium swallow that establishes not only the presence or absence of aspiration but also the etiology of the swallowing disorder—necessary information for treatment and planning (12).

A new method of assessment has been described for 5 patients. The authors used gelatin capsules filled with barium to assess esophageal lumen diameter and to permit grading of dysphagia (23). Further research is needed with larger samples of patients.

3. MANAGEMENT OPTIONS

A. Nonoral Management Nonoral management is indicated if the results of the videofluoroscopy evaluation reveal aspiration (particularly if the aspiration exceeds 10% of the bolus), severe oral motility problems, absent or delayed pharyngeal swallow, or impaired pharyngeal peristalsis or if oral and pharyngeal transit times exceed 10 seconds (12).

B. Oral Management An oral feeding program may be initiated if zero to minimal (10%) aspiration is observed. If the examiner is able to utilize compensatory strategies during the evaluation to minimize observed aspiration, oral feeding may be begun (12). If aspiration occurs, small amounts can be resorbed by the lungs without causing pneumonia (15).

Staff and caregivers responsible for feeding the patient need to be trained to understand appropriate foods, feeding positions, and techniques.

POSSIBLE ADVERSE REACTIONS

1. GASTROINTESTINAL REFLUX

The use of milk-thickening agents such as carob bean gum preparations made from St.-John's-bread were recommended in the past to treat gastrointestinal reflux in infants. The use of these milk-thickening agents in 6-to-8-week-old babies with esophageal reflux has been questioned (24). New data suggest that esophageal motility in such infants is not always developed enough to clear thickened acid gastric content. Although there is a clinical impression of improvement, duration of the reflux episodes, possibly related to esophagitis, actually increases (24).

2. ASPIRATION PNEUMONIA

Videofluoroscopic studies document that certain bolus consistencies and textures may be more easily aspirated than others. Thin liquids, crumbly foods that tend to fall apart, and sticky or bulky items are frequently implicated. Recurrent aspiration pneumonia may indicate that the patient is not safely ingesting the present diet, but the condition may not preclude all oral intake.

3. NASAL REGURGITATION

The soft palate elevates during a normal swallow and approximates the pharyngeal wall, closing off the nasal passage. The escape of foods and liquids into the nasal sinus indicates soft palate weakness or incoordination. Many patients with this problem are observed using their napkins to wipe their nose more often than their mouth.

CONTRAINDICATIONS

Milk thickeners may be contraindicated for 6-to-8-week-old infants (21). Thickening agents are contraindicated for any patient who may have an esophageal obstruction. Tube feedings, particularly nasogastric and gastrostomy feedings, may also be contraindicated in certain patients (2). The diet is not intended for long-term use except in instances when the patient is regularly reevaluated to reconfirm the need for current restrictions.

CLINICAL ASSESSMENT

As part of the routine diet history, the dietitian should screen for dysphagia, oral dentition, history of weight loss or aspiration pneumonia, and other nutritional risk factors.

The dietitian should also determine patient food preferences and tolerances and look for clinical signs of malnutrition. Within 48 hours of patient admission, the dietitian should observe potential dysphagia patients at mealtime.

The dietitian should assess the outcome of the nutrition care plan by making calorie counts of oral and tube-feeding intake at least 2 times a week for all patients participating in the dysphagia

program and by monitoring weight, intake, and output records.

BIOCHEMICAL ASSESSMENT

Pertinent lab data, such as total proteins, albumin, and, if available, prealbumin and retinol-binding protein, should be reviewed to ensure that the patient's protein needs are being met. Hydration status should be considered in evaluation of laboratory results, because these patients have a propensity to become dehydrated as a result of difficulty in swallowing fluids. Particular attention should be paid to indices of anemia, as described in Chapter 1.

ASSESSMENT OF POTENTIAL DRUG INTERACTIONS

1. CALCIUM CHANNEL BLOCKERS

Drugs that interfere with the entry of calcium into smooth muscle cells have been shown to decrease the contraction pressure in the body of the esophagus significantly. These compounds, including verapamil, nifedipine, and diltiazem have

been suggested as potential therapeutic agents for the treatment of esophageal motility disorders. Some patients with achalasia (impaired esophageal peristalsis) respond to regular therapy with nifedipine (25–27).

2. SPECIFIC DRUG-NUTRIENT INTERACTIONS

Specific nutritional interactions of drugs used by dysphagic patients are given in table 6.7.

IMPLEMENTATION AND EDUCATION

1. KNOWLEDGE OF TERMINOLOGY AND PHYSIOLOGY

The dietitian should have a current understanding of terminology used by other team members to describe swallowing and evaluation techniques. A comprehensive medical review of dysphagia and its treatment is beyond the scope of this book. Dietitians involved in a rehabilitation setting should refer to other published resources to assure that they understand the physiology involved.

TABLE 6.7. SPECIFIC POTENTIAL NUTRITIONAL INTERACTIONS WITH CERTAIN DRUGS USED BY DYSPHAGIC PATIENTS

Drug	Nutritional implications	Recommended action
Diltiazem HCl (Cardizem)	May cause altered taste, nausea, constipation, edema, hyperglycemia, dizziness, dry mouth, and anorexia (26); increases serum levels of alkaline phosphatase, SGOT, SGPT, LDH, and CPK (creatine phosphokinase)	Take drug 1 hour before or 2 hours after meals (28). Diet should be low in sodium, without excessive calories (28).
Nifedipine (Procardia)	May decrease glucose tolerance; may cause edema; increases serum alkaline phosphatase, SGOT, SGPT, and LDH	Take after meals; monitor blood chemistries; avoid sodium excesses (29).
Verapamil HCl (Calan, Isoptin)	Increases SGOT, SGPT, and alkaline phosphatase; may cause constipation and nausea	Take on empty stomach; increase fiber in diet if possible; monitor drug levels (29).

2. TEST TRAYS

Following the dysphagia team's initial assessment, the speech therapist will usually specify foods to be included in a test tray. This tray has a variety of food textures—from liquid to solid forms—for testing the patient's ability to swallow. A typical test tray would include ice chips, a pureed food such as applesauce, a thick liquid such as nectar, a thin liquid such as water or juice, and soft solids such as banana, soft bread, or crackers.

The results of the test tray may indicate a need to further define the problem by videofluoroscopy. Another test tray will be designed for this procedure, using similar foods to which a radiopaque label has been added. Following the diagnosis, a feeding program is recommended by the team. The dietitian should institute a tray setup that incorporates the patient's preferences and allows sequential feeding.

3. THE TEAM APPROACH

Initially the test tray should be prepared only for meals when a member of the dysphagia team is available to monitor the patient. The diet is progressed as the patient's swallowing improves. The dietitian's intervention is significant in the recognition and assessment of dysphagic patients, in the structuring of the tray service, and in the provision of appropriate nutritional support to the patient. In some medical centers, liquids may be given to some patients via a percutaneous endoscopic gastrostomy (PEG) tube or a percutaneous endoscopic jejunostomy (PEJ) while the oral diet provides the solids. To enhance patient mobility, the PEG or PEJ feedings can be administered during the evening, freeing the patient for daily activities (30).

The speech pathologist is usually responsible for assessment of the patient and for determination of appropriate food consistencies and feeding or swallowing techniques. Speech therapists and occupational therapists may teach the pa-

MENU PLANNING

SAMPLE MENU FOR THE CONTROLLED-CONSISTENCY, MODIFIED-FLUID DIET (FOR A MALE, AGE 25–50)

BREAKFAST
Orange juice	½ cup
With Thick-It	3 tbsp.
Pureed scrambled egg	1 large
Cream of Wheat	1 cup
Ensure Plus	1 cup
With Thick-It	8 tbsp.

LUNCH
Pureed beef and vegetable stew	1 cup
Mashed potatoes	1 cup
Pureed carrots	½ cup
With Thick-It	1 tbsp.
Pureed peaches	½ cup
With Thick-It	1 tbsp.
Ensure Plus	½ cup
With Thick-It	4 tbsp.

DINNER
Pureed spaghetti with meat sauce	2 cups
Pureed green beans	1 cup
With Thick-It	2 tbsp.
Forta pudding	½ cup
Ensure Plus	½ cup
With Thick-It	2 tbsp.

Approximate Nutrient Analysis
Energy	2,908 kcal
Protein	104.7 g (14% of kcal)
Fat	86.3 g (27% of kcal)
Polyunsaturated fat	19.4 g
Monounsaturated fat	5.4 g
Saturated fat	25.0 g
Cholesterol	464 mg
Carbohydrate	425.0 g (58% of kcal)
Vitamin A	22,866 IU
	1,570 RE
Thiamine	2.59 mg
Riboflavin	2.74 mg
Niacin	36.1 mg
Folate	458 mcg
Vitamin B-12	5.36 mcg
Vitamin B-6	2.45 mg
Vitamin C	278.8 mg
Calcium	1,080 mg
Phosphorus	1,607 mg
Iron	33.1 mg
Copper	1.63 mg
Zinc	12.0 mg
Magnesium	313 mg
Sodium	4,475 mg
Potassium	5,013 mg

tient various exercises and techniques to improve swallowing. The dietitian develops a meal plan that meets the patient's nutritional needs and utilizes foods allowed on the prescribed diet, incorporating the patient's preferences. Recipes, preparation methods, portion sizes, and actual food items are evaluated for nutritional content and standardization. All team members monitor patient acceptance of meals as served and communicate necessary adjustments to the rest of the team. Through this team venture, risk of aspiration is reduced, intake by mouth is sufficient to support nutrient requirements, and quality of life is enhanced (30).

4. PATIENT EDUCATION

The final goal of the dietitian is to provide the most appropriately advanced diet for the patient's use upon discharge. There should be a method of teaching and demonstrating to the patient or caretaker the actual food preparation techniques necessary. The caretaker should then demonstrate the technique, so that problems with home preparation are avoided. Cookbooks are available to aid with special recipes (31).

5. FOOD PREPARATION TECHNIQUES

Each container of food should be labeled with the patient's name, date prepared, and type of food. It is important to refrigerate all foods after they have been pureed and to measure portions as specified on special diets (31, 32).

Water will dilute the flavor of foods. It should be used only when other liquids are not appropriate or if recipe directions call for water. In place of water, liquid drained from canned fruits and vegetables, fruit juices, nectars, gravies, milk, syrups, or tomato or barbecue sauces may be used to provide the appropriate consistency. Such liquids will improve nutritional content as well as flavor.

Canned foods should be drained thoroughly, pureed alone, and thinned with reserved liquid or thickened with the appropriate thickening agent, according to the desired consistency. Cookies, graham crackers, and cakes should be pureed to fine crumbs, checked for pieces that are not fine enough, and combined with other foods as indicated in the recipe.

Meats and fish may be pureed until smooth, adding gravy, tomato sauce, barbecue sauce, or other liquids to moisten and form the desired consistency. Approximately 1 oz. of liquid per serving of meat will be needed. Bread or cheese may be added to obtain the desired thickness.

When combining smooth foods— e.g., gelatin desserts and pudding— neither should be pureed. Instead they should be folded together.

PRIORITIES FOR QUALITY ASSURANCE

1. SUPERVISION AT MEALS

Particularly during the early stages of oral feeding, nursing supervision is necessary at meals when the therapist or dietitian is not present, to avoid possible adverse reactions. A quality assurance monitor can be developed to document the supervision as well as the other care provided.

2. PERIODIC REEVALUATION

One dysphagia evaluation is not enough. The patient should be regularly reevaluated to determine progress and the appropriateness of changes in fluid or bolus consistency.

3. CALORIE COUNTS

Particularly if a patient is on a tube feeding and is being trained to improve swallowing, tube feedings should not be discontinued until adequate nutrient intakes via oral food have been documented through nutrient analysis of calorie counts (12).

REFERENCES

1. American Dietetic Association: Manual of clinical dietetics. Chicago: American Dietetic Association, 1988.

2. Sitzmann, J. V.: Nutritional support of the dysphagic patient: Methods, risks and complications of therapy. JPEN 14:60, 1990.

3. Vaneck, A. W., and Diamant, N. E.: Responses of the human esophagus to paired swallows. Gastroenterology 92:643, 1987.

4. Dooley, C. P., Schlossmacher, B., and Valenzuela, J. F.: Effects of alteration in bolus viscosity on esophageal peristalsis in humans. Am J Physiol 254:8, 1988.

5. Kaye, M. D., Kilby, A. E., and Harper, P. C.: Changes in distal esophageal function in response to cooling. Dig Dis Sci 32:22, 1987.

6. Dooley, C. P., Schlossmacher, B., and Valenzuela, J. F.: Modulation of esophageal peristalsis by alterations of body position: Effect of bolus viscosity. Dig Dis Sci (in press).

7. Bilder, C. R., Dooley, C. P., and Valenzuela, J. F.: Effect of bolus osmolality on human esophageal function. Am J Gastroenterol 84:611, 1989.

8. Nasrallah, S. M., and Hendrix, E. A.: Comparison of hypertonic glucose to other provocative tests in patients with noncardiac chest pain. Am J Gastroenterol 82:406, 1987.

9. Glickstein, J. K., ed.: Focus on geriatric care and rehabilitation. Rockville, Md.: Aspen, 1989.

10. Loustau, A.: Dealing with the dangers of dysphagia. Nursing 15 (2):47, 1985.

11. Tripp, F., and Cordero, O.: Dysphagia and nutrition in the acute care geriatric patient. Top Clin Nutr 6 (2):60, 1991.

12. Milazzo, L. S., Buchard, J., and Lund, D. A.: The swallowing process: Effects of aging and stroke. In Erickson, R. V.: Medical management of the elderly stroke patient. Phys Med Rehab 3:489, 1989.

13. Veis, S., and Logemann, J.: Swallowing disorders in persons with cerebrovascular accidents. Arch Phys Med Rehabil 66:373, 1985.

14. Matthews, L. E.: Techniques for feeding the person with dysphagia. J Nutr Elderly 8:59, 1988.

15. Stern, J.: Dysphagia: The role of the dietitian in its management. Dir Appl Nutr 1 (10):1, 1987.

16. Houck, H.: Updated comparison of dysphagia thickening agents. Network: DPMR 8 (5):7, 1989.

17. Vartan, K.: Tackling the problem that's hard to swallow. Issues, Dietary Managers Assoc 26 (4):1, 1990.

18. Hill, J. W., and DeLuca, S. A.: Achalasia. Am Fam Physician 37 (3):201, 1988.

19. San Roman, A. L., Buzon, L., et al.: Dysphagia and the human immunodeficiency virus: Endoscopy is not a first step. Am J Gastroenterol 84:1461, 1989.

20. Triadafilopoulos, C.: Nonobstructive dysphagia in reflux esophagitis. Am J Gastroenterol 84:614, 1987.

21. Laub, N., and Patter, E.: Dysphagia team protocols. Network: DPMR 8 (2):1, 1989.

22. Horner, J., and Massey, E. W.: Silent aspiration following stroke. Neurology 38:317, 1988.

23. Goldschmidt, S., Brown, J. I., et al.: A new objective measurement of esophageal lumen patency. Am J Gastroenterol 84:1255, 1989.

24. Vanderplas, Y., and Sacre, L.: Milk thickening agents as a treatment of gastroesophageal reflux. Clin Pediatr 26:66, 1987.

25. Wood, P., and Kintzer, T.: Dysphagia management. Network: DPMR 8 (5):3, 1989.

26. Richter, J. E., and Castell, D. O.: Esophageal disease as a cause of noncardiac chest pain. Adv Intern Med 33:311, 1988.

27. Tabibian, N.: Calcium channel blockers in dysphagia secondary to esophageal dysmotility. Am J Gastroenterol 84:668, 1989.

28. Powers, D. E., and Moore, A. O.: Food/medication interactions. 6th ed. Phoenix: 1988 (self-published).

29. Signore, J., and Erickson, R. V.: Nutritional assessment of the stroke patient. In Erickson, R. V.: Medical management of the elderly stroke patient. Phys Med Rehab 3:501, 1989.

30. Vadilloa, M., Kincaid, P. J., and Musson, M. A.: Dietitian intervention with the dysphagic patient in a long-term care setting. Network: DPMR 8 (3):3, 1989.

31. Brenner, R. V., and Anderson, M. V.: Blended diets: Applied preparation and feeding techniques. Sugar Land, Tex.: Anderson Brenner Associates, 1989.

32. Yankelson, S.: Procedure for preparation of dysphagia diets. Network: DPMR 3 (6):7, 1987.

7.

MODIFIED FIBER DIETS: TABLES AND DEFINITIONS

Types of fiber are described in table 7.1. Components of dietary fiber are outlined according to food source in tables 7.2 and 7.3. Analysis of the fiber content of selected foods is provided in tables 7.4 and 7.5.

It is difficult to find methods to determine the dietary fiber content of foods accurately, because the definition of dietary fiber is physiological. Historically, food composition tables listed only crude fiber values. Such values grossly underestimate the actual fiber content of foods, however. The diverse nature of dietary fiber requires complex analytical techniques. Dietary fiber is most commonly determined by using the neutral detergent fiber (NDF) method to estimate water-insoluble fiber and adding values for soluble fibers such as pectin. Other estimates include enzymatic and sequential methods (6).

Values for the dietary fiber content of a food may vary because of different methods of analysis, variation between laboratories even when they use the same method, differences between genetic varieties and maturity of plant foods, and the type and extent of food processing (7, 8). The type of fiber recovered with each method of analysis is outlined in table 7.6 (9).

The effects of different classes of dietary fiber on gastrointestinal function are summarized in table 7.7.

DEFINITIONS

1. CRUDE FIBER

That portion of a feeding material that remains after treatment with boiling sulfuric acid, alkali, water, alcohol, and

TABLE 7.1. CHEMICAL CLASSIFICATION OF FIBER TYPES

Fiber	Main chain	Side chain	Description
Polysaccharides			
Cellulose	Glucose	None	Main structural component of plant cell wall. Insoluble in concentrated alkali; soluble in concentrated acid.
Noncellulose			
Hemicellulose	Xylose Mannose Galactose Glucose	Arabinose Galactose Glucuronic acid	Cell-wall polysaccharides containing backbone of 1,4-linked pyranoside sugars. Vary in degree of branching and uronic acid content. Soluble in dilute alkali.
Pectic substances	Galacturonic acid	Rhamnose Arabinose Xylose Fucose	Components of primary cell wall and middle lamella. Vary in methyl ester content. Generally water soluble and gel-forming.
Mucilages	Galactose-mannose Glucose-mannose Arabinose-xylose Galacturonic acid–rhamnose	Galactose	Synthesized by plant secretory cells; prevent desiccation of seed endosperm. Food industry use, hydrophilic, stabilizer (e.g., guar).
Gums	Galactose Glucuronic acid–mannose Galacturonic acid–rhamnose	Xylose Fucose Galactose	Secreted at site of plant injury by specialized secretory cells. Food and pharmaceutical use (e.g., karaya gum).
Algal polysaccharides	Mannose Xylose Glucuronic acid Glucose	Galactose	Derived from algae and seaweed. Vary in uronic acid content and presence of sulphate groups. Food and pharmaceutical use (e.g. carrageenan, agar).
Lignin	Sinapyl alcohol Coniferyl alcohol *p*-Coumaryl alcohol	3-D structure	Noncarbohydrate cell-wall component. Complex cross-linked phenyl propane polymer. Insoluble in 72% sulphuric acid. Resists bacterial degradation.

Source: Mendeloff, A. I. (1).

ether. It is mainly a measure of the cellulose content of food, although it may include some largely insoluble hemicellulose-like materials (11–13). Prior to the 1970s, crude fiber was the form of fiber measured in foods, because of the lack of a more scientific method of analysis.

2. DIETARY FIBER

Plant material of diverse chemical and morphological structure that is resistant to the actions of human digestive enzymes (4, 14). It is the sum of lignin and the non-alpha-glucan (nonstarch) polysaccharides in foods (4, 14). Dietary fiber has been divided into 3 basic components, as follows (6, 15–17):

- Structural nonpolysaccharides: Predominantly lignin
- Structural polysaccharides: Associated with the cell wall; includes noncellulose polysaccharides (18)—i.e., hemicellulose and some pectins—and cellulose
- Nonstructural polysaccharides: Includes gums and mucilages secreted by cells and polysaccharides from algae and seaweed

Figure 7.1 clarifies the various categories of dietary fiber.

3. LIGNIN

A noncarbohydrate encrusting substance of the plant cell wall.

4. POLYSACCHARIDES

Complex carbohydrates that can be further divided into 2 classes: starches and nonstarch polysaccharides (NSPs). Starch is digested and is therefore not a component of dietary fiber. NSPs are principally the cell wall polysaccharides of plant foods (19).

5. NONSTARCH POLYSACCHARIDES

All the carbohydrate fractions and types of dietary fiber (soluble and insoluble), pectins, gums, hemicelluloses, cellu-

TABLE 7.2. COMPONENTS OF DIETARY FIBER

Main components of a mixed diet	Tissue types	Main constituent groups of DF polymers[a]
Fruits and vegetables	Mainly parenchymatous	Pectic substances (e.g., arabinans and methyl-esterfied rhamnogalacturonans), cellulose, hemicellulosic polymers (e.g., xyloglucans), and some proteins[b] and phenolics
	Partially lignified vascular tissues	Cellulose, hemicelluloses (e.g., glucuronoxylans), lignin, and some pectin substances and proteins[b]
	Cutinized epidermal tissues	Cutin and waxes
Cereals and products	Parenchymatous (endosperm and aleurone layer)	Hemicelluloses (e.g., arabinoxylans and/or β-D-glucans) and some cellulose, proteins,[b] and phenolics
	Partially lignified seed	Hemicelluloses (e.g., glucuronoarabinoxylans), cellulose, lignin, phenolics, and some proteins[b]
Seeds other than cereals (e.g., legume seeds)	Parenchymatous (e.g., pea cotyledons)	Cellulose, pectin substances, hemicelluloses (e.g., xyloglucans), and some proteins[b]
	Cells with thickened endosperm walls (e.g., guar seed splits)	Galactomannans and some cellulose, pectin substances, and proteins[b]
Seed husk of *Plantago ovata* (ispaghul husk)	Mucilage of epidermal cells	Mainly highly branched acidic arabinoxylans
Polysaccharide food additives	—	Food gums—gum arabic, alginates, carrageenan, guar gum, carboxymethylcellulose, modified starches, and so forth

Source: Selvendran, R. R., Stevans, B. J. H., and Dupont, M. S. (2).
[a]The polymers are listed in approximately decreasing order of amounts.
[b]Most of the proteins are present as components of glycoproteins or proteoglycans.

lose, beta-glucans, and noncellulosic polysaccharides. Because NSP represents a more chemical definition rather than a functional definition of dietary fiber, certain groups have recommended that it replace the term *dietary fiber*. At the present time, however, controversy exists as to whether or not lignin—or, more properly stated, substances measuring as lignin—and certain forms of resistant starch should be included in this definition (19, 20).

TABLE 7.3. FIBER COMPONENTS AND FOOD SOURCES

Water-soluble fibers are hydrated, resulting in gel-like or viscous substances, and are fermented by colonic bacteria.

Water-soluble fibers	Foods containing water-soluble fibers include the following:
Gum	
Mucilages	Fruits, vegetables
Pectin	Barley, legumes, oats, and oat bran
Some hemicellulose	

Water-insoluble fibers remain essentially unchanged during digestion.

Water-insoluble fibers	Foods containing water-insoluble fibers include the following:
Cellulose	
Lignin	Fruits, vegetables
Some hemicellulose	Cereals, whole wheat products, wheat bran

Source: American Dietetic Association (3).

6. NONCELLULOSIC POLYSACCHARIDES

The same as NSPs minus cellulose (4). Abbreviated as NCP.

7. RESISTANT STARCH

A form of retrograded amylose that is difficult to remove from food samples by normal enzymatic hydrolysis. The resistant starch content of a food depends upon food processing and method of preparation. Because some resistant starch escapes hydrolysis and enters the large bowel, it has been suggested by some people and disputed by others that resistant starch be included in the

TABLE 7.4. PROVISIONAL DIETARY FIBER TABLE

Food	Analytical method[a]	Fiber (g)/100 g	Calories/ 100 g	Serving size	Fiber (g)/serving	Calories/ serving
Breakfast cereals						
All-Bran	1	29.9	249	⅓ cup (1 oz.)	8.5	71
Bran Buds	1	27.7	258	⅓ cup (1 oz.)	7.9	73
Bran Chex	1	16.2	319	⅔ cup (1 oz.)	4.6	91
Cheerios-type	1	3.8	391	1¼ cup (1 oz.)	1.1	111
Corn Bran	1	19.0	346	⅔ cup (1 oz.)	5.4	98
Cornflakes	1	1.1	389	1¼ cup (1 oz.)	0.3	110
Cracklin' Bran	1	15.1	382	⅓ cup (1 oz.)	4.3	108
Crispy Wheats n' Raisins	1	4.6	349	¾ cup (1 oz.)	1.3	99
40% Bran–type	1	13.4	325	¾ cup (1 oz.)	4.0	93
Frosted Mini-Wheats	1	7.6	359	4 biscuits (1 oz.)	2.1	102
Graham Cracko's	1	6.1	361	¾ cup (1 oz.)	1.7	102
Grape Nuts	1	4.8	357	¼ cup (1 oz.)	1.4	101
Heartland Natural Cereal, plain	1	4.7	434	¼ cup (1 oz.)	1.3	123
Honey Bran	1	11.1	341	⅞ cup (1 oz.)	3.1	97
Most	1	12.4	337	⅔ cup (1 oz.)	3.5	95
Nutri-Grain, barley	1	5.8	372	¾ cup (1 oz.)	1.7	106
Nutri-Grain, corn	1	6.2	381	¾ cup (1 oz.)	1.8	108
Nutri-Grain, rye	1	6.4	359	¾ cup (1 oz.)	1.8	102
Nutri-Grain, wheat	1	6.3	360	¾ cup (1 oz.)	1.8	102
100% Bran Flakes	1	29.6	269	½ cup (1 oz.)	8.4	76
100% Natural Cereal; plain	1	3.7	470	¼ cup (1 oz.)	1.0	133
Raisin Bran–type	1	11.3	312	¾ cup (1 oz.)	4.0	115
Rice Krispies	1	0.2	395	1 cup (1 oz.)	0.1	112
Shredded Wheat	1	9.3	359	⅔ cup (1 oz.)	2.6	102
Special K	1	0.8	390	1⅓ cup (1 oz.)	0.2	111
Sugar Smacks	1	0.9	373	¾ cup (1 oz.)	0.4	106
Tasteeos	1	3.5	393	1¼ cup (1 oz.)	1.0	111
Total	1	7.2	352	1 cup (1 oz.)	2.0	100

(continued)

TABLE 7.4. *CONTINUED*

Food	Analytical method[a]	Fiber (g)/100 g	Calories/ 100 g	Serving size	Fiber (g)/serving	Calories/ serving
Wheat 'n' Raisin Chex	1	6.6	343	¾ cup (1⅓ oz.)	2.5	130
Wheat Chex	1	7.4	367	⅔ cup (1⅓ oz.)	2.1	104
Wheaties	1	7.0	349	1 cup (1 oz.)	2.0	99
Oatmeal, regular, quick, and instant, cooked	4, 5	0.9	62	¾ cup (1 oz.)	1.6	108
Wheat germ	1	14.3	386	¼ cup (2 oz.)	3.4	108
Fruits						
Apple (with skin)	2	2.5	59	1 medium	3.5	81
Apple (without skin)	2, 3, 4	2.1	57	1 medium	2.7	72
Apricot (fresh)	2, 3	1.7	48	3 medium	1.8	51
Apricot, dried	6	8.1	238	5 halves	1.4	42
Banana	2, 4	2.1	92	1 medium	2.4	105
Blueberries	2	2.7	51	½ cup	2.0	39
Cantaloupe	3	1.0	24	¼ melon	1.0	30
Cherries, sweet	2, 3	1.2	72	10	1.2	49
Dates	3, 4	7.6	275	3	1.9	68
Grapefruit	2, 3, 4	1.3	32	½	1.6	38
Grapes	3, 4	1.3	63	20	0.6	30
Orange	2, 4	2.0	47	1	2.6	62
Peach (with skin)	4	2.1	43	1	1.9	37
Peach (without skin)	2, 3	1.4	43	1	1.2	37
Pear (with skin)	4	2.8	59	½ large	3.1	61
Pear (without skin)	2, 3, 4	2.3	59	½ large	2.5	61
Pineapple	2, 3	1.4	49	½ cup	1.1	39
Plums, damson	2, 4	1.7	60	5	0.9	33
Prunes	3, 4	11.9	239	3	3.0	60
Raisins	3, 4	8.7	300	¼ cup	3.1	108
Raspberries	3, 4	5.1	57	½ cup	3.1	35
Strawberries	2, 3	2.0	30	1 cup	3.0	45
Watermelon	2	0.3	26	1 cup	0.4	42
Juices						
Apple	2	0.3	47	½ cup (4 oz.)	0.4	56
Grape	2	0.5	51	½ cup (4 oz.)	0.6	64
Grapefruit	2	0.4	41	½ cup (4 oz.)	0.5	51
Orange	2	0.4	45	½ cup (4 oz.)	0.5	56
Papaya	2	0.6	57	½ cup (4 oz.)	0.8	71
Vegetables						
Cooked						
Asparagus, cut	2, 3	1.5	20	½ cup	1.0	15
Beans, string, green	2, 3, 4	2.6	25	½ cup	1.6	16
Broccoli	2, 4	2.8	26	½ cup	2.2	20
Brussels sprouts	2, 3	3.0	36	½ cup	2.3	28
Cabbage, red	4	2.0	20	½ cup	1.4	15
Cabbage, white	4	2.0	20	½ cup	1.4	15
Carrots	2, 3, 4	3.0	31	½ cup	2.3	24
Cauliflower	3, 4	1.7	22	½ cup	1.1	14
Corn, canned	2, 3	2.8	83	½ cup	2.9	87
Kale leaves	3	2.6	34	½ cup	1.4	22
Parsnip	3, 4	3.5	66	½ cup	2.7	51
Peas	2, 3, 4	4.5	71	½ cup	3.6	57

(*continued*)

TABLE 7.4. *CONTINUED*

Food	Analytical method[a]	Fiber (g)/100 g	Calories/ 100 g	Serving size	Fiber (g)/serving	Calories/ serving
Potato (with skin)	4	1.7	93	1 medium	2.5	106
Potato (without skin)	3, 4	1.0	93	1 medium	1.4	97
Spinach	2, 4	2.3	23	½ cup	2.1	21
Squash, summer	2, 4	1.6	14	½ cup	1.4	13
Sweet potatoes	2, 3	2.4	141	½ medium	1.7	80
Turnip	3, 4	2.2	23	½ cup	1.6	17
Zucchini	4	2.0	12	½ cup	1.8	11
Raw						
Bean sprouts, soy		2.6	46	½ cup	1.5	13
Celery, diced	3, 4	1.5	8	½ cup	1.1	10
Cucumber	3, 4	0.8	15	½ cup	0.4	8
Lettuce, sliced	3, 4	1.5	12	1 cup	0.9	7
Mushrooms, sliced	3	2.5	28	½ cup	0.9	10
Onions, sliced	3, 4	1.3	23	½ cup	0.8	33
Pepper, green, sliced	3, 4	1.3	23	½ cup	0.5	9
Spinach	2	4.0	26	1 cup	1.2	8
Tomato	3, 4	1.5	22	1 medium	1.5	20
Legumes						
Baked beans, tomato sauce	3	7.3	121	½ cup	8.8	155
Dried peas, cooked	3, 4	4.7	115	½ cup	4.7	115
Kidney beans, cooked	3	7.9	118	½ cup	7.3	110
Lentils, cooked	3	3.7	97	½ cup	3.7	97
Lima beans, cooked/canned	2	5.4	75	½ cup	4.5	64
Navy beans, cooked	6, 3	6.3	118	½ cup	6.0	112
Breads, pastas, and flours						
Bagels	1	1.1	264	1 bagel	0.6	145
Bran muffins	1	6.3	263	1 muffin	2.5	104
Cracked wheat	1	4.1	246	1 slice	1.0	62
Crisp bread, rye	1	14.9	376	2 crackers	2.0	50
Crisp bread, wheat	1	12.9	376	2 crackers	1.8	50
French bread	1	2.0	291	1 slice	0.7	102
Italian bread	1	1.0	278	1 slice	0.3	83
Mixed grain	1	3.7	235	1 slice	0.9	59
Oatmeal	1	2.2	253	1 slice	0.5	63
Pita bread (5-inch)	1	0.9	273	1 piece	0.4	123
Pumpernickel bread	1	3.2	207	1 slice	1.0	66
Raisin bread	1	2.2	267	1 slice	0.6	67
White bread	1, 4	1.6	279	1 slice	0.4	78
Whole wheat bread	1, 4	5.7	243	1 slice	1.4	61
Pasta and rice, cooked						
Macaroni	1, 5	0.8	111	1 cup	1.0	144
Rice, brown	3, 5	1.2	119	½ cup	1.0	97
Rice, polished	1, 4, 5	0.3	109	½ cup	0.2	82
Spaghetti (regular)	1, 5	0.8	111	1 cup	1.1	155
Spaghetti (whole wheat)	1, 5	2.8	111	1 cup	3.9	155
Flours and grains						
Bran, corn	4	62.2				
Bran, oat	3	27.8				
Bran, wheat	1, 3, 4, 5	41.2				

(continued)

TABLE 7.4. *CONTINUED*

Food	Analytical method[a]	Fiber (g)/100 g	Calories/ 100 g	Serving size	Fiber (g)/serving	Calories/ serving
Rolled oats	4, 5	5.7				
Rye flour (72%)[b]	4	4.5	350			
Rye flour (100%)[b]	4	12.8	335			
Wheat flour						
Wholemeal (100%)[b]	3, 4	8.9	318			
Brown (85%)[b]	3, 4	7.3	327			
White (72%)[b]	3, 4	2.9	333			
Nuts						
Almonds	4	7.2	627	10	1.1	79
Filberts	3	6.0	634	10	0.8	90
Peanuts	3	8.1	568	10	1.4	105

Source: Lanza, E., and Butrum, R. R. (4).

Note: Dietary fiber values are averages compiled from literature sources. Users of the table are advised to read the accompanying manuscript to understand fully the derivation and meaning of the values.

[a]The numbers in this column refer to the analytical method used to obtain the mean dietary fiber value. The method and a reference or references describing the method are as follows:

1. Neutral detergent fiber (Approved methods of the AACC. St. Paul: American Association of Cereal Chemists, 1983.)
2. Neutral detergent fiber plus water-soluble fraction, such as (Zyrene, J., Elkins, E. R., et al.: Fiber contents of selected raw and processed vegetables, fruits and fruit juices as served. J Food Sci 48:600, 1983.)
3. Southgate procedure (Southgate, D. A. T.: Determination of food carbohydrates. London: Applied Science, 1976.)
4. Total dietary fiber procedure ([1] Englyst, H.: Determination of carbohydrate and its composition in plant material. In James, W. P. T., and Theander, O.: The analysis of dietary fibers in foods. New York: Marcel Dekker, 1981. [2] Schweizer, T. F., and Wursch, P.: Analysis of dietary fibre. J Sci Food Agric 30:613, 1979. [3] Furda, I.: Simultaneous analysis of soluble and insoluble dietary fiber. In James, W. P. T., and Theander, O.: The analysis of dietary fiber in food. New York: Marcel Dekker, 1981. [4] Prosky, L., Asp, N., et al.: Determination of total dietary fiber in foods and food products: Collaborative study. J Assoc Off Anal Chem 68:677, 1985. [5] Theander, O., and Aman, P.: Studies on dietary fibre: A method for the chemical characterization of total dietary fibre. J Sci Food Agric 33:340, 1982. [6] Englyst, H., Wiggins, H. S., and Cummings. J.: Determination of the non-starch polysaccharides in plant foods by gas-liquid chromatography of constituent sugars as alditol acetates. Analyst 107:307, 1982. [7] Varo, P., Laine, R., et al.: Dietary fiber and available carbohydrates in Finnish cereal products. J Agric Sci Finland 56:39, 1984.)
5. Englyst, nonstarch polysaccharide, or NSP (Englyst, H., Anderson, V., and Cummings, J. H.: Standard and non-starch polysaccharides in some cereal foods. J Sci Food Agric 34:1434, 1983.)

[b]The number in parentheses refers to the extraction rate of the flour. White-type breads and household flour are made with 72% flour; 85% extraction flour was consumed in the United States before World War II.

definition of dietary fiber. When certain foods with resistant starch are cooked first and then eaten, the resistant amylose reverts back to digestible starch (20, 21).

8. INSOLUBLE FIBER

Components of fiber that are insoluble in water, including cellulose, hemicellulose, and lignin (8).

9. SOLUBLE FIBER

Components of fiber that are soluble in water, including pectins, gums, and mucilages (8).

10. RESIDUE

The total feces made up of undigested and unabsorbed food and metabolic products. This term does not really describe foods, because it includes bacteria and cells as well as undigested foodstuffs (22).

TABLE 7.5. DIETARY FIBER CONTENT OF SELECTED FOODS

	g/100 g dry weight						
	TDF	TNSP	SNSP	INCP	CELL	LIG	% water
Cereal products							
All-Bran[a]	31.60	28.43	5.24	16.94	6.25	3.17	2.7
Bran, corn	85.19	82.87	1.16	59.38	22.33	2.32	4.3
Bran, oat	15.72	14.49	7.84	5.86	0.79	1.56	8.4
Bread, white	3.22	3.08	1.58	0.98	0.52	0.15	36.9
Bread, whole wheat	9.26	8.15	2.03	4.39	1.72	1.12	40.8
Cornflakes[a]	1.65	1.06	0.48	0.41	0.18	0.59	4.4
Crackers, graham	2.47	2.29	1.22	0.89	0.18	0.19	3.3
Crackers, saltine	3.08	2.62	1.75	0.71	0.16	0.46	3.4
Crackers, snack	13.04	11.77	3.78	6.59	1.40	1.26	5.2
Fiber 1	44.02	40.98	3.10	28.22	9.67	3.03	3.7
Flour, white	3.96	3.68	1.70	1.38	0.61	0.27	8.0
Flour, whole wheat	12.39	11.09	2.07	6.61	2.40	1.30	11.8
40% bran flakes	15.88	14.25	2.79	7.63	3.83	1.63	3.5
Grape Nuts	10.41	9.76	3.07	3.43	3.27	0.65	3.1
Grits	2.41	2.04	0.41	1.32	0.32	0.37	8.8
Macaroni	3.37	3.07	1.81	1.09	0.17	0.30	10.4
Oats, rolled	10.51	9.47	5.43	3.30	0.74	1.04	9.2
Product 19	4.47	3.87	1.08	1.37	1.41	0.60	2.3
Puffed rice	1.40	1.19	0.41	0.47	0.31	0.21	6.5
Puffed wheat	7.20	6.68	3.40	2.04	1.24	0.52	0
Rice, brown	ND	2.87	0.89	1.37	0.61	ND	5.1
Rice, white	ND	1.40	0.92	0.29	0.19	ND	2.0
Rice Krispies	1.21	0.81	0.32	0.32	0.16	0.40	1.2
Spaghetti, white	ND	3.47	1.82	1.41	0.23	ND	5.2
Spaghetti, whole wheat	10.36	9.54	1.85	5.42	2.27	0.82	8.5
Special K	3.24	2.24	0.60	1.17	0.47	1.00	1.9
Wheaties	8.29	7.29	2.43	3.48	1.38	1.00	0.3
Vegetables							
Asparagus, canned	32.23	27.36	5.80	7.04	14.52	4.87	92.7
Beets, canned	24.27	23.67	7.50	6.95	9.22	0.60	89.3
Broccoli, frozen	30.40	28.94	13.63	6.43	8.88	1.46	90.8
Brussels sprouts, frozen	26.94	26.32	10.86	7.17	8.29	0.62	83.2
Cabbage, raw	23.24	22.41	8.68	5.39	8.34	0.83	91.0
Carrots, raw[a]	23.76	22.75	11.32	3.62	7.81	1.01	86.5
Cauliflower, frozen	26.70	26.06	8.92	7.19	9.95	0.64	90.4
Corn, canned, whole kernel	9.43	8.88	1.24	5.20	2.44	0.55	80.3
Kale, frozen	33.48	30.12	9.94	8.39	11.79	3.36	88.6
Lettuce, raw	21.02	19.00	4.70	5.64	8.66	2.02	95.8
Potato, white, raw	9.48	8.58	4.91	1.34	2.33	0.90	79.0
Potato, sweet, canned	7.08	6.81	2.71	1.20	2.90	0.27	82.7
Spinach, frozen[a]	28.75	24.65	6.56	9.23	8.86	4.10	92.4
Squash, frozen	19.79	17.87	7.39	4.82	5.66	1.92	94.7
Tomato, raw	13.13	11.44	2.13	2.73	6.58	1.69	93.7
Legumes							
Garbanzo beans, canned	10.21	9.16	1.18	5.42	2.56	1.05	65.6
Green beans, canned	33.97	31.42	8.13	8.30	14.99	2.55	91.2
Kidney beans, canned	20.90	17.53	5.26	6.85	5.42	3.37	70.4

(*continued*)

TABLE 7.5. *CONTINUED*

	g/100 g dry weight						
	TDF	TNSP	SNSP	INCP	CELL	LIG	% water
Lima beans, canned	14.40	13.59	3.75	4.35	5.49	0.81	75.3
Navy beans, dried, cooked	23.02	21.80	7.76	7.08	6.96	1.22	ND
Pinto beans, canned[a]	19.11	15.86	4.47	5.10	6.29	3.26	73.3
Pinto beans, dried, cooked[a]	24.10	21.42	7.52	7.91	5.99	2.68	71.2
Pinto beans, dried, raw	21.18	19.60	8.15	7.72	3.73	1.58	8.2
Pork and beans, canned[a]	15.67	14.88	7.70	3.29	3.90	0.79	73.5
White beans, canned[a]	20.97	19.55	6.30	6.97	6.28	1.43	73.6
White beans, dried, cooked	18.16	17.21	5.29	6.74	5.18	0.95	ND
White beans, dried, raw[a]	18.31	17.27	4.54	8.60	4.14	1.04	3.6
Lentils, dried, cooked	15.73	12.60	1.69	5.49	5.42	3.13	66.5
Lentils, dried, raw	12.71	10.61	1.32	5.14	4.15	2.10	9.9
Black-eyed peas, canned	11.06	8.87	1.19	3.68	4.00	2.19	65.0
Green peas, canned	21.30	20.40	3.00	4.62	12.78	0.90	82.2
Fruits							
Apple, raw	12.73	10.50	4.48	2.45	3.57	2.23	84.3
Applesauce, canned	13.29	12.36	5.12	2.86	4.38	0.93	87.9
Banana, raw	7.35	4.13	2.14	0.96	1.03	3.22	73.9
Grapefruit, raw, Florida yellow	11.80	11.38	7.24	1.91	2.23	0.42	89.5
Orange, raw, seedless, California navel	11.45	11.14	6.70	1.97	2.47	0.31	87.9
Peach, canned	18.80	17.06	7.60	3.72	5.74	1.74	91.6
Pear, canned	32.18	27.24	6.89	8.48	11.87	4.94	90.6
Pineapple, canned	9.54	9.33	1.22	3.90	4.21	0.21	82.7
Plum, purple, canned	22.81	19.71	9.92	3.98	5.81	3.10	90.4

Source: Anderson, J. W., and Bridges, S. R. (5). Copyright © 1988, *American Journal of Clinical Nutrition,* American Society for Clinical Nutrition.

Note: TDF, total dietary fiber; TNS, total nonstarch polysaccharides; SNSP, soluble nonstarch polysaccharides; INCP, insoluble noncellulose polysaccharides; CELL, cellulose; LIG, lignin; ND, values not determined.

[a] Values are means of 2 or more determinations.

TABLE 7.6. SUMMARY OF ANALYTICAL METHODS FOR DIETARY FIBER AND FIBER

Analytic measurement	Outline of method and fraction actually measured	Nature of fraction measured
Dietary fiber (= unavailable carbohydrates)		
Total (23)	Preparation of residue insoluble in alcohol; measurement of starch and protein and deduction of these from the residue	All components of dietary fiber in 1 fraction
As the components (24)	Sequential extraction and hydrolysis of residue insoluble in alcohol	Noncellulosic polysaccharides as component hexoses, pentoses, and uronic acids; Cellulose as glucose; Lignin as the residue insoluble in 72% (weight-for-weight) H_2SO_4
Total (25)	Enzymatic digestion of defatted residue to remove protein and starch	All components of dietary fiber in 1 fraction (minus some soluble fiber)
Fiber		
Crude (26)	Extraction of food with boiling acid and alkali; measurement of organic matter in residue	Cellulose plus lignin (incompletely in many foods)
Acid detergent (ADF) (27)	Extraction of food with boiling acid detergent solution; measurement of organic matter in residue	Cellulose plus lignin
Neutral detergent (NDF) (27)	Extraction of food with boiling neutral detergent and weighing of residue	Cell-wall materials less water-soluble components

Source: Jenkins, D. J. A. (9); *adapted from* Southgate, D. A. T., Bailey, B., et al. (28).

TABLE 7.7. EFFECTS OF DIETARY FIBER CLASSES ON GASTROINTESTINAL FUNCTION

Region of gastrointestinal tract	Total dietary fiber		
	Insoluble fiber (neutral detergent fiber)	Soluble fiber (gums, pectin)	Phenolics (lignin, tannin, Maillard products)
General	Hydration sponge effect of coarse particles	Gellation	Binding of lipids, ions, proteins and enzyme inhibitors (?)
Stomach	Minimal delay in emptying	Moderate delay in emptying	None
Small intestine	Binding of minerals and enzymes	↑ thickness of un-stirred layer ↓ absorption rate of lipids, glucose, amino acids	Ion exchange Bile salt binding Toxin binding
Colon	Fermentable: go to volatile fatty acids and bacteria Nonfermentable: go to fecal bulk passage	Very fermentable: go to volatile fatty acids and bacteria Slowly fermentable: go to fecal bulk passage	Unfermentable: go to fecal bulk passage

Source: McPherson, R.: Classification of fibre types (16); *adapted from* VanSoest (10).

FIG. 7.1. CATEGORIZATION OF TOTAL DIETARY FIBER.

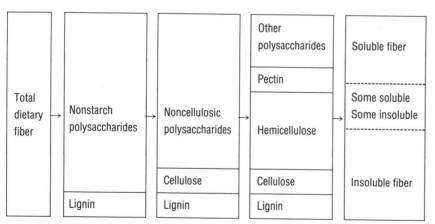

Source: Food and Nutrition Board (8), copyright © 1989 by the National Academy of Sciences; reprinted by permission.

Note: Total dietary fiber can be categorized as shown. For example, total dietary fiber can be divided into nonstarch polysaccharides and lignin; nonstarch polysaccharides can be further divided into noncellulosic polysaccharides and cellulose. Cellulose, lignin, and most hemicelluloses are not soluble in water, whereas pectins and other polysaccharides (such as gums and mucilages) are water soluble.

REFERENCES

1. Mendeloff, A. I.: Dietary fiber in 1985: Reasonable expectations. In Bowen, P. E., Connell, A. M., et al.: The clinical role of fibre. Toronto: Medical Education Services, 1985.

2. Selvendran, R. R., Stevans, B. J. H., and Dupont, M. S.: Dietary fiber: Chemistry, analysis and properties. Adv Food Research 31:117, 1987.

3. American Dietetic Association: Manual of clinical dietetics. Chicago: American Dietetic Association, 1988.

4. Lanza, E., and Butrum, R. R.: A critical review of food fiber analysis and data. J Am Diet Assoc 86:732, 1986.

5. Anderson, J. W., and Bridges, S. R.: Dietary fiber content of selected foods. Am J Clin Nutr 47:440, 1988.

6. Slavin, J. L.: Dietary fiber: Classification, chemical analyses and food sources. J Am Diet Assoc 87:1164, 1987.

7. Marlett, J. A., Chesters, J. G., et al.: Recovery of soluble dietary fiber is dependent on the methods of analysis. Am J Clin Nutr 50:479, 1989.

8. Food and Nutrition Board, National Research Council—National Academy of Sciences: Diet and health: Implications for reducing chronic disease risk. Report of the Committee on Diet and Health. Washington, D.C.: National Academy Press, 1989.

9. Jenkins, D. J. A.: Carbohydrates— dietary fiber. In Shils, M. E., and Young, V. R.: Modern nutrition in health and disease. 7th ed. Philadelphia: Lea & Febiger, 1988.

10. VanSoest, P. J.: Some physical characteristics of dietary fiber and their influence on the microbial ecology of the human colon. Proc Nutr Soc 43:25, 1984.

11. Cummings, J. H.: Progress report: Dietary fiber. Gut 14:69, 1973.

12. Southgate, J. A.: The definition and analysis of dietary fiber. Nutr Rev 35:31, 1977.

13. Theander, O.: The chemistry of dietary fibers. Nutr Rev 35:23, 1977.

14. Anderson, J. W.: Fiber and health: An overview. Am J Gastroenterol 81:892, 1986.

15. Southgate, D. A. T.: Definitions and terminology of dietary fiber. In Vahouny, G. V., and Kritchevsky, D.: Dietary fiber in health and disease. New York: Plenum Press, 1982.

16. McPherson, R.: Classification of fibre types. In Bowen, P. E., Connell, A. M., et al.: The clinical role of fibre. Toronto: Medical Education Services, 1985.

17. Schneeman, B. O.: Dietary fiber: Physical and chemical properties, methods of analysis and physiological effects. Food Technol 40:104, 1986.

18. Kritchevsky, D.: Diet, nutrition and cancer: The role of fiber. Cancer 58:1830, 1986.

19. Cummings, J. H.: Dietary fiber. Am J Clin Nutr 45:1040, 1987.

20. Bingham, S.: Definitions and intakes of dietary fiber. Am J Clin Nutr 45:1226, 1987.

21. Englyst, H. N., Trowell, H., et al.: Dietary fiber and resistant starch: A human colon. Proc Nutr Soc 43:25, 1984.

22. Kramer, P. The meaning of high and low residue diets. Gastroenterology 47:649, 1964.

23. McCance, R. A., Widdowson, E. M., and Shackleton, L. R. B.: Spec Rep Scr Med Res Coun Lond 213. London: HMSO, 1936.

24. Southgate, D. A. T.: Determination of carbohydrates in foods. J Sci Food Agric 20:326, 1969.

25. Prosky, L., Asp, N., et al.: In Determination of total dietary fiber in foods, food products and ingredients: Collaborative study. Unpublished.

26. Horwitz, W., ed.: Official methods of analysis. 11th ed. Washington, D.C.: Association of Official Analytical Chemists, 1970.

27. Van Soest, P. J.: J Assoc Off Agric Chem 46:825, 1963.

28. Southgate, D. A. T., Bailey, B., et al.: A guide to calculating intakes of dietary fibre. J Hum Nutr 30:303, 1976.

8.

FIBER-RESTRICTED DIET

DEFINITION

A diet that contains a minimum of dietary fiber and connective tissue. Until more-complete and more-accurate tables of composition are published regarding the dietary fiber content of all commonly used foods (not just high-fiber foods), this diet must be provisionally described in qualitative terms. In general, most of the foods on the high-fiber diet with more than 1.4 g of dietary fiber per serving should be avoided.

PURPOSE OF THE DIET

To prevent the formation of an obstructing bolus of high-fiber foods in patients with narrowed intestinal or esophageal lumens or to reduce the frequency of painful stools in acute phases of diverticulitis or inflammatory bowel disease.

EFFECTS OF THE DIET

Low-fiber diets—most particularly those with decreased amounts of insoluble fibers, such as bran and other cereal fibers—decrease the weight and bulk of the stool and lead to delayed intestinal transit. A low-fiber diet is not necessarily synonymous with a low-residue diet, however. Some low-fiber foods, such as milk and prune juice, actually increase colonic residue and stool weight by mechanisms other than dietary fiber (1).

PHYSIOLOGY, FOODS, AND NUTRIENTS

To achieve a low-fiber intake, indigestible carbohydrates are reduced by using limited amounts of well-cooked or canned vegetables; ripe, canned, or well-cooked fruits; and certain raw fruits and vegetables low in dietary fiber content. Tender meat or meat made tender in the cooking process is used to decrease the intake of connective tissue.

The nutritional consequences of long-term dietary fiber restriction are just beginning to be elucidated. The pH of the intestinal environment is altered. Activity of certain pancreatic enzymes and hormones—such as glucagon, which inhibits motility of the small and large bowels—is increased. Bacterial flora and their metabolic activities are altered. Short-chain fatty acid metabolism is changed. The concentration of bile acids in the aqueous phase of feces (fecal water) is increased within 4 days. Also, nutritional adequacy is more difficult to achieve, because of the limitations on fruit and vegetable intake (2–6).

INDICATIONS FOR USE

Low-fiber diets are indicated during acute phases of diverticulosis, infectious enterocolitis, ulcerative colitis, or Crohn's disease when the bowel is markedly inflamed, fixed radiological strictures are present, or the intestinal lumen is narrowed. Barring such complications or acute situations, there is little evidence to support the long-term use of a fiber-restricted diet for any condition, including duodenal ulcers or Crohn's disease (7–9).

The diet may also be useful for a short period in the transition between a completely liquid diet and a normal diet with patients convalescing from surgery, trauma, or other illnesses. It should be individualized to suit specific patient tolerances, depending upon the type of surgery or illness.

POSSIBLE ADVERSE REACTIONS

1. CONSTIPATION

Fiber-deficient diets are associated with prolonged intestinal transit and small infrequent stools. It has been suggested that continued use of a low-fiber diet with large amounts of highly refined carbohydrates may be associated with diverticular disease of the colon. According to this theory, the reduced bulk of the diet eventually results in the narrowing of the colonic lumen. The small compact stool produced by low-fiber diets causes the colon to contract more tightly around it, thus decreasing the size of the lumen and increasing intraluminal pressures. These pressure increases may lead to herniation of the colonic muscle and the characteristic diverticula of the disorder (10).

2. GALLSTONE DISEASE

Recently, epidemiological and case control studies have linked low-fiber intake with gallstone disease. A possible mechanism for this, as yet unproven, may involve the fact that bran supplements increase the proportion of chenodeoxycholic acid in the circulating bile salt pool and that wheat bran reduces the lithogenic (calculi-forming) index of bile (11–14).

3. CANCER OF THE COLON

A low-fiber diet results in increased concentrations of bile acids in fecal water, which are associated with increased cytotoxicity of the feces and an increased risk of colon cancer. Fecal bile acid concentration is a factor in carcinogenesis of the rectosigmoid but not of the right colon. Deoxycholic and lithocholic acids, produced by bacterial enzyme action on bile acids, are potential tumor promoters (1, 5, 6, 15, 16).

CONTRAINDICATIONS

A low-fiber diet may actually aggravate symptoms and is contraindicated in irritable bowel syndrome or diverticulosis, except in acute phases when the lumen of the colon is narrowed or stenosed (10).

There is no longer any justification for a fiber-restricted diet in the routine treatment of duodenal ulcers or Crohn's disease. Lifting of low-fiber-diet restrictions in these conditions has been shown to have no adverse effect and some benefits to patients (8, 17).

CLINICAL ASSESSMENT

Depending on the site of inflammation, lactose intolerance and fat malabsorption may require additional modifications of the diet (18).

Priorities for the nutritional assessment of these patients include calorie counts that evaluate the percentage of the Recommended Dietary Allowances met daily. Stool frequency and constipation problems should also be assessed.

BIOCHEMICAL ASSESSMENT

In the patient with gastrointestinal disease, the assessment should involve nutritional surveillance for the resolution of leukocytosis and an increased sedimentation rate, which accompany an acute inflammatory phase.

The presence of occult blood in the stool due to mucosal bleeding, with an accompanying fall in serum proteins, indicates the need for an increased protein intake.

TABLE 8.1. NUTRITIONAL IMPLICATIONS OF DRUGS COMMONLY USED IN CONJUNCTION WITH A FIBER-RESTRICTED DIET

Drug	Nutritional implications	Recommended action
Prednisone (Deltasone, Orasone, Prednisone) (19, 20)	May take with food; need foods high in pyruvate, vitamins C and D, folate, calcium, and phosphorus; may cause GI distress; may cause poor growth, osteoporosis, disordered carbohydrate metabolism, hyperglycemia, and weight gain due to edema	Check weight for height, then monitor weight; check x-rays for bone density; monitor levels of blood glucose and glycosylated hemoglobin; reduce dose and give calcium supplement if osteoporosis occurs; if sodium retention and weight gain occur, reduce caloric and sodium intake; lower dose if patient is diabetic.
Sulfasalazine (Azulfidine) (18–20)	May induce folate deficiency; may cause anorexia and altered taste; may increase urinary protein; may cause abdominal pain	Give with 8 oz. water after meals; monitor CBC, serum, and RBC folate; if folate deficiency occurs, stop drug and give folic acid.
Diphenoxylate with atropine (Lomotil) (19, 20)	May cause dry mouth, sore and swollen gums, nausea, vomiting, and bloating; may increase serum amylase	For dry mouth, give ice to suck; patient should avoid alcohol.
Loperamide (Immodium) (20)	May cause abdominal pains, constipation, bloating, dry mouth, nausea, vomiting, and electrolyte imbalance	Monitor electrolytes; stop drug if they are abnormal.

ASSESSMENT OF POTENTIAL DRUG INTERACTIONS

When the diet is used in acute phases of ulcerative colitis or Crohn's disease in combination with corticosteroids, calcium metabolism and protein synthesis may be adversely affected, requiring increases in dietary calcium and protein intake. If the drug sulfasalazine is used, folate utilization may be affected (18).

Cholestyramine, used to treat secondary fat malabsorption, may interfere with metabolism of fat-soluble vitamins (3). See table 8.1 for further interactions.

IMPLEMENTATION AND EDUCATION

Patients with gastrointestinal disorders may need a great deal of supportive help from the dietitian, particularly when the diet is transitional and the patient must be gradually weaned into a more normal diet.

If a low-residue diet is indicated, all fruits and vegetables, including prune juice, should be eliminated except white potatoes without skin and strained fruit and vegetable juices. There is limited evidence that milk, which contains no crude fiber, may indirectly contribute to fecal residue. Thus, with certain patients it may be wise to restrict milk to 2 cups per day. The diet should be individualized according to the patient's specific food tolerances.

PRIORITIES FOR QUALITY ASSURANCE

Every attempt should be made to liberalize restrictions in fiber intake whenever possible. When the diet is used as a transitional diet in the hospital setting, patients should be evaluated periodically, e.g., after a certain number of days on the diet.

TABLE 8.2. FOOD LIST AND DAILY AMOUNTS FOR THE FIBER-RESTRICTED DIET

Food group	Serving size and number of servings	Foods allowed	Foods excluded
Beverages	Allowed foods are virtually free of fiber. Amount allowed: as desired	Coffee, tea, milk, carbonated beverages, fruit drinks	Any containing raw egg, or fruit or vegetable pulp
Breads	Allowed foods contain approximately 1.0 g fiber or less per 1-oz. serving or 1 slice. Amount allowed: limit to 3 servings daily	Refined breads, rolls, biscuits, muffins, crackers, pancakes, waffles, plain pastries, raisin bread	Any made with whole-grain flour, bran, seeds, nuts, coconut, or raw or dried fruit (with the exception of raisin bread); cornbread, graham crackers; any containing more than 1.0 g fiber per serving
Cereals	Allowed foods contain approximately 1.0 g fiber or less per ½- to ¾-cup serving. Amount allowed: limit to 1 serving daily	Refined cooked cereals, such as Cream of Wheat, Cream of Rice, Malt-O-Meal, grits, and farina; refined dry cereals, such as Cheerios, cornflakes, Rice Krispies, puffed rice, puffed wheat, Special K, Kix, and Sugar Smacks	Oatmeal; any whole-grain, bran, or granola cereals; any containing seeds, nuts, coconut, or dried fruit; any containing more than 1.0 g fiber per serving
Desserts and sweets	Allowed foods contain approximately 1.0 g fiber or less per serving. Amount allowed: limit to 1 serving daily	Plain cakes and cookies; pie made with allowed foods	Any made with whole-grain flour, bran, seeds, nuts, coconut, or dried fruit; any containing more than 1.0 g fiber per serving
	These foods are virtually free of fiber. Amount allowed: as desired	Plain sherbet, fruit ice, ice cream, yogurt, custard; fruit-flavored or unflavored gelatin; Popsicles, sugar, honey, jelly, plain hard candy, marshmallows	
Fats	Allowed foods are virtually free of fiber. Amount allowed: as desired	Margarine, butter, cream, salad oils, mayonnaise, cream, bacon, plain gravies and salad dressings	Any containing whole-grain flour, bran, seeds, nuts, coconut, or dried fruit
Fruits	Allowed foods contain approximately 2.0 g fiber or less per ½-cup serving. Amount allowed: limit to 1 serving daily	Canned or cooked—apple slices, applesauce, cherries, grapefruit, grapes, oranges, peaches, pineapple, plums; canned fruit cocktail; raw—banana, cherries, grapefruit, grapes, melon, orange, peach, pineapple	Dried fruit; all berries; raw fruit except that allowed; all fruit not listed as allowed
	Allowed foods contain approximately 0.5 g fiber per ½-cup serving. Amount allowed: limit to 2 servings daily	Fruit juice or vegetable juice without pulp	Fruit juice or vegetable juice with pulp
Meat and substitutes	Allowed foods do not contain fiber. Amount allowed: as desired	All meat, fish, or poultry; eggs, plain cheeses	Any made with whole-grain ingredients, seeds, or nuts; dried beans, peas, lentils, legumes, nuts, peanut butter
Potato and substitutes	Allowed foods contain 2.0 g fiber or less per ½-cup serving. Amount allowed: limit to 1 serving daily	Cooked white and sweet potatoes without skin; white rice; refined pasta	All others

(continued)

TABLE 8.2. *CONTINUED*

Food group	Serving size and number of servings	Foods allowed	Foods excluded
Soups	Allowed foods contain approximately 1.0 g fiber per 6-oz. serving. Amount allowed: limit to 1 serving daily	Bouillon, broth, or cream soups made with allowed vegetables, noodles, rice, or flour	All others
	These soups are free of fiber. Amount allowed: as desired	Plain bouillon, broth, or consommé	
Vegetables	Allowed foods contain approximately 2.0 g fiber or less per ½-cup serving. Amount allowed: limit to 2 servings daily	Frozen, canned, cooked or raw— asparagus, green beans, yellow beans, bean sprouts, beets, cabbage,[a] carrots, cauliflower,[a] celery, cucumber,[a] eggplant (pared); collard, dandelion, or mustard greens; green pepper,[a] lettuce, mushrooms, onion,[a] rutabaga,[a] spinach, summer squash, tomato, turnip, zucchini; tomato paste, sauce, and puree	Dried beans, peas, lentils, legumes; sauerkraut, winter squash, peas; vegetables not listed as allowed
Miscellaneous		Salt, pepper, sugar, spices, herbs, gravy, vinegar, ketchup, mustard	Nuts, coconut, seeds, popcorn

Source: Revord, J. (21).
[a]Some individuals may not tolerate these vegetables; omit if they cause discomfort.

MENU PLANNING

A list of foods allowed and excluded and the daily amounts of allowed foods is provided in table 8.2.

SAMPLE MENU FOR THE FIBER-RESTRICTED DIET (FOR A MALE, AGE 25–50)

BREAKFAST

Orange juice	½ cup
Poached or soft-cooked egg	1 large
Pancakes	2
Margarine	2 tsp.
Syrup	2 tbsp.
Cornflakes	¾ cup
Low-fat milk	1 cup
Coffee	1 cup
Sugar	1 tsp.

LUNCH

Chicken rice soup	8 oz.
Baked chicken breast	3 oz.
Well-cooked asparagus	½ cup
White bread	1 slice
Margarine	2 tsp.
Banana	1 large
Low-fat milk	1 cup
Orange sherbet	1 cup

(continued)

| Tea | 1 cup |
| Sugar | 1 tsp. |

DINNER

Lean broiled sirloin steak	4 oz.
Baked potato without skin	1 small
Sour cream	2 tbsp.
Tender cooked spinach	½ cup
White toast	1 slice
Margarine	3 tsp.
Low-fat fruit yogurt	1 cup
Tea	1 cup
Sugar	1 tsp.

EVENING SNACK

Cranberry juice cocktail	1 cup
Vanilla wafers	6
Low-fat cottage cheese	½ cup

Approximate Nutrient Analysis

Energy	2,911 kcal
Protein	141.9 g (20% of kcal)
Fat	86.3 g (27% of kcal)
Polyunsaturated fat	12.4 g
Monounsaturated fat	26.4 g
Saturated fat	30.7 g
Cholesterol	587 mg
Carbohydrate	398.2 g (55% of kcal)
Vitamin A	13,569 IU
	2,100 RE
Thiamine	1.94 mg
Riboflavin	3.74 mg
Niacin	31.3 mg
Folate	504 mcg
Vitamin B-12	7.88 mcg
Vitamin B-6	3.49 mg
Vitamin C	213.4 mg
Calcium	1,809 mg
Phosphorus	2,242 mg
Iron	19.2 mg
Copper	1.48 mg
Zinc	16.5 mg
Magnesium	388 mg
Sodium	3,843 mg
Potassium	4,850 mg

REFERENCES

1. Kramer, P.: The meaning of high and low residue diets. Gastroenterology 47:649, 1964.
2. Connell, A. M.: The role of fibre in the gastrointestinal tract. In Bowen, P. E., Connell, A. M., et al.: The clinical role of fibre. Toronto: Medical Education Services, 1985.
3. Jenkins, D. A., Jenkins, A. L., et al.: Cancer risk: Possible protective role of high carbohydrate high fiber diets. Am J Gastroenterol 81:931, 1986.
4. Salyers, A. A., Kuritza, A. P., and McCarthy, R. E.: Influence of dietary fiber on the intestinal environment. Proc Soc Exp Biol Med 180:415, 1985.
5. Rafter, J., Child, P., et al.: Cellular toxicity of fecal water depends upon diet. Am J Clin Nutr 45:559, 1987.
6. Allinger, V. G., Johansson, G. K., et al.: Shift from a mixed to a lactovegetarian diet: Influence on acidic lipids in fecal water—a potential risk factor for colon cancer. Am J Clin Nutr 50:992, 1989.

7. Levi, A. J.: Diet in the management of Crohn's disease. Gut 26:985, 1985.
8. Levenstein, S., Prantera, C., et al.: Low residue or normal diet in Crohn's disease: A prospective controlled study in Italian patients. Gut 26:989, 1985.
9. Malhotra, S. L.: A comparison of unrefined wheat and rice diets in the management of duodenal ulcer. Postgrad Med J 54 (Jan.):6, 1978.
10. Painter, N. S., and Burkitt, D. P.: Diverticular disease of the colon: A deficiency disease of Western civilization. Br Med J 2:450, 1971.
11. Jenkins, D. A., Jenkins, A. L., et al.: Fiber and starch foods: Gut function and implications in disease. Am J Gastroenterol 81:920, 1986.
12. Heaton, K. W.: Gallstones. In Vahoney, G. V., and Kritchevsky, D.: Dietary fiber: Basic and clinical aspects. New York: Plenum Press, 1986.
13. McDougall, R. M., Yakymyshym, L., and Walker, K.: The effect of wheat bran on serum lipoproteins and biliary lipids. Can J Surg 21:433, 1978.
14. Alessandriui, A., Fusco, M., and Batti, E.: Dietary fibers and cholesterol gallstones—a case control study. Ital J Gastroenterol 14:156, 1982.
15. Eastwood, M.: Dietary fiber and the risk of cancer. Nutr Rev 45:93, 1987.
16. Galloway, D. J., Jarrett, F., et al.: Morphological and cell kinetic effects of dietary manipulation during colorectal carcinogenesis. Gut 28:754, 1987.
17. Rydning, A., and Berstad, A.: Fiber diet and antacids in the short-term treatment of duodenal ulcer. Scand J Gastroenterol 20:1078, 1985.
18. American Dietetic Association: Manual of clinical dietetics. Chicago: American Dietetic Association, 1988.
19. Powers, D. E., and Moore, A. O.: Food/medication interactions. 6th ed. Phoenix: 1988 (self-published).
20. Roe, D. A.: Handbook on drug and nutrient interactions. 4th ed. Chicago: American Dietetic Association, 1989.
21. Revord, J.: Fiber restricted diet. In ServiceMaster diet manual. 2d ed. Chicago: ServiceMaster Food Management Services, ServiceMaster Co., 1988.

HIGH-FIBER DIET

DEFINITION

A diet that contains increased amounts of soluble and insoluble dietary fiber (1).

Quantitative recommendations for a high-fiber diet vary. The American Diabetes Association, the National Cancer Institute, and others have suggested similar ranges of optimal and maximal intake for preventive and therapeutic purposes. The American Dietetic Association recommends daily consumption of a high-carbohydrate, low-fat diet containing 20 to 35 g of dietary fiber from a variety of food sources (2–6).

PURPOSE OF THE DIET

High-fiber diets are directed toward one or more of the following aims.

1. INCREASED FECAL BULK AND REDUCED INTESTINAL TRANSIT TIME

Cereal fiber is most effective in increasing fecal bulk and weight of residue reaching the distal colon. Fruit and vegetable fiber increases cell mass but not necessarily bulk (7, 8). Increased bulk and lower transit times combine to prevent constipation.

2. DECREASED INTRALUMINAL COLONIC PRESSURES

Wheat bran fiber may provide relief from symptoms of diverticular disease by decreasing intraluminal pressures. Such a decrease would help to maintain the normal size of the colonic lumen and prevent further segmentation. Controlled studies have not demonstrated this effect conclusively, however (7).

3. DECREASED RISK OF COLON CANCER

Colon cancer is the result of a complex interaction of carcinogens, cocarcinogens, tumor promoters, and tumor inhibitors. A high-fat diet may result in increased production of bile acids, which may damage DNA and have been implicated in the etiology of colon cancer. Bile acids may act as direct tumor promoters or may be converted by colonic bacteria to secondary bile acids, which are also promoters. One study demonstrated that cellulose may act as a catalyst to promote polyesterification of bile acids to a biologically inactive form and thus prevent DNA damage (9, 10).

Dietary fiber is thought to reduce the risk for colon cancer through the following mechanisms (9):

- Increasing the amount of feces passed, thereby reducing the concentration of carcinogenic substances in the bowel
- Reducing transit time through the colon, thereby reducing contact time between fecal carcinogens and the colonic mucosa
- Altering bacterial metabolism to decrease carcinogen production

4. DECREASED SERUM CHOLESTEROL LEVELS

The addition of fiber to controlled diets has been estimated to lower elevated serum cholesterol levels by 6% to 19% (2). In general, the water-soluble viscous polysaccharide types of dietary fiber appear to be the most effective in lowering plasma cholesterol and LDL-cholesterol.

Fiber intake has been found to be inversely related to mortality from ischemic heart disease in a group of 859 individuals (11–13).

5. DECREASED GLUCOSE ABSORPTION RATE

Both soluble and insoluble fibers delay glucose absorption from the gastrointestinal tract. Water-soluble fiber supplements from legumes, guar, and pectin decrease the postprandial glycemic response more than insoluble wheat fiber supplements (8, 14).

EFFECTS OF THE DIET

The physicochemical, physiological, and clinical aspects of fiber are summarized in table 9.1.

1. IN THE MOUTH

High-fiber foods take longer to chew which may reduce meal size (1).

2. IN THE STOMACH

A. Prolonged Gastric Filling High-fiber bulkier foods require longer periods for ingestion (16).

B. Delayed Gastric Emptying The effect of fiber on gastric emptying depends upon the physical properties of the particular type of fiber, such as viscosity. The soluble viscous fibers, such as guar and pectin, delay gastric emptying, whereas the insoluble particulate fibers, such as bran, may enhance gastric emptying rate (1, 7, 14, 17).

TABLE 9.1. PHYSICOCHEMICAL, PHYSIOLOGIC, AND CLINICAL ASPECTS OF FIBER

Physicochemical property	Type of fiber	Physiologic effect	Clinical implication
Viscosity	Gums, mucilages, pectins	↓ gastric emptying, ↑ mouth-to-cecum transit, ↓ rate of small intestinal absorption (e.g., of glucose, bile acids)	Dumping syndrome Diabetes Hypercholesterolemia
Particle formation and water-holding capacity	e.g., Wheat bran, pentosan content, polysaccharide-lignin mixtures	↑ gastric emptying, ↓ mouth-to-cecum transit, ↓ total GI transit time, ↓ colonic intraluminal pressure, ↑ fecal bulk	Peptic ulcer Constipation Diverticular disease Dilute potential carcinogens
Adsorption and nonspecific effects	Lignin, pectin, mixed fibers	↑ fecal steroids output, ↑ fecal fat and N losses (small)	Hypercholesterolemia Cholelithiasis
Cation exchange	Acidic polysaccharides (e.g., pectins)	↑ small-intestinal losses of minerals (±), trace elements (±), heavy metals	Negative mineral balance, probably compensated for by colonic salvage and antitoxic effect
Antioxidant	Lignin (reducing phenolic groups)	↓ free radicals in digestive tract	Anticarcinogenesis?
Degradability (colonic bacteria)	Polysaccharides (free of lignin)	↑ Production of gas and short-chain fatty acids, ↓ cecal pH	Flatus, energy production

Source: Jenkins, D. J. A. (37); *adapted from* Eastwood, M. A., and Kay, R. M. (86), and Kay, R. M., and Strasberg, S. M. (87). Copyright © 1979, *American Journal of Clinical Nutrition,* American Society for Clinical Nutrition.

C. Increased Postprandial Satiety
Foods high in wheat fiber take longer to eat and provide less energy per unit weight than do most low-fiber foods; satiety, or the sense of fullness, tends to be higher after their ingestion. Gum and combination fiber supplements may decrease appetite and lower energy intake (8, 9, 18, 19).

D. Decreased Gastric Acidity One report that warrants further investigation suggests that the ingestion of refined low-fiber grain products results in a greater increase in gastric acidity than does the ingestion of unrefined grains (16).

3. IN THE SMALL INTESTINE

A. Intestinal Transit Time Insoluble fiber speeds intestinal transit, whereas breath hydrogen studies indicate that soluble fiber delays it. Wholemeal bread increases the rate of intestinal transit. When compared with gel-like soluble fibers such as oat bran and citrus flour, the insoluble fibers wheat and corn bran produced a greater increase in the rate of intestinal transit (14, 16, 20, 21).

B. Decreased Rate of Digestion Dietary fiber delays digestion by decreasing the surface area of starch and other nutrients that is exposed to hydrolytic enzymes and by inhibiting enzyme activity.

The presence of fiber in a food can provide a physical barrier to enzyme penetration. The higher the amylose content of a starch, the less rapidly it is digested and the less it raises the blood sugar. Processed foods are digested at a faster rate than unprocessed foods, ground foods are digested faster than whole foods, and foods subjected to the sterilization heat of the canning process are more readily hydrolyzed than those that are not (1, 7, 8, 22–25).

The rate of digestion of a fiber containing starch depends upon the physical form of the food, the degree of processing, the type and amount of fiber, and the amount of amylase-resistant starch, phytate, lectins, tannins, saponins, and enzyme inhibitors (17, 22, 26, 27).

C. Decreased Rate of Nutrient Absorption   Fiber sources, primarily those containing viscous polysaccharides, slow the rate at which nutrients are absorbed from the small intestine, but they do not necessarily affect the total amount absorbed. One postulated mechanism for this finding is the increase in the volume and viscosity of the aqueous phase of the intestinal contents caused by viscous fibers such as pectin or guar gum (1, 16).

D. Decreased Glucose Absorption Rate   The total sugar absorption after administration of various test foods compared with a standard, usually bread, has been termed the glycemic index (GI). The concept of the glycemic index was introduced by Jenkins et al. to overcome the difficulty in predicting the physiological effects of starchy foods and to classify foods in terms of their glycemic response (23).

Glycemic index =

$$\frac{\text{blood glucose from food}}{\text{blood glucose from standard carbohydrate (glucose or bread)}} \times 100$$

The flattened glycemic response noted to foods with a high-fiber content is probably due to an increase in the thickness of the unstirred water layer of the aqueous phase of the intestinal contents (23).

Factors other than the amount and type of dietary fiber content of the food affect the glycemic index. Legumes, high in soluble fiber, have a low GI, whereas bread and most other cereals high in insoluble fiber have a high GI. In mixed diets, however, the soluble fiber content of a food may not be a reliable indicator of its GI. Other factors that affect GI include the nature of the carbohydrate; the presence of antinutrients such as lectins, phytates, saponins, and enzyme inhibitors; starch-nutrient interac-

tions; and ripeness, processing, cooking, and storage of the food (28, 29).

Several foods low in fiber, such as spaghetti and other pastas, also have low glycemic indices. Rice with a high amylase content raises the blood glucose less than rice with a higher amylopectin content, and whole rice has a lower GI than ground rice (28, 29).

The practicality and clinical utility of the glycemic index have been questioned. Predictions of improvement in long-term glucose control in the diabetic are complicated by the fact that the glycemic response to single foods does not necessarily resemble the results obtained when they are incorporated into meals (30–32).

4. ON THE EXOCRINE PANCREAS

In one study the effect of 20 g of fiber added to the diet in the form of fiber-supplemented biscuits led to an increase in lipase concentration. Conversely, in vitro studies have demonstrated that dietary fiber inhibits pancreatic enzymes (33, 34).

5. IN THE COLON

A. Production of Volatile Fatty Acids
Foods high in fiber content, particularly hemicellulose and to a lesser extent cellulose, can be broken down by intestinal bacteria to volatile fatty acids that act as potent cathartics (35).

B. Increased Stool Bulk   Certain types of fiber imbibe water or act as hygroscopic agents. Water-holding capacity may be of importance in reducing colonic transit time as well as overall transit time, because most of the water holding is accomplished in the colon. Hemicellulose, cellulose, a number of mucilaginous gums, and bran can absorb water. Bran can absorb 3 times its weight in water—one reason that it produces an increase in fecal weight. Particle size is a determinant of the water-holding capac-

ity of dietary fiber. Coarse bran will hold more water than fine bran (7, 36–38).

C. Cation Exchange   The weak cation-exchange-resin property of fiber suggests that the electrolyte content of the stool may be controlled by diet (39).

D. Colorectal Cancer   A high-fiber diet lowers total fecal bile acids and neutral animal sterol concentrations. The ratio of fecal coprostanol to total neutral animal sterols is also lower. Several mechanisms by which dietary fiber may reduce the risk of colorectal cancers have been proposed, including bulking action to reduce the concentration of mutagens or carcinogens in the luminal contents; an increase in the rate of intestinal transit and a reduction in the contact time between the potential carcinogens and the mucosa; fermentation by intestinal microbes to short-chain fatty acids that influence proliferation and differentiation of colonic epithelial cells in such a way as to reduce tumor development; and acidification of luminal contents by short-chain fatty acids, which inhibits microbial production of carcinogens (40, 41).

The strongest physiological relationship between colonic cancer and fiber in the diet is in the fecal bulking action of fiber and its potential ability to dilute toxic or undesirable materials. The National Research Council (NRC) of the National Academy of Sciences reports, "There is no conclusive evidence to indicate that total dietary fiber exerts a protective effect against colorectal cancer in humans. Both epidemiological and laboratory reports suggest that if there is such an effect, specific components of fiber, rather than total fiber, are most likely to be responsible." The latest data from the NRC state that in animals, wheat bran appears to inhibit tumor development more consistently than other fiber sources do. Evidence available from the Melbourne colorectal cancer study suggests, however, that all forms of fiber, including vegetable and cereal fiber, have a protective effect and that there may be an interaction between fiber intake and vegetable intake in the protection provided (11, 42–48).

6. OTHER GENERAL EFFECTS

A. Improved Glucose Tolerance

High-carbohydrate, high-fiber diets providing 55% to 60% of energy as carbohydrate, 15% to 20% as protein, and 20% to 25% as fat, and including up to 50 g of dietary fiber daily, improve glucose metabolism without increasing insulin. The mechanisms by which dietary fiber reduces postprandial hyperglycemia or improves glucose tolerance are believed to include delayed gastric emptying, altered rate of nutrient absorption, and altered rate of nutrient utilization. In nondiabetic as well as diabetic subjects, high-fiber diets lower fasting serum insulin values and serum insulin responses to glucose administration. Insulin-receptor binding to circulating monocytes is increased by high-fiber diets, as is insulin sensitivity of peripheral tissues such as muscle (15, 49).

In normal healthy adults, high-carbohydrate, high-fiber diets may improve carbohydrate economy by enhanced peripheral sensitivity to insulin. In diabetics on high-fiber diets, the urinary excretion of C-peptides, a parameter of endogenous insulin secretion, is not increased. This finding probably means that the improvement in glycemic control is related not to increased endogenous insulin secretion but to improved utilization of insulin (15, 50).

B. Decreased Gastrointestinal Peptides

A diet high in cereal fibers has been demonstrated to result in decreased plasma glucagon levels. Glucagon has a hyperglycemic effect and is also a known potent inhibitor of small-bowel and large-bowel motility. Pectin has also been demonstrated to decrease serum levels of glucagon and gastric inhibitory polypeptide (GIP), hormones that regulate insulin secretion. Similar responses in plasma gastric inhibitory polypeptide but not glucagon have been observed with guar gum. The effects on gastric inhibitory polypeptide have been disputed by other investigators who reported that pectin lowers serum gastrin levels. Soy polysaccharide, a gel-forming water-soluble fiber, has been reported to decrease glucagon levels, and decreased serum levels of gastrin and GIP have been attributed to the water-soluble fiber xanthan gum. More research is needed on the effect of a mixed diet on gastrointestinal peptides (7, 16, 49, 51–53).

C. Decreased Blood Pressures

Vegetarians with twofold higher intakes of dietary fiber have lower average blood pressures than matched control groups. Because a vegetarian diet includes dietary changes other than an increased fiber intake, more research is needed to determine the exact role played by fiber in observed decreases in blood pressure (8, 11, 54).

D. Absorption of Organic Molecules Such as Bile Acids

Dietary fiber binds bile acids and bile salts. The extent of this effect varies with the type of fiber and the bile acid or salt under study. Prevention of bile acid reabsorption is one way to decrease serum cholesterol. If bile acids are bound and excreted, less cholesterol will be absorbed and less will appear in the circulation. Cellulose binds almost no bile acid, bran binds a small amount, and alfalfa binds bile acids to a significant extent. Soluble fibers such as pectin, guar gum, and psyllium consistently enhance bile acid output (51, 55, 56).

E. Reduced Serum Cholesterol Levels

A diet containing fiber may inhibit lymphatic absorption or reabsorption of cholesterol, leading to lowered serum levels. According to one theory, an increased flux of short-chain fatty acids formed by colonic bacteria from fiber polysaccharides has been suspected to inhibit cholesterol synthesis. Bacteria in the colon ferment soluble fiber almost completely into short-chain fatty acids, methane, carbon dioxide, hydrogen, and water. These fatty acids—primarily acetate, propionate, and butyrate—are absorbed into the body and may mediate changes in glucose and lipid metabolism. According to one author, propionate inhibits hepatic and peripheral cholesterol synthesis and accelerates LDL-cholesterol clearance. Oat bran and beans, rich in soluble fiber, have a significant lowering effect on total and LDL-cholesterol, whereas wheat fiber supplements have little impact on cholesterol levels over short periods of time (1, 8, 14, 51, 56, 57).

In a comparative study of the effects of oat bran and low-fiber wheat on serum lipoprotein levels and blood pressure, oat bran had little effect on either blood pressure or serum lipoproteins in 20 healthy individuals on a low-cholesterol diet. The authors speculated that beneficial effects observed by others may be due to the replacement of dietary fats by the oat bran in the diet. The results of this study should not be extrapolated to patients with hyperlipidemia, because they were excluded (58).

A more recent study involving hypercholesterolemic men and a diet that included 25 g of oat bran daily found that the diet lowered serum total cholesterol and serum LDL-cholesterol concentrations significantly—by 5.4% and 8.5%, respectively (59).

F. Possible Effects on Serum Triglyceride Levels

Evidence that fiber may have a role in the management of hypertriglyceridemia warrants further research. Whereas low-fiber, high-carbohydrate diets increase fasting serum triglycerides of nondiabetic and diabetic individuals, inclusion of fiber in these diets results in reductions of average fasting serum triglyceride values. Dietary fiber may have a protective effect against sucrose-induced hypertriglyceridemia (2, 8, 57).

PHYSIOLOGY, FOODS, AND NUTRIENTS

1. DIET CHARACTERISTICS

Emphasis is placed on modifying the normal diet by increasing the intake of whole-grain breads and cereals and of fruits and vegetables that are high in fiber content. The intake of highly refined carbohydrates is reduced to the extent that they are replaced by unrefined foods. The caloric content is not substantially different from that of a normal diet.

2. FOOD SOURCES

The diet described herein includes increased amounts of both soluble and insoluble forms of fiber, which have different physiological effects upon the body. Vegetables, wheat, and most grains are good sources of insoluble fiber, whereas fruits, oats, barley, and legumes provide more soluble fiber. Oat bran and legumes are especially good sources of soluble fiber (14).

High levels of cellulose are found in root and leafy vegetables, legumes, and some fruits, such as pears and apples. Lignin content is highest in fruits, particularly strawberries and peaches. Pectin levels are highest in citrus fruits and apples. Cereals and grains contain high levels of the insoluble fibers cellulose and hemicelluloses. The fiber content of canned vegetables may be higher than that of fresh vegetables, because browning reactions may occur with cooking and water is lost from the plant during cooking (5, 11). Food sources of various fiber components are presented in table 9.2.

TABLE 9.2. FOOD SOURCES OF VARIOUS FIBER COMPONENTS

Cellulose	*Hemicellulose*	*Pectin*
Whole wheat flour	Bran	Apples
Bran	Cereals	Citrus fruits
Cabbage family	Whole grains	Strawberries
Peas and beans	*Gums*	*Lignin*
Apples	Oatmeal	Mature vegetables
Root vegetables	Dried beans	Wheat
	Other legumes	

Source: Slavin J. L. (5). Copyright © 1987 by the American Dietetic Association.

3. FIBER SUPPLEMENTS VERSUS HIGH-FIBER DIET

Clear effects on cholesterol and bile acid have been observed in studies of purified fibers such as guar gum and pectin. These polysaccharides lower LDL-cholesterol and increase fecal bile acid excretion. When fiber is fed as part of a food, these changes are less consistent and are not great when compared with those associated with other dietary components, such as fat (60, 61).

4. RESEARCH

Nutritional research on dietary fiber is in its infancy, with the development of complete and accurate tables of composition with dietary fiber content of American foods lagging far behind the documentation of clinical applications for their use. The development of such data should be a priority for researchers in fiber nutrition.

INDICATIONS FOR USE

Increasing dietary fiber intake from a high-fiber diet may be beneficial in atonic constipation, uncomplicated diverticular disease, irritable bowel syndrome, diabetes, and hyperlipidemia (2, 7, 14, 15, 17, 23, 62–69).

A high-fiber diet may possibly be beneficial in prevention of other conditions. If further research verifies the benefits, a high-fiber diet would be indicated for the general population. Although high-fiber diets are not recommended for treatment of ulcers, their use may have a preventive effect. The fiber most recommended in that case is particulate bran, which encourages rapid gastric emptying. A high-fiber diet may also protect against colorectal cancer (9, 11, 17, 37, 40–48, 70).

POSSIBLE ADVERSE REACTIONS

1. OSMOTIC DIARRHEA

Volatile fatty acids produced by the action of bacteria on large amounts of fiber in the intestine may result in an irritating osmotic diarrhea and increased flatus production (7).

2. DECREASED NUTRIENT AVAILABILITY

Excessive use of foods high in phytate, and to a lesser extent oxalate, to increase dietary fiber intake may have undesirable nutritional consequences. Even a diet that includes fruit and vegetable fiber may cause some decrease in nutrient availability. Mineral balances have been reported for men and women consuming a mixed high-fiber diet that provided 50% of the calories in the form of carbohydrates and 40 g of neutral detergent fiber per day. Calcium and magnesium balances were generally negative, especially in women, even though intakes were adequate. Bran and breads made from unprocessed flour have been reported to lower serum levels of calcium, zinc, and iron. The addition of ascorbic acid to a meal with fiber will improve iron absorption. A recent clinical review of the research in this area concludes that even a combination of fiber and phytic acid does not appear to affect mineral balance unless unrefined cereal intakes are high and mineral intakes are low. Also, the body may be able to adjust to the decreased availability of minerals by increased absorption of those available. Oxalic acid may result in decreases in mineral availability if consumed with a high-fiber diet, but the decrease may be transient (71–76).

3. BEZOAR FORMATION AND INTESTINAL DAMAGE

Massive doses of particulate fiber may result in rare occurrences of damage to the villous structure of the small bowel. There have also been reports of the formation of bezoars—physical obstacles created by tangles of fibrous material in the gastrointestinal tract that may cause dangerous gastrointestinal obstructions—following increased fiber intakes in some. Diabetics who suffer from gastroparesis should be monitored closely for such potential adverse effects (71).

CONTRAINDICATIONS

The high-fiber diet is contraindicated in cases of inflammation, stenosis, or narrowing of the intestinal lumen (77).

CLINICAL ASSESSMENT

The medical and dietary histories should elicit information on dietary fiber, fluid, and nutrient intake, as well as the identification of risk factors for disease (2). For individuals with gastrointestinal disease, a medical workup should include medical documentation of any suspected

intolerances. For example, milk should not be eliminated from the diet without a lactose tolerance test.

BIOCHEMICAL ASSESSMENT

Complaints of diarrhea should be followed by a medical workup to identify the specific cause. No food should be incriminated without medical proof implicating the food as the cause of the problem. Patients with hyperlipidemia should be evaluated according to guidelines in Chapter 26, and those with diabetes should be evaluated according to the guidelines for the diet in Chapter 28.

ASSESSMENT OF POTENTIAL DRUG INTERACTIONS

Assessment should include information on drugs that affect the gastrointestinal tract, such as antibiotics that cause diarrhea (see Chapter 13); analgesic agents, tranquilizers, and anti-anxiety drugs that decrease motility and cause constipation; and Reglan, which is used for gastroparesis in the diabetic (see Chapter 28). Nutritional implications of selected drugs are given in table 9.3. Known effects of various types of high-fiber diet on nutrient absorption are summarized in table 9.4.

IMPLEMENTATION AND EDUCATION

Fiber should be added to the diet gradually in increments of 5 to 10 g to allow adaptation of gastrointestinal function and flora (2). Patients should be encouraged to consume liberal amounts of fluids, at least 8 to 12 cups per day.

One approach has been to incorporate dry beans and oat products as sources of soluble fiber. This regimen is implemented by the daily inclusion of 1 bowl of oat cereal (such as oatmeal, oat bran, or dry oat cereal) along with 2 oat bran muffins or 50 g of dry pinto, navy, or

kidney beans. This inclusion provides 6 g of soluble fiber (81).

Putting high-fiber, high-carbohydrate, low-fat diets into practice may require coordination between dietitians and other health care providers. Because such diets lower insulin requirements, insulin dose is usually decreased about 10% when the diet is instituted. Oral-agent dose may be decreased by one-third to one-half. Home blood-glucose monitoring permits faster adjustments until satisfactory glycemic control is achieved.

To facilitate the implementation of the dietary guidelines to reduce the risk of cancer published by the National Research Council of the National Academy of Sciences, guidelines to food selection and special recipes have been formulated (82–85).

PRIORITIES FOR QUALITY ASSURANCE

Data on the health benefits of dietary fiber and the value of fresh as opposed to processed fruit and vegetable fiber come at a time when cost containment measures in hospital and long-term-care settings have affected food budgets in dietary departments. It is tempting to substitute less expensive canned fruit and vegetables in place of fresh or to serve baked products for dessert. With elderly patient populations a common justification is poor patient tolerance, either real (dysphagia secondary to stroke; lack of or improperly fitted dentures) or imagined (drug-induced diarrhea falsely attributed to diet). A quality assurance program that includes a monitor on dietary fiber intake of patients and on the appropriateness of pureed, soft, or low-fiber diet may in the long run save money if it results in an increased dietary fiber intake with less reliance on stool softeners, laxatives, and other expensive components of hospital bowel regimens. Analysis of menus in the health care setting should include estimations of dietary fiber to ensure adequate intake.

TABLE 9.3. NUTRITIONAL IMPLICATIONS AND RECOMMENDATIONS FOR SELECTED DRUGS

Drug	Nutritional implications	Recommended action
Diazepam (Valium)	An antianxiety drug; may cause nausea, vomiting, constipation, and increased appetite and weight; may cause dry mouth and a reduced food intake if given in high doses	Patient should take with food or water and avoid alcohol. If dry mouth occurs, reduce dose.
Imipramine (Tofranil)	May cause nausea, vomiting, constipation, epigastric distress, cramps, stomatitis, anorexia, altered taste, dry mouth, and inappropriate ADH (antidiuretic hormone) syndrome	If GI distress occurs, give with food. If riboflavin depletion occurs, increase intake of foods high in riboflavin. Monitor erythrocyte glutathione reductase test on RBC.
Phenolphthalein (Correctol, Ex-Lax, Feen-A-Mint)	May decrease absorption of vitamins D and C; may cause steatorrhea, electrolyte imbalance, osteomalacia, hypokalemia, and weight loss	Patient should take on empty stomach with 8 oz. water and chew tablet well. Encourage fluids. Test fecal fat excretion for presence of steatorrhea; if fat intake is excessive (see low-fat diet for guidelines), reduce intake. Monitor serum potassium, and if hypokalemia occurs, stop drug and give IV potassium.
Psyllium gum (Metamucil)	A bulk-forming laxative; may decrease riboflavin absorption; may cause anorexia, bloating, steatorrhea, decreased serum cholesterol, and altered transport of electrolytes	Patient should take with large amounts of fluids. Monitor weight and erythrocyte glutathione reductase; increase intake of foods high in riboflavin; monitor fecal fat excretion.

Sources: Powers, D. E., and Moore, A. O. (78); Roe, D. A. (79).

TABLE 9.4. EFFECT OF HIGH-FIBER DIET ON NUTRIENT ABSORPTION

Diet components	Effect on nutrient absorption
High-fiber diet with pectin, guar gum, or acarbose	Delays sugar absorption
High-fiber diet with coarse bran	Enhances riboflavin absorption
High-fiber diet with psyllium	Reduces riboflavin absorption

Source: Roe, D. A. (80).

MENU PLANNING

DAILY MEAL PLAN FOR THE HIGH-FIBER DIET[a]

Food and serving size	Grams of fiber	Number of servings
Breads and starches		
Whole-grain or rye bread (1 slice)	2	5 (plus 0–5 refined
Whole-grain bagel or pita bread (½)		breads and
Oat bran muffin (½)		starches)
Corn or flour tortilla (1)		
Graham crackers, rice cakes, crisp breads (2)		
Whole-grain pasta, corn, peas (½ cup)		
Brown rice, sweet potato (⅓ cup)		
Air-popped popcorn (3 cups)		
Potato with skin (1 small)		
Cereals		
Whole-grain or bran cold cereals (1 oz.)	4	1
Oatmeal, oat bran, grits (⅓ cup dry)		
Vegetables		
Cooked: asparagus, green beans, broccoli, cabbage, carrots, cauliflower, greens, onions, snow peas, spinach, squash, tomatoes (½ cup)	2	3 (plus 0–2 other vegetables or juices)
Raw: broccoli, cabbage, carrots, cauliflower, leafy lettuce, squash, tomatoes (1 cup)		
Fruits		
Apple, nectarine, orange, peach (1 medium)	2.5	2 (plus 0–2 other fruits or juices)
Banana, grapefruit, pear (½)		
Berries, melons (1 cup)		
Beans		
Garbanzo beans, kidney beans, lentils, lima beans, split peas, pinto beans, other beans and peas (½ cup)	5	1
Milk		
Milk, yogurt (1 cup)	0	2–3 for men
		3–4 for women
		2 or more for children
		4 or more for teens or pregnant or lactating women
Proteins		
Meat, fish, poultry (1 oz.)	0	4–6
Eggs (1)		
Tofu (2½ oz.)		
Fats		
Margarine, butter, oil, mayonnaise (1 tsp.)	0	Avoid excess
Clear salad dressing (1 tbsp.)		

[a]This plan provides approximately 30 g of dietary fiber, depending on actual foods chosen (85).

SAMPLE MENU FOR THE HIGH-FIBER DIET (FOR A MALE, AGE 25–50)

BREAKFAST

Grapefruit	½ medium
Oat-flake cereal	1 cup
Low-fat milk	1 cup
Whole wheat bread	2 slices
Peanut butter	2 tbsp.
Coffee	1 cup
Sugar	1 tsp.

LUNCH

Bean-and-barley soup	1 cup
Whole wheat bread	2 slices
White turkey meat	3 oz.
Lettuce	2 leaves
Mayonnaise	2 tbsp.
Fresh pear	½ medium
Low-fat milk	1 cup
Tea	1 cup
Sugar	1 tsp.

AFTERNOON SNACK

Low-fat fruit yogurt	1 cup
Raisins	2 tbsp.

DINNER

Lean roast beef round	3 oz.
Baked potato with skin	1 large
Steamed broccoli	½ cup
Romaine lettuce	½ cup
Grated carrots	¼ cup
Tomato	1
Olive oil	2 tsp.
Cider vinegar	2 tsp.
French bread	2 slices
Margarine	4 tsp.
Honeydew melon	1 cup
Tea	1 cup
Sugar	1 tsp.

EVENING SNACK

Plain popcorn	3 cups
Mineral water	1 cup

Approximate Nutrient Analysis

Energy	2,765 kcal
Protein	131.2 g (19% of kcal)
Fat	83.3 g (27% of kcal)
Polyunsaturated fat	19.5 g
Monounsaturated fat	31.2 g
Saturated fat	21.4 g
Cholesterol	191 mg
Carbohydrate	391.0 g (57% of kcal)

(continued)

Vitamin A	15,246 IU
	2,283 RE
Thiamine	2.58 mg
Riboflavin	3.10 mg
Niacin	36.1 mg
Folate	526 mcg
Vitamin B-12	8.22 mcg
Vitamin B-6	3.42 mg
Vitamin C	192.0 mg
Calcium	1,396 mg
Phosphorus	2,176 mg
Iron	32.1 mg
Copper	2.12 mg
Zinc	16.4 mg
Magnesium	447 mg
Sodium	3,014 mg
Potassium	5,662 mg

REFERENCES

1. Schneeman, B. O.: Dietary fiber and gastrointestinal function. Nutr Rev 45:129, 1987.
2. Floch, M. H., Maryniuk, M. D., et al.: Practical aspects of implementing increased dietary fiber intake. Am J Gastroenterol 81:936, 1986.
3. American Dietetic Association: Position of the American Dietetic Association: Health implications of dietary fiber. J Am Diet Assoc 88:216, 1988.
4. American Diabetes Association: Nutritional recommendations and principles for individuals with diabetes mellitus, 1986. Diabetes Care 10:126, 1987.
5. Slavin, J. L.: Dietary fiber: Classification, chemical analyses and food sources. J Am Diet Assoc 87:1164, 1987.
6. National Institutes of Health: Diet nutrition and cancer prevention: A guide to food choices. NIH Publication no. 87-2878. Bethesda, Md., 1987.
7. Connell, A. M.: The role of fibre in the gastrointestinal tract. In Bowen, P. E., Connell, A. M., et al.: The clinical role of fibre. Toronto: Medical Education Services, 1985.
8. Anderson, J. W.: Health implications of wheat fiber. Am J Clin Nutr 41:1103, 1985.
9. Greenwald, P., Lanza, E., and Eddy, G. A.: Dietary fiber in the reduction of colon cancer risk. J Am Diet Assoc 87:1178, 1987.
10. Cheah, P. Y., and Bernstein, H.: Colon cancer and dietary fiber: Cellulose inhibits the DNA-damaging ability of bile acids. Nutr Canc 13:51, 1990.
11. Food and Nutrition Board, National Research Council—National Academy of Sciences: Diet and health: Implications for reducing chronic disease risk. Report of the Committee on Diet and Health. Washington, D.C.: National Academy Press, 1989.
12. Schneeman, B. O., and Lefeure, M.: Effects of fiber on plasma lipoprotein composition. In Vahouny, G. V., and Kritchevsky, D.: Dietary fiber: Basic and clinical aspects. New York: Plenum Press, 1986.
13. Khaw, K. T., and Barrett-Connor, E.: Dietary fiber and reduced ischemic heart disease mortality rates in men and women: A 12-year prospective study. Am J Epidemiol 126:1093, 1987.
14. Anderson, J. W.: Fiber and health: An overview. Am J Gastroenterol 81:892, 1986.
15. Anderson, J. W., and Bryant, C. A.: Dietary fiber and obesity. Am J Gastroenterol 81:898, 1986.
16. Vahouny, G. V., and Cassidy, M. M.: Dietary fibers and absorption of nutrients. Proc Soc Exp Biol Med 180:432, 1985.
17. Jenkins, D. J. A., Jenkins, A. L., et al.: Fiber and starchy foods: Gut function and implications in disease. Am J Gastroenterol 81:920, 1986.
18. Stevens, J., Levitsky, D. A., et al.: Effect of psyllium gum and wheat bran on spontaneous energy intake. Am J Clin Nutr 46:812, 1987.
19. Duncan, K. H., Bacon, J. A., and Weinsier, R. I.: The effect of high and low energy density diets on satiety, energy intake and eating time of obese and nonobese subjects. Am J Clin Nutr 37:763, 1983.
20. Eastwood, M. A., Elton, R. A., and Smith, J. H.: Long term effect of whole wheat bread on stool weight, transit time, fecal bile acids, fats and neutral sterols. Am J Clin Nutr 43:343, 1986.
21. Hanson, C. F., and Winterfeldt, E. A.: Dietary fiber effects on passage rate and breath hydrogen. Am J Clin Nutr 42:44, 1985.
22. Schneeman, B. O., and Gallagher, D.: Effects of dietary fiber on digestive enzyme activity and bile acids in the small intestine. Proc Soc Exp Biol Med 180:409, 1985.
23. Jenkins, D. J. A., Jenkins, A. L., et al.: Simple and complex carbohydrates. Nutr Rev 44:44, 1986.
24. Brand, J. C., Nicholson, P. L., et al.: Food processing and the glycemic index. Am J Clin Nutr 42:1192, 1985.
25. Wong, S., Traianedes, K., and O'Dea, K.: Factors affecting the rate of hydrolysis of starch in legumes. Am J Clin Nutr 42:38, 1985.
26. Englyst, H. N., and Cummings, J. H.: Digestion of polysaccharides of potato in the small intestine of man. Am J Clin Nutr 45:423, 1987.
27. Englyst, H. N., and Cummings, J. H.: Digestion of the polysaccharides of some cereal foods in the human small intestine. Am J Clin Nutr 42:778, 1985.
28. Jenkins, D. J. A., and Jenkins, A. L.: Dietary fiber and the glycemic response. Proc Soc Exp Biol Med 180:422, 1985.
29. Mann, J.: Complex carbohydrates: Replacement energy for fat or useful in their own right? Am J Clin Nutr 45:1202, 1987.
30. Reaven, G. M.: Effect of dietary carbohydrate on metabolism of patients with non-insulin diabetes mellitus. Nutr Rev 44:65, 1986.
31. Szostak, W. B., and Cybulska, B.: Dietary carbohydrates in the prevention and treatment of metabolic diseases of major public health importance. Am J Clin Nutr 45:1207, 1987.
32. Hollenbeck, C. B., Coulston, A. M., and Reaven, G. M.: Glycemic effects of carbohydrates: A different perspective. Diabetes Care 9:641, 1987.
33. Dukehart, M. R., Dutta, S. K., and Vaeth, J.: Dietary fiber supplementation: Effect on exocrine pancreatic secretion in man. Am J Clin Nutr 50:1023, 1989.
34. Selvendran, R. R., Stevens, H. J. H., and Du Pont, M. S.: Dietary fiber: Chemistry, analysis, and properties. Adv Food Research 31:117, 1987.
35. Hoverstad, T.: Studies of short chain fatty acid absorption in man. Scand J Gastroenterol 21:257, 1986.
36. Stephen, A. M., Wiggins, H. S., et al.: The effect of age, sex and level of intake of dietary fiber from wheat on large bowel function in thirty healthy subjects. Br J Nutr 56:349, 1986.
37. Jenkins, D. J. A.: Carbohydrates—dietary fiber. In Shils, M. E., and Young, V. R.: Modern nutrition in health and disease. 7th ed. Philadelphia: Lea & Febiger, 1988.
38. Armstrong, E. F., and Eastwood, M. A.: Fiber and the distribution of

water in the colon. J Clin Gastroenterol 9:378, 1987.

39. Southgate, D. A. T.: Minerals, trace elements, and potential hazards. Am J Clin Nutr 45:1256, 1987.

40. McKeigue, P. M., Adelstein, A. M., et al.: Diet and fecal steroid profile in a South Asian population with a low colon-cancer rate. Am J Clin Nutr 50:151, 1989.

41. Fleming, S. E., Fitch, M. D., and Chansler, M. W.: High-fiber diets: Influence on characteristics of cecal digesta including short-chain fatty acid concentrations and pH. Am J Clin Nutr 50:93, 1989.

42. Jenkins, D. J. A., Jenkins, A. L., et al.: Cancer risk: Possible protective role of high carbohydrate high fiber diets. Am J Gastroenterol 81:931, 1986.

43. Kritchevsky, D.: Diet, nutrition, and cancer: The role of fiber. Cancer 58:1830, 1986.

44. Higginson, J.: Cancer, carbohydrates and fiber. Nutr Canc 8:14, 1986.

45. Salyers, A. A., Kuritza, A. P., and McCarthy, R. E.: Influence of dietary fiber on the intestinal environment. Proc Soc Exp Biol Med 180:415, 1985.

46. Hill, M. J.: Bile, bacteria and bowel cancer. Gut 24:871, 1983.

47. Palmer, S.: Dietary considerations for risk reduction. Cancer 58:1949, 1986.

48. Kune, G., and Kune, S.: The nutritional causes of colorectal cancer: An introduction to the Melbourne study. Nutr Canc 9:1, 1987.

49. Tsai, A. C., Vinik, A. J., et al.: Effects of soy polysaccharide on postprandial plasma glucose, insulin, glucagon, pancreatic polypeptide, somatostatin, and triglyceride in obese, diabetic patients. Am J Clin Nutr 45:596, 1987.

50. Fugawa, N. K., Anderson, J. W., et al.: High carbohydrate–high fiber diets increase peripheral insulin sensitivity in healthy, young and old adults. Am J Clin Nutr 52:524, 1990.

51. Kritchevsky, D.: Geriatric diabetes: Latest research on the role of dietary fiber. Geriatrics 41:117, 1986.

52. Flourie, B., Vidon, N., et al.: Effect of increased amounts of pectin on a solid-liquid meal digestion in healthy man. Am J Clin Nutr 42:495, 1987.

53. Osilesi, O., Trout, D. L., et al.: Use of xanthan gum in dietary management of diabetes mellitus. Am J Clin Nutr 42:597, 1985.

54. Rouse, I. L., Beilin, L. J., et al.: Nutrient intake, blood pressure, serum and urinary prostaglandins and serum thromboxane B-2 in a controlled trial with a lacto-ovo-vegetarian diet. Am J Hypertens 4:241, 1986.

55. Hodges, R. E., and Rebello, T.: Dietary changes and their possible effect on blood pressure. Am J Clin Nutr 41:1155, 1985.

56. Miettinen, T. A.: Dietary fiber and lipids. Am J Clin Nutr 42:1237, 1987.

57. Albrink, M. J., and Ullrich, I. H.: Interaction of dietary sucrose and fiber on serum lipids in healthy young men fed high carbohydrate diets. Am J Clin Nutr 43:419, 1986.

58. Swain, J. F., Rouse, I. L., et al.: Comparison of the effects of oat bran and low-fiber wheat on serum lipoprotein levels and blood pressure. N Engl J Med 322:147, 1990.

59. Henderson, J. W., Spencer, D. B., et al.: Oat-bran lowers serum total and LDL cholesterol in hypercholesterolemic men. Am J Clin Nutr 52:495, 1990.

60. Williams, P. T., Krauss, R. M., et al.: Relationship of dietary fat, protein, cholesterol and fiber intake to atherogenic lipoprotein in men. Am J Clin Nutr 44:788, 1986.

61. Cummings, J. H.: Dietary fiber. Am J Clin Nutr 45:1040, 1987.

62. Jenkins, D. J. A., Wolever, T. M. S., et al.: Low glycemic index carbohydrate foods in the management of hyperlipidemia. Am J Clin Nutr 42:604, 1985.

63. Corazziari, E., Materia, E., et al.: Laxative consumption in chronic non-organic constipation. J Clin Gastroenterol 9:427, 1987.

64. Loening-Baucke, V.: Factors determining outcome in children with chronic constipation and faecal soiling. Gut 30:999, 1989.

65. Castle, S. C.: Constipation—a pressing issue. Arch Intern Med 147:1702, 1987.

66. Jenkins, D. J. A., Dewey Peterson, R., et al.: Wheat fiber and laxation: Dose response and equilibration time. Am J Gastroenterol 82:1259, 1987.

67. Floch, M. H.: The pharmacology of dietary fiber for laxation. Am J Gastroenterol 82:1295, 1987.

68. Vanderpool, D. M.: Dietary fiber: Its role in preventing gastrointestinal disease. South Med J 79:1201, 1986.

69. Mendeloff, A. I.: Dietary fiber in 1985: Reasonable expectations. In Bowen, P. E., Connell, A. M., et al.: The clinical role of fibre. Toronto: Medical Education Services, 1985.

70. Rydning, A., and Berstad, A.: Fiber diet and antacids in the short-term treatment of duodenal ulcer. Scand J Gastroenterol 20:1078, 1985.

71. Slavin, J. L.: The availability of minerals in fiber diets. In Bowen, P. E., Connell, A. M., et al.: The clinical role of fibre. Toronto: Medical Education Services, 1985.

72. Hallfrisch, J., Powell, A., et al.: Mineral balances of men and women consuming high fiber diets with complex or simple carbohydrate. J Nutr 117:48, 1987.

73. Hallberg, L., Rossander, L., and Britt-Skanberg, A.: Phytates and the inhibitory effect of bran on iron absorption in man. Am J Clin Nutr 45:988, 1987.

74. Mackler, B. P., and Herbert, V.: The effect of raw wheat bran, alfalfa meal and alpha-cellulose on iron ascorbate chelate and ferric chloride in three binding solutions. Am J Clin Nutr 42:618, 1987.

75. Cook, J. D., Noble, N. L., et al.: Effect of fiber on nonheme iron absorption. Gastroenterology 85:1354, 1983.

76. Kelsay, J. L.: Effects of fiber, phytic acid, and oxalic acid in the diet on mineral bioavailability. Am J Gastroenterol 82:983, 1987.

77. Bowen, P. E., Connell, A. M., et al.: Panel discussion. In Bowen, P. E., Connell, A. M., et al.: The clinical role of fibre. Toronto: Medical Education Services, 1985.

78. Powers, D. E., and Moore, A. O.: Food/medication interactions. 6th ed. Phoenix: 1988 (self-published).

79. Roe, D. A.: Diet and drug interactions. New York: Van Nostrand Reinhold, 1988.

80. Roe, D. A.: Handbook on drug and nutrient interactions. 4th ed. Chicago: American Dietetic Association, 1989.

81. Anderson, J. W., and Tietyen-Clark, J.: Dietary fiber, hyperlipidemia, hypertension, and coronary heart disease.

Am J Gastroenterol 81:907, 1986.

82. National Research Council, National Academy of Sciences: Diet, nutrition and cancer. Washington, D.C.: National Academy Press, 1982.

83. Chen, M. C., and Meguid, M. M.: Postulated cancer prevention diets: A guide to food selection. Surg Clin North Am 66:931, 1986.

84. Chen, M. C., and Meguid, M. M.: The anti-cancer lifestyle. In press.

85. Anderson, J. W.: HCF exchanges: A

sensible plan for healthy eating. HCF Nutrition Research Foundation, P.O. Box 22124, Lexington, KY 40502, 1989.

86. Eastwood, M. A., and Kay, R. M.: An hypothesis for the action of dietary fiber along the gastrointestinal tract. Am J Clin Nutr 32:364, 1979.

87. Kay, R. M., and Strasberg, S. M.: Origin, chemistry, physiological effects and clinical importance of dietary fibre. Clin Invest Med 1:9, 1978.

10.

BLAND DIET

DEFINITION

A diet that eliminates foods containing caffeine, alcohol, pepper, spice (is "CAPS free"), and other foods that are assumed to be irritating to the intestinal mucosa or that promote gastric acid secretion. The bland diet is often combined with a low-fiber diet. The efficacy of the bland diet in the treatment of peptic and duodenal ulcers and hiatal hernia has never been scientifically validated.

PHYSIOLOGY, FOODS, AND NUTRIENTS

1. PEPTIC AND DUODENAL ULCERS

The physiological purpose of gastric acid secretion is to activate pepsinogen and thus to initiate protein digestion; to facilitate the absorption of calcium and iron; and to defend the highly specialized absorption and secretory cells of the lower alimentary tract against ingested organisms (1, 2).

Both acid or peptic activity and impaired mucosal defense must occur in order for an ulcer to develop. Breaks in mucosal integrity and sloughing of epithelial cells occur continuously. The normal process is rapid healing; breaks in the mucosa become clinically relevant only when the reseal process fails (3).

Several factors have been implicated in instances of peptic ulcer relapse: defective gastric mucus, reduced duodenal bicarbonate secretion, altered synthesis of prostaglandin E and other prostaglandins, decreased salivary secretion of epidermal growth factor, gastric *Campylobacter pylori* infections, thermal injury as a result of drinking hot liquids,

increased acid secretion due to mental stress, and poor patient compliance with drug therapy (4–9).

Smoking is associated with an increased incidence of duodenal ulcers and with an adverse outcome in both healing and relapse. It also lowers esophageal sphincter pressure and causes esophageal reflux (10–11).

The possibility that milk has a beneficial effect on ulcers unrelated to gastric acid secretion has not been disproved. Prostaglandins E-1 and E-2, which have been discovered in significant quantities in whole milk, heavy cream, and yogurt, are prime candidates for this postulated cytoprotective role of milk. In duodenal ulcers, loss of such a cytoprotective mechanism in the mucosa, due to defective prostaglandin synthesis, may be a causative factor (12–15).

Alcoholic and caffeinated beverages (coffee, tea, and cola) stimulate gastric acid secretion. Decaffeinated coffee, red pepper, and even caffeine-free carbonated beverages also have this effect. Additives such as food coloring or monosodium glutamate have no effect on gastric acid secretion. Beyond this knowledge, little new information has been forthcoming to incriminate any food as a gastric irritant (3, 13, 16–21).

2. HIATAL HERNIA

Transient lower esophageal relaxation is the major mechanism underlying gastroesophageal reflux. The following foods have been documented to cause decreased lower esophageal sphincter pressure or to have an irritating effect on the esophageal mucosa: tomatoes, to-

mato juice, citrus juices, chocolate, peppermint, and excessively fatty foods. Decreased pressure on the lower esophageal sphincter causes the sphincter to open more readily, allowing acid from the stomach to reflux back into the esophagus, causing esophageal irritation (22–26).

In normal individuals, raw onions have no effect on esophageal reflux. In individuals with gastroesophageal reflux, however, raw onions cause an increase in the symptoms of reflux and irritation (27).

POSSIBLE ADVERSE REACTIONS

Various types of aversive and restrictive bland diets continue to be in use despite the absence of any scientific basis (28, 29). Not only has the clinical value of the traditional bland, fiber-restricted diet in ulcer therapy never been proven, but it may also have adverse effects.

1. MILK EXCESSES

A. Milk-Alkali Syndrome The ingestion of excessive amounts of milk along with antacids can lead to the milk-alkali syndrome, a form of hypercalcemia differentiated from primary hyperparathyroidism by a low to normal serum phosphate level and a positive response to dietary calcium restrictions. Milk-alkali syndrome may be caused by an intake of 2 or more quarts of milk plus 1.4 g of calcium carbonate daily (30).

B. Increased Gastric Acid Secretion Because of its protein and calcium content, milk results in increased gastric acid secretion, which often coincides with the onset of postprandial pain in persons with ulcers. A 12-oz. glass of milk stimulates the production of as much gastric acid as does a 12-oz. glass of beer (17, 31–33).

2. PUREED FOODS

Homogenization, mincing, or pureeing of foods may actually increase rather than decrease gastric acid secretion (15).

3. DIETARY FIBER RESTRICTIONS

Fiber restrictions may do more harm than good to the patient with ulcers. The effectiveness of a fiber-restricted diet as compared with a high fiber diet in preventing ulcer recurrence was evaluated in a group of 75 individuals with recently healed duodenal ulcers. At the end of the study, 80% of the individuals on a fiber-restricted diet experienced recurrence of their disease, whereas only 45% of individuals who followed a high-fiber diet developed new ulcers. Similarly, in patients with active duodenal ulcers being treated with antacids and ranitidine, no beneficial effect could be documented for a fiber-restricted diet. The ulcer healed in 67.5% of the individuals who followed a high-fiber diet and in 60% of the adherents to a low-fiber diet (34–36).

CLINICAL ASSESSMENT

A thorough diet history will reveal foods the patient believes to be irritating. This information provides a basis for education if the patient is misinformed. It will also highlight potential dietary deficiencies or excesses due to self-imposed dietary restrictions.

ASSESSMENT OF POTENTIAL DRUG INTERACTIONS

Drug therapy has obviated the need for restrictive bland diets. The emergence of H-2 receptor agents, with their potent parietal-cell antisecretory properties, marked a turning point in the medical treatment of ulcers. One of the first of such agents, metiamide, was quickly followed by cimetidine and then ranitidine. Ranitidine can be effectively administered in a single bedtime dose, providing maximal protection at night, when ulcer patients have inappropriately high gastric acid secretion. It also avoids hypochlorhydria at times of the day when the patient is eating and may be more susceptible to an infection (1, 2, 29, 45–47).

Omeprazole is a drug that controls gastric acid secretion by inhibiting the gastric proton pump in parietal cells, thereby controlling the final step of gastric acid production. Clinical trials indicate that it may be even more effective than ranitidine in healing duodenal ulcers (48).

The thrust of current research is in the area of the development of drugs that provide a mucosal defense or have cytoprotective effects on gastrointestinal mucosal cells. Sucralfate, a sulphated disaccharide, acts as a local protective barrier to the ulcer and possibly as a cytoprotective agent. There has recently been renewed interest in the use of low doses of calcium carbonate as a treatment for ulcers (29, 49–51).

Current pharmaceutical alternatives to the bland diet and their nutritional implications are summarized in Table 10.1.

IMPLEMENTATION AND EDUCATION

The best nutritional advice for an ulcer patient is to eat a well-balanced diet with adequate amounts of protein and other nutrients to permit healing. Any foods that are known to increase gastric acid secretion or that cause discomfort to the individual patient should be avoided.

Meals should be served at regular times in pleasant, unhurried surroundings amid a lifestyle in which stresses are effectively managed and ulcerogenic drugs, alcohol, and smoking are avoided. Late dinners close to bedtime should be avoided because they may increase nocturnal gastric acidity. Eating dinner early may reduce nocturnal gastric acidity. Fortunately for the patients, current medical therapy for ulcers is based upon pharmacological, not nutritional, treatments (37–49).

PRIORITIES FOR QUALITY ASSURANCE

In the clinical setting, orders for bland diet should be investigated. Appropriate alternatives should be recommended and documented in the medical record.

TABLE 10.1. PHARMACEUTICAL ALTERNATIVES TO THE BLAND DIET

Drug	Action	Nutritional implications
Hydrogen (H₂) receptor agents and other related drugs		
Cimetidine (Tagamet) (40, 41, 43, 52)	Inhibits secretion of gastric acid by acting on H_2 receptor cells of parietal glands of gastrointestinal mucosa to block the normal secretory response to histamine secretion	Diarrhea, impaired release of vitamin B-12 from animal foods, decreased serum B-12 levels, reduced metabolism of vitamin D
Ranitidine (Zantac) (42–47, 53)	Same as above, except effect is more prolonged and drug can be given less frequently	Nausea, constipation, abdominal pain, decreased serum vitamin B-12, increased urinary protein
Omeprazole (48)	Controls gastric acid secretion by selectively inhibiting the enzyme hydrogen-potassium-stimulated adenosine triphosphatase, the gastric proton pump in parietal cells that controls the final step of gastric acid production	
Antacids		
Aluminum hydroxide (Alternagel, Amphojel) (54, 55)	Initial neutralization of acid	Decreased vitamin absorption, constipation, decreased absorption of phosphate, hypophosphatemic osteomalacia, milk alkali syndrome
Magnesium hydroxide (Milk of Magnesia) (56)	Initial neutralization of acid	Increased magnesium levels in renal failure, mental and respiratory changes as well as hypotension due to magnesium absorption, diarrhea
Calcium carbonate (Tums, Os-Cal, Titralac) (30, 33, 38, 51–57)	Initial neutralization of acid; stimulates production of bicarbonate ion in gastric mucosa, providing a mucosal barrier unrelated to acid neutralization	Calcium stimulates production of gastrin, which increases acid rebound, nausea, decreased absorption of iron, and milk alkali syndrome; used as a calcium supplement, low doses may be effective in increasing mucosal resistance
Aluminum hydroxide, alginic acid, sodium bicarbonate, magnesium trisilicate (Gaviscon, Gaviscon Extra Strength) (29, 53, 57)	Forms a viscous barrier in the stomach that impedes esophageal reflux	Should be taken 1 to 3 hours after meals; may decrease absorption of vitamin A, cause constipation, inactivate thiamine, and cause weight loss and anorexia; should not be taken with a low-sodium diet
Anticholinergics		
Propantheline (Pro-Banthine) (40, 54)	Decreased gastrointestinal secretion and motility by acting on the central nervous system to block the action of acetylcholine on nerves; contraindicated in hiatal hernia	Causes a feeling of fullness and early satiety and increased fluid intake
Glycopyrrolate (Robinul)	Same as above	Same as above
Belladonna alkaloids (Donnatol) (54)	Same as above	Same as above, plus decreased iron absorption, bitter taste, and dry mouth; should be administered ½ hour before meals
Pirenzepine (43)	Tricyclic compound that has greater effects on the exocrine glands than on smooth muscle; although the effectiveness and indications for use of other anticholinergics have been questioned, this drug has more-promising effects	Not yet clearly defined

TABLE 10.1. *CONTINUED*

Drug	Action	Nutritional implications
Cytoprotective agents		
Sucralfate (Carafate)	Accelerates healing of duodenal ulcers, reacts with protein exudates found in ulcer base, and blocks passage of pepsin and gastric acid to ulcer site	Slight constipation due to its aluminum content
Carbenoxolone sodium (not currently available in U.S.) (29)	A mucosal barrier that prevents hydrogen ion back-diffusion into the mucosa and stimulates mucosal production, which is implicated in ulcer healing	Not clearly defined
Colloidal bismuth (not currently available in U.S.)	Accelerates healing by action on base of ulcer	Not clearly defined
Parasympathomimetic agents (drugs used for gastroesophageal reflux)		
Bethanechol (Urecholine, Myotonachol, Duvoid) (40, 57)	A cholinergic stimulant that increases the resting pressure in the lower esophageal sphincter, thus helping to prevent reflux; used with some success in reflux esophagitis	Nausea, diarrhea, cramps
Metoclopramide (Reglan) (40, 53)	A parasympathomimetic that acts by sensitizing gastrointestinal muscle to effects of acetylcholine	Should be taken ½ hour before meals; may cause nausea, diarrhea, and fluid retention
Cisapride (40, 58)	A new prokinetic drug that increases lower esophageal sphincter pressure and is effective in gastroesophageal reflux	Not clearly identified

REFERENCES

1. Howden, C., and Hunt, R.: Relationship between gastric secretion and infection. Gut 28:96, 1987.
2. Alsted, E., Ryan, F., et al.: Ranitidine in the prevention of gastric and duodenal ulcer relapse. Gut 24:418, 1983.
3. Soll, A. H.: Peptic ulcer diseases: Perspectives on pathophysiology and therapy. J Clin Gastroenterol 11 (Supp 1):S1, 1989.
4. Freston, J. W.: Mechanisms of relapse in peptic ulcer disease. J Clin Gastroenterol 11 (Supp 1):S34, 1989.
5. Colin-Jones, D. G.: *Campylobacter pylori:* An advance in understanding of dyspepsia and gastritis. J Clin Gastroenterol 11 (Supp 1):S39, 1989.
6. Taha, A. S., Boothman, P., et al.: Gastric mucosal prostaglandin synthesis in the presence of *Campylobacter pylori* in patients with gastric ulcers and non-ulcer dyspepsia. Am J Gastroenterol 85:47, 1990.
7. Pearson, R. C., and McCloy, R. F.: Preference for hot drinks is associated with peptic disease. Gut 30:1201, 1989.
8. Holtmann, G., Singer, M. V., et al.: Differential effects of acute mental stress on interdigestive secretion of gastric acid, pancreatic enzymes, and gastroduodenal motility. Dig Dis Sci 34:1701, 1989.
9. Baber, J. P., and Stanescu, L.: Problems with patients' compliance in peptic ulcer therapy. J Clin Gastroenterol 11 (Supp 1):S25, 1989.
10. Chiverton, S. G., and Hunt, R. H.: Smoking and duodenal ulcer disease. J Clin Gastroenterol 11 (Supp 1):S29, 1989.
11. Kahrilas, P. J., and Gupta, R. R.: Mechanisms of acid reflux associated with cigarette smoking. Gut 31:4, 1990.
12. Spiro, H.: Clinical gastroenterology. 3d. ed. New York: Macmillan, 1983.
13. Materia, A., Jaffe, B., et al.: Prostaglandins in commercial milk preparations. Arch Surg 119:290, 1984.
14. Ahlquist, D., Doxois, R., et al.: Duodenal prostaglandin synthesis and acid load in health and in duodenal ulcer disease. Gastroenterology 85:522, 1983.
15. Hunt, D., and Forrest, A.: The role of the antrum in determining the acid secretory response to meals of different consistency. Gut 16:774, 1975.
16. Goldschmiedt, M., Redfern, J. S., and Feldman, M.: Food coloring and monosodium glutamate: Effects on the cephalic phase of gastric acid secretion and gastrin release in humans. Am J Clin Nutr 51:794, 1990.
17. McArthur, K., Hogan, D., and Isenberg, J.: Relative stimulatory effects of commonly ingested beverages on gastric acid secretion in humans. Gastroenterology 83:199, 1982.
18. Lenz, H. J., Ferrari-Taylor, J., and Isenberg, J. I.: Wine and five per cent ethanol are potent stimulants of gastric acid secretion in humans. Gastroenterology 85:1082, 1983.
19. Solanke, T.: The effect of red pepper (*Capsicum frutescens*) on gastric acid secretion. J Surg Res 15:385, 1973.
20. Groisser, D.: A study of caffeine in tea. 1. A new spectophotometric micro method. 2. Concentration of caffeine in various strengths, brands, blends and types of teas. Am J Clin Nutr 31:1727, 1978.
21. Dubey, P., Sundram, K., and Nundy, S.: Effect of tea on gastric acid secretion. Dig Dis Sci 29:202, 1984.
22. Wang, J. C., Castell, D. O., et al.: Does sleeping on a waterbed promote gastroesophageal reflux? Dig Dis Sci 34:1585, 1989.
23. Holloway, R. H., Wyman, J. B., and Dent, J.: Failure of transient lower oesophageal sphincter relaxation in response to gastric distension in patients with achalasia: Evidence for neural mediation of transient lower oesophageal sphincter relaxations. Gut 30:762, 1989.
24. Castell, D. O.: Medical measures that influence the gastroesophageal junction. South Med J 71 (Supp 1):26, 1978.
25. Jamieson, G. G., Beauchamp, G., and Duranceau, A. C.: The physiologic basis for the medical management of gastroesophageal reflux. Surg Clin N Am 63:841, 1983.
26. Cohen, S., and Booth, G. H.: Gastric acid secretion and lower esophageal sphincter pressure in response to coffee and caffeine. N Engl J Med 293:897, 1975.
27. Allen, M. L., Mellow, M. H., et al.: The effect of raw onions on acid reflux and reflux symptoms. Am J Gastroenterol 85:377, 1990.
28. Ingelfinger, F., Ebert, R., et al.: Controversy in internal medicine. Vol. 2. Philadelphia: W. B. Saunders, 1974.
29. Bonnevie, O.: Developments in the treatment of peptic ulcer. Scand J Gastroenterol 22 (Supp 127):51, 1987.
30. Carroll, P., and Clark, O.: Milk-alkali syndrome: Does it exist and can it be differentiated from primary hyperparathyroidism? Ann Surg 197:427, 1983.
31. Ippoliti, A., Maxwell, V., and Isenberg, J. I.: The effect of various forms of milk on gastric acid secretion: Studies in patients with duodenal ulcer and normal subjects. Ann Intern Med 84:286, 1974.
32. Behar, J., Hitchings, M., and Smyth, R.: Calcium stimulation of gastrin and gastric acid secretion: Effect of small doses of calcium carbonate. Gut 18:442, 1977.
33. Christiansen, J., Kirkegaard, P., et al.: Interaction of calcium and gastrin on gastric acid secretion in duodenal ulcer patients. Gut 25:174, 1984.
34. Rydning, A., Berstad, A., et al.: Prophylactic effect of dietary fiber in duodenal ulcer disease. Lancet 2:736, 1982.
35. Rydning, A., and Berstad, A.: Fiber diet and antacids in the short-term treatment of duodenal ulcer. Scand J Gastroenterol 20:1078, 1985.
36. Rydning, A., and Berstad, A.: Prophylactic effect of dietary fiber in duodenal ulcer. Lancet 2:736, 1982.
37. Nasiry, R., McIntosh, J., et al.: Prognosis of chronic duodenal ulcer: A prospective study of the effects of demographic and environmental factors and ulcer bleeding. Gut 28:533, 1987.

38. Armstrong, C., and Blower, A.: Non-steroidal anti-inflammatory drugs and life threatening complications of peptic ulceration. Gut 28:527, 1987.

39. Duroux, P., Bauerfeind, P., et al.: Early dinner reduces nocturnal gastric acidity. Gut 30:1063, 1989.

40. Freston, J. W.: Cimetidine: II. Adverse reactions and patterns of use. Ann Intern Med 97:728, 1982.

41. Barr, G., Kang, J., et al.: A two year prospective controlled study of maintenance cimetidine and gastric ulcer. Gastroenterology 85:100, 1983.

42. Gledhill, T., Howard, O., et al.: Single nocturnal dose of a H-2 receptor antagonist for the treatment of duodenal ulcer. Gut 24:904, 1983.

43. Piper, D.: Drugs for the prevention of peptic ulcer recurrence. Drugs 26:439, 1983.

44. Jorde, R., Burhol, P., and Hansen, T.: Ranitidine 150 mg at night in the prevention of gastric ulcer relapse. Gut 28:460, 1987.

45. Chambers, J., Pryce, D., et al.: Effect of bedtime ranitidine dose on overnight gastric acid output and intragastric pH: Dose/response study and comparison with cimetidine. Gut 28:294, 1987.

46. Elsborg, L.: Esophageal reflux disease. Scand J Gastroenterol 22 (Supp 127):101, 1987.

47. Dobrilla, G., De Pretis, G., et al.: Comparison of once-daily bedtime administration of famotidine and ranitidine in short-term treatment of duodenal ulcer. Scand J Gastroenterol 22 (Supp 134):21, 1987.

48. McFarland, R. J., Bateson, M. C., et al.: Omeprazole provides quicker symptom relief and duodenal ulcer healing than ranitidine. Gastroenterology 98:278, 1990.

49. Glise, H., Carling, L., et al.: Treatment of acute duodenal ulcer—a Swedish multicenter study. Scand J Gastroenterol 22 (Supp 127):61, 1987.

50. Aarimma, M.: Medical and surgical prophylaxis for duodenal ulcer: The role of sucralfate. Scand J Gastroenterol 22 (Supp 127):81, 1987.

51. Texter, E. C.: A critical look at the clinical use of antacids in acid-peptic disease and gastric acid rebound. Am J Gastroenterol 84:97, 1989.

52. Roe, D. A.: Diet and drug interactions. New York: Van Nostrand Reinhold, 1988.

53. Powers, D. E., and Moore, A. O.: Food/medication interactions. 6th ed. Phoenix: 1988 (self-published).

54. Roe, D. A.: Handbook: Interactions of selected drugs and nutrients in patients. 3d ed. Chicago: American Dietetic Association, 1982.

55. Decker, E.: Drug and food interactions, gastrointestinal drugs. RD 1 (3):1, 1981.

56. Port, J., Kirshner, J., and Lopes, R.: Antacid therapy: Calcium vs. Al, Mg. JAMA 248:2045, 1982.

57. Novak, F., and Clinton-Texter, J. E.: Gastrointestinal reflux. Arch Intern Med 145:329, 1985.

58. Cucchiara, S., Staiano, A., et al.: Effects of cisapride on parameters of oesophageal motility and on the prolonged intraoesophageal pH test in infants with gastro-oesophageal reflux disease. Gut 31:21, 1990.

11.

ENTERAL FEEDING BY TUBE

DEFINITIONS

1. ENTERAL FEEDING

Feeding via the gastrointestinal tract either orally or by tube. The term *enteral* does not necessarily imply feeding by tube.

2. TUBE FEEDINGS

Diets of liquid formula or blenderized foods designed to provide essential nutrients in a form that will easily pass through a tube.

PURPOSE OF THE DIET

The purpose of tube feeding is to provide essential nutrients in a form that will easily pass through a tube for patients with a functional gastrointestinal tract and an impaired ability to ingest, digest, or absorb nutrients. Tube feedings can also serve as transitional feedings when parenteral support is being discontinued or as a supplement to oral intake when nutritional needs cannot be met by oral intake alone.

EFFECTS OF THE DIET

The physiological response to enteral feeding is determined by the patient's health status, the rate of formula infusion, and the composition of the formula (1). Enteral tube feedings should fulfill the basic requirements of providing adequate protein and calories, preserving electrolyte and mineral balance, and maintaining adequate hydration.

1. NUTRITIONAL STATUS

Tube feedings may be used to preserve nutritional status in the nourished patient or to improve nutritional status in the undernourished or catabolic patient. In either situation, adequate energy intake is essential to allow protein to be utilized for tissue repair and anabolism. Protein is used as an energy source if energy intake is insufficient, resulting in a negative nitrogen balance. Nitrogen equilibrium or positive nitrogen balance can be achieved if both energy and protein requirements are met.

Serum vitamin levels can also be maintained by enteral nutrition formulas, provided that the volume meets the required Recommended Dietary Allowances (2). The catabolic or undernourished patient may require vitamin supplements, depending on the degree of protein-energy malnutrition and clinical condition.

2. IMMUNE FUNCTION

It is well documented that immune function is compromised by protein-calorie malnutrition, either alone or in combination with stress. Nutrition support via the enteral route protects the gastrointestinal tract and stimulates immune response, thereby shortening hospital stays, reducing sepsis, and lowering mortality rates. The specific effects of the composition of nutrient intake on the immune response is beyond the scope of this chapter and is currently undergoing investigation.

3. MUCOSAL INTEGRITY AND FUNCTION

Delivering nutrients via an enteral route offers numerous physiologic advantages when compared with intravenous feeding. The most significant advantage is maintenance of the structure and function of the intestinal mucosa, due to the presence of nutrients in the intestinal lumen. Additional advantages include preservation of hormonal balance, mucosal enzyme activity, and nutrient utilization. Furthermore, nutrients may be more efficiently used when the physiologic sequence of nutrient absorption, metabolism, and utilization prior to delivery to peripheral tissues is maintained. Although parenteral nutrition bypasses the liver, nutrients ingested enterally are processed by the liver prior to systemic distribution. Thus the liver is allowed to mediate metabolism of nutrient substrates and maintain its function as the central distributing organ.

The presence of glutamine or glutamate found in enteral formulas provides an essential fuel for the gastrointestinal tract and minimizes villous atrophy, a common consequence of prolonged parenteral alimentation (3). Because enteral feeding "feeds the gut," bacteria present in the luminal contents are kept within the lumen of the gut, enhancing the patient's ability to withstand a septic insult (4).

PHYSIOLOGY, FOODS, AND NUTRIENTS

1. FEEDING ROUTE

Feeding tubes can be introduced into the gastrointestinal tract at various points, using a surgical or nonsurgical approach.

TABLE 11.1. ADVANTAGES AND DISADVANTAGES OF THE VARIOUS ENTERAL FEEDING ROUTES

Feeding route	Advantages	Disadvantages
Nasogastric	1. Placement is rapid and requires minimal equipment. 2. Feedings can be initiated immediately following confirmation of tube placement and bowel sounds. 3. Formula can be delivered by continuous or intermittent infusion. 4. The route is appropriate for short-term or long-term use.	1. Tubes can be easily removed by a disoriented or combative patient (12, 13). 2. Anomalies in the nose and neck area such as a deviated septum, nasopharyngeal or esophageal tumors, and esophageal strictures may complicate or prevent tube placement. 3. The tube can be inadvertently inserted into the tracheobronchial tree, especially in individuals with neurological deficits and impaired gag reflexes (13, 14)
Nasoduodenal or nasojejunal	1. The risk for aspiration may be decreased in patients with neuromotor deglutition disorders (9). 2. Patients with poor tolerance to gastric feedings due to gastric retention or reflux tend to display improved tolerance. 3. The presence of functioning gastroesophageal and pyloric sphincters aids in preventing regurgitation of formula. 4. Nasojejunal access permits enteral feeding in patients with partial gastric outlet obstruction or duodenal fistula (15).	1. Accidental dislodgment of the tube into the stomach by coughing or vomiting is fairly common and increases the risk for aspiration in patients with altered gastric motility (16). 2. Administration of the feeding is usually limited to continuous delivery of formula, because the small intestine tolerates bolus feeding and sudden rate changes poorly (17–20).
Cervical pharyngostomy	1. The surgical procedure can be performed under local anesthesia and does not require an opening into the abdominal wall (21). 2. Feeding can begin immediately after tube insertion. 3. Because the abdomen is not opened, the risk of wound dehiscence, intraabdominal anastomotic leakage, and peritonitis is avoided. 4. The route allows for enteral feeding in patients with trauma or congenital anomalies of the maxillofacial region, cervical or maxillofacial surgeries, radiotherapy for partially obstructing esophageal tumors, and oral pharyngeal lesions (22).	1. The route requires surgery and formation of a stoma, which must be carefully maintained. 2. Complications include irritation of the surrounding skin, wound infections, and development of excessive granulation tissue around the stoma (22). 3. Accidental dislodgment of the tube is common, requiring prompt replacement of the tube to prevent closure of the stoma.
Gastrostomy or percutaneous endoscopic gastrostomy (PEG)	1. The method takes advantage of the stomach's natural functions of adjusting osmolarity, mixing, and serving as a reservoir. 2. It ensures that the nutrients provided are allowed maximal opportunity for absorption, and it closely simulates natural delivery of nutrients into the stomach. 3. Formula can be administered by continuous or intermittent infusion. 4. Nasal or esophageal irritation caused by the feeding tube is eliminated. 5. Risk for aspiration may be slightly reduced because of complete closure of the gastroesophageal sphincter.	1. Complications of a conventional gastrostomy include leakage of gastric contents around the tube, wound dehiscence, gastrointestinal bleeding, aspiration, and erosion of the abdominal wall by the tube (25). 2. PEG placement may be contraindicated in patients into whom an endoscope cannot be passed or in patients with marked obesity (26). 3. Leakage at the tube entry site can create problems such as wound infection and erosion of the feeding tube through the stoma.

(continued)

TABLE 11.1. *CONTINUED*

Feeding route	Advantages	Disadvantages
	6. The tube is unobtrusive. 7. PEG placement can be performed under local anesthesia and is significantly less expensive than a surgical gastrostomy (23, 24). 8. PEG feedings can be initiated after about 24 hours, whereas surgical gastrostomy patients are generally kept NPO up to 72 hours. 9. The PEG can be converted to a jejunostomy by endoscopic techniques if aspiration is a concern (10, 11).	
Jejunostomy	1. The route permits enteral feeding in patients with an upper gastrointestinal tract obstruction, esophageal reflux, inability to protect the airway from aspiration, ulcerative or neoplastic disease of the stomach, and impaired gastric emptying. 2. Feeding into the jejunum reduces gastroesophageal reflux and the risk for aspiration pneumonia associated with intragastric feeding (27). 3. Early postoperative feeding is possible because the jejunum rapidly resumes its function, within 12 to 24 hours (28).	1. A surgical procedure is required, involving the risk for postoperative complications. 2. Ambulatory patients may find jejunal feeding limiting because of the need for delivery of formula by continuous infusion (17–20).

A. Nasogastric The insertion of a tube through the nose to the stomach is the simplest and most widely used initial approach to enteral feeding.

B. Nasoduodenal or Nasojejunal A longer, weighted feeding tube is placed via the nose into the stomach and then passed through the pylorus into the duodenum or jejunum. The tube may be initially placed in the stomach and allowed to advance by peristalsis; this method may require from 4 to 48 hours for tube passage, however, and requires x-ray confirmation of tube placement (5). Fluoroscopic placement eliminates the need to wait for peristaltic passage into the small intestine and provides immediate confirmation of tube placement (6).

C. Cervical Pharyngostomy A surgically created stoma is formed at the upper border of the neck just below the hyoid bone, allowing placement of a tube into the oropharynx for feeding.

D. Gastrostomy A feeding tube is surgically placed into the stomach, bypassing the intrathoracic portion of the gastrointestinal tract. This procedure involves the formation of a feeding stoma, which may be temporary or permanent.

E. Percutaneous Endoscopic Gastrostomy Percutaneous endoscopic gastrostomy (PEG) is a nonsurgical procedure in which an endoscope, a needle, and a guide wire are used to pass a small catheter feeding tube percutaneously into the stomach (7–9). In situations in which intestinal feedings are more appropriate, the tube can be advanced into the jejunum to create a percutaneous endoscopic jejunostomy (PEJ) (10, 11).

F. Jejunostomy Jejunostomy is a surgical procedure in which an opening is created into the jejunum to allow placement of a tube for feeding. In some cases, a jejunal stoma may be created that can be intermittently catheterized.

The advantages and disadvantages of the various feeding routes are summarized in table 11.1.

2. TYPES OF TUBE-FEEDING FORMULAS

Tube-feeding preparations vary from a homogenized or blenderized mixture of foods selected from a normal diet to nutrient combinations carefully formulated to meet specific therapeutic needs. Formulas may be nutritionally complete, providing the total nutrient needs in a specified volume of formula; modular, providing one or more nutrients to supplement a diet or formula; or combined to meet specific nutritional needs.

Formulas may be categorized according to various classification systems. Examples include categorization by caloric density, protein content, nutrient sources or quality, or use for specific disease states. In table 11.2 the available enteral formulas are classified into 8 broad categories, and the characteristics of the categories are summarized.

3. NUTRIENT COMPOSITION

Before a formula can be selected, knowledge of formula composition and normal digestive processes is essential. The forms and sources of carbohydrate, protein, and fat play an important role in dictating the tolerance and effectiveness of enteral tube feeding. See tables 11.3 through 11.5 for summaries of the sources of carbohydrate, protein, and fat.

A. Carbohydrate   Most commercial formulas contain carbohydrate as the largest calorie source. With the exception of lactose, carbohydrate is the most easily digested and absorbed component of commercial formulas. Digestion and absorption rely on the action of pancreatic and intestinal enzymes and the integrity of the small bowel. Enteral formulas differ mainly in the form and concentration of carbohydrate. The form of carbohydrate contributes to the osmolality, sweetness, and digestibility of a formula. As the glucose chain length decreases, the osmolality and sweetness increase, and digestion is more rapid.

B. Protein   Protein is generally the smallest contributor to total calories in an enteral formula but plays an extremely important role in the majority of bodily functions and in maintaining body cell mass. Protein in enteral formulas may be in the form of intact protein or crystalline amino acids, or it may be partially hydrolyzed into smaller polypeptide fragments (referred to as oligopeptides, tripeptides, and dipeptides). Digestion begins in the stomach and continues into the proximal small intestine by action of specific pancreatic enzymes. Protein must be in the form of small peptides and free amino acids before it can be absorbed. Therefore, intact protein and some hydrolysates require further digestion to an absorbable form. The quality

TABLE 11.2. GENERAL CHARACTERISTICS OF ENTERAL TUBE FEEDINGS, BY CATEGORY

Tube feeding	Characteristics
Standard polymeric formulas	Provide approximately 1.0 to 1.2 kcal/cc and 14% to 16% of total calories as protein Provide intact macronutrients In composition of total nutrients, mimic a standard American diet Are usually lactose free Have low osmolality Are generally well tolerated Supply the RDAs in volumes of 1,080 to 2,000 cc/day
High-nitrogen polymeric formulas	Provide approximately 1.0 to 2.0 kcal/cc and >15% of total calories as protein Provide intact macronutrients Are lactose free Have low to moderate osmolality Are designed to meet increased protein demands at standard or elevated calorie levels Supply the RDAs in volumes of 950 to 2,000 cc/day
Concentrated polymeric formulas	Provide approximately 1.5 to 2.0 kcal/cc and 14% to 17% of total calories as protein Provide intact macronutrients Are lactose free Have moderate to high osmolality Are designed to meet calorie and protein demands in a reduced volume of formula Supply the RDAs in volumes of 900 to 1,200 cc/day
Blenderized formulas	Have characteristics similar to those of standard polymeric formulas except usually contain lactose Are composed of a blenderized mixture of ordinary foods, including meat, fruit, vegetable, nonfat dry milk solids, and added carbohydrate, oils, vitamins, and minerals Have high viscosity Have moderate osmolality Supply the RDAs in volumes of 1,500 cc or less per day
Fiber-containing formulas	Provide approximately 1.0 to 1.2 kcal/cc and 14% to 17% of total calories as protein Provide intact macronutrients Contain fiber from natural food sources or from added soy polysaccharide Are lactose free Have low osmolality Supply the RDAs in volumes of 1,320 to 1,500 cc/day
Predigested or elemental formulas	Provide 1.0 to 1.3 kcal/cc and 8% to 17% of total calories as protein Provide partially or fully hydrolyzed nutrients Are usually hyperosmolar Are lactose free

(continued)

TABLE 11.2. CONTINUED

Tube feeding	Characteristics
	Are generally low in total fat and may contain branched-chain amino acids
	Have unpleasant taste
	Are more expensive than standard formulas with intact nutrients
Modular formulas	Are composed of single nutrients (i.e., protein, carbohydrate, and fat)
	Are used to modify existing formulas or foods or are combined to produce a unique formulation tailored to meet an individual's specific nutrient demands
Specialty formulas	Are designed to meet specialized nutrient demands for a specific disease state, such as renal failure, liver failure, diabetes, or pulmonary disease
	Have varying characteristics, depending on intended function and formulation of modular components
	May require supplementation with vitamins, minerals, or trace elements
	Some are unpalatable
	Most are very expensive

of protein found in an enteral formula should be considered when selecting an enteral formula, especially for infants and children. Protein quality depends on the amino acid profile—i.e., the content of essential amino acids—and is often measured in terms of biological value, or BV (29). BV is defined as the measure of nitrogen retained in the body for growth and maintenance. A protein source with a low biological value is interpreted as a protein containing a higher proportion of nonessential amino acids. See Table 11.6 for a comparison of the biological values of major protein sources in enteral feedings.

C. Fat The major role of fat in an enteral formula is to provide a source of concentrated energy and essential fatty acids and a carrier for fat-soluble vitamins. Fat in enteral formulas may be in the form of long-chain triglycerides (LCTs), medium-chain triglycerides (MCTs), lecithin, monoglycerides, or diglycerides. Digestion and absorption are complex processes and require the action of bile salts and pancreatic lipase prior to the absorption of materials into the intestinal cell. Transportation of the reesterified free fatty acids and monoglycerides to the bloodstream occurs via the lymphatic circulation. MCTs differ from LCTs in that they do not require the actions of bile salts and pancreatic lipase for absorption, and transportation into the bloodstream occurs directly via the portal system. Monoglycerides and diglycerides are partially hydrolyzed fats that can be absorbed into the intestinal cell with little or no digestion required.

4. PHYSICAL PROPERTIES OF ENTERAL FORMULAS

In addition to consideration of formula characteristics, a review of the physical qualities of enteral formulas is important to facilitate optimal tolerance and effectiveness.

A. Microbiological Safety Commercial formulas are prepared and packaged under sterile conditions to reduce the risk of contamination. Once the formula container is opened, however, adherence to storage and handling protocols is essential to minimize opportunities for microbiological contamination and growth.

B. Osmolality Osmolality is an important physical quality to consider in selecting a formula. The number and size of molecular and ionic particles present in a given volume determine the osmolality. The particles may be electrolytes, minerals, carbohydrates, and proteins. Generally, large-molecular-weight particles exert less osmotic pressure than their corresponding hydrolysates. Thus, the more predigested the formula, the higher the osmolality. Most manufacturers provide osmolality data for their formulas. Osmolality of a modular formula or a combination of enteral formulas can also be calculated (31).

The implications of formulas with differing osmolality are critical for 3 reasons. First, formulas with osmolalities higher than 200 mOsm tend to slow gastric emptying (32). As osmolality increases, the inhibitory effect also increases. As a result, gastric retention, nausea, and vomiting may occur when hypertonic formulas are fed into the stomach, particularly by bolus.

Second, hyperosmolar formulas are adjusted to isotonic levels by changes in their water content in the duodenum. This adjustment may result in large fluid shifts into the small bowel, with subsequent diarrhea, electrolyte depletion, and dehydration, particularly in the poorly functioning gut or with rapid administration of a hypertonic formula (33).

Third, the osmolality of a formula will affect hydration status by direct influence on the renal solute load. Renal solute load is determined by the constituents of a formula that must be diluted and excreted by the kidneys: urea as the breakdown product of protein; sodium; potassium; and chloride. As was previously mentioned, these constituents also contribute largely to formula osmolality. Hyperosmolar formulas, which often tend to be concentrated, require adequate water administration to prevent dehydration caused by the obligatory loss of water as the kidneys attempt to dilute and excrete waste products. The kidneys will adapt by concentrating the urine, but this ability is limited and can lead to clinical dehydration if additional water is not provided. Dehydration caused by this hyperosmolar syndrome has been associated with high-protein tube feedings in a number of studies (34–38). In most of the reported cases, dehydration was due to an increased renal solute load caused by a very high protein intake and insufficient fluid intake. Water loss is not limited to this hyperosmolar syndrome; therefore other clinical conditions causing water loss should be evaluated before incriminating the tube feedings.

C. Nutritional Adequacy and Balance

Tube feedings should provide not only carbohydrate, protein, and fat in appropriate concentrations but also adequate amounts of vitamins and minerals, especially when indicated for the long term. In calculating the volume of formula required to meet estimated calorie and protein demands, it is also important to determine if the Recommended Daily Allowances (RDAs) are being met by the calculated volume. Enteral formulas differ considerably in volume required to meet RDAs, and the ability of one formula to meet RDAs in a volume lower than that of a comparable formula may often be a deciding factor in formula selection. If an appropriate formula cannot be selected that will provide adequate vitamins and minerals in the required volume to meet calorie and protein needs, administration of a multivitamin may be indicated. The electrolyte content of formulas should also be considered and supplementary electrolytes administered if

TABLE 11.3. CHARACTERISTICS OF TYPES OF CARBOHYDRATES

Type	Characteristics	Sources
Starch	Is composed of glucose chains in straight (amylose) and branched (amylopectin) configurations Is hydrolyzed by pancreatic enzymes to dextrin, maltose, and isomaltose Contributes little to the osmolality of a formula, because of its high molecular weight Is generally well tolerated and easily digested Is difficult to use in enteral formulas because of its relative insolubility	Hydrolyzed cereal solids Pureed green beans, carrots, and peas Modified food starch Tapioca starch
Glucose polymers	Result from the partial hydrolysis of cornstarch Are more soluble than starch Are rapidly hydrolyzed in the small intestine by pancreatic enzymes Contribute more to the osmotic load than starch but 5 times less than pure glucose, allowing higher concentrations of calories without the side effects associated with hypertonicity Intolerance is rare, although final hydrolysis to glucose depends upon brush-border enzyme activity and small-intestine function	Glucose polysaccharides Glucose oligosaccharides Glucose polymers Maltodextrins Corn syrup Corn syrup solids
Disaccharides	Require activity of specific disaccharidase enzymes in the brush border of the small-intestinal mucosa Are hydrolyzed to their monosaccharide components before being absorbed Sucrose and maltose hydrolysis is rapid, whereas lactose hydrolysis takes almost twice as long Contribute more to the osmotic load than glucose polymers do Primary disaccharidase deficiency is rare	Sucrose (glucose-fructose) Lactose (glucose-galactose) Maltose (glucose-glucose)
Monosaccharides	Formulas containing pure glucose are very sweet and hypertonic Hydrolysis is not required; thus utilization of glucose is unaffected by digestive capacity Impaired absorptive capacity of the small intestine may reduce tolerance, making glucose polymers more desirable	Glucose (dextrose) Fructose

TABLE 11.4. CHARACTERISTICS OF TYPES OF PROTEIN

Type	Characteristics	Sources
Intact protein	Requires normal levels of pancreatic enzymes for complete digestion Must be hydrolyzed to smaller peptides and amino acids for absorption Contributes very little to formula osmolality	Pureed beef Egg white solids Soy protein isolates Casein isolates Lactalbumin Whey Nonfat and whole dry milk Sodium and calcium caseinates
Protein hydrolysates	Result from enzymatic hydrolysis of intact protein to peptides of varying lengths and free amino acids Often require addition of free amino acids to enhance protein quality Dipeptides, tripeptides, and free amino acids can be absorbed directly into the bloodstream Are useful in conditions in which absorptive surface area is reduced, in exocrine pancreatic insufficiency, and in selective disorders of amino acid transport Contribute more to the osmotic load as the protein molecules become smaller	Casein Whey, soy, or meat protein Lactalbumin Collagen
Crystalline amino acids	Do not require the action of pancreatic enzymes and are absorbed via active transport Contribute largely to the osmotic load because of their small size Adversely affect taste Are best utilized in conditions of hepatic or renal failure	L-Amino acids

serum deficiencies are found to be due to inadequate provision from the formula.

Modular feedings generally provide a single nutrient (carbohydrate, protein, or fat) and may be used to fortify or enhance an existing formula or to construct an individualized formula. They can be useful in the hands of a skilled practitioner with a small number of patients who have specific metabolic or fluid imbalances that preclude the administration of standard formula (39). It is important to note, however, that modular components do not contain vitamins, minerals, or electrolytes; thus they require addition of these nutrients in appropriate concentrations specific to the clinical condition to make the modular formula nutritionally complete. Use of modular components is time-consuming and costly. It should be attempted only for patients who can be evaluated frequently with serial nutritional assessments and serum biochemistries to determine the tolerance to the modular formula.

D. Calorie-Nutrient Density   The calorie and nutrient density of a tube-feeding formula can also influence the gastric emptying rate, thus affecting patient tolerance. Gastric emptying rate is slowed as caloric density (kcal/mL) increases. The total fat content also reduces gastric emptying rate by the inhibitory effect of fat on gastric motility (32). A delay in gastric emptying rate may be desirable for some patients, but it may be a problem for others, particularly in neurologically impaired patients whose risk for aspiration is high.

In addition, patients whose gastrointestinal tracts have not been used for an extended period or who have experienced mucosal damage or disease may display improved tolerance with a diluted or low-calorie formula. The rationale for using such a formula is to allow the gastrointestinal tract time for gradual restoration of tissue integrity and repletion of enzyme concentrations.

E. Calorie-to-Nitrogen Ratio   A high-protein diet will not necessarily result in a positive nitrogen balance, because extra protein without extra calories may result in the utilization of protein as an energy source (40). For a normal active person, the most efficient ratio of kilocalories to grams of nitrogen is approximately 300:1. During illness and injury, a lower ratio is more appropriate (41). For the stressed patient, tube feedings with a ratio between 120:1 and 180:1 have been recommended (42). A ratio above 200:1 may provide inadequate protein. A ratio of less than 100:1 may provide too much protein in relation to calorie content and may result in increased levels of blood urea nitrogen and ammonia as well as subsequent dehydration due to the increased solute load (43).

F. Flow Rate   Viscosity, caloric density, osmolality, and type and amount of protein all affect flow rate of formulas. Blenderized diet feedings have been reported to sediment particulate matter in the tube and may require a slightly larger

TABLE 11.5. CHARACTERISTICS OF TYPES OF FAT

Type	Characteristics	Source
Long-chain triglycerides (LCTS)	Provide essential fatty acids and serve as carriers for fat-soluble vitamins Require emulsification and hydrolysis by both bile salts and pancreatic enzymes Are transported to the bloodstream via lymphatic circulation Do not contribute significantly to formula osmolality	Butterfat Corn, soy, safflower, or sunflower oil
Medium-chain triglycerides (MCTS)	Are composed of triglycerides of 6 to 12 carbons long Provide 8.2 to 8.4 kcal/g Are water soluble Hydrolysis in the intestinal lumen is more rapid and complete than hydrolysis of LCTS, causing a rapid increase in osmotic concentration Require little or no pancreatic lipase or bile salts for absorption Are indicated in disorders of fat absorption and lymphatic drainage	MCT oil (fractionated coconut or palm kernel oil)

bore or internal diameter of the Silastic or polyurethane tube (44).

G. Cost   Cost controls are best achieved when products are categorized according to their therapeutic applicability in a formulary system (45, 46). A comparative analysis can then be made within each product category to determine the most cost-effective formulation.

5. MECHANICAL CONSIDERATIONS

Characteristics of various tubes and systems are presented in table 11.7. Internal and external tube diameters are depicted in figure 11.1.

INDICATIONS FOR USE

Tube feeding may be used as a sole source of nutrition or as a supplement to oral intake. In either case, the need for nutrition support should be determined by a thorough nutritional assessment and identification of conditions indicating the need

for enteral tube feeding (table 11.8). Figures are provided to assist the practitioner in determining the need for enteral tube feeding (fig. 11.2), choosing the appropriate enteral formula category (fig. 11.3), and making the transition from parenteral to enteral nutrition support (fig. 11.4).

Given the marked increase in commercially available tube-feeding formulas and the wide range of clinical conditions indicating enteral alimentation by tube, there is no ideal tube feeding to fit all needs. In choosing an enteral formula, the composition of the formula must be consistent with the nutritional needs of the patient as influenced by disease state and effects on the patient's ability to digest, absorb, and utilize the nutrients. Tube-feeding selection should be preceded by a nutritional assessment that identifies individual nutritional demands, preexisting deficits, and specific intolerances. Once the indication for tube

feeding is identified and the formula category is determined, the specific enteral formula can be chosen using the criteria provided in table 11.9.

Selection of the method of tube-feeding administration is dependent on several criteria: patient risk for aspiration, goals of therapy, patient comfort, tube placement, and pathology of the gastrointestinal tract. Enteral formulas can be administered by 1 of 4 infusion methods: intermittent bolus, intermittent gravity, continuous infusion, or cyclic continuous infusion. Generally, the method of administration is dictated by the type of enteral access.

Bolus feedings are primarily used when the tip of the tube rests in the stomach (74). Formula is infused over a short time by a large syringe or feeding bag in volumes of approximately 250 to 450 mL several times per day (75, 76). This method is relatively inexpensive compared with pump-assisted enteral feeding, permits greater mobility and flexibility, and mimics normal nutrient ingestion. Bolus feedings may create a higher risk for aspiration, however, and may be poorly tolerated in some individuals.

TABLE 11.6. BIOLOGICAL VALUE OF MAJOR PROTEIN SOURCES IN ENTERAL FEEDINGS

Protein source	Biological value
Lactalbumin with methionine	130
Egg, whole	100
Milk, cow	90
Fish	85
Lactalbumin	84
Beef	76
Soybeans	75
Casein	72

Source: Oser, B. L. (30).

TABLE 11.7. TUBE CHARACTERISTICS AND CONSIDERATIONS

	Thinnest wall, or largest flow of lumen per outside diameter (O.D.)	*Ease of insertion*	*Kinking*	*Ease of aspirating gastric residuals*	*Patient comfort*	*Durability over time*	*Strength (breaking, rupturing)*
1. Material							
PVC	Good	Stiff, no need for stylet; but there may be patient resistance because of size and stiffness	Virtually none	Excellent	Poor	Poor (embrittles; is uncomfortable)	Very strong but can embrittle or split
Silicone	Better	Too soft for easy insertion?	Prone to kink and collapse on aspiration	Fair	Best	Excellent	Weak
Polyurethane	Best	Adequate stiffness, smallest O.D. per French size	Some	Good	Good	Excellent	Strong
Latex	Poor	Similar to PVC	Virtually none	Good	Poor	Poor	Very strong but can crack

2. Weights

Do weights . . .
- facilitate tube placement?
- help keep tubes positioned properly?
- assist in transpyloric passage?

Tungsten
- Presents no disposal problems
- Is inert
- Is heavy (specific gravity = 19)
- Comes as pellets, segments, or powder
- Shorter segments provide more flexibility than longer segments do

3. Tip size and shape

Bolus vs. smooth
- Smooth tips are easier than bolus shapes to insert
- Do bolus shapes assist peristalsis in transpyloric passage and/or in tube retention?

Water-activated lubricant coating
- Assists in passage through the nares

4. Eyelets

Location of eyes in rigid tip
- Help prevent tube kinking and occlusion
- Help prevent tube collapse during aspiration
- Help prevent accidental exit of stylet

Size and shape
- Should have cross-sectional area equal to cross-sectional area of the tube lumen
- If holes are as large as tube lumen, flow is controlled by size of tube lumen, not by number of holes
- Do oblong holes or slotted ports contribute to occlusion by coagulated feeding material or medications?

(continued)

TABLE 11.7. *CONTINUED*

5. Tube length	• Color coding of hub assists in tube-length identification in situ • Centimeter markings are important to monitor position and to assist in tube placement • 36-inch length for gastric, 43-inch length for intestinal
6. Stylets Steel wire vs. plastic	• Wire is stiff and straight; provides for good insertion but presents the potential for tissue perforation • Plastic is very soft; coils and takes a "set" in package • Wire can provide for duodenal placement under fluoroscopy
Ease of removal	• Water-activated lumen lubricants facilitate removal • Wire stylets are more easily removed than plastic? • Silicone tubes tend to "accordion" during stylet removal?
Potential for misplacement	• Stylets should not be replaced with tube in situ, regardless of stylet design • Stylets can accidentally exit eyelets in any tube that has the eyelets in the tube wall
External vs. internal	• External stylets minimize perforation potential • External stylets cause more discomfort during intubation
No stylet	• Minimizes potential for perforation • If tube is stiff, it may cause discomfort during intubation • Causes long-term discomfort for duration of intubation • Probably best for short-term bolus administration • Potential for misplacement
7. Tube clogging	• Need for irrigation every 4 hours • Never use stylet to unclog • Location, shape, and size of hole contributes to occlusion? • Always use syringes that are 50 mL or larger
8. Administration set connectors	• Hard Luers cannot "pop off" from syringes or administration sets if pressure in line exceeds the rupture threshold of silicone or urethane feeding tubes • Soft Luers separate from the set or syringe under excessive pressure • Combination Luer/irrigation adapters provide maximum flexibility and convenience for irrigation and/or addition of medication • Color coding helps identify tube length in situ
9. Cost	• Cost per day is insignificant for long-term intubation with silicone or urethane tubes • Can tube be reinserted if removed?

10. French size considerations	• Type of patient
	  • Neonate
	  • Pediatric
	  • Adult
	• Duration of feeding
	• Viscosity of solution
	• Gravity vs. pump administration
	• Patient pathology
	• Potential for mucosal irritation

Source: Lysen, L. K. (47).

FIG. 11.1. COMPARISON OF INTERNAL AND OUTER DIAMETERS OF TUBES BY FRENCH SIZE.

Brand:		Silk	Prima	Silk		Silk		Silk	Biosearch		PVC	Silicone
Material:	PVC	PU	PVC	PU	PVC	PU	Silicone	PU	PU	PVC		
Size:	5 Fr	5 Fr	6 Fr	6 Fr	8 Fr	8 Fr	9.6 Fr	10 Fr	12 Fr	12 Fr	14 Fr	14 Fr

Inner diameter:	0.96 mm	1.1 mm	1.1 mm	1.37 mm	1.55 mm	2.03 mm	1.98 mm	2.61 mm	2.71 mm	2.51 mm	3.12 mm	2.64 mm
Outer diameter:	1.65 mm	1.65 mm	2.1 mm	2.1 mm	2.67 mm	2.79 mm	3.18 mm	3.30 mm	4.06 mm	4.01 mm	4.62 mm	4.88 mm
Internal area:	0.72 mm^2	0.95 mm^2	0.95 mm^2	1.47 mm^2	1.89 mm^2	2.98 mm^2	3.08 mm^2	5.30 mm^2	5.77 mm^2	4.95 mm^2	7.64 mm^2	5.46 mm^2

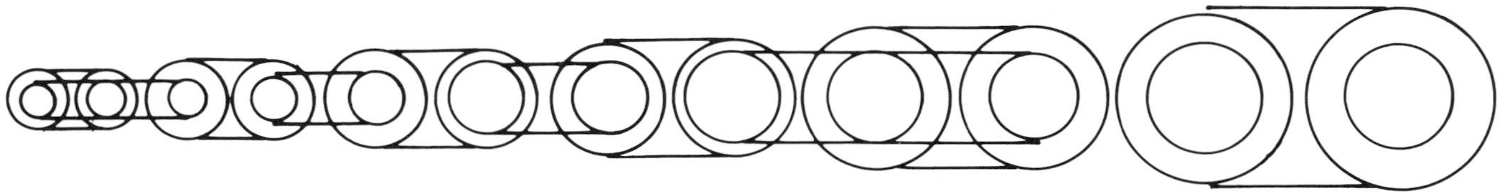

Source: Lysen, L. K. (47).

TABLE 11.8. CONDITIONS INDICATING TUBE FEEDING

Conditions	Type of disorder
Impaired swallowing	Central nervous system disorders
	Cerebrovascular accidents
	Neoplasms affecting central nervous system
	Trauma
	Inflammation
	Demyelinating diseases
	Coma
	Certain types of paralysis
	Cerebral palsy
Oropharyngeal-esophageal disorders	Oropharyngeal-esophageal neoplasms
	Inflammation
	Fractures or other types of trauma
	Head and neck radiation
	Palliative chemotherapy
	Radical head and neck surgery
Psychiatric disorders	Severe depression
	Anorexia nervosa
	Dementia or Alzheimer's disease
Type I glycogen storage disease (48)	Continuous feeding may help to control hypoglycemia
Increased nutritional losses or needs (49–53)	Fever and infection
	Sepsis (54)
	Surgically or medically related stress
	Cancer (55, 56)
	Kwashiorkor
	Marasmus
	Cachexia (57, 58)
Gastrointestinal disorders	Bile-acid-induced diarrhea (59)
	Gastrointestinal fistulas
	Pancreatitis after ileus (60)
	Inflammatory bowel disease (61)
	Short-bowel syndrome (61–63)
	Gastrointestinal diseases associated with malabsorption (61)
	Crohn's disease
Early postoperative feeding (64, 65)	Jejunal feeding with gastric decompression
Specialized nutritional needs	Renal failure (66)
	Liver failure (61)
	Postoperative protein synthesis in trauma patients (67)
Chronic obstructive pulmonary disease	Cystic fibrosis (1)
	Respirator-dependent patients
	Carbon dioxide retention
Decubiti, risk of decubiti (68, 69)	Hypoalbuminemia
	Impaired nutritional status
	Inadequate oral intake
	Institutionalized elderly

Intermittent gravity feedings are infused several times a day over a longer period than bolus feedings, using a feeding bag. This method of administration is appropriate for patients who do not require a precisely regulated flow rate and who demonstrate poor tolerance to bolus feedings. Administration is fairly simple and inexpensive, although mobility is more limited and tolerance may be poor.

Continuous feedings are required when the tube is placed in the duodenum or jejunum but can also be used when feeding into the stomach (76, 77). Bolus feedings and sudden rate changes are poorly tolerated when the tube tip rests in the small intestine; thus continuous infusion by pump is indicated for controlled and accurate delivery of nutrients (78). Continuous feeding into the small intestine offers the advantage of reducing the risk for aspiration because both the lower esophageal and pylorus sphincters act as natural barriers in helping to prevent reflux. In addition, feeding continuously into the duodenum or jejunum can prevent or lessen bowel distention, abnormal fluid and electrolyte shifts, and diarrhea. In patients with delayed gastric emptying—as occurs with diabetic gastroparesis, partial gastric-outlet obstruction, or pancreatitis—continuous feedings advanced at a slow rate are indicated to avoid the risk of gastric dilatation and aspiration (79). Following gastrectomy, continuous feedings may minimize symptoms of dumping syndrome. Continuous infusion by pump is more expensive than other feeding methods and restricts patient mobility.

In cycled feedings, formula is usually infused by pump for 6 or more hours. This method is an option for patients who require continuous feedings but do not wish to be attached to a pump 24 hours a day or who require close supervision during feeding. Nutritional needs may be partially or fully met by the tube feeding, depending on the patient's ability to consume nutrients by mouth. Noc-

FIG. 11.2. DECISION TREE FOR AN ENTERAL FEEDING ROUTE.

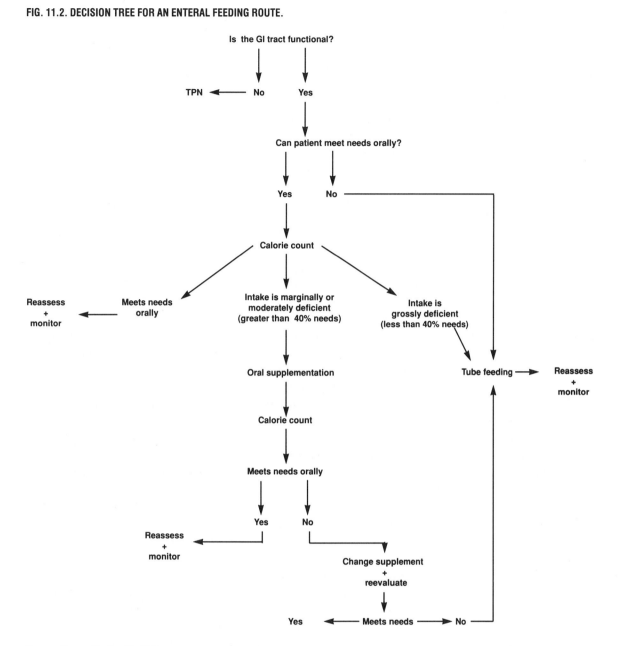

Source: Touger-Decker, R. (70).

turnal cyclic feedings may be used to facilitate increased oral intake during the
day and provide more flexibility for ambulatory patients. Daytime cyclic feedings are indicated for patients who may
require close supervision during formula
infusion, such as patients at high risk for
aspiration.

The hormonal and metabolic effects of
bolus or intermittent feedings versus
continuous feedings should also be considered in choosing a formula administration method. This consideration is especially important with the critically ill
patient. Continuous feedings may enable
more-rapid achievement of the caloric

goal and have been shown to reduce
stool frequency in adult burn patients
(80). Evidence also suggests that maintenance energy requirements are reduced
during continuous feedings when compared with isocaloric intermittent feedings (81, 82). Extra calories are burned
when feedings are given by bolus, be-

cause of intraprandial and postprandial thermogenesis caused by the specific dynamic action of food. This process reduces energy available from the bolus (or meal) to be used for healing and anabolism, a reduction that is especially significant for patients whose calculated energy requirements are very high. Disadvantages of continuous feedings include decreased nitrogen retention, an elevated respiratory quotient, and reduced mobilization of fat (83). Reduced fat mobilization occurs as a result of the constant stimulation for insulin secretion from the pancreas produced by the continuous administration of a carbohydrate load. A constant high serum level of insulin prevents mobilization of fatty acids from adipose stores, limiting the use of this nutrient as an alternative energy source.

POSSIBLE ADVERSE REACTIONS

Of the relatively few clinically significant complications of enteral alimentation, most can be easily treated and prevented when patients are properly monitored. Complications can be of metabolic, gastrointestinal, or mechanical origin. Some of the possible complications of tube feedings and the typical management strategies for each are summarized in table 11.10.

Ideally, management of the tube-fed patient should involve a multidisciplinary team of health professionals for optimal care. The dietitian's role includes evaluation of nutrient needs, selection of the appropriate formula, close monitoring of tube-feeding tolerance, and identification of possible causes of adverse reactions to tube feeding. Although the dietitian may not actually perform the management strategies provided here, it is important that the dietitian be able to evaluate the potential cause of complications and to provide recommendations appropriate for their prevention or treatment.

CONTRAINDICATIONS

Enteral tube feeding is contraindicated for individuals with intestinal obstructions, paralytic ileus, gastrointestinal hemorrhage, intractable vomiting, or certain jejunal fistulas (89). Diarrhea with or without malabsorption may contraindicate enteral feeding but may also be managed by an adjustment in flow rate or change in formula.

CLINICAL ASSESSMENT

Clinical determinations are a prerequisite for tube-feeding selection and as a routine means of evaluating the efficacy of nutritional interventions in tube-fed patients.

The condition of the skin and the presence or absence of edema may indicate fluid and electrolyte imbalance. Patients with a decrease in body fluid have decreased skin turgor and dry mucous membranes. Dry sticky membranes may reflect sodium excess.

Bowel function should be monitored regularly especially during the initial period of tube feeding. Stool frequency and consistency in addition to the presence of bowel sounds, nausea, vomiting, and distention should be assessed on a daily basis. The existence of diarrhea as an adverse reaction is described in table 11.10, and its specific characteristics are clues to its cause. Antidiarrheal medications (table 11.11) can be used in cases in which the diarrhea is not caused by infection.

Measurement of gastric residuals allows for assessment of gastric emptying and can be used as an indicator for advancement of feeding rate or volume. Measurement of residuals cannot be performed during intestinal feedings or when a small-bore collapsible tube is used.

Regular weights are important because they reflect fluid balance as well as changes in lean body mass. Rapid weight gain or loss may be a sign of fluid imbalance and indicates the need for close monitoring of fluid intake and output.

The dietary interview also reveals important data for a clinical evaluation of nutritional status, e.g., information about previous gastrointestinal problems, allergies, and long-term use of medications. Skinfold measurements and midarm muscle circumference estimations provide data on the effects of interventions on skeletal protein stores, particularly in the long-term setting, in which serial measurements can be taken over a period of time.

BIOCHEMICAL ASSESSMENT

Regular monitoring of pertinent laboratory and biochemical data is an essential part of the ongoing assessment and follow-up protocol. The frequency of biochemical monitoring of tube-fed patients varies depending on patient acuity, feeding duration, and hospital protocol.

Serum proteins such as albumin, prealbumin, and transferrin should be evaluated every 3 to 4 weeks and more frequently for the acute patient. Electrolyte and mineral status, including blood urea nitrogen (BUN) and creatinine, should be monitored 2 to 3 times weekly until it is stable, and more frequently if problems are suspected. Parameters of fluid balance such as serum levels of sodium, BUN, and hemoglobin should be monitored regularly. In addition, records of fluid intake and output can be helpful in evaluating fluid balance and prescription of adequate fluids. Glucose levels in urine or blood should be measured regularly in the acute patient when sepsis may be a concern and in the patient with diabetes or glucose intolerance. Nitrogen balance studies can be a useful tool for evaluating protein utilization; the results can be influenced by many variables, however, limiting its usefulness. Care should be taken in interpreting laboratory

TABLE 11.9. CRITERIA FOR TUBE-FEEDING SELECTION

Product category	Patient indications
Standard polymeric	Functional GI tract Normal nutrient needs Nothing by mouth <7 days (73)
High-nitrogen polymeric	Functional GI tract Malnourished Catabolic Presence or risk of pressure sores
Concentrated	Fluid restriction Intolerance to large volumes of formula
Blenderized	Normal intact GI tract Lactose tolerant Normal fiber needs Tube of sufficient bore size to permit flow of formula
Fiber-containing	Abnormal bowel regulation Dumping syndrome
Predigested or elemental	Partially functioning GI tract Impaired digestive capacity Reduced absorptive ability Pancreatic insufficiency Bile salt deficiency Nothing by mouth >7 days (73)
Specialty	Organ failure Pulmonary compromise
Modular	Specialized nutrient, electrolyte, and fluid needs that cannot be met with a conventional formula

and biochemical values, because factors other than nutritional status can influence their results.

ASSESSMENT OF POTENTIAL DRUG INTERACTIONS

The use of enteral feedings, particularly in critically ill patients, has expanded dramatically over recent years. Reports of complications caused by the administration of medications via feeding tubes have also increased. When a medication is administered concurrently with an enteral feeding, the bioavailability of either the drug or the nutrients in the solution may be affected (91–93; see table 11.12). In addition, the combination of certain drugs with enteral formulas can result in serious physical and metabolic side effects (table 11.13).

The stomach dissolves medications to prepare them for uptake by the gastrointestinal tract. A drug administered beyond the stomach directly into the small intestine must be in solution to be effective. Guidelines for pharmacies in the proper preparation of drugs not commercially available in liquid form have been published elsewhere. If the viscosity of the drug impedes its passage, it should be diluted with 15 to 20 mL of lukewarm water to facilitate its delivery into the small bowel (100). Flushing the tube with 30 mL warm water before and after administering medications clears the tube for drug delivery and facilitates passage of the drug.

Some drugs simply cannot be mixed with formulas. When added to enteral products, they cause an increase in viscosity or particle size, tackiness, clumping, and occlusion of the tube feeding. A common practice—and one that should be avoided—when administering solid-dosage forms via feeding tube is to crush the medication, mix it with water, and force it through the tube using a syringe. This practice should be avoided not only because particles of the drug block the holes at the tip of the feeding tube but also because many medications, when crushed, are no longer effective as designed (91). Crushing slows release, and enteric coating of the drug destroys the drug's integrity and may alter the desired absorption rate. Liquid forms of medication should be used when possible, and a pharmacist consulted to determine which medications can be safely crushed. The increase in osmolality caused by the addition of medications to enteral feedings has also been identified as a possible cause of gastrointestinal complications (101).

Some drugs can affect the rate of gastric emptying, which in turn affects tube-feeding tolerance. Certain medical conditions can also decrease gastric emptying time. The drug metoclopramide may be useful to increase gastric motility, and thus gastric emptying time, in tube-fed patients. It has also been used to facilitate the transpyloric placement of weighted feeding tubes, but with mixed reviews on its effectiveness (102–104).

The addition of calcium to tube feedings in amounts of 130 mEq or above compromises the stability of the solution (91). Syrups, especially those with a pH of less than 4, may cause problems that necessitate the alternative use of suspensions and elixirs (97).

FIG. 11.3. ENTERAL PRODUCT SELECTION.

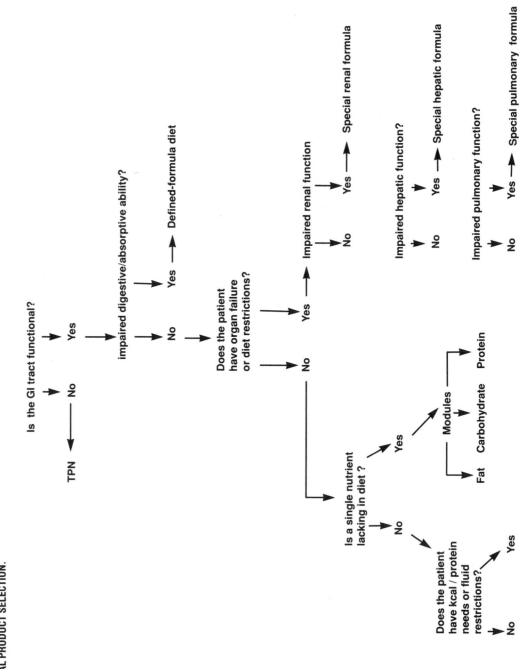

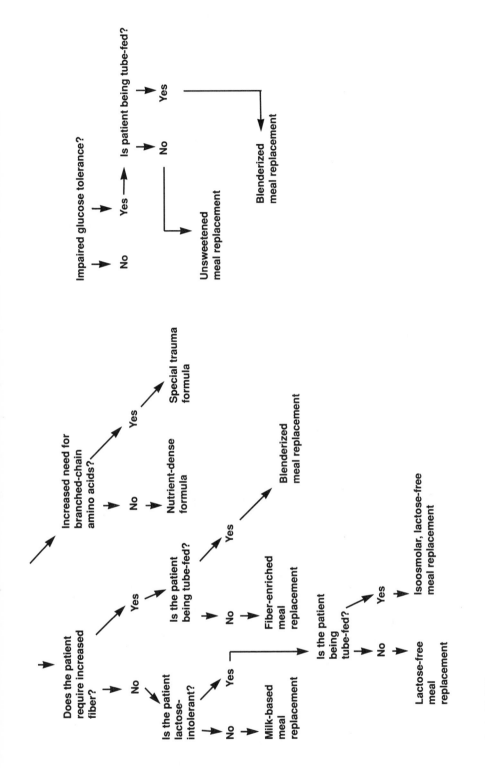

Does the patient require increased fiber?

Yes → Increased need for branched-chain amino acids?
- Yes → Special trauma formula
- No → Nutrient-dense formula

No → Is the patient lactose-intolerant?
- Yes → Is the patient being tube-fed?
  - Yes → Blenderized meal replacement
  - No → Fiber-enriched meal replacement
- No → Milk-based meal replacement

Is the patient being tube-fed?
- Yes → Isoosmolar, lactose-free meal replacement
- No → Lactose-free meal replacement

Impaired glucose tolerance?
- No → Is patient being tube-fed?
- Yes → Is patient being tube-fed?
  - No → Unsweetened meal replacement
  - Yes → Blenderized meal replacement

Source: Irwin, C. (71).

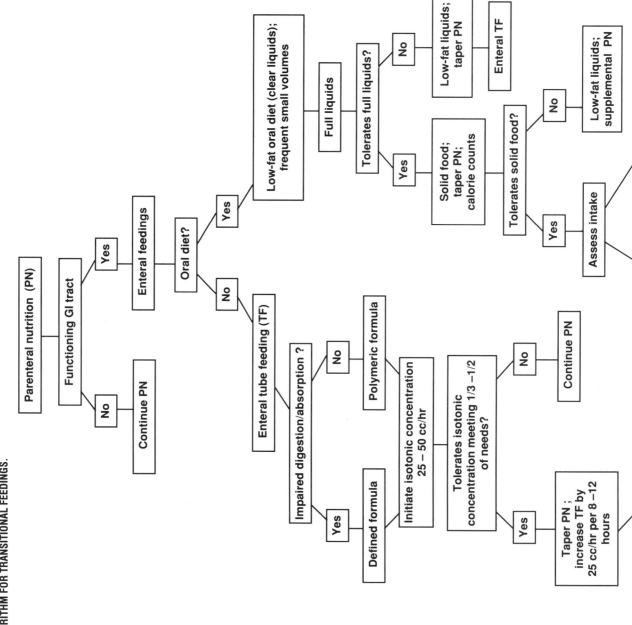

FIG. 11.4. ALGORITHM FOR TRANSITIONAL FEEDINGS.

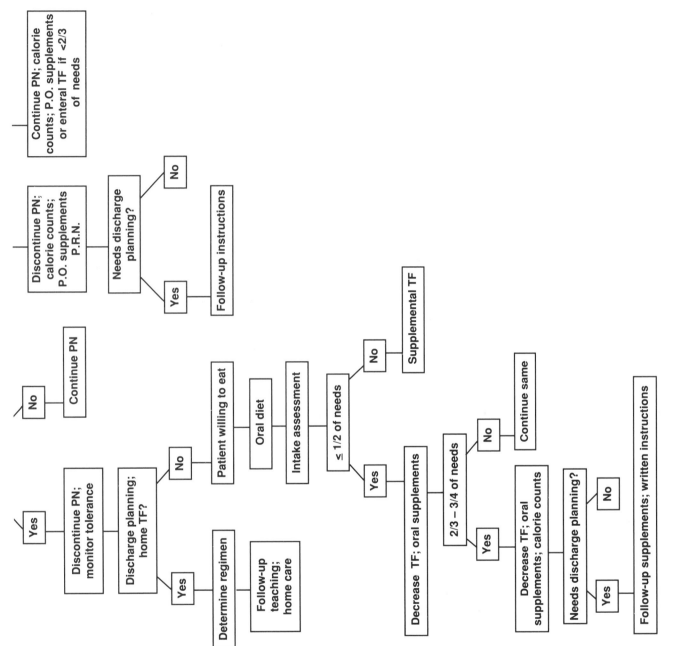

Source: Shronts, E. P. (72).

TABLE 11.10. POSSIBLE ADVERSE REACTIONS TO TUBE FEEDINGS

Problem	Possible causes	Management strategy
Mechanical complications		
Tube displacement	Coughing, vomiting	Replace tube and confirm placement.
	Dislodgment by patient	Replace tube; restrain patient if necessary; consider alternate feeding route.
	Inadequate taping of tube	Position tube properly and tape correctly.
Tube obstruction or clogging	Improperly crushed medications	Use liquid medications when possible.
	Medications mixed with incompatible formulas	Follow drug nutrient interaction guidelines, and flush tube before and after addition of medications.
	Formula residue adhering to tube; failure to irrigate properly (84)	Flush tube with 20 to 50 mL water before starting and after stopping feeding. Flush tube at least every 4 hours during continuous infusion.
Gastric retention; aspiration pneumonia	Delayed gastric emptying	Re-position tube into small intestine.
	Patient lying flat during infusion	Elevate head of bed to 30° or more during and for 2 hours after infusion.
	Displaced feeding tube	Monitor and confirm tube placement before feeding.
Nasopharyngeal irritation; mucosal erosion; otitis media	Large bore vinyl or rubber feeding tubes for prolonged time periods	Consider use of soft, small-bore feeding tubes or feeding by tube enterostomy.
	Improper positioning or placement	Position tube properly and tape correctly; choose tube of correct size for patient.
	Decreased salivary secretions due to lack of chewing; mouth breathing	Keep mouth and lips moist. Allow chewing of sugarless gum, gargling, or sucking on anaesthetic lozenges if appropriate.
Gastrointestinal complications		
Nausea and vomiting; cramping; distention	Improper location of tube	Periodically confirm tube position.
	Rapid increase in rate, volume, or concentration	Return to slower rate, and advance by smaller increments. Advance only when tolerated at current rate.
	High osmolality	Dilute to isotonic strength if gastric residuals are consistently high. Increase concentration over several days. Consider change to isotonic formula.
	Delayed gastric emptying	Check gastric residuals every 4 to 6 hours on continuous feedings or prior to each bolus. Monitor for drugs or disease states that may influence gastric or intestinal motility.
	Lactose intolerance	Change to lactose-free formula.
	Cold formula	Warm to room temperature before use.
	Obstruction	Stop formula feeding immediately.
	Excessive fat in formula	Switch to lower-fat formula. Reduce fat in modular feedings.
Constipation	Inadequate fiber or fluid intake	Monitor intake and output; add free water if intake is not greater than output by 500 to 1,000 mL/day (85). Use formula with added fiber.
	Medications	Evaluate medication side effects; suggest stool softener or bulk-forming laxative.
	Inactivity	Increase patient activity if possible.

(continued)

TABLE 11.10. *CONTINUED*

Problem	Possible causes	Management strategy
Diarrhea; defined as passage of more than 200 g of stool per 24 hours or the passage of liquid stools (86)	Protein-energy malnutrition; decreased oncotic pressure due to serum albumin below 3.0 g/dL (87, 88)	Use isotonic or elemental formula at slow rate initially. If severe, suggest antidiarrheal therapy or parenteral nutrition.
	Infectious origin; microbial contamination of formula	Confirm with stool, blood, or formula cultures. Review tube-feeding handling and infection control procedures.
	Malabsorption of fat or other nutrients	Evaluate for pancreatic insufficiency; use pancreatic enzyme replacements if indicated. Change to low-fat or elemental formula.
	Bolus feeding; dumping syndrome	Change to continuous feeding, or decrease bolus volume and increase frequency of feeding.
	Hyperosmolar formula	Reduce rate and increase gradually; dilute formula or change to isotonic product.
	Medications	Consider antidiarrheal agents such as Kaopectate, paregoric, or Lomotil. Change to fiber-containing formula.
Metabolic complications		
Hyperosmolar dehydration	Administration of hypertonic formula with inadequate water	Initiate hypertonic feedings at reduced rates; dilute; or consider use of isotonic formula.
Fluid overload or overhydration	Refeeding of patients with PEM; common in patients with cardiac, renal, or hepatic disease	Restrict fluids; use concentrated formula.
	Prolonged use of over dilute formula	Advance formula concentration as tolerated.
Hyponatremia	Congestive heart failure, cirrhosis, hypoalbuminemia, edema, ascites	Apply diuretic therapy; restrict fluids. Use concentrated formula.
	Excess gastrointestinal losses	Monitor serum levels and hydration status, and replace sodium as needed.
Hypernatremia	Dehydration	Assure adequate fluid intake.
Hypokalemia	Acidosis, insulin administration, diarrhea, marked malnutrition, diuretic therapy	Monitor electrolytes daily; supplement potassium as needed.
Hyperkalemia	Renal insufficiency	Perform frequent biochemical monitoring. Use formula containing low levels of potassium.
Other serum electrolyte or mineral abnormalities	Various	Monitor serum levels regularly, making individualized adjustments as needed.
Essential fatty acid (EFA) deficiency	Formula with low levels of EFA used over prolonged time periods	Provide a minimum of 4% of the caloric intake from EFAS. Add 5 mL safflower oil daily.
Glucose intolerance; hyperglycemic hyperosmolar nonketotic coma	Diabetes mellitus; or temporary insulin resistance caused by trauma or sepsis	May need to stop feeding and to rehydrate patient. Monitor blood sugar frequently, making adjustments in insulin dose. Avoid formulas high in simple sugars.
Increased respiratory quotient; excess CO_2 production; respiratory insufficiency	Overfeeding of calories, especially in the form of carbohydrates	Reduce the respiratory quotient by balancing the calories provided from fat, protein, and carbohydrate. Increase the percentage of calories provided as fat by using high-fat formula or adding modular fat.

TABLE 11.11. ANTIDIARRHEAL MEDICATIONS FOR USE WITH TUBE FEEDINGS

Medication	Effects	Dosage
Kaopectate (kaolin-pectin)	Adsorbs bacteria and toxins, reduces water loss, consolidates stool	30 mL 3 or 4 times daily
Immodium (loperamide)	Slows GI motility	1 or 2 capsules up to 5 times daily, not to exceed 8 capsules/day
Lomotil (diphenoxylate-atropine)	Slows GI motility	5 mL 3 or 4 times daily
Parepectolin (Kaopectate-paregoric)	Adsorbs bacteria and toxins, reduces water loss, consolidates stool, slows GI motility	15 to 30 mL per dose, up to 4 doses in 12 hours
Paregoric (0.04% morphine)	Slows GI motility	10 mL 3 or 4 times daily
Opium tincture	Slows GI motility	0.3 to 1.0 mL up to 4 times daily

Source: Matthews-Antosiewicz, L. (90); *adapted from* The United States Pharmacopeia (124), Physicians' Desk Reference (125).

Phenytoin (Dilantin) may increase the viscosity of certain tube feedings by as much as 30% (97). In addition, phenytoin absorption and seizure control may be compromised by administration of the drug during continuous infusion (105). Studies suggest that the tubing should be flushed and clamped for 2 hours before and 2 hours after the phenytoin dose, a procedure that permits a lower phenytoin dose and reduces the risk of toxicity (106). Increasing the phenytoin dose to compensate for the decreased absorption has also been suggested; however, the risk for drug toxicity if the feeding is stopped outweighs the potential benefits of this method (107). The drug has also been found to adhere to the feeding tube, warranting frequent water flushes of the tube to assure proper dosage. Regardless, serum phenytoin concentrations of patients on a tube feeding must be closely monitored to assure that desired serum levels are achieved (91). If possible, phenytoin should be given by oral capsule or intravenously.

When administered with a high-protein tube feeding, aluminum and/or magnesium hydroxide antacids have been reported to result in a gelatinous mass that can potentially occlude the feeding tube. The same reaction did not occur with a feeding containing a low-molecular-weight peptide (108).

IMPLEMENTATION AND EDUCATION

Priorities for education within the hospital setting should include in-service sessions for food service personnel involved in formula preparation, labeling, and delivery and for nursing staff on the types of formulas, clinical indications for tube feeding, and possible adverse reactions attributable to enteral feedings. Problems identified in quality assurance audits should be addressed in the hospital's in-service education programs, whether they involve infection-control policies, administration techniques, or any unsafe or unsound practice.

Patients and caretakers who are able should be involved in tube-feeding routines. Patients who rely on tube feedings to meet their nutritional needs are often distressed by feelings of dependency, loss of control over their own food intake, disruption of the normal psychosocial aspects of eating, loss of ability to satisfy oral cravings, changes in body image, and feelings of being isolated and dehumanized. Acceptance of the feeding can be facilitated by addressing these problems. By involving the patient in tube-feeding care and decision making, a feeling of control is fostered. Depending upon the scope of their problems, tube-feeding patients may need specialized counseling that focuses on helping them to work through their own particular needs (109–112).

For the ambulatory patient, it may be possible to confine the feeding to nighttime hours, thus permitting daytime freedom for physical activity or other therapies. This schedule may also have psychological advantages, particularly if the patient is being weaned from the tube feeding or has started small oral feedings during the day (113).

A growing number of individuals can be managed on tube feedings at home. They have created a need for specialized nutrition counseling on the techniques of tube-feeding insertion, administration, selection, and care, which the registered dietitian is uniquely qualified to perform. For the patient and family who are not candidates for this type of training, home health care agencies can provide home enteral nutrition care. Third-party reimbursement is available for at least part of these costs (112). Guidelines have been published on the priorities and strategies of a home enteral training program, as have patient-oriented booklets to simplify techniques for patients. Discharge planning should begin early enough to

TABLE 11.12. SUMMARY OF REPORTED NUTRIENT-DRUG INTERACTIONS

Drug	Interaction	Intervention
Antacids containing aluminum or magnesium	Bind phosphorus in the gut, preventing phosphorus absorption.	Monitor phosphorus levels, supplementing if necessary; change the antacid.
Tetracycline hydrochloride	Divalent and trivalent cations inactivate tetracycline by chelation.	Stop feedings 1 hour before and 1 hour after each dose of tetracycline.
Corticosteroids	Decrease glucose tolerance.	Use caution in advancing enteral formulas; monitor glucose frequently.
Warfarin sodium	Vitamin K in enteral formulas is a warfarin antagonist.	Adjust warfarin dose, and monitor partial thromboplastin time; select another enteral formula.
Phenytoin	Enteral feeding may decrease phenytoin absorption by 70%.	Stop feedings 1 hour before and 1 hour after each dose of phenytoin, or increase dose.

Source: Skipper, A. (94). Copyright © 1987 by Aspen Publishers, Inc.

permit proper identification of home care candidates and sufficient time for the educational program to be successful.

PRIORITIES FOR QUALITY ASSURANCE

In the large acute-care medical center, quality assurance safeguards can be readily addressed by the nutrition support service or by the critical nutrition specialist and nursing specialist working together. Standards are just as important in smaller institutions with fewer nutritional support patients and should be a collaborative effort of all professionals responsible for the tube feeding of these patients. Parameters for evaluation could include the following criteria.

1. TUBE-FEEDING ADMINISTRATION

The head of the bed should be elevated to 30° to 45° at all times during feeding and for at least 2 hours following in-termittent or bolus feeding (114). Gastric residuals should be measured every 4 hours or prior to each bolus feeding; feeding should be stopped if the residual amount exceeds 100 mL for bolus feeding or 115% of the hourly rate for continuous feeding. Adequate fluid should be provided to tube-fed patients to maintain hydration status and tube patency.

2. STANDARDIZATION OF FORMULARY

Categories of tube feedings and nutrient composition data should form the basis for the development of a formulary system (115). Forms can be printed that not only identify the products but also provide data for handling and storage (116). Therapeutic duplications can be avoided, and products can be purchased, stored, dispensed, and administered by the category or type of feeding they represent. Dietitians must update data and forms as new products become available.

3. INFECTION CONTROL

Microbiological contamination and growth is a hazard of enteral nutrition solutions (117). Although many tube feedings require no mixing and may be sterile when packaged, they can become contaminated by unsanitary handling and administration practices (118).

The tube-feeding preparation area should be separate from other food preparation areas. Care should be taken that tube feedings are not prepared on the same table used to process raw fruits and vegetables. Blenders used in the preparation of tube feedings can be a source of contamination and should be sterilized after each use. The blender used for mixing tube-feeding formulas should not be used for anything else.

Institutions that prepare large amounts of tube feedings should have a quality assurance program that includes a microbiological safety monitor. An excellent quality control program has been published that involves periodic bacterial cultures of feeding solutions to identify the presence of known food pathogens in feedings (119).

The washing of hands should be stressed, as well as the use of sanitary techniques in transferring formula to feeding containers. The containers should be designed and utilized in a manner that facilitates infection control and hinders the growth of the airborne organisms. Warming opened tube feedings or leaving them exposed at room temperature for long periods of time is unsafe and unwarranted. An alternate approach is utilizing formulas packaged in a closed enteral feeding system, thereby reducing the risk of contamination (120).

Once opened, formulas should be kept refrigerated until used and should be allowed to hang no more than 8 hours (115, 117, 121). If a longer infusion time is needed, the bag should be changed or should have an ice pouch. Formulas

TABLE 11.13. EFFECTS OF CERTAIN DRUGS WHEN ADMINISTERED WITH TUBE FEEDINGS

Effect	Drug type	Drug examples
Nausea, vomiting, diarrhea, or delayed gastric emptying (95)	Cholinergic blocking agents	Anistropine Atropine Glycopyrrolate Mepenzolate Psyphencyclimine Trihexyphenidyl
	Adrenergic agents	Isoproterenol Metaproterenol
	Drugs causing decreased motility	Aspirin in large doses Codeine Morphine Pentazocine
	Anti-infective agents	Erythromycin Griseofulvin Oxacillin (steatorrhea) Penicillin Piperazine Pyrantel
Nephrotoxic increases in creatinine, BUN (95)		Amphotericin B Capreomycin Cephalexin Colistimethate-colistin Cycloserine
Hypokalemia	Certain antibiotics	Capreomycin Clindamycin Para-aminosalicylic acid Penicillin Vimycin
Malabsorption	Certain antibiotics	Gentamicin Kanamycin Neomycin Paromomycin
Absorption of drug impaired by feedings with calcium, magnesium, and iron	An antibiotic	Tetracycline
Altered absorption and excretion of drug by tube feeding (96)		Captopril Carbamazepine Dicumarol Digoxin Griseofulvin Hydralazine Hydrochlorothiazide Isoniazid Metoprolol

(continued)

should never be opened and then left out to reach room temperature. Feeding administration sets should be changed daily (115).

4. ACTUAL NUTRIENT INTAKE

Patients' actual intake should be periodically evaluated and compared with the 1989 Recommended Dietary Allowances (122). Hospitalized patients do not always get the amount of tube feedings actually ordered. One study in a university hospital found that nasoenteric-tube-fed patients received only 61% of their mean caloric goals over a 6-week period (123). This underfeeding was due partially to physicians' ordering calculated energy needs only 75% of the time. Other reasons for halting infusion were tests, therapies, or complications.

TABLE 11.13. *CONTINUED*

Effect	Drug type	Drug examples
		Nitrofurantoin
		Penicillin
		Phenacitin
		Phenytoin suspension
		Procainamide
		Propranolol
		Rifampin
		Tetracycline
		Theophylline
Feeding problems if not added slowly and mixed vigorously (97)		Decadron elixir
		Elixophyllin
		Furadantin suspension
		Haldol liquid or drops
		Isoprel elixir
		Lomotil liquid
		Navane concentrate
		Sumycin syrup
		Theolair liquid
Drugs that will clog tubes if mixed with soy- or casein-based feedings (97)		Bactrim suspension
		Benadryl elixir
		Benadryl syrup
		Cephulac syrup
		Mellaril solution
		Mylicon drops
		Phenergan syrup
		Thorazine concentrate
Interactions with feedings that contraindicate their combination with tube feedings in any way		Cibalith-S syrup
		Dimetane elixir
		Dimetapp elixir
		Feosol elixir
		KCl 10% and 20% liquid
		Klorvess syrup
		Lanoxin syrup
		Mandelamine suspension (98)
		Mellaril oral solution (99)
		Neo-Calglucon syrup
		Organidin elixir
		Robitussin expectorant
		SSKI (potassium iodide oral solution)
		Sudafed syrup

REFERENCES

1. Kane, R. E., Hobbs, P. J., and Black, P. G.: Comparison of low, medium and high carbohydrate formulas for nighttime enteral feedings in cystic fibrosis patients. JPEN 14:47, 1990.
2. Berner, Y., Morse, R., et al.: Vitamin plasma levels in long-term enteral feeding patients. JPEN 13:525, 1989.
3. Souba, W. W., Smith, R. J., and Wilmore, D. W.: Glutamine metabolism by the intestinal tract. JPEN 9:608, 1985.
4. Deitch, E. A., and Bridge, R. M.: Effect of stress and trauma on bacterial translocation from the gut. J Surg Res 42:536, 1987.
5. Whatley, K., Turner, W., et al.: Transpyloric passage of feeding tubes. Nutr Supp Ser 3 (July):18, 1983.
6. Grant, J., Curtas, M., and Kelvin, F.: Fluoroscopic placement of nasojejunal feeding tubes with immediate feeding using a non-elemental diet. JPEN 7:300, 1983.
7. Kirby, D., Craig, R., et al.: Percutaneous endoscopic gastrostomies: A prospective evaluation and review of the literature. JPEN 10:155, 1987.
8. Ponsky, J. L., Gauderer, M. W., et al.: Percutaneous approaches to enteral alimentation. Am J Surg 149:102, 1985.
9. Ho, C. S., Gray, R. R., et al.: Percutaneous gastrostomy for enteral feeding. Radiology 156:349, 1985.
10. Gottried, E. B., and Plumser, A. B.: Endoscopic gastrojejunostomy: A technique to establish small bowel feeding without laparotomy. Gastrointest Endosc 30:355, 1984.
11. Chung, R. S.: Percutaneous endoscopic gastrostomy and jejunostomy by a single pass of the endoscope. Am J Surg 154:541, 1987.
12. Meer, J.: Inadvertent dislodgment of nasoenteral feeding tubes: Incidence and prevention. JPEN 11:187, 1987.
13. Raff, M., Cho, S., and Dale, R.: A technique for positioning nasoenteral feeding tubes. JPEN 11:210, 1987.
14. Culpepper, J., Veremakis, C., and Guntupalli, K.: Malpositioned naso-gastric tube causing pneumothorax and bronchopleural fistula. Chest 81:389, 1982.
15. Ryan, J., and Page, C.: Intrajejunal feeding: Development and current status. JPEN 8:187, 1984.
16. Methany, N., Eisenberg, P., and Spies, M.: Monitoring patients with nasally placed feeding tubes. Heart Lung 14:285, 1985.
17. Orr, G., Wade, J., et al.: Alternatives to total parenteral nutrition in the critically ill patient. Crit Care Med 8:29, 1980.
18. Rombeau, J. L., and Barot, L. R.: Enteral nutrition therapy. Surg Clin N Am 61:605, 1981.
19. Dobbie, R. P., and Butterick, O. D., Jr.: Continuous pump tube enteral hyperalimentation: Use in esophageal disease. JPEN 1:100, 1977.
20. Evans, D., Di Sipio, M., et al.: Comparison of gastric and jejunal tube feedings. JPEN 4:79, 1980.
21. Rhode, C. L., and Braum, T. M.: Home enteral/parenteral nutrition therapy. Chicago: American Dietetic Association, 1986.
22. Rombeau, J. L., and Palacio, J. C.: Feeding by tube enterostomy. In Rombeau, J. L., and Caldwell, M. D.: Enteral and tube feeding. Philadelphia: W. B. Saunders, 1990.
23. Wills, J., Oglesby, J., and Burke, W.: Percutaneous gastrostomy: A safe, cost-effective alternative to surgical gastrostomy and intravascular hyperalimentation. Nutr Supp Ser 6 (Feb.):10, 1986.
24. Tanker, M. S., Scheinfeldt, B. D., et al.: A prospective randomized study comparing surgical gastrostomy and percutaneous endoscopic gastrostomy. Gastrointest Endosc 32:144, 1986.
25. Shellito, P. C., and Malt, R. A.: Tube gastrostomy: Techniques and complications. Ann Surg 201:180, 1985.
26. Deveney, K. E.: Endoscopic gastrostomy and jejunostomy. In Rombeau, J. L., and Caldwell, M. D.: Enteral and tube feeding. Philadelphia: W. B. Saunders, 1990.
27. Ryan, J. A., and Page, C. P.: Intraje-junal feeding: Development and current status. JPEN 8:187, 1984.
28. Sagar, S., Harland, P., and Shield, R.: Early postoperative feeding with elemental diet. Br Med J 66:727, 1979.
29. Mitchell, H. H.: A method of determining the biological value of protein. J Biol Chem 58:873, 1924.
30. Oser, B. L.: Method for integrating essential amino acid content in the nutritional evaluation of protein. J Am Diet Assoc 27:396, 1951.
31. Krey, S. H., and Lockett, G. M.: Enteral nutrition: A comprehensive overview. In Krey, S. H., and Murray, R. L.: Dynamics of nutrition support: Assessment, implementation, evaluation. East Norwalk, Conn.: Appleton-Century-Crofts, 1986.
32. Davenport, H. W.: Physiology of the digestive tract. 4th ed. Chicago: Year Book Medical Publishers, 1977.
33. Macburney, M. M., Russell, C., and See Young, L.: Formulas. In Rombeau, J. L., and Caldwell, M. D.: Enteral and tube feeding. Philadelphia: W. B. Saunders, 1990.
34. Wilson, W. S., and Meinert, J. K.: Extracellular hyperosmolarity secondary to high protein nasogastric tube feeding. Ann Intern Med 47:585, 1957.
35. Engel, F. L., and Jaeger, C.: Dehydration with hypernatremia, hyperchloremia, and azotemia complicating nasogastric tube feeding. Am J Med 17:196, 1954.
36. Cramer, L. M., Haverback, C. Z., and Smith, R. R.: Hypertonic dehydration complicating high protein nasogastric tube feeding. Med Ann D C 27:331, 1958.
37. Gault, M. H., Dixon, M. E., et al.: Hypernatremia, azotemia, and dehydration due to high protein tube feeding. Ann Intern Med 68:778, 1968.
38. Bell, S. J., Pasulka, P. S., and Blackburn, G. L.: Enteral formulas. In Skipper, A.: Dietitian's handbook of enteral and parenteral nutrition. Rockville, Md.: Aspen, 1989.
39. Krey, S. H., and Murray, R. L.: Modular and transitional feedings.

In Rombeau, J. L., and Caldwell, M. D.: Enteral and tube feeding. Philadelphia: W. B. Saunders, 1990.

40. Calloway, D., and Spector, H.: Nitrogen balance as related to caloric and protein intake in active young men. Am J Clin Nutr 2:405, 1954.

41. Matarese, L.: Enteral alimentation. In Fischer, J. E.: Surgical nutrition. Boston: Little, Brown, 1983.

42. Margen, S.: Evaluation of efficacy. In Fischer, J. E.: Surgical nutrition. Boston: Little, Brown, 1983.

43. Bell, S. J., Pasulka, P. S., and Blackburn, G. L.: Enteral formulas. In Skipper, A.: Dietitian's handbook of enteral and parenteral nutrition. Rockville, Md.: Aspen, 1989.

44. Hearne, B., Besser, P., et al.: In vitro flow rates of enteral solutions through nasoenteric tubes. JPEN 8:456, 1984.

45. Hopeful, A., and Herrman, V.: Developing a formulary for enteral nutrition products. Am J Hosp Pharm 39:1514, 1982.

46. Heff, N.: Enteral tube feeding system: A benefit to all concerned. Nutr Supp Ser 3 (Jan.):25, 1983.

47. Lysen, L. K.: Enteral feeding tubes. Port St. Lucie, Fla.: 1990 (self-published).

48. Burr, I., O'Niel, J., et al.: Comparison of the effects of total parenteral nutrition, continuous intragastric feeding, and portacaval shunt on a patient with type I glycogen storage disease. J Pediatr 85:792, 1974.

49. Taylor, K. B., and Anthony, L. E.: Clinical nutrition. New York: McGraw-Hill, 1983.

50. Silberman, H., and Eisenberg, D.: Parenteral and enteral nutrition for the hospitalized patient. East Norwalk, Conn.: Appleton-Century-Crofts, 1983.

51. Del Rio, O., Williams, K. and Miller, B.: Handbook of enteral nutrition. El Segundo, Calif.: Medical Specifics, 1982.

52. Dean, R. E.: Enteral feeding: A practical approach. Chicago: Pluribus Press, 1983.

53. MacFadyen, B., Copeland, E., III, and Dudrick, S. J.: Surgery and oncology. In Schneider, H. A., Anderson, C. E., and Coursin, D. B.: Nutritional support of medical practice. 2d ed. Philadelphia: Harper and Row, 1983.

54. Carpenter, Y. A.: Indications for nutritional support. Gut 27 (Supp 1):14, 1986.

55. Sigal, R. K., and Daly, J. M.: Enteral nutrition in the cancer patient. In Rombeau, J. L., and Caldwell, M. D.: Enteral and tube feeding. Philadelphia: W. B. Saunders, 1990.

56. Fearon, K., and Calman, K.: Methods of nutritional support for cancer patients. Clin Oncol 5:319, 1986.

57. Raymond, J.: The nutritional care of Barney Clark: A case study. Summerville, N.J.: Biosearch Medical Products, 1983.

58. Heymsfield, S. B.: Cardiac cachexia. Paper presented at the 4th Clinical Congress of the American Society for Parenteral and Enteral Nutrition, Jan. 1979, and at "Malnutrition in Hospitalized Patients," Harvard Medical School, Boston, May 13, 1980.

59. Nelson, L., Carmichael, H., et al.: Use of an elemental diet (Vivonex) in the management of bile acid induced diarrhea. Gut 18:792, 1977.

60. Keith, R.: Effect of a low fat elemental diet on pancreatic secretion during pancreatitis. Surg Gynecol Obstet 151:337, 1980.

61. Howard, L. J., Michalek, A. V., and Alger, S. A.: Enteral nutrition and gastrointestinal, pancreatic, and liver disease. In Rombeau, J. L., and Caldwell, M. D.: Enteral and tube feeding. Philadelphia: W. B. Saunders, 1990.

62. May, R., Nath, B., and Schapir, R.: Altered gut absorption in disease. In Fischer, J. E.: Surgical nutrition. Little, Brown, 1983.

63. Koretz, R. L.: Nutritional support: How much for how much? Gut 27 (Supp 1): 85, 1986.

64. Dunn, E., Moore, E., and Jones, T.: Nutritional support of the critically ill patient. Surgery 153:45, 1981.

65. Moore, E.: Enteral elemental nutrition in major trauma. Contemp Surg 28:18, 1986.

66. Hirschberg, R. R., and Kopple, J. D.: Enteral nutrition and renal disease. In Rombeau, J. L., and Caldwell, M. D.: Enteral and tube feeding. Philadelphia: W. B. Saunders, 1990.

67. Cerra, F., Upson, B., et al.: Branched chains support postoperative protein synthesis. Surgery 92:192, 1982.

68. Pinchcofsky-Devin, G., and Kaminshki, M. V.: Correlation of pressure sores and nutritional status. J Am Geriatr Soc 34:335, 1986.

69. Holmes, R., Macchiano, et al.: Combating pressure sores nutritionally. Am J Nurs 130:1, 1987.

70. Touger-Decker, R.: Development of an enteral formulary. Dietitians Nutr Supp 9 (4):5, 1988.

71. Irwin, C.: The decision making process for choosing an enteral formula. Dietitians Nutr Supp 9 (6):4, 1988.

72. Shronts, E. P.: Nutrition support dietetics—core curriculum, 1989. Silver Spring, Colo.: American Society for Parenteral and Enteral Nutrition, 1989.

73. Berezin, S., Medow, M. S., et al.: Home teaching of nocturnal nasogastric feeding. JPEN 12:392, 1988.

74. Heitkemper, M. E., Martin, D. L., et al.: Rate and volume of intermittent enteral feeding. JPEN 5:125, 1981.

75. Guenter, P., Jones, S., et al.: Administration and delivery of enteral nutrition. In Rombeau, J. L., and Caldwell, M. D.: Enteral and tube feeding. Philadelphia: W. B. Saunders, 1990.

76. Jones, B. S., Payne, S., and Silk, D. B.: Indications for pump assisted enteral feeding. Lancet 1:1057, 1980.

77. Jones, B. J. M.: Enteral feeding: Techniques of administration. Gut 27 (Supp 1):47, 1986.

78. Hiebert, J. M., Brown, A., et al.: Comparison of continuous versus intermittent tube feedings in adult burn patients. JPEN 5:73, 1981.

79. Gordon, A. M.: Enteral nutritional support: guidelines for tube feeding selection and placement. Postgrad Med 70 (5):155, 1981.

80. Rolandelli, R. H., DePaula, J. A., et al.: Critical illness and sepsis. In Rombeau, J. L., and Caldwell, M. D.: Enteral and tube feeding.

Philadelphia: W. B. Saunders, 1990.

81. Heymsfield, S. B., Hill, J. O., et al.: Energy expenditure during continuous intragastric infusion of fuel. Am J Clin Nutr 45:526, 1987.

82. Heymsfield, S. B., Casper, K., and Grossman, G. D.: Bioenergetic and metabolic response to continuous intermittent nasogastric feeding. Metabolism 36:570, 1987.

83. Grant, A., and DeHoog, S.: Nutritional assessment and support. 3d ed. Seattle: 1985 (self-published).

84. Wilson, M.: Cranberry juice or water? A comparison of feeding-tube irrigants. Nutr Supp Ser 7 (July):23, 1987.

85. McCrae, J. D., and Hall, N. H.: Current practices for home enteral nutrition. J Am Diet Assoc 89:233, 1989.

86. Silk, D. B. A.: Progress report: Fibre and enteral nutrition. Gut 30:246, 1989.

87. Brinson, R. R., and Kalts, B. E.: Hypoalbuminemia as an indicator of diarrhea incidence in critically ill patients. Crit Care Med 15:506, 1987.

88. Pesola, G. C., Hogg, J. E., et al.: Isotonic nasogastric tube feedings: Do they cause diarrhea? Crit Care Med 17:1151, 1989.

89. Shils, M. E.: Enteral nutrition by tube. Cancer Res 37:2432, 1977.

90. Matthews-Antosiewicz, L.: Antidiarrheal medications for use with tube feedings. Dietitians Nutr Supp 9 (4):9, 1988.

91. LaFrance, R. J., Miyagawa, C. I., and Youngs, C. H. F.: Pharmacotherapeutic considerations in enteral and parenteral therapy. In Lang, C. E.: Nutritional support in critical care. Rockville, Md.: Aspen, 1987.

92. Gora, M. L., Tschampel, M. M., and Visconti, J. A.: Considerations of drug therapy in patients receiving enteral nutrition. Nutr Clin Prac 4:101, 1989.

93. Ross Laboratories: Administering oral medications through an enteral feeding tube. Columbus, Ohio: Ross Laboratories, 1986.

94. Skipper, A.: Monitoring and complications of enteral feeding. In Skipper, A.: Dietitian's handbook of enteral

and parenteral nutrition. Rockville, Md.: Aspen, 1989.

95. Roe, D. A.: Handbook on drug and nutrient interaction. 4th ed. Chicago: American Dietetic Association, 1989.

96. Wright, B.: Enteral feeding tubes as drug delivery systems. Nutr Supp Ser 6 (Feb.):33, 1986.

97. Altman, E., and Cutie, A.: Compatibility of enteral products with commonly employed drug additives. Nutr Supp Ser 4 (Dec.):8, 1984.

98. Egging, P.: Enteral nutrition from a pharmacist's perspective. Nutr Supp Ser 7 (Apr.):17, 1987.

99. Olsen, K., Hiller, C., et al.: Effect of enteral feedings on oral phenytoin absorption. Nutr Clin Prac 4:176, 1989.

100. Melnik, G.: Pharmacologic aspects of enteral nutrition. In Rombeau, J. L., and Caldwell, M. D.: Enteral and tube feeding. Philadelphia: W. B. Saunders, 1990.

101. Niemier, P., Vanderveen, T., et al.: Gastrointestinal disorders caused by medication and electrolyte solution osmolality during enteral nutrition. JPEN 7:387, 1983.

102. Whatley, K., Turner, W., and Deys, M.: When does metoclopramide facilitate transpyloric intubation of weighted feeding tubes? JPEN 8:679, 1984.

103. Seifert, C., Cuddy, P., et al.: A randomized trial of metoclopramide's effects on the transpyloric intubation of weighted feeding tubes. Nutr Supp Ser 7 (July):11, 1987.

104. Kalfarentzos, F., Panagopoulos, K., and Androulakis, J.: Nasoduodenal intubation with the use of metoclopramide. Nutr Supp Ser 7 (Sept.):33, 1987.

105. Bauer, L.: Interference of oral phenytoin absorption by continuous nasogastric feedings. Neurology 34:132, 1984.

106. Saklad, J. J., Graves, R. H., and Sharp, W. P.: Interaction of oral phenytoin with enteral feedings. JPEN 10:322, 1986.

107. Ozuna, J., and Friel, P.: Effect of enteral tube feeding on serum phenytoin levels. J Neurosurg Nurs 16:289, 1984.

108. Valli, C., Schulthess, K., et al.: In-

teraction of nutrients with antacids: A complication during enteral tube feeding [letter]. Lancet 1:747, 1986.

109. Bauers, C.: Counseling the nutrition support patient. Nutr Supp Ser 3 (July):6, 1983.

110. Block, A.: Special needs of the home enteral patient. Nutr Supp Ser 3 (July):8, 1983.

111. Adams, M., and Wirsching, R.: Guidelines for planning home enteral feedings. J Am Diet Assoc 84:58, 1984.

112. Piepmeyer, J., Lichenstein, V., et al.: Tube feeding at home: A manual of instruction for home tube feeding care. Evansville, Ind.: Mead Johnson, 1982.

113. Allison, S. P.: Some psychological and physiological aspects of enteral nutrition. Gut 27 (Supp 1):18, 1986.

114. Heymsfield, S., Bethel, R., et al.: Enteral hyperalimentation: An alternative to central venous hyperalimentation. Ann Intern Med 90:63, 1979.

115. Matarese, L. E.: Standardized enteral nutritional support. Nutr Supp Ser 3 (Aug.):27, 1983.

116. Heff, N.: Enteral tube feeding system: A benefit to all concerned. Nutr Supp Ser 3 (Jan.):25, 1983.

117. Hostetler, C., Lipman, T., et al.: Bacterial safety of reconstituted continuous drip tube feeding. JPEN 6:232, 1982.

118. Mandal, J. M., Hamilton, B. W., et al.: A study of microbial contamination of enteral nutrient solutions. Nutr Supp Ser 5 (Apr.):58, 1985.

119. Fagerman, K., Davis, A., and Dean, R.: Quality control program for hospital-based enteral feeding solutions. Nutr Supp Ser 5 (Nov.):30, 1985.

120. Pemberton, L. B., Lyman, B., et al.: An evaluation of a closed enteral feeding system. Nutr Supp Ser 5 (Apr.):36, 1985.

121. Stegmayer, P.: Tube feeding hang times: HCFA, region IX, interim guidelines as of September 1987. U.S. Department of Health and Human Resources, Division of Health Standards and Quality, HS-207, Region IX, 100 Van Ness Ave., San Francisco, Calif., 1987.

122. Food and Nutrition Board, National Research Council: Recommended Dietary Allowances. 10th ed. Washington, D.C.: National Academy of Sciences, 1989.

123. Abernathy, G. B., Heizer, W. D., et al.: Efficacy of tube feeding in supplying energy requirements of hospital patients. JPEN 13:387, 1989.

124. The United States pharmacopeia, DI. 5th ed. Rockville, Md.: United States Pharmacopeial Conventions, 1985.

125. Physicians' desk reference. 40th ed. Oradell, N.J.: Medical Economics Co., 1986.

12.

PARENTERAL NUTRITION

SHEILA M. CAMPBELL, M.S., R.D., AND DIANA F. BOWERS, PH.D., R.D.

INTRODUCTION

The era of parenteral nutrition (PN) began in the late 1960s when Dudrick successfully adapted a technique of intravenous fluid infusion into large-diameter veins for delivery of nutritional solutions (1, 2). Before then, provision of adequate parenteral nutrients was not possible, because hypertonic nutritional solutions damage small peripheral veins. Since that initial innovation, continuing improvements in techniques, solutions, catheters, and devices have enhanced PN so that now the technique is commonly used in most hospitals. Many individuals in a variety of alternate-care and outpatient settings also benefit from PN.

INDICATIONS

1. CONDITIONS INDICATING USE OF PARENTERAL NUTRITION

Conditions in which PN has been used include protein-calorie malnutrition, malabsorption syndromes, neoplastic disease, major organ failure, enterocutaneous fistulas, and hypermetabolic states (3). Parenteral nutrition is frequently used when the gastrointestinal (GI) tract is dysfunctional because of obstruction or ileus following surgery, trauma, disease, or infection. Patients with a depressed gag reflex, resulting in an increased risk for pulmonary aspiration of gastric contents, also have traditionally been candidates for PN. Improvements in enteral feeding devices and techniques, however, plus development of specialized enteral formulas, fa-

cilitate enteral feeding of many patients who previously would not have tolerated enteral nutritional support (4–9). Recent evidence shows that the enteral route has benefits beyond simply providing adequate nutrients. Enterally administered nutrients help maintain GI mass and function (10, 11), minimize secretion of catabolic hormones (10, 11), attenuate stress-induced elevations in resting metabolic expenditure (10, 12), and help maintain immunocompetence (10–13). Because of these nonnutritional effects, enteral feeding should be used whenever possible.

In spite of this, PN remains the method of choice when adequate nutrients cannot be delivered by the enteral route, such as in patients with extreme short-bowel syndrome or severe malabsorption. Other indications for PN include conditions that require long-term gut rest. Patients suffering total obstruction of the GI tract or distal small-bowel fistulas may require PN. Other patients who may benefit from PN include individuals who cannot be safely intubated, such as persons with depressed levels of consciousness; patients in whom feeding tubes cannot be placed beyond the stomach; or patients with extremely edematous or friable bowel, precluding placement of feeding tubes during abdominal surgery. Additionally, patients suffering intractable vomiting or severe diarrhea due to medical condition or therapy may require PN (14). Finally, health care professionals should consider the parenteral route whenever enteral nutrition cannot be established or maintained within a period of 7 to 10 days (14).

2. CONDITIONS INDICATING THAT PARENTERAL NUTRITION IS UNNECESSARY OR UNDESIRABLE

Because of the known benefits of enteral feeding, PN should be reserved for patients who do not have functioning GI tracts or who cannot receive adequate nutrients enterally. Enteral nutrition remains the method of choice for patients with GI tract obstruction when feeding tubes can be placed distal to the obstruction.

Parenteral nutrition is undesirable immediately following injury, when energy needs are relatively low (the ebb phase) and the primary goal is patient stabilization. Parenteral nutrition also should not be considered when it cannot contribute to positive outcome.

A. Ebb Phase Cuthbertson characterized the metabolic response to sepsis or trauma as 2 distinct phases: the early ebb, or shock, phase, and the following flow, or catabolic, phase (15). During the ebb phase, glucose and fat mobilization occurs, associated with increased glucose oxidation, depressed fat oxidation, and depressed energy expenditure (table 12.1). Nordenstrom and Persson (16) concluded that, because of depressed energy expenditure, the ebb phase is not a problem of nutrition, so provision of hypocaloric 5% glucose in water suffices during this period. The ebb phase generally lasts 4 to 7 days following injury (15). If enteral feeding cannot be initiated, parenteral nutrition may be indicated during the flow phase, which is marked by significantly increased energy expenditure and fat oxidation.

TABLE 12.1. SUBSTRATE FLUX DURING EBB AND FLOW PHASES FOLLOWING INJURY

Process	Ebb phase	Flow phase
Energy expenditure	−	+
Glucose mobilization	++	+
Glucose oxidation	+	−
Fat mobilization	+	+
Fat oxidation	−	+

B. No Benefit to the Patient Patient outcome depends on a number of factors that must be considered when planning PN. When considering PN, clinicians must recognize the influence of the underlying disease. Poor clinical prognosis prior to initiation of PN may reduce the time patients can receive PN, thus decreasing their opportunity to achieve therapeutic benefit (18). Other factors, such as age, psychological state, available therapy, PN-associated risks, and the ability of PN to maintain or restore nutritional status, must be considered prior to initiation of sophisticated nutritional therapy (14, 19, 20).

i. Parenteral Nutrition of Less than 5 Days' Duration The use of PN for less than 5 to 10 days cannot improve nutritional status. During extremely short-term PN, the risks outweigh the benefits (14, 19, 20). Parenteral nutrition should not be instituted when the course of therapy is known to be less than 5 days.

ii. Terminal Illness Difficult ethical issues arise in regard to the use of PN for terminally ill patients. Shils states that PN has no place in prolonging life for the hopelessly ill patient (19), but each practitioner must make the decision to withhold or discontinue PN according to existing laws, patient comfort and wishes, and aggressiveness of medical therapy (17, 21). For these reasons, we cannot overemphasize the importance of thorough patient evaluation and of development of realistic nutritional goals for each patient prior to initiating PN.

ROUTE OF INTRAVENOUS ACCESS

Clinicians have defined 2 types of access for PN. Short-term catheters are intended for use during a period of days or up to 3 weeks. Long-term catheters are used for months to years, are made of different materials, and are placed using techniques different from those used for short-term catheters (22).

1. CENTRAL ACCESS

A. Percutaneous Catheters Percutaneous placement of single-lumen plastic catheters into the superior vena cava via the jugular or subclavian vein is a common method of obtaining short-term access for PN. Double- and triple-lumen central venous catheters, which allow simultaneous infusion of multiple solutions, are also available. Use of multiple-lumen catheters is increasing, especially for critically ill patients who often need more than one central line (23).

A major advantage of short-term catheters is ease of insertion. Physicians usually insert short-term central venous catheters, using local anesthesia during a bedside procedure. But because percutaneous catheters can serve as foci for infection, many clinicians limit their use to relatively short periods of time and specify that their use be limited to infusion of PN solutions (24).

B. Right-Atrial Indwelling Catheters Patients who require PN for longer periods need catheters especially designed to reduce complications and to withstand long-term use. Single- and double-lumen right-atrial indwelling catheters, commonly called Hickman or Hickman-Broviac catheters, were developed to provide vascular access for patients requiring long-term intravenous (IV) therapies. These catheters, made of biocompatible materials such as silicone or polyurethane, are less thrombogenic than catheters of other materials. Silicone and polyurethane resist bacteria and reduce the likelihood of catheter-associated infection. These catheters must be inserted by surgeons. In the operating room, surgeons tunnel the catheters subcutaneously for a distance prior to entering systemic circulation, thereby creating a physical barrier to infection. Right-atrial indwelling catheters feature cuffs that serve as mechanical barriers to the entrance of bacteria into systemic circulation. Tissue engrafts to the cuff, forming a seal that helps maintain the skin's protective barrier.

C. Implantable Infusion Ports Physicians use total implantable infusion ports to administer chemotherapy and long-term IV antibiotics (25). Some clinicians also use these devices to deliver long-term PN, because they believe that implanted ports have less potential for infection than conventional catheters. Some patients prefer infusion ports over indwelling catheters because the ports are small, easily concealed, comfortable, and simple to use (26).

Physicians can insert implantable infusion ports under local anesthesia, but proper placement of the catheter portion requires fluoroscopic visualization. Parenteral nutritional solutions are infused through a needle placed into the port's inlet system.

2. PERIPHERAL ACCESS

The availability of safe lipid emulsions makes delivery of PN through peripheral veins feasible. Isotonic lipid emulsions are less likely than hypertonic glucose solutions to sclerose small veins.

During peripheral PN, isotonic lipid emulsions are a major energy source. Ordinarily, during peripheral PN, lipid emulsions are infused simultaneously with amino acid–glucose solutions. Intravenous lipid emulsions are extremely concentrated sources of calories; 10% and 20% lipid emulsions provide 1.1 and 2.0 kcal/mL, respectively. This concentration is desirable because it keeps the total volume required to meet nutritional needs within tolerable limits.

Peripheral PN is desirable only for short-term support because peripheral access is more difficult to maintain than centrally delivered PN. Peripheral access sites must be frequently changed to prevent infiltration of solutions into subcutaneous tissue and to reduce incidence of phlebitis. Peripheral PN may not be ideal for malnourished patients, because they often do not have adequate peripheral veins for delivery of PN (27). Moreover, the cost-benefit ratio of peripheral PN may be difficult to justify, considering the associated complications, requirements for nursing care, and the high cost of lipid calories relative to the cost of glucose calories (28).

TEAM MANAGEMENT

The disciplines most consistently represented on teams responsible for nutritional support include medicine, surgery, clinical dietetics, nursing, and pharmacy. Representatives from social services, physical and occupational therapy, and other services may also participate in team management of patients.

In the past the roles of team members were clearly delineated. The team leader, usually a physician, had responsibility for directing and supervising team activities, evaluating candidates for nutritional therapy, placing catheters, and coordinating the development, implementation, and evaluation of nutritional therapy. The team dietitian performed nutritional assessments, estimated nutrient requirements, coordinated enteral nutrition, and documented nutrient intake. The team nurse was responsible for coor-

dinating nursing care, caring for venous and enteral access sites, and providing patient education and discharge planning. The pharmacist was accountable for safe, accurate, and efficient formulation of parenteral solutions and for monitoring drug therapy (29–31).

As Agriesti-Johnson (32) noted, however, nutrition support professionals have difficulty applying these narrowly defined role descriptions in their daily practice because responsibilities are not so clearly defined in the clinical setting. Controversies frequently occur when discipline functions overlap (33); "turf disputes" were relatively common during the formative years of many nutrition support teams. In spite of these issues, the nutrition support team has outlived any other multidisciplinary health care team (34). This longevity may be credited to the particular evolution experienced by nutrition support teams.

Individuals practicing on initial nutrition support teams began, out of necessity, to exchange information. They discovered that, for optimal functioning of the team, each member must have a practical working knowledge of nutritional and metabolic issues commonly encountered in the practice of nutrition support. Researchers have discerned that each member brings an important, discipline-specific process to the team, and all team members contribute to management of specialized nutritional support (35, 36). Successful teams consist of individuals who have a common core of knowledge and effectively share information to facilitate optimal patient care and team functioning.

Today nutrition support team dietitians must be able to perform a number of technical functions (37; see table 12.2). In addition, effective dietitians understand the team concept and contribute to team success and growth by communicating and readily sharing information with their nutrition support colleagues.

TABLE 12.2. FUNCTIONS PERFORMED BY NUTRITION SUPPORT TEAM DIETITIANS

Perform and evaluate nutritional assessments
Identify and interpret nutritional deficiencies
Assess energy and protein needs
Recommend mode of therapy
Prescribe enteral formulas
Formulate special enteral solutions
Determine composition of parenteral solutions
Obtain food tolerances and preferences
Monitor food intake
Coordinate transitional feedings
Monitor and recommend changes in nutritional therapy
Relate drugs to nutritional care
Evaluate nutrition products and devices
Develop standards and procedures for nutritional care
Participate in research

FORMULA DESIGN

1. DIFFERENCES IN NUTRIENT METABOLISM BETWEEN PARENTERAL AND ENTERAL ADMINISTRATION

The GI tract performs important functions of metabolic regulation, including nutrient digestion and absorption, secretion of hormones, control of intraorgan substrate flux, and enhancement of cell-mediated immunity. Through these processes, the GI tract protects the body from nutrient toxicities, inefficient use of substrates, and transfer of potential pathogens into systemic circulation. Because PN delivers nutrients directly into central veins, many of the GI tract's protective and regulatory functions are bypassed. The success of PN and of subsequent enteric refeeding depends largely on recognizing and understanding the alterations in metabolic processes and the effects of bypassing the GI tract (38–43).

A. Loss of First-Pass Effect   The liver is the primary organ responsible for processing, storing, and releasing nutrients. Given the liver's important role in nutrient metabolism, it is not surprising that it is the first organ in the GI tract located downstream in the portal blood supply (42). In a single pass, the liver normally extracts more than 75% of nutrients in the portal blood, allowing it to process all available nutrients. Parenterally administered nutrients, delivered directly into systemic circulation, prevent the first-pass effect. When this effect is bypassed, all organs have equal opportunity for nutrient uptake and utilization without benefit of hepatic detoxification, alteration, or metabolism of nutrients.

B. Absence of Regulatory Effect of Digestion and Absorption The GI tract regulates nutrient absorption. The small intestine absorbs amino acids and glucose via 3 mechanisms: simple diffusion, facilitated diffusion, and active transport (44). The gut also regulates the uptake of vitamins and minerals by specific absorptive mechanisms. The potential for nutrient toxicity exists with PN because the GI tract cannot regulate nutrient uptake. Moreover, lack of enteric stimulation leads to atrophy of intestinal mucosa, decreased mucosal mass (45), and reduced levels of mucosal digestive enzymes (38, 46, 47). The jejunum appears to be most affected by disuse atrophy (38). Gut hypoplasia associated with PN can apparently be minimized, however, by even token feeding of enteral formulas (47, 48).

C. The Gut as Endocrine Organ Researchers recognize that the gut is a major endocrine organ. Approximately 22 hormones secreted by the gut have been identified. Many of them respond to the presence of intraluminal nutrients by preparing the body for nutrient influx and regulating homeostatic control of nutrient metabolism (49, 50). When intraluminal nutrients are absent, as is usually the case during PN, the GI tract's hormo-

nal response is attenuated. When lack of hormonal response is combined with pancreatic hyposecretion, the potential for wide variations in homeostatic control, especially of levels of glucose and amino acids, is created (40, 51).

D. Pancreatic Hyposecretion Researchers have described pancreatic hyposecretion in patients receiving long-term PN (45, 52). Atrophy of pancreatic acinal cells and decreased secretion of pancreatic enzymes increase the potential for protein and fat malabsorption during enteral refeeding.

During PN the pancreas cannot be forewarned by the GI tract of impending substrate influx. Therefore, the insulin response to PN may be delayed and of varying intensity (40, 53). This phenomenon often makes control of serum glucose difficult as PN infusion rates change.

E. Parenteral Nutrition–Induced Stress Gastritis and Ulceration Intravenous infusion of amino acids significantly increases gastric acid production (54, 55), although simultaneous infusion of lipid emulsions reduces the effects of amino acids on gastric acid secretion (45). The combination of increased gastric acid production and decreased gastric mucosal thickness during PN increases the potential for stress gastritis and ulceration. Therefore, prophylactic therapy to neutralize intragastric acid is an important consideration during PN (45).

F. Immune Function Enteral feeding appears to protect immune response to septic challenge (56, 57). The presence of intraluminal nutrients is important in maintaining secretory immunoglobulin A (IgA), the principal component of the gut immune system (43). Secretory IgA prevents the uptake of enteric antigens and the binding of enterotoxins and microorganisms to intestinal microvilli.

PN eliminates enteral stimulation of the gut immune response and has been associated with depressed lymphocyte reactivity in rats (43, 58). Deitch has proposed that translocation of gut flora through atrophied gut mucosa into systemic circulation may be responsible for some bacteremias seen in patients on PN (59).

2. MACRONUTRIENTS

A. Protein Protein in PN is a mixture of essential and nonessential crystalline amino acids. Clinicians recommend that 40% of total amino acids be essential amino acids (60), and a balanced supply of nonessential amino acids should provide the remaining 60% for patients with normal kidney and liver function.

Amino acid solutions are available in concentrations ranging from 5.0% to 15% solutions. When combined with 500 mL of glucose and water solution to make 1 L of final PN solution, these amino acid concentrations supply from 27.5 to 50 g of protein/L, respectively. (Parenteral protein provides 4 kcal/g.)

Although exact nitrogen content varies among manufacturers, generally the nitrogen content of PN solutions can be calculated by dividing g protein/L by 6.25. The amount of nitrogen required varies according to metabolic state. Hill and Church found that 0.3 g nitrogen/kg body weight/day sufficiently spared body protein in patients following major elective surgery or moderate trauma (61).

Provision of adequate calories is a major factor in nitrogen utilization. The body catabolizes amino acids for energy, excreting the nitrogen when insufficient nonprotein calories are provided. Optimal calorie : nitrogen ratios vary with disease state and metabolic expenditure, although research suggests that a ratio of 150 : 1 meets the needs of most patients (62). Conversely, provision of nitrogen beyond the amount needed to achieve nitrogen balance does not enhance protein synthesis (63, 64) and may increase energy expenditure via diet-induced thermogenesis (65).

The benefits of specific amino acids in various conditions continue to be an area of active research. The ability of formulas enriched with branched-chain amino acids (BCAAS) to improve outcome in stress and trauma is controversial (66–69). Brennan and colleagues suggested that the benefits of using BCAA-enriched solutions in humans must be more clearly demonstrated before their use can be endorsed (69). Other areas of research include elucidation of optimal concentrations of taurine, glutamine, arginine, and alpha-keto analogues (70–74).

Amino acid solutions are available with and without added electrolytes. Amino acid solutions without electrolytes allow nutrition support practitioners greater flexibility in prescribing electrolytes when formulating PN solutions for critically ill patients.

B. Carbohydrate Monohydrous glucose, the most common parenteral carbohydrate source, provides 3.4 kcal/g. The hypertonicity of 50% glucose in water—2,525 milliosmoles (mOsm)—necessitates infusion of PN into large central veins (64, 75). Glucose may be used effectively as the only energy source (61, 76) or in varying concentrations with lipid emulsions (16, 77).

Hyperglycemia, hypoglycemia, hyperosmolar dehydration, hypophosphatemia, and essential-fatty-acid deficiency have been reported when glucose is used as the sole energy source (16, 60, 78). High concentrations of glucose may also induce fatty liver infiltration, increase production of carbon dioxide, and elevate catecholamine excretion (16). The sole use of glucose as an energy source may be contraindicated for patients with essential-fatty-acid deficiency, volume

overload, poorly controlled diabetes, or respiratory failure with hypercapnia (76).

Healthy adults need 2 g glucose/kg body weight/day. Glucose requirements approach 3 to 4 g/kg/day for acutely ill patients (16). Manufacturers recommend that the maximum infusion rate of hypertonic glucose not exceed 84 g/kg body weight/hr (75).

C. Lipid Lipid emulsions provide essential fatty acids and a concentrated energy source. Essential-fatty-acid deficiency can be prevented when as little as 8% of total nonprotein calories are provided by lipid (79). Commercially available lipid emulsions, prepared from safflower or soybean oil, provide only long-chain fatty acids (LCFAS) and are rich sources of linoleic and linolenic acids. Egg phospholipid is added as an emulsifying agent, and hypertonic glycerol is added to prevent the final solution from being hypotonic (80). Emulsions of 10% and 20% lipid are nearly isotonic and provide 1.1 and 2.0 kcal/mL, respectively. Lipid calories are between 5 to 15 times more expensive than glucose calories (28, 60, 76, 79). Because essential-fatty-acid deficiency takes approximately 3 weeks to develop, some clinicians delay administration of relatively costly lipid emulsions until the 3d week of PN (81).

In 1983 the Food and Drug Administration approved the addition of lipid emulsions to glucose–amino acid preparations (82). The resulting solutions are called total nutrient admixtures (TNAS). Prior to 1983, patients received lipid emulsions through peripheral veins or by simultaneous infusion with glucose–amino acid solutions into central venous lines.

The efficacy of substrate use, microbial safety, admixture limitations, and cost of TNA have been extensively studied (16, 28, 80, 83). Use of TNA avoids

the need for peripheral lines, eliminates central-line violations for lipid infusion, allows lipid infusion over 24 hours, decreases carbon dioxide production, and reduces hepatic accumulations of fat induced by long-term use of glucose (82).

Lipid emulsions may supply 30% to 50% of nonprotein calories, with glucose supplying the remainder. A minimum of 30% of total calories provided by glucose is required for efficient metabolism of fat. Clinicians often design PN solutions in which some carbohydrate calories are replaced by fat calories for patients who are hypercapnic or have abnormal glucose tolerance. The daily dosage of lipid should not exceed 2.5 g/kg body weight/day (84).

Alternate intravenous lipid emulsions are the subject of research. Parenteral administration of medium-chain triglycerides (MCTS) is currently being investigated (85–88). Unlike LCFAS, MCTS are readily transported into the mitochondria independent of carnitine and are not stored in adipose tissue (80). Fish-oil emulsions represent another potential lipid source for PN (80).

D. Energy Patients receiving PN rarely need more than 40 kcal/kg body weight/day (16, 60, 89, 90). Overfeeding has been associated with metabolic complications and contributes to the cost of PN (28, 91).

Reports have indicated that the Harris-Benedict equation may not be reliable for predicting energy needs in malnourished patients (92, 93). Likewise, indirect calorimetry may not be a useful method of energy assessment for some hospitalized patients (28, 94), possibly because of technical and logistical difficulties (95). Some authors believe that body weight is the best predictor of resting metabolic expenditure (93, 96). Regardless of the method used for initial estimation of energy needs, nutritional support professionals must routinely reassess caloric dose and make adjustments based on nitrogen balance, weight status, and progress toward therapeutic goals.

E. Computing Macronutrient Composition of PN Solutions The macronutrient content of conventional amino acid–dextrose PN solutions has a final concentration of 25% glucose and 4.25% crystalline amino acids.

i. Carbohydrate

- Check PN order sheet to determine the concentration of carbohydrate in the *final* solution (e.g., if 500 mL of 50% glucose is used to prepare 1 L of PN solution, the concentration of carbohydrate in the final PN solution is 25%). Glucose concentrations often used in PN solutions include 20%, 50%, and 70%.
- Multiply the volume of PN infused (in mL) and the concentration of carbohydrate in the PN solution to get grams of carbohydrate. For example, if a patient receives 1,225 mL of a PN solution that is 25% carbohydrate, approximately 306 g of carbohydrate will be provided (1,225 mL × 0.25 g carbohydrate/mL = 306.25 g carbohydrate).

The caloric content of carbohydrate is usually considered to be 4 kcal/g. Because the carbohydrate source of PN solutions is monohydrous glucose, however, a value of 3.4 kcal/g is used to compute its caloric contribution. Using the example of the standard PN solution described above, the carbohydrate calories provided in 1 L can be computed by multiplying the grams of carbohydrate by 3.4 kcal/g:

250 g carbohydrate/L × 3.4 kcal/g = 850 carbohydrate kcal/L

ii. Protein Grams of protein provided in 1 L of standard PN solution can be computed similarly

- Check PN order sheet to determine the concentration of amino acids in the *final* solution (e.g., if 500 mL of 8.5% amino acid solution is used to prepare 1 L of PN solution, the concentration of amino acids in the final PN solution is 4.25%). Amino acid concentrations often used in PN solutions include 5.5%, 8.5%, and 10%.
- Multiply the volume of PN infused (in mL) and the concentration of amino acids in the PN solution to get grams of amino acids. For example, if a patient receives 1,225 mL of a PN solution that is 4.25% amino acids, approximately 52 g of protein will be provided (1,225 mL × 0.0425 g protein/mL = 52.06 g protein).

The caloric content of protein is 4 kcal/g.

iii. Lipid Intravenous lipid emulsions are sources of concentrated calories and essential fatty acids. Lipid emulsions can be infused separately from glucose–amino acid PN solutions, or they can be added to the PN solution. Lipid emulsions are commercially available in 500-mL volumes in 10% and 20% concentrations. Emulsions of 10% lipid provide 1.1 kcal/mL; 20% lipid emulsions provide 2.0 kcal/mL. Dietitians can compute the caloric contribution of 500 mL of 10% lipid emulsion by multiplying the volume infused and the caloric density/mL:

500 mL of 10% lipid emulsion × 1.1 kcal/mL = 550 kcal

or

500 mL of 20% lipid emulsion × 2.0 kcal/mL = 1,000 kcal

Dietitians can compute the grams of fat provided by lipid emulsions by dividing calories the lipid emulsion provides by 9 kcal/g fat. For example:

$$\frac{550 \text{ kcal}}{9 \text{ kcal/g fat}} = 61.1 \text{ g fat}$$

3. MICRONUTRIENTS

A. Vitamins Vitamins are vital cofactors in metabolic pathways involved in nutrient use, protein synthesis, and maintenance of host defenses. Initially, clinicians supplemented PN solutions with varying amounts of vitamins. In 1979 the Nutritional Advisory Group (NAG) of the American Medical Association published guidelines for intravenous vitamin dosages in response to reports of deficiencies and concern over potential toxicities (97). These vitamin doses (table 12.3) are based on the Recommended Dietary Allowances (RDAS) but also consider the possibility of increased needs or toxicities. The NAG recommendations do not exceed 2 times the RDA of the vitamins. Some clinicians have questioned the adequacy of these doses for malnourished, critically ill patients (98). But because the medical literature contains little information on vitamin needs during stress, hypermetabolism, anabolism, or PN in general,

TABLE 12.3. DAILY INTRAVENOUS VITAMIN DOSAGES RECOMMENDED BY NAG

Vitamin	Dosage
Vitamin A	3300.0 IU
Vitamin D	200.0 IU
Vitamin E	10.0 IU
Thiamine	3.0 mg
Riboflavin	3.6 mg
Niacin	40.0 mg
Pantothenic acid	15.0 mg
Pyridoxine	4.0 mg
Vitamin C	100.0 mg
Folic acid	400.0 mcg
Vitamin B-12	5.0 mcg
Biotin	60.0 mcg

Source: American Medical Association, Department of Foods and Nutrition (97). Copyright © 1979 by the American Society of Parenteral and Enteral Nutrition.

the NAG guidelines are almost universally applied.

A variety of conditions can affect vitamin needs of patients, necessitating alteration in vitamin dosages. Fat-soluble vitamins may require supplementation when malabsorption, pancreatic insufficiency, or resection of the GI tract interfere with absorption and metabolism. Acute illness, infection, negative nitrogen balance, adsorption of vitamins to tubing, and use of fat as a calorie source may also elevate need for fat-soluble vitamins (99–101). Patients with renal failure may require less than the NAG-suggested dosage of vitamin A (102) and vitamin D (103), because of the kidney's impaired function.

Dosages of many water-soluble vitamins are related to energy and protein intake. But patients suffering from pre-existing malnutrition, disease, injury, infection, resection of the GI tract, and excessive fluid losses from wounds or fistulas may require amounts that vary from the NAG recommendations (104–106).

B. Electrolytes   When planning doses of calcium, magnesium, phosphorus, acetate, chloride, potassium, and sodium, nutrition support professionals must consider nutritional needs, nonrenal fluid losses, and replacement of pre-existing deficits (107). Because electrolyte needs are dynamic, appropriate dosing requires careful monitoring of serum chemistries and correlation with fluid, renal, and clinical status.

Rudman et al. have suggested optimal electrolyte : nitrogen ratios to promote anabolism (108). Every gram of nitrogen retained must be accompanied by 800 mg phosphorus, 3.9 mEq sodium, 3.0 mEq potassium, 2.5 mEq chloride, and 1.2 mEq calcium (108). Suggested amounts of parenteral electrolytes are given in table 12.4.

TABLE 12.4. SUGGESTED DAILY INTRAVENOUS ELECTROLYTE DOSAGES

Electrolyte	Dosage (mEq/24 hours)
Calcium	6–25
Magnesium	10–45
Phosphorus	30–60
Acetate	20–40
Chloride	105–125
Potassium	100–120
Sodium	70–120

C. Trace Elements and Conditionally Essential Nutrients   Iodine, cobalt, zinc, copper, and possibly chromium and manganese are essential micronutrients for humans. Selenium, molybdenum, vanadium, nickel, tin, and silicon are also found in small amounts in human tissue (109). The essentiality of many trace elements was proved when they were not included in early PN solutions and deficiency syndromes resulted. In 1979 the NAG published recommended intravenous dosages for trace elements (110; see table 12.5). The NAG based its guidelines on established oral requirements for trace elements and on the amount normally absorbed from the GI tract. Under conditions of excessive loss

TABLE 12.5. DAILY INTRAVENOUS TRACE ELEMENT DOSAGES RECOMMENDED BY NAG

Trace element	Dosage
Zinc	2.5–4.0 mg
Copper	0.5–1.5 mg
Chromium	10.0–15.0 mcg
Manganese	0.15–0.8 mg

Source: American Medical Association, Department of Foods and Nutrition (110). Copyright © 1979 by the American Medical Association.

or need or in the case of some pathological processes, nutrition support professionals may need to provide doses that differ from the NAG recommendations.

i. Zinc   Zinc deficiency was the first and most frequently reported trace element deficiency. Symptoms of zinc deficiency—anorexia, diarrhea, dermatitis, psychological changes, and alopecia—can develop within 4 to 8 weeks. Patients may require more than the NAG-suggested dose for zinc during acute illness, injury, and anabolism and especially in the face of marginal zinc nurture or large diarrheal or GI fluid losses (111, 112). Because GI fluids are rich in zinc, their zinc content should be measured to facilitate replacement. When losses can't be quantified, clinicians may use the amounts given in table 12.6 as guides (112). Zinc is toxic in amounts more than 50 times the recommended dosage.

ii. Copper   Patients rarely develop copper deficiency unless their PN solutions contain no copper or they have excessive GI losses. Deficiency symptoms include anemia, leukopenia, and neutropenia resistant to iron, folate, or B-12 supplementation. The NAG suggested a range for parenteral copper dosage of 500 to 1,500 mcg/day. Some researchers believe that 300 mcg/day is a more appro-

TABLE 12.6. SUGGESTED DOSAGES FOR ZINC REPLACEMENT

Condition	Zinc dosage
Catabolism	+ 2.0 mg/day
Small-bowel losses	+ 12.2 mg/L small-bowel fluid/day
Stool or ileostomy losses	+ 17.1 mg/kg stool/day

priate copper dose. Because copper is stored and excreted mainly by the liver, patients with cholestatic liver disease should receive less than the NAG-suggested dosages (113).

iii. Chromium Chromium deficiency is rare. Symptoms of chromium deficiency—glucose intolerance, weight loss, and neuropathy—may take as long as 2 to 3 years to appear (114).

iv. Manganese Only one case of manganese deficiency has been reported (115). Symptoms of deficiency—low prothrombin, low clotting times, and hair, skin, and nail changes—appeared after 4 months of feeding solely a chemically defined enteral diet. Manganese toxicity following injection has been reported (116). Patients with hepatic disease should be closely monitored because bile is the major excretory route for manganese (114).

v. Selenium Clinicians did not recognize selenium as an essential trace element when the NAG issued its recommendations in 1979. Now health care professionals recognize that patients on long-term nutritional support require selenium supplementation in the range of 40 to 160 mcg/day (117, 118). Fistula, urinary, and wound losses increase selenium requirements (119). Cardiomyopathy and muscle pain, which are symptoms of selenium deficiency, may appear following 6 to 24 months of deficient intake. Selenium toxicity has been reported, and because selenium is excreted mainly in the urine, patients with kidney dysfunction should be closely monitored (119).

vi. Conditionally Essential Nutrients Researchers have postulated that some nutrients are conditionally essential. They suggest that, in some pathologic conditions or in cases of unusual need,

nutrients normally synthesized by the body must be supplied by exogenous sources (119). Tyrosine, cysteine, taurine, choline, and carnitine have been classified as conditionally essential nutrients (120, 121).

PROBLEM SOLVING

Complications associated with PN can be categorized as mechanical, metabolic, and septic. Improvements in catheter design and in methods of insertion and care, plus increased experience, have reduced the incidence of complications associated with PN.

1. MECHANICAL COMPLICATIONS

Clinicians have termed the mechanical problems arising from catheter insertion as technical complications (table 12.7) because these problems appear secondary to difficulties encountered during catheter placement (122). Technical complications may occur because physicians insert catheters without the benefit of visualization. Injury to the adjacent structures may occur during cathe-

TABLE 12.7. TECHNICAL COMPLICATIONS ASSOCIATED WITH CATHETER PLACEMENT

Catheter malposition
Pneumothorax
Hemothorax
Hydrothorax
Chylothorax
Air embolism
Catheter embolism
Thrombosis
Artery laceration
Arteriovenous fistula
Injury to the phrenic, vagus, brachial
    plexus, or laryngeal nerves
Cardiac arrhythmias
Cardiac perforation with tamponade

ter placement because of their proximity to the point of insertion (123).

Other mechanical difficulties are associated with relatively long-term use of catheters. These difficulties include in vivo catheter breakage and separation, hub fracture, formation of fibrin sheaths, thrombogenesis, catheter compression, and occlusion (23, 124–128).

Physicians note that the incidence of technical complications depends largely on clinician experience and familiarity with techniques of catheter insertion (122). Adequately preparing the patient prior to catheter placement and using direct visualization whenever possible facilitate atraumatic insertion. Physicians frequently place central lines during emergency situations for resuscitation and monitoring, but more technical complications are likely to occur during emergency insertions than during elective catheter placement (129). For these reasons, PN should be initiated only after the patient has been stabilized.

Many problems associated with in vivo catheter breakage, cracking, and separation have been solved by catheter redesign. Changes in procedures for placement and care have also reduced the frequency of these problems (23, 129).

The formation of fibrin sheaths and thrombi is of concern because of their association with pulmonary emboli and catheter occlusion. Thrombogenesis during PN is related to the presence of catheters in the venous system. Catheter material, size, and softness; PN pH, osmolarity, and composition of solution; duration of infusion; and presence of bacteria contribute to thrombogenesis (130–131). Host factors implicated in thrombus formation include immobilization, congestive heart failure, sepsis, and the hypercoagulability of malignant disease (132). Using routine heparin flushes, adding heparin to the infusate, and avoiding placement of catheters through the relatively small cephalic vein, help reduce the potential of thrombogenesis (126–134).

Treatment of central venous thrombosis includes removal of the catheter and, if symptoms persist, anticoagulation therapy (122). Some authors have reported successful use of streptokinase to restore function to catheters occluded by fibrin sheaths (127).

2. METABOLIC COMPLICATIONS

Metabolic complications frequently arise from an excess or deficiency of substrates and from disorders of glucose metabolism. The composition and administration of PN solutions have improved as a result of increased understanding of nutrient metabolism in disease states. Thus many previously reported metabolic complications do not occur. In addition, improved patient monitoring by nutrition support teams has helped reduce the occurrence and severity of metabolic complications (135–137). An example of a monitoring schedule for patients receiving PN is given in table 12.8.

The etiology, prevention, and treatment of some of the most common metabolic complications are described in this section.

A. Glucose Patients with normal insulin response metabolize 0.4 to 1.2 g glucose/kg/hr (135, 136). Normally, insulin production increases 4 to 6 times over basal production within 6 hours after initiating glucose infusion. When PN infusion rates are slowly advanced, patients can tolerate up to 1,500 g of glucose per day (136).

Diabetes mellitus, sepsis, shock, elective operations, major trauma, and advanced age decrease glucose tolerance. Unchecked hyperglycemia due to abnormal glucose tolerance can lead to hyperglycemic, hyperosmolar, nonketotic

coma. This condition results from dehydration due to osmotic diuresis. Symptoms include disorientation, stupor, and convulsions, leading to coma and death. During this condition, serum glucose levels may exceed 1,000 mg/dL, with serum osmolarities greater than 350 mOsm/L. If hyperglycemic, hyperosmolar, nonketotic coma develops, PN should be stopped immediately, and a solution of hypoosmolar saline and regular insulin begun. The goal is to slowly reduce serum glucose levels, allowing equilibration of body fluids (136).

Hyperglycemia can be controlled by reducing infusion rate, using appropriate substrates, and, if necessary, giving exogenous insulin. Replacing some carbohydrate calories with fat calories is a useful strategy. Exogenous insulin can be given as a separate, continuous infusion, as a component of the PN solution, or on a sliding-scale basis (138, 139).

Glucose tolerance should be monitored by frequently evaluating blood glucose levels and serum osmolality. Blood glucose levels should be measured frequently until the caloric goal is reached and blood sugar levels are stable. Patients receiving exogenous insulin require frequent monitoring until the final PN solution, infusion rate, and insulin dosage are achieved. The avail-

ability of bedside capillary blood glucose monitoring obviates reliance on urine glucose measurements. Serum osmolality should be measured initially and evaluated frequently until patients are stable.

Patients may become hypoglycemic following abrupt discontinuation of PN. Serum glucose levels can drop below normal within 30 to 60 minutes after stopping PN. Clinical symptoms of hypoglycemia include headache, sweating, thirst, disorientation, paresthesias, convulsions, and eventual coma (136). Treatment of hypoglycemia includes administration of 50% glucose in water until symptoms subside. Tapering the PN flow rate prior to discontinuation facilitates a decrease in endogenous insulin secretion, preventing hypoglycemia. Exogenous insulin should also be adjusted along with the rate of PN infusion when discontinuing PN (135, 136).

B. Potassium Potassium is required to maintain intracellular tonicity, nerve transmission, cardiac muscle contraction, renal function, glucose uptake and metabolism, and anabolism. A potassium : nitrogen of 3.5 : 1 to 4.0 : 1 is required for optimal protein synthesis (140). Patients suffering from starvation, alcoholism, or excessive diarrheal, intestinal, biliary, or renal fluid losses, as

TABLE 12.8. SUGGESTED MONITORING SCHEDULE FOR PARENTERAL NUTRITION

Parameter	Frequency[a]
Blood glucose	Every 6 hours
Vital signs	Every 8 hours
Serum electrolytes, BUN, serum creatinine, and serum calcium and phosphorus	Daily
Serum magnesium, liver enzymes, and bilirubin	Every other day
Serum triglycerides, cholesterol, and albumin; 24-hour urinary urea nitrogen	Once weekly
Estimation of nutrient intake	Daily
Fluid intake and output	Daily
Body weight	Daily

[a]Frequency can be decreased once patient has stabilized.

well as individuals treated with diuretics, corticosteroids, L-dopa, and potassium-wasting antibiotics (penicillin, ampicillin, carbenicillin, nafcillin, and tricarcillin) have potential for hypokalemia. Serum potassium levels are significantly influenced by shifts in acid-base balance. Metabolic and respiratory acidosis reduce renal potassium excretion, causing serum potassium levels to increase, whereas the opposite result is seen with metabolic and respiratory alkalosis. Correction of underlying acid-base disorders contributes to improved serum potassium levels.

Clinical symptoms of hypokalemia appear when serum potassium levels reach 3 mEq/L. Common clinical symptoms include vomiting, peritoneal distension, acute muscle weakness, reduced reflexes, paralysis, paresthesia, dyspnea, hypotension, cardiac arrhythmias, decreased glomerular filtration, and polydipsia (141). Treatment of hypokalemia requires correction of the underlying cause and replacement of potassium.

Potassium requirements can be evaluated from serum potassium, although urinary potassium concentration provides a more accurate estimation of total body potassium status. The kidney normally excretes 40 mEq potassium/L. Lower concentrations indicate a deficit.

C. Phosphate   Glucose metabolism and the synthesis of protein, ATP, DNA, and membrane components increase phosphate requirements during PN. Patients who have chronic weight loss, abuse alcohol, or receive chronic antacid or diuretic therapy are more likely to be phosphate depleted. They require repletion prior to initiating PN (136, 142). Symptoms of hypophosphatemia—progressive lethargy, muscle weakness, anorexia, paresthesias, and long-bone pain—begin when serum phosphate levels fall below 1 mg/dL (135, 136). Hypophosphatemia causes increased oxygen-to-hemoglobin affinity, decreased

tissue oxygen transfer, shortened survival of red blood cells and platelets, and reduced myocardial function. Impaired white-blood-cell chemotaxis and phagocytosis caused by hypophosphatemia may increase host susceptibility to infection (135–137). Hypophosphatemia may also worsen fatty liver infiltration (142).

Hypophosphatemia may be avoided during PN by repleting serum phosphorus levels prior to beginning nutritional support (143). Initially, serum phosphorus should be monitored at least 3 times per week. The frequency of testing can be reduced after achieving the optimal PN rate.

D. Magnesium   Synthesis of new tissue increases magnesium requirements. Persons normally require 0.3 to 0.35 mEq magnesium/kg/day. During PN, 0.5 mEq of magnesium is needed for each gram of nitrogen used for protein synthesis (136, 137). When serum magnesium levels fall below 1 mEq/L, clinical symptoms may develop. Symptoms of hypomagnesemia include muscle weakness, depression, apathy, nausea, vomiting, and irritability (134, 135). Magnesium deficiency can be avoided by providing at least 0.35 to 0.45 mEq/kg/day.

Excessive magnesium can produce symptoms such as drowsiness, weakness, nausea, vomiting, and cardiac arrhythmias. Severe hypermagnesemia may cause hypotension, coma, and cardiac arrest. To prevent toxicity or deficiency, magnesium levels should be monitored once a week. Patients with renal failure require evaluation twice weekly.

E. Carbon Dioxide Retention   Carbon dioxide is a normal product of metabolism. Patients with sepsis or impaired pulmonary function, however, may be unable to clear carbon dioxide adequately (136). These patients may develop hypercapnia when they are overfed or when glucose is their only

energy source. Elevated serum carbon dioxide levels result in compensatory increase in minute ventilation. Increases in minute ventilation may exacerbate pulmonary dysfunction or impede weaning from mechanical ventilation (135). Carbon dioxide production may be minimized by providing 40% to 50% of calories as fat and by prudently estimating total energy need.

F. Azotemia   Although a number of aberrations in protein metabolism have been reported (135, 136, 144), the most common is azotemia. Prerenal azotemia occurs when excessive amounts of amino acids are infused without sufficient calories. In these cases, amino acids are used for energy rather than for protein synthesis. When that occurs, the body excretes the nitrogen from amino acids and uses the remaining carbon skeleton for energy. Dehydration worsens azotemia, and vice versa. Patients with azotemia and dehydration may develop progressive lethargy and eventually coma. Prerenal azotemia can be prevented by maintaining appropriate calorie : nitrogen ratios and adequate hydration. Monitoring body weight, fluid balance, and serum blood urea nitrogen is useful in preventing prerenal azotemia.

G. Complications of Fat Metabolism
Essential-fatty-acid deficiency (EFAD) can develop within 3 to 6 weeks of initiating fat-free PN. The well-described symptoms of EFAD include scaliness and dryness of the skin, hair loss, impaired wound healing, hepatomegaly, and bone changes (136). Biochemical findings include low serum levels of linoleic and arachidonic acids and increased eicosatrienoic acid. The serum triene : tetraene ratio becomes greater than 0.4 with EFAD. Provision of a minimum of 4% of total calories as fat, or 500 mL of 10% lipid emulsion once or twice a week can prevent EFAD (135, 136).

Fat overload syndrome has been described during use of lipid emulsions.

Symptoms include hyperlipidemia, respiratory distress, hemolytic anemia, platelet dysfunction, and renal failure (136, 145, 146). Sepsis and stress can significantly alter the ability to metabolize exogenous fat. Therefore serum triglyceride and cholesterol concentrations (indices of fat mobilization and utilization) should be interpreted considering clinical condition (147). Regular monitoring of plasma triglyceride and cholesterol concentrations before and after lipid infusions is recommended (147).

H. Liver Enzymes   Changes in liver enzyme levels are sometimes seen in patients receiving PN. Elevations in serum glutamic-oxaloacetic transaminase (SGOT), serum glutamic-pyruvic transaminase (SGPT), alkaline phosphatase, and sometimes bilirubin may occur within 5 to 7 days after initiation of PN (135, 136, 148). The etiology of the changes is unclear, although they are probably multifactorial in origin. Several pathogenic mechanisms have been proposed. Excessive glucose or lipid administration, EFAD, impaired bile flow, or deficiency of specific amino acids may play a role (135). Excessive carbohydrate infusion or an imbalance between glucose and amino acid content of PN solutions has caused fatty infiltration of the liver in animals (142, 149). Ineffective lipid disposal due to abnormalities in transport lipoproteins, often seen in protein malnutrition, can exacerbate fatty infiltration of the liver.

Administration of balanced PN solutions that provide appropriate caloric doses may help prevent elevations in liver enzymes. Serum liver enzyme levels should be monitored at least once a week during PN.

3. SEPTIC COMPLICATIONS

In an excellent review of infection control related to PN, Williams (150) described factors responsible for sepsis associated with PN. Catheter-related factors include direct entry of microorganisms on the skin to systemic circulation, and "seeding" of the intravascular portion of the catheter from distant infections. Bacteria from distant infections may also colonize the fibrin sheath that often forms on the distal intravascular catheter.

Using PN catheters for other procedures requiring central venous access significantly increases the potential for catheter-related sepsis (151). Critically ill patients frequently require more than one central line, and the development of multilumen catheters has obviated the need to place bilateral central lines or violate PN catheters in these patients. Unfortunately, the infection rate associated with use of multiple-lumen catheters is 3 times that with use of single-lumen catheters (152, 153). This increased infection rate may be due to the number of ports available for manipulation (154).

Microbial contamination of PN solutions is another potential source of infection. Parenteral nutritional solutions can become contaminated at any point from compounding to administration.

Prevention of septic complications is best accomplished by a team approach to patient selection, catheter insertion and care, administration of PN solutions, and monitoring of therapy. Development and adherence to standard protocols for catheter placement, patient care, and maintenance of the PN administration system, along with meticulous quality control during and after admixture, are vital to maintaining infection rates to within tolerable limits (150).

HOME PARENTERAL NUTRITION

An increasing number of patients who are unable to meet their nutritional requirements either orally or enterally for a prolonged period of time are receiving parenteral nutrition at home. This approach is used for patients with severe forms of short-bowel syndrome, Crohn's disease, radiation enteritis, disturbed intestinal motility, certain malignancies, congenital bowel disease, fistulas, intestinal obstruction, and malabsorptive and diarrheal disorders. It should be used only if the GI tract is not functional or usable and the patient is otherwise well enough to be managed at home. The patient or family must be able to carry out the various procedures necessary in administering PN (155–157).

Home administration of PN can greatly reduce medical costs as compared with inpatient care. It also allows long-term patients to live in their home environment. Education of the patient and caregiver is of vital importance to minimize complications. Frequently, monitoring is also still necessary to tailor PN to individual and changing needs (158).

TRANSITION TO ENTERAL AND ORAL FEEDING

Feeding via the GI tract is safer, easier to administer, and more economical than PN (48). It also confers physiological benefits not seen with PN (10–13). Enteric feeding should begin as soon as GI function allows. The presence of bowel sounds, passage of flatus and/or stool, and decreased gastric residuals indicate readiness for enteral feeding. Intestinal disuse atrophy, pancreatic hyposecretion, and altered hormone secretion and action resulting from the absence of intraluminal nutrients have a major impact on initial tolerance of enteric feedings. The GI tract quickly responds to enteric refeeding. Ideally, patients should be weaned from PN gradually as enteric feeding progresses, to ensure continued adequate intake during the transition period.

Gastric motility may be decreased in patients maintained on PN, despite the return of bowel function (159). This delay may be due to decreased secretions of gut hormones into the gastric antrum and proximal duodenum, central nervous system disorders, or drug therapy such as digoxin, morphine, or other narcotics (159). Symptoms of reduced gastric motility include abdominal distention, anorexia, mild emesis, or severe reflux with possible pulmonary aspiration. Because endotracheal intubation does not prevent pulmonary aspiration of gastric contents, gastric residuals should be frequently monitored. Tube-fed patients with gastric dysmotility should be positioned upright at least 30° during and 1 hour following formula infusion to prevent pulmonary aspiration. Duodenal or jejunal feeding should be used whenever possible. Feeding a low-fat formula, decreasing feeding volume or frequency, or using metaclopramide may improve gastric motility.

Diarrhea often occurs with enteric refeeding. Osmotic diarrhea may occur because of malabsorption resulting from reductions in pancreatic or mucosal fluids (159). Increased water flux across the bowel wall due to decreased plasma oncotic pressure (160) or drug therapy may also cause osmotic diarrhea. Secretory diarrhea most frequently occurs because of bacterial enterotoxins but can also result from neoplasms or from the presence of bile acids in the large bowel due to ileal resection or use of stimulatory laxatives. If diarrhea develops, stool assays for electrolytes and osmolality should be obtained to determine the type of diarrhea (161).

Secretory diarrhea due to bacterial enterotoxins is usually treated with specific antibiotics (162). The management of osmotic diarrhea requires further investigative work to determine the etiology. Osmolality of formula and the rate and site of administration influence the appearance of osmotic diarrhea resulting from disuse atrophy of the intestine and from pancreatic hyposecretion. Enteric refeeding rapidly reverses mucosal atrophy; mucosal proliferation has been demonstrated as early as 4 hours following refeeding (38), with return to

normal within 30 hours of enteric refeeding (163).

Successful refeeding by tube results from careful initiation, monitoring, and progression. During oral refeeding, patients may benefit from numerous, low-fat, small meals to reduce symptoms due to reduced gastric motility. Metaclopramide may enhance gastric emptying during oral refeeding. Until intestinal enzymes and pancreatic secretions normalize, an ideal oral diet consists of bland foods that are low in residue, lactose, and fat. Commercial lactose-free supplements can be used to enhance the nutrient content of the diet. Dietary progression can advance fairly rapidly, according to patient tolerance. Patients benefit from frequent monitoring of tolerance of and progress with enteric refeeding.

Hypoproteinemia and hypoalbuminemia may precipitate diarrhea associated with enteral feeding (164–166). Hypoalbuminemia contributes to decreases in plasma oncotic pressure, allowing secretory filtration of fluid and proteins into the intestinal lumen. Animal studies have shown that administration of hydrolyzed enteral formulas significantly reduce diarrhea associated with hypoalbuminemia (160). Other therapies for hypoalbuminemia-associated diarrhea include use of hypoosmolar, isotonic, or fiber-supplemented formulas and use of stool bulking agents. Intravenous administration of albumin has also been suggested until endogenous synthesis can recover (167). Albumin concentration is only one of many contributors to oncotic pressure. Albumin administration should be closely monitored to assess its therapeutic benefit. If no positive outcome is observed within 2 days, this expensive treatment should be discontinued.

Many necessary drug therapies cause diarrhea unrelated to the refeeding process. Manipulation of enteric feeding in these cases has little impact in resolving diarrhea. Diarrheal loss of nutrients may

be reduced, however, by altering feeding schedules so that feedings are not given immediately before or after administration of diarrhea-inducing medications.

SUMMARY

Dr. Stanley Dudrick is credited with innovations in the late 1960s that made PN a viable method of nutritional support. Inpatients and outpatients who cannot consume adequate nutrients by the enteric route—e.g., persons with severe malabsorption syndromes—may benefit from PN. PN is useful when long-term gut rest is required, as in the case of inflammatory bowel disease, total obstruction of the GI tract, and distal small-bowel fistulas. Additionally, PN is useful for patients who need nutritional support but for whom enteral nutrition cannot be established or maintained within a period of 7 to 10 days.

Methods of parenteral access include those acceptable for short-term access and those for long-term access. Central lines can be placed percutaneously or in the operating room. Clinicians use peripheral lines mainly for short-term PN because peripheral access sites must be frequently changed to prevent phlebitis.

The macronutrient sources in PN solutions include protein in the form of amino acids. Amino acid solutions are commercially available in 5% to 15% solutions. Hypertonic glucose (providing 3.4 kcal/g) and 10% or 20% lipid emulsions (providing 1.1 and 2.0 kcal/g, respectively) are the major energy sources in PN solutions. Vitamins and trace elements are usually added in amounts consistent with NAG guidelines. When planning electrolyte dosages, nutrition support professionals must consider nutritional needs, nonrenal fluid losses, and replacement of preexisting deficits.

A team approach facilitates patient management. Cooperation between a variety of disciplines—including medicine, surgery, clinical dietetics, nursing, pharmacy, and other allied health professions—reduces mechanical, metabolic, and septic complications associated with PN. Routine monitoring of patients receiving PN also reduces complications and facilitates evaluation of progress toward nutritional goals.

Refeeding via the GI tract requires a careful dietary approach known as transitional feeding. This regimen is necessary to prevent GI symptoms of intolerance arising from reduced nutrient absorptive surface and reduced production of digestive enzymes associated

with prolonged NPO periods.

PN can be a life-saving therapy, but it is associated with complications that are best managed through a team approach and routine monitoring of tolerance to therapy and progress toward nutritional goals.

REFERENCES

1. Dudrick, S. J., Wilmore, D. W., et al.: Long-term total parenteral nutrition with growth, development and positive nitrogen balance. Surgery 64:134, 1968.
2. Dudrick, S. J., Wilmore, D. W., et al.: Can intravenous feeding as the sole means of nutrition support growth in the child and restore weight loss in an adult? An affirmative answer. Ann Surg 169:974, 1969.
3. Grant, J.: Handbook of total parenteral nutrition. Philadelphia: W. B. Saunders, 1980.
4. Gallo, S., Ramirez, A., et al.: Endoscopic placement of enteral feeding tubes. JPEN 9:747, 1985.
5. Nelson, R., and Nyhus, L. M.: A new tube for simultaneous gastric decompression and jejunal alimentation. Surg Gynecol Obstet 160:369, 1985.
6. Chernoff, R.: Enteral nutritional support. In Finn, S. C.: Nutritional support systems. Hosp Material Man Quart (Feb.):26, 1986.
7. Skipper, A.: Specialized formulas for enteral nutrition support. J Am Diet Assoc 86:654, 1986.
8. Pagana, K. D.: Preventing complications in jejunostomy tube feedings. Dimen Crit Care Nurs 6:28, 1987.
9. Kelly, K. M., Lewis, B., et al.: Use of percutaneous gastrostomy in the intensive care patient. Crit Care Med 16:62, 1988.
10. Mochizuki, H., Trocki, O., et al.: Mechanism of prevention of postburn hypermetabolism and catabolism by early enteral feeding. Ann Surg 200:297, 1984.
11. Saito, H., Trocki, O., et al.: The effect of route of nutrient administration on the nutritional state, catabolic hormone secretion, and gut mucosal integrity after burn injury. JPEN 11:1, 1987.
12. McArdle, A. H., Palmason, C., et al.: Protection from catabolism in major burns: A new formula for the immediate enteral feeding of burn patients. J Burn Care Rehabil 4:245, 1983.

13. Dominioni, L., Trocki, O., et al.: Prevention of severe postburn hypermetabolism and catabolism by immediate intragastric feeding. J Burn Care Rehabil 5:106, 1984.
14. ASPEN Board of Directors: Guidelines for use of total parenteral nutrition in the hospitalized adult patient. JPEN 10:441, 1986.
15. Cuthbertson, D. P.: Observations on the disturbance of metabolism produced by injury to the limbs. Quart J Med 1:233, 1932.
16. Nordenstrom, J., and Persson, E.: Energy supply during total parenteral nutrition—how much and what source? Acta Anaesthesiol Scand 29:95, 1985.
17. Abbott, W. C., Echenique, M. M., et al.: Nutritional care of the trauma patient. Surg Gynecol Obstet 157:585, 1983.
18. Chang, R. W. S., Hatton, I., et al.: Total parenteral nutrition: A four year audit. Br J Surg 73:656, 1986.
19. Shils, M. E.: Guidelines for total parenteral nutrition. JAMA 220:1721, 1972.
20. Goodgame, J. T.: A critical assessment of the indications for total parenteral nutrition. Surg Gynecol Obstet 151:433, 1980.
21. Steinbrook, R., and Lo, B.: Artificial feeding—solid ground, not a slippery slope. N Engl J Med 318:286, 1988.
22. Wachs, T., Watkins, S., and Hickman, R. O.: "No more pokes": A review of parenteral access devices. Nutr Supp Ser 7 (June):12, 1987.
23. Kaufman, J. L., Rodriguez, J. L., et al.: Clinical experience with the multiple lumen central venous catheter. JPEN 10:487, 1986.
24. McCarthy, M. C., Shives, J. K., et al.: Prospective evaluation of single and triple lumen catheters in total parenteral nutrition. JPEN 11:259, 1987.
25. Ross, M. N., Haase, G. M., et al.: Comparison of totally implanted reservoirs with external catheters as venous access devices in pediatric oncologic patients. Surg Gynecol Obstet 167:141, 1988.
26. Beck, S. L., Rose, N. R., and Zago-

ren, A. J.: Home total parenteral nutrition utilizing implantable infusion ports: A retrospective review. Nutr Clin Prac 2:26, 1987.
27. Fleming, R. C., and Nelson, J.: Nutritional options. In Kinney, J. M., Jeejeebhoy, K. N., et al.: Nutrition and metabolism in patient care. Philadelphia: W. B. Saunders, 1988.
28. Mirtallo, J. M., Powell, C. R., et al.: Cost-effective nutrition support. Nutr Clin Prac 2:142, 1987.
29. Grant, J.: Handbook of total parenteral nutrition. Philadelphia: W. B. Saunders, 1980.
30. Niemiec, P. W.: The nutrition support team structure at the Medical University of South Carolina. In Chernoff, R.: Interrelationships of dietary and pharmacy services in nutrition support. Report of the 4th Ross Roundtable on Medical Issues. Columbus, Ohio: Ross Laboratories, 1983.
31. Driscoll, D. F., Galvin, M., et al.: Nutritional support teams and services. In Finn, S. C.: Nutritional support systems. Hosp Material Man Quart (Feb.):16, 1986.
32. Agriesti-Johnson, C.: Nutrition-support team survey. In Training for dietitians working in critical care. Report of the 6th Ross Roundtable on Medical Issues. Columbus, Ohio: Ross Laboratories, 1985.
33. Thobaben, M.: Nurse/social worker home care. Home Healthcare Nurse 6:37, 1988.
34. Luther, R. W.: Evolution of the nutrition support team. In Chernoff, R.: Interrelationships of dietary and pharmacy services in nutrition support. Report of the 4th Ross Roundtable on Medical Issues. Columbus, Ohio: Ross Laboratories, 1983.
35. Johnson, C., Steinbaugh, M., and Dwyer, K.: Shared functions of nutritional support team members. Nutr Supp Ser 7 (Aug.):24, 1987.
36. Agriesti-Johnson, C., Dwyer K., and Steinbaugh, M.: Nutrition support practice: A study of factors inherent in the delivery of nutrition support services. JPEN 12:130, 1988.
37. ASPEN: Standards of practice for nu-

trition support dietitians. Nutr Clin Prac 5:74, 1990.

38. Bristol, J. B., Williamson, R. C. N., and Chir, M.: Nutrition, operations, and intestinal adaptation. JPEN 12:299, 1988.

39. Buchan, A. M. J., Green, K. A., et al.: The effect of total parenteral nutrition in the rat on a sub-group of enteroendocrine cells. Reg Peptides 11:347, 1985.

40. Greenberg, G. R., Wolman, S. L., et al.: Effect of total parenteral nutrition on gut hormone release in humans. Gastroenterology 80:988, 1981.

41. Souba, W. W.: The gut as a nitrogen-processing organ in the metabolic response to critical illness. Nutr Supp Ser 8 (May):15, 1988.

42. Souba, W. W., Smith, R. J., and Wilmore, D. W.: Glutamine metabolism by the intestinal tract. JPEN 9:608, 1985.

43. Alverdy, J., Chi, H. S., and Sheldon, G. F.: The effect of parenteral nutrition on gastrointestinal immunity; the importance of enteral stimulation. Ann Surg 202:681, 1985.

44. Stevens, B. R., Kaunitz, J. D., and Wright, E. M.: Intestinal transport of amino acids and sugars: Advances using membrane vesicles. Ann Rev Physiol 46:417, 1984.

45. Levine, G. M., Deren J. J., et al.: Role of oral intake in maintenance of gut mass and disaccharidase activity. Gastroenterology 67:975, 1974.

46. Wilson, J.: Gastrointestinal dysfunction in the critically ill: Nutritional implications. Compr Ther 11:45, 1985.

47. Roche, A. F., ed.: The gastrointestinal response to injury, starvation, and enteral nutrition. Report of the 8th Ross Conference on Medical Research. Columbus, Ohio: Ross Laboratories, 1988.

48. Heymsfield, S. B., Bethel, R. A., et al.: Enteral hyperalimentation: An alternative to central venous hyperalimentation. Ann Intern Med 90:63, 1979.

49. Roehrig, K. L.: Carbohydrate biochemistry and metabolism. Westport, Conn.: AVI, 1984.

50. Johnson, L. R.: The trophic action of gastrointestinal hormones. Gastroenterology 70:278, 1976.

51. McIntyre, N., Holdsworth, C. D., and Turner, D. S.: Intestinal factors in the control of insulin secretion. J Clin Endocrinol Metab 25:1317, 1965.

52. Kotler, D. P., and Levine, G. M.: Reversible gastric and pancreatic hyposecretion after long-term total parenteral nutrition. N Engl J Med 300:241, 1979.

53. Burt, M. E., Gorschboth, C. M., and Brennan, M. F.: A controlled, prospective, randomized trial evaluating the metabolic effects of enteral and parenteral nutrition in the cancer patient. Cancer 49:1092, 1982.

54. Isenberg, J. I., and Maxwell, V. M.: Intravenous infusion of amino acids stimulates gastric acid secretion in man. N Engl J Med 298:27, 1978.

55. American Academy of Pediatrics, Committee on Nutrition: Commentary on parenteral nutrition. Pediatrics 71:547, 1983.

56. Kudsk, K. A., Carpenter, G., et al.: Effect of enteral and parenteral feeding in malnourished rats with *E. coli*–hemoglobin adjuvant peritonitis. J Surg Res 31:105, 1983.

57. Kudsk, K. A., Stone, J. M., et al.: Enteral and parenteral feeding influences mortality after hemoglobin–*E. coli* peritonitis in normal rats. J Trauma 23:605, 1983.

58. Birkhahn, R. H., and Renk, C. M.: Immune response and leucine oxidation in oral and intravenous fed rats. Am J Clin Nutr 39:45, 1984.

59. Deitch, E. A.: Systemic translocation of gut bacteria: A mechanism of nosocomial infection. Paper presented at the 11th Clinical Congress of the American Society for Parenteral and Enteral Nutrition, New Orleans, Feb. 1987.

60. Macfie, J.: Towards cheaper intravenous nutrition. Br Med J 292:107, 1986.

61. Hill, G. L., and Church, J.: Energy and protein requirements of general surgical patients requiring intravenous nutrition. Br J Surg 71:1, 1984.

62. Long, C. L., Schaffel, N., et al.: Metabolic response to injury and illness: Estimation of energy and protein needs from indirect calorimetry and nitrogen balance. JPEN 3:452, 1979.

63. Ang, S. D., Leskiw, M. J., and Stein, T. P.: The effect of increasing total parenteral nutrition on protein metabolism. JPEN 7:525, 1983.

64. Veech, R. L.: The toxic impact of parenteral solutions on the metabolism of cells: A hypothesis for physiological parenteral therapy. Am J Clin Nutr 44:519, 1986.

65. Stanier, M. W., Mount, L. E., and Bligh, J.: Energy balance and temperature regulation. Cambridge: Cambridge University Press, 1984.

66. Blackburn, G. L., Moldawer, L. L., et al.: Branched chain amino acid administration and metabolism during starvation, injury, and infection. Surgery 86:307, 1979.

67. Downey, R. S., Karl, I. E., and Bier, D. M.: Branched-chain amino acid interactions in skeletal muscle: Isoleucine and L-alloisoleucine. JPEN 10:456, 1986.

68. Cerra, F. B., Mazuski, J. E., et al.: Branched chain metabolic support. Ann Surg 199:286, 1984.

69. Brennan, M. F., Cerra, F., et al.: Report of a research workshop: Branched-chain amino acids in stress and injury. JPEN 10:446, 1986.

70. Geggel, H. S., Ament, M. E., et al.: Nutritional requirements for taurine in patients receiving long-term parenteral nutrition. N Engl J Med 312:142, 1985.

71. Rassin, D. K., and Malloy, M. H.: Taurine requirement with parenteral nutrition. N Engl J Med 313:120, 1985.

72. Hwang, T. L., O'Dwyer, T. S., et al.: Preservation of small bowel mucosa using glutamine-enriched parenteral nutrition. Surg Forum 37:56, 1986.

73. Barbul, A., Wasserkrug, H. L., et al.: Optimal levels of arginine in maintenance intravenous hyperalimentation. JPEN 8:281, 1984.

74. Walser, M.: Rationale and indications for the use of alpha-keto analogues. JPEN 8:37, 1984.

75. Hypertonic dextrose injection, USP. Package insert. McGraw Laboratories, New York, Aug. 1977.

76. Clouse, R. E., and Alpers, D. H.: Energy sources for total parenteral nutrition patients: Would sugar suffice? Gastroenterology 87:226, 1984.

77. Baker, J. P., Detsky, A. S., et al.: Randomized trial of total parenteral nutrition in critically ill patients: Metabolic effects of varying glucose-lipid ratios as the energy source. Gastroenterology 87:53, 1983.

78. Harper, P. H., Royle, G. T., et al.: Total parenteral nutrition: Value of a standard feeding regimen. Br Med J 286:1323, 1983.

79. Adult parenteral nutrition: Which preparation? Drug Ther Bull 18:85, 1981.

80. Trimbo, S. L., and Valicenti, A. J.: What's new in parenteral lipids. Nutr Supp Ser 6 (May):18, 1986.

81. Roberts, D., Thelen, D., and Weinstein, S.: Parenteral and enteral nutrition—a cost benefit audit. Minn Med 65:707, 1982.

82. Driscoll, D. F., Bistrian, B. R., et al.: Practical considerations regarding the use of total nutrient admixtures. Am J Hosp Pharm 43:416, 1986.

83. Driscoll, D. F., Bistrian, B. R., et al.: Base solution limitations and patient-specific TPN admixtures. Nutr Clin Prac 2:160, 1987.

84. Intralipid 10% IV fat emulsion. Package insert. KabiVitrum, Alameda, Calif., 1987.

85. Cotter, R., Taylor, C. S., et al.: A metabolic comparison of a pure long-chain triglyceride lipid emulsion (LCT) and various medium-chain triglycerides (MCT-LCT) combination emulsions in dogs. Am J Clin Nutr 45:927, 1987.

86. Bradley, J. E., Brown, C., and Brown, R. O.: Use of intravenous fat emulsions during total parenteral nutrition in glucose-intolerant patients. Nutr Clin Prac 1:136, 1986.

87. Record, K. E., Kolpeck, J. H., and Rapp, R. P.: Long chain versus medium chain length triglycerides. Nutr Clin Prac 1:129, 1986.

88. Wicklmayr, M., Rett, K., et al.: Comparison of metabolic clearance rates of MCT/LCT and LCT emulsions in diabetes. JPEN 12:68, 1988.

89. Askanzi, J., Carpentier, Y. A., et al.: Influence of total parenteral nutrition on fuel utilization in injury and sepsis. Ann Surg 191:40, 1980.

90. Barot, L. R., Rombeau, J. L., et al.: Caloric requirements in patients with inflammatory bowel disease. Ann Surg 195:214, 1982.

91. Weinsier, R. L., and Krumdieck, C. L.: Death resulting from overzealous total parenteral nutrition: The refeeding syndrome revisited. Am J Clin Nutr 34:393, 1980.

92. Roza, A. M., and Shizgal, H. M.: The Harris-Benedict equation reevaluated: Resting energy requirements and the body cell mass. Am J Clin Nutr 40:168, 1984.

93. Quebbeman, E. J., and Ausman, R. K.: Estimating energy requirements in patients receiving parenteral nutrition. Arch Surg 117:1281, 1982.

94. Livesey, G., and Elia, M.: Estimation of energy expenditure, net carbohydrate utilization and net fat oxidation and synthesis by indirect calorimetry: Evaluation of errors with special reference to the detailed composition of fuels. Am J Clin Nutr 47:608, 1988.

95. Campbell, S. M., and Kudsk, K. A.: "High tech" metabolic measurements: Useful in daily clinical practice? JPEN 12:610, 1988.

96. De Boer, J. O., van Es, A. J. H., et al.: Energy requirements and energy expenditure of lean and overweight women, measured by indirect calorimetry. Am J Clin Nutr 46:13, 1987.

97. American Medical Association, Department of Foods and Nutrition: Multivitamin preparations for parenteral use: A statement by the Nutritional Advisory Group. JPEN 3:260, 1979.

98. Dempsey, D. T., Mullen, J. L., et al.: Treatment effects of parenteral vitamins in total parenteral nutrition patients. JPEN 11:229, 1987.

99. Lowry, S. F., Goodgame, J. T., et al.: Parenteral vitamin requirements during intravenous feeding. Am J Clin Nutr 31:2149, 1978.

100. Lowry, S. F.: Vitamin requirements of intravenously fed man. J Environ Pathol Toxicol Oncol 5:91, 1985.

101. Riggle, M. A., and Brandt, R. B.: Decrease of available vitamin A in parenteral nutrition solutions. JPEN 10:388, 1986.

102. Gleghorn, E. E., Eisenberg, L. D., et al.: Observations of vitamin A toxicity in three patients with renal failure receiving parenteral alimentation. Am J Clin Nutr 44:107, 1986.

103. Satomura, K., Seino, Y., et al.: Renal 25-hydroxyvitamin D3-1-hydroxylase in patients with renal disease. Kidney Internat 34:712, 1988.

104. Inculet, R. I., Norton, J. A., et al.: Water soluble vitamins in cancer patients on parenteral nutrition: A prospective study. JPEN 11:243, 1987.

105. Nicholds, G. E., Meng, H. C., and Caldwell, M. D.: Vitamin requirements in patients receiving total parenteral nutrition. Arch Surg 112:1061, 1977.

106. Hoffman, F. A.: Micronutrient requirements of cancer patients. Cancer 55:295, 1985.

107. Mirtallo, J. M.: Parenteral therapy. In Lang, C. E.: Nutritional support in critical care. Rockville, Md.: Aspen, 1987.

108. Rudman, D., Millikan, W. J., et al.: Elemental balances during intravenous hyperalimentation of underweight adult subjects. J Clin Invest 55:94, 1975.

109. Burch, R. E., Millikan, W. J., et al.: Trace elements in human nutrition. Med Clin N Am 63:1057, 1979.

110. American Medical Association, Department of Foods and Nutrition: Guidelines for essential trace elements for parenteral use. JAMA 241:2050, 1979.

111. Takagi, Y., Okada, A., et al.: Clinical studies on zinc metabolism during total parenteral nutrition as related to zinc deficiency. JPEN 10:195, 1986.

112. Wolman, S. L., Anderson, H., et al.: Zinc in total parenteral nutrition: Requirements and metabolic effects.

Gastroenterology 76:458, 1979.

113. Solomons, N. W.: Biochemical, metabolic, and clinical role of copper in human nutrition. J Am Coll Nutr 4:83, 1985.

114. Danford, D. A.: Essential trace elements in total parenteral nutrition. Clin Cons Nutr Supp 4:1, 1984.

115. Doisy, E. A.: Effects of deficiency in manganese upon plasma levels of clotting proteins and cholesterol in man. In Hoekstra, W. G., Suttie, J. U., et al.: Trace elements: Metabolism in animals. Baltimore: University Park Press, 1974.

116. National Nutrition Consortium: Vitamin-mineral safety, toxicity, and misuse. Chicago: American Dietetic Association, 1978.

117. Shils, M. E.: Historical aspects of minerals and vitamins in parenteral nutrition. Fed Proc 43:1412, 1984.

118. Lane, H. W., Lotspeich, C. A., and Moore, E. C.: The effect of selenium supplementation on selenium status of patients receiving chronic total parenteral nutrition. JPEN 11:177, 1987.

119. Hunt, D. R., Lane, H. W., et al.: Selenium depletion in burn patients. JPEN 8:695, 1984.

120. Rudman, D., and Feller, A.: Evidence for deficiencies of conditionally essential nutrients during total parenteral nutrition. J Am Coll Nutr 5:101, 1986.

121. Bailey, L. B.: Carnitine. In Baumgartner, T. G.: Clinical guide to parenteral micronutrition. Melrose Park, Ill.: Educational Publications, 1984.

122. Warner, B. W., and Bower, R. H.: Complications of therapy. In Lang, C. E.: Nutritional support in critical care. Rockville, Md.: Aspen, 1987.

123. Fischer, J. E.: Nutritional support in the seriously ill patient. Curr Probl Surg 17:527, 1980.

124. Rubenstein, R. B., Alberty, R. E., et al.: Hickman catheter separation. JPEN 9:754, 1985.

125. Fleming, C. R., Barham, S. S., et al.: Analytical assessment of broviac catheter occlusion. JPEN 9:314, 1985.

126. Fabri, P. J., Mirtallo, J. M., et al.: Incidence and prevention of thrombosis of the subclavian vein during total parenteral nutrition. Surg Gynecol Obstet 155:238, 1982.

127. Cassidy, F. P., Zajko, A. B., et al.: Noninfectious complications of long-term central venous catheters: Radiologic evaluation and management. Am J Roentgenology 149:671, 1987.

128. Rubenstein, R. B., Alberty, R. E., et al.: Hickman catheter separation. JPEN 9:754, 1985.

129. Bernard, R. W., and Stahl, W. M.: Subclavian vein catheterizations: A prospective study. 1. Non-infectious complications. Ann Surg 173:184, 1971.

130. Di Constanzo, J., Sastre, B., et al.: Mechanism of thrombogenesis during total parenteral nutrition: Role of catheter composition. JPEN 12:190, 1988.

131. Di Constanzo, J., Cano, N., et al.: Venous thrombosis during total parenteral nutrition with central venous catheters: Role of nutritive solutions. Clin Nutr 1:201, 1982.

132. MacDonough, J. J., and Altmeier, W. A.: Subclavian venous thrombosis secondary to indwelling catheters. Surg Gynecol Obstet 133:397, 1971.

133. Padberg, F. T., Ruggiero, J., et al.: Central venous catheterization for parenteral nutrition. Ann Surg 193:264, 1981.

134. Takasugi, J. K., and O'Connell, T. X.: Prevention of complications in permanent central venous catheters. Surg Gynecol Obstet 167:6, 1988.

135. Ladefoged, K., and Jarnum, S.: Metabolic complications to total parenteral nutrition. Acta Anaesthesiol Scand 29:89, 1985.

136. Ang, S. D., and Daly, J. M.: Potential complications and monitoring of patients receiving total parenteral nutrition. In Rombeau, J. L., and Caldwell, M. D.: Clinical nutrition, vol. 2: Parenteral nutrition. Philadelphia: W. B. Saunders, 1986.

137. Knochel, J. P.: Complications of total parenteral nutrition. Kidney Int 27:489, 1985.

138. Woolfson, A. M. J.: An improved method for blood glucose control during nutritional support. JPEN 5:436, 1981.

139. Sajbel, T. A., Durto, M. P., and Radway, P. R.: Use of separate insulin infusions with total parenteral nutrition. JPEN 11:97, 1987.

140. Beal, J. M., Frost, P. M., and Smith, J. L.: The influence of caloric and potassium intake on nitrogen retention in man. Ann Surg 138:842, 1953.

141. Freitag, J. J., and Miller, L. W., eds. Manual of medical therapeutics. 23d ed. Boston: Little, Brown, 1980.

142. Keim, N. L.: Nutritional effectors of hepatic steatosis induced by parenteral nutrition in the rat. JPEN 8:137, 1984.

143. Thompson, J. S., and Hodges, R. E.: Preventing hypophosphatemia during total parenteral nutrition. JPEN 8:137, 1984.

144. Kushner, R. F.: Total parenteral nutrition–associated metabolic acidosis. JPEN 10:306, 1986.

145. Taylor, R. F., and Buckner, C. D.: Fat overload from 10 percent soybean oil emulsion in a marrow transplant recipient. West J Med 136:345, 1982.

146. Campbell, A. N., Freedman, M. H., et al.: Bleeding disorder from the "fat overload" syndrome. JPEN 8:447, 1984.

147. Carpentier, Y. A., and Thonnart, N.: Parameters for evaluation of lipid metabolism. JPEN 11:104S, 1987.

148. Al-Kawas, F.: Pathogenesis of parenteral nutrition–associated liver injury. Paper presented at the 12th Clinical Congress of the American Society for Parenteral and Enteral Nutrition, Las Vegas, Nev., Jan. 1988.

149. Bower, R. H.: Hepatic complications of parenteral nutrition. Sem Liv Dis 3:216, 1983.

150. Williams, W. W.: Infection control during parenteral nutrition therapy. JPEN 9:735, 1985.

151. Ryan, R. A., Abel, R. M., et al.: Catheter complications in total parenteral nutrition: A prospective study of 200 consecutive patients. N Engl J Med 290:757, 1974.

152. Pemberton, L. B., Lyman, B., et al.: Sepsis from triple- vs single-lumen

catheters during total parenteral nutrition in surgical or critically ill patients. Arch Surg 121:591, 1986.

153. Powell, C., Fabri, P. J., and Kudsk, K. A.: Risk of infection accompanying the use of single-lumen vs double-lumen subclavian catheters: A prospective randomized study. JPEN 12:127, 1988.

154. Wolfe, R. M., Ryder, M. A., et al.: Complications of parenteral nutrition. Am J Surg 152:93, 1986.

155. ASPEN Board of Directors: Guidelines for use of home total parenteral nutrition. JPEN 11:342, 1987.

156. American Society for Parenteral and Enteral Nutrition: Standards for home nutrition support. Nutr Clin Prac 3:202, 1988.

157. Position of the American Dietetic Association: Nutrition monitoring of the home parenteral and enteral patient. J Am Diet Assoc 89:263, 1989.

158. Gouttebel, M. C., Saint-Aubert, B., et al.: Ambulatory home total parenteral nutrition. JPEN 11:475, 1987.

159. Wilson, J. P.: Gastrointestinal dysfunction in the critically ill: Nutritional implications. Compr Ther 11:45, 1985.

160. Granger, D. N., and Brinson, R. R.: Intestinal absorption of elemental and standard enteral formulas in hypoproteinemic (volume expanded) rats. JPEN 12:278, 1988.

161. Shiau, Y., Feldman, G. M., et al.: Stool electrolyte and osmolality measurements in the evaluation of diarrheal disorders. Ann Intern Med 102:772, 1985.

162. Mitchell, J. E., and Skelton, M. M.: Diarrheal infections. Am Fam Physician 37:195, 1988.

163. Biasco, G., Callegari, C., et al.: Intestinal morphological changes during oral refeeding in a patient previously treated with total parenteral nutrition for small bowel resection. Am J Gastroenterol 79:585, 1984.

164. Brinson, R., Guild, R., and Kolts, B.: Diarrhea and hypoalbuminemia in a medical intensive care unit. Gastroenterology 88:1336, 1986.

165. Durr, E. D., Hunt, D. R., et al.: Hypoalbuminemia and gastrointestinal intolerance to enteral feeding in head injured patients. Gastroenterology 90:1401, 1986.

166. Moss, G.: Malabsorption associated with extreme malnutrition: Importance of replacing plasma albumin. J Am Coll Nutr 1:89, 1982.

167. Kohn, C. L., and Keithley, J. K.: Techniques for evaluating and managing diarrhea in the tube-fed patient: A review of the literature. Nutr Clin Prac 2:250, 1987.

PART III

MODIFICATIONS IN PROTEIN CONTENT

13.

HIGH-PROTEIN, HIGH-CALORIE DIET

DEFINITION

A diet that provides a level of total calories and protein substantially above that which is normally required. A typical high-protein, high-calorie diet for an adult may include 1,000 or more supplemental calories daily. It should provide a minimum of 1.5 g of protein per kilogram of body weight. For the adult the usual range is between 100 and 120 g of protein daily. The Recommended Dietary Allowance for protein for adults is 0.8 g/kg of body weight. The RDAs for protein for various age groups are summarized in table 13.1 (1).

PURPOSE OF THE DIET

The diet has 2 purposes: to provide for nutritional repletion of the protein- and energy-malnourished patient and to prevent weight loss and tissue wasting in conditions under which normal protein and calorie requirements are greatly increased.

EFFECTS OF THE DIET

1. REVERSAL OF WEIGHT LOSS AND TISSUE WASTING

If continued for a sufficient period of time, a high-protein, high-calorie diet will reverse the effects of weight loss and tissue wasting associated with protein-energy malnutrition (PEM). Metabolic responses to PEM and its treatment are summarized in figure 13.1.

2. IMPROVED IMMUNE FUNCTION

The diet also has a partially restorative effect on immune responses altered by

TABLE 13.1. RECOMMENDED ALLOWANCES OF REFERENCE PROTEIN AND U.S. DIETARY PROTEIN

Category	Age (years) or condition	Weight (kg)	Derived allowance of reference protein[a] (g/kg)	(g/day)	Recommended Dietary Allowance (g/kg)[b]	(g/day)
Both sexes	0–0.5	6	2.20[c]		2.2	13
	0.5–1	9	1.56		1.6	14
	1–3	13	1.14		1.2	16
	4–6	20	1.03		1.1	24
	7–10	28	1.00		1.0	28
Males	11–14	45	0.98		1.0	45
	15–18	66	0.86		0.9	59
	19–24	72	0.75		0.8	58
	25–50	79	0.75		0.8	63
	51+	77	0.75		0.8	63
Females	11–14	46	0.94		1.0	46
	15–18	55	0.81		0.8	44
	19–24	58	0.75		0.8	46
	25–50	63	0.75		0.8	50
	51+	65	0.75		0.8	50
Pregnancy	1st trimester			+1.3		+10
	2d trimester			+6.1		+10
	3d trimester			+10.7		+10
Lactation	1st 6 months			+14.7		+15
	2d 6 months			+11.8		+12

Source: Food and Nutrition Board (1), copyright © 1989 by the National Academy of Sciences; reprinted by permission.

[a]*Data from* World Health Organization (53).

[b]Amino acid score of typical U.S. diet is 100 for all age groups, except young infants. Digestibility is equal to reference proteins. Values have been rounded upward to 0.1 g/kg.

[c]For infants 0 to 3 months of age, breast-feeding that meets energy needs also meets protein needs. Formula substitutes should have the same amount and composition of amino acids as human milk does, corrected for digestibility if appropriate.

FIG. 13.1. METABOLIC RESPONSES TO PROTEIN-ENERGY MALNUTRITION AND ITS TREATMENT.

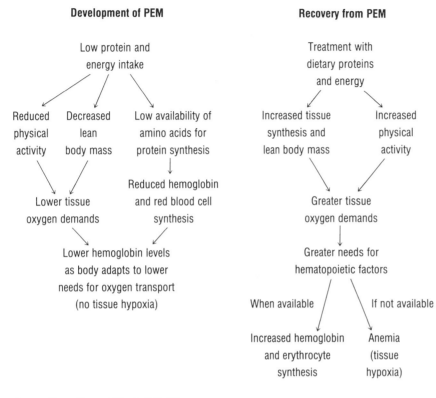

Source: Torun, B., and Viteri, F. E. (2).

severe malnutrition. If protein and energy deficits are severe and prolonged, weight loss and protein wasting will progress to atrophy of the thymus gland, delayed hypersensitivity reactions, and altered cell-mediated immune responses. Nonspecific immunity is impaired, particularly adherence and chemotaxis of phagocytes. PEM impairs lymphocyte function, reduces total lymphocyte count, and also affects IgG antibodies. Hypoalbuminemia results in generalized hypoplasia, leading to depressed bone-marrow activity, decreased numbers of stem cells able to differentiate into T and B cells, and atrophy of lymphoid organs, mucous membranes, and the gastrointestinal tract. As a result, the patient is at high risk for infections (3–6).

In one study involving very young infants, high-protein, high-calorie diet therapy partially but not completely normalized immune responses that had been depressed by severe malnutrition (5). The specific effects of protein depletion on immune responses in man remains obscure and controversial, however.

3. IMPROVED WOUND HEALING

The relationship between nutritional state and wound healing was examined in 66 adult surgical patients. Wound-healing response was assessed by measuring the collagen (hydroxyproline) content of Gore-Tex inserted subcutaneously along standardized needle-track arm wounds. After 7 days the tubes were removed, and a higher hydroxyproline content was found in the tubing of well-nourished individuals than in the tubing of individuals with PEM (2, 7).

4. REVERSAL OF HORMONAL CHANGES

Protein-energy malnutrition adversely affects hormonal activities, resulting in various metabolic effects (table 13.2).

With nutritional recovery these changes are reversed.

PHYSIOLOGY, FOODS, AND NUTRIENTS

1. DIET CHARACTERISTICS

The diet is essentially a normal one supplemented with high-protein, high-calorie foods. It is important that caloric intake is increased as well as protein to ensure that added protein is not used as an energy source. Additional servings of milk, meat or meat alternates, and eggs are included, and special high-protein, high-calorie proprietary liquid supplements may also be utilized. When calories must be increased to inordinately high levels, as for the severely burned patient, it is inevitable that the diet will be high in carbohydrate and fat as well as protein.

2. ESSENTIAL AMINO ACIDS

Nine amino acids—histidine, isoleucine, leucine, lysine, methionine, phenylalanine, threonine, tryptophan, and valine—are not synthesized by mammals and are therefore essential or indispensable nutrients. Estimates of amino acid requirements are provided in table 13.3.

INDICATIONS FOR USE

1. PROTEIN-ENERGY MALNUTRITION

Replenishment of nutritional reserves via a high-calorie, high-protein diet adjusted to the needs and tolerances of the individual is indicated in many forms of primary or secondary PEM. In constructing these diets, attention should be paid to the relationship between nonprotein calories and protein nitrogen. A high-calorie, low-protein diet will distort body composition, whereas a high-protein diet without extra calories from nonprotein sources will result in much of the nitrogen's being wasted. The optimal kcal : N ratio is approximately 100 to

TABLE 13.2. SELECTED HORMONAL CHANGES AND THEIR MAIN METABOLIC EFFECTS USUALLY SEEN IN SEVERE PEM

| Hormone | Influenced in PEM by | Hormonal activity in | | Metabolic effects of changes in PEM |
		Energy deficit	Protein deficit	
Insulin	Low food intake ($\downarrow$ glucose) ($\downarrow$ amino acids)	Decreased	Decreased	$\downarrow$ muscle protein synthesis $\downarrow$ lipogenesis $\downarrow$ growth
Growth hormone	Low protein intake ($\downarrow$ amino acids) Reduced somatomedin synthesis	Normal or moderately increased	Increased	$\uparrow$ visceral protein synthesis $\downarrow$ urea synthesis $\uparrow$ lipolysis
Somatomedins	Low protein intake?	Variable	Decreased	$\downarrow$ muscle and cartilage protein synthesis $\downarrow$ collagen synthesis $\downarrow$ lipolysis $\downarrow$ growth $\uparrow$ production of growth hormone
Epinephrine	Stress of food deficiency, infections ($\downarrow$ glucose)	Normal but can increase	Normal but can increase	$\uparrow$ lipolysis $\uparrow$ glycogenolysis inhibits insulin secretion
Glucocorticoids	Stress of hunger Fever ($\downarrow$ glucose)	Increased	Normal or moderately increased	$\uparrow$ muscle protein catabolism $\uparrow$ visceral protein turnover $\uparrow$ lipolysis $\uparrow$ gluconeogenesis
Aldosterone	$\downarrow$ blood volume $\uparrow$ extracellular K? $\downarrow$ serum Na?	Normal	Increased	$\uparrow$ sodium retention and $\uparrow$ water retention contribute to appearance of edema
Thyroid hormones	?	T_4 normal or decreased; T_3 decreased	T_4 usually decreased; T_3 decreased	$\downarrow$ glucose oxidation $\downarrow$ basal energy expenditure $\uparrow$ reverse T_3
Gonadotropins	Low protein intake? Low energy intake?	Decreased	Decreased	Delayed menarche

Source: Torun, B., and Viteri, F. E. (2).

Note: $\downarrow$ = low or reduced; $\uparrow$ = high or increased.

200 kcal/g of nitrogen intake. A commonly used kcal : N ratio is 150 nonprotein kilocalories per gram of nitrogen (2, 9, 10).

In long-term progressive malnutrition, tissue proteins are depleted before changes in serum albumin are detectable. Therefore, the need for a high-calorie, high-protein diet should be anticipated before blood changes have occurred. The diet may be indicated especially in the preparation of a nutritionally wasted patient for surgery. Surgical procedures often result in a catabolic loss of body nitrogen, and the protein status of many surgical patients is poor. Animal studies, although inconclusive, have suggested that nutrition plays an important role in the adaptation of the small intestine after massive resection, that the protein and caloric content of the diet may influence response to the hemorrhagic shock of surgery, and that malnutrition severely impairs colonic healing (9–15). According to one author, a serum albumin below 3 g/100 mL indicates a state of malnutrition so severe that it should be corrected by diet before elective surgery is attempted (12).

2. HYPERMETABOLIC OR CATABOLIC STATES

Additional protein and calories should be provided in conditions such as fevers, sepsis, postsurgical states, or thyrotoxicosis (8, 16).

3. BURNS

A high-protein, high-calorie diet is also

TABLE 13.3. ESTIMATES OF AMINO ACID REQUIREMENTS

Amino acid	Requirements, mg/kg per day, by age group			
	Infants, age 3 to 4 months[a]	Children, age ~2 years[b]	Children, age 10 to 12 years[c]	Adults[d]
Histidine	28	?	?	8–12
Isoleucine	70	31	28	10
Leucine	161	73	42	14
Lysine	103	64	44	12
Methionine plus cystine	58	27	22	13
Phenylalanine plus tyrosine	125	69	22	14
Threonine	87	37	28	7
Tryptophan	17	12.5	3.3	3.5
Valine	93	38	25	10
Total without histidine	714	352	214	84

Source: Food and Nutrition Board (1); *estimates from* World Health Organization (53). Copyright © 1989 by the National Academy of Sciences; reprinted by permission.

[a]Based on amounts of amino acids in human milk or cow-milk formulas fed at levels that supported good growth. *Data from* Fomon, S. J., and Filer, L. J., Jr.: Amino acid requirements for normal growth. In Nyhan, W. L.: Amino acid metabolism and genetic variation. New York: McGraw-Hill, 1967.

[b]Based on achievement of nitrogen balance sufficient to support adequate lean tissue gain (16 mg N/kg per day). *Data from* Pineda, O. B., Torun, F. E., et al.: Protein quality in relation to estimates of essential amino acid requirements. In Bodwell, C. E., Adkins, J. S., and Hopkins, D. T.: Protein quality in humans: Assessment and in vitro estimation. Westport, Conn.: AVI, 1981.

[c]Based on upper range of requirements for positive nitrogen balance. *Original data from* Nakagawa, I., Takahashi, T., et al.: Amino acid requirements of children: Nitrogen balance at the minimum level of essential amino acids. J Nutr 83:115, 1964; *recalculated by* Williams, H. H., Harper, A. E., et al.: Nitrogen and amino acid requirements. In Improvement of protein nutriture: Report of the Committee on Amino Acids, Food and Nutrition Board. Washington, D.C.: National Academy of Sciences, 1974.

[d]Based on highest estimate of requirement to achieve nitrogen balance. Data from several investigators (*reviewed in* Food and Agriculture Organization/World Health Organization: Energy and protein requirements: Report of a joint FAO/WHO ad hoc expert committee. Technical Report Series, no. 552; FAO Nutrition Meetings Report Series, no. 52. Rome: World Health Organization, 1973).

indicated for the severely burned patient in order to compensate for greatly increased nutritional requirements and losses of protein, electrolytes, and fluids from the burn site (17–19). A combination of several forms of nutritional support may be necessary to achieve the required intakes of protein and calories. The optimum diet for a severely burned patient should contain 2,000 to 2,200 kcal per square meter of body surface area and 15 g of nitrogen (approximately 94 g of protein) per square meter daily, as well as supplemental vitamins (17).

Among all hospitalized patients, burned patients have been shown to have the greatest increase in metabolic demand. Estimates of the caloric and protein needs of burned patients are provided in tables 13.4 and 13.5, and vitamin, mineral, and electrolyte needs are given in table 13.6. In general, protein needs are in the range of 2.5 to 3.0 g/kg body weight. Except for the child under 1 year of age, burns that cover more than 10% of total body surface area should be treated with a diet that provides at least 20% of calories from protein. For infants under 1 year of age, the RDA should be the guideline. Higher protein intakes may increase renal solute loads beyond the infant's tolerance level (20, 21).

4. CANCER

Some, but not all, cancer patients have been noted to have protein kinetics similar to those of patients in the catabolic phase of severe trauma, sepsis, or chronic infection. When the catabolic rate exceeds the synthetic rate persistently, depletion of body protein occurs. In severely affected children with Wilms' tumor, use of total parenteral nutrition for the first 5 weeks of treatment is recommended because enteral nutrition alone is ineffective in preventing further depletion during this time. Nutritional problems associated with neoplastic diseases are presented in table 13.7. Consequences of cancer treatment predisposing to nutritional problems are listed in table 13.8 (22, 23).

Nutritional support of the malnourished cancer patient leads to weight gain, improved serum protein status, and immunocompetence. The role of protein metabolism in cancer has been described in detail elsewhere (24–27).

5. SHORT-BOWEL SYNDROME

Patients with short-bowel syndrome need 35 to 40 kcal/kg/day in order to counteract increased losses. They also require at least 80 to 100 g of protein per day in order to maintain a positive nitrogen balance. If the patient has been stable for 1 year, there is usually no need to restrict fat intake. Oral supplements of calcium,

TABLE 13.4. METHODS TO ESTIMATE THE CALORIC NEEDS OF BURNED PATIENTS

Source	Formula	
Curreri	Adults: caloric intake = $(25 \times W) + (40 \times \text{TBSA})$	
	Children: caloric intake = $(B \times W) + (40 \times \text{TBSA})$	
Boston Group	Caloric intake = $2 \times$ predicted BMR	
Long	Males: BMR = $(66.47 + 13.75W + 5.0H - 6.76A) \times$ (activity factor) $\times$ (injury factor)	
	Females: BMR = $(55.10 + 9.56W + 1.85H - 4.68A) \times$ (activity factor) $\times$ (injury factor)	
	Activity factor: Confined to bed	1.2
	Out of bed	1.3
	Injury factor: Severe thermal burn	2.10
	Skeletal trauma	1.35
	Major sepsis	1.60
	Minor operation	1.20
Wilmore	Caloric intake = $2,000 \times$ BSA	
Davies and Lilijedahl	Adults: 20 kcal/kg/day + 70 kcal/TBSA/day	
	Children: 60 kcal/kg/day + 35 kcal/TBSA/day	

Source: Bell, S. J., and Wyatt, J. (20), copyright © 1986 by the American Dietetic Association; *adapted from* Molnar, J. A., Wolfe, R. R., and Burke, J. F. (54).
Note: W, weight (kg); TBSA, total body surface area burned (%); B, 100 at 1 year of age, decreases gradually to 25 at age 15; BMR, basal metabolic rate; H, height (cm); A, age (years); BSA, body surface area (m²).

TABLE 13.5. ESTIMATIONS OF PROTEIN NEEDS OF BURNED PATIENTS

Source	Formula
Curreri	3 g protein/kg
Wolfe and Burke	1.5 to 2.5 g/kg/day (children and adults)
Wilmore	15 g nitrogen/m² body surface area
Davies and Lilijedahl	Adults: 1 g/kg/day + 3 g/TBSA/day
	Children: 3 g/kg/day + 1 g/TBSA/day

Source: Bell, S. J., and Wyatt, J. (20).
Note: TBSA, total body surface area burned (%).

magnesium, and zinc may be necessary (28).

6. ACQUIRED IMMUNE DEFICIENCY SYNDROME (AIDS)

The clinical course of 71 patients with AIDS was evaluated to determine the relationship between nutritional status, gas-trointestinal symptoms, and survival. Weight loss was present in 98% of the patients, and hypoalbuminemia occurred in 83%. Both serum albumin level and the magnitude of body weight loss were strongly associated with survival rates. The author concluded that nutritional status is a major determinant of survival in AIDS. The rate of albumin decrease may define a limiting factor for survival of individual patients with this condition (29).

Immunocompromised patients tend to have increased needs because of opportunistic infections as well as poor food intakes. Poor food intake further compromises immunity in a downward cycle that is difficult to break.

7. DECUBITI

Approximately 3% of patients in acute-care hospitals and up to 49% in chronic-care hospitals develop decubiti. In 1984 the median length of hospital stays for patients with decubiti was 46 days, at a total cost of $27,000 per patient. Reductions of serum albumin levels from the normal 3.5 to 4.5 g/100 mL to as low as 1.6 g/100 mL are increasingly closely correlated to formation of pressure sores (30–32).

Both sufficient calories and protein are essential to normal wound healing. A high-protein diet alone is not effective, because some protein would then be utilized for energy. A high-calorie diet with insufficient protein will delay healing (31). The person who has lost weight or cannot restore normal weight should be on a high-carbohydrate, high-protein, moderate-fat diet that provides no less than 2,500 to 3,500 calories daily.

8. ANOREXIA NERVOSA

Restoration of proper nutrition is associated with a reversal of leukopenia, elevated blood urea nitrogen, and correction of some of the other abnormalities associated with anorexia nervosa (33). A high-protein, high-calorie diet will avert a medical crisis in a severely malnourished patient, but a team approach, including psychotherapy, is necessary for long-term recovery.

9. ORGAN TRANSPLANT RECIPIENTS

Following organ transplant, a high-protein, high-calorie diet may be indicated because of pretreatment malnutrition,

TABLE 13.6. VITAMIN, MINERAL, AND ELECTROLYTE REQUIREMENTS FOR BURNED PATIENTS

Micronutrient	Adults	Children	Infants (0–9 months)
Electrolytes (sodium and potassium)	Provided as determined by serum and urine data and fluid requirements		
Water-soluble vitamins (B-complex, folate, biotin, and B-12)	2 × RDA, 2 × AMA	2 × RDA, 2 × AMA	RDA, AMA
Vitamin C	1 to 2 g/day	500 mg	250 mg
Fat-soluble vitamins (A, D, and E)	RDA, AMA	RDA, AMA	RDA, AMA
Zinc	2 × RDA, 2 × AMA-TE	2 × RDA, 2 × AMA-TE	RDA, AMA-TE
Trace elements (copper, manganese, chromium, and iodine)	RDA, AMA-TE	RDA, AMA-TE	RDA, AMA-TE
Minerals	RDA[a]	RDA[b]	RDA[b]
Iron[c]	—	—	—

Source: American Dietetic Association (21).

Note: Recommended guidelines are for enteral and parenteral diets. RDA, Recommended Dietary Allowances, enteral use; AMA, parenteral guidelines from American Medical Association for vitamins; AMA-TE, parenteral guidelines from American Medical Association for trace elements.

[a]No national guidelines for adult parenteral mineral supplementation are published. Amounts provided vary with the clinician.

[b]Poole, R. L.: Electrolyte and mineral requirements. In Kerner, J. A.: Manual of pediatric parenteral nutrition. New York: John Wiley and Sons, 1983.

[c]Routine iron supplementation should be avoided during acute injury, particularly when associated with infection.

catabolic stresses of surgery, and high-dose steroid therapy.

10. OTHER DISEASE STATES

Surgery, sepsis, trauma, ruptured aneurysms, pancreatitis, and infections may initiate a catabolic response and trigger the need for a high-protein, high-calorie diet (34).

POSSIBLE ADVERSE REACTIONS

1. ELEVATED SERUM LIPIDS

The diet is high in total fat, saturated fat, cholesterol, and lactose and may produce elevated levels of serum lipids in susceptible individuals if continued over a long period of time. Adjustments can be made, however, to lower intake of lipids and simple sugars, if necessary.

2. NEGATIVE CALCIUM BALANCE

Very-high-protein diets adversely affect calcium balance, resulting in increased urinary calcium excretion and negative calcium balances in some instances. The mechanism of the calciuretic effect of dietary protein is unknown but may be related to alterations of calcium absorption in the gastrointestinal tract (35, 36).

3. VITAMIN A DEFICIENCY

Under certain conditions, protein supplements given to patients with kwashiorkor may provoke symptoms of vitamin A deficiency. A high-protein diet results in a greater demand by the body for vitamin A. Those patients with kwashiorkor whose liver stores of vitamin A are low should not be treated solely with nonfat milk supplements that are low in vitamin A. The increased dietary protein will increase the requirement for vitamin A, precipitating vitamin A deficiency. The vitamin A content of the high-protein, high-calorie diet presented here is adequate. Any adjustments made by dietitians in diet, however, should be made in such a manner as to ensure a sufficient intake of vitamin A.

4. HEPATIC COMA

In a few susceptible individuals with severe liver disease, usually those with massive necrosis, a high-protein diet may induce hepatic coma (37).

5. RENAL INSUFFICIENCY

A high-protein intake increases renal perfusion and renal solute load and may accelerate decline in renal function.

TABLE 13.7. NUTRITIONAL PROBLEMS ASSOCIATED WITH THE PRESENCE OF NEOPLASTIC DISEASE

1. Anorexia with progressive weight loss and undernutrition
2. Taste changes causing depressed or altered food intake
3. Alterations in protein, carbohydrate, and fat metabolism
4. Hypermetabolism in a variable number of patients
5. Impaired food intake and malnutrition secondary to bowel obstruction at any level
6. Malabsorption associated with the following:
   a. Deficiency or inactivation of pancreatic enzymes
   b. Deficiency or inactivation of bile salts
   c. Failure of food to mix with digestive enzymes (e.g., enzyme dilution; pancreaticocibal asynchrony)
   d. Fistulous bypass of small bowel
   e. Infiltration of small bowel or lymphatics and mesentery by malignant cells
   f. Blind-loop syndrome occurring with depressed gastric secretion or partial upper small-bowel obstruction leading to bacterial overgrowth
   g. Malnutrition-induced villous hypoplasia
7. Protein-losing enteropathy with various malignancies
8. Hormonal abnormalities induced by tumors
   a. Hypercalcemia induced by increased serum calcitriol and other hormones or by osteoclastic processes
   b. Osteomalacia with hypophosphatemia often associated with depressed serum calcitriol
   c. Hypoglycemia of insulin-secreting tumors
   d. Hyperglycemia, e.g., with islet glucagonoma or somatostatinoma
9. Anemia of chronic blood loss
10. Electrolyte and fluid problems with the following:
    a. Persistent vomiting with intestinal obstruction or intracranial tumors
    b. Intestinal fluid losses through fistulas or diarrhea
    c. Intestinal secretory abnormalities with hormone-secreting tumors (e.g., carcinoid syndrome, Zollinger-Ellison syndrome [gastrinoma], Verner-Morrison syndrome, increased calcitonin, villous adenoma)
    d. Inappropriate antidiuretic hormone secretion associated with certain tumors (e.g., lung carcinomas)
    e. Hyperadrenalism with tumors producing corticotropin or corticosteroid
11. Miscellaneous organ dysfunction with nutritional implications, e.g., intractable gastric ulcers with gastrinomas, Fanconi's syndrome with light-chain disease, coma with brain tumors

Source: Shils, M. E. (22).

6. INTERFERENCE WITH ACTION OF L-DOPA

A high protein intake can impair absorption of L-dopa (5). This drug should not be taken with meat, high-protein food, or protein hydrolysates.

CONTRAINDICATIONS

The diet is contraindicated for patients with hepatic coma or hyperammonemia (a blood ammonia level above 150 mcg/100 mL), uremia, or any condition in which the renal glomerular rate has been seriously impaired. Despite weight loss, delayed maturation, and delayed growth associated with certain inborn errors of protein metabolism, such as methylmalonic aciduria, arginosuccinic aciduria, proprionic acidemia, hyperammonemia, and maple syrup urine disease, a high-protein diet is contraindicated. Treatment of choice is either selective amino acid– or protein-restricted diets (22, 38–43).

CLINICAL ASSESSMENT

For all patients on this diet, weights should be measured at least every other day. Midarm muscle circumference measurements should be taken periodically to assess improvement in skeletal muscle status. Dietary intake should be analyzed at least twice weekly. The tables in Chapter 1 should be used to evaluate clinical signs of malnutrition.

Calorie counts should be taken daily in patients with major burns and 3 times a week in patients with minor burns (21). Calorie counts are also used to determine the adequacy of oral intake when deciding whether nutrition support should be initiated or may be withdrawn. The intake of vitamins and minerals should also be evaluated. A child who is undergoing a rapid rate of catch-up growth on the diet has increased needs for vitamins and minerals. Unless the child is given adequate amounts of all essential nutrients, deficiency states may occur (6).

BIOCHEMICAL ASSESSMENT

1. PROTEIN AND IRON

Total protein, albumin, and, if possible, transferrin, retinol-binding protein, and prealbumin should be evaluated regularly. Parameters of iron status such as hemoglobin, hematocrit, mean corpuscular volume (MCV), mean corpuscular hemoglobin (MCH), and mean corpuscular hemoglobin concentration (MCHC) should also be measured.

TABLE 13.8. CONSEQUENCES OF CANCER TREATMENT PREDISPOSING TO NUTRITION PROBLEMS

Radiation treatment
1. Radiation of oropharyngeal area
   a. Destruction of sense of taste
   b. Xerostomia and odynophagia
   c. Loss of teeth
2. Radiation to lower neck and mediastinum
   a. Esophagitis with dysphagia
   b. Fibrosis with esophageal stricture
3. Radiation of abdomen and pelvis: bowel damage, acute and chronic, with diarrhea, malabsorption, stenosis and obstruction, fistulization

Surgical treatment
1. Radical resection of oropharyngeal area: chewing and swallowing difficulties
2. Esophagectomy
   a. Gastric stasis and hypochlorhydria secondary to vagotomy
   b. Steatorrhea secondary to vagotomy
   c. Diarrhea secondary to vagotomy
   d. Early satiety
   e. Regurgitation
3. Gastrectomy (high subtotal or total)
   a. Dumping syndrome
   b. Malabsorption
   c. Achlorhydria and lack of intrinsic factor and R protein
   d. Hypoglycemia
   e. Early satiety
4. Intestinal resection
   a. Jejunum: decreased efficiency of absorption of many nutrients
   b. Ileum
      • Vitamin B-12 deficiency
      • Bile salt losses with diarrhea or steatorrhea
      • Hyperoxaluria and renal stone
      • Calcium and magnesium depletion
      • Malabsorption of fat and fat-soluble vitamins
   c. Massive bowel resection
      • Life-threatening malabsorption
      • Malnutrition
      • Metabolic acidosis
      • Dehydration
   d. Ileostomy and colostomy: complications of salt and water balance
5. Blind-loop syndrome: vitamin B-12 malabsorption
6. Pancreatectomy
   a. Malabsorption
   b. Diabetes mellitus

Drug treatment
1. Corticosteroids
   a. Fluid and electrolyte problems
   b. Nitrogen and calcium losses
   c. Hyperglycemia
2. Sex hormone analogues: may induce nausea and vomiting
3. Immunotherapy with interleukin-2:
   a. Azotemia
   b. Hypotension
   c. Fluid retention
4. Antimetabolites, alkylating agents, and other drugs

Source: Shils, M. E. (22).

Nitrogen balance should be checked periodically in all patients on the diet, using the procedure described in Chapter 1. Nitrogen balance may be interpreted with the aid of table 13.9.

2. BURNS

Nutrition status cannot be interpreted from total protein and albumin determinations during the burn recovery period, because of major fluid shifts, protein losses through the burn wound, and multiple transfusions given to the patient. In the recovery phase, the burn patient's total protein and albumin should be monitored weekly. Retinol-binding protein and/or prealbumin should be monitored weekly in the recovering patient. Serum transferrin concentrations and recall skin antigen testing help to identify burn patients who are at high risk of developing infectious complications (21, 26, 44, 45).

3. POTASSIUM

Serum potassium levels as well as potassium intake should be regularly monitored. Potassium and protein coexist in each tissue in a relatively constant ratio, and potassium depletion can depress protein synthesis. In muscle, the ratio is approximately 3 mEq of potassium per gram of nitrogen. In normal, healthy individuals, the potassium balance is usually zero. In protein-malnourished patients, however, when new body protein is being synthesized in the anabolic phase of recovery, additional potassium is required. Normally 3 mEq of potassium are required for each gram of nitrogen retained. A potassium : nitrogen ratio (mEq potassium to grams of nitrogen) of 6 : 1 produces the most efficient utilization of nitrogen during the acute catabolic and early recovery phases following severe burn injury (46). During late convalescence the ratio should be 4 : 1.

TABLE 13.9. INTERPRETATION AND MANAGEMENT OF NITROGEN BALANCE RESULTS

Nitrogen balance result	Interpretation of net body protein change	Management
Zero	Breakdown equals synthesis: normal state for healthy adults	Continue same protein intake unless anabolism or repletion is indicated (pregnancy, wound healing, and so forth)
Negative (i.e., less than zero)	Breakdown exceeds synthesis: undesirable state in all cases	Confirm that protein is of high quality and that calories are adequate; then increase protein intake by 6.25 g for each gram of N_2 under desired balance
Positive (i.e., greater than zero); anabolism goal: positive (4 to 6 g of N_2 per day)	Synthesis exceeds breakdown: desirable in growth, pregnancy, anabolic states, and repletion states of stress and disease	Continue current nutritional support; monitor tolerance of increased protein intake

Source: Hedberg, A. M., and Garcia, N. (34). Copyright © 1987 by Aspen Publishers, Inc.

ASSESSMENT OF POTENTIAL DRUG INTERACTIONS

1. L-DOPA

A high-protein diet impairs the entry of L-dopa into the central nervous system without affecting its absorption from the gut. When patients receiving L-dopa were given oral protein loads, motor performance declined despite maintenance of plasma L-dopa levels. These findings suggest that competition for L-dopa carrier-mediated transport by amino acids is more important at the blood-brain barrier than across the gut mucosa. Consequently, high protein intakes limit the effectiveness of the L-dopa (47). Some patients delay intake of major dietary protein sources until the evening meal. This allows increased effectiveness of the drug and improved functional ability during the day.

2. RAMIPRIL

High dietary protein intakes accelerate the progression of renal disease. In animals the angiotensin converting enzyme (ACE) inhibitor Ramipril significantly reduced albuminuria produced by a high-protein diet. Further study is needed to determine whether or not this drug may have a protective effect on kidney function in patients on a high-protein diet (48).

3. CHEMOTHERAPY

The effects of chemotherapy on the alimentary tract are summarized in table 13.10. Cyclophosphamide is often used to treat breast cancer in combination with 5-fluorouracil and methotrexate. One of the side effects of cyclophosphamide is hemorrhagic cystitis. In rats, a low-protein diet markedly increases the incidence of hemorrhagic cystitis.

A high-protein, high-calorie diet may therefore be useful in this regard as well as in countering weight loss due to anorexia, nausea, vomiting, and diarrhea.

4. AZIDOTHYMIDINE (AZT)

Azidothymidine or zidovudine, used to treat AIDS, is not greatly affected by the ingestion of food or milk. The drug does, however, cause severe headaches, nausea, abdominal pain, anorexia, rash, and taste alterations (49).

TABLE 13.10. EFFECTS OF CANCER CHEMOTHERAPEUTIC AGENTS ON THE ALIMENTARY TRACT

Drug	Effect[a]
AMSA	N, V, D, M
Asparaginase	A, N, V
Bleomycin	N, V, D, M
Busulfan	N, V
Carmustine (BiCNU)	A, N, V
Cisplatin	A, N, V
Cyclophosphamide (Cytoxan)	A, N, V, P
Cytarabine	N, V, M
Dacarbazine	N, V
Dactinomycin	A, N, V, D, M, P
Daunorubicin	A, N, V, M
Doxorubicin (Adriamycin)	A, N, V, M
Fluorouracil	N, V, M
Gallium nitrate	N, V
Hydroxyurea	N, V, M, D
Methotrexate	A, N, U, P, M
Methyl GAG	N, V, D, E, M
Mitomycin	N, V, D
Procarbazine	A, N, U
Streptozocin	N, V, D
Vinblastine	N, V, P, O
Vincristine	N, V, P, O
Vindesine (DVA)	O, N, V

Source: Shils, M. E. (22).
[a]A, anorexia; D, diarrhea; E, esophagitis; M, mucositis; N, nausea; P, abdominal pain; O, obstipation; V, vomiting; U, intestinal ulceration.

IMPLEMENTATION AND EDUCATION

1. PLANNING THE DIET

At least one-half of the day's protein allowance should be selected from complete protein foods, including some at each meal. An excellent vegetarian high-protein diet has been published for persons who prefer to exclude animal proteins (50).

Severely burned patients or patients whose intakes must be extremely high may need to use commercial supplemental formulas. Extra powdered milk may be added to creamed potatoes, cream soups, gravies, and cottage cheese, provided that the vitamin A content of the diet is kept at a high level in patients with low vitamin A stores.

Glucose polymers may be used as a sweetening agent instead of glucose. Particularly in a polymerized form, glucose is less sweet than sucrose; thus more glucose may be incorporated in foods to increase the caloric content without making them too sweet.

Distribution of meals should be planned for maximum food consumption by the specific patient. In some instances, an increased number of feedings may be indicated. In others, fewer feedings may result in a better appetite. Supplemental tube feedings may be given nocturnally so as to prevent interference with meals.

2. BARRIERS TO ADEQUATE INTAKE

Patients may have oral problems that prevent them from eating the diet as planned. These problems may include poorly fitting dentures, sensitive teeth, inability to chew, or oral infections such as thrush, especially in AIDS patients.

Patients who are malnourished are frequently lethargic and take little initiative in ingesting a high-calorie, high-protein diet. Malnourished patients may also have diarrhea, which tends to be stimulated by intake. This condition may lead to voluntary restriction of meals and should therefore be identified during nutritional assessment.

During rehabilitation, calories and protein should be increased gradually to the required level over a period of several days. Individual preferences and tolerance of specific foods should be reassessed frequently.

The diet must be individualized to promote adherence in patients for whom eating may not be pleasurable. Encouraging them to consume the recommended types and amounts of foods and monitoring their intake via food diaries, calorie counts, and/or meal rounds are of great importance.

3. CANCER PATIENTS

Anorexia is a common phenomenon in cancer. The existence of a central food-intake regulating system in the body has been proposed, and it is hypothesized that the system is altered in cancer. It has been suggested that tryptophan, the serotonin precursor, is more readily available for transport into the brain in cancer patients complaining of loss of appetite. Some drugs, such as cyproheptadine, a serotonin receptor antagonist, have been associated with appetite stimulation and weight gain in cancer patients (51, 52).

Radiation therapy of the head and neck results in dry mouth usually during the first week. Other side effects such as mucositis, sore throat, pain in swallowing, alterations of taste and smell, and decreased appetite start about 1 week later. "Mouth blindness" (loss of taste), mouth sores, dryness of the mouth (xerostomia), and malaise result in complete lack of interest in foods. To compensate, the focus should be on the aesthetic aspects of the diet, such as the arrangement or appearance of the food, meals served in a pleasant atmosphere, and eating with others, as well as use of seasonings and addition of supplements to increase calories (52). See also table 6.3.

PRIORITIES FOR QUALITY ASSURANCE

Whenever possible, specific protocols for nutritional intervention should be developed for use. They should be correlated with staging of the disease. Cancer protocols can be set up by stages of each type of cancer, for example. Decubiti protocols should correspond with the 4 stages of decubitus development.

A test tray or trial tray of several alternative supplements can be used to help patients choose the supplement they prefer.

Calorie counts and meal rounds should be used to determine how much of the diet, as provided, the patient is actually consuming.

Protocols should include monitoring plans for effectiveness of specific interventions and documenting outcome effects, such as wound healing, weight gain, or improved serum albumin.

MENU PLANNING

DAILY MEAL PLAN FOR THE HIGH-PROTEIN, HIGH-CALORIE DIET

Food	Minimum amount
Whole milk, equivalent dairy products, or commercial supplemental formula	4 cups
Medium-fat meat, fish, poultry, cheese, or alternate	8 oz. (cooked weight)
Eggs	2
Vegetables:	4 servings:
Green or yellow	1 serving
Potato or substitute	1–2 servings
Other vegetable	1–2 servings
Fruits, including 1 citrus	3 servings
Whole-grain or enriched cereal	1 serving
Whole-grain or enriched bread	6 servings
Butter or fortified margarine	5 tsp.
Other foods	As desired

SAMPLE MENU FOR THE HIGH-PROTEIN, HIGH-KILOCALORIE DIET (FOR A MALE, AGE 25–50)[a]

BREAKFAST	
Orange juice	1 cup
Farina	1 cup
Scrambled eggs	2 large
Whole wheat bread	2 slices
Margarine	2 tsp.
Jam	1 tbsp.
Whole milk	1 cup
Coffee	1 cup
Sugar	1 tsp.
MORNING SNACK	
Vanilla wafers	6
Apple juice	1 cup
LUNCH	
Roast turkey	3 oz.
Whole wheat bread	2 slices
Mayonnaise	2 tsp.
Sliced tomato	1
French dressing	1 tbsp.
Fruit cocktail	½ cup
Whole milk	1 cup
Coffee	1 cup
Sugar	1 tsp.
AFTERNOON SNACK	
Low-fat fruit yogurt	1 cup
DINNER	
Round steak	4 oz.
Baked potato	1 large
Cooked spinach	½ cup
Whole-kernel corn	½ cup

(continued)

Whole wheat bread	2 slices
Margarine	2 tsp.
Banana	1 medium
Whole milk	1 cup
Coffee	1 cup
Sugar	1 tsp.

EVENING SNACK

Whole milk	1 cup
Whole wheat bread	2 slices
Low-fat mozzarella cheese	1 oz.
Mustard	2 tsp.

Approximate Nutrient Analysis

Energy	3,302 kcal
Protein	165.2 g (20% of kcal)
Fat	107.3 g (29% of kcal)
Polyunsaturated fat	16.6 g
Monounsaturated fat	33.0 g
Saturated fat	41.0 g
Cholesterol	764 mg
Carbohydrate	435.5 g (53% of kcal)
Vitamin A	12,147 IU
	1,783 RE
Thiamine	2.23 mg
Riboflavin	4.07 mg
Niacin	28.1 mg
Folate	381 mcg
Vitamin B-12	8.90 mcg
Vitamin B-6	3.71 mg
Vitamin C	169.4 mg
Calcium	2,279 mg
Phosphorus	2,848 mg
Iron	23.7 mg
Copper	1.82 mg
Zinc	19.1 mg
Magnesium	528 mg
Sodium	3,838 mg
Potassium	6,705 mg

[a]Some individuals may prefer a regular diet supplemented by commercial supplemental formulas to this diet with its larger quantities of food.

REFERENCES

1. Food and Nutrition Board, National Research Council: Recommended Dietary Allowances. 10th ed. Washington, D.C.: National Academy Press, 1989.
2. Torun, B., and Viteri, F. E.: Protein-energy malnutrition. In Shils, M. E., and Young, V. R.: Modern nutrition in health and disease. 7th ed. Philadelphia: Lea & Febiger, 1988.
3. Worthington, B. S.: Effect of nutritional status on immune phenomena. J Am Diet Assoc 65:123, 1974.
4. Schlesinger, L., and Stekel, A.: Impaired cellular immunity in marasmic infants. Am J Clin Nutr 27:614, 1974.
5. Garre, M. A., Boles, J. M., and Youinou, P. Y.: Current concepts in immune derangement due to undernutrition. JPEN 11:309, 1987.
6. Vitale, J. J.: Impact of nutrition on immune function. In Vitale, J. J., and Broctman, S. A.: Advances in human clinical nutrition. London: John Wright, PSG, 1982.
7. Haydock, D. A., and Hill, G. L.: Impaired wound healing in surgical patients with varying degrees of malnutrition. JPEN 10:550, 1986.
8. Moore, F. D., and Brennan, M. F.: Surgical injury: Body composition and neuroendocrinology. In Bollinger, W. F., Collins, J. A., et al.: Manual of surgical nutrition. Philadelphia: W. B. Saunders, 1975.
9. Kinney, J. M.: Calories, nitrogen, disease and injury relationships. In White, P. L., and Nagy, M. E.: Total parenteral nutrition. Acton, Mass.: Publishing Sciences Group, 1974.
10. Mason, E. E.: Parenteral fluids, electrolyte and nutrient therapy in surgery. Philadelphia: Lea & Febiger, 1974.
11. O'Keefe, S. J., Sender, P. M., and James, W. P. T.: "Catabolic" loss of body nitrogen in response to surgery. Lancet 2:1035, 1974.
12. Bistrian, B. R., Blackburn, G. L., et al.: Protein status of general surgical patients. JAMA 230:858, 1974.
13. Wilmore, D. W., Dudrick, S. J., et al.: The role of nutrition in the adaptation of the small intestine after massive re-section. Surg Gynecol Obstet 132:673, 1971.
14. Drucker, W. R., Howar, P. L., and McCoy, S.: The influence of diet on response to hemorrhagic shock. Ann Surg 181:698, 1975.
15. Irwin, T. T., and Hunt, T. K.: Effect of malnutrition on colonic healing. Ann Surg 180:765, 1974.
16. Kluger, J. J.: Body temperature changes during inflammation: Their mediation and nutritional significance. Proc Nutr Soc 48:337, 1989.
17. Wilmore, D. W.: Nutrition and metabolism following thermal injury. Clin Plast Surg 1:603, 1974.
18. Curreri, P. W., Richmond, D., et al.: Dietary requirements of patients with major burns. J Am Diet Assoc 65:415, 1974.
19. Love, R. T.: Nutrition in the burned patient. J Miss State Med Assoc 13:391, 1972.
20. Bell, S. J., and Wyatt, J.: Nutrition guidelines for burned patients. J Am Diet Assoc 86:648, 1986.
21. American Dietetic Association: Manual of clinical dietetics. Chicago: American Dietetic Association, 1988.
22. Shils, M. E.: Nutrition and diet in cancer. In Shils, M. E., and Young, V. R.: Modern nutrition in health and disease. 7th ed. Philadelphia: Lea & Febiger, 1988.
23. Rickard, K. A., Jaeger-Godshall, B., et al.: Integration of nutrition support into oncologic treatment protocols for high and low nutritional risk children with Wilms' tumor. Cancer 64:491, 1989.
24. Burgess, J.: Cancer therapy. In Skipper, A.: Dietitian's handbook of enteral and parenteral nutrition. Rockville, Md.: Aspen, 1989.
25. Kurzer, M., and Meguid, M. M.: Cancer and protein metabolism. Surg Clin N Am 66:969, 1986.
26. Lundholm, K. G.: Body compositional changes in cancer patients. Surg Clin N Am 66:1013, 1986.
27. Westin, T., Ahlbom, E., et al.: Circulating levels of selenium and zinc in relation to nutritional status in patients with head and neck cancer. Arch Oto-laryngol Head Neck Surg 115:1079, 1989.
28. Woolf, G. M., Miller, C., et al.: National absorption in short bowel syndrome—evaluation of fluid, calorie, and divalent cation requirements. Dig Dis Sci 32:8, 1987.
29. Chlebowski, R. T., Grosvenor, M. B., et al.: Nutritional status, gastrointestinal dysfunction, and survival in patients with AIDS. Am J Gastroenterol 84:1288, 1989.
30. Nurse, B. A., and Collins, M. C.: Skin care and decubitus ulcer management in the elderly stroke patient. In Erickson, R. V.: Medical management of the elderly stroke patient. Phys Med Rehab 3:549, 1989.
31. Natow, A. B.: Nutritional factors in the etiology and treatment of pressure sores. J Nutr Elderly 3:17, 1983.
32. Durr, E. D.: Nutritional intervention for patients with pressure sores. Nutr Supp Ser 10 (Oct.):28, 1986.
33. Silverman, J. A.: Anorexia nervosa: Clinical observations in a successful treatment plan. J Pediatr 84:68, 1974.
34. Hedberg, A. M., and Garcia, N.: Macronutrient requirements. In Skipper, A.: Dietitian's handbook of enteral and parenteral nutrition. Rockville, Md.: Aspen, 1989.
35. Rekha Anand, C., and Linkswiler, H. M.: Effect of protein intake on calcium balance of young men given 500 mg calcium daily. J Nutr 104:695, 1974.
36. Margen, S., Chu, J. Y., et al.: Studies in calcium metabolism. 1. The calciuretic effect of dietary protein. Am J Clin Nutr 27:584, 1974.
37. Davidson, C. W.: Diseases of the liver. In Goodhart, R. S., and Shils, M. E.: Modern nutrition in health and disease. 5th ed. Philadelphia: Lea & Febiger, 1973.
38. Burton, B. T.: Current concepts of nutrition and diet in diseases of the kidney. J Am Diet Assoc 65:623, 1974.
39. Scriver, C. R., and Rosenberg, L. E.: Amino acid metabolism and its disorders. Philadelphia: W. B. Saunders, 1973.
40. Lancaster, G., Mamer, O. A., and Scriver, C. R.: Branched-chain alpha-

keto acids isolated as oxime derivatives: Relationship to the corresponding hydroxy acids and amino acids in maple syrup urine disease. Metabolism 23:257, 1974.

41. Nyhan, W. L., Fawcett, N., et al.: Response to dietary therapy in B-12 unresponsive methylmalonic acidemia. Pediatrics 51:539, 1973.

42. Brandt, I. K., Hsia, E. Y., et al.: Proprionicacidemia (ketotic hyperglycinemia): Dietary treatment resulting in normal growth and development. Pediatrics 53:391, 1974.

43. Hartlage, P. L., Coryell, M. E., et al.: Argininosuccinic aciduria: Perinatal diagnosis and early dietary management. J Pediatr 85:86, 1974.

44. DelSavio, N.: Nutrition support for thermally injured patients: The role of the dietitian. Nutr Supp Ser 4 (Oct.):10, 1984.

45. Jensen, T. G., Long, J. M., et al.: Nutritional assessment indications of post burn complications. J Am Diet Assoc 85:68, 1985.

46. Ross Laboratories: Protein in health and disease. Columbus, Ohio: Ross Laboratories, 1983.

47. Frankel, J. P., Kempster, P. A., et al.: The effects of oral protein on the absorption of intraduodenal levodopa and motor performance. J Neurol Neurosurg Psych 52:1063, 1989.

48. O'Brien, R. C., Cooper, M. E., et al.: Ramipril reduces albuminuria in diabetic rats fed a high protein diet. Clin Exp Pharmacol Physiol 16:675, 1989.

49. McEvoy, G. K., ed.: AHFS Drug Information. 30th ed. Bethesda, Md.: American Society of Hospital Pharmacies, 1988.

50. Beckner, A., Hayasaka, R., et al.: Diet manual utilizing a vegetarian diet plan. 7th ed. Loma Linda, Calif.: Seventh-Day Adventist Dietetic Association, 1990.

51. Soeters, P. B., and Von Meyenfeldt, M. F.: Mechanisms of anorexia in cancer and potential ways for intervention. Clin Oncol 5:293, 1986.

52. McKenzie-Korezowski, M.: Food intake and the cancer patient. Nutr Supp Ser 5 (Nov.):15, 1985.

53. World Health Organization: Energy and protein requirements: Report of a joint FAO/WHO/UNU expert consultation. Technical Report Series, no. 724. Geneva: World Health Organization, 1985.

54. Molnar, J. A., Wolfe, R. R., and Burke, J. F.: Metabolism and nutritional therapy in thermal injury. In Schneider, H. S., Anderson, C. E., and Coursin, D. B.: Nutritional support in medical practice. 2d ed. Hagerstown, Md.: Harper and Row, 1983.

14.

POSITION OF THE AMERICAN DIETETIC ASSOCIATION: NUTRITION INTERVENTION IN THE TREATMENT OF HUMAN IMMUNODEFICIENCY VIRUS INFECTION, 1989

Acquired immune deficiency syndrome (AIDS) has become a major health problem, and the number of individuals infected with the human immunodeficiency virus continues to increase. The need for nutrition intervention and education for those individuals should be a primary concern among health professionals. In addition, research in the area of nutrition and AIDS is vital.

Since the early 1980s, acquired immune deficiency syndrome (AIDS) has become a major health problem. The virus responsible for this disease has been named human immunodeficiency virus (HIV). Its

Approved by the House of Delegates on February 17, 1989, as Position Paper No. 89-03 to be in effect until May 3, 1992, unless it is reaffirmed or withdrawn as directed in the position development procedures of the House of Delegates. The American Dietetic Association authorizes republication of this position, in its entirety, provided full and proper credit is given.

Recognition is given to the following for their contributions. Organization units: Dietitians in Nutrition Support DPG, Nutrition Research DPG, Public Health Nutrition DPG, and Association Position Committee. Authors: Candy Collins, M.Ed., R.D., L.D.; and Maria E. Garcia, M.P.H., R.D., L.D. Reviewers: Carla Bouchard, M.S., R.D.; Steve Bowen, M.D.; Mary Anne Bryan, R.D.; Helene Kent, M.P.H., R.D.; Susan Resler, M.S., R.D.; and Faye Wong, M.P.H., R.D.

attack on the individual's T cells results in a decreased ability to fight foreign organisms, thus increasing the victim's susceptibility to a variety of opportunistic infections, as well as certain neoplasms. Because of the severity of the disease, health care for individuals infected with HIV is an issue that deserves special attention. Nutrition intervention can be important in preventing the weight loss and malnutrition seen in HIV infection and AIDS (1).

Position
It is the position of the American Dietetic Association that nutrition intervention and education be a component of the total health care provided to individuals infected with human immunodeficiency virus. This intervention should be implemented at all stages of the disease. The American Dietetic Association also supports nutrition research related to the spectrum of human immunodeficiency virus infection.

The early surveillance definition of AIDS, as established by the Centers for Disease Control (CDC), included a reliably diagnosed disease that was indicative of an underlying cellular immunodeficiency with no known cause for the immunological defect (2). In 1987 the case definition was revised in order to better describe the conditions associated with HIV infection and to simplify reporting of cases (3). In the new definition, changes included the addition of HIV wasting syndrome, which is characterized by emaci-

ation and weight loss. As a result of the increasing knowledge about the etiological retrovirus, a classification system was developed by CDC in 1986 (4). The system classifies the manifestation of the infection into 4 groups: acute infection, asymptomatic infection, persistent generalized lymphadenopathy, and other diseases, which include the constitutional disease, neurologic disease, secondary infectious diseases, secondary cancers, and other HIV conditions.

In 1987, 20,620 new cases of AIDS were reported, a 58.5% increase over the number of cases in 1986 (5). Some of the increase could be attributed to the new reporting definition. In January 1988, the number of diagnosed cases of AIDS passed 50,000, with deaths totaling more than 28,000 since the beginning of CDC surveillance. As of the beginning of 1989, more than 87,000 cases had been reported; nearly 50,000 patients had died (6). Various epidemiological models for estimating future cases of AIDS have been proposed. They predict that approximately 365,000 cumulative cases will be diagnosed by the end of 1992 (7).

Nutrition intervention is necessary at all stages of HIV infection. During the asymptomatic period, the goal of nutrition counseling is to promote an adequate, balanced diet for weight maintenance and prevention of vitamin and mineral deficiencies (8–10). In the later stages of the disease, nutrition recommendations may involve enteral or parenteral nutrition support (11, 12).

Patients with other HIV-related infections also require individual nutrition intervention and education. The constitutional disease is characterized by fever, diarrhea, and weight loss. Nutrition counseling for dietary modification of such nutrients as carbohydrate, fat, and fiber may help reduce the severity of the diarrhea. In addition, maintaining adequate hydration and changing the frequency and timing of meals may be beneficial (8, 9, 13). When diarrhea is present for long periods, assessment for protein, folic acid, and minerals may be needed.

It has been hypothesized that a malnourished, HIV-infected individual may develop AIDS more quickly because of the effect of the immunodeficient state plus the presence of the HIV infection (14). Protein-calorie malnutrition and deficiencies of iron, zinc, pyridoxine, folic acid, and vitamins B-12 and A are associated with compromised immune function (15, 16). The effects of nutritional repletion or maintenance of optimal nutritional status on the progression of the disease remain undefined, however; further research is needed. The intervention should be aimed at relieving disease symptoms or those secondary to the complications of the disease. This should be done in an effort to improve the quality of life for HIV-infected individuals.

HIV diseases can be infectious or malignant in nature. The former are usually viral, protozoan, fungal, or bacterial. The malignancies are usually in the form of Kaposi's sarcoma, B-cell lymphomas, or squamous-cell carcinomas. Identification of appropriate nutrition intervention depends on the nature of the problem, the organ system involved, and the specific side effects resulting from therapy (17–21).

Malnutrition, characterized by severe weight loss and depletion of somatic and visceral proteins, is almost always present in persons with AIDS (22–26). It is the result of decreased oral intake, increased nutrition needs, and malabsorption. Gastrointestinal infections can result in damage to the mucosal lining and result in impairment of nutrient absorption (18). In addition, fever secondary to infection results in a hypermetabolic state. Nausea, vomiting, anorexia, dysphagia, and odynophagia can occur when oral, esophageal, and/or gastric lesions are present (27).

Frequently, an individual with AIDS may be placed on several medications to alleviate a variety of illnesses. Antibiotics and chemotherapy have become integral parts of therapy for AIDS patients. Nutritional disorders associated with those therapies are managed no differently from such disorders associated with non-AIDS cases. Because of the lack of knowledge in the use of experimental drugs, it is important when interviewing a patient to be aware of and to document possible drug-induced nutritional disorders. A specific example of this phenomenon is the effect of pentamidine. This drug is currently used in the therapeutic and prophylactic treatment of *Pneumocystis carinii* pneumonia. Hypoglycemia may result from the treatment because of the drug's possible toxicity for the beta islet cells in the pancreas (28). Pancreatitis and diabetes mellitus may also occur as a result of treatment with pentamidine. As new forms of pentamidine become available, this toxicity may no longer be seen. Other disorders resulting from drug therapy for AIDS may include appetite suppression, alteration in taste and smell, impairment of nutrient absorption, and vitamin-mineral antagonism.

Mechanical problems with eating are also common in neurological disease, often referred to as AIDS encephalopathy. Special attention to food consistency, eating utensils, and monitoring during meals is needed. If the neurological complications result in dementia, confusion, and poor motor function, assistance in eating and/or enteral intubation may be necessary (29).

Modification in diet texture, nutrients, and delivery of nutrition support may need to be changed frequently during the course of the disease in an effort to provide adequate nutrition support. Frequent monitoring of nutritional status is imperative. Currently accepted nutrition assessment parameters, except for total lymphocyte count and skin hypersensitivity testing, can be applied to this population (22). Obtaining a baseline nutrition assessment during the early stages of the disease is essential (13). Subsequent assessments should be compared with values at baseline as well as with currently accepted standards.

Other factors to consider include the social and economic situation of the individual. Loss of income and insurance coverage can cause economic hardships, sometimes preventing access to health care and medical supplies. Furthermore, emotional responses to HIV infection can affect food intake (30).

It is important that equitable and quality routine care not be denied to persons with AIDS. Food service delivery becomes an issue worth addressing in this area. Hospitalized patients with AIDS do not require disposable utensils, plateware, or trays (31). Individual hospital isolation policies for such conditions as tuberculosis and hepatitis must be adhered to, however. Like non-AIDS patients, patients with AIDS prefer personal menu selection and discussion with food service personnel about specific problems with respect to their diets.

Education regarding food service care for persons with AIDS is essential for food service workers. This education is primarily for the purpose of reducing possible fears concerning contact with AIDS patients. Another consideration for food service facilities is maintenance of quality assurance standards for sanitation. Routine sanitation standards for food storage, preparation, and serving must be maintained, as well as appropriate dishwashing and cleaning procedures, to prevent opportunistic infections (31). It is also necessary for the food service department to be involved in policy-making with regard to isolation policies and procedures. To date, CDC has not documented any cases of HIV infection transmitted through food or handling of trays and silverware. Many persons with HIV infection are concerned about transmission of other infections as a result of improper cleaning or food preparation methods. It is important to educate those individuals about proper preparation, cleaning, and storage of food (32, 33). Food poisoning, especially salmonellosis, can lead to serious infection and death for someone who is HIV-infected (34). Some clinicians have gone as far as recommending a low-microbial diet and avoidance of raw fruits and vegetables, cold cuts, and products with raw eggs for high-risk patients because of their increased susceptibility to infection (35).

Nutrition services can also be provided in the community. Many organizations and health care services in the community provide educational programs for individuals with HIV infection and AIDS. The programs include counseling and support groups, such as foundations dedicated to the care of individuals with AIDS. Because misinformation and nutrition myths are prevalent in the population with AIDS, it can be helpful to provide correct and appropriate nutrition information in such group settings. Many foundations or organizations provide free food through pantries, meal service in homes, or advice on applying for food stamps.

Home care is another area in which nutrition needs to be addressed. Providing health care to homebound AIDS patients has become a common practice. The dietitian must be actively involved with the discharge planning team. It is important to discuss the care plan with a patient's family and/or significant other.

In addition, communication directly with home health care representatives or home visits by the dietitian can help in providing continuity of care. Caring for an individual with AIDS in an outpatient setting can help decrease the total cost. In 1988 it was estimated that the life cost of caring for 1 person with AIDS was $57,000. An increase to $61,800 is expected by 1991 (36).

The use of self-prescribed, potentially harmful diets and/or nutritional supplements is a common practice in this patient population (37). It is imperative that dietitians develop and maintain good rapport with HIV-infected individuals. Dietitians should discuss possible harmful effects of such self-prescribed therapy, the unnecessary expense, and possible compromise to the individual's medical treatment. Discussion of inappropriate diets and unnecessary supplements requires an open, nonjudgmental approach. Inappropriate or inadequate self-prescribed diets may include macrobiotic, yeast-free, and special immune-boosting diets and vitamin-mineral megadosing. Other varieties of inappropriate diets that may exist are usually specific to regional areas in the United States.

Because AIDS is a disease with a high mortality rate, providing care to the terminally ill patient has become an additional issue worth addressing. Nutrition support will most likely be a factor when a decision is made to continue or cease therapy. A helpful guide in this area is the position statement of the American Dietetic Association that specifically addresses care for the terminally ill (38). It is important that the wishes of the individual as well as those of the family and significant others be taken into consideration. In addition, other medical, social, religious, and economic factors may need to be addressed.

Providing nutrition care for individuals with HIV infection or AIDS is an essential part of the total health care of the patient. Individualized care is required with respect to nutrition assessment, nutrient modification, nutrition support, home care, and advice on inappropriate nutrition practices. Many of the current practices in nutrition care already in place can be applied to caring for persons with HIV infection and AIDS. Nutrition assessment and counseling require timely follow-up in order to adjust for changes in nutritional status.

Currently, there is a limited amount of research in the area of nutrition and AIDS. When federal and state governments appropriate funds for research or care of patients with AIDS, provision should be made for dietitians to be included for nutrition assessment and counseling. It is necessary that dietitians become more involved in ongoing research in both the clinical and the public health areas. Research needs to be directed at defining the relationship between maintenance of optimal nutritional status and nutritional repletion and the progression of the disease.

The possibility exists that if malnutrition is controlled during the early stages of infection, the immune system, which is suppressed in the presence of HIV infection, may function better. Research should also be directed at estimating caloric requirement by stage of disease. Furthermore, the relationship between nutritional repletion and frequency and severity of infections, frequency and severity of complications, length of hospital stay, tolerance and response to treatment, and life expectancy needs to be investigated.

REFERENCES

1. Chlebowski, R. T.: Significance of altered nutritional status in acquired immune deficiency syndrome (AIDS). Nutr Canc 7:85, 1985.

2. Centers for Disease Control: Update: Acquired immunodeficiency syndrome (AIDS)—United States. MMWR 32:389, 1983.

3. Centers for Disease Control: Revision of the Centers for Disease Control surveillance definition for acquired immunodeficiency syndrome. MMWR 36 (Supp 1):3S, 1987.

4. Centers for Disease Control: Classification system for human T-lymphadenopathy virus type III/lymphadenopathy-associated virus infections. MMWR 35:334, 1986.

5. CDC AIDS Weekly (Jan. 18):6, 1988.

6. AIDS-HIV Record 3 (2 and 3):12, 1989.

7. Heyward, W. L., and Curran, J. W.: The epidemiology of AIDS in the U.S. Sci Am 259 (4):72, 1988.

8. Collins, C. L.: AIDS and nutritional care. RD 7 (3):6, 1987.

9. Collins, C. L.: Nutrition care in AIDS. Diet Curr 15 (3):11, 1988.

10. Beach, R. S.: Altered folate metabolism in early HIV infection. JAMA 259:519, 1988.

11. Domaldo, T. L., and Natividad, L. S.: Nutritional management of patients with AIDS and *Crytosporidium* infection. Nutr Supp Ser 6 (Apr.):30, 1986.

12. Budd, C. B.: Nutritional care of patients with *Pneumocystis carinii* pneumonia. Nutr Supp Ser 2 (Dec.):12, 1982.

13. Garcia, M. E., Collins, C. L., and Mansell, P. W. A.: The acquired immune deficiency syndrome nutritional complications and assessment of body weight status. Nutr Clin Prac 2:108, 1987.

14. Jain, V. K., and Chandra, R. K.: Does nutrition deficiency predispose to acquired immunodeficiency syndrome? Nutr Res 4:537, 1984.

15. Cunningham, R. S.: Effects of nutritional status on immunologic function. Am J Clin Nutr 35:1202, 1982.

16. Beisel, W. R., Edelman, R., et al.: Single-nutrient effects on immunologic functions. JAMA 245:53, 1981.

17. Cone, L. A., Woodard, D. R., et al.: An update on the acquired immunodeficiency syndrome (AIDS) associated disorders of the alimentary tract. Dis Colon Rectum 29 (1):60, 1986.

18. Gillian, J. S., Shike, M., et al.: Malabsorption and mucosal abnormalities of the small intestine in the acquired immunodeficiency syndrome. Ann Intern Med 102:619, 1985.

19. Kotler, D. P., Gatz, H. P., and Lange, M.: Enteropathy associated with the acquired immunodeficiency syndrome. Ann Intern Med 101:421, 1984.

20. Lefkowitch, J. H.: AIDS and the liver. Endo Rev (Nov./Dec.):43, 1986.

21. Pardo, V., Aldana, M., et al.: Glomerular lesions in the acquired immunodeficiency syndrome. Ann Intern Med 101:429, 1984.

22. Kotler, D. P., Wang, J., and Pierson, R. N.: Body composition studies in patients with the acquired immunodeficiency syndrome. Am J Clin Nutr 42:1255, 1985.

23. O'Sullivan, P., Linke, R. A., and Dalton, S.: Evaluation of body weight and nutritional status among AIDS patients. J Am Diet Assoc 85:1483, 1985.

24. Brinson, R. R.: Hypoalbuminemia, diarrhea and acquired immunodeficiency syndrome. Ann Intern Med 102:413, 1985.

25. Beach, R. S., and Laura, P. F.: Nutrition and the acquired immunodeficiency syndrome. Ann Intern Med 99:565, 1983.

26. Gray, R. H.: Similarities between AIDS and PCM. Am J Public Health 73:1332, 1983.

27. Barr, C. E., and Torosian, J. P.: Oral manifestations in inpatients with AIDS or AIDS-related complex. Lancet 2:288, 1986.

28. Stahl-Bayliss, C. M., Kalman, C. M., and Laskin, O. L.: Pentamidine-induced hypoglycemia in patients with the acquired immune deficiency syndrome. Clin Pharmacol Ther 39:271, 1986.

29. Resler, S. S.: Nutrition care of AIDS patients. J Am Diet Assoc 88:828, 1988.

30. Detmer, W. M., and Lu, F. G.: Neuropsychiatric complications of AIDS: A literature review. Int J Psychiatry Med 16:21, 1986–1987.

31. Centers for Disease Control: Recommendations for preventing transmission of infection with human T-lymphotropic virus type III/lymphadenopathy-associated virus in the workplace. MMWR 34:681, 1985.

32. Bennett, J. A.: AIDS beyond the hospital. Am J Nurs 86:1015, 1986.

33. Dhundale, K., and Hubbard, P. M.: Home care for AIDS patient: Safety first. Nursing 16 (9):34, 1986.

34. Profeta, S., Forrester, C., et al.: Salmonella infections in patients with acquired immunodeficiency syndrome. Arch Intern Med 145:670, 1985.

35. Aker, S. N., and Cheney, C. L.: The use of sterile and low microbial diets in ultraisolation environments. JPEN 7:390, 1983.

36. CDC AIDS Weekly (June 27):19, 1988.

37. Pike, J. T.: Alternative nutritional therapies: Where is the evidence? AIDS Patient Care (Feb.):31, 1988.

38. Position of the American Dietetic Association: Issues in feeding the terminally ill adult. J Am Diet Assoc 87:78, 1987.

15.

DIETS TO CONTROL PROTEIN, SODIUM, POTASSIUM, PHOSPHORUS, AND FLUIDS (RENAL DIETS)

DEFINITIONS

1. DIET TO CONTROL PROTEIN, SODIUM, POTASSIUM, PHOSPHORUS, AND FLUIDS

A diet in which the dietary protein, sodium, potassium, phosphorus, and fluids are carefully regulated from day to day according to the clinical condition of the patient.

2. AZOTEMIA

The retention of nitrogenous products such as urea, creatinine, and uric acid in the blood (1).

3. PRERENAL AZOTEMIA

A decrease in glomerular filtration rate resulting from a decrease in renal perfusion pressure and or intense vasoconstriction. Volume depletion or an improvement in cardiac function will reverse prerenal azotemia but not acute renal failure (1).

Prerenal azotemia is caused by volume depletion due to excessive diuresis; hemorrhage; gastrointestinal losses; third-space losses from burns, traumatized tissue, peritonitis, or pancreatitis; or cardiac and vascular disorders such as congestive heart failure, acute myocardial infarction, pericardial effusion with tamponade, acute pulmonary embolism, or renal artery emboli, thrombosis, or stenosis.

4. ANURIA

An absence of urine production (1).

5. OLIGURIA

A significant reduction of urinary volume below 500 mL per day (1).

6. UREMIA

The specific clinical and biochemical findings and symptoms that result when kidney function fails. It is the result of toxins and hormonal, fluid, and electrolyte abnormalities. Symptoms include loss of appetite, fatigue, apathy or mental dullness, rise in blood pressure, decreased urine output, edema of the feet or face, nausea, vomiting, metallic taste, twitching, restlessness, itching, and seizures. It occurs rapidly over a period of days or hours in acute renal failure and slowly and insidiously over a period of years in chronic renal failure (1–3).

7. HEMODIALYSIS

A technique that filters an individual's blood in an artificial kidney or hemodialyzer. Blood and dialysate solution are separated by a semipermeable membrane through which the excess fluid and other waste products are filtered (2). Dialysis involves 2 processes: diffusion and ultrafiltration.

A. Diffusion The uniform dispersement or spreading of particles or molecules that are in constant motion throughout a solution. The rate of the spread depends upon the concentration, size, and electric charge of the particles. Substances move along a concentration gradient from the blood to the dialysate solution or vice versa. Low-molecular-weight materials, such as urea and potassium, are removed by diffusion (2, 4, 5).

B. Ultrafiltration The process of fluid removal whereby substances are swept along with water by convection. During dialysis, ultrafiltration removes excess water from the blood. In this instance, a hydraulic pressure gradient is the primary force promoting solute movement across the dialysis membrane from the blood to the dialysate (4). By increasing the hydrostatic pressure, water and dissolved solutes are transported across the membrane and out of the patient's blood.

8. CONTINUOUS ARTERIOVENOUS HEMOFILTRATION (CAVH)

A process that continuously filters an individual's blood in a small external hemofilter. Fluid, electrolytes, and small to medium-sized molecules are removed from the patient by ultrafiltration, using the force of the patient's own blood pressure. The replacement solution infused into the patient can be tailored to his or her serum electrolyte profile. Unlike regular hemodialysis, filtration rate decreases when the patient's blood pressure decreases, lessening the risks of complications in patients with unstable blood pressure. This process is indicated in acute renal failure for critically ill, hemodynamically unstable surgical patients who may have multiple organ failure or severe fluid overload (6–8).

9. PERITONEAL DIALYSIS

The removal of body waste products and water within the peritoneal cavity, using the peritoneal membrane as a filter. Access is provided by a permanent Silastic catheter, such as the Tenckhoff catheter, through which dialysate is delivered. The uremic toxins are removed by passive movement or diffusion from the peritoneal capillaries into the dialysate. Excess extracellular fluid is removed from the blood by ultrafiltration, which is achieved by rendering the dialysate solution hypertonic with dextrose. By adjusting the osmolality of the dialysate solution, ultrafiltration can be controlled with considerable precision (9, 10). The 3 types of peritoneal dialysis are as follows.

A. Intermittent Peritoneal Dialysis (IPD)
The use of the peritoneum and peritoneal cavity for the diffusion and ultrafiltration of blood through a process that is repeated for 8 to 10 hours, 3 or 4 days per week. IPD usually requires that the catheter be attached to an automatic proportioning machine called a cycler, which warms and automatically delivers the dialysate either from bottles or bags. Use of the cycler for IPD has also been referred to as automated peritoneal dialysis, or APD (3–5, 11).

Up to 3 L of peritoneal dialysate are infused into the abdominal cavity and left there for 20 minutes, during which time toxins diffuse into the dialysate. The solution is then drained from the patient (9, 11).

B. Continuous Ambulatory Peritoneal Dialysis (CAPD)
The use of the peritoneum and peritoneal cavity for the diffusion and ultrafiltration of blood through a manual process that permits the patient to be ambulatory (5). CAPD differs from IPD in that the solution remains in the abdominal cavity for 4 to 6 hours, not 20 minutes, before being drained out of the abdomen. This process of instillation, dwelling, and drainage is repeated 4 or 5 times per day, 6 or 7 days per week.

C. Cycler Continuous Peritoneal Dialysis (CCPD)
A process similar to CAPD except that 3 or 4 exchanges are done, usually at night, by an automatic cycler. Specifically, this procedure involves exchanging 6 to 8 L of peritoneal fluid during the night and leaving 2 L of peritoneal fluid in the abdominal cavity during the day. The procedure allows for more daytime freedom from exchanges (4, 9).

10. ARTERIOVENOUS FISTULA

The surgical joining, or anastamosis, usually of the radial artery and cephalic vein at the wrist to provide a vascular access route for hemodialysis (11). This internal connection of an artery and a vein will eventually become large enough to permit entry of large dialysis needles. After 6 to 12 weeks, hypertrophy, or "arterialization," of the venous limb of the fistula occurs, and dialysis can be started.

11. BOVINE OR GORTEX GRAFT

A device of special material that connects an artery and a vein (3). Both the fistula and the graft are under the skin, allowing normal activity but requiring venipuncture for access to the patient's blood for dialysis.

12. ARTERIOVENOUS SHUNT

A biocarbon port grafted to a polytetrafluoroethylene arteriovenous graft. The port has a special plug connected to 2 tubes. During dialysis, needles are inserted into the tubes, one to send blood to the hemodialyzer and the other to return the blood to the patient. After dialysis, the connecting tubing is removed, and a protective cap is placed over the plug (11). The junction of the 2 tubes, or cannulas, is on the outside of the skin. Because it is open to the outside of the body, it is more prone to develop infections and clots.

REFERENCES

1. Gutch, C. F., and Stoner, M. H.: Review of hemodialysis for nurses and dialysis personnel. 4th ed. St. Louis: C. V. Mosby, 1983.
2. Anthony, L. E., and Taylor, K. B.: Clinical nutrition. New York: McGraw-Hill, 1983.
3. Harum, P.: Nutritional management of the adult hemodialysis patient. In Gillet, D., Stover, J., and Spinozzi, N.: A clinical guide to nutrition care in end stage renal disease. Chicago: American Dietetic Association, 1987.
4. Rosansky, S. J.: Choosing therapy for end stage renal disease. Am Fam Physician 28 (1):115, 1983.
5. Binkley, L. S.: Keeping up with peritoneal dialysis. Am J Nurs 84:729, 1984.
6. McGuire, W., and Anderson, R.: Continuous arteriovenous hemofiltration in the intensive care unit. J Crit Care 1:54, 1986.
7. Goldstein, J.: Continuous arteriovenous hemofiltration: Nutritional considerations. Renal Dietitians Newsletter 6 (2):1, 1987.
8. Bartlett, R., Mault, J., et al.: Continuous arteriovenous hemofiltration: Improved survival in surgical acute renal failure? Surgery 100:400, 1986.
9. McCann, L.: Peritoneal dialysis and nutritional considerations. In Gillet, D., Stover, J., and Spinozzi, N.: A clinical guide to nutrition care in end stage renal disease. Chicago: American Dietetic Association, 1987.
10. Milutinovic, J.: Peritoneal dialysis. Dial Transplant 9 (6):576, 1980.
11. Nissenson, A. R.: Dialytic techniques in renal failure. In Bricker, N. S., and Kirschenbaum, M. A.: The kidney: Diagnosis and management. New York: John Wiley and Sons, 1984.

DIET IN CHRONIC RENAL FAILURE

DEFINITION

CHRONIC RENAL FAILURE

The presence of irreversible nephron damage characterized by a slow, progressive worsening of renal function. A typical patient with progressive renal disease may pass through several stages, arbitrarily defined as follows (1):

- mild renal insufficiency, in which renal function is reduced to 40% to 80% of normal
- moderate renal insufficiency, in which renal function is reduced to 15% to 40% of normal
- severe renal insufficiency, in which renal function is reduced to 2% to 20% of normal

PURPOSE OF THE DIET

Although diet therapy cannot be considered a cure for chronic renal failure, modifications in intake can have significant impacts on nutritional and health status:

- Reduction in workload of the diseased kidney by reducing the urea, uric acid, creatinine, and electrolytes (especially potassium, sodium, and phosphate) that must be excreted (2–4)
- Replacement of lost substances, such as protein lost in dialysis, or correction of deficits (5)
- Prevention of acceleration of nephron damage produced by excessive protein intake (prior to dialysis) and calcification secondary to renal osteodystrophy (6–9)
- Prevention of renal osteodystrophy, control of dietary phosphorus intake, and maintenance of the serum calcium-phosphorus product below 70 (5)
- Maintenance of lean body mass and optimal nutritional status; prevention of muscle wasting and growth retardation (5, 10–13)
- Maintenance of blood urea nitrogen (BUN) below the level at which azotemia induces clinical symptoms of uremic toxicity such as gastrointestinal disturbances (10)
- Maintenance of normal extracellular fluid volume, pH, and osmolality (10)
- Promotion of a feeling of well-being in the patient (5)
- Postponement of initiation of dialysis (5)
- Reduction of complications of glucose intolerance, common in uremia because the peripheral insulin-sensitive tissues of the patient become insulin resistant as a result of postreceptor defects in muscle, adipose tissue, and liver cells; in advanced renal failure, decreased insulin degradation may result in hypoglycemia (14)
- Control of blood pressure (15)

EFFECTS OF THE DIET

1. PROTEIN RESTRICTION

The degree of azotemia is markedly reduced by protein restriction. A low-protein diet may retard the progression of mild and moderate renal insufficiency. Even in healthy individuals, increases in protein intake increase the glomerular filtration rate, possibly mediated by renal prostaglandins. The increased glomerular capillary blood flows and hydraulic pressures associated with unrestricted protein intake may accelerate hemodynamically mediated glomerular injury. By limiting capillary perfusion, dietary protein restriction may help to preserve glomerular structure and function (5, 8–10, 16–26).

Protein restriction may also reduce renal hypertrophy in remnant nephrons and prevent some of the changes that may lead to progressive disease, such as increased oxygen consumption and the toxic oxygen radicals that accompany it. By decreasing glomerular filtration rate, protein restriction decreases tubular cell metabolism and the generation of toxic radicals (27, 28).

An increased protein intake, with its resulting increased ammonia production, may harm the renal interstitium. Conversely, protein restriction may interfere with the progression of the disease by reducing the dietary acid load and the production of ammonia in the surviving nephrons (27, 29).

Protein restriction reduces serum urea and phosphate concentrations. Moderate dietary protein restriction early in the course of the disease reduces serum urea and phosphate concentrations and urinary phosphate and protein excretion. Phosphorus-calcium deposition may play a role in the progression of renal disease, and a decrease in protein intake may decrease the load of phosphorus and decrease renal damage (21, 27, 29).

An 18-month study of 64 patients with serum creatinine levels between 350 and 1,000 μmol per liter showed that 27% of those on a regular diet and 6% of patients on a diet of 0.4 g protein per kilogram of body weight developed end-stage renal disease. The authors concluded that dietary protein restriction is effective in slowing the rate of progressive renal failure. The treatment group lost weight on the diet, however, and often did not consume all the calories allotted to them from energy-dense foods such as fats and simple carbohydrates. They also had a much poorer quality of life than patients on a regular diet. In another study involving restriction of protein to 0.8 g/kg/day, the authors concluded that the type of underlying disease influenced progression of renal failure more than did the protein intake (30, 31).

Preservation of peripheral nerve function in severe uremia has been attributed to a low-protein, high-calorie diet supplemented with essential amino acids. Gastrointestinal symptoms often improve with dietary protein restriction. Pruritus may improve with protein restriction and/or with dietary measures that improve secondary hyperparathyroidism. Protein restriction also aids maintenance of internal homeostasis by decreasing the intake of potassium and phosphate and the production of fixed, nonmetabolizable organic acids (5, 9, 32).

In the case of the diabetic patient with nephropathy, preliminary results suggest a beneficial effect of protein restriction, but these results need to be confirmed. As nephropathy progresses in the diabetic, hyperglycemia leads to expansion of extracellular fluid volume as well as to changes in vasoactive neurohormones. As a result, vasodilation of the retinal, peripheral, and renal capillaries occurs. Renal capillary pressures and flows then increase, and structural damage to the kidney occurs (33, 34).

2. SODIUM AND FLUID

Control of sodium and water balance augments control of blood pressure (35).

3. PHOSPHORUS

Dietary phosphate restrictions, combined with phosphate-binding drugs, help prevent or control renal osteodystrophy and to retard the progression of renal disease. It has been further suggested that phosphate restrictions early in the course of the disease may retard its progression. Emerging evidence argues strongly that a low-phosphorus diet or agents that reduce phosphorus absorption preserve renal function. Conversely, dietary phosphorus appears to be strongly detrimental to residual renal function. Dialysis alone is not adequate to control serum phosphate levels in most patients. In one study a dietary phosphorus intake reduced by 50% to 21 mg/kg body weight/day for 6 months resulted in improved growth, a sharp decline in serum and urinary phosphorus, and suppression of secondary hyperparathyroidism (35–39).

4. LIPIDS

Conflicting results have been reported on the effect of a protein-restricted diet on serum lipids. In a group of 15 patients with chronic renal failure on a diet that averaged 20 g of protein, 120 g of fat, and 273 g carbohydrate or 50% of total calories as carbohydrate, including 94 g of sucrose daily, no change was noted in serum lipid levels, apolipoprotein levels, or lipolytic activities (40).

When the proportion of carbohydrate in the diet is reduced in predialysis or dialysis patients, hypertriglyceridemia diminishes. Increasing the ratio of polyunsaturated to saturated fats in the diet has a similar effect, as does exercise. In predialysis and hemodialysis, a reduction of the total carbohydrate intake from 50% to 35% of total calories and an increase in the ratio of polyunsaturated to saturated fatty acids to 2.0 have been demonstrated to produce a decrease in serum triglyceride levels. A diet high in carbohydrates (mainly complex starches) and low in fat (20% of total calories) and saturated fat, with 100 mg cholesterol, has also been recommended to reduce elevated triglycerides (41–45).

The effect of a fish oil called MAX EPA, rich in polyunsaturated fatty acids such as eicosapentaenoic acid, on the lipid abnormalities of 13 hemodialysis patients was studied over a 2-month period. The result was a significant decrease in serum triglyceride levels and apolipoprotein B (46). Further studies are needed in larger groups over a more extended period of time.

5. GROWTH RATES IN CHILDREN

Provided that minimum nutrient needs are met and that adequate calories are provided, the diet will improve previously abnormal growth rates in uremic children. Diet counseling and prevention of renal acidosis and osteodystrophy help to minimize growth retardation. The use of recombinant human growth hormone

has been shown to produce acceleration of growth velocity in a small group of growth-retarded children with renal failure. Infants with end-stage renal disease are usually severely growth retarded and developmentally delayed. Early nutritional intervention and dialysis can yield much improved results (12, 47–51).

PHYSIOLOGY, FOODS, AND NUTRIENTS

Nutritional management of the patient with chronic renal failure is correlated with renal status, in particular the degree of nephron damage, the glomerular filtration rate, and the degree of remaining renal function. The patient's overall clinical condition and nutritional status per assessment and the specific form of medical treatment being provided will also affect the prescribed level of each restricted nutrient.

The diet is based upon specialized lists of exchanges (table 15.7), which in turn are based on the amounts of protein, sodium, potassium, and phosphorus each food contains. It permits the substitution of other food items within a list, as long as the total protein, sodium, potassium, phosphorus, and fluids do not exceed the limits of the diet prescription. Particularly at lower levels of protein intake, protein-containing foods of high biological value, such as milk and eggs, are preferentially used over other sources.

Nutrients that may need to be controlled usually include protein, energy, sodium, fluid, potassium, calcium, and phosphorus, but may also include vitamins, other minerals, fat, carbohydrate, and fiber. The diet prescription must be individualized according to biochemical and functional indices. Suggested intakes of critical nutrients in various stages of renal failure are summarized in table 15.1.

1. PROTEIN

A. Protein Wasting Chronic renal failure is of itself a form of malnutrition

TABLE 15.1. SUGGESTED INTAKES OF CRITICAL NUTRIENTS IN VARIOUS STAGES OF RENAL FAILURE

Nutrient	Acute renal failure	Predialysis	Hemodialysis	Peritoneal dialysis	Transplantation	Diabetes
Kilocalories	30–50 kcal/kg body weight (52) or use BEE (15)	35 kcal/kg body weight for maintenance (9, 15); 25–35 kcal/kg for weight loss (53); 40–50 kcal/kg for protein malnutrition (54); 45 kcal/kg for weight gain (55); for children, 10 kcal/cm standing height (15) or use BEE (15)	35–55 (7, 54) kcal/kg body weight, depending on individual; 35 kcal/kg for weight maintenance; 25–30 for weight loss; 40–50 for weight gain (53)	35–42 kcal/kg body weight (56) or 20–50, depending on condition of patient and type of dialysis (see text)	35–40 kcal/kg body weight (57) or use BEE to estimate; or 30–35 for maintenance, 40–45 for repletion, 20–25 for weight reduction (58); may need to restrict calories in individuals on steroids (57)	35 kcal/kg body weight (57, 59) or amount needed to maintain ideal body weight (60)
Protein	If UNA < 4–5 g, give 0.3–0.4 g essential amino acids/kg body weight; with higher UNA give essential and nonessential amino acids; in TPN, use either 2 : 1 or 4 : 1 ratio of essential to nonessential amino acids (52)	0.6 g/kg body weight (10, 55), or if GFR = 20 mL per min or less, give 0.55–0.60 g/kg body weight (9, 15); maximum = 45 g/day; if GFR = 20–25, give 40–50 g/day (9) or use UNA (9)	1.0–1.2 g/kg body weight (9); for children, at least 0.3 g/cm statural height (61)	1.2–1.3 g/kg body weight for maintenance, 1.5 for repletion, 1.2 for reduction (16)	Unrestricted once transplant is functioning; increase to 1.5 g/kg if steroid use has caused negative N balance	Same as without diabetes (60)
Sodium	Not clearly established; in TPN, 50 mEq/L or as per demonstrated individual patient need	1–3 g/day (9) when GFR = 4–10 mL/min; or 2–3 g (55)	1.0–3.0 g/day (53) or limit to amount needed to keep blood pressure and weight under control; no more than 2-kg gains between dialyses	3–4 g/day (16)	2–4 g/day (58) as necessary due to sodium-retaining effects of steroids (57)	2–3 g/day (59)
Fluid	In TPN, infusion at 20 to 100 mL/hr; in oliguria, add mL of urine, mL fluid losses from wounds, gastric suction, and diarrhea, and 300 mL for insensible loss (62)	500 mL + previous day's urinary and other losses	750–1,500 mL/day (9, 56); or 500 mL and urinary losses (53)	2,000–3,000 mL/day (9, 63)	Individualized, usually unrestricted (57, 64), or 800 mL/day + urine volume (65)	500 mL + previous day's urine output

(continued)

TABLE 15.1. *CONTINUED*

Nutrient	Acute renal failure	Predialysis	Hemodialysis	Peritoneal dialysis	Transplantation	Diabetes
Potassium	Individualized; varies depending upon degree of metabolism	No more than 70 mEq or 2,730 mg/day (35); unrestricted unless serum K > 5.5 mEq/L (55) or urine < 1,000 mL	1,500–3,000 mg/day (53)	Unrestricted unless serum K is elevated; if it is, then 2–3 g/day	Usually not restricted unless patient on cyclosporine or serum K > 6.0 mEq/L	2.0–2.5 g (59)
Phosphorus	Not established	600–800 mg/day (55) or 15 mg phosphorus per g protein; keep serum level at 3–4 mg/100 mL (9); Ca/P product no higher than 70 (5, 9)	600–1,200 mg/day (9, 53); keep serum level at maximum of 4–6 mg/100 mL (53); Ca/P product no higher than 70 (5, 9)	800–1,200 mg (63) or 1,000–1,200 mg (16); maximum of 6 mg/100 mL (17)	Unrestricted (57, 63); may need supplements (58)	600–700 mg/day (66)
Calcium	Not established	1,200–1,600 mg (56) or 1,000–1,500 mg (55)	1–2 g/day (53, 67) to keep levels between 10.5 and 11.0 mg/L (53)	1,000–1,400 mg/day (63)	Should at least meet RDA	Same as without diabetes (60)
Vitamin C		70–100 mg (55)	100 mg (53)	100 mg (16)	Should at least meet RDA	Same as without diabetes (60)
Vitamin B-6		5 mg (55)	10 mg (9, 68); 5–10 mg (53)	10–15 mg (68)	Should at least meet RDA	Same as without diabetes (60)
Thiamine		1.5 mg (55)	10 mg (9, 69)	3–4 mg (69)	Should at least meet RDA	Same as without diabetes (60)
Folate		1 mg (55)	1 mg (53)	1 mg (16)	Should at least meet RDA	Same as without diabetes (60)

as evidenced by its abnormalities of body composition and of plasma and intracellular amino acid patterns and by its growth retardation in children (13, 20, 70–73). Wasting in chronic renal disease has multiple causes.

Dietary intake is often inadequate, particularly with regard to energy and protein needs. The cause may be anorexia, depression, superimposed medical complications or illnesses, or a response to dialysis therapy (9, 74).

In a study of uremic patients, reduced levels of intracellular glycolytic-regulating enzymes, pyruvate kinase, phosphofructokinase, free amino acids, and protein synthesis indicated cellular malnutrition. Cellular nutrition of children on CAPD was reduced but was normal in adults. Cellular nutrition of nondialyzed uremics was the worst of all groups (75).

Protein synthesis is reduced because of the metabolic acidosis of uremia, which increases muscle-protein degradation and increases the requirements for essential amino acids. When metabolic acidosis is corrected, tissue wasting is reduced and nitrogen balance improves (76).

Other postulated causes of wasting include altered hormonal concentrations, particularly elevated glucagon and parathyroid hormone levels; impaired activity of insulin and somatomedin; decreased synthesis of erythropoietin; disordered kidney metabolism, which results in decreased synthesis or degradation of certain amino acids and hormones; elevated serum and tissue levels of uremic toxins;

and blood losses from gastrointestinal bleeding, sequestration of blood in the hemodialyzer, and excessive blood drawing for tests (9).

B. Protein Intake

i. Predialysis Ideally, essential amino acids should be provided in amounts sufficient to permit positive nitrogen balance without inordinately increasing the blood urea nitrogen levels. Protein consumption must be titrated to meet individual needs without exceeding individual tolerance levels. A minimum of 0.6 g of protein per kilogram of body weight is usually required to maintain nitrogen balance. When the diet is limited to only those proteins containing high proportions of essential amino acids, as little as 0.35 g of protein per kilogram of body weight will usually maintain nitrogen balance. In theory, excess urea in the blood can be used by the body to synthesize nonessential amino acids. In practice, however, it appears that the total amount of urea recycled in this way is limited (9–12).

ii. Hemodialysis Adults who are hemodialyzed 3 times a week need 1.0 to 1.2 g of protein per kilogram of desirable body weight per day. Approximately 6 to 7 g or as much as 10 g of amino acids and 3 to 4 g of peptides are lost in a single hemodialysis treatment in a nonfasting patient. Because 30% to 40% of the amino acids lost are essential amino acids, 50% of the daily protein intake should be from sources with high biological value. Furthermore, when glucose-free dialysate is used, the loss of 20 to 50 g of glucose that occurs with each hemodialysis alters protein metabolism to further increase protein needs (3, 12, 53).

In children undergoing maintenance hemodialysis, a positive nitrogen balance can be achieved at a protein intake of 0.3 g per centimeter of height and at an energy intake of 10 kcal/cm without an increase in dialysis requirements (61).

TABLE 15.2. USE OF UREA KINETICS TO DETERMINE PROTEIN CATABOLIC RATE DURING PREDIALYSIS STAGE OF END-STAGE RENAL DISEASE

Urea kinetics data needed	*Measurements necessary to perform calculations*
1. Residual renal urea clearance, or KrU (mL/min) $$KrU = \frac{urine\ urea}{BUN} \times \frac{urine\ volume}{time}$$	1. 24-hour urine urea in mg/mL (at least 24 hours) 2. 24-hour urine volume in mL 3. BUN in mg/mL (if reported in mg/100 mL or in mg/dL, divide by 100) 4. Time in minutes of collection (if 24 hours, time = 1,440 minutes)
2. Calculation of urea generation rate, or GU (mg/min), for nutritionally stable patient[a] GU = KrU (mL/min) × BUN (mg/mL)	1. KrU (from urea clearance calculation above) 2. BUN in mg/mL (already determined above in calculation for urea clearance)
3. Protein catabolic rate (g/day) PCR = 9.35(GU) + 11	1. GU in mg/min (determined above)
4. Comparison of 1- to 3-day dietary intake record and PCR	1. Request that dietary intake records be kept for an interval preceding the urine collection, with completion on the ending day of the urine collection.

Example:

Mr. S is a 45-year-old teacher with the following nutritional profile:

Height = 5'7"
Weight = 67 kg (medium frame)
Protein intake = 50-g-protein diet (minimum 0.6 g protein/kg or 44–55 g per creatinine clearance of 10–15)
kcal/day = 2,300 (35 kcal/kg desirable weight)
24-hour urine volume = 2,000 mL
24-hour urine urea = 5,800 mg in the entire 2,000-mL collection, or 290 mg/100 mL (5,800/200), or 2.9 mg/mL
Urinary creatinine in mg/mL = 0.45 mg/mL, or 45 mL/100 mL
BUN = 85 mg/100 mL, or 0.85 mg/mL
Serum creatinine = 6 mg/100 mL
3-day nutrient intake: day 1 = 49 g protein, 2,300 kcal
                     day 2 = 49 g protein, 2,200 kcal
                     day 3 = 48 g protein, 2,400 kcal

1. $KrU = \dfrac{urine\ urea}{BUN} \times \dfrac{urine\ volume}{time}$

    $= \dfrac{2.9\ mg/mL}{0.85\ mg/mL} \times \dfrac{2,000\ mL}{1,440\ min}$

    $= 4.7\ mL/min$

2. GU = KrU × BUN
    = 4.7 mL/min × 0.85 mg/mL
    = 4.0 mg/min

(continued)

TABLE 15.2. *CONTINUED*

3.   PCR $= 9.35(GU) + 11$
            $= 9.35(4.2 \text{ mg/min}) + 11$
            $= 48 \text{ g protein per day}$

4. Comparison of intake and protein catabolic rate: Protein catabolic rate is 48 g a day, and patient is on a 50-g-protein diet with an intake averaging 49 g per day. Therefore protein intake matches protein catabolic rate, and patient is in zero nitrogen balance.

Source: Denny, M. E., Kelley, M. P., and O'Regan Esrey, T. (204).
[a]This formula is not applicable in the nutritionally unstable patient. See source (204) for calculation of the urea generation rate in the nutritionally unstable patient (non-zero nitrogen balance).

To reduce morbidity, the National Cooperative Dialysis Study (NCDS) recommended that the protein catabolic rate be between 0.8 and 1.4 g/kg body weight/day and that the BUN not exceed 50 mg/100 mL (77).

iii. Peritoneal Dialysis The peritoneal dialysis patient needs from 1.2 to 1.5 g of protein per kilogram body weight per day, depending on his or her protein nutriture. Protein as amino acids and albumin is lost in peritoneal dialysate at the rate of 13 g per 10 hours of intermittent peritoneal dialysis. Losses of 6 to 10 g per 24 hours of CAPD have been reported. Up to 40 g per day can be lost during infection or peritonitis (9, 16, 63, 78, 79).

Of the 3 types of peritoneal dialysis, IPD treatments result in the greatest hourly losses. A major determinant of morbidity is the nutritional status of the patient, as indicated by the protein catabolic rate (PCR). In turn, the PCR is directly dependent upon the amount and type of dialysis received (27, 51). The PCR should be used to determine ideal daily protein intake. A method for calculation of the protein catabolic rate is given in table 15.2 (55).

Because CAPD involves more actual hours of dialysis, the total weekly losses are greater than losses induced by IPD alone. Spontaneous protein intake of patients on CAPD decreases over time, and the use of dialysate containing amino acids has been reported to be beneficial in those patients unable to ingest adequate amounts of protein (4, 10, 80, 81).

2. ENERGY

The diet will not be effective unless adequate calories are provided. Nitrogen balance is influenced by energy and protein intake. When protein intake is low, high caloric intakes are necessary to maintain a neutral or positive nitrogen balance. Low-protein foods that are high in complex carbohydrates or fat may provide adequate calories (7, 12, 61).

A. Predialysis To maintain weight, 35 kcal/kg/day is needed, and up to 45 kcal/kg/day in the patient who is protein malnourished or who needs to gain weight. When energy intake is low, there is a tendency for body mass and creatinine : height ratio to decrease (9, 54, 55, 82, 83).

B. Hemodialysis Caloric needs are similar to those required for predialysis. Even with obese patients, weight reduction should begin gradually in a manner that conserves nitrogen, providing 20 to 30 kcal/kg ideal body weight (10, 41, 84).

C. Peritoneal Dialysis Daily caloric recommendations for adults treated with peritoneal dialysis are provided in table 15.3. Because glucose is absorbed from the dialysate, calorie intake from food may need to be reduced to prevent undesirable weight gain. Individuals will vary in the amount of glucose they absorb, depending on peritoneal permeability (16). A method for estimating calories absorbed from dialysate fluid is given in figure 15.1.

For children with renal failure, a normal growth rate requires a daily energy intake of at least 108% of the RDA. Whether lower-protein diets supplemented with essential amino acids can improve growth rates and help restore renal metabolic function is under investigation (61, 85).

3. SODIUM

When the glomerular filtration rate is 4 to 10 mL/min or less, sodium intake must usually be restricted. Appropriateness of sodium intake can be monitored from body weight and blood pressure. In a patient who is not edematous or hypertensive, a reduction in body weight or blood pressure may indicate a need for a higher sodium intake. On the other hand, edema or an unexplained increase in body weight or hypertension may indicate a need to reduce sodium intake (9, 86–89).

Tolerance for extremes of sodium intake, both high and low, is reduced in proportion to the reduction in renal func-

TABLE 15.3. DAILY CALORIC RECOMMENDATIONS FOR ADULTS RECEIVING DIALYSIS

Type of dialysis	*Caloric recommendation (kcal/kg)*		
	Weight maintenance	*Repletion*	*Weight loss*
IPD	35	45	20–25
CAPD	25–35	35–50	20–25
CCPD	35	35–50	20–25

Source: McCann, L. (16).

FIG. 15.1. ESTIMATING ABSORPTION OF GLUCOSE FROM DIALYSATE.

Dialysis solutions:

   1.5% solution contains 15 g glucose per liter

   2.5% solution contains 25 g glucose per liter

   4.25% solution contains 42.5 g glucose per liter

Glucose (g/L) × volume (L) = total glucose (g)

   Example: A 2-L exchange of 1.5% solution = 30 g glucose

Total glucose (g) × absorption rate (approximately 80%) = glucose absorbed (g)

   Example: 30 g glucose × 80% = 24 g glucose absorbed

Glucose absorbed (g) × 3.7 kcal/g glucose = kcal absorbed

   Example: 24 g × 3.7 kcal/g = 88.8 kcal

Therefore, a 2-L exchange of 1.5% solution adds 89 kcal to the patient's caloric intake.

Source: McCann, L. (16, in the section "Diet in Chronic Renal Failure").
Note: Because each patient differs in absorption rate, these figures are estimates at best.

tion (87). In end-stage renal disease, sodium excretion may be markedly reduced, resulting in sodium retention, edema, hypertension, or congestive heart failure.

Although sodium retention is a characteristic feature of renal failure, some patients may also have a decreased capacity to conserve sodium normally. More than 99% of the sodium filtered by the normal kidney is reabsorbed. As renal failure advances, the percentage of sodium reabsorbed decreases progressively. If sodium intake is not sufficient to replace urinary losses, extracellular blood volume will decrease, followed by a decrease in the flow of blood through the kidney. The result is further decreases in glomerular filtration rate. Thus acute reductions in sodium intake may actually reduce renal function (9, 87).

In a small number of patients, the ability to conserve sodium is so impaired that their clinical state has been referred to as a salt-losing nephropathy. This condition produces severe volume and sodium depletion, most likely caused by tubulointerstitial renal disease such as medullary cystic disease, polycystic disease, chronic interstitial nephritis, or partial urethral obstruction. The condition can be demonstrated by a urinary sodium excretion greater than 80 mEq or 3,120 mg per day despite volume depletion (88, 90).

Volume depletion is difficult to identify. Patients with advanced renal failure who do not have heart failure, edema, or hypertension should be given a carefully monitored trial sodium load to determine if the extra sodium will improve their glomerular filtration rate. In most uremic patients, the daily sodium intake should be maintained at a minimum of 960 mg or 30 mEq sodium (7, 9).

A. Predialysis Most patients will require 1 to 3 g of sodium daily (18).

B. Hemodialysis As in predialysis, sodium needs depend upon urinary output: The more urine produced, the more sodium may be eliminated via the urine. Sodium intake generally must be restricted to approximately 1 to 3 g per day. Sodium and fluid intake should be controlled so that gain in weight does not exceed 2 kg between dialyses or 1 to 2 lbs. per 24 hours (53, 62).

Blood pressure control is achieved by normalization of body-fluid compartments. Over several weeks, postdialysis weight is progressively reduced by 1 to 2 lbs. each dialysis until the predialysis blood pressure is normal. Excessive interdialytic weight gains, edema, shortness of breath, and increased thirst are clinical indications that the patient needs to reduce sodium and fluid intake. Persistent hypertension may require more aggressive ultrafiltration and antihypertensive medication. Hypotension with little or no weight gain between treatments signals the need to liberalize sodium and fluid intake and/or antihypertensive medication (35, 53).

C. Peritoneal Dialysis In patients undergoing CAPD, it is easier to remove sodium and water, and a more liberal sodium of 3 to 4 g per day may be tolerated. Sodium balance and blood pressure can be well controlled on CAPD and CCPD. By liberalizing the amount of sodium and water permitted, the quantity of fluid removed from the patient, and hence the daily dialysate outflow volume, can be increased. For some CAPD patients an even higher sodium and water intake (e.g., 6 to 8 g per day of sodium and 3 L per day of water) may be possible, removing more fluid through more-hypertonic glucose exchanges. At the same time, the amount of glucose and calories absorbed from the dialysate is increased. Sodium may have to be restricted, however, in patients who use fewer high-dextrose exchanges (16, 63).

Hyponatremia has been reported in 2 anemic infants on peritoneal dialysis. It occurred because the sodium losses from ultrafiltration were greater than the sodium content of the infant formulas (91).

4. FLUID

In the early stages of renal disease, in prerenal azotemia, and in certain instances of mild renal insufficiency, a severe fluid restriction is contraindicated because it may actually worsen the condition. On the other hand, in end-stage renal disease, fluid intake may have to be curtailed to as low as 500 mL, a level that would mean even the draining of fruits and vegetables.

A. Predialysis When sodium balance is well maintained, the patient's thirst mechanism will usually serve to regulate water balance appropriately. When the GFR falls below 2 to 5 mL per minute, however, it may be necessary to monitor water intake, as well as sodium intake. Under these conditions, the development of overhydration is a risk. The amount of urine that the patient is able to produce is often used as an indicator for the adjustment of fluid intake. The attainment of an optimal quantity of body water is indicated by normal or near normal blood pressure, absence of edema, and a normal level of serum sodium. After an optimal quantity of body water is attained, daily fluid intake may be allowed to exceed the previous day's urine output by 500 mL to replace unmeasured losses. Most nondialyzed patients will retain balance with a fluid intake of 1,500 to 3,000 mL per day (9).

B. Hemodialysis In oliguric dialysis patients, fluid intake must be restricted to 750 to 1,500 mL per day. In hemodialysis, urine volume per 24 hours plus 500 mL for insensible water losses will limit weight gain to about 1 to 2 lbs. per day (53).

C. Peritoneal Dialysis During CAPD, fluid intake can be liberalized to 2,000 to 3,000 mL per day. Most patients can ultrafilter at least 2 L a day, and fluid may not need to be restricted at all on CAPD or CCPD. Fluid balance can also be adjusted by altering the quantity or strength of the hypertonic solution (16).

5. POTASSIUM

Hyperkalemia involves several risks that the diet aims to prevent. Uncontrolled hyperkalemia can lead to cardiac arrhythmias and cardiac arrest. Hyperkalemia can suppress the normal renal adaptation to chronic respiratory acid-

osis. An increased serum potassium concentration results in decreased renal ammonia production, decreased hydrogen ion excretion, and acidosis. In hyporenemic hypoaldosteronism, hyperkalemia occurs frequently. Approximately 50% of these patients with hyperkalemia have acidosis. Diabetics with nephropathy may also become hyperkalemic with only moderate reductions (20 to 80 mL/min) in the glomerular filtration rate (5, 92).

Correction of metabolic acidosis in chronic renal failure has been shown to improve potassium balance (93).

Dietary potassium may need no restriction as long as renal function is 15% or more of normal and urinary output is at least 1,000 mL per day, unless dietary potassium intake is excessive, acidosis or hypoaldosteronism occurs, or a catabolic illness or surgery supervenes (87).

During infections or following stress or severe exercise, hyperkalemia may result from a catabolic or acidotic state. Two mechanisms act to reduce the likelihood of hyperkalemia. First, as long as oliguria is not present, renal clearance of potassium falls proportionately less than glomerular filtration rate and tubular secretion of potassium by each functioning nephron increases. Second, an increase of fecal potassium excretion per unit of dietary potassium intake increases. However, fecal potassium excretion is variable from one patient to another (9, 62, 87).

A. Predialysis Potassium is often unrestricted (unless serum levels are very elevated), with intake set to maintain normal serum levels (55).

B. Hemodialysis Most patients can handle approximately 2,340 mg of potassium or 60 mEq per day and should receive no more than 2,730 mg per day. Diets that provide between 1.5 and 3 g of potassium per day permit most patients to maintain normal serum levels (between 3.5 and 5.5 mEq/L). If predialysis

serum potassium concentrations exceed 6.0 mEq/L in a patient being dialyzed 3 times weekly, dietary compliance should be evaluated (15, 53, 56, 62).

C. Peritoneal Dialysis In CAPD, intakes of 2,730 to 3,120 mg (70 to 80 mEq) per day, or 2 to 3 g, have been recommended. When daily intake is well distributed throughout the day, CAPD patients may not need potassium restrictions at all (16, 63).

6. CALCIUM AND PHOSPHORUS

Uremia is often accompanied by a group of bone disorders known as renal osteodystrophy: osteomalacia, osteoporosis, osteitis fibrosa cystica, and osteosclerosis. These disorders are accompanied by hyperphosphatemia, hypocalcemia, secondary hyperparathyroidism, and vitamin D deficiency (62).

When the glomerular filtration rate falls below 20 mL/min, serum levels of phosphate are increased. Hyperphosphatemia is harmful because of its contribution to secondary hyperparathyroidism and to an increased calcium-phosphorus product in the kidney (53). A calcium-phosphorus product greater than 70 increases calcium phosphate deposition in soft tissues, which results in metastatic calcification, further damage to the kidney, and acceleration of the progress of the disease. Calcium deposits in the skin may cause the itching or pruritus seen in advanced uremia.

The kidney plays a pivotal role in the regulation of calcium and phosphorus metabolism. It is the site of the synthesis of the metabolically active form of vitamin D and of the tubular reabsorption of calcium and phosphorus. As renal function deteriorates, serum phosphate increases and serum calcium decreases. This effect increases the secretion of parathyroid hormone, stimulating osteoclasts (bone cells) to draw calcium out of existing bone and return it to the circulation. The result is thinned-out bones characteristic of osteitis fibrosa cystica. Secondary hyperparathyroidism contributes to anemia, impotence, metastatic calcification, and renal osteodystrophy. The total amount of bone structure is also reduced by endocrine imbalances, nutritional deficiencies, and lack of physical exercise, all of which promote osteoporosis (5, 10, 62, 94, 95).

Two opposing theories exist on the cause of renal osteodystrophy. One theory is that the impairment in the metabolism of vitamin D in renal disease occurs early in the course of the disease, resulting in vitamin D deficiency. The lack of vitamin D then becomes the precipitating event in the cycle of consequent hypocalcemia, hyperphosphatemia, and demineralization of bone (96).

The second theory states that hyperphosphatemia is the primary cause. Other contributing factors are reduced calcium intake and decreased synthesis of 1,25-dihydroxycholecalciferol, the active form of vitamin D (15, 97–100).

In both children and adults, control of renal osteodystrophy requires maintaining serum phosphate levels below 6 mg/100 mL, maintaining plasma calcium between 10 and 11 mg/100 mL, and monitoring plasma parathormone levels and bone mineralization in order to prevent or treat renal osteodystrophy, especially in children (48). In children, the problem is more compelling, because bones are growing, and mineralization should be increasing. Vitamin D stimulates growth and may be needed earlier in children.

Impaired absorption leads to an increased requirement for dietary calcium. The need for calcium is magnified by low-protein and low-phosphorus diets, which are also low in calcium.

No attempt should be made to normalize serum calcium levels until the serum phosphorus level is controlled. Metastatic calcification may occur when the solubility product of calcium and phosphate is above 70. It is not safe to administer oral calcium supplements, dihydrotachysterol, or 1,25-dihydroxycholecalciferol until serum phosphate levels are down to at least 3.5 to 4.5 mg per 100 mL (35).

Although serum phosphate is better controlled by continuous ambulatory peritoneal dialysis than by hemodialysis, CAPD alone cannot correct the altered calcium-phosphate metabolism. CAPD controls serum phosphate levels, but it does not prevent the loss of vitamin D metabolites and the onset of hypocalcemia. Plasma phosphate levels are correlated with BUN levels such that when BUN levels are high, plasma phosphate levels are high. Reduced dialyzer clearances of phosphate will override effects of phosphate-binding agents and a phosphate-restricted diet and will raise serum phosphate levels (36, 37, 79).

Hyperphosphatemia or hyperparathyroidism may accelerate the rate of progression of renal failure. Limitations in phosphorus intake early in renal failure will prevent surreptitious elevations in serum phosphorus levels, complexing of serum calcium, and stimulation of parathyroid hormone secretion (36, 69, 101).

A. Predialysis Recent recommendations suggest that dietary phosphate should be restricted to 0.6 g per kilogram of body weight per day (101, 102).

In the predialysis state, 1,200 to 1,600 mg of calcium is often required to maintain calcium balance. One author has recommended from 1 to 3 g of calcium, preferably in a form such as calcium carbonate, which will also buffer metabolic acidosis (5, 56).

B. Hemodialysis In patients undergoing hemodialysis, phosphorus is usually restricted to 600 to 1,200 mg per day (53).

Despite a net calcium uptake during dialysis, patients receiving maintenance hemodialysis should receive a calcium supplement of 1.0 to 2.0 g per day of elemental calcium. The goal of therapy is to achieve serum calcium levels between 10.5 and 11.0 mg/100 mL (53, 56).

C. Peritoneal Dialysis Because of the need for phosphate-containing proteins, dietary phosphate intake cannot realistically be restricted to less than 1,000 to 1,200 mg per day. Phosphate binders are often required (16).

The recommended calcium intake in continuous peritoneal dialysis is 1,000 to 1,400 mg per day (63).

7. VITAMIN D

Although vitamin D increases phosphate absorption, various forms of it have been used in renal failure to increase intestinal calcium absorption. It has also been used to suppress secondary hyperparathyroidism and to prevent or treat renal osteodystrophy, particularly osteitis fibrosa cystica and osteomalacia. Vitamin D can be given in the form of its most active metabolite, 1,25-dihydroxycholecalciferol or one of the less potent but similarly effective forms such as the 1-hydroxylated forms or dihydrotachysterol (10, 69).

In the predialysis state, vitamin D use is controversial, and vitamin D use in the hypocalcemic dialysis patient is not safe unless serum phosphate levels have been reduced to 3.5 to 4.5 mg per 100 mL. If given when serum phosphate levels are elevated, these drugs may increase the serum calcium-phosphorus product and promote soft-tissue calcification, particularly in the kidney (10, 35).

Initial doses of 1,25-dihydroxy-vitamin-D range from 0.25 to 0.50 mcg per day. If the response is inadequate, the dose may be slowly increased, usually by no more than 0.25 mcg per day every 4 to 8 weeks (9).

8. OTHER VITAMINS AND MINERALS

The causes of vitamin and mineral deficiencies include insufficient dietary intake, altered metabolism due to uremia, antagonism of vitamins by medications, and losses during dialysis (9).

A. Ascorbic Acid   Dietary restrictions in uremia may lower vitamin C intake below the RDA, and losses also occur in dialysis, whereas stresses such as infection may increase requirements. At least 60 mg—preferably 100 mg—a day and 100 to 200 mg in continuous ambulatory peritoneal dialysis are recommended (41, 68, 69).

B. Thiamine   Erythrocyte transketolase activity, an indicator of thiamine status that was previously reported to be normal in hemodialysis, has been found to be decreased in CAPD patients. A daily supplement of 30 to 40 mg has been recommended (68).

C. Pyridoxine   Pyridoxine metabolism is altered in uremia, and deficiencies are likely to develop. The abnormal amino acid patterns, altered immune responses, and altered plasma lipid patterns in uremia may be due to pyridoxine deficiency. Assertions have been made that 300 mg daily administered to a group of hemodialysis patients improved amino acid patterns, response to an immune challenge, and serum levels of high-density lipoproteins. Present recommendations are 5 mg per day of pyridoxine hydrochloride in the predialysis state, 10 mg in hemodialysis, and 10 to 15 mg in continuous peritoneal dialysis (9, 41, 68, 69, 103).

D. Folic Acid   Hyperphosphatemia can inhibit folate uptake into the cells. Also, foods rich in folic acid often have to be restricted because of their potassium content, and leaching or prolonged cooking of foods to lower potassium content also lowers folic acid content. An estimated 30 to 150 mcg of folate are lost in dialysis. In maintenance hemodialysis and in peritoneal dialysis, 1 mg per day is recommended (16, 56, 68, 69).

E. Biotin   Biotin is loosely bound to serum proteins and is lost from the blood to the dialysate during hemodialysis (53).

F. Vitamin E   There is no evidence that uremic individuals need vitamin E supplementation. Although erythropoiesis is impaired in vitamin E–deficient animals, vitamin E supplements had no effect on the anemia of uremia (104).

G. Vitamin A   In chronic renal failure, retinol may not be converted to retinoic acid in the kidney and excreted in the urine in the normal way. Excessive amounts of unmetabolized vitamin A may be found in the liver and plasma of these patients and may result in vitamin A toxicity. Thus, vitamin A supplements are contraindicated. Recently the use of routine supplementation even of the B vitamins has been questioned, and supplementation of any kind should be accompanied by periodic monitoring of blood levels (53, 105).

H. Vitamin K   Vitamin K supplements are not recommended (53).

I. Iron   A low or falling serum ferritin (below 80 mg/100 mL) may indicate iron deficiency. Bleeding from the gastrointestinal tract, sequestration in the dialyzer, protein-restricted diets, and menstrual losses of the young female are common causes. An acute reduction in hematocrit of greater than 5% may be due to the presence of chloramine in the dialysate (5, 35).

For most patients, the anemia is not due to iron deficiency, and iron supplementation has no value. Except for the elderly, severe cardiac problems, or acute overt blood loss, routine blood transfusions are discouraged because of the risk of hepatitis and iron overload (35).

Red cells have a shortened life span in uremia, and there is a lack of the blood-forming hormone erythropoietin, normally synthesized in the kidney. In addition, bone marrow of uremic patients is less responsive to erythropoietin. A new form of recombinant human erythropoietin produced by genetic engineering

has been found to shorten bleeding times and increase hematocrits in these patients. However, iron demand is significantly increased, and supplementation may be necessary if iron stores are not adequate. In long-term dialysis patients, erythropoietin has been used to reduce iron overload in conjunction with ferritin (7, 62, 106–110).

Coagulation defects and bleeding states are common. A platelet abnormality that involves failure to produce the thromboplastic substance factor III has been implicated (62).

J. Zinc   A reduction in the plasma zinc concentration with an increase in zinc concentrations in red cells, the brain, and the heart has been noted in dialysis. In CAPD, serum zinc concentrations are also low, whereas red cell concentrations are increased. In a recent study, dialysis-associated hypogeusia and uremic polyneuropathy responded to long-term zinc supplementation. A positive response to zinc supplementation is the best criterion of zinc deficiency (111, 112).

Hemodialyzed patients are at greater risk for zinc deficiency. A zinc intake of 10 mg a day permitted positive zinc balance in normal controls. The same diet caused negative zinc balance in hemodialysis patients. The study demonstrated that augmented fetal zinc excretion in the presence of hypozincemia contributes to the negative zinc balance in hemodialyzed uremic patients (113).

K. Selenium   Selenium is an essential trace element for glutathianine peroxidase activity. Selenium deficiency has been found with hemodialysis in association with skeletal and cardiac myopathy and may increase the risk for cardiovascular disease and cancer. When compared with normal controls, hemodialysis patients had much lower levels of plasma selenium, plasma glutathianine peroxidase, and erythrocyte glutathione peroxidase (114).

L. Magnesium   Hypermagnesemia is more likely to occur in renal patients than is magnesium deficiency, particularly in patients taking magnesium antacids, because magnesium balance is regulated in the kidney. Most patients with uremia should avoid the use of laxatives, enemas, or phosphate binders containing magnesium. An intake of 200 mg of magnesium per day will maintain balance in most patients. The diet used to treat chronic renal failure is usually low in magnesium—100 to 300 mg per day on a diet of 40 g protein (35, 53).

M. Aluminum   The use of aluminum hydroxide phosphate-binding gels to control hyperphosphatemia can lead to aluminum toxicity, osteomalacia, encephalopathy, and a microcytic anemia. Aluminum toxicity secondary to dialysis leads to a microcytic anemia, which is reversible after deionization of the water supply (115–121).

The use of an alkalinizing citrate, Shohl's solution, enhances aluminum absorption. Serum aluminum levels in renal patients increase with age. Citrate may cause encephalopathy, especially in the elderly. Shohl's solution and aluminum hydroxide should not be used in renal disease (122).

N. Fluoride   Fluoride levels in adult hemodialysis patients have been reported to be twice the normal levels. The most critical vulnerability to excess fluoride for the permanent teeth occurs at age 2. Infants who are on peritoneal dialysis may be at particular risk for fluoride loading and the complications of excessive fluoride exposure. Factors that contribute to elevated levels include the consumption of fluoride in water, severe renal insufficiency, and the scant removal of fluoride through dialysis. Infants with renal disease should not receive fluoride supplements (123).

9. LIPIDS

Abnormalities of carbohydrate and fat metabolism are common in uremic di-alysis and nondialysis patients. Hyperlipidemia begins to appear when creatinine clearance falls to 50 mL/min, and it may affect the progression of the disease (41, 42, 124–129).

There is a high incidence of hyperlipidemia with reduced plasma levels of high-density lipoprotein and elevated plasma levels of very-low-density lipoprotein in chronically uremic patients and those undergoing maintenance hemodialysis. It is the major lipid disorder in patients with chronic renal failure, affecting 30% of patients. Reduced lipolysis of triglyceride-rich proteins may be the major defect (42, 126, 129).

The association between lipoprotein and apolipoprotein levels has been investigated. The progression of renal insufficiency was accompanied by marked increases in total triglycerides and low-density and high-density lipoproteins. Alterations were present even in early stages of renal disease (130). There is some concern that these changes cause deterioration of renal function via atherosclerosis of the kidney. These changes are associated with an increased incidence of ischemic heart disease, although doubt has been cast as to whether lipid abnormalities actually accelerate atheromatous disease in uremic patients and whether hypertriglyceridemia is a risk factor (42, 127).

A. Hemodialysis   Patients on long-term dialysis have a high incidence of cardiovascular events. There is a 56% mortality rate in hemodialysis, with half of the deaths related to consequences of atherosclerosis, such as myocardial infarction. Dialysis patients have lower levels of apolipoprotein B than do controls. The catabolic rate of this apoprotein is also decreased. These changes all contribute to accelerated atherogenesis (131).

Carnitine deficiency can provoke hyperlipidemia, and patients undergoing dialysis, particularly hemodialysis, often have reduced plasma and muscle car-nitine levels, all of which may be ameliorated by carnitine supplements. L-Carnitine is a metabolite of lysine and methionine that functions as the transport vehicle for long-chain fatty acids. It is lost in the dialysis bath. In a group of hemodialysis patients with hypertriglyceridemia and low serum levels of high-density lipoprotein cholesterol, carnitine supplementation reduced serum levels of triglyceride and increased serum levels of high-density lipoprotein cholesterol (132–134).

In a study of children on hemodialysis, a daily dose of 5 mg of carnitine per kilogram of body weight resulted in marked reductions in serum triglyceride levels. In another study of hemodialysis patients, fatty acid abnormalities, including a depletion of essential fatty acids, were reversed by carnitine supplementation. Treatment should avoid high doses of carnitine, which have adverse antiketogenic effects. If serum triglycerides are elevated, serum carnitine should be measured. If serum carnitine is low, patients may receive a trial of L-carnitine— 0.5 to 1.0 g per day for nondialyzed patients with chronic renal failure and for maintenance dialysis patients. Alternatively, hemodialysis patients may be given 1.5 g of L-carnitine at the end of each dialysis (135, 136).

B. Peritoneal Dialysis   CAPD is associated with a loss of all plasma lipoproteins into the dialysate through a molecular sieving effect of the peritoneal membrane. There is a continuous loss of plasma HDL in CAPD patients. This loss, along with the hypertriglyceridemia that occurs, suggests increased catabolism as well as defective metabolism of HDL (128).

Diminished lipoprotein lipase activity, perhaps related to decreased insulin sensitivity, results in hypertriglyceridemia. Many peritoneal dialysis patients, particularly those who do not get the routine heparin therapy given in hemodialysis (which tends to clear triglycerides), have increased serum levels of triglycerides. In CAPD an added cause of hypertriglyceridemia is probably continuous glucose absorption from the dialysate bath, with resultant insulin release. There is also some evidence that an increase in the synthesis of very-low-density lipoproteins contributes to hypertriglyceridemia (16, 54, 124, 128, 130, 137, 138).

10. CARBOHYDRATE AND FIBER

The action of many hormones that normally play a regulatory role in lipoprotein metabolism is disturbed in chronic renal failure. The kidney plays a central role in the production and metabolism of many hormones, such as insulin and glucagon, and renal failure changes the internal environment that affects many of these hormones. The rate of degradation and removal from the circulation of hormones such as insulin, glucagon, gastrin, and prolactin is decreased. The result is carbohydrate intolerance in nondiabetics, increased insulin requirements in diabetics, enhanced gluconeogenesis from the amino acid serine, increased peripheral resistance to insulin, diminished lipoprotein lipase activity, thyroid dysfunction, and glucagon hypersensitivity. In advanced renal failure, diminished catabolism of endogenous and exogenous insulin by the diseased kidney decreases insulin requirements (15, 62, 127, 137–139).

It has been suggested that certain forms of fiber may reduce serum urea and creatinine concentrations via the inhibition of ammonia generation (140).

Constipation is a problem in many dialysis patients because of medications, fluid restrictions, and lack of exercise. Foods high in insoluble fiber such as whole grains and wheat bran should be encouraged. Because these foods are often high in potassium and phosphorus, they should be carefully incorporated into the exchange system, e.g., by replacing high-potassium fruits with low-potassium fruits.

INDICATIONS FOR USE

1. PLASMA UREA AND CREATININE

When creatinine clearance is less than 25 mL per minute or blood urea nitrogen exceeds 100 mg per 100 mL, protein restriction is indicated. Elevations of plasma urea and creatinine occur rapidly once 50% to 70% of glomerular filtration has been lost. In view of the potentially damaging effect of high protein intakes and the possibility that the progression of the disease may be accelerated, protein excesses should be avoided (5, 15).

2. UREMIC SYMPTOMS

The timing of the decision to intervene with dietary therapy also depends upon the appearance of symptoms. The appearance of anorexia, nausea, diarrhea, and vomiting is also indication for protein restriction (5).

3. SERUM CALCIUM AND PHOSPHORUS LEVELS

Calcium and phosphorus blood levels should be under surveillance, with dietary interventions whenever phosphorus exceeds normal limits (5). Calcium supplementation should always await modification of the serum calcium-phosphorus product to 70 or less.

4. URINARY OUTPUT

Sodium restrictions are usually initiated when the glomerular filtration rate drops to 4 to 10 mL per minute, whereas potassium restrictions are usually not indicated until urinary output is less than 1,000 mL per day (15).

POSSIBLE ADVERSE REACTIONS

Failure to meet caloric and minimum protein needs in children can result in growth failure. Overzealous protein restriction may result in negative nitrogen balance, protein deficiency, muscle wasting, and growth retardation, par-

ticularly when energy intakes are 75% below the Recommended Dietary Allowances. The importance of early diagnosis and treatment cannot be overemphasized. Even a few months' delay in proper dietary therapy can result in growth retardation that cannot be made up in later years and that could have been prevented (8, 11, 12, 19, 141).

Inadequate energy intake in adults also contributes to muscle wasting, weight loss, and decline in nutritional status.

Unnecessary fluid restrictions in the early stages of renal insufficiency in the absence of any signs of hyponatremia and in patients without decreased urinary output will diminish blood flow through the kidney. This condition further decreases the rate of glomerular filtration and kidney function.

Calcium supplementation in a patient with high levels of serum phosphate can promote soft-tissue calcification and renal osteodystrophy (15).

There is a propensity for protein-calorie malnutrition with long-term use. Although generally well nourished, patients with a glomerular filtration rate (GFR) of 24 mL/min/1.73 m^2 or lower had a low intake energy of about 23 kcal/kg/day after years on a low-protein diet. The energy intake was lower as GFR decreased, and there was a tendency for creatinine-height ratio and body mass to decrease as the years progressed and GFR continued to fall (83).

CONTRAINDICATIONS

The diet is not indicated for use with conditions other than renal failure, such as hypernatremia or elevated blood urea nitrogen values, which reflect dehydration rather than renal disease. Successful nutritional intervention presupposes that the diet is individualized to the clinical, biochemical, and nutritional profile of the patient and that adjustments are made frequently, based upon changes in the patient (142–149).

CLINICAL ASSESSMENT

Anthropometry is important in chronic renal failure and should include at least height, weight, triceps, and subscapular skinfold thickness, percent body fat, midarm muscle circumference estimations, and percentages of standard values. Predictions of adult height are important in children.

Standardization is vital in order for measurements to be valid. Serial measurements done by the same person are more valuable than a single estimation or measurements taken by different practitioners, particularly if they have not standardized their techniques. For dialysis patients, percentage of relative dry body weight and weight change as percentage of usual weight are also important. Whenever possible, estimations of lean body mass and evaluation of body composition provide useful information to the routine nutritional assessment procedures (69, 150–153).

Estimations of nutrient intake that include total calories, protein, nitrogen, dietary fiber, sodium, potassium, calcium, phosphorus, and amount and type of fat and carbohydrate should be done periodically. Whenever serum potassium levels exceed 6.0 mEq per liter, nutrient intakes should be estimated to monitor the level of dietary compliance. Diet diaries, 1- to 3-day recalls, and nutrition histories targeted for the uremic population and timed to identify intake during the periods between dialyses are all useful clinical nutritional assessment tools when administered and interpreted by a trained dietitian. A sample diet history for use in end-stage renal disease has been published elsewhere (150).

Other important clinical determinations are the actual physical appearance of the patient, including skin and skin turgor, as well as urine volume, blood pressure, and activity level (154, 155).

BIOCHEMICAL ASSESSMENT

Blood chemistries will be affected by the timing of the sample drawing in relation to dialysis. The most useful information will be provided by samples taken just before dialysis. If the procedure is interrupted due to complications such as hypotension, the blood chemistries will not provide accurate information. Changes in the composition of the dialysate solution will also change the blood biochemistries. For example, the calcium content of dialysate can be varied from 0 to 4.5 mEq per liter, and the potassium content can vary from 0 to 4 mEq per liter (56).

The dietitian should also monitor urine output and clearance tests. Changes in kidney function call for changes in the diet.

1. BLOOD UREA NITROGEN

Sometimes referred to or measured as serum urea nitrogen (SUN), blood urea nitrogen (BUN) correlates well with dietary intake, except when accompanied by inadequate dialysis periods, blood flow rates, or techniques; blood loss into the gastrointestinal tract; protein catabolism; or hyperosmolar dehydration. BUN values below 40 mg per 100 mL suggest malnutrition, whereas values above 100 mg per 100 mL are often accompanied by dietary noncompliance and symptoms such as nausea, vomiting, sleepiness, and taste changes (156).

2. SERUM CREATININE

Serum creatinine values are not affected by diet but are proportional to muscle mass. Provided that muscle mass is not declining, they are an indicator of renal function.

3. CREATININE CLEARANCE ESTIMATIONS

One way to estimate optimum protein intake is based upon creatinine clearance, which is properly done via a 24-hour urine estimation. In patients in whom urine output remains constant, a 2-hour creatinine clearance test may be useful (157). In instances in which a 24-hour urine collection has not been done, the following formula may be used to estimate creatinine clearance from lean body mass, serum creatinine, and age (158).

In men:
$$\text{Creatinine clearance} = \frac{(140 - \text{age}) \times \text{body weight (kg)}}{72 \times \text{serum creatinine}}$$

In women:
$$\text{Creatinine clearance} = \frac{(140 - \text{age}) \times \text{body weight (kg)}}{72 \times \text{serum creatinine}} \times 0.85$$

Example: If serum creatinine = 2.0 in a 70-kg, 60-year-old-male, then creatinine clearance would be calculated as follows:

$$\frac{(140 - 60) \times 70}{72 \times 2.0} = \frac{5,600}{144} = 32$$

This method of determination is not valid for patients receiving dialysis, patients with acute renal failure, or patients in a catabolic state in which muscle mass is being destroyed (159).

The creatinine clearance parallels the glomerular filtration rate and is a useful parameter with which to predict individual levels of protein tolerance and to set the level of the protein prescription. In the predialysis state, an adult with a glomerular filtration rate of 4 to 10 mL per minute should have a diet that provides 0.55 to 0.60 g of protein per kilogram of body weight per day. For a man who weighs 70 kg, this formula provides an intake of 40 g of protein per day, about two-thirds of which should be provided by high-quality proteins. High-quality proteins provide a high content of essential amino acids in proportions that are similar to the daily requirements for humans. For women, and for men under 130 lbs., protein intake may be closer to 35 g per day and should include approximately 20 g of high-quality protein (9).

4. RELATIONSHIP BETWEEN BLOOD UREA NITROGEN, SERUM CREATININE, AND DIETARY PROTEIN INTAKE

In men during predialysis, there is a direct relationship between dietary protein intake and the ratio of blood urea nitrogen to creatinine concentration. Equations based upon that relationship permit an estimate of the optimal protein intake needed to maintain a specific BUN level (9):

$$y = 0.13x + 0.77$$

and

$$x = \frac{(y - 0.77)}{0.13}$$

where y = BUN level (mg/100 mL) divided by serum creatinine concentration and x = estimated protein needs (g/day).

Example: In a man with a serum creatinine concentration of 10, it is desired to maintain the BUN level at 60 mg/100 mL. Optimal protein intake would be estimated as follows:

$$y = \frac{\text{BUN level}}{\text{serum creatinine concentration}}$$
$$= \frac{60}{10} = 6$$
$$x = \frac{(6 - 0.77)}{0.13} = 40 \text{ g per day}$$

Optimal protein intake to maintain BUN level at 60 mg/100 mL is 40 g per day.

This relationship can also be used to estimate the patient's average protein intake and the level of dietary compliance to protein restriction. Uremic symptoms do not usually appear until the BUN is above 90 mg/100 mL, and it has been recommended that protein intake not exceed the amount required to maintain the BUN level below 90 mg/100 mL (9).

There are limitations to the use of this estimate. For women, the relationship between the BUN : creatinine ratio and protein intake has not been well defined, and this equation should not be used in the manner described above. Other factors that can alter the predictability of the BUN : creatinine ratio include mild oliguria, catabolic stress, and decreased

muscle mass, each of which will increase the ratio (9).

5. UREA KINETICS

Nitrogen balance is not an accurate measure of protein nutriture in renal failure. The use of urea kinetics to estimate protein balance of the nutritionally unstable patient allows the dietitian to guide protein intake into the optimal range for minimized catabolite accumulation and maximized nutritional status. The protein catabolic rate (PCR), or the amount of protein catabolized to waste products per day in grams, is calculated from the rate of urea nitrogen generation (GU) (55, 160, 161). Guidelines and sample calculations are provided in table 15.2.

Because urea is the major nitrogenous product of protein and amino acid metabolism, urea nitrogen appearance correlates closely with, and can be used to estimate, total nitrogen output or net protein degradation in both nondialyzed chronically uremic patients and hemodialysis patients (150). It permits estimation of nitrogen balance and has other practical applications in renal disease that are discussed in the Appendix (see "Using Urea Nitrogen Appearance in Nutritional Assessment").

6. ALBUMIN

The usefulness of serum albumin determinations in nutritional assessment is limited, in part because they are influenced by hydration status. However, for the uremic individual who is not edematous, they can be an adjunct to other tests in evaluating the adequacy of the protein intake. Uremia may affect albumin metabolism and thus serum levels. Low serum albumin levels also occur in CAPD, particularly in children whose increased protein requirements for CAPD and growth are not being met (63, 159, 162, 163).

In hemodialysis patients, prealbumin levels are highly correlated with nutritional status and outcome. Serum prealbumin levels in hemodialysis patients

are normally higher than in healthy volunteers. The higher levels may be due to the formation of a complex that is a combination of prealbumin and retinol-binding protein (164).

Abnormal urinary albumin excretion can be used to predict the development of clinically significant nephropathy in insulin-dependent diabetes. It is not an accurate enough measure, however, at the present time to permit its use on a large scale for screening. A new technique, the measurement of immunoglobulin subclasses in the urine, appears to be a promising parameter to characterize and subgroup diabetic patients with preclinical diabetic nephropathy (165, 166).

7. IMMUNOLOGICAL ASSAYS

Malnutrition and uremia have profound effects upon immune function. Poor nutritional status may be a cause of impaired lymphocyte function, as measured by counts of number and type of lymphocytes, tests of antibody production, and delayed cutaneous hypersensitivity using *Candida* and purified protein derivative (PPD) (167–169).

8. SERUM SODIUM

For the most part, serum sodium values reflect fluid and hydration status, not whether the patient is taking in too much or too little sodium. Serum sodium values alone are not an indication for the dietitian to recommend either an increase or a decrease in sodium intake in the renal patient.

For example, clinical assessment of extracellular fluid volume to confirm its depletion requires an evaluation of both the urine sodium and chloride concentrations. Even in instances when a low serum sodium level actually does represent depleted total-body sodium stores, such an identification cannot be made on the basis of serum sodium values alone. In renal sodium wasting, more than 20 mEq per liter of sodium is excreted in a 24-hour urine collection. Some patients who have low serum sodium values actually have increased amounts of total body sodium. Such is the situation in nephrotic syndrome and in congestive heart failure. Whenever hyponatremia is suspected, it is also important to determine serum and urine osmolality as well as 24-hour urinary sodium excretion in order to ascertain the cause and the best dietary intervention (88, 170).

Serum sodium levels may drop during the period between dialyses, because fluid is retained along with extra weight. A decreased serum sodium level in a patient who is gaining weight may indicate too much sodium and water intake, not too little. If serum sodium concentration remains in the normal range, interdialytic weight gain is a relatively accurate measure of sodium intake. A weight gain of 1 kg is equal to an extracellular fluid (ECF) expansion of 1 L and a sodium intake of 130 to 140 mEq. Patients using salt in excess quantities in the interdialytic period experience chronic overexpansion of the ECF and become hypertensive (170).

If serum sodium falls significantly below normal (less than 120 mEq per liter), it may also reflect the dilution effect of a high concentration of plasma lipids, rather than representing an actual decrease in body sodium content. Sodium is dissolved only in plasma water, which is displaced by the lipids. This form of hyponatremia is also referred to as euosmolar artifactual hyponatremia because it is associated with a normal plasma osmolality (86, 156).

Hyperosmolar hyponatremia means there is an elevated serum osmolality and cellular dehydration. It may be due to mannitol infusions or may occur in the diabetic with severe hyperglycemia (88). The presence of substances such as mannitol and glucose in the extracellular fluid result in the drawing out of water from the intracellular fluid into the extracellular fluid. The extra fluid dilutes the plasma and results in a low serum sodium level. Similarly, a rise in blood glucose from 100 to 800 mg/100 mL will reduce the plasma sodium concentration from 140 to 129 mEq per liter.

A low serum sodium level accompanied by a low serum osmolality means hypoosmolar hyponatremia and often reflects the inability of the kidney to excrete adequate amounts of fluid (88).

Symptoms of true sodium depletion, as may accompany excess sodium and fluid removal from dialysis, include a sudden drop in blood pressure, nausea, weakness, and muscle cramps.

The optimum dietary sodium intake can be ascertained more precisely by examining the maximum and minimum capacity of the kidney to excrete or conserve sodium. The technique involves sodium loading and sodium dietary restrictions to specific known levels over a period of several days. During the test period, 24-hour urinary sodium excretion rates, body weight, blood pressure, and serum sodium concentrations are monitored (9).

9. SERUM BICARBONATE

Bicarbonate is the major extracellular buffer of hydrogen ions in the body. Hydrogen ions are generated from the breakdown of sulfur amino acids and nuclear proteins and the incomplete oxidation of carbohydrates and fats. In renal disease, bicarbonate reabsorption is decreased by fluid retention and hyperkalemia. Expansion of extracellular fluid volume is the most important hindrance to bicarbonate reabsorption. When the glomerular filtration rate of a failing kidney falls to 5 to 10 mL per minute, the kidney's ability to excrete excess hydrogen ions and to regenerate bicarbonate may be impaired to the point of acidosis. If serum bicarbonate levels fall, sodium and fluid may need to be restricted to prevent volume expansion. The intake of acid-producing proteins may also need to be limited (47, 171).

10. SERUM POTASSIUM

Hypokalemia or hyperkalemia can lead to cardiac arrest. In instances of persistent hyperkalemia, 1 g of the exchange resin Kayexalate will bind 1 mEq of potassium, and it will be excreted in the stool. Because the process involves sodium retention by the body of 1 mEq sodium for every mEq of potassium lost in the stools, the use of this drug has obvious limitations for the person on a sodium-restricted diet. Hyperkalemia is caused by excessive intake, fever, infection, surgery, or gastrointestinal bleeding (159).

11. SERUM CALCIUM AND PHOSPHORUS

Even before hypocalcemia occurs in chronic renal failure, urinary calcium excretion falls. Even in the presence of a normal serum calcium level, a high serum alkaline phosphatase level may indicate that calcium is being withdrawn from bones in an effort to maintain serum calcium at a normal level. Symptoms of hypocalcemia include tingling fingers, abdominal cramps, convulsions, tetany, and cardiac or respiratory arrest (159, 172).

The most accurate and reliable way to measure the serum calcium level is with an ionized calcium analyzer, although there is another less accurate method that takes advantage of the fact that most of the protein-bound calcium is bound to albumin. Alterations in the serum protein concentrations will affect the level of total calcium. For every fall in serum albumin of 1 g per liter, the total serum calcium will decrease by 0.8 mg per 100 mL. The relationship between the total serum calcium and the serum albumin concentration is often useful in the interpretation of the total calcium concentration. A low albumin level will lower the serum total calcium. Ionized calcium may be very roughly estimated from serum or plasma total calcium and total protein by the following formula (158, 173, 174).

Ionized calcium (mg/100 mL) = {[total calcium (mg/100 mL) × 6] − [total protein (g/100 mL) × 3]} ÷ total protein

In instances of continued high levels of serum phosphate, despite phosphate binders, the dietitian should scrutinize the diet for hidden sources of phosphate in the form of food additives—e.g., additives in certain soft drinks (175). In addition, the timing of the use of phosphate binders in relationship to meals should be ascertained in the diet history; they can do nothing to help phosphate absorption if taken before or after rather than with meals. A low serum phosphorus level may indicate excessive use of phosphate-binding drugs.

12. IRON, HEMOGLOBIN, AND HEMATOCRIT

High levels of serum iron usually reflect multiple blood transfusions. Serum ferritin levels should be evaluated before any form of iron supplementation is recommended. Normal ferritin levels indicate adequate iron stores. In renal disease, anemia is caused by decreased production of red blood cells, a lack of erythropoietin, hemolysis of red blood cells, gastrointestinal blood loss, and frequent blood sampling (159). A low serum hemoglobin level or hematocrit taken just before dialysis in a patient who has gained a considerable amount of weight may actually reflect hemodilution from the fluid retention to a certain extent. These indicators should be remeasured when the patient is at dry weight.

13. SERUM COPPER

Hypercupremia occurs in uremia before the onset of dialysis and continues independently of the mode of dialysis (176). The cause is not known.

14. CHOLESTEROL AND TRIGLYCERIDES

In contrast to the general population, a much greater percentage of individuals with renal failure have hyperlipidemia, and their serum cholesterol and triglyceride levels should be monitored at least monthly. There may be a reduction in the catabolism of lipoproteins. In patients with elevated serum triglyceride levels who are at minimal dry weight for height, maintenance of dry weight should take priority over any attempt to further restrict calories in order to lower serum triglycerides.

15. SERUM GLUCOSE

Because of decreased insulin removal from the circulation of the renal diabetic, insulin requirements are often decreased (59). On the other hand, peritoneal dialysis involves absorption of considerable amounts of glucose, which must be taken into account as a source of calories.

16. SERUM URIC ACID

Serum uric acid levels may be elevated, precipitating an attack of gout in individuals with a history of the disorder (177, 178). Most foods high in protein are already restricted on the diet, so that no additional restrictions are necessary.

17. OTHER LABORATORY TESTS

Among other biochemical indices of nutritional assessment are serum transferrin (estimated from total iron-binding capacity), total protein, and creatinine height index in nondialyzed patients (56).

ASSESSMENT OF POTENTIAL DRUG INTERACTIONS

1. PHOSPHATE BINDERS

Drugs such as aluminum hydroxide gels are intended to increase the fecal excretion of phosphorus. They must be taken with meals in order to be effective but

should not be taken at the same time as iron or calcium supplements because they may bind and excrete the iron and the calcium. Possible gastrointestinal side effects include nausea, vomiting, anorexia, and constipation. Antacids containing magnesium are contraindicated because they can lead to excessive blood magnesium levels, which cause depression of the central nervous system. Aluminum hydroxide gel inhibits the absorption of tetracyclines, barbiturates, digoxin, and anticholinergics. Aluminum contamination of dialysate water and excessive use of aluminum hydroxide phosphate binders can result in deposition of the metal in bones, as well as a form of encephalopathy. Calcium alginate is an aluminum-free phosphate binder used in CAPD. It is a good alternative to aluminum-containing phosphate binders because it does not lead to hyperaluminemia, it prevents aluminum intoxication, and it has no serious side effects (179–182).

Calcium carbonate in high doses has been shown to be as effective as aluminum hydroxide for the control of hyperphosphatemia and hyperparathyroidism. Calcium carbonate may be preferable to aluminum compounds for preventing hyperaluminemia. Use of phosphate binders should be geared toward producing the lowest 24-hour urinary phosphate excretion achievable. A rule of thumb is to achieve phosphate excretion in milligrams that is 7 times the clearance rate of creatinine in mL/min (38, 183).

A mixture of ketoacids is also effective in lowering increased serum phosphate and serum parathyroid levels. Recent studies to clarify the underlying mechanisms reveal that ketoacids act as phosphate binders (184).

2. CALCIUM SUPPLEMENTS

Calcium impairs the absorption of ferrous salts and tetracycline, whereas steroid administration interferes with calcium absorption (179). Calcium is lost as a soap as a result of steatorrhea.

If given when serum phosphorus levels are elevated, calcium supplements will enhance soft-tissue calcification of the kidney. Possible side effects of their use are constipation, anorexia, flatulence, nausea, vomiting, polyuria, and thirst (179).

3. ANABOLIC ANDROGENIC HORMONES

Used to treat anemias in renal failure, androgens promote retention of fluid, sodium, potassium, nitrogen, and phosphorus and excretion of calcium. They also promote weight gain, increased appetite, nausea, vomiting, diarrhea, and elevation of serum triglyceride levels (179).

4. ANTIARRHYTHMIC DRUGS

The antiarrhythmic activity of bretylium, lidocaine, phenytoin, and procainamide may be enhanced by a state of hyperkalemia. An elevated blood urea nitrogen level is a potential side effect of atenolol, metoprolol, nadolol, propranolol, and timolol (179).

5. ANTIBIOTICS

Penicillin G is high in sodium and potassium and should be avoided in renal disease. Penicillin V potassium may cause hyperkalemia (179).

6. DRUGS USED TO TREAT HYPERLIPIDEMIA

Several drugs are used and are discussed in the section on fat-controlled diets. A combination of bile-acid sequestrants and hydroxymethylglutaryl coenzyme-A (HMG-CoA) reductase is most effective (129).

7. ERYTHROPOIETIN

Before the clinical availability of recombinant human erythropoietin, the only treatment for symptomatic anemic patients was blood transfusion. Five chil-

dren on peritoneal dialysis responded to recombinant human erythropoietin with an increase in the hemoglobin levels to normal and total elimination of the need for subsequent transfusions. However, the treatment is not yet available for all children. Another study has found that recombinant human erythropoietin not only helps erythropoiesis but also corrects amino acid problems seen in renal failure, such as the decreased tyrosine-to-phenylalanine ratio and decreased glutamine levels (48, 185).

8. OTHER DRUGS

Anticonvulsants reduce calcium absorption by facilitating the conversion of vitamin D to inactive metabolites. An increase in calcium intake may decrease phenytoin absorption (179).

Sodium bicarbonate, prochlorperazine, and thrimethobenzamide are used to treat severe metabolic acidosis (serum bicarbonate level below 15 to 18 mEq per liter) in renal failure, and prochlorperazine and trimethobenzamide are used to treat nausea (97). Prochlorperazine (Compazine) may cause constipation and increased serum glutamic-oxaloacetic transaminase (SGOT), serum glutamic-pyruvic transaminase (SGPT), lactic dehydrogenase (LDH), and alkaline phosphatase. It may increase the need for riboflavin and may cause dry mouth, blurred vision, and, if given intravenously, extensive dizziness.

Pruritus due to hyperparathyroidism is treated with ultraviolet light, diphenylhydramine, or activated charcoal. It causes dry mouth and altered taste (97, 186).

Prazosin and propranolol work together to lower blood pressure and serum lipids in hemodialysis patients. Minipress may cause dry mouth and gastrointestinal distress. Propranolol may mask symptoms of hyperglycemia in diabetics. It results in decreased serum levels of glucose and HDL and increased serum

levels of potassium, triglycerides, BUN, uric acid, SGOT, SGPT, LDH, and alkaline phosphatase (186, 187).

Diazepam (Valium) is used to treat severe muscle cramps and myoclonic spasms or twitches that do not respond to dietary protein restriction (97). It may cause fatigue and increased appetite.

Rheumatic symptoms may be treated with phenylbutazone (Butazolidin). It results in hyperglycemia, gastrointestinal distress, altered taste, and decreased absorption of folate, tryptophan, and amino acids (97, 186).

9. DRUG INTERFERENCE WITH LABORATORY TESTS IN NEPHROLOGY

Increases in serum creatinine levels are produced by cephalosporins, trimethoprim and cimetidine, and acetylsalicylic acid. Acetohexamide increases serum urea nitrogen levels. Ascorbic acid, salicylates, acetaminophen, aminophylline, and methyldopa increase serum uric acid levels (188).

False positive urinary protein determinations are produced by aminosalicylic acid, acetylsalicylic acid, cephalosporins, penicillins, sulfonamides, acetazolamide, tolbutamide, and tolmetin (188).

A more complete description of drug use in renal disease and the necessary adjustments in dialysis has recently been published (189). Other effects of drugs used in renal disease on blood tests are given in table 15.4. The mineral content of drugs may be a factor in considering total intake. The mineral content of selected drugs is given in table 15.5.

IMPLEMENTATION AND EDUCATION

1. CLIENT COMPREHENSION

Renal management is a difficult balancing act between tolerance levels and needs for a number of nutrients whose intake is controlled by the diet prescription. Simplified diet exchange booklets and educational materials that make extensive use of graphics to communicate complex concepts are available. Some patients do not respond well to any type of exchange list and become confused; for them a set of specific menus written from actual food composition data may be best. For other patients such a system may be too confining and may not provide the desired level of variety (102, 191–193).

For dietitians who have access to a personal computer, several nutritional analysis programs lend themselves well to formulating a set of menus or meal plans. Renal cookery classes and cookbooks that focus on maintenance of adequate calories or the specialized needs of different types of patient are also useful in increasing compliance (193–195).

2. ETHNIC DIETS

Because diet is culturally determined, it is important to evaluate it as such. For example, there is no "black diet" as such. However, certain eating patterns that are characteristic of blacks in this country are important to consider in the impact of diet on renal disease. Approximately 53% of the black population lives in the South. Food preparation methods include frying, smothering and barbecuing meats, and using black pepper, hot sauces, ham hocks, and salt pork as essential flavorings. Fewer blacks than whites consume milk, yogurt, cheese, and beef. Blacks in general have higher intakes of meat, eggs, vitamin A, and salty foods (196).

Dietary compliance in black dialysis patients is only 30%. Cultural food preferences of blacks have a negative impact on the renal diet. Greens caused increased serum K levels in 26% of patients studied, and french fries have caused more instances of elevated serum K levels than any other food in blacks (197).

Practical guidelines can be given to

TABLE 15.4. EFFECTS OF SELECTED DRUGS ON BLOOD TESTS

Blood test	Increased by	Decreased by
Potassium	Triamterene Spironolactone Amiloride Salt substitutes Penicillin G potassium Phosphorus replacements (Fleet's Phospho-Soda, K-Phos-Neutral Tablets, Neutra-Phos, Neutra-Phos-K) Anabolic androgenic hormones	Penicillin G sodium Laxatives Corticosteroids Furosemide Ethacrynic acid Licorice IV sodium bicarbonate Hypertonic glucose and insulin IV Hydrochlorothiazide Kayexalate
Calcium	Aluminum hydroxide gel Basic aluminum carbonate gel Vitamin D preparations Calcium replacements Triamterene Spironolactone Amiloride Hydrochlorothiazide Anabolic androgenic hormones	Tetracycline Corticosteroids Furosemide Ethacrynic acid Dilantin Phosphorus replacements Kayexalate Antacids containing phosphorus and aluminum Anabolic androgenic hormones
Phosphorus	Phosphorus replacements Vitamin D preparations Anabolic androgenic hormones	Aluminum hydroxide gel Basic aluminum carbonate gel Furosemide Ethacrynic acid Hydrochlorothiazide Dilantin Oral calcium Vitamin D Glucose
Creatinine	Anabolic androgenic hormones Diazoxide Guanethidine Minoxidil Nipride	
Urea nitrogen	Corticosteroids Furosemide Ethacrynic acid Vitamin D preparations Anabolic androgenic agents Licorice Tetracycline Beta-blockers Diazoxide Guanethidine Minoxidil	Glucose

(continued)

TABLE 15.4. *CONTINUED*

Blood test	Increased by	Decreased by
Iron	Iron preparations Ascorbic acid Sorbitol Vitamin E Amino acids (especially cysteine)	Cimetidine Clofibrate Aluminum hydroxide gel Basic aluminum carbonate gel Phosphorus replacements Antacids containing phosphorus Calcium carbonate Sodium bicarbonate Magnesium hydroxide Tetracyclines
Glucose	Corticosteroids Furosemide Glucagon HCl Hydrochlorothiazide Diazoxide Dilantin	Insulin Bisacodyl (Dulcolax) Clofibrate

Lipids (cholesterol,
  triglyceride)
	Allopurinol
	Anabolic androgenic hormones
	Corticosteroids
	Dilantin
	Vitamin D preparations
	Some beta-blockers
		Clofibrate (Atromid-S)
		Cholestyramine (Questran)
		Colestipol hydrochloride
		  (Colestid)
		Gemfibrozil (Lopid)
		Probucol (Lorelco)
		Niacin

Source: Mitchell-Wright, P. (190).

the patient to help bridge the gap. Collard greens may be allowed if restricted to a ½-cup serving once a week, but they cannot be prepared with salted cured meats and bacon fat. Potatoes can be allowed, but they must be soaked overnight to leach out the potassium. Watermelon must be restricted to a ½-cup serving a day. Extra effort must be spent on teaching these patients to avoid high-sodium fast foods. Fried chicken, barbecued ribs, chitterlings, and pigs' feet are allowed on the diet as long as they are prepared without salt (197).

3. FACILITATION OF COMPLIANCE TO A CHANGING DIET PRESCRIPTION

At times patients may just become overwhelmed by alterations in lifestyle, deprivations imposed by treatment, and physical incompetences and become noncompliant (198). Tips for increasing compliance in patients who have excessive interdialytic weight gains are available (199). Dietary hazards in the patient's lifestyle and environment should be considered in meal planning, as well as the environmental assets that the patient can call upon to prevent noncompliance. For example, the talents of an interested family member who has baking skills can make a tremendous difference, as can the individualization of the diet to allow for specific lifestyle or ethnic preferences.

The very nature of the disease means that the diet designed to control symptoms is never static but must change to match the internal milieu whose homeostasis the kidney is no longer able to manage. Today's predialysis low-protein diet becomes tomorrow's high-protein diet in the CAPD patient.

In predialysis, when the care of the patient may require protein intakes of 40 g of a mixed diet or 20 g of a high-biological-protein diet to which amino acid supplements are added, specialized low-protein foods, including low-protein bread, low-protein cake, and gelatin desserts, are necessary to maintain caloric intake and prevent protein wasting. More information, along with a nutrient analysis of various products, is available in table 15.6.

4. STUDIES OF DIETARY COMPLIANCE

A study of compliance for 9 years determined the reasons for noncompliance, as follows (200):

- Physiological and nutritional needs—Many patients failed to comply with their diet because it made them feel hungry and fatigued.
- Psychological and normalcy needs—Certain patients who cheated on their diet said they did it to feel normal because a renal diet is just too different from a normal diet.
- Social and interactional needs—Patients alluded to the difficulty of having to be concerned about providing special foods, especially on social occasions such as holidays or outings with friends.

In one study in which noncompliance was a serious problem, there was no mention of a dietitian's having any involvement in the diet instructions. There was a gradual decrease in nursing implementation of behavioral management techniques to restrict fluid intake. The author's conclusion that this decrease was due to nursing burnout was not supported by any facts supplied. The nursing staff may simply have had enough nursing tasks to accomplish without assuming the role of dietitian as well (201).

TABLE 15.5. MINERAL CONTENT OF SELECTED DRUGS

Classification of drugs	Dose	K^+ (mg)	PO_4^{3-} (mg)	Na^+ (mg)	$Mg(OH)_2$ (mg)	Ca^{++} (mg)	$Al(OH)_3$ (mg)	$Al(CO_3)_3$ (mg)
Aluminum hydroxide or carbonate								
Alternagel, suspension	5 mL			<2.5			600	
Alu-Cap	1 capsule			2.0			475	
Amphojel								
0.3 g	1 tablet			1.8			300	
0.6 g	1 tablet			3.0			600	
Suspension	5 mL			2.3			320	
Basaljel								
Tablet	1 tablet			28.3				608
Extra-strength	5 mL			23.0				1,000
Capsule	1 capsule			2.8				608
Suspension	5 mL			3.0				400
Dialume	1 capsule			1.2			500	
Nephrox, suspension	5 mL			10.0			320	
Magnesium oxide or hydroxide								
Gelusil	1 tablet			1.6	200		200	
	5 mL			0.69	200		200	
Maalox	1 tablet				200		220	
	5 mL				200		205	
Mylanta	1 tablet				200		200	
	5 mL				200		200	
Phillips' Milk of Magnesia	5 mL			0.6	405			
Miscellaneous								
Alka-Seltzer								
Regular	1 tablet			311				
Extra-strength	1 tablet			588				
Kayexalate	1 tsp.			345				
Metamucil								
Instant	1 packet	285–305		2.0				
Powder	1 dose	31		1.0				
Rolaids								
Sodium-free	1 tablet				64	127		
Regular	1 tablet			53		134		
Sodium bicarbonate	1 tablet			177				

Source: Adapted from Mitchell-Wright, P. (190).

Results of another study found that it is very difficult to achieve strict compliance to a diet providing 0.5 to 0.6 g of protein/kg body weight and 6 to 9 mg of phosphorus/kg ideal body weight per day, with potassium restrictions ranging from 700 to 2,200 mg/day and sodium intake between 112 and 782 mg/day. The level of compliance is about 58%. Dietary compliance improved with time (perhaps because of better understanding of the diet), improved emotional acceptance, and an onset of symptoms. The most common deviations were higher protein intake, lower caloric intake, or both, showing that the dietitian needs to take an aggressive approach in teaching caloric needs (202).

PRIORITIES FOR QUALITY ASSURANCE

1. MEETING MEDICARE REQUIREMENTS

Federal regulations for mandated minimum requirements for outpatient dialysis have been published in the *Federal Register.* All laboratory tests for chronic dialysis patients are classified as either routine (listed below) or nonroutine.

TABLE 15.6. NUTRITIONAL ANALYSIS OF LOW-PROTEIN PRODUCTS

Product	Serving	Protein (g)	Calories	Na (mg)	K (mg)	Ca (mg)	P (mg)
Cal Plus[a]							
High-calorie	100 g	0	400	110	7	25	10
Supplement	¼ cup	0	128	36	2	7	3
Low-protein products[a]							
Wheat starch (4-lb. bag)	1 oz.	0.1	100	17	3	3	13
Baking mix (4-lb. bag)	1 oz.	0.1	110	12	3	3	15
Bread	1 slice (1.8 oz.)	0.3	83	10	13	3	7
Chocolate chip cookies	1	0.1	70	30	12	5	5
Butterscotch chip cookies	1	0.1	70	20	8	4	4
Aproten products[a]							
Anellini (cooked)	1 cup	0.3	196	15	5		
Ditalini (cooked)	1 cup	0.3	114	10	5		
Rigatini (cooked)	1 cup	0.3	114	10	5		
Tagliatelle (cooked)	1 cup	0.3	214	15	5		
Rusks	1 slice (10 g)	0.1	43	3	5		
Prono gelled dessert[a]							
Orange	⅓ cup	0.02	55	9	69	24	0
Lime	⅓ cup	0.02	55	8	97	39	0
Strawberry	⅓ cup	0.02	55	8	91	23	0
Cherry	⅓ cup	0.02	55	7	67	30	0
Wel-Plan[b]							
Baking mix	100 g	7.0	600	0	0	N/A	0
Sweet cookies (variety)	1 cookie	0–0.5	22–49	2	1.5	N/A	N/A
Pasta	100 g	0.5	335	15	10.0	N/A	10
Brown bread	1 slice	0.4	75	113	43.3	N/A	N/A
Crackers	1 cracker	0.03	30	30	1.0	N/A	N/A

Source: Denny, M. E., Kelly, M. P., and O'Regan Esrey, T. (55).
[a] Additional information may be obtained from Dietary Specialties, P.O. Box 227, Rochester, NY 14601.
[b] Additional information may be obtained from Anglo-Dietetics Ltd., P.O. Box 333, Wilton, CT 06897, (203) 762-2504.

Medical justification according to specific formats must accompany all nonroutine tests performed at frequencies greater than those listed. Documentation of nutritional problems or needs as they occur will help to form an ongoing data base for justification by the physician of lab tests that must be performed more often than routinely. Failure to provide the medical justification often means that the facility itself must pay the cost of these tests. Routine laboratory testing recognized as such by the Health Care Financing Administration includes the following:

Per dialysis   Hematocrit

Weekly   Prothrombin time (patients on anticoagulant therapy)
Serum creatinine
BUN

Monthly   Serum calcium
Serum potassium
Serum chloride
Complete blood count (CBC)
Serum bicarbonate
Serum phosphorus
Total protein
Serum albumin
Alkaline phosphatase
SGOT
LDH

2. CONTINUITY OF CARE

Process and outcome criteria that incorporate many of the principles of management outlined in this chapter have been presented in a problem-solving format elsewhere (97). Nowhere is the new emphasis on monitoring efforts in quality assurance more important than in treating renal disease. Guidelines useful to the development of quality assurance programs for hospitalized children, adults, and transplant patients are published by the American Dietetic Association (150). Individuals who start the course of renal disease in an acute-care setting may return to the same setting for dialysis or they may have home dialysis. Governmental regulations now encourage decreased lengths of stay in hospitals in an effort to control costs. Against this background there are an increasing number of instances of superimposed illnesses or complications of renal disease, such as respiratory insufficiency, diabetes, hypertension, heart disease, stroke, myocardial infarction, or other problems (142–149). Some individuals may require a short period of time in a respiratory, cardiac, or stroke rehabilitation health care facility before returning home or being admitted to an extended-care facility. Nutritional rehabilitation is often required and frequently affects the outcome of other treatments.

To avoid unnecessary blood drawing and duplications of laboratory tests that probably will not be covered by Medicare, results of laboratory tests performed in one facility, such as the dialysis unit, should be routinely and quickly communicated to the nursing home or rehabilitation unit. Sharing of data will help to cut costs. Patient care goals for renal disease should be communicated to facilities actually performing the care, such as the rehabilitation center or nursing home, and incorporated into the overall plan of care for other patient problems. At least part of the nutritional assessment could be performed in the rehabilitation center, and shared with the dialysis unit. No less important than routine monitoring of dietary potassium, sodium, protein, and phosphate compliance is the monitoring of discharge plans and communication tools between health care facilities and other parameters of the continuity of renal dietary management.

MENU PLANNING

Nutritional analysis, food groups, steps for calculating the renal diet, and a sample diet prescription and meal plan are given in tables 15.7 through 15.10.

TABLE 15.7. NUTRITIONAL ANALYSIS OF LOW-SODIUM SEASONINGS

Product	Portion	Protein (g)	Calories	Sodium (mg)	Potassium (mg)	Phosphorus (mg)
Mrs. Dash Seasoning Blend	1 tsp.	0.4	12	4.4	38	8
Mrs. Dash Seasoning Blend, low-pepper, no garlic	1 tsp.	0.4	12	4.4	49	10
Mrs. Dash Coating Mix	¼ envelope	4.8	63	3.3	229	0
Mrs. Dash Steak Sauce	1 tbsp.	0.3	17	7.5	70	0
Med Diet All-Purpose	1 tsp.	0	0	0	22	N/A
Med Diet Seafood Blend	1 tsp.	0	0	0	23	N/A
Med Diet Herb	1 tsp.	0	0	0	13	N/A
Med Diet Salad Blend	1 tsp.	0	0	9.7	20	N/A
Lemon Flavor Crystals (Diamond Crystal Salt Co.)	1 package	0	3	0	0	N/A
Chef Seasoning (Diamond Crystal Salt Co.)	1 package	0	0	3	4	N/A
	1 tsp.	0	6	15	24	N/A
Italian (Diamond Crystal Salt Co.)	1 tsp.	0	6	17	24	N/A
French (Diamond Crystal Salt Co.)	1 tsp.	0	8	15	22	N/A
Bar-B-Q (Diamond Crystal Salt Co.)	1 tsp.	0	6	19	17	N/A

Source: Denny, M. E., Kelly, M. P., and O'Regan Esrey, T. (55).

TABLE 15.8A. AVERAGE NUTRIENT VALUES OF FOOD GROUPS FOR PROTEIN-CONTROLLED DIETS

Food group	Protein (g)	Fluid (cc)	Sodium (mg)	Potassium (mg)	Phosphorus (mg)	Kilocalories
Milk	4.0	40–120	40–60	175	110	80–200
Fruit	0.5	90	2.0	Group A: 95	25	80
				Group B: 175	25	
				Group C: 300	25	
Vegetables	2.0	90	15.0	Group A: 110	35	35
				Group B: 185	35	
				Group C: 310	35	
Bread, cereal, and desserts						
Regular (A)	2.0	10	130	25	25	70
Low-sodium (B)	2.0	10–85	7	25	25	70
Meat	7.0	15	25	120	70	75
Egg	6.0	35	60	70	90	75
Fats						
Regular	Trace	—	50	—	0–10	45
Low-sodium	Trace	—	0	—	0–10	45
Calorie supplement A	Trace	Trace	Trace	Trace	Trace	60
Calorie supplement B	Trace	see group	10	25	50	50–70
Other beverage	0	150	0	40	7	0
Salt item (Count as other food group item plus sodium.)			400			

Source: Chicago Dietetic Association and South Suburban Dietetic Association (203).
Note: Serving sizes for each group are specified in table 15.8b.

TABLE 15.8B. FOOD GROUPS FOR LOW-PROTEIN DIET PLANS

	Amount per serving	Grams per serving

MILK GROUP
Avoid commercially prepared milk drinks and all milk products not listed.
Each serving is equivalent to ½ cup (120 cc) of milk and contains approximately
  4 g protein
 60 mg sodium
175 mg potassium
110 mg phosphorus
 80 to 200 kcal

Milk		
Whole, 2%, low-fat, skim	½ cup	120
Condensed	¼ cup	60
Evaporated	¼ cup	60
Dry powdered, whole or skim	2 tbsp.	15
Cream		
Light coffee or table	½ cup	120
Half-and-half	½ cup	120
Heavy whipping cream	¾ cup	180
Sour cream	½ cup	120

(continued)

TABLE 15.8B. *CONTINUED*

	Amount per serving	Grams per serving
Ice cream	½ cup	70
Yogurt, all varieties	½ cup	120
Custard	¼ cup	60
Pudding	½ cup	120

FRUIT GROUP
Fruit listed is fresh or frozen unless otherwise specified.
Group A
Each serving contains approximately
0.5 g protein
2 mg sodium
95 mg potassium
25 mg phosphorus
80 kcal

	Amount per serving	Grams per serving
Applesauce, canned sweet	½ cup	128
Blackberries	½ cup	72
Blueberries	½ cup	73
Boysenberries, raw	½ cup	128
Gooseberries, raw	¼ cup	38
Raspberries, raw	½ cup	64
Strawberries	⅓ cup	50
Cranberries	1 cup	96
Cranberry juice cocktail, bottled	½ cup	128
Cranberry sauce		
Jellied, canned	½ cup	138
Whole, canned	2 oz.	57
Figs, canned, heavy syrup	3 w/liquid	83
Fruit cocktail, canned, heavy syrup	½ cup	128
Mixed fruit, canned, heavy syrup	½ cup	128
Fruit salad, canned, heavy syrup	½ cup	128
Fruit salad, tropical, heavy syrup	¼ cup	64
Grapes, adherent skin, raw	10	50
Grape juice, canned, bottled, or frozen concentrate	½ cup	127
Lemon, fresh	1	58
Lime, fresh	1	67
Nectar—apricot, pear, peach	½ cup	125
Mandarin oranges, canned, w/syrup	½ cup	126
Peach, canned, w/syrup	2 halves	162
Pear, canned, w/syrup	½ cup	128
Pineapple, raw	½ cup	78
Pineapple, canned, w/syrup	⅓ cup	85
Plums, canned, w/syrup	2	90

(continued)

TABLE 15.8B. *CONTINUED*

	Amount per serving	*Grams per serving*
Group B		
Each serving contains approximately		
0.5 g protein		
2 mg sodium		
175 mg potassium		
25 mg phosphorus		
80 kcal		
Apple	1 small	138
Apple juice	½ cup	124
Apricots, canned, heavy syrup	4 halves	90
Apricots	2 medium	70
Cherries	10	68
Cherries, canned, w/syrup	½ cup	129
Figs, raw	1 medium	50
Grapefruit, pink, red, white	½ medium	120
Grapefruit, canned, w/syrup	½ cup	127
Grapefruit juice, canned or frozen concentrate	½ cup	124
Peach	1 small	87
Pineapple juice, canned	½ cup	125
Plums	1	66
Rhubarb, frozen, cooked	½ cup	100
Tangerine	1	84
Watermelon	1 cup diced	80
Group C		
Each serving contains approximately		
0.5 g protein		
2 mg sodium		
300 mg potassium		
25 mg phosphorus		
80 kcal		
Avocado	¼	50
Apricots	3 medium	105
Banana	½	57
Figs, dried	2	38
Apricots, dried	5	18
Dates, dried	5	42
Prunes, dried	5	42
Raisins, seedless	¼ cup	36
Guava	1	90
Kiwi fruit	1 medium	76
Cantaloupe	½ cup	134
Casaba	¾ cup cubed	128

(continued)

TABLE 15.8B. *CONTINUED*

	Amount per serving	Grams per serving
Honeydew	½ cup	85
Mango	1	207
Nectarine	1 medium	136
Orange, navel	1 medium	140
Orange juice, fresh, canned, or frozen concentrate	½ cup	124
Papaya	⅓ medium	102
Pomegranate	½ medium	75
Prunes, canned	5	86
Prune juice, canned or bottled	⅓ cup	80
Tangelo	1 medium	170

VEGETABLE GROUP

Vegetables listed are fresh or are frozen and cooked unless otherwise specified. Pickles, pickle relish, olives, sauerkraut, and all other pickled vegetables should be avoided if there is a sodium restriction. Vegetables should be cooked in a large amount of water and drained well before using if there is a potassium restriction.

Group A

Each serving contains approximately

  2.0 g protein

  15 mg sodium

110 mg potassium

  35 mg phosphorus

  35 kcal

Bamboo shoots, canned	½ cup	60
Bean sprouts, mung	1¾ oz.	50
Bean sprouts, soybean	½ cup	62
Beans, green, snap, canned, cooked, frozen	½ cup	68
Beans, green, fresh cooked	¼ cup	34
Beans, wax, cooked	½ cup	68
Cabbage, all varieties	½ cup	35
Cauliflower, raw	½ cup	50
Celery, raw	½ stalk	25
Celery, cooked, diced	⅓ cup	50
Cucumber	½ cup sliced	52
Eggplant, cooked, 1″ cubes	½ cup	48
Hominy, grits, cooked	½ cup	123
Leek	½ cup	52
Lettuce, romaine, raw, shredded	1 oz.	30
Lettuce, iceberg	1¾ oz.	50
Watercress, chopped	1¾ oz.	30
Mushroom, raw	2½ small	25
Onion, all varieties	½ cup	105
Pepper, jalapeño, canned, solid	½ cup	68
Pepper, sweet, raw	½ cup	148

(*continued*)

TABLE 15.8B. *CONTINUED*

	Amount per serving	*Grams per serving*
Radish, raw	3 small	30
Turnip	½ cup	78
Water chestnuts, canned	8	56

Group B
Each serving contains approximately
   2.0 g protein
  15 mg sodium
185 mg potassium
  35 mg phosphorus
  35 kcal

Artichoke, cooked	1 medium	60
Artichoke hearts, frozen, cooked	⅓ cup	50
Asparagus, canned, cooked	½ cup	100
Asparagus, frozen	¼ cup	50
Beets, cooked	½ cup	83
Brussels sprouts, cooked	3–4 medium	50
Carrots	⅔ cup	100
Corn, sweet, cooked	½ cup	82
Corn on cob, sweet	½ ear	77
Greens: Collard, mustard, turnip, kale, dandelion	½ cup	85
Mixed vegetables	½ cup	141
Okra, frozen, cooked, sliced	½ cup	92
Peas	½ cup	80
Rutabaga	½ cup	85
Squash, summer, all varieties, cooked	½ cup	90

Group C
Each serving contains approximately
   2.0 g protein
  15 mg sodium
310 mg potassium
  35 mg phosphorus
  90 cc fluid
  35 kcal

Beet greens	1¾ oz.	50
Broccoli	⅔ cup	100
Kohlrabi, raw	½ cup	70
Kohlrabi, cooked	½ cup	82
Parsnips, cooked	½ cup	78
Potato, cooked without skin	½ cup	78
Potato, frozen, french-fried, home or restaurant	10 strips	50
Pumpkin, cooked or canned	½ cup	122
Spinach	½ cup	28

(continued)

TABLE 15.8B. *CONTINUED*

	Amount per serving	Grams per serving
Squash, winter, all varieties, baked	½ cup cubed	102
Sweet potato	½ cup	128
Yam, cooked or baked	⅓ cup	68
Tomato, raw	1 small	123
Tomato, canned whole	½ cup	120
Tomato juice, unsalted	½ cup	122
Vegetable juice cocktail, unsalted	½ cup	121

BREAD, CEREAL, AND DESSERT GROUP

Avoid excessive amounts of chocolate, nuts, and coconut in baking, because they are high in potassium. Refer to "Salt List," below, for foods high in sodium that may be planned into the diet.

Group A—Regular
Each serving contains approximately
  2 g protein
130 mg sodium
  25 mg potassium
  25 mg phosphorus
  70 kcal (values vary)

Bread, any	1 slice	25
Biscuit or muffin	1 small	35
Roll, any	1 small or ½ large	35
Cornbread	2″ square	30
Saltine crackers	3	20
Graham crackers	2 squares	20
Melba toast	5 slices	20
Ry-krisp	2 slices	20
Dry cereal, any	¾ cup	30
Homemade pancakes or waffles	1	50
Tortilla	1 (6″)	30
Danish pastry, doughnut, sweet roll	1 small or ½ large	30
Cookies, any	2 medium	30
Cupcake, any	1 medium	30
Brownies	1 (2×2×¾″)	30
Angel food cake, sponge cake, layer cake, pound cake, any kind	⅒ of small cake or 1 small slice	30
Hamburger or hot dog bun	1 small or ½ large	30
Nondairy creamer	1 cup	240

Group B—Low-Sodium
Each serving contains approximately
  2 g protein
  7 mg sodium
25 mg potassium

(continued)

TABLE 15.8B. *CONTINUED*

	Amount per serving	Grams per serving
25 mg phosphorus 70 kcal (values vary)		
Low-sodium bread	1 slice	25
Low-sodium crackers	5	20
Low-sodium melba toast	5 slices	20
Holland rusk, regular	1	20
Hot-water cornbread without salt	2″ square	30
Hot cooked cereal without salt (do not use "quick" or "instant")	½ cup	100
Cold cereals: Puffed Rice, Puffed Wheat, Shredded Wheat, low-sodium cereals, Sugar Smacks, Muffets, Puffa Puffa Rice, Frosted Mini Wheats	¾ cup or 4 biscuits	30
Macaroni, noodles, spaghetti, rice cooked without salt	½ cup	100
Homemade unsalted fruit pie (omit ½ fruit)	⅛ of 9″ pie	125
Low-sodium cookies	2 medium	30
Low-sodium pound cake, sponge cake, or angel food cake	⅒ of cake	30
Flour, cornmeal, tapioca, cornstarch	2½ tbsp.	20
Uncooked barley	1½ tbsp.	30
Popcorn, popped, unsalted	1½ cup	30
Sherbet	¾ cup	150

MEAT GROUP

Refer to "Salt List," below, for foods high in sodium that may be planned into the diet.
Each serving contains approximately
   7 g protein
  25 mg sodium
120 mg potassium
 70 mg phosphorus
 75 kcal (values vary widely)

	Amount per serving	Grams per serving
Egg (6 g protein, 60 mg Na, 90 mg P, 70 mg K, 35 cc fluid)	1	50
Cheese, low-sodium	1 oz.	30
Meat or poultry	1 oz.	30
Fish		
Fresh	1 oz.	30
Low-sodium salmon or tuna	¼ cup	30
Shellfish: fresh clams, oysters, shrimp	5 small or ¼ cup	30
Scallops	1 oz.	30
Peanut butter (246 mg K, 118 mg P)	2 tbsp.	30
Soybean curd (tofu) (21 mg K, 63 mg P)	½ cup	100

(continued)

TABLE 15.8B. *CONTINUED*

	Amount per serving

FAT GROUP

Each serving provides

 0 g protein

50 mg sodium (regular fat choice)

 0 mg sodium (salt-free fat choice)

 0 mg potassium

 0–10 mg phosphorus

45 kcal

The following may be regular or low-sodium:

Butter	1 tsp.
Margarine	1 tsp.
Mayonnaise	2 tsp.
Salad dressing:	
French	1 tsp.
Roquefort/Blue Cheese	1 tsp.
Thousand Island	1 tsp.
Italian, low-sodium	2 tsp.
Cooking oil	1 tsp.
Lard	1 tsp.
Salad oil	1 tsp.
Vegetable shortening	1 tsp.

CALORIE SUPPLEMENT GROUP A

An asterisk indicates that the food item is considered a fluid.

Each serving provides

Negligible protein

Negligible potassium

Negligible sodium

Negligible phosphorus

60 kcal

Arrowroot flour	2 tbsp.
*Beverages, alcoholic: vodka, whiskey, rum, gin	¾ oz.
Supplements	
Polycose	1 tbsp.
Controlyte	2 tbsp.
Butterballs	1 medium
Butterscotch drops	3 pieces
Chewing gum	6 sticks
Cornstarch	2 tbsp.
Cotton candy	2 cups
Gumdrops	2 large
Gumdrops	15 small
Hard candy	2 pieces
Jelly beans	10
Lollipop	1 small
Marshmallows	3 large
Mints	2 medium

(*continued*)

TABLE 15.8B. *CONTINUED*

	Amount per serving
*Popsicle	1 average
Sugar, granulated	4 tsp.
Sugar, confectioners'	1 tbsp.
Syrup, corn, light	1 tbsp.
Syrup, flavored (not chocolate)	2 tbsp.

CALORIE SUPPLEMENT GROUP B
An asterisk indicates that the food item is considered a fluid.
Each serving provides
Negligible protein
25 mg potassium
10 mg sodium
50 mg phosphorus
50–70 kcal

*Beverages, artificially flavored fruit drinks	6 oz.
*Beverages, carbonated: cola type, lemon-lime, root beer	6 oz.
Cranberries, raw	¼ cup
*Ginger ale	1 cup
Honey	1 tbsp.
Jam	1 tbsp.
Jelly	1 tbsp.
*Lemonade	½ cup
Marmalade	1 tbsp.
*Tang orange drink	⅓ cup

OTHER BEVERAGE GROUP
An asterisk indicates that the food item is considered a fluid.
Each serving provides
 0 protein
40 mg potassium
 7 mg phosphorus
 0 sodium
 0 kcal

*Coffee, instant	5 oz.
*Coffee, instant, decaffeinated	5 oz.
*Tea, medium strength	5 oz.
*Tea, herbal	5 oz.
*Tea, decaffeinated	5 oz.

SALT LIST
Each item contains approximately 1 g salt (400 mg sodium).

Miscellaneous items
 ¼ tsp. salt, scant
 1 tsp. soy sauce
 4 tsp. Worcestershire sauce

(*continued*)

2⅓ tbsp. catsup

2 tbsp. mustard, chili sauce, or barbecue sauce

4⅔ tbsp. tartar sauce

4⅔ tbsp. mayonnaise

4 tbsp. Thousand Island salad dressing

3 tbsp. Russian salad dressing

2 tbsp. French salad dressing

1⅓ tbsp. Italian salad dressing

4 medium, 3 extra-large, or 2 giant green olives (16 g)

4 tbsp. sweet pickle relish (60 g) (deduct 1 fruit)

Meat items

1 small hot dog or 1 slice lunchmeat (not braunschweiger, liverwurst, or salami, because they are higher in phosphorus) (deduct 1 oz. meat)

4 slices bacon (deduct 1 oz. meat)

1½ oz. cooked pork sausage (deduct 1½ oz. meat)

1½ oz. ham or corned beef (deduct 1½ oz. meat)

1½ oz. regular canned tuna (deduct 1½ oz. meat)

3 oz. regular canned salmon (deduct 3 oz. meat)

1½ oz. regular canned crab (deduct 1 oz. meat)

¾ cup cottage cheese (deduct 3 oz. meat)

2 oz. cheese (deduct 2 oz. meat)

Bread, cereal, and dessert items

20 small pretzels

3 medium twisted pretzels

1 Dutch or soft pretzel

Vegetable items

2 servings (½ cup each) regular canned vegetables (deduct 2 vegetables)

⅓ cup canned regular sauerkraut, drained (deduct ½ vegetable)

½ dill pickle (30 g) (deduct ½ vegetable)

Approximately 20 potato chips (1 oz.) (deduct 1 vegetable)

Soup items (count as fluid)

All soups listed are canned soups diluted with equal amounts of *water*.

⅔ cup beef broth or vegetable vegetarian

½ cup bisque of tomato, clam chowder (Manhattan style), chicken gumbo, cream of asparagus, cream of celery, golden vegetable noodle

⅓ cup cream of mushroom

LOW-PROTEIN, LOW-ELECTROLYTE SUPPLEMENTS

The following may be used freely to supply needed calories:

1. High-carbohydrate, high-fat, high-calorie supplements, such as Polycose, Moducal,
   Nutrisource Carbohydrate, and Sumacal.
2. Low-protein starch products, such as low-protein breads and pastas, may be used to
   supply additional calories (i.e., Aproten bread products and cookies).

Source: Chicago Dietetic Association and South Suburban Dietetic Association (203).

TABLE 15.9. CALCULATING THE RENAL DIET

1. Determine the amount of protein of high biological value for the patient by multiplying the amount of protein ordered by 66%.
2. Divide the high-biological-value protein between the dairy products group and the meat group.
3. Divide the remaining protein between the bread, cereal, and dessert group and the vegetable group.
4. Add the amount of potassium available from foods supplying protein. Subtract this amount of potassium from the total potassium allowed in the diet.
5. Divide the remaining potassium between the fruit groups and other beverages.
6. Adjust for prescribed sodium level.
7. Adjust for caloric level with use of allowed foods.
8. Modify for fluid level as prescribed.

Source: Chicago Dietetic Association and South Suburban Dietetic Association (203).

TABLE 15.10. SAMPLE DIET PRESCRIPTION AND MEAL PLAN

PRESCRIPTION

60 g protein; 2 g Na; 2 g K; less than 1,000 mg P; between 2,800 and 3,000 kcal; less than 1.5 liters of fluid per day.

MEAL PLAN

Food group	Number of servings	Protein (g)	Fluid (cc)	Na+ (mg)	K+ (mg)	P (mg)	Kilocalories
Milk	1	4	120	60	175	110	85
Egg	1	6	35	60	70	90	75
Meat	4	28	15	100	480	280	300
Bread, cereal, and desserts (A)	7	14	70	910	175	175	490
Vegetables							
Group A	1	2	90	15	112	35	35
Group B	1	2	90	15	184	35	35
Group C	1	2	90	15	307	35	35
Fruit							
Group A	2	1	180	4	192	50	160
Group B	1	0.5	90	2	176	25	80
Fats (regular)	16			800			720
Calorie supplement A	9						540
Calorie supplement B	4			40	100	200	240
Other beverage	1		150		40	7	0
Total		59.5	930	2,021	2,011	1,042	2,795

Source: Adapted from Chicago Dietetic Association and South Suburban Dietetic Association (203).

SAMPLE MENU FOR DIET IN CHRONIC RENAL FAILURE, WITH 60 g PROTEIN, 2,000 mg SODIUM, 2,000 mg POTASSIUM, 1,000 mg PHOSPHORUS, AND 1,500 cc FLUIDS (FOR A MALE, AGE 25–50)ª

BREAKFAST

Grapefruit sections	½ cup
Cornflakes	¾ cup
Sugar	2 tbsp.
Whole milk	½ cup
Fried egg	1 large
Margarine	1 tsp.
Whole wheat toast	2 slices
Margarine	2 tsp.
Jelly	2 tbsp.
Coffee	½ cup
Sugar	2 tsp.

LUNCH

Low-sodium vegetable soup	⅔ cup
Lean hamburger patty	2 oz.
Hamburger bun	1 whole
Mayonnaise	2 tsp.
Lettuce	1 leaf
Sliced tomato	1 medium
Salt-free Thousand Island dressing	3 tsp.
Canned fruit salad	½ cup
Marshmallows	6 large
Lemonade	½ cup

DINNER

Broiled chicken	2 oz.
White rice	½ cup
Steamed carrots	½ cup
Margarine	1 tsp.
Hard dinner roll	1
Margarine	2 tsp.
Lettuce-and-cucumber salad	1 cup
Oil-and-vinegar dressing	1 tbsp.
Baked apple	1 medium
Margarine	2 tsp.
Sugar	4 tsp.
Ginger ale	1 cup
Mints	2 medium

SNACKS THROUGHOUT DAY

Gumdrops	2 large
Jelly beans	10
Popsicle	1

Approximate Nutrient Analysis

Energy	2,718 kcal
Protein	70.2 g (10% of kcal)
Fat	84.4 g (28% of kcal)
Polyunsaturated fat	18.3 g
Monounsaturated fat	28.9 g
Saturated fat	20.4 g

(*continued*)

Cholesterol	342 mg
Carbohydrate	433.0 g (64% of kcal)
Fluid	1,490 cc
Vitamin A	24,121 IU
	3,042 RE
Thiamine	1.34 mg
Riboflavin	1.57 mg
Niacin	24.2 mg
Folate	214 mcg
Vitamin B-12	2.44 mcg
Vitamin B-6	1.73 mg
Vitamin C	97.3 mg
Calcium	428 mg
Phosphorus	802 mg
Iron	14.0 mg
Copper	0.69 mg
Zinc	6.2 mg
Magnesium	134 mg
Sodium	2,025 mg
Potassium	2,033 mg

[a]All food should be unsalted and prepared without salt. Fruits and vegetables should be drained. This menu is adequate in all nutrients except calcium, magnesium, and zinc.

REFERENCES

1. Coburn, J. W.: General concepts and management of chronic renal failure. In Bricker, N. S., and Kirschenbaum, M. A.: The kidney: Diagnosis and management. New York: John Wiley and Sons, 1984.
2. Burton, P., and Walls, J.: Selection-adjusted comparison of life-expectancy of patients on continuous ambulatory peritoneal dialysis, hemodialysis and renal transplantation. Lancet 1:1115, 1987.
3. Kopple, J.: Nutritional management. In Massry, S., and Glassock, R.: Textbook of nephrology. Vol. 2. Baltimore: Williams and Wilkens, 1983.
4. Heide, B., Pierratos, A., et al.: Nutritional status of patients undergoing continuous ambulatory peritoneal dialysis. Perit Dial Bull (July–Sept.), 1983.
5. Burton, B. T., and Hirschman, G. H.: Current concepts of nutritional therapy in chronic renal failure: An update. J Am Diet Assoc 82:359, 1983.
6. Meyer, T. W., Lawrence, W. E., and Brenner, B. M.: Dietary protein and the progression of renal disease. Kidney Internat Supp 16:S243, 1983.
7. Klahr, S., Buerkert, J., and Purkerson, M. L.: Role of dietary factors in the progression of chronic renal disease. Kidney Internat 24:579, 1983.
8. Barsotti, G., Morelli, E., et al.: Restricted phosphorus and nitrogen intake to slow the progression of chronic renal failure: A controlled trial. Kidney Internat Supp 16:S278, 1983.
9. Kopple, J. D.: Significance of diet and parenteral nutrition in chronic renal failure. In Bricker, N. S., and Kirschenbaum, M. A.: The kidney: Diagnosis and management. New York: John Wiley and Sons, 1984.
10. Walser, C. M., Limbembo, A. L., et al.: Nutritional management: The Johns Hopkins handbook. Philadelphia: W. B. Saunders, 1984.
11. Kleinknecht, C., Broyer, M., et al.: Growth and development of non-dialyzed children with chronic renal failure. Kidney Internat Supp 15:S40, 1983.
12. Arnold, W. C., Danford, D., and Holliday, M. A.: Effects of caloric supplementation on growth in children with uremia. Kidney Internat 24:205, 1983.
13. Barrett, T., Broyer, M., et al.: Assessment of growth. Am J Kidney Dis 7:340, 1986.
14. Hager, S. R.: Insulin resistance of uremia. Am J Kidney Dis 14:272, 1989.
15. Anthony, L. E., and Taylor, K. B.: Clinical nutrition. New York: McGraw-Hill, 1983.
16. McCann, L.: Peritoneal dialysis and nutritional considerations. In Gillet, D., Stover, J., and Spinozzi, N.: A clinical guide to nutrition care in end-stage renal disease. Chicago: American Dietetic Association, 1987.
17. Cameron, J., and Challah, S.: Treatment of end stage renal failure due to diabetes in the United Kingdom, 1975–1984. Lancet 1:962, 1986.
18. Alvestrand, A., Ahlberg, M., and Bergstrom, J.: Retardation of the progression of renal insufficiency in patients treated with low-protein diets. Kidney Internat Supp 16:S268, 1983.
19. Maschio, G., Oldrizzi, L., et al.: Early dietary protein and phosphorus restriction is effective in delaying progression of chronic renal failure. Kidney Internat Supp 16:S273, 1983.
20. Wassner, S., Bergstrom, J., et al.: Protein metabolism in renal failure: Abnormalities and possible mechanisms. Am J Kidney Dis 7:285, 1986.
21. Rosman, J. B., Meijer, S., et al.: Prospective randomized trial of early dietary protein restriction in chronic renal failure. Lancet 2:291, 1984.
22. Giordano, C.: Protein restriction in chronic renal failure. Kidney Internat 22:401, 1982.
23. Walser, M.: Conservative management of the uremic patient. In Brenner, B., and Rector, F. D.: The kidney. Philadelphia: W. B. Saunders, 1981.
24. Wiseman, W., Hunt, R., et al.: Dietary composition and renal function in healthy subjects. Nephron 46:37, 1987.
25. Hunt, J., Zhou, J., et al.: Dynamic aspects of whole-body nitrogen metabolism in uremic patients on dietary therapy. Nephron 44:288, 1986.
26. Brouhard, B. H., and LaGrone, L.: Effect of indomethacin on the glomerular filtration rate after a protein meal in humans. Am J Kidney Dis 13:232, 1989.
27. Klahr, S.: Effects of protein intake on the progression of renal disease. Ann Rev Nutr 9:87, 1989.
28. Nath, K. A., Wooley, A. C., and Hostetter, T. H.: O_2 consumption and oxidant stress in the remnant nephron. Clin Res 35:553A, 1987.
29. Nath, K. A., Hostetter, M. K., and Hostetter, T. H.: Pathophysiology of chronic tubulo-interstitial disease in rats: Interactions of dietary acid load, ammonia and complement component C3. J Clin Invest 76:667, 1985.
30. Ihle, B. U., Becker, G. J., et al.: The effect of protein restriction on the progression of renal insufficiency. N Engl J Med 321:1773, 1989.
31. Hannedouche, T., Chauveau, P., et al.: Effect of moderate protein restriction on the rate of progression of chronic renal failure. Kidney Internat Supp 27:S91, 1989.
32. Bergstrom, J., Lindblom, T., and Noree, L. O.: Preservation of peripheral nerve function in severe uremia during treatment with low protein, high calorie diet and surplus of essential amino acids. Acta Neurol Scand 51:99, 1975.
33. Zeller, K. R., and Jacobson, H.: Reducing dietary protein intake to retard progression of diabetic nephropathy. Am J Kidney Dis 13:17, 1989.
34. Brenner, B. M., and Anderson, S.: Glomerular function in diabetes mellitus. Adv Nephrol 19:135, 1990.
35. Comty, C. M., and Collins, A. J.: Dialytic therapy in the management of chronic renal failure. Med Clin N Am 68:399, 1984.

36. Harter, H. R., Laird, N. M., and Teehan, B. P.: Effects of dialysis prescription on bone and mineral metabolism: The National Cooperative Dialysis Study. Kidney Internat Supp 13:S73, 1983.

37. Rickers, H., Christensen, M., and Rodbro, P.: Bone mineral content in patients on prolonged maintenance hemodialysis: A three year follow-up study. Clin Nephrol 20:302, 1983.

38. Lau, K.: Phosphate excess and progressive renal failure: The precipitation-calcification hypothesis. Kidney Internat 36:918, 1989.

39. McCrory, W. W., Gertner, J. M., et al.: Effects of dietary phosphate restriction in children with chronic renal failure. J Pediatr 111:410, 1987.

40. Attman, P. O., Gustafson, A., et al.: Effect of protein reduced diet on plasma lipids, apolipoproteins and lipolytic activities in patients with chronic renal failure. Am J Nephrol 4:92, 1984.

41. Walser, M.: Nutrition in renal failure. Ann Rev Nutr 3:125, 1983.

42. Golper, T. A.: Therapy for uremic hyperlipidemia. Nephron 38:217, 1984.

43. Sanfellippo, M. L., Swenson, R. S., and Reaven, G. M.: Reduction of plasma triglycerides by diet in subjects with chronic renal failure. Kidney Internat 11:54, 1977.

44. Sanfellippo, M. L., Swenson, R. S., and Reaven, G. M.: Response of plasma triglycerides to dietary change in patients on hemodialysis. Kidney Internat 14:180, 1977.

45. Gokal, R., Mann, J. I., et al.: Dietary treatment of hyperlipidemia in chronic hemodialysis patients. Am J Clin Nutr 31:1915, 1978.

46. Azar, R., Dequiedt, F., et al.: Effects of fish oil rich in polyunsaturated fatty acids on the hyperlipidemia of hemodialysis patients. Kidney Internat Supp 27:S239, 1989.

47. Sigstrom, L., Attman, P. O., et al.: Growth during treatment with low-protein diet in children with renal failure. Clin Nephrol 21:152, 1984.

48. Fine, R. N.: Recent advances in the management of the infant, child and adolescent with chronic renal failure. Ped Rev 11:277, 1990.

49. Koch, V. H., Lippe, B. M., and Nelson, P. A.: Accelerated growth following recombinant human growth hormone treatment of children with chronic renal failure (CRF). J Pediatr 115:365, 1989.

50. Tonshoff, B., Mehls, O., et al.: Improvement of uremic growth failure by recombinant human growth hormone. Kidney Internat Supp 27:S201, 1989.

51. Warady, B. A., Kriley, M., et al.: Growth and development of infants with end-stage renal disease receiving long-term peritoneal dialysis. J Pediatr 112:714, 1988.

52. Kopple, J., and Cianciaruso, B.: Nutritional management of acute renal failure. In Fischer, J. E.: Surgical nutrition. Boston: Little, Brown, 1983.

53. Harum, P.: Nutritional management of the adult hemodialysis patient. In Gillet, D., Stover, J., and Spinozzi, N.: A clinical guide to nutrition care in end stage renal disease. Chicago: American Dietetic Association, 1987.

54. Walser, M.: Nutrition in renal failure. Ann Rev Nutr 3:125, 1983.

55. Denny, M. D., Kelly, M. P., and O'Regan Esrey, T.: Pre–end stage renal disease: A guide for the professional nutritionist. Council on Renal Nutrition of National Kidney Foundation, Northern California and Northern Nevada, 1986.

56. Kopple, J. D.: Nutritional therapy in kidney failure. Nutr Rev 39:193, 1981.

57. Zeman, F. J.: Clinical nutrition and dietetics. Lexington, Ky.: Collamore Press, 1983.

58. Shah, R.: Nutritional management of renal transplant patients. In Gillet, D., Stover, J., and Spinozzi, N.: A clinical guide to nutrition care in end stage renal disease. Chicago: American Dietetic Association, 1987.

59. Levine, S. E.: Nutritional care of patients with renal failure and diabetes. J Am Diet Assoc 81:226, 1982.

60. Davis, M.: Nutritional management of the diabetic patient. In Gillet, D., Stover, J., and Spinozzi, N.: A clinical guide to nutrition care in end stage renal disease. Chicago: American Dietetic Association, 1987.

61. Grupe, W. E., Harmon, W. E., and Spinozzi, N. S.: Protein and energy requirements in children receiving chronic hemodialysis. Kidney Internat Supp 15:S6, 1983.

62. Gutch, C. F., and Stoner, M. H.: Review of hemodialysis for nurses and dialysis personnel. 4th ed. St. Louis: C. V. Mosby Company, 1983.

63. Kopple, J. D., and Blumenkrantz, M. J.: Nutritional requirements for patients undergoing continuous ambulatory peritoneal dialysis. Kidney Internat Supp 16:S295, 1983.

64. Liddle, V. R., and Johnson, H. K.: Dietary therapy in renal transplantation. Proc Clin Dial Transplant Forum 9:219, 1979.

65. Whitter, F., Evans, D., et al.: Nutrition in renal transplantation. Am J Kidney Dis 6:405, 1985.

66. Jensen, T., Stender, S., et al.: Partial normalization by dietary cod-liver oil of increased microvascular albumin leakage in patients with insulin-dependent diabetes and albuminuria. N Engl J Med 321:1572, 1989.

67. Varcoe, A. R., Halliday, D., et al.: Anabolic role of urea in renal failure. Am J Clin Nutr 31:1601, 1978.

68. Blumberg, A., Hanck, A., and Sander, G.: Vitamin nutrition in patients on continuous ambulatory peritoneal dialysis (CAPD). Clin Nephrol 20:244, 1983.

69. Airaghi, J. A., Bhola, A. C., et al.: Vitamin/mineral nutrition in hemodialysis: Recommendations for supplementation in adults. Cincinnati: Cincinnati/Dayton Council on Renal Nutrition, National Kidney Foundation, 1982.

70. Wassner, S. J., Abitbol, C., et al.: Nutritional requirements for infants with renal failure. Am J Kidney Dis 7:300, 1986.

71. Holliday, M., Kulin, H., and Lock-

wood, D.: The endocrine control of growth in children with chronic renal failure. Am J Kidney Dis 7:262, 1986.

72. Rizzoni, G., Broyer, M., et al.: Growth retardation in children with chronic renal disease: Scope of the problem. Am J Kidney Dis 7:256, 1986.

73. Holliday, M. A.: Nutrition therapy in renal disease. Kidney Internat Supp 19:S3, 1986.

74. Feinstein, E. I., Kopple, J. D., et al.: Total parenteral nutrition with high or low nitrogen intakes in patients with acute renal failure. Kidney Internat Supp 16:S319, 1983.

75. Metcoff, J., Scharer, K., et al.: Energy production, intracellular amino acid pools, and protein synthesis in chronic renal disease. J Am Coll Nutr 8:271, 1989.

76. Mitch, W. E., May, R. C., et al.: Protein and amino acid metabolism in uremia: Influence of metabolic acidosis. Kidney Internat Supp 27:S205, 1989.

77. Lair, N. M., Berky, C. S., and Lowrie, E. G.: Modeling success or failure of dialysis therapy: The National Cooperative Dialysis Study. Kidney Internat Supp 13:S103, 1983.

78. Binkley, L. S.: Keeping up with peritoneal dialysis. Am J Nurs 84:729, 1984.

79. Ramos, J. M., Gokal, R., et al.: Continuous ambulatory peritoneal dialysis: Three years' experience. Quart J Med 206:165, 1983.

80. Lindsay, R. M., and Spanner, E.: A hypothesis: The protein catabolic rate is dependent upon the type and amount of treatment in dialyzed uremic patients. Am J Kidney Dis 13:382, 1989.

81. Khanna, R., Wu, G., et al.: Use of amino acid containing solution in CAPD patients. Perit Dial Bull (Supp):121, 1984.

82. Gretz, N., Lasserre, J., and Strauch, M.: Caloric supplements for patients on low-protein diets? Nephron 50:129, 1988.

83. Kopple, J. D., Berg, R., et al.: Nutri-tional status of patients with different levels of chronic renal insufficiency: Modification of Diet in Renal Disease (MDRD) Study Group. Kidney Internat Supp 27:S184, 1989.

84. Slomowitz, G. A., Monteon, F. J., et al.: Effect of energy intake on nutritional status in maintenance hemodialysis patients. Kidney Internat 35:704, 1989.

85. Holliday, M., Chesney, R., and Silverman, W.: Children with renal disease: A commentary. Am J Kidney Dis 7:350, 1986.

86. Levy, Mortimer: The edematous patient. In Schrier, R. W.: Manual of nephrology. Boston: Little, Brown, 1981.

87. Holliday, M. A.: Renal disease. In Schneider, H. A., Anderson, C. E., and Coursin, D. B.: Nutritional support of medical practice. 2d ed. Philadelphia: Harper and Row, 1983.

88. Kurokawa, K., and Gordon, E. M.: Abnormalities of sodium and water metabolism. In Bricker, N. S., and Kirschenbaum, M. A.: The kidney: Diagnosis and management. New York: John Wiley and Sons, 1984.

89. Sherman, R. A., and Eisinger, R. P.: Urinary sodium and chloride during renal salt retention. Am J Kidney Dis 3:121, 1983.

90. Uribarri, J., Oh, M. S., and Carroll, H. J.: Salt losing nephropathy. Am J Nephrol 3:193, 1983.

91. Paulson, W. D., Bock, G. H., et al.: Hyponatremia in the very young chronic peritoneal dialysis patient. Am J Kidney Dis 14:196, 1989.

92. Krapf, R., and Cogan, M. G.: Hyperkalemia suppresses the renal adaptation to chronic respiratory acidosis. Am J Kidney Dis 14:158, 1989.

93. Papadoyannakis, N. J., Stefanidis, C. J., and McGeown, M.: The effect of the correction of metabolic acidosis on nitrogen and potassium balance of patients with chronic renal failure. Am J Clin Nutr 40:623, 1984.

94. Holick, M. F.: Vitamin D and the kidney. Kidney Internat 32:912, 1987.

95. Chesney, R. W., Hamstra, A. J., et al.: Vitamin D metabolites in renal insufficiency and other vitamin D disorders of children. Kidney Internat Supp 15:S63, 1983.

96. Walser, M.: Renal disease. In Paige, D. M.: Manual of clinical nutrition. Pleasantville, N.J.: Nutrition Publications, 1983.

97. Gillet, D.: Overview: The normal and diseased kidney. In Gillet, D., Stover, J., and Spinozzi, N.: A clinical guide to nutrition care in end stage renal disease. Chicago: American Dietetic Association, 1987.

98. Teehan, B. P., Laird, N. M., and Harter, H. R.: Influences of dialysis prescription on electrolyte and acid-base metabolism: The National Cooperative Dialysis Study. Kidney Internat Supp 13:S66, 1983.

99. Buccianti, G., Bianchi, M. L., and Valenti, G.: Progress of renal osteodystrophy during continuous ambulatory peritoneal dialysis. Clin Nephrol 22:279, 1984.

100. Kraut, J. A., Gordon, E. M., et al.: Effect of chronic metabolic acidosis on vitamin D metabolism in humans. Kidney Internat 24:644, 1983.

101. Plante, G. E.: Urinary phosphate excretion determines the progression of renal disease. Kidney Internat Supp 27:S128, 1989.

102. Brooks, L., and Snetselaar, L.: Modification of diet in renal disease study. Renal Dietitians Newsletter 6 (1):1, 1987.

103. Ross, E. A., Shah, G. M., et al.: Vitamin B-6 requirements of patients on chronic peritoneal dialysis. Kidney Internat 36:702, 1989.

104. Drake, J. R., Leavitt, J. N., et al.: Lack of effect of vitamin E therapy on the anemia of patients receiving hemodialysis. Am J Clin Nutr 39:223, 1984.

105. Ramirez, G., Chen, M., et al.: Longitudinal follow-up of chronic hemodialysis patients without vitamin supplementation. Kidney Internat 30:99, 1986.

106. Moia, M., Vizzotto, L., et al.: Improvement in the hemostatic defect of uremia after treatment with recombi-

nant human erythropoietin. Lancet 2:1227, 1987.

107. Lutton, J. D., Solangi, K. B., et al.: Inhibition of erythropoiesis in chronic renal failure: The role of parathyroid hormone. Am J Kidney Dis 3:380, 1984.

108. Adamson, J. W., and Eschbach, J. W.: Treatment of the anemia of chronic renal failure with recombinant human erythropoietin. Ann Rev Med 41:349, 1990.

109. Bergmann, M., Grutzmacher, P., et al.: Iron metabolism under rEPO therapy in patients on maintenance hemodialysis. Int J Artif Organs 13 (2):109, 1990.

110. Lazarus, J. M., Hakim, R. M., and Newell, J.: Recombinant human erythropoietin and phlebotomy in the treatment of iron overload in chronic hemodialysis patients. Am J Kidney Dis 16:101, 1990.

111. Sprenger, K. B., Bundschu, D., et al.: Improvement of uremic neuropathy and hypogeusia by dialysate zinc supplementation: A double-blind study. Kidney Internat Supp 16:S315, 1983.

112. Wallaeys, B., Cornelis, R., et al.: Trace elements in serum, packed cells, and dialysate of CAPD patients. Kidney Internat 30:599, 1986.

113. Mahajan, S. K., Bowersox, E. M., et al.: Factors underlying abnormal zinc metabolism in uremia. Kidney Internat Supp 27:S269, 1989.

114. Saint-Georges, M. D., Bonnefont, D. J., et al.: Correction of selenium deficiency in hemodialyzed patients. Kidney Internat Supp 27:S274, 1989.

115. Touam, M., Martinez, F., et al.: Aluminum induced, reversible microcytic anemia in chronic renal failure: Clinical and experimental studies. Clin Nephrol 19:295, 1983.

116. Meyer, J. L., and Thomas, W. C., Jr.: Aluminum and aluminum complexes: Effect on calcium phosphate precipitation. Kidney Internat Supp 18:S20, 1986.

117. Committee on Nutrition, American Academy of Pediatrics: Aluminum toxicity in infants and children. Pediatrics 78:1150, 1986.

118. Larsen, E., Ash, S., et al.: Phosphate binding gels: Balancing phosphate adsorption and aluminum toxicity. Kidney Internat 29:1131, 1986.

119. Milliner, D., Malekzader, M., et al.: Plasma aluminum levels in pediatric dialysis patients: Comparison of hemodialysis and continuous ambulatory peritoneal dialysis. Mayo Clin Proc 62:269, 1987.

120. Altmann, P., Al-Salihi, F., et al.: Serum aluminum levels and erythrocyte dihydropteridine reductase activity in patients on hemodialysis. N Engl J Med 317:80, 1987.

121. Bia, M. J., Cooper, K., et al.: Aluminum induced anemia: Pathogenesis and treatment in patients on chronic hemodialysis. Kidney Internat 36:852, 1989.

122. Bakir, A. A., Hryhorck, D. O., et al.: Hyperaluminemia in renal failure: The influence of age and citrate intake. Clin Nephrol 31:40, 1989.

123. Warady, B. A., Koch, M., et al.: Plasma fluoride concentration in infants receiving long-term peritoneal dialysis. J Pediatr 115:435, 1989.

124. Rubin, J., Walsh, D., and Bower, J.: Diabetes, dialysate losses, and serum lipids during continuous ambulatory peritoneal dialysis. Am J Kidney Dis 10:104, 1987.

125. Keane, W., Kaiske, B., and O'Donnell, M.: Hyperlipidemia and the progression of renal disease. Am J Clin Nutr 47:157, 1988.

126. McLeod, R., Reeve, E., and Frohlich, J.: Plasma lipoproteins and lecithin: Cholesterol acyltransferase distribution in patients on dialysis. Kidney Internat 25:683, 1984.

127. Drueke, T., Lacour, B., et al.: Recent advances in factors that alter lipid metabolism in chronic renal failure. Kidney Internat Supp 16:S134, 1983.

128. Kagan, A., Bar-Khayim, Y., et al.: Kinetics of peritoneal protein loss during CAPD: 2. Lipoprotein leakage and its impact on plasma lipid levels. Kidney Internat 37:980, 1989.

129. Grundy, S. M.: Management of hyperlipidemia of kidney disease. Kidney Internat 37:847, 1990.

130. Grutzmacher, P., Marz, W., et al.: Lipoproteins and apolipoproteins during the progression of chronic renal disease. Nephron 50:103, 1988.

131. Chan, P. C. K., Persaud, J., et al.: Apolipoprotein B turnover in dialysis patients: Its relationship to pathogenesis of hyperlipidemia. Clin Nephrol 31:88, 1989.

132. Moorthy, A. V., Rosenblum, M., et al.: A comparison of plasma and muscle carnitine levels in patients on peritoneal or hemodialysis for chronic renal failure. Am J Nephrol 3:205, 1983.

133. Vacha, G. M., Giorcelli, G., et al.: Favorable effects of L-carnitine treatment on hypertriglyceridemia in hemodialysis patients: Decisive role of low levels of high density lipoprotein cholesterol. Am J Clin Nutr 38:532, 1983.

134. Walser, M.: Nutritional support in renal failure: Future directions. Lancet 1:340, 1983.

135. Gloggler, A., Bulla, M., and Furst, P.: Effect of low dose supplementation of L-carnitine on lipid metabolism in hemodialyzed children. Kidney Internat Supp 27:S256, 1989.

136. Ahmad, S., Dasgupta, A., and Kenny, M. A.: Fatty acid abnormalities in hemodialysis patients: Effect of L-carnitine administration. Kidney Internat Supp 27:S243, 1989.

137. Mooradian, I., and Morley, J. E.: Endocrine dysfunction in chronic renal failure. Arch Intern Med 144:351, 1984.

138. DeFronzo, R. A., Smith, D., and Alvestrand, A.: Insulin action in uremia. Kidney Internat Supp 16:S102, 1983.

139. Riegel, W., Stepinski, J., et al.: Effect of serine on gluconeogenic ability of hepatocytes in acute uremia. Kidney Internat Supp 16:S48, 1983.

140. Rampton, D. S., Cohen, S. L., et al.: Treatment of chronic renal failure with dietary fiber. Clin Nephrol 21:159, 1984.

141. Laouari, D., Kleinknecht, C., et al.: Adverse effect of proteins on remnant kidney: Dissociation from that of other nutrients. Kidney Internat Supp 16:S248, 1983.

142. Drukker, A., Hurwich, B. J., et al.: Acute osteolytic lesions following pancreatitis in a dialysis patient. Am J Nephrol 3:220, 1983.

143. Glassock, R. J., Goldstein, D. A., et al.: Diabetes mellitus, moderate renal insufficiency and hyperkalemia. Am J Nephrol 3:233, 1983.

144. Russell, R. P., and Whelton, P. K.: Hypertension in chronic renal failure: Clinical presentation, prognosis, pathophysiology and treatment. Am J Nephrol 3:185, 1983.

145. Sica, D. A., Harford, A. M., and Zawada, E. T.: Hypercalcemic hypertension in hemodialysis. Clin Nephrol 22:102, 1984.

146. D'Elia, J. A., Kaldany, A., et al.: The management of the diabetic patient with renal disease. Compr Ther 10:39, 1984.

147. Felsenfeld, A. J., Harrelson, J. M., et al.: Osteomalacia after parathyroidectomy in patients with uremia. Ann Intern Med 96:34, 1982.

148. Bush, A., and Gabriel, R.: Cancer in uremic patients. Clin Nephrol 22:77, 1984.

149. Rostand, S. G., Kirk, K. A., and Rutsky, E. A.: Dialysis associated ischemic heart disease: Insights from coronary angiography. Kidney Internat 25:653, 1984.

150. Wilkins, K., ed.: Suggested guidelines for nutrition care of renal patients. Chicago: Renal Dietitians Practice Group, American Dietetic Association, 1986.

151. Schoenfeld, P. Y., Henry, R. R., et al.: Assessment of nutritional status of the National Cooperative Dialysis Study population. Kidney Internat Supp 13:S80, 1983.

152. Gilli, G., Mehls, O., et al.: Prediction of adult height in children with chronic renal insufficiency. Kidney Internat Supp 15:S48, 1983.

153. Cohn, S. H., Brennan, L., et al.: Evaluation of body composition and nitrogen content of renal patients on chronic dialysis as determined by total body neutron activation. Am J Clin Nutr 38:52, 1983.

154. Goldberg, A. P., Geltman, E. M., et al.: Therapeutic benefits of exercise training for hemodialysis patients. Kidney Internat Supp 16:S303, 1983.

155. Hagberg, J. M., Goldberg, A. P., et al.: Exercise training improves hypertension in hemodialysis patients. Am J Nephrol 3:209, 1983.

156. Frederico, C. B., and Martin, B. R.: Practical applications of nutrition assessment in the chronic hemodialysis population. Am J Intraven Ther Clin Nutr 10:10, 1983.

157. Wilson, R. F., and Soullier, G.: The validity of two-hour creatinine clearance studies in critically ill patients. Crit Care Med 8:281, 1980.

158. Shils, M. E., and Alcock, N. W.: Clinical nutrition. In Halsted, J. A., and Halsted, C. H.: The laboratory in clinical medicine. 2d ed. Philadelphia: W. B. Saunders, 1981.

159. Norwood, K.: Nutritional assessment in chronic renal failure. In Gillet, D., Stover, J., and Spinozzi, N.: A clinical guide to nutrition care in end stage renal disease. Chicago: American Dietetic Association, 1987.

160. Bennett, N.: Urea kinetics in the nutritional management of patients with renal failure. Nutr Supp Ser 4:21, 1984.

161. Acchiardo, S. R., Moore, L. W., and Latour, P. A.: Malnutrition as the main factor in morbidity and mortality of hemodialysis patients. Kidney Internat Supp 16:S199, 1983.

162. Broyer, M., Niaudet, P., et al.: Nutritional and metabolic studies in children on continuous ambulatory peritoneal dialysis. Kidney Internat Supp 15:S106, 1983.

163. Salasky, I., Fine, R., et al.: Nutritional status of children undergoing peritoneal dialysis. Am J Clin Nutr 38:599, 1983.

164. Cano, N., DiCostanzo-Dufetel, J., et al.: Prealbumin-retinol-binding-protein-retinol complex in hemodialysis patients. Am J Clin Nutr 47:664, 1987.

165. Bennett, P. H.: Microalbuminuria and diabetes: A critique-assessment of urinary albumin excretion and its role in screening for diabetic nephropathy. Am J Kidney Dis 13:29, 1989.

166. DiMario, U., Morani, S., et al.: New parameters to monitor the progression of diabetic nephropathy. Am J Kidney Dis 13:45, 1989.

167. Glassock, R. J.: Nutrition, immunology, and renal disease. Kidney Internat Supp 16:S194, 1983.

168. Wolfson, M., Strong, C. J., et al.: Nutritional status and lymphocyte function in maintenance hemodialysis patients. Am J Clin Nutr 37:547, 1984.

169. Bansal, V. K., Popli, S., et al.: Protein calorie malnutrition and cutaneous anergy in hemodialysis maintained patients. Am J Clin Nutr 33:1608, 1980.

170. Kamel, K. S., Magner, P. O., et al.: Urine electrolytes in the assessment of extracellular fluid volume contraction. Am J Nephrol 9:344, 1989.

171. Sabatini, S.: The acidosis of chronic renal failure. Med Clin N Am 67:845, 1983.

172. Berner, J. J.: Effects of diseases on lab tests. Philadelphia: J. B. Lippincott, 1983.

173. Agus, Z. S., Goldfarb, S., and Wasserstein, A.: The patient with disorders of serum calcium and phosphate. In Schrier, R. W.: Manual of nephrology. Boston: Little, Brown, 1981.

174. Conceicao, S. C., Weightman, D., et al.: Serum ionised calcium concentration: Measurement versus calculation. Br Med J 1:1103, 1978.

175. Massey, L. K.: Soft drink consumption, phosphorus intake and osteoporosis. J Am Diet Assoc 80:581, 1982.

176. Sondheimer, J. H., Mahajan, S. K., et al.: Elevated plasma copper in chronic renal failure. Am J Clin Nutr 47:896, 1988.

177. Bricker, N. S.: Consequences of pro-

gressive nephron loss. In Bricker, N. S., and Kirschenbaum, M. A.: The kidney: Diagnosis and management. New York: John Wiley and Sons, 1984.

178. Klinenberg, J. R.: Uric acid and diseases of the kidney. In Bricker, N. S., and Kirschenbaum, M. A.: The kidney: Diagnosis and management. New York: John Wiley and Sons, 1984.

179. Mitchell, P. J., and Butler, C. D.: Renal disease: Interactions of nutrients and drugs and their effect on the gastrointestinal tract. St. Louis: Missouri-Kansas Council on Renal Nutrition, 1983.

180. Kaye, M.: Oral aluminum toxicity in a nondialyzed patient with renal failure. Clin Nephrol 20:208, 1983.

181. Boyce, B. F., Elder, H. Y., et al.: Hypercalcemic osteomalacia due to aluminum toxicity. Lancet 2:1009, 1982.

182. Passlick, J., Wilhelm, M., et al.: Calcium alginate, an aluminum-free phosphate binder, in patients on CAPD. Clin Nephrol 32:96, 1989.

183. Moriniere, P., Hocine, C., et al.: Long term efficacy and safety of oral calcium as compared to aluminum hydroxide as phosphate binders. Kidney Internat 36 Supp 27:S133, 1989.

184. Schaefer, K., Erley, C. M., et al.: Calcium salts of ketoacids as a new treatment strategy for uremic hyperphosphatemia. Kidney Internat Supp 27:S136, 1989.

185. Reidel, E., Hampl, H., et al.: Correction of amino acid metabolism by recombinant human erythropoietin therapy in hemodialysis patients. Kidney Internat Supp 27:S216, 1989.

186. Powers, D. E., and Moore, A. O.: Food/medication interactions. 6th ed. Phoenix: 1988 (self-published).

187. Meltzer, V. N., Goldberg, A. P., et al.: Effects of prazosin and propranolol on blood pressure and plasma lipids in patients undergoing chronic hemodialysis. Am J Cardiol 53:40A, 1984.

188. Bennett, W. M.: Approach to drug use in the azotemic patient. In Schrier, R. W.: Manual of nephrology. Boston: Little, Brown, 1981.

189. Bennett, W. M., Aronoff, G. R., et al.: Drug prescribing guidelines for adults. Am J Kidney Dis 3:155, 1983.

190. Mitchell-Wright, P.: Drugs, diet and dialysis. In Gillet, D., Stover, J., and Spinozzi, N.: A clinical guide to nutrition care in end-stage renal disease. Chicago: American Dietetic Association, 1987.

191. Falciglia, G., Nelson, E., et al.: Evaluation of an educational program for dialysis patients. J Am Diet Assoc 81:928, 1984.

192. Greene, M., and Michelis, M.: The gourmet renal nutrition cookbook. New York: Lenox Hill Hospital, 1980.

193. Lidinsky, D. J.: To eat or not to eat—a guide for the person with end stage renal disease: A simple way to tell a complicated story. P.O. Box 1562, Hobe Sound, FL 33455.

194. Mayfield, M., and Nicol, A.: Sodium controlled recipes especially for renal patients. Council on Renal Nutrition of National Kidney Foundation, Northern California and Northern Nevada. Lanexa, Kans.: Cookbook Publishers, 1983.

195. Mayfield, M., and Nicol, A.: Carbohydrate and sodium controlled recipes especially for diabetic and CAPD renal patients. Council on Renal Nutrition of National Kidney Foundation, Northern California and Northern Nevada. Lanexa, Kans.: Cookbook Publishers, 1983.

196. Smith, S. A.: The black diet versus the renal diet: Bridging the gap. Transplant Proc 21:3989, 1989.

197. Jones, W. O.: Bridging the gap between black food preferences and the renal diet. Transplant Proc 21:3990, 1989.

198. Gardner, J.: Hyperdietism: Its prevention, control and relation to compliance in dialysis patients. In Gillet, D., Stover, J., and Spinozzi, N.: A clinical guide to nutrition care in end stage renal disease. Chicago: American Dietetic Association, 1987.

199. Brown, E.: Appendix C: Helpful hints for common patient problems. In Gillet, D., Stover, J., and Spinozzi, N.: A clinical guide to nutrition care in end stage renal disease. Chicago: American Dietetic Association, 1987.

200. O'Brien, M. E.: Compliance behavior and long term maintenance dialysis. Am J Kidney Dis 15:209, 1990.

201. Tucker, C. M.: The effects of behavioral intervention with patients, nurses, and family members on dietary noncompliance in chronic hemodialysis patients. Transplant Proc 21:3985, 1989.

202. Cianciaruso, B., Capuani, A., et al.: Dietary compliance to a low protein and phosphate diet in patients with chronic renal failure. Kidney Internat Supp 27:S173, 1989.

203. Chicago Dietetic Association and South Suburban Dietetic Association: Manual of clinical dietetics. Chicago: American Dietetic Association, 1988.

204. Gee, C., and Schroepfer, C.: Urea kinetics in the nutritional management of the pre-ESRD patient. In Denny, M. D., Kelly, M. P., and O'Regan Esrey, T.: Pre–end stage renal disease: A guide for the professional nutritionist. Council on Renal Nutrition of National Kidney Foundation, Northern California and Northern Nevada, 1986.

DIET IN ACUTE RENAL FAILURE

DEFINITION

Acute renal failure is a functional disturbance of the kidneys that is severe enough to cause a substantial change in the plasma biochemistry. It develops over a period of days or at most weeks and may be associated with oliguria and anuria. In contrast to chronic renal failure, acute renal failure occurs more suddenly and is often reversible (1, 2).

PURPOSE OF THE DIET

Provision of sufficient nonprotein energy sources to permit maintenance of vital functions and to reduce the catabolism of body proteins is a priority. Preservation of body cell mass, particularly visceral protein status, is especially important. Net protein breakdown in acute renal failure can be massive, with daily net losses of 150 to 200 g. Protein catabolism may enhance the rate of rise of plasma potassium, phosphorus, and nitrogenous metabolites and the fall of blood pH. An adequate caloric intake will minimize catabolism. However, individuals who are hypercatabolic in response to trauma, infection, or surgery may continue to catabolize endogenous protein at an excessive rate despite caloric supplements (3, 4).

Protein lost via dialysis or wasting must be replaced, and the net catabolism of endogenous protein must be reduced. In addition to nonprotein calories, exogenous essential amino acids may be provided with or without nonessential amino acids. Although still somewhat controversial, studies suggest that a combination of essential and nonessential amino acids may be preferable to essential amino acids alone (4–6).

Maintenance of the extracellular fluid volume and body fluid osmolality as close as possible to normal by the control of sodium and fluid intake is also important.

Hypercalcemia is not very common in acute renal failure. In patients with nonparathyroid malignancies, control of hypercalcemia can be achieved by agents that prevent bone resorption, such as diphosphonates, which are pyrophosphate analogues that bind to hydroxyapatite in bone and inhibit bone resorption (7).

PHYSIOLOGY, FOODS, AND NUTRIENTS

1. CAUSES

Acute tubular necrosis (ATN) is the cause in 75% of cases of acute renal failure. It can be due to any of the following:

- Posttraumatic or surgical shock: A failure of renal blood perfusion or decreased renal blood supply may cause transient ischemic anoxia, a temporary loss of oxygen supply. The precipitating event is usually a significant fall in blood pressure for at least 5 minutes during or after major surgery, severe trauma, burns or hemorrhage, septic abortion, preeclampsia, or septicemia (1).
- Toxic effects of metals: The therapeutic use of gold or the accidental ingestion of chromium or mercury salts can cause acute renal failure (1).
- Organic compounds or drugs: Organic compounds such as methanol and carbon tetrachloride or other halogenated hydrocarbons, some of which are used as anesthetic agents, can provoke renal failure. Sulfonamides and rarely antibiotics such as neomycin, polymyxin, and methicillin can also damage the kidney, as can radiographic contrast media (1).

ATN follows a 3-phase course. The oliguric phase may last 7 to 21 days, during which less than 400 mL of urine is produced per day. The phase is characterized by fluid overload, nausea, vomiting, lethargy, and increased BUN, creatinine,

phosphorus, and potassium levels. At this stage the mortality rate improves with dialysis and good nutrition. The diuretic phase, lasting 7 to 14 days, follows. Biochemistries improve, and the diet can be liberalized. Urinary output may be excessive, and care must be taken to lift previous fluid restrictions. Over the next 2 to 6 months the patient will go through a convalescent phase.

Acute renal failure may also have prerenal or postrenal causes. Prerenal azotemia may be caused by hypovolemia (dehydration, diarrhea, vomiting, hemorrhage, or diuretic abuse), cardiovascular failure, or obstruction of the renal artery. Postrenal azotemia may be due to obstruction of the ureter, urethra, or renal vein. In these cases dietary treatment is not indicated, and kidney function is restored with removal of the cause.

2. DIETARY PARAMETERS IN ATN

Dietary restrictions are summarized in table 15.1.

A. Protein Protein needs are often greatly increased by hypercatabolic states such as sepsis, hemorrhage, or open, draining wounds. The anorexia, nausea, and vomiting that often occur in acute renal failure prevent the ingestion of adequate protein and calories and frequently necessitate the use of parenteral nutrition (3, 4).

Patients who are unable to consume adequate calories by the enteral route and who have a urea nitrogen appearance (UNA) of 4 to 5 g per day or less and are not very wasted should be given 0.30 to 0.40 g per kilogram of body weight per day of essential amino acids parenterally. With a higher UNA, more nitrogen is needed, and both essential and nonessential amino acids are given. Evidence supports the concept that in the hypercatabolic patient, mixtures of essential and nonessential amino acids are handled better than essential amino acids alone. When high-nitrogen intakes are needed, it has been suggested that histidine and nonessential amino acids such as arginine, tyrosine, alanine, glycine, proline, and serine should also be given. In contrast to the 1 : 1 ratio of essential to nonessential amino acids used in total parenteral nutrition, a 2 : 1 or 4 : 1 ratio may be preferable. A recent study found no advantage to using increased amounts of nonessential amino acids for acute renal failure rather than using an equal ratio of essential to nonessential amino acids (4, 5, 8).

It has also been suggested that a higher proportion of the essential amino acids be supplied in the form of branched-chain amino acids. A new amino acid formula for intravenous use is B5695, produced by Boehringer-Biochemia-Robin of Italy. Designed to reverse amino acid abnormalities in renal patients, it contains histidine, a higher percentage of valine and threonine, and a lower percentage of methionine and phenylalanine than the standard formula by Rose (4, 9).

B. Energy   If possible, energy expenditure should be measured in patients with postoperative multiple organ failure that includes renal failure. Energy needs may be increased by as much as 35%. Patients may need from 30 to 50 kcal/kg/day (4, 10).

C. Fluid   In acute renal failure with oliguria, total fluid loss may be calculated by adding the measured urine volume (usually minimal), plus other losses such as from wounds, gastric suction, and diarrhea. Normal breakdown of tissues produces about 400 mL of preformed water each day. This quantity is produced even when there is no intake of food and water each day. To this is added estimated insensible fluid loss of about 300 mL per day (1).

In early stages, when feeding is by the parenteral route, the fluid infusion rate is initially about 20 mL per hour, or 480 mL

per day. Depending upon the patient's size, this rate is gradually increased, over a period of 2 to 4 days, to a limit of 70 to 100 mL per hour. In acute renal failure with oliguria, fluid is restricted to less than 1 L per day (11, 12).

D. Potassium   The aims of potassium control are to reverse hyperkalemic-induced membrane abnormalities, to reverse the transmembrane K gradient by moving potassium back into the cells, and to remove any excess potassium from the body. Potassium requirements vary in acute renal failure, depending upon the degree of hypermetabolism caused by stress, infection, fever, and pain and upon hemodynamic status.

Acidosis due to diminished renal hydrogen ion excretion or a coexistent metabolic abnormality may complicate acute renal failure and potentiate hyperkalemia. Acidosis shifts potassium from the intracellular to the extracellular space and produces hyperkalemia without an actual increase in total body potassium.

Although acute renal failure is usually associated with hyperkalemia, occasionally hypokalemia may occur. It is most commonly seen in the diuretic phase of acute tubular necrosis. It is also seen during the diuresis that may follow relief of urinary tract obstruction, because of the potassium loss associated with increased urinary volume (13).

E. Calcium and Phosphorus   Phosphorus needs to be restricted in acute renal failure, as does magnesium, to prevent its accumulation. The total parenteral solution recommended by Kopple for acute renal failure includes 5 mmol calcium and 8 mmol phosphorus per liter (13).

BIOCHEMICAL ASSESSMENT

Biochemical indices of acute renal failure include the following (8):

- Increased serum phosphate and other products of nitrogen metabolism: urea indoles, uric acid, sulfate, and hydrogen ions
- Decreased serum bicarbonate and pH
- Decreased serum calcium in some patients
- Hyperkalemia (may occur in oliguric renal failure)

In prerenal failure there is a disproportionate elevation of blood urea nitrogen as compared with the serum creatinine, as well as decreased urine volume, low urinary sodium values, and high urinary osmolality, all of which can help distinguish it from intrarenal failure (14). Biochemical indices in prerenal failure and ATN are compared in table 15.11.

IMPLEMENTATION AND EDUCATION

Because dietary restrictions are usually temporary, it may not be necessary to provide a complete diet instruction. However, for a nauseated patient and an anxious family, dietary compliance may be improved by an explanation of the importance of nutritional adequacy and restrictions. Consideration should be given to the preferences of the patient, who will probably need much encouragement to consume adequate calories. In-service education of nursing staff can also help to reinforce the importance of nutrition. Because of lack of appetite, nausea, and vomiting, nutrition support may be indicated.

PRIORITIES FOR QUALITY ASSURANCE

In acute renal failure the patient's status may change over a period of hours. Frequent monitoring of biochemistries and clinical condition and daily adjustment of the diet are important. Special attention should be paid to the appropriateness of fluid restrictions, especially as the patient enters the diuretic phase.

TABLE 15.11. BIOCHEMICAL INDICES IN PRERENAL FAILURE VERSUS ATN

	Prerenal failure	*ATN*
Urine sodium	<20	>40
Urine chloride	<20	>40
Urine creatinine	>40 mg/dL	<20 mg/dL
Urine osmolarity	>500	<400
BUN : serum creatinine	10 : 1	>10 : 1

REFERENCES

1. Gutch, C. F., and Stoner, M. H.: Review of hemodialysis for nurses and dialysis personnel. 4th ed. St. Louis: C. V. Mosby, 1983.

2. Gillet, D.: Overview: The normal and diseased kidney. In Gillet, D., Stover, J., and Spinozzi, N.: A clinical guide to nutrition care in end stage renal disease. Chicago: American Dietetic Association, 1987.

3. Walser, C. M., Limbembo, A. L., et al.: Nutritional management: The Johns Hopkins handbook. Philadelphia: W. B. Saunders, 1984.

4. Kopple, J., and Cianciaruso, B.: Nutritional management of acute renal failure. In Fischer, J.: Surgical nutrition. Boston: Little, Brown, 1983.

5. Feinstein, E. I., Kopple, J. D., et al.: Total parenteral nutrition with high or low nitrogen intakes in patients with acute renal failure. Kidney Internat Supp 16:S319, 1983.

6. Whitney, E. N., and Cataldo, C. B.: Understanding normal and clinical nutrition. St. Paul: West Publishing Co., 1983.

7. Gibson, S. M., and Kimmel, P. L.: Relative hypercalcemia in acute renal failure. Am J Kidney Dis 14:419, 1989.

8. Anthony, L. E., and Taylor, K. B.: Clinical nutrition. New York: McGraw-Hill, 1983.

9. Torgo, G., Situlin, R., et al.: Effect of intravenous supplementation of a new essential amino acid formulation in hemodialysis patients. Kidney Internat Supp 27:S278, 1989.

10. Soop, M., Forsberg, E., et al.: Energy expenditure in postoperative multiple organ failure with acute renal failure. Clin Nephrol 31:139, 1989.

11. Binkley, L. S.: Keeping up with peritoneal dialysis. Am J Nurs 84:729, 1984.

12. Meyer, T. W., Lawrence, W. E., and Brenner, B. M.: Dietary protein and the progression of renal disease. Kidney Internat Supp 16:S243, 1983.

13. Kopple, J. D.: Nutrition, diet and the kidney. In Shils, M. E., and Young, V. E.: Modern nutrition in health and disease. 7th ed. Philadelphia: Lea & Febiger, 1988.

14. Berner, J. J.: Effects of diseases on lab tests. Philadelphia: J. B. Lippincott, 1983.

DIET IN NEPHROTIC SYNDROME

DEFINITION

Nephrotic syndrome is a kidney disorder characterized by losses of large quantities of protein in the urine (at least 3.0 g per day), low serum albumin concentration, high blood levels of certain fats, and severe edema (1, 2).

PURPOSE OF THE DIET

The diet aims to control hypertension, minimize edema, decrease urinary albumin loss, offset protein malnutrition, slow progression of renal disease, prevent muscle catabolism, and supply adequate energy. Control of hyperlipidemia is a secondary concern.

EFFECTS OF THE DIET

In rat studies, there was no therapeutic benefit to a high-protein diet in treating protein losses in the urine of rats with nephrotic syndrome. Yet another study in rats suggested that the benefits of dietary protein restrictions in nephrotic syndrome with progressive renal damage are outweighed by severe nutritional disadvantages. Obviously, more study is needed in this area in humans (3, 4).

A sodium restriction to 60 to 90 mEq (1,380 to 2,070 mg) per day is usually effective in controlling blood pressure and edema, often in conjunction with medication (5).

Because LDL serum cholesterol is severely elevated, dietary therapy alone will not normalize serum cholesterol levels. A decrease in intakes of saturated fatty acids and cholesterol, along with weight reduction in obese patients, is a reasonable first step in the management of nephrotic syndrome hypercholesterolemia. Reduction of saturated fat to less than 10% of total calories and of dietary cholesterol to less than 300 mg per day will lower LDL-cholesterol levels by 30

to 40 mg/100 mL. Bile-acid sequestrants will also lower LDL-cholesterol. The recommended therapy is a combination of bile-acid sequestrants and HMG CoA inhibitors (6). This treatment is likely to be tolerated by most patients and has the advantage of producing a greater reduction in LDL-cholesterol than either the diet alone or one drug with the diet (1, 6).

PHYSIOLOGY, FOODS, AND NUTRIENTS

1. PROTEIN AND ENERGY

Nephrotic syndrome is caused by diseases that increase glomerular permeability to protein. Patients are often wasted with protein malnutrition and edema because of large protein losses and poor appetite. Deficiencies of nutrients normally bound to plasma proteins are also common.

Until recently, because the large protein losses in urine result in a decreased plasma protein concentration, physicians generally prescribed a high-protein diet for nephrotic syndrome. This policy is now debatable because of the potential hazards of high protein intakes on the progression of renal insufficiency. Loss of albumin in the urine of nephrotic patients is due to increased catabolism, not decreased protein synthesis. It is postulated that a low-protein diet, which decreases catabolism, may be more beneficial than a high-protein diet for nephrotic syndrome.

In a study using a 0.6 g protein/kg body weight diet/day, the authors concluded that the dietary intake was not adequate to maintain normal muscle and visceral protein in patients with renal insufficiency who had been on a low-protein diet for 10 years. However, caloric intake was found to be inadequate in both intervention and control groups. (Controls consumed a normal diet.) Although the protein restriction did seem to delay progression of the disease to a certain extent, the poor calorie intake in

both groups caused serious nutritional problems. The authors suggest that more attention needs to be paid to persuading patients to consume adequate calories in their diet (7).

The effect of dietary protein restriction to 0.8 g protein/kg/day, plus treatment with angiotensin converting enzyme (ACE) inhibitors, on protein metabolism has been studied. Plasma amino acid levels and nitrogen balance were used as parameters. Results of this short-term study were that neither moderate protein restriction nor treatment with an ACE inhibitor over a 3-week period had any unfavorable effects in patients with nephrotic syndrome (8).

Until more information is available, it is recommended that patients be given 0.6 g protein per kilogram ideal body weight daily, plus replacement of urinary protein losses with high-biologic-value protein (1).

2. SODIUM AND FLUID

Fluid restriction is not necessary. A sodium restriction to 60 to 90 mEq (1,380 to 2,070 mg) is recommended to control blood pressure and edema, in conjunction with pharmacological therapy (5).

3. LIPIDS

Hyperlipidemia with increased levels of serum cholesterol and low-density lipoproteins and decreased levels of high-density lipoproteins is seen in nephrotic syndrome. Hyperlipidemia in nephrotic syndrome may be due to overproduction of hepatic lipoproteins, triggered by hypoalbuminemia. Two patients with nephrotic syndrome showed loss of HDL and apoproteins I and II in the urine. Further studies are needed in a larger population. Serum apolipoproteins A (Apo A) and B (Apo B) were measured before and after steroid treatment for nephrotic syndrome. Untreated patients had significantly decreased concentrations of Apo A and lecithin cholesterol acyl transferase (LCAT). High triglyceride levels occur late in the disease (6, 9–14).

CLINICAL ASSESSMENT

Calorie counts are helpful in determining the adequacy of the patient's intake. Body weight is usually not reliable, because of edema.

BIOCHEMICAL ASSESSMENT

Low levels of serum albumin in the presence of proteinuria (3 to 5 g of protein in the urine daily plus an albumin of 2.5 mL/100 mL or less), hypertension, and edema are diagnostic of nephrotic syndrome (5, 15). Urine sodium concentration often falls to below 1 mEq/mL, urine potassium is usually high, and the sodium : potassium ratio is greater than 1. In nephrotic syndrome, elevated serum cholesterol levels may indicate the need for a fat-controlled diet.

IMPLEMENTATION AND EDUCATION

Patients with nephrotic syndrome often need encouragement to eat adequate energy. Every effort should be made to accommodate patient preferences within protein and sodium restrictions.

REFERENCES

1. Kopple, J. D.: Nutrition, diet and the kidney. In Shils, M. E., and Young, V. E.: Modern nutrition in health and disease. 7th ed. Philadelphia: Lea & Febiger, 1988.
2. Olmer, M., Pain, C., et al.: Protein diet and nephrotic syndrome. Kidney Internat Supp 27:S152, 1989.
3. Feehally, J., Baker, F., and Walls, J.: Dietary protein manipulation in experimental nephrotic syndrome. Nephron 50:247, 1988.
4. Kaysen, G. A., Davies, R. W., and Hutchison, N.: Effect of dietary protein intake and angiotensin converting enzyme inhibition in Heymann nephritis. Kidney Internat 36 Supp 27:S154, 1989.
5. Kaufman, C. E.: Fluid and electrolyte abnormalities in nephrotic syndrome. Postgrad Med 76:135, 1984.
6. Grundy, S. M.: Management of hyperlipidemia of kidney disease. Kidney Internat 37:847, 1990.
7. Guarnieri, G. F., Toigo, G., et al.: Nutritional state in patients on long-term low-protein diet or with nephrotic syndrome. Kidney Internat Supp 27:S195, 1989.
8. Don, B. R., Wada, L., et al.: Effect of dietary protein restriction and angiotensin converting enzyme inhibition on protein metabolism in the nephrotic syndrome. Kidney Internat Supp 27:S163, 1989.
9. Rubies, K., Espinel, E., et al.: High-density lipoprotein cholesterol subfractions in chronic uremia. Am J Kidney Dis 9:60, 1987.
10. Valeri, A., Gelfand, J., et al.: Treatment of the hyperlipidemia of the nephrotic syndrome: A controlled trial. Am J Kidney Dis 8:368, 1986.
11. Short, C., Durrington, P., et al.: Serum and urinary high density lipoproteins in glomerular disease with proteinuria. Kidney Internat 29:1224, 1986.
12. Wheeler, D. C., Varghese, Z., and Moorhead, J. F.: Hyperlipidemia in nephrotic syndrome. Am J Nephrol 9 (Supp 1):78, 1989.
13. Saku, K., Mendoza, S. G., et al.: High-density lipoprotein apolipoprotein AI and AII turnover in moderate and severe proteinuria. Nephron 50:112, 1988.
14. Nayak, S. S., Bhaskaranand, N., et al.: Serum apolipoproteins A and B, lecithin: Cholesterol acyl transferase activities and urinary cholesterol levels in nephrotic syndrome patients before and during steroid treatment. Nephron 54:234, 1990.
15. Stewart, D. W., Gordon, J. A., and Schoolwerth, A. C.: Evaluation of proteinuria. Am Fam Physician 29:218, 1984.

DIET FOLLOWING RENAL TRANSPLANT

PURPOSE OF THE DIET

Following renal transplantation it is necessary to provide adequate energy and protein to promote wound healing while modifying the diet according to renal function and side effects of immunosuppressive drugs.

1. PROMOTION OF POSITIVE NITROGEN BALANCE

In addition to the patient's increased protein needs due to surgery, steroid therapy promotes negative nitrogen balance secondary to protein catabolism (1–3).

2. PREVENTION OF SODIUM RETENTION

Steroid therapy promotes sodium retention, sometimes leading to edema and hypertension (1).

3. PREVENTION OF CUSHINGOID FEATURES

Cushingoid facial features are seen in transplant patients on high steroid doses. A high-protein, low-carbohydrate diet may prevent these effects by increasing and redistributing lean body mass (1–3).

4. PREVENTION OF POTASSIUM AND PHOSPHORUS DEPLETION

Steroids enhance potassium and phosphorus excretion, necessitating increased phosphorus and potassium intakes.

5. IMPROVEMENT IN LIPID METABOLISM

Lipid metabolism is altered by steroids and is treated by decreasing saturated-fat intake (4).

EFFECTS OF THE DIET

Renal transplant patients have corticosteroid-induced hypercholesterolemia in addition to hypertriglyceridemia. In a group of transplant patients, serum cholesterol and triglycerides were reduced to normal with a diet that provided less than 500 mg cholesterol, 35% of total calories from fat, limited alcohol consumption, and a polyunsaturated-to-saturated-fat ratio of more than 1 (5).

The American Heart Association's Step One Diet resulted in a reduction of total cholesterol, HDL-cholesterol, and triglycerides in hyperlipidemia following renal transplantation (6).

PHYSIOLOGY, FOODS, AND NUTRIENTS

1. PROTEIN

Recent evidence indicates that a diet high in protein and low in carbohydrate with at least 1.3 g of protein per kilogram of body weight per day will permit a positive nitrogen balance. Other researchers have recommended from 1 to 2 g of protein per kg (1, 7).

2. ENERGY

Energy requirements following renal transplantation are given in table 15.1. Calories may need to be restricted to prevent excessive weight gain in patients taking steroids (8).

3. SODIUM

Sodium intake is limited to 2 to 4 g per day (1).

4. FLUID

One author has described a diet that includes 800 mL of water a day plus an amount equal to the daily urine volume (3). Fluid does not usually have to be restricted at all if the new kidney is not rejected and is functioning well.

5. POTASSIUM

Potassium is usually not restricted unless cyclosporin A, which causes hyperkalemia, is used or rejection is occurring. In any instance in which serum potassium levels exceed 6.0 mg/100 mL, potassium restriction is indicated (1).

6. CALCIUM AND PHOSPHORUS

Hyperphosphatemia has been reported in some renal transplant patients. In addition, in a small number of transplant patients who do not have normal parathyroid hormone levels, renal osteodystrophy has developed. Calcium intakes should at least meet the RDA and may need to be increased if there is a preexisting calcium lack (1, 4, 9).

7. ZINC

Taste and zinc abnormalities persist up to 12 months after renal transplant and may be related to increased urinary losses in the transplant patient (10).

ASSESSMENT OF POTENTIAL DRUG INTERACTIONS

Immunosuppressive drugs used following renal transplantation include cyclosporine A, azathioprine, prednisolone, chlorambucil, and cyclophosphamide.

Cyclosporine is a potent immunosuppressant drug, and its effectiveness in pediatric renal transplantation is well established. Enthusiasm for use of this drug, however, has been tempered by potential nephrotoxicity and aggravated posttransplant hypertension (11, 12).

It has been advised that to prevent irreversible nephrotoxicity in the transplanted kidney, patients be taken off cyclosporine and put on a combination of azathioprine and prednisolone. This change actively improves function of the transplant. If given, cyclosporine A should be given as an oral solution. It should be mixed at room temperature and diluted with milk, chocolate milk, or orange juice and should be taken at the same time each day. It may cause anemia, hyperglycemia, gum inflammation, anorexia, decreased levels of serum magnesium, and increased levels of SGPT, alkaline phosphatase, SGOT, bilirubin, amylase, potassium, and uric acid. Cyclosporine A can adversely affect glucose metabolism and may be diabetogenic (13–15).

Azathioprine (Imuran) should be taken with food. It may cause diarrhea, stomach pain, altered taste, blood dyscrasia, decreased serum albumin, decreased serum and urinary uric acid, and increased serum levels of SGOT, SGPT, bilirubin, alkaline phosphatase, and amylase (13).

Corticosteroids are given to renal transplant patients as part of immunosuppressive therapy. The drugs decrease glucose tolerance as well as the absorption of calcium and phosphorus. They may also increase protein catabolism, serum triglycerides, and cholesterol levels and deplete body potassium, calcium, zinc, and vitamins B-6 and C. Methylprednisolone (Depo-Medrol or Medrol) should be taken with food. Patients should consume foods high in pyridoxine, vitamins C and D, and folate (13, 16).

Chlorambucil (Leukeran) should be taken with chilled liquid. Increased fluid intake should be encouraged. Acidic foods, hot foods, and spices should be avoided. The drug may cause gastrointestinal pain, leukemia, mouth sores, sore throat, metallic taste, and increased serum and urinary uric acid (13).

Cyclophosphamide (Cytoxan) should be taken after meals, and increased fluid intake should be encouraged. The drug may cause anorexia and mucosal ulceration (13).

IMPLEMENTATION AND EDUCATION

The patient is usually looking forward to a less restrictive diet and freedom from dialysis. During rejection, extra encouragement will be necessary to facilitate compliance with a return to renal restrictions. The patient should be reminded that sodium intake should still be controlled, even following successful transplantation.

MENU PLANNING

SAMPLE MENU FOR THE RENAL TRANSPLANT DIET (FOR A MALE, AGE 25–50)

BREAKFAST

Orange juice	½ cup
Special K	1 cup
Skim milk	1 cup
Banana	1 small
Whole wheat toast	2 slices
Margarine	2 tsp.
Coffee or tea	1 cup

LUNCH

Minestrone soup	1 cup
Saltine crackers	6
Whole wheat bread	2 slices
Tuna salad	½ cup
Fresh apple	1 medium
Coffee or tea	1 cup

AFTERNOON SNACK

Vanilla wafers	6
Fresh grapes	10
Skim milk	1 cup

DINNER

Roast chicken breast	4 oz.
Baked potato	1 large
Steamed broccoli spears	½ cup
Margarine	1 tsp.
Garden salad	1 cup
Italian dressing	1 tbsp.
Dinner roll	1 small
Margarine	2 tsp.
Fresh strawberries	1 cup
Tea	1 cup

EVENING SNACK

Whole wheat bread	2 slices
Peanut butter	2 tbsp.
Jelly	1 tbsp.
Skim milk	1 cup

Approximate Nutrient Analysis

Energy	2,486 kcal
Protein	127.3 g (20% of kcal)
Fat	73.9 g (27% of kcal)
Polyunsaturated fat	21.5 g
Monounsaturated fat	23.9 g
Saturated fat	14.7 g
Cholesterol	141 mg
Carbohydrate	347.1 g (56% of kcal)
Vitamin A	9,356 IU
	1,600 RE

(*continued*)

Thiamine	1.93 mg
Riboflavin	2.51 mg
Niacin	45.2 mg
Folate	354 mcg
Vitamin B-12	4.45 mcg
Vitamin B-6	3.50 mg
Vitamin C	262.3 mg
Calcium	1,333 mg
Phosphorus	2,088 mg
Iron	20.1 mg
Copper	1.76 mg
Zinc	10.8 mg
Magnesium	387 mg
Sodium	3,749 mg
Potassium	5,414 mg

REFERENCES

1. Shah, R.: Nutritional management of renal transplant patients. In Gillet, D., Stover, J., and Spinozzi, N.: A clinical guide to nutrition care in end stage renal disease. Chicago: American Dietetic Association, 1987.

2. Liddle, V. R., and Johnson, H. K.: Dietary therapy in renal transplantation. Proc Clin Dial Transplant Forum 9:219, 1979.

3. Whitter, F., Evans, D., et al.: Nutrition in renal transplantation. Am J Kidney Dis 6:405, 1985.

4. Wilkins, K., ed.: Suggested guidelines for nutrition care of renal patients. Chicago: Renal Dietitians Practice Group, American Dietetic Association, 1986.

5. Shen, S. Y., Lukens, C. W., et al.: Patient profile and effect of dietary therapy on post-transplant hyperlipidemia. Kidney Internat Supp 16:S147, 1983.

6. Moore, R. A., Callahan, M. F., et al.: The effect of the American Heart Association Step One Diet on hyperlipidemia following renal transplantation. Transplantation 49:60, 1990.

7. Khanna, R., Wu, G., et al.: Use of amino acid containing solution in CAPD patients. Perit Dial Bull (Supp):121, 1984.

8. Zeman, F. J.: Clinical nutrition and dietetics. Lexington, Ky.: Collamore Press, 1983.

9. Alsina, J., Gonzalez, M. T., et al.: Long-term evolution of renal osteodystrophy after renal transplantation. Transplant Proc 21:2151, 1989.

10. Mahajan, S. K., Abraham, J., et al.: Zinc metabolism and taste acuity in renal transplant recipients. Kidney Internat Supp 16:S310, 1983.

11. Hannedouche, T. P., Delgado, A. G., et al.: Nephrotoxicity of cyclosporine in autoimmune diseases. Adv Nephrol 19:169, 1990.

12. Ogborn, M. R., Crocker, J. F. S., et al.: Cyclosporine A and hypertension in pediatric renal transplant patients. Transplant Proc 21:1705, 1989.

13. Powers, D. E., and Moore, A. O.: Food/medication interactions. 6th ed. Phoenix: 1988 (self-published).

14. Hall, B. M., Tiller, D. J., et al.: Comparison of three immunosuppressive regimens in cadaver transplantation: Long-term cyclosporine, short-term cyclosporine followed by azathioprine and prednisolone, and azathioprine and prednisolone without cyclosporine. N Engl J Med 318:1499, 1988.

15. Smith, W. G. J., Thomas, S., et al.: Comparative effects of immunosuppressive therapy on glucose metabolism. Transplant Proc 21:1502, 1989.

16. Mitchell, P. J., and Butler, C. D.: Renal disease: Interactions of nutrients and drugs and their effect on the gastrointestinal tract. St. Louis: Missouri-Kansas Council on Renal Nutrition, 1983.

16.

GLUTEN-FREE (GLIADIN-FREE) DIET

DEFINITIONS

1. GLUTEN-FREE (GLIADIN-FREE) DIET

A diet free of gliadin or glutens, such as those in wheat, rye, oat, and barley protein and malt (a derivative of barley). Gliadin and glutens are toxic to individuals with gluten-sensitive enteropathy (1).

2. CELIAC DISEASE

(Nontropical Sprue, Gluten Enteropathy, Celiac Sprue) A chronic intestinal malabsorption disorder caused by intolerance to gluten and characterized by a flat jejunal mucosa with clinical and histologic improvement following withdrawal of dietary gluten.

PURPOSE OF THE DIET

The diet is intended to eliminate toxic glutens, or more specifically the toxic fraction, gliadin. Its aim is to ameliorate the symptoms of diarrhea, abdominal distension, and failure to thrive (2, 3).

EFFECTS OF THE DIET

1. IMPROVEMENT IN SYMPTOMS

Dramatic improvement of the symptoms of the disease follows the institution of a gluten-restricted diet, although recovery may take up to 6 months in some patients. The majority of patients demonstrate a rapid symptomatic response. Complaints such as abdominal discomfort, diarrhea, and malaise usually show marked improvement in just a few days. Objective evidence of improvement (de-

crease in steatorrhea and weight gain) follows the symptomatic improvement (4).

Failure to respond to the diet indicates a misdiagnosis, undetected sources of gliadin, or other concomitant food sensitivities (2, 3, 5, 6).

2. IMPROVEMENT IN THE INTESTINAL LESION

Patients have a characteristic, if not specific, lesion of the jejunal mucosa and may have altered but reversible disaccharide enzyme activity secondary to the lesion. Long-term adherence to the diet will produce at least partial restoration of the normal mucosal surface (2, 3, 7).

Prior to dietary treatment, small lymphocytes and plasma cells, often IgA producing, infiltrate the jejunal mucosa. Mucosal mast cells increase in number, and local tissue density of intraepithelial lymphocytes (IELs) is increased (8–15).

After adherence to the diet, many of the cellular changes are reversed. The rapid clinical response to diet is not immediately reflected by an improvement in biopsy appearance. The speed and eventual degree of histological improvement is unpredictable. Although an increase in enterocyte height may be evident within 1 week of gluten avoidance, the return of villous architecture toward normal takes considerably longer and may not be evident on rebiopsy for 2 or 3 months (4, 6, 11–15).

In general, adherence to the diet is followed by a gradual improvement in most if not all of the histological abnormalities seen in the untreated disease. Although a return to complete normality can occur, especially in children, usually minor de-

grees of villous blunting and some increase in the numbers of intraepithelial lymphocytes persist. A gluten-free diet has been documented to improve both jejunal mucosal histology and serum reticulum and gliadin antibody titers (4, 16).

3. CATCH-UP GROWTH

In a recent study, children with celiac disease had a normal intestinal mucosa after 1 year on a gluten-restricted diet. Also, bone age increased more rapidly than chronological age. At the beginning of the study the children had an average chronological age of 8.9 years and a bone age of 6.6 years. At the end of the study they had an average chronological age of 12.5 and a bone age of 11.3 years. In another study, of children who were from 18 to 36 months of age and were treated with a gluten-free diet, growth accelerated, and height at 3 years of age was almost the same as for healthy children (17–19).

PHYSIOLOGY, FOODS, AND NUTRIENTS

1. TOXICITY OF GLUTENS

Each cereal grain has a characteristic gluten. Glutens in wheat, rye, triticale, barley, and often oats cause characteristic symptoms in patients with celiac disease (20–21). Cereals containing glutens that produce no ill effects in susceptible individuals are not restricted.

2. TOXIC FRACTION OF GLIADIN

Gluten is the protein that remains after the starch has been removed from the grain. Gluten consists of 4 classes of protein: gliadin, glutenins, albumins, and globulins. Gliadin, the protein that is toxic to individuals with celiac disease, has about 4 components, all of which have been shown to be toxic to different degrees (2, 22).

3. DISEASE ETIOLOGY

There are 2 major theories as to the etiology of celiac disease. The immunological model proposes increased antibodies to gliadin. The biochemical model proposes not increased antibodies but alterations in the cell membrane and in prostaglandin E-2. Enhanced jejunal prostaglandin E-2 synthesis may be involved in the pathophysiological processes initiated when gluten is introduced into the diet of individuals with celiac disease. After gliadin challenge of individuals with celiac disease, a significant increase in prostaglandin E-2 secretion has been documented. An abnormal response to gluten is characteristic, leading to damage to gastrointestinal and epithelial cells (2, 23–31).

4. SYMPTOMS

Celiac disease manifests itself with steatorrhea, with or without vomiting and occasional crampy abdominal pain that can occur anytime after the introduction of foods containing toxic glutens during the first or second year of life of children with the disease. It may also manifest itself late in adulthood (4).

5. INCIDENCE

Gluten must be present for the disease to appear. It is therefore more common in countries where wheat is a staple and thus where incidence may range from 1 in 300 to 1 in 6,000. Celiac disease is more common in Ireland than in North America and in adult patients with insulin-dependent diabetes mellitus (2, 4, 32).

The increased incidence of the disease in the 1950s and 1960s has been attributed to the practice of introducing ce-

reals at an increasingly early age, often at 4 to 6 weeks of age, whereas the decrease in incidence since 1974 has been ascribed to the reversal of this practice. Gluten antibodies are found in many patients with untreated disease and, according to one theory, were formed as a result of a sensitization reaction due to increased permeability of the gut to macromolecules (12).

6. INHERITANCE

Gluten enteropathy, or celiac disease, is inherited in a multifactorial fashion. The disease can occur in more than one member of the family. The histocompatibility antigen HLA-B8 occurs in 80% of patients and can be used as a marker for the disease (12).

7. BONE MASS DEFICIENCY

Patients in whom the diagnosis is not made early in life and who follow a normal diet have significantly lower bone mass than patients treated early in life with a gluten-restricted, gliadin-free diet. After 12 months of treatment, bone turnover markers decrease. The exact mechanism of the bone derangement is not known. Prompt diagnosis and early treatment are extremely important in preventing bone mass deficiencies (33–35).

8. DENTAL ENAMEL DEFECTS

Enamel defects (hypoplasia) found in celiac disease correlate significantly with gluten ingestion and with the severity of symptoms in children with celiac disease. Catch-up growth in dental tissues and bone occur after gluten-free (gliadin-free) nutritional therapy. It is recommended that the enamel defects be examined visually under proper lighting and after the teeth have been cleaned and dried. The use of the gluten challenge in children should also be restricted. It should not be made before the age of 3 years, it should be of short duration, and it should preferably be instituted after 7 years of age when all the crowns of per-

manent teeth, except third molars, have developed (36).

INDICATIONS FOR USE

1. DIAGNOSIS

A definitive diagnosis of gluten-sensitive enteropathy requires a jejunal biopsy in which flattened mucosal villi and other characteristic changes are noted. The biopsy is repeated between 3 months and 2 years later to confirm the diagnosis. A subsequent gluten challenge may be performed if the original biopsy was not obtained or if diagnosis is in question. Patients may have abnormal responses to clinical tests for malabsorption (4, 21, 24–29, 37–39).

2. MONITORING

Clinical symptoms and antibody testing are used to monitor response and compliance to diet (4).

3. DURATION OF DIETARY TREATMENT

Primary gluten-sensitive enteropathy is a permanent condition requiring lifelong gluten restriction. One study has suggested that even as little as 0.5 g of gluten can interfere with recovery. Children who have been rechallenged with gluten after a period of time responded with decreased growth rates and changes in intestinal biopsies. Even in symptomless patients, the diet is required for life (9, 21, 40–42).

POSSIBLE ADVERSE REACTIONS

Constipation may be encountered because wheat fiber is excluded from the diet. Alternative sources of insoluble fiber and roughage need to be employed to prevent the problem (4).

CONTRAINDICATIONS

No contraindications have been reported.

CLINICAL ASSESSMENT

A primary aim of treatment is to enable patients to achieve and maintain normal growth velocities (4). Untreated children are at higher risk of short stature. Thus, determination of height and weight in relation to ideal weight and estimation of bone age are priority measures for the prevention of delayed growth. Skinfold measurements and midarm muscle circumference estimations will provide clues to skeletal muscle abnormalities due to protein malnutrition.

Secondary malabsorption of fat and protein may result in foul-smelling bulky stools, as well as weight loss, irritability, and delayed growth and development. Edema may result from low levels of serum albumin in the protein-malnourished child (43). Muscle cramps, tetany, and weakness may signal calcium malabsorption, and rickets may indicate vitamin D malabsorption.

BIOCHEMICAL ASSESSMENT

1. IRON AND FOLATE STATUS

Individuals with gluten-sensitive enteropathy should be evaluated regularly for iron and folate status as well as for coagulation factors via periodic determinations of hemoglobin, MCV, MCH, and MCHC. Routine hematological or biochemical tests may unearth subclinical deficiency states, attributable to celiac enteropathy, often in the complete absence of gastrointestinal symptoms. Iron deficiency is common in the untreated disease, and in children a microcytic, hypochromic anemia is frequently found. In adults, iron deficiency also occurs, but concomitant folic acid deficiency is more likely to be evident, and a reduction in serum folate is a sensitive indicator of celiac malabsorption (4).

2. VISCERAL PROTEIN STATUS

Serum albumin and total protein are helpful in determining visceral protein status. Hypoalbuminemia is usually found in patients with severe and prolonged malabsorption (4).

3. OTHER VITAMINS AND MINERALS

Steatorrhea is associated with malabsorption of the fat-soluble vitamins. Malabsorption of vitamin D and calcium is particularly likely to occur, though with earlier diagnosis, clinically evident osteomalacia and rickets are now seldom encountered. Scurvy or deficiencies of B vitamins are rare (4).

Prothrombin time may be delayed if vitamin K is being malabsorbed. Abnormalities of coagulation, reversed by the administration of vitamin K, may occur but are mild and seldom result in hemorrhagic complications (4).

ASSESSMENT OF POTENTIAL DRUG INTERACTIONS

The mucosal damage that occurs in gluten-sensitive enteropathy results in alterations in pH, which disrupt the absorption of drugs and nutrients such as iron, folate, vitamin D, and calcium (21).

Corticosteroids such as prednisolone have been useful in the treatment of severely affected individuals. Their use permits relaxation of dietary restrictions. Both dietary treatment and steroids produce reversal of mucosal changes. However, steroids, unlike diet therapy, also stimulate protein catabolism; depress protein synthesis; decrease calcium and phosphorus absorption; increase urinary excretion of calcium, potassium, zinc, nitrogen, and ascorbic acid; and decrease serum levels of proteins, zinc, triglycerides, and glucose. The diet lacks any of the above adverse side effects and thus is the treatment of choice except in severe "refractory sprue" or in instances of celiac crisis (43–45).

Drugs used for celiac patients must be gluten-free and gliadin-free. None of the drugs manufactured by Beecham Laboratories contains gluten, and all of the alcohol in consumable products (ethanol) is from petroleum, not grain, sources. The pharmacist should always be consulted as to the gluten content of medications.

IMPLEMENTATION AND EDUCATION

1. PARENTAL KNOWLEDGE AND NETWORKING

Families with members who have gluten-sensitive enteropathy share a number of common problems and concerns to which there are no easy answers. Associations such as the National Celiac Sprue Society, the Midwestern Celiac Sprue Association, and the Gluten Intolerance Group foster networking as a means of achieving common goals and facilitating compliance. According to one study, to increase dietary compliance, parents of children with celiac disease should be guided mainly by enhancing their subjective evaluation of their own knowledge of celiac disease, improving their practical ability to handle a menu, and increasing their level of concern regarding possible long-term adverse effects of dietary noncompliance (46).

2. FOOD-COMPOSITION SURVEILLANCE SYSTEM

Some manufacturers have adopted a special symbol, a crossed ear of wheat, to designate products that do not contain toxic glutens. The composition of some foods is uncertain, however. Even when the content is clearly discernible from the label, a manufacturer may change ingredients without notice. Support-group newsletters are a good way to keep abreast of such changes, as well as of new products. Periodic follow-up by a dietitian is important. A carefully taken diet history in conjunction with a gluten antibody test is a useful way of detecting the inadvertent ingestion of gluten from less obvious dietary sources. The most common reason for failure of the patient to respond to the diet is the continued intentional or inadvertent ingestion of toxic glutens (4, 41, 47, 48).

A rapid gluten test kit has been developed that could be used by practitioners and patients. This qualitative, semiquantitative test to detect gluten would be invaluable in determining the safety of suspect foods (49).

Family members, including affected children, must be taught with a positive approach in order to avoid emotional problems. They must learn to scrutinize labels on all foods before bringing them into the house. They must be able to question the content of foods and to refuse those with forbidden ingredients. They must acquire special planning skills and exercise foresight to circumvent environmental situations in which there is no alternative to gliadin-containing meals. Previewing a menu before going to a restaurant and reviewing the menu there are prerequisites to safe restaurant dining. In the case of family picnics or parties, a gliadin-free homemade TV dinner, boxed lunch, or snack can be made ahead. A gluten-free cake or homemade gluten-free ice cream cake is an appealing alternative to a wheat-flour birthday cake (50).

3. GLIADIN-FREE CUISINE

A. Home Management Skills An accurate and complete listing of the gliadin content of any and all foods to be eaten is a prerequisite to the effective management of gluten-sensitive enteropathy. Other home management skills that promote compliance include the reorganization of the kitchen to facilitate gliadin-free baking and cooking and the elimination of hazards such as foods with hidden sources of gluten. If space permits, a separate cabinet that is reserved for gliadin-free supplies and staples will reduce the risk of inadvertent use of gliadin-containing products. If possible, a separate mixing board or countertop

should be used to avoid traces of sandwich breads or wheat flours. A second set of measuring cups, spoons, and other utensils is also helpful.

B. Special Baking Tips Cooking and baking for the gliadin-free diet is an important part of successful nutritional counseling. Flours of arrowroot, corn, potatoes, rice, and soybeans may be used in place of wheat flour. Their use will produce unsatisfactory results, however, unless adjustments in other ingredients and baking techniques are made to account for their unique properties. For example, rice flour and cornmeal have a grainy texture. Boiling these grains in liquid prior to their combination with other ingredients will improve their texture. For best results, soy flour should be mixed with some other gliadin-free flour rather than being used by itself. The use of coarse meals and flours often increases the amount of leavening needed. Although the use of these special products adds to weekly grocery expenses, the diet cannot be nutritionally adequate without substitutes for wheat-flour products. Expenses that exceed those of a regular diet are tax-deductible, provided there is a physician prescription and accurate record keeping (50–55).

C. Xanthan Gum Xanthan gum is the cell coating of an organism called *Xanthomonas campestris*. If the organism is grown in a laboratory, large amounts of this cell coat can be removed by a chemical process, dried, and milled to form a powder called xanthan gum. It is a polysaccharide joined by links that the human intestine cannot split apart. Because xanthan gum is not readily absorbed, few of the sugar units can be used by the body for energy. Thus xanthan gum is low in calories, providing only 0.5 kcal per gram, or 8 kcal per tablespoon. The special strength of the cell coat makes xanthan gum useful in foods. It is added to salad dressings, canned gravies and

sauces, and even ice cream to give these foods a smoother texture. It also has the ability to hold the particles of a food together, making it a good stabilizer and a good substitute for gluten in yeast breads.

The following proportions of xanthan gum to gluten-free flour give the most satisfying results:

Product	Amount of xanthan gum per cup of gluten-free flour
Cake	¼ tsp.
Bread	1 tsp.
Pizza crust	2 tsp.

Xanthan gum is available commercially in 100-lb. units or in ½-lb. and 1-lb. units from the Gluten Intolerance Group, P.O. Box 23053, Seattle, WA 98102-0353.

4. SECONDARY DISORDERS

Untreated celiac patients show increased small-intestinal permeability, which may account for the increased serum levels of antibodies to a variety of food proteins, such as casein and ovalbumin. Secondary sucrose and lactose intolerance may occur in individuals whose intestinal lesions are severe because of delayed diagnosis or repeated gluten challenges. In such instances, temporary lactose and sucrose restriction is necessary but may often be relaxed once the intestinal surface changes are reversed. Significant lactase deficiencies have been found in biopsy specimens from patients with untreated celiac disease. Lactose should be restricted as for lactose intolerance, and after 6 months it may be slowly added back (4, 56, 57).

In patients with untreated celiac disease, even small doses of sorbitol are malabsorbed and cause severe diarrhea. It is recommended that the use of sorbitol be eliminated in celiac disease (58).

Gluten restriction can never be relaxed and represents a lifelong commitment for the patient with gluten-sensitive enteropathy.

PRIORITIES FOR QUALITY ASSURANCE

Quality assurance monitors should be developed by professionals responsible for providing quality medical and nutritional care to patients with either primary or secondary gluten intolerance. They should be designed to meet at least the following criteria.

1. IDENTIFICATION OF AFFECTED INDIVIDUALS

Other diseases that also affect the intestinal mucosa should be ruled out. In other cases of mucosal injury, such as gastrointestinal milk allergy or inflammatory bowel disease, the patient may have symptoms that suggest he or she might benefit from temporary gluten restriction because of a secondary and transitory gluten intolerance.

2. ACCURACY OF THE DIET

In the hospital or institutional setting, all sources of gluten in the food supply should be identified. Adequate data to identify gluten-containing foods both in the institution and in the local food supply of patients should be acquired. The administrative section of the department should have adequate information to make correct purchasing choices. Group buying practices for gluten-restricted products should be planned with adequate safeguards against inadvertent substitution of gluten-containing foods.

3. NUTRITIONAL ADEQUACY

Each individual diet should be planned to meet the caloric needs, as well as any extraordinary needs of catch-up growth in children or vitamin and mineral deficiencies caused by malabsorption. There should be enough variety in the diet to promote dietary compliance with recipes made from wheat-flour substitutes. Regular dietary follow-up should be planned to monitor compliance (47).

MENU PLANNING

Clinical experience has shown that bread wheat, durum wheat, triticale, and rye are highly toxic. Barley is less toxic but should still be avoided. Wheat starch is safe for most celiacs, provided the total protein content is low. Maize and rice are nontoxic and are safe to eat. Other cereals, such as millet, buckwheat, amaranth, and sorghum, have been suggested as alternatives for celiacs. They are taxonomically closer to maize than to wheat and therefore should be suitable, although it would be wise for patients to refrain from using these cereals until controlled studies have been conducted (49).

Foods allowed and foods to avoid in the gluten-free (gliadin-free) diet are listed in tables 16.1 and 16.2. Additional gliadin-free additives are listed in table 16.3. Sources of special products are provided in table 16.4.

SAMPLE MENU FOR GLUTEN-FREE (GLIADIN-FREE) DIET (FOR A CHILD, AGE 7–10)

BREAKFAST	
Orange juice	½ cup
Cream of Rice cereal	1 cup
Low-fat milk	1 cup
Gliadin-free brown toast[a]	½-inch slice
Margarine	2 tsp.
Gliadin-free preserves	1 tsp.
Soft-cooked egg	1 large
LUNCH	
Tacos:	
Corn tortillas	2
Cooked ground beef	2 oz.
Shredded lettuce	2 leaves
Chopped tomato	1 medium
Grated cheddar cheese	1 oz.
Sour cream	2 tbsp.
Banana	1 medium
Low-fat milk	½ cup

(continued)

DINNER

Baked chicken	2 oz.
Baked potato	1 small
Cooked spinach	½ cup
Gliadin-free brown bread[a]	½-inch slice
Margarine	2 tsp.
Canned apricots	1 cup
Low-fat milk	½ cup

EVENING SNACK

Rice pudding	½ cup
Raisins	2 tbsp.

Approximate Nutrient Analysis

Energy	1,993 kcal
Protein	80.5 g (16% of kcal)
Fat	67.1 g (30% of kcal)
Polyunsaturated fat	9.4 g
Monounsaturated fat	24.1 g
Saturated fat	25.1 g
Cholesterol	179 mg
Carbohydrate	276.1 g (55% of kcal)
Vitamin A	12,362 IU
	1,629 RE
Thiamine	0.92 mg
Riboflavin	1.93 mg
Niacin	23.8 mg
Folate	300 mcg
Vitamin B-12	3.89 mcg
Vitamin B-6	2.64 mg
Vitamin C	128.5 mg
Calcium	1,278 mg
Phosphorus	1,282 mg
Iron	19.6 mg
Copper	1.50 mg
Zinc	11.0 mg
Magnesium	350 mg
Sodium	1,252 mg
Potassium	3,870 mg

[a]Welplan brand, from Dietary Specialties, P.O. Box 227, Rochester, NY 14601.

TABLE 16.1. GLUTEN-RESTRICTED, GLIADIN-FREE FOODS

Food group and suggested daily intake	Foods allowed	Foods to avoid
Milk: 2 or more cups	Fresh, dry, evaporated, or condensed milk; cream, sour cream,[a] whipping cream; yogurt[a]	Malted milk; some commercial chocolate drinks; some nondairy creamers[b]
Meat, fish, poultry: 2 or more servings	All kinds of fresh meats, fish, other seafood, poultry; fish canned in oil or brine; some prepared meat products, such as hot dogs and lunch meats[b]	Prepared meats that contain wheat, rye, oats, or barley, such as some sausages, hot dogs, bologna, luncheon meats, chili con carne;[b] bread-containing products, such as Swiss steak, croquettes, meat loaf; tuna canned in hydrolyzed protein[b] and turkey with hydrolyzed vegetable protein injected as part of the basting solution
Cheeses (can be used for meat and milk groups)	All aged cheeses, such as cheddar, Swiss, Edam, Parmesan; cottage cheese,[a] cream cheese,[a] pasteurized processed cheese[a,b]	Any cheese product containing oat gum as an ingredient
Eggs	Plain or in cooking	Eggs in sauce made from gliadin-containing ingredients, such as a regular, wheat-based white sauce
Potato or other starch: 1 or more servings	White and sweet potatoes, yams, hominy, rice, wild rice, special gliadin-free noodles (Aproten and other brands),[c] some oriental rice and bean noodles	Regular noodles, spaghetti, macaroni; most packaged rice mixes[b]
Vegetables: 3 or more servings	All plain, fresh, frozen, or canned vegetables; dry peas and beans; lentils; some commercially prepared vegetables[b]	Creamed vegetables;[b] vegetables canned in sauce;[b] some canned baked beans;[b] commercially prepared vegetables and salads[b]
Fruits: 2 or more servings	All fresh, frozen, canned, or dried fruits; all fruit juices; some canned pie fillings	Thickened or prepared fruits; some pie fillings[b]
Breads: 4 or more servings	Specially prepared breads made from only allowed flours (examples that are commercially available: Ener-G Foods brown rice bread, white rice bread, and xanthan gum bread[c])	All others containing wheat, rye, oat, or barley flours; breads made with "carob-soy flour" (Sterling Food Co., Seattle), which contains 80% wheat flour
Cereals: 1 or more servings of enriched cereal	Hot cereals made from cornmeal, Cream of Rice, hominy, or rice; cold cereals as follows: puffed rice, Corn Pops (Kellogg), Fruity and Chocolate Pebbles (Post), special cereals made without malt, Kenmei, Sun Flakes (corn and rice flakes only)	All others containing wheat, rye, oats, or barley; bran; graham; wheat germ; malt; kasha; bulgur; buckwheat,[d] millet,[d] amaranth,[d] spelt,[d] quinoa,[d] teff[d]
Flours and thickening agents[e]	Arrowroot starch (A), corn bran (B), corn flour (B, C, D),[c] corn germ (B), cornmeal (B, C, D), cornstarch (A), potato flour (B, C, E),[c] potato starch flour (B, C, E), rice bran (B), rice flours [plain, brown (B, C, D, E), sweet (A, B, C, F)], rice polish (B, C, G),[c] rice starch (A), soy flour (B, C, G),[c] tapioca starch (A)	Wheat starch; all flours containing wheat, rye, oats, or barley; "carob-soy flour" (Sterling Food Co., Seattle), which contains 80% wheat flour Substances needing additional testing: amaranth, buckwheat, millet, quinoa, spelt, and teff
Crackers and snack foods	Rice wafers; rice crackers; pure cornmeal tortillas; popcorn; some crackers and chips[b]	All others containing wheat, rye, oats, or barley

TABLE 16.1. *CONTINUED*

Food group and suggested daily intake	Foods allowed	Foods to avoid
Fats	Butter; margarine; vegetable oil; nuts; peanut butters; hydrogenated vegetable oils; some salad dressings;[b] mayonnaise[b]	Some commercial salad dressings[b]
Soups	Homemade broth and soups made with allowed ingredients; some commercially canned soups[b]	Most canned soups and soup mixes;[b] bouillon and bouillon cubes with hydrolyzed vegetable protein (HVP; the term *flavoring* is often used to represent HVP)
Desserts	Cakes, quick breads, pastries, puddings prepared with allowed ingredients; cornstarch, tapioca, and rice puddings; gelatin desserts; custard; vanilla and coffee-flavored ice cream from Arden, Carnation, Darigold, Foremost, and Lucerne;[b] some pudding mixes;[b] most Häagen-Dazs ice cream and sherbets[b]	Commercial cakes, cookies, pies, etc., made with wheat, rye, oats, or barley; prepared mixes;[b] ice cream cones; puddings;[b] Jell-O instant pudding
Beverages	Instant and ground coffee; instant tea; tea; carbonated beverages;[b] pure cocoa powder; U.S. wines; rums; some root beers;[b] vodka distilled from grapes or potatoes	Ovaltine; malted milk; ale; beer; gin; whiskeys;[f] vodka distilled from grain; flavored coffees;[b] some herbal teas with malted barley[b]
Sweets	Jelly; jam; honey; brown and white sugar; molasses; most syrups;[b] some candy;[b] chocolate; pure cocoa; coconut	Some commercial candies (with such ingredients as flour and malt or where wheat flour is dusted on the conveyor belts during processing), chocolate-coated nuts, which are often rolled in flour
Miscellaneous	Salt, pepper, herbs, extracts,[g] food coloring, cloves, ginger, nutmeg, cinnamon, chili powder, tomato puree and paste, olives, pickles,[f] cider, rice and wine vinegar, yeast, bicarbonate of soda, baking powder, cream of tartar, dry mustard, some other condiments,[b] monosodium glutamate (MSG),[h] soy sauce and tamari made without wheat	Some curry powder,[b] some dry seasoning mixes,[b] some gravy extracts,[b] some meat sauces,[b] some catsup,[b] some mustard,[b] horseradish,[b] most soy sauce,[b] chip dips,[b] some chewing gum,[b] distilled white vinegar[f]

Source: Hartsook, E. I. (51).

Note: Additional information on celiac sprue and dermatitis herpetiformis may be obtained from the Gluten Intolerance Group of North America, P.O. Box 23053, Seattle, WA 98102-0353.

[a]Check vegetable gum used.

[b]Consult label and contact manufacturer to clarify questionable ingredients, especially the source of flavorings in meat and poultry products.

[c]See table 16.4 for availability and ordering information.

[d]Although botanically different from other gliadin-containing grains, this cereal cannot be cleared until additional information is gathered.

[e]A, good thickening agent; B, good combined with other flours; C, best combined with milk and eggs in baked product; D, grainy-textured products; E, drier product than with other flours; F, moister product than with other flours; G, adds distinct flavor to product—use in moderation.

[f]Distilled white vinegar uses grain as a starting material. Whiskeys, including "corn whiskey," use wheat, rye, oats, or barley in their mash. According to chemistry professors consulted, in large-scale distillation processes such as are used in the manufacture of whiskey and vinegar, it is possible that a very small amount of protein may be carried over into the distillate. The presence of such a small amount of gliadin must be tested via immunoassay, an expensive and complex technique using laboratory animals to produce a gliadin-antibody. Currently, gliadin-intolerant persons are advised to avoid all whiskeys and to use cider vinegar and wine vinegar in food preparation, such as making salad dressings and pickles, and in cooking.

[g]Alcohol-free extracts are available; see table 16.4.

[h]MSG is made in the United States from sugar beets; starting materials of MSG from other sources should be checked.

TABLE 16.2. QUESTIONABLE INGREDIENTS

Ingredient (as appears on label)	Allowed	To be avoided
"Hydrolyzed vegetable protein"[a]	Soy, corn	Mixtures of wheat, corn, and soya (soy)
"Flour" or "cereal products"	Rice flour, corn flour, cornmeal, potato flour, soy flour	Wheat, rye, oats, barley
"Vegetable protein"	Soy, corn	Wheat, rye, oats, barley
"Flavoring"	In meat and poultry products this can be hydrolyzed vegetable protein (HVP).	
"Malt" or "malt flavoring"	Those derived from corn	Those derived from barley or barley malt syrup
"Starch"	When listed as such on a U.S. manufacturer's ingredient list, it is corn starch and therefore is allowed.	
"Modified starch" or "modified food starch"	Arrowroot, corn, potato, tapioca, waxy maize, maize	Wheat starch
"Vegetable gum"	Carob bean, locust bean, cellulose gum, guar gum, gum arabic, gum acacia, gum tragacanth, xanthan gum	Oat gum
"Soy sauce" or "soy sauce solids"	Those that *do not* contain wheat, such as Chun King	Those that *do* contain wheat
Monoglycerides and diglycerides	Those using a gliadin-free carrier	Those using a wheat-starch carrier
Monosodium glutamate (MSG)	Made in the U.S. from sugar beets	Imports for which the starting material is unknown

Source: Hartsook, E. I. (51).

Note: Gliadin-intolerant persons should always check with the manufacturer of the questionable ingredients listed here before eating any product containing them. When writing the manufacturer, request information on the specific starting material(s) used in the questionable ingredient. For example, if "modified food starch" appears as a labeling ingredient, ask for the specific type of starch used, i.e., potato starch, tapioca starch, etc.

[a]A combination of wheat, corn, and soya is primarily used as starting material for hydrolyzed vegetable protein (HVP) and thus is not allowed in a gluten-free diet. When wheat protein is 'hydrolyzed,' its large amino acid chains are broken down into smaller chains. Some protein researchers believe that the same sequences of amino acids found in these smaller chains contain the same toxicity as the intact gliadin subfraction of the gluten protein. Thus, HVP made from wheat is not recommended for use on a gliadin-free diet.

TABLE 16.3. ADDITIONAL GLIADIN-FREE ADDITIVES

Adipic acid	Mannitol
Ascorbic acid	Microcrystalline cellulose
BHA	Niacin
BHT	Niacinamide
Beta carotene	Polyglycerol
Biotin	Polysorbate 60
Calcium chloride	Polysorbate 80
Calcium pantothenate	Potassium citrate
Calcium phosphate	Potassium iodide
Carboxymethylcellulose	Propylene glycol monostearate
Carrageenan	Propylgallate
Citric acid	Pyridoxine hydrochloride
Corn sweetener	Riboflavin
Corn syrup solids	Sodium acid pyrophosphate
Demineralized whey	Sodium ascorbate
Dextrimaltose	Sodium benzoate
Dextrins	Sodium caseinate
Dextrose	Sodium citrate
Dioctyl sodium sulfosuccinate	Sodium hexametaphosphate
Folic acid	Sodium nitrate
Folacin	Sodium silicoaluminate
Fructose	Sorbitol
Fumaric acid	Sucrose
Gums: acacia, arabic, carob bean, cellulose,	Sulfosuccinate
guar, locust bean, tragacanth, xanthan	Tartaric acid
Invert sugar	Thiamine hydrochloride
Lactic acid	Tricalcium phosphate
Lactose	Vanillin
Lecithin	Vitamins and minerals
Magnesium hydroxide	Vitamin A (palmitate)
Malic acid	

Medications: prescription and over-the-counter drugs

All medications have fillers or dispersing agents added. These agents are usually lactose or cornstarch, but wheat starch may also be used. *Before taking any medication,* gliadin-intolerant persons must check with the manufacturer to make sure the product is gliadin free. When calling or writing the drug company, be able to provide the lot number of the product.

Source: Hartsook, E. I. (51).
Note: The above list is not exhaustive.

TABLE 16.4. SOURCES OF GLIADIN-FREE PRODUCTS

Manufacturer	Product information
AlpineAire Foods P.O. Box 926 Nevada City, CA 95959 (916) 272-1971	Freeze-dried foods for backpacking and camping. All foods are vacuum-packed and contain no preservatives, no added sugar, and no artificial flavors or colors. *Note:* The "vegetable pasta" listed in the Pasta Roma and Vegetable Pasta Stew *contains wheat flour* as its major ingredient. Mail orders are accepted.
Bickford Laboratories Co. 282 S. Main St. Akron, OH 44308 (216) 762-4666	A complete line of alcohol-free flavoring agents.
Cook Flavoring Co. P.O. Box 890 Tacoma, WA 98401	Pure vanilla powder. Also carried by regular food stores and Ener-G Foods.
DeBoles Garden City Park, NY 11040	Corn pasta products, including ribbon noodles, macaroni, and spaghetti.
Dietary Specialties P.O. Box 227 Rochester, NY 14601 1-800-544-0099	Dietary Specialties, Wel-Plan, and Aproten brands. Gluten-free bread, crackers, cookies and pasta. Mixes for bread, cakes, muffins, and brownies. Mail orders are accepted.
El Molino Mills 345 N. Baldwin Park Blvd. City of Industry, CA 91746 (213) 962-7167	A variety of gluten-free cereals and flours. Available through local distributors only; no retail mail sales. Company will forward name and address of nearest distributor, as well as product ingredient information.
Ener-G Foods, Inc. P.O. Box 84487 Seattle, WA 98124-5787 (206) 767-6660 1-800-331-5222	Jolly Joan gluten-free flours and flour mixes; company will ship gluten-free flours in bulk also. Variety of baked products including breads, cinnamon rolls, cookies, pizza crusts, pasta, and crackers. Mail orders are accepted. Write for complete product information.
Fearn Soya Foods Division of Richard Foods Corp. Melrose Park, IL 60160 (312) 345-2335	Variety of gluten-free flours, baking mixes, and other baking ingredients (Fearn brand). Mail orders are accepted.
Gluten Intolerance Group P.O. Box 23053 Seattle, WA 98102-0353	Xanthan gum for stabilization of homemade brown and white rice flour yeast bread. Variety of publications dealing with celiac sprue. *GIG Cookbook* also available.
NuVita Foods, Inc. 7524 S.W. Macadam Portland, OR 97219 (503) 246-5433	Lange's "Mello Gold" gluten-free flours. Mail orders are accepted.

(continued)

TABLE 16.4. *CONTINUED*

Manufacturer	Product information
Red Mill Farms, Inc. Gluten-Free Products Division 290 S. 5th St. Brooklyn, NY 11211 (718) 384-2150	Gluten-free, lactose-free dutch chocolate cake, banana-nut cake, and coconut macaroons—all vacuum-packed. Excellent products. Mail orders only.
Van Brode's Milling Co. Clinton, MA 01510	Gluten-free cold breakfast cereals. Write for complete product listing and distribution information.

Source: Hartsook, E. I. (51).

REFERENCES

1. Sleisinger, M., Rynbergen, H., et al.: Wheat-rye and oat free diet. J Am Diet Assoc 33:1137, 1957.
2. Strober, W.: Gluten-sensitive enteropathy: A nonallergic immune hypersensitivity of the gastrointestinal tract. J Allergy Clin Immunol 78:202, 1986.
3. Westergaard, H.: Southwestern internal medicine conference: The sprue syndromes. Am J Med Sci 290:249, 1985.
4. Kelly, C. P., Feighery, C. F., et al.: Diagnosis and treatment of gluten-sensitive enteropathy. Adv Intern Med 35:341, 1990.
5. Van de Kamer, J., and Weijers, H.: Coeliac disease. 5. Some experiments on the cause of the harmful effect of wheat gliadin. Acta Paediatr Scand 44:465, 1955.
6. Colaco, J., Egan-Mitchell, B., et al.: Compliance with gluten free diet in coeliac disease. Arch Dis Child 62:706, 1987.
7. Vuoristo, M., and Miettinen, T.: Serum cholesterol precursor sterols in coeliac disease: Effects of gluten free diet and cholestyramine. Gut 27:1312, 1986.
8. Farthing, M., Rees, L., et al.: Male gonadal function in coeliac disease. 2. Sex hormones. Gut 24:127, 1983.
9. Ferguson, R., Holmes, G., and Cooke, W.: Coeliac disease, fertility and pregnancy. Scand J Gastroenterol 17:65, 1982.
10. Shanahan, F., Aburajab, A., et al.: Factor V deficiency and its reversal with gluten restriction. Arch Intern Med 143:2009, 1983.
11. Crofton, R., Glover, S., et al.: Zinc absorption in celiac disease and dermatitis herpetiformis: A test of small intestinal function. Am J Clin Nutr 38:706, 1983.
12. Chandra, R., and Sahni, S.: Immunological aspects of gluten intolerance. Nutr Rev 39:117, 1981.
13. Ferguson, A., Blackwell, J., and Barnetson, R.: Effects of additional dietary gluten on the small intestinal mucosa of volunteers and of patients with dermatitis herpetiformis. Scand J Gastroenterol 22:543, 1987.
14. Strobel, S., Busuttil, S., and Ferguson, A.: Human intestinal mast cells: Expanded population in untreated coeliac disease. Gut 24:222, 1983.
15. Marsh, M. N.: Grains of truth: Evolutionary changes in small intestinal mucosa in response to environmental antigen challenge. Gut 31:111, 1990.
16. Collin, P., Hallstrom, O., et al.: Atypical coeliac disease found with serologic screening. Scand J Gastroenterol 25:245, 1990.
17. DeLuca, F., Astori, M., et al.: Effects of gluten free diet on catch up growth and height prognosis in children with growth retardation recognized after the age of 5. Eur J Pediatr 147:188, 1988.
18. Karlberg, J., Henter, J. T., et al.: Longitudinal analysis of infantile growth in children with celiac disease. Acta Paediatr Scand 77:516, 1988.
19. Barr, D., Schmerling, D., and Prader, A.: Catchup growth in malnutrition: Studies in celiac disease after institution of a gluten free diet. Pediatr Res 6:521, 1972.
20. Hjortland, M., Abowd, M., et al.: Low gluten diet with tested recipes. Ann Arbor: University of Michigan Medical Center, 1969.
21. Cooke, W., and Holmes, G.: Coeliac disease, inflammatory bowel disease and food intolerance. In Lessof, M. H.: Clinical reactions to food. New York: John Wiley and Sons, 1983.
22. Cornell, H., and Townley, R.: The toxicity of certain glutens in celiac disease. Gut 15:862, 1974.
23. Lavo, B., Knutson, L., et al.: Gliadin challenge–induced jejunal prostaglandin E-2 secretion in celiac disease. Gastroenterology 99:703, 1990.
24. Stahlberg, M., Savilahti, E., and Viander, M.: Antibodies to gliadin by ELISA as a screening test for childhood celiac disease. J Pediatr Gastroenterol Nutr 5:726, 1986.
25. Volta, R., Lazzari, F., et al.: Antibodies to dietary antigens in coeliac disease. Scand J Gastroenterol 21:935, 1986.
26. Husby, S., Foged, N., et al.: Serum IgG subclass antibodies to gliadin and other dietary antigens in children with coeliac disease. Clin Exp Immunol 64:526, 1986.
27. Sikkud, I., Kohlberg, J., et al.: Antibodies to wheat germ agglutinin in coeliac disease. Clin Exp Immunol 63:95, 1986.
28. Friis, S., and Hoyer, G.: Screening for coeliac disease in adults by simultaneous determination of IgA and IgG gliadin antibodies. Scand J Gastroenterol 21:1058, 1986.
29. Demarchi, M., Carbonara, A., et al.: HLA-DR 3 and DR 7 in coeliac disease: Immunological and clinical aspects. Gut 24:706, 1983.
30. Ciclitira, P., Nelufer, J., et al.: The effect of gluten on HLA-DR in the small intestinal epithelium of patients with coeliac disease. Clin Exp Immunol 63:101, 1986.
31. Mearin, M., Biemond, I., et al.: HLA-DR 3 and DR 7 in coeliac disease. Gut 24:532, 1983.
32. Collin, P., Salmi, O., et al.: High frequency of celiac disease in adult patients with Type I diabetes. Scand J Gastroenterol 24:81, 1987.
33. Troncone, R., Auricchio, S., et al.: An analysis of cereals that react with serum antibodies in patients with celiac disease. J Pediatr Gastroenterol Nutr 6:346, 1987.
34. Molteni, N., Caraceni, M. P., et al.: Bone mineral density in adult celiac patients and the effect of gluten-free diet from childhood. Am J Gastroenterol 85:51, 1990.
35. Caraceni, M. P., Molteni, N., et al.: Bone and mineral metabolism in adult celiac diseases. Am J Gastroenterol 83:274, 1988.
36. Aine, L.: Dental enamel defects and dental maturity in children and adolescents with celiac disease. Proc Finn Dent Soc 82 (4):227, 1986.
37. Gawkrodger, J., Blackwell, J., et al.: HLA antigens and atopy in children with coeliac disease. Gut 24:306, 1983.
38. Scott, H., Fausa, O., et al.: Measurements of serum IgA and IgG activities

to dietary antigens. Scand J Gastroenterol 25:287, 1990.

39. Greco, L., Troncone, R., et al.: Discriminant analysis for the diagnosis of childhood celiac disease. J Pediatr Gastroenterol Nutr 6:538, 1987.

40. Valletta, E. A., Trevisiol, D., and Mastella, G.: IgA anti-gliadin antibodies in the monitoring of gluten challenge in celiac disease. J Pediatr Gastroenterol Nutr 10:169, 1990.

41. Hamilton, J., and McNiel, L.: How long should a celiac child stay on a gluten free diet? Lancet 1:175, 1983.

42. Dissanayake, A., Truelove, S., and Whitehead, R.: Jejunal mucosal recovery in coeliac disease in relation to the degree of adherence to a gluten free diet. Quart J Med 43:161, 1974.

43. Falchuk, Z. M.: Gluten sensitive enteropathy. Clin Gastroenterol 12:475, 1983.

44. Editor: Response of gluten sensitive enteropathy to corticosteroids. Nutr Rev 39:132, 1981.

45. Roe, D. A.: Handbook: Interactions of selected drugs and nutrients in patients. 3d. ed. Chicago: American Dietetic Association, 1982.

46. Anson, O., Weizman, Z., and Zeevi, N.: Celiac disease: Parental knowledge and attitudes of dietary compliance. Pediatrics 85:98, 1990.

47. Editor: An evaluation of children with gluten sensitive enteropathy: Clinical and laboratory data compared with jejunal biopsy findings. Nutr Rev 39:365, 1981.

48. Hartsook, E. I.: Flavored and herbal teas. GIG Newsletter 15 (1):8, 1989.

49. Skerritt, J. H., Devery, J. M., and Hill, A. S.: Gluten intolerance: Chemistry, celiac-toxicity, and detection of prolamins in foods. Cereal Foods World 35:638, 1990.

50. Weiss, M., Davis, J., and Smith, A.: Pointers for parents coping with celiac sprue. Chicago: Children's Memorial Hospital, 1982.

51. Hartsook, E.: Gluten-restricted, gliadin-free diet instruction (wheat, rye, oat, and barley free): The Gluten Intolerance Group of North America. P.O. Box 23053, Seattle, WA 98102-0353, 1987.

52. Krause, M. V., and Mahan, L. K.: Food, nutrition, and diet therapy. Philadelphia: W. B. Saunders, 1984.

53. Baking for people with food allergies. Home and Garden Bulletin no. 145. Rev. ed. Washington, D.C.: U.S. Department of Agriculture, 1979.

54. Allergy recipes. Chicago: American Dietetic Association, 1979.

55. Carpenter, C. B.: Luncheon with Laurie. Rock Hill, S.C.: Carolyn Busbee Carpenter, 1973.

56. Roggero, P., Ceccatelli, M. P., et al.: Extent of lactose absorption in children with active celiac disease. J Pediatr Gastroenterol Nutr 9:920, 1989.

57. Dahlquist, A., and Semenza, G.: Disaccharidase of small intestinal mucosa. J Pediatr Gastroenterol Nutr 4:857, 1985.

58. Corazza, G. R., Strocchi, A., et al.: Sorbitol malabsorption in normal volunteers and in patients with coeliac disease. Gut 29:44, 1988.

17.

PHENYLALANINE-RESTRICTED DIET

JOANNE FAUST FRIEDMAN, M.A., R.D.

Phenylketonuria (PKU) was discovered by Asbjorn Folling in 1934 when he noticed a musty odor in the urine of 2 mentally retarded siblings. This musty odor was caused by the presence of phenylketones, abnormal breakdown products that result when the amino acid phenylalanine cannot be adequately converted to the amino acid tyrosine because of a defect in, or an absence of, phenylalanine hydroxylase. Phenylalanine hydroxylase is an enzyme normally present in hepatocytes (fig. 17.1). Individuals with PKU usually have phenylalanine hydroxylase activity less than 1% of normal (1, 2).

In the 1950s it was discovered that a phenylalanine-restricted diet can benefit children with PKU. Unfortunately, many children were not diagnosed until the consequences of untreated PKU—developmental delay and mental retardation—were present. Seizures, hypotonia, hyperkinesis, eczema, and pigment dilution are other characteristics of untreated individuals (2).

A tremendous breakthrough in the treatment of phenylketonuria occurred in 1961 when Robert Guthrie invented a bacterial inhibition assay screening test to detect PKU in newborns (3). Now infants throughout much of the world are screened for PKU, and the diet can begin soon after birth.

Not all individuals with hyperphenylalaninemia have PKU. Other, milder forms occur when an individual has higher phenylalanine hydroxylase activity, i.e., more than 5% of normal (1, 2). A cofactor—tetrahydrobiopterin (pteridine-H4 or BH4)—and dihydropteridine reductase (DHPR) are required, in addition to phenylalanine hydroxylase, for the conversion of phenylalanine to tyrosine (fig. 17.1). Deficiencies in either the cofactor or the reductase will cause a malignant form of hyperphenylalaninemia, characterized by progressive neurologic disease despite phenylalanine restriction. Additional treatment is now in use to treat these deficiencies.

Incidence varies with the population, and many ethnic groups are affected, some more than others. The general incidence of the hyperphenylalaninemias are as follows: PKU—100 per million live births; milder hyperphenylalaninemia—50 per million; and biopterin deficiencies—1 per million (1).

DEFINITIONS

1. HYPERPHENYLALANINEMIA

A disease characterized by a plasma phenylalanine value above 2 mg/dL (120 μmol/L).

2. PHENYLKETONURIA (PKU)

A form of hyperphenylalaninemia characterized by plasma values above 20 mg/dL (1,200 μmol/L) in its untreated state; an autosomal recessive inborn error of metabolism.

3. MATERNAL PHENYLKETONURIA (MPKU)

The name given to phenylketonuria or hyperphenylalaninemia when a woman with the disease becomes pregnant. Her hyperphenylalaninemia can cause intrauterine phenylalanine excess, which in turn can have teratogenetic effects on her fetus.

4. PHENYLALANINE-RESTRICTED DIET

A diet in which the intake of phenylalanine is limited to a prescribed level governed by individual tolerance.

PHYSIOLOGY, FOODS, AND NUTRIENTS

1. MENTAL FUNCTIONING

High blood phenylalanine levels have 2 effects on mental functioning: the early developmental effect of retarding brain growth, and a reduced mental efficiency due to an intoxication effect (1, 4).

A. Brain Damage   In the first 3 years of life, permanent structural brain damage occurs with untreated PKU. Hyperphenylalaninemia interferes with central nervous system development by the accumulation of phenylalanine or its metabolites, by a deficiency of tyrosine or its products, or by a combination of these circumstances (5). Efficient transmission of electric signals is not provided, because the myelin sheath around parts of nerve cells is inadequately formed. Myelination occurs throughout adolescence. Branching of dendrite parts of nerve cells is reduced, slowing the formation of complex associations among ideas, feelings, memories, and motor impulses. Dendritic branching continues for approximately 60 years (4).

B. Mental Efficiency   Hyperphenylalaninemia produces an intoxication effect that is due to altered neurotransmitter production and function (1, 4). Neu-

FIG. 17.1. METABOLISM OF AROMATIC AMINO ACIDS.

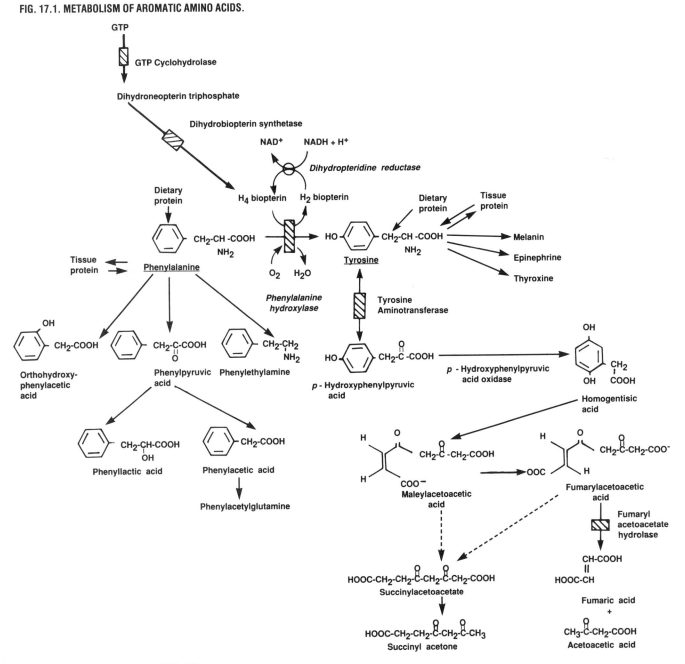

Source: Elsas, L. J., and Acosta, P. B. (5).
Note: The metabolic flow and nutrient interaction in disorders of phenylalanine and tyrosine are sche-
matized. Crosshatched bars represent impaired enzymes involved in biopterin biosynthesis, phenylketonuria, and tyrosinemia.

rotransmitters are responsible for the
way in which electrical impulses are
passed from one nerve cell to another.
The phenylalanine-restricted diet often
reverses this biochemical impairment of
transmission. Mental efficiency may improve, even if the individual has never

been on the diet before or has been off
the diet for several years (4).

2. MATERNAL PKU

Retrospective surveys have indicated
that maternal hyperphenylalaninemia
with a plasma phenylalanine value of 20

mg/dL (1,200 μmol/L) or greater is associated with a high rate of mental retardation (92%), microcephaly (73%),
congenital heart defects (12%), and low
birth weight (40%) among non-PKU offspring of women with PKU (6–8). Lower
maternal phenylalanine levels are associ-

ated with reduced frequencies of abnormalities.

In maternal PKU syndrome, the fetus is exposed to a greater concentration of phenylalanine than exists in the maternal circulation (6). The placenta normally concentrates amino acids in pregnancy. In MPKU there is a positive transplacental gradient of phenylalanine from mother to fetus of between 1.25 and 2.5, with an average fetal phenylalanine exposure of 1.5 times greater than the mother's level (8). For this reason, treatment goals for MPKU are phenylalanine levels that are no higher than 2 to 6 mg/dL (120 to 360 μmol/L) and that may be approximately 2 to 4 mg/dL (100 to 300 μmol/L) (9, 10).

Pregnancy outcome is optimal if the diet begins before conception and is maintained diligently throughout pregnancy (6, 11). The Maternal PKU Collaborative Study, including PKU programs throughout the country, is currently studying pregnancy outcome. Goals of PKU centers are to identify young women with any degree of hyperphenylalaninemia and to provide dietary support, psychosocial services, and metabolic monitoring (12, 13).

PURPOSE OF THE DIET

One purpose of the diet is to maintain serum phenylalanine levels within treatment goals to allow the greatest development of intellectual potential. Treatment goals were traditionally defined as 2 to 10 mg/dL (120 to 600 μmol/L) by the National PKU Collaborative Study, a joint effort by many PKU centers (14). Advances in plasma quantitation, as well as studies of individuals with PKU, have led experts to suggest lower treatment ranges of 2 to 5 mg/dL (100 to 300 μmol/L or 120 to 300 μmol/L), 2 to 6 mg/dL (120 to 360 μmol/L), or 2 to 8 mg/dL (120 to 480 μmol/L) for the older child and nonpregnant adult (2, 10, 15–17).

Other purposes of the diet are to provide enough protein, tyrosine, and energy for the promotion of growth and development and to meet vitamin, mineral, and fluid needs of the individual (10).

EFFECTS OF THE DIET

In the absence of treatment, the majority of individuals lose more than 60 IQ points, leaving them in the 30 to 50 IQ range (4). Approximately 2% lose very little IQ and remain of average intelligence (1, 4).

The benefits of the phenylalanine-restricted diet during infancy and childhood have been well documented by the National PKU Collaborative Study and others (18–23). Cognitive development of treated children with PKU is only slightly diminished, with near-normal intelligence quotient levels of about 100, although levels are somewhat lower than in unaffected siblings (16, 24–26). Performance deficits in conceptual, visuospatial, and language skills (1, 27), decreased attention span (25), and behavior problems (28) indicate that early dietary treatment cannot solve all problems. Some practitioners have lowered their treatment range in the hope of ameliorating these sequelae (2, 16). Children with PKU may have a tendency toward lower self-esteem (29). Family functioning may be adversely affected by the impact of childhood chronic disease (30).

Early practitioners believed that the diet could be discontinued during childhood because 90% of brain growth is completed by 4 to 5 years of age (4) and because untreated individuals placed on the diet after age 3 showed no improvement in IQ. More-recent evidence indicates that some individuals taken off the diet at an early age experience performance deficits, including decline in IQ scores (24–26, 31, 32), deviant electroencephalograph patterns (33), decreased neurotransmitter synthesis (33), mild neurological impairment (34), abnormalities in magnetic resonance image

(34), losses in social quotient (35), and behavior problems (28). Which individuals will be affected cannot be predicted, so it is recommended that all individuals with PKU remain on their diet. Adults who began treatment early in childhood seem to function productively in society (36).

FOODS AND NUTRIENTS

The phenylalanine-restricted diet should begin immediately after the diagnosis is confirmed. The first step is establishing a dietary prescription for phenylalanine, tyrosine, protein, energy, and fluid needs (see table 17.1). Phenylalanine is an essential amino acid. Tyrosine becomes an essential amino acid in phenylketonuria, and adequate quantities must be provided in the diet to meet the individual's needs for growth and repair of body tissue. Adequate tyrosine is required for synthesis of protein, thyroxine, neurotransmitters, and melanin (2).

Once the dietary prescription is established, it must be filled. A special formula low in phenylalanine or phenylalanine-free must be given. In commercial formulas for normal infants, the ratio of phenylalanine to tyrosine is approximately 1 : 1. In special formula for PKU, the absolute amount of tyrosine should be equal to the sum of phenylalanine and tyrosine provided by commercial formula for normal infants (2). This amount ensures that a possible deficiency of tyrosine will not develop.

The current formulas, or "medical foods," for infants available in the United States are Analog XP (Ross) and Lofenalac and PKU 1 (both made by Mead Johnson). Lofenalac is a casein hydrolysate and is the only special PKU formula that contains small amounts of phenylalanine. All other formulations are composed of L-amino acids and contain no phenylalanine (see table 17.2).

Rapid decline in blood phenylalanine level may be accomplished by initially

TABLE 17.1. RECOMMENDED DAILY NUTRIENT INTAKES (AVERAGE AND RANGE) FOR INFANTS WITH PKU

Age (months)	*Nutrients*			
	Phenylalanine[a] *(mg/kg)*	*Protein*[b] *(g/kg)*	*Energy*[b] *(kcal/kg)*	*Fluid*[c] *(mL/kg)*
0–3	55 (70–25)	3.00–2.50	120 (145–95)	150–125
3–6	35 (55–20)	3.00–2.50	115 (145–95)	160–130
6–9	30 (50–15)	2.50–2.25	110 (135–80)	145–125
9–12	25 (45–15)	2.50–2.25	105 (135–80)	135–120

Source: Acosta, P. B. (10). Copyright © 1989 by Ross Laboratories.

Note: Values in parentheses indicate variation in requirements.

[a]*Modified from* [1] Elsas, L. J., and Acosta, P. B.: Nutrition support of inherited metabolic disorders. In Shils, M. E., and Young, V. R.: Modern nutrition in health and disease. 7th ed. Philadelphia: Lea & Febiger, 1988; [2] Acosta, P. B.: The contribution of therapy of inherited amino acid disorders to knowledge of amino acid requirements. In Wapnir, R. A.: Congenital metabolic diseases: Diagnosis and treatment. New York: Marcel Dekker, 1985.

[b]*Modified from* Food and Nutrition Board, Committee on Dietary Allowances: Recommended Dietary Allowances. 9th ed. Washington, D.C.: National Academy of Sciences, 1980.

[c]Under normal circumstances, at least 1 mL of fluid should be prescribed for each kcal prescribed. *Data from* Behrman, R. E., and Vaughan, V. C.: Nelson textbook of pediatrics. 12th ed. Philadelphia: W. B. Saunders, 1983.

giving an infant a formula free of phenylalanine or low in phenylalanine (5). Once treatment goals are reached, a maintenance diet is begun. Phenylalanine and tyrosine not provided by the special PKU formula should be added by using commercial infant formula, breast milk, evaporated milk, or solid foods. Methods for breast-feeding an infant with PKU have been described (37, 38).

When the diet prescription is filled, the diet should be evaluated by the dietitian for nutritional adequacy, osmolality, and, for infants, renal solute load (10, 39). This stepwise progression of establishing diet prescription, filling it, and evaluating nutritional adequacy must be repeated frequently in response to the individual's plasma phenylalanine levels and nutritional needs. Excellent protocols for nutrition support are available to the PKU nutritionist (10).

As babies mature, they should gradually change to a special formula suitable for children. The change is made when table food (fruit, vegetables, grains) provide all of the added phenylalanine. Products specially formulated for children include Maxamaid XP (Ross) and Phenyl-Free and PKU 2 (both made by Mead Johnson). For composition of medical foods and for recommended daily nutrient intakes, see tables 17.2 and 17.3. Specially prepared low-protein products such as bread, pasta, cookies, and baking mixes are important adjuncts to the phenylalanine-restricted diet.

Adolescents pose a difficult challenge to nutritionists. Because of the former clinical practice of removing children from their diet, many are now off diet. The longer individuals are off diet, the harder it is for them to resume it (40). Reintroduction of diet should be gradual.

Particular attention to the psychosocial needs of this age group is necessary for effective treatment (2, 41).

An important reason for adequate control in female adolescents is the possibility of pregnancy and the need to have young women within treatment goals prior to conception. Products used for management of maternal PKU include Maxamum XP (Ross) and Phenyl-Free and PKU 3 (both Mead Johnson products). See table 17.2 for composition of medical foods and table 17.4 for recommended daily nutrient intakes. Maxamum XP and PKU 3, although intended for pregnant women, may also be useful for adolescents and adults (42). A protocol for nutrition support of maternal PKU is available to the PKU nutritionist (43).

INDICATIONS FOR USE

1. PHENYLKETONURIA

The phenylalanine-restricted diet is required for dietary treatment of infants, children, and adolescents with phenylketonuria. It is indicated for treatment of adults and is essential in the prevention of teratogenetic effects of maternal PKU. Recent evidence suggests that in some cases, the phenylalanine-restricted diet is effective in improving behavior and intellectual performance of late-treated mentally retarded individuals with PKU (4, 17).

2. NON-PKU HYPERPHENYLALANINEMIA

Phenylalanine restriction during early childhood in individuals with nonphenylketonuric hyperphenylalaninemia has not been shown to have any beneficial effect (44). It is important that females with non-PKU hyperphenylalaninemia be monitored, because maternal PKU may become a problem resulting from higher levels of phenylalanine in the uterine environment than in the mother's plasma (44).

TABLE 17.2. COMPOSITION OF MEDICAL FOODS FOR INFANTS, CHILDREN, AND ADULTS WITH PKU

Nutrients per 100 g powder	Analog XP[b] # 350	Lofenalac	PKU 1
Energy (cal)	475	460	280
Weight (g)	100	100	100
Protein equivalent (g)	13.0	15	50
% of total calories	11	13	72
Source	L-Amino acids	Enzymatically hydrolyzed casein, L-amino acids	L-Amino acids
Amino acids (g)			
Cystine	0.38	0.06	1.4
Histidine	0.59	0.48	1.4
Isoleucine	0.90	0.87	3.4
Leucine	1.55	1.67	5.7
Lysine	1.06	1.65	4.0
Methionine	0.25	0.54	1.4
Phenylalanine	Trace	0.075	Trace
Threonine	0.76	0.78	2.7
Tryptophan	0.30	0.195	1.0
Tyrosine	1.37	0.80	3.4
Valine	0.99	1.38	4.0
Fat (g)	20.9	18	0
% of total calories	39	35	0
Source	Peanut oil, refined animal fat (pork), coconut oil	Corn oil	None added
Linoleic acid (g)	2.85	9.2	0
Carbohydrate (g)	59.0	60	19
% of total calories	50	52	28
Source	Corn syrup solids	Corn syrup solids, modified tapioca starch	Sucrose
Minerals			
Calcium (mg)	325	430	2,400
Phosphorus (mg)	230	320	1,860
Magnesium (mg)	34	50	520
Iron (mg)	7.0	8.6	34
Zinc (mg)	5.0	3.6	26
Manganese (mg)	0.60	0.14	2.4
Copper (mg)	0.45	0.43	6.7
Iodine (mcg)	47	32	230
Sodium [mg (mEq)]	120 (5.2)	220 (9.6)	1,070 (47)
Potassium [mg (mEq)]	420 (10.7)	470 (12)	2,300 (59)
Chloride [mg (mEq)]	290 (8.2)	320 (9.0)	1,650 (46)
Chromium (mcg)	15	None added	None added
Selenium (mcg)	15	None added	None added
Molybdenum (mcg)	35	None added	None claimed

Maxamaid XP^c #344—Orange #363—Unflavored	Phenyl-Free	PKU 2	Maxamum XP^d #346—Orange #369—Unflavored	PKU 3
350	410	300	340	290
100	100	100	100	100
25	20	67	39	68
29	20	90	46	95
L-Amino acids	L-Amino acids	L-Amino acids	L-Amino acids	L-Amino acids
0.71	0.35	1.8	1.11	1.8
1.27	0.47	1.8	1.71	1.8
1.70	1.10	4.5	2.66	4.5
2.91	1.73	7.6	4.56	7.6
2.22	1.89	5.4	3.49	5.4
0.48	0.63	1.8	0.73	1.8
Trace	Trace	Trace	Trace	Trace
1.42	0.94	3.6	2.23	3.6
0.57	0.28	1.4	0.89	1.4
2.56	0.94	4.5	4.03	6.0
1.85	1.26	5.4	2.92	5.4
<1	6.8	0	<1.0	0
0	15	0	0	0
None added	Corn and coconut oils	None added	None added	None added
0	N/A	0	0	0
62	66	7	45	3
71	65	10	54	5
Sucrose, hydrolyzed cornstarch	Sucrose, corn syrup solids, modified tapioca starch	Sucrose	Sucrose, hydrolyzed cornstarch	Sucrose
810	510	1,310	670	1,310
810	510	1,010	670	1,010
200	152	156	285	540
12	12.2	15	23.5	21
13	7.1	7.8	13.6	24
1.3	1.02	0.7	1.7	4.8
2.0	0.61	2.0	1.4	3.6
134	46	120	107	143
580 (25)	410 (17.8)	640 (28)	560 (24)	640 (28)
840 (22)	1,370 (35)	1,330 (34)	700 (18)	1,330 (34)
450 (13)	930 (26)	990 (28)	560 (16)	1,000 (28)
None added	None added	None added	50	None added
None added	6.1	None added	50	None added
60	None added	None claimed	110	None claimed

(continued)

TABLE 17.2. *CONTINUED*

Nutrients per 100 g powder	Analog XP[b] # 350	Lofenalac	PKU 1
Vitamins			
Vitamin A [IU (mcg RE)]	1,760 (530)	1,430 (430)	9,300 (3,000)
Vitamin D [IU (mcg)]	340 (8.5)	290 (7.3)	1,000 (25)
Vitamin E [IU (mg α-TE)]	4.9 (3.3)	14.3 (9.6)	34 (23)
Vitamin K (mcg)	21	72	167
Thiamine (vitamin B-1, mg)	0.50	0.36	2.70
Riboflavin (vitamin B-2, mg)	0.60	0.43	4.00
Vitamin B-6 (mg)	0.52	0.29	2.2
Vitamin B-12 (mcg)	1.25	1.43	7.9
Niacin [mg (mg NE)]	4.5 (9.5)	5.8 (9.1)	54.0 (71)
Folic acid (folacin, mcg)	38	72	340
Pantothenic acid (mg)	2.65	2.2	25.0
Biotin (mcg)	26	36	100
Vitamin C (ascorbic acid, mg)	40	37	230
Choline (mg)	50	61	430
Inositol (mg)	100	22	500
Other nutrients			
Carnitine (mg)	9.5	9	0
Taurine (mg)	19	27	0
Water (g)	3	3.8	2
Osmotic characteristics			
Renal solute load (mOsm)[a]	76.1	91	350
Osmolality [mOsm (unflavored)]	243	360 mOsm/kg H$_2$O	N/A

Source: Composition of medical foods for infants, children, and adults with metabolic disorders (60); *reviewed by* Mead Johnson (Evansville, Ind.), with minor changes made in information about its products. Copyright © 1989 by Ross Laboratories.

[a]Estimated potential renal solute load = [protein (g) × 4] + [Na (mEq) + K (mEq) + Cl (mEq)].

[b]Approximate weights of Analog Powder measured in level U.S. standard dry measures: 1 tbsp. = 8 g powder; ¼ cup = 30 g powder; ½ cup = 55 g powder; 1 cup = 115 g powder.

[c]Approximate weights of Maxamaid Powder measured in level U.S. standard dry measures: 1 tbsp. = 10 g powder; ¼ cup = 40 g powder; ½ cup = 75 g powder; 1 cup = 155 g powder.

[d]Approximate weights of Maxamum Powder measured in level U.S. standard dry measures: 1 tbsp. = 10 g powder; ¼ cup = 40 g powder; ½ cup = 75 g powder; 1 cup = 150 g powder.

3. BIOPTERIN DEFICIENCIES

Treatment of dihydropteridine reductase (DHPR) deficiency involves controlling hyperphenylalaninemia by dietary restriction of phenylalanine and restoring neurotransmitter homeostasis by oral administration of L-dopa, 5-hydroxytryptophan, and other agents. Folate therapy is often used (1, 45).

Tetrahydrobiopterin (BH4) deficiency has 2 forms. Guanosine triphosphate–cyclohydrolase deficiency may be treated early with BH4 to lessen progression of the disease. The recommended treatment for 6-pyruvoyltetrahydropterin synthase (6-PTS) deficiency is to use pterin plus restriction of phenylalanine, with oral L-dopa, 5-hydroxytryptophan, and carbidopa (1).

POSSIBLE ADVERSE REACTIONS

Phenylalanine, protein, or energy deficiency may result from overaggressive management. Phenylalanine deficiency is first manifested as a low plasma phenylalanine level. Blood phenylalanine level will rise as muscle protein degradation occurs. As phenylalanine deficiency continues, body protein stores are cata-

Maxamaid XP[c] #344—Orange #363—Unflavored	Phenyl-Free	PKU 2	Maxamum XP[d] #346—Orange #369—Unflavored	PKU 3
1,000 (300)	1,220 (370)	5,200 (1,560)	2,350 (705)	4,000 (1200)
480 (12)	152 (3.8)	1,310 (33)	320 (8)	480 (12)
6.5 (4.4)	10.2 (6.8)	18 (12)	7.8 (5.2)	12 (8)
0	102	167	70	167
1.10	0.61	1.40	1.4	1.80
1.20	1.02	2.00	1.4	1.80
1.0	0.91	1.50	2.1	3.20
4.0	2.5	3	4.0	5
12.0 (21.5)	8.1 (12.8)	24 (47)	13.6 (28.4)	18 (41)
150	127	400	500	950
3.7	3	11.0	5.0	8.3
120	30	300	140	179
135	53	80	90	100
110	86	260	320	260
56	30	300	86	300
0	0	0	19	0
0	0	0	140	0
3	3.2	2	3	2
160	160	360	214	360
516 (392)	790 mOsm/kg H$_2$O	N/A	599 (548)	N/A

bolized, energy stores are depleted, and "active" membrane functions are impaired (5). Mental retardation, growth retardation, and eventually death occur if the deficiency is not corrected. Inadequate protein or energy intake also results in hyperphenylalaninemia due to tissue catabolism, because tissue protein has approximately a 5.5% phenylalanine content (5). These deficiencies are easily remedied by the addition of phenylalanine from food ingested, protein from special PKU formula, and energy from nonprotein or low-protein foods. Fever also causes catabolism and consequently elevated phenylalanine levels. It should be treated promptly by the use of high-carbohydrate fluids and food to provide adequate energy and fluids (42).

Because chemically defined medical food (formula) is used for prolonged periods of time, there has been interest in trace mineral status. Lowered blood selenium and chromium levels (46–48) in PKU individuals have led one formula manufacturer to add these minerals to some of its products. Vitamin K and molybdenum are absent from some products (39). Refer to table 17.2.

Essential fatty acids must be provided

TABLE 17.3. RECOMMENDED DAILY NUTRIENT INTAKES (AVERAGE AND RANGE) FOR CHILDREN, ADOLESCENTS, AND ADULTS WITH PKU

	Nutrients					
Age (years)	*Phenylalanine*[a] *(mg/day)*	*Tyrosine*[a] *(g/day)*	*Protein (g/day)*	*Fat*[b] *(% of energy)*	*Energy (kcal/day)*	*Fluid*[c] *(mL/day)*
Female and male						
1–4	325 (200–450)	2.80 (1.40–4.20)	25	45–40	1,300 (900–1,800)	900–1,800
4–7	425 (225–625)	3.15 (1.75–4.55)	35	40–35	1,700 (1,300–2,300)	1,300–2,300
7–11	450 (250–650)	3.50 (2.10–4.90)	40	35–30	2,400 (1,650–3,300)	1,650–3,300
Females						
11–15	500 (300–700)	3.85 (2.45–5.25)	55	35–30	2,200 (1,500–3,000)	1,500–3,000
15–19	475 (275–675)	3.50 (1.40–5.60)	55	35–30	2,100 (1,200–3,000)	1,200–3,000
≥19	475 (275–675)	3.50 (1.58–5.40)	50	30–25	2,100 (1,400–2,500)	1,400–2,500
Males						
11–15	550 (350–750)	4.55 (2.45–6.65)	50	35–30	2,700 (2,000–3,700)	2,000–3,700
15–19	550 (350–750)	4.20 (2.10–8.10)	65	35–30	2,800 (2,100–3,900)	2,100–3,900
≥19	500 (300–700)	3.85 (2.10–5.60)	65	30–25	2,900 (2,000–3,300)	2,000–3,300

Source: Acosta, P. B. (10). Copyright © 1989 by Ross Laboratories.

Note: Values in parentheses indicate variation in requirements.

[a]*Modified from* [1] Elsas, L. J., and Acosta, P. B.: Nutrition support of inherited metabolic disorders. In Shils, M. E., and Young, V. R.: Modern nutrition in health and disease. 7th ed. Philadelphia: Lea & Febiger, 1988; [2] Acosta, P. B.: The contribution of therapy of inherited amino acid disorders to knowledge of amino acid requirements. In Wapnir, R. A.: Congenital metabolic diseases: Diagnosis and treatment. New York: Marcel Dekker, 1985.

[b]*Modified from* Food and Nutrition Board, Committee on Dietary Allowances: Recommended Dietary Allowances. 9th ed. Washington, D.C.: National Academy of Sciences, 1980.

[c]Under normal circumstances, at least 1 mL of fluid should be prescribed for each kcal prescribed. *Data from* Behrman, R. E., and Vaughan, V. C.: Nelson textbook of pediatrics. 12th ed. Philadelphia: W. B. Saunders, 1983.

during pregnancy (10, 48). Most of the medical foods (formula) provide no cholesterol, and cholesterol levels should be monitored. "Conditionally essential" nutrients such as carnitine and taurine are not provided by some formulas (39).

None of the medical foods for phenylketonuria contain fluoride. Fluoride supplements should be provided to infants and children in areas without fluoridated water (49).

CONTRAINDICATIONS

There are no known contraindications to the phenylalanine-restricted diet if used as prescribed.

CLINICAL ASSESSMENT

Height and weight should be monitored at least monthly in infancy and pregnancy and every 3 to 6 months otherwise. Height and weight should remain in appropriate percentiles. Protein and energy prescriptions may be increased 5% to 10% if a child falls below usual growth channels (10). Head circumference should be measured and recorded (49).

Medical and physical status and developmental and psychological status should be assessed by the physician and the psychologist, respectively.

BIOCHEMICAL ASSESSMENT

Plasma phenylalanine and tyrosine levels should be measured often, with exact frequency to be determined by the PKU program. Diet prescription must be serially revised based on serum phenylalanine levels. Tyrosine supplements may be necessary, especially during pregnancy. Tyrosine levels below 0.8 mg/dL

TABLE 17.4. RECOMMENDED DAILY NUTRIENT INTAKES (AVERAGE AND RANGE) FOR PREGNANT WOMEN WITH PKU

Trimester and age (years)	*Nutrients*					
	Phenylalanine[a] *(mg/day)*	*Tyrosine*[a] *(g/day)*	*Protein (g/day)*	*Fat (% of energy)*	*Energy*[b] *(kcal/day)*	*Fluid*[c] *(mL/day)*
Trimester 1						
15–19	500 (200–800)	3.50 (1.40–5.60)	75	30–35	2,400 (1,500–3,300)	1,500–3,000
≥19	500 (225–775)	3.50 (1.58–5.40)	75	30–35	2,400 (1,900–2,800)	1,900–2,800
Trimester 2						
15–19	800 (350–1,250)	4.80 (2.10–7.50)	75	30–35	2,400 (1,500–3,300)	1,500–3,300
≥19	750 (300–1,200)	4.50 (1.80–7.20)	75	30–35	2,400 (1,900–2,800)	1,900–2,800
Trimester 3						
15–19	1,300 (700–1,900)	7.80 (4.20–11.40)	75	30–35	2,400 (1,500–3,300)	1,500–3,300
≥19	1,250 (650–1,850)	7.50 (3.90–11.10)	75	30–35	2,400 (1,900–2,800)	1,900–2,800

Source: Acosta, P. B. (10). Copyright © 1989 by Ross Laboratories.

Note: Actual requirements may vary considerably. See values in parentheses.

[a]*From* Rohr, F. J., Doherty, L. B., et al.: New England maternal PKU project: Prospective study of untreated and treated pregnancies and their outcomes. J Pediatr 110:391, 1987.

[b]For the 15- to 19-year-old, energy intake should never be less than 45 kcal/kg of ideal pregnancy weight. For women ≥19 years of age, energy intake should never be less than 35 kcal/kg of ideal pregnancy weight (Oldham, H., and Sheft, B. B.: Effect of caloric intake on nitrogen utilization during pregnancy. J Am Diet Assoc 27:847, 1951). *For ideal pregnancy weight gain, see* Rosso, P.: A new chart to monitor weight gain during pregnancy. Am J Clin Nutr 41:644, 1985. *Data modified from* Food and Nutrition Board, Committee on Dietary Allowances: Recommended Dietary Allowances. 9th ed. Washington, D.C.: National Academy of Sciences, 1980.

[c]At least 1 mL fluid per each kcal prescribed is recommended.

(44 μmol/L) in the first trimester or 0.5 mg/dL (28 μmol/L) in the second and third trimesters require supplementation (11).

Additional parameters to be assessed include protein status (plasma albumin and/or prealbumin) and iron status (plasma ferritin, and hemoglobin and/or hematocrit). Erythrocyte folate should be evaluated during each trimester of pregnancy (10).

ASSESSMENT OF POTENTIAL DRUG INTERACTIONS

Although not technically a drug, aspartame is a concern to individuals with phenylketonuria. L-aspartyl-L-phenylalanine methyl ester is degraded in the intestinal lumen to methanol and its 2 amino acids, phenylalanine and aspartic acid (50). Aspartame is sold as an artificial sweetener (Equal) and as an ingredient in food products (NutraSweet) by the NutraSweet Company (51).

One study indicated that an estimated average dose of aspartame may safely be consumed by individuals with hyperphenylalaninemia who are *not* on a phenylalanine-restricted diet. Individuals who *are* on a phenylalanine-restricted diet must avoid aspartame-containing foods and beverages and the sweetener itself, because plasma phenylalanine concentration may exceed acceptable limits (50).

IMPLEMENTATION AND EDUCATION

Individuals with hyperphenylalaninemia must be referred to a PKU program for diagnosis and treatment. Because the prevalence of the disorder is low in the general population, it is in the individual's best interest to be treated by a team of professionals expert in the disease, its diagnosis, and its complex regimen. A list of PKU programs has been published (52).

Education of the family is an ongoing process. Parents must be able to achieve

exact measurements when preparing formula and food, by using a gram scale
or standardized measuring equipment.
Food intake records are a necessary tool
for daily phenylalanine calculation as
well as an evaluation technique for the
dietitian.

The success of early diet management
rests with the parents and their ability to
understand and cope with the diet. Later,
the child's understanding of the diet and
his or her ability to assume responsibility
for it are essential. Parent-child power
struggles may be diffused by the medical
team, particularly the psychologist (53).
Adolescent peer pressure should be addressed. Families need to be made aware
of maternal PKU issues early on. The social worker is essential in solving social
problems that would otherwise detract
from medical care. The family would
benefit from a parents' guide available
by order (54).

PRIORITIES FOR QUALITY ASSURANCE

Suggested quality assurance criteria for
phenylketonuria have been provided by
the Dietitians in Pediatric Practice Group
of the American Dietetic Association
(49).

MENU PLANNING

Foods allowed on the phenylalanine-
restricted diet include fruits, vegetables,
small amounts of bread and cereal, fats,
and "free foods" (predominantly sugar
and oil containing foods). Milk and eggs
may be added in special circumstances,
primarily late pregnancy. The composition per serving of items in food lists for
phenylalanine-restricted diets is provided
in table 17.5. Portion sizes must be carefully measured.

There are several methods of planning
and calculating the diet. One is an exchange system, with interchangeable
foods with similar phenylalanine and
tyrosine content grouped together (10).

TABLE 17.5. CONTENT PER SERVING IN FOOD LISTS FOR PHENYLALANINE-RESTRICTED DIETS

List	Content per serving				
	Phenylalanine (mg)	Tyrosine (mg)	Protein (g)	Fat (g)	Energy (kcal)
Breads and cereals	30	20	0.6	0	30
Fats	5	4	0.1	5.0	60
Fruits	15	10	0.5	0	60
Vegetables	15	10	0.5	0	10
Free foods A	5	4	0.2	0	65
Free foods B	0	0	0	Varies	55
Milk, whole (100 mL)[a]	160	160	3.4	3.4	62
Egg, whole (1 lg/50 g)[a]	343	253	6.1	5.6	79

Source: Acosta, P. B. (10). Copyright © 1989 by Ross Laboratories.

Note: Food lists are given in table 17.6. Except for milk and egg, *data from* Elsas, L. J., and Acosta, P. B.: Nutrition support of inherited metabolic disorders. In Shils, M. E., and Young, V. R.: Modern nutrition in health and disease. 7th ed. Philadelphia: Lea & Febiger, 1988.

[a]*From* Posati, L. P., and Orr, M. L.: Composition of foods: Dairy and egg products: Raw, processed, prepared. Agricultural Handbook no. 8-1. Rev. ed. Washington, D.C.: U.S. Department of Agriculture, Agricultural Research Service, 1976.

Calculations are more exact using this
method. Measuring food in terms of
equivalents, where 1 equivalent = 15
mg of phenylalanine (55), is less restrictive. Food lists using the exchange
method are provided in table 17.6. Other
excellent food lists are available (55–
57). Cookbooks written by professionals
and parents provide variety and family
enjoyment (58, 59).

TABLE 17.6. FOOD LISTS FOR PHENYLALANINE-RESTRICTED DIETS

Food	Amount	Weight (g)	Phenylalanine (mg)	Tyrosine (mg)	Protein (g)	Energy (kcal)
BABY AND JUNIOR FOODS (GERBER)[a]						
Breads and cereals						
Dry						
Barley	1 tbsp. + 1 tsp.	4.7	30	19	0.6	18
Mixed	1 tbsp. + 1 tsp.	4.7	29	22	0.8	18
Mixed/banana	1 tbsp. + 1 tsp.	4.7	27	19	0.5	18
Oatmeal	1 tbsp.	3.6	28	20	0.6	14
Oatmeal/banana	1 tbsp.	3.6	27	16	0.5	14
Rice	2 tbsp.	7.1	26	24	0.6	27
Rice/banana	2 tbsp.	7.1	31	19	0.7	28
Jarred						
Mixed/apples and bananas						
Strained	3 tbsp.	43	32	23	0.6	25
Junior	2 tbsp. + 2 tsp.	38	30	22	0.6	21
Rice/apples and bananas	5 tbsp. + 1 tsp.	76	32	33	0.7	54
Rice/mixed fruit	3½ tbsp.	50	30	34	0.8	36
Vegetables						
Creamed corn	3 tbsp.	43	30	28	0.6	27
Creamed spinach	1 tbsp. + 1 tsp.	19	27	23	0.5	8
Sweet potato	2 tbsp. + 2 tsp.	38	30	22	0.5	23
Fruits and juices						
Strained and junior fruits						
Applesauce and apricots	10 tbsp.	143	15	9	0.4	69
Apricots with tapioca	7 tbsp.	100	17	9	0.4	64
Bananas with tapioca	7 tbsp.	100	14	9	0.4	77
Bananas with pineapple and tapioca	10 tbsp.	143	15	12	0.4	72
Peaches	7 tbsp.	100	19	16	0.6	65
Pears	7 tbsp.	100	13	4	0.5	52
Pears and pineapple	7 tbsp.	100	11	8	0.4	52
Plums with tapioca	10 tbsp.	143	13	5	0.6	97
Prunes with tapioca	7 tbsp.	100	13	5	0.6	72
Strained juices						
Mixed fruit	4.2 oz.	—	15	10	0.5	70
Orange	2.1 oz.	—	15	8	0.5	35
Orange-apple	4.2 oz.	—	16	10	0.5	70
Orange-apricot	2.1 oz.	—	17	9	0.5	35
Orange-pineapple	3.0 oz.	—	18	12	0.6	57
Vegetables						
Beets	⅓ cup	71	17	24	0.9	26
Carrots	⅓ cup	71	14	12	0.5	18
Creamed green beans	1 tbsp. + 2 tsp.	24	16	14	0.3	10
Garden vegetables	1 tbsp.	14	16	12	0.3	5
Green beans	2 tbsp.	29	17	13	0.4	7
Mixed vegetables	2 tbsp.	29	19	14	0.4	12
Squash	¼ cup	57	18	15	0.5	15
Vegetable and meat combinations, *strained only*						
Vegetables and bacon	2 tbsp.	29	18	16	0.5	22

(*continued*)

TABLE 17.6. *CONTINUED*

Food	Amount	Weight (g)	Phenylalanine (mg)	Tyrosine (mg)	Protein (g)	Energy (kcal)
Vegetables and beef	2 tbsp.	29	16	12	0.5	19
Vegetables and chicken	1 tbsp. + 1 tsp.	19	17	13	0.4	9
Vegetables and ham	1 tbsp. + 1 tsp.	19	12	9	0.3	11
Vegetables and turkey	1 tbsp. + 2 tsp.	24	16	13	0.4	12
Free foods						
Fruits						
Apple-blueberry	¼ cup	57	5	3	0.1	54
Applesauce	7 tbsp.	100	5	4	0.2	46
Applesauce with pineapple	7 tbsp.	100	6	5	0.2	46
Mango with tapioca	¼ cup	57	6	3	0.2	77
Juices						
Apple	4.2 oz.	—	3	3	0.1	60
Apple-banana	3.0 oz.	—	6	4	0.2	43
Apple-cherry	3.0 oz.	—	5	4	0.2	43
Apple-grape	4.2 oz.	—	3	3	0.1	60
Apple-peach	4.2 oz.	—	7	6	0.3	60
Apple-plum	4.2 oz.	—	6	4	0.3	60
Apple-prune	4.2 oz.	—	6	4	0.3	60
Strained tropical fruit						
Guava with tapioca	14 tbsp.	200	2	8	0.6	134
TABLE FOODS						
Breads and cereals						
Cereals, cooked						
Corn grits						
Regular and quick, plain	3 tbsp.	45	33	28	0.6	28
Instant, plain	¼ packet	34	27	22	0.5	20
Instant with artificial cheese flavor	¼ packet	36	36	29	0.7	27
Cream of Rice	⅓ cup	81	30	40	0.7	42
Cream of Wheat						
Regular	2 tbsp.	31	26	15	0.5	17
Quick	2 tbsp.	30	25	14	0.4	16
Instant	2 tbsp.	30	30	18	0.6	19
Mix'n Eat, plain	¼ packet	36	37	22	0.7	26
Mix'n Eat, flavored	¼ packet	38	33	20	0.6	33
Farina	3 tbsp.	44	34	20	0.6	22
Maltex	2 tbsp.	31	33	19	0.7	22
Malt-o-Meal	3 tbsp.	45	31	18	0.7	23
Maypo oat cereal	2 tbsp.	30	34	20	0.7	21
Oats, regular, quick, and instant	1½ tbsp.	22	31	20	0.6	14
Pettijohns	2 tbsp.	30	24	14	0.5	20
Ralston	2 tbsp.	32	32	19	0.7	17
Rice, brown	3 tbsp.	28	36	41	0.7	33
Rice, white	3 tbsp.	28	28	32	0.6	31
Roman Meal, plain	1½ tbsp.	22	31	22	0.6	14
Wheatena	2 tbsp.	30	29	17	0.6	22
Whole wheat hot natural cereal	2 tbsp.	30	29	17	0.6	19
Cereals, ready-to-eat						
All-Bran	1 tbsp.	6	34	25	0.8	14

(continued)

TABLE 17.6. *CONTINUED*

Food	Amount	Weight (g)	Phenylalanine (mg)	Tyrosine (mg)	Protein (g)	Energy (kcal)
Alpha-Bits	¼ cup	7	29	20	0.6	28
Apple Jacks	⅓ cup	9	26	18	0.5	37
Bran Buds	1 tbsp.	6	33	24	0.8	15
Bran Chex	2 tbsp.	6	24	18	0.6	20
C. W. Post, Plain	1 tbsp.	6	29	21	0.5	27
C. W. Post with Raisins	1 tbsp.	6	28	21	0.6	28
Cap'n Crunch	¼ cup	9	25	19	0.5	39
Cap'n Crunch's Crunch Berries	¼ cup	9	24	18	0.4	36
Cap'n Crunch's Peanut Butter	¼ cup	9	33	26	0.6	38
Cheerios	3 tbsp.	4	35	23	0.6	17
Cocoa Krispies	⅓ cup	12	27	36	0.6	46
Cocoa Pebbles	½ cup	16	33	42	0.7	66
Cookie-Crisp	½ cup	15	37	30	0.8	60
Corn Bran	¼ cup	9	32	26	0.6	31
Corn Chex	¼ cup	7	26	21	0.5	28
Cornflakes	⅓ cup	7	29	24	0.6	28
Crispy Rice	⅓ cup	9	26	34	0.6	37
Crispy Wheats'n Raisins	¼ cup	11	37	21	0.8	38
Fortified Oat Flakes	1 tbsp.	3	29	21	0.6	11
40% bran flakes (Post)	2 tbsp.	6	30	20	0.7	19
Froot Loops	⅓ cup	9	29	20	0.6	37
Frosted Mini-Wheats	1 biscuit	8	38	22	0.8	28
Frosted Rice Krinkles	½ cup	16	34	44	0.8	62
Frosted Rice Krispies	½ cup	14	28	37	0.6	54
Fruity Pebbles	½ cup	16	27	37	0.6	66
Golden Grahams	¼ cup	10	28	22	0.6	38
Grape Nuts Flakes	2 tbsp.	4	22	13	0.4	15
Honey Nut Cheerios	3 tbsp.	6	35	24	0.7	23
Honeycomb	½ cup	11	33	26	0.6	43
King Vitamin	½ cup	10	28	22	0.6	42
Kix	⅓ cup	6	27	21	0.5	23
Life	1 tbsp.	3	28	21	0.5	10
Lucky Charms	3 tbsp.	6	30	20	0.5	23
Nutri-Grain Barley	2 tbsp.	5	31	19	0.6	19
Nutri-Grain Corn	3 tbsp.	8	33	27	0.6	30
Nutri-Grain Rye	3 tbsp.	8	31	14	0.7	27
Nutri-Grain Wheat	3 tbsp.	8	33	19	0.7	30
Product 19	3 tbsp.	6	30	22	0.6	24
Quisp	6 tbsp.	11	30	23	0.6	46
Raisin bran (Post)	2 tbsp.	7	26	17	0.6	22
Rice Chex	½ cup	13	29	38	0.7	50
Rice Krispies	⅓ cup	9	27	36	0.6	37
Rice, puffed	¾ cup	10	28	38	0.7	42
Special K	2 tbsp.	3	22	19	0.5	14
Sugar Frosted Flakes	⅓ cup	12	31	25	0.6	44
Sugar Pops	½ cup	14	36	29	0.7	54
Sugar Smacks	¼ cup	9	32	23	0.6	34
Sugar Sparkled Flakes	½ cup	13	35	29	0.7	64
Super Sugar Crisp	¼ cup	8	28	16	0.5	31
Team	¼ cup	10	32	31	0.7	41

(*continued*)

TABLE 17.6. *CONTINUED*

Food	Amount	Weight (g)	Phenylalanine (mg)	Tyrosine (mg)	Protein (g)	Energy (kcal)
Toasties	⅓ cup	7	29	24	0.6	27
Total	3 tbsp.	6	30	18	0.6	22
Trix	⅓ cup	9	27	21	0.5	36
Wheat Chex	2 tbsp.	6	26	15	0.6	21
Wheat, puffed	⅓ cup	4	30	18	0.6	15
Wheat, shredded	1 tbsp.	6	30	18	0.6	20
Wheaties	¼ cup	7	33	20	0.7	25
Crackers						
Animal	5	10	33	19	0.7	43
Graham (2″ × 2″)	1	7	19	15	0.6	27
Ritz	3	10	33	19	0.7	54
Rye Thins	3	8	27	12	0.6	39
Saltine	2	6	29	14	0.5	26
Soda	1	7	35	19	0.7	30
Sugar Wafers (Nabisco)	5	16	30	16	0.6	75
Tortilla chips	1	8	36	29	0.7	27
Tortilla, corn (¼″ × 6″ diameter)	1	8	36	29	0.7	27
Tortilla, flour (¼″ × 6″ diameter)	1	8	33	19	0.7	27
Vanilla wafers	4	13	32	16	0.6	60
Wheat Thins	5	9	29	17	0.6	45
Miscellaneous						
Cake flour	1 tbsp.	7	28	16	0.6	29
Chocolate sauce (Hershey's)	1 tbsp.	20	25	18	0.5	49
Corn, cooked	2 tbsp.	21	26	21	0.5	17
Corn on cob (medium ear)	⅙	17	31	25	0.6	16
Jell-O	⅓ cup	80	30	3	0.6	65
Macaroni, cooked	2 tbsp.	18	31	16	0.6	19
Marshmallows (60/lb.)	2	15	38	2	0.4	50
Noodles, cooked	2 tbsp.	20	40	22	0.8	25
Popcorn, popped, plain	⅓ cup	5	31	16	0.6	19
Spaghetti, cooked	2 tbsp.	19	33	17	0.6	21
Potatoes						
Baked, no skin	¼ cup	30	27	22	0.6	28
Boiled in skin	¼ cup	39	32	27	0.7	34
Boiled, no skin	¼ cup	39	30	25	0.7	34
Canned	¼ cup	45	28	24	0.3	27
Chips (2″ diameter)	6	12	29	18	0.7	68
French fries (½″ × ½″ × 2″)	3	15	26	15	0.6	47
Microwaved in skin	3 tbsp.	29	27	23	0.6	29
Hash browns, cooked from frozen	2 tbsp.	20	26	16	0.6	42
Pan-fried from raw	3 tbsp.	29	30	18	0.7	61
Sweet potatoes						
Baked in skin (mashed)	2½ tbsp.	31	32	22	0.5	32
Boiled, no skin (mashed)	1½ tbsp.	31	30	21	0.5	32
Canned, syrup pack	3 tbsp.	37	27	20	0.5	40
Yams, baked or boiled	⅓ cup	42	30	17	0.6	49
Fats						
Butter	2 tsp.	10	4	4	0.1	72

(continued)

TABLE 17.6. *CONTINUED*

Food	Amount	Weight (g)	Phenylalanine (mg)	Tyrosine (mg)	Protein (g)	Energy (kcal)
Dessert topping with sodium caseinate						
Frozen	2 tbsp.	8	6	6	0.1	26
Pressurized	2 tbsp.	8	4	4	0.1	22
Margarine, stick or brick	2 tsp.	9	4	4	0.1	68
Margarine, soft, tub	2 tsp.	9	4	4	0.1	67
Margarine, liquid	1 tsp.	5	4	4	0.1	34
Nondairy creamers						
with sodium caseinate, liquid	2 tsp.	10	6	4	0.1	14
Salad dressing (commercial)						
French	1 tbsp.	16	4	3	0.1	67
Italian	1 tbsp.	15	4	3	0.1	69
Mayonnaise	2 tsp.	9	5	4	0.1	66
Thousand Island	1 tbsp.	16	4	3	0.1	59
Fruits						
Apricots						
Canned	¼ cup	64	14	8	0.3	54
Dried	3 halves	10	16	9	0.4	25
Frozen, sweet	¼ cup	60	16	9	0.4	60
Nectar	3 oz.	94	15	8	0.4	54
Raw	1	35	18	10	0.5	17
Avocado, mashed	1½ tbsp.	22	15	11	0.4	35
Banana, sliced	3 tbsp.	42	16	10	0.4	39
Blackberries[c]						
Canned[b]	2 tbsp.	32	12	8	0.4	59
Raw	½ cup	72	15	10	0.5	37
Blueberries						
Canned[b]	¼ cup	64	15	5	0.4	56
Frozen, sweet	½ cup	115	16	6	0.5	94
Raw	½ cup	72	17	6	0.5	41
Boysenberries, canned[b,c]	¼ cup	64	18	13	0.6	56
Cherries[c]						
Sour, red, canned[b]	¼ cup	64	13	9	0.5	58
Sweet, canned[b]	⅓ cup	86	15	10	0.5	67
Raw	¼ cup	72	13	9	0.4	26
Dates	3	25	14	8	0.5	68
Figs						
Canned[b]	½ cup	130	12	20	0.5	114
Dried	1	19	14	25	0.6	48
Raw (large)	1	64	12	20	0.5	47
Fruit cocktail, canned[b]	½ cup	128	14	10	0.5	93
Fruit salad, canned[b]	½ cup	128	14	10	0.4	94
Grapefruit, red, pink, and white[c]						
Canned[d]	⅓ cup	85	14	10	0.5	51
Juice, canned, unsweetened	4 oz.	124	19	13	0.6	48
Raw, sections	⅓ cup	77	14	10	0.5	25
Grapes						
Adherent skin, raw	¾ cup	120	16	12	0.8	86
Juice, canned	½ cup	126	15	4	0.7	78

(continued)

TABLE 17.6. *CONTINUED*

Food	Amount	Weight (g)	Phenylalanine (mg)	Tyrosine (mg)	Protein (g)	Energy (kcal)
Slip skin, raw	1 cup	92	12	10	0.6	58
Thompson, seedless, canned[b]	½ cup	128	13	10	0.6	94
Mango, raw, sliced	½ cup	82	14	9	0.4	54
Melon						
Cantaloupe, cubed	⅓ cup	53	14	9	0.5	19
Casaba, cubed	⅓ cup	57	15	10	0.5	15
Honeydew, cubed	½ cup	85	11	8	0.4	30
Nectarines, raw, sliced	½ cup	69	19	13	0.6	34
Oranges						
Juice, canned	1 cup	249	17	7	1.5	105
Juice, frozen, diluted	¾ cup	187	15	8	1.3	84
Raw, sections	¼ cup	45	14	7	0.4	21
Papaya, raw, cubed	1 cup	140	13	7	0.9	54
Peaches						
Canned, sliced[b]	½ cup	128	18	16	0.6	95
Dried	½	13	15	12	0.5	31
Frozen, sweet	⅓ cup	83	17	13	0.5	78
Nectar	¾ cup	187	16	13	0.5	100
Spiced, canned[b]	½ cup	121	16	13	0.5	90
Raw, sliced	½ cup	85	18	16	0.6	37
Pears						
Canned[b]	1 cup	255	13	5	0.5	188
Dried	2 halves	35	17	6	0.7	92
Raw, sliced	1 cup	165	17	5	0.6	97
Persimmons, Japanese, raw	⅓	56	15	9	0.4	39
Pineapple						
Canned, chunks, tidbits, crushed[b]	¾ cup	191	17	15	0.8	149
Frozen, sweet, chunks	½ cup	122	15	16	0.5	104
Juice, canned	½ cup	125	13	13	0.4	70
Raw, cubed	¾ cup	116	14	14	0.4	58
Plantains, cooked, sliced	⅓ cup	51	14	10	0.4	60
Plums						
Purple, canned[b]	¾ cup	194	16	6	0.7	172
Raw	½ cup	82	14	5	0.6	46
Prunes						
Dried	3	25	14	2	0.7	60
Juice	½ cup	128	17	6	0.8	90
Raisins, dried seedless	2 tbsp.	18	12	10	0.6	54
Raspberries[c]						
Canned[b]	¼ cup	64	15	11	0.5	58
Frozen, red, sweet	⅓ cup	83	17	12	0.6	85
Raw	½ cup	62	16	11	0.6	30
Rhubarb, cooked, sweet	½ cup	120	14	9	0.5	139
Strawberries						
Frozen, sweet, sliced	⅓ cup	85	13	15	0.5	82
Raw, sliced	½ cup	74	13	16	0.5	23
Tangerines						
Canned[b]	⅓ cup	84	13	7	0.4	51
Juice, canned, sweet	1 cup	249	15	7	1.2	125

(continued)

TABLE 17.6. *CONTINUED*

Food	Amount	Weight (g)	Phenylalanine (mg)	Tyrosine (mg)	Protein (g)	Energy (kcal)
Juice, frozen, diluted	1 cup	241	12	5	1.0	110
Raw, medium-sized	1	84	18	9	0.5	37
Watermelon, diced	¾ cup	120	18	14	0.7	38
Vegetables, drained before measuring if canned or cooked						
Asparagus						
Canned, green	2 tbsp.	30	15	9	0.6	6
Canned, white	2 spears	38	19	13	0.6	7
Fresh or frozen, cooked	1½ spears	22	16	10	0.6	6
Raw	1½ spears	21	16	10	0.7	5
Bamboo shoots, canned	3 tbsp.	25	15	12	0.4	5
Beans, snap (green)						
Canned	¼ cup	34	15	9	0.4	7
Fresh, cooked	2 tbsp.	16	14	9	0.4	7
Frozen, cooked	¼ cup	34	17	11	0.5	9
Beans, yellow wax						
Canned	¼ cup	50	17	13	0.7	12
Frozen, cooked	¼ cup	33	14	11	0.6	9
Bean sprouts, mung, seed attached to sprout						
Cooked	2 tbsp.	16	14	6	0.3	3
Raw	2 tbsp.	13	15	7	0.4	4
Bean sprouts, soy						
Cooked	1 tbsp.	8	13	12	0.4	3
Raw	1 tbsp.	6	12	11	0.4	3
Beet greens, cooked	2 tbsp.	18	12	7	0.5	5
Beets, red, sliced						
Cooked, from fresh or canned	⅓ cup	50	15	12	0.5	15
Pickled	⅓ cup	50	15	12	0.5	15
Broccoli, fresh or frozen						
Cooked	2 tbsp.	20	18	13	0.6	6
Raw	3 tbsp.	16	14	7	0.3	3
Brussels sprouts						
Cooked, from fresh or frozen	1	21	16	12	0.5	8
Cabbage						
Cooked, shredded	⅓ cup	52	12	7	0.6	10
Raw, shredded	½ cup	35	14	7	0.4	8
Cabbage, Chinese (pakchoi)						
Cooked, shredded	3 tbsp.	32	15	10	0.5	4
Raw, shredded	½ cup	35	15	10	0.5	5
Cabbage, red						
Cooked, shredded	¼ cup	37	13	7	0.4	8
Raw, shredded	½ cup	35	15	8	0.5	10
Carrots						
Canned	½ cup	73	15	9	0.5	17
Cooked	¼ cup	39	14	8	0.4	18
Raw, shredded	7 tbsp.	46	15	9	0.5	20
Cauliflower						
Cooked	3 tbsp.	23	16	9	0.4	6
Frozen, cooked	2 tbsp.	22	13	8	0.4	4
Raw	¼ cup	25	18	11	0.5	6

(continued)

TABLE 17.6. *CONTINUED*

Food	Amount	Weight (g)	Phenylalanine (mg)	Tyrosine (mg)	Protein (g)	Energy (kcal)
Celery						
Cooked, diced	½ cup	75	11	5	0.4	11
Raw, diced	½ cup	60	11	5	0.4	9
Chard, cooked	1 tbsp.	11	12	5	0.2	2
Chayote fruit, cooked	¼ cup	40	14	10	0.2	10
Collards, chopped						
Fresh, cooked	¼ cup	48	18	15	0.5	6
Frozen, cooked	1 tbsp.	11	11	8	0.3	4
Cucumber, pared, sliced	1 cup	104	16	10	0.7	14
Eggplant						
Cooked, cubed	½ cup	48	17	11	0.4	13
Raw, cubed	6 tbsp.	31	14	9	0.3	8
Kale						
Cooked, fresh	2 tbsp.	16	6	11	0.3	5
Cooked, frozen	1 tbsp.	8	12	8	0.2	3
Kohlrabi						
Cooked, sliced	¼ cup	41	17	21	0.7	12
Raw, sliced	¼ cup	35	14	17	0.6	10
Lettuce						
Boston or Bibb	4 leaves	30	16	10	0.4	4
Cos or romaine	2 leaves	20	14	8	0.3	4
Mushrooms, *Agaricus bisporus*						
Cooked or canned, pieces	2 tbsp.	20	16	9	0.4	5
Raw	1	18	15	8	0.4	5
Mushrooms, shiitake						
Cooked, pieces	2 tbsp.	18	12	8	0.3	10
Dried	1	4	17	12	0.3	11
Okra, cooked, from fresh or frozen, 2 pods or sliced	2 tbsp.	23	16	21	0.5	8
Onions						
Cooked	⅓ cup	75	15	15	0.7	20
Raw, chopped	5 tbsp.	50	15	15	0.6	15
Peas, green, cooked, canned, frozen	1 tbsp.	10	17	10	0.5	7
Peppers, green						
Cooked	1	74	14	9	0.4	13
Raw	1	74	19	13	0.6	18
Pumpkin, canned	3 tbsp.	46	16	21	0.5	15
Radish, red, small	15	67	15	9	0.4	10
Radish, white icicle, raw, sliced	½ cup	50	18	11	0.6	7
Rutabagas						
Cooked, mashed	¼ cup	60	17	13	0.7	20
Raw, cubed	⅓ cup	44	14	10	0.5	16
Sauerkraut	¼ cup	40	12	8	0.4	8
Shallots, raw, chopped	2 tbsp.	20	16	14	0.5	14
Spinach						
Cooked, from fresh or frozen	1 tbsp.	12	16	13	0.4	2
Raw, chopped	¼ cup	14	18	15	0.4	3
Squash, summer, all varieties						
Cooked, from fresh or frozen	¼ cup	45	15	11	0.4	9
Raw, slices	¼ cup	33	14	10	0.4	7

(continued)

TABLE 17.6. *CONTINUED*

Food	Amount	Weight (g)	Phenylalanine (mg)	Tyrosine (mg)	Protein (g)	Energy (kcal)
Squash, winter						
Acorn						
Baked, cubes	3 tbsp.	38	17	15	0.4	21
Boiled, mashed	¼ cup	61	16	14	0.4	20
Butternut						
Baked, cubes	¼ cup	51	18	16	0.5	20
Boiled, mashed	2 tbsp.	30	15	12	0.4	12
Hubbard						
Baked, cubes	2 tbsp.	26	15	13	0.6	13
Boiled, mashed	2 tbsp.	30	17	15	0.4	9
Spaghetti, cooked	½ cup	78	19	16	0.5	23
Taro, cooked, sliced	½ cup	66	18	13	0.3	94
Taro leaves, cooked	2 tbsp.	18	20	18	0.5	4
Tomatoes						
Catsup	3 tbsp.	45	16	12	0.9	48
Cooked, from fresh or canned	¼ cup	60	17	12	0.7	15
Juice	3 oz.	92	15	5	0.7	16
Marinara sauce	3 tbsp.	47	16	10	0.8	32
Paste	1 tbsp.	16	13	8	0.6	14
Puree	3 tbsp.	47	16	10	0.8	19
Raw, small	½	66	14	9	0.5	12
Sauce, regular, with onions, green pepper, and celery (canned)	¼ cup	61	17	11	0.8	19
Turnip greens						
Canned	2 tbsp.	25	17	10	0.4	4
Cooked, from fresh or frozen	2 tbsp.	18	12	8	0.2	4
Turnip root						
Cooked, diced	½ cup	78	11	9	0.6	14
Raw, diced	½ cup	65	11	8	0.6	18
Soups, Campbell's condensed, *measured before diluting (dilute with water only)*						
Asparagus, Cream of	1 tbsp.	16	12	9	0.3	11
Celery, Cream of	2 tbsp.	31	20	14	0.4	22
Chicken Gumbo	1 tbsp.	16	12	9	0.3	7
Chicken Vegetable	1 tbsp.	16	17	12	0.5	9
Mushroom, Cream of	1 tbsp.	16	12	9	0.3	16
Potato, Cream of	1½ tbsp.	24	16	12	0.3	14
Tomato	2 tbsp.	32	18	11	0.5	21
Tomato Bisque	2 tbsp.	32	19	15	0.6	31
Vegetarian Vegetable	1 tbsp.	15	12	6	0.3	9
Free foods A: Limit to prescribed servings.						
Aproten low-protein products[f]						
dp Chocolate chip cookies	2	28	4	4	0.2	140
Low-protein bread (½″ slice)	½ slice	16	5	4	0.1	42
Rusks	1 slice	—	2	2	0.1	43
Pastas, cooked						
Anellini	½ cup	110	4	3	0.2	98
Ditalini	1 cup	130	4	3	0.2	114
Rigatini	1 cup	130	4	3	0.2	114

(*continued*)

TABLE 17.6. *CONTINUED*

Food	Amount	Weight (g)	Phenylalanine (mg)	Tyrosine (mg)	Protein (g)	Energy (kcal)
Semolino	1 cup	267	3	2	0.1	91
Tagliatelle	½ cup	120	4	3	0.2	107
Fruits and Juices						
Apples						
Canned, sliced, sweet	½ cup	102	5	3	0.2	68
Dehydrated	¼ cup	15	6	4	0.2	54
Dehydrated, cooked	¼ cup	48	4	2	0.1	36
Juice, frozen (diluted)	¼ cup	120	4	3	0.2	56
Raw, small	½ cup	100	5	4	0.2	59
Applesauce, canned, sweet	1	128	6	4	0.2	97
Cranberry sauce, canned	¼ cup	69	4	3	0.1	104
Lemonade	½ cup	125	4	2	0.1	55
Papaya nectar	6 oz.	187	4	2	0.3	108
Peach nectar	2 oz.	62	5	4	0.2	34
Pear nectar	6 oz.	187	5	1	0.2	114

Free foods B: May be used as desired if child is not overweight and they do not depress appetite for prescribed foods.[e]

Food	Amount	Weight (g)	Phenylalanine (mg)	Tyrosine (mg)	Protein (g)	Energy (kcal)
Beverages						
Apple juice, canned	4 oz.	124	2	2	0.1	60
Carbonated beverages, caffeine-free	4 oz.	113	0	0	0	52
Cranberry juice cocktail	4 oz.	126	1	1	0	72
Gatorade	4 oz.	125	0	0	0	25
Kool-Aid, sweet	4 oz.	125	0	0	0	48
Limeade, sweet	4 oz.	125	0	0	0	51
Tang	4 oz.	125	0	0	0	59
Candy						
Butterscotch	1 piece	5	0	0	0	21
Fondant, mint-flavored	1	11	0	0	0	4
Gumdrop, large	1	10	0	0	0	33
Hard candy (1″ × 1½″ rolls)	2	10	0	0	0	38
Jelly beans	10	28	0	0	0	66
Lollipop, medium-sized	1	28	0	0	0	108
Fruit and fruit products						
Fruit butters	1 tbsp.	20	3	2	0.1	37
Fruit ices	½ cup	—	0	0	Trace	69
Guava, raw	1	90	2	9	0.7	45
Guava sauce	½ cup	119	1	5	0.4	43
Jams	1 tbsp.	20	3	2	0.1	55
Jellies	1 tbsp.	20	0	0	0	50
Miscellaneous						
Cornstarch	1 tbsp.	8	0	0	Trace	29
Rich's topping, unwhipped	1 tbsp.	—	0	0	0	42
Shortening, vegetable	1 tbsp.	13	0	0	0	113
Wheat starch	1 tbsp.	8	1	1	Trace	25
Sugars and sweets						
Corn syrup	1 tbsp.	20	0	0	0	57
Danish dessert	½ cup	—	0	0	0	123
dp butterscotch chip cookies (Aproten)[f]	1	14	1	1	0	70
Honey	1 tbsp.	20	3	2	0.1	64

(continued)

TABLE 17.6. *CONTINUED*

Food	Amount	Weight (g)	Phenylalanine (mg)	Tyrosine (mg)	Protein (g)	Energy (kcal)
Maple syrup	1 tbsp.	20	0	0	0	50
Popsicle, per twin bar	1	—	0	0	0	95
Prono[f]	⅓ cup	14[g]	0	0	0	55
Sugar						
Brown	1 tbsp.	14	0	0	0	52
Granulated	1 tbsp.	12	0	0	0	46
Powdered	1 tbsp.	11	0	0	0	42

Source: Acosta, P. B. (10); *data from* Douglas, J. S., Matthews, R. H., and Hepburn, F. N. (61); Gebhardt, S. E., Cutrufelli, R., and Matthews, R. H. (62); Haytowitz, D. B., and Matthews, R. H. (63); Marsh, A. C. (64); Pennington, J. A. T., and Church, H. N. (65). Copyright © 1989 by Ross Laboratories.

[a]*Data derived from* nutrient values. Fremont, Mich.: Gerber Baby Food, 1981, 1982, 1985, 1987.

[b]Fruit is packed in heavy syrup.

[c]Phenylalanine is calculated as 2.9% of protein; tyrosine, as 2.0% of protein.

[d]Fruit is packed in light syrup.

[e]These foods contain little or no phenylalanine or tyrosine.

[f]Available from Dietary Specialties, PO Box 277, Rochester, NY 14601, (716) 263-2787.

[g]Weight is before water is added.

REFERENCES

1. Scriver, C. R., Kaufman, S., and Woo, S. L. C.: The hyperphenylalaninemias. In Scriver, C. R., Beaudet, A. L., et al.: The metabolic basis of inherited disease. 6th ed. New York: McGraw-Hill Professional Division, 1989.
2. Matalon, K. M., and Matalon, R.: Nutrition support of infants, children, and adolescents with phenylketonuria. Met Curr 2 (2):1, 1989.
3. Levy, H. L.: Problems of newborn screening for inborn errors of metabolism. Met Curr 3 (2):1, 1990.
4. Yannicelli, S., Davidson, A. J., and Van Doorninck, W.: Diet intervention for the late-treated adult with PKU. Inherited Metabolic Diseases Clinic, University of Colorado Health Sciences Center, Campus Box C-233, 4200 E. Ninth Ave., Denver, CO 80262, 1990.
5. Elsas, L. J., and Acosta, P. B.: Nutrition support of inherited metabolic diseases. In Shils, M. E., and Young, V. E.: Modern nutrition in health and disease. 7th ed. Philadelphia: Lea & Febiger, 1988.
6. Levy, H. L.: Maternal phenylketonuria. In Scarpelli, D. G., and Migaki, G.: Transplacental effects on fetal health. New York: John Wiley and Sons, 1988.
7. Rohr, F. J., Doherty, L. B., et al.: New England Maternal PKU Project: Prospective study of untreated and treated pregnancies and their outcomes. J Pediatr 110:391, 1987.
8. Friedman, E. G., and Koch, R.: Report from the Maternal PKU Collaborative Study. Met Curr 1 (1):4, 1988.
9. Rohr, F.: Maternal phenylketonuria: A new challenge in the dietary treatment of phenylketonuria. Top Clin Nutr 2 (3):44, 1987.
10. Acosta, P. B.: Ross metabolic formula system: Nutrition support protocols. Columbus, Ohio: Ross Laboratories, 1989.
11. Rohr, F.: Maternal PKU. Met Curr 1 (1):1, 1988.
12. Guthrie, R.: Maternal PKU—a con-

tinuing problem. Am J Public Health 78:771, 1988.
13. Waisbren, S. E., Doherty, L. B., et al.: The New England Maternal PKU Project: Identification of at-risk women. Am J Public Health 78:789, 1988.
14. Acosta, P. B., and Wenz, E.: Diet management of PKU for infants and preschool children. U.S. Department of Health, Education and Welfare. Publication no. (HSA) 78-5209. Washington, D.C., 1978.
15. Michals, K., and Matalon, R.: Phenylalanine metabolites, attention span and hyperactivity. Am J Clin Nutr 42:361, 1985.
16. Smith, I., Beasley, M. G., and Ades, A. E.: Intelligence and quality of dietary treatment in phenylketonuria. Arch Dis Child 65:472, 1990.
17. Yannicelli, S., Davidson, A. J., and Van Doorninck, W. J.: Nutrition support for the late-treated adult with phenylketonuria. Met Curr 3 (1):1, 1990.
18. Smith, I., and Wolff, O. H.: Natural history of phenylketonuria and influence of early treatment. Lancet 2:540, 1974.
19. Dobson, J. C., Kushida, E., et al.: Intellectual performance of 36 phenylketonuria patients and their nonaffected siblings. Pediatrics 58:53, 1976.
20. Williamson, M., Dobson, C., and Koch, R.: Collaborative study of children treated for phenylketonuria: Study design. Pediatrics 60:815, 1977.
21. Dobson, J. C., Williamson, M. L., et al.: Intellectual assessment of 111 four-year-old children with phenylketonuria. Pediatrics 60:822, 1977.
22. Williamson, M. L., Koch, R., et al.: Correlates of intelligence test results in treated phenylketonuric children. Pediatrics 68:161, 1981.
23. Koch, R., Azen, C., et al.: Paired comparisons between early treated PKU children and their matched sibling controls on intelligence and school achievement test results at eight years of age. J Inher Metab Dis 7:86, 1984.
24. Waisbren, S. E., Mahon, B. E., et al.: Predictors of intelligence quotient and intelligence quotient change in persons

treated for phenylketonuria early in life. Pediatrics 79:351, 1987.
25. Brunner, R. L., Berch, D. B., and Berry, H.: Phenylketonuria and complex spatial visualization: An analysis of information processing. Dev Med Child Neurol 29:460, 1987.
26. Levy, L. H.: Phenylketonuria—1986. Ped Rev 7:269, 1986.
27. Pennington, B. F., and Van Doorninck, W. J.: Neuropsychological deficits in early treated phenylketonuric children. Am J Ment Defic 89:467, 1985.
28. Smith, I., Beasley, M. G., et al.: Behavior disturbance in 8-year-old children with early treated phenylketonuria. J Pediatr 112:403, 1988.
29. Moen, J. L., Wilcox, R. D., and Burns, J. K.: PKU as a factor in the development of self-esteem. J Pediatr 90 (6):1027, 1977.
30. Kazak, A. E., Reber, M., and Snitzer, L.: Childhood chronic disease and family functioning: A study of phenylketonuria. Pediatrics 81:224, 1988.
31. Michals, K., Azen, C., et al.: Blood phenylalanine levels and intelligence of 10-year-old children with PKU in the National Collaborative Study. J Am Diet Assoc 88:1226, 1988.
32. Holtzman, N. A., Krohmal, R. A., et al.: Effect of age at loss of dietary control on intellectual performance and behavior of children with phenylketonuria. N Engl J Med 314:593, 1986.
33. Lou, H. C., Guttler, F., et al.: Decreased vigilance and neurotransmitter synthesis after discontinuation of dietary treatment of phenylketonuria in adolescents. Eur J Pediatr 144:17, 1985.
34. Thompson, A. J., Smith, I., et al.: Neurological deterioration in young adults with phenylketonuria. Lancet 336:602, 1990.
35. Matthews, W. S., Barabas, G., et al.: Social quotients of children with phenylketonuria before and after discontinuation of dietary therapy. Am J Ment Defic 91:92, 1986.
36. Koch, R., Yusin, M., and Fishler, K.: Successful adjustment to society by adults with phenylketonuria. J Inher

Metab Dis 8:209, 1985.

37. Yannicelli, S.: Breastfeeding the infant with phenylketonuria: A practical approach. Top Clin Nutr 2 (3):25, 1987.

38. Ernest, A. E., Yannicelli, S., et al.: Guide to breast feeding the infant with PKU. U.S. Department of Health and Human Services Publication no. (HSA) 79-5110. National Maternal and Child Health Clearinghouse, 38th and R Streets, N.W., Washington, DC 20057, 1980.

39. Martin, S. B., and Acosta, P. B.: Osmolalities of selected enteral products and carbohydrate modules used to treat inherited metabolic disorders. J Am Diet Assoc 87:48, 1987.

40. Michals, K.: Diet therapy for phenylketonuria: New challenges. Top Clin Nutr 2 (3):40, 1987.

41. Rees, J. M., and Trahms, C. M.: The adolescent and phenylketonuria: Promoting self-management. Top Clin Nutr 2 (3):35, 1987.

42. Martin, S. B., and Acosta, P. B.: Nutrition support of phenylketonuria and maple syrup urine disease. Top Clin Nutr 2 (3):9, 1987.

43. Acosta, P. B., Castiglioni, L., et al.: Protocol for nutrition support of maternal phenylketonuria. 1985.

44. Lang, M. J., Koch, R., et al.: Non-phenylketonuric hyperphenylalaninemia. AJDC 143:1464, 1989.

45. Kaufman, S.: Unsolved problems in diagnosis and therapy of hyperphenylalaninemia caused by defects in tetrahydrobiopterin metabolism. J Pediatr 109:572, 1986.

46. Gropper, S. S., Acosta, P. B., et al.: Trace element status of children with PKU and normal children. J Am Diet Assoc 88:459, 1988.

47. Rottoli, A., Lista, G., et al.: Plasma selenium levels in treated phenylketonuric patients. J Inher Metab Dis 8 (Supp 2):127, 1985.

48. Acosta, P. B., and Stepnick-Gropperr, S.: Problems related to diet management of maternal phenylketonuria. J Inher Metab Dis 9 (Supp 2):183, 1986.

49. Rohr, F.: Inborn errors of metabolism. In Wooldridge, N. H.: Quality assurance criteria for pediatric nutrition conditions: A model. Chicago: Quality Assurance Committee, Dietitians in Pediatric Practice, American Dietetic Association, 1988.

50. Caballero, B., Mahon, B. E., et al.: Plasma amino acid levels after single-dose aspartame consumption in phenylketonuria, mild hyperphenylalaninemia, and heterozygous state for phenylketonuria. J Pediatr 109:668, 1986.

51. Thomas-Doberson, D.: Calculation of aspartame intake in children. J Am Diet Assoc 89:831, 1989.

52. Schuett, V.: National survey of treatment programs for PKU and selected other metabolic diseases. DHHS Publication no. HRS-M-CH-89-5. National Maternal Child Health Clearinghouse, 38th and R Streets, N.W., Washington, DC 20057, 1990.

53. Jahn, D.: Inside, looking out: One mother's view on phenylketonuria. Top Clin Nutr 2 (3):87, 1987.

54. Acosta, P. B., Fernhoff, P. M., and Rappaport, A.: The parents guide to the child with PKU. Florida State University, Institute of Science and Public Affairs, Center for Family Services, 103 Sandels Bldg., Tallahassee, FL 32306, 1982.

55. Schuett, V.: Low protein food list. Madison: University of Wisconsin Press, 1984.

56. Roberts, R. S., and Meyer, B. A.: Lopro diet guide. Metabolism Office, Room A-36, James Whitcomb Riley Hospital for Children, 702 Barnhill Dr., Indianapolis, IN 46223, 1987.

57. Hunt, M. M.: The phenylalanine, protein and calorie content of selected foods. Division of Inborn Errors of Metabolism, Children's Hospital Research Foundation, Elland and Bethesda Avenues, Cincinnati, OH 45229, 1977.

58. Schuett, V.: Low protein cookery for phenylketonuria. Madison: University of Wisconsin Press, 1988.

59. Lorimer, C.: Low protein cuisine. 128 E. Drummond Ave., Glendale Heights, IL 60139, 1990.

60. Composition of medical foods for infants, children, and adults with metabolic disorders. Columbus, Ohio: Ross Laboratories, 1989.

61. Douglass, J. S., Matthews, R. H., and Hepburn, F. N.: Composition of foods: Breakfast cereals: Raw, processed, prepared. Agricultural Handbook no. 8-8. Washington, D.C.: U.S. Department of Agriculture, Agricultural Research Service, 1982.

62. Gebhardt, S. E., Cutrufelli, R., and Matthews, R. H.: Composition of foods: Fruits and juices: Raw, processed, prepared. Agricultural Handbook no. 8-9. Washington, D.C.: U.S. Department of Agriculture, Agricultural Research Service, 1982.

63. Haytowitz, D. B., and Matthews, R. H.: Composition of foods: Vegetables and vegetable products: Raw, processed, prepared. Agricultural Handbook no. 8-11. Washington, D.C.: U.S. Department of Agriculture, Agricultural Research Service, 1984.

64. Marsh, A. C.: Composition of foods: Soups, sauces and gravies: Raw, processed, prepared. Agricultural Handbook no. 8-6. Washington, D.C.: U.S. Department of Agriculture, Agricultural Research Service, 1980.

65. Pennington, J. A. T., and Church, H. N.: Bowe's and Church's food values of portions commonly used. 14th ed. New York: Harper and Row, 1985.

18.

GOUT AND THE PURINE-RESTRICTED DIET

DEFINITIONS

1. PURINE-RESTRICTED DIET

A diet in which uric acid, its purine precursors, and foods that promote endogenous purine production are limited. Sources of purines include organ meats, dried legumes, lentils, and meat extracts. In strict traditional purine-restricted diets these sources are prohibited and other meats and fish are restricted to 4 oz. weekly, reducing the daily intake of uric acid equivalent to approximately 35 mg/day. The diet has been prescribed with the aim of lowering serum uric acid levels in the treatment of hyperuricemia and gout (1, 2).

2. GOUT

Increased serum uric acid levels leading to formation of monosodium urate crystals in synovial fluid in joint tissues, producing a severe inflammatory reaction and pain (3).

3. ASYMPTOMATIC HYPERURICEMIA

An elevated serum urate level in which arthritic symptoms, tophi (deposits of uric acid crystals), or uric acid stones have not yet appeared.

4. ACUTE GOUTY ARTHRITIS

Acute occurrences of throbbing or crushing joint pain, swelling, inflammation, and tenderness in individuals with gout, precipitated by overindulgence in food or alcohol, minor trauma, fatigue, emotional stress, infection, or certain drugs. Attacks may involve single or multiple joints, most commonly in the lower ex-

tremities. Mild attacks may last only a few hours, severe attacks several weeks. Early in the course of untreated disease, attacks may be several months apart, but this interval will usually decrease as the disease progresses (4).

5. INTERCRITICAL GOUT

Intercritical periods are the asymptomatic intervals between gouty attacks. Most patients experience a second attack within 6 months to 2 years of the initial occurrence (4).

6. CHRONIC TOPHACEOUS GOUT

Visible appearance of tophi, usually between 3 and 42 years after the initial gouty attack. Rate of urate deposition in and around the joints depends mainly on the serum urate level. Incidence of tophaceous gout has declined with increased drug treatment. Tophi themselves are relatively painless but may lead to deformities and progressive crippling (4).

7. PRIMARY HYPERURICEMIA OR GOUT

Those cases that appear to be innate—neither secondary to another acquired disorder nor a subordinate manifestation of an inborn error that leads initially to a major disease unlike gout. Some cases of primary gout have a genetic basis; others do not.

8. SECONDARY HYPERURICEMIA OR GOUT

Those cases that develop in the course of another disease or as a consequence of drug therapy.

9. IDIOPATHIC HYPERURICEMIA OR GOUT

Those cases in which a more precise classification cannot be assigned. Further subclassification is based on overproduction, underexcretion, or both, as responsible for the hyperuricemia.

10. URIC ACID CALCULI AND URATE NEPHROPATHY

Renal stones may result from excessive uric acid excretion or increased urine acidity. Urate nephropathy is caused by deposition of monosodium urate crystals in the renal interstitial tissue because of chronic hyperuricemia and may lead to renal failure (4).

PHYSIOLOGY, FOODS, AND NUTRIENTS

1. PHYSIOLOGY

Gout refers to a heterogeneous group of diseases of disordered purine metabolism characterized by hyperuricemia (serum uric acid levels above 7 mg/dL in males and 6 mg/dL in females), recurrent attacks of acute inflammatory arthritis, and tophi in joints, cartilage, and kidneys. Acute gouty attacks may be precipitated by any break in the patient's daily routine, such as overindulgence in alcohol, food, or exercise, or conversely by fasting, surgery, major illnesses, or thiazide diuretics (5–10). Gout is most common in men, accounting for about 95% of cases. Most female cases are postmenopausal.

2. DRUG THERAPY

Drug therapy has largely replaced diet

therapy in the treatment of gout. Acute attacks are best treated with nonsteroidal anti-inflammatory agents such as phenylbutazone, indomethacin, naproxen, piroxicam, azapropazone, and colchicine. Long-term medical management is directed toward serum urate reduction and lessening of the inflammatory response. Allopurinol inhibits uric acid production by interfering with the action of the enzyme xanthine oxidase. Serum urate is also reduced by the promotion of uric acid excretion by probenecid. The inflammatory response is reduced via such drugs as colchicine. A possible single alternative to the combined use of allopurinol and colchicine is azapropazone, a drug with both uricosuric and anti-inflammatory properties. Research with a new enzymic drug offers hope for enzymatic reduction of serum and urinary uric acid concentrations. In rare instances of allopurinol allergy, oxypurinol is a less effective yet acceptable substitute. Dietary measures play a secondary role in the therapy of hyperuricemia (5, 9–14).

3. CONTROVERSIAL DIETARY RESTRICTIONS

A. Purines and Protein Dietary restrictions reduce only exogenous sources of nucleoproteins, which account for less than half the uric acid found in the blood. The diet does not appreciably affect the endogenous production of uric acid. In addition to the uric acid available from the metabolism of nucleic acids, the body can synthesize purines from the simplest carbon and nitrogen compounds, such as carbon dioxide, acetic acid, and the amino acid glycine, which contributes the carbon and nitrogen chain around which the purine skeleton is assembled. Any source of these materials, such as carbohydrate, fat, or protein, will evoke uric acid production. In the fasting state or in the protein-malnourished individual with compromised visceral or skeletal

proteins, cellular breakdown of tissues results in uric acid production. A high protein intake will also promote an increase in urinary urate excretion (15–17).

Purine restrictions have been justified on the basis that dietary purine excesses can contribute substantially to the serum and urinary uric acid concentrations. When a purine-restricted diet was compared with a normal diet in a group of healthy individuals, the purine-restricted diet resulted in a significant decrease in both serum uric acid levels and urinary urate excretion. However, alcohol consumption was a major factor in the diets of these patients, and some of the adverse effects attributed to dietary purine overindulgence could have been caused by alcohol (16, 18).

In patients on purine-restricted diets, serum uric acid levels generally decrease between 0.5 and 1.5 mg/dL, although one author has reported decreases of greater than this on a diet that permitted up to 1 g protein per kilogram of ideal body weight. In general, rigid protein-restricted diets that eliminate or sharply curtail meat consumption are unrealistic, of little value, and unnecessary (15, 19–23).

Excesses in protein, purines, calcium, oxalate, and vitamin C and deficiencies in magnesium, phosphate, and calcium can alter solute load and the states of saturation for particular crystal systems (22). In addition, eating large meals, particularly late in the evening, may add a factor of stress for stone formation (22).

While it is prudent to avoid excesses and correct deficiencies, there is no evidence to support drastic dietary protein or purine reductions. Drastic reductions in protein or purine intakes are also ineffective against uric acid calculi. On a low-protein diet, some individuals with hyperuricosuria do not decrease their urate excretion to the same levels as do normal individuals, suggesting a defect in the renal handling of uric acid (24).

Stone formation in some but not all

cases may be the result of a persistently acid urine due to a defect in ammonium excretion; in these instances, treatment includes the use of agents that alkalinize the urine and the ingestion of large volumes of fluids (20, 25).

There are, however, certain individuals in whom excessive uric acid excretion appears to play a causal role in calcium oxalate stone formation. The frequent finding of hyperuricosuria in patients with recurrent calcium nephrolithiasis has been related to purine overingestion. Excessive excretion of uric acid could also be due to excessive uric acid production or an impairment in the renal handling of uric acid. In a recent study of these individuals, a purine-free diet normalized uric acid excretion in 4 out of 9 patients while the other 5 continued to have persistent hyperuricosuria. This suggests in the latter instance that the cause was not dietary purine excesses. Excessive dietary purine intake, i.e., up to 425 mg/day, was noted to be a major factor in producing hyperuricosuria in another group of 10 such patients (26–28).

A more rational alternative to a very low purine diet is to limit only foods extremely high in purines ($\geq$ 150 mg per 100 g) in order to avoid any unnecessary metabolic stress on the body and to identify persons prone to huge excesses of dietary protein or purine (19, 20, 28).

B. RNA Foods high in purines related to deoxyribonucleic acid (DNA) affect serum uric acid levels to a much lesser degree than those high in ribonucleic acid (RNA). Oral administration of the purines hypoxanthine, adenine, adenosine-5′-monophosphate (AMP), guanosine-5′-monophosphate (GMP), and inosine-5′-monophosphate (IMP) to individuals with hyperuricemia has been shown to produce elevations in serum uric acid levels. Conversely, guanine, of which only 30% to 50% is absorbed, and xanthine have no effect. Very little is known about the precise identity and quantity of purines in foods. Only a limited number of foods have been analyzed for their RNA and specific purine content, and the lack of more comprehensive tables makes it impossible to take advantage of these findings in planning diets. Because individual purines have different effects on urate metabolism, total purine nitrogen-composition tables are invalid for the assessment of the impact of specific foods, particularly cooked foods, upon urate metabolism. Lentils and organ meats are high in adenine and hypoxanthine, while anchovies and sardines provide very little (29–31).

C. Coffee, Tea, and Cocoa Patients with gout have in the past been advised to eliminate coffee, tea, and cocoa from their diets because these foods contain the methylxanthines theobromine, theophylline, and caffeine. This recommendation was based on misinterpreted animal studies, which wrongly concluded that humans can convert methylxanthines to uric acid. The development of more-sensitive enzymatic methods of analysis and the use of investigative animals that more closely resemble humans in their purine metabolism have led other investigators to the conclusion that theobromine, theophylline, and caffeine are metabolized to methyl urates, not urates, and are not deposited in the gouty tophus. Therefore, there is no scientific evidence to support the elimination or restriction of coffee, tea, and cocoa on a purine-restricted diet (32–34).

CURRENT DIETARY RECOMMENDATIONS

1. FLUID INTAKE

The patient should be encouraged to increase the intake of fluids to a minimum of 3 qts. per day. A large fluid intake is helpful in eliminating uric acid, preventing renal calculi, and retarding the progressive involvement of the kidney. The volume of fluid ingested should be suffi-

cient to keep the patient from experiencing thirst at any time and also enough to necessitate voiding at least once during the night. A treatment plan that includes increased fluid intake, urinary alkalanizing agents, and allopurinol has proven to be very effective in the management of uric acid calculi. Patients should also be encouraged to enjoy a liberal intake of fruits and vegetables, which serve to alkalinize the urine (10, 25, 34, 35).

2. WEIGHT REDUCTION

Obesity is often associated with gout and may be a contributory factor in the onset of the disease. In addition, high-calorie diets are often high-fat diets, which may promote renal retention of uric acid. In such cases, weight reduction will have a beneficial effect on urate metabolism. The reduction in weight should be gradual; fasting or drastic dieting will increase serum uric acid levels. The mechanism by which serum uric acid levels are increased may involve the production of ketones, which inhibit uric acid secretion (16, 25, 35–37).

3. PURINE AND PROTEIN RESTRICTIONS

Excesses of dietary protein and purine should be avoided. Those foods high in purines or those that contain more than 150 mg per 100 g should be eliminated from the diet. Specifically, anchovies, shrimp, sardines, organ meats, meat extracts, and dried legumes (high in adenine) should be excluded, in order to avoid any additional metabolic stress on the body. The purine content of foods is given in table 18.1. It has also been recommended that daily protein intake not exceed 1 g per kilogram of ideal body weight. Meat consumption should not exceed 3 to 4 oz. at a meal (22, 23, 30, 39).

4. RESTRICTION OF ALCOHOLIC BEVERAGES

Overindulgence in alcoholic beverages is a common precipitating factor in acute

gouty attacks. In addition, the combined effects of alcohol and fasting may lead to an attack. In a study of 200 individuals with gout, 50% had a minimum intake of a liter of wine daily (6). In another study, over 40% of 61 patients consumed more than 60 g of ethanol daily, with beer the most frequently consumed alcohol beverage (30). In a trial in which subjects consumed 2.8 L of beer daily, the beer promoted accentuation of urate clearance, increased serum lactate and reduced urinary pH (40). Excessive intake of alcohol results in the accumulation in the body of lactic acid, which inhibits the renal secretion of urates. Adverse effects that have been attributed to purines in food in many instances may actually have been a result of excess alcohol indulgence and not the result of diet. One other possible explanation for ethanol-induced hyperuricemia is increased urate synthesis by the enhancement of adenine nucleotide degradation. Fructose intake can produce hyperuricemia, but the trial study did not address any possible contribution of the fructose in the 1 to 1.7 L of grapefruit juice consumed to the hyperuricemic effect of the beverage and attributed the effect to the alcohol alone (40).

Moderate alcohol consumption, on the other hand, such as 100 g of an 86-proof whiskey, when consumed with food will produce only minor changes in uric acid metabolism. On this basis, alcohol is best taken in a diluted form and in moderation by the patient with gout. While the definition of moderation in this instance is debatable, one author has categorized a daily ethanol intake of 50–60 mL, or 40–50 g of absolute alcohol, the amount present in 4 to 5 oz. of an 86-proof beverage, as representing a moderate intake. Forty grams of alcohol in men and 20 g in women also represents the amount above which there is a detectable increase in cirrhosis of the liver. Liquor labels should be used to determine the daily amount of any alcoholic beverage

TABLE 18.1. PURINE-YIELDING FOODS

Foods highest in purines (150–825 mg/100 g)
Anchovies (363 mg/100 g)
Brains
Kidney (beef—200 mg/100 g)
Game meats
Gravies
Herring
Liver (calf/beef—233 mg/100 g)
Mackerel
Meat extracts (160–400 mg/100 g)
Sardines (295 mg/100 g)
Scallops
Sweetbreads (825 mg/100 g)

Foods high in purines (50–150 mg/100 g)
Asparagus
Breads and cereals, whole-grain
Cauliflower
Eel
Fish, fresh and saltwater
Legumes—beans/lentils/peas
Meat—beef/lamb/pork/veal
Meat soups and broths

Foods high in purines (continued)
Mushrooms
Oatmeal
Peas, green
Poultry—chicken/duck/turkey
Shellfish—crab/lobster/oysters
Spinach
Wheat germ and bran

Foods lowest in purines (0–50 mg/100 g)
Beverages—coffee/tea/sodas
Breads and cereals (except whole-grain)
Cheese
Eggs
Fats
Fish roe
Fruits and fruit juices
Gelatin
Milk
Nuts
Sugars, syrups, sweets
Vegetables (except those listed above)
Vegetable and cream soups

Source: Pennington, J. A. T. (38).

that represents a moderate intake. The value given for proof on each label represents double the percentage of alcohol content by volume. In other words, 100-proof alcohol is 50% alcohol by volume (and 42.5% by weight). The percentage values designated on labels, unless otherwise specified, indicate alcohol percentage by volume rather than weight. Forty grams by weight of alcohol represents about 1 L of beer that is 3.6% alcohol, or 15½ oz. of a table wine that is 15% alcohol (37, 41).

5. OTHER RESTRICTIONS

Portion sizes should be investigated to ensure that meals are moderate in size, because large meals are stress factors for uric acid stone formation. Large, heavy meals should especially be avoided late in the evening. Appropriate dietary measures should be undertaken for any asso-ciated disorders, such as renal insufficiency, hypertension, cardiovascular disease, or hyperlipoproteinemia. Preliminary reports indicate that a diet high in fructose may be harmful. Fructose increases uric acid excretion and production (22, 42, 43).

CLINICAL ASSESSMENT

In light of the relationship between gout and obesity, as discussed above, the identification of the overweight patient is a priority in the nutritional assessment of hyperuricemia. Equally important is a complete nutritional history that focuses on daily fluid, protein, purine, oxalate, fructose, alcohol, fat, and calorie intake and meal size. Dietary diaries kept for 3 or more days by individuals with hyper-uricosuria and analyzed for their kilo-calorie, protein, purine, and oxalate con-tent are very useful clinical tools that help to identify those individuals who need more stringent dietary measures. Individuals on drugs that have the potential to cause malabsorption should be regularly evaluated.

BIOCHEMICAL ASSESSMENT

Because 2% to 50% of individuals with diabetes have hyperuricemia, serum glucose levels should be determined in gout. While uric acid levels may be lower in patients with diabetes rather than higher, owing to the uricosuric effect of high blood glucose levels, recent animal studies suggest that uric acid inhibits insulin secretion. Seventy-five to 84% of patients with gout also have hypertriglyceridemia. Therefore, screening for hyperlipidemia, particularly triglyceride abnormalities, should be routine and the results should be part of the patient's nutritional profile. The pH of the urine should be determined regularly, as these patients, particularly if prone to renal stones, have an acid urine, which favors uric acid calculi formation (25).

ASSESSMENT OF POTENTIAL DRUG INTERACTIONS

1. ALLOPURINOL

Allopurinol is indicated for use in gout patients who overexcrete uric acid. This includes cases of uric acid overproduction, states of increased cell turnover (e.g., leukemia, lymphoma, myeloproliferative disorders, polycythemia vera, psoriasis, or therapy with cytoxic drugs), cases of tophaceous gout, and instances when uricosuric agents are contraindicated, as in chronic renal insufficiency and nephrolithiasis. Patients who underexcrete uric acid may be managed with a uricosuric agent such as probenecid (3, 44–46).

TABLE 18.2. NUTRITIONAL EFFECTS OF DRUGS USED IN TREATMENT OF GOUT

Drug	Action	Potential effects	Recommendations
Colchicine	Increases uric acid excretion (51)	Nausea, vomiting, diarrhea (53) Burning throat, decreased appetite, altered taste (54) Abdominal distension Decreased absorption of cobalamin because of functional changes in ileal mucosa (54) Decreased absorption of vitamin A, folate, vitamin K, fat, sodium, nitrogen, and lactose (54) Decreased serum cholesterol, vitamin A, vitamin B-12 (54); hyponatremia (25) Increased serum alkaline phosphatase and SGOT (54) Inhibition of insulin secretion (25) Inhibition of renal response to ADH (25) Increased risk of bone marrow and neuromuscular toxicity when renal function is reduced (51, 55)	Take with water, drink 10–12 glasses per day (54) Avoid high doses of ascorbic acid (56)
Probenicid (Benemid)	Increases uric acid excretion	Gastrointestinal distress (52) Decreased absorption of riboflavin and amino acids (54) Decreased serum uric acid and increased urinary uric acid (54) Increased urinary riboflavin, calcium, magnesium, sodium, potassium, chloride (54) Decreased urinary pantothenic acid (54) Increased false-positive urinary glucose tests (54)	Take with food to avoid gastric irritation (54) Avoid high doses of ascorbic acid (56) More effective in alkaline urine (54)
Allopurinol (Lopurin, Zyloprim)	Inhibits uric acid production (53)	Nausea, vomiting, abdominal pain Decreased iron absorption (56) Increased serum alkaline phosphatase, SGOT, SGPT (54) Decreased serum uric acid and increased urinary uric acid (54) Decreased risk of xanthine calculi with alkaline urine (54)	Take with meals with fluids (54) Use 10–12 glasses fluid per day to produce 2 L urine in 24 hours (54) Iron supplementation may be necessary with long-term use (56)
Indomethacin (Indocin)	Anti-inflammatory agent	Nausea, vomiting, erosive gastritis, steatorrhea Dizziness, headache, weight gain (54) Increased rate of gastric emptying (56) Gastrointestinal bleeding with secondary anemia (54) Decreased absorption of amino acids (54) Hyperglycemia, hyperkalemia (54) Increased BUN, serum creatinine, SGOT, SGPT (54) Decreased serum vitamin C, urinary sodium, urinary potassium (54, 56) Sodium retention (52) Increased urinary glucose and protein (56)	Take with food to decrease gastrointestinal distress (54, 56) Ensure adequate dietary ascorbic acid (56)
Phenylbutazone (Azolid, Butazolidin)	Anti-inflammatory agent	Nausea, vomiting, erosive gastritis, steatorrhea Altered taste, decreased thyroid activity (54) Decreased absorption of amino acids (54) Hyperglycemia (54) Decreased serum ascorbic acid levels (56)	Take with water (54) Take with food to decrease gastrointestinal distress (54) Ensure adequate dietary ascorbic acid (56) May need sodium-restricted diet (54)
Naproxen (Anaprox, Naprosyn)	Anti-inflammatory agent	Nausea, vomiting, erosive gastritis, steatorrhea Stomatitis (54) Hypoglycemia (54) Decreased serum ascorbic acid levels (56) Increased BUN, serum creatinine, SGOT, SGPT (54)	Take with water (54) Take with food to decrease gastrointestinal distress (54) Ensure adequate dietary ascorbic acid (56)

2. CYCLOSPORINE

Hyperuricemia is a metabolic consequence of cyclosporine therapy. Gouty arthritis has been reported in renal transplant patients (47) and heart transplant patients on cyclosporine. Some of the mechanisms that cause the drug's nephrotoxicity may also be responsible for the hyperuricemia. The combination of cyclosporine-induced renal insufficiency, hypertension, and use of diuretics also predisposes these patients to toxic reactions to allopurinol (48–50).

3. SPECIFIC DRUG INTERACTIONS

Nutritional effects and recommendations for drugs used in the treatment of gout are described in table 18.2. Drugs that may increase serum uric acid levels are listed in table 18.3.

TABLE 18.3. DRUGS THAT MAY INCREASE SERUM URIC ACID LEVELS

Acetazolamide
Furosemide[a]
Hydrochlorothiazide[a]
Oxtriphylline
Probucol
Propoxyphene napsylate combined with
    acetaminophen
Theophylline
Cyclosporine (Seromycin)
Chlorambucil
Cyclophosphamide
Nicotinic acid
Aspirin (blocks the uricosuric effect of
    probenicid and sulfinpyrazone)

Sources: Kelley, W. N., Fox, I. H., and Palella, T. D. (4); West, C., Carpenter, B. J., and Hakula, T. R. (47); Kahl, L. E., Thompson, M. E., and Griffith, B. P. (48); Kelley, W., and Palella, T. D. (52); Powers, D. E., and Moore, A. O. (54).
[a]Any diuretic that produces volume depletion may lead to tubular reabsorption of uric acid (53).

IMPLEMENTATION AND EDUCATION

Gout is a disease surrounded by dietary misinformation, due in part to misinterpretation of animal research. The dietitian must be able to translate current research into clear and specific guidelines. As the majority of patients have such nutritionally related diseases as obesity and hypertension or, less frequently, diabetes and hyperlipidemia compliance may be increased by an approach that incorporates purine restrictions into other food lists, such as the exchange lists in Chapter 28.

Counseling strategies should focus on moderation and integration. The concept of moderation in all food choices as the underlying basis of change of eating behaviors should be established, stressing the importance of moderation in protein and alcohol consumption. A coordinated approach combining all dietary instructions into one integrated set of written guidelines should be utilized. The importance of an adequate fluid intake should be stressed, and the benefits of weight reduction versus the dangers of fasting should be made clear to the client.

REFERENCES

1. Turner, D.: Handbook of diet therapy. 5th ed. Chicago: University of Chicago Press, 1970.
2. Bartels, E. C.: Successful treatment of gout. Ann Intern Med 18:21, 1943.
3. Zell, S., and Carmichael, J. M.: Evaluation of allopurinol use in patients with gout. Am J Hosp Pharm 46:1813, 1989.
4. Kelley, W. N., Fox, I. H., and Palella, T. D.: Gout and related disorders of purine metabolism. In Kelly, W. N., Harris, E. D., Jr., et. al.: Textbook of rheumatology. 3d ed. Philadelphia: W. B. Saunders, 1989.
5. Seegmiller, J. E.: Diseases of purine and pyrimidine metabolism. In Bondy, P. K., and Rosenberg, L. E.: Metabolic control and disease. 8th ed. Philadelphia: W. B. Saunders, 1980.
6. Spaccarelli, A., Giacomello, A., et al.: Clinical survey of 200 patients with gout. In De Bruyn, C., Simmonds, H., and Muller, M.: Purine metabolism in Man—IV. Part A: Clinical and therapeutic aspects; regulatory mechanisms. Adv Exp Biol Med 165A:115, 1984.
7. Darlington, L. G.: Lean, dry gout patients. In De Bruyn, C., Simmonds, H., and Muller, M.: Purine metabolism in man—IV. Part A: Clinical and therapeutic aspects; regulatory mechanisms. Adv Exp Biol Med 165A:129, 1984.
8. Gibson, T., Waterworth, R., et al.: Hyperuricemia in young New Zealand Maori men. In De Bruyn, C., Simmonds, H., and Muller, M.: Purine metabolism in man—IV. Part A: Clinical and therapeutic aspects; regulatory mechanisms. Adv Exp Biol Med 165A:123, 1984.
9. Hart, F. D.: Diagnosis and management of gout. Practitioner 227:1089, 1983.
10. Rodnan, G. P., Robin, J. A., et al.: Allopurinol and gouty hyperuricemia, efficacy of a single dose. JAMA 231:1143, 1975.
11. Gibson, T., Simmonds, H. A., et al.: Azapropazone—a treatment for hyperuricaemia and gout? Br J Rheum 23:44, 1944.
12. Fitzgerald, O., Fitzpatrick, D. A., and McGerney, K. F.: Urate oxidase treatment for hyperuricemia. Lancet 1:525, 1975.
13. Earll, J. M., and Saavedra, M.: Oxypurinol therapy in allopurinol-allergic patients. Am Fam Physician 28:147, 1983.
14. Coe, F. L., Moran, E., and Kavalich, A. G.: The contribution of dietary purine overconsumption to hyperuricosuria in calcium oxalate stone formers. J Chron Dis 29:793, 1976.
15. Mayer, J.: Nutrition and gout. Postgrad Med 45:277, 1969.
16. Seegmiller, J. E.: Diseases of purine and pyrimidine metabolism. In Bondy, P. K., and Rosenberg, L. E.: Metabolic control and disease. 8th ed. Philadelphia: W. B. Saunders, 1980.
17. Yu, T. F., and Roboz, J.: Incorporation of 15-N from glycine into uric acid in gout: A follow-up study. In De Bruyn, C., Simmonds, H., and Muller, M.: Purine metabolism in man—IV. Part A: Clinical and therapeutic aspects; regulatory mechanisms. Adv Exp Biol Med 165A:119, 1984.
18. Stafford, W., and Emmerson, B. T.: Effect of purine restriction on serum and urine urate in normal subjects. In De Bruyn, C., Simmonds, H., and Muller, M.: Purine metabolism in man—IV. Part A: Clinical and therapeutic aspects; regulatory mechanisms. Adv Exp Biol Med 165A:309, 1984.
19. Salmon, S. E., Schrier, R. W., and Smith, L. H.: Hyperuricemia pathogenesis and treatment. Calif Med 116:38, 1972.
20. Mikkelsen, W. M., and Robinson, W. D.: Physiologic and biochemical basis for the treatment of gout and hyperuricemia. Med Clin N Am 53:1331, 1969.
21. Thier, S. O.: An approach to disorders of uric acid metabolism. Arch Intern Med 134:579, 1974.
22. Smith, L. H.: The pathophysiology and medical treatment of urolithiasis. Sem Nephrol 10:31, 1990.
23. Talbott, J. H., and Yu, T. F.: Gout and uric acid metabolism. New York: Stratton Intercontinental Medical Book Corp., 1976.
24. Williams, A. W., and Wilson, D. M.: Uric acid metabolism in humans. Sem Nephrol 10:9, 1990.
25. Wyngaarden, J. B., and Kelly, W. N.: Gout. In Stanbury, J. B., Wyngaarden, J. B., and Frederickson, D. S.: The metabolic basis of inherited disease. 5th ed. New York: McGraw-Hill, 1983.
26. Anton, F. M., Puig, J. G., et al.: Renal handling of uric acid in patients with recurrent calcium nephrolithiasis and hyperuricosuria. Nephron 123:1984.
27. Coe, F. L.: Uric acid and calcium oxalate nephrolithiasis. In Kidney Internat 24:392, 1983.
28. Coe, F. L., Moran, E., and Kavalach, A. G.: The contribution of dietary purine over-consumption to hyperuricosuria in calcium oxalate stone formers. J Chron Dis 29:793, 1976.
29. Clifford, A., Riumallo, J. A., et al.: Effect of oral purines on serum and urinary uric acid of normal hyperuricemic and gouty humans. J Nutr 106:428, 1976.
30. Mann, A. V., Rodgers, H. A., et al.: Controlled study of diet in patients with gout. Ann Rheum Dis 42:123, 1983.
31. Clifford, A. J., and Story, D. L.: Levels of purines in foods and their metabolic effects in rats. J Nutr 106:435, 1976.
32. Buchanan, O. H., Christman, A. A., and Block, W. D.: The metabolism of the methylated purines. II. Uric acid excretion following the ingestion of caffeine, methylated purines. J Biol Chem 157:189, 1945.
33. Wolfson, W. Q., Huddlestun, B., and Levine, R.: The transport and excretion of uric acid in man. II. The endogenous uric acid like chromogen of biological fluids. J Clin Invest 26:995, 1947.
34. Thier, S. O., M.D.: Pers. comm. Yale School of Medicine, New Haven, Conn., 1975.
35. Smith, L. H., Van Den Berg, C. J., and Wilson, D. M.: Nutrition and urolithiasis. N Engl J Med 298:87, 1978.
36. Emmerson, B. T.: Alteration of urate metabolism by weight reduction. Aust N Z J Med 3:410, 1973.
37. Maclachlan, M. J., and Rodnan, G. P.:

Effects of food, fast and alcohol on serum uric acid and acute attacks of gout. Am J Med 42:38, 1967.

38. Pennington, J. A. T.: Bowes and Church's food values of portions commonly used. 15th ed. Philadelphia: J. B. Lippincott, 1989.

39. Yu, T. F.: Nephrolithiasis in patients with gout. Postgrad Med 63:166, 1978.

40. Faller, J., and Fox, I.: Ethanol-induced hyperuricemia. Evidence for increased urate production by activation of adenine nucleotide turnover. N Engl J Med 26:1598, 1984.

41. Lieber, C. S.: To drink moderately or not to drink. N Engl J Med 310:846, 1984.

42. Emmerson, B. T.: Effect of oral fructose on urate production. Ann Rheum Dis 33:276, 1974.

43. Raivio, K. O., Becker, M. A., et al.: Stimulation of human purine synthesis de novo by fructose infusion. Metabolism 24:861, 1975.

44. Emmerson, B. T.: Therapeutics of hyperuricemia and gout. Med J Aust 141:31, 1984.

45. Lo, B.: Hyperuricemia and gout. West J Med 142:104, 1985.

46. Palella, T. D., and Kelly, W. N.: An approach to hyperuricemia and gout. Geriatrics 39:89, 1984.

47. West, C., Carpenter, B. J., and Hakula, T. R.: The incidence of gout in renal transplant patients. Am J Kidney Dis 10:369, 1987.

48. Kahl, L. E., Thompson, M. E., and Griffith, B. P.: Gout in the heart transplant recipient: Physiologic puzzle and therapeutic challenge. Am J Med 87:289, 1989.

49. German, D. C., and Holmes, E. W.: Hyperuricemia and gout. Med Clin N Am 70:419, 1986.

50. Lin, H., Rocker, L. L., et al.: Hyperuricemia in cyclosporine treated renal allograft recipients. Evidence for un-

dersecretion of urate. Arthritis Rheum 31:S109, 1988.

51. Roberts, W., Liang, M., and Stern, S. H.: Colchicine in acute gout. Reassessment of risks and benefits. JAMA 257:1920, 1987.

52. Kelly, W., and Palella, T. D.: Gout and other disorders of purine metabolism. In Harrison's principles of internal medicine. New York: McGraw-Hill, 1987.

53. Decker, E. R. Drugs adversely affecting the gastrointestinal tract. RD 1:4, 1981.

54. Powers, D. E., and Moore, A. O.: Food/medication interactions. 6th ed. Phoenix: 1988 (self-published).

55. Kunci, R. W., Duncan, G., et al.: Colchicine myopathy and neuropathy. N Engl J Med 316:1562, 1987.

56. American Dietetic Association: Manual of clinical dietetics. Chicago: American Dietetic Association, 1988.

19.

TYRAMINE-RESTRICTED DIET

DEFINITION

A diet in which foods containing dopamine are eliminated and those containing tyramine are restricted, so that tyramine intake is limited to 2 to 5 mg daily (1, 2).

PURPOSE OF THE DIET

To prevent the occurrence of serious side effects from the ingestion of the monoamines tyramine and dopamine in individuals treated with monoamine oxidase inhibitor (MAOI) drugs.

EFFECTS OF THE DIET

The diet prevents a serious hypertensive drug-nutrient interaction between MAOI drugs and pressor amines, tyramine and dopamine, in food. Normally these amines are oxidized to harmless metabolites by monoamine oxidase (MAO), but this enzyme is inhibited by certain drugs.

PHYSIOLOGY, FOODS, AND NUTRIENTS

1. RATIONALE AND PHYSIOLOGY

The monoamine-MAOI interaction results in the release of norepinephrine from the nerve endings, which, instead of being oxidized, is absorbed into the bloodstream. Following systemic absorption of large amounts of tyramine, there may be a rapid, massive displacement and release of norepinephrine from adrenergic neurons. This causes constriction of blood vessels and an abnormal elevation of blood pressure, which in some instances leads to excruciating headaches,

intracranial hemorrhages, and death (3, 4).

Monoamines are pressor substances normally detoxified and rendered harmless by oxidizing enzymes such as MAO. They become a potential hazard only when a drug interferes with the action of the enzymes that provide protection from toxicity. The pressor effect of tyramine may be enhanced 100-fold by medications that interfere with its metabolism (5–7).

The severity of the hypertensive reaction depends upon the amount of tyramine ingested, the type and dose of MAOI administered, the time elapsed between the dose and the ingestion of tyramine-containing foods, and the individual patient. Ingestion of 6 mg of tyramine results in a mild elevation of blood pressure, whereas 25 mg produces a hypertensive crisis (8).

2. FOODS ELIMINATED

Recommendations for food restrictions have been the subject of much discussion. Some argue that questionable foods should be avoided because of the potential severity of the reaction. Others suggest that the diet should not be overly restrictive of foods not implicated by case reports (9). Evidence for restriction of foods based on case reports and tyramine content is compared in table 19.1. Most agree that it is best to err on the side of safety.

Eliminated from the diet are those foods with any dopamine and sufficient tyramine to create a dangerous rise in blood pressure even when consumed in small quantities. The tyramine content of

TABLE 19.1. EVIDENCE FOR RESTRICTION OF FOODS

	Case reports[a]	Tyramine content[b]
Aged cheese	+++	+++
Marmite	++	++
Sauerkraut	−	+++
Aged meats	−	++
Alcohol	+	++
Pickled herring[a]	+	−
Liver[c]	+	−

Source: Shulman, K. I., Walker, S. E., et al. (9). Copyright © 1989 by Williams and Wilkins.
[a]Case reports: +++, multiple; ++, moderate; +, few.
[b]Tyramine content: +++, >10 mg; ++, 1–10 mg; +, <1 mg.
[c]Freshness must be ensured.

selected foods and beverages is given in tables 19.2, 19.3, and 19.4. Serotonin (5-hydroxytryptamine) and histamine are also vasoactive amines and should be eliminated. The presence of other amines in the food, particularly phenylethamine and histamine, may compound the effect on blood pressure (2). Biologically active amines are listed in table 19.5.

Fermented or aged foods that rely on protein breakdown to enhance flavor are excluded, as they contain bacteria capable of forming amines from amino acid precursors. These bacteria have been found in sauerkraut, certain sausages, and cheeses with tyrosine decarboxylase,

TABLE 19.2. TYRAMINE CONTENT OF MISCELLANEOUS FOODS

Food	Tyramine concentration (μg/g)	Tyramine content per serving (mg)
Fish		
Pickled herring brine	15.1 μg/mL	
Lump fish roe	4.4	0.2 mg/50 g
Sliced schmaltz herring in oil	4.0	0.2 mg/50 g
Pickled herring	Nil	
Smoked carp	Nil	
Smoked salmon	Nil	
Smoked white fish	Nil	
Meat and sausage (per 30 g)		
Salami	188	5.6
Mortadella	184	5.5
Air-dried sausage	125	3.8
Chicken liver (day 5)	51	1.5
Bologna	33	1.0
Aged sausage	29	0.9
Smoked meat	18	0.5
Corned beef	11	0.3
Kolbasa sausage	6	0.2
Liverwurst	2	0.1
Smoked sausage	1	<0.1
Sweet Italian sausage	1	<0.1
Pepperoni sausage	Nil	Nil
Chicken liver (day 1)	Nil	Nil
Paté (per 30 g)		
Salmon mousse	22	0.7
Country style	3	0.1
Peppercorn	2	0.1
Fruit		
Banana peel	51.7	1.424 mg/peel
Avocado	Nil	Nil
Ripe avocado	Nil	Nil
Banana	Nil	Nil
Raisins (California seedless)	Nil	Nil
Figs, California Blue Ribbon	Nil	Nil
Yeast extracts		
Marmite concentrated yeast extract	645	6.45 mg/10 g
Brewer's yeast tablets (Drug Trade Company)		191.27 μg/400 mg
Brewer's yeast tablets (Jamieson)		66.72 μg/400 mg
Brewer's yeast flakes (Vegetrates)		9.36 μg/15 g
Brewer's yeast debittered (Maximum Nutrition)		Nil
Other		
Sauerkraut (Krakus)	55.47	13.87
Beef bouillon mix (Bovril)		231.25 μg/package
Beef bouillon (Oetker)		102.00 μg/cube
Soya sauce	18.72 μg/mL	0.2 mg/10 mL
Beef gravy (Franco American)	0.858 μg/mL	<0.1 mg/30 mL
Chicken gravy (Franco American)	0.46 μg/mL	<0.1 mg/30 mL
Chicken bouillon mix (Maggi)	Nil	Nil
Vegetable bouillon mix	Nil	Nil
Yogurt	Nil	Nil
Fava beans	Nil	Nil

Source: Shulman, K. I., Walker, S. E., et al. (9). Copyright © 1989 by Williams and Wilkins.

which produces tyramine from tyrosine. Any food rich in aromatic amino acids can become high in tyramine if aging, contamination, prolonged storage (even under refrigeration), or spoilage occurs. Attention should be focused on the choice of fresh, fresh-frozen, or canned foods that are handled, prepared, stored, and served in a manner that maximizes freshness. As a rule, all protein-rich foods that have been aged, dried, fermented, pickled, smoked, or bacterially contaminated should be avoided. Heat does not destroy tyramine (1, 5, 10).

3. STATUS OF SPECIFIC FOODS

A. Dairy Products Cheeses with organisms with a high tyrosine decarboxylase activity are especially rich in tyramine. Cheese varies in tyramine content. All hard and aged cheeses, and cheese spreads made from them, are high in tyramine and should not be eaten, either alone or as an ingredient in other foods. Processed cheese, farmer cheese, ricotta, and sour cream are low in tyramine and are safe. Fresh and cottage cheeses have no detectable tyramine. The tyramine content of various cheeses is given in table 19.4. Cultured dairy products such as sour cream, yogurt, buttermilk, and acidophilus milk should be limited to ½ cup per day. Fresh and canned milks are acceptable (1, 2, 5, 8, 11).

B. Meats and Meat Substitutes Pickled or aged chicken or beef, dry and fermented sausage and smoked or pickled fish such as herring are major sources of tyramine. Processed meats, including luncheon meats, smoked meats, bacon, ham, hot dogs, and corned beef, should also be avoided. On the other hand, fresh meat, game, poultry, fish, shellfish, eggs, and beans are safe. Fish roe (caviar) and pâté should be restricted to 1 oz. per day. Fermented soybean products, such as tofu and miso, contain histamine and are prohibited (8, 11).

TABLE 19.3. TYRAMINE CONTENT OF CHEESES

Type	Tyramine content (μg/g)	Tyramine content per serving (mg)[a]
English Stilton	1,156.91	17.3
Blue cheese	997.79	15.0
3-year-old white	779.74	11.7
Extra-old	608.19	9.1
Old cheddar	497.90	7.5
Danish blue	369.47	5.5
Danish blue	294.67	4.4
Mozzarella	158.08	2.4
Cheese spread, Handisnack	133.81	2.0
Swiss Gruyere	125.17	1.9
Muenster, Canadian	101.69	1.5
Old Coloured, Canadian	77.47	1.2
Feta	75.78	1.1
Parmesan, grated (Italian)	74.57	1.1
Gorgonzola (Italian)	55.94	0.8
Blue-cheese dressing	39.20	0.6
Medium (Black Diamond)	37.64	0.6
Mild (Black Diamond)	34.75	0.5
Swiss Emmenthal	23.99	0.4
Brie (M-C) with rind	21.19	0.3
Cambozola Blue Vein (germ)	18.31	0.3
Parmesan, grated (Kraft)	15.01	0.2
Brie (d'OKA) without rind	14.65	0.2
Farmers, Canadian plain	11.05	0.2
Cream cheese (plain)	9.04	0.1
Cheez Whiz (Kraft)	8.46	0.1
Brie (d'OKA) with rind	5.71	0.1
Brie (M-C) without rind	2.82	<0.1
Sour cream (Astro)	1.23	<0.1
Boursin	0.93	<0.1
Havarti, Canadian	Nil	Nil
Ricotta	Nil	Nil
Processed cheese slice	Nil	Nil
Bonbel	Nil	Nil
Cream cheese (Philadelphia)	Nil	Nil

Source: Shulman, K. I., Walker, S. E., et al. (9). Copyright © 1989 by Williams and Wilkins.
[a]Based on a 15-g serving (single slice).

C. Fruits and Vegetables Italian green beans (also known as fava beans, bean pods, or broad beans) contain enough dopamine to warrant their exclusion from the diet. A nonfatal tyramine-MAOI reaction was documented in a patient who had ingested large amounts of avocado and guacamole, which are allowed only in small quantities. Pickled or fermented vegetables such as sauerkraut are also un-safe. Banana, raspberries, raisins, figs, and avocado should be limited to ½ cup per day because of their dopamine content. Banana peel and overripe or spoiled fruit should be avoided (8, 10–12).

D. Breads Commercially prepared breads are safe. Sourdough and fresh, homemade yeast-leavened breads may contain high levels of histamine and should be avoided (11).

E. Fats Margarine, butter, oil, mayonnaise, nuts, peanut butter, salad dressing, and cream cheese are safe. Care should be taken to avoid salad dressings or spreads containing hard cheeses (11).

F. Desserts Chocolate and foods containing chocolate contain histamine and should be limited to 1 serving per day (11).

G. Beverages Excessive caffeine intake may result in central nervous system stimulation, which may exacerbate a hypertensive crisis associated with MAOI therapy. It has been suggested that caffeinated beverages be limited to two 8-oz. servings per day (8, 11, 13).

H. Alcohol The claim that red wine has more tyramine than white wine because it is made from the grape pulp has been questioned. Chianti wine has from 1.76 to 25.4 mcg per mL and is excluded from this diet because a 120-mL glass of Chianti could have as much as 3 mg tyramine. Other red wines are not excluded. However, all wine and beer should be limited to 1 drink per day because of their histamine content (2, 5, 6, 11, 14).

I. Miscellaneous Products Brewer's yeast, which is used in Great Britain as a spread or beverage, contains too much tyramine to be allowed. Yeast and meat extracts, which may be found in soups and bouillon cubes as well as in protein supplements, should be avoided. Meat tenderizers also should be avoided. Adverse reactions to soy sauce are more

TABLE 19.4. TYRAMINE CONTENT OF ALCOHOLIC BEVERAGES

	Brewer	Color	Type	Country	Tyramine concentration (μg/mL)	Tyramine content per serving (mg)[a]
Beer					4.52	1.54
Amstel	Amstel				3.79	1.29
Export Draft	Molson				3.42	1.16
Blue Light	Labatts				3.37	1.15
Guinness Extra Stout	Labatts				3.32	1.13
Old Vienna	Carling				3.01	1.03
Canadian	Molson				2.91	0.99
Miller Light	Carling				2.78	0.95
Export	Molson				1.81	0.62
Heineken	Holland				1.80	0.61
Blue	Labatts				1.45	0.49
Coors Light	Molson				1.15	0.39
Carlsberg Light	Carling				0.98	0.33
Michelob	Anheuser Busch				0.86	0.29
Genesee Cream	Genesee				0.78	0.27
Stroh's	Stroh's					
Wine						
Rioja (Siglo)		Red		Spain	4.41	0.53
Ruffino		Red	Chianti	Italy	3.04	0.36
Blue Nun		White		Germany	2.70	0.32
Retsina		White		Greece	1.79	0.21
La Colombaia		Red	Chianti	Italy	0.63	0.08
Brolio		Red	Chianti	Italy	0.44	0.05
Beau-Rivage		White	Bordeaux	France	0.39	0.05
Beau-Rivage		Red	Bordeaux	France	0.35	0.04
Maria Christina		Red		Canada	0.20	0.02
Cinzano		Red	Vermouth	Italy	Nil	Nil
Le Piazze		Red	Chianti	Italy	Nil	Nil
Other						
Harvey's Bristol Cream					2.65	0.32 mg/4 oz.
Dubonnet					1.59	0.19 mg/4 oz.
London distilled dry gin (Beefeater)					Nil	Nil
Vodka					Nil	Nil
Rare blended scotch whiskies					Nil	Nil

Source: Shulman, K. I., Walker, S. E., et al. (9). Copyright © 1989 by Williams and Wilkins.

[a]For beer, based on a 341-mL serving (1 bottle); for wine, based on a 120-mL (4 oz.) serving.

likely related to monosodium glutamate sensitivity than to tyramine-MAOI interactions, because it would take 6 L of soy sauce to provide the minimum amount of tyramine required to produce a reaction. However, it is wise to limit soy or teriyaki sauce to ¼ cup per day (11).

INDICATIONS FOR USE

1. MAOI DRUGS

The tyramine- and dopamine-restricted diet is indicated whenever one of the MAOI drugs (see table 19.6) is administered (2).

Of the MAOI drugs used in the United States, 3 are antidepressants, 2 are antihypertensives, and 1 is an antineoplastic agent. The drugs vary in the speed and degree of MAO suppression, with procarbazine a weak inhibitor and tranylcypromine a rapid acting inhibitor. New

TABLE 19.5. CLASSIFICATION OF BIOLOGICALLY ACTIVE AMINES BY FUNCTION

Psychoactive (neurotransmitters)
  Norepinephrine
  Dopamine
Vasoactive amines (pressor amines)
  Tyramine
  Isoamylamine
  Phenylethylamine
  Serotonin
  Histamine

Source: McCabe, B. (6). Copyright © 1986 by the American Dietetic Association.

forms of antidepressants are under development, as well as biochemical tests which may be able to identify clearly the specific chemical imbalance in the brain that causes depression. Until such time as these efforts are successful, MAOI therapy and a concomitant tyramine-restricted diet will play a role in the treatment of certain forms of depression (2, 6).

2. DURATION OF DIET THERAPY

Resynthesis of monoamine oxidase occurs slowly, and reactions may occur for up to 3 weeks after the drug has been discontinued. The diet should be started when drug therapy is initiated and continued for 4 weeks after the drug is withdrawn (6, 15, 16).

3. COMBINATION DRUG THERAPY

Newer forms of treatment, in which a tricyclic antidepressant such as amitriptyline is combined with the action of an MAOI, seem to prevent some of the more severe adverse reactions of MAOI therapy. This form of therapy can protect against the dangers of inadvertent ingestion of tyramine-containing foods. However, it is not recommended that patients on such therapy follow a regular diet, because large amounts of tyramine may be absorbed in certain instances (16–18).

POSSIBLE ADVERSE REACTIONS

The diet is nutritionally adequate, and there have been no adverse reactions attributable to its use. Conversely, it is intended to protect the body against the side effects of drug therapy.

CONTRAINDICATIONS

None are known.

CLINICAL ASSESSMENT

An accurate diet history that includes the types of foods consumed (processed versus fresh), the length of time foods are stored, and the methods of handling, storage, and preparation is critical in alerting the patient and the dietitian to potentially hazardous practices.

BIOCHEMICAL ASSESSMENT

As for patients on a normal diet.

ASSESSMENT OF POTENTIAL DRUG INTERACTIONS

A very complete patient profile should be developed, which lists all drugs the patient is taking, the dose, and the time relationship to all foods consumed. Some of the more severe reactions have been due to the combination of tyramine-containing foods, the MAOI, and the use of other drugs that contain pressor amines, such as bronchodilators or over-the-counter diet, cough, cold, or allergy medications (e.g., ephedrine, isoproterenol, orciprenaline, phenylephrine, phenylpropanolamine, amphetamine, metaamphetamine, and methylphenidate).

MAOIs also potentiate the effects of hypoglycemics, anticholinergics, hypotensives, barbiturates, anesthetics, narcotics, and alcohol. Particularly when consuming foods from among those that should be used with caution, patients should be strongly warned against self-medication and advised to read labels of anything they consume and to consult a

TABLE 19.6. MONOAMINE OXIDASE INHIBITOR (MAOI) DRUGS CURRENTLY PRODUCED

Generic name	Trademark and producer	General use
Tranylcypromine sulfate	Parnate Smith, Kline & French Laboratories	Antidepressant
Phenelzine sulfate	Nardil Warner-Lambert Co.	Antidepressant
Isocarboxazid	Marplan Roche Laboratories	Antidepressant
Furazolidone	Furoxone Eaton Laboratories	Antimicrobial
Procarbazine[a]	Matulane Roche Laboratories	Antineoplastic
Pargyline hydrochloride	Eutonyl Abbott Laboratories	Antihypertensive
Pargyline hydrochloride and methylclothiazine	Eutron Abbott Laboratories	Antihypertensive

Source: McCabe, B. (6); *adapted from* Jalon, M., Santos-Buegla, C., et al. (13).
[a]Administered as "MOPP" program of mechlorethamine, vincristine, procarbazine, and prednisone.

physician before taking any new medication (8, 19).

IMPLEMENTATION AND EDUCATION

Compliance with the diet has been reported to be poor, leading one author to suggest that a more liberalized approach may improve the results. Nutritional counseling should include a clear description in nonmedical terms of the exact nature of the potential adverse reaction, followed by written descriptions and guidelines. Instructions should include a list of all drugs that may compound the reaction. The use of a medic-alert bracelet is also helpful (6, 8).

Given that most reactions are dose related, portion sizes should be a focus of diet counseling. The client should demonstrate accurate use of portion sizes in meal choices. Because 6 mg tyramine is sufficient to cause a tyramine-MAOI interaction, intake should be no higher than 2 to 5 mg per day. Counseling should be initiated before drug therapy is administered, and patient compliance should be monitored with regular nutritional follow-up.

Only foods at their peak of freshness should be used, and any food that is aged or fermented or has a questionable remaining shelf life should not be consumed. Patients must be instructed to read labels and to be wary of hidden ingredients in commercial and mixed dishes, such as cheese in casseroles and yeast extracts in sauces. Weight control powders and nutritional supplements may also contain tyramine. Foods should not be eaten if the ingredients are uncertain.

It is recommended that counseling begin before the initiation of drug therapy and that adherence to the diet continue for 4 weeks beyond drug treatment (6).

PRIORITIES FOR QUALITY ASSURANCE

In the hospital setting it is important to

MENU PLANNING

SAMPLE MENU FOR TYRAMINE-RESTRICTED, DOPAMINE-FREE DIET (FOR A MALE, AGE 25–50)

BREAKFAST
Orange juice	1 cup
Grapefruit	½ medium
All-bran cereal	1 cup
Low-fat milk	1 cup
Whole wheat bread	2 slices
Margarine	2 tsp.
Jam	1 tbsp.
Decaffeinated coffee	1 cup

LUNCH
Homemade minestrone soup (no pea pods)	1 cup
Whole wheat bread	2 slices
Water-packed tuna	3 oz.
Mayonnaise	2 tbsp.
Lettuce	1 leaf
Tomato	½ medium
Apple	1 medium
Low-fat milk	½ cup

AFTERNOON SNACK
Fresh pineapple	1 cup

DINNER
Chicken breast	3 oz.
Sesame seeds	1 tsp.
Corn oil	2 tsp.
Baked potato	1 large
Cooked spinach	1 cup
Pumpernickel bread	3 slices
Margarine	4 tsp.
Low-fat milk	½ cup
Angel food cake	1 slice
Sliced strawberries	½ cup

EVENING SNACK
Oatmeal cookies	2
Herbal tea	1 cup
Honey	1 tsp.

Approximate Nutrient Analysis
Energy	2,634 kcal
Protein	121.7 g (18% of kcal)
Fat	71.7 g (24% of kcal)
Polyunsaturated fat	23.1 g
Monounsaturated fat	19.1 g
Saturated fat	17.2 g
Cholesterol	135 mg
Carbohydrate	422.7 g (64% of kcal)
Vitamin A	24,106 IU
	3,605 RE
Thiamine	3.11 mg

(continued)

Riboflavin	3.72 mg
Niacin	49.1 mg
Folate	757 mcg
Vitamin B-12	4.50 mcg
Vitamin B-6	4.32 mg
Vitamin C	309.8 mg
Calcium	1,469 mg
Phosphorus	2,637 mg
Iron	37.0 mg
Copper	2.67 mg
Zinc	18.4 mg
Magnesium	771 mg
Sodium	4,365 mg
Potassium	6,734 mg

be aware of ingredients of menu items, so that patients can be instructed and menus checked appropriately. Each time the menu is changed, the various menu items, especially entrées, soups, sauces, and vegetables, should be evaluated for suitability for patients on MAOI drugs.

REFERENCES

1. Lovenberg, W.: Some vasoactive and psychoactive substances in food: Amines, stimulants, depressants, and hallucinogens. Committee on Food Protection, Food and Nutrition Board, National Academy of Sciences: Toxicants Occurring Naturally in Foods. 2d ed. Washington, D.C.: National Academy of Sciences, 1973.

2. Diet and MAOs: Updated guidelines. Biol Ther Psychiatry 6:43, 1983.

3. American Society of Hospital Pharmacists: American Hospital Formulary Service: Drug information. Bethesda, Md.: American Society of Hospital Pharmacists, 1987.

4. Blackwell, B., Marley, E., et al.: Hypertensive crisis in a patient on MAOI antidepressants following a meal of beef liver. Can Med Assoc J 102:1394, 1970.

5. Horwitz, D., Lovenberg, W., et al.: Monoamine oxidase inhibitors, tyramine and cheese. JAMA 188:1108, 1964.

6. McCabe, B.: Dietary tyramine and other pressor amines in MAOI regimens: A review. J Am Diet Assoc 86:1059, 1986.

7. Ziscook, S. A.: A clinical overview of monoamine oxidase inhibitors. Am Fam Physician 34:113, 1986.

8. Walker, J. I., Davidson, J., and Zung, W. K.: Patient compliance with MAO inhibitor therapy. J Clin Psychiatry 45:78, 1984.

9. Shulman, K. I., Walker, S. E., et al.: Dietary restriction, tyramine, and the use of monoamine oxidase inhibitors. J Clin Psychopharmacol 9:397, 1989.

10. Maxell, M.: Re-examining the dietary restrictions with procarbazine. Cancer Nurs 3:451, 1980.

11. Registered dietitians, food and nutrition services: Tyramine controlled meal plan. Chicago: Northwestern Mem. Hosp., Sept. 1990.

12. Folks, D.: Monoamine oxidase inhibitors: Reappraisal of dietary considerations. J Clin Psychopharmacol 3:249, 1983.

13. Jalon, M., Santos-Buegla, C., et al.: Tyramine in cocoa and derivatives. J Food Sci 48:545, 1983.

14. Rivas-Gonzalo, J., Santos-Hernandez, J., and Marine-Font, A.: A study of the evolution of tyramine content during the vinification process. J Food Sci 48:417, 1983.

15. McCabe, B., and Tsuang, M.: Dietary considerations in MAOI regimens. J Clin Psychiatry 43:177, 1982.

16. Davidson, J., Zung, W. K., and Walker, I.: Practical aspects of MAO inhibitor therapy. J Clin Psychiatry 45:81, 1984.

17. White, K., and Simpson, G.: The combined use of MAOIs and tricyclics. J Clin Psychiatry 45:67, 1984.

18. Pare, C. M. B., Hallstrom, C., et al.: Will amitriptyline prevent the "cheese" reaction of monoamine oxidase inhibitors? LANCET 2:183, 1982.

19. Ziscook, S.: Side effects of isocarboxazid. J Clin Psychiatry 45:53, 1984.

PART IV

MODIFICATIONS IN CARBOHYDRATE CONTENT

20.

CARBOHYDRATE-CONTROLLED DIET FOR MANAGEMENT OF POSTGASTRECTOMY DUMPING SYNDROME

DEFINITION

A diet used in the medical management of the triad of gastrointestinal, vasomotor, and metabolic symptoms that constitute postgastrectomy dumping syndrome. The diet provides small, frequent feedings; withholds liquids from 1 hour before to 1 hour after meals; avoids simple sugars; and provides an increased intake of complex carbohydrates, particularly those high in soluble fiber. Caffeine is excluded, and protein and fat are tailored to individual needs and tolerances (1, 2).

PURPOSE OF THE DIET

The purpose is to prevent the occurrence of dumping syndrome following gastric surgery.

EFFECTS OF THE DIET

1. EFFECT ON SYMPTOMS

Such forms of carbohydrate as soluble fiber have a beneficial effect in delaying gastric emptying. The rationale for the more traditional form of dietary management of dumping syndrome, which restricted total carbohydrate, is no longer tenable. The dramatic improvement in symptoms attributed to the diet is due to the exclusion of sucrose and glucose precursors with a high glycemic index, restriction of fluid with meals, limitation of meal size, and use of high-fiber meals containing pectin and guar gum which delay carbohydrate absorption and minimize any stimulus to release of insulin.

Thus, the feeding of a dry, solid meal low in simple sugars but high in complex carbohydrates and pectin slows the output of liquid gastric contents (2–6).

2. FACTORS THAT AFFECT GASTRIC EMPTYING

A. Fat Fat delays gastric emptying but has no effect on small-bowel transit time. It is less effective in delaying gastric emptying following vagotomy. Fat is valuable in increasing calorie intake, although large amounts may result in steatorrhea. Some patients may benefit from inclusion of medium-chain triglycerides (MCT) for additional energy (1, 7, 8).

B. Osmolality In general, the more hypertonic the solution, the more rapidly it may dump. However, osmolality is not the only determinant, and some researchers dispute the osmotic load hypothesis for early dumping symptoms, claiming that dumping is due to intestinal hypermotility. Gastric emptying is biphasic: It has a liquid phase and a solid phase. The proximal or upper portion of the stomach regulates the emptying of liquids, while the distal section of the stomach near the pylorus regulates the emptying of solids. One report suggests that dumping is more likely to occur in vagotomies with drainage procedures, but this has been disputed. Even when the nerves to the gastric antrum, where solids are processed, are not damaged, dumping has been reported. This suggests that loss of receptive relaxation in the denervated proximal stomach or re-

duction of hydrogen ion may also play a role (9–15).

C. Temperature The temperature of a liquid meal has no effect on gastric secretion, serum gastrin, or gastric emptying. The practice of warming cold liquids to room temperature or higher in the hope that this will facilitate digestion or otherwise affect the rate of gastric emptying has been refuted by 2 current research reports (16, 17).

D. Trituration and Peristalsis Intragastric grinding of foods by the stomach (called trituration) and the peristaltic action of the stomach both affect the rate of gastric emptying. These functions should be distinguished, because they may be driven by separate dietary factors with different influences on dumping syndrome (7, 8, 18).

PHYSIOLOGY, FOODS, AND NUTRIENTS

1. NORMAL FUNCTIONS OF THE STOMACH

A. Reservoir After a meal, the proximal stomach (fundus and body) relaxes to accommodate the increased volume of food. It can hold up to 1 L of food at a time and can accommodate large meals at infrequent intervals (5).

B. Trituration The distal stomach mixes and grinds solid food to a particle size of about 1 to 2 cm. Only then does emptying of solid particles occur.

C. Controlled Release In the stomach

the food is diluted to an isotonic state before it enters the duodenum. The increased pressure within the fundus of the stomach accelerates the rate at which liquids, but not solids, are emptied. Gastric emptying is controlled by interactions between pressure and resistance. In addition, omnireceptors in the duodenum and caloric density both affect emptying. Liquid meals with different caloric densities all empty at the rate of 2.3 kcal per minute (5).

D. Digestion of Protein   Acid and pepsin break down protein. Acid reduction has to be extremely severe before it can cause symptoms of dumping. The pancreatic secretions can complete hydrolysis of food even when gastric digestion is impaired. However, the reduced acid plus stasis in the afferent loop of the intestine can cause bacterial growth and a stagnant loop syndrome (5).

E. Intrinsic Factor and R Protein   Intrinsic factor secreted by parietal cells in the fundus of the stomach combines with vitamin B-12 to facilitate its absorption in the terminal ileum. Another substance called R protein also binds to vitamin B-12. Pancreatic protease releases it from vitamin B-12, which then binds to intrinsic factor again in order to permit vitamin B-12 to be absorbed from the terminal ileum. Postgastrectomy patients should therefore be assessed for anemia and especially for vitamin B-12 status (5).

2. SURGICAL PROCEDURES

A number of surgical procedures for peptic ulcer, reflux esophagitis, and gastric cancer may result in dumping syndrome. Gastric surgery attacks the neural phase of gastric secretion via vagotomy, or the hormonal phase via a partial or complete gastrectomy. The effect of a gastrectomy depends on the amount and section of stomach removed and on individual differences in the ability of re-

maining sections to adapt and compensate.

There are 3 types of vagotomies (1):

- *Truncal Vagotomy* All nerves to the stomach and other abdominal organs are severed. The resting time of stomach is altered and liquid emptying accelerates (5).
- *Total Gastric or Selective Vagotomy* Nerves to the entire stomach are severed. Emptying of liquids is rapid, but the effect on solid gastric emptying is variable (5).
- *Proximal or Superselective Vagotomy* Only nerves to the upper or proximal part of stomach are severed. Liquid emptying is only slightly accelerated, and the emptying of solids is not affected (5).

It is important for the dietitian to know which type of vagotomy has been performed. A superselective vagotomy minimizes the risk of dumping, but in practice this procedure is less common. In all 3 types of vagotomies the proximal stomach develops higher pressures and empties more, and fatty meals are less effective in slowing gastric emptying. Thus, even proximal vagotomies can contribute to dumping syndrome, which is the most common nutritional side effect of gastric surgery.

3. POSTGASTRECTOMY SYMPTOMS

Three types of postgastrectomy dumping symptoms have been described (1, 5, 7–12, 18–25).

A. Gastrointestinal   Approximately 20 to 90 minutes after a meal, the patient develops gastrointestinal symptoms of abdominal pain, distention, and oversatiety and may become nauseated and vomit. Then, after the vasomotor symptoms described below, the patient may have a copious diarrhea. These symptoms are related to distention of the proximal jejunum by hyperosmolar simple

carbohydrates emptying rapidly into the jejunum and saturating the small intestine's absorbent capacity.

Fecal chenodeoxycholic acid output is elevated in dumping syndrome. Excessive bile-acid output into the colon may also be a contributing factor to postvagotomy diarrhea (5).

Even on a high-fat diet, steatorrhea rarely exceeds 20 g per day, unless patients have short-bowel syndrome. Postvagotomy diarrhea is now uncommon, because surgical treatment of peptic ulcer diseases is rarely needed and highly selective vagotomy has superseded truncal vagotomy and drainage (5).

B. Vasomotor   The presence of unabsorbed carbohydrate in the distal small intestine causes the release of such hormones as neurotensin, nonpancreatic glucagon, bradykinin (a vasodilator believed to cause some of these symptoms), serotonin (a vasoconstrictor), gastric inhibitory polypeptide (GIP), and substance P. These are at least partially responsible for symptoms of weakness, flushing, palpitations, sweating, dizziness, hypotension, and tachycardia. It is believed that some vasomotor symptoms are caused in part by extravascular fluid depletion as fluid is drawn into the intestine from the blood to restore osmolality. This is not the cause of all symptoms, however. Some symptoms persist despite simultaneous expansion of vascular and extracellular fluid volume by intravenous infusions (5, 26, 27).

C. Metabolic   Some patients experience metabolic symptoms of hypoglycemia, owing to a rapid fall in blood sugar that occurs 2 to 3 hours after a meal. These symptoms probably are also hormonally mediated. Glucose may be a stimulus for hypersecretion of GIP. GIP is proposed to stimulate insulin release, which brings about the drop in blood sugar (1, 13, 28).

A decrease in hydrogen ion concentration may also play a role in the onset of symptoms (27).

4. RESTRICTION OF SIMPLE CARBOHYDRATES

Simple carbohydrates are restricted because they are more rapidly hydrolyzed to osmotically active substances than are proteins and fats. Thus, sugar, cookies, pies, pastries, and other concentrated sweets, as well as alcohol, are eliminated in favor of more slowly absorbed complex carbohydrates, particularly foods high in soluble fiber such as barley and lentils, which produce much less of a glycemic response (1–4, 19, 20).

5. MEAL SIZE, FREQUENCY, AND LIQUIDS

In patients who have had major gastric resections, small, frequent feedings are provided in order to accommodate the reduced capacity of the stomach as a reservoir and to prevent jejunal overloading. The withholding of liquids until 1 hour after the meal will slow gastric transit. Unless weight reduction is indicated for the patient, the intake of protein and fat-containing food is increased in order to provide an adequate caloric intake (29).

6. CAFFEINE

Caffeine is a vasodilator and a stimulant to the central nervous system. Caffeine may increase the concentration of epinephrine, a stimulus to the glucose-producing hormone glucagon, by as much as 50%. Because catecholamines have been implicated in the gastrointestinal phase of dumping syndrome, excesses of caffeine should be avoided (21, 30).

INDICATIONS FOR USE

1. SURGICAL CONDITIONS

The diet may be indicated following a vagotomy, partial or total gastrectomy, or other surgeries that either interfere with the pyloric sphincter or compromise the effectiveness of the stomach as a reservoir. Symptoms of dumping follow the rapid stomach emptying of such easily hydrolyzed foods as monosaccharides and the resulting hyperosmolar solution in the jejunum. The most difficult patients to manage are those with a small gastric remnant, severe dumping, malabsorption, and total gastrectomy. In the patient with cancer, with weight loss exceeding 25% of body weight, tube feeding or total parenteral nutrition may be necessary (5, 22–24, 31).

2. IDENTIFICATION OF DUMPING SYNDROME

The best way to evaluate gastric emptying and determine the degree of dumping is by radioisotope labeled test meals. These are commonly used in most hospitals and are the current state-of-the-art technique. Emptying of solids is evaluated by the use of technetium 99m–labeled solid foods, usually 1-cm cubes of chicken liver, mixed with 8 oz. of untagged beef stew and 2 crackers. The gastric emptying of liquids is evaluated with indium 111 in 100 mL of water. The patient is then scanned with a gamma camera, which records the emptying rates (32).

Radioisotope techniques now permit evaluation of liquids and solids at the same time. These techniques provide the best tolerated and most accurate means of diagnosing clinically significant gastric emptying disorders and studying the effects of drugs on gastric emptying (33).

The serum glucose level is also a modulator of gastric motility (34).

POSSIBLE ADVERSE REACTIONS

Care should be taken not to increase the protein or fat content of the diet more than necessary. Antidumping diets that drastically curtail total carbohydrate intake regardless of the type are often a hazard to the normal serum lipid profile. The high protein content of the diet may not be well tolerated in individuals with impaired glomerular filtration rates, nor in cases of impending hepatic encephalopathy.

Bolus tube feedings are usually not well tolerated. A continuous infusion with a pump is usually necessary. The regulation of the infusion avoids peak loading of the jejunum with hypertonic fluids (29).

CONTRAINDICATIONS

The diet as presented is contraindicated in the presence of any accompanying condition in which increases in protein or fat intake may be harmful—i.e., certain forms of liver, renal, or cardiovascular disease—or in individuals who have undergone massive ileal resections and are intolerant of fat. There is no need for the diet in operations that do not affect the vagus nerves and that preserve the pyloric sphincter (32).

CLINICAL ASSESSMENT

The dietary evaluation should relate onset of specific symptoms to the type and amount of carbohydrate consumed, the timing and volume of meals, alcohol and caffeine intake, fluid intake, and the amount of calories and protein provided. If malabsorption is suspected, particularly if there is also small-bowel disease, evaluation should include nutrient intake analysis for fat, protein, iron, folate, vitamin B-12, vitamin D, and calcium.

Significant weight loss of up to 25% to 30% of body weight is not uncommon after a gastrectomy. It is helpful to use anthropometrics, including weight, and serial midarm muscle circumference measurements to quantify this degree of weight loss and depletion of skeletal muscle mass and to evaluate the outcome of nutritional interventions.

BIOCHEMICAL ASSESSMENT

1. SERUM LIPID PROFILES

Particularly in individuals using a high-fat diet to provide adequate calories to reverse weight loss, long-term effects on serum cholesterol and triglycerides should be periodically evaluated. While cholesterol may be low initially, especially if the patient is protein malnourished, this is no guarantee that hypercholesterolemia will not occur once the patient has been eating well and gaining weight steadily.

2. FAT, PROTEIN, AND ENERGY UTILIZATION

If documented descriptions of stool suggest fat malabsorption, a 72-hour stool fat test may be helpful. Visceral protein status should be periodically assessed via total lymphocyte counts, total protein, and serum albumin. Nitrogen balance studies may be helpful in the protein-malnourished patient who is not meeting goals set for the return of visceral proteins to normal. Serum glucose determinations are of particular value in individuals who exhibit late dumping hypoglycemic symptoms.

3. IDENTIFICATION OF ANEMIA

Iron deficiency is common in these patients, particularly in menstruating women. Release of ferrous iron from coated tablets taken after meals may be inadequate, owing to decreased gastric acid secretion (5). Serum iron, hemoglobin, hematocrit, MCV, MCH, and MCHC determinations will permit identification of the patient with anemia. If anemia is iron related, the MCV will be below normal, indicating a microcytic state, whereas if it is related to folate or B-12, the MCV will be increased, indi-

cating a megaloblastic state. Patients who have had a Bilroth II partial gastrectomy are particularly susceptible to the development of anemia from inadequate dietary folate, malabsorption of iron, decreased intrinsic factor causing a vitamin B-12 deficiency, or inadequate ingestion of bound vitamin B-12.

4. CALCIUM METABOLISM

It is important to identify patients with abnormalities of calcium metabolism, which are common after gastric surgery. Many of these patients have metabolic bone disease. Osteomalacia has also been observed, but the cause is not known, because steatorrhea is often absent and vitamin D metabolism is normal (5).

ASSESSMENT OF POTENTIAL DRUG INTERACTIONS

1. DRUGS USED AS AN ADJUNCT TO DIET IN DUMPING SYNDROME

Drugs are now available as an adjunct to diet to control dumping syndrome in instances in which diet alone does not effectively reduce symptoms. Because the output of bile salts increases after gastric surgery and may cause choleraic diarrhea, administration of a bile salt–binding agent such as cholestyramine is useful. Cholestyramine taken with meals will reduce steatorrhea if fat malabsorption exists. Some patients, especially those with a truncal vagotomy and pyloroplasty who have a severe diarrhea refractory to dietary management, may benefit from such drugs as codeine and loperamide, or diphenoxylate. Codeine or diphenoxylate should be taken 30 minutes before meals. Patients who take loperamide may have a dry mouth (1, 35, 36).

Tolbutamide has been used with limited success to prevent the rapid rise of blood glucose that initiates late dumping.

A glucoside-hydrolase inhibitor of microbial origin produces symptomatic improvement. Acarbose, by interacting with sucrose to delay its absorption, has been shown to reduce the stimulus of sucrose-induced hyperglycemia on the pancreatic cells. When administered before a 50-g sucrose test meal, it improved both the hyperglycemic and the hypoglycemic phases of plasma glucose levels and greatly reduced the rise in plasma levels of gastric inhibitory polypeptide and insulin (37, 38).

Soluble or viscous dietary fiber has been shown to be effective by slowing intestinal transit. Fifty grams of the soluble fiber pectin taken before meals tends to reduce the hypovolemic phase by impeding the effect of osmotically active contents of the small intestine. Thus, dietary fiber gives a more sustained rate of absorption, less intestinal hurry, a lower insulin response, and less of a lag phase to the blood glucose response. The addition of the viscous fiber guar gum to meals will also slow gastric emptying (2, 6).

2. DRUGS THAT ARE CONTRAINDICATED

A. Metoclopramide The advent of the procainamide derivative metoclopramide, with its combined cholinergic and dopamine-antagonizing effects, provided a new therapeutic approach to the treatment of delayed gastric emptying. Its use should be avoided in anyone with dumping syndrome (33).

B. Domperidone This drug has been shown to increase the rate of liquid emptying in diabetic gastroparesis, and it should be avoided in dumping syndrome (33).

3. EFFECTS OF REPRESENTATIVE MEDICATIONS ON GASTRIC EMPTYING

See table 20.1.

4. OTHER DRUGS THAT AFFECT GASTRIC EMPTYING

See table 20.2.

TABLE 20.1. REPRESENTATIVE MEDICATIONS SHOWING THEIR MODE OF ACTION AND EFFECT ON GASTRIC EMPTYING (GE)

Medication	Therapeutic use	GE	Mode of action
Cardiovascular			
Potassium salts	Electrolyte balance	Delay	Not known
Dopamine	Antishock vasopressor	Slow	Via dopamine receptor
L-Dopa	Parkinson's disease	Delay	Via dopamine receptor
Nifedipine	Antihypertensive, antianginal	Delay or no effect	Calcium channel blocker
Respiratory			
Isoproterenol	Asthma	Delay	β-Adrenergic
Theophylline	Asthma	Not known	Smooth muscle relaxant
Gastrointestinal			
Sucralfate	Peptic ulcer	Delay or no effect	Mucosal coating and antacid
Aluminum OH	Peptic ulcer	Delay	Antacid
Propantheline	Peptic ulcer	Delay	Anticholinergic
Cimetidine	Peptic ulcer	No effect	H_2-blocker
Metoclopramide	Gastroparesis, dyspepsia	Accelerate	Cholinergic, antidopaminergic
Domperidone	Gastroparesis	Accelerate	Antidopaminergic
Cisapride	Gastroparesis	Accelerate	Cholinergic
Bulk laxatives	Constipation	Accelerate	Gastric distention
Opiates	Diarrhea	Delay	Increased smooth muscle tone
Psychiatric			
Chlordiazepoxide	Anxiety	No effect	
Tricyclic compounds	Depression	Delay	Anticholinergic, norepinephrine-enhancing
Phenothiazine	Psychosis	Delay	Anticholinergic
Diazepam	Anxiety	Accelerate	Spasmolytic
Nonsteroidal anti-inflammatory drugs			
Indomethacin	Anti-inflammatory	No effect	PG inhibitor
Miscellaneous			
Synthetic estrogen compounds	Hormonal therapy	Delay	(?) gastric sex hormone receptors
Acetaminophen	Antipyretic, analgesic	Not known	PG synthetase inhibitor

Source: Chaudhuri, T. K., and Fink, S. (33). Copyright © 1990 by the American College of Gastroenterology.

IMPLEMENTATION AND EDUCATION

1. PERIODIC REEVALUATIONS AND LIBERALIZATION OF THE DIET

Most patients with dumping syndrome will improve considerably within 1 year of beginning treatment (1). The diet should be gradually liberalized as symptoms permit. Patients should be reassured that symptoms are likely to improve with time and cautioned against unnecessarily rigid dietary restrictions.

Especially in the initial stages, the outcome of the diet should be regularly re-evaluated and adjustments made in caloric, protein, and nutrient intake on the basis of the individual patient's response. For example, results of nitrogen balance studies may indicate nitrogen losses higher than originally anticipated, suggesting the need to increase protein or energy intake.

2. SECONDARY LACTOSE INTOLERANCE

A secondary and usually temporary form of lactose intolerance may develop in certain individuals with intestinal mucosal damage. Milk and milk products should be added to the diet slowly and in small amounts. If they produce symptoms of lactose intolerance, they should be withdrawn until a later date. Lactose-hydrolyzed milk may be better tolerated. As clinical symptoms of dumping subside and the patient improves, milk products may again be introduced. The use of calcium supplements may be necessary (39).

3. PECTIN SUPPLEMENTS

Pectin supplements can be used to add to the unabsorbable carbohydrate intake in

TABLE 20.2. OTHER DRUGS THAT AFFECT GASTRIC EMPTYING

Drug	Effect on gastric emptying	Mechanism
Cholecystokinin	Delay	Inhibits proximal gastric contractions, despite increased antral motor activity
Gastrin	Delay	Inhibits movement of solids into duodenum by inhibition of migrating motor (MM) complex, or interdigestive myoelectric complex, a cycle of electromechanical activity
Sex steroid hormones	Variable inhibitory effects	Not known. Occurs in men and in premenopausal and postmenopausal women
Morphine and other narcotic analgesics	Delay	Increases tone of smooth muscle and interferes with normal peristalsis

Sources: Chaudhuri, T. K., and Fink, S. (33); Powers, D. E., and Moore, A. O. (36).

Nursing and physician notes describing stool patterns may provide a clue to malabsorption. Patients with anemia and any abnormality in calcium metabolism should be identified. Vitamin B-12 injections should routinely be given to all patients who have had a total gastrectomy (29).

instances of poor tolerance. A dosage of 10 g or two 5-g packets taken daily with meals as a supplement to the diet has proven to be effective. The packets can be made into a fruit or vegetable conserve and added to cooked foods. If they are incorporated into recipes, patients must be cautioned that the packet should be mixed with only the amount that can be realistically consumed in 1 portion, so that the full amount of the pectin is taken. When liquids are given after meals, the packets may also be mixed with the liquids, especially fruit juices (40).

4. TUBE-FEEDING FORMULAS

Continuous drip feeding will usually prevent dumping, unless the rate is excessive. For malnourished patients, it is usually possible to use a high nitrogen formula, provided it is administered slowly. Compleat modified (Sandoz) has less simple sugar than other formulas and may therefore be better tolerated. Tube feedings containing fiber may also be beneficial.

5. SPECIAL TECHNIQUES

For individuals whose major problem is late dumping syndrome or hypoglycemia

2 hours after a meal, some of the meal should be withheld to be consumed 90 minutes later. Acarbose with or without pectin and guar gum is also effective. The addition of guar gum to meals will help slow gastric emptying, bind bile acids, and reduce the initial hyperglycemia and hyperinsulinemia that produces the late hypoglycemia (1, 41–43).

6. SURGICAL TREATMENT

If the diet fails, surgical treatment designed to slow small-bowel transit may be needed. Good results have been reported by use of a distal onlay reversed ileal graft procedure. This procedure creates a passive nonpropulsive segment some 30 cm from the ileocecal junction. It has been used successfully in severe postvagotomy diarrhea that is refractory to dietary treatment (43).

PRIORITIES FOR QUALITY ASSURANCE

Screening should identify the patient who is underweight by reason of poor intake because he or she fears the symptoms of dumping syndrome, as well as the patient who is underweight because of significant malabsorption of nutrients.

MENU PLANNING

FOOD LIST FOR THE CARBOHYDRATE-CONTROLLED DIET FOR MANAGEMENT OF POSTGASTRECTOMY DUMPING SYNDROME

Food group	Foods allowed	Foods excluded
Beverages	Whole, low-fat, or skim milk or buttermilk (if well tolerated by patient), decaffeinated coffee, tea, and dietetic carbonated beverages	Alcohol, sugar-sweetened or caffeinated carbonated beverages, sweetened cocoa, sweetened milk products, sweetened fruit drinks, regular coffee and tea, sweetened cereal beverages
Breads and cereals	Unsweetened or diet frosted cereals, plain breads, crackers and rolls, starchy vegetables—e.g., corn, lima beans, parsnips, peas, potato, pumpkin, winter, acorn or butternut squash, yam or sweet potato, rice, pasta, dried beans, or other high-fiber starches	Sugar-frosted or sweetened cereals, or those packaged with dates, raisins and brown sugar, honey, or other concentrated sources of sugar; "natural" cereals (e.g., granola)
Meat and meat substitutes	Any type	None
Vegetables	Any vegetable prepared with other allowed foods without added sugar	Any to which sugar has been added
Fruits	Unsweetened fruits and fruit juices, particularly high-fiber fruits, such as apples	Sweetened canned fruits and juices; fruit juice in excess of ½ cup at any one meal
Desserts	Fruit-based products or other desserts made without simple sugars or concentrated sweets; unsweetened gelatin, specially made pies with whole wheat crust and artificially sweetened custards and junkets	Cakes or cookies, ice cream, sherbet, glazed or sugar-frosted doughnuts or rolls, danish pastries, regular pies, candy, sweetened custards except as noted
Fats	All	None
Miscellaneous	Soups made from allowed foods, broth, gravies, nuts, spices, condiments, artificial sweeteners	Honey, jams, jellies, syrups

(*continued*)

SAMPLE MEAL PLAN AND MENU FOR THE CARBOHYDRATE-CONTROLLED DIET FOR MANAGEMENT OF POSTGASTRECTOMY DUMPING SYNDROME (FOR A MALE, AGE 25–50)

Food	Serving size	Exchange[a]
7:00 a.m.		
Tea	1 cup	—
Artificial sweetener	1 packet	—
BREAKFAST *(8:00 a.m.)*		
Scrambled egg	1 large	1 meat
Margarine	1 tsp.	1 fat
Oatmeal	1 cup	2 breads
9:00 a.m.		
Low-fat milk	1 cup	1 milk
Decaffeinated coffee	½ cup	—
Artificial sweetener	1 packet	—
MORNING SNACK *(10:00 a.m.)*		
Rye wafers	8	2 breads
Ricotta cheese	2 oz.	2 meats
Fresh orange sections	½ cup	1 fruit
11:00 a.m.		
Broth	1 cup	—
LUNCH *(noon)*		
Sliced turkey breast	3 oz.	3 meats
Whole wheat bread	2 slices	2 breads
Lettuce	2 leaves	—
Mayonnaise	1 tbsp.	3 fats
Cooked spinach	1 cup	2 vegetables
Margarine	1 tsp.	1 fat
1:00 p.m.		
Tea	1 cup	—
Artificial sweetener	1 packet	—
2:00 p.m.		
Low-fat milk	1 cup	1 milk
AFTERNOON SNACK *(3:00 p.m.)*		
Rye wafers	4	1 bread
Lean ham	1 oz.	1 meat
Apple	1 small	1 fruit
4:00 p.m.		
Diet soda	1 cup	—
DINNER *(6:00 p.m.)*		
Roast beef	4 oz.	4 meats
Baked potato	1 large	2 breads
Whole wheat roll	1 small	1 bread
Cooked carrots	½ cup	1 vegetable
Margarine	3 tsp.	3 fats

(continued)

7:00 p.m.

Tea	½ cup	—
Artificial sweetener	1 packet	—
Low-fat milk	½ cup	½ milk

EVENING SNACK *(8:00 p.m.)*

Banana	1 medium	2 fruits
Rye wafers	8	2 breads
Peanut butter	2 tbsp.	2 meats

9:00 p.m.

Low-fat milk	1 cup	1 milk

Approximate Nutrient Analysis

Energy	2,700 kcal
Protein	154.3 g (23% of kcal)
Fat	87.5 g (29% of kcal)
Polyunsaturated fat	17.6 g
Monounsaturated fat	32.6 g
Saturated fat	27.6 g
Cholesterol	427 mg
Carbohydrate	346.3 g (51% of kcal)
Vitamin A	31,436 IU
	3,742 RE
Thiamine	2.31 mg
Riboflavin	3.51 mg
Niacin	27.9 mg
Folate	516 mcg
Vitamin B-12	8.32 mcg
Vitamin B-6	3.53 mg
Vitamin C	129.4 mg
Calcium	1,839 mg
Phosphorus	2,858 mg
Iron	24.2 mg
Copper	1.85 mg
Zinc	16.3 mg
Magnesium	592 mg
Sodium	6,964 mg
Potassium	6,566 mg

ªSee Part V for exchanges.

REFERENCES

1. Radziuk, J., and Bondy, D.: Gastric surgery. In Jeejeebhoy, K. N.: Current therapy in nutrition. Philadelphia: B. C. Decker, 1988.
2. Jenkins, D., and Jenkins, L.: Dietary fiber. In Jeejeebhoy, K. N.: Current therapy in nutrition. Philadelphia: B. C. Decker, 1988.
3. Jenkins, D., Wolever, T., et al.: Glycemic index of foods: A physiological basis for carbohydrate exchange. Am J Clin Nutr 34:362, 1981.
4. Jenkins, D., Wolever, T., and Jenkins, A.: Starchy foods and glycemic index. Diabetes Care 11:150, 1988.
5. Desai, M. B., and Jeejeebhoy, K. N.: Nutrition and diet in management of diseases of the gastrointestinal tract. A. Esophagus, stomach, and duodenum. (4) Surgery for peptic ulcer. In Shils, M. E., and Young, V. E., eds.: Modern nutrition in health and disease. 7th ed. Philadelphia: Lea & Febiger, 1988.
6. Leichter, S.: Alimentary hypoglycemia: A new appraisal. Am J Clin Nutr 32:2104, 1979.
7. Valenzuela, J., and Defilippi, C.: Inhibition of gastric emptying in humans by secretin, the octapeptide of cholecystokinin and intraduodenal fat. Gastroenterology 81:898, 1981.
8. Read, N. W., Cammack, J., et al.: Is transit time of a meal through the small intestine related to the rate at which it leaves the stomach? Gut 23:824, 1982.
9. Ruppin, H., Bar-Meir, S., et al.: Effects of liquid formula diets on proximal gastrointestinal function. Dig Dis Sci 26:202, 1981.
10. Houghton, L., Hickson, F., and Read, N.: Effect of food consistency on gastric emptying in man. Gut 28:1584, 1987.
11. Siegel, J., Urbain, J., et al.: Biphasic nature of gastric emptying. Gut 29:85, 1988.
12. Fisher, R.: Gastroduodenal motility disturbances in man. Scand J Gastroenterol 20 (Supp 109):59, 1985.
13. Snook, J. A., Wells, A. D., et al.: Studies on the pathogenesis of the early dumping syndrome induced by intraduodenal instillation of hypertonic glucose. Gut 30:1716, 1989.
14. Ebied, I., Ralphs, D., et al.: Dumping syndromes after vagotomy treated by reversal of pyloroplasty. Br J Surg 69:527, 1982.
15. Kauskik, S., Ralphs, D., and Hobsley, R.: Gastric emptying and dumping after proximal gastric vagotomy. Am J Gastroenterol 77:363, 1982.
16. Sun, W., Houghton, L., et al.: Effect of meal temperature on gastric emptying of liquids in man. Gut 29:302, 1988.
17. McArthur, K. E., and Feldman, M.: Gastric acid secretion, gastrin release, and gastric emptying in humans as affected by liquid meal temperature. Am J Clin Nutr 49:51, 1989.
18. Holt, S., Reid, J., et al.: Gastric emptying of solids in man. Gut 23:292, 1982.
19. Pittman, A., and Robinson, F.: Dumping syndrome—control by diet. J Am Diet Assoc 34:596, 1968.
20. Pittman, A., and Robinson, F.: Dietary management of the dumping syndrome. J Am Diet Assoc 40:108, 1962.
21. Shemerdiak, W., Abramson, E., et al.: Catecholamines in the early dumping syndrome. Clin Chem 28:722, 1982.
22. Smith, F., and Jeffries, G.: Late and persistent postgastrectomy problems. In Sleisinger, M. H., and Fordtran, J. S.: Gastrointestinal disease. Philadelphia: W. B. Saunders, 1973.
23. Welch, C.: Late effects of gastrectomy. JAMA 228:1287, 1974.
24. Pemberton, C. M., and Gastineau, C. F.: Mayo Clinic diet manual—a handbook of dietary practices. 5th ed. Philadelphia: W. B. Saunders, 1981.
25. Desai, M. B., and Jeejeebhoy, K. N.: Nutrition and diet in management of diseases of the gastrointestinal tract. A. Esophagus, stomach, and duodenum. (4) Nutrition and surgery for peptic ulcer. In Shils, M. E., and Young, V. R.: Modern nutrition in health and disease. 7th ed. Philadelphia: Lea & Febiger, 1988.
26. Becker, H. D.: Hormonal changes after gastric surgery. Clin Gastroenterol 9:755, 1980.
27. Wong, P., Talamo, R., et al.: Kallikrein-kinin system in postgastrectomy dumping syndrome. Ann Intern Med 80:577, 1974.
28. Shultz, K., Neelon, F., et al.: Mechanism of postgastrectomy hypoglycemia. Arch Int Med 128:240, 1971.
29. Desai, M. B., and Jeejeebhoy, K. N.: Peptic ulcer. In Kinney, J. M., Jeejeebhoy, K. N., et al.: Nutrition and metabolism. Philadelphia: W. B. Saunders, 1988.
30. Ritchie, J. M.: Central nervous system stimulants. Xanthines. In Goodman, L. S., and Gilman, A.: The pharmacologic basis of therapeutics. 5th ed. New York: Macmillan, 1975.
31. Berk, J.: The dumping syndrome. Arch Surg 102:88, 1971.
32. Ricci, D., and McCallum, R.: Diagnosis and treatment of delayed gastric emptying. Adv Intern Med 33:357, 1988.
33. Chaudhuri, T. K., and Fink, S.: Update: Pharmaceuticals and gastric emptying. Am J Gastroenterol 85:223, 1990.
34. Barnett, J., and Owyang, C.: Serum glucose concentration as a modulator of interdigestive gastric motility. Gastroenterology 94:739, 1988.
35. O'Brien, J., Thompson, D., et al.: Effect of codeine and loperamide on upper intestinal transit and absorption in normal subjects and patients with postvagotomy diarrhea. Gut 29:312, 1988.
36. Powers, D. E., and Moore, A. O.: Food/medication interactions. 6th ed. Phoenix: 1988 (self-published).
37. McLoughlin, J., Buchanan, K., and Alam, M.: A glucosidehydrolase inhibitor in treatment of dumping syndrome. Lancet 2:603, 1979.
38. Taylor, R., Jenkins, D., et al.: Effect of acarbose on the 24-hour blood glucose profile and pattern of carbohydrate absorption. Diabetes Care 5:92, 1982.
39. Pirk, F., Skala, I., and Vulterinova, M.: Milk intolerance after gastrec-

tomy. Digestion 9:130, 1973.

40. Jenkins, D., Gassull, M., et al.: Effect of dietary fiber on complications of gastric surgery: Prevention of post-prandial hypoglycemia by pectin. Gastroenterology 73:215, 1973.

41. Harju, E., Heikkila, J., and Larmi, T.: Effect of guar gum on gastric emptying after gastric resection. JPEN 8:18, 1984.

42. Harju, E., and Nordback, I.: Postprandial hyperglycemia after different carbohydrates in patients with total gastrectomy. Surg Gynecol Obstet 165:41, 1987.

43. Cushieri, A.: Surgical treatment of severe intractable postvagotomy diarrhea. Br J Surg 73:981, 1986.

21.

LACTOSE-FREE DIET

DEFINITIONS

LACTOSE-FREE DIET

A diet that virtually eliminates all known sources of the disaccharide lactose.

CONGENITAL LACTASE DEFICIENCY

An extremely rare, life-threatening condition due to a genetic defect, which manifests itself at birth as a virtual absence of the enzyme lactase (1–4). If the condition is not diagnosed soon after birth, symptoms may lead to death.

PRIMARY ADULT LACTASE DEFICIENCY

An acquired condition involving age-related developmental decreases in intestinal lactase concentrations, which by adolescence may be only 5% to 10% of the amount present at birth. The World Health Organization (WHO) has proposed that the term *lactase nonpersistence* be used instead of the term *primary adult lactase deficiency*. Certain racial and ethnic groups may be more genetically susceptible to these lactase decreases than others. Exact occurrence rates, however, must await widespread testing with more standardized tests and parameters. Generally, about 80% of individuals with adult lactase deficiency can drink up to a glass of milk (the equivalent of 12 g of lactose) without experiencing symptoms of lactose intolerance (5–11).

SECONDARY LACTASE DEFICIENCY

A temporary state of lactase deficiency occurring in previously lactose-tolerant individuals—i.e., those who have normal intestinal lactase levels, referred to as "lactase persistence" by the WHO (7). It is the result of mucosal injury, which can occur from many causes, including sprue, infectious gastroenteritis, or protein-energy malnutrition.

LACTOSE INTOLERANCE

The experience of symptoms of gastrointestinal discomfort: nausea, gas in the abdomen or intestines, abdominal cramping and distension, belching or flatulence, and/or watery stools after ingestion of lactose, either in milk, in other dairy foods, or as the sugar itself (12).

LACTOSE MALDIGESTION

The incapacity to digest or break down an oral dose of lactose into its constituent simple sugars—glucose and galactose—during its passage through the small intestine (12).

PURPOSE OF THE DIET

The diet is intended to prevent the life-threatening consequences of lactose ingestion by infants with congenital lactose intolerance. Total exclusion of dietary lactose is necessary in severely affected individuals, who have almost no lactase enzyme at all (1–2).

The absence of lactase results in the inability to hydrolyze lactose to glucose and galactose. Undigested lactose, because it cannot be absorbed, remains in the intestinal lumen; there it ferments and causes abdominal cramps, increased motility, distension, and an irritating osmotic diarrhea. Nutrient absorption may be affected, as evidenced by the presence of large amounts of protein, calcium, magnesium, and phosphate in the ileum of lactase-deficient individuals (3).

EFFECTS OF THE DIET

Symptoms resolve within a few days of institution of the lactose-free diet.

PHYSIOLOGY, FOODS, AND NUTRIENTS

The diet excludes milk and milk products, as well as foods prepared from milk or to which whey has been added. In addition, all foods that either naturally contain lactose or to which lactose is added during processing are eliminated from the diet. Some of the nondairy, lactose-containing foods include breads, some prepared and processed foods, and commercial sauces and gravies (13). Lactate, lactic acid, and lactalbumin do not contain lactose.

INDICATIONS FOR USE

Primary lactase deficiency occurs as a congenital abnormality in the intestinal mucosa. The Holzel syndrome and the Durand syndrome are both rare, primary disorders of infancy that are managed with lactose-free diet therapy. Sensitivity to milk protein, as opposed to milk sugar, should be considered in forming the diagnosis. Milk-protein sensitivity may also be accompanied by skin and respiratory tract symptoms (1, 2, 4, 14, 15).

1. CLINICAL SYMPTOMS

As soon as an affected infant is breast-fed or receives a milk-based formula, symptoms of flatulence, colic, diarrhea, and lack of weight gain occur (4). In children, an acidic stool pH of less than 5 or 6, the presence of more than 10 g/100 mL lactose in the stool, and a therapeutic response to lactose withdrawal are also helpful clues.

2. INTESTINAL BIOPSY

The single most reliable and definitive diagnosis is made from an intestinal biopsy. A special capsule attached to an endoscope is used to obtain a biopsy of the intestinal mucosa, which is then analyzed for its lactase activity. This is, however, an invasive procedure with inherent risks of its own, which is now reserved for those cases in which an inborn error of carbohydrate metabolism or celiac disease is suspected, or in which symptoms persist despite removal of the suspected offending foods (4).

3. BREATH HYDROGEN TEST

One of the more recently used diagnostic tools for carbohydrate malabsorption is the breath hydrogen test. If it is performed after an oral dose of lactose (2 g/kg body weight) mixed with water, it provides an analysis of lactose absorption. The test is based on the principle that gaseous hydrogen is released when unabsorbed carbohydrate is fermented by intestinal bacterial flora. Some of the intestinal hydrogen is absorbed into the bloodstream and excreted by the lungs. Expiratory breath samples are collected during fasting and at 30-minute intervals over a period of 2 to 3 hours and assayed for the presence of hydrogen, using a chromatographic method. A rise of >20 ppm above baseline is considered indicative of some form of malabsorption (4, 10, 13, 16).

The test has some limitations that affect its reliability, particularly when compared to the more definitive intestinal biopsy. There have been other reports of elevated breath hydrogen in fasting individuals. False positive results have been reported in patients with bacterial overgrowth, as well as in individuals who consumed legumes, beans, or whole-grain breads or other unabsorbable carbohydrates before the test. For example, smoking interferes with the test by increasing the peak of hydrogen production. False negative results have been reported in patients on broad-spectrum antibiotics, which destroy the normal hydrogen-producing flora. Overall, however, it has been claimed that if properly performed and interpreted, the breath hydrogen test is more reliable than the lactose tolerance test, particularly in diabetics or in conditions where gastric emptying is delayed or in "intestinal hurry" (4, 17–20).

4. LACTOSE TOLERANCE TEST

Prior to more recent use of the breath hydrogen test, lactose intolerance was evaluated by the lactose tolerance test. After a 50-g dose of lactose, blood samples are taken at about every 15 minutes up to 120 minutes after the test and analyzed for glucose, a breakdown product of lactose. Lactose malabsorption should be suspected if the blood glucose level increases less than 25 mg/100 mL. The test involves several invasive blood samples, and the lactose load is an unphysiological one that has often provoked severe symptoms. According to one investigator, this test results in an unacceptable level of false negative as well as false positive results and should be replaced by the breath hydrogen test (20, 21).

POSSIBLE ADVERSE REACTIONS

Prolonged adherence to a lactose-free diet may result in a calcium deficiency. Calcium supplements are needed to ensure adequate intake. Lactose has been shown to enhance calcium absorption in postmenopausal women. Consequently, its absence from the diet may affect the calcium content of the body. A recent review of several studies on the effect of lactose on calcium absorption stated that the majority of evidence indicates either a neutral or favorable effect of lactose on calcium absorption in both lactose digesters and maldigesters (22, 23).

CONTRAINDICATIONS

The diet is very restrictive and should only be used when it is absolutely necessary, as in congenital lactase deficiency. Individuals with adult lactase deficiency usually do not need such a severe restriction.

CLINICAL ASSESSMENT

Periodic 3-day diaries should be analyzed and compared to the RDAs to ensure key nutrients such as protein, calcium, and phosphorus are being provided in the amounts required. Height and weight should be taken at least every month in all infants and children on lactose-free diets. Growth curves should be kept and compared to standard curves to evaluate growth and development.

BIOCHEMICAL ASSESSMENT

Positive diagnosis is made by intestinal biopsy and assay of intestinal enzyme activity. In individuals in whom such an invasive procedure is too risky, a breath hydrogen test should be done. A totally lactose-free diet should not be prescribed solely on the basis of clinical symptoms, diet history, and blood glucose testing, which may be nonspecific for the exact carbohydrate being malabsorbed (21). Initially, the pH of the stool, although not conclusive by itself (an acid pH is simply an indication of intolerance to some form of carbohydrate) is a simple and inexpensive assessment tool.

Serum proteins should be evaluated to

determine if the loss of carbohydrate calories in the diarrheal stool has compromised visceral protein status by the diversion of protein calories for energy needs. Repeated intestinal challenges of lactose in these individuals may temporarily damage the intestinal mucosa and produce temporary malabsorption of other nutrients as well.

Serum calcium levels and alkaline phosphatase levels should be periodically evaluated in these patients.

ASSESSMENT OF POTENTIAL DRUG INTERACTIONS

Medications should be considered as a source of lactose in individuals who suffer relapses without obvious dietary indiscretions. Lactose is added to many drugs (e.g., lithium carbonate) as a filler (24, 25). Lists of drugs containing lactose are available, but the pharmacist should always be consulted because formulations may change.

IMPLEMENTATION AND EDUCATION

1. FORMULAS FOR CONGENITAL LACTASE DEFICIENCY

Severely affected infants with congenital lactase deficiency may need a formula free of simple carbohydrate. For example, Product 3232A (Mead Johnson) is a casein hydrolysate free of monosaccharides and disaccharides and with tapioca starch, to which simple carbohydrate is added to meet the individualized needs and tolerances of the infant. When prepared by mixing 81 g of the formula base with about 59 g of a tolerated carbohydrate and 1 qt. of water, it provides 20 cal per ounce. Particularly if diagnosis has been delayed and there has been mucosal injury from continued lactose consumption, there may be temporary intolerances to other disaccharides and monosaccharides as well. Initially, while the patient is recovering from the

MENU PLANNING

FOOD LIST FOR THE LACTOSE-FREE DIET

Food group	Foods allowed	Foods excluded
Beverages	Isomil (Ross Laboratories), Isomil SF (Ross Laboratories), Mocha Mix (Presto Food Products), Nutramigen (Mead Johnson), Pregestimil (Mead Johnson), Product 3232 A (Mead Johnson), RCF (Ross Laboratories), carbonated drinks, coffee, freeze-dried coffee, Lidolac (Lidano), lactose-free enteral formulas such as Ensure (Ross Laboratories), Citrotein (Sandoz Nutrition), Isocal (Mead Johnson), Osmolyte (Ross Laboratories), Sustacal (Mead Johnson), Nutri 1000 LF (Cutter Laboratories), and others (see discussion of enteral feeding and infant formula for complete list)	All untreated milk of any species and all products containing milk (except lactose-free milk), e.g., skim, dried, evaporated, or condensed milk; yogurt; ice cream; sherbet; malted milk; Ovaltine (Ovaltine Products), hot chocolate; some cocoas and instant coffees (read labels); powdered soft drinks with lactose; whey; casein milk that has been treated with lactobacillus/acidophilus culture rather than lactase, e.g., Nutrish (Ross Laboratories)
Breads and cereals	Breads and rolls made without milk, Italian bread, some cooked cereals and prepared cereals (read labels), macaroni, spaghetti, soda crackers, rice	Prepared mixes, e.g., muffins, biscuits, waffles, pancakes; some dry cereals, e.g., Total (General Mills), Special K (Kellogg), and Cocoa Krispies (Kellogg) (read labels carefully); Instant Cream of Wheat (Nabisco), commercial breads and rolls to which milk solids have been added; zwieback, French toast made with milk

(continued)

Meat and meat substitutes	Plain beef, chicken, fish, turkey, lamb, veal, pork, and ham; strained or junior meats and vegetables and meat combinations that do not contain milk or milk products; kosher frankfurters and cold cuts	Creamed or breaded meat, fish, or fowl; sausage products, such as weiners, liver sausage, cold cuts containing nonfat milk solids; cheese
Soups	Clear soups, vegetable soups, consommés, cream soups made with Mocha Mix or nondairy creamers	Cream soups unless made only with allowed ingredients; chowders; commercially prepared soups containing lactose
Desserts	Water and fruit ices; gelatin; angel food cake; homemade cakes, pies, cookies made from allowed ingredients, puddings made with water	Commercial cakes and cookies and mixes, custard, puddings, sherbet, ice cream made with milk, any containing chocolate, pie crust made with butter or margarine, gelatin made with carrageen
Eggs	All	Omelets, soufflés, and other dishes containing milk
Fats	Margarines and salad dressings that do not contain milk or milk products, oils, shortening, bacon, Rich's Whip Topping (Rich Products), some nondairy creamers (read labels), nut butters, nuts	Margarines and dressing containing milk or milk products, butter, cream, cream cheese, peanut butter with milk solid fillers, salad dressings containing lactose
Fruits	All fresh, canned, or frozen fruits that are not processed with lactose	Any canned or frozen fruits processed with lactose
Vegetables	Fresh, canned, or frozen artichokes, asparagus, broccoli, cabbage, carrots, cauliflower, celery, chard, corn, cucumber, eggplant, green beans, kale, lettuce, mustard, okra, onions, parsley, parsnips, pumpkin, rutabaga, spinach, squash, tomatoes, white and sweet potatoes, yams, lima beans, beets	Any to which lactose is added during processing; creamed, breaded, or buttered vegetables; instant potatoes, corn curls, frozen french fries if processed with lactose

(continued)

acute symptoms of lactose intolerance, the formula may need to contain less carbohydrate and can be instituted with 30 g carbohydrate and 10 cal per ounce.

RCF (Ross Laboratories) is a carbohydrate-free formula with a soy protein isolate base. When mixed with 12 oz. water to 13 oz. formula base plus 52 g tolerated carbohydrate, it provides 20 kcal per ounce.

2. FOOD LABELS

Manufacturers often simply use the word *sugar* on their labels without specifying which sugar, and they may in fact change the specific sugar without warning as cost or availability varies. Mothers should be warned to use only those foods they are sure do not contain lactose. Recipes for foods permitted on galactose-free diets may be used for lactase deficiency. Those intended for children with allergies to milk protein, rather than with lactose intolerance, may not be used unless no other source of lactose is present (26–28).

PRIORITIES FOR QUALITY ASSURANCE

A diagnostic priority is the use of standardized techniques in the performance of the breath hydrogen lactose test, particularly in cutoff criteria used as parameters to make the diagnosis. Symptom assessment alone has been noted to be a poor predictor of lactose malabsorption. Too often milk- or lactose-containing foods are eliminated from diets on the basis of nonspecific symptoms of unproven lactose intolerance. In any institution in which children may be placed on milk-free diets, a quality assurance monitor could be set up that simply documents the number of all milk-free or lactose-free diets ordered, backed up by a diagnostic test that substantiates the need for the diet (10, 21).

Conversely, some adult lactose malabsorbers are unaware that certain symptoms may be related to lactose malabsorption (21).

Miscellaneous	Soy sauce, carob powder, popcorn, olives, pure sugar candy, jelly or marmalade, sugar, corn syrup, carbonated beverages, gravy made with water, baker's cocoa, pickles, pure seasonings and spices, wine, molasses (beet sugar), pure monosodium glutamate, instant coffees that do not contain lactose, Tofutti frozen dessert (Tofutti Brands), Sweet 'n Low artificial sweetener (NIFDA)	Chewing gum, chocolate, some cocoas, toffee, peppermint, butterscotch, caramels; some instant coffees, dietetic preparations (read labels), certain drugs and certain vitamin and mineral preparations; spice blends if they contain milk products, monosodium glutamate extender, artificial sweeteners containing lactose, e.g., Equal (L. G. Searle) and Wee Cal (Domino Amstar), some nondairy creamers (read labels)

SAMPLE MENU FOR THE LACTOSE-FREE DIET (FOR A CHILD, AGE 7–10)[a]

BREAKFAST	
Orange	1 small
Cream of Rice cereal	½ cup
Nondairy creamer	½ cup
Vienna bread, toasted	1 slice
Milk-free margarine	1 tsp.
Grape jelly	1 tsp.
Grape juice	½ cup
LUNCH	
Sliced turkey	2 oz.
Vienna bread	2 slices
Lettuce	1 leaf
Milk-free margarine	1 tsp.
Pear	1 medium
Oatmeal cookies	2
DINNER	
Hamburger	2 oz.
Lactose-free hard roll	1
Sliced tomato	1 medium
Lactose-free mayonnaise	1 tbsp.
Oven-browned potato strips	1 cup
with olive oil	1 tsp.
Cooked spinach	½ cup
Milk-free margarine	1 tsp.
Banana	½ medium
BEDTIME	
Vanilla wafers	6
Apple juice	1 cup

(continued)

Approximate Nutrient Analysis

Energy	1,965 kcal
Protein	54.9 g (11% of kcal)
Fat	59.1 g (27% of kcal)
Polyunsaturated fat	13.7 g
Monounsaturated fat	15.3 g
Saturated fat	13.4 g
Cholesterol	99 mg
Carbohydrate	314.6 g (64% of kcal)
Vitamin A	9,248 IU
	1,024 RE
Thiamine	1.35 mg
Riboflavin	1.24 mg
Niacin	19.2 mg
Folate	295 mcg
Vitamin B-12	2.52 mcg
Vitamin B-6	2.41 mg
Vitamin C	188.7 mg
Calcium	358 mg
Phosphorus	748 mg
Iron	14.9 mg
Copper	1.46 mg
Zinc	6.1 mg
Magnesium	270 mg
Sodium	2,202 mg
Potassium	3,903 mg

[a]A calcium supplement is necessary to supply the RDAs for calcium and zinc. For a lactose-restricted diet, use regular margarine, whole wheat or white bread, and lactose-hydrolyzed milk instead of non-dairy creamer and juice.

REFERENCES

1. Lindquist, B., and Meeuwisee, G.: Diets in disaccharidase deficiency and defective monosaccharide absorption. J Am Diet Assoc 48:307, 1966.

2. Herber, R.: Disaccharide deficiency in health and disease. Calif Med 116:23, 1972.

3. Scrimshaw, N. E., and Murray, E. B.: The acceptability of milk and milk products in populations with a high prevalence of lactose intolerance. Am J Clin Nutr 48 (Supp):1083, 1988.

4. Bayless, T. M.: Disaccharidase deficiency. J Am Diet Assoc 60:478, 1972.

5. Newcomer, A. D., and McGill, D. B.: Lactose intolerance. Clin Nutr 3:53, 1984.

6. Lebenthal, E., and Rossi, T. M.: Correlation between lactase deficiency and lactose intolerance. In Lifshitz, T.: Carbohydrate intolerance in infancy. New York: Marcel Dekker, 1982.

7. World Health Organization. Sponsored workshop on lactose malabsorption. Moscow, USSR, June 10–11, 1985.

8. Newcomer, A., Gordon, H., et al.: Family studies of lactase deficiency in the American Indian. Gastroenterology 62:234, 1977.

9. Roggero, P., Offrendi, M., and Mosca, F.: Lactose absorption in healthy Italian children: Do the quantity of malabsorbed sugar and the small bowel transit time play roles in symptom production? J Pediatr Gastroenterol Nutr 4:82, 1985.

10. Solomons, N., and Barillas, C.: The cut-off criterion for a positive hydrogen breath test in children: A reappraisal. J Pediatr Gastroenterol Nutr 5:920, 1986.

11. Newcomer, A., and McGill, D.: Clinical importance of lactase deficiency. N Engl J Med 310:42, 1984.

12. Solomons, N. W.: An update on lactose intolerance. Nutr News 49:1, 1986.

13. Beaudette, T., and Strickland, R.: Lactose intolerance. Chicago: American Dietetic Association, 1985.

14. Heycock, E., Heatley, V., et al.: An in vitro test for cow's milk protein intolerance? Scand J Gastroenterol 21:1245, 1986.

15. Matsura, T., Kuroume, T., and Amada, K.: Close relationship between lactose intolerance and allergy to milk protein. J Asthma Res 9:13, 1971.

16. Salyers, A.: Breakdown of polysaccharides by human intestinal bacteria. In Calabrese, E., and Scherr, G.: Advances in human nutrition. Vol. 2. Park Forest, Ill.: Chem Orbital, 1985.

17. Saavedrea, J. M., and Perman, J. A.: Current concepts in lactose malabsorption and intolerance. Ann Rev Nutr 9:475, 1989.

18. Barr, R. G.: Limitations of the breath hydrogen test and other techniques for predicting incomplete lactose absorption. In Paige, D., and Bayless, T.: Lactose digestion: Clinical and nutritional implications. Baltimore: Johns Hopkins University Press, 1981.

19. Hermann-Zaidens, M.: Malabsorption in adults: Etiology, evaluation, and management. J Am Diet Assoc 86:1171, 1986.

20. Caspary, W.: Diarrhea associated with carbohydrate malabsorption. Clin Gastroenterol 15:631, 1986.

21. DiPalma, J., and Narvaez, R.: Prediction of lactose malabsorption in referral patients. Dig Dis Sci 33:303, 1988.

22. Grieesen, M., Cochet, B., et al.: Calcium absorption from milk in lactase deficient subjects. Am J Clin Nutr 49:377, 1989.

23. Scrimshaw, N. E., and Murray, E. B.: The acceptability of milk and milk products in populations with a high prevalence of lactose intolerance. 9. Lactase deficiency and the absorption of nutrients. Am J Clin Nutr 48 (Supp):1126, 1988.

24. Lieb, J., and Kazienko, D. J.: Lactose filler as a cause of "drug induced" diarrhea. N Engl J Med 299:314, 1978.

25. Goodman, L. S., and Gilman, A.: The pharmacological basis of therapeutics. 6th ed. New York: Macmillan, 1980.

26. Rudoff, C.: The allergy cookie jar. Menlo Park, Calif.: Prologue Publications, 1985.

27. Rudoff, C.: The allergy baker. Menlo Park, Calif.: Prologue Publications, 1985.

28. Beaudette, T., and Strickland, R.: Lactose intolerance. Chicago: American Dietetic Association, 1985.

22.

LACTOSE-RESTRICTED DIET

DEFINITION

A diet limited in its content of the disaccharide lactose. It provides an amount of lactose small enough to avoid recurrence of symptoms in mild forms of lactose intolerance, usually less than 8 to 12 g of lactose daily.

PURPOSE OF THE DIET

To prevent the occurrence of symptoms in patients with adult primary or secondary lactase deficiency (1).

EFFECTS OF THE DIET

Within a few days of institution of the diet in cases of primary lactose intolerance, symptoms resolve. A patient with proven lactose intolerance who does not experience relief of abdominal pain and diarrhea may have lactose intolerance secondary to another disorder that requires treatment, such as celiac disease, regional enteritis, or postgastrectomy dumping syndrome (2).

PHYSIOLOGY, FOODS, AND NUTRIENTS

1. FACTORS AFFECTING INDIVIDUAL TOLERANCE

The lactose-restricted diet should be specialized to accommodate individual tolerance levels. Wide variations exist among lactase-deficient persons as to the amount of lactose tolerated. Some persons with adult onset lactase deficiency may be asymptomatic except when they consume large quantities of milk, while a small number of others cannot tolerate any milk at all. In such cases milk beverages, creamed foods, and ice cream may have to be avoided.

Foods with equivalent amounts of lactose may vary widely in their effects on lactose intolerant individuals. For example, some individuals may be able to tolerate chocolate milk better than whole milk, for reasons other than lactose content. Chocolate milk has a higher caloric density than whole milk, which may cause a delay in gastric emptying time (3, 4). The longer the time before lactose reaches the intestine and is exposed to intestinal lactase, the more readily it will be digested and absorbed.

Other factors that have an effect on an individual's tolerance to a given amount of lactose include the form of the food, intestinal transit time, the degree of compensation by the colon, and the person's age. Consuming milk with solid food delays gastric emptying, thereby favoring lactose absorption. Lactose consumed in a food containing fat—e.g., whole milk—is better tolerated than lactose in skim milk. Lactose in skim milk is better tolerated than lactose in water. An aqueous solution of lactose, as is used in the lactose tolerance test, empties from the stomach faster than lactose in foods containing protein and fats. For this reason, it has been proposed that whole milk, rather than an aqueous solution of lactose, be used to test for lactose intolerance (5, 6).

The nature of the microflora and absorptive capacity of the colon affect the rate of lactose fermentation in the colon and thus the appearance of such symptoms of lactose intolerance as cramps and diarrhea. Fewer symptoms occur when milk is consumed along with other solid foods in a meal than when milk is taken alone. This may be due to delayed gastric emptying caused by hyperosmolality of the meal with the solid foods. Or the solid foods consumed along with the milk may slow the rate of intestinal transit and decrease the rate of colonic fermentation. Although ice cream and ice milk result in lactose malabsorption in susceptible individuals, they are better tolerated than milk (6–9).

For a given amount of available lactase activity and a given load of lactose, the longer the time over which the substrate is presented to the absorptive surface, the greater the likelihood of adequate hydrolysis and therefore better tolerance. The rate at which substrate is delivered to the stomach or small intestine can be important. For example, tube feedings delivered by continuous drip enhance the chances for carbohydrate hydrolysis and absorption, as indicated by breath hydrogen tests, when compared with bolus feedings (7).

2. LACTOSE FORMULAS IN PROTEIN-ENERGY MALNUTRITION

Concern has been expressed over the use of regular milk supplements in the feeding of children at risk for undernutrition (10). Milk based formulas and supplements have been used extensively in the past in the rehabilitation of severely malnourished children with protein-energy malnutrition. Because reduced lactase activity frequently accompanies protein-calorie malnutrition, there has been concern that recovery formulas based on cow's milk will worsen diarrhea, abdominal cramps, and overall nutritional status. A second concern is related to the possibility of impaired absorption of such essential nutrients as dietary protein, fat, and calcium, induced by the malabsorption of lactose.

As a result, low-lactose milk has been given as an alternative to lactose-containing milk products. In a 45-day trial, one group of investigators compared a lactose-containing cow's milk with the same formula pretreated with beta-galactosidase to hydrolyze the lactose. No differences were found in the rate of growth, body protein repletion, or absorption of nutrients, nor in the incidence of abdominal discomfort or diarrhea (2, 9).

Another study demonstrated that low dose milk supplements can be well tolerated when consumed with other foods by certain lactose malabsorbers. Before calling for the avoidance of milk by groups in whom the incidence of lactose intolerance is high, a milk tolerance test should be done. A more recent study confirms the finding that there are no adverse effects from milk feeding in protein-energy nutrition, that the lactose has little effect on the degree of calcium absorption, and that in fact the milk supplements are a necessary part of treatment (10–12).

3. FERMENTED MILK PRODUCTS

Some fermented milk products, such as aged Swiss and cheddar cheeses, contain less lactose than fresh milk products. This is because of the separation of the whey (which contains most of the lactose) from the curds in manufacturing. Additionally, some of the lactose is converted to lactic acid. Fermented forms of milk that have only a small amount of their lactose converted to lactic acid are yogurt and buttermilk (13).

Of all the fermented milk products recommended, yogurt (which is produced by fermentation of milk with *Lactobacillus bulgaricus* and *Streptococcus thermophilus*) has shown the most promise. Some individuals with lactose intolerance who cannot take milk can con-

sume lactose-containing yogurt with impunity. The lactose in yogurt seems to be better absorbed than that in other foods because the bacteria responsible for yogurt fermentation release a form of lactase called beta-galactosidase in the stomach. However, beta-galactosidase levels in yogurt vary significantly, owing to differences in pH and microbial cell integrity (3, 4, 14, 15). According to one researcher, yogurt does not increase or alter the residual lactase enzyme in the small intestine. Its improved absorption is due to an intraluminal process (16).

One study compared the lactase activity and/or lactose absorbability of yogurt; lactose-hydrolyzed milk prepared with LactAid enzyme (LactAid, Sugar Lo Co., Pleasantville, N.J.); a tablet form of lactase enzyme (LactAid); and sweet acidophilus milk. Yogurt showed the highest lactase activity. In contrast, cultured buttermilk and sweet acidophilus milk do not significantly change the extent of lactose digestion in lactase-deficient adults. The beta-galactosidase in acidophilus milk appears not to be available for lactose digestion (14, 17, 18).

If lactose from fresh yogurt is absorbed in the small intestine, as indicated by low hydrogen production, determined by the breath hydrogen test, this absorption occurs only in the lower part of the organ, where beta-galactosidase activity may be stimulated by progressively increasing pH levels. Flavored yogurts, which have added fruit, sweeteners, and flavorings, are less well tolerated than unflavored yogurts. Current methods for the production of frozen yogurts produce a product with no microbial beta-galactosidase that is not well tolerated by lactase deficient individuals. Pasteurized yogurt is not well tolerated, owing to the destruction of the organism that produces the beta-galactosidase. Of a group of several yogurts, the Dannon brand has the highest lactase activity (14, 15, 19, 20).

A dried, low-fat milk, fermented by

yogurt microorganisms, has been used successfully as an alternative to fresh yogurt in countries where it is difficult to store foods at the low temperature required for fresh yogurt (21).

4. LACTOSE-HYDROLYZED MILK AND LACTASE ENZYME INGESTION

Lactose-hydrolyzed milk (milk incubated with the lactase enzyme) is better tolerated than regular milk in certain populations. There is some evidence that under certain conditions, lactase enzymes which are added to milk just before mealtime also effectively reduce lactose maldigestion. Much more of the lactose appears to be hydrolyzed at higher temperatures of incubation, i.e., 37° C to 38° C. The use of higher temperatures is impractical, because milk must be stored at lower temperatures to maintain its bacteriological safety (22–24).

Another report has also demonstrated the efficacy of oral enzyme-replacement therapy. The beta-galactosidase Lactrase (Kremers, Urban Co., Milwaukee), taken orally in capsule form in high doses, after milk digestion, temporarily reversed lactose malabsorption, as evidenced by improvement in symptoms and in results of breath hydrogen tests. Another study evaluated the use of Lactrase just before lactose ingestion and demonstrated a dose-dependent reduction in breath hydrogen excretion, bloating, and flatus (25, 26).

INDICATIONS FOR USE

1. LACTOSE-RESTRICTED VERSUS LACTOSE-FREE DIET

Restriction of dietary lactose rather than its total exclusion is usually indicated in most forms of lactose intolerance. Lactase deficiency is rarely absolute, and individuals vary in their tolerance of lactose-containing foods. Tolerance may decrease with age and degree of gastrointestinal disease. Treatment of the more severe manifestations of congenital intolerance—e.g., the Durand syndrome—may require adherence to a lactose-free diet indefinitely (27). Lactose intolerance occurring secondary to intestinal damage or surgery may be improved with rigorous therapy of the underlying disorder that causes the damage. Therapy that is effective to the point that there is mucosal and brush-border restoration may permit elimination of all lactose restrictions.

2. POPULATION GROUPS AFFECTED

Lactose intolerance occurs in Italians and in Chinese in significant numbers (28, 29). Current evidence indicates that low intestinal lactase levels are probably present in the majority of adults in most population groups in the world, except northern European Caucasians. Most probably inherited as an autosomal recessive trait, lactose nonpersistence is particularly prevalent in adult white persons of Western European origin and in a majority of Asians, African and American blacks, and Mediterraneans.

3. ENVIRONMENTAL FACTORS

Such environmental factors as diet, nutrition, and subclinical intestinal disease are also important determinants in some patients. Lactase is the disaccharidase most sensitive to intestinal damage and is uniformly depressed in intestinal disease (30).

POSSIBLE ADVERSE REACTIONS

See lactose-free diet.

CONTRAINDICATIONS

There are none if the diet is properly planned. The use of lactose-hydrolyzed milk in which much of the lactose has been converted to glucose and galactose may, however, be contraindicated in uncontrolled diabetes mellitus because of the high free glucose content, especially if taken without solid food to delay gastric emptying. Lactose-hydrolyzed milk is contraindicated in infants with galactosemia because of its high level of galactose. It is also contraindicated in severely affected infants with congenital forms of lactase deficiency, who should be following a lactose-free, as opposed to a lactose-restricted, diet.

CLINICAL ASSESSMENT

For individuals who do not have the more severe congenital form of the disorder, it should be ascertained whether the disorder is primary, or secondary and reversible. A secondary form is due to a disease that adversely affects the intestinal mucosa wherein lies the lactase enzyme; this may occur, for example, in celiac disease, postgastric surgery, or gastroenteritis. Through diet history and review of lactose tolerance and breath hydrogen test results, it should be determined how much milk or lactose-containing foods can be tolerated by the patient without provoking symptoms. In some cases, giving milk and milk-containing foods in smaller, divided doses improves tolerance.

In a hospital setting, nursing notes should be reviewed for objective changes in such symptoms as the incidence of abdominal cramps and the frequency, consistency, and color of stools prior to nutritional intervention and then periodically after the intervention of a lactose-restricted diet, to determine the outcome of the treatment.

BIOCHEMICAL ASSESSMENT

Biochemical parameters of calcium nutriture, for example as serum total calcium and serum alkaline phosphatase, should be priorities in patients diagnosed later in life, who may have been self-limiting their consumption of milk without assuring an adequate calcium intake.

ASSESSMENT OF POTENTIAL DRUG INTERACTIONS

Any drug documented to cause severe gastrointestinal irritation (e.g., methotrexate), used in significant doses over a length of time, may provoke a secondary lactose intolerance. In patients with other primary conditions who suddenly present with abdominal cramps and bulky, frothy, light-colored acid diarrhea, gastrointestinal side effects of their medications should be reviewed as possible causative agents.

IMPLEMENTATION AND EDUCATION

The majority of individuals with lactase non-persistence can consume small amounts of milk without any symptoms. Limiting milk to 4-oz. portions with meals and increasing the total number of servings may help to improve tolerance in individuals who cannot tolerate an 8-oz. portion. Tolerance can also be improved by ingesting a meal that delays gastric emptying, such as milk, cornflakes, and a hard-boiled egg. The use of lactose-hydrolyzed milk or the addition of beta-galactosidases to milk at mealtime permits liberalization of the diet (5, 23).

Education of these patients should include lactose-free and lactose-restricted shopping guides, a list of lactose-containing drugs for severely affected individuals, and supermarket training in how to scrutinize labels for hidden sources of lactose. Lactose-free cookery should be included in diet counseling (31).

PRIORITIES FOR QUALITY ASSURANCE

In addition to the breath hydrogen test, the need for a lactose-restricted diet may be confirmed by a standardized milk tolerance test, which provides a more physiologically appropriate load than the traditional lactose tolerance test and which is not based merely on the body's response to an aqueous solution of lactose (5, 11).

MENU PLANNING

See lactose-free diet.

REFERENCES

1. Scrimshaw, N. S., and Murray, E. B.: The acceptability of milk and milk products in populations with a high prevalence of lactose intolerance. Am J Clin Nutr 48 (Supp):1083, 1988.
2. Greenburger, N. J.: Diagnostic approach to the patient with a chronic diarrheal disorder. Dis Month 36 (3):1990.
3. Newcomer, A., and McGill, D.: Clinical importance of lactase deficiency. N Engl J Med 310:42, 1984.
4. Martini, M., Bollweg, G., et al.: Lactose digestion by yogurt beta-galactosidase: Influence of pH and microbial cell integrity. Am J Clin Nutr 45:432, 1987.
5. Solomons, N., Guerrero, A., and Torun, B.: Dietary manipulation of postprandial colonic lactose fermentation. I. Effect of solid foods in a meal. Am J Clin Nutr 41:199, 1985.
6. Sategna-Guidetti, C., Cruto, E., and Capobianco, P.: Breath hydrogen excretion after lactose and whole milk ingestion. J Clin Gastroenterol 11:287, 1989.
7. Saavedra, J. M., and Perman, J. A.: Current concepts in lactose malabsorption and intolerance. Ann Rev Nutr 9:475, 1989.
8. Martini, M., and Saviano, D.: Reduced intolerance symptoms from lactose consumed during a meal. Am J Clin Nutr 47:57, 1988.
9. Martini, M., Smith, D., and Savaiano, D.: Lactose digestion from flavored and frozen yogurts, ice milk, and ice cream by lactase-deficient persons. Am J Clin Nutr 46:636, 1987.
10. Brown, K., Khatun, M., et al.: Nutritional consequences of low dose milk supplements consumed by lactose malabsorbing children. Am J Clin Nutr 33:1054, 1980.
11. DeVilliers, F.: A standardized milk tolerance test. J Clin Gastroenterol 9:320, 1987.
12. Caballero, B., Solomons, N., et al.: Calcium metabolism in children recovering from severe protein-energy malnutrition. J Pediatr Gastroenterol Nutr 5:740, 1986.
13. Gallagher, C., Molleson, A., and Caldwell, J.: Lactose intolerance and fermented dairy products. J Am Diet Assoc 65:418, 1974.
14. Onwulata, C. I., Ramkishan-Rao, D., and Vankinemi, P.: Relative efficiency of yogurt, sweet acidophilus milk, lactose-hydrolyzed milk, and a commercial lactase tablet in alleviating lactose maldigestion. Am J Clin Nutr 49:1233, 1989.
15. Wystock, D., and DiPalma, J.: All yogurts are not created equal. Am J Clin Nutr 47:454, 1988.
16. Lerebours, E., Adam, C. N., et al.: Yogurt and fermented-then-pasteurized milk: Effects of short-term and long-term ingestion on lactose absorption and mucosal lactase activity in lactase-deficient subjects. Am J Clin Nutr 49:823, 1989.
17. Savaiano, D., ElAnour, A., et al.: Lactose malabsorption from yogurt, pasteurized yogurt, sweet acidophilus milk and cultured milk in lactase deficient individuals. Am J Clin Nutr 40:1219, 1984.
18. Payne, D., Welsh, J., et al.: Effectiveness of milk products in dietary management of lactose malabsorption. Am J Clin Nutr 34:2711, 1980.
19. Food sensitivity and dairy products. Dairy Council Digest 60 (5), 1989.
20. Pochart, G., Dewit, O., et al.: Viable starter culture, beta-galactosidase activity, and lactose in duodenum after yogurt ingestion in lactase deficient humans. Am J Clin Nutr 49:828, 1989.
21. Gendrel, D., Dupont, C., et al.: Feeding lactose intolerant children with a powdered fermented milk. J Pediatr Gastroenterol Nutr 10:44, 1990.
22. Lisker, R., Aguilar, L., et al.: Double blind study of milk lactose intolerance in a group of rural and urban children. Am J Clin Nutr 33:1049, 1980.
23. Barillas, C., and Solomons, N.: Effective reduction of lactose maldigestion in preschool children by direct addition of beta-galactosidases to milk at mealtime. Pediatrics 79:786, 1987.
24. Schneider, R. E., Corona, E., et al.: Effect of temperature on the lactose hydrolytic capacity of *Kluyveromyces lactis*. Am J Clin Nutr 51:197, 1990.
25. Moskovitz, M., Curtis, C., and Gavaler, J.: Does oral enzyme replacement therapy reverse intestinal lactose malabsorption? Am J Gastroenterol 82:632, 1987.
26. DiPalma, J. A., and Collins, M. S.: Enzyme replacement for lactose malabsorption using a beta-D-galactosidase. J Clin Gastroenterol Nutr 11:290, 1989.
27. Holzel, A.: Sugar malabsorption and sugar intolerance in childhood. Proc Roy Soc Med 61:1095, 1968.
28. Ting, C. W., Hwang, B., and Wu, T. C.: Developmental changes of lactose malabsorption in normal Chinese children: A study using breath hydrogen test with a physiological dose of lactose. J Pediatr Gastroenterol Nutr 7:848, 1988.
29. Ceriani, R., Zuccato, E., et al.: Lactose malabsorption and recurrent abdominal pain in Italian children. J Pediatr Gastroenterol Nutr 7:852, 1988.
30. Gray, G. M.: Intestinal disaccharidase deficiencies and glucose-galactose malabsorption. In Stanbury, J. B., Wyngaarden, J. B., et al.: The metabolic basis of inherited disease. 5th ed. New York: McGraw-Hill, 1983.
31. Beaudette, T., and Strickland, R.: Lactose intolerance. Chicago: American Dietetic Association, 1985.

23.

GALACTOSE-FREE DIET

DEFINITIONS

1. GALACTOSE-FREE DIET

A diet free of all sources of the monosaccharide galactose (1). The diet is also lactose free, because galactose is a component of the disaccharide lactose.

2. GALACTOSEMIA

Elevated levels of blood galactose, caused most commonly by galactose-1-phosphate uridyl transferase deficiency.

PURPOSE OF THE DIET

The diet is intended to manage galactosemia and prevent or minimize the following (1–14).

1. ACUTE PROBLEMS

Vomiting, failure to thrive, liver damage, and death due to *E. coli* sepsis.

2. CHRONIC PROBLEMS

Mental retardation, visual and perceptual learning disorders, cataract formation, and premature ovarian failure.

EFFECTS OF THE DIET

The galactose-free diet causes a striking regression of all signs and symptoms of the toxicity syndrome. Liver abnormalities, galactosuria, proteinuria, and aminoaciduria disappear. Cataracts regress, and those visible with the ophthalmoscope may revert to small lesions seen only on slit lamp examination (5).

The degree of mental development depends on the level of dietary compliance and the age of the child at the time of institution of the diet. Children treated within the first month of life maintain the highest level of intellectual progress, with a mean IQ of 95. When the diet is not started before 1 month, IQ levels are lower (2, 6, 9).

PHYSIOLOGY, FOODS, AND NUTRIENTS

1. ENZYME AND TRANSPORT DISORDERS

Galactose metabolism is driven by several enzymes. The lack of adequate activity of any one of them renders an individual unable to convert galactose to glucose in a normal way, resulting in galactosemia. The various enzyme deficiencies are inherited as an autosomal recessive trait. Each has a specific set of clinical manifestations, requiring dietary treatment. The forms are as follows (1–18):

- Galactose-1-phosphate uridyl transferase deficiency galactosemia
- Galactokinase deficiency galactosemia
- Galactose-4-epimerase deficiency galactosemia

The term *galactosemia* is usually used to refer to galactose-1-phosphate uridyl transferase deficiency, which is the most common. This is the form for which newborns are screened.

2. MENTAL DEVELOPMENT

Mental retardation may be caused by an altered uridine diphosphate (UDP) galactose; by a UDP-glucose ratio that may influence cellular oxidation by neural cells and myelin formation; by inhibition of brain protein synthesis by galactose and galactose-1-phosphate; or by increased levels of galactitol in the brain.

Phosphatidylinositol is an integral constituent of cell membranes, and galactitol inhibits the incorporation of inositol into essential lipids of neural cell membranes. Inhibition of synthesis of nerve cell membrane (myelin) may lead to permanently altered function.

The measurement of IQ alone does not reveal the entire mental picture. Many children with normal IQs have learning disabilities involving spatial relationships and mathematics and are 1 or more grades behind in school. Behavioral problems occur frequently, owing to a short attention span. Psychological problems that have been demonstrated include inadequate drive, shyness and withdrawal, and speech and language deficits. According to one group of investigators, it is the lack of UDP galactose that causes ovarian failure, speech defects, and retarded mental functioning. The level of visual perceptual skills achieved also correlates well with the degree of dietary control. In a group of children treated between the ages of 4 and 11 months, not one child had normal visual perceptual skills (19, 20).

INDICATIONS FOR USE

1. GALACTOSE-1-PHOSPHATE URIDYL TRANSFERASE DEFICIENCY

Galactosemia is inherited as an autosomal recessive trait resulting from a lack of any 1 of 4 distinct enzymes involved in the metabolism of galactose. Galactose-1-phosphate uridyl transferase deficiency is the classical form of the disorder, resulting from the lack of the enzyme of the same name, which converts galactose-1-phosphate to uridine diphosphate galactose. Because the missing enzyme cannot be replaced, treatment is based upon exclusion of dietary galactose (5).

The term *galactosemia* refers to a toxicity syndrome with clinical manifestations that are the result of exposure to a high blood-galactose environment. The abnormal accumulation of galactose metabolites derived from alternative pathways of galactose metabolism causes characteristic changes in tissues. The ability to form glucose-1-phosphate is severely impaired, with a corresponding tissue accumulation of galactose-1-phosphate (1, 4–7, 13, 15, 21).

If the diet is not instituted soon after birth, affected infants may present with failure to thrive, vomiting, hepatomegaly, jaundice, brain damage, or death. In the lens of the eye, the conversion of galactose to its alcohol galactitol causes osmotic changes that result in cataracts. Hyperbilirubinemia is present, owing to toxic injury to liver cells by galactose-1-phosphate, delayed maturation of glucuronyl transferase, mild hemolysis, and bleeding. Prolonged neonatal jaundice at 4 to 10 days is common. Bleeding diatheses, *E. coli* sepsis, and shock are catastrophic events that may occur during the neonatal period. The most life-threatening complication is sepsis due to *E. coli* bacteria (1–10, 12, 15, 22).

There are several variant forms of galactosemia, detected by electrophoresis.

A. Duarte Variant In the past, individuals with the Duarte variant of transferase deficiency galactosemia were thought to have a benign form of the disorder in which dietary management is not necessary. More recently the diet has been recommended, at least during the first few months of life, as a result of documented abnormalities arising from high blood-galactose levels in affected individuals and in heterozygous carriers of the Duarte variant gene (23–25).

B. Black Variant A variant of the transferase disorder occurs in blacks, characterized by an absence of the enzyme transferase in red blood cells. A unique feature of this variant is the ability to metabolize significant amounts of galactose despite the absence of the enzyme in red blood cells. Unlike other transferase-deficient patients, these patients have some residual amount of transferase enzyme in their visceral tissues, which may be just enough to prevent the symptoms of toxicity (19).

C. Indiana Variant, German Variant, and Heterozygous Carriers Individuals with the Indiana and German variants require a galactose-free diet. It has been suggested that heterozygous carriers of the galactokinase gene are at risk for the development of cataracts. Carriers should be evaluated as to the need for dietary management, along with anyone with increased serum levels of aldose reductase, the enzyme which converts galactose to galactitol in the lens of the eye (26, 27).

Two other variants are the Los Angeles variant, in which galactose metabolism is normal, and the Chicago variant, which requires diet restrictions (19).

2. GALACTOKINASE DEFICIENCY

Galactokinase is the enzyme required for the first step in the metabolism of galactose: the conversion of galactose to galactose-1-phosphate. Cataracts may be the first and only clinical finding. Mental retardation has been reported in this disorder, although the extent and nature of neurological involvement in galactokinase deficiency is controversial (5, 14, 19, 28).

3. URIDINE DIPHOSPHATE GALACTOSE-4-EPIMERASE DEFICIENCY

Lack of this enzyme, which converts uridine diphosphate galactose to uridine diphosphate glucose, produces the disorder also known as epimerase deficiency galactosemia. It was initially thought to be a benign disorder, because a report of 3 affected families described healthy individuals with normal galactose tolerance. We now know that there are 2 forms of epimerase deficiency; the more common is benign, and the rarer produces both clinical and biochemical manifestations (16–19).

The benign form involves only red and white blood cells without deranged metabolism in other tissues. It can be detected by screening procedures that assay red cell galactose-1-phosphate. The rarer form, which responds to a galactose-free diet, presents with symptoms resembling transferase deficiency. In contrast to the benign form, there is a loss of enzyme activity in the liver and other tissues. A lack of this enzyme also affects the synthesis of uridine diphosphate galactose, which is a constituent of gangliosides in the brain. Some dietary galactose is necessary for the formation of the uridine diphosphate galactose, which is essential in certain metabolic processes (18, 19).

The treatment of this disorder may require a different strategy from that of transferase deficiency. It is theorized that epimerase is required for the formation of UDP galactose from UDP glucose. In this case, a complete absence of galactose from the diet and the absence of the endogenous formation of UDP galactose would result in the inability to form complex carbohydrates and galactolipids that require UDP galactose for synthesis. Thus, the focus of therapy would not be complete exclusion of dietary galactose, but rather the provision of just enough galactose (1.5 to 4 g per day) for the synthesis of galactoprotein and galactolipids without provoking toxicity symptoms. This theory needs verification in clinical trials (18, 19).

4. PREGNANT WOMEN WITH GALACTOSEMIA

The diet may be indicated in pregnant women with galactosemia, not only for the mother, but for the fetus, who may be homozygous for the disease. It may also be indicated in women who have already produced one child with galactosemia. Prenatal diagnosis can be performed by direct enzyme assay of galactose-1-phosphate uridyl transferase on amniotic culture cells. One case has also been diagnosed by chorionic villi sampling. Unfortunately, placing heterozygous females on a galactose-restricted diet has not brought about decreased levels of galactose-1-phosphate in the fetus, possibly because of endogenous production of galactose-1-phosphate by the fetus (29–35).

5. DURATION OF DIET THERAPY

One report, which promotes a relaxed attitude toward dietary treatment in school-age children in order to promote social acceptability, is not based on properly controlled clinical trials. Because there is evidence that the abnormalities of galactosemia do not improve with age, dietary restrictions should be lifelong (19, 21, 27, 36).

POSSIBLE ADVERSE REACTIONS

Some studies indicate that growth and development may be subnormal for certain groups of patients if the diet is not skillfully planned and implemented (5).

CONTRAINDICATIONS

None, provided the proper diagnosis is made.

CLINICAL ASSESSMENT

Clinical determinations such as height, weight, growth rates, midarm muscle circumference estimates, and other anthropometric measurements are tools useful to the dietitian in assessing the effect of diet on growth and development. Poor dietary control is associated with poor growth. Physical or developmental problems may be related to deficiencies

of protein, calories, and other critical nutrients (19).

Prior to discharge following the first admission, parents of children with galactosemia should meet with the clinical nutritionist specializing in inborn errors of metabolism and should be taught all the details needed to accurately record food intake over a 3-day period. Recall booklets should be given to patients before each checkup. These should be subjected to computerized nutrient analysis and evaluated for nutritional adequacy.

BIOCHEMICAL ASSESSMENT

1. DIAGNOSIS

The diagnosis is suggested by the detection of galactose in the blood or urine. The finding of a reducing substance in urine that does not react with glucose oxidase reagents such as Clinistix is consistent with the presence of galactose. An assay of red blood cell enzyme activity provides definitive diagnosis of transferase deficiency galactosemia, galactokinase deficiency galactosemia, or epimerase deficiency galactosemia. In most states, newborns are screened by measuring activity of the transferase enzyme. Patients with a positive Beutler and a positive E. coli bacteriophage test should have all the lactose and galactose removed from their diet while enzyme diagnosis and family workup proceed. Both the patient and the family should be evaluated for genotype and form of impaired enzyme activity (5, 22).

2. DIETARY MONITORING

For monitoring dietary compliance, determination of erythrocyte galactose-1-phosphate levels is the preferred parameter as well as an important quality control measure. The diet must maintain acceptable limits of red blood cell galactose-1-phosphate while meeting nutrient needs for normal growth and development. Red blood cell galactose-1-phos-

phate levels range from 10 to 100 mg/dL in untreated individuals, less than 5 mg/dL in treated individuals, and less than 1 mg/dL in normal individuals (5, 15, 36).

ASSESSMENT OF POTENTIAL DRUG INTERACTIONS

Because galactosemia is not treated with drugs, there are no documented drug-nutrient interactions except for the inadvertent ingestion of galactose or galactose-containing lactose fillers used in medications and in vitamin and mineral supplements. While it may be necessary to provide the child with a supplement to ensure the adequacy of nutrient intake, this should only be done if it is certain that the product contains no galactose. The pharmacist should be consulted as to the galactose content of medications.

IMPLEMENTATION AND EDUCATION

1. SPECIAL FORMULAS

Human milk contains 6% to 8% lactose, cow's milk contains 3% to 4%, and many infant proprietary formulas contain 7%. Milk intake must therefore be replaced by special formulas such as Nutramigen (Mead Johnson), Pregestimil (Mead Johnson), Alimentum (Ross Laboratories), Isomil (Ross Laboratories), and Prosobee (Mead Johnson). Nutramigen, Pregestimil, and Alimentum are casein hydrolysates. Because casein is made from milk, it may contain small amounts of lactose as a contaminant, but this does not compromise the efficacy of the product in cases of galactosemia. When a baby is severely ill with failure to thrive, Nutramigen or Pregestimil may be preferable, but once good weight gain is achieved, a less expensive soy formula may be used (5, 22).

2. CORRELATION WITH THE LACTOSE-FREE DIET

The composition of the galactose-free

diet is similar to that of the lactose-free diet. All foods excluded on a lactose-free diet are also eliminated from the galactose-free diet. Fermented dairy products and aged cheese are not completely lactose free and should not be used on the galactose free diet. Special milks in which the lactose has been reduced by enzymes or bacterial fermentation still contain galactose and should be avoided.

3. SPECIFIC FOODS

Such organ meats as liver, pancreas, and brain contain galactose. Peas have been documented to contain free galactose. Sugar beets, peas, lima beans, and soybeans contain the oligosaccharides raffinose and stachyose; these are alpha galactosides, which may release galactose upon digestion. Formulas containing soy protein isolate have about 14 mg galactose per liter in the form of raffinose and stachyose. However, humans lack the necessary enzymes for the hydrolysis of raffinose and stachyose. Therefore, while peas are excluded from the diet, sugar beets, lima beans, and soybeans are permitted (1, 3, 21, 37).

Any food or drug to which lactose has been added in processing must be avoided. Monosodium glutamate and soy sauce may have lactose added as extenders (3). Also, because galactose may be released during fermentation in the production of soy sauce, only unfermented soy sauce should be used. Bread often contains unsafe ingredients (except Italian or French breads made without milk). Unless the consumer can be positively assured by the manufacturer that the product is free of lactose and galactose, it should be excluded from the diet.

4. NUTRITIONAL COUNSELING

Family members require training in food diary techniques and in dietary-galactose surveillance, particularly in the detection of galactose from less obvious food sources. Parents should be instructed to

MENU PLANNING

FOOD LIST FOR THE GALACTOSE-FREE DIET[a]

Food group	Foods allowed	Foods excluded
Milk and milk products	None	Breast milk, cow's milk, goat's milk, or any other animal milk in any form; whole, low-fat, nonfat (skim), evaporated, dried, or condensed milk or buttermilk; most brands of imitation or filled milk; yogurt, frozen yogurt; cream, sour cream; ice cream, ice milk, milk shakes; all types of cheese
Milk substitutes	Galactose-free infant formulas, e.g., Nutramigen (Mead Johnson), Pregestimil (Mead Johnson), Alimentum (Ross Laboratories), Isomil (Ross Laboratories), and Prosobee (Mead Johnson); nondairy creamers free of milk or milk derivative	Milk-based infant formulas; nondairy products containing lactose, galactose, lactostearin, casein, sodium caseinate, curds, whey, dry milk solids
Beverages	Carbonated soft drinks, fruit juices, fruit drinks, punch; regular and instant coffee and tea; plain alcoholic beverages	Chocolate drinks made with milk chocolate or with milk; cocoa mix, malt or malted drink mixes; premixed alcoholic drinks with prohibited ingredients
Breads and cereals	Any that do not contain milk or milk products; rice, pasta; bread, crackers, hot and cold cereals (read labels carefully)	Breads, rolls, crackers, or cereals made with milk or milk products; prepared mixes such as muffins, biscuits, waffles, and pancakes
Meat and meat substitutes	Any meat, fish, or poultry (except liver, pancreas, and brain) that has been processed without milk and milk products; eggs	Creamed or breaded meat, fish, or poultry; processed meats, e.g., luncheon meats or hot dogs, containing prohibited ingredients; liver, pancreas, brain; eggs prepared with milk or milk products; all types of cheese

(continued)

Vegetables	Any vegetable (except green peas) that has not been processed with lactose or prepared with milk or milk products	Green (English) peas; creamed, breaded, or buttered vegetables; canned or frozen vegetables to which lactose has been added during processing; vegetables with cheese, butter, or sauces containing dairy products or lactose; commercial french fries, instant mashed potatoes, chips to which lactose has been added during processing
Fruits	All fresh, canned or frozen fruits that are not processed with lactose	Any canned or frozen fruit processed with lactose
Desserts	Fruit ices, gelatin, angel food cake; homemade cakes, pies, and cookies using allowed ingredients; homemade pudding made with milk substitute or water; Popsicles, fruit slushes	Most commercial cakes, cookies, and dessert mixes; custards, ice cream, ice milk, sherbet, yogurt
Fats	Oils, shortenings, and dressings that do not contain milk or milk products; bacon, lard, margarines made without milk solids (some diet margarines and kosher margarines)	Butter, cream, sour cream, cream cheese, dressings containing milk or milk products, margarines containing milk solids
Soups	Clear soups, vegetable soups, consommés, and "cream" soups made with allowed milk substitutes	Regular cream soups, commercially prepared soups that contain lactose
Miscellaneous	Nuts, peanut butter, unbuttered popcorn, olives, pickles, relishes, mushrooms, tomato sauce, catsup, mustard, vinegar, Tabasco sauce, Worcestershire sauce, monosodium glutamate, pure spices, herbs, condiments, flavorings, artificial extracts	Some spice brands (read labels carefully)

(continued)

look not only for milk, butter, cream, or cheese in foods but also for other forms of milk that contain lactose, such as non-fat dry milk, whey, or casein. Because manufacturers often switch ingredients without warning, the importance of label reading cannot be overemphasized (22).

The entire family should be involved in nutritional counseling sessions with the goal of gradually developing in the child skills that will enable him or her to assume control of the diet. By the age of 3, the child should develop some sense of responsibility for his or her own diet (4, 15).

Successful control and proper development require periodic and timely follow-up visits in which food diaries are assessed by the dietitian, not only for the absence of galactose but also for the presence of adequate amounts of essential nutrients.

5. CALCIUM SUPPLEMENTS

Calcium supplements may be necessary because of decreased intake of calcium-rich foods. This is especially true in the older child who no longer consumes infant formula.

PRIORITIES FOR QUALITY ASSURANCE

The first priority is to monitor the effectiveness of nutritional intervention in meeting the goals of the diet. Serial anthropometric measurements should be a part of the patient's nutritional profile to be used in the monitoring of growth and development.

Biochemical monitoring of blood galactose levels is important in evaluation of the results of the treatment program.

Sugar, honey, corn syrup, pure sugar candy, cotton candy, jelly, chewing gum, unsweetened cocoa, unsweetened cooking chocolate, semisweet chocolate	Toffee, peppermints, butterscotch, caramels, molasses candies, milk chocolate, cocoa with skim milk powder added
Foods and beverages, including carbonated drinks, presweetened with artificial sweeteners	Powdered artificial sweeteners (often contain lactose as a filler)
Wheat germ, unsweetened coconut	
Gravy made with water	Gravy or sauces made with milk or milk products

Source: Adapted from Roberts, S. R., and Meyer, B. A. (38).

Daily Meal Plan

Galactose-free formula	24–32 oz. for infants
	16–24 oz. for children
Meat, fish, poultry, eggs, peanut butter, nuts or legumes	4–6 oz.
Fruits and vegetables, including	4 servings
citrus, tomatoes, pineapple or green peppers	1 serving
dark yellow or dark green leafy vegetables	1 serving
Whole-grain or enriched bread without milk	4 slices or servings

Other foods to be added as desired to meet caloric needs:
• Margarines, oils, and salad dressing without milk
• Soy milk ice creams, to ensure an adequate intake of milk substitutes

SAMPLE MENU FOR THE GALACTOSE-FREE DIET (FOR A CHILD, AGE 4–6)

BREAKFAST	
Orange juice	½ cup
Poached egg	1 large
Toasted French bread	1 slice
Lactose-free margarine	2 tsp.
Oatmeal	½ cup
Galactose-free formula	8 oz.
LUNCH	
Lean hamburger	2 oz.
Lactose-free hamburger bun	1
Tomato, sliced	1 medium
Lettuce	2 leaves
Cooked spinach	⅓ cup
Banana	1 medium
Galactose-free formula	6 oz.

(continued)

DINNER

Sliced roast turkey	2 oz.
Baked potato	1 small
Lactose-free margarine	2 tsp.
Cooked carrots	⅓ cup
Galactose-free formula	6 oz.

EVENING SNACK

Angel food cake	1 slice
Sliced frozen strawberries	½ cup
Galactose-free formula	4 oz.

Approximate Nutrient Analysis

Energy	1,761 kcal
Protein	68.4 g (16% of kcal)
Fat	66.3 g (34% of kcal)
Polyunsaturated fat	16.6 g
Monounsaturated fat	19.2 g
Saturated fat	20.3 g
Cholesterol	294 mg
Carbohydrate	227.8 g (52% of kcal)
Vitamin A	18,136 IU
	2,430 RE
Thiamine	1.54 mg
Riboflavin	1.99 mg
Niacin	23.0 mg
Folate	366 mcg
Vitamin B-12	5.44 mcg
Vitamin B-6	2.33 mg
Vitamin C	212.2 mg
Calcium	867 mg
Phosphorus	1,165 mg
Iron	22.2 mg
Copper	1.72 mg
Zinc	11.6 mg
Magnesium	259 mg
Sodium	1,848 mg
Potassium	3,166 mg

REFERENCES

1. Donnell, G., Bergen, W., and Bergen, N.: Galactosemia. Biochem Med 1:29, 1967.

2. Waggoner, D. D., Buist, N. R. M., and Donnell, G. N.: Long term prognosis in galactosemia: Results of a survey of 350 cases. J Inher Metab Dis 13:802, 1990.

3. Fanning, A.: Dietary treatment of galactosemia and other inherited disorders of carbohydrate metabolism. Top Clin Nutr 2 (3):64, 1987.

4. Cohn, R., and Segal, S.: Galactose metabolism and its regulation. Metabolism 22:627, 1973.

5. Segal, S.: Disorders of galactose metabolism. In Stanbury, J. B., Wyngaarden, J. B., and Frederickson, D. S.: The metabolic basis of inherited disease. 5th ed. New York: McGraw-Hill, 1983.

6. Donnell, G. N., Koch, R., et al.: Clinical aspects of galactosaemia. In Burman, D., Holton, J. B., and Pennock, C. A.: Inherited disorders of carbohydrate metabolism. Lancaster, England: MTP Press, Falcon House, 1980.

7. Koch, R., Acosta, P., Donnell, G., et al.: Nutritional therapy of galactosemia. Clin Pediatr 4:571, 1965.

8. Fishler, K., Koch, R., et al.: Developmental aspects of galactosemia from infancy to childhood. Clin Pediatr 19:38, 1980.

9. Simoons, F. J.: A geographic approach to senile cataracts: Possible links with milk consumption, lactose activity and galactose metabolism. Dig Dis Sci 27:257, 1982.

10. Beutler, E., Matsumotu, F., et al.: Galactokinase deficiency as a cause of cataracts. N Engl J Med 288:1203, 1973.

11. Olanbiwonau, N., McVie, R., et al.: Galactokinase deficiency in twins: Clinical and biochemical studies. Pediatrics 53:314, 1974.

12. Kaufman, F. R., Xu, Y. K., et al.: Correlation of ovarian function with galactose-1-phosphate uridyl transferase levels in galactosemia. J Pediatr 112:754, 1988.

13. Gitzelmann, R., and Hansen, R. G.: Galactose metabolism, hereditary defects and their clinical significance. In Burman, D., Holton, J., and Pennock, C.: Inherited disorders of carbohydrate metabolism. Lancaster, England: MTP Press, Falcon House, 1980.

14. Segal, S., Rutman, J., and Frimpter, G. W.: Galactokinase deficiency and mental retardation. J Pediatr 95:750, 1979.

15. Acosta, P. B., and Elsas, L. J.: Dietary management in inherited metabolic disease: Phenylketonuria, galactosemia, tyrosinemia, homocystinuria, maple syrup urine disease. Atlanta: ACELMU Publishers, 1976.

16. Skalka, H., and Pachal, J.: Presenile cataract formation and decreased activity of galactosemic enzyme. Arch Ophthalmol 98:269, 1980.

17. Gitzelmann, R., Steinmann, B., et al.: Uridine diphosphate galactose-4-epimerase deficiency. Helv Paediatr Acta 31:441, 1976.

18. Holton, J., Gillett, M., et al.: Galactosemia: A new severe variant due to uridine diphosphate galactose-4-epimerase deficiency. Arch Dis Child 56:885, 1982.

19. Segal, S.: Disorders of galactose metabolism. In Scriver, C. R., Beaudet, A. L., et al.: The metabolic basis of inherited disease. 6th ed. New York: McGraw-Hill, 1989.

20. Nu, W. G., Xu, Y. K., et al.: Deficit of uridine diphosphate galactose in galactosemia. J Inher Metab Dis 12:257, 1989.

21. Turner, J. F.: Physiology of pea fruits. Austr J Biol Sci 22:1145, 1969.

22. Elsas, L. J., and Acosta, P.: Nutrition support of inherited metabolic diseases. In Shils, M. E., and Young, V. R.: Modern nutrition in health and disease. 7th ed. Philadelphia: Lea & Febiger, 1988.

23. Cornblath, M., and Schwartz, R.: Disorders of carbohydrate metabolism in infancy. 2d ed. Philadelphia: W. B. Saunders, 1976.

24. Kelly, S.: Significance of the Duarte classical genetic compound. J Pediatr 94:937, 1979.

25. Schwarz, H., Zuppinger, K., et al.: Galactose intolerance in individuals with double heterzygosity for Duarte variant and galactosemia. J Pediatr 100:704, 1982.

26. Chacko, C., Christian, J., and Nadler, H.: Unstable galactose-1-phosphate uridyl transferase: A new variant of galactosemia. J Pediatr 78:454, 1971.

27. Wenz, E., and Mitchell, M.: Galactosemia. In Palmer, S., and Ekvall, S.: Pediatric nutrition in developmental disorders. Springfield, Ill.: Charles C. Thomas, 1978.

28. Xu, Y. K., Ng, W. G., et al.: Uridine nucleotide sugars in erythrocytes of patients with galactokinase deficiency. J Inher Metab Dis 12:445, 1989.

29. Donnell, G. N., Koch, R., and Bergen, W. R.: Observations on results of management of galactosemic patients. In Hsia, D. Y.: Galactosemia. Springfield, Ill.: Charles C. Thomas, 1969.

30. Holton, J. B., and Raymart, C. M.: Prenatal diagnosis of classical galactosemia. In Burman, D., Holton, J., and Pennock, C.: Inherited disorders of carbohydrate metabolism. Lancaster, England: MTP Press, Falcon House, 1980.

31. Mahoney, M.: Prenatal diagnosis of inborn errors of metabolism. Clin Perinatol 6:255, 1979.

32. Elsas, S., and Simpson, J. L.: Amniocentesis. In Milunsky, A.: Genetic disorders of the fetus. New York: Plenum, 1986.

33. Shulman, L. P.: Chorionic villus sampling. Pediatr Ann 18:714, 1989.

34. Irons, M., Levy, H., and Pueschel, S.: Accumulation of galactose-1-phosphate in the galactosemic fetus despite maternal milk avoidance. J Pediatr 107:261, 1985.

35. Sardharwall, K. B., Komrower, G. M., and Schwarz, V.: Pregnancy in classical galactosemia. In Burman, D., Holton, J., and Pennock, C.: Inherited disorders of carbohydrate metabolism. Lancaster, England: MTP Press, Falcon House, 1980.

36. Komrower, G. M.: Galactosemia: Thirty years or the experience of a gen-

eration. J Inher Metab Dis 96 (Supp 2):104, 1982.

37. Gitzelman, R., and Auricchio, S.: The handling of soy alpha-galactosides in a normal and a galactosemia child. Pediatrics 36:231, 1965.

38. Roberts, S. R., and Meyer, B. A.: Living with galactosemia: A handbook for families. Indianapolis: Metabolism Clinic, James Whitcomb Riley Hospital for Children, 1983.

24.

SUCROSE-RESTRICTED DIET

DEFINITIONS

1. SUCROSE-FREE DIET

A diet that eliminates all known sources of sucrose.

2. SUCROSE-RESTRICTED DIET

A diet that excludes all foods containing more than 2% sucrose and limits the intake of other sucrose-containing foods. Depending on food choices, it provides approximately 5 to 15 g of sucrose daily. The sucrose level can be tailored to individual tolerance, and more may be tolerated by older patients than by infants and children.

PURPOSE OF THE DIET

The diet is intended to ameliorate or prevent symptoms of primary or secondary sucrase–alpha-dextrinase (isomaltase) deficiency (1, 2).

EFFECTS OF THE DIET

Symptoms of sucrase-isomaltase deficiency disappear within 24 hours after the diet is instituted (1, 2). Substitution of foods high in fructose for those high in sucrose may have a beneficial effect upon sucrase enzyme activity. Specifically, it has been reported that high-fructose diets result in small increases in enzyme activity of certain patients with sucrase-isomaltase deficiency (1–5).

PHYSIOLOGY, FOODS, AND NUTRIENTS

1. PHYSIOLOGY

Sucrase-isomaltase is an enzyme found in the small-intestinal brush border, which hydrolyzes dietary sucrose as well as some of the products of starch digestion. In the absence of adequate enzyme activity, isomaltose is not metabolized to glucose, and sucrose is not metabolized to glucose and fructose. Gastric emptying is delayed, partially compensating for accelerated duodenal-ileal transit by the action of the undigested sucrose. The osmotic action of the unabsorbed sucrose causes fluid to move into the intestine of the untreated patient. Abdominal distension, cramps, and increased gastrointestinal motility result (6, 7).

In the colon, the undigested sucrose is fermented by bacteria to short-chain fatty acids—e.g., lactic and acetic acids—which increase osmolarity, lower pH, interfere with the reabsorption of fluid, and produce a sour odor. The carbon dioxide and hydrogen produced by the fermentation probably also contribute to bloating and frothy diarrhea (8).

Sucrase-isomaltase deficiency is a genetic defect inherited as an autosomal recessive trait. It is rare (0.2%) in North America but more common in Eskimos and in the population of Greenland (4–10%). Children usually first develop symptoms at about 4 months of age, or at the time when fruits and prepared sweetened foods are added to the diet. Occasionally, sucrase deficiency may be masked early in life and may present later in adult life. The disorder resembles, and may be misdiagnosed as, celiac disease (9–12).

2. FOODS

All foods that naturally contain sucrose or to which it has been added in processing are either eliminated or restricted. Cakes, cookies, pastries, and pies prepared with sucrose are prohibited. Corn syrup should be avoided, because it contains sucrose. Glucose, lactose, or, preferably, fructose are used as substitute sweetening agents. Because of the high sucrose concentration of many fruits and vegetables, only a limited variety are permitted on the diet. When total abstinence from all dietary sucrose is indicated, virtual exclusion of all fruits and vegetables becomes a necessity.

Intolerance to isomaltose, a derivative of starch, is less of a problem in these patients than is sucrose intolerance. Starch is less osmotically active than sucrose, owing to its high molecular weight. The enzyme glucoamylase hydrolyzes the alpha linkages in starch and frees about half of its potentially available glucose for absorption. Amylose yields only a small amount of isomaltose on hydrolysis, and such starches as corn and rice, which contain mainly amylose, are well tolerated. On the other hand, starch with an appreciable amount of amylopectin has a high percentage of nonhydrolyzable linkages, yielding large amounts of isomaltose on digestion, and is not so well tolerated (1, 10, 13–16).

Treatment in the first years of life may require a complete elimination of sucrose, glucose polymers, and starch, but after 2 to 3 years starch intake can be liberalized (7).

3. EXPERIMENTAL THERAPIES

A. Enzyme Replacement Therapy
An enzyme substitute is available that may augment the effect of sucrose restriction. When taken before meals, the

enzyme glucoamylase permits most patients to progress to the more liberal sucrose-restricted diet, as opposed to total abstinence from sucrose. Tolerance to sucrose may increase with age in some patients but not others (1, 16, 17).

B. Baker's Yeast Following a sucrose load of 2-g per kg body weight, 8 children with the disorder were treated with baker's yeast or *Saccharomyces cerevisiae*. The treatment resulted in a 70% reduction in hydrogen production and improvement in or disappearance of symptoms (18).

INDICATIONS FOR USE

1. FLAT SUCROSE TOLERANCE TEST AND LOW STOOL PH

In congenital or acquired sucrase-isomaltase deficiency, sucrose intake must be restricted or eliminated. The diet should be prescribed in the presence of a low stool pH (normal is 6.3 or higher) and a flat sucrose tolerance test, followed within hours by gastrointestinal symptoms and watery, acid diarrhea (1, 2).

2. ABNORMAL BREATH HYDROGEN TEST RESULTS

Hydrogen breath analysis, which is based on the release of hydrogen from malabsorbed sucrose by colonic bacteria, is more reliable than the sucrose tolerance test as a diagnostic tool. In addition, the breath hydrogen test permits the use of a small sucrose dose and reduces the risk of sucrose-related side effects. The test is performed by taking a breath sample followed by administration of 2 g sucrose per kilogram of body weight, or a maximum of 50 g in a 10% aqueous solution. Breath samples are collected every half-hour for 2 to 3 hours (5, 19, 20).

Unless bacteria cultivate the small bowel, hydrogen is normally produced only in the colon. Therefore, abnormally increased concentrations of hydrogen in

the breath indicate that a portion of the ingested carbohydrate being tested has not been absorbed by the small bowel. A rise in hydrogen concentration exceeding 20 parts per million (ppm) above fasting baseline indicates malabsorption. If the increase in hydrogen is less than 10 ppm, the test is considered negative, with values between 10 and 20 being equivocal (19, 20).

3. DEFICIENT ENZYME ACTIVITY IN INTESTINAL BIOPSY TISSUE

The presumptive diagnosis may be confirmed by analysis of intestinal biopsy specimens which reveal deficient enzyme activity. There is no test to identify heterozygotes or gene carriers. Symptoms are indistinguishable from those of lactase deficiency, except that they are provoked by table sugar rather than milk (1, 10).

4. SECONDARY FORMS OF SUCRASE-ISOMALTASE DEFICIENCY

The diet may also be indicated in any disease that involves secondary damage to the small-intestinal mucosa, which decreases the activity of the sucrase-isomaltase enzymes (21). For example, the disorder has been reported as a post-operative complication in Hirschsprung's disease and in severe gastroenteritis.

POSSIBLE ADVERSE REACTIONS

1. POTENTIAL VITAMIN AND MINERAL DEFICIENCIES

Continued use of an unsupplemented sucrose-free diet may provoke deficiencies of ascorbic acid and folic acid, because the diet is inadequate in these nutrients. Deficiencies in thiamine, riboflavin, and iron are also possible. In the late 1970s, 2 carbohydrate-free formulas used for this disorder were withdrawn from the market because of their inadequate chloride content, which led to failure to thrive and to hypochloremic

acidosis. Provided they are consumed in adequate quantities, currently available formulas meet mineral and electrolyte requirements.

2. INTOLERANCE TO CORN SYRUP SOLIDS OR GLUCOSE POLYMERS

A few patients may have difficulty tolerating the corn syrup solids that are used as the base for sucrose-free formula, for 2 reasons. First, corn syrup solids contain some amylopectin with alpha 1–6 linkages, which may require isomaltase. Glucose polymers or oligosaccharides are now the primary source of carbohydrate in "hypoallergenic formulas." Second, the short-chain oligosaccharides in corn syrup solids require alpha glucoamylase. Intestinal mucosal injury (usually reversible) in the individual with sucrase-isomaltase deficiency may provoke maltase-glucoamylase deficiency and a resulting glucose-polymer intolerance (22–24).

CONTRAINDICATIONS

No contraindications have been described among individuals with proven sucrase-isomaltase deficiency. Further research is needed on long-term effects in larger populations.

CLINICAL ASSESSMENT

Assessment of potential physical signs of nutritional deficiencies should be conducted at each follow-up visit. Height, weight, growth curves and midarm muscle circumference measurements in older children will facilitate the monitoring of growth and development. In both initial and follow-up visits, the dietary evaluation should focus on the provision of calories from other sources to replace sucrose-derived calories, as well as the detection of hidden sources of sucrose in the diet. Without some form of regular assessment and reevaluation, affected individuals may become noncompliant and relapse into old symptoms (17).

BIOCHEMICAL ASSESSMENT

Parameters of visceral protein status such as total protein, serum albumin, and total lymphocyte count should be measured regularly as well as stool pH, serum carotene, serum and erythrocyte folate, serum and leukocyte ascorbic acid, hemoglobin, hematocrit, MCV, MCHC, and MCH to ensure that dietary restrictions not only are effective in preventing the acid diarrhea that may occur but also facilitate normal nutritional status, growth, and development.

Patients must be instructed at the time of the breath hydrogen analysis test following the sucrose load to avoid all forms of dietary carbohydrate intake for at least 12 hours before the test in order to prevent false-positive baseline readings (20).

ASSESSMENT OF POTENTIAL DRUG INTERACTIONS

The sucrose content of any drug, whether over-the-counter or prescription, should be identified to prevent inadvertent consumption of significant amounts of sucrose. Patients should be instructed to ask the pharmacist about the sucrose content of any medication.

False-negative breath hydrogen tests for sucrose intolerance will result when the normal intestinal flora is lost, as in acute enteritis, in patients taking antibiotics, or when increased acidity of stool inhibits hydrogen evolution by bacteria.

IMPLEMENTATION AND EDUCATION

Infants with sucrase-isomaltase deficiency should be started on a sucrose-free diet on presentation and gradually advanced to one that is sucrose-restricted after about 1 week (1). Sucrose-containing foods should be added gradually,

MENU PLANNING
FOOD LIST FOR THE SUCROSE-FREE DIET

Food group	Foods allowed	Foods excluded
Beverages	CHO-Free infant formula (Borden's), whole milk, skimmed milk, evaporated milk, buttermilk; diet sodas not sweetened with sucrose	Chocolate milk and drink, condensed milk, flavored yogurt or any beverage made with sweetened fruit; milk shakes, ice cream, sherbet, regularly sweetened carbonated beverages
Meat and meat substitutes	Beef, pork, lamb, veal, chicken, turkey, and other meats and poultry prepared without the addition of sugar (e.g., sucrose or corn syrup); eggs; cream cheese, cottage cheese, other plain unprocessed cheeses; fish	Frankfurter, cold cuts to which sucrose has been added as a filler, commercially prepared infant meat and vegetable dinners to which sucrose has been added; some processed cheese spreads
Vegetables	None	All
Fruits	None	All
Fats	Butter, margarine, vegetable oils, sour cream, cream cheese, cream	Mayonnaise, salad dressings, peanut butter
Desserts	Custard, vanilla pudding made with allowed ingredients without sugar, plain or artificially sweetened yogurt	Commercially prepared gelatin desserts sweetened with sucrose; cakes, cookies, pies, or pastries containing sucrose or wheat germ
Miscellaneous	Aspartame, acesulfame-K, saccharin, sugars and artificial sweeteners that are free of sucrose (e.g., Sweet 'n Low, Sugar Twin, Sucaryl, Equal, Sweet One); pure spices, herbs	Allspice; cane sugar, molasses, honey; most pickles, catsup, carob powder; almonds, chestnuts, coconut and coconut milk, macadamia nuts, pecans; jams, jellies, preserves made with sucrose, corn syrup, invert sugar

Source: Adapted from Ament, M., and Esther, L. (1).

Additional Foods for the Sucrose-Restricted Diet

Food	Number of servings
Fruits and fruit juices containing 1% or less sucrose Gooseberries, loganberries, blackberries, cranberries, currants, lemons, rhubarb, pomegranates	Limit to 3–4 servings (½ cup) daily

(continued)

Fruits and fruit juices containing more than 1% but less than 2% sucrose

Boysenberries, bing cherries, figs, Tokay or Thompson seedless grapes, guava, lime juice, pears, raspberries, strawberries	Limit to 1 serving (½ cup) daily

Vegetables containing 1% or less sucrose

Snap, string, or green beans; cabbage, cauliflower, celery, corn, eggplant, lettuce, potato white, pumpkin, radishes, hubbard, butternut or crookneck squash, tomatoes, tomato juice	Limit to 3–4 servings (½ cup) daily

Grains, cereals, nuts, and miscellaneous items containing 1% or less sucrose

Cornmeal, puffed rice, whole wheat cereals and crackers, patent wheat flour, brown or white rice, macaroni, spaghetti; Kraft mayonnaise, Kraft Salad Bowl Mayonnaise, commercial salad dressings, pecans, honey	As desired

Source: Adapted from Ament, M., Perea, D., and Esther, L. (1).

however, particularly in patients not receiving an oral enzyme substitute.

Isomil SF (Ross Laboratories), Prosobee (Mead Johnson), Pregestimil (Mead Johnson), and Product 3232A (Mead Johnson) are sucrose-free infant formulas that provide 40% of their calories as carbohydrate in the form of corn syrup solids. Corn syrup–intolerant individuals can use a carbohydrate-free soy protein isolate formula called RCF (Ross Laboratories) to which a well-tolerated form of carbohydrate, such as fructose, must be added. Approximately 52 g of a carbohydrate such as fructose must be mixed with 13 oz. formula and 13 oz. water before use (23).

Sucrose is now added to many different commercially prepared foods, especially pureed baby foods. Mothers of sucrose-intolerant children should be instructed to read labels carefully and eliminate less obvious sources of sucrose in the diet. Where appropriate substitutes are not available, it may be necessary to instruct the mother in the homemade preparation of certain pureed foods suitable for infant feeding. Manufacturers

change ingredients often; therefore, label reading should be a regular part of grocery shopping.

When rigid adherence to a sucrose-free diet necessitates the omission of all fruits and vegetables, vitamin and mineral supplements should be provided according to individual needs. References are available to assist the dietitian in guiding patient food selection (25, 26).

PRIORITIES FOR QUALITY ASSURANCE

Medical centers dealing with children need screening programs for inborn errors, including quality-assurance monitors that focus on the sensitivity and specificity of tests used in their protocols. They also need follow-up programs to monitor the effectiveness of treatment.

Periodic food diaries serve as a monitor of nutritional adequacy as well as of compliance.

Screening for clinical signs of nutritional deficiencies should be regularly performed, especially for the major nutrients in omitted foods, such as folic acid and vitamin C.

MENU PLANNING

SAMPLE MENU FOR THE SUCROSE-RESTRICTED DIET (FOR A CHILD, AGE 4–6)

BREAKFAST

Diet cranberry juice cocktail	4 oz.
Puffed rice	1 cup
Low-fat milk	1 cup
Scrambled egg	1 large
Whole wheat toast made with fructose	1 slice
Margarine	1 tsp.

LUNCH

Hamburger	2 oz.
Hamburger bun	1
Sliced tomato	1 medium
Corn kernels	½ cup
Margarine	1 tsp.
Fresh strawberries	1 cup
Plain nonfat yogurt	½ cup
Fructose	2 tsp.
Low-fat milk	½ cup

DINNER

Ribeye steak	3 oz.
Mashed potato	½ cup
Butternut squash	½ cup
Whole wheat bread made with fructose	1 slice
Margarine	1 tsp.
Bing cherries	½ cup
Low-fat milk	1 cup

EVENING SNACK

Whole wheat toast made with fructose	1 slice
Margarine	1 tsp.
Sugar-free pudding	½ cup

Approximate Nutrient Analysis

Energy	1,838 kcal
Protein	98.0 g (21% of kcal)
Fat	72.0 g (35% of kcal)
Polyunsaturated fat	7.9 g
Monounsaturated fat	25.0 g
Saturated fat	25.7 g
Cholesterol	396 mg
Carbohydrate	211.1 g (46% of kcal)
Vitamin A	10,844 IU
	1,523 RE
Thiamine	1.36 mg
Riboflavin	2.55 mg
Niacin	19.4 mg
Folate	173 mcg
Vitamin B-12	7.62 mcg
Vitamin B-6	1.58 mg

(*continued*)

Vitamin C	182.3 mg
Calcium	1,250 mg
Phosphorus	1,520 mg
Iron	13.8 mg
Copper	0.71 mg
Zinc	14.3 mg
Magnesium	256 mg
Sodium	2,318 mg
Potassium	3,822 mg

REFERENCES

1. Ament, M., Perea, D., and Esther, L.: Sucrase-isomaltase deficiency—a frequently misdiagnosed disease. J Pediatr 83:721, 1973.
2. Ament, M., and Bill, A.: Persistent diarrhea due to sucrase-isomaltase deficiency in a postoperative child with Hirschsprung's disease. J Pediatr Surg 8:543, 1973.
3. Greene, H., Stifel, F., and Herman, R.: Dietary stimulation of sucrase in a patient with sucrase-isomaltase deficiency. Lancet 1:651, 1971.
4. Greene, H., Stifel, F., and Herman, R.: Dietary stimulation of sucrase in a patient with sucrase-isomaltase deficiency. Biochem Med 6:409, 1972.
5. Rosenweig, N.: Diet and intestinal enzyme adaptation. Am J Clin Nutr 28:648, 1975.
6. Lloyd, M., and Olsen, W.: A study of the molecular pathology of sucrase-isomaltase deficiency. N Engl J Med 316:438, 1987.
7. Semenza, G., and Auricchio, S.: Small-intestinal disaccharidases. In Scriver, C. R., Beaudet, A. L., et al.: The metabolic basis of inherited disease. 6th ed. New York: McGraw-Hill, 1989.
8. Bayless, T.: Disaccharidase deficiency. J Am Diet Assoc 60:478, 1973.
9. Spiller, R. C., and Silk, D. A.: Malabsorption. In Kinney, J. M., Jeejeebhoy, K. N., et al.: Nutrition and metabolism in patient care. Philadelphia: W. B. Saunders, 1988.
10. Gray, G. M.: Intestinal disaccharidase deficiencies and glucose-galactose malabsorption. In Stanbury, J. B., Wyngaarden, J. B., et al.: The metabolic basis of inherited disease. 5th ed. New York: McGraw-Hill, 1983.
11. Desai, M. B., and Jeejeebhoy, K. N.: Nutrition and diet in management of diseases of the gastrointestinal tract. C. Small intestine. (1) Effects of intestinal disease on digestion and absorption. In Shils, M. E., and Young, V. R.: Modern nutrition in health and disease. 7th ed. Philadelphia: Lea & Febiger, 1988.
12. Neale, G., Clark, M., and Levin, B.: Intestinal sucrose intolerance in adult life. Br Med J 2:1203, 1988.
13. Newcomer, A.: Disaccharidase deficiencies. Mayo Clin Proc 48:648, 1974.
14. Skovbjerg, H., and Krasilnikoff, P.: Maltase-glucoamylase and residual isomaltase in sucrose intolerant patients. J Pediatr Gastroenterol 5:365, 1986.
15. Lindquist, B., and Meeuwise, G.: Diets in disaccharidase deficiency and defective monosaccharide absorption. J Am Diet Assoc 48:307, 1966.
16. Fomon, S. J.: Infant nutrition. 2d ed. Philadelphia: W. B. Saunders, 1974.
17. Kelby, A., Burgess, A., et al.: Sucrase-isomaltase deficiency—a follow up report. Arch Dis Child 53:677, 1978.
18. Harms, H., Bertele-Harms, R., and Bruer-Kleis, D.: Enzyme-substitution therapy with the yeast *Saccharomyces cerevisae* in congenital sucrase-isomaltase deficiency. N Engl J Med 516:1306, 1987.
19. Perman, J., Barr, R., and Watkins, J.: Sucrose malabsorption in children: Noninvasive diagnosis by interval breath hydrogen determination. J Pediatr 93:17, 1978.
20. Kerzner, B., and Sloan, H.: Carbohydrate malabsorption. In Rudolph, A., and Hoffman, J.: Pediatrics. 18th ed. East Norwalk, Conn.: Appleton & Lange, 1987.
21. Herber, R.: Disaccharidase deficiency in health and disease. Calif Med 116:23, 1972.
22. Clark, J., Bullock, L., and Fitzgerald, J.: Dietary fructose in the management of intractable diarrhea of infancy. J Pediatr Gastroenterol 5:81, 1986.
23. Ross Laboratories: Product handbook. Columbus, Ohio: Ross Laboratories, 1989.
24. Lebenthal, E., and Lee, P.: Glucoamylase and disaccharidase activities in normal subjects and in patients with mucosal injury of the small intestine. J Pediatr 97:389, 1980.
25. Hardinge, M., Swarner, J., and Crooks, H.: Carbohydrates in foods. J Am Diet Assoc 46:197, 1965.
26. Eheart, J., and Mason, B.: Sugar and acid in the edible portion of fruits. J Am Diet Assoc 50:130, 1967.

PART V

MODIFICATIONS IN FAT CONTENT

25.

FAT-RESTRICTED DIET

DEFINITIONS

1. FAT-RESTRICTED DIET

A diet that limits all types of fat ingested, regardless of the source, to less than 50 g per day (1).

2. MALDIGESTION

Maldigestion may result from exocrine pancreatic insufficiency or from aberrations in the release and activity of pancreatic enzymes and bile acids, which impair the digestion of nutrients. Pancreatic steatorrhea does not occur until pancreatic function is less than $\frac{1}{10}$ of normal. Maldigestion can be caused by pancreatic cancer, alcoholic pancreatitis, cystic fibrosis, and other forms of pancreatic insufficiency that decrease enzyme production. Maldigestion may also follow surgery, particularly if it severs the vagus nerve, as in esophagectomies and gastrectomies. Postvagotomy steatorrhea and diarrhea may occur from rapid gastric emptying and transit through the small bowel of a large hyperosmolar load of partially digested food. The dysmotility that occurs inhibits enzyme secretion (2–4).

3. MALABSORPTION

The failure to assimilate or absorb nutrients in the intestinal tract. Primary malabsorption occurs as a result of a disorder of the small intestine. The small intestine plays a key role in lipid metabolism by absorbing fat and synthesizing lipoproteins. Fat malabsorption secondary to intestinal disease results in abnormalities of lipoprotein concentrations. Impairments in the synthesis of apoprotein B may occur as well as deficiencies of essential fatty acids and fat-soluble vitamins (5).

Secondary malabsorption refers to a failure to absorb nutrients that is secondary to their unavailability at the absorptive site, due to maldigestion.

PURPOSE OF THE DIET

The diet is intended to relieve symptoms of diarrhea, steatorrhea, and nutrient losses caused by the ingestion of a high-fat diet in individuals with maldigestion or malabsorption.

The goal is to make the best possible use of the remaining digestive and absorptive functions, by giving the types of foods that are most readily absorbed and avoiding those that are not. Where distal ileal damage is serious, oxalate intake may have to be restricted, when the colon is present, to prevent the occurrence of oxalate renal stones (6).

Another important goal of the diet is to replace lost substances. Because steatorrhea and diarrhea reduce the absorption of fat-soluble vitamins, calcium, magnesium, and iron, increased amounts of these substances need to be provided daily. Iron may have to be given intramuscularly if diarrhea is severe and iron deficiency is acute (6).

Fat-modified diets for the prevention of cardiovascular disease may be found in Chapter 26.

EFFECTS OF THE DIET

1. IMPROVEMENTS IN STEATORRHEA

Steatorrhea is improved, resulting in a decrease in the amount of fat being lost in the stool and an accompanying amelioration of such symptoms as abdominal cramps, nausea, and diarrhea. In instances of weight loss, long-term use of the diet permits weight gain. Nitrogen losses in the stool are decreased, followed by an increase in serum albumin, serum calcium, and serum carotene and a decrease in alkaline phosphatase.

Once fat intake is decreased, steatorrhea will diminish whatever the cause. The pathogenesis of diarrhea involves the formation of hydroxy-fatty acids in the colon. If fewer fatty acids reach the colon, diarrhea will be lessened, and colonic absorption of products of bacterial fermentation will increase (7).

2. REDUCED POSTPRANDIAL ESOPHAGEAL REFLUX

High-fat meals reduce the pressure of the lower esophageal sphincter and cause gastrointestinal esophageal reflux (GER) and heartburn in certain susceptible individuals. Low-fat meals are associated with an increase in esophageal sphincter pressure, which tends to maintain sphincter closure and reduce the incidence of reflux. High-fat meals increase postprandial acid exposure in patients with GER who are in a supine position (8).

3. LIPOPROTEIN METABOLISM AND ESSENTIAL FATTY ACIDS

The low fat intake results in decreased formation of chylomicrons, the lipoprotein particles in which ingested dietary fat is packaged for delivery through the bloodstream. Because fats are a source of essential fatty acids, the intake of essential fatty acids may be significantly decreased on a low-fat diet. The provision in the diet of 1% to 2% of total calories in the form of linoleic acid will meet the Recommended Dietary Allowance, or 3 to 7 g linoleic acid. Good sources of linoleic acid include mayonnaise, margarine, safflower oil, sunflower oil, corn oil, soybean oil, and cottonseed oil. Linoleic acid is a precursor of prostaglandins, and a diet low in fat and low in linoleic acid will also affect prostaglandin synthesis (9, 10).

4. HORMONAL MILIEU OF PREMENOPAUSAL WOMEN

Nutritional factors may affect 1 or more of the processes leading to breast cancer by altering hormonal or immunological balance. Several investigators have found that premenopausal women with high plasma prolactin, high 17-beta-estradiol, or low progesterone levels appear to have an elevated risk of breast cancer. There is some evidence in animals that a high-fat diet increases the levels of 17-beta-estradiols. In one study in humans, however, in which fat intake was increased from 28 to 51 g per 1,000 kcal, there were no substantial differences in prolactin, 17-beta-estradiols, or the overall hormonal milieu. Controversy over the validity of the claims regarding a high-fat diet in breast cancer has caused the National Cancer Institute to cancel a $300 million trial of this hypothesis (11, 12).

PHYSIOLOGY, FOODS, AND NUTRIENTS

1. FAT MALABSORPTION

Causes of maldigestion and malabsorption are presented in table 25.1. Fat absorption is a multistep process involving the coordinated participation of several organs as well as luminal, secretory, mucosal, and lymphatic or portal venous transport phases (14).

The intraluminal phase requires hormonal coordination of pancreatic secre-

TABLE 25.1. CAUSES OF MALDIGESTION AND MALABSORPTION

Problem	Site	Mechanism	Example
Maldigestion	Gastric	Precipitate emptying Lack of intrinsic factor Excess acid secretion	Postgastrectomy dumping Pernicious anemia Zollinger-Ellison syndrome
	Pancreatic	Inadequate enzyme and bicarbonate secretion	Cystic fibrosis; chronic pancreatitis; carcinoma of pancreas
	Biliary	Defective micelle formation	Chronic biliary obstruction; primary biliary cirrhosis; massive ileal resection; cholestyramine
	Small bowel	Isolated brush border enzyme defects	Lactase insufficiency; congenital alactasia; sucrase-isomaltase deficiency; glucose-galactose malabsorption
Malabsorption	Small bowel	Loss of absorptive surface/damaged enterocyte	Celiac disease; tropical sprue; giardiasis; small-bowel resection; Crohn's disease; radiation enteritis; contaminated-small-bowel syndrome
		Impaired postabsorptive fat transport	Lymphangiectasia; abetalipoproteinemia
		Drugs	Alcohol; neomycin

Source: Spiller, R. C., and Silk, D. A. (13).

tion with the presence of bile salts and lipid in the small intestine. Cholecystokinin-pancreozymin responds to the presence of fat and protein, causes gallbladder contraction, and synchronizes bile salt secretion. The release of secretin by gastric acid stimulates pancreatic fluid and bicarbonate secretions and increases pH to the level where the pancreatic enzymes are activated. Pancreatic insufficiency is one example of intraluminal fat malabsorption (5, 14).

The secretory phase involves the passage of acidic contents into the duodenum, which stimulates release of pancre-

atic enzymes. Small-bowel resection may cause hypergastrinemia and gastric hypersecretion, with subsequent inactivation and/or dilution of pancreatic enzymes, intraluminal hyperosmolarity, and rapid transit (4).

The mucosal phase involves the uptake of micellar lipids and in many instances their reesterification. Any condition that results in a reduced concentration of bile salts within the intestinal lumen will impair micellar solubilization of lipid. If biliary flow is obstructed by cirrhosis or a tumor, fat emulsification and micelle formation will not occur. One example of impaired micelle formation leading to steatorrhea is that attributed to ileal resection (3, 5, 15).

The lymphatic or portal venous transport phases involve chylomicron formation and secretion into lymph. Although intestinal lymph is probably the major pathway of absorption of cholesterol and fat-soluble vitamins, some absorption may occur via the portal vein (5).

2. SMALL-BOWEL RESECTION

After small-bowel resection, 4 major factors influence the degree of malabsorption. The first is the extent of bowel resection. The exact minimum length of bowel needed to maintain nutritional status is not known and may differ from individual to individual, owing to variations in the degree of intestinal hypertrophy and adaptation of the remaining bowel. Ileal resections have the most severe nutritional and metabolic consequences because the jejunum is unable to assume several ileal functions, such as slowing the rate of transit. Also, it is in the ileum that bile salts and vitamin B-12 are absorbed, and when unabsorbed bile salts and hydroxy-fatty acids are lost into the colon they behave as cathartics. The ileum has a greater capacity to hypertrophy than other parts of the intestine, with steatorrhea occurring only when more bile salts are lost than the liver has the capacity to synthesize (when more than 100 cm ileum is resected) (3).

The second major factor to affect the degree of malabsorption subsequent to ileal resections is the presence of the ileocecal valve. This valve regulates the flow rate from the small intestine, and malabsorption is worse when this valve is lost.

The third factor is gut adaptation. After intestinal resections, particularly duodenal or jejunal resections, such structural changes as villous hyperplasia occur over a 1- to 2-year period that increase the absorptive surface of the remaining

bowel. These changes are mediated by the presence of food and gastrointestinal hormones (16, 17). The fourth factor determining ileal resection–induced malabsorption is the function of the remaining gastrointestinal tract. Prior gastrointestinal surgery or an active disease process (e.g., cancer) may affect digestive and absorptive capacity.

3. CHRONIC PANCREATITIS

Fat is the single most potent stimulus to pancreatic secretion, and long-chain fatty acids are more potent stimulants than medium-chain fatty acids. The pancreas secretes more than a dozen enzymes and isoenzymes, of which lipase is responsible for hydrolysis of triglycerides to monoglycerides and free fatty acids. Emulsification by bile salts is necessary for optimal lipase activity. Lipase is susceptible to inactivation by gastric juice, which has led to the use of H-2 receptor antagonists in the management of pancreatic insufficiency to reduce postprandial acidity and increase the effectiveness of pancreatic enzyme replacements (18).

Individuals with pancreatic insufficiency may have some of the highest levels of fecal fat excretion among the fat malabsorption syndromes. In order to promote weight gain and maximum nutrient intake, the patient should be given the greatest amount of fat that can be tolerated without an increase in steatorrhea or pain. The individual with chronic pancreatitis can compensate for weight loss and steatorrhea by increasing caloric and fat intake, but at the expense of more abdominal cramping associated with more-voluminous diarrhea (19–21).

4. GALLBLADDER DISEASE

Gallstones can be composed of either pigment or cholesterol and can be detected in very early stages by ultrasonography. Alterations in biliary motility have been implicated in the development

of gallstones and postcholecystectomy symptoms. Deoxycholic acid has also been implicated in the pathogenesis of cholesterol-rich gallstones. This is probably because high concentrations of deoxycholic acid in the circulating bile salt pool promote hepatic secretion of cholesterol and supersaturation of bile, both of which increase the occurrence of gallstones. One study suggests that patients with gallstones may have a decreased intracellular degradation of protein and/or mucin. Cholesterol-saturated bile, gallbladder stasis, an increased concentration of calcium within the gallbladder lumen, and the stimulation of the gallbladder mucosa by calcium and prostaglandins to secrete mucus into the bile are the building blocks of gallstone formation. Hypertriglyceridemia is a risk factor for gallstone formation in both men and women, but high-fat diets and hypercholesterolemia have not been proven to be risk factors (22–29).

A significant percentage of patients have postcholecystectomy symptoms. Many of these individuals turn out to have other problems unrelated to gallstones (30).

There is a greater incidence of increased biliary production of cholesterol, and thus of cholesterol gallstones, in obesity. The presence of gallstones is positively associated with body mass index in women, and it has been claimed that obese individuals do not empty their gallbladder effectively. The claim has been challenged by other investigators, whose research does not support a role for impaired gallbladder emptying in gallstone formation in obese individuals whose weight is in a steady state (28, 31, 32).

Some liquid low-calorie meal substitutes used in semifasting weight reduction regimens have low concentrations of the amino acids phenylalanine and tryptophan, which stimulate the release of the hormone cholecystokinin; this in turn stimulates the gallbladder to contract and empty. The use of such liquid low-calorie products in semifasting may result in gallbladder stasis, decreased gallbladder contractions, increased gallbladder volume, and increased risk of gallstones (28, 33).

On the other hand, slow but consistent weight reduction with well-balanced, nutritionally adequate low-calorie meals may diminish biliary cholesterol saturation and the risk of gallstones (29, 34).

There is a high incidence of cholelithiasis and cholecystitis, owing to gallbladder stasis, in individuals on total parenteral nutrition with no oral feedings. Physical activity, coffee consumption, and diabetes are not statistically related to gallstone disease, but smoking is (32–35).

INDICATIONS FOR USE

1. DIAGNOSTIC CLUES

Tests should be able to distinguish between malabsorption from an intestinal disease and maldigestion due to lack of pancreatic enzymes, and to quantify the amount of fat being malabsorbed (2).

A. 72-Hour Stool Fat Test   The quantitative chemical determination of stool fat over a 24-hour period is still the method that most accurately measures the amount of fat malabsorption. The validity of the 72-hour fecal fat test has been reconfirmed. The fecal excretion of more than 5 to 6 g fat per day over a 3-day period in patients receiving a known amount of fat per day is considered to be quantitative evidence of fat malabsorption in most laboratories. The test does not have to be conducted as a balance study. All that is required is that the quantity of fat ingested be quantified, along with the quantity of fat excreted in the stool (2, 36–38).

According to one author, severe steatorrhea of 40 g or more of fecal fat per day indicates defective lipolysis, often from chronic pancreatitis, carcinoma of

the pancreas, or massive bowel resection. Moderate steatorrhea of 25 to 35 g per day is suggestive of such intestinal mucosal diseases as celiac sprue, and mild steatorrhea of less than 25 g of fecal fat per day is commonly seen with defects in micelle formation. One investigation has tested the usefulness of the 72-hour stool fat test in identifying the underlying cause of malabsorption by the variations in the amount of fat excreted. Results indicated that the 72-hour stool fat test can identify the total amount of fat lost daily but does not provide accurate qualitative information that differentiates between pancreatic and intestinal steatorrhea (7, 36, 39).

B. Sudan Stain of Fecal Fat   Positive results from a Sudan stain of stool for fat and a serum carotene level of less than 60 mcg per 100 mL suggest fat malabsorption but are not definitive (2).

If used properly with newer methods that permit identification of triglycerides and fatty acids, the Sudan stain for fecal fat can be used to provide information about the type of fat malabsorbed. These data provide a source of qualitative information to augment the more quantitative type of information provided by the 72-hour stool fat test (40).

C. Other Tests   One approach described is the fatty meal test. A description, including cost effectiveness, of a number of different tests for malabsorption has been published elsewhere. One qualitative test involves administering radioactive fat and then measuring carbon dioxide in the breath. Results may be invalid in anyone with delayed gastric emptying or with an abnormal retention of carbon dioxide, or falsely negative in individuals with bile acid–induced diarrhea (2, 38, 41, 42).

In a comparative review of the efficacy of several tests for fat malabsorption, it was noted that the new C-14 triglyceride breath test is not sufficiently sensitive, does not provide quantitative

information, and must be done in 2 separate versions on 2 separate days. The serum C-14 triolein/H-3 oleic acid test is not sufficiently sensitive nor quantitative to be useful in clinical practice (2).

2. SHORT-BOWEL SYNDROME

Treatment of short-bowel syndrome has been categorized into 3 stages, the first 2 of which involve very rigid fat restrictions. In many of these patients, the steatorrhea in response to fat ingestion diminishes markedly after 4 to 13 months (37).

Initially, the patient is kept NPO to reduce any osmotic component. H-2 blockers are used to reduce gastric acid secretion. Opiates are used to slow bowel motility, including loperamide, which acts locally, and if necessary, codeine or diphenoxylate (43).

For patients who have more than 60 to 80 cm of their bowel remaining (greater than 15% to 20% of normal length), refeeding should be progressive, liberalizing the diet as gut adaptation permits. Some patients may require restrictions—e.g., lactose or moderate fat restrictions—depending on tolerance. In individuals whose only remaining small bowel is the duodenum, small liquid feedings are given in addition to total parenteral nutrition (44). Feeding considerations depend on the length and site of resection.

A. Jejunal Resection   Patients with jejunal resections but intact ileum and colon can be fed normally and rarely have any problems (44). A low-oxalate diet may be necessary (see chapter 35).

B. Ileal Resections   Patients with resection of less than 100 cm ileum have choleraic diarrhea and need approximately 4 g cholestyramine 3 times daily to bind bile salts. If vitamin B-12 absorption studies are abnormal, 200 mcg per month of parenteral vitamin B-12 should be given. If hyperoxaluria occurs, the patient should receive cholestyramine to reduce bile salt enhancement of colonic absorption of oxalates, as well as a low-oxalate diet (44).

If 100 to 200 cm ileum are resected, bile salts enter the colon and produce steatorrhea. Cholestyramine is indicated, in combination with a low-fat diet. If they occur, hyperoxaluria and vitamin B-12 deficiency should be treated as previously discussed (44).

Patients who undergo resection of greater than 200 cm of small bowel or lesser resection associated with colectomy are initially NPO, with H-2 blockers and opiates. Parenteral feeding may be needed initially. As the intestine adapts, a chemically defined diet may be used. Eventually, depending upon the degree of intestinal adaptation and the amount of bowel left, gradually increasing the oral feedings and separating liquids from solids may be tolerated, with a low-fat, low-oxalate diet as needed.

Following extensive resections leaving less than 60 cm of small bowel and/or only a duodenum, patients need parenteral nutrition on an indefinite basis. The infusion rate can be adjusted as the patient gradually becomes able to maintain weight. The decision to reduce intravenous feeding should be based on a nutritional assessment that determines that the rate of weight gain is excessive and that the reduced infusion rate will not result in electrolyte and fluid imbalance (44).

C. Ileal versus Jejunal

Resections Extensive small-bowel resection often leaves diseased intestine to perform digestive functions. As previously discussed, ileal resections produce greater metabolic derangements than resections of an equivalent amount of jejunum, owing to the impact of the ileum on bile salt reabsorption and fat absorption. Removal of the ileocecal valve and a partial colectomy produce even greater diarrhea. Because the ileum is involved in reabsorption of vitamin D

metabolites and vitamin B-12, and fat is excreted in the form of calcium and magnesium soaps, fat malabsorption also affects these nutrients, as well as fat-soluble vitamins E and K (17, 21, 45, 46).

D. Adaptation of the Remaining Gastrointestinal Tract Adaptation of the remaining gastrointestinal tract plays a significant role in nutrient absorption and maintenance of adequate nutrition. In a comparison in 8 patients of a 60% fat diet versus a 60% carbohydrate diet with 18% of the carbohydrate as simple sugars, no differences could be demonstrated in fecal fat losses, zinc, calcium, magnesium, or electrolyte balances. On the basis of these findings, the authors have questioned the rationale for a low-fat diet in individuals whose bowel disease has been in remission for 6 months or longer. These conclusions have been questioned by others, however, because of the heterogeneous characteristics of the medical conditions of patients studied, the length of the study time, and other factors (45, 47, 48).

3. CHRONIC PANCREATITIS

Chronic pancreatitis may give rise to or be associated with various hepatobiliary disorders. The diet may serve as an adjunct to enzyme replacement in controlling pancreatic steatorrhea and its accompanying fat and fat-soluble vitamin losses. Pancreatic enzyme replacement remains the primary treatment for steatorrhea associated with chronic pancreatitis; however, alterations in dietary fat intake may bring additional benefit (38, 49).

Fat intake should be reduced to 50 g per day or less and gradually increased until the patient reaches the limit of tolerance. Medium-chain triglycerides may be a better tolerated source of fat. In azotorrhea (greater than 2.5 g of fecal nitrogen per day on a daily diet of about 120 g protein), fat intake should be lim-

ited to 20% to 25% of calories ingested (19, 20, 50, 51).

Patients with severe pancreatic insufficiency have impaired gallbladder emptying in response to duodenal fat, which can be overcome by the use of pancreatic enzymes (52). The value of various methods of nutritional support in chronic pancreatic insufficiency is given in table 25.2.

4. HYPERTRIGLYCERIDEMIA

In patients with plasma triglycerides above 500 mg per 100 mL and chylomicronemia, a very low fat intake of 10% to 20% of total calories is indicated to prevent pancreatitis. (See Chapter 26.) The need to maintain the diet at all times must be emphasized.

5. YELLOW NAIL SYNDROME

The underlying pathology of the yellow nail syndrome is probably that of a lymphatic abnormality. Patients have abnormal lymphatic histology of the pleura, abnormal lymphangiograms of the lower limbs, chylous ascites, and yellow nails. The chylous ascites is probably caused by the oozing of lymph from the lymphangiectatic intestinal wall. Treatment involves a very low-fat diet supplemented with at least 50 mL medium-chain triglycerides (MCT) daily and diuretics. Long-chain triglycerides (LCT) are absorbed into the lacteals whereas MCT are absorbed directly into the portal system. Replacing LCT with MCT reduces the load on the lymph system (54).

6. INTESTINAL LYMPHANGIECTASIA

Dilated lymphatics are a major pathophysiological feature of intestinal lymphangiectasia. Such patients frequently have a generalized defect in their lymphatic system, often presenting with peripheral edema, chylous pleural or ascitic effusions, and hypoalbuminemia. Lymphangiograms show generalized abnormalities, with atresia in some areas and blocked dilated lymphatics in other

TABLE 25.2. VALUE OF VARIOUS METHODS OF NUTRITIONAL SUPPORT IN CHRONIC PANCREATIC INSUFFICIENCY

Method	Value
Dietary alterations	High-calorie intake; high-protein, high-carbohydrate medium-chain triglycerides
Nutrient supplements	Fat-soluble vitamins (A, D, K); vitamin B-12 may also be necessary Pancreatic enzyme supplements
Enteral nutrition[a]	Polymeric diets require digestive capability from pancreas but may improve nutritional status if given with pancreatic enzyme supplements "Elemental" diets, improve nutritional status without requiring exocrine pancreatic function
Intravenous nutrition	Rarely necessary, but effective if required

Source: Desai, M. B., and Jeejeebhoy, K. N. (53).
[a]Usually by tube feedings.

sites. A low-fat diet or a diet based on medium-chain rather than long-chain fatty acids may benefit some patients. The rationale for such a diet is to reduce the postprandial rise in lymphatic flow, which is especially large after meals containing long-chain fatty acids (13).

7. RADIATION ENTERITIS

This is a functional disturbance of the gastrointestinal tract caused by radiation treatment of the abdomen. Malabsorption may occur because of morphologic changes in the mucosa that decrease its absorptive power, reduce enzymatic digestion in both lumen and cell, proliferate a pathologic flora, or increase gastrointestinal motility (6, 13).

In addition to malabsorption of fat, there may be malabsorption of water, minerals, and other nutrients. It frequently begins early in the course of treatment and intensifies during the course. If chronic changes occur, it may not end when treatment is over. It may also appear months or years after treatment, due to intestinal stricture or fistula (6, 13).

8. COMPLICATIONS FOLLOWING GASTRIC SURGERY

A small number of individuals undergoing gastric surgery, particularly vagotomies, may have fat malabsorption. There is also some evidence that fat malabsorption occurs after total gastrectomy. After vagotomy, the proximal stomach develops higher pressures and empties more quickly. Inhibitory reflexes mediated by the vagus nerve are also affected. Fatty meals are less effective in slowing emptying, and the stomach empties more rapidly in the upright position, with loss of some neural reflexes (55–57).

Fat loss is usually limited to 10% to 12% of the daily fat ingested, or 10 to 12 g of fat per day. In most patients, total fat lost in the stool does not exceed 20 g per day unless there is another primary disease, such as sprue. In instances in which steatorrhea is more severe, the diet used for management of dumping syndrome may need to be combined with a low-fat MCT substituted diet (55).

9. BLIND LOOP SYNDROME

Deconjugation of bile salts leads to steat-

orrhea. The low-fat diet should be a temporary measure only and not a substitute for therapy directed at the primary disorder, such as antibiotics or corrective surgery (55).

10. FAT MALABSORPTION SECONDARY TO CELIAC DISEASE

The severity of the fat malabsorption that may exist in celiac disease can be correlated with ileal morphology. It is only after the loss of ileal function that fat will escape absorption into the large intestine. There may also be malabsorption and maldigestion due to delayed and reduced pancreatic and biliary secretions, which probably reflects cholecystokinin release. Fecal fat is further elevated by increased endogenous fat losses, presumably from desquamated cells. Once the primary disorder is controlled by a gluten-restricted, gliadin-free diet, fat absorption may improve enough to relax or even remove fat restrictions (13).

11. ALCOHOLIC CIRRHOSIS COMPLICATED BY PANCREATITIS

Impaired fat absorption has been noted in patients with alcoholic cirrhosis, as evidenced by modest increases in fecal fat output. Pancreatitis and neomycin administration are probably the major causes of the malabsorption, although small intestinal changes have been noted by electron microscopy. A minor cause may be the reduced bile salt pool (58).

12. HYPEROXALURIA

Untreated steatorrhea increases the risk of increased renal oxalate excretion and oxalate renal stones. When the amount of unabsorbed fatty acids in the colon is high, calcium is bound to the fatty acids to form insoluble calcium soaps. As a result, less calcium is available for the precipitation of unabsorbed dietary oxalate as calcium oxalate. The oxalate remains in solution and is ultimately excreted in the urine. Therefore, anyone with an intact colon and steatorrhea will exhibit hyperoxaluria (greater than 40 to 50 g per day of urinary oxalate). Four approaches recommended to correct the hyperoxaluria are low dietary oxalate intake, a diet low in long-chain triglycerides, pancreatic enzyme supplementation, and increased intake of either calcium (2 to 3 g per day) or aluminum (3.5 g per day) in the form of antacids. Vitamin C supplements should be avoided, because ascorbic acid is converted to oxalic acid (19).

Dietary oxalate should be restricted in all cases. If the degree of steatorrhea is severe, with more than 30 g of fat excreted in the feces daily, 1 or more of the other measures should be used in addition (19).

13. CYSTIC FIBROSIS

Patients with cystic fibrosis who do not receive pancreatic supplements excrete large amounts of bile acids in their stools. The decrease of the bile acid pool in the duodenum adversely affects micelle formation. Pancreatic extracts in cystic fibrosis help maintain normal biliary composition and prevent gallstones. Children with the disorder may develop deficiencies of fat-soluble vitamins and have low serum concentrations of albumin and urea nitrogen (59, 60).

If the 72-hour stool fat test in patients on pancreatic enzymes still documents severe steatorrhea, a trial of a low-fat diet with MCT should be instituted. The focus, however, should be on the correction of the cause of the steatorrhea as well as its nutritional consequences. In the past, too much emphasis was placed on controlling the symptoms of malabsorption even if this required limitation of dietary fat. When children with cystic fibrosis begin wasting, dietary fat must be increased, or growth rate may be decreased over a period of time (61).

Now that effective pancreatic replacements are available, normal fat intakes appear to improve the growth rate and are thus recommended for children with cystic fibrosis. A study confirms that

most of these children who comply with proper enzyme intake can tolerate a normal fat intake (62–64).

14. CROHN'S DISEASE

Some patients with Crohn's disease have severe steatorrhea, particularly when they have had intestinal resections. Fatty acids and their hydroxylated derivatives exert a cathartic effect upon the colonic mucosa. In addition, there is a direct correlation between the loss of fat in the stool and the loss of calcium, magnesium, and possibly zinc. Also related is the excessive absorption of uncomplexed oxalate, hyperoxaluria, and the increased risk of calcium oxalate renal stones. A low-fat diet will provide symptomatic improvement of steatorrhea. The use of MCT will also help symptoms of steatorrhea, while glucose polymers permit addition of needed calories (65).

15. GALLBLADDER DISEASE

A fat-restricted diet is believed by some physicians to be of benefit for the symptomatic patient with gallbladder disease. The purpose of the diet is to prevent biliary colic by lessening fat-induced gallbladder contractions. In these instances, moderate restriction of dietary fat to 25% of total kilocalories, or 45 to 75 g per day, is usually deemed sufficient (46, 66–68).

Although fatty foods stimulate the gallbladder to contract by liberating cholecystokinin, amino acids have the same effect. The hypothesis that symptoms of cholecystitis are precipitated by the ingestion of fatty foods may be invalid. Such foods as fried chicken, ice cream, cabbage, and eggs were once cited as precipitating factors without convincing evidence. It has now been suggested that patients with gallbladder disease are no less tolerant of fried foods than are normal persons. The only new data that implicate any food in causing the gallbladder to contract are found in a study incriminating both regular and decaffein-

ated coffee and suggesting restrictions in these beverages (69–72).

Although the fat as well as the protein in some of these foods may cause the gallbladder to contract, unless a gallstone is located within the duct system, contraction of the gallbladder is unlikely to produce symptoms. For patients with vague symptoms such as fullness, belching, slight nausea, and dull aching in the right upper quadrant, dietary changes have little or no value (70).

Cholecystectomy is still the most popular treatment for cholelithiasis, but alternatives exist as well. Currently available nonsurgical therapy for gallstones includes oral dissolution of the stones, extracorporeal shock wave lipotripsy, and choledocholithiasis (in vivo stone dissolution using methyl tertiary butyl ether, MTBE) (73–81).

16. OTHER DISORDERS INVOLVING FAT MALABSORPTION

Fat malabsorption may occur as a complication of cirrhosis, extrahepatic biliary obstruction, alcoholism, intrahepatic biliary tract disease with or without jaundice, jejunal bacterial overgrowth, and as a secondary occurrence in other diseases, as discussed previously. It should be remembered, however, that low-fat diets are used to control symptoms, not to reverse abnormal physiology of the underlying disease that resulted in fat malabsorption (21, 46, 82).

POSSIBLE ADVERSE REACTIONS

A low-fat diet with a high proportion of polyunsaturated fats may increase the risk of gallstones. Some, but not all, patients develop saturated bile on polyunsaturated fats, owing to the increased output of biliary cholesterol (29).

Preliminary studies indicate that the presence of fat in food has trophic effects on the small intestine, and some fat may be necessary in tube feedings to enhance mucosal hyperplasia following short-bowel syndrome (83).

Weight loss caused by inadequate caloric intake is common on low-fat diets. Low-fat oral supplements can be prescribed if unintended weight loss occurs. Adverse reactions of the diet can be avoided by the provision of adequate calories, adequate but not excessive amounts of essential fatty acids, and supplements deemed necessary on the basis of nutritional assessment.

CONTRAINDICATIONS

Restriction of fat in certain liver diseases, such as uncomplicated hepatitis, has been found to be based on fallacious assumptions. There is no need to restrict fat intake in patients ill with hepatitis, unless the condition is complicated by a diminished supply of bile salts from the liver in the intestine. While high-fat diets are not necessary, a modicum of fat, in the range of 30% to 40% of the calories per day, adds palatability to the diet, carries fat-soluble vitamins, and is generally well tolerated (84, 85).

CLINICAL ASSESSMENT

Patients with fat malabsorption present with a well-defined clinical picture, including weight loss and alterations in the composition, color, consistency, and odor of the stool.

If the diet is used in fat malabsorption associated with pancreatitis, the dietary interview should include a detailed assessment of alcohol intake as well as the relationship of symptoms to the timing and composition of meals. Prior to dietary adjustments, information should be solicited as to the effect of the diet on symptoms in an effort to determine the limits of the patient's fat tolerance, as well as protein and calcium intakes. Physical signs of hyperlipidemia may be noted in individuals with pancreatitis. Height, weight, and other anthropomet-

ric measurements should be evaluated at regular intervals.

BIOCHEMICAL ASSESSMENT

1. PANCREATITIS

Steatorrhea may be associated with decreased serum cholesterol, serum folate, vitamin B-12, iron, calcium, and magnesium, and prolonged prothrombin time. Patients should also be assessed for possible iron deficiency and a megaloblastic anemia resulting from lack of vitamin B-12. Despite pancreatic enzyme replacements, fat-soluble vitamin stores have been found to be diminished in these patients, and they may need supplements. Absorption of vitamin A is disturbed and that of vitamin E is occasionally decreased (19, 51).

Serum amylase levels are often elevated in pancreatitis, and this is one of the biochemical determinations used to identify this condition. In instances of extremely high levels, enteral feedings may need to be temporarily postponed, although there are some physicians who allow the patient to eat as soon as he or she is free from pain or discomfort (86).

Blood glucose levels may be elevated, owing to transient release of excess glucagon from alpha cells of the pancreas (19).

A disturbance in the absorption of vitamin D and calcium causes hypocalcemia, with skeletal demineralization. The binding of calcium to fatty acids in the stool contributes to transient hypocalcemia. Calcium–fatty acid binding is also related to a decrease in serum albumin levels, due to loss of nitrogen in the stool. A decreased serum calcium should be a warning to check oxalate intake in order to lessen the risk of hyperoxaluria and oxalate stones (51).

In the patient with a low serum calcium, alkaline phosphatase levels may be increased. This is accompanied by decreased mineralization and increased

mobilization of calcium from bones in an attempt to raise serum calcium levels. Serum calcium levels should gradually increase as the patient improves. Serum magnesium levels may also be low in the patient who has steatorrhea and is forming magnesium–fatty acid complexes in the stool.

2. SHORT-BOWEL SYNDROME

As discussed above, individuals with short-bowel syndrome due to massive intestinal resections or other causes should have serum levels of calcium, alkaline phosphatase, albumin, and glucose assessed, as well as undergoing 72-hour stool fat determinations. Alteration in calcium status may be accompanied by lower levels of vitamin D, since the intestine is important in the absorption of vitamin D, which then affects calcium absorption. Absorption of vitamins A, E, and K may be impaired and affect serum levels as well as absorption of the vitamin B-12 intrinsic factor complex, leading to a macrocytic anemia with a characteristic change in bone marrow, hematocrit, hemoglobin, MCH, and MCHC. An increased prothrombin time may be indicative of a vitamin K deficiency (46, 87).

ASSESSMENT OF POTENTIAL DRUG INTERACTIONS

1. NEOMYCIN, CHOLESTYRAMINE, AND COLCHICINE

The antibiotic neomycin (Mycifraden), the hypocholesterolemic agent cholestyramine, and the anti-inflammatory agent colchicine may all cause fat malabsorption (88).

Neomycin is used to alter intestinal bacterial flora to inhibit ammonia production in hepatic encephalopathy. It inhibits lipase action, decreases the absorption of lipids, and flattens intestinal villi. A daily dose of 8 to 12 g results in approximately 20 g of fat lost in the stool daily. It also inhibits lactase and other disaccharidases and decreases absorption of cholesterol, carotene, glucose, lactose, sucrose, sodium, calcium, iron, vitamin A, vitamin D, vitamin K, folic acid, and vitamin B-6. It may cause a sore mouth, increased serum creatinine levels, increased BUN levels, and increased urinary protein levels (46, 89).

Cholestyramine (Questran) is an anion exchange resin that binds bile acids, which are metabolites of cholesterol, in the intestinal lumen so that they are not available for micellar solubilization. Cholestyramine acts like a sponge or a magnet, trapping the cholesterol-containing bile and carrying it out in the stool. The extent of steatorrhea depends upon the amount used, with 15 g of fat excreted daily with a dose of 24 to 36 g per day. With or without fat restrictions, the drug will help control bile acid–induced diarrhea in patients with ileal resections. Cholestyramine powder should always be mixed with water or pureed foods; it should never be taken in its dry form (20, 89).

The most common side effects of this drug are indigestion, bloating, gas, and constipation; these occur because bile, a natural laxative, is bound and therefore less available. In most patients, the body adapts after a few weeks or months and symptoms may diminish or disappear completely. Other potential side effects of the drug include weight loss, altered taste acuity, edema, osteomalacia, hyperchloremic acidosis, and decreased absorption of calcium, vitamin A, vitamin D, vitamin K, vitamin B-12, folic acid, MCT, and glucose. With long-term use, iron reserves may be diminished. Serum levels of triglycerides, alkaline phosphatase, SGOT, SGPT, phosphorus, and chloride are increased, while serum levels of cholesterol, low-density lipoproteins, calcium, potassium, and sodium are decreased (89, 90).

Colchicine has an effect on intestinal epithelial cell function, and doses of 2 to 4 g per day result in a mild steatorrhea of about 10 g lost fat each day. Colchicine may cause decreased absorption of vitamin A, folic acid, vitamin K, sodium, nitrogen, and lactose, decreased serum levels of cholesterol, vitamin A, vitamin B-12, alkaline phosphatase, and SGOT, and altered taste (20, 89). Additional drug-nutrient information about the drug is found in Chapter 18.

2. AMILORIDE (MIDAMOR)

Cholesterol gallstones exist only when bile has a high lipid and cholesterol content. Two prerequisites to the formation of cholesterol-containing gallstones are cholesterol-saturated and calcium-saturated bile. The concentration of calcium within the gallbladder lumen appears to be a critical determinant. Prostaglandins and biliary calcium reduce the solubility of cholesterol and stimulate the secretion of mucus glycoproteins found in the gallstone matrix. The magnesium-sparing diuretic amiloride lowers the intraluminal concentrating ability of the gallbladder mucosa and reduces the incidence of stone formation. The drug should not be used in hepatic disease, or on anyone with a BUN over 40 mg/100 mL. It may cause fluid retention and hyperkalemia. In individuals also taking digoxin, cortisone, lithium, or cardiac glycosides, it may decrease serum levels of these drugs (27, 91).

3. PANCREATIC ENZYME REPLACEMENTS, CIMETIDINE, ANTACIDS, AND OTHER DRUGS

Treatment of pancreatic insufficiency involves the use of commercially available enzyme replacements, such as pancreatin (Viokase) or pancrelipase (Cotazym), with meals in order to abolish steatorrhea. Pancreatin is most often used in cystic fibrosis. It is available as a powder that can be sprinkled on food, in tablet form, or in capsules (51, 82, 86).

Cimetidine (Tagamet) may be useful in the patient with intestinal resection and gastric hypersecretion. It lowers the pH and thus inactivates the pancreatic enzymes. The use of caffeine should be limited with this drug. Effects of the drug include increased serum creatinine, SGOT, and SGPT (39, 92). See Chapter 10 for additional information on this drug.

The use of antacids to alter the pH in favor of pancreatic enzyme activity in pancreatitis has yielded mixed results. Whereas aluminum hydroxide improves fat malabsorption, calcium carbonate and magnesium aluminum hydroxide have been reported to make it worse. See Chapter 10 for more information about these drugs (85).

Now available are microspheres or coated pancreatic granules that are designed to release their contained enzymes when the pH rises toward neutrality (Creon, Pancrease, pancreatin granules). Compared with more-traditional pancreatin preparations that are frequently ineffective in controlling pH, granular preparations have been shown to increase enzyme levels and to diminish steatorrhea in patients with chronic pancreatitis. Effects have been seen when 10 to 20 mL of granules (Pankreon or pancreatin granules) were taken with each meal. Long-term use of the granules also leads to weight gain (86).

IMPLEMENTATION AND EDUCATION

Fat intake should be increased gradually to the patient's level of tolerance. It must be stressed to patients with pancreatic insufficiency and cystic fibrosis that enzyme replacements should be taken with meals. Pancreatin has an unpleasant taste and smell, which limits compliance for preparations without an enteric coat. Dietitians should do all they can to support patients and encourage their compliance, particularly for adolescent patients who are still in school (93).

The most important recommendation for patients with chronic pancreatitis secondary to alcoholism is complete abstinence from alcohol. This one measure can lead to relief of fat malabsorption and pancreatic pain in as many as half of those who suffer from it. Dietary fat should be reduced to less than 25% of total calories in order to avert steatorrhea and avoid undue stimulation of the gland. In patients with severe exocrine insufficiency, it may be necessary to increase dietary protein intake if patients are malnourished or in order to compensate for poor absorption. Diabetes complicates chronic pancreatitis in a small number of patients; in such case, the diabetes exchange list must be modified to call for further decreases in fat intake. In individuals with alcoholism, education on the effects of alcohol should be part of an overall multidisciplinary approach that also treats the psychological causes of alcohol abuse (82, 86).

The addition of high-fiber foods such as fresh fruits, vegetables, legumes, and whole grains to the diet will minimize the constipation that is caused by cholestyramine (90). Caloric intake can be boosted, if necessary, by the addition of medium-chain triglycerides to foods. The replacement of long-chain triglycerides with medium-chain ones may prevent weight loss. The nutritional advantages of MCT over LCT in the area of digestion and absorption are related to the greater solubility in water and in body solutions, easier hydrolysis despite pancreatic lipase or bile salt deficiencies, transport without requiring chylomicron formation, and transport directly to the liver via the portal vein, bypassing the lymphatic system. MCT can be used in cooking, on foods in place of oil, butter, or margarine, or (when frozen) as a spread, but it must be introduced gradually into the diet to avoid side effects (94).

PRIORITIES FOR QUALITY ASSURANCE

The diet prescription should be based on a definitive diagnosis that establishes fat malabsorption, distinguishes between primary malabsorption and secondary malabsorption arising from maldigestion, and quantifies the amount of fat malabsorbed. Terminology used in the diet prescription should be accurate so that there is no confusion with other diets, e.g., a fat-controlled diet for heart disease.

Fat restriction should be used to control symptoms and not as a substitute for medical or surgical therapy—for instance, antibiotics in blind loop syndrome, or surgery, in the case of cholelithiasis. The diet should provide at least 1% to 2% of calories as essential fatty acids, as recommended by the Food and Nutrition Board (9). Fat restrictions should not be achieved at the expense of protein and kilocalorie intake. The discharge plan should include supermarket strategies and low fat cookery tips as well as the daily meal plan.

MENU PLANNING

FOOD LIST FOR FAT-RESTRICTED DIET

Food group	Foods allowed	Foods excluded
Breads and cereals High-fiber, whole-grain breads and cereal, 4 or more servings per day	Whole-grain breads (non-fat), (1 slice); enriched breads (1 slice), saltines, soda crackers (6), cold cereals (¾ cup), cooked cereals (½ cup); whole-grain cereal, except granola-type (½ cup); unbuttered popcorn (3 cups)	Biscuits; breads containing egg or cheese; sweet rolls, pancakes, French toast, doughnuts, waffles, fritters, buttered popcorn, or muffins, if made with fat; granola-type cereals or breads to which extra fat is added; popovers; snack crackers with added fat; snack chips; stuffing
Dairy products Skim milk and skim-milk dairy products, 2 or more servings per day	Skim milk (1 cup); buttermilk made with skim milk (1 cup); powdered skim milk (⅓ cup); evaporated skim milk (½ cup); yogurt made from skim milk (1 cup); cottage cheese (1% fat), (¼ cup); cottage cheese (dry curd), (¼ cup); skim farmer's cheese (1 oz.); parmesan cheese (3 tbsp. or ½ oz.); feta cheese (1 oz.); part-skim mozzarella cheese (1 oz.); part-skim ricotta cheese (¼ cup); low-fat cheeses (with less than 55 kcal/oz.) (1 oz.); ice milk (chocolate, ⅔ cup; strawberry, ⅔ cup; vanilla, ¾ cup); nonfat frozen yogurt (1 cup)	Whole milk; buttermilk made with whole milk; chocolate milk; 2% and low-fat milk; cream, evaporated milk, yogurt made from whole milk, or sour cream or cream cheese (in excess of amounts allowed in "Fats" category list); high-fat cheese, e.g., cheddar, American, blue, Brie, Edam, limburger, romano, monterey, provolone, Swiss, muenster, roquefort, brick, Colby, Gouda; ice cream
Desserts In moderation	Sherbet made with skim milk; fruit ice; gelatin; plain angel food cake, vanilla wafers, ladyfingers, arrowroot cookies, graham crackers; meringues, junket, pudding made with skim milk (rice or tapioca); fruit whips made with gelatin or egg whites; fat-free commercial baked items or frozen desserts	All other cakes, cookies, pies, doughnuts, puddings made with whole milk and egg yolks or eggs, cream puffs, turnovers

(continued)

Fats
Amount listed equals 1
fat equivalent
3–5 equivalents per day
Polyunsaturated fats are
recommended

Polyunsaturated fats:
Margarine, diet (1 tbsp.) or
soft tub (1 tbsp.); may-
onnaise, diet (1 tbsp.) or
regular (1 tsp.); mayon-
naise-type dressing, low-
calorie (1 tbsp.) or regular (2 tsp.); salad dressing, low-calorie (2 tbsp.)
or regular (1 tbsp.); vegetable oil, corn (1 tsp.),
cottonseed (1 tsp.), saf-
flower (1 tsp.), soybean
(1 tsp.), or sunflower (1
tsp.); dry-roasted al-
monds (6 whole); dry-
roasted cashews (1 tbsp.
or 2 whole), pecans (2
whole), peanuts (20
small or 10 large),
cashew butter (2 tsp.),
walnuts (2 whole),
pistachios (18 whole),
other nuts (1 tbsp.);
seeds, sesame (1 tbsp.),
sunflower (1 tbsp.),
pumpkin (2 tsp.)

Saturated fats:
Bacon (1 strip), bacon fat
(1 tsp.), butter (1 tsp.),
coconut (½ oz.), dried
(2 tbsp.) or fresh (1″ ×
1″ × ⅜″); cream cheese
(1 tbsp.); lard (1 tsp.);
filberts (5 nuts or 1
tbsp.); coconut oil, palm
oil, or shortening (1
tsp.); sour cream (2
tbsp.); or whipped butter
(2 tsp.)

Other fats:
Olive oil or peanut oil (1
tsp.); olives (10 large or
5 small); peanut butter
(2 tsp.); or avocado (⅛
medium or 2 tbsp.)

Fruits
2 or more total servings
per day, with at least 1
source rich in vitamin
C

Fresh, frozen, canned, or
dried fruit; fruit juices

Any in excess of amounts
prescribed on diets; all
others not listed

(*continued*)

Meat and meat substitutes 6 oz. of lean meat per day Recommended preparation methods are broiling, roasting (on rack), grilling, or boiling Weigh meat after cooking	Cornish hen, chicken, or turkey, without skin; veal (all cuts); lean beef (USDA good or choice cuts, i.e., round, sirloin, flank steak, tenderloin, or chopped beef); roast (rib, chuck, rump); steak (cubed, porterhouse, T-bone); meat loaf made with extra-lean ground beef; lean pork (fresh ham; canned, cured, or boiled ham; Canadian bacon; tenderloin; chops; loin roast; Boston butt; cutlets); lean lamb (chops, leg, roast); fish, fresh, frozen, or canned in water (crab, lobster, scallops, shrimp, clams, oysters); tuna canned in water; herring (uncreamed or smoked); sardines (canned, drained); salmon (canned in water); 95% fat-free luncheon meat; legumes cooked without added fat; tofu; tempeh; natto; egg whites, egg substitutes with less than 55 kcal per ¼ cup; eggs, poached, soft, or hard cooked; scrambled egg that is not fried in fat (1 egg = 1 oz. of meat count as part of daily meat allowance)	Any fried, fatty, or heavily marbled meat, fish, or poultry; most USDA prime cuts of beef, ribs, corned beef; spareribs, ground pork, pork sausage (patty or link), ham hocks, pigs' feet, chitterlings; lamb patties (ground lamb); bologna, salami, pimiento loaf; Polish or Italian sausage, knockwurst, smoked bratwurst, frankfurter; duck, goose; tuna or salmon packed in oil; legumes cooked with added fat; eggs fried in fat
Potatoes and substitutes 2–3 servings	Potatoes, rice, barley, noodles, spaghetti, macaroni, other pastas (½ cup)	Fried potatoes; fried rice; potato chips; chow mein noodles
Soups As desired	Fat-free broth; fat-free vegetable soup; cream soup made with skim milk; packaged dehydrated soups	All others
Sweets In moderation	Sugar, honey, jelly, jam, marmalade, molasses, maple or chocolate syrup; sour balls, gum drops, jelly beans, marshmallows, hard candy; cocoa powder	Chocolate or chocolate candy; candy made with cream, cocoa fats, nuts, coconut

(continued)

Vegetables 3 or more servings per day, including 1 green or yellow per day	All fresh, frozen or canned vegetables prepared without fats, oil, or fat-containing sauces (1 cup raw or ½ cup cooked)	Buttered, au gratin, creamed, or fried vegetables unless made with allowed fat
Spices As desired	All herbs and seasonings except those specifically excluded	Herbs and seasonings with added fat
Miscellaneous	Catsup, chili sauce, vinegar, pickles, vanilla, unbuttered popcorn; white sauce made with skim milk	Olives and nuts in excess of specified portions; peanut butter, apple butter, cream sauces, gravies, buttered popcorn

Source: Adapted from American Dietetic Association (1).

DAILY MEAL PLAN FOR THE DIET OF 50-g FAT[a]

Food	Amount	Fat (g)
Skim milk	2 or more cups	—
Lean or medium-fat meat, fish, poultry	6 oz.	18–30
Whole egg	2 per week	2
Vegetables (at least 1 dark green or deep yellow)	3 or more servings	—
Fruit (at least 1 citrus)	2 or more servings	—
Fats	3 servings	15
Breads, cereals, starches	6 or more servings	Trace
Desserts and sweets from permitted list	As desired	—
Total fat		35–47

[a]See American Dietetic Association exchange lists in Chapter 28.

SAMPLE MENU FOR THE FAT-RESTRICTED DIET (FOR A MALE, AGE 25–50)

BREAKFAST	
Stewed dried apricots	½ cup
Sugar	1 tbsp.
Orange juice	1 cup
Cornflakes	1 cup
Skim milk	1 cup
Whole wheat toast	2 slices
Margarine	2 tsp.
Jam	2 tbsp.
Coffee	1 cup
MORNING SNACK	
Pretzels	1 oz.
Apple juice	1 cup
LUNCH	
Vegetable soup	1 cup
Lean hamburger patty	3 oz.
Hamburger bun	1

(continued)

Sliced tomato	1 medium
Lettuce	2 leaves
Angel food cake	1 slice
Sliced strawberries	½ cup
Skim milk	1 cup
Tea	1 cup

AFTERNOON SNACK

Nonfat fruit yogurt	¾ cup
Grapenuts	¼ cup
Raisins	2 tbsp.

DINNER

V-8 juice	½ cup
Broiled skinless chicken breast	3 oz.
Herbed rice	½ cup
Steamed broccoli	½ cup
Whole wheat bread	1 slice
Margarine	1 tsp.
Banana	1
Tea	1 cup

EVENING SNACK

| Fruit sherbet | ½ cup |
| Pear | 1 medium |

Approximate Nutrient Analysis

Energy	2,833 kcal
Protein	121.2 g (17% of kcal)
Fat	45.2 g (14% of kcal)
Polyunsaturated fat	6.6 g
Monounsaturated fat	15.8 g
Saturated fat	12.9 g
Cholesterol	173 mg
Carbohydrate	502.9 g (71% of kcal)

Vitamin A	14,709 IU
	2,187 RE
Thiamine	2.20 mg
Riboflavin	3.29 mg
Niacin	37.0 mg
Folate	446 mcg
Vitamin B-12	7.47 mcg
Vitamin B-6	3.55 mg
Vitamin C	271.4 mg

Calcium	1,603 mg
Phosphorus	2,039 mg
Iron	18.4 mg
Copper	1.46 mg
Zinc	13.5 mg
Magnesium	370 mg
Sodium	4,131 mg
Potassium	6,065 mg

REFERENCES

1. American Dietetic Association: Manual of clinical dietetics. Chicago: American Dietetic Association, 1988.
2. Pedersen, N.: Fat digestion tests. Digestion 37:25, 1987.
3. Hermann-Zaidens, M.: Malabsorption in adults: Etiology, evaluation and management. J Am Diet Assoc 86:1171, 1986.
4. Lodas, S., Issacs, P., et al.: The role of the small intestine in postvagotomy diarrhea. Gastroenterology 85:1088, 1983.
5. Thompson, G. R.: Lipid related consequences of intestinal malabsorption. Gut 29:34, 1989.
6. Desai, M. B., and Jeejeebhoy, K. N.: Nutrition and diet in the management of diseases of the gastrointestinal tract. C. Small intestine. (1) Effects of intestinal disease on digestion and absorption. In Shils, M. E., and Young, V. R.: Modern nutrition in health and disease. 7th ed. Philadelphia: Lea & Febiger, 1988.
7. Alpers, D. H.: Dietary management and vitamin-mineral replacement therapy. In Sleisinger, M. H., and Fordtran, J. S.: Gastrointestinal disease. 3d ed. Philadelphia: W. B. Saunders, 1983.
8. Becker, D. J., Sinclair, J., et al.: A comparison of high and low fat meals on postprandial esophageal acid exposure. Am J Gastroenterol 84:782, 1990.
9. Food and Nutrition Board, National Research Council: Recommended Dietary Allowances. 10th ed. Washington, D.C.: National Academy of Sciences, 1989.
10. Cunningham, J.: Introduction to nutritional physiology. Philadelphia: George F. Stickley, 1983.
11. Hagerty, M. A., Howie, B. J., et al.: Effect of low and high fat intakes on the hormonal milieu of premenopausal women. Am J Clin Nutr 47:653, 1988.
12. Musey, P. I., Collins, D. C., et al.: Effect of diet on oxidation of 17-beta-estradiol in vivo. J Clin Endocrinol Metab 65:792, 1987.
13. Spiller, R. C., and Silk, D. A.: Malabsorption. In Kinney, J. M., Jeejeebhoy, K. N., et al.: Nutrition and metabolism in patient care. Philadelphia: W. B. Saunders, 1988.
14. Glickman, R.: Fat absorption and malabsorption. Clin Gastroenterol 12:323, 1983.
15. Dobbins, W.: When and how to evaluate the patient with malabsorption. Pract Gastroenterol 4:36, 1980.
16. Ostrov, A., and Balint, J.: Management of the short bowel syndrome. Pract Gastroenterol 4:14, 1980.
17. Weser, E.: Nutritional aspects of malabsorption: Short gut adaptation. Clin Gastroenterol 12:443, 1983.
18. Greenberg, G. R.: Nutrition and diet in management of diseases of the gastrointestinal tract. B. Pancreas: Nutrient interactions with function and structure. In Shils, M. E., and Young, V. R.: Modern nutrition in health and disease. 7th ed. Philadelphia: Lea & Febiger, 1988.
19. Grendell, J.: Nutrition and absorption in disease of the pancreas. Clin Gastroenterol 12:551, 1983.
20. Losowsky, M., Walker, B., and Kelleher, J.: Malabsorption in clinical practice. Edinburgh: Livingstone Churchill, 1974.
21. Iber, F.: Treatment of pancreatic insufficiency. Johns Hopkins Med J 122:172, 1968.
22. Bruckstein, A. H.: Nonsurgical management of cholelithiasis. Arch Intern Med 150:960, 1990.
23. Cucchiaro, G., Rossitch, J. C., et al.: Clinical significance of ultrasonographically detected coincidental gallstones. Dig Dis Sci 35:417, 1990.
24. Grace, P. A., Poston, G. J., and Williamson, R. C. N.: Biliary motility. Gut 31:571, 1989.
25. Marcus, S. N., and Heaton, K. W.: Deoxycholic acid and the pathogenesis of gallstones. Gut 29:522, 1988.
26. Sahlin, S., Ahlberg, J., et al.: Quantitative ultrastructural studies of gallbladder epithelium in gallstone free subjects and patients with gallstones. Gut 31:100, 1989.
27. Jacyna, M. R.: Interactions between gallbladder bile and mucosa: Relevance to gallstone formation. Gut 31:568, 1990.
28. Marzio, L., Capone, F., et al.: Gallbladder kinetics in obese patients. Effect of a regular meal and low-calorie meal. Dig Dis Sci 33:4, 1988.
29. Einarsson, K., and Angelin, B.: Hypolipoproteinemia, hypolipidemic treatment, and gallstone disease. Bile Acids Atheroscl 15:67, 1986.
30. Ros, E., and Zambon, D.: Postcholecystectomy symptoms: A prospective study of gallstone patients before and two years after surgery: Gut 28:1500, 1987.
31. Howard, B. V.: Obesity, cholelithiasis and lipoprotein metabolism in man. Bile Acids Atheroscl 15:169, 1986.
32. Jorgensen, T.: Gallstones in a Danish population. Relation to weight, physical activity, smoking, coffee consumption and diabetes mellitus. Gut 30:528, 1989.
33. Hanyu, N., Dodds, W. J., et al.: Cholecystokinin-induced contraction of opossum sphincter of Oddi—mechanism of action. Dig Dis Sci 35:567, 1990.
34. Liddle, R. A., Goldstein, R. B., and Saxton, J.: Gallstone formation during weight-reduction dieting. Arch Intern Med 149:1750, 1989.
35. Holzbach, R. T.: Gallbladder stasis: Consequence of long term parenteral hyperalimentation and risk factor for cholelithiasis. Gastroenterology 84:1055, 1984.
36. Bai, J. C., Andrush, A., et al.: Fecal fat concentration in the differential diagnosis of steatorrhea. Am J Gastroenterol 84:27, 1989.
37. Wright, H. K., and Tilson, M. D.: Postoperative disorders of the gastrointestinal tract. New York: Grune and Stratton, 1973.
38. Westergaard, H., and Dietscht, J.: Normal mechanisms of fat absorption and derangements induced by various gastrointestinal diseases. Med Clin N Am 58:1513, 1974.
39. Ryan, M., and Olsen, W.: A diagnostic approach to malabsorption syndromes: A pathophysiologic approach.

Clin Gastroenterol 12:533, 1983.

40. Khouri, M. R., Huang, G., and Shiau, Y. F.: Sudan stain of fecal fat: New insight into an old test. Gastroenterology 96:421, 1989.

41. Goldstein, R., Blondheim, O., et al.: The fatty meal test: An alternative to stool fat analysis. Am J Clin Nutr 38:763, 1983.

42. Steinberg, W., and Toskes, P.: A practical approach to evaluating maldigestion and malabsorption. Geriatrics 2:73, 1978.

43. Desai, M. B., and Jeejeebhoy, K. N.: Nutrition and diet in management of diseases of the gastrointestinal tract. C. Small intestine. (5) Nutritional support of patients with short bowel syndrome and malabsorption. In Shils, M. E., and Young, V. R.: Modern nutrition in health and disease. 7th ed. Philadelphia: Lea & Febiger, 1988.

44. Jeejeebhoy, K. N.: Short bowel syndrome. In Kinney, J. M., Jeejeebhoy, K. N., et al.: Nutrition and metabolism in patient care. Philadelphia: W. B. Saunders, 1988.

45. Morris, J., Selivanov, V., and Sheldon, G.: Nutritional management of patients with malabsorption syndrome. Clin Gastroenterol 12:463, 1983.

46. Gray, G. M.: Maldigestion and malabsorption: Clinical manifestations and specific diagnosis. In Selisenger, M. H., and Fordtran, J. S.: Gastrointestinal disease. 3d ed. Philadelphia: W. B. Saunders, 1983.

47. Woolf, G., Miller, C., et al.: Diet for patients with a short bowel: High fat or high carbohydrate? Gastroenterology 84:823, 1983.

48. Young, E.: Short bowel syndrome: High fat versus high carbohydrate diet. Gastroenterology 84:872, 1982.

49. Wilson, C., Auld, C. D., et al.: Hepatobiliary complications in chronic pancreatitis. Gut 30:520, 1989.

50. Taubin, H., and Spiro, H.: Nutritional aspects of chronic pancreatitis. Am J Clin Nutr 26:367, 1973.

51. Lankisch, P.: Conservative treatment of pancreatitis. Digestion 37:48, 1987.

52. Masclee, A. A. M., Jansen, M. B. M. J., et al.: Reversible gallbladder dys-

function in severe pancreatic insufficiency. Gut 30:866, 1989.

53. Russell, R. J.: Nutrition and diet in management of diseases of the gastrointestinal tract. B. The pancreas. (2) Nutritional support of patients with pancreatic diseases. In Shils, M. E., and Young, V. R.: Modern nutrition in health and disease. 7th ed. Philadelphia: Lea & Febiger, 1988.

54. Tan, W. C.: Dietary treatment of chylous ascites in yellow nail syndrome. Gut 30:1622, 1989.

55. Wolman, S.: Nutrition and diet in management of diseases of the gastrointestinal tract. A. Esophagus, stomach, and duodenum. (2) Nutritional effects of disease of the stomach and duodenum. In Shils, M. E., and Young, V. R.: Modern nutrition in health and disease. 7th ed. Philadelphia: Lea & Febiger, 1988.

56. Walther, B., Clementsson, C., et al.: Fat malabsorption in patients before and after total gastrectomy, studied by the triolein breath test. Scand J Gastroenterol 24:309, 1989.

57. Radziuk, J., and Bondy, D. C.: Gastric surgery. In Jeejeebhoy, K. N.: Current therapy in nutrition. Philadelphia: B. C. Decker, 1988.

58. Blendis, L. M., and Jenkins, D. J. A.: Nutrition and diet in management of diseases of the gastrointestinal tract. E. Liver. (1) Nutritional support in liver disease. In Shils, M. E., and Young, V. R.: Modern nutrition in health and disease. 7th ed. Philadelphia: Lea & Febiger, 1988.

59. Huang, N. N., Schidlow, D. V., et al.: Cystic fibrosis. In Kinney, J. M., Jeejeebhoy, K. N., et al.: Nutrition and metabolism in patient care. Philadelphia: W. B. Saunders, 1988.

60. Russell, R. J.: Nutrition and diet in management of diseases of the gastrointestinal tract. B. Pancreas. (2) Nutritional support of patients with pancreatic diseases. In Shils, M. E., and Young, V. R.: Modern nutrition in health and disease. 7th ed. Philadelphia: Lea & Febiger, 1988.

61. Patrick, J., and Boland, M. P.: Cystic fibrosis. In Jeejeebhoy, K. N.: Current

therapy in nutrition. Philadelphia: B. C. Decker, 1988.

62. Goodchild, M.: Nutritional management of cystic fibrosis. Digestion 1:62, 1987.

63. Daniels, L., Davidson, G., and Martin, A.: Comparison of the macronutrient intake of healthy controls and children with cystic fibrosis on low or nonrestricted fat diets. J Pediatr Gastroenterol Nutr 6:381, 1987.

64. Waters, D. L., Dorney, S. F., et al.: Pancreatic function in infants identified as having cystic fibrosis in a neonatal screening program. N Engl J Med 322:303, 1990.

65. Rosenberg, I. H.: Nutrition and diet in management of diseases of the gastrointestinal tract. C. Small intestine. (4) Nutritional support of inflammatory bowel disease. In Shils, M. E., and Young, V. R.: Modern nutrition in health and disease. 7th ed. Philadelphia: Lea & Febiger, 1988.

66. Morrissey, K., and Eisenmenger, W.: Medical aspects of diseases of the gallbladder and biliary tree. Am J Med 51:542, 1971.

67. Robins, R. E., and Trueman, G. E.: The gallbladder and extra-hepatic bile ducts. In Boguch, A.: Gastroenterology. New York: McGraw-Hill, 1974.

68. Wintrobe, M. M., Thorn, W. W., et al., eds.: Harrison's principles of internal medicine. 7th ed. New York: McGraw-Hill, 1974.

69. Williams, C.: Diet and diseases of the gastrointestinal tract. N S Med Bull 52:211, 1973.

70. Hodges, R. E., and Adelamn, R. D.: Nutrition in medical practice. Philadelphia: W. B. Saunders, 1980.

71. Price, W.: Gallbladder dyspepsia. Br Med J 2:138, 1963.

72. Douglas, B. R., Jansen, J., et al.: Coffee stimulation of cholecystokinin release and gallbladder contraction in humans. Am J Clin Nutr 52:533, 1990.

73. Gilliland, T. M., and Traverso, L. W.: Modern standards for comparison of cholecystectomy with alternative treatments for symptomatic cholelithiasis with emphasis on long term relief of symptoms. Surg Gynecol Obstet

170:40, 1990.

74. Way, L. W., and Sleisinger, M. H.: Cholelithiasis and cholecystitis. In Sleisenger, M. H., and Fordtran, J. S.: Gastrointestinal disease. 3d ed. Philadelphia: W. B. Saunders, 1983.

75. Breckstein, A. H.: Nonsurgical management of cholelithiasis. Arch Intern Med 150:960, 1990.

76. Lanzini, A., and Northfield, T. C.: Hepatic biliary lipid secretion and gallbladder biliary lipid mass in gallstone patients: Effect of ursodeoxycholic acid. Gut 31:226, 1990.

77. Fromm, H., and Malavolti, M.: Dissolving gallstones. Arch Intern Med 33:409, 1988.

78. Bouchier, I. A. D.: Non-surgical treatment of gallstones: Many contenders but who will win the crown? Gut 29:137, 1988.

79. Sackman, M., Delius, M., et al.: Shock wave lithotripsy of gallbladder stones—the first 175 patients. N Engl J Med 318:393, 1988.

80. Herberer, G., Sachmann, M., et al.: The place of lithotripsy and surgery in the management of gallstone disease. Arch Surg 23:291, 1990.

81. Murray, W. R., Laferla, G., and Fullarton, G. M.: Choledocholithiasis—in vivo stone dissolution using methyl tertiary butyl ether (MTBE). Gut 29:143, 1988.

82. Sandberg, A.: Enzyme substitution in pancreatic disease. Digestion 37:35, 1987.

83. Maxton, D. G., Cynk, E. U., et al.: Effect of dietary fat on the small intestinal mucosa. Gut 30:1252, 1989.

84. Crew, R., and Faloon, W.: The fallacy of a low fat diet in liver disease. JAMA 181:754, 1962.

85. Davidson, C. S.: Diseases of the liver. In Goodhart, R. S., and Shils, M. E.: Modern nutrition in health and disease. 6th ed. Philadelphia: Lea & Febiger, 1980.

86. McMahon, M. J.: Diseases of the exocrine pancreas. In Kinney, J. M., Jeejeebhoy, K. N., et al.: Nutrition and metabolism in patient care. Philadelphia: W. B. Saunders, 1988.

87. Bikle, D.: Calcium absorption and vitamin D metabolism. Clin Gastroenterol 12:379, 1983.

88. Roe, D. A.: Drug induced nutritional deficiencies. Westport, Conn.: AVI, 1980.

89. Powers, D. E., and Moore, A. O.: Food/medication interactions. 6th ed. Phoenix: 1988 (self-published).

90. Mead Johnson Pharmaceuticals: Cholesterol, Questran and you. Evansville, Ind.: Bristol-Myers, 1987.

91. Skidmore-Roth, L.: Medication cards for clinical use. East Norwalk, Conn.: Appleton & Lange, 1985.

92. Wallach, J.: Interpretation of diagnostic tests. 4th ed. Boston: Little, Brown, 1986.

93. Wilson-Goodman, V., Taylor, M. L., and Mueller, D.: Factors affecting the dietary habits of adolescents with cystic fibrosis. J Am Diet Assoc 90:429, 1990.

94. Signore, J.: Ketogenic diet containing medium-chain triglycerides. J Am Diet Assoc 62:285, 1973.

26.

NATIONAL CHOLESTEROL EDUCATION PROGRAM FAT-CONTROLLED DIET

DEFINITIONS

1. NATIONAL CHOLESTEROL EDUCATION PROGRAM (NCEP) FAT-CONTROLLED 2-STEP DIET

A diet that limits total fat intake to less than 30% of total calories, and that limits saturated fat and cholesterol in 2 phases, known as the Step-One and Step-Two diets (1, 2). The composition of these diets is shown in table 26.1.

2. CORONARY HEART DISEASE (CHD)

A disorder caused by narrowing of the coronary arteries (arteries that supply oxygen and nutrients directly to the heart muscle). It is caused by atherosclerosis, thickening and hardening of arterial walls with deposits of lipids and other compounds, which decreases the blood supply to the heart muscle. The inadequate intake of oxygen-rich blood and nutrients may damage the heart muscle and can lead to chest pain, heart attack, and death (3, 4).

3. LIPOPROTEINS

Complexes of proteins and lipids (cholesterol, triglycerides, and phospholipids), which circulate in the bloodstream. Five specific lipoproteins have been identified based on density, each containing different concentrations of lipids: chylomicrons, VLDL, LDL, IDL, and HDL (see below). These protein-coated lipid packages allow fat and cholesterol to be transported in the bloodstream. In general, the larger and lighter a lipoprotein particle is, the more triglyceride it contains (3, 5–7).

TABLE 26.1. DIETARY THERAPY OF HIGH BLOOD CHOLESTEROL

Nutrient	Recommended intake	
	Step-One diet	Step-Two diet
Total fat	Less than 30% of total calories	
Saturated fatty acids	Less than 10% of total calories	Less than 7% of total calories
Polyunsaturated fatty acids	Up to 10% of total calories	
Monounsaturated fatty acids	10% to 15% of total calories	
Carbohydrates	50% to 60% of total calories	
Protein	10% to 20% of total calories	
Cholesterol	Less than 300 mg/day	Less than 200 mg/day
Total calories	To achieve and maintain desirable weight	

Source: National Cholesterol Education Program (2).

4. CHYLOMICRONS

The largest particles of the 5 classes of lipoproteins. These triglyceride-rich particles are made in the intestines, reach the circulation via the lymphatic system, and carry dietary triglycerides to adipose tissue and muscle (8).

5. VERY LOW-DENSITY LIPOPROTEIN (VLDL)

The next largest lipoprotein is responsible for transport of endogenous triglycerides and is synthesized mainly in the liver. VLDL carries triglycerides made in the body to adipose tissue and muscle. Its rate of synthesis is influenced by the amount of carbohydrate and alcohol in the diet; the body fat percentage; and the excess of calories ingested over calories expended. Contained in VLDL are several apolipoproteins, including apolipopro-

tein B-100, which is involved in cholesterol and triglyceride metabolism (9–11).

6. LOW-DENSITY LIPOPROTEIN (LDL)

Lipoprotein that contains the largest amount of cholesterol in the blood. LDL is responsible for depositing cholesterol in the artery walls. High levels of LDL are associated with an increased risk of heart disease. Approximately 70% of LDL is removed from the plasma via hepatic LDL receptors (3).

7. LIPOPROTEIN (A)

Lipoprotein (a), or Lp(a), is a cholesterol-rich plasma lipoprotein similar to LDL but with a different protein composition. It contains 2 apoproteins covalently linked together, apolipoprotein (a) and apolipoprotein B-100. The apoprotein

B-100 is the lipoprotein found in LDL. Individuals with increased concentrations of Lp(a) have an increased independent risk for early myocardial infarction. The increase in risk is unrelated to age, sex, smoking status, or serum levels of total cholesterol, triglycerides, or HDL-cholesterol (12–21).

Lipoprotein (a) is structurally very similar to plasminogen and may have thrombogenic (clot-promoting) properties, as well as atherogenic ones (promoting plaque formation). An increased concentration of lipoprotein (a) means an increased risk for atherosclerotic disease in both the native coronary vessels and the saphenous vein grafts of coronary bypass patients (13–21).

8. INTERMEDIATE-DENSITY LIPOPROTEIN (IDL)

IDL is an intermediary protein that is formed in the catabolism of VLDL to LDL.

9. HIGH-DENSITY LIPOPROTEIN (HDL)

Lipoprotein synthesized by the liver that contains a large proportion of protein and a small amount of cholesterol. It transports cholesterol from body cells and tissues to the liver (3, 8, 22–26).

Low levels of HDL are associated with increased risk of coronary heart disease. Therefore, the higher the HDL level, the better (3, 26).

10. APOPROTEINS

The protein fractions of lipoproteins have been given letters and numbers, e.g., apoprotein A-I and apoprotein A-II. Each class of lipoprotein contains a variety of apolipoproteins in differing proportions, with the exception of LDL, which contains only apo-B (22, 25).

11. LIPIDS

Fatty substances, including cholesterol and triglycerides, that are present in blood and body tissues (3, 26).

12. CHOLESTEROL

A waxy lipid, made in sufficient quantity by the body for normal functions, including the manufacture of hormones, bile acid, and vitamin D (3, 26).

13. BLOOD CHOLESTEROL

Cholesterol that is manufactured in the liver or absorbed from food and is carried in the blood for use by all parts of the body. A high level of blood cholesterol leads to atherosclerosis and coronary heart disease (3, 26).

14. DIETARY CHOLESTEROL

Cholesterol found in food. It is present only in foods of animal origin, not in foods from plants. The role of dietary cholesterol in raising blood cholesterol is uncertain and may vary in different individuals (3, 26).

15. LOW-DENSITY LIPOPROTEIN (LDL) CHOLESTEROL

Cholesterol attached to LDL, which transports it in the blood and deposits it in the artery walls. LDL-cholesterol levels exceeding 130 mg/dL are associated with an increased risk of heart disease (3).

16. HIGH-DENSITY LIPOPROTEIN (HDL) CHOLESTEROL

Cholesterol attached to HDL. HDL-cholesterol levels lower than 35 mg/dL are associated with an increased risk of heart disease. Low HDL-cholesterol levels constitute another risk factor (along with hypertension or smoking) to be considered in the assessment of overall coronary risk (1, 2).

17. TRIGLYCERIDES

The predominant type of lipid in the body, which forms the bulk of adipose tissue. It is carried in the bloodstream in lipoproteins and is composed of a glyc-

erol skeleton to which 3 fatty acids are attached.

18. TOTAL FAT

The sum of the saturated, monounsaturated, and polyunsaturated fats present in food. A mixture of all 3 in varying amounts is found in most food (3, 26).

19. SATURATED FAT

A type of fat found in greatest amounts in foods from animals, such as meat, poultry, and whole-milk dairy products (e.g., cream, milk, ice cream, and cheese). Other examples of saturated fat include butter, marbling and fat along the edges of meat, and lard. The saturated fat content is high in some vegetable oils, e.g., coconut, palm kernel, and palm oils. Hydrogenated or partially hydrogenated oils also contain saturated fat. Saturated fat raises blood cholesterol more than anything else in the diet (3, 26).

20. UNSATURATED FAT

A type of fat that is usually liquid at refrigerator temperature. Monounsaturated fat and polyunsaturated fat both come under the heading of unsaturated fat (3, 26).

21. MONOUNSATURATED FAT

A slightly unsaturated fat that is found in greatest amounts in foods from plants, including olive and canola (rapeseed) oil. When substituted for saturated fat, monounsaturated fat helps reduce blood cholesterol (3, 26).

22. POLYUNSATURATED FAT

A highly unsaturated fat found in greatest amounts in foods from plants, including safflower, sunflower, corn, and soybean oils. When substituted for saturated fat, polyunsaturated fat helps reduce blood cholesterol (3, 26).

23. HYPERLIPIDEMIA

An elevation of the concentration of 1 or more of the lipids in the blood (5).

24. HYPERCHOLESTEROLEMIA

An elevation of the level of serum cholesterol above 200 mg/dL (1, 2).

25. HYPERLIPOPROTEINEMIA

Increased concentrations of 1 or more of the lipoproteins in the blood. There have been 5 distinct types of hyperlipoproteinemia identified, on the basis of the characteristics of the specific lipoprotein abnormality (6, 7).

26. HYPERTRIGLYCERIDEMIA

An elevation of the level of serum triglycerides above 500 mg/dL, according to the National Institutes of Health Consensus Development Conference on the treatment of hypertriglyceridemia. Levels in the range of 250 to 500 mg/dL constitute "borderline hypertriglyceridemia" (27).

27. XANTHOMA

A visible deposit of lipid and cholesterol in skin and tendons (5–7).

PURPOSE OF THE DIET

Prevention of vascular disease is the ultimate goal of hyperlipidemia treatment. The treatment begins with dietary therapy. Although the goal is to lower the LDL-cholesterol concentration specifically, measurement of total serum cholesterol can be used to monitor the response to diet. A total cholesterol of 240 mg/dL corresponds to a fasting LDL-cholesterol level of approximately 160 mg/dL. If the patient is found to have hypertriglyceridemia or an extremely high or low HDL-cholesterol level, total cholesterol cannot be used to estimate LDL-cholesterol (2, 28).

The goals and protocols for dietary intervention are shown in figure 26.1.

EFFECTS OF THE DIET

1. EFFECT OF LDL-CHOLESTEROL LOWERING ON CHD RISK

The issue of whether to lower LDL-cholesterol levels by dietary and drug intervention has been addressed in more than a dozen randomized clinical trials. One of the largest was the Coronary Primary Prevention trial, which substantiates the decrease in overall mortality that follows reduction of LDL-cholesterol levels. A more recent angiographic study showed that cholesterol-lowering dietary and drug therapy slowed the progression and produced regression of coronary atherosclerosis in men with bypass grafts. Intervention is also effective in preventing a second myocardial infarction (2, 29–35).

For individuals with initial blood cholesterol levels in the range of 250 to 300 mg/dL, each 1% reduction in serum cholesterol level yields approximately 2% reduction in CHD rates; in other words, a 10% to 15% reduction of blood cholesterol will reduce risk by 20% to 30% (2).

2. USE OF FISH OILS HIGH IN OMEGA-3 FATTY ACIDS

Fish oils high in omega-3 fatty acids have demonstrated triglyceride-lowering effects. However, most experts agree that omega-3 fatty acids are not effective for lowering LDL-cholesterol levels. Any benefits of fish oils may be related to effects on platelet aggregation, in which they improve the balance between the production of substances that promote blood clotting and the production of prostacyclins, which inhibit blood clotting (28, 36–38).

One study indicated that fish oils have

a beneficial effect on the myocardium itself, which warrants further investigation. Data are also available on other pharmacological and physiological effects of these substances that may provide some protection against coronary artery disease, but these must first be evaluated in human clinical trials. As to use of fish oil capsules as supplements, further investigations to assess safety and efficacy are needed. Meanwhile, patients should be encouraged to increase their consumption of fish (28, 39, 40).

Research is limited regarding the persistence of the hypotriglyceridemic effect of fish oils. The potentially reduced efficacy during prolonged therapy and lack of beneficial effect on apolipoprotein and LDL-cholesterol levels may limit the usefulness of fish oil treatment of hypertriglyceridemia. Long-term clinical trials are needed to elucidate and confirm the effects of fish oil prior to widespread recommendations for its use (41, 42).

3. EFFECTS OF REDUCING BODY WEIGHT

Obesity is not only associated with increased LDL-cholesterol, increased VLDL-cholesterol, and lower HDL-cholesterol levels. It is an independent risk factor for CHD. Obesity often coexists with other CHD risks, including hypertension and diabetes mellitus. Evidence exists that truncal or central obesity may be an additional risk for CHD, independent of body mass index (BMI) (43). The control of obesity should be a priority for the reduction of CHD risk by dietary means. Weight loss may lower serum triglycerides and LDL-cholesterol; and weight loss achieved with exercise may raise HDL levels (2).

4. ADDITIVE EFFECTS OF EXERCISE ON DIET INTERVENTIONS

Most studies have shown that exercise has little effect on total serum cholesterol

FIG. 26.1. DIETARY TREATMENT FOR CONTROL OF CHOLESTEROL.

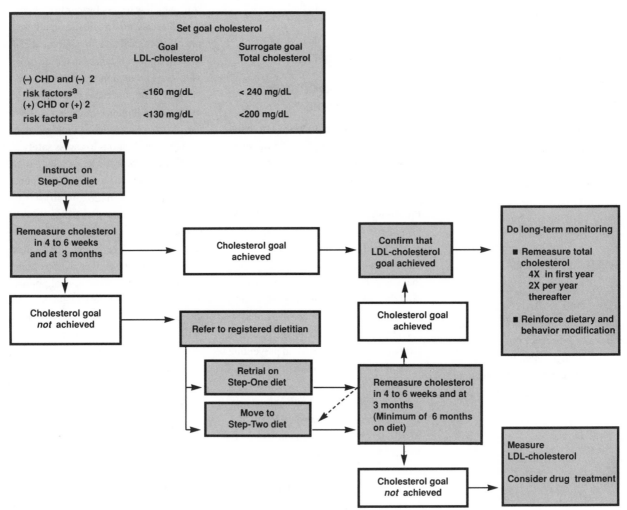

Source: National Cholesterol Education Program (2).
[a]One of which can be male sex (see table 26.3).

or LDL-cholesterol. However, HDL-cholesterol tends to be higher in active and athletic men than in sedentary individuals; this in turn produces a higher ratio of HDL to LDL and a less atherogenic lipid profile. The elevation in HDL demonstrates a dose-response relationship: the greater the energy expended in exercise, the greater the increase in HDL. It appears that a threshold of energy expenditure in exercise of 1,000 kcal per week is needed, with no further benefit above 4,500 kcal per week. Endurance-type exercise is effective, whereas power or speed-type exercise training has little, if any effect on plasma lipoprotein concentrations (44, 45–47).

5. EFFECT OF SATURATED FATTY ACID INTAKE

Epidemiological, clinical, and experimental studies have demonstrated a strong relationship between saturated fatty acid intake and hypercholesterolemia. The saturated fatty acids lauric (C12:0), myristic (C14:0), and palmitic (C16:0), found largely in dairy products and tropical oils, seem to be the most potent in raising cholesterol levels. However, it has been shown that stearic acid (C18:0), found largely in meat, does not have this effect (48, 49).

Saturated fat intake is usually reduced when total fat intake is decreased. Pre-

dictive equations have been developed to determine the expected magnitude of change in blood cholesterol in response to a given change in fatty acid composition of the diet. It is predicted that the plasma cholesterol–raising effect of saturated fatty acids is about twice the lowering effect of polyunsaturated fatty acids (50, 51).

6. EFFECT OF DIETARY CHOLESTEROL INTAKE

The significance of dietary cholesterol as a contributor to hypercholesterolemia continues to be debated. While large increases in dietary cholesterol levels result in elevated plasma cholesterol levels and in reduced catabolism of plasma LDL, studies of the effect of modest changes in dietary cholesterol and LDL metabolism indicate that such effects are minimal and less significant than the effect of changes in the type and amount of dietary fat. Results of another study indicate that an increase in dietary cholesterol can significantly elevate plasma LDL-cholesterol and apolipoprotein B in certain normolipidemic, healthy men, even when they are exercising regularly and consuming a moderately fat-restricted diet low in saturated fat. Dietary cholesterol restriction may be justifiable even when other dietary measures and lifestyle changes are undertaken, to minimize blood cholesterol levels (44).

7. EFFECT OF ALCOHOL CONSUMPTION ON HDL

Moderate alcohol consumption in a group of 100 healthy individuals resulted in a significant increase in plasma HDL-cholesterol. The authors point out, however, that under the conditions of the study, there is no proof that this effect is protective against heart disease and that there is no basis to recommend increased alcohol intake to raise HDL levels. Most other studies have shown that moderate alcohol intake raises HDL-cholesterol and apoprotein A-I while lowering levels of LDL-cholesterol and apoprotein B. The benefits of the rise in HDL-cholesterol have been questioned, however, because the predominant increase appears to be in the HDL-3 subfraction rather than the protective HDL-2 subfraction. Furthermore, the known risks of alcohol, including liver disease and stroke, limit its usefulness (28, 52, 53).

8. EFFECTS OF COFFEE AND CAFFEINE

Research on the effects of coffee consumption on plasma lipids is complicated by many confounding variables, including dietary habits, age, sex, BMI, exercise, smoking, alcohol consumption, estrogen use, ethnicity, occupation, stress,

use of drugs, and baseline plasma total cholesterol level. Moreover, the type of coffee used, the method of preparation, and even the kind of water used affect outcomes. Epidemiological and clinical studies have given conflicting results, but the emerging consensus is that coffee consumption may elevate plasma lipids. The effects of caffeine in other forms are also unclear. Awaiting further research, it has been suggested that dietitians assess the coffee and caffeine intake of individual patients and intervene in cases of high risk or high consumption (54–56).

9. EFFECTS OF DIETARY FIBER ON SERUM LIPIDS

There is evidence that water-soluble fibers (gums, pectins, oat bran) but not insoluble fibers (wheat bran, cellulose) lower LDL-cholesterol and triglycerides (28).

Currently, there are several theories defining the mechanism of action for soluble fibers. The most common is that soluble fibers may increase the excretion of fecal bile acid, resulting in a potential increase in LDL receptors and increased uptake of LDL-cholesterol from the blood. Soluble fiber does not seem to affect HDL levels. Scientists believe that the major cholesterol-lowering component in oats is a water-soluble polysaccharide beta-glucan gum, also found in barley (57).

In a free-living population, the addition of 2 oz. of oatmeal per day to a fat-modified diet in place of other carbohydrate foods caused a further reduction in total serum cholesterol of 2% to 3% over 6 to 8 weeks (58, 59). Also, in a double-blind trial, psyllium supplements were found to reduce total serum cholesterol by 14.8%, whereas the placebo group had only a 3.6% drop over an 8-week period (60). This demonstrates a beneficial effect of adding moderate amounts of soluble fiber to the diet without the ad-

verse reactions of drug therapy. However, longer studies are needed to evaluate the duration of progressive reduction, or the potential adaptation (with loss of treatment effect).

Corn bran, rice bran, carrots, and several citrus fruits have been investigated for their cholesterol-lowering ability, but more research is needed before specific claims can be made for their efficacy.

PHYSIOLOGY, FOODS, AND NUTRIENTS

1. HYPERCHOLESTEROLEMIA AND DIET

Evidence is now overwhelming that coronary heart disease is causally related to hypercholesterolemia and elevated levels of LDL-cholesterol. Coronary risk rises progressively with cholesterol levels, especially when cholesterol exceeds 200 mg/dL. High serum cholesterol levels constitute a risk factor for sudden death. Even in individuals aged 40 to 69 years with preexisting cardiovascular disease, total cholesterol levels and LDL and HDL levels are predictive of subsequent mortality. There is also substantive evidence that lowering total cholesterol and LDL-cholesterol levels will reduce the risk of heart disease (1, 2, 29–34, 61–78).

The incidence of hypercholesterolemia increases with age to a plateau at age 50, with a higher prevalence in older women. Beginning at age 20, mean total cholesterol and LDL-cholesterol levels increase about 40 mg/dL during the next 2 decades of life. The strategy recommended by the Cholesterol Consensus Development Conference for making clinical decisions about patients 20 to 39 years of age is to use cutoff points that correspond to the age-specific 75th and 90th percentile values. Adults 20 to 29 years of age would be considered to have high blood cholesterol if their level exceeds 200 mg/dL. Individuals aged 30 to 39 would be in this category if total cholesterol exceeds 220 mg/dL. Giving dietary treatment to the top 25% of the young adult population has been recommended in order to prevent the development of atherosclerosis at an earlier stage (1). Diagnosing genetic disorders helps clarify the etiology and management of LDL-cholesterol elevations in affected individuals and emphasizes the desirability of measuring cholesterol in first-degree relatives (1).

Whether or not individuals over 60 years old benefit from intervention is controversial. While there is some disagreement on the predictive value of serum cholesterol as a risk factor in the elderly, new data support the view of the NCEP. It has also been suggested that it may be wise to follow up the finding of a total cholesterol over 200 mg/dL in the individual over 60 years of age with determinations of LDL-cholesterol and HDL-cholesterol before imposing treatment. Furthermore, in this age group, a 6-month-minimum trial of dietary treatment is now recommended prior to the institution of drug treatment, and active medical management should be limited to those most likely to benefit from it. The risk of CHD increases in the later decades of life, which means that the absolute magnitude of the potential beneficial effects is substantial (69, 70, 79, 80).

2. OVERALL GOALS OF NCEP

The National Cholesterol Education Program was established by an expert panel on detection, evaluation, and treatment of high blood cholesterol in adults under the National Heart, Lung and Blood Institute of the National Institutes of Health. The recommendations are built on the work of the 1984 Consensus Development Conference on lowering blood cholesterol to prevent heart disease to reflect the current state of knowledge about cholesterol and coronary heart disease in 1988 (2). NCEP has 2 goals:

Goal I: A Patient-Based Approach
To establish criteria that define candidates for medical intervention and to

provide guidelines on how to detect, set goals for, treat, and monitor these patients. These criteria seek to identify individuals at high risk who will benefit from intensive intervention efforts (1, 2).

Goal II: A Public Health Strategy
To shift the distribution of cholesterol levels in the entire population to a lower range (1, 2).

3. USE OF POLYUNSATURATED FATS

There are 2 categories of polyunsaturated fatty acids, commonly known as omega-6 and omega-3. Linoleic acid is an omega-6 fatty acid which, when substituted for saturated fat in the diet, lowers serum cholesterol (81). Good sources of linoleic acid include mayonnaise, margarine, safflower oil, sunflower oil, corn oil, soybean oil, and cottonseed oil.

Good sources of omega-3 fatty acids are certain fish oils. The major fatty acids in this class are eicosapentanoic acid (EPA) and docosahexanoic acid (DHA), which in high doses lower serum triglycerides and VLDL lipoproteins, prolong bleeding times, reduce platelet aggregation, and lower blood pressure. No recommendations for the use of these products to prevent CHD should be made without more study on their immediate and long-term effects (82–84).

Polyunsaturated fats, despite their benefits, are also a concentrated source of calories, and when consumed in larger amounts than recommended may lead to weight gain (2).

4. USE OF MONOUNSATURATED FATS

Recent evidence suggests that such monounsaturated fatty acids as oleic acid may have an effect on LDL-cholesterol similar to that of polyunsaturated fatty acids. The advantage of substituting monounsaturated fatty acids (rather than polyunsaturates) for saturated fatty acids in the diet is that they do not tend to lower the HDL-cholesterol level. Oleic acid is the principal fatty acid in olive oil, rapeseed (canola) oil, and high-oleic-acid sunflower seed and safflower oils. The Seven Countries Study showed an inverse association between oleic acid intake and CHD. Research continues on whether oleic acid may be preferred over linoleic acid when substituting for saturated fatty acids (9, 85).

INDICATIONS FOR USE

1. INITIAL CLASSIFICATION

Criteria for treatment of hyperlipidemia via the Step-One and Step-Two diets and by drugs have recently been standardized in the report of the expert panel on detection, evaluation, and treatment of high blood cholesterol in adults (2).

Indications for Step-One and Step-Two diets are summarized in figure 26.1. It is recommended that total cholesterol be routinely measured in all adults over age 20. The measurement of total cholesterol may be made in the nonfasting state (1, 2). The initial classification based on total cholesterol and the recommended follow-up are shown in table 26.2. Levels should

TABLE 26.2. INITIAL CLASSIFICATION BASED ON TOTAL CHOLESTEROL

Total cholesterol	Classification
<200 mg/dL	Desirable blood cholesterol
200–239 mg/dL	Borderline-high blood cholesterol
≥240 mg/dL	High blood cholesterol

Source: National Cholesterol Education Program (2).

not be measured during weight loss or pregnancy or within 3 months of a myocardial infarction. The incidence of coronary heart disease rises sharply when serum cholesterol exceeds 240 mg/dL.

2. CHD RISK FACTORS

The presence of other risk factors or definite coronary heart disease warrants treatment to lower LDL-cholesterol levels and the setting of lower LDL-cholesterol goals (1). Other CHD risk factors that may be present are listed in table 26.3.

3. RECOMMENDED FOLLOW-UP

Individuals with high blood cholesterol levels (≥ 240 mg/dL) should have serum lipoprotein analysis and be classified according to their LDL-cholesterol (see below). Individuals with desirable blood cholesterol levels (≤ 200 mg/dL) should receive general dietary advice and educational materials on CHD risk reduction, and should have the measurement repeated within 5 years. Those with borderline high blood cholesterol (200 to 240 mg/dL) should be counseled on the Step-One diet and reevaluated annually (see table 26.4).

4. CLASSIFICATION BY LDL-CHOLESTEROL

Once someone is identified as requiring lipoprotein analysis, attention should switch from total cholesterol to LDL-cholesterol in order to meet the goal of identifying and lowering LDL-cholesterol levels. Lipoprotein analysis requires 3 measurements in the fasting state: total cholesterol, total triglycerides, and HDL-cholesterol. From these values LDL-cholesterol is calculated as follows (1):

LDL-cholesterol = total cholesterol −
                  HDL-cholesterol −
                  (triglycerides)/5

Example:

Total cholesterol = 260 mg/dL; HDL-

TABLE 26.3. RISK STATUS BASED ON PRESENCE OF CHD RISK FACTORS OTHER THAN LDL-CHOLESTEROL

The patient is considered to have a high risk status if he or she has one of the following:

Either
Definite CHD—the characteristic clinical picture and objective laboratory findings of either one of the following:
• Definite prior myocardial infarction
• Definite myocardial ischemia, such as angina pectoris

Or
Two other CHD risk factors:
• Male sex[a]
• Family history of premature CHD (definite myocardial infarction or sudden death before age 55 in a parent or sibling)
• Cigarette smoking (currently smokes more than 10 cigarettes per day)
• Hypertension
• Low HDL-cholesterol concentration (below 35 mg/dL confirmed by repeat measurement)
• Diabetes mellitus
• History of definite cerebrovascular or occlusive peripheral vascular disease
• Severe obesity (≥30% overweight)

Source: National Cholesterol Education Program (2).
[a]Male sex is considered a risk factor in this scheme because the rates of CHD are 3 to 4 times higher in men than in women in the middle decades of life and roughly 2 times higher in the elderly. Hence, a man with 1 other CHD risk factor is considered to have a high-risk status, whereas a woman is not so considered unless she has 2 other CHD risk factors.

TABLE 26.4. RECOMMENDED FOLLOW-UP BASED ON TOTAL CHOLESTEROL

Cholesterol level	Follow-up
Total cholesterol <200 mg/dL	Repeat within 5 years
Total cholesterol 200–239 mg/dL	
Without definite CHD or 2 other risk factors (one of which can be male sex)	Dietary information and recheck annually
With definite CHD or 2 other risk factors (one of which can be male sex)	Lipoprotein analysis; further action based on LDL-cholesterol level
Total cholesterol ≥240 mg/dL	

Source: National Cholesterol Education Program (2).

cholesterol = 25 mg/dL; and triglycerides = 270 mg/dL.

LDL-cholesterol = 260 − 25 − 270/5 = 181 mg/dL

When serum triglycerides exceed 400 mg/dL, the formula becomes less accurate. One report, which suggests dividing the triglycerides by 6 rather than 5, awaits substantiation by others. The predictive value of the original formula has been reconfirmed (1, 86, 87).

LDL-cholesterol should be determined after an overnight fast. Two measurements should be taken, 1 to 8 weeks apart, and the average used. Patients with desirable LDL-cholesterol (≤ 130 mg/dL) are treated like those with desirable total cholesterol and are given general educational materials and tested again within 5 years. Similarly, those with borderline high LDL-cholesterol (130 to 159 mg/dL) are instructed in the Step-One diet and reevaluated annually. However, if they also have CHD or 2 other risk factors (table 26.3), they are treated in the same manner as the high-risk LDL-cholesterol group (≥ 160 mg/dL), who undergo clinical evaluation (history, physical exam, and laboratory tests) and begin a cholesterol-lowering treatment program (2).

Classification and treatment decisions based on LDL-cholesterol are shown in table 26.5. The process of identifying individuals requiring Step-One and Step-Two diets is summarized in figures 26.2 and 26.3.

5. HDL-CHOLESTEROL

The level of HDL-cholesterol is inversely related to coronary heart disease rates. Although there is no direct experimental evidence that raising HDL-cholesterol reduces the risk of coronary heart disease, lifestyle interventions that increase HDL levels—e.g., reducing obesity, exercising, and giving up smoking—are good advice in themselves for CHD risk reduction as well as for other health benefits.

TABLE 26.5. CLASSIFICATION AND TREATMENT DECISIONS BASED ON LDL-CHOLESTEROL

Classification

<130 mg/dL	Desirable LDL-cholesterol
130–159 mg/dL	Borderline-high-risk LDL-cholesterol
≥160 mg/dL	High-risk LDL-cholesterol

Dietary treatment

	Initiation level	Minimal goal
Without CHD or 2 other risk factors[a]	≥160 mg/dL	<160 mg/dL[b]
With CHD or 2 other risk factors[a]	≥130 mg/dL	<130 mg/dL[c]

Drug treatment

	Initiation level	Minimal goal
Without CHD or 2 other risk factors[a]	≥190 mg/dL	<160 mg/dL
With CHD or 2 other risk factors[a]	≥160 mg/dL	<130 mg/dL

Source: National Cholesterol Education Program (2).

[a]Patients have a lower initiation level and goal if they are at high risk because they already have definite CHD, or because they have any 2 of the following risk factors: male sex, family history of premature CHD, cigarette smoking, hypertension, low HDL-cholesterol, diabetes mellitus, definite cerebrovascular or peripheral vascular disease, or severe obesity.

[b,c]Roughly equivalent to total cholesterol <240 mg/dL ([b]) or <200 mg/dL ([c]) as goals for monitoring dietary treatment.

Research in the measurement of HDL subfractions may help to clarify specific effects of HDL (88–94).

POSSIBLE ADVERSE REACTIONS

None, provided the diet is adequately planned and implemented.

CONTRAINDICATIONS

None, if guidelines are followed and if no more than 10% of total calories is provided as polyunsaturated fat (2). Diets outside these critical limits may have adverse reactions.

CLINICAL ASSESSMENT

A thorough assessment of patient's diet history and current eating habits is useful in implementation of dietary change. The assessment should include a periodic recording of patient's height and weight

at various times and under varying conditions. Desirable weight and, whenever possible, percentage of body fat should be estimated. A predominance of truncal or abdominal fat has a poorer prognosis than does fat distributed elsewhere on the body, and the use of waist to hip circumference should be used to measure the amount of truncal fat. A screening form for the clinical assessment of dietary fat intake has been published along with information for scoring and coding. The dietary interview should address number of meals, preparation techniques, and fat sources in the diet (95, 96).

The influence of other diseases or drugs and presence of familial lipid disorders should also be determined. Hypothyroidism, nephrotic syndrome, diabetes mellitus, obstructive liver disease, progestins, and anabolic steroids may all increase LDL-cholesterol. Consideration of the patient's clinical status, total coronary risk, and age and sex are prerequisites to the setting of treatment goals.

FIG. 26.2. INITIAL CLASSIFICATION BASED ON TOTAL CHOLESTEROL.

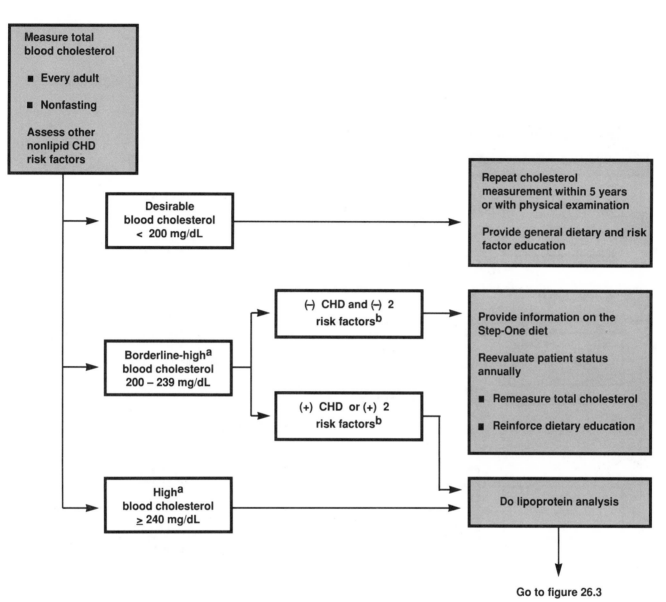

Source: National Cholesterol Education Program (2).
[a]Must be confirmed by repeat measurement; use average value.
[b]One of which can be male sex (see table 26.3).

BIOCHEMICAL ASSESSMENT

Levels of total cholesterol, and if indicated, LDL-cholesterol should be monitored according to guidelines presented here. The biochemical evaluation should include basic laboratory tests, such as urinalysis, complete blood count (CBC),

serum thyroid-stimulating hormone (TSH), glucose, alkaline, phosphatase, and albumin. For more complete data, see Chapter 1.

ASSESSMENT OF POTENTIAL DRUG INTERACTIONS

1. DRUGS THAT INCREASE SERUM CHOLESTEROL LEVELS

Such drugs include chlorthalidone, lev-arterenol corticosteroids, oral con-

FIG. 26.3. CLASSIFICATION BASED ON LDL-CHOLESTEROL.

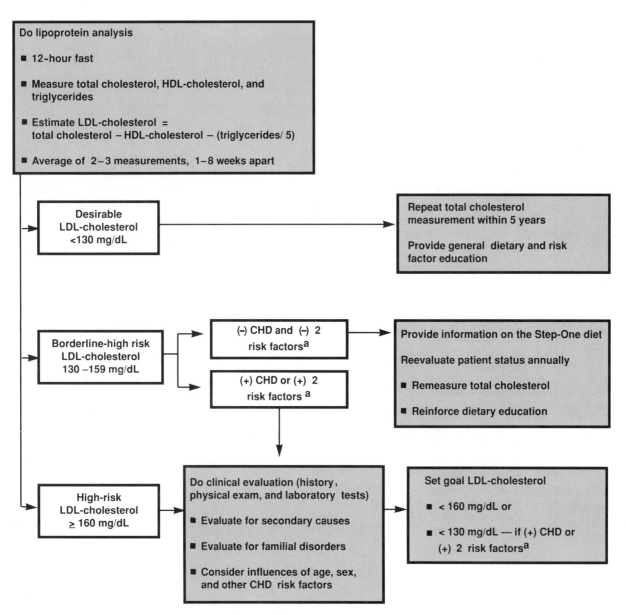

Source: National Cholesterol Education Program (2).
[a]One of which can be male sex (see table 26.3).

traceptives, disulfiram, miconazole, epinephrine, penicillamine, ether, phenothiazines, furosemide, thiazides, and levodopa (97, 98).

2. DRUG THERAPY FOR REDUCTION OF SERUM LIPIDS

Maximum efforts should be made to lower cholesterol levels by dietary, non-pharmacological means. LDL-cholesterol is the best parameter to use in making the decision to use drugs and in monitoring the response to drug therapy. A decision tree for adding drug therapy to diet therapy is given in figure 26.4. Drug therapy is not a substitute for dietary modifications, and patients should be encouraged

to continue to comply with their prescribed diet. The major drugs for consideration include bile acid sequestrants (cholestyramine, colestipol), nicotinic acid, HMG-CoA reductase inhibitors (lovastatin), gemfibrozil, and probucol (99–101). Drugs used in lowering serum cholesterol are described in tables 26.6 and 26.7.

FIG. 26.4. THE ADDITION OF DIET THERAPY TO DRUG THERAPY.

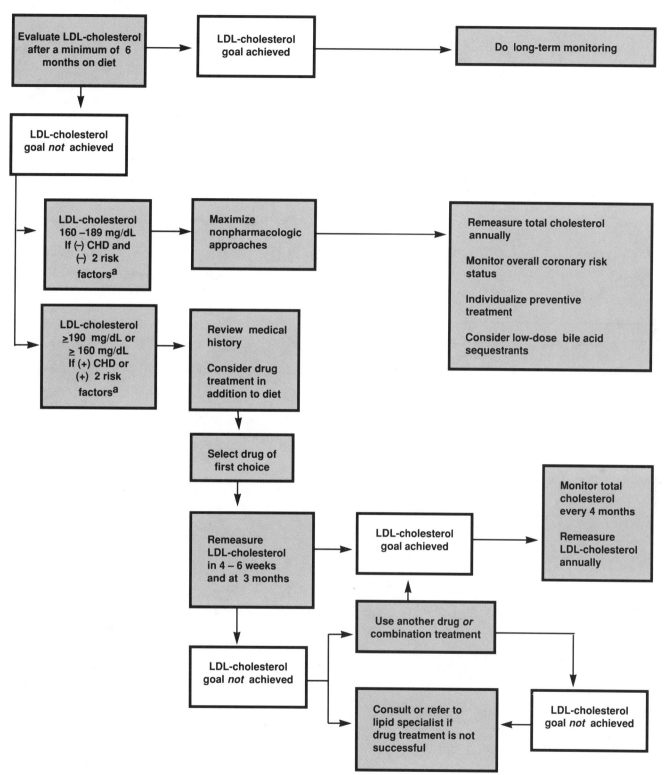

Source: National Cholesterol Education Program (2).
aOne of which can be male sex (see table 26.3).

TABLE 26.6. SUMMARY OF MAJOR CHOLESTEROL-LOWERING DRUGS

Drug	Reduce CHD risk	Long-term safety	Maintaining adherence	LDL-cholesterol lowering	Special precautions
Cholestyramine Colestipol	Yes	Yes	Requires considerable education	15%–30%	Can alter absorption of other drugs. Can increase triglyceride levels and should not be used in patients with hypertriglyceridemia.
Nicotinic acid	Yes	Yes	Requires considerable education	15%–30%	Test for hyperuricemia, hyperglycemia, and liver function abnormalities.
Lovastatin[a]	Not proven	Not established	Relatively easy	25%–45%	Monitor for liver function abnormalities, and possible lens opacities.
Gemfibrozil[b]	Not proven	Preliminary evidence	Relatively easy	5%–15%	May increase LDL-cholesterol in hypertriglyceridemic patients. Should not be used in patients with gallbladder disease.
Probucol	Not proven	Not established	Relatively easy	10%–15%	Lowers HDL-cholesterol; significance of this has not been established. Prolongs QT interval.

Source: National Cholesterol Education Program (2).

[a]Recently approved by the FDA for marketing.

[b]Not FDA-approved for routine use in lowering cholesterol. The results of the Helsinki Heart Study should be available soon to define the effect on CHD risk and long-term safety.

TABLE 26.7. DRUGS HIGHLY EFFECTIVE IN LOWERING LDL-CHOLESTEROL

Drug	Starting dose	Maximum dose	Usual time and frequency	Side effects	Monitoring
Cholestyramine Colestipol	4 g twice daily 5 g twice daily	24 g/day 30 g/day	Twice daily, within an hour of major meals	Dose-dependent upper and lower gastrointestinal	Dosing schedules of coadministered drugs
Nicotinic acid	100–250 mg as single dose	3 g/day; rarely, doses up to 6 g are used	Three times a day, with meals to minimize flushing	Flushing, upper gastrointestinal and hepatic	Uric acid, liver function, glucose
Lovastatin	20 mg once daily with evening meal	80 mg/day	Once (evening) or twice daily with meals	Gastrointestinal and hepatic; miscellaneous, including muscle pain	Liver function, CPK, lens

Source: National Cholesterol Education Program (2).

A. Bile Acid Sequestrants These are the drugs of first choice for patients without hypertriglyceridemia (101); the second choice is nicotinic acid (2). They reduce LDL-cholesterol and CHD risk and are generally safe (2).

Bile acid sequestering agents bind bile acids in the intestinal lumen and prevent their reabsorption in the terminal ileum. In addition, their interruption of the enterohepatic recirculation of bile acids affects lipoprotein metabolism. They activate the enzyme cholesterol 7-alpha hydroxylase (which promotes the conversion of cholesterol to bile acids). Cholestyramine and colestipol are both powders that must be mixed with water or fruit juice and taken in 2 or 3 divided doses with meals. The patient may prefer one or the other drug on the basis of taste and palatability. Cholestyramine is now available as a candy bar. Some patients cannot tolerate a full dose. Constipation may be handled by increased use of water, bran, or, if needed, stool softeners (2, 102, 103).

Cholestyramine and colestipol may interact with other drugs, which are best taken at least 1 hour before the sequestrants or 4 hours after them. Bile acid sequestrants may interfere with absorption of digoxin, warfarin, thyroxine, thiazide diuretics, beta blockers, fat-soluble vitamins and folic acid. Biochemical side effects may include increased plasma triglyceride concentrations and a transient increase in alkaline phosphatase and transaminase (2).

Both alone and with other drugs, the bile acid sequestrants cholestyramine and colestipol are excellent agents for lowering LDL-cholesterol levels. They have been shown to lower the incidence of coronary events and to retard the progression of atherosclerosis (104).

B. Nicotinic Acid Nicotinic acid lowers serum triglyceride levels and is preferred in hypertriglyceridemia. It lowers LDL-cholesterol levels, lowers total cholesterol by about 25%, and increases HDL levels. The usual dose required to achieve hypolipidemic action is 2 to 7 g per day. Hyperglycemia, gastrointestinal side effects, and flushing may occur. With higher doses of the drug, hyperuricemia and abnormal liver function may occur (2, 102).

C. HMG-CoA Reductase Inhibitors The discovery of specific competitive inhibitors of the rate limiting enzyme in cholesterol biosynthesis (HMG-CoA reductase) has opened up a new avenue of therapy for patients with primary hypercholesterolemia. HMG-CoA reductase inhibitors inhibit the rate limiting enzyme for cholesterol synthesis, which in turn stimulates the production of LDL receptors in the liver, increasing the rate of removal of LDL from the plasma. Thus, these drugs reduce LDL-cholesterol by about 25% to 45%. Lovastatin, formerly known as mevinolin, is the prototype drug in this class and may lower LDL by 35% to 45%. Triglyceride levels are lowered modestly, by 15% to 20%, and HDL-cholesterol levels increase by 5% to 10%. Other drugs in this class, Simvastatin and Pravastatin, are not currently available but are undergoing clinical trials. A rare, but troubling, side effect is myositis presenting as muscle pain and associated with an elevated creatinine phosphokinase level. Acute renal failure is also possible when the drug is taken in combination with gemfibrozil or nicotinic acid. Studies have also shown beneficial effects of this drug on lipid levels in diabetics (2, 99, 102, 105).

D. Other Drugs Gemfibrozil is highly effective in lowering serum triglycerides. The primary action of these triglycerides enhances the activity of lipoprotein lipase and may interfere with the hepatic synthesis of VLDL-triglyceride. In the Helsinki study, gemfibrozil moderately reduced serum levels of total and LDL-cholesterol, reduced triglycerides, increased HDL-cholesterol levels, and reduced the incidence of CHD in hypercholesterolemic men by about 34%. The drug may be particularly useful to patients with high-risk LDL-cholesterol levels who also have borderline hypertriglyceridemia and low HDL-cholesterol levels. It potentiates the action of Coumadin, and if combined with lovastatin, it may cause myositis (2, 102, 106).

Probucol is an antioxidant that is carried within the LDL particle. It reduces LDL-cholesterol by about 8% to 15% and may produce regression of xanthomas in severely hypercholesterolemic patients but also reduces HDL-cholesterol levels (2, 102).

Clofibrate is useful primarily in lowering serum triglyceride levels to reduce the risk of pancreatitis. It is used infrequently because long-term use is associated with some toxicity (2).

E. Combination Drug Therapy Combinations of various drugs may be more effective than 1 drug alone in some instances. In the Stockholm Heart Disease Secondary Prevention Study, CHD risk reduction was achieved with combination of clofibrate and nicotinic acid (105, 107–109). Research and experience will provide more information as to the efficacy and possible adverse effects of drug combinations.

IMPLEMENTATION AND EDUCATION

1. THE PHYSICIAN'S ATTITUDE

The physician should prepare the patient for diet counseling by presenting in a very positive way the role of diet and drug therapy in the treatment of disease.

2. IMPLEMENTATION STRATEGIES

Diet therapy should proceed by means of the Step-One and Step-Two diets. These are designed to limit total fat intake, to reduce progressively the intake of saturated fatty acids and cholesterol, and to promote weight loss in overweight patients by eliminating excess calories.

A. Step-One Diet This diet involves an intake of total fat that accounts for less than 30% of calories, saturated fatty acids less than 10% of calories, and cholesterol less than 300 mg per day. The focus should be on reducing the intake of foods that are major sources of saturated fatty acids, particularly those with butterfat and fatty meats. Each of the major food groups should be discussed as presented in table 26.8, with suggestions of foods to increase and decrease. The use of high-fat processed meats, candies, and other snacks high in simple sugars and saturated fats should be discouraged. Patient response should be monitored at 4 to 6 weeks and after 3 months, using blood cholesterol determinations. Appropriate cooking techniques and recipes should be provided. If target goals for total cholesterol levels are met, LDL-cholesterol determinations should be used as confirmation and regular cholesterol education reinforcement set up on a long-term basis.

B. Step-Two Diet Depending on the degree of response of serum lipids, if goals are not met, the patient can progress directly to the Step-Two diet or another 3-month trial of the Step-One diet. The Step-Two diet specifies a further reduction in saturated fatty acids to 7% of calories and a reduction in cholesterol to less than 200 mg per day. The focus of instruction should be a meal plan with suggested numbers of servings of foods from a list of food groups that identifies saturated fat, polyunsaturated fat, and caloric content, as in table 26.9. If goals are met after 3 more months, long-term monitoring should be planned. If goals are not met, it may be necessary to extend the trial period to a maximum of 1 year or to institute drug therapy (2).

3. NUTRITIONAL ADEQUACY

A prerequisite to this or any other therapeutic diet is that it must be nutritionally adequate, provide a variety of different foods, and be palatable.

4. REDUCTION IN TOTAL FAT INTAKE

Except for patients with hypertriglyceridemia and hyperchylomicronemia who need to follow a very low-fat diet (10% to 20% fat) to prevent pancreatitis, more drastic reductions in dietary fat intake are unnecessary and may compromise both the palatability of the diet and the patient's ability to comply. One study comparing 3 cholesterol-lowering diets demonstrated no significant differences in lipid lowering effects between a diet providing 20% of the calories as fat and one providing 30% (2, 110).

5. INCREASED INTAKE OF COMPLEX CARBOHYDRATES AND SOLUBLE FIBERS

Oat bran and beans are rich sources of a soluble fiber called beta-glucan, which is a hypolipidemic agent. Pectin is also a soluble fiber, found in fruits and certain vegetables, that lowers serum lipids. Patients should be instructed in the choice and cookery of foods high in soluble fibers, such as legumes, oats, fruits, and vegetables (2).

6. ALCOHOL

Alcohol increases serum triglyceride levels, and its use should be discouraged.

7. THE PATIENT'S UNDERSTANDING

Many patients and consumers are confused by terms used in association with cholesterol-lowering diets. The difference between fat and cholesterol and between serum and dietary cholesterol should be highlighted. Patients may not be aware of common misunderstandings or may be unwilling to ask; the practitioner should therefore be careful to define all terms used.

8. BEHAVIOR MODIFICATION

Long-term adherence to the diet requires changes in eating behavior. The most effective strategies are ones that the patient has helped to develop. It is sometimes useful to make desired changes gradually, in a series of steps. One way to involve the patient in developing goals and setting a personalized timetable to achieve them is some sort of written contract between the patient and the practitioner, which outlines those interventions for which the patient has agreed to assume responsibility.

There is some evidence that vascular lesions can recur after coronary bypass operations and that the drugs used to treat rejection in heart transplant patients tend to raise serum lipid levels. For these reasons, dietary treatment should continue after bypass grafts and after heart transplant operations. The diet should be followed even after myocardial infarctions, to prevent recurrences (111, 112).

9. FOOD LABELS AND NEW PRODUCTS

Dietitians should alert patients to misleading labels, which may promote the cholesterol-lowering advantages of a high soluble-fiber content while failing to mention the disadvantages of a high saturated fat content. New food labeling legislation will help prevent misleading nutritional claims.

With the ever-increasing commercial availability of fat-modified food products, close scrutiny of these products and the identification of those which are nutritionally inferior is an important priority for quality assurance.

10. EVALUATING EFFICACY

After 3 months of the Step-One diet, the serum total cholesterol level should be measured and adherence to the diet assessed. If goals are met, an LDL-cholesterol level should be determined to assure the LDL goal is achieved. The

TABLE 26.8. RECOMMENDED DIET MODIFICATION: THE STEP-ONE DIET

Food group	Choose	Decrease
Fish, chicken, turkey, and lean meats	Fish, poultry without skin, lean cuts of beef, lamb, pork or veal, shellfish	Fatty cuts of beef, lamb, pork; spare ribs, organ meats, regular cold cuts, sausage, hot dogs, bacon, sardines, roe
Skim and low-fat milk, cheese, yogurt, and dairy substitutes	Skim or 1%-fat milk (liquid, powdered, evaporated); buttermilk	Whole milk (4% fat): regular, evaporated, condensed; cream, half-and-half, 2% milk, imitation milk products, most non-dairy creamers, whipped toppings
	Nonfat (0% fat) or low-fat yogurt	Whole-milk yogurt
	Low-fat cottage cheese (1% or 2% fat)	Whole-milk cottage cheese (4% fat)
	Low-fat cheeses, farmer, or pot cheeses (all of these should be labeled no more than 2–6 g fat/oz.)	All natural cheeses (blue, Roquefort, Camembert, cheddar, Swiss); low-fat or "light" cream cheese; low-fat or "light" sour cream; cream cheeses; sour cream
	Sherbet; sorbet	Ice cream
Eggs	Egg whites (2 whites = 1 whole egg in recipes), cholesterol-free egg substitutes	Egg yolks
Fruits and vegetables	Fresh, frozen, canned, or dried fruits and vegetables	Vegetables prepared in butter, cream, or other sauce
Breads and cereals	Homemade baked goods using unsaturated oils sparingly; angel food cake, low-fat crackers, low-fat cookies	Commercial baked goods: pies, cakes, doughnuts, croissants, pastries, muffins, biscuits, high-fat crackers, high-fat cookies
	Rice, pasta	Egg noodles
	Whole-grain breads and cereals (oatmeal, whole wheat, rye, bran, multigrain, etc.)	Breads in which eggs are major ingredient
Fats and oils	Baking cocoa	Chocolate
	Unsaturated vegetable oils: corn, olive, rapeseed (canola oil), safflower, sesame, soybean, sunflower; margarine or shortening made from one of those unsaturated oils; diet margarine	Butter, coconut oil, palm oil, palm kernel oil, lard, bacon fat
	Mayonnaise; salad dressings made with unsaturated oils listed above; low-fat dressings	Dressings made with egg yolk
	Seeds and nuts	Coconut

Source: National Cholesterol Education Program (2).

TABLE 26.9. FAT AND CHOLESTEROL COMPARISON CHART

MEATS

When following a cholesterol-lowering diet, select the meats that are lowest in saturated fat (i.e., saturated fatty acids) and cholesterol. The information on total fat, percent calories from fat, and calories should be helpful if you are trying to lose weight.

The following foods within each category (veal, lamb, beef, pork) are ranked from low to high in saturated fat. To reduce the saturated fat in your diet, select the leaner cuts from the upper portion of each category. Trimming the visible fat will reduce the fat content even more. Since meats contribute a significant amount of saturated fat and cholesterol to your diet, you should eat smaller portions (no more than 6 oz. per day).

Product (3½ oz., cooked)[a]	Saturated fatty acids (g)	Cholesterol (mg)	Total fat[b] (g)	Calories from fat[c] (%)	Total calories
Beef					
Kidneys, simmered[d]	1.1	387	3.4	21	144
Liver, braised[d]	1.9	389	4.9	27	161
Round, top round, lean only, broiled	2.2	84	6.2	29	191
Round, eye of round, lean only, broasted	2.5	69	6.5	32	183
Round, tip round, lean only, roasted	2.8	81	7.5	36	190
Round, full cut, lean only, choice, broiled	2.9	82	8.0	37	194
Round, bottom round, lean only, braised	3.4	96	9.7	39	222
Short loin, top loin, lean only, broiled	3.6	76	8.9	40	203
Wedge-bone sirloin, lean only, broiled	3.6	89	8.7	38	208
Short loin, tenderloin, lean only, broiled	3.6	84	9.3	41	204
Chuck, arm pot roast, lean only, braised	3.8	101	10.0	39	231
Short loin, T-bone steak, lean only, choice, broiled	4.2	80	10.4	44	214
Short loin, porterhouse steak, lean only, choice, broiled	4.3	80	10.8	45	218
Brisket, whole, lean only, braised	4.6	93	12.8	48	241
Rib eye, small end (ribs 10–12), lean only, choice, broiled	4.9	80	11.6	47	225
Rib, whole (ribs 6–12), lean only, roasted	5.8	81	13.8	52	240
Flank, lean only, choice, braised	5.9	71	13.8	51	244
Rib, large end (ribs 6–9), lean only, broiled	6.1	82	14.2	55	233

(continued)

patient should progress to the Step-Two diet if LDL goals are not met after 6 months on the Step-One diet. Total cholesterol levels again should be determined after a further 3 months. Drug therapy should be considered if LDL-cholesterol goals are not achieved after an aggressive 1 year trial with diet.

PRIORITIES FOR QUALITY ASSURANCE

The NCEP report gives clear criteria that can be applied to each institution as monitors of quality assurance. Examples include the percentage of diet orders reflecting application of the principles outlined in the report, adequate supplies of appropriate instructional materials to implement the diets and properly counsel patients, and response of patients in the institution to the Step-One and Step-Two diets.

TABLE 26.9. *CONTINUED*

Product (3½ oz., cooked)[a]	Saturated fatty acids (g)	Cholesterol (mg)	Total fat[b] (g)	Calories from fat[c] (%)	Total calories
Chuck, blade roast, lean only, braised	6.2	106	15.3	51	270
Corned beef, cured, brisket, cooked	6.3	98	19.0	68	251
Flank, lean and fat, choice, braised	6.6	72	15.5	54	257
Ground, lean, broiled medium	7.2	87	18.5	61	272
Round, full cut, lean and fat, choice, braised	7.3	84	18.2	60	274
Rib, short ribs, lean only, choice, braised	7.7	93	18.1	55	295
Salami, cured, cooked, smoked, 3–4 slices	9.0	65	20.7	71	262
Short loin, T-bone steak, lean and fat, choice, broiled	10.2	84	24.6	68	324
Chuck, arm pot roast, lean and fat, braised	10.7	99	26.0	67	350
Sausage, cured, cooked, smoked, about 2	11.4	67	26.9	78	312
Bologna, cured, 3–4 slices	12.1	58	28.5	82	312
Frankfurter, cured, about 2	12.0	61	28.5	82	315
Lamb					
Leg, lean only, roasted	3.0	89	8.2	39	191
Loin chop, lean only, broiled	4.1	94	9.4	39	215
Rib, lean only, roasted	5.7	88	12.3	48	232
Arm chop, lean only, braised	6.0	122	14.6	47	279
Rib, lean and fat, roasted	14.2	90	30.6	75	368
Pork					
Cured, ham steak, boneless, extra lean, unheated	1.4	45	4.2	31	122
Liver, braised[d]	1.4	355	4.4	24	165
Kidneys, braised[d]	1.5	480	4.7	28	151
Fresh, loin, tenderloin, lean only, roasted	1.7	93	4.8	26	166
Cured, shoulder, arm picnic, lean only, roasted	2.4	48	7.0	37	170
Cured, ham, boneless, regular, roasted	3.1	59	9.0	46	178
Fresh, leg (ham), shank half, lean only, roasted	3.6	92	10.5	44	215

(continued)

TABLE 26.9. *CONTINUED*

Product (3½ oz., cooked)[a]	Saturated fatty acids (g)	Cholesterol (mg)	Total fat[b] (g)	Calories from fat[c] (%)	Total calories
Fresh, leg (ham), rump half, lean only, roasted	3.7	96	10.7	43	221
Fresh, loin, center loin, sirloin, lean only, roasted	4.5	91	13.1	49	240
Fresh, loin, sirloin, lean only, roasted	4.5	90	13.2	50	236
Fresh, loin, center rib, lean only, roasted	4.8	79	13.8	51	245
Fresh, loin, top loin, lean only, roasted	4.8	79	13.8	51	245
Fresh, shoulder, blade, Boston, lean only, roasted	5.8	98	16.8	59	256
Fresh, loin, blade, lean only, roasted	6.6	89	19.3	62	279
Fresh, loin, sirloin, lean and fat, roasted	7.4	91	20.4	63	291
Cured, shoulder, arm picnic, lean and fat, roasted	7.7	58	21.4	69	280
Fresh, loin, center loin, lean and fat, roasted	7.9	91	21.8	64	305
Cured, shoulder, blade roll, lean and fat, roasted	8.4	67	23.5	74	287
Fresh, Italian sausage, cooked	9.0	78	25.7	72	323
Fresh, bratwurst, cooked	9.3	60	25.9	77	301
Fresh, chitterlings, cooked	10.1	143	28.8	86	303
Cured, liver sausage, liverwurst	10.6	158	28.5	79	326
Cured, smoked link sausage, grilled	11.3	68	31.8	74	389
Fresh, spareribs, lean and fat, braised	11.8	121	30.3	69	397
Cured, salami, dry or hard	11.9	—	33.7	75	407
Bacon, fried	17.4	85	49.2	78	576
Veal					
Rump, lean only, roasted	—	128	2.2	13	156
Sirloin, lean only, roasted	—	128	3.2	19	153
Arm steak, lean only, cooked	—	90	5.3	24	200
Loin chop, lean only, cooked	—	90	6.7	29	207

(continued)

TABLE 26.9. *CONTINUED*

Product (3½ oz., cooked)[a]	Saturated fatty acids (g)	Cholesterol (mg)	Total fat[b] (g)	Calories from fat[c] (%)	Total calories
Blade, lean only, cooked	—	90	7.8	33	211
Cutlet, medium fat, braised or broiled	4.8	128	11.0	37	271
Foreshank, medium fat, stewed	—	90	10.4	43	216
Plate, medium fat, stewed	—	90	21.2	63	303
Rib, medium fat, roasted	7.1	128	16.9	70	218
Flank, medium fat, stewed	—	90	32.3	75	390

POULTRY

When following a cholesterol-lowering diet, select poultry low in saturated fat (i.e., saturated fatty acids) and cholesterol. Choosing poultry lower in total fat, calories, and percent calories from fat will also help you lose weight.

This table ranks poultry from low to high in saturated fat. Select the lower-fat poultry from the upper portion of the table. In general, poultry, especially poultry with the skin removed, is lower in saturated fat than most cuts of meat. To reduce the saturated fat in your diet even more, eat smaller servings (no more than 6 oz. per day).

Product (3½ oz., cooked)[a]	Saturated fatty acids (g)	Cholesterol (mg)	Total fat[b] (g)	Calories from fat[c] (%)	Total calories
Turkey, fryer-roasters, light meat without skin, roasted	0.4	86	1.9	8	140
Chicken, roasters, light meat without skin, roasted	1.1	75	4.1	24	153
Turkey, fryer-roasters, light meat with skin, roasted	1.3	95	4.6	25	164
Chicken, broilers or fryers, light meat without skin, roasted	1.3	85	4.5	24	173
Turkey, fryer-roasters, dark meat without skin, roasted	1.4	112	4.3	24	162
Chicken, stewing, light meat without skin, stewed	2.0	70	8.0	34	213
Turkey roll, light and dark	2.0	55	7.0	42	149
Turkey, fryer-roasters, dark meat with skin, roasted	2.1	117	7.1	35	182
Chicken, roasters, dark meat without skin, roasted	2.4	75	8.8	44	178

(*continued*)

TABLE 26.9. *CONTINUED*

Product (3½ oz., cooked)ᵃ	Saturated fatty acids (g)	Cholesterol (mg)	Total fatᵇ (g)	Calories from fatᶜ (%)	Total calories
Chicken, broilers or fryers, dark meat without skin, roasted	2.7	93	9.7	43	205
Chicken, broilers or fryers, light meat with skin, roasted	3.0	84	10.9	44	222
Chicken, stewing, dark meat without skin, stewed	4.1	95	15.3	53	258
Duck, domesticated, flesh only, roasted	4.2	89	11.2	50	201
Chicken, broilers or fryers, dark meat with skin, roasted	4.4	91	15.8	56	253
Goose, domesticated, flesh only, roasted	4.6	96	12.7	48	238
Turkey bologna, about 3½ slices	5.1	99	15.2	69	199
Chicken frankfurter, about 2	5.5	101	19.5	68	257
Turkey frankfurter, about 2	5.9	107	17.7	70	226

FISH AND SHELLFISH

When following a cholesterol-lowering diet, you may want to eat more fish and shellfish, which in general have a lot less saturated fat (i.e., saturated fatty acids) and cholesterol than meat and poultry. However, some shellfish is relatively high in cholesterol and should be eaten less often. Fish and shellfish also contain less total fat and calories than meat and poultry. Use the information on total fat, percent calories from fat, and calories to help you lose weight.

This table ranks fish and shellfish within each category (finfish, crustaceans, mollusks) from low to high in saturated fat. You will want to select the lower-fat and lower-cholesterol fish and shellfish from the upper portion of the table. To reduce the amount of saturated fat in your diet even more, eat smaller portions (no more than 6 oz. per day).

Omega-3 fatty acid (fish oil) is a type of polyunsaturated fat found in the greatest amounts in fattier fish. Evidence is mounting that omega-3 fatty acids in the diet may help lower high blood cholesterol. Since their potential benefit is not fully understood, the use of fish oil supplements is not recommended. However, eating fish is beneficial because it not only contains omega-3 fatty acids but, more important, is low in saturated fat.

Product (3½ oz., cooked)ᵃ	Saturated fatty acids (g)	Cholesterol (mg)	Omega-3 fatty acids (g)	Total fatᵇ (g)	Calories from fatᶜ (%)	Total calories
Finfish						
Haddock, dry heat	0.2	74	0.2	0.9	7	112
Cod, Atlantic, dry heat	0.2	55	0.2	0.9	7	105

(continued)

TABLE 26.9. *CONTINUED*

Product (3½ oz., cooked)[a]	Saturated fatty acids (g)	Cholesterol (mg)	Omega-3 fatty acids (g)	Total fat[b] (g)	Calories from fat[c] (%)	Total calories
Pollock, walleye, dry heat	0.2	96	1.5	1.1	9	113
Perch, mixed species, dry heat	0.2	42	0.3	1.2	9	117
Grouper, mixed species, dry heat	0.3	47	—	1.3	10	118
Whiting, mixed species, dry heat	0.3	84	0.9	1.7	13	115
Snapper, mixed species, dry heat	0.4	47	—	1.7	12	128
Halibut, Atlantic and Pacific, dry heat	0.4	41	0.6	2.9	19	140
Rockfish, Pacific, dry heat	0.5	44	0.5	2.0	15	121
Sea bass, mixed species, dry heat	0.7	53	—	2.5	19	124
Trout, rainbow, dry heat	0.8	73	0.9	4.3	26	151
Swordfish, dry heat	1.4	50	1.1	5.1	30	155
Tuna, bluefin, dry heat	1.6	49	—	6.3	31	184
Salmon, sockeye, dry heat	1.9	87	1.3	11.0	46	216
Anchovy, European, canned	2.2	—	2.1	9.7	42	210
Herring, Atlantic, dry heat	2.6	77	2.1	11.5	51	203
Eel, dry heat	3.0	161	0.7	15.0	57	236
Mackerel, Atlantic, dry heat	4.2	75	1.3	17.8	61	262
Pompano, Florida, dry heat	4.5	64	—	12.1	52	211
Crustaceans						
Lobster, northern	0.1	72	0.1	0.6	6	98
Crab, blue, moist heat	0.2	100	0.5	1.8	16	102
Shrimp, mixed species, moist heat	0.3	195	0.3	1.1	10	99
Mollusks						
Whelk, moist heat	0.1	130	—	0.8	3	275
Clam, mixed species, moist heat	0.2	67	0.3	2.0	12	148
Mussel, blue, moist heat	0.9	56	0.8	4.5	23	172
Oyster, Eastern, moist heat	1.3	109	1.0	5.0	33	137

(continued)

TABLE 26.9. *CONTINUED*

DAIRY AND EGG PRODUCTS

When following a cholesterol-lowering diet, select dairy products low in saturated fat (i.e., saturated fatty acids) and cholesterol. Whole-milk dairy products are relatively high in both when compared ounce for ounce with meat, poultry, and seafood. If you are trying to lose weight on your cholesterol-lowering diet, choose dairy products low in total fat, calories, and percent calories from fat.

The following foods within each category (milk, yogurt, cheese) are ranked from low to high in saturated fat. In general, the hard cheeses are much higher in saturated fat and cholesterol than yogurt and most soft cheeses. You will want to select foods from the upper portion of each category.

Product	Saturated fatty acids (g)	Cholesterol (mg)	Total fat[b] (g)	Calories from fat[c] (%)	Total calories
Milk (8 oz.)					
Skim milk	0.3	4	0.4	5	86
Buttermilk	1.3	9	2.2	20	99
Low-fat milk, 1% fat	1.6	10	2.6	23	102
Low-fat milk, 2% fat	2.9	18	4.7	35	121
Whole milk, 3.3% fat	5.1	33	8.2	49	150
Yogurt (4 oz.)					
Plain yogurt, low-fat	0.1	2	0.2	3	63
Plain yogurt	2.4	14	3.7	47	70
Cheese					
Cottage cheese, low-fat, 1% fat, 4 oz.	0.7	5	1.2	13	82
Mozzarella, part-skim, 1 oz.	2.9	16	4.5	56	72
Cottage cheese, creamed, 4 oz.	3.2	17	5.1	39	117
Mozzarella, 1 oz.	3.7	22	6.1	69	80
Sour cream, 1 oz.	3.7	12	5.9	87	61
American processed cheese spread, pasteurized, 1 oz.	3.8	16	6.0	66	82
Feta, 1 oz.	4.2	25	6.0	72	75
Neufchatel, 1 oz.	4.2	22	6.6	81	74
Camembert, 1 oz.	4.3	20	6.9	73	85
American processed cheese food, pasteurized, 1 oz.	4.4	18	7.0	68	93
Provolone, 1 oz.	4.8	20	7.6	68	100
Limburger, 1 oz.	4.8	26	7.7	75	93
Brie, 1 oz.	4.9	28	7.9	74	95
Romano, 1 oz.	4.9	29	7.6	63	110
Gouda, 1 oz.	5.0	32	7.8	69	101
Swiss, 1 oz.	5.0	26	7.8	65	107
Edam, 1 oz.	5.0	25	7.9	70	101
Brick, 1 oz.	5.3	27	8.4	72	105
Blue, 1 oz.	5.3	21	8.2	73	100

(*continued*)

TABLE 26.9. *CONTINUED*

Product	Saturated fatty acids (g)	Cholesterol (mg)	Total fat[b] (g)	Calories from fat[c] (%)	Total calories
Gruyere, 1 oz.	5.4	31	9.2	71	117
Muenster, 1 oz.	5.4	27	8.5	74	104
Parmesan, 1 oz.	5.4	22	8.5	59	129
Monterey Jack, 1 oz.	5.5	25	8.6	73	106
Roquefort, 1 oz.	5.5	26	8.7	75	105
Ricotta, part-skim, 4 oz.	5.6	25	9.0	52	156
American processed cheese, pasteurized, 1 oz.	5.6	27	8.9	75	106
Colby, 1 oz.	5.7	27	9.1	73	112
Cheddar, 1 oz.	6.0	30	9.4	74	114
Cream cheese, 1 oz.	6.2	31	9.9	90	99
Ricotta, whole-milk, 4 oz.	9.4	58	14.7	67	197
Eggs					
Egg, chicken, white	0	0	Trace	0	16
Egg, chicken, whole	1.7	274	5.6	64	79
Egg, chicken, yolk	1.7	272	5.6	80	63

FROZEN DESSERTS

When following a cholesterol-lowering diet, select frozen desserts low in saturated fat (i.e., saturated fatty acids) and cholesterol. This table ranks frozen desserts from low to high in saturated fat. Select the lower-fat desserts from the upper portion of the list. If you are also trying to lose weight on your cholesterol-lowering diet, the calories will be of special interest to you. Although some frozen desserts are lower in fat than others, they may be just as high in calories as the higher fat products because of their sugar content. You will want to select those desserts not only low in fat but also low in calories.

Product (1 cup)	Saturated fatty acids (g)	Cholesterol (mg)	Total fat[b] (g)	Calories from fat[c] (%)	Total calories
Fruit Popsicle, 1 bar	—	—	0	0	65
Fruit ice	—	—	Trace	0	247
Fudgsicle	—	—	0.2	2	91
Frozen yogurt, fruit-flavored	—	—	2.0	8	216
Sherbet, orange	2.4	14	3.8	13	270
Pudding pops, 1 pop	2.5	1	2.6	25	94
Ice milk, vanilla, soft-serve	2.9	13	4.6	19	223
Ice milk, vanilla, hard	3.5	18	5.6	28	184
Ice cream, vanilla, regular	8.9	59	14.3	48	269
Ice cream, French vanilla, soft-serve	13.5	153	22.5	54	377
Ice cream, vanilla, rich, 16% fat	14.7	88	23.7	61	349

(*continued*)

TABLE 26.9. *CONTINUED*

FATS AND OILS

This table compares the fat content of selected fats and oils, going from those with a low saturated fat (i.e., saturated fatty acids) content to those with a high saturated fat content. When following a cholesterol-lowering diet, you will limit the amount of fat and oil in your diet and when necessary use those fats which are lower in saturated fat, in the upper portion of the table. All fats and oils are high in calories (115–120 calories per tbsp.).

Product (1 tbsp.)	Saturated fatty acids (g)	Cholesterol (mg)	Polyunsaturated fatty acids (g)	Monounsaturated fatty acids (g)
Rapeseed oil (canola oil)	0.9	0	4.5	7.6
Safflower oil	1.2	0	10.1	1.6
Sunflower oil	1.4	0	5.5	6.2
Peanut butter, smooth	1.5	0	2.3	3.7
Corn oil	1.7	0	8.0	3.3
Olive oil	1.8	0	1.1	9.9
Hydrogenated sunflower oil	1.8	0	4.9	6.3
Margarine, liquid, bottled	1.8	0	5.1	3.9
Margarine, soft, tub	1.8	0	3.9	4.8
Sesame oil	1.9	0	5.7	5.4
Soybean oil	2.0	0	7.9	3.2
Margarine, stick	2.1	0	3.6	5.1
Peanut oil	2.3	0	4.3	6.2
Cottonseed oil	3.5	0	7.1	2.4
Lard	5.0	12	1.4	5.8
Beef tallow	6.4	14	0.5	5.3
Palm oil	6.7	0	1.3	5.0
Butter	7.1	31	0.4	3.3
Cocoa butter	8.1	0	0.4	4.5
Palm kernel oil	11.1	0	0.2	1.5
Coconut oil	11.8	0	0.2	0.8

NUTS AND SEEDS

When following a cholesterol-lowering diet, you will be selecting foods low in saturated fat (i.e., saturated fatty acids) and cholesterol. This table ranks nuts and seeds from low to high in saturated fat. Choose those from the upper portion of the list. Most nuts and seeds would appear to be appropriate foods to eat because they contain little saturated fat. However, except for chestnuts, they are all high in total fat and consequently high in calories. Thus, if you are also trying to lose weight, you should limit the use of nuts and seeds in your diet.

Product (1 oz.)	Saturated fatty acids (g)	Cholesterol (mg)	Total fat[b] (g)	Calories from fat[c] (%)	Total calories
European chestnuts	0.2	0	1.1	9	105
Filberts or hazelnuts	1.3	0	17.8	89	179
Almonds	1.4	0	15.0	80	167
Pecans	1.5	0	18.4	89	187
Sunflower seed kernels, roasted	1.5	0	1.4	77	165

(continued)

TABLE 26.9. *CONTINUED*

Product (1 oz.)	Saturated fatty acids (g)	Cholesterol (mg)	Total fat[b] (g)	Calories from fat[c] (%)	Total calories
English walnuts	1.6	0	17.6	87	182
Pistachio nuts	1.7	0	13.7	75	164
Peanuts	1.9	0	14.0	76	164
Hickory nuts	2.0	0	18.3	88	187
Pine nuts, pignolia	2.2	0	14.4	89	146
Pumpkin and squash seed kernels	2.3	0	12.0	73	148
Cashew nuts	2.6	0	13.2	73	163
Macadamia nuts	3.1	0	20.9	95	199
Brazil nuts	4.6	0	18.8	91	186
Coconut meat, un-sweetened	16.3	0	18.3	88	187

BREADS, CEREALS, PASTA, RICE, AND DRIED PEAS AND BEANS

When following a cholesterol-lowering diet, you will be selecting foods low in saturated fat (i.e., saturated fatty acids) and cholesterol. To lose weight on your cholesterol-lowering diet, choose foods that are lower in total fat, percent calories from fat, and calories.

Each of the following categories (breads, cereals, pasta, rice, and dried peas and beans) is ranked from low to high in saturated fat. To reduce the saturated fat in your diet, select the products from the upper portion of each category.

Product	Saturated fatty acids (g)	Cholesterol (mg)	Total fat[b] (g)	Calories from fat[c] (%)	Total calories
Breads					
Melba toast, 1 plain	0.1	0	Trace	0	20
Pita, ½ large shell	0.1	0	1.0	5	165
Corn tortilla	0.1	0	1.0	14	65
Rye bread, 1 slice	0.2	0	1.0	14	65
English muffin	0.3	0	1.0	6	140
Bagel, 1, 3½″ diameter	0.3	0	2.0	9	200
White bread, 1 slice	0.3	0	1.0	14	65
Rye Krisp, 2 triple crackers	0.3	0	1.0	16	56
Whole wheat bread, 1 slice	0.4	0	1.0	13	70
Saltines, 4	0.5	4	1.0	18	50
Hamburger bun	0.5	Trace	2.0	16	115
Hot dog bun	0.5	Trace	2.0	16	115
Pancake, 1, 4″ diameter	0.5	16	2.0	30	60
Bran muffin, 1, 2½″ diameter	1.4	24	6.0	43	125
Corn muffin, 1, 2½″ diameter	1.5	23	5.0	31	145
Plain doughnut, 1, 3¼″ diameter	2.8	20	12.0	51	210
Croissant, 1, 4½″ × 4″	3.5	13	12.0	46	235
Waffle, 1, 7″ diameter	4.0	102	13.0	48	245

(*continued*)

TABLE 26.9. *CONTINUED*

Product	Saturated fatty acids (g)	Cholesterol (mg)	Total fat[b] (g)	Calories from fat[c] (%)	Total calories
Cereals (1 cup)					
Cornflakes	Trace	—	0.1	0	98
Cream of Wheat, cooked	Trace	—	0.5	3	134
Corn grits, cooked	Trace	—	0.5	3	146
Oatmeal, cooked	0.4	—	2.4	15	145
Granola	5.8	—	33.1	50	595
100% Natural Cereal with raisins and dates	13.7	—	20.3	37	496
Pasta (1 cup)					
Spaghetti, cooked	0.1	0	1.0	6	155
Elbow macaroni, cooked	0.1	0	1.0	6	155
Egg noodles, cooked	0.5	50	2.0	11	160
Chow mein noodles, canned	2.1	5	11.0	45	220
Rice (1 cup cooked)					
Rice, white	0.1	0	0.5	2	225
Rice, brown	0.3	0	1.0	4	230
Dried peas and beans (1 cup cooked)					
Split peas	0.1	0	0.8	3	231
Kidney beans	0.1	0	1.0	4	225
Lima beans	0.2	0	0.7	3	217
Black-eyed peas	0.3	0	1.2	5	200
Garbanzo beans	0.4	0	4.3	14	269

SWEETS AND SNACKS

When following a cholesterol-lowering diet, select foods low in saturated fat (i.e., saturated fatty acids) and cholesterol. To lose weight on your cholesterol-lowering diet, see the information on total fat, percent of calories from fat, and calories. Since the foods in this table may be sweet even if they are low in fat, they could be high in calories. Fruits, vegetables, and breads provide tasty, low-fat, low-calorie alternatives.

The following foods within each category (beverages, candy, cookies, cakes and pies, snacks, and pudding) are ranked from low to high in saturated fat. To reduce the saturated fat in your diet, select the products from the upper portion of each category.

Product	Saturated fatty acids (g)	Cholesterol (mg)	Total fat[b] (g)	Calories from fat[c] (%)	Total calories
Beverages					
Ginger ale, 12 oz.	0	0	0	0	125
Cola, regular, 12 oz.	0	0	0	0	160
Chocolate shake, 10 oz.	6.5	37	10.5	26	360
Candy (1 oz.)					
Hard candy	0	0	0	0	110
Gum drops	Trace	0	Trace	Trace	100

(continued)

TABLE 26.9. *CONTINUED*

Product	Saturated fatty acids (g)	Cholesterol (mg)	Total fat[b] (g)	Calories from fat[c] (%)	Total calories
Fudge	2.1	1	3.0	24	115
Milk chocolate, plain	5.4	6	9.0	56	145
Cookies					
Vanilla wafers, 5 cookies, 1¾″ diameter	0.9	12	3.3	32	94
Fig bars, 4 cookies 1⅝″ × 1⅝″ × ⅜″	1.0	27	4.0	17	210
Chocolate brownie with icing, 1½″ × 1¾″ × ⅞″	1.6	14	4.0	36	100
Oatmeal cookies, 4 cookies, 2⅝″ diameter	2.5	2	10.0	37	245
Chocolate chip cookies, 4 cookies, 2¼″ diameter	3.9	18	11.0	54	185
Cakes and pies					
Angel food cake, 1/12 of 10″ cake	Trace	0	Trace	Trace	125
Gingerbread, 1/9 of 8″ cake	1.1	1	4.0	21	175
White layer cake with white icing, 1/16 of 9″ cake	2.1	3	9.0	32	260
Yellow layer cake with chocolate icing, 1/16 of 9″ cake	3.0	36	8.0	31	235
Pound cake, 1/17 of loaf	3.0	64	5.0	41	110
Devils food cake with chocolate icing, 1/16 of 9″ cake	3.5	37	8.0	31	235
Lemon meringue pie, 1/6 of 9″ pie	4.3	143	14.0	36	355
Apple pie, 1/6 of 9″ pie	4.6	0	18.0	40	405
Cream pie, 1/6 of 9″ pie	15.0	8	23.0	46	455
Snacks					
Popcorn, air-popped, 1 cup	Trace	0	Trace	Trace	30
Pretzels, stick, 2¼″, 10 pretzels	Trace	0	Trace	Trace	10
Popcorn with oil and salted, 1 cup	0.5	0	3.0	49	55
Corn chips, 1 oz.	1.4	25	9.0	52	155
Potato chips, 1 oz.	2.6	0	10.1	62	147
Pudding					
Gelatin	0	0	0	0	70
Tapioca, ½ cup	2.3	15	4.0	25	145
Chocolate pudding, ½ cup	2.4	15	4.0	24	150

TABLE 26.9. *CONTINUED*

MISCELLANEOUS

Product	Saturated fatty acids (g)	Cholesterol (mg)	Total fat[b] (g)	Calories from fat[c] (%)	Total calories
Gravies (½ cup)					
Au jus, canned	0.1	1	0.3	3	80
Turkey, canned	0.7	3	2.5	37	61
Beef, canned	1.4	4	2.8	41	62
Chicken, canned	1.7	3	6.8	65	95
Sauces (½ cup)					
Sweet-and-sour	Trace	0	0.1	<1	147
Barbecue	0.3	0	2.3	22	94
White	3.2	17	6.7	50	121
Cheese	4.7	26	8.6	50	154
Sour cream	8.5	45	15.1	53	255
Hollandaise	20.9	94	34.1	87	353
Bearnaise	20.9	99	34.1	88	351
Salad dressings (1 tbsp.)					
Russian, low-calorie	0.1	1	0.7	27	23
French, low-calorie	0.1	1	0.9	37	22
Italian, low-calorie	0.2	1	1.5	85	16
Thousand Island, low-calorie	0.2	2	1.6	59	24
Imitation mayonnaise	0.5	4	2.9	75	35
Thousand Island, regular	0.9	—	5.6	86	59
Italian, regular	1.0	—	7.1	93	69
Russian, regular	1.1	—	7.8	92	76
French, regular	1.5	—	6.4	86	67
Blue cheese	1.5	—	8.0	93	77
Mayonnaise	1.6	8	11.0	100	99
Other					
Olives, green, 4 medium	0.2	0	1.5	90	15
Nondairy creamer, powdered, 1 tsp.	0.7	0	1.0	90	10
Avocado, Florida	5.3	0	27.0	72	340
Pizza, cheese, ⅛ of 15" diameter	4.1	56	9.0	28	290
Quiche lorraine, ⅛ of 8" diameter	23.2	285	48.0	72	600

Source: National Cholesterol Education Program (2); *from* Composition of foods: Beef products (113); Composition of foods: Pork products (114); Nutritive value of foods (115); Composition of foods: Poultry products (116); Composition of foods: Finfish and shellfish products (117); Composition of foods: Dairy and egg products (118); Pennington and Church (119); Composition of foods: Fats and oils (120); Composition of

TABLE 26.9. *CONTINUED*

foods: Legumes and legume products (121); Composition of foods: Nut and seed products (122); Composition of foods: Breakfast cereals (123); Composition of foods: Soups, sauces, and gravies (124).

[a]3½ oz. = 100 g (approximately).

[b]Total fat = saturated fatty acids plus monounsaturated fatty acids plus polyunsaturated fatty acids.

[c]Percent calories from fat = (total fat calories divided by total calories) multiplied by 100; total fat calories = total fat (g) multiplied by 9.

[d]Liver and most organ meats are low in fat, but high in cholesterol. If you are eating to lower your blood cholesterol, you should consider your total cholesterol intake before selecting an organ meat.

MENU PLANNING

SAMPLE MENU FOR THE STEP-ONE DIET (FOR A MALE, AGE 25–50)

BREAKFAST

Pineapple juice	1 cup
Oatmeal	1 cup
Banana	½ medium
Low-fat milk (1% fat)	1 cup
Whole wheat toast	2 slices
Margarine	2 tsp.

LUNCH

Lean hamburger	3 oz.
Part-skim mozzarella cheese	1 oz.
Hamburger bun	1
Mayonnaise	2 tsp.
Lettuce	1 leaf
Tomato	1 slice
Carrot sticks	½ cup
Raw broccoli florets	1 cup
Fresh pear	1 medium
Low-fat milk (1% fat)	1 cup

AFTERNOON SNACK

Nonfat fruit yogurt	1 cup

DINNER

Broiled salmon	3 oz.
Margarine	2 tsp.
Rice	1 cup
Steamed snow peas, tomato wedges, and onions	1 cup
Fresh cantaloupe	½ small
Dinner rolls	2 small
Margarine	2 tsp.
Fruit ice or sherbet	⅔ cup

EVENING SNACK

Air-popped popcorn	6 cups
Melted margarine	2 tsp.
Lemonade	1 cup

Approximate Nutrient Analysis

Energy	2,972 kcal
Protein	120.6 g (16% of kcal)
Fat	87.4 g (26% of kcal)
Polyunsaturated fat	15.8 g
Monounsaturated fat	32.3 g
Saturated fat	24.9 g
Cholesterol	210 mg
Carbohydrate	438.7 g (59% of kcal)
Vitamin A	24,969 IU
	3,030 RE
Thiamine	2.15 mg
Riboflavin	2.54 mg
Niacin	22.8 mg

(continued)

Folate	338 mcg
Vitamin B-12	10.17 mcg
Vitamin B-6	2.34 mg
Vitamin C	309.5 mg
Calcium	1,564 mg
Phosphorus	2,093 mg
Iron	16.1 mg
Copper	1.48 mg
Zinc	14.4 mg
Magnesium	402 mg
Sodium	2,364 mg
Potassium	4,932 mg

SAMPLE MENU FOR THE STEP-TWO DIET (FOR A MALE, AGE 25–50)

BREAKFAST
Apple juice	1 cup
Cornflakes	1 cup
Banana	1 medium
Skim milk	1 cup
Whole wheat toast	2 slices
Peanut butter	2 tbsp.

LUNCH
Roast turkey breast	2 oz.
Whole wheat bread	2 slices
Mayonnaise	3 tsp.
Lettuce	1 leaf
Tomato	1 medium
Green pepper rings	½ medium
French dressing	2 tbsp.
Fresh nectarine	1 medium
Graham crackers	6 squares
Skim milk	1 cup

DINNER
Lean roast beef	4 oz.
Pasta	1 cup
Margarine	1 tsp.
Steamed green beans	1 cup
Steamed yellow squash with onions	½ cup
Margarine	1 tsp.
Whole wheat bread	2 slices
Margarine	2 tsp.
Fruit ice or sherbet	⅔ cup

EVENING SNACK
Plain nonfat yogurt	1 cup
Orange slices	1 medium
Raisins	2 tbsp.
Grapenuts	⅓ cup

Approximate Nutrient Analysis
Energy	2,779 kcal
Protein	129.4 g (19% of kcal)

(*continued*)

Fat	78.0 g (25% of kcal)
Polyunsaturated fat	20.3 g
Monounsaturated fat	23.1 g
Saturated fat	17.5 g
Cholesterol	155 mg
Carbohydrate	415.4 g (60% of kcal)
Vitamin A	6,212 IU
	1,163 RE
Thiamine	2.00 mg
Riboflavin	3.36 mg
Niacin	32.7 mg
Folate	363 mcg
Vitamin B-12	7.76 mcg
Vitamin B-6	2.92 mg
Vitamin C	188.1 mg
Calcium	1,498 mg
Phosphorus	2,242 mg
Iron	20.9 mg
Copper	1.37 mg
Zinc	16.2 mg
Magnesium	378 mg
Sodium	4,663 mg
Potassium	5,611 mg

REFERENCES

1. National Cholesterol Education Program: Report of the expert panel on detection, evaluation and treatment of high blood cholesterol in adults. Arch Intern Med 148:36, 1988.

2. National Cholesterol Education Program: Report of the expert panel on detection, evaluation and treatment of high blood cholesterol in adults. Bethesda, Md.: National Heart, Lung and Blood Institute, Public Health Service, National Institutes of Health, 1988.

3. National Cholesterol Education Program: Eating to lower your high blood cholesterol. Bethesda, Md.: National Heart, Lung and Blood Institute, Public Health Service, National Institutes of Health, 1988.

4. Mabuchi, H., Koizumi, J., et al.: Development of coronary heart disease in familial hypercholesterolemia. Circulation 79:225, 1989.

5. Frederickson, D. S., Levy, R. I., et al.: The dietary management of hyperlipoproteinemia: A handbook for physicians and dietitians. Washington, D.C.: Government Printing Office, 1978.

6. Tamir, I., Rifkind, B. M., and Levy, R. I.: Measurement of lipids and evaluation of lipid disorders. In Henry, J. B.: Clinical diagnosis and management by laboratory methods. Philadelphia: W. B. Saunders, 1979.

7. Bierman, E. L., and Chait, A.: Nutrition and diet in relation to hyperlipidemia and atherosclerosis. In Shils, M. E., and Young, V. R.: Modern nutrition in health and disease. 7th ed. Philadelphia: Lea & Febiger, 1988.

8. Gotto, A.: Classification and structure of lipoproteins. Am J Cardiol 56:20, 1985.

9. Gotto, A., Jones, P., and Scott, L.: The diagnosis and management of hyperlipidemia. Dis Month 32:245, 1986.

10. Gordon, D. J., and Rifkind, B. M.: High-density lipoprotein—the clinical implications of recent studies. N Engl J Med 321:1311, 1989.

11. Kane, J. P., and Molloy, M. J.: When to treat hyperlipidemia. Adv Intern Med 33:143, 1988.

12. Sandkamp, M., Funke, H., et al.: Lipoprotein (a) is an independent risk factor for myocardial infarction at a young age. Clin Chem 36:20, 1990.

13. Seed, M., Hoppichler, F., et al.: Relation of serum lipoprotein (a) concentration and apolipoprotein (a) phenotype to coronary heart disease in patients with familial hypercholesterolemia. N Engl J Med 322:1494, 1990.

14. Miles, L. A., Fless, G. M., et al.: A potential basis for the thrombotic risks associated with lipoprotein (a). Nature 339:301, 1989.

15. Hajjar, K. A., Gavish, D., et al.: Lipoprotein (a) modulation of endothelial cell surface fibrinolysis and its potential role in atherosclerosis. Nature 339:303, 1989.

16. McClean, J. W., Thomlinson, J. E., et al.: DNA sequence of human apolipoprotein (a) is homologous to plasminogen. Nature 330:132, 1987.

17. Dahlen, G. H., Guyton, J. R., et al.: Association of levels of lipoprotein (a) Lp (a), plasma lipids and other lipoproteins with coronary artery disease documented by angiography. Circulation 74:758, 1986.

18. Hoff, H. F., Beck, G. K., et al.: Serum Lp (a) level as a predictor of vein graft stenosis after coronary artery bypass surgery in patients. Circulation 77:1238, 1988.

19. Cushing, G. L., Gaubatz, J. W., et al.: Quantification and localization of apolipoproteins (a) and B in coronary artery bypass vein grafts resected at re-operation. Arteriosclerosis 9:593, 1989.

20. Rath, M., Niendorf, A., et al.: Detection and quantification of lipoprotein (a) in the arterial wall of 107 coronary bypass patients. Arteriosclerosis 9:579, 1988.

21. Utermann, G.: The mysteries of lipoprotein (a). Science 246:904, 1989.

22. Reinhart, R. A., Gani, K., et al.: Apolipoproteins A-1 and B as predictors of angiographically defined coronary artery disease. Arch Intern Med 150:1629, 1990.

23. Grundy, S. M., and Vega, G. L.: Role of apolipoprotein levels in clinical practice. Arch Intern Med 150:1579, 1990.

24. Cohn, J. S., McNamara, J. R., et al.: Postprandial plasma lipoprotein changes in human subjects of different ages. J Lipid Res 29:469, 1988.

25. Grundy, S. M., and Vega, G. L.: Causes of high blood cholesterol. Circulation 81:412, 1990.

26. National Cholesterol Education Program: So you have high blood cholesterol. Bethesda, Md.: National Heart, Lung and Blood Institute, Public Health Service, National Institutes of Health, 1988.

27. National Institutes of Health: Consensus development conference: Treatment of hypertriglyceridemia. JAMA 251:1196, 1984.

28. Margolis, S., and Dobs, A. S.: Nutritional management of plasma lipid disorders. J Am Coll Nutr 8:33s, 1989.

29. Cholesterol lowering and the reduction of coronary heart disease risk. JAMA 256:2873, 1986.

30. National Institutes of Health: Consensus conference: Lowering blood cholesterol to prevent heart disease. JAMA 253:2080, 1985.

31. Castelli, W. P., Garrison, R. J., et al.: Incidence of coronary heart disease and lipoprotein cholesterol levels: The Framingham study. JAMA 256:2835, 1986.

32. Lipid Research Clinics Program: The lipid research clinics coronary primary prevention trial results. I. Reduction in incidence of coronary heart disease. JAMA 251:351, 1984.

33. Lipid Research Clinics Program: The lipid research clinics coronary primary prevention trial results. II. The relationship of reduction in incidence of coronary heart disease to cholesterol lowering. JAMA 251:365, 1984.

34. Martin, M., Hulley, S., et al.: Serum cholesterol, blood pressure and mortality: Implications from a cohort of 361,662 men. Lancet 2:933, 1986.

35. Blankenhorn, D. H., Nessim, S. A., et al.: Beneficial effects of combined colestipol-niacin therapy on coronary atherosclerosis and coronary venous bypass grafts. JAMA 257:3233, 1987.

36. Connor, W. E., and Connor, S. L.: Diet, atherosclerosis and fish oil. Adv Intern Med 35:139, 1990.

37. DeLany, J. P., Vivian, V. M., et al.: Effects of fish oil on serum lipids in men during a controlled feeding trial. Am J Clin Nutr 52:477, 1990.

38. Flaten, H., Hostmark, A. T., et al.: Fish-oil concentrate: Effects on variables related to cardiovascular disease. Am J Clin Nutr 52:300, 1990.

39. Mclennan, P. L., Abeywardena, M. Y., and Charnock, J. S.: Reversal of the arrhythmogenic effects of long term saturated fatty acid intake by dietary n-3 and n-6 polyunsaturated fatty acids. Am J Clin Nutr 51:53, 1990.

40. Leaf, A.: Cardiovascular effects of fish oil: Beyond the platelet. Circulation 82:624, 1990.

41. Schectman, G., Kaul, S., et al.: Can the hypotriglyceridemic effect of fish oil concentrate be sustained? Ann Intern Med 110:346, 1989.

42. Fisher, M., Levine, P. H., and Leaf, A.: N-3 fatty acids and cellular aspects of atherosclerosis. Arch Intern Med 149:1726, 1989.

43. Donahue, R., Bloom, E., et al.: Central obesity and coronary heart disease in men. Lancet 1:822, 1987.

44. Johnson, C., and Greenland, P.: Effects of exercise, dietary cholesterol and dietary fat on blood lipids. Arch Intern Med 150:137, 1990.

45. Haskell, W. L.: Exercise-induced changes in plasma lipids and lipoproteins. Prev Med 13:23, 1984.

46. Wood, P. D., Stefanick, M. L., et al.: Changes in plasma lipids and lipoproteins in overweight men during weight loss through dieting as compared with exercise. N Engl J Med 318:1173, 1988.

47. Despres, J. P., Moorjani, S., et al.: Heredity and changes in plasma lipids and lipoproteins after short-term exercise training in men. Arteriosclero-sis 8:402, 1988.

48. Keys, A.: Coronary heart disease in seven countries. Circulation 41:1, 1970.

49. Bonanome, A., and Grundy, S. M.: Effect of dietary stearic acid on plasma cholesterol and lipoprotein levels. N Engl J Med 318:1244, 1988.

50. Keys, A., Anderson, J. T., and Grande, F.: Serum cholesterol response to changes in the diet. IV: Particular saturated fatty acids in the diet. Metabolism 14:776, 1965.

51. Hegsted, D. M., McGandy, R. B., et al.: Quantitative effects of dietary fat on serum cholesterol in man. Am J Clin Nutr 17:281, 1965.

52. Moderate alcohol consumption increases plasma high-density lipoprotein cholesterol. Nutr Rev 45:1, 1987.

53. Hartung, G. H., Foreyt, J. P., et al.: Effect of alcohol dose on lipoprotein subfractions and lipolytic enzyme activity in active and inactive men. Metabolism 39:81, 1990.

54. Astrup, A., Toubro, S., et al.: Caffeine: A double-blind, placebo-controlled study of its thermogenic, metabolic and cardiovascular effects in healthy volunteers. Am J Clin Nutr 51:759, 1990.

55. Bak, A., and Grobee, D. E.: The effect on serum cholesterol levels of coffee brewed by filtering or boiling. N Engl J Med 321:1432, 1989.

56. Kris-Etherton, P. M., ed.: Cardiovascular disease: Nutrition for prevention and treatment. Chicago: American Dietetic Association, 1990.

57. Kantor, M. A.: Nutrition, cholesterol and heart disease. IV: The role of dietary fiber. Nutr Forum 6 (4):1, 1989.

58. Van Horn, L. V., Liu, K., et al.: Serum lipid response to oat product intake with a fat-modified diet. J Am Diet Assoc 86:759, 1986.

59. Van Horn, L., Emidy, L. A., et al.: Serum lipid response to a fat-modified, oatmeal-enhanced diet. Prev Med 17:377, 1988.

60. Anderson, J. W., Zettwoch, N., et al.: Cholesterol-lowering effects of psyllium hydrophilic mucilloid for hypercholesterolemic men. Arch Intern Med 148:292, 1988.

61. Taking on the fat of the land: Cholesterol and health. JAMA 257:2873, 1986.

62. Lowering serum cholesterol: It is time to proceed. Arch Intern Med 148:34, 1988.

63. Commentary on the published results of the lipid research clinic coronary primary prevention trial. JAMA 253:2091, 1985.

64. Grundy, S.: Cholesterol and coronary heart disease: A new era. JAMA 256:2849, 1986.

65. Slikelle, R., Shryock, A., et al.: Diet, serum cholesterol and death from coronary heart disease: The Western Electric study. N Engl J Med 304:65, 1981.

66. American Heart Association: Dietary guidelines for healthy American adults: A statement for physicians and health professionals by the Nutrition Committee, American Heart Association. Circulation 74:1465A, 1986.

67. Kromhout, D., Bosschieter, E. B., et al.: Serum cholesterol and 25-year incidence of and mortality from myocardial infarction and cancer: The zutphen study. Arch Intern Med 148:1051, 1988.

68. Suhonen, O., Reunanen, A., et al.: Risk factors for sudden and non-sudden coronary death. Acta Med Scand 223:19, 1988.

69. Alfred, J. B., Gallagher-Alfred, C. R., and Bowers, D. F.: Elevated blood cholesterol: A risk factor for heart disease that decreases with advanced age. J Am Diet Assoc 90:574, 1990.

70. Benfante, R., and Reed, D.: Is elevated serum cholesterol a risk factor for coronary heart disease in the elderly? JAMA 263:393, 1990.

71. Chilian, W. M., Dellsperger, K. C., et al.: Effects of atherosclerosis on the coronary microcirculation. Am J Physiol 258:H529, 1990.

72. Andersen, P., Nilsen, D. W. T., et al.: Increased fibrinolytic potential af-

ter diet intervention in healthy coronary high risk individuals. Acta Med Scand 223:499, 1988.

73. U.S. Preventative Task Force: Screening for high blood cholesterol. Am Fam Physician 41 (2):503, 1990.

74. Shekelle, R. B., and Stamler, J.: Dietary cholesterol and ischemic heart disease. Lancet 1:1177, 1989.

75. Gordon, D. J., Probstfield, J. L., et al.: High density lipoprotein cholesterol and cardiovascular disease: Four prospective American studies. Circulation 79:8, 1989.

76. Kaplan, K. M.: Critical comments on recent literature: The cholesterol campaign: American aggressiveness and British reservations. Am J Hypertens 2:941, 1989.

77. Hamsten, A.: Apolipoproteins, dyslipoproteinemia and premature coronary heart disease. Acta Med Scand 223:389, 1989.

78. Lekkanen, J., Linn, S., et al.: Ten-year mortality from cardiovascular disease in relation to cholesterol level among men with and without preexisting cardiovascular disease. N Engl J Med 322:1700, 1990.

79. Denke, M. A., and Grundy, S. M.: Hypercholesterolemia in elderly persons: Resolving the treatment dilemma. Ann Intern Med 112:781, 1990.

80. Feinlieb, M., and Gillum, R.: CHD in the elderly. The magnitude of the problem in the U.S. In Wenger, N. K., Furberg, C. D., and Pitt, E.: CHD in the elderly. New York: Elsevier, 1986.

81. Winterfeldt, E.: Diet and coronary heart disease. Top Clin Nutr 2 (Apr. 3):1, 1988.

82. Ballard-Barbash, R., and Callaway, W.: Marine fish oils: Role in prevention of coronary artery disease. Mayo Clin Proc 62:113, 1987.

83. Mehta, J., Lopez, L., et al.: Dietary supplementation with omega-3 polyunsaturated fatty acids in patients with stable coronary heart disease. Am J Med 84:45, 1988.

84. Rylance, P., Gordge, M., et al.: Fish oil modifies lipids and reduces plate-let aggregability in hemodialysis patients. Nephron 43:202, 1986.

85. Keyes, A.: Diet and blood cholesterol in population surveys—lessons from analysis of the data from a major survey in Israel. Am J Clin Nutr 48:1161, 1988.

86. DeLong, D., DeLong, E., and Wood, P.: A comparison of methods for the estimation of plasma low and very low density lipoprotein cholesterol: The lipid research clinics prevalence study. JAMA 256:2372, 1986.

87. McNamara, J. R., Cohen, J. S., et al.: Calculated values for low density lipoprotein cholesterol in the assessment of lipid abnormalities and coronary disease risk. Clin Chem 36:36, 1990.

88. Kantor, M. A., Cullinane, E. M., et al.: Exercise acutely increases high density lipoprotein-cholesterol and lipoprotein lipase activity in trained and untrained men. Metabolism 36:188, 1987.

89. Schwartz, R. D.: The independent effect of dietary weight loss and aerobic training on high density lipoproteins and apolipoprotein A-1 concentrations in obese men. Metabolism 36:165, 1987.

90. Superko, H. R., Haskell, W. L., and Wood, P. D.: Modification of plasma cholesterol through exercise: Rationale and recommendations. Hyperlipidemia 78:64, 1985.

91. De Parscau, L., and Fielding, C. J.: Abnormal plasma cholesterol metabolism in cigarette smokers. Metabolism 35:1070, 1986.

92. Krauss, R. M.: Relationship of intermediate and low-density lipoprotein subspecies to risk of coronary artery disease. Am Heart J 113:578, 1987.

93. Miller, N. E.: Associations of high-density lipoprotein subclasses and apolipoproteins with ischemic heart disease and coronary atherosclerosis. Am Heart J 113:589, 1987.

94. Griffin, B. A., Skinner, E. R., and Maughan, R. J.: Plasma high density lipoprotein subfractions in subjects with different coronary risk indices as assessed by plasma lipoprotein con-centrations. Atherosclerosis 70:165, 1988.

95. Ostlund, R. E., Staten, M., et al.: The ratio of waist-to-hip circumference, plasma insulin level, and glucose intolerance as independent predictors of the HDL-2 cholesterol level in older adults. N Engl J Med 322:229, 1990.

96. Block, G., Clifford, C., et al.: A brief dietary screen for high fat intake. J Nutr Education 21:199, 1989.

97. Cutler, R.: Effect of antihypertensive agents on lipid metabolism. Am J Cardiol 51:628, 1983.

98. Hansten, P. D.: Drug interactions. 4th ed. Philadelphia: Lea & Febiger, 1979.

99. Lovastatin Study Group II: Therapeutic response to lovastatin (mevinolin) in nonfamilial hypercholesterolemia: A multicenter trial. JAMA 256:2829, 1986.

100. Steinberg, D.: Studies on the mechanism of action of probucol. Am J Cardiol 57:16H, 1986.

101. Illingworth, D. R.: Lipid-lowering drugs: An overview of indication and optimum therapeutic use. Drugs 33:259, 1987.

102. Witztum, J. L.: Current approaches to drug therapy for the hypercholesterolemic patient. Circulation 80:1101, 1989.

103. Shepherd, J.: Mechanism of action of bile acid sequestrants and other lipid lowering drugs. Cardiology 76 (Supp 1):65, 1989.

104. LaRosa, J.: Review of clinical studies of bile acid sequestrants for lowering plasma lipid levels. Cardiology 76 (Supp 1):55, 1989.

105. Roberts, W. C.: Cardiology. Boston: Butterworths, 1989.

106. Frick, M. H., Elo, L., and Happa, K.: Helsinki heart study: Primary prevention trial with gemfibrozil in middle aged men with dyslipemia-safety of treatment, changes in risk factors and incidence of coronary heart disease. N Engl J Med 317:1237, 1937.

107. Brown, W. V.: Review of clinical studies of fenofibrate in combination with currently approved lipid-lower-

ing drugs. Cardiology 76 (Supp 1):45, 1989.

108. Witztum, J. L., Simmons, D., et al.: Intensive combination drug therapy of familial hypercholesterolemia with lovastatin, probucol, and colestipol hydrochloride. Circulation 79:16, 1989.

109. Carlson, L. A., and Rosenhamer, G.: Reduction of mortality in the Stockholm ischemic heart disease secondary prevention study by combined treatment with clofibrate and nicotinic acid. Acta Med Scand 223:405, 1988.

110. Grundy, S., Nix, D., et al.: Comparison of three cholesterol-lowering diets in normolipidemic men. JAMA 256:2351, 1986.

111. Atger, V., Cambilau, M., et al.: Serum lipid abnormalities in heart transplant patients: Predominance of HDL-2 like particles in the HDL pattern. Atherosclerosis 81:103, 1990.

112. DeFaire, U.: Time for reestablishment of serum lipid lowering after myocardial infarction. Acta Med Scand 223:385, 1988.

113. Composition of foods: Beef products—raw, processed, prepared. Agriculture Handbook no. 8-13. Washington, D.C.: U.S. Department of Agriculture, Human Nutrition Information Service, 1986.

114. Composition of foods: Pork products—raw, processed, prepared. Agriculture Handbook no. 8-10. Washington, D.C.: U.S. Department of Agriculture, Human Nutrition Information Service, 1983.

115. Nutritive value of foods. Home and Garden Bulletin no. 72. U.S. Department of Agriculture, Human Nutrition Information Service, 1986.

116. Composition of foods: Poultry products—raw, processed, prepared. Agriculture Handbook no. 8-5. Washington, D.C.: U.S. Department of Agriculture, Science and Education Administration, 1979.

117. Composition of foods: Finfish and shellfish products—raw, processed, prepared. Agriculture Handbook no. 8-15. Washington, D.C.: U.S. Department of Agriculture, Human Nutrition Information Service, 1987.

118. Composition of foods: Dairy and egg products—raw, processed, prepared. Agriculture Handbook no. 8-1. Washington, D.C.: U.S. Department of Agriculture, Agricultural Research Service, 1976.

119. Pennington, J., and Church, H.: Bowes and Church's food values of portions commonly used. 14th ed. Philadelphia: J. B. Lippincott, 1985.

120. Composition of foods: Fats and oils—raw, processed, prepared. Agriculture Handbook no. 8-4. Washington, D.C.: U.S. Department of Agriculture, Science and Education Administration, 1979.

121. Composition of foods: Legumes and legume products—raw, processed, prepared. Agriculture Handbook no. 8-16. Washington, D.C.: U.S. Department of Agriculture, Human Nutrition Information Service, 1986.

122. Composition of foods: Nut and seed products—raw, processed, prepared. Agriculture Handbook no. 8-12. Washington, D.C.: U.S. Department of Agriculture, Human Nutrition Information Service, 1984.

123. Composition of foods: Breakfast cereals—raw, processed, prepared. Agriculture Handbook no. 8-8. Washington, D.C.: U.S. Department of Agriculture, Human Nutrition Information Service, 1982.

124. Composition of foods: Soups, sauces, and gravies—raw, processed, prepared. Agriculture Handbook no. 8-6. Washington, D.C.: U.S. Department of Agriculture, Science and Education Administration, 1980.

27.

MEDIUM-CHAIN-TRIGLYCERIDES-BASED KETOGENIC DIET

DEFINITIONS

1. MCT-BASED KETOGENIC DIET

A high-fat, low-carbohydrate diet that induces ketosis in the body, used in the prophylactic treatment of some types of epilepsy in children. It provides approximately 50% to 70% of the total kilocalories in the form of medium-chain triglycerides (MCT), a maximum of 19% from carbohydrates, a maximum of 29% from protein and carbohydrates combined, and a minimum of 11% from fats exclusive of MCT (1).

2. MEDIUM-CHAIN TRIGLYCERIDES (MCT)

Glycerol esters of medium-chain fatty acids or fats composed almost entirely of fatty acids containing 8 and 10 carbon atoms—i.e., caprylic or octanoic acid (C8) and capric or decanoic acid (C10). MCT are liberated from coconut oil by steam hydrolysis and provide 8.3 kcal/g (1–5).

3. LONG-CHAIN TRIGLYCERIDES (LCT)

Naturally occurring glycerol esters of long-chain fatty acids or fat composed of fatty acids containing 12 or more carbon atoms, mainly lauric (C14), palmitic (C16), stearic (C18), oleic (C18), and linoleic (C18.2) acids.

PURPOSE OF THE DIET

Ketogenic diets have a therapeutic effect on certain epileptic seizures. The aim of the ketogenic diet is to induce and maintain a state of ketosis in the body in order to achieve an anticonvulsant effect. The effectiveness of the diet has been corroborated by more than 1 group of re-

searchers. The exact mechanism of the anticonvulsant action of the diet is uncertain. MCT are reported to be more ketogenic than other fats. The use of MCT oil also makes the diet more palatable and easier to implement (6–12).

EFFECTS OF THE DIET

1. KETOSIS

Major effects of the ketogenic diet are to change the balance of energy substances presented to cells and to reduce blood glucose concentrations. However, complete oxidation of fats is dependent on the presence of a certain level of glucose precursors (6, 7, 9, 10, 13).

Ketones (acetoacetate and betahydroxybutyric acid) are produced whenever large amounts of fat are metabolized in the absence of carbohydrate. Until recently, these ketones were thought of as detrimental because of their role in diabetic ketoacidosis. But during starvation, the body of a nondiabetic normally produces ketones, and the metabolism adapts to supply the central nervous system with its high calorie requirements. This requirement is ordinarily met by glucose in the nonstarving state (5, 14–17).

MCT are more ketogenic than equivalent amounts of LCT. Therefore, a diet based on the use of MCT rather than LCT will maintain ketosis while providing less total fat and more carbohydrate and protein (17–18).

2. SIGNIFICANT ANTICONVULSANT EFFECT

It has been postulated that the beneficial

effects of a ketogenic diet in epilepsy result from an enforced change in neuronal metabolism. That neurons are able to metabolize ketone bodies is supported by studies of obese, starving individuals. One possible theory is that a ketone body may behave as an inhibitory neurotransmitter, thereby producing the anticonvulsant effect of the diet (7, 8, 16).

Clinical evidence of the anticonvulsant effect, including EEG findings, correlates with the degree of elevation of blood levels of the ketone bodies, betahydroxybutyrate and acetoacetate. Children with mean beta-hydroxybutyrate levels above 2 mM (millimoles) per liter achieve good to excellent seizure control in a significantly greater proportion of cases than children with blood levels of less than 2 mM per liter. Plasma levels of betahydroxybutyrate and acetoacetate in children maintained on a 3 : 1 ratio ketogenic diet (87% total fat) were noted to be similar to those in children receiving a 60% MCT diet (72% total fat). It has been suggested that the anticonvulsant effectiveness of MCT is due not only to ketosis, but also to increased blood concentrations of octanoic and decanoic acids (7, 9, 18).

3. CHANGES IN SERUM LIPIDS

MCT produces increases in serum lipids and lipoproteins. Somewhat lower levels of serum cholesterol have been reported on the MCT ketogenic diet than on the traditional 3 : 1 ratio ketogenic diet (1, 19, 20).

4. EFFECTS ON BLOOD GLUCOSE

A slight depression in blood glucose levels has been noted. This is not accompanied by clinical hypoglycemia and does not correlate with the anticonvulsant effect (7).

5. COMA IN INFANTS WITH CERTAIN INBORN ERRORS OF METABOLISM

In infants in whom beta oxidation is limited by inborn errors of metabolism, large doses of MCT precipitate coma, with a substantial urinary excretion of omega-1-hydroxy and dicarboxy fatty acids. This indicates that the omega oxidation role is a detoxification process. Therefore, infants with defects in beta oxidation should not be placed on a ketogenic diet (21).

6. DICARBOXYLIC ACIDURIA

Dicarboxylic aciduria has been causally related to a diet high in MCT. Dicarboxylic aciduria was reported in 4 infants 2 to 9 months of age who were fed a formula high in MCT, and in 1 adult on oral MCT. This condition has also been observed in low–birth weight infants on formulas high in MCT and in individuals with inherited defects in carnitine and fatty acid metabolism (21–26).

PHYSIOLOGY, FOODS, AND NUTRIENTS

1. FLEXIBILITY OF THE DIET

The use of diabetes exchange lists in the calculating of the ketogenic meal pattern using MCT permits greater flexibility and is less time-consuming than methods used to calculate traditional ketogenic diets. Accurate weighing of foods served is not necessary, and household measures may be used. The intake of noncaloric fluids need not be restricted (27).

When compared calorie-to-calorie with most other diets, the MCT ketogenic diet provides less bulk and less total volume.

2. CHARACTERISTICS OF MCT

Compared with LCT, MCT is relatively soluble in water, is liquid at room tem-

perature, and has a lower smoke point. When heated above 150° to 160° C, MCT is oxidized and its taste becomes less acceptable. MCT oil contains no essential fatty acids and provides 8.3 kcal/g (3, 4).

MCT oil softens or splits containers made of such plastics as polyethylene and polystyrene, but not polypropylene. Therefore, it is recommended that MCT be stored in metal, glass, or ceramic containers (3, 28). The relatively small molecular weight and the water solubility of MCT facilitate the action of the digestive enzymes in the intestinal lumen, and consequently the hydrolysis of MCT is both faster and more complete than that of LCT. MCT are not incorporated into chylomicrons, presumably because of their great water solubility. They are selectively transported into the mesenteric portal blood as a free fatty acid complex with albumin (21).

MCT are hydrolyzed to free fatty acids in the intestinal lumen at a rate 5 times faster than the hydrolysis of LCT. The MCT-derived free fatty acids are absorbed by the intestinal cell at a rate twice that of LCT-derived fatty acids. MCT-derived fatty acids, unlike those from LCT-derived fatty acids, cross the intestinal epithelial cell without reesterification to a triglyceride. The efficiency with which MCT are used as a metabolic fuel is demonstrated, as well, by the rapid appearance of beta-hydroxybutyric acid. The presence of ketones owing to MCT should be viewed as an indication of rapid utilization of the medium-chain fatty acids as a metabolic fuel, rather than as a deleterious effect (5, 21, 28–30).

A gastric lipase hydrolyzes MCT in the stomach. New evidence suggests that MCT is absorbed in the stomach of infants and children and that the absorption rate improves with age (31). With newer methods of lipid analysis it has been reported that MCT has been found in the adipose tissue of infants who receive it orally (32–34).

INDICATIONS FOR USE

1. CONTROL OF EPILEPSY

The MCT ketogenic diet is prescribed for its anticonvulsant effect. It may be indicated for the control of akinetic and myoclonic seizures in children who are resistant to treatment by anticonvulsant medications or in whom side effects have developed. The diet is most effective in children below about 5 years of age. Older children respond to the diet with less marked ketonuria and do not achieve as high levels of serum betahydroxybutyric acid (2, 6, 7).

2. POSSIBLE SURGICAL APPLICATIONS

The metabolic changes that occurred in a group of children on the traditional ketogenic diet during anesthesia and surgery suggest that the use of ketogenic diets should be investigated as a means of preventing seizures during surgery or presurgical conditions. Furthermore, the common practice of postsurgical glucose infusions should be reevaluated in epileptic patients, in whom they cause a fall in plasma ketones and a loss of seizure control (8, 13).

3. PYRUVATE DEHYDROGENASE DEFICIENCY

A ketogenic diet has been reported successful in the management of pyruvate dehydrogenase deficiency. Higher plasma levels of betahydroxybutyric acid (giving evidence of a greater ketogenic effect) were demonstrated when a ketogenic diet supplemented with MCT was used, as opposed to a ketogenic diet with no MCT (35).

POSSIBLE ADVERSE REACTIONS

1. NAUSEA, VOMITING, AND ABDOMINAL CRAMPS

Nausea, vomiting, and abdominal cramps are possible side effects related to the rapid hydrolysis of MCT and the resulting high concentrations of free fatty acids in the stomach and small intestine. Such a hyperosmolar solution can cause an influx of large amounts of fluid, which can be irritating to the bowel. Many of these symptoms can be prevented by eating the MCT-containing food more slowly. Also, the MCT should never be ingested alone but instead should be eaten with other foods (2).

2. ESSENTIAL FATTY ACID DEFICIENCY

An essential fatty acid deficiency has been reported in humans receiving MCT and no source of linoleic acid. Improperly planned MCT ketogenic diets that do not include adequate amounts of food sources of linoleic acid can be expected to have similar effects (36).

3. DISORDERED MINERAL METABOLISM

Disordered mineral metabolism has been reported in ketogenic diet therapy, including vitamin D deficiency osteomalacia, decreased serum 25-hydroxy-vitamin-D, decreased serum calcium concentrations, elevated serum alkaline phosphatase and parathyroid hormone concentrations, decreased urinary calcium excretion, increased urinary hydroxyproline excretion, and decreased bone mass. Vitamin D supplements should be given to prevent these changes in patients who manifest biochemical evidence of vitamin D deficiency (37).

4. IMPAIRED NEUTROPHIL FUNCTION

It has been reported that the diet may have an adverse effect on granulocyte function. Specifically, a significant neutrophil dysfunction that impairs phagocytosis and bactericidal capacity has been found in patients on the MCT ketogenic diet. Neutrophil function improved when the MCT ketogenic diet was discontinued. While the mechanism of this effect is not fully understood, it appears to be related to serum metabolites that have an effect on the early events in the pro-

cess of phagocytosis. If serious bacterial infections develop on the diet, it may have to be discontinued (45).

CONTRAINDICATIONS

Large amounts of MCT should not be used in cases of diabetes, particularly in the patient with a hyperosmolar diabetic syndrome. It is also contraindicated in other conditions associated with ketosis or acidosis. The diet is of little value in the treatment of grand mal seizures (4, 6).

CLINICAL ASSESSMENT

Because the diet is aimed at the preschool child, nutritional assessments should include growth curves, height and weight, midarm muscle circumference estimates, bone age, and other appropriate clinical parameters of growth and development. The diet should be evaluated at least every 6 months in order to determine nutrient intakes that may be below those recommended in the Recommended Dietary Allowances (38). A follow-up program should include periodic nutritional assessments, in which the level of compliance and the effect of the diet on nutritional status are measured.

Parents should be encouraged to keep a food intake diary. The significance of appropriate portion sizes should be stressed. The diet should be evaluated at least every 6 months in order to identify marginal intakes of nutrients, particularly protein, calcium, and vitamin D.

BIOCHEMICAL ASSESSMENT

1. PLASMA OCTANOIC AND DECANOIC ACIDS

The presence of relatively high quantities of octanoic and decanoic acid in the plasma of children on an MCT ketogenic diet may contribute to seizure control.

Octanoic acid is a straight-chain isomer of the well-known anticonvulsant Depakene. Other data indicate that L- and D-carboxylic acids are necessary to protect experimental animals from certain drug-induced seizures. New chromatographic methods for the determination of octanoic and decanoic acid levels in the plasma of children have been described, which may prove helpful in the investigations of the specific anticonvulsant effect of the MCT ketogenic diet. The serum levels of betahydroxybutyrate and acetoacetate are biochemical parameters of the degree of ketosis achieved that will also help to detect episodes of noncompliance (17–20, 32, 33).

2. OTHER PARAMETERS

The effect of the diet on blood lipids should be assessed regularly. Hemoglobin, hematocrit, and other parameters of iron status and serum folate should be periodically evaluated. Total lymphocyte counts, creatinine height index, serum albumin, total protein, albumin/globulin ratio, prealbumin, and retinol-binding protein measurements are parameters of protein status that may be useful.

Biochemical parameters of vitamin D deficiency osteomalacia should be periodically reviewed, including serum levels of 25-hydroxy-vitamin-D, calcium, alkaline phosphatase, parathyroid hormone, and urinary levels of calcium and hydroxyproline (37). Patients on carbamazepine should have periodic liver function tests and baseline CBC and platelets checked every 2 weeks (39).

ASSESSMENT OF POTENTIAL DRUG INTERACTIONS

1. DIET AND ANESTHESIA

Some forms of anesthesia, for example, phencyclidine and ketamine, are contraindicated in epileptic children because of their potential to cause seizures. Other drugs may produce an anticonvulsant toxic reaction by increasing blood levels of anticonvulsant medication. The ideal anesthetic should maintain low blood glucose concentrations and ketonemia throughout the surgery (13).

2. ANTICONVULSANT DRUGS

See table 27.1.

IMPLEMENTATION AND EDUCATION

While the MCT ketogenic diet is more liberal than the traditional ketogenic diet, potential impediments to compliance exist and must be addressed. The target patient population is young children, in whom snacking on concentrated sweets is common. Candy bars, cakes, cookies, and lollipops must not be used as reinforcements for desired behaviors, rewards for "being good," or simply cooperating with the doctor in a medical exam. Neighbors, schoolchildren, teachers, friends, and all caretakers must be informed of the hazards of carbohydrate-containing snacks and their effect on seizure control.

MCT can be added to the diet in a number of ways. It may be incorporated into casseroles, tomato sauce, pizza, milk shakes, and ice cream with relative ease. MCT oil is usually divided into 3 or 4 servings, depending on the patient's needs. Some children respond more favorably when a bedtime feeding with MCT is provided.

PRIORITIES FOR QUALITY ASSURANCE

It is important that seizure control not compromise the child's growth, development, or mineral status. With such a large proportion of the total kilocalories provided from one nutrient source, meals should be planned to provide foods of high nutrient density. Food diaries should be used whenever possible to ensure that parents are using proper amounts and that essential foods such as milk and meat

are provided. Appropriate supplements should be provided to meet the Recommended Dietary Allowances for all vitamins and minerals. The portions of food other than MCT are not large; therefore, amounts of leftovers that are insignificant in a regular diet assume a greater importance in the MCT ketogenic diet. To reduce the risk of vitamin D deficiency, vitamin D–fortified milk should be used.

Pediatric hospital units in which neurology patients are periodically admitted for MCT ketogenic diet therapy should have standardized protocols for the procurement, mixing, food preparation, and administration of MCT, written by the dietitian in consultation with nursing. Protocols should be used in the education of staff and should also include provisions for alterations in the diet during illness, and alternatives to high-sugar liquid diets.

MENU PLANNING

The following calculations for a 1- to 3-year-old child weighing 13 kg illustrate the calculation of a typical MCT ketogenic diet.

1. *Establish caloric needs,* using Recommended Dietary Allowances.
   For a child 1 to 3 years old weighing 13 kg, the RDA is 1,300 kcal.
2. *Determine the amount of MCT oil.* Depending on the amount needed to induce ketosis in the individual child, MCT oil should account for 50% to 70% of total kilocalories.
   60% of 1,300 = 780 kcal from MCT
   1 g MCT = 8.3 kcal
   780 / 8.3 = approximately 94 g MCT
   15 mL (1 tbsp.) MCT = 14 g
   94 / 14 = 6.7 tbsp. (6 tbsp. + 2 tsp.) MCT
3. *Determine kilocalories to be provided by other foods.*
   1,300 − 780 = 520 kcal
4. *Estimate maximum carbohydrate kilocalories.*

19% of 1,300 = maximum 247 kcal
247 kcal / 4 = maximum 61 g carbohydrate

5. *Estimate maximum combined protein and carbohydrate kilocalories.*
   29% of 1,300 = maximum 377 kcal from protein + carbohydrate
6. *Establish protein intake,* based on Recommended Dietary Allowances and patient's desires or needs.
   1.2 g per kg body weight; e.g., 15.6 g (rounded off in RDA to 16) for a 13-kg child
   This is a minimum. Many children need extra protein, and high-protein foods increase palatability of the diet.
   377 − 247 = 130 kcal from protein = 32.5 g protein
7. *Estimate minimum fat kilocalories exclusive of MCT oil.*
   11% of 1,300 = minimum 143 kcal from other fats
   143 / 9 = minimum 16 g fat exclusive of MCT
8. *Summarize results.*
   This sample diet will consist of the following:
   1,300 kcal
   6.7 tbsp. MCT
   61 g carbohydrate
   32.5 g protein
   16 g fat exclusive of MCT
9. *Calculate the dietary pattern using diabetes exchange lists.* See table 27.2.

TABLE 27.1. POTENTIAL INTERACTIONS BETWEEN DIET AND ANTICONVULSANT DRUGS

Drug	Effects			Recommendations
	Appetite	Gastrointestinal	Metabolic	
Carbamazepine (Tegretol) (39-41)	Nausea, altered taste, anorexia	Vomiting, abdominal pain, dry mouth, glossitis, stomatitis	Decreased serum folate and B vitamins Increased serum alkaline phosphatase, brom-osulphalein (BSP), HDL-cholesterol Blood dyscrasias Water intoxication, hyponatremia Syndrome of inappropriate artidiuretic hormone secretion (SIADH) Increased BUN, SGOT, SGPT, bilirubin, urinary glucose and albumin Decreased serum calcium, T-3 and T-4	Take with food to avoid gastrointestinal effects.
Clonazepam (Klonopin) (41)	Nausea, anorexia	Constipation, diarrhea, coated tongue, dry mouth, sore mouth	Increased serum SGOT, SGPT, alkaline phosphatase	Avoid alcohol.
Ethotoin (40)	Nausea	Vomiting, diarrhea		
Mephobarbital (40)			Megaloblastic anemia Rickets, deranged vitamin D metabolism	
Ethosuximide (Zarontin) (39-41)	Nausea	Hiccups, swollen tongue, vomiting, cramps, diarrhea	Decreased serum 25-OH-vitamin-D, osteomalacia	Take with food and milk to avoid gastrointestinal effects.
Metharbital (40)		Gastric distress	Vitamin K deficiency in infants of women who take it during pregnancy	
Methsuximide (40)	Nausea, anorexia, weight loss	Vomiting, diarrhea, epigastric pain, abdominal pain, constipation		
Phenacemide (40)	Anorexia, weight loss	Gastrointestinal disturbances		
Phenobarbital (40, 42, 43)			Increased serum HDL Decreased serum folate, B vitamins, pyridoxine, 25-hydroxy-vitamin-D, calcium, magnesium Decreased cerebrospinal fluid levels of vitamin B-12 and folate	Alcohol ingestion should be avoided (potentiates central nervous system effects). Toxicity is more likely in protein deficiency.

(continued)

TABLE 27.1. *CONTINUED*

Drug	Effects			Recommendations
	Appetite	*Gastrointestinal*	*Metabolic*	
			Increased turnover of vitamins D and K Decreased bone density, osteomalacia Megaloblastic anemia	
Phenytoin (Dilantin) (39-41, 43-44)	Decreased	Decreased taste acuity, gum hypertrophy; constipation; calcium supplements decrease bioavailability of both drug and mineral	Increased turnover of vitamins D and K Rickets, anemia, hyperglycemia Decreased serum folate, vitamin B-12, pyridoxine, vitamin D, calcium, magnesium, 25-hydroxy-vitamin-D Increased serum copper, glucose, alkaline phosphatase, GGT Mildly elevated transaminases, especially gamma-glutamyl transpeptidase and alkaline phosphatase	Pyridoxine or folate supplements decrease anticonvulsant effects. Take with food or milk. Swallow extended-release tablets whole. Avoid excessive fluid intake. Never mix with tube feedings (adheres to tube). Alcohol consumption may cause seizures. May cause minor anomalies in infants of mothers who take it during pregnancy.
Prinidone (Nysoline) (40, 41, 43)	Nausea	Vomiting	Decreased serum folate, vitamin B-12, pyridoxine, and bilirubin Decreased absorption of calcium and vitamin D Increased turnover of vitamins D and K Osteomalacia, megaloblastic anemia Impaired folate metabolism	Folate supplements can interfere with action.
Sulthiamine (40)				May cause peripheral neuritis.
Trimethadione (40)	Nausea, anorexia, weight loss	Hiccups, vomiting, abdominal pain, gastric distress		
Valproic acid (Depakene) (39, 41)		Abdominal pain, constipation, diarrhea	Increased serum HDL Decreased serum LDL Anemia Increased serum alkaline phosphatase, SGOT, SGPT, bilirubin, LDH Produces urinary ketones	Take after meals to avoid gastrointestinal distress. Swallow capsules whole. Do not take oral solution with carbonated beverages. Avoid alcohol.

TABLE 27.2. DAILY FOOD EXCHANGES FOR A CHILD, AGE 1–3

Food	Amount (exchanges)	Protein (g)	Protein (kcal)	Fat (g)	Fat (kcal)	Carbohydrate (g)	Carbohydrate (kcal)
Skim milk	1½	12	48			18	72
Meat, medium-fat	2	14	56	10	90		
Fruit	1½					23	92
Bread	1	3	12			15	60
Vegetable	1	2	8			5	20
Fat	1½			8	72		
Total g		31		18		61	
Total kcal			124		162		244

Kilocalories from foods exclusive of MCT = 124 + 162 + 244 = 530.
Total kilocalories (including MCT) = 1,302.

**MEAL PLAN AND SAMPLE MENU FOR THE MCT-BASED KETOGENIC DIET
(FOR A CHILD, AGE 1–3)**

Food	Exchange[a]
Breakfast	
¼ cup orange juice	½ fruit
½ scrambled egg	½ medium-fat meat[b]
½ tsp. margarine	½ fat
¼ cup Cream of Wheat	½ bread
1 oz. skim milk (for cereal)	1 oz. skim milk
3 oz. skim milk	3 oz. skim milk
2 tbsp. MCT oil (blenderized with milk)	2 tbsp. MCT oil
Lunch	
½-oz. turkey frankfurter	½ high-fat meat[b]
5 french-fried potato strips	½ bread + ½ fat
Salad:	½ vegetable
2 leaves lettuce, ¼ cup raw spinach, ½ raw diced carrot, 1 tsp. low-calorie Italian dressing	
3 oz. skim milk	3 oz. skim milk
2 tbsp. MCT oil (blenderized with milk)	2 tbsp. MCT oil
Dinner	
1 oz. cooked round steak	1 lean meat[b]
¼ cup cooked green beans	½ vegetable
½ tsp. margarine	½ fat
⅝ cup fresh strawberries and 1 tbsp. raisins	1 fruit
3 oz. skim milk	3 oz. skim milk
2 tbsp. MCT oil (blenderized with milk)	2 tbsp. MCT oil
Evening snack	
2 oz. skim milk	2 oz. skim milk
2 tsp. MCT oil (blenderized with milk)	2 tsp. MCT oil

Approximate Nutrient Analysis

Energy	1,293 kcal
Protein	30.2 g (9% of kcal)
Fat	110.3 g (77% of kcal)
Polyunsaturated fat	5.1 g
Monounsaturated fat	5.9 g
Saturated fat	5.0 g
Cholesterol	145 mg
Carbohydrate	64.2 g (20% of kcal)
Vitamin A	12,562 IU
	1,476 RE
Thiamine	0.49 mg
Riboflavin	1.00 mg
Niacin	4.4 mg
Folate	129 mcg
Vitamin B-12	2.60 mcg
Vitamin B-6	0.67 mg
Vitamin C	91.7 mg
Calcium	617 mg
Phosphorus	1,645 mg
Iron	5.9 mg
Copper	0.30 mg
Zinc	4.1 mg
Magnesium	120 mg
Sodium	761 mg
Potassium	1,645 mg

[a]Artificial flavorings—e.g., strawberry, vanilla—may be used if desired. Salad dressing should have less than 6 kcal per teaspoon.
[b]For 2 medium-fat meat exchanges, it is permissible to substitute 1 lean meat exchange plus ½ high-fat and ½ medium-fat exchange.

REFERENCES

1. Senior, J.: Medium chain triglycerides. Philadelphia: University of Pennsylvania Press, 1968.

2. Signore, J.: Ketogenic diet containing medium-chain triglycerides. J Am Diet Assoc 62:285, 1973.

3. Sucher, K.: Medium chain triglycerides: A review of their enteral use in clinical nutrition. Nutr Clin Prac 1:146, 1986.

4. Bach, A., and Babayan, V.: Medium chain triglycerides: An update. Am J Clin Nutr 36:950, 1982.

5. Cotter, R., and D'Alleinne, C. D.: Medium chain triglycerides—a preclinical perspective. In Kinney, J. M., and Borum, P. R.: Perspectives in clinical nutrition. Baltimore: Urban and Schwarzenberg, 1989.

6. Huttenlocher, P., Wilborn, A., and Signore, J.: Medium chain triglycerides as a therapy for intractable childhood epilepsy. Neurology 21:1097, 1971.

7. Huttenlocher, P.: Ketonemia and seizures: Metabolic and anticonvulsant effects of two ketogenic diets. Pediatr Res 10:536, 1976.

8. Isom, J.: Treatment of minor motor seizures. Paper presented at the annual meeting of the Child Neurology Society, October 10–12, 1974.

9. Stephenson, J., House, F., and Stronberg, P.: Medium chain triglycerides in a ketogenic diet. Dev Med Child Neurol 19:693, 1977.

10. Berman, W.: Ketogenic diet and clonazepam in the treatment of childhood myoclonic epilepsy. Dev Med Child Neurol 18:819, 1976.

11. Schwartz, R. H., Eaton, J., et al.: Ketogenic diets in the treatment of epilepsy: Short-term clinical effects. Dev Med Child Neurol 31:145, 1989.

12. Schwartz, R. H., Boyes, S., and Aynsley-Green, A.: Metabolic effects of three ketogenic diets in the treatment of severe epilepsy. Dev Med Child Neurol 31:152, 1989.

13. Hinton, W., Schwartz, R., and Loach, A.: Diet induced ketosis in epilepsy and anaesthesia. Anaesthesia 37:39, 1982.

14. Aftergood, L., and Alfin-Slater, R.: Absorption, digestion and metabolism of lipids. In Wohl, M., and Goodhart, R.: Modern nutrition in health and disease. 4th ed. Philadelphia: Lea & Febiger, 1968.

15. Freund, G.: The caloric deficiency hypothesis of ketogenesis tested in man. Metabolism 14:985, 1965.

16. Freund, G., and Weinsier, R.: Standardized ketosis following medium chain triglyceride ingestion. Metabolism 15:980, 1966.

17. Pi-Sunyer, F., Hashin, S., and Van Itallie, R.: Insulin and ketone responses to ingestion of medium and long chain triglycerides in man. Diabetes 18:96, 1969.

18. Haldukewych, D., Forsythe, W., and Sills, M.: Monitoring octanoic and decanoic acids in plasma from children with intractable epilepsy treated with medium chain triglyceride diet. Clin Chem 26:642, 1982.

19. Heldenberg, D., Harel, S., et al.: The effect of chronic anticonvulsant therapy on serum lipids and lipoproteins in epileptic children. Neurology 33:510, 1983.

20. Dekaban, A.: Plasma lipids in epileptic children treated with the high fat diet. Arch Neurol 15:177, 1966.

21. Lima, L. A. M.: Neonatal parenteral nutrition with medium chain triglycerides—rationale for research. JPEN 13:312, 1989.

22. Mortensen, P. B., and Gregersen, N.: Medium chain triglyceride medication as a pitfall in the diagnosis of nonketotic C6-C10 dicarboxylic acidurias. Clin Chem Acta 103:33, 1980.

23. Whyte, R. K., Whelan, D., et al.: Excretion of dicarboxylic and omega-1-hydroxy fatty acids by low birth infants fed with medium chain triglycerides. Pediatr Res 20:122, 1986.

24. Henderson, M. J., and Dear, P. R. F.: Dicarboxylic aciduria and medium chain triglyceride supplemented milk. Arch Dis Child 61:610, 1986.

25. Dupont, C., Rocchioccioli, F., and Bougneres, P. F.: Urinary excretion of dicarboxylic acids in term newborns fed with 5% medium chain triglycerides enriched formula. J Pediatr Gastroenterol Nutr 6:610, 1986.

26. Mortensen, P. B.: Dicarboxylic acids and the lipid metabolism. Dan Med Bull 31:121, 1984.

27. American Dietetic Association and American Diabetes Association: Meal planning with exchange lists. Chicago: American Dietetic Association, 1986.

28. Mead Johnson Co.: The enteral nutritional management system: Product handbook. Evansville, Ind., 1985.

29. Jensen, G., Mascioli, E. A., et al.: Parenteral infusion of medium chain triglyceride (MCT) and reticulo-endothelial system (RS) function in man. Am J Clin Nutr 47:786, 1988.

30. Mascioli, E. A., Porter, K. A., et al.: Metabolic response to MCT. In Kinney, J. M., and Borum, P. R.: Perspectives in clinical nutrition. Baltimore: Urban and Schwarzenberg, 1989.

31. Faber, J., Goldstein, R., et al.: Absorption of medium chain triglycerides in the stomach of the human infant. J Pediatr Gastroenterol Nutr 7:189, 1988.

32. LePage, C., and Roy, C.: Direct transesterification of all classes of lipids in a one step reaction. J Lipid Res 27:114, 1986.

33. Dietary medium chain fatty acids in adipose tissue of infants. Nutr Rev 45:202, 1987.

34. Sarda, P., Lepage, G., et al.: Storage of medium chain triglycerides in adipose tissue of orally fed infants. Am J Clin Nutr 45:399, 1987.

35. Falk, R., Cederbaum, S., et al.: Ketonic diet in the management of pyruvate dehydrogenase deficiency. Pediatrics 58:713, 1976.

36. Hirona, H., Suzuki, H., et al.: Essential fatty acid deficiency induced by total parenteral nutrition and by medium chain triglyceride feeding. Am J Clin Nutr 30:1670, 1977.

37. Hahn, T., Halstead, L., and Devivo, D.: Disordered mineral metabolism produced by ketogenic diet therapy.

Calcif Tissue Int 28:17, 1979.

38. Food and Nutrition Board, National Research Council: Recommended Dietary Allowances. 10th ed. Washington, D.C.: National Academy of Sciences, 1989.

39. Knoben, J. E., and Anderson, P. O.: Handbook of clinical drug data. 6th ed. Hamilton, Ohio: Drug Intelligence Publications, 1989.

40. Roe, D.: Handbook: Interactions of selected drugs and nutrients in patients. 3d ed. Chicago: American Dietetic Association, 1979.

41. Powers, D. E., and Moore, A. O.: Food/medication interactions. 6th ed. Phoenix: 1988 (self-published).

42. Bleck, T. F.: Epilepsy. Dis Month 33 (11):1, 1988.

43. American Dietetic Association: Manual of clinical dietetics. Chicago: American Dietetic Association, 1988.

44. Gaily, E., Granstrom, M-L., et al.: Minor anomalies in offspring of epileptic mothers. J Pediatr 112:520, 1988.

45. Woody, R. C., Steele, R. W., et al.: Impaired neutrophil function in children with seizures treated with the ketogenic diet. J Pediatr 115:427, 1989.

PART VI

MODIFICATIONS IN KILOCALORIE CONTENT

28.

KILOCALORIE- AND NUTRIENT-CONTROLLED DIET FOR DIABETES

CHRISTINE A. BEEBE, M.S., R.D., C.D.E.

DEFINITIONS

1. DIABETES

Diabetes mellitus is a group of genetically and clinically related disorders characterized by blood glucose levels above defined limits (table 28.1). Diverse etiological and pathological mechanisms contribute to a relative or absolute deficiency of insulin, a hormone secreted by pancreatic beta cells. Significant clinical complications are associated with the hyperglycemia of diabetes:

- Macrovascular disease—2 to 6 times greater risk than the general population (2).
  - Heart disease
  - Stroke
  - Peripheral vascular disease
- Microvascular disease
  - Nephropathy
  - Retinopathy
- Neuropathy
  - Peripheral
  - Autonomic

The development of these complications is believed to be correlated to the level of blood glucose control maintained throughout the diabetic individual's life span (3). This assumption continues to be investigated (4). However, even individuals with impaired glucose tolerance are subject to increased incidence of macrovascular complications (5). Generally, complications do not appear until diabetes has been present for more than 15 to 20 years. Genetic and environmental factors also play a role in the development of the complications associated with the disease.

Individuals with diabetes are classified into 2 primary categories according to their etiology and subsequent treatment needs (table 28.2). Nearly 90% of individuals with diabetes have non-insulin-dependent diabetes mellitus (NIDDM); 5% to 10% have insulin-dependent diabetes mellitus (IDDM). Other classifications of glucose intolerance include gestational diabetes and impaired glucose tolerance (6).

2. AMERICAN DIABETES ASSOCIATION (ADA) DIET

The diet recommended by the American Diabetes Association is essentially the same healthy diet recommended by the American Dietetic Association, American Heart Association, American Cancer Institute, and the United States surgeon general (7). In principle the diet is low in fat and cholesterol, high in fiber-rich carbohydrates, and modest in protein content (table 28.3) (8). A weight-loss regimen is the primary dietary component for nearly 80% of all persons with diabetes, given that obesity is the primary risk factor for the disease.

Because of the heterogeneous nature of diabetes, the diet must be individu-

TABLE 28.1. NORMAL BLOOD GLUCOSE VALUES AND VALUES THAT ARE DIAGNOSTIC FOR DIABETES MELLITUS AND IMPAIRED GLUCOSE TOLERANCE (IGT)

	Glucose concentration		
	Venous plasma (mg/dL)	Venous whole blood (mg/dL)	Capillary whole blood (mg/dL)
Normal values			
Fasting	<115	<100	<100
½, 1, 1½ hours	<200	<180	<200
2 hours	<140	<120	<140
Diabetes[a]			
Fasting[b]	≥140	≥120	≥120
2 hours[c]	≥200	≥180	≥200
IGT[d]			
Fasting	<140	<120	<120
½, 1, 1½ hours	≥200	≥180	≥200
2 hours	140–199	120–179	140–199

Source: Beebe, C. A., and Rubenstein, A. H. (1), copyright © 1987 by Aspen Publishers, Inc.; *adapted from* National Institutes of Health (6), copyright © 1979 by the American Diabetes Association.
[a]A plasma value at any time ≥200, plus classic symptoms, is diagnostic.
[b]Noted value on more than one occasion.
[c]Noted value after OGTT at 2 hours and one other time from 0–2 hours is diagnostic.
[d]During OGTT, criteria for 3 time periods must be met.

TABLE 28.2. CLASSIFICATION OF DIABETES AND OTHER CATEGORIES OF GLUCOSE INTOLERANCE

Classification	Former terms	Characteristics
Diabetes		
Insulin-dependent diabetes mellitus (IDDM), Type I	Juvenile-onset diabetes Ketosis-prone diabetes Brittle diabetes	Low or absent endogenous insulin Onset generally in youth Dependent on exogenous insulin for life Ketosis-prone
Non-insulin-dependent diabetes mellitus (NIDDM), Type II Obese Nonobese	Adult-onset diabetes Maturity-onset diabetes Ketosis-resistant diabetes Stable diabetes	Insulin levels normal, elevated, or depressed Not ketosis-prone Onset generally after age 40 Majority obese Insulin resistant May require OHA or insulin for control of symptoms
Diabetes associated with certain conditions or syndromes	Secondary diabetes	Hyperglycemia present at a level diagnostic of diabetes Diabetes may be result of drugs, pancreatic disease, hormonal disease, or unknown cause
Gestational diabetes (GDM)	Gestational diabetes	Elevated glucose with onset in pregnancy Associated with increased risk of congenital malformations Increased risk for later developing DM
Impaired glucose tolerance (IGT)	Borderline diabetes Chemical diabetes	Defined by plasma glucose criteria and OGTT Plasma glucose levels greater than normal, but less than diabetic
Previous abnormality of glucose tolerance (Prev AGT)	Subclinical diabetes Prediabetes Latent diabetes	Previous hyperglycemia or IGT, but currently has normal glucose tolerance May develop DM
Potential abnormality of glucose tolerance (Pot AGT)	Prediabetes Potential diabetes	Never had IGT or DM, but is at greater risk Strong family history of DM or obesity

Source: Beebe, C. A., and Rubenstein, A. H. (1), copyright © 1987 by Aspen Publishers, Inc.; *adapted from* National Institutes of Health (6), copyright © 1979 by the American Diabetes Association.

alized and must be evaluated and altered as lifestyles and personal factors change. A preprinted diet is unacceptable for appropriate diabetes management.

PURPOSE OF THE DIET

The purposes of the diet in diabetes are to achieve optimal blood glucose concentrations throughout the day; to meet individual nutritional needs for overall health, including normal growth and development; to attain or maintain a reasonable body weight; and to achieve optimal lipid and nutrient levels to prevent or delay complications.

PHYSIOLOGY, FOODS, AND NUTRIENTS

Normally, fasting blood glucose levels are maintained within a very narrow range of 60 to 120 mg/dL. Rarely do postprandial blood glucose levels rise above 160 mg/dL. Such metabolic homeostasis is orchestrated by the hormone insulin in synergy with its antagonist glucagon. The purpose of such precision is to maintain a constant and adequate supply of glucose to the central nervous system. The brain, in particular, is very much dependent on glucose, requiring about 6 g per hour under normal conditions (144 g per day). Because the brain cannot store glucose, it is important that glucose always be available in the blood.

Glucose available in the bloodstream comes from food and from endogenous production by the liver. In the normally fed individual, shortly after eating, glucose is derived from ingested carbohydrates, protein, and fat. After about 2 to 4 hours most of these nutrients have been metabolized and stored, at which time the body shifts into a fasting state. Glucose in the blood is then derived from the breakdown of stored nutrients. This shift between the fed and fasting states occurs unconsciously as insulin levels rise and fall in response to incoming glucose loads. In cases of diabetes, how-

TABLE 28.3. TARGET NUTRITION GOALS FOR PEOPLE WITH DIABETES

Calories

Sufficient to achieve and maintain reasonable weight.

Carbohydrate

May be up to 55%–60% of total calories. Liberalized; individualized; emphasis on unrefined carbohydrate with fiber; modest amounts of sucrose and other refined sugars may be acceptable, contingent on metabolic control.

Protein

Usual intake of protein in most Americans is double the amount needed; exact ideal percentage of total calories is unknown. Usual recommendation for people with diabetes is 12%–20% of total calories. Recommended daily allowance is 0.8 g/kg body weight for adults; intake is modified for children, pregnant and lactating women, the aged, and individuals with special medical conditions, e.g., renal complications.

Fiber

Up to 40 g/day; 25 g/1,000 kcal for low-calorie intakes.

Fat

Ideally <30% of total calories. However, this needs to be individualized, because 30% may be unachievable for some individuals.

- Polyunsaturated fats, up to 10%
- Saturated fats, <10%
- Monounsaturated fats, remaining percentage (10%–15%)

Cholesterol

<300 mg/day.

Alternative sweeteners

Use is acceptable.

Sodium

Not to exceed 3,000 mg/day; modified for special medical conditions.

Alcohol

Occasional use; limit to 1–2 alcohol equivalents 1–2 times per week.

Vitamins and minerals

No evidence that diabetes causes increased need.

Source: American Diabetes Association and American Dietetic Association (8); *adapted from* American Diabetes Association (7).

Note: Each goal needs to be individualized. The above goals should serve as a guide for establishing short- and long-term goals.

ever, this shift between the fed and fasting states does not occur, largely because insulin secretion and function are diminished.

1. IDDM

A person who is diagnosed with insulin-dependent diabetes mellitus has usually lost, by the time of diagnosis, 80% to 90% of beta cell function. Insulin-producing beta cells are destroyed by a progressive autoimmune response that may occur over several months to a few years. The process is believed to result from a combination of genetic predisposition and environmental or unknown stimuli (9). Occasionally, once metabolic derangements are corrected with insulin therapy, pancreatic insulin secretion may

actually increase. This is known as the "honeymoon phase" and rarely lasts more than a year (10). Insulin therapy requirements are usually very low during this time. Eventually, however, beta cell reserves are exhausted, and by 5 to 10 years after diagnosis the patient is totally dependent on exogenous insulin.

2. NIDDM

Non-insulin-dependent diabetes mellitus can occur as early as the teen years if obesity and a family history of the disorder are present as cofactors, although it is more common after age 45. The primary abnormality in NIDDM is insulin resistance, or the failure of body cells to respond to insulin in a normal fashion (11). The resistance occurs at the pe-

ripheral level as insulin receptors on muscle cells, in particular, fail to respond to insulin. This "receptor defect" means that glucose cannot enter cells. A "post-receptor" defect, in which insulin cannot be metabolized once it does enter the cells, is considered the primary problem of NIDDM, as insulin-sensitive reactions fail to occur.

Insulin resistance also occurs in the liver as insulin fails to shut off glucose production. Indeed, one of the hallmarks of NIDDM is a high fasting level of glucose as a result of nighttime hepatic glucose production.

Normal and elevated levels of circulating insulin are found in most patients with NIDDM but are misleading. In reality, insulin levels are less than adequate in relation to the amount of glucose present in the blood. Low insulin levels are usually present in thin patients with NIDDM or those with diabetes of long duration.

Family history and obesity are the 2 strongest risk factors for NIDDM. Obesity itself is an insulin-resistant state, whereby beta cells are forced to produce excessive amounts of insulin to overcome insulin resistance. Not all obese people develop diabetes, however. The genetic propensity for diabetes leads some obese individuals eventually to beta cell exhaustion and frank hyperglycemia. Upper body obesity has been identified as being an even stronger risk factor for diabetes than degree of obesity (12). Patients with a waist-to-hip ratio greater than 0.8 are at greater risk not only for diabetes but also for heart disease and hypertension. The risk increases as degree of obesity increases.

Clinically, NIDDM patients do not usually present with the characteristic symptoms of diabetes (polyuria, polyphagia, polydipsia). However, they may present with the signs of diabetes complications. Because of the slow, progressive nature of NIDDM, patients may have diabetes many years before diagnosis. It is not uncommon to be diagnosed after a heart attack, stroke, or neuropathic problems.

3. GDM

Gestational diabetes mellitus is a form of glucose intolerance that has its onset during pregnancy and is resolved on parturition. Nearly 2% of pregnancies result in GDM. Because fetal abnormalities and mortality are increased in the presence of hyperglycemia, all pregnant women should be screened between the 24th and 28th week of pregnancy. Nearly 40% of women with GDM eventually develop NIDDM (6). Guidelines for nutrition and monitoring of diabetic pregnancies have been published (8).

EFFECTS OF THE DIET

The outcome from dietary modification in diabetes is influenced by such individual factors as type of diabetes, age, lifestyle, coexisting medical conditions, and extent of adherence. Even when the diet is followed explicitly, blood glucose control may fluctuate, because diet is only one of several factors affecting blood glucose levels.

1. CALORIES

Calories should be modified to provide for growth and development in children and pregnant women; maintain normal weight in adults; and promote weight loss in overweight adults.

Normal growth and development in children with diabetes requires frequent evaluations of caloric needs, i.e., yearly and as activity levels change. Blood glucose levels can be expected to be erratic during puberty as hormone surges raise blood glucose. Hypoglycemic reactions can occur frequently in childhood and teen years as activity is often unpredictable. Blood glucose goals may need to be relaxed to weather the teen years.

Normal-weight adults with diabetes should be provided with enough calories

to maintain weight and support physical exercise. Blood glucose and insulin requirements can be expected to increase with weight gain. Evidence of weight gain should be quickly evaluated and calories adjusted (see the discussion of hypoglycemia under "Possible Adverse Reactions").

Obese adults placed on a hypocaloric diet should expect an improvement in blood glucose with the loss of as little as 10 to 20 lbs. (13). Weight reduction improves the primary problem in NIDDM, i.e., insulin resistance, by enhancing muscle glucose uptake and reducing hepatic glucose output. NIDDM patients placed on very low-calorie diets demonstrate a rapid drop in blood glucose that appears to maximize within the first 2 weeks of caloric restriction (14). Blood glucose response to calorie restriction appears correlated to the duration of diabetes. Individuals who begin caloric restriction early in the course of the disease are more likely to respond favorably.

Pregnant women with diabetes should receive sufficient calories to maintain fetal and maternal tissue development. Because of the teratogenic nature of ketones, enough calories should be provided to prevent ketone production. Ketones should be monitored daily and calories adjusted if necessary.

Because many pregnant women with gestational diabetes are overweight, minimizing weight gain should be a goal in this group. A current recommendation is 30 kcal/kg of actual weight for pregnant women of normal weight and for those with up to 120% of desirable weight, and 24 kcal/kg for women greater than 120% of desirable weight (15).

2. CARBOHYDRATES

The recommendation of the American Diabetes Association to liberalize carbohydrate intake to 55% to 60% of total calories is aimed for the most part at reducing fat intake. Because the risk of

cardiovascular disease is 4 to 6 times greater in people with diabetes than in the general population, reducing serum lipid levels is a priority of dietary management. Generally, serum LDL-cholesterol and triglycerides are elevated in diabetes, and HDL-cholesterol is less than normal. Both LDL-cholesterol and triglycerides increase as blood glucose levels increase. Improving diabetes control tends to improve lipid levels (16, 17).

For the most part, concentration of glucose in the blood following a meal is dependent on the amount of carbohydrate consumed and on factors that affect the rate at which the food is digested and absorbed. The inclusion of fat, protein, or fiber with carbohydrate tends to slow down digestion and absorption, leading to a blunted glucose response. While studies have shown this to be true in both control and diabetic subjects, individual variability suggests that this may not always be the case. For example, adding peanut butter to bread did not change the glycemic response in IDDM subjects as it did in normal and NIDDM subjects (18).

Such factors as the nature of a carbohydrate—i.e., wheat, corn, rye, or potato starch—affect digestibility and subsequent blood glucose response (19, 20). Even the form in which a carbohydrate is consumed can affect glycemic response. Wheat starch consumed as pasta, for example, gives a flatter glucose curve than wheat starch consumed as bread (21). Cooking and processing can also affect glycemic response, although inconsistently (22). Cooking potatoes increases the glycemic response, because the starch is made more easily digestible by the cooking process. In contrast, cooking carrots does not change the response (23).

The presence of a previous meal may also influence glycemic response; some studies indicate that blood glucose values are blunted when food consumption is preceded by another meal (24). Time of day is also a factor: Glycemic response to a given meal or food is greatest at the end of the day (25).

Avoiding sugar was once considered a necessary precaution in the diet recommended for diabetes. Sugar was thought to produce a blood glucose response that was faster and higher than that for more complex carbohydrates, e.g., bread or potatoes. Recent research, however, has shown this to be a misconception. When equal amounts of carbohydrate from various foods are compared for their effect on blood glucose, there are no distinguishing characteristics between simple and complex carbohydrate sources (26).

This finding has led to the recognition that sugar may be included in the diet of a person with diabetes. The general recommendation is that sugar may comprise up to 5% of carbohydrate calories without detrimental effects (7). Generally, such high-sugar foods as cookies, ice cream, and candy are substituted for breads in the diabetic exchange system. The large amounts of fat contained in most of these foods should be of more concern to the practitioner than their sugar content.

High-carbohydrate diets, in which carbohydrates make up 50% or more of total calories, increase insulin receptors and enhance insulin sensitivity in subjects without diabetes and in subjects with diabetes characterized by mild hyperglycemia (27). A high-carbohydrate diet is thought to improve glycemia in these individuals. In contrast, there are data obtained from individuals with diabetes that show a worsening of glycemia on high-carbohydrate diets (28). Some individuals with moderate to severe hyperglycemia may be incapable of secreting enough insulin to compensate for large glucose loads.

High-carbohydrate diets rich in dietary fiber have been shown to reduce blood glucose levels and insulin require-

ments (29). Non-insulin-dependent diabetic subjects treated with less than 30 units of insulin daily to achieve glycemic control have been able to stop insulin therapy, in one set of studies (30). Diets used in these and other successful studies have been very high in carbohydrate (nearly 70%) and fiber (65 g per day). Investigators are unsure whether the improvements seen in these studies are truly due to the fiber content or the high carbohydrate content of the diets. One group did find that high-fiber, high-carbohydrate diets improve blood glucose to a greater degree than high-carbohydrate, low-fiber diets (31).

Others argue that while the data strongly support increasing the fiber content of the diet, it is unrealistic to expect most people to see great improvements in blood glucose control. In one study, a high-carbohydrate, high-fiber diet utilizing typical fiber-rich foods, such as fruits, vegetables and grains, failed to affect blood glucose control in NIDDM patients (20).

Soluble fibers (guar, pectins, oat bran, legumes, barley) have the greatest impact on blood glucose response. Their viscous nature appears to slow gastric emptying, intestinal digestion, and absorption and to result in a blunting of the blood glucose curve following a meal (32). In addition, soluble fibers have been shown to reduce serum cholesterol levels (33). Insoluble fibers (cellulose-type) have not been shown to reduce glycemic response or affect cholesterol, yet are beneficial from an overall health standpoint because they enhance gut motility.

The recommendation of the American Diabetes Association for daily fiber intake is 25 g/1,000 kcal up to 50 g per day. Average intake in the United States is 13 to 19 g per day. Simple substitutions of whole wheat for white bread should not be expected to have an impact on blood glucose control or lipid levels

in patients with diabetes. Oats, barley, and legumes should be consumed to produce benefits in either blood glucose or serum lipids. Oats and oat bran are now added to many foods but may not be present in significant amounts. Patients should be trained to read labels of such foods to determine the fiber content.

Although it would appear that a high-carbohydrate, high-fiber diet would benefit all persons with diabetes, this recommendation is not without controversy. The idiosyncratic nature of diabetes dictates that diet recommendations be individualized. While a high-carbohydrate diet may be best for IDDM patients, individuals with NIDDM may need to be treated differently.

Most patients with NIDDM have hypertriglyceridemia. The National Institutes of Health Consensus Development Conference on Treatment of Hypertriglyceridemia defines this condition as a fasting triglyceride level exceeding 500 mg/dL. Hepatic very low-density lipoprotein (VLDL) production is increased in both NIDDM and obesity. This is probably caused by hyperinsulinemia and insulin resistance, which characterize both states. Several studies suggest that hypertriglyceridemia, including that found in NIDDM, is worsened by high-carbohydrate diets (34, 35). The increased triglyceride production seen following carbohydrate intake was once thought to be a transient response. More recent evidence suggests the contrary, as studies demonstrate triglycerides can remain elevated for as much as 4 months (36).

Some investigators are suggesting that part of the carbohydrate in the diet for NIDDM patients should be replaced with monounsaturated fat (36–38). A study (39) demonstrated a decrease in triglycerides in NIDDM patients placed on a diet containing 47% carbohydrate and 38% fat. Monounsaturated fat contributed 18% of calories in this study. Others have demonstrated similar results to support these data (37, 38). Blood glucose control in these studies either remained the same or was improved.

Such controversy illustrates the importance of individualization when designing the diet for a person with diabetes. Only through close follow-up is it possible to observe the effects of a selected nutrition approach and to make alterations if necessary. Given that most Americans consume a diet close to 40% fat, it is possible that an aggressive fat reduction to 30% of calories would be difficult to implement. A more modest reduction in fat, to between 35% and 38%, while increasing monounsaturates could be an acceptable approach. A gradual reduction of the fat content to 30% may be the eventual goal for most NIDDM patients.

Gestational diabetes represents another situation in which a high-carbohydrate diet may not be preferred. Tight control of blood glucose, both pre- and postprandially, is required during pregnancy. In one set of clinical trials, optimal blood glucose results were obtained by restricting carbohydrate intake to 40% of calories (15). This reduces postprandial rises in blood glucose yet provides enough carbohydrate to prevent fasting ketonemia.

3. FAT

Restricting fat intake in the diet of a person with diabetes is of utmost importance to help reduce the increased risk of cardiovascular disease. Cardiovascular disease and death is 3 to 6 times greater in diabetic individuals than in the general population (2). Hyperlipidemia is common among diabetic patients. Most patients with NIDDM are also obese, and more than 50% are hypertensive. Because cardiovascular risk factors are additive, even mild degrees of hyperlipidemia may be harmful to the person with diabetes.

Poor diabetes control raises low-density lipoprotein (LDL) and VLDL (40).

LDL uptake by peripheral tissues is reduced as LDL receptors become glycosylated in the presence of elevated blood glucose. VLDL production by the liver is increased in NIDDM patients because of insulin resistance, which prevents cells from taking up glucose. As a result, cells switch to using free fatty acids. Large quantities of free fatty acids are released into the circulation and provide substrate for VLDL production by the liver.

Improving daily blood glucose values should be a priority if the maximum response from dietary fat restriction is to be expected. Recommended fat and cholesterol restrictions should produce expected results in patients with diabetes. Concern has been raised, however, that low-fat, high-carbohydrate diets lower high-density lipoprotein (HDL) cholesterol levels and raise triglyceride levels (see the discussion of carbohydrates in this section). Increasing monounsaturated fats to 14% of total caloric intake has been recommended, as HDL levels are either maintained or increased slightly and triglycerides are reduced (36–38).

Clinical judgment based on frequent follow-up of the patient is the only way to determine which approach works best with individual patients. By this means, fat can be lowered gradually and fiber can be increased gradually. Monounsaturates can be increased if the expected result from lowering fat is not achieved.

Omega-3 fatty acids have been recommended to control the hypertriglyceridemia of NIDDM. Clinical trials (40, 41) have shown promising results from high doses of omega-3 fatty acids (as much as 15 g per day), yet supplementation is generally not recommended except in extreme hypertriglyceridemia. One of the drawbacks to supplementation with omega-3 fatty acids is that blood glucose control worsens. For individuals requiring insulin therapy, this may necessitate an increase in insulin dose. For others it may produce a need for exogenous in-

sulin, which is generally to be avoided when possible. An additional drawback to supplementation is the large doses required to be therapeutic. For the average person with diabetes, increasing consumption of fish to 2 to 3 servings per week will supply approximately the 8 g of eicosapentenoic acid that most epidemiological data suggest is preventive.

All overweight NIDDM patients should be placed on some degree of caloric restriction to promote weight loss. Relative body weight is strongly correlated with hypertriglyceridemia and other forms of hyperlipidemia. For the obese NIDDM patient, losing weight should be the first therapeutic step to control both blood glucose and serum lipids.

4. PROTEIN

Most nutrition experts agree that Americans consume much more protein than they need. The recommendation of the American Diabetes Association to reduce protein intake to the Recommended Dietary Allowance (0.8 g/kg) is in part an effort to help reduce dietary fat intake. Many high-protein foods are also major sources of fat, saturated fat, and cholesterol.

Evidence is accumulating to suggest that low-protein diets may help to maintain renal function and reduce proteinuria in patients with renal insufficiency (42). Lower-protein diets could therefore be of benefit to the person with diabetes; as many as 40% of patients on dialysis require the procedure because of diabetic nephropathy.

Studies conducted in patients with diabetes have found a reduction in proteinuria to occur during protein restrictions of 40 to 60 g per day (43, 44). While protein restriction may prove to be helpful in preventing or delaying the onset of chronic renal failure in diabetes, there is a lack of consensus on this issue. More research is required. In the meantime a prudent approach to protein intake is recommended, and every effort should be made to use the RDA as a goal for most individuals. Unfortunately the RDA for protein is so restrictive to most Americans that adherence becomes difficult.

Growing children, pregnant and lactating women, and the elderly, who may be in a compromised nutritional state, will require greater levels of protein (see RDAS).

5. MODIFYING FOOD INTAKE PATTERN

The eating patterns of a person with diabetes may influence blood glucose response and can thus be modified to optimize glucose values. Patients with IDDM are required to inject insulin and therefore have abnormal levels of insulin circulating in their bodies at specific times. Because their insulin dose is matched to a specific quantity of food and carbohydrate at specific times of the day, any deviation from that pattern of intake will produce a deviation in blood glucose.

Generally, meals must be eaten on time and should be consistent in the quantity of food and carbohydrate consumed from day to day. If a meal is to be delayed more than 45 to 60 minutes, a fruit or starch serving (carbohydrate source) should be borrowed from that meal and consumed at the regular meal time to avoid a hypoglycemic reaction. Knowing the blood glucose level at the time the meal is delayed can make this decision easier. If the blood glucose is 140 mg/dL or higher, the meal most likely can be delayed without adverse effects. This varies with each individual and the circumstances.

Between-meal snacks may be consumed by patients with IDDM to prevent hypoglycemia between meals or simply as a preference. They should not be considered a requirement. Each person will vary in this regard.

Patients with NIDDM have a problem releasing and using insulin effectively. If they are not taking insulin, consistency in meal timing and composition are not crucial. Spacing meals 4 to 5 hours apart may help normalize blood glucose. Snacks may be useful to prevent hunger but may also keep blood glucose levels elevated and thus be undesirable in some NIDDM patients (45). Maintaining calories at or below caloric requirements is the best approach, given that the majority of NIDDM patients are obese.

There is some question as to whether calories should be divided equally between meals to minimize postprandial responses, but this has never been confirmed. There is evidence to the contrary, that as long as calories are appropriate, as much as 70% of caloric intake may be consumed at the evening meal without increasing 24-hour glucose values (45).

6. ALTERNATIVE SWEETENERS

Alternative sweeteners can be of benefit to the person with diabetes. They should not be substituted for nutrients required to maintain a healthy diet. Alternate sweeteners are either noncaloric or caloric (8).

Noncaloric sweeteners include saccharin, aspartame (Equal or Nutrasweet), and acesulfame-K (Sunette). Noncaloric sweeteners themselves provide virtually no calories and do not raise blood glucose. Caloric sweeteners include fructose, sorbitol, and mannitol. Although these contain calories (4 cal/g), they are absorbed more slowly or metabolized differently so that they have a lesser impact on blood sugar levels. These sweeteners are often used in products that have considerable calories and fat in themselves. Frequently, as is the case with sorbitol-sweetened candies and food products, additional fat is added to the product to increase solubility and palatability. Large doses of sorbitol may have a laxative effect.

Blood sugar may be increased considerably by some products that contain other forms of carbohydrate, including flour, fruit, and milk. It is not unusual for some "sugar-free" products to have more calories than their "sugar-sweetened" counterparts. As a result, patients should be taught how to fit artificially sweetened products into their meal plan. In general, products that contain less than 20 cal per serving can be used freely, whereas others must be counted as fruits or starches in the exchange diet. Many times, using an artificially sweetened product is of no value to the patient.

7. ALCOHOL

Alcoholic beverages can be used by persons with diabetes who are able to control their intake. The same precautions that apply to the general population for use of alcoholic beverages also apply to persons with diabetes. The risk of hypoglycemia in patients who take insulin or oral hypoglycemic agents is a problem. The metabolism of alcohol interferes with gluconeogenesis and prevents the necessary increase in blood glucose that would ordinarily follow a low blood-sugar reaction. Therefore, specific precautions should be followed (46):

- Alcohol should be used in moderation, defined as not more than 1 to 2 alcohol equivalents once or twice per week. One equivalent is defined as the amount of alcohol in 4 oz. of wine; 12 oz. of beer; or 1½ oz. of distilled beverage.
- Alcohol should be consumed with food to avoid hypoglycemia.
- Alcohol is metabolized like fat and is substituted as fat in an exchange diet: One equivalent equals 90 calories or 2 fat exchanges.
- Caloric mixers such as juice or tonic water should be calculated into the meal plan.
- Alcohol should not be used in cases of hypertriglyceridemia, pancreatitis, gastritis, or certain renal and cardiac disorders.

INDICATIONS FOR USE

Diet therapy is indicated for any person diagnosed with diabetes (IDDM, NIDDM, or GDM) or documented glucose intolerance. A diet plan should be instituted as soon as possible after diagnosis. The choice of meal plan from among several different approaches should be made by the patient and the dietitian together.

POSSIBLE ADVERSE REACTIONS

1. WEIGHT GAIN

Body weight should be monitored carefully in all patients with diabetes. Patients on insulin who are in very good control of their diet risk weight gain as the frequency of reactions increases and the loss of glucose calories in the urine diminishes (47). Weight gain tends to increase insulin requirements and may be problematic to the patient as blood glucose and lipids increase. Calories should be adjusted routinely if necessary.

2. HYPOGLYCEMIA

Hypoglycemia may occur when circulating insulin levels are elevated, producing a precipitous fall in blood glucose to below the normal level of 70 mg/dL. The most frequent causes are too much insulin, too much exercise, or too little food. Occasionally patients will inadvertently increase their insulin dose. The most common cause is skipping or delaying food intake. An unexpected increase in physical activity is frequently the cause, especially in children.

Exercise can often result in hypoglycemia in the person with IDDM and is best regulated by the self-monitoring of blood glucose. Because exercise utilizes glucose and generally lowers glucose concentration in the blood, food intake must be increased or else insulin dose must be reduced, in order to prevent hypoglycemia. Guidelines for making food adjustments for exercise have been developed (table 28.4).

If a person is utilizing exercise to assist in weight loss, it is preferable to re-duce the dose of insulin rather than to increase food intake. The time of day at which exercise is performed will influence which insulin dose to reduce; i.e., if exercise is performed before the evening meal, the morning dose of NPH insulin would be reduced. One study has suggested that insulin should be reduced by one-third prior to exercise, although this will vary with each individual (48).

Exercising muscles remain sensitive to insulin for as much as 24 to 48 hours after the activity. Hypoglycemia can occur during, immediately following, or several hours after exercise. IDDM patients should be instructed to consume an evening snack larger than normal on days on which they exercise, to prevent nocturnal hypoglycemia. Exercising NIDDM patients on insulin or oral agents will usually not need supplementary food following exercise.

Overweight patients who are dieting and take insulin or oral hypoglycemic agents (OHA) may experience hypoglycemia as they reduce their caloric intake and lose weight. Because this is counterproductive to weight loss, insulin doses should be reduced for patients when they begin a weight-loss diet.

Tight control of blood glucose may produce frequent blood glucose reactions. This phenomenon was observed in the early phases of the Diabetes Control and Complications Trial (47). Weight gain can be a sign of frequent reactions, because patients consume extra calories when treating reactions.

If hypoglycemia is suspected, it should be identified by a blood glucose test and treated quickly and appropriately. In the event that self-testing of blood glucose is not feasible, treatment should be given anyway. Most patients quickly learn to identify the symptoms of hypoglycemia: headache, sweating, shaking, blurred vision, and confusion. Some individuals with diabetes of long duration lose their ability to detect reactions, and the hypo-glycemic attack may go untreated until the patient becomes unconscious. Frequent blood glucose monitoring and relaxing goals for blood glucose control are generally required in this situation. The 15/15 rule is recommended when treating reactions:

- Consume 15 g of carbohydrate (table 28.5).
- Wait 10 to 15 minutes and test blood glucose.
- Repeat 15 g of carbohydrate if blood glucose is below 80 mg/dL.

Severe blood glucose reactions may require 30 g or more of carbohydrate. It is wise to avoid overtreating a reaction, because this may lead to rebound hyperglycemia.

3. HYPERGLYCEMIA OF ILLNESS

During periods of illness and surgery, blood glucose is elevated and diabetes control may worsen. Counterregulatory hormones (epinephrine, norepinephrine, glucagon, and cortisol), stimulated by infection, illness, injury, or stress, increase hepatic production of glucose. This in turn raises insulin requirements. Because food intake generally decreases during illness, many patients mistakenly stop or decrease insulin therapy. In reality, most patients need to increase their dose.

The goals of diet therapy during illness are to prevent dehydration and provide adequate nutrition to promote recovery. Carbohydrate intake can be maintained with liquids and easily digested soft foods. Patients should be taught to follow specific guidelines during illness (table 28.6).

CONTRAINDICATIONS

Because the American Diabetes Association diet is a healthy, well-balanced diet, there are no contraindications. Such medical conditions as renal failure may require altering the diet.

TABLE 28.4. GUIDELINES FOR MAKING FOOD ADJUSTMENTS FOR EXERCISE FOR PEOPLE WITH IDDM

Type of exercise	Examples of exercise	If blood glucose (in mg/dL) is:	Increase food intake by:	Suggested foods to use
Short duration of low to moderate intensity	Walking ½ mile or leisurely bicycling for <30 minutes	<80–99	10–15 g carbohydrate/hour	1 fruit or 1 bread exchange
		>100	Not necessary to increase food	
Moderate intensity	1 hour of tennis, swimming, jogging, leisurely bicycling, gardening, golfing, or vacuuming	<80–100	25–50 g carbohydrate before exercise	½ meat sandwich with 1 milk and/or 1 fruit exchange
		100–180	10–15 g carbohydrate/hour of exercise	1 fruit or 1 bread exchange
		180–300[a]	Not necessary to increase food	
		>300[a]	Do not begin exercise until blood glucose levels are within target range	
Strenuous activity or exercise	~1–2 hours of football, hockey, racquetball, or basketball games; strenuous bicycling or swimming; shoveling heavy snow	<80–100	50 g carbohydrate; monitor blood glucose carefully	1 meat sandwich (2 slices bread) with 1 milk or fruit exchange
		100–180	25–50 g carbohydrate, depending on intensity and duration	½ meat sandwich with 1 milk and/or fruit exchange
		180–300[a]	10–15 g carbohydrate/hour of exercise	1 fruit or 1 bread exchange
		>300[a]	Do not begin exercise until blood glucose levels are within target range	

Source: American Diabetes Association and American Dietetic Association (8); *adapted from* Franz, M. J. (57).
Note: During period of exercise, individuals need to be sure to increase fluid intake. Self-monitoring of blood glucose is essential for all people to determine actual carbohydrate needs.
[a]Some individuals will experience hyperglycemia with preexercise values of ~250 mg/dL.

CLINICAL ASSESSMENT

Nutritional assessment must take into account the patient's age, gender, lifestyle, socioeconomic conditions and cultural and religious beliefs (table 28.7). Diet is identified by patients with diabetes as the most difficult self-management task associated with the disease. Dietary adherence can only be accomplished with a careful consideration for the patient's needs, learning abilities, and willingness to make necessary adjustments. The diet in diabetes is not temporary. It is a lifelong adjustment that should be made gradually.

A 24-hour or 3-day diet recall is a must to observe usual patterns of intake as well as specific composition. The dietitian will want to look at the quality of the diet from the standpoint of macronutrient composition and calories. Problems with digestion, nausea, diarrhea, or constipation should be evaluated. The times of day at which food is usually consumed, as well as work and exercise times, are important when evaluating what changes need to be made.

The goal of insulin therapy in diabetes is to mimic physiologic insulin delivery.

TABLE 28.5. CHARACTERISTICS OF FOODS OR GLUCOSE SOURCES ROUGHLY EQUIVALENT TO 15 G CARBOHYDRATE

Food/glucose source	Amount	Glucose (g)[a]	Carbohydrate (g)	Calories
Gelatin, regular, prepared	½ cup	6.0	17	71
Hard candy (Life Savers), flavored	5	0[b]	15	50
Honey	1 tbsp.	7.1	17.3	64
Juice, apple	½ cup	3.1	14.5	58
Juice, orange	½ cup	6.6	12.8	54
Milk, skim	1 cup	0	12	86
Raisins	2 tbsp.	5.6	14.2	54
Soft drinks, regular				
Cola	½ cup	5	12.8	50
Ginger ale	¾ cup	5.6	15.9	62
Sugar, granulated[a]	4 tsp.	0	15.5	61
Sugar, ½″ cubes[a]	6	0	14.5	57
Syrup, corn	1 tbsp.	4.4	15	44
Thirst quencher (Gatorade)	1 cup	5.8	15.2	60
Glucose tablets	3	15	15	60
Glutose, 80-g bottle	½	16	16	64
Insta Glucose, 31-g tube	½	6.4	12.5	50
Insulin Reaction Gel, 25-g packets	1½	15	17	69

Source: American Diabetes Association and American Dietetic Association (8).
[a]This is the amount of glucose found in food before digestion and metabolism. For example, common table sugar is the disaccharide sucrose. Sucrose consists of the 2 monosaccharides glucose and fructose joined by a glycosidic linkage. Consequently, digestion and metabolism need to occur before glucose in sucrose is available. *Values from* Matthews, R. H., Pehrsson, P. R., and Farhat-Sabet, M.: Sugar content of selected foods: Individual and total foods. USDA/HNIS/Home Economics Research Report no. 48. Washington, D.C., 1987.
[b]Glucose is known to be present, but there is a lack of reliable data.

TABLE 28.6. SICK-DAY GUIDELINES

1. Monitor blood glucose at least 4 times per day (before each meal and at bedtime).
2. Test urine for ketones if blood glucose is >240 mg/dL.
3. If regular foods are not tolerated, carbohydrates in the meal plan should be replaced with liquid, semiliquid, or soft foods. The carbohydrate source is not of major concern; more important is what the patient can tolerate (e.g., sugar-containing liquids may be the only food source tolerated). A good rule of thumb:
   • Every 1–2 hours, ~15 g carbohydrate (e.g., ½ cup juice or ½ cup applesauce) should be consumed, or every 3–4 hours, 50 g (e.g., 1 cup juice and ¾ cup applesauce or 10 saltine crackers, 1 cup soup, and ½ cup juice) should be consumed.
   • If blood glucose is >240 mg/dL, individuals may not need to consume the entire amount.
4. Each hour, 8 to 12 oz. fluid (e.g., water, broth, tea) should be taken. A carbohydrate source could also be the fluid source, i.e., ½ cup (4 oz.) apple juice diluted with ½ cup (4 oz.) water.
5. If vomiting, diarrhea, or fever occurs, small amounts of salted foods and liquids should be taken more frequently to replace lost electrolytes.

Source: American Diabetes Association and American Dietetic Association (8); *adapted from* Franz, M. J., and Jaynes, J. O. (58).

This can be accomplished in a variety of ways. In IDDM, in which insulin reserve is virtually zero, the only way to provide insulin in a physiologic manner is to use multiple injections of insulins of various types. Most of the time, this is done with 2 injections per day—before breakfast and before the evening meal (fig. 28.1-A) of a combination of short- and intermediate-acting insulin (table 28.8). If this fails to produce acceptable pre- and postprandial blood glucose levels, a more aggressive approach of 3 or more shots of short-acting insulin before each meal can be used. This is generally accompanied by an injection before bedtime of an intermediate or long-acting insulin.

Insulin doses are generally derived by considering insulin reserve and body weight. On average, the pancreas secretes approximately 1 unit of insulin per kg body weight per hour. Insulin dose per injection should be provided in accordance with food intake, and not the other way around. Dietary adherence is best promoted when the fewest possible changes are required. Thus, a person who normally eats a very small breakfast can continue to do so after diagnosis, because the morning dose of regular insulin can be adjusted to the meal size.

Individuals with NIDDM may require insulin in order to optimize blood glucose control. Occasionally this can be done with a single injection, but more than likely 2 will be necessary. A common problem with 1 injection is that it delivers large amounts of intermediate-acting insulin, which peaks late in the afternoon and frequently produces bouts of hunger and/or hypoglycemia. This is

TABLE 28.7. NUTRITION ASSESSMENT CHECKLIST

It is helpful to have this information before nutrition counseling begins. The form in which it is collected should be adapted for the convenience of the counselor or institution.

Medical and clinical data
- Type of diabetes (IDDM, NIDDM, impaired glucose tolerance, gestational)
- Onset of diabetes
- Diabetes treatment regimen (diet alone, type/amount/schedule of insulin, oral hypoglycemic agent)
- Medications other than for diabetes
- Glucose/ketone monitoring methods
- Health history, including medical problems in addition to diabetes, e.g., allergies, cancer, ulcers
- Medical problems associated with diabetes, e.g., renal, hypertension, lipidemia
- Family medical history (e.g., other members with diabetes, hypertension, cardiovascular disease, obesity)

Biochemical data
- Blood glucose values
- Lipids (cholesterol [low- and high-density lipoproteins], triglycerides)
- Glycosylated hemoglobin
- Blood pressure values
- Proteinuria
- Other (e.g., creatinine values)

Anthropometric data
- Age (birth date for children), sex
- Height
- Weight
- Frame size
- Growth rate (for children and pregnant women)

Nutrition data
- Previous diets and diet instructions
- Weight history
- Use of vitamin and mineral supplements
- Exercise or activity level
- Current daily schedule (workdays and weekends) or school schedule
- Meal frequency
- Allergies
- Alcohol use
- Physical factors affecting nutrition (e.g., dentition, swallowing problems, sense of smell and taste, diarrhea, constipation)
- Meals away from home

Psychosocial and economic data
- Patient's expectations and goals
- Family situation/living situation (e.g., who prepares meals, for how many people)
- Financial situation
- Educational background
- Employment (type of job, hours) or school schedule
- Cooking facilities, food refrigeration, etc.
- Ethnic or religious considerations

Source: American Diabetes Association and American Dietetic Association (8).

counterproductive for the majority of these patients, who need to lose weight.

Occasionally patients will be given combination therapy, i.e., insulin injections combined with OHA. The rationale for this approach is that OHA improve insulin resistance at the peripheral and hepatic levels, thereby enhancing insulin therapy.

Oral hypoglycemic agents function to lower blood glucose by stimulating insulin release from the pancreas and overcoming insulin resistance at the peripheral level (table 28.9). Obviously, insulin must be present in the pancreas in order for this therapy to be useful. Patients with IDDM cannot, therefore, use OHA therapy alone.

BIOCHEMICAL ASSESSMENT

The initial diabetes assessment should include fasting blood glucose and lipid levels, including LDL- and HDL-cholesterol, as well as triglycerides. Renal function should be evaluated with serum urea and creatinine determinations, accompanied by a urinalysis for protein-uria. Repeat values should be obtained at regular intervals, and a 24-hour urine should be collected yearly to quantitate total protein excretion.

1. OVERALL GLUCOSE CONTROL

Glucose can attach to hemoglobin and other proteins by a continuous reaction that is a function of the duration of contact between glucose and the protein. This is an irreversible process. The amount of glucose attached to a protein, for instance hemoglobin, can be measured and used to indicate average glycemic control over the preceding 4 to 8 weeks (the life span of the red blood cell). Glycosylated hemoglobin has become the "gold standard" in assessment of diabetes control, because it is a better indicator of overall glucose control than is a single fasting glucose performed at an office visit. Glycosylated hemoglobin should be performed at regular intervals. Normal values vary with the laboratory technique but are typically 4% to 6%; 6% to 8% is considered good control, 8% to 10% fair, and greater than 10% poor (50).

Glycosylated albumin (fructosamine) is becoming a popular measure of average glycemic control. This value reflects blood glucose levels over the preceding 7 to 10 days. Results of changes in diet can be evaluated quickly. This is particularly valuable in pregnancy complicated by diabetes.

2. DAILY GLUCOSE CONTROL

Self-monitoring of blood glucose (SMBG) is one of the most useful assessment tools in diabetes management. Accurate glucose values can be obtained quickly from a single drop of capillary blood, using a small portable blood glucose meter. Patients are taught to perform this test several times a day if necessary (fig. 28.2). The frequency of testing varies depending on the type of diabetes, state of metabolic control, physical dexterity, and

FIG. 28.1. GENERAL SCHEMES FOR INSULIN DELIVERY.

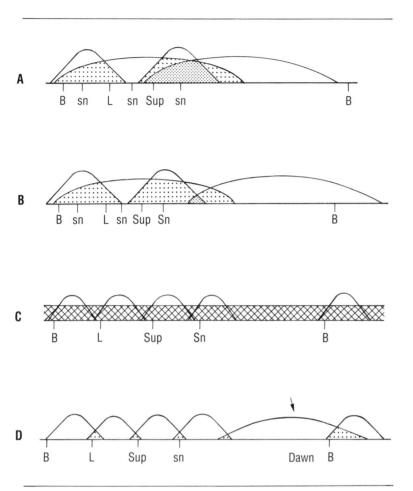

Source: American Diabetes Association (9). Copyright © 1988 by the American Diabetes Association.

Note: Regimens as shown are not individualized for meal plan, exercise, or lifestyle.

A, Standard twice-daily insulin regimen (e.g., intermediate and short acting). *B,* 3-times-daily insulin regimen, suggested for patients with early-morning hypoglycemia followed by rebound hyperglycemia or for patients with early-morning hyperglycemia (dawn phenomenon). *C,* Multidose insulin regimen; 4 injections/day (short-acting insulin before meals and long-acting at bedtime). *D,* Alternative multidose regimen consisting of 5 injections (short-acting insulin premeal and intermediate-acting insulin at bedtime). *Shaded areas* illustrate overlap between insulin peaks.

willingness (including financial capability) to perform the test.

Generally, IDDM patients perform the test 4 times per day (before meals and bedtime). Patients who may be beginning a new insulin regimen or are trying to maintain tight blood glucose control may test as much as 7 to 8 times per day

(before meals and bed, 2 hours after meals, and between 2:00 and 3:00 A.M.).

Patients with NIDDM may test only 1 to 2 times per day, because dramatic glucose fluctuations in this population are less common. It is best to have these patients change their testing times from day to day. At the end of a week they will

have a complete profile of blood glucose values from various times of the day, without having had to monitor as frequently. SMBG test results are recorded by patients and used by the health care team to modify insulin dose, OHA dose, diet, and exercise routine.

Self-monitoring of blood glucose is the most important evaluative tool for the dietitian working with patients with diabetes. Blood glucose records can be evaluated at each counseling visit and observations made regarding blood glucose responses to particular types and quantities of food, as well as the effect of meal spacing and caloric distribution. Meal plans can be modified to improve blood glucose control.

Hypoglycemic reactions should be documented with SMBG so that their cause can be pinpointed and the diet, medication, or exercise regimen modified to prevent reactions. Frequency of monitoring should be increased during illness, when blood glucose tends to rise quickly. Monitoring is also important for any IDDM patient embarking on an exercise program.

ASSESSMENT OF POTENTIAL DRUG INTERACTIONS

Both prescribed (table 28.10) and over-the-counter drugs, as well as recreational drugs (table 28.11), can affect blood glucose concentration. Their use should be assessed and the benefits and risks considered. Thiazide diuretics, in particular, should be avoided by people with diabetes. Beta blockers can lead to unawareness of hypoglycemia and should be used with caution and only if really necessary in patients using insulin.

IMPLEMENTATION AND EDUCATION

The goal of nutrition education is to facilitate positive behavior changes, not simply to transfer knowledge. The nutrition counselor should be aware that at the

TABLE 28.8. ONSET, PEAK, AND DURATION OF DIFFERENT INSULINS

	Onset	*Peak*	Duration	
			Therapeutic[a]	*Pharmaceutic*[b]
Rapid-acting (Regular, Semilente)	½ hour to 1 hour	2–4 hours	6–8 hours	5–12 hours
Intermediate-acting (NPH, Lente)	1–4 hours	8±2 hours	10–16 hours	16–24 hours
Long-acting (PZI, Ultralente)	4–6 hours	18 hours	24–36 hours	36+ hours

Source: American Association of Diabetes Educators (49); *adapted from* Campbell, R. K. (59), and Diabetes Treatment Center (60).

[a]Therapeutic (or effective duration of action): the amount of active insulin needed to keep blood glucose levels in normal limits.

[b]Pharmaceutic (or pharmacokinetic): the action of insulin on "entrance" into and "exit" from the body.

TABLE 28.9. CHARACTERISTICS OF SULFONYLUREA AGENTS

Generic name	*Brand name*	*Daily dosage range (mg)*	*Duration of action (hours)*	*Comments*
Tolbutamide	Orinase (generic)	500–3,000	6–12	Metabolized by liver to an inactive product; given 2 to 3 times per day
Chlorpropamide	Diabinese (generic)	100–500	60	Metabolized by liver (~70%) to less-active metabolites and excreted intact (~30%) by kidneys; can potentiate ADH action; given once per day
Acetohexamide	Dymelor	250–1,500	12–18	Metabolized by liver to active metabolite; given 1 to 2 times per day
Tolazamide	Tolinase (generic)	100–1,000	12–24	Metabolized by liver to both active and inactive products; given 1 to 2 times per day
Glipizide	Glucotrol	5–40	12–24	Metabolized by liver to inert products; given 1 to 2 times per day
Glyburide	Diabeta Micronase	2.5–20	16–24	Metabolized by liver to mostly inert products; give 1 to 2 times per day

Source: American Diabetes Association (5). Copyright © 1988 by the American Diabetes Association.

same time the person with diabetes is encouraged to change familiar patterns of eating, he or she is also being asked to inject insulin several times per day, monitor blood glucose several times per day, exercise daily, use proper foot care, and control stress.

The process of teaching individuals with diabetes about nutrition and meal planning is gradual and progressive, building on previous knowledge and skills. Because over 90% of patients with diabetes are adults, principles of adult learning should be applied. Most adults learn only what they perceive they need to learn at the time. Thus, it is important to focus only on what is pertinent to the individual at the time of learning.

The American Diabetes Association has defined 2 levels of education in diabetes (53): initial or survival skills, and continuing or in-depth education. Initial education involves teaching individuals the basics, i.e., beginning-level concepts and skills to suffice while they learn to cope with the disease and the behavior changes required. Examples include eating 3 meals per day, eating on time, and avoiding sugared soft drinks or eating at night. For some patients, initial skills may include decreasing fat intake by limiting fried foods or cheese to once per week or by eating a high-fiber cereal daily.

Examples of more in-depth education may be the use of an exchange system for meal planning, adjusting insulin to food intake, or counting carbohydrates. The goal of in-depth education is to add flexibility in lifestyle and to promote self-management.

Meaningful education can best be accomplished by establishing a trusting relationship with the patient and developing realistic goals. Both short-term and long-term goals should be established by mutual agreement between the individual with diabetes and the dietitian. Individualized goals must be realistic and measurable. This provides the patient

FIG. 28.2. BLOOD GLUCOSE TESTING REGIMEN.

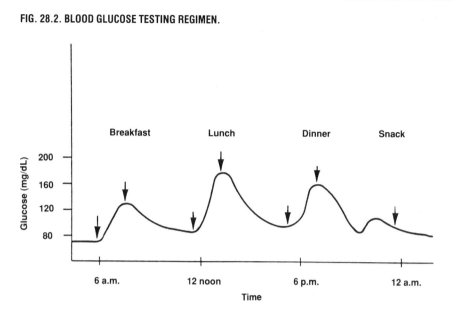

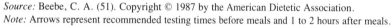

Source: Beebe, C. A. (51). Copyright © 1987 by the American Dietetic Association.
Note: Arrows represent recommended testing times before meals and 1 to 2 hours after meals.

with the impetus and confidence to continue working toward broader goals and also promotes a positive self-image, which is important in dealing with the day-to-day issues of diabetes.

Maintaining dietary changes can be difficult, particularly for the obese NIDDM patient. Support from the diabetes health-care team and from other individuals with diabetes is important. Patients should be encouraged to join support groups and weight loss groups when appropriate. Regular follow-up is essential to maintain and promote dietary change in diabetes. Diet should be evaluated yearly in most normal-weight patients, and as frequently as weekly in the obese.

Follow-up visits should focus on the patient's agenda, i.e., it should deal with specific problems that exist at the time. It is of no value, for example, to discuss the treating of hypoglycemia if the pa-

TABLE 28.10. DRUG INTERACTIONS

Drugs that may decrease blood glucose levels	Drugs that may increase blood glucose levels
Alcohol	L-Asparaginase
Allopurinol	Caffeine (large
Anabolic steroids	doses)
Bishydroxycoumarin	Calcium channel
Cimetidine	blockers
Clofibrate	(possibly)
Insulin	Corticosteroids
Monoamine oxidase	Diazoxide
inhibitors	Estrogen
Phenylbutazone	Furosemide
Potassium salts	Nicotine
Probenecid	Phenobarbital
Propranolol (beta-	Phenytoin
blockers)	Rifampin
Salicylates (large	Thiazides
doses)	Thyroids
Sulfonamides	

Source: Campbell, R. K. (61).

TABLE 28.11. EFFECT OF RECREATIONAL DRUGS ON BLOOD GLUCOSE

Drug	Effect on blood glucose
Alcohol	Increase or decrease dependent on quantity ingested, status of liver glycogen stores, whether accompanied by food or drink, etc.
Opiates	
Heroin	Increase
Morphine	Increase
Cocaine	Increase; although may impair appetite, causing a resultant decrease in intake and blood glucose levels.
Amphetamines	Increase
Caffeine (large amounts)	Increase
Sedatives, hypnotics, psychedelics (i.e., LSD)	Increase or decrease dependent on mental processes. If intake decreases, blood glucose may also decrease.
Marijuana	High doses may decrease. Use may also cause "the munchies" (urge to eat frequently), thereby causing an increase.

Source: Robles, F. (52).

tient is not on insulin or an OHA. Sometimes a change in pattern or routine can help to renew interest in following a diet plan. Changing from an exchange diet to counting calories, for example, may be a welcome variation for the obese NIDDM patient not on insulin. Occasionally the health professional has to allow the patient a brief "vacation" from the diet plan to allow the patient to refocus or relax. In many instances this can help to foster motivation at a later time.

PRIORITIES FOR QUALITY ASSURANCE

Several sources of quality assurance standards have been published. One that can easily be rewritten into quality assurance monitors is the American Diabetes Association Standards of Medical Care for Patients with Diabetes Mellitus (54). National standards for the education of diabetes patients have been established by the American Diabetes Association, and review criteria have been published (55). Diabetes education programs that meet these criteria may apply and achieve recognition from the American Diabetes Association.

Parameters for quality nutritional care in acute care settings focus on specifics of the initial patient evaluation; the diet prescription and meal plan and its individualization with regard to calorie level, meal distribution, adjustments for complications, meal replacements, insulin administration, and type or classification of diabetes; documentation in the medical record; and specific skills demonstrated or verbalized at the time of discharge. These parameters should be included in the educational curriculum of diabetes teaching programs.

TABLE 28.12. CALORIE NEEDS FOR CHILDREN AND YOUNG ADULTS

Age	kcal required/ lb. body weight	kcal required/ kg body weight
Children		
0–12 months	~55	~120
1–10 years	45–36[a]	100–80
Young women		
11–15 years	~17	~35
≥16 years	~15	~30
Young men		
11–15 years	36–20 (30)	80–50 (65)
16–20 years		
Medium active	~18	~40
Very physically active	~22	~50
Sedentary	~15	~30

Source: American Diabetes Association and American Dietetic Association (8).

Note: Numbers in parentheses are means.

[a]Gradual decline in kilocalories per pound as age increases.

TABLE 28.13. HELPFUL HINTS FOR CALCULATING MEAL PLANS AND USE OF EXCHANGE LISTS

- Round off nutrition history calorie level to the nearest 50 or 100. Calculations of food intake are not accurate enough to allow more precision, and patients may consume an extra 50–60 cal/day from free foods; therefore, some dietitians and nutrition counselors round up rather than down.
- The type of milk the patient uses should be calculated into the meal plan. Skim and low-fat milks are recommended rather than whole milk.
- Foods in the starch/bread and skim/very low-fat milk exchange lists contain, on average, slightly <1 g fat/serving. A "trace" of fat is used in the *Exchange Lists,* below, to make it easier to teach the exchange concept to patients; however, nutrition counselors should use 1 g fat in their calculations to yield the appropriate calorie level for the exchange group. If the counselor knows the patient uses very few food choices that have ~1 g fat, then it is appropriate to use a lesser value of 0 and adjust the calorie value for the exchange.
- When calculating grams of fat per meat serving, use the fat value that best represents the patient's actual intake. However, encourage individuals to eat lean meats as often as desired. People do not need to add or subtract fat exchanges when using the different meat categories.
- For calculating protein amounts for renal diabetic diets, use the average value of 2.5 g protein per starch/bread exchange or the average grams of protein for each subcategory on the starch/bread list.
- Most diets calculated with the 1976 exchange values will be 100–200 cal lower than the same diets calculated with the 1986 exchange values. Calorie intakes were previously underestimated.
- In converting nutrition labels and recipes into exchanges, it is important to make it as easy as possible for people to use the product. Thus, it is recommended not to use ¼ or ⅓ exchanges and to avoid the use of ½ exchanges whenever possible. The following recommendations could be used for carbohydrate rounding off in the starch/bread and fruits groups.

  1–5 g: do not count
  6–10 g: ½ exchange
  11–15 g: 1 exchange

  In addition, a range of ±20 cal can be used to round off, as well as ±5 g protein and ±2 g fat.
- Although some foods have been placed in one particular exchange food group, they could just as appropriately fit into another group. For example, beans and lentils are listed in the starch/bread group; however, they also may be used in the vegetarian diet as a meat substitute. If so, 1 cup dried beans, peas, or lentils (cooked) is equal to 2 starch/bread exchanges and 1 lean-meats exchange. Another example is sugar-free pudding, which is in the combination foods list as a starch/bread exchange but could also be used as a skim/very low-fat milk exchange. During in-depth/continuing education, these variations can be discussed with the patient. The exchange system serves as an excellent guide to making food selections. The nutrition counselor should, however, work closely with those patients who want more flexibility.
- A 1-cup serving of most casserole or stew dishes is 2 starch/bread exchanges, 2 medium-fat meat exchanges, and 1 fat exchange. These are the same exchange equivalents that are used for many sandwiches.
- Fruits, starch/bread, and milk exchanges have similar carbohydrate content and may be interchanged. Self-monitoring of blood glucose can be used to determine the effects of the substitution. If regular substitution of fruits or starches for milk is made, calcium status may be compromised. Conversely, regularly choosing milk instead of fruits or starches may result in inadequate fiber intake.

Source: American Diabetes Association and American Dietetic Association (8).

TABLE 28.14. SUMMARY OF EXCHANGE LISTS (1986)

Exchange list	Carbohydrate (g)	Protein (g)	Fat (g)	Calories
Starch/bread	15	3	1[a]	80
Meats				
Lean		7	3	55
Medium-fat		7	5	75
High-fat		7	8	100
Vegetables	5	2		25
Fruits	15			60
Milk				
Skim	12	8	1[a]	90
Low-fat	12	8	5	120
Whole	12	8	8	150
Fats			5	45

Source: American Diabetes Association and American Dietetic Association (8).

[a]In *Exchange Lists,* trace is listed. For calculation purposes, 1 g can be used. If patient always uses skim milk that is 0 fat and 80 cal, calculate it as such. If starches with >1 g fat are usually selected, then the nutrition counselor has the option of calculating with a different fat value if desired.

TABLE 28.15. SAMPLE MEAL PLANS FOR VARIOUS CALORIC REQUIREMENTS AND SPECIFIC SITUATIONS

1,500-kcal Sample Meal Plan for Person with NIDDM *Who Does Not Require Snacks*

Food group	Breakfast 7:00	Snack	Lunch 12:00	Snack	Dinner 6:00	Snack	Total servings/ day	CHO (g)	Protein (g)	Fat[a] (g)	Kilocalories
Starch/ bread	2		2		2		6	15 / 90	3 / 18	1 / 6	80 / 480
Meats/ substitutes			1		3		4		7 / 28	5 / 20	75 / 300
Vegetables			0–1		2		2	5 / 10	2 / 4		25 / 50
Fruits	1		1				2	15 / 30			60 / 120
Milk	½		½		1		2	12 / 24	8 / 16	1 / 2	90 / 180
Fats	1		1		1		3			5 / 15	45 / 135
Total								154	66	43	
Kilocalories								× 4 = 616	× 4 = 264	× 9 = 387	Total = 1,267
% calories								50	20	30	

TABLE 28.15. *CONTINUED*

1,800-kcal Sample Meal Plan for Person who Desires a Small Breakfast[b]

Food group	Breakfast 7:00	Snack 9:30	Lunch 12:00	Snack 3:00	Dinner 6:30	Snack 10:30	Total servings/ day	CHO (g)	Protein (g)	Fat[a] (g)	Kilocalories
Starch/ bread	1	1 (or 1 fruit)	3		2	1	8	15 / 120	3 / 24	1 / 8	80 / 640
Meats/ substitutes			2		3		5		7 / 35	5 / 25	75 / 375
Vegetables			0–1	OK	2		2	5 / 10	2 / 4		25 / 50
Fruits	1		1	1	1	1	5	15 / 75			60 / 300
Milk			1		1		2	12 / 24	8 / 16	1 / 2	90 / 180
Fats	1		1		2	0–1	5			5 / 25	45 / 225
Total								229	79	60	
Kilocalories								× 4 = 916	× 4 = 316	× 9 = 540	Total = 1,772
% calories								52	18	30	

1,800-kcal Sample Meal Plan for Person Who Desires a Large Breakfast

Food group	Breakfast 6:30	Snack	Lunch 11:30	Snack 3:00	Dinner 6:00	Snack 10:00	Total servings/ day	CHO (g)	Protein (g)	Fat[a] (g)	Kilocalories
Starch/ bread	3		2		2	1	8	15 / 120	3 / 24	1 / 8	80 / 640
Meats/ substitutes	1		2		3		6		7 / 42	5 / 30	75 / 450
Vegetables			0–1	OK	2		2	5 / 10	2 / 4		25 / 50
Fruits	1		1	1	1	1	5	15 / 75			60 / 300
Milk	1		1				2	12 / 24	8 / 16	1 / 2	90 / 180
Fats	1		1		1	0–1	4			5 / 20	45 / 180
Total								229	86	60	
Kilocalories								× 4 = 916	× 4 = 344	× 9 = 540	Total = 1,800
% calories								51	19	30	

TABLE 28.15. *CONTINUED*

1,800-kcal Sample Meal Plan With Snacks

Food group	Breakfast 7:30	Snack	Lunch 1:30	Snack 3:30	Dinner 7:00	Snack 10:00	Total servings/day	CHO (g)	Protein (g)	Fat[a] (g)	Kilocalories
Starch/ bread	3		2	1 (or 1 fruit) 2	2	1	9	15 / 135	3 / 27	1 / 9	80 / 720
Meats/ substitutes			2	3			5		7 / 35	5 / 25	75 / 375
Vegetables			0–1	2			2	5 / 10	2 / 4		25 / 50
Fruits	1		1	1	1		4	15 / 60			60 / 240
Milk	1		1				2	12 / 24	8 / 16	1 / 2	90 / 180
Fats	1			2	0–1		4			5 / 20	45 / 180
Total								229	82	56	
Kilocalories								× 4 = 916	× 4 = 328	× 9 = 504	Total = 1,748
% calories								52	19	29	

Source: American Diabetes Association and American Dietetic Association (8).

[a]Calculations are based on medium-fat meats and skim/very low-fat milk. If diet is predominantly low-fat meats, use factor 3 instead of 5; if predominantly high-fat meats, use factor 8. If low-fat (2%) milk is used, use factor 3, if whole milk is used, use factor 5.

[b]Although current recommendations suggest that up to 55%–60% of calories come from carbohydrates and ≤30% from fat, the more important emphasis is the need for individualization. Not every meal plan will meet the recommendations. An 1,800-kcal meal plan is shown calculated 3 different ways to emphasize that the meal plan needs to be individualized.

MENU PLANNING

The meal plan for the person with diabetes should be as individualized and flexible as possible. The exchange system is included here but does not represent the method of choice for all individuals with diabetes. Several other approaches for meal planning exist and should be considered (56). Examples include calorie counting, carbohydrate counting, basic guidelines for reducing fat and sugar, high-fiber diets, the point system, and supplemental fasting (very low-calorie diet therapy). The meal plan should be considered a continuum in that it may constantly change throughout the life span of the individual.

The following is an example of how to calculate an exchange meal plan:

1. Determine current food intake and eating pattern.
   a. Using a 24-hour or 3-day recall, determine the usual pattern of intake.
   b. Categorize intake into exchanges at each meal and each snack.
   c. Translate into calories.
2. Determine caloric prescription.
   a. Caloric needs vary depending on age, weight, and activity level. When calculating for children, refer to table 28.12. For adults, several ways are possible (see Chapter 1.) Whichever method is used, the correct intake should be substantiated with a 24-hour recall.
   b. Subtract calories if weight loss is desired. Because 1 lb. of fat is approximately equal to 3,500 kcal, daily consumption must be cut by 500 kcal to produce a 1-lb. loss per week, or by 1,000 kcal to produce a 2-lb. loss per week. For example, 2,800 − 1,000 = 1,800 kcal per day.
3. Translate 1,800 kcal into exchange diet.
   a. Begin by categorizing current diet into exchanges, staying as close to the current pattern of intake as possible.
   b. Calculate grams of carbohydrate, protein, and fat from exchanges

and determine percentages of carbohydrate, protein, and fat (table
28.14):

$$\frac{\text{grams of carbohydrate} \times 4}{\text{total kilocalories}}$$

$$\frac{\text{grams of protein} \times 4}{\text{total kilocalories}}$$

$$\frac{\text{grams of fat} \times 4}{\text{total kilocalories}}$$

c. Adjust exchanges as needed to
reach goal percentages for each
macronutrient.
d. Adjustments should be made with
the patient (table 28.13).

A variety of 1,800-kilocalorie sample
meal plans for patients with diabetes is
given in table 28.15.

SAMPLE MENU, USING EXCHANGES, FOR THE 1,800-kcal DIABETIC DIET (FOR WEIGHT REDUCTION FOR A MALE, AGE 25–50)

Food	Amount	Exchange
BREAKFAST		
Orange juice	½ cup	1 fruit
Whole-grain flaked cereal	1½ cups	2 starches
Banana	½ medium	1 fruit
Skim milk	1 cup	1 milk
Whole wheat toast	1 slice	1 starch
Margarine	1 tsp.	1 fat
Coffee or tea	1 cup	Free
LUNCH		
Whole wheat bread	2 slices	2 starches
Turkey breast	2 oz.	2 lean meats
Mustard	1 tbsp.	Free
Sliced tomato	1 medium	1 vegetable
Apple	1 small	1 fruit
Coffee, tea, or diet soda	1 cup	Free
Chocolate chip cookies	2 small	1 starch
AFTERNOON SNACK		
Pretzels	¾ oz.	1 starch
Mineral water	1 cup	Free
DINNER		
Lean round steak	3 oz.	3 lean meats
Baked potato	1 large	2 starches
Margarine	2 tsp.	2 fats
Steamed broccoli	1 cup	2 vegetables
Rye bread	1 slice	1 starch
Margarine	1 tsp.	1 fat
Melon cubes	1 cup	1 fruit
Coffee or tea	1 cup	Free
EVENING SNACK		
Air-popped popcorn	3 cups	1 bread
Mineral water or diet soda	1 cup	Free

Approximate Nutrient Analysis

Energy	1,821 kcal
Protein	80 g (18% of kcal)
Fat	57 g (28% of kcal)
Polyunsaturated fat	6.0 g
Monounsaturated fat	10.4 g
Saturated fat	8.1 g
Cholesterol	98 mg
Carbohydrate	247 g (54% of kcal)
Vitamin A	6,280 IU
	1,233 RE
Thiamine	1.78 mg
Riboflavin	1.93 mg
Niacin	27.3 mg

(continued)

Folate	364 mcg
Vitamin B-12	6.26 mcg
Vitamin B-6	3.00 mg
Vitamin C	295.1 mg
Calcium	659 mg
Phosphorus	1,352 mg
Iron	19.1 mg
Copper	1.39 mg
Zinc	8.3 mg
Magnesium	298 mg
Sodium	2,836 mg
Potassium	4,385 mg

REFERENCES

1. Beebe, C. A., and Rubenstein, A. H.: Classification, diagnosis and treatment of diabetes. In Powers, M.: Handbook of diabetes nutritional management. Rockville, Md.: Aspen, 1987.

2. Barrett-Connor, E., and Orchard, T.: Diabetes and heart disease. In Harris, M. I., and Mannan, R. F.: Diabetes in America. National Diabetes Data Group Publication no. 85-1468. Bethesda, Md.: U.S. Department of Agriculture, 1985.

3. Raskin, P., and Rosenstock, J.: Blood glucose control and diabetic complications. Ann Intern Med 105:254, 1986.

4. The Diabetes Control and Complications Trial (DCCT): Design and methodologic considerations for the feasibility phase. Diabetes 35:530, 1986.

5. American Diabetes Association: Physician's guide to non-insulin dependent (Type II) diabetes: Diagnosis and treatment. 2d ed. Alexandria, Va.: American Diabetes Association, 1988.

6. National Institutes of Health, National Diabetes Data Group: Classification and diagnosis of diabetes mellitus and other categories of glucose intolerance. Diabetes 28:1039, 1979.

7. American Diabetes Association: Position statement: Nutritional recommendations and principles for individuals with diabetes mellitus. Diabetes Care 10:126, 1987.

8. American Diabetes Association and American Dietetic Association: Nutrition guide for professionals: Diabetes education and meal planning. Chicago: American Diabetes Association and American Dietetic Association, 1988.

9. American Diabetes Association: Physician's guide to insulin dependent (Type I) diabetes: Diagnosis and treatment. Alexandria, Va.: American Diabetes Association, 1988.

10. Hocking, M. D., Rayner, P. W. H., and Nattrass, M.: Residual insulin secretion in adolescent diabetics after remission. Arch Dis Child 62:1144, 1987.

11. Roth, J., and Muggeo, M.: Insulin receptors and hyperglycemia. In Rifkin, H.: Diabetes mellitus. Vol. 5. New York: McGraw-Hill, 1983.

12. Kissebah, A. H., Vydelingum, N., et al.: Relation of body fat distribution to metabolic complications of obesity. J Clin Endocrinol Metab 54:254, 1982.

13. Wing, R., Koeske, R., et al.: Long term effects of modest weight loss in Type II diabetic patients. Arch Intern Med 147:1749, 1987.

14. Henry, R. R., Wiest, L., and Schaffer, L.: Metabolic consequences of very low calorie diet therapy in obese NIDDM and non-diabetic subjects. Diabetes 35:155, 1986.

15. Jovanovic, L., Peterson, C., and Fuhrmann, K.: Diabetes and pregnancy. New York: Praeger, 1986.

16. Reaven, G. S.: Non-insulin-dependent diabetes mellitus, abnormal lipoprotein metabolism, and atherosclerosis. Metabolism 36:1, 1987.

17. American Diabetes Association, Consensus Panel: Role of cardiovascular risk factors in prevention and treatment of macrovascular disease in diabetes. Diabetes Care 12:573, 1989.

18. Wolever, T. M. S., Jenkins, D. J. A., et al.: Glycemic index of foods in individual subjects. Diabetes Care 13:126, 1990.

19. Wolever, T. M. S., Csima, A., et al.: The glycemic index: Variation between subjects and predictive difference. J Am Coll Nutr 8:235, 1989.

20. Coulston, A., Hollenbeck, C., et al.: Effect of source of dietary carbohydrate on plasma glucose and insulin responses to mixed meals in subjects with NIDDM. Diabetes Care 10:395, 1987.

21. Wong, S., and O'Dea, K.: Importance of physical form rather than viscosity in determining the rate of starch hydrolysis in legumes. Am J Clin Nutr 37:66, 1983.

22. Bornet, F. R. J., Cloarec, D., et al.: Pasta cooking time: Influence on starch digestion and plasma glucose and insulin responses in healthy subjects. Am J Clin Nutr 51:421, 1990.

23. Vaaler, S., Hanssen, K. F., and Aagenaes, O.: The effect of cooking upon the blood glucose response to ingested carrots and potatoes. Diabetes Care 7:221, 1984.

24. Jenkins, D. J. A., Wolever, R. M. S., et al.: Slow release dietary carbohydrate improves second meal tolerance. Am J Clin Nutr 35:1339, 1982.

25. Polonsky, K. S., Given, B. D., et al.: Abnormal patterns of insulin secretion in non-insulin dependent diabetes mellitus. N Engl J Med 318:1231, 1988.

26. Crapo, P. A., Reaven, G., and Olefsky, J. M.: Plasma glucose and insulin responses to orally administered simple and complex carbohydrates. Diabetes 25:741, 1976.

27. Brunzell, J. D., Lesner, R. L., et al.: Improved glucose tolerance with high carbohydrate feeding in mild diabetes. N Engl J Med 284:531, 1971.

28. Coulston, A., Hollenbeck, C., and Swislocki, A.: Deleterious effects of high carbohydrate, sucrose containing diets in patients with noninsulin dependent diabetes mellitus. Am J Med 82:213, 1987.

29. Anderson, J. W.: Physiological and metabolic effects of dietary fiber. Fed Proc 44:2902, 1985.

30. Anderson, J. W., and Ward, K.: Long-term effects of high carbohydrate, high-fiber diets on glucose and lipid metabolism: A preliminary report on patients with diabetes. Diabetes Care 1:77, 1978.

31. Riccardi, G., Rivellese, A., et al.: Separate influence of dietary carbohydrate and fiber on the metabolic control in diabetes. Diabetologia 26:116, 1984.

32. Simpson, H. C. R., Simpson, R. W., et al.: High carbohydrate leguminous fibre diet improves all aspects of diabetic control. Lancet 1:1, 1981.

33. Anderson, J. W., Gustafson, N. J., et al.: Dietary fiber and diabetes: A comprehensive review and practical application. J Am Diet Assoc 87:1189, 1987.

34. Coulston, A., Hollenbeck, C., and Donner, C.: Metabolic effects of added dietary sucrose in individuals with noninsulin-dependent diabetes mellitus (NIDDM). Metabolism 34:962, 1985.

35. Rivellese, A. A., Giacco, R., et al.:

Effects of changing amount of carbohydrate in diet on plasma lipoproteins and apolipoproteins in Type II diabetic patients. Diabetes Care 13:446, 1990.

36. Coulston, A. M., Hollenbeck, C. B., et al.: Persistence of hypertriglyceridemic effect of low-fat high carbohydrate diets in NIDDM patients. Diabetes Care 12:94, 1989.

37. Garg, A., Bonanome, A., et al.: Comparison of a high-carbohydrate diet with a high-monounsaturated fat diet in patients with NIDDM. N Engl J Med 319:829, 1988.

38. Abbott, W. G. H., Boyce, V. L., et al.: Effects of replacing saturated fat with complex carbohydrate in diets of subjects with NIDDM. Diabetes Care 12:102, 1989.

39. Ginsberg, H. N., Barr, S. L., et al.: Reduction of plasma cholesterol levels in normal men on an American Heart Association Step 1 diet or a Step 1 diet with added monounsaturated fat. N Engl J Med 322:574, 1990.

40. Garg, A., and Grundy, S. M.: Management of dyslipidemia in NIDDM. Diabetes Care 13:153, 1990.

41. Friday, K. E., Childs, M. T., et al.: Elevated plasma glucose and lowered triglyceride levels from omega-3 fatty acid supplementation in Type II diabetes. Diabetes Care 12:276, 1989.

42. Alvestrand, A., Ahlberg, M., and Bergstrom, J.: Retardation of the progression of renal insufficiency in patients treated with low-protein diets. Kidney Internat 24:268, 1983.

43. Ciavarella, A., Gianfranco, D. M., et al.: Reduced albuminuria after dietary protein restrictions in insulin dependent diabetic patients with clinical nephropathy. Diabetes Care 10:407, 1987.

44. Evanoff, G. V., Thompson, C. S., et al.: The effect of dietary protein restriction on the progression of diabetic nephropathy. Arch Intern Med 147:492, 1987.

45. Beebe, C. A., VanCauter, E. V., et al.: Effects of temporal distribution of calories on diurnal patterns of glucose levels and insulin secretion in NIDDM. Diabetes Care 13:748, 1990.

46. Franz, M. J.: Alcohol and diabetes. Diabetes Spectrum 3:136, 1990.

47. The DCCT Research Group: Weight gain associated with intensive therapy in the Diabetes Control and Complications Trial. Diabetes Care 11:567, 1988.

48. Schiffrin, A., and Parikh, S.: Accommodating planned exercise in Type I diabetic patients on intensive treatment. Diabetes Care 8:337, 1985.

49. American Association of Diabetes Educators: Diabetes education: A core curriculum for health professionals. Chicago: American Association of Diabetes Educators, 1988.

50. Nathan, D. M., Singer, D. E., et al.: The clinical information value of the glycosylated hemoglobin assay. N Engl J Med 310:341, 1984.

51. Beebe, C. A.: Self blood glucose monitoring: An adjunct to dietary and insulin management of the patient with diabetes. J Am Diet Assoc 87:61, 1987.

52. Robles, F.: Medications used in diabetes treatment. On the Cutting Edge (DCEPG newsletter) 10 (6):2, 1989.

53. American Diabetes Association: Goals for diabetes education. Alexandria, Va.: American Diabetes Association, 1989.

54. American Diabetes Association: Position statement: Standards of medical care for patients with diabetes mellitus. Diabetes Care 12:365, 1989.

55. American Diabetes Association: Standards for diabetes patient education and review criteria. Diabetes Care 9:4, 1986.

56. Green, J. A., and Holler, H. J.: Diabetes Care and Education Practice Group, American Dietetic Association: Meal planning approaches in the nutrition management of the person with diabetes. Chicago: American Dietetic Association, 1987.

57. Franz, M. J.: Diabetes and exercise: Guidelines for safety and enjoyable activity. Minneapolis: Diabetes Center, 1987.

58. Franz, M. J., and Jaynes, J. O.: Diabetes and brief illness. Minneapolis: Diabetes Center, 1984.

59. Campbell, R. K.: Diabetic management: Insulin, oral agents, and intensified insulin therapy (module 9). Chicago: American Association of Diabetes Educators Continuing Education Self-Study Program, 1985.

60. Diabetes Treatment Center: Care and control of your diabetes. Wichita, Kans.: St. Joseph Medical Center, 1988.

61. Campbell, R. K.: How oral agents are used in the treatment of type II diabetes. Pharmacy Times 53 (10):32, 1987.

29.

KILOCALORIE-RESTRICTED DIET

DEFINITIONS

1. KILOCALORIE-RESTRICTED DIET

A diet that limits total kilocalories to a prescribed level significantly below normal requirements and is used in the treatment of overweight and obesity.

2. VERY LOW-CALORIE WEIGHT-LOSS DIET (VLCD)

A diet that limits calories to the range of 400 to 800 kcal per day. Current diets may consist of special formulas or conventional foods and may contain relatively large proportions of protein and little fat or carbohydrate; they are supplemented to meet Recommended Dietary Allowances for vitamins, minerals, and electrolytes. VLCDs do lead to fast, significant weight loss, which may be crucial for morbidly obese individuals, but also carry some risks (1). See Chapter 30 for the position statement of the American Dietetic Association on very low-calorie weight-loss diets.

3. OBESITY AND OVERWEIGHT

Obesity refers to a condition of excess body fat. *Overweight* refers to excess body weight, which may reflect increases in body fat or in lean body mass. Because the 2 conditions are often associated and body weight is considerably easier to measure than body fat content, overweight is more frequently studied and defined than obesity. However, it is important to understand the difference.

There is currently no standard definition of obesity based on the degree of excess body fat at which health risks to individuals begin to increase. At present,

arbitrary criteria are based on percentage of body fat, skinfold measurements, waist-to-hip ratio, weight-for-height measurements, or BMI (2). (For more information on these measurements, see Chapter 1.)

Definitions of obesity depend upon their use. As defined by the general public, obesity is based on subjective criteria and is frequently a basis for discrimination. Statistical definitions are useful in population studies and may, for instance, classify the upper 5% to 20% of the population as obese and the upper 5% as superobese. An operational definition is based on mortality and morbidity and will therefore vary according to race and sex (3). It is important for dietitians to realize that their basis for defining obesity may differ from that of their patients.

The following are commonly used criteria for obesity and overweight.

A. Desirable or Normal Weight   The National Institutes of Health (NIH) have defined desirable weight as the midpoint of the recommended weight range at a specified height for persons of medium build, according to the 1983 Metropolitan Life Insurance table. This table is based on measurements from subjects wearing shoes and light clothing. This criterion for desirable weight corresponds to a BMI of 22.0 for men and 21.5 for women (4, 5).

B. Overweight   The NIH defines overweight as greater than 120% of desirable weight as specified above. This corresponds to a BMI of 27.2 for males and 26.9 for females (4, 5). The National Center

for Health Statistics (NCHS) has classified individuals with BMI at or above the 85th percentile for 20- to 29-year-olds, as measured in the National Health and Nutrition Examination Survey II (NHANES II), as overweight. This is equivalent to a BMI of 27.8 for males and 27.3 for females, similar to the NIH values (4, 6). The use of the data for 20- to 29-year-olds is based on the rationale that weight gained later in life represents largely a gain in fat mass. However, the relevance of this criterion for elderly subjects, in whom excess weight may contribute less to health risk, has been challenged (7).

C. Severe Overweight   The NIH defines severe overweight as greater than 140% of desirable weight (2). The NCHS classifies individuals with BMI at or about the 95th percentile for 20- to 29-year-olds in NHANES II as severely overweight. This corresponds to a BMI of 31.1 for males and 32.3 for females. Again, NIH and NCHS values are similar (4).

D. Obesity   According to the NCHS, obesity is defined as a sum of triceps and subscapular skinfolds greater than the 85th percentile for 20- to 29-year-olds using NHANES II data. This is equivalent to 45.5 mm in males and 70.1 mm in females. Using the same data, severe obesity is attributed to individuals above the 95th percentile (4, 8, 9). Another approach, using cutoffs from the 1959 Metropolitan Life Insurance table, classifies mild obesity as 120% to 140%, moderate obesity as 141% to 200%, and severe obesity as greater than 200% of desirable body weight (1). The NIH has defined extreme or morbid obesity as 200% of desirable body weight, or 45 kg (100 lbs.) over desirable body weight (5). Extreme or morbid obesity has also been used to refer to individuals with a BMI of 50 and over (10).

E. Abdominal (Android, Apple, Upper Body, Truncal, or Central) Obesity A form of obesity in which the excess fat is found predominantly in the abdominal area. It is characterized by a waist-to-hip ratio of over 0.8 in women and over 1.0 in men (2). In men a criterion of 0.95 may be used, above which the risks of cardiovascular disease and of non-insulin-dependent diabetes mellitus are thought to increase (1). Obese men usually have abdominal obesity, whereas women may have either abdominal or peripheral obesity (11–15).

F. Peripheral (Gynoid, Pear, Lower Body, Gluteal, or Femoral) Obesity A form of obesity usually found only in women, and associated with excess fat distribution in the hip region and in the thighs. The distribution of fat in the female hip or femoral region seems to be controlled by steroid hormones and reproductive history. It is the area that is primarily increased during pregnancy and that provides energy stores for lactation. Fat in this region is controlled by the fat-storing enzyme lipoprotein lipase. Obesity here is more benign than abdominal obesity (16, 17).

4. BODY MASS INDEX (BMI) OR QUETELET'S INDEX

Body mass index is derived by dividing the weight (in kilograms) by the height (in meters) squared [BMI = wt/(ht²)]. The NIH recommends that physicians adopt the BMI as an assessment tool in evaluating obese patients (8, 10, 16).

5. WAIST-TO-HIP RATIO (WHR)

A term used to describe the ratio between the circumference of the waist and the circumference of the hip. The ratio is calculated by dividing the minimal waist circumference by the maximal hip circumference. It is used to identify individuals with abdominal obesity (see the definition above) (2).

6. NORMAL WEIGHT METABOLIC OBESITY

A form of obesity that develops in individuals of normal weight and is characterized by increased fat mass, increased fat cell size, and decreased lean body mass; these are all findings that occur with aging in sedentary people. Although of normal weight, these individuals may develop metabolic abnormalities characteristic of obesity, including hypertriglyceridemia, increased plasma insulin levels, glucose intolerance, and hypertension (10).

7. EATING DISORDERS

For more information on eating disorders see the position statement of the American Dietetic Association on nutrition intervention in the treatment of anorexia nervosa and bulimia nervosa in Chapter 31.

A. Compulsive Overeating Compulsive overeaters are obese individuals who place a disproportionate amount of importance on eating and body weight, have a distorted relationship with food, and have lost the ability to control their food intake. Their sense of self-esteem is dependent on weight loss. Most dietary intervention will fail in such cases, unless it is administered with concurrent psychiatric and medical treatment (18, 19).

B. Anorexia Nervosa Anorexia nervosa is defined as intentional weight loss of at least 15% of desirable weight and refusal to maintain body weight over a minimal normal weight for age and height. This is combined with distorted body image, an intense fear of becoming fat, and amenorrhea in women (20).

C. Bulimia Nervosa Bulimia nervosa is characterized by a minimum average of 2 binge eating episodes (rapid consumption of a large amount of food in a discrete period of time) per week for at least 3 months. The individual frequently experiences depression, feelings of inadequacy, and self-deprecating thoughts. Regular purges (self-induced vomiting, use of laxatives or diuretics, strict dieting or fasting, or vigorous exercise) and distorted body image are common (20, 21).

PURPOSE OF THE DIET

1. REASONABLE RATE OF WEIGHT LOSS OR WEIGHT MAINTENANCE

The diet is intended to provide an individualized means of weight loss at a reasonable rate, and to provide just enough caloric restriction to maintain that weight once the goal is achieved. The goal may be based on desirable weight (see definitions above) or a higher but more realistic weight for a given individual, as determined by that individual and the dietitian or health-care team.

2. LOSS OF ADIPOSE TISSUE WITH PRESERVATION OF LEAN BODY MASS

The development of excess fat is associated with a certain degree of formation of lean body mass structures, which are necessary to support the fat. Excess body weight is composed of 22% to 38% lean body mass in supporting structures, and 62% to 78% body fat. While the diet should not permit loss of lean body mass not associated with excess fat, it is not unreasonable for some loss of lean body mass to occur by attrition of the supporting structures associated with the excess fat. For example, during weight gain, more muscle, blood, extracellular fluid, connective tissue, and skin are needed to support and maintain the increased adipose tissue mass. Thus, a reasonable goal is to permit loss of lean body mass not to exceed 25% of the total weight lost, and to permit a slightly negative nitrogen balance in order to achieve that loss. It should not be forgotten, however, that lean body mass has a higher metabolic rate than fat, and for this reason loss of lean body mass should be as low as possible (10, 22).

3. AMELIORATION OF UNDESIRABLE EFFECTS OF OBESITY

The diet should reduce any such risk factors as abdominal fat, hypertriglyceridemia, hyperinsulinemia, and hypercholesterolemia. It should help to reduce hypertension, occlusive arterial lesions, peripheral venous status abnormalities, and sleep disorders (23).

4. LIFE-LONG BEHAVIOR CHANGE

Dietary interventions should include the teaching of skills and behaviors for making lifelong food choices to maintain healthful weight loss. The client's understanding of the importance of the diet, the diet structure, food types, amounts, purchasing, preparation methods, and eating management all need to be addressed as the plan is developed by the dietitian. Weight loss should be viewed in terms of lifestyle and food habits, rather than in the rigid context of a short-term diet. Both the client and the dietitian must cooperate in identifying problems in behavioral patterns, strategies for change, and reinforcement of the new behavior in order for it to be sustained (24).

EFFECTS OF THE DIET

1. WEIGHT LOSS

A. Predictions Using Caloric Deficit A reduction in caloric intake of 3,500 kcal is required in order to bring about the loss of 1 lb. of body weight. For example, if the diet is designed to provide 500 kcal less than the person requires to maintain current weight, the person would have to follow the diet for 7 days in order to lose 1 lb.: 3,500 divided by 500 equals 7.

B. Rate of Weight Loss and Metabolic Rate The best predictor of weight loss in a patient on a strictly controlled reducing diet is the basal metabolic rate. The frequency and duration of previous diets also affect the rate of weight loss. The amount of weight loss occurring in the first week has been noted to be less in individuals who were already following a weight-loss diet than in those who were not (9, 25).

Dieting and weight loss cause a decrease in body mass, which then reduces caloric requirements. In addition, there is some evidence that dieting eventually lowers the resting metabolic rate. It is still a matter of debate whether the metabolic rate declines more or less than would be expected for the change in body mass. However, it does seem that reductions are less significant during moderate caloric restrictions than during very low-calorie diets (10, 22, 26–32).

C. Proportions of Protein, Fat, and Carbohydrate Several studies have indicated that diet composition may be more closely correlated with adiposity than energy intake. Obese individuals have been found to obtain a greater percentage of their energy from fat, and less from carbohydrate, than do lean individuals. It has been generally accepted that the increased caloric density of a high-fat diet results in hyperphagia and that this results in obesity. However, many researchers have shown that neither absolute nor relative energy intakes are greater in obese subjects than they are in lean subjects (33).

It appears that carbohydrate oxidation is related to carbohydrate intake, but fat oxidation is not related to fat intake. Therefore, extra calories ingested in the form of fat are more likely to be deposited in adipose tissue, whereas extra carbohydrate calories are more likely to be oxidized. This may be related to the difference in size of carbohydrate (glycogen) and fat (adipose tissue) stores in the body. Glycogen stores reach a maximum level, whereas adipose tissue has great capacity for expansion (34, 35).

A 10-week study of 3 different diets of 1,200 kcal composed of 25%, 45%, or 75% carbohydrates, concluded that there was no difference among the diets as to total amount of weight lost, body composition, serum cholesterol, triglycerides, blood urea nitrogen, percent body fat, uric acid, or nutrient intake (36). However, this study has been criticized, because it is possible that the individuals on the high-fat regimen did not consume the entire 1,200 kcal. The fact that they did not have greater weight loss than the other groups would confirm that dietary carbohydrate is more easily oxidized than fat (37).

Another study using much lower caloric intakes—i.e., 12 kcal/kg ideal body weight—measured carbohydrate-induced responsiveness to growth hormone. (Growth hormone stimulates fat mobilization.) The results indicated that when caloric restriction is severe, carbohydrate intake becomes a major determinant of growth-hormone responsiveness. An adequate amount of dietary carbohydrate is necessary in order for the effects of growth hormone on weight loss to be demonstrated (38).

D. Exercise Combined with a Kilocalorie-Restricted Diet Most but not all studies claim that weight loss is greater when exercise is added to the diet. A study of nonobese women found that the subjects ate less after strenuous exercise. Furthermore, resistance weight-training during caloric restriction enhances lean body weight maintenance. However, resting energy expenditure (REE) undergoes a decrease in response to caloric restriction, and exercise training of sufficient intensity to substantially increase

$\dot{V}O_2$ max does not reverse the dietary-induced depression of REE. However, exercise does tend to increase use of fat, rather than carbohydrate, as the metabolic fuel, and this use could contribute to weight loss (26, 34, 39–42).

E. Weight Cycling There is some evidence that repetitive weight loss followed by weight gain and reloss progressively lowers resting metabolic rate. There may be adaptive metabolic changes during refeeding following caloric restriction that favor fat storage. However, to date research on this point is not conclusive. Many studies have been conducted on rats and on male wrestlers, but relatively few on obese dieters. Results are confounded by the effects of exercise, fitness and training, dehydration, difficulty in correcting for fat-free weight, and age-related declines in resting metabolic rate and in the thermic effect of physical activity (43–47).

2. METABOLIC CHANGES

Weight loss decreases production of very low-density lipoproteins (VLDL) and thus lowers serum triglycerides. After a 500-calorie diet and a 26% weight loss, followed by 6 months of a low-fat maintenance diet, a group of obese individuals had significant decreases in serum triglycerides and low-density lipoproteins (LDL) and increases in high-density lipoprotein (HDL) cholesterol. Greater reductions in serum triglycerides and LDL-cholesterol occurred in younger individuals, those who lost the most weight, and those who had more abnormal values at the onset of the study (48, 49).

A loss of 10% to 15% of body weight will produce significant improvements in blood pressure, glucose tolerance, sleep disorders, respiratory function, and lipid profiles in 90% of patients (10, 23). After a 10-kg weight loss, women with abdominal obesity had greater decreases in serum lipids and blood glucose than

women with peripheral obesity (50).

A reduced thermic response and impaired activation of the sympathetic nervous system have been reported after the ingestion of oral glucose in human obesity. Hyperinsulinemia down-regulates insulin receptors in the liver and muscle. In addition, free fatty acid flux stimulates hepatic synthesis and the release of triglycerides and VLDL. Thus, hypertrophic abdominal adipocytes that develop as a consequence of relative overnutrition are a significant factor in the development of glucose intolerance, hyperinsulinemia, and hypertriglyceridemia associated with abdominal or android obesity. After a 30-lb. weight loss, the lipid and glucose profiles of 8 obese patients were markedly improved, but their impairment in glucose-induced thermogenesis was not. These results suggest that a defective sympathetic nervous system may be a contributing factor in obesity (51, 52).

3. DECREASED ADIPOSITY

In one study, obese women were placed on a 544-kcal high-protein diet for 4 weeks. Weight loss was associated with a decrease in the waist-to-hip ratio and significantly higher emptying of abdominal than gluteal fat cells (53). Another study found that while women with lower-body obesity lost more fat than women with upper-body obesity, the latter experienced greater reductions in waist-to-hip ratio. This is encouraging, in that the smaller fat losses in women with android obesity can be expected to have more impact on health risk factors via a more favorable relative distribution of fat (54).

4. BLOOD PRESSURE

Hyperinsulinemia and high blood pressure occur in obesity. It has been suggested that insulin affects blood pressure through its action on renal tubular sodium reabsorption (55).

Weight reduction decreases plasma

noradrenaline levels, serum renin activity, serum aldosterone levels, and blood pressure. The blood pressure reduction occurs even before normal weight is achieved. There is a greater fall in blood pressure in individuals who reduce their waist-to-hip ratio (56). Even a short-term fast of 48 hours, reduces weight and blood pressure (57). In one study, the use of a fiber supplement caused a decrease in diastolic blood pressure that was independent of the effects of weight reduction (58).

5. MYOCARDIAL ENERGY METABOLISM

Obese individuals with angina pectoris treated with a low-fat, low-calorie diet for 3 months had a considerably reduced coronary sinus blood flow and myocardial oxygen consumption. These and other improvements, including a reduction in lactate release during pacing, a reduction in citrate release during recovery, a reduction in alanine output during rest and recovery, and a lower uptake of glutamate, point to an improvement in myocardial energy metabolism (59).

6. SLEEP-DISORDERED BREATHING

In morbid obesity, improvements in sleep-disordered breathing as well as in oxygen desaturation occur as a result of weight reduction. In mild to moderately obese individuals with obstructive sleep apnea, even a moderate weight loss of 7 kg resulted in alleviation of the sleep apnea, improvement in sleep "architecture," and a decrease in daytime hypersomnolence (60).

PHYSIOLOGY, FOODS, AND NUTRIENTS

1. THEORIES ON THE ETIOLOGY OF OBESITY

A complete review of all existing theories of obesity is beyond the scope of this section. A brief summary of the most popular theories follows. The causes of obesity include heredity, overeating, altered metabolism of adipose tissue, defective or decreased thermogenesis, decreased physical activity, and certain prescribed medications. However, each of these factors and their interactions are incompletely understood. All studies to date are somewhat inconclusive and indicate the need for further research (2).

A. Genetic Factors The relative contributions of environment and heredity to obesity continue to be debated. At present, no genetic marker for obesity has been found, although population, adoption, and twin studies suggest that the tendency for obesity is inherited. Even in well-designed studies it is difficult to separate genetics from cultural and environmental contributions (2).

B. Overeating While overeating is clearly a factor in obesity, studies have failed to demonstrate that obese persons consume more calories per unit weight than lean individuals. The possibility that results are skewed by underreporting of food intake by the obese cannot be ruled out (2).

Feeding behavior is governed by complex biologic and behavioral controls. Biological factors are integrated mainly by the hypothalamus and include neurotransmitters, nervous impulses, circulating levels of nutrients, and hormones. It is possible that irregularities in any of these mechanisms may contribute to overeating.

One hypothesis suggests that serotonin may be involved in the mechanism of short-term satiety. A small caloric preload of a mixture of amino acids that included tryptophan, a precursor of serotonin, had the effect of reducing food intake in overweight individuals. In animals, the neurotransmitter tryptophan increases brain serotonin levels, as does a carbohydrate meal (61). A precursor of tryptophan, 5-hydroxytryptamine, may be decreased in obese diabetics. The effect of this decrease in 5-hydroxytryp-

tamine and tryptophan is a craving for sweet, carbohydrate-rich foods. Consumption of high-carbohydrate foods by obese individuals classified as carbohydrate cravers results in an increase in the brain's synthesis of serotonin. Whether an obese individual ingests large amounts of carbohydrate or of protein has an effect on mood. Carbohydrates seem to have a calming effect, and there is some evidence that carbohydrates with a high glycemic index have a greater serotoninergic effect than those with a low glycemic index. This may explain carbohydrate binges in certain obese individuals (62–64).

Appetite is also induced by the presence of food, especially highly palatable foods high in fat and sugar and low in fiber. But it has been shown, too, that foods low in fat and high in fiber tend to promote satiety at lower calorie intakes (62–64).

Psychological and behavioral influences on eating behavior are difficult to define. It has been suggested that obese persons may be more dependent on external cues than internal, physiological hunger signals or may tend to be more restrained, leading to compensatory overeating. In the clinical setting this distinction has not always been useful. Moreover, the effects of peer pressure have not been clearly described (2).

C. Altered Adipose Cell Metabolism
Excess fat accumulation is associated with increased fat cell size (hypertrophy). In extreme obesity, fat cell numbers are also increased (hyperplasia). When compared with lean controls of similar lean body mass, obese individuals exhibit normal resting energy expenditure but impaired thermogenic response to a meal (8, 65).

It is possible that a metabolic error in energy balance in obese individuals causes an unusually high proportion of dietary calories to be stored. Elevated levels of the enzyme lipoprotein lipase in

adipose tissue may cause overremoval of triglyceride from the bloodstream so that other tissues are deprived, leading to overeating. Increased lipoprotein lipase has been documented in adipose tissue of obese individuals who are losing weight, and it may contribute to rapid regain of weight. However, results are inconsistent; other workers have shown a decrease in lipoprotein lipase with caloric restriction, followed by an increase with a return to a higher caloric intake (2).

During exercise and stress, the hormones epinephrine and norepinephrine are probably the main activators of lipolysis. Epinephrine-stimulated lipolysis appears to have a genetic component, which may account for the failure of some obese persons to lose weight with exercise. Elevated blood levels of insulin as well as insulin resistance are common in obesity, and weight reduction is often accompanied by improvements in glucose tolerance. Overfeeding in infancy may lead to excessive secretion of insulin and growth hormone and to increases in fat cell size and number (2, 66).

D. Altered Thermogenesis

i. Set Points According to this theory, individuals with obesity have an internal regulatory system which keeps their weight at a predetermined set point. When weight reaches this set point, further weight loss is extremely difficult. Exercise may be required to alter the set point and bring it to a lower level (67).

ii. Metabolic Rate Basal metabolic rate (BMR) is the energy needed by the body when the subject is at complete rest, before rising in the morning and 12 or more hours after the last meal. Resting metabolic rate (RMR) is a measure of the energy needed for the body's essential functions, obtained at rest several hours after eating or physical activity. RMR is slightly higher than BMR but provides a reasonable estimation and is more convenient to measure. At stable body weight, BMR and RMR are higher in obese individuals, owing to increased body size. However, it is uncertain whether metabolic rate is the same or lower when expressed in terms of lean body mass (2).

iii. Diet-Induced Thermogenesis Diet-induced thermogenesis is the metabolic energy generated during digestion. Adaptive thermogenesis is the increase in RMR that occurs with increased food intake. Persons of normal weight experience increased thermogenesis following a meal, in proportion to meal size and macronutrient content. Protein, carbohydrate, and fat have been estimated to have thermogenic effects of 25%, 10%, and 3% of calories ingested, respectively. When compared with lean controls of similar lean body mass, obese subjects exhibit normal resting energy expenditure but impaired thermogenic response to a meal. Postprandial thermogenesis is blunted in obese individuals, as compared with lean persons. The increase in metabolic rate after a caloric load, individualized to each person's resting metabolic rate, is significantly lower in obese men than in lean men. Postprandial thermic responses are significantly lower in obese men (2, 65, 67, 68).

iv. Futile Cycles Adenosine Triphosphate (ATP) Theory It has been theorized that obese individuals use calories more efficiently than nonobese individuals and store their caloric savings as fat. Humans have a hypothetical catecholamine-mediated throttle, which permits them to utilize ATP to burn off extra calories and prepare for stress by accelerating metabolic pathways (spinning the metabolic wheels). This theory has been disputed (69–72).

v. Brown Fat Theory Body fat is composed of both brown fat and white fat. White fat cells form the majority and are energy repositories each made up of

1 large droplet of triglyceride. Brown fat consists of triglycerides localized in smaller droplets surrounding numerous mitochondria. Extensive vascularization and densely striated mitochondria give the tissue its brown appearance, and its impressive oxidative capacity is the basis for its major function: heat production. Brown fat provides heat to the body by diet-induced thermogenesis. It minimizes weight gain because excess calories are dissipated as heat rather than being stored (73).

According to the brown fat theory, obesity is the result of a malfunction in brown fat. The debate over brown fat continues; researchers have discovered that brown fat actually contributes little to metabolic rate in human beings. Current research is focused on the search for agents that may metabolically turn on brown fat to enable individuals to waste extra calories (73).

E. Lack of Exercise Several studies have documented shorter life expectancy with physical inactivity. However, it is difficult to show that obesity is directly linked to inactivity, partly because methodology for measurement of physical inactivity is poor, most studies depending on questionnaires. Some studies have shown relationships between activity level and leanness, and between time spent in sedentary activities (such as watching television) and degree of overweight. Involuntary movement, meaning spontaneous fidgeting or moving, may also make an important contribution to energy expenditure. Cumulative effects of exercise and spontaneous activity could be important in weight management (2).

F. Prescribed Medications See "Assessment of Potential Drug Interactions," below.

2. NUTRIENT DENSITY OF KILOCALORIE-RESTRICTED DIETS

Most foods are restricted, and highly

concentrated sources of kilocalories, especially high-fat and high-sugar foods, are eliminated. Exchange lists similar to those used for the diabetic diet may be used (74). Low-nutrient-density foods, which provide small amounts of nutrients at a high caloric cost, are avoided in favor of high-nutrient-density foods, which provide high levels of nutrients per unit of energy. Given the caloric density of dietary fat, a low-calorie diet is often a low-fat diet and vice versa (75). Hypocaloric diets designed to meet the needs of the individual patient should be combined with appropriate exercise, as well as with behavioral changes in eating habits.

3. AGE-RELATED CHANGES

With advancing age, body composition shifts toward an increased proportion of body fat and decreased lean body mass. These changes result in a decrease in resting energy expenditure of 2% to 3% per decade. Also, energy expended in activity tends to decline with age (76).

4. SMOKING AND CAFFEINE

Smokers have less body fat than nonsmokers. The reason may be that cigarette smoking stimulates thermogenesis. Coffee and tea contain caffeine, which has also been shown to stimulate thermogenesis (77, 78).

5. FAT REPLACEMENTS AND SUGAR SUBSTITUTES

Simplesse is a protein-based fat replacement, which provides the taste and texture of fat in foods. It is made by microparticulation of egg white, skim milk, or whey protein. It has been approved for use in frozen desserts and is suitable for use in any product that does not require cooking. It provides only 1 to 2 kcal/g.

Sucrose polyester is a synthetic lipid under experimental use that has physical properties similar to triglycerides. It inhibits dietary lipid absorption and thus promotes weight loss, inhibits cholesterol absorption, and lowers serum cholesterol and LDL (79).

Polysiloxane is a noncaloric, nonabsorbable liquid oil that is now being studied as a fat substitute (80).

See Chapter 28 for a discussion of sugar substitutes.

INDICATIONS FOR USE

1. OBESE OR SIGNIFICANTLY OVERWEIGHT INDIVIDUALS

A calorie-restricted diet should be part of an overall program of weight reduction in any person who is obese or significantly overweight, as determined by skinfold thickness measurements or by BMI (see the definitions at the beginning of this chapter) (7).

2. CRITERIA FOR DEFINING OVERWEIGHT AND OBESITY

Caution must be used with the use of the term *ideal weight,* either to identify abnormalities in body weight or composition or as the sole basis for weight-loss recommendations. Such an approach has neither a statistical nor a biological rationale. The lowest mortality rates are associated with *average* weights for age and sex, which are higher than ideal weights. In children, triceps and subscapular skinfolds seem to correlate better with estimates of total body fat than weight or weight-height ratios. An index for estimating adiposity in children, based upon a study of longitudinal growth, has been published. An evaluation of 5 indices of relative body weight for use with children found that the most reliable measurement was a weight-for-length index (81–83).

Health risks associated with overweight in the elderly have been found to be less significant than for younger individuals. A BMI greater than or equal to 27.8 in men and 27.3 in women has not been found to be a risk factor for significantly increased mortality among 55- to 74-year olds. The relevance of health-based criteria that were established from younger populations has therefore been challenged in older adults (7).

3. CLINICAL HEALTH RISKS

Weight reduction of the significantly overweight individual is specifically indicated in instances of hyperlipidemia, hypertension, instances in which there are 1 or more risk factors for cardiovascular disease, osteoarthritis, pickwickian syndrome, sleep apnea, gallbladder disease, glucose intolerance, diabetes mellitus, rupture of intravertebral disks, intermittent claudication, or problems with knees, hip, or other leg joints.

A. Hypertension and Diabetes Levels of blood pressure vary with levels of obesity in a continuous manner. In a study of men less than 45 years of age, subjects with a BMI greater than 26.6 had higher systolic and diastolic blood pressures than age- and weight-matched men with lower BMI. Early in the course of obesity, insulin levels are elevated and are associated with insulin resistance and insulin receptor and postreceptor defects. Eventually, long-term obesity may result in exhaustion of the pancreatic beta cells and insulinopenia (75, 84, 85).

The risks of hypertension, hypercholesterolemia, and diabetes are greater in overweight adults aged 20 to 45 years of age than in overweight persons aged 45 to 75 (4).

B. Breast Cancer Obesity has been linked by epidemiological data to breast cancer. When preliminary data were followed by an actual prospective clinical trial, however, the finding was that obesity did not increase the risk for breast cancer (9).

C. Abdominal Versus Peripheral Fat Distribution In women, the risk for impaired carbohydrate metabolism and diabetes is correlated with abdominal obesity but not with obesity per se. As waist-to-hip ratio (WHR) increases in obese women, plasma insulin and plasma glucose levels increase. Women equally obese but with normal WHR (gynoid or peripheral obesity) do not show this impairment of blood glucose metabolism (16). Such data argue strongly for regional fat distribution rather than obesity as a risk factor for diabetes and coronary artery disease. Centrally obese individuals are at increased risk of coronary artery disease, independent of BMI (11, 86–88).

Abdominal distribution of fat seems to be important even in the absence of significant obesity. Intraabdominal fat deposition constitutes a greater cardiovascular risk than obesity alone, possibly owing to hyperinsulinemia (11–14).

Abdominal obesity tends to be associated with hypertension. Even a moderate accumulation of fat in the abdominal region increases the risk for hypertension. Hypertension may occur in abdominal obesity because of an excess production of free fatty acids from lipolytically active depots. The health risk is increased in abdominal obesity because abdominal fat cells are more metabolically active than fat cells in other areas. Reduced hepatic insulin uptake may result in peripheral hyperinsulinemia, insulin resistance, diabetes mellitus, and hypertension (7, 8, 15).

In summary, a high WHR is associated with large, centrally located adipose cells and is a risk factor for ischemic heart disease, hypertension, stroke, diabetes mellitus, and death (89).

D. Other Health Risks An excess of abdominal fat tends to be associated with a decrease in serum HDL-cholesterol. In obese women, increased intraabdominal fat is significantly correlated with plasma lipoprotein levels, independent of total fatness (14, 90).

The risk for gallbladder disease is higher as obesity increases and is greater for women than for men. An increased body fat reservoir tends to be associated with increased cholesterol production. As a result, greater biliary excretion of cholesterol increases the cholesterol concentrations in bile, which can enhance cholesterol stone formation (27). A form of arthritis in which the weight-bearing joints are affected, called osteoarthritis, is also a risk of obesity (76). In addition, as weight increases, serum uric acid levels increase. The incidence of gouty attacks is higher in obese individuals (76).

4. EATING DISORDERS

The incidence of eating disorders is increasing. Attention has been drawn to the fact that patients with these disorders need both medical and psychiatric treatment, and there is a need for therapists and medical practitioners to become familiar with the potential medical sequelae of eating disorders. One dietary approach is to provide a structured, kilocalorie-controlled plan based on nutritional needs, with 3 meals and 3 snacks daily (21, 91). For more information on eating disorders see Chapter 31, the position statement of the American Dietetic Association on nutrition intervention in the treatment of anorexia nervosa and bulimia nervosa.

POSSIBLE ADVERSE REACTIONS

1. MARGINAL INTAKES OF VITAMINS AND MINERALS

Iron and thiamine may be marginal even on a well-balanced diet. Unbalanced fad diets that exclude major groups of foods with essential nutrients can cause deficiencies (92). Clients need to be taught to choose foods of high nutrient density to provide maximal nutrients within the decreased energy intake. Similarly, caloric restriction should be achieved, where possible, by limiting foods that contain significant calories but few nutrients.

2. GROWTH RETARDATION

In children, the goal of a weight-reduc-tion program must take into account normal growth and development. Lean body mass must be preserved. Severe caloric restriction in growing individuals is inappropriate, because it means an intolerable psychological stress and a decrease in lean body mass with arrested linear growth. While some reduction in growth velocity is related to the amount of weight loss, diets should be planned so that growth is maintained within the normal range. If possible, weight should be maintained as height increases, until normal weight-for-height is reached (93, 94).

CONTRAINDICATIONS

A kilocalorie-restricted diet is contraindicated in the obese pregnant woman. Severe caloric restrictions during pregnancy, even in an obese woman, may compromise the well-being of both the developing fetus and the mother, particularly if the caloric level is so low that protein is used for energy rather than for growth. Despite the added risk of obesity, weight-reduction regimens should not be used during pregnancy (95).

CLINICAL ASSESSMENT

1. DIETARY EVALUATION

A. Basic Data The dietary evaluation should include data as to the number and timing of meals and their composition. A diet history, or at least a 24-hour recall and a completed food frequency questionnaire, are minimum requirements. Carbohydrate and other cravings and sensitivity and preference for sweetness should be assessed. Use of nutritive and non-nutritive sweeteners, use and nature of condiments, occurrence and characteristics of binges, relationship of binging to hunger, hunger patterns, the meaning of food to the patient, psychological and sociological determinants of eating behavior, the use of food in dealing with stress, vitamin and mineral supplement use, and smoking-eating patterns should also be addressed (96, 97).

B. Smoking Cessation Smoking has a thermogenic effect. On average, smokers weigh less than nonsmokers, and weight gain is often an aftermath of smoking cessation. Weight reduction should not be instituted concurrently with smoking cessation programs. The smoker should complete the cessation program prior to institution of a weight-control program (98).

C. Problems with Dietary Evaluation Tools Problems exist with many common dietary evaluation techniques. The use of data from dietary recalls to estimate energy intake has been reported to result in a 20% degree of error. An analysis of the accuracy of food records in obese, dieting clients concluded that there were huge errors in the estimates of food quantities consumed, and many entries in food records were not specific enough to permit an objective evaluation of calories consumed. Error rates were similar in obese and normal-weight recorders (99–101).

New methods have been proposed, including the use of telephones and tape recorders in the assessment of children's intakes. In the development of new or improved techniques to estimate nutrient intake, it is important periodically to validate the technique for accuracy and to identify intermediate steps that clients use in estimating their food intake behavior (102, 103).

2. BODY MASS INDEX (BMI)

One of the simplest and most useful measures of body weight is body mass index. It represents the weight (in kilograms) divided by the height (in meters) squared. It deemphasizes the effect of stature on body weight and also correlates closely with adiposity (8). Tables for its use as well as more information about it are found in Chapter 1 and in the definitions at the beginning of this chapter.

3. BODY FRAME SIZE

Height-weight tables, which are based upon arbitrary norms for body frame size and shape, have been criticized. More objective measures of body frame size e.g., elbow breadth, have been proposed. While certain applications of the use of wrist circumference measurements have fallen into disrepute, a recent study reaffirms the usefulness of the wrist circumference technique as proposed by Grant. Accurate use of frame size measurements presupposes minimal association of the technique with body fatness and the provision of an estimate of fat-free mass. If the actual measurements do not support these assumptions, then they will not accurately estimate frame size. Comparisons of 2 wrist circumference techniques and the elbow breadth technique indicate that the elbow breadth technique was correlated with body fatness; the wrist circumference technique, by Grant, was more accurate, because it had little association with body fatness (104–108).

4. SKINFOLD THICKNESS

These techniques and the procedures for their use are discussed more fully in Chapter 1. Subscapular and triceps skinfold measurements are useful in the estimation of body fat. The percentiles provided by the NCHS for use in the interpretation of skinfold thickness measurements should be derived from a single measurement, and interpretations based upon them should be made with caution in children. Skinfold measurements are a useful means of judging obesity in the early phase of Prader-Willi syndrome (8, 109).

5. ESTIMATING CALORIC NEEDS

A complete review of procedures and techniques for estimating basal energy and resting energy needs under a variety

of different conditions are discussed in Chapter 1. Caloric requirements of men have been reappraised. The effect of body size and composition on caloric needs has been reviewed, and equations depicting the relationship between energy intake and lean body mass have also been published. New predictive equations for basal caloric requirements (C) derived from the data of Boothby, Berkson, and Dunn are as follows (110–112):

For men 20 through 74 years of age:
$$C/m^2/hr = 43.66 - (0.1329 \times \text{age [years]})$$

For women 20 through 74 years of age:
$$C/m^2/hr = 38.65 - (0.0909 \times \text{age [years]})$$

BIOCHEMICAL ASSESSMENT

Parameters of visceral protein status such as serum albumin, total lymphocyte counts, pre-albumin, and creatinine height indices should be monitored during all types of treatment for weight loss (113). Serum potassium measurements are of particular importance, because skeletal muscle potassium levels are decreased by obesity (114–117).

ASSESSMENT OF POTENTIAL DRUG INTERACTIONS

1. DRUGS THAT CONTRIBUTE TO WEIGHT GAIN

Many drugs used in treatment of other clinical problems may cause weight gain. Medications such as propranolol and clonidine, prescribed for hypertension and other cardiovascular diseases, may change metabolic rates and decrease levels of energy expenditure. Hypertrophic obesity may be caused by such adrenal steroids as prednisone, prescribed as an anti-inflammatory agent. Also, tranquilizers such as amitriptyline and diazepam, antihistamines such as cyproheptadine, and birth control pills may

lead to weight gain in some individuals (2).

2. IDEAL ANTI-OBESITY AGENTS

Safe and efficacious drugs are sought to accelerate weight loss and to prevent its regain once ideal body weight has been reached. Such agents should be used as an adjunct to diet therapy, behavior modification, and exercise. Characteristics of the ideal anti-obesity agent are sustained reduction of body weight through a selective reduction of body fat stores, prevention of rebound weight gain once other forms of therapy are no longer effective, improved efficacy as an adjunct to caloric restriction, and absence of the potential for abuse or for serious adverse reactions (79).

3. AMPHETAMINES (BENZEDRINE)

Amphetamines appear to reduce the *frequency* of eating, but not the *rate* at which food is consumed. They appear to act by enhancing the release of norepinephrine. They should be taken 6 hours or more before bedtime because of their stimulant effects. Side effects include addiction, central nervous system stimulation, dry mouth, light-headedness, tachycardia, palpitations, sweating, elevation of blood pressure, nausea and vomiting, diarrhea or constipation, metallic taste, blurred vision, and depression and paranoid psychosis on cessation of therapy. Because of their side effects, particularly addiction, these drugs are not recommended for use as anorectic agents now that other, less dangerous drugs are available (79, 118–120).

4. MAZINDOL (SANOREX)

Mazindol is a tricyclic compound that appears to inhibit the uptake of norepinephrine. It reduces appetite and has central nervous system–stimulating side effects similar to those of the amphetamines. The potential side effects include dry mouth, nausea, vomiting, constipation, dizziness, drowsiness, unpleasant taste, blurred vision, and weakness (120).

5. DIETHYLPROPRION (TENUATE, TEPANIL)

This drug has an amphetamine-like action but is much less severe. The last dose should be taken 6 hours before bedtime to avoid sleeplessness. It may adversely affect blood glucose levels in individuals with diabetes and should not be taken with caffeine or alcohol. It may result in dry mouth, altered sense of taste, bloating, confusion (especially in the elderly), dizziness, and drowsiness (118, 120).

6. PHENTERMINE-HYDROCHLORIDE (FASTIN) AND PHENTERMINE RESIN (LONAMIN)

These drugs seem to act in a manner similar to the amphetamines, but to a lesser degree. Phentermine resin should be swallowed whole, and its unpleasant taste may be masked with fruit juice. Caffeine intake should be limited. Potential side effects include gastrointestinal distress, constipation, alteration of the effects of insulin in a diabetic, dizziness, tremors, dry mouth, unpleasant taste, tachycardia, and elevated blood pressure (119, 120).

7. FENFLURAMINE HYDROCHLORIDE (PONDIMIN)

Fenfluramine acts through the serotonergic system. It appears to have a specific effect on carbohydrate metabolism and reduces cravings in obese individuals who specifically crave carbohydrate. The drug has no effect on obese individuals who are not carbohydrate cravers. This specificity highlights the importance of a dietary evaluation that is geared to differentiate among individuals. Major clinical advantages of fenfluramine hydrochloride are its lack of nervous system stimulation and its potential usefulness for obese individuals

with hypertension. The drug, even when it does not achieve weight loss, seems to reduce serum triglycerides and LDL-cholesterol levels, and thus may reduce the risk of cardiovascular disease in hyperlipidemic obese individuals. Side effects include dyspepsia, constipation, nausea and vomiting, heartburn, dry mouth, and thirst. The drug also may increase levels of serum glutamic-oxalo-acetic transaminase, LDH, alkaline phosphatase, and blood urea nitrogen (118–123).

8. FLUOXETINE HYDROCHLORIDE (PROZAC)

Fluoxetine is a chemically unique antidepressant, with selective inhibition of serotonin uptake, that decreases appetite and consistently causes weight loss. Individuals classified as carbohydrate cravers lose more weight on this drug than do noncarbohydrate cravers. It is one of the most effective of the anorectic agents. It should be taken in the morning, and excessive intake of foods high in tryptophan should be avoided, because tryptophan increases its effects. It may cause nausea, diarrhea, dry mouth, headache, tremors, and drowsiness (79, 120, 124).

9. PHENYLPROPANOLAMINE (ACUTRIM, CONTROL, DEXATRIM, PROLAMINE)

Nonprescription drugs have increased in popularity. Many contain phenylpropanolamine as well as caffeine. Phenylpropanolamine increases the concentration of cyclic adenosine monophosphate (cAMP), and caffeine enhances its action. Caffeinated coffee produces an increase in energy expenditure of 16% over a 2-hour period, as compared with decaffeinated coffee. Caffeine and coffee both stimulate the metabolic rate (125, 126).

Phenylpropanolamine should be swallowed whole and taken several hours before bedtime. It can cause drowsiness, dry mouth, and headache. Excessive use of the drug increases blood pressure,

owing to increased systemic vascular resistance and cardiac output. Several cases of intracranial hemorrhage have been reported in individuals taking the drug. There has also been published a case report of cerebral vasculitis and hemorrhage in an adolescent who took 5 pills of a product called Diet Aid. The pills contained 75 mg each, or a total of 375 mg, of phenylpropanolamine. As a result of these cases it has been recommended that the daily dosage not exceed 75 mg, or preferably 50 mg, to avoid side effects (120, 127–130).

10. BULKING AGENTS

Another approach to reducing appetite has been bulking agents such as methylcellulose. These have been used to inhibit food intake but have not been proven effective in reducing hunger. The actual methylcellulose content of several over-the-counter preparations is insignificant (119).

11. ANESTHETICS

Several diet candies that promise to decrease appetite are based on anesthetics. They supposedly dull the person's sense of taste. Long-term investigations of the effect of anesthetics as reducing agents are not available (118, 119).

12. DRUGS IN EXPERIMENTAL USE

Aspirin alone has no effect, but when combined with ephedrine, it enhances and activates ephedrine-induced thermogenesis and causes weight loss. More studies are needed on the long-term combined effects of aspirin-ephedrine combinations (131).

There are several drugs being tested as anorectic agents. Studies of cholecystokinin thus far indicate it has no practical use in appetite suppression. Studies of the beta-adrenoreceptor agonist BRL 26830 A indicate that it does not lead to any weight loss in obese individuals (132).

IMPLEMENTATION AND EDUCATION

1. USE OF ALTERNATIVE SWEETENERS

The use of alternative sweeteners enhances dietary compliance with a kilocalorie-restricted diet. The use of fructose as a sweetener, as compared to aspartame, glucose, or water results in the lowest caloric intake in obese individuals (133). Alternative sweeteners have been discussed in detail in Chapter 28.

2. LOW-CALORIE FOODS

The use of commercial foods that are low in calories helps with compliance. The Food and Drug Administration has set forth regulations for the labeling of foods with regard to descriptions of calories. A food labeled "low calorie" may contain no more than 40 kcal per serving. A food may be called "reduced calorie" only if its caloric content is at least one-third lower than a similar food for which it can substitute. Foods normally low in calories—e.g., celery—cannot use the term *low calorie* immediately before the name of the food. In order for a food to be labeled as "sugar free," "sugarless," or "no sugar," it must also be accompanied by the statement "not a reduced-calorie food," unless it fits the category for a low-calorie or reduced-calorie food (134).

3. NUTRITIONAL COUNSELING STRATEGIES

A. Goal Setting A fundamental skill that forms the foundation for other interventions is goal assessment. Using goal assessment, nutrition counselors can help patients to attain goals by breaking down complex behaviors into a series of small, successive steps. This approach focuses on the patient's strengths and fosters commitment to change. The process includes 4 basic steps: goal identification, goal importance assessment, goal roadblock analysis, and goal attainment (135).

B. Validity of Popular Quick Weight-Loss Schemes Once the dietitian has helped the patient grasp the mechanics of his or her own individualized meal plan, information should be provided on the validity or nonvalidity of popular weight loss regimens, including any dangers inherent in their use.

C. Identifying Compliant Patients It has been claimed that older subjects are more likely to change than younger ones and females are more likely to change than males. Six variables help differentiate the changers from the nonchangers (136):

- Perception of personal susceptibility to diet-related diseases
- Perception of benefits from taking preventive health actions
- Overall health concern
- Beliefs of those important to the survey recipients
- Cues to action
- Chance locus of control (patients' belief either that the locus of health control is internalized within themselves, giving them some control over outcome, or that it is external, occurring by chance or arising from external circumstances)

The nutritionist should assess the client's readiness to learn, including such factors as information-processing capacity, affective state, prior learning and experience, and most effective methods of learning (137).

D. Self-Identification Training Self-motivation is enhanced by supplementary behavioral therapy in the use of positive, coping self-statements. An exercise in self-identification designed to increase self-motivation has been published. An analysis of its use suggests that health education is more effective when treatment practices are supplemented with the teaching of self-actualization characteristics (138).

4. BEHAVIOR MODIFICATION THERAPY

Behavioral approaches to weight loss base their effect on an accurate assessment and modification of idiosyncratic eating habits of obese individuals, and on relapse-prevention strategies to help clients through difficult situations. Behavioral modification focuses on overt behaviors or habits rather than on hypothetical emotional causes. The strategy implies that the symptoms or behavior problems themselves may be the root of the disturbance and that the modification of problematic eating behaviors cures the problem (139, 140). Behavioral or lifestyle change needs to be an integral part of any successful weight-management plan (24).

In a weight control program in the corporate setting, changes in behavior most often associated with success by patients were regular aerobic exercise, recording of food intake, and counting calories. A review by the California Dietetic Association on the effectiveness of different weight-control approaches concluded that characteristics associated with poor outcome include the use of extremely low-calorie diets, extremes of macronutrient restriction, and reliance on formula diets or special products (141).

An evaluation of a program that includes a behavioral modification approach to the formulation and use of a shopping list determined that the program had a strong effect on the amounts and types of foods purchased after the training. It has been recommended that long-term evaluations should be conducted to gauge the effectiveness of commercial programs in keeping weight off (142, 143).

A. Self-Monitoring The patient should be instructed to keep a detailed record of all instances of eating, detailing the amounts and specific nature of the food consumed as well as patient's subjective feelings at the time and the environment in which the food was consumed.

B. Stimulus Control and Environmental Management Surroundings are changed in order to break the learned association between particular environmental cues and eating.

C. Positive Reinforcement The presentation of some kind of reward follows the occurrence of a specified behavior.

D. Contingency Contracting An agreement is made between the therapist and the patient, specifying the problem behaviors to be changed.

E. Aversive Conditioning A procedure is employed to develop a negative or unpleasant association to a previously positively conditioned stimulus (144).

PRIORITIES FOR QUALITY ASSURANCE

Quality assurance monitors are vital for any program of weight reduction. While there is no method of weight reduction that is applicable to all individuals, the method most likely to succeed for most people most of the time is a 4-way approach, which includes a food plan based on the science and art of nutrition; a program of increased physical activity; a series of eating management skills (behavior change); and a positive support system (145). The following are minimal standards that should be applied to all weight-control programs.

Prior to the institution of any program based on a kilocalorie level, the diet should be planned to include all food groups and should be subjected to a computerized nutrient analysis to identify any potential inadequacies or excesses. An exchange system should be used that presents foods of similar nutrient content within specific categories, allowing for variety, moderation, and portion control (145).

Alternatives to the exchange system should be available to those individuals who do not do well with exchanges— e.g., the ADA Healthy Food Choices pamphlets (96) and other such tools, as presented in the discussion of meal planing for diabetes in Chapter 28.

The energy deficit induced by a kilocalorie-restricted diet (other than monitored, very low-calorie diet programs) should allow a safe, progressive weight loss of 1 to 2 lbs. per week. Macronutrients should be provided in amounts specified in the RDAS (146).

There should be an awareness of cholesterol, sodium, and fat sources. It is recommended that 30% of the kilocalories come from fat, which should be one-third each of saturated, monounsaturated, and polyunsaturated (145).

A group of foods listing optional calories should be provided. This is a daily allowance of extra calories that can be "banked" or "spent," to enhance recipe development and to make possible the enjoyment of such social situations as dining out, brunches, and holiday meals, with foods not usually on weight-control plans (145).

The program should include a weekly menu planner that outlines specific foods in specific amounts, to provide structure and at the same time freedom and flexibility for individual lifestyles (145). A system of individualization in the form of "personal choice selections" should be included to enhance adherence and to introduce maintenance strategies early in the weight-loss program (145). Also important are relapse-prevention strategies such as identification of individual high-risk situations, development of coping skills for high-risk situations and cognitive coping strategies for use immediately after a lapse, practice in the use of these skills, and the development of a more balanced lifestyle (147).

MENU PLANNING

SAMPLE MENU, USING EXCHANGES, FOR THE 1,200-kcal DIET (FOR A FEMALE, AGE 25–50)

Food	Amount	Exchange
BREAKFAST		
Oatmeal	½ cup	1 bread/starch
Skim milk	1 cup	1 milk
Whole wheat toast	1 slice	1 bread/starch
Margarine	1 tsp.	1 fat
Banana	½ medium	1 fruit
Coffee or tea	1 cup	Free
LUNCH		
Turkey breast	2 oz.	2 meats
Whole wheat bread	2 slices	1 breads/starches
Mayonnaise	1 tsp.	1 fat
Sliced tomato	1 medium	1 vegetable
Skim milk	1 cup	1 milk
Coffee or tea	1 cup	Free
DINNER		
Lean ground beef	2 oz.	2 meats
Spaghetti	½ cup	1 bread/starch
Spaghetti sauce	½ cup	1 vegetable
Spinach salad	1 cup	1 vegetable
Oil-and-vinegar dressing	1 tbsp.	1 fat
Fresh orange	1 medium	1 fruit
Coffee or tea	1 cup	Free

Approximate Nutrient Analysis

Energy	1,113 kcal
Protein	64.5 g (23% of kcal)
Fat	34.9 g (28% of kcal)
Polyunsaturated fat	8.5 g
Monounsaturated fat	12.5 g
Saturated fat	9.0 g
Cholesterol	83 mg
Carbohydrate	144.9 g (52% of kcal)
Vitamin A	7,227 IU
	954 RE
Thiamine	0.99 mg
Riboflavin	1.41 mg
Niacin	16.3 mg
Folate	238 mcg
Vitamin B-12	4.30 mcg
Vitamin B-6	1.53 mg
Vitamin C	134.9 mg
Calcium	855 mg
Phosphorus	1,150 mg
Iron	9.3 mg
Copper	0.75 mg
Zinc	7.5 mg

(*continued*)

Magnesium	263 mg	
Sodium	2,692 mg	
Potassium	3,299 mg	

SAMPLE MENU, USING EXCHANGES, FOR THE 1,500-kcal DIET (FOR A MALE, AGE 25–50)

Food	Amount	Exchange
BREAKFAST		
Oatmeal	½ cup	1 bread/starch
Skim milk	1 cup	1 milk
Whole wheat toast	1 slice	1 bread/starch
Margarine	1 tsp.	1 fat
Banana	½ medium	1 fruit
Coffee or tea	1 cup	Free
LUNCH		
Turkey breast	2 oz.	2 meats
Whole wheat bread	2 slices	2 breads/starches
Mayonnaise	1 tsp.	1 fat
Sliced tomato	1 medium	1 vegetable
Melon cubes	1 cup	1 fruit
Skim milk	1 cup	1 milk
Coffee or tea	1 cup	Free
DINNER		
Lean ground beef	2 oz.	2 meats
Spaghetti	½ cup	1 bread/starch
Spaghetti sauce	½ cup	1 vegetable
Spinach salad	1 cup	1 vegetable
Oil-and-vinegar dressing	1 tbsp.	1 fat
Dinner roll	1 small	1 bread/starch
Margarine	1 tsp.	1 fat
Fresh orange	1 medium	1 fruit
Coffee or tea	1 cup	Free
EVENING SNACK		
English muffin	½	1 bread/starch
Mozzarella cheese	1 oz.	1 meat

Approximate Nutrient Analysis

Energy	1,457 kcal
Protein	80.0 g (22% of kcal)
Fat	45.5 g (28% of kcal)
Polyunsaturated fat	9.8 g
Monounsaturated fat	15.3 g
Saturated fat	12.7 g
Cholesterol	108 mg
Carbohydrate	192.6 g (53% of kcal)
Vitamin A	12,705 IU
	1,566 RE
Thiamine	1.31 mg
Riboflavin	1.69 mg
Niacin	19.3 mg

(continued)

Folate	268 mcg
Vitamin B-12	4.71 mcg
Vitamin B-6	1.76 mg
Vitamin C	202.5 mg
Calcium	1,088 mg
Phosphorus	1,372 mg
Iron	11.6 mg
Copper	0.82 mg
Zinc	8.9 mg
Magnesium	280 mg
Sodium	3,158 mg
Potassium	3,805 mg

REFERENCES

1. Position of the American Dietetic Association: Very-low-calorie weight loss diets. J Am Diet Assoc 90:722, 1990.
2. U.S. Department of Health and Human Services: The Surgeon General's report on nutrition and health. DHHS (PHS) Publication no. 88-50210. Washington, D.C.: U.S. Government Printing Office, 1988.
3. National Center for Health Statistics: Obese and overweight adults in the United States. DHHS (PHS) Publication no. 83-1680. Washington, D.C.: U.S. Government Printing Office, 1983.
4. Van Itallie, T. B.: Health implication of overweight and obesity in the United States. Ann Intern Med 103:983, 1985.
5. Position of the American Dietetic Association: Optimal weight as a health promotion strategy. J Am Diet Assoc 89:1814, 1989.
6. London, S. J., Colditz, G. A., et al.: Prospective study of relative weight, height, and risk of breast cancer. JAMA 262:2853, 1989.
7. Tayback, M., Kumanylka, S., and Chee, E.: Body weight as a risk factor in the elderly. Arch Intern Med 150:1065, 1990.
8. National Institutes of Health: Health implications of obesity—National Institutes of Health consensus development conference statement. Ann Intern Med 103:1077, 1985.
9. Najjar, M. F., and Rowland, M.: Anthropometric reference data and prevalence of overweight, United States, 1976–1980. DHHS Publication no. DHS-87; Vital Health Statistics ser. 11, no. 238, p. 1688. Washington, D.C.: U.S. Government Printing Office, 1987.
10. Lerman, R. H., and Cave, D. R.: Medical and surgical management of obesity. Adv Intern Med 34:127, 1989.
11. Donahue, R. P., Abbott, R. D., et al.: Central obesity and coronary heart disease in men. Lancet 1:821, 1987.
12. Fujioka, S., Matsuzawa, Y. M., et al.: Contribution of intra-abdominal fat accumulation to the impairment of glucose and lipid metabolism in human obesity. Metabolism 36:54, 1989.
13. Peiris, A., Sothmann, M., et al.: Adiposity, fat distribution and cardiovascular risk. Ann Intern Med 110:867, 1989.
14. Despres, J. P., Moorjani, S., et al.: Adipose tissue distribution and plasma lipoprotein levels in obese women—importance of intra-abdominal fat. Arteriosclerosis 9:203, 1989.
15. Bjorntorp, P.: Hypertension and other complications in human obesity. J Clin Hypertens 2:163, 1986.
16. Greenwood, M. R. C., and Pittman-Waller, V.: Weight control: A complex, various and controversial problem. In Frankle, R. T., and Yang, M. U.: Obesity and weight control. Rockville, Md.: Aspen, 1988.
17. Rebuffe-Scrive, M., Enk. L., and Crona, N.: Fat cell metabolism in different regions in women. J Clin Invest 75:1873, 1985.
18. Hollis, J.: Fat is a family affair. Center City, Minn.: Hazelden, 1985.
19. American Dietetic Association: Nutrition intervention in the treatment of anorexia nervosa and bulimia nervosa: Technical support paper. J Am Diet Assoc 88:69, 1988.
20. American Psychiatric Association: Diagnostic and statistical manual of mental disorders. 3d ed. Washington, D.C.: American Psychiatric Association, 1987.
21. American Dietetic Association: Manual of clinical dietetics. Chicago: American Dietetic Association, 1988.
22. Yang, M. U.: Body composition and resting metabolic rate in obesity. In Frankle, R. T., and Yang, M. U.: Obesity and weight control. Rockville, Md.: Aspen, 1988.
23. Blackburn, G. L., and Kanders, B. S.: Medical evaluation and treatment of the obese patient. Am J Cardiol 60:55G, 1987.
24. Dalton, S.: Eating management: A tool for the practitioner. In Frankle, R. T., and Yang, M. U.: Obesity and weight control. Rockville, Md.: Aspen, 1988.
25. Garrow, J. S., Durrant, M. L., et al.: Factors determining weight loss in a metabolic ward. Int J Obesity 2:441, 1978.
26. Hill, J. O., Sparling, P. B., et al.: Effects of exercise and food restriction on body composition and metabolic rate in obese women. Am J Clin Nutr 46:622, 1987.
27. Garrow, J. S., and Webster, J. D.: Effects of weight and metabolic rate of obese women on a 3.4 MJ (800-kcal) diet. Lancet 1:1429, 1989.
28. Weigle, D. S.: The contribution of decreased body mass to diminished thermic effect of exercise in reduced-obese men. Int J Obesity 12:567, 1988.
29. Foster, G. D., Wadden, T. A., et al.: Controlled trial of the metabolic effects of a very-low-calorie diet: Short- and long-term effects. Am J Clin Nutr 51:167, 1990.
30. Heshka, S., Yang, M. U., et al.: Weight loss and change in resting metabolic rate. Am J Clin Nutr 52:981, 1990.
31. de Groot, L. C., van Es, A. J. H., et al.: Energy metabolism of overweight women 1 mo. and 1 y. after an 8-wk. slimming period. Am J Clin Nutr 51:578, 1990.
32. Wadden, T. A., Foster, G. D., et al.: Long-term effects of dieting on resting metabolic rate in obese outpatients. JAMA 264:707, 1990.
33. Miller, W. C., Lindeman, A. K., et al.: Diet composition, energy intake, and exercise in relation to body fat in men and women. Am J Clin Nutr 52:426, 1990.
34. Flatt, J. P.: Importance of nutrient balance in body weight regulation. Diabetes/Metabolism Rev 4 (6):571, 1988.
35. Abbott, W. G. H., Howard, B. V., et al.: Short-term energy balance: Relationship with protein, carbohydrate, and fat balances. Am J Physiol 255:E332, 1988.

36. Alford, B. B., Blankenship, A. C., and Hagen, R. D.: The effects of variations in carbohydrate, protein, and fat content upon weight loss, blood values, and nutrient intake of adult obese women. J Am Diet Assoc 90:534, 1990.

37. Canty, D. J.: Letter to the editor. J Am Diet Assoc 90:1371, 1990.

38. Snyder, D. K., Clemmons, D. R., and Underwood, L. E.: Dietary carbohydrate content determines responsiveness to growth hormone in energy-restricted humans. J Clin Endocrinol Metab 69:745, 1989.

39. Ballor, D., Katch, V. L., et al.: Resistance weight training during caloric restriction enhances lean body weight maintenance. Am J Clin Nutr 47:19, 1988.

40. Poehlman, E. T., Melby, C. L., and Badylak, S. F.: Resting metabolic rate and postprandial thermogenesis in highly trained and untrained males. Am J Clin Nutr 47:793, 1988.

41. Henson, L. C., Poole, D. C., et al.: Effects of exercise training on resting energy expenditure during caloric restriction. Am J Clin Nutr 46:893, 1987.

42. Kissileff, H. F., Pi-Sunyer, F. X., et al.: Acute effects of exercise on food intake in obese and non obese women. Am J Clin Nutr 52:240, 1990.

43. Dulloo, A. G., and Giarardier, L.: Adaptive changes in energy expenditure during refeeding following low-calorie intake: Evidence for a specific metabolic component favoring fat storage. Am J Clin Nutr 52:415, 1990.

44. Melby, C. L., Schmidt, W. D., and Corrigan, D.: Resting metabolic rate in weight-cycling collegiate wrestlers compared with physically active, noncycling control subjects. Am J Clin Nutr 52:409, 1990.

45. Blackburn, G. L., Wilson, G. T., et al.: Weight cycling: The experience of human dieters. Am J Clin Nutr 49:1105, 1989.

46. Steen, S. N., Opplinger, R. A., and Brownell, K. D.: Metabolic effects of repeated weight loss and regain in adolescent wrestlers. JAMA 260:47, 1988.

47. van Dale, D., and Saris, W. H. M.: Repetitive weight loss and weight regain: Effects on weight reduction, resting metabolic rate, and lipolytic activity before and after exercise and/or diet treatment. Am J Clin Nutr 49:93, 1989.

48. Winston, M.: Heart disease—a review. In Frankle, R. T., and Yang, M. U.: Obesity and weight control. Rockville, Md.: Aspen, 1988.

49. Stevenson, D. W., Darga, L. L., et al.: Variable effects of weight loss on serum lipids and lipoproteins in obese patients. Int J Obesity 12:495, 1988.

50. Vansant, G., Den Besten, C., et al.: Body fat distribution and the prognosis for weight reduction: Preliminary observations. Int J Obesity 12:133, 1988.

51. Astrup, A., Anderson, T., et al.: Impaired glucose-induced thermogenesis and arterial norepinephrine response persist after weight reduction in obese humans. Am J Clin Nutr 51:331, 1990.

52. Owen, O. E.: Obesity. In Kinney, J. M., Jeejeebhoy, K. N., et al.: Nutrition and metabolism in patient care. Philadelphia: W. B. Saunders, 1988.

53. Krotkiewski, M., Grimby, G., et al.: Increased muscle dynamic endurance associated with weight reduction on a very low calorie diet. Am J Clin Nutr 51:321, 1990.

54. Wadden, T. A., Stunkard, A. J., et al.: Body fat deposition in adult obese women. II. Changes in fat distribution accompanying weight reduction. Am J Clin Nutr 47:229, 1988.

55. Mancini, M., and Strazzullo, P.: Energy balance and blood pressure regulation—update and future perspectives. J Clin Hypertens 2:148, 1986.

56. Eliahou, H. E., Iaina, A., et al.: Body weight reduction necessary to attain normotension in the overweight hypertensive patient. Int J Obesity 1 (Supp):157, 1981.

57. Andersson, B., Wallin, G., et al.: Acute effects of short term fasting on blood pressure, circulating noradrenaline and efferent sympathetic nerve activity. Acta Med Scand 223:485, 1988.

58. Rossner, S., Andersson, I. L., and Ryttig, K.: Effects of a dietary fiber supplement to a weight reduction program on blood pressure. Acta Med Scand 223:353, 1988.

59. Thuesen, L., Nielsen, T. T., et al.: Beneficial effect of a low fat, low calorie diet on myocardial energy metabolism in patients with angina pectoris. Lancet 1:59, 1984.

60. Smith, P. L., Gold, A. R., et al.: Weight loss in mildly to moderately obese patients with obstructive sleep apnea. Ann Intern Med 103:850, 1985.

61. Butler, R. N., Davies, M., et al.: The effect of preloads of amino acid on short term satiety. J Am Diet Assoc 34:2045, 1981.

62. Ashley, D. V. M., Fleury, M., et al.: Evidence for diminished brain 5-hydroxytryptamine biosynthesis in obese diabetic and non-diabetic human. Am J Clin Nutr 42:1240, 1985.

63. Lieberman, H., Wurtman, J. J., and Chew, B.: Changes in mood after carbohydrate consumption among obese individuals. Am J Clin Nutr 44:772, 1986.

64. Lyons, P. M., and Truswell, A. S.: Serotonin precursor influenced by type of carbohydrate meal in healthy adults. Am J Clin Nutr 47:433, 1988.

65. Lean body mass and food-induced thermogenesis in obesity. Nutr Rev 45:264, 1987.

66. Morris, S. S., Farrier, S. C., et al.: Feeding behaviors, food attitudes and body fatness in infants. J Am Diet Assoc 80:330, 1982.

67. Vasselli, J. R., and Maggio, C. A.: Mechanisms of appetite and body-weight regulation. In Frankle, R. T., and Yang, M. U.: Obesity and weight control. Rockville, Md.: Aspen, 1988.

68. Segal, K. R., Edano, A., et al.: Comparison of thermic effects of constant and relative caloric loads in lean and obese men. Am J Clin Nutr 51:14,

1990.

69. Newsholme, E. A.: A possible metabolic basis for the control of body weight. N Engl J Med 302:400, 1980.

70. Cahill, G.: Metabolic memory. N Engl J Med 302:396, 1980.

71. Deluise, M., Blackburn, G. L., and Filer, J. S.: Reduced activity of the red-cell sodium potassium pump in human obesity. N Engl J Med 303:1017, 1980.

72. Bray, G. A., Kral, J., and Bjuorntorp, P.: Hepatic sodium potassium dependent ATPase in obesity. N Engl J Med 304:1580, 1981.

73. Olmstead-Schulz, L.: Brown adipose tissue: Regulation of thermogenesis and implications for obesity. J Am Diet Assoc 87:761, 1987.

74. American Diabetes Association and American Dietetic Association: Exchange lists for weight management. Chicago: American Dietetic Association and American Diabetes Association, 1989.

75. Lissner, L., Levitsky, D. A., et al.: Dietary fat and the regulation of energy intake in human subjects. Am J Clin Nutr 46:886, 1987.

76. Xavier Pi-Sunyer, F.: Obesity. In Shils, M. E., and Young, V. R.: Modern nutrition in health and disease. 7th ed. Philadelphia: Lea & Febiger, 1988.

77. Klesges, R. C., Eck, L. H., et al.: Smoking status: Effects on the dietary intake, physical activity, and body fat of adult men. Am J Clin Nutr 51:784, 1990.

78. Kromhout, D., Saris, W. H. M., and Horst, C. H.: Energy intake, energy expenditure, and smoking in relation to body fatness: The Zutphen study. Am J Clin Nutr 47:668, 1988.

79. Nauss-Karol, C., and Sullivan, A. C.: Pharmacological approaches to the treatment of obesity. In Frankle, R. T., and Yang, M. U.: Obesity and weight control. Rockville, Md.: Aspen, 1988.

80. Bracco, E. F., Baba, N., and Hashim, S. A.: Polysiloxane: Potential non-caloric fat substitute; effects on body composition of obese Zucker rats. Am

J Clin Nutr 46:784, 1987.

81. Callaway, W.: Obesity: A "culture bound" syndrome. Mayo Clin Proc 57:327, 1982.

82. Owen, G. M., and Paige, D. M.: Obesity in infants and children. Clin Nutr 1:9, 1982.

83. Rolland-Cachera, M. F., Sempe, M., et al.: Adiposity indices in children. Am J Clin Nutr 36:178, 1982.

84. Egan, B. M., Schork, J., and Weder, A. B.: Regional hemodynamic abnormalities in overweight men—focus on alpha adrenergic vascular responses. Am J Hypertens 2:428, 1989.

85. Felber, A., Golay, A., et al.: The metabolic consequences of long term human obesity. Int J Obesity 12:377, 1988.

86. Bjorntorp, P.: Hypertension and other complications of human obesity. J Clin Hypertens 2:163, 1986.

87. Den Besten, C., Vansant, G., et al.: Resting metabolic rate and diet induced thermogenesis in abdominal and gluteal-femoral obese women before and after weight reduction. Am J Clin Nutr 47:840, 1988.

88. Evans, D. J., Barth, J. H., and Burke, C. W.: Body fat topography in women with androgen excess. Int J Obesity 12:157, 1988.

89. Messerli, F. H.: Overweight and sudden death—increased ventricular ectopy in cardiopathy of obesity. Arch Intern Med 147:1725, 1987.

90. Despres, J. P., Tremblay, A., et al.: Abdominal adipose tissue and serum HDL-cholesterol association independent from obesity and serum triglyceride concentration. Int J Obesity 12:1, 1988.

91. Palla, B., and Litt, I. F.: Medical complications of eating disorders in adolescents. Pediatrics 81:613, 1985.

92. Morgan, S. L.: Rational weight loss programs: A clinician's guide. J Am Coll Nutr 8:186, 1989.

93. Hager, A.: Nutritional problems in adolescence—obesity. Nutr Rev 39:89, 1981.

94. Dietz, W.: Childhood and adolescent obesity. In Frankle, R. T., and Yang,

M. U.: Obesity and weight control. Rockville, Md.: Aspen, 1988.

95. Subcommittee on Nutritional Status and Weight Gain during Pregnancy, Institute of Medicine, National Academy of Sciences: Nutrition during pregnancy. Part I. Weight gain. Washington, D.C.: National Academy Press, 1990.

96. Green, J. A., and Holler, H. J.: Meal planning approaches in the nutrition management of the person with diabetes. Chicago: American Dietetic Association, 1987.

97. Grommet, J. K.: Assessment of the obese person. In Frankle, R. T., and Yang, M. U.: Obesity and weight control. Rockville, Md.: Aspen, 1988.

98. Wack, J. T., and Rodin, J.: Smoking and its effects on body weight and the systems of caloric regulation. Am J Clin Nutr 35:366, 1982.

99. Acheson, K. J., Campbell, I. T., et al.: The measurement of food and energy intake in man—an evaluation of some techniques. Am J Clin Nutr 33:1147, 1980.

100. Lansky, D., and Brownell, K. O.: Estimates of food quantity and calories: Errors in self-reporting among obese patients. Am J Clin Nutr 35:727, 1982.

101. Blake, A. T., Guthrie, H. A., and Smicklas-Wright, H.: Accuracy of food portion estimation by overweight and normal-weight subjects. J Am Diet Assoc 89:962, 1990.

102. VanHorn, L. V., Gernhofer, N., et al.: Dietary assessment in children using electronic methods: telephones and tape recorders. J Am Diet Assoc 90:412, 1990.

103. Larkin, F., Metzner, H. L., et al.: Comparison of estimated nutrient intakes by food frequency and dietary records in adults. J Am Diet Assoc 90:215, 1990.

104. Katch, V. L., and Freedson, P. S.: Body size and shape: Derivation of the "Hat" frame size model. Am J Clin Nutr 36:669, 1982.

105. Frisancho, A. R., and Flegel, P. N.: Elbow breadth as a measure of frame size for U.S. males and females. Am

J Clin Nutr 37:311, 1983.

106. Garm, S. M., Pesick, S. D., and Hawthorne, V. M.: The bony chest breadth as a frame size standard in nutritional assessment. Am J Clin Nutr 37:315, 1983.

107. Himes, J. H., and Bouchard, C.: Do the new Metropolitan Life Insurance weight-height tables correctly assess the body frame size and body fat relationships? Am J Public Health 75:1076, 1985.

108. Novasconem, M. A., and Smith, E. P.: Frame size estimation: A comparative analysis of methods based on height, wrist circumference, and elbow breadth. J Am Diet Assoc 89:964, 1989.

109. Butler, M. G., Butler, R. L., and Meaney, F. J.: The use of skinfold measurements to judge obesity during the early phase of Prader-Labhart-Willi syndrome. Int J Obesity 12:417, 1988.

110. Owen, O. E., Holup, J. L., et al.: A reappraisal of the caloric requirements of men. Am J Clin Nutr 46:875, 1987.

111. Forves, G. B., and Brown, M. R.: Energy need for weight maintenance in human beings: Effect of body size and composition. J Am Diet Assoc 89:499, 1989.

112. Staats, B. A., Gastineau, G. F., and Offord, K. P.: Predictive equations for basal energy requirement derived from the data of Boothby, Berkson, and Dunn. Mayo Clin Proc 63:409, 1988.

113. Scalfi, L., Laviano, A., et al.: Albumin and labile-protein serum concentrations during very low calorie diets with different compositions. Am J Clin Nutr 51:338, 1990.

114. Kral, J.: Surgery for obesity. In Frankle, R. T., and Yang, M. U.: Obesity and weight control. Rockville, Md.: Aspen, 1988.

115. Booylan, L. M., Sugarman, H. J., and Diskell, J. A.: Vitamin E, vitamin B-6, vitamin B-12 and folate status of gastric bypass surgery patients. J Am Diet Assoc 88:579, 1988.

116. Andersen, T., and Larsen, U.: Dietary outcome in obese patients treated with a gastroplasty program. Am J Clin Nutr 50:1328, 1990.

117. Landin, K., Lindgarde, F., et al.: Decreased skeletal muscle potassium in obesity. Acta Med Scand 223:507, 1988.

118. Calesnick, B.: Nonprescription anorexiants. Am Fam Physician 26:206, 1982.

119. Friedman, R. B., Kindy, P., and Reinke, J.: What to tell patients about weight loss. 2. Drugs. Postgrad Med 72:85, 1982.

120. Powers, D. E., and Moore, A. O.: Food/medication interactions. 6th ed. Phoenix: 1988 (self-published).

121. Wurtman, J., Wurtman, R., et al.: D-Fenfluramine selectively suppresses carbohydrate snacking by obese subjects. Int J Eating Dis 4:89, 1984.

122. Wurtman, J., Wurtman, R., et al.: Fenfluramine suppresses snack intake among carbohydrate cravers but not among noncarbohydrate cravers. Int J Eating Dis 6:687, 1987.

123. Brun, L. D., Bielmann, P., et al.: Effects of fenfluramine in hypertriglyceridemic obese subjects. Int J Obesity 12:423, 1988.

124. Knoben, J. E., and Anderson, P. O.: Handbook of clinical drug data. 6th ed. Hamilton, Ill.: Drug Intelligence Publications, 1988.

125. Hollands, M. A., Arch, J. R. S., et al.: A simple apparatus for comparative measurements of energy expenditure in human subjects: The thermic effect of caffeine. Am J Clin Nutr 34:2291, 1981.

126. Acheson, K. J., Zahorska-Markiewicz, B., et al.: Caffeine and coffee: Their influence on metabolic rate and substrate utilization in normal weight and obese individuals. Am J Clin Nutr 33:989, 1980.

127. Pentel, P. R., and Eisen, T.: Effects of phenylpropanolamine and isometric exercise on blood pressure. Int J Obesity 12:199, 1988.

128. Bale, J. F., Fountain, M. T., and Shaddy, R.: Phenylpropanolamine associated CNS complications in children and adolescents. Am J Dis Child 138:683, 1985.

129. Forman, H. P., Levin, S., et al.: Cerebral vasculitis and hemorrhage in an adolescent taking diet pills containing phenylpropanolamine: Case report and review of the literature. Pediatrics 83:737, 1989.

130. Weiner, N.: Norepinephrine, epinephrine and the sympathomimetic amines. In Gilman, A. G., Goodman, L. S., and Rall, T. W.: The pharmacological basis of therapeutics. 6th ed. New York: Macmillan, 1985.

131. Dulloo, A. G., and Miller, D. S.: Aspirin as a promoter of ephedrine induced thermogenesis: Potential use in the treatment of obesity. Am J Clin Nutr 45:564, 1987.

132. Chapman, B. J., Farquahar, D. L., et al.: The effects of a new beta-adrenoceptor agonist BRL 26830 A in refractory obesity. Int J Obesity 12:119, 1988.

133. Rodin, J.: Comparative effects of fructose, aspartame, glucose and water preloads on calorie and macronutrient intake. Am J Clin Nutr 51:428, 1990.

134. Calorie labeling. Cons Register 8 (21):1, 1978.

135. Laquatra, I., and Danish, S. J.: A primer for nutritional counseling. In Frankle, R. T., and Yang, M. U.: Obesity and weight control. Rockville, Md.: Aspen, 1988.

136. Contento, I. R., and Maksymowicz-Murphy, B.: Psycho-social factors differentiating people who reported making desirable changes in their diets from those who did not. J Nutr Education 22:6, 1990.

137. Achterberg, C.: Factors that influence learner readiness. J Am Diet Assoc 88:1426, 1988.

138. Moore, S. A., Marlow, R., and Merrell, A. N.: Comparing effects of two types of weight-control counseling on motivation and weight loss. J Am Diet Assoc 88:60, 1988.

139. Gardner, F. S.: Patient education for weight loss: Comparing strategies. J Am Diet Assoc 80:432, 1982.

140. Holli, B. B.: Using behavior modi-

fication in nutritional counseling. J Am Diet Assoc 88:1530, 1988.

141. Rock, C. R., and Coulston, A. M.: Weight control approaches: A review by the California Dietetic Association. J Am Diet Assoc 88:44, 1988.

142. Beneke, W. M., Davis, C. H., and Vandertuig, J. G.: Effects of a weight-loss program on food purchases: Instructions to shop with a list. Int J Obesity 12:335, 1988.

143. Fatis, M., Weiner, A., et al.: Follow-ing up on a commercial weight loss program: Do the pounds stay off after your picture has been in the newspaper? J Am Diet Assoc 89:547, 1989.

144. Bukoff, M., and Carlson, S.: Diet modifications and behavioral changes for bariatric gastric surgery. J Am Diet Assoc 78:158, 1981.

145. Frankle, R. T.: Weight control for the adult and the elderly. In Frankle, R. T., and Yang, M. U.: Obesity and weight control. Rockville, Md.: Aspen, 1988.

146. Food and Nutrition Board, National Research Council: Recommended Dietary Allowances. 10th ed. Washington, D.C.: National Academy of Sciences, 1989.

147. Morton, C. J.: Weight loss maintenance in relapse prevention. In Frankle, R. T., and Yang, M. U.: Obesity and weight control. Rockville, Md.: Aspen, 1988.

30.

POSITION OF THE AMERICAN DIETETIC ASSOCIATION: VERY LOW-CALORIE WEIGHT-LOSS DIETS, 1989

A very low-calorie weight-loss diet (VLCD) can produce large and rapid weight loss. Current VLCDs are safe when administered appropriately; however, dieters must be adequately warned of the limitations and risks involved with the VLCD and understand that it is no magic cure. Careful monitoring by a physician and a registered dietitian is essential.

Diets that severely limit calories to the range of 400 to 800 kcal/day became popular in the early 1970s and, with major changes in composition, are in continued use today. The current diets contain relatively large amounts of protein while limiting fat and carbohydrate and are supplemented to meet Recommended Dietary Allowances (RDAS) for vitamins, minerals, and electrolytes. They may be in the form of special formulas or conventional foods. These diets—usually

Approved by the House of Delegates on October 21, 1989, to be in effect until December 31, 1994, unless it is reaffirmed or withdrawn as directed in the position development procedures of the House of Delegates. The American Dietetic Association authorizes republication of this position, in its entirety, provided full and proper credit is given.

Recognition is given to the following for their contributions. Organization unit: Diabetes Care and Education. Author: Barbara K. Paulsen, M.S., R.D.; Reviewers: Anne Coulston, M.S., R.D.; Dawn C. Laine, M.P.H., R.D.; Carol Lang, R.D.; Myrlene Staten, R.D., M.D.

referred to as very low-calorie diets, or VLCDS—do promote a large and rapid weight loss, which may be lifesaving for individuals 100 lbs. or more overweight, but they also carry some risks (1).

Position

It is the position of the American Dietetic Association that while very low-calorie diets promote rapid weight loss and may be beneficial for certain individuals, such diets have health risks and should be undertaken only with the supervision of a multidisciplinary health team with monitoring by a physician and nutrition counseling by a registered dietitian.

The obese person is at increased risk for a number of health problems, including cardiovascular disease, hypertension, non-insulin-dependent diabetes mellitus (NIDDM, or Type II diabetes), gallbladder disease, and possibly some types of cancer (1–3). Bone and joint problems, pulmonary difficulties, and increased surgical risk are also more likely to occur in the obese. One study (2), in investigating mortality rates of severely obese men, showed all age categories to have a higher mortality rate than the normal U.S. population. The younger the man, the higher the mortality rate, with the highest mortality in men aged 25 to 34 years. The rate of mortality relates to the degree of obesity as well as to age. Rapid weight loss is most urgent for the obese person with serious health problems such as diabetes, hypertension, or sleep apnea (4) or those requiring surgery.

HISTORICAL PERSPECTIVE

In the late 1950s and early 1960s, total starvation was evaluated as a method of weight reduction for the massively obese. The advantages of this method were the rapid weight loss and the relative ease with which the dieter could maintain the fast once initiated. However, because the total fasts resulted in large protein and potassium losses (5, 6) and some deaths (4, 7), additional studies on semistarvation were conducted, in which researchers observed that administering even small amounts of protein during the fast dramatically reduced the protein and potassium losses observed earlier (7, 8). This observation led to the development of the protein-modified fast, or very low-calorie weight-loss diet (VLCD).

The first commercial venture with the VLCD marketed by several companies was the liquid-protein-modified-fast formula, which was popular in 1976 and 1977. The recommended formulas often did not include any type of vitamin, mineral, or electrolyte supplementation and contained 300 to 400 kcal, primarily from collagen hydrolysate, an incomplete protein low in biologic value. More than 100,000 individuals used these products, and by the end of 1977, a total of 60 deaths attributable to this diet had been reported to the Centers for Disease Control (9). In 17 of the cases, there was no underlying health problem, and sufficient evidence was available to implicate the diet as the basis for the cardiac arrhythmias that led to death (10). Examination of the data available about these 17 individuals provided valuable information. A positive relationship was observed between pre-diet body mass index (or amount of obesity) and survival on the diet (11). Those with the highest percentage of body fat survived the longest, presumably because they were better able to conserve body protein, especially myocardial muscle.

Drastic reduction in caloric intake at the onset of the VLCD resulted in marked diuresis and sodium loss (12). Without supplementation, the balance of a number of electrolytes and minerals—including sodium, potassium, calcium, magnesium, and zinc—became negative (12). Potassium is the primary electrolyte associated with cardiac arrhythmias (13), although a number of other minerals, such as sodium, calcium, magnesium, phosphorus, iron, zinc, and copper, are known to affect cardiac function (12). A common feature among 9 of the 17 deaths related to the liquid-protein-modified-fast was an alteration in the electrocardiogram (11). The cause of these alterations was related to a number of interacting factors, and the complete etiology is not known. However, undesirable changes in a patient's electrocardiogram should be viewed as a danger signal (14). The deaths attributable to the early VLCDs and the information learned from them prompted the medical community to recommend continued research and only carefully controlled clinical use of the VLCD (9, 15).

CURRENT PERSPECTIVE

The VLCDs in use today are very different from those used in the late 1970s. These dietary regimens contain complete proteins of high biologic value, with recommended intake levels at 50 to 100 g/day (16, 17). Some programs provide a set amount of protein based on sex: 55 g for women and 75 g for men (17). Others provide a protein intake based on kilograms of ideal body weight, usually 1.5

g/kg ideal body weight per day (18). There is no absolute guide because protein needs appear to vary considerably among individuals on a VLCD (16, 19–21).

The dietary regimen may be a semisynthetic preparation or consist of real foods. Most of the current VLCD programs use a product in powder form with protein from an egg or milk base. These are mixed with water before use. Supplementation with vitamins, minerals, and electrolytes up to 100% of the RDAs is recommended (16, 22, 23).

The diets usually also contain some carbohydrate. Considerable research has been done to evaluate the precise combination of protein, carbohydrate, and total calories needed to minimize protein tissue loss during a VLCD; however, the ideal combination is not known at this time. Currently, the carbohydrate level in the VLCDs on the market ranges from 30 to 45 g/day, although some may contain higher levels. The addition of carbohydrate at this level has been shown to lessen sodium losses and decrease the incidence of orthostatic hypotension while having no adverse effect on nitrogen balance (protein tissue loss) (24, 25).

The current VLCDs are safe when administered appropriately. Numerous studies have been conducted to evaluate safety, and under clinical and outpatient conditions the diets have not been found to have any serious adverse effects (8, 19, 26, 27).

BENEFITS OF VLCDS

Weight losses on the VLCD are rapid, especially in the early phases. This initial rapid weight loss, which is due to diuresis and sodium loss, may provide psychological benefits and incentive to proceed. Although weight dependent, weight loss averages 0.78 kg/day during the first week of fasting and falls to about 0.28 kg/day by the third week of the fast (12). Total weight losses during treatment vary, depending on duration of

treatment, sex of the dieter, and compliance (26, 28, 29). Health benefits that may occur include significantly reduced serum total cholesterol and triglycerides (16, 27, 30), improved glucose tolerance, and, in persons with NIDDM, lowered plasma glucose levels (19, 27, 30). Other benefits are lowered blood pressure in persons with hypertension, improved breathing in those with pulmonary problems, and diminished surgical risk for those needing surgery (1, 2, 8, 16, 26, 27, 30, 31).

RISKS OF VLCDS

Body protein and potassium losses resulting from a VLCD are of major concern. Such losses are lower with the VLCD than with total fasting, and the extent of the losses varies among individuals (12, 16, 20, 21). Adequate supplementation with sodium, potassium, and the RDA for major and trace minerals is essential for maintenance of health and normal physiologic function during the diet (22). Weight-loss-associated protein and potassium losses are higher in men than in women and are related to the amount of initial body weight and lean tissue (12). The ratio of nitrogen (body protein) loss to total weight loss is inversely related to body fat content. Thus, the more obese person loses relatively less body protein than the less obese person—approximately 20 g/kg weight loss in the nonobese and 10 g/kg weight loss in those overweight by 50 kg or more (32, 33).

Other less serious side effects that have been noted in association with the VLCD are cold intolerance, fatigue, lightheadedness, nervousness, euphoria, constipation or diarrhea, dry skin, thinning reddened hair, anemia, and menstrual irregularities (31, 34).

LONG-TERM RESULTS

High dropout rates and poor long-term maintenance are discouraging aspects of

VLCDs. In one study (28), 55% of the dieters starting the program did not complete the VLCD phase of the program. For those who did complete the program, much of the weight lost was regained. Other studies have shown equally discouraging completion rates and long-term weight maintenance (30, 34, 35). The use of other treatment modalities in conjunction with the VLCD, such as nutrition counseling, increased exercise, relaxation techniques, and behavior modification, offers hope for better weight loss maintenance (35–37) and produces a comprehensive treatment program.

CRITERIA FOR SELECTING AN APPROPRIATE TREATMENT POPULATION

Because of the potentially life-threatening nature of some of the side effects of the VLCD, candidates should be carefully selected for this regimen. Screening should include evaluations by several members of the health care team: physician, registered dietitian, and behavior therapist. Factors to evaluate include medical necessity, degree of overweight, overall health status, psychological status, initial nutritional status, projected length of time on the VLCD, repeated failure with previous attempts at weight loss, compliance with previous programs, and ability to understand and comply with the diet regimen.

Potential users of a VLCD need to see the diet as one component of a comprehensive weight management program. The VLCD plays an important role in actual weight loss. The other components of the program, i.e., nutrition counseling, exercise, and behavior therapy, are equally important aspects and are critical to the long-term success of the program. Potential dieters need to be adequately informed about the time and effort they will need to expend to be successful in such a program. Success on a VLCD and maintenance of weight loss has been shown to relate to the dieter's ability to

complete weight loss and maintenance training regimens (26, 28, 36).

One of the prime considerations in determining who should use a VLCD is the degree of obesity of the dieter. Experience with the VLCDs in the 1970s demonstrated an increased danger of cardiac problems in lighter individuals (11). Research examining body protein losses has shown a higher rate of body protein loss in lighter individuals as well (32, 33). Because of these factors, the VLCD should only be used with dieters who are at least 30% to 40% overweight (18, 34, 38). Van Itallie recommends a body mass index (BMI = weight in kg/[height in m]^2) of 32 or higher (39).

Overall health status may influence the advisability of a VLCD. VLCDs should not be undertaken by infants, children, adolescents, pregnant or lactating women, elderly persons, or persons with any of the following conditions: cardiac failure or myocardial infarction within the past 6 months, active cancer, hepatic disease, renal failure, or severe psychological disturbances (7, 18, 34). A VLCD program requires a high level of patient involvement over an extended period. Severe psychological problems, in particular those requiring drug therapy, may hinder the dieter's ability to follow guidelines and complete the program and may be a reason for exclusion from a VLCD program (16, 26, 34, 35). The list below presents some guidelines that can be used to determine contraindications for use of the VLCD.

1. Absolute contraindications
   A. Malignant arrhythmias
   B. Unstable angina
   C. Protein wasting diseases (e.g., lupus, Cushing's syndrome)
   D. Major system failure (e.g., liver failure, renal failure)
   E. Drug therapy causing protein wasting (steroids, antineoplastic agents)
   F. Body weight less than 20% over "desirable" (body mass index—

weight in kg/[height in m]^2—less than 25)
   G. Pregnancy or lactation
2. Relative contraindications
   A. Congestive heart failure
   B. Drug therapy with potassium wasting diuretics, adrenergic stimulating agents
   C. History of failure of compliance with medical regimens
   D. Body weight less than 30% over "desirable" (body mass index less than 30)
   E. Substance abuse
3. Cautions
   A. Angina or history of heart disease
   B. Presence of systemic disease
   C. History of psychiatric or emotional disorder
   D. Chronic drug therapy (insulin, oral hypoglycemics, anti-inflammatory agents, psychotropic agents, etc.)

Source: Adapted from Atkinson, R. (40).

Individuals vary in the amount of body protein loss they experience while on a VLCD. It is difficult to determine which dieters on a VLCD may continue to lose body protein over an extended period. To reduce the risk of adverse complications related to body protein losses, in particular cardiac problems, total time on the VLCD should be monitored. Researchers and physicians experienced in the use of VLCDs recommend that the time on a VLCD be limited to 12 to 16 weeks (12, 34, 38). As individuals continue on a VLCD and lose more and more body fat, their ability to conserve body protein is compromised. For this reason, dieters on a VLCD the full 12 to 16 weeks should probably increase their caloric intake as they lose large amounts of weight (38, 39).

DIET PROTOCOL

Eating pattern guidelines should be included before and after the reduced-calorie diet period as well as during the VLCD period for reasons of safety and practicality.

The VLCD should be preceded by 2 to 4 weeks on a well-balanced 1,200-kcal diet, which allows time for the body to adjust to the caloric deprivation and promotes a gradual diuresis instead of the rapid sodium and water loss seen with abrupt introduction of the VLCD (16, 34). The pre-VLCD period also provides the health care team administering the program a chance to evaluate the dieter's ability to adhere to program guidelines, which may have particular relevance to the maintenance of weight loss following the VLCD.

The VLCD should be followed by a gradual refeeding period of 2 to 4 weeks. Foods need to be reintroduced slowly. Simple sugars need to be added to the diet gradually to prevent a rapid fluid weight gain (16, 34). Dieters should continue some type of follow-up or maintenance program. Research has shown that completion of a maintenance training program significantly improves maintenance of weight loss (26, 36, 37). The length of the maintenance program will vary from individual to individual. Therefore, maintenance training should be considered completed only when the dieter can demonstrate specific behaviors, such as a voluntary restriction of eating, particularly during stress, a return to a normal eating pattern, and a sense of well-being (36). Most dieters will need some type of maintenance support for at least 12 months. Some dieters may need ongoing support even after the maintenance program has ended.

MONITORING BY THE HEALTH CARE TEAM

Because of the serious risks associated with the VLCD, supervision by a qualified health care team is essential. Most dieters can be monitored on an outpatient

basis (29), but individuals with diabetes who are taking insulin may need to be hospitalized initially until their exogenous insulin dosages are reduced or eliminated (34).

Medical monitoring should be done by a physician experienced in the use of a VLCD and trained in clinical nutrition, especially in such areas as body composition, cardiac function during severe caloric restriction, and lipid and energy metabolism (38). Monitoring should include a complete blood chemistry workup, in particular a profile of electrolyte levels, and a physical examination done initially and every 1 to 2 weeks while on the VLCD. An electrocardiogram (ECG) should be ordered initially to establish a baseline and repeated at approximately 4-week intervals or after each 12-kg weight loss (34) while the dieter is on the VLCD to identify any early changes in cardiac function. Patient complaints of palpitations or heart flutters also necessitate an ECG (30).

The amount and composition of weight lost should be closely monitored throughout the program to help assess body protein losses. Periodic anthropometric measurements can help in this area. Nutrition counseling by a registered dietitian is important throughout the program and is of particular importance for guidance on refeeding and the establishment of healthy eating habits that will enable the dieter to maintain the weight loss achieved. Individual or group sessions should be held weekly to provide assistance to the dieter on food choices, menu planning, grocery shopping, eating on special occasions, and nutrition education (41). These skills are essential if the dieter is to have long-term success, i.e., to maintain the new weight.

The effectiveness of behavioral techniques in conjunction with moderate dietary restrictions is well documented (42–44). The inclusion of a behavior

modification component in conjunction with the VLCD appears to significantly improve maintenance of weight lost. In a study of 17 dieters using behavior modification with the VLCD, those who received behavioral training over a 6-month period had regained only 2.1 kg of their original loss at 1-year follow-up (37). A larger study with 59 subjects (36) also reported significantly better maintenance of weight loss in the group that received behavioral training.

A study of 400 dieters using a VLCD and behavior modification gave mixed results (28). Patients who completed treatment lost a mean of 83.9% of excess weight but regained an average of 59% to 82% of the initial excess weight by 30 months posttreatment. This study did show, however, that weight maintenance was best for dieters who completed treatment, who did not have to repeat treatment, and who weighed less at the onset of treatment.

It is important to note that these behavioral programs were developed and administered by individuals highly trained in the use of behavioral techniques. The effectiveness of these techniques could be very different if administered by untrained individuals; therefore, ongoing training of patient educators is essential.

Adding an exercise component to a VLCD program has been hypothesized to provide a number of beneficial effects. Studies of the impact of aerobic exercise in conjunction with a VLCD have not shown any difference in weight loss as a result of adding exercise (45–48). However, exercise has been shown to have an effect on the composition of the weight loss, with an increased percentage of the lost weight being fat in the exercising group (48, 49).

It has also been demonstrated in a number of studies (47–51) that persons on a VLCD can successfully participate in aerobic exercise such as brisk walking. The composition of the VLCD may have an effect on endurance during exercise.

Studies indicate that patients on a diet without carbohydrate supplementation have reduced endurance (51). However, patients on these diets do adapt and are able to maintain a normal blood glucose level (50, 51).

An additional benefit of exercise was demonstrated in a study of the long-term effects of exercise in a VLCD program utilizing behavior modification (45). At 2-year follow-up, the group that participated in an aerobic exercise program had significantly better weight maintenance than the non-exercise group. When to initiate an exercise component within a VLCD program is a matter best determined by the practitioner on a case-by-case basis.

Potential dieters should evaluate carefully the program and personnel for any VLCD they plan to use. The program should include medical monitoring by a physician with experience in this form of treatment, a nutrition counseling component conducted by a registered dietitian, a behavioral component taught by a person specifically trained in the use of behavioral techniques for weight loss, and participation by an exercise physiologist in the development and monitoring of an exercise component.

SUMMARY

It has been well documented that a VLCD can produce large and rapid weight loss. A number of studies using appropriate levels of high biologic value protein, vitamin and mineral supplementation, and careful monitoring have shown that the VLCD can be safe (17–19, 26, 36). Careful monitoring by a physician experienced in such programs and by a registered dietitian is essential. The maintenance of weight loss must be of key importance throughout the program, necessitating the skills of a multidisciplinary team with medical, nutritional, and behavioral training. It must be recognized that the VLCD is only one part of a total weight management program. The complete program is needed for long-term success. Insurance reimbursement for the services of all members of the health care team, including dietitians, facilitates and supports the multidisciplinary team approach.

Potential candidates for this program and health professionals must realize that VLCDs are not for everyone and can be harmful for persons who do not meet the following selection criteria:

- At least 30% overweight, with a minimum body mass index of 32
- Free from contraindicated medical conditions: pregnancy or lactation, active cancer, hepatic disease, renal failure, active cardiac dysfunction, or severe psychological disturbances
- Committed to establishing new eating and lifestyle behaviors that will assist the maintenance of weight loss
- Committed to taking the time to complete both the treatment and the maintenance components of a program

Dieters must receive careful medical and nutritional monitoring throughout the program and should continue with nutrition, exercise, and behavioral counseling after cessation of the VLCD until sound eating and lifestyle habits can be established. The length of time an individual is on the VLCD must be carefully monitored and the VLCD discontinued immediately if medical tests and/or weight loss indicate increased health risks to the client.

Finally, potential clients must be adequately warned that there are limitations and risks involved with the VLCD. A VLCD is no magic cure. It requires considerable effort and commitment on the part of both practitioners and participants to ensure the program's success.

REFERENCES

1. National Institutes of Health: Health implications of obesity: National Institutes of Health Consensus Development Conference Statement. Ann Intern Med 103:1073, 1985.
2. Bray, G. A.: Effects of obesity on health and happiness. In Brownell, K. D., and Foreyt, J. P.: Handbook of eating disorders. New York: Basic Books, 1986.
3. U.S. Department of Health and Human Services: The Surgeon General's Report on Nutrition and Health—Summary and Recommendations. DHHS Publication no. (PHS) 88-50210. Washington, D.C.: U.S. Government Printing Office, 1988.
4. Atkinson, R. L.: Issues and opinions in nutrition. J Nutr 116:918, 1986.
5. Drenick, E. J., Swendseid, M. E., et al.: Prolonged starvation as treatment for severe obesity. JAMA 187:140, 1964.
6. Scheck, J., Spencer, H., et al.: Mineral and protein losses during starvation. J Am Diet Assoc 49:211, 1966.
7. Apfelbaum, M., Fricker, J., and Igoin-Apfelbaum, L.: Low- and very-low-calorie diets. Am J Clin Nutr 45 (Supp):1126, 1987.
8. Genuth, S. M., Castro, J., and Vertes, V.: Weight reduction in obesity by outpatient semistarvation. JAMA 230:987, 1974.
9. Felig, P.: Editorial retrospective: Very-low-calorie protein diets. N Engl J Med 310:589, 1984.
10. Isner, J. M., Sours, H. E., et al.: Sudden, unexpected death in avid dieters using the liquid-protein-modified-fast diet. Circulation 60:1401, 1979.
11. Van Itallie, T. B., and Yang, M.: Cardiac dysfunction in obese dieters: A potentially lethal complication of rapid, massive weight loss. Am J Clin Nutr 39:695, 1984.
12. Fisler, J. S., and Drenick, E. J.: Starvation and semistarvation diets in the management of obesity: Ann Rev Nutr 7:465, 1987.
13. Fisch, C.: Relation of electrolyte disturbances to cardiac arrhythmias. Circulation 47:408, 1973.
14. Sours, H. E., Frattali, V. P., et al.: Sudden death associated with very low calorie weight reduction regimens. Am J Clin Nutr 34:453, 1981.
15. Lantigua, R. A., Amatruda, J. M., et al.: Cardiac arrhythmias associated with a liquid protein diet for the treatment of obesity. N Engl J Med 303:735, 1980.
16. Wadden, T. A., Stunkard, A. J., and Brownell, K. D.: Very low calorie diets: Their efficacy, safety, and future. Ann Intern Med 99:675, 1983.
17. Apfelbaum, M.: Effects of very restrictive high-protein diets with special reference to the nitrogen balance. Int J Obesity 5:209, 1981.
18. Bistrian, B. R.: Clinical use of a protein-sparing modified fast. JAMA 240:2299, 1978.
19. Henry, R. R., Wiest-Kent, T. A., et al.: Metabolic consequences of very-low-calorie diet therapy in obese non-insulin-dependent diabetic and non-diabetic subjects. Diabetes 35:155, 1986.
20. Yang, M., and Van Itallie, T. B.: Variability in body protein loss during protracted severe caloric restriction: Role of triiodothyronine and other possible determinants. Am J Clin Nutr 40:611, 1984.
21. Fisler, J., Drenick, E., et al.: Nitrogen economy during very low calorie reducing diets: Quality and quantity of dietary protein. Am J Clin Nutr 35:471, 1982.
22. Amatruda, J. M., Biddle, T. L., et al.: Vigorous supplementation of a hypocaloric diet prevents cardiac arrhythmias and mineral depletion. Am J Med 74:1016, 1983.
23. Phinney, S. D., Bistrian, B. R., et al.: Normal cardiac rhythm during hypocaloric diets of varying carbohydrate content. Arch Intern Med 143:2258, 1983.
24. DeHaven, J., Sherwin, R., et al.: Nitrogen and sodium balance and sympathetic-nervous-system activity in obese subjects treated with a low-calorie protein or mixed diet. N Engl J Med 302:477, 1980.
25. Yang, M., Barbosa-Saldivar, J. L., et al.: Metabolic effects of substituting carbohydrate for protein in a low-calorie diet: A prolonged study in obese patients. Int J Obesity 5:231, 1981.
26. Palgi, A., Read, J. L., et al.: Multidisciplinary treatment of obesity with a protein-sparing modified fast: Results in 668 outpatients. Am J Public Health 75:1190, 1985.
27. Amatruda, J. M., Richeson, J. F., et al.: The safety and efficacy of a controlled low-energy ("very-low-calorie") diet in the treatment of non-insulin-dependent diabetes and obesity. Arch Intern Med 148:873, 1988.
28. Hovell, M. F., Koch, A., et al.: Long-term weight loss maintenance: Assessment of a behavioral and supplemented fasting regimen. Am J Public Health 78:663, 1988.
29. Vertes, V., Genuth, S. M., and Hazelton, I. M.: Supplemented fasting as a large-scale outpatient program. JAMA 238:2151, 1977.
30. Kirschner, M. A., Schneider, G., et al.: An eight-year experience with a very-low-calorie formula diet for control of major obesity. Int J Obesity 12:69, 1987.
31. Genuth, S. M., Vertes, V., and Hazelton, J.: Supplemented fasting in the treatment of obesity. In Bray, G.: Recent advances in obesity research: II Proceedings of the Second International Congress on Obesity. London: Newman Publishing, 1977.
32. Forbes, G. B., and Drenick, E. J.: Loss of body nitrogen on fasting. Am J Clin Nutr 32:1570, 1979.
33. Forbes, G. B.: Lean body mass-body fat interrelationships in humans. Nutr Rev 45:225, 1987.
34. Smoller, J. W., Wadden, T. A., and Brownell, K. D.: Popular and very-low-calorie diets in the treatment of obesity. In Frankle, R. T., and Yang, M.: Obesity and weight control. Rockville, Md.: Aspen, 1988.
35. Wadden, T. A., and Stunkard, A. J.: Controlled trial of very low calorie diet, behavior therapy, and their combination in the treatment of obesity. J Consult Clin Psychol 54:482, 1986.
36. Lindner, P. G., and Blackburn, G. L.:

Multidisciplinary approach to obesity utilizing fasting modified by protein-sparing therapy. Obesity/Bariatric Med 5:198, 1976.

37. Wadden, T. A., Stunkard, A. J., et al.: Treatment of obesity by behavior therapy and very low calorie diet: A pilot investigation. J Consult Clin Psychol 52:692, 1984.

38. Wadden, T. A., Van Itallie, T. B., and Blackburn, G. L.: Responsible and irresponsible use of very-low-calorie diets in the treatment of obesity. JAMA 263:83, 1990.

39. Van Itallie, T. B.: Obesity. In Jeejeebhoy, K. N.: Current therapy in nutrition. Burlington, Ontario: B. C. Decker, 1988.

40. Atkinson, R.: Medical management of VLCD in NIDDM. Diabetes Care and Educ Pract Group 9 (Nov.):3, 1988.

41. Waggoner, C. R.: Nutrition management during VLCD and refeeding. Diabetes Care and Educ Pract Group 9 (Nov.):5, 1988.

42. Stuart, R. B.: Behavioral control of overeating. Behav Res Ther 5:357, 1967.

43. Paulsen, B. K., Lutz, R. N., et al.: Behavior therapy for weight control: Long term results of two programs with nutritionists as therapists. Am J Clin Nutr 29:880, 1976.

44. Jeffery, R. W., Wing, R. R., and Stunkard, A. J.: Behavioral treatment of obesity: The state of the art 1976. Behav Ther 6:189, 1978.

45. Sikand, G., Kondo, A., et al.: Two-year follow-up of patients treated with a very-low-calorie diet and exercise training. J Am Diet Assoc 88:487, 1988.

46. Phinney, S. D., LaGrange, B. M., et al.: Effects of aerobic exercise on energy expenditure and nitrogen balance during very low calorie dieting. Metabolism 37:758, 1988.

47. Davis, P.: The role of physical activity in VLCD programs. Diabetes Care and Educ Pract Group 9 (Nov.): 8, 1988.

48. Hill, J. O., Sparling, P. B., et al.: Effects of exercise and food restriction on body composition and metabolic rate in obese women. Am J Clin Nutr 46:622, 1987.

49. Pavlou, K. N., Steffee, W. P., et al.: Effects of dieting and exercise on lean body mass, oxygen uptake, and strength. Med Sci Sports Exercise 17:466, 1985.

50. Phinney, S. D., Horton, E. S., et al.: Capacity for moderate exercise in obese subjects after adaption to a hypocaloric, ketogenic diet. J Clin Invest 66:1152, 1980.

51. Bogardus, C., LaGrange, B. M., et al.: Comparison of carbohydrate-containing and carbohydrate-restricted hypocaloric diets in the treatment of obesity: Endurance and metabolic fuel homeostasis during strenuous exercise. J Clin Invest 68:399, 1981.

31.

POSITION OF THE AMERICAN DIETETIC ASSOCIATION: NUTRITION INTERVENTION IN THE TREATMENT OF ANOREXIA NERVOSA AND BULIMIA NERVOSA, 1987

Anorexia nervosa and bulimia nervosa require a multidisciplinary approach to treatment in order to address the diverse needs of persons with those complex eating disorders. It is essential that nutrition intervention and education be included as part of the team treatment approach to that population.

Position
It is the position of the American Dietetic Association that nutrition intervention and education be integrated into the team treatment of patients with anorexia nervosa and bulimia nervosa during the assessment and treatment phases of outpatient and/or inpatient therapy.

Approved by the House of Delegates on October 18, 1987, to be in effect until October 1992 unless it is reaffirmed or withdrawn as directed in the position development procedures of the House of Delegates. The American Dietetic Association authorizes republication of this position, in its entirety, provided full and proper credit is given.

Recognition is given to the following for their contributions. Organization units: Dietitians in Pediatric Care, and Dietetics in Developmental and Psychiatric Disorders. Authors: Carole DoCouto, M.Ed., R.D., L.D.; Dan Reiff, M.P.H., R.D.; Elaine Stewart, R.D.; and Kim Lampson-Reiff, Ph.D. Reviewers: Joy Armillay, Ed.D., R.D.; Lisa Beckley, R.D.; Barbara R. Dale, R.D.; Diane M. Huse, R.D.; Lynn Magnuson, R.D.; Mary Taylor Montgomery, R.D.; and Philip Olverd, R.D.

Concerns about the most effective treatment modalities for patients with anorexia nervosa and/or bulimia nervosa continue to be explored. A multidisciplinary approach appears to be most effective because it provides a pool of expert knowledge, a supportive treatment network, shared responsibility for patient treatment, and a model of collaborative relationships for patients. The registered dietitian (R.D.) or other qualified nutrition professional is a key member of the team who can provide expertise in nutrition intervention and education.

Nutrition intervention focuses on helping patients understand how the psychological and medical aspects relate to their food and weight behaviors and should be seen as part of the team treatment goals. Nutrition intervention involves establishing an alliance with patients concerning their food fears and eating behaviors, followed by gradual implementation of change. Involving the patient's family members in the process enhances their understanding of the eating disorder and increases their support for the treatment.

Outpatient nutrition intervention involves a long-term collaborative relationship with patients and their therapists in the management and resolution of food behaviors and body image. It involves planning food and behavior strategies that include self-care and self-monitoring as ways for patients to gain a greater sense of control in their lives. Nutrition education helps the patient understand how behavior is altered by restricted intake, provides individualized information on nutrient needs for growth and weight control, and helps the patient make appropriate food choices.

Although most anorectic and bulimic patients respond well to outpatient treatment, there are some for whom hospitalization is necessary. The decision to hospitalize a patient for treatment of an eating disorder is predicated on team findings of medical and/or psychiatric crises. When a hospitalized patient is treated, nutrition intervention is usually required before psychotherapy can be effective. The nutrition care plan should clearly define the method and rate of nutritional rehabilitation and weight restoration and identify methods for decreasing purging behaviors. Setting limits on exercise eliminates the potential to abuse exercise as a form of purging, helps in weight restoration, and balances caloric intake within the context of healthful energy expenditures. Nutrition repletion methods, such as nasogastric tube feeding and peripheral intravenous feeding, carry increased medical and psychological risks. Use of such methods should be limited to stabilizing the health status of medically precarious patients.

The development of an eating disorder is often based on a distorted body image and may include the use of unsafe rigid diets, unproven diet products, and arbitrary weight standards. The R.D. or other qualified nutrition professional should identify and inform the professional and lay public about dangerous diets and diet products and educate the public about healthy weight ranges and weight stabilization methods. Such interventions may play a significant part in the prevention and treatment of eating disorders.

POSITION OF THE AMERICAN DIETETIC ASSOCIATION: NUTRITION INTERVENTION IN THE TREATMENT OF ANOREXIA NERVOSA AND BULIMIA NERVOSA—TECHNICAL SUPPORT PAPER

The diagnostic criteria for anorexia nervosa and bulimia nervosa are based on one or more of the following nutrition-related problems: dramatic weight loss, distorted body image, preoccupation with food and weight gain, chaotic eating patterns, and purging behavior (1). It is essential that issues concerning food intake patterns, food behaviors, body image and weight regulation be addressed to facilitate recovery (2). Research regarding the most effective treatment modalities for patients with anorexia nervosa and bulimia nervosa continue to be explored in the literature. One of the most consistent recommendations is a team treatment model that offers individualized care to this complex population.

It is the position of the American Dietetic Association that nutrition intervention and education be integrated into the team treatment of patients with anorexia nervosa and bulimia nervosa during the assessment and treatment phases of outpatient and/or inpatient therapy.

Because of the complex etiology of eating disorders, a multidisciplinary approach appears to be the most effective method of treating patients with anorexia nervosa and bulimia nervosa. This approach provides a sound basis for differential diagnosis and treatment plan-

ning (1–4). The advantages of the team treatment method include pooled knowledge, team support, and shared responsibility for patient care and a model of collaborative relationships for the patient. The challenges of the treatment method are to maintain open lines of communication, avoid replication of family dynamics, recognize individual team members' strengths and limitations, and avoid power struggles that limit collaborative treatment.

It is important that the team be identified as a cohesive treatment network with a consistent approach (2, 5–7). The R.D. or other qualified nutrition professional is a key member of the treatment team, which ideally will include trained professionals to address the medical, psychiatric, dental, psychological, and nutritional needs of the patient (3, 4, 8).

Weight modification and/or control of bulimic behaviors are important but are not the only objectives of treatment. Nutrition intervention should involve the psychological and nutritional aspects of eating disorders throughout the recovery process. Maintaining a focus on team treatment goals rather than on one aspect of care helps patients understand how the psychological and medical concerns relate to their food and weight behaviors.

Nutrition intervention involves forming a therapeutic alliance with patients that will enable them to resolve their food fears and develop realistic goals for weight and behavior change. The initial nutrition interview and history can be a therapeutic experience, because it allows the patient to discuss secretive behaviors and food fears openly with someone who is a supportive and understanding health care provider. The interview should be performed in a nonjudgmental manner to help establish trust and collaboration with the patient (8–10).

Nutritional assessment of this heterogeneous population should include a comprehensive history of weight changes, eating and exercise patterns,

and purging behaviors. A detailed history helps the R.D. or other qualified nutrition professional quantify behaviors and nutrient intake patterns, identify the impact of behavior on patient lifestyle, and direct treatment plans and goals (5, 6, 8, 9).

The treatment team may direct patients to supportive self-help groups, psychotherapy, medical, and/or psychopharmacological interventions during the initial stages of treatment. After developing a relationship with the therapist, a patient may be able to tolerate the lengthy and variable process of nutrition change. A patient's ability to make changes in food intake, weight, and behaviors may decrease substantially when emotionally painful issues surface during the course of therapy. If the nutrition professional has been identified as supportive during the assessment phase, then a patient can feel comfortable about leaving and reentering nutrition therapy, a process that may be influenced by therapy progress and medical needs.

Eating behaviors are influenced by the social context in which they occur (11). Involving family members in the recovery process will increase their understanding of the eating disorder and their support for treatment. The R.D. or other qualified nutrition professional can help decrease family frustration at mealtimes by relieving the family of the responsibility for monitoring food intake or changing food-related behaviors. Concrete suggestions on meal planning, nutrient needs, and strategies for dealing with inappropriate food- and weight-related behaviors should be offered cautiously in conjunction with therapy. That allows the family to work toward a supportive rather than a confrontational environment around food.

Outpatient treatment alone is sufficient for the recovery of most persons with eating disorders. The key to nutrition intervention for the outpatient population is a very gradual change of food intake patterns and food- and weight-related be- haviors. Patients should be discouraged from adherence to rigid meal plans, rig- orous exercise routines, or immediate cessation of purging. Those are unrealis- tic goals that only mimic patients' prior diet efforts and typically result in bing- ing for the bulimic patient. The R.D. or other qualified nutrition professional can help the patient become aware of the complexities of an eating disorder and that a period of "purge-free" behavior does not mean *recovery*. That can help patients accept "setbacks" if and when they do occur in the course of treatment.

The patient with anorexia nervosa may be overwhelmed by rapid diet changes and experience his or her ultimate fear of uncontrolled weight gain (7). Proceeding too quickly with nutrition change may cause the patient to become defensive and withdraw from therapy and may do much to discredit the value of nutri- tion intervention. Requesting too many changes too quickly only reinforces the patient's perceived inability to control the environment, further undermining self- esteem.

Nutrition intervention sessions are in- tended to be the forum for planning food and behavior strategies, thus freeing therapy sessions for psychological explo- ration. Nutrition intervention strategies might include tailoring regimens to pa- tients' medical concerns, which will im- prove their sense of self-sufficiency, since patients can demonstrate to them- selves that they are capable of self-care. Possible strategies are including high- potassium foods to help correct an elec- trolyte imbalance and adding high-cal- cium foods for patients with low bone density. Behavior change efforts are most effective when coupled with an ed- ucational intervention. An effective way to decrease laxative abuse might be to contract with the patient to decrease the use of laxatives by a specified amount while increasing fiber and fluid intake and concurrently to provide education

about the limited value of laxatives in weight loss (12). Behavior change is often easier for less entrenched behav- iors. A possible intervention would be to help patients with anorexia nervosa grad- ually add back to their daily food intakes the foods that they had most recently omitted from their diets.

Self-monitoring techniques may be helpful with some patients to quantify progress, identify problems, and help patients gain control. Monitoring tech- niques can include keeping complete food and behavior records, counting the number of laxatives and diuretics used in specified periods of time, or identifying the frequency of binging and vomiting or the number of minutes food is retained. Recording the amount of money spent on binging or completing food and behavior contracts are also ways of monitoring patient progress and identifying prob- lems (5). Some patients are obsessive and over-involved in the records. With patients for whom these methods are ineffective or counterproductive, less structured supportive methods may work well.

Although most patients with anorexia nervosa and bulimia nervosa respond well to outpatient treatment, there are some for whom hospitalization is neces- sary. The decision to hospitalize a patient for treatment of an eating disorder is predicated on team findings of medical and/or psychiatric crisis, which may in- clude weight loss greater than 30% of ideal body weight over 3 months, severe metabolic disturbances, severe depres- sion or suicide risk, severe binging and purging (with risk of aspiration), psy- chosis, family crisis, or lack of response to outpatient treatment programs (4, 13).

The hospital setting can provide a safe, controlled environment for initiat- ing or reestablishing medical, psycho- logical, and nutrition rehabilitation (7, 14, 15). A defined nutrition care plan for each variant of eating disorder should specify parameters of nutrition rehabili-

tation. The care plan may identify daily caloric intake, rate of weight gain, a weight-range goal, food choices, and su- pervision of meals. Limits on activity may be useful in ensuring weight gain in patients with low body weight (16). Upon admission of a patient, the R.D. or other qualified nutrition professional may find it useful to obtain a detailed diet, weight, and behavior history. Such information can be used to individualize treatment goals and help staff anticipate problems with compliance to inpatient protocols. As with outpatient assess- ment, the initial interview performed in a supportive and nonjudgmental manner can be used to establish an alliance with the patient.

Nutrition repletion methods, such as nasogastric tube feedings and peripheral intravenous feeding, carry increased medical and psychological risks. Their use should be limited to stabilizing the health status of medically precarious patients who are unable to consume suf- ficient calories orally (14, 16). The med- ical risks associated with the more ag- gressive forms of nutrition repletion in very underweight patients include fluid retention, electrolyte changes, and hypo- phosphatemia (17). The psychological risks may include the patient's perceived loss of control, loss of identity, increased body distortion, and mistrust of the treat- ment team. Both of the feeding methods may be potentially lifesaving medical treatments but should not be used as pun- ishment for recalcitrant patients (18, 19).

The treatment team should involve the patient's family throughout the hospital- ization to help the family understand treatment goals and to learn about the eating disorder and the function it serves for both patient and family (20). It is es- sential that no one be blamed for the dis- order but that the family learn to commu- nicate verbally rather than through food (11). The extent of involvement of fam- ily members should be assessed by the therapist and discussed with the patient.

The R.D. or other qualified nutrition professional plays an important role in educating the family and significant others on the nutrition needs of the patient and the effect of starvation on patient behavior (21). Arranging for outpatient follow-up is essential, since transition from a structured hospital to the choices and responsibilities of outpatient care can be difficult and frightening. It should be emphasized that the responsibility for eating behaviors and weight management belongs to the patient.

Nutrition education is an important component of inpatient and outpatient treatment. Educational interventions on physiological and psychological responses to starvation help the patient, family, and staff understand how behavior is altered by restricted food intake. The R.D. or other qualified nutrition professional can provide nutrition and behavior interventions to restructure the cognitive distortions concerning food.

Providing education to patients on nutrient needs for growth and weight control and helping patients make appropriate food choices will promote recovery. Encouraging regular mealtimes, variety and moderation of intake, and the gradual reintroduction of feared foods will increase patient confidence in food selection and weight control (6, 8–10, 22).

The development of eating disorder behaviors typically includes the use of unsafe diets, unproven diet products, and arbitrary standards of ideal weight, in addition to an underlying psychopathology. As legitimate purveyors of diet and health information, R.D.s and other qualified nutrition professionals should identify and inform the professional and lay public of the dangers of fad diets and diet products and educate the public regarding healthy weight ranges and weight stabilization methods. Such interventions may play a significant part in the treatment and prevention of eating disorders (4, 7, 23).

REFERENCES

1. Diagnostic and statistical manual of mental disorders. 4th ed. Washington, D.C.: American Psychiatric Association, 1987.
2. Reiff, D.: Nutrition therapy in treatment of anorexia nervosa and bulimia nervosa. Presented at Anorexia/Bulimia Nervosa Symposium on Theories of Treatment, Bergan, Norway, February 1984. Universitetsforlaget As 1985.
3. Health and Public Policy Committee, American College of Physicians: Position paper on eating disorders: Anorexia nervosa and bulimia. Ann Intern Med 105:5, 1986.
4. Herzog, D. B., and Copeland, P. M.: Eating disorders. N Engl J Med 313:295, 1985.
5. Huse, D. M., and Lucas, A. R.: Dieting patterns in anorexia nervosa. Am J Clin Nutr 40:251, 1984.
6. Willard, S. G., Anding, R. H., and Winstead, D. K.: Nutritional counseling as an adjunct to psychotherapy in bulimia treatment. Psychosomatics 86:6, 1983.
7. Garrow, J. S.: Dietary management of obesity and anorexia nervosa. J Hum Nutr 34:137, 1980.
8. Storey, M.: Nutrition management and the dietary treatment of bulimia. J Am Diet Assoc 86:4, 1986.
9. Gannon, M. A., and Mitchell, J. E.: Subjective evaluation of treatment methods by patients treated for bulimia. J Am Diet Assoc 86:4, 1986.
10. Huse, D. M., and Lucas, A. R.: Dietary treatment of anorexia nervosa. J Am Diet Assoc 83:6, 1983.
11. Bayer, L., Bauers, C., and Kapp, S.: Psychosocial aspects of nutritional support. Nurs Clin N Am 1:1, 1983.
12. Bo-Linn, G. W., Santa Anna, C. A., and Morawski, B. A.: Purging and caloric absorption in bulimic patients and normal women. Ann Intern Med 99:1, 1983.
13. Anderson, A. E., Morse, C., and Santmyer, K.: In-patient treatment for anorexia nervosa. In Garner, D. M., and Garfinkel, P. E.: Anorexia nervosa and bulimia. New York: Guilford Press, 1985.
14. Tolstrup, K.: The treatment of anorexia nervosa in childhood and adolescence. J Child Psychol Psychiatry 16:75, 1975.
15. Gwirstsman, H. E., George, D. T., et al.: Constructing an in-patient treatment program for bulimia. In Kaye, W. H., and Gwirstsman, H. E.: A comprehensive approach to the treatment of normal weight bulimia. Washington, D.C.: American Psychiatric Press, 1985.
16. Garfinkel, P. E., and Garner, D. M.: Anorexia nervosa: A multidimensional perspective. New York: Brunner, Mazel, 1982.
17. Krause, M. V., and Mahan, L. K.: Food, nutrition and diet therapy. 6th ed. Philadelphia: W. B. Saunders, 1979.
18. Claggett, M. S.: Anorexia nervosa: A behavioral approach. Am J Nurs 80:147, 1980.
19. Maloney, M. J., and Farrell, M. K.: Tubefeeding for very low weight anorectic patients [letter to the editor]. Am J Psychiatry 137:11, 1980.
20. Garfinkel, P. E., Garner, D. M., and Kennedy, S.: Special problems of inpatient management. In Garner, D. M., and Garfinkel, P. E.: Anorexia nervosa and bulimia. New York: Guilford Press, 1985.
21. Garner, D. M., Rockett, W., et al.: Psychoeducational principles in the treatment of bulimia and anorexia nervosa. In Garner, D. M., and Garfinkel, P. E.: Anorexia nervosa and bulimia. New York: Guilford Press, 1985.
22. Beaumont, P. J. V., Chambers, T. L., et al.: The diet composition and nutritional knowledge of patients with anorexia nervosa. J Hum Nutr 35:265, 1981.
23. Kirkley, B. G.: Bulimia: Clinical characteristics, development, and etiology. J Am Diet Assoc 86:468, 1986.

PART VII

MODIFICATIONS IN MINERAL CONTENT

32.

SODIUM-RESTRICTED DIET

DEFINITIONS

1. SODIUM-RESTRICTED DIET

A diet in which the sodium content is limited to a prescribed level.

TABLE 32.1. CLASSIFICATION OF BLOOD PRESSURE[a] IN ADULTS AGE 18 YEARS OR OLDER

Range (mm Hg)	Category[b]
Diastolic	
<85	Normal blood pressure
85–89	High normal blood pressure
90–104	Mild hypertension
105–114	Moderate hypertension
≥115	Severe hypertension
Systolic, when diastolic blood pressure is <90	
<140	Normal blood pressure
140–159	Borderline isolated systolic hypertension
≥160	Isolated systolic hypertension

Source: National High Blood Pressure Education Program, National Heart, Lung and Blood Institute (3).
[a]Classification based on the average of 2 or more readings on 2 or more occasions.
[b]A classification of borderline isolated systolic hypertension (SBP 140–159 mm Hg) or isolated systolic hypertension (SBP ≥160 mm Hg) takes precedence over high normal blood pressure (diastolic blood pressure, 85–89 mm Hg) when both occur in the same person. High normal blood pressure (DBP 85–89 mm Hg) takes precedence over a classification of normal blood pressure (SBP <140 mm Hg) when both occur in the same person.

2. HYPERTENSION

Hypertension is defined by the National Research Council as sustained elevated arterial blood pressure measured indirectly by an inflatable cuff and pressure manometer (1). The National Research Council, the World Health Organization, and the National Heart, Lung, and Blood Institute have published similar charts defining hypertension (1–3). Those reproduced in tables 32.1 and 32.2 are from the National Heart, Lung, and Blood Institute.

PURPOSE OF THE DIET

The primary purpose of a sodium-restricted diet is to restore normal sodium balance to the body by effecting loss of excess sodium and water from extracellular fluid compartments.

1. IN HYPERTENSION

When the diet is prescribed for the person with essential hypertension, the goal of treating patients is to prevent cardiovascular morbidity and mortality associated with high blood pressure, especially strokes. The objective is to reduce diastolic blood pressure to below 90 mm Hg and to achieve and maintain arterial blood pressure below 140/90 mm Hg (3, 5).

2. IN ASCITES ASSOCIATED WITH LIVER DISEASE

The accumulation of massive quantities of fluid in the peritoneal cavity, ascites, with or without edema, is a frequent complication of cirrhosis. Therapy aimed at reducing ascites should be gen-

tle and incremental. The goal is the loss of no more than 1.0 kg daily if both ascites and peripheral edema are present and no more than 0.5 kg daily in patients with ascites alone (6, 7).

3. IN ADRENOCORTICAL THERAPY

The diet is intended to prevent or reverse the sodium retention, potassium loss, edema, and hypertension that accompany the use of adrenocorticoids. Caloric restriction to prevent weight gain and supplemental potassium may also be needed. Consideration should be given to the provision of supplemental vitamin D and calcium when osteoporosis occurs (8, 9).

4. IN CONGESTIVE HEART FAILURE

Poor cardiac function or limited fluid access can cause hypernatremia and edema. The diet is used in congestive heart failure to ameliorate the sodium retention and edema that occur as a result of inadequate cardiac output (10, 11).

EFFECTS OF THE DIET

1. PREVENTION OF HYPERTENSION IN INDIVIDUALS WITH HIGH NORMAL BLOOD PRESSURE

A 5-year trial in 201 men and women with high normal blood pressure has demonstrated the ability of "nutritional hygiene" measures to prevent hypertension or reduce its incidence (12). The nutritional hygiene measures included restricting sodium to 1,800 mg, controlling fat intake, limiting alcohol to 26 g (2 drinks), and reducing energy to approx-

TABLE 32.2. CLASSIFICATION OF HYPERTENSION IN THE YOUNG BY AGE GROUP[a]

	≥95th percentile (mm Hg)	≥99th percentile (mm Hg)
Newborns		
7 days	SBP ≥ 96	SBP ≥106
8–30 days	SBP ≥104	SBP ≥110
Infants (≤2 years)	SBP ≥112	SBP ≥118
	DBP ≥ 74	DBP ≥ 82
Children (3–5 years)	SBP ≥116	SBP ≥124
	DBP ≥ 76	DBP ≥ 84
Children (6–9 years)	SBP ≥122	SBP ≥130
	DBP ≥ 78	DBP ≥ 86
Children (10–12 years)	SBP ≥126	SBP ≥134
	DBP ≥ 82	DBP ≥ 90
Children (13–15 years)	SBP ≥136	SBP ≥144
	DBP ≥ 86	DBP ≥ 92
Adolescents (16–18 years)	SBP ≥142	SBP ≥150
	DBP ≥ 92	DBP ≥ 98

Source: National High Blood Pressure Education Program, National Heart, Lung and Blood Institute (3); *adapted from* American Academy of Pediatrics (147). Copyright © 1987 by the American Academy of Pediatrics.
[a]Hypertension should not be diagnosed on the basis of a single measurement. As in adults, children require repeated measurements to determine the stability or lability of blood pressure elevation. Attention should be given to using proper equipment and technique. The widest cuff that will comfortably encircle the arm without covering the antecubital fossa should be used. For infants in whom the accuracy of measurements by auscultation is uncertain, an electronic device using a Doppler technique can be used. Whenever possible, measurements should be obtained while patients are seated in quiet, nonstressful surroundings.

The higher the blood pressure and the younger the child, the greater the possibility of secondary hypertension. A careful medical history and physical examination are essential. The laboratory tests warranted for young patients are generally similar to those recommended for adults.

imately 500 kcal less than the usual daily intake. Isotonic exercise for at least 30 minutes 3 times per week was also required.

Only 13% of the intervention group actually achieved and maintained the 1,800-mg sodium intake. The actual dietary sodium intake decreased from a baseline of 4,000 mg per day to an average of 3,000 mg per day in the intervention group. Potassium intake went from 2,700 mg per day to 2,665 mg per day. The incidence of hypertension was 8.8%

in the intervention group and 19.2% in the untreated group. This study demonstrates that although the sodium restriction did not decrease to prescription levels, even a modest reduction of 1,000 mg per day was beneficial.

2. DECREASED BLOOD PRESSURE IN HYPERTENSIVES NOT RECEIVING PHARMACOLOGICAL THERAPY

By definition, salt-sensitive hypertensives lower their blood pressure by at least 10 mm Hg in response to sodium

restriction. Older studies demonstrating the beneficial effect of sodium restriction on blood pressure have been reported. Sodium restriction in one study produced a 50% reduction in urinary sodium excretion (urinary sodium excretion parallels, and is used to corroborate, intake), indicating that dietary adherence is feasible (13–15). In the Chicago Coronary Prevention Evaluation Program, 70 out of 101 men were able to maintain a significant decrease in blood pressure for 5 to 10 years, demonstrating the feasibility of achieving long-term dietary effects (16).

These reports have been corroborated by some, but not all, of the later trials. On the basis of available evidence, the NIH has concluded that some patients with mild or moderate blood pressure elevations may achieve control through moderate sodium restriction to 70 to 100 mEq per day (1,500 to 2,500 mg sodium, or 4 to 6 g of salt) (3).

More recently Langford restudied a group of patients whose blood pressure had been controlled in an earlier trial. Patients from the first trial were randomized into control and "discontinued medication" groups, with and without dietary interventions. Interventions were weight loss or sodium reduction to 40 mEq (920 mg) sodium per day. Both dietary interventions, continued for 56 weeks, increased the likelihood of remaining normotensive without medication. The highest success rate was obtained in nonoverweight, mild hypertensives on sodium restriction. This reaffirms the effect of earlier studies showing a beneficial effect of sodium restriction on blood pressure in hypertensives (17, 18).

The Intersalt Study was an international analysis of the relationship between electrolyte excretion and blood pressure, conducted on 200 patients in 32 countries throughout the world. This study found that sodium excretion is significantly related to blood pressure, independent of body mass index and alcohol intake, indicating that lower average sodium intakes have a favorable influence on blood pressure, on change of blood pressure with age, and hence on cardiovascular mortality. Populations with low sodium excretion (reflecting low sodium intake) had low medium blood pressures, low prevalence of hypertension, and either a decrease or only a small increase in blood pressure with aging (19, 20).

There are 3 essential differences between studies that report a low-sodium diet reduces blood pressure in hypertension and those that do not (21). Studies in which a beneficial effect is demonstrated report higher baseline sodium intakes and lower actual achieved intakes, higher initial blood pressures, and shorter study duration.

3. AUGMENTATION OF THE EFFECTIVENESS OF ANTIHYPERTENSIVE PHARMACOLOGICAL THERAPY

In the hypertensive patient, sodium-restricted diets have a mechanism of action similar to that of diuretic drugs. Both forms of therapy produce a negative salt and water balance during long-term treatment and prevent sodium retention. Consequently, they both result in volume depletion and short- and long-term hemodynamic adjustments that produce arterial blood pressure reduction (14, 22, 23).

Some forms of hypertension, however, respond to sodium restrictions more favorably than others. Salt-sensitive patients, including those with primary aldosteronism, hypervolemic essential hypertension, and hypertension associated with chronic renal parenchymal disease, benefit from the induction of a negative sodium and water balance (23).

Salt restriction appears useful in salt-sensitive patients who receive beta blockers, diuretics, angiotensin-converting enzyme inhibitors, or centrally acting drugs. An evaluation of the response to

salt restriction in hypertensive subjects receiving drugs revealed that by having their sodium intake restricted to less than 80 mEq (1,840 mg) sodium daily for 3 months, 50% of the patients reaching goal compliance were able to discontinue diuretics. Sodium restriction has been noted to augment the hypotensive effects of chlorthalidone and also beta blockers (24).

One study involved 100 pairs of hypertensive subjects treated on antihypertensive drugs who were instituted on an 80-mEq (1,840 mg) sodium diet, whose baseline intakes at the start of the study averaged 170 mEq (3,900 mg) and whose actual achieved intakes were about 2,200 mg sodium per day. The study found a significant reduction in blood pressure, which permitted one-third of the patients to reduce blood-pressure medications. This study documents the value of sodium-restricted diet therapy as an adjunct to hypertensive medications (25).

A sodium intake of 100 mEq per day caused a much greater decrease in blood pressure in response to a single dose of the angiotensin-converting enzyme (ACE) drug captopril than did a 200 mEq per day sodium intake. Even a reduction of sodium intake from 170 mEq to 150 mEq augmented the response to a twice-daily dose of 25 mg captopril in a group of patients by an average of 4 mm Hg systolic and 3 mm Hg diastolic blood pressure (24, 26).

The more sodium an individual ingests, the more potassium is lost. Hypertensives treated with diuretics seem to develop an increased appetite for salt and, unless persuaded to do otherwise, will increase their sodium intake. This has several adverse effects, including increased excretion of sodium and potassium in the urine, hypokalemia, and decreased effectiveness of the diuretic in lowering blood pressure (16, 27).

Individuals on diuretic therapy will experience 3 benefits from a concomitant

sodium restriction. The sodium restriction effects a modest but definite reduction in blood pressure, minimizes potassium loss and possibly obviates the need for a potassium supplement or a more expensive potassium-sparing diuretic, and augments the antihypertensive action of the drug in such a way that the drug dosage may be able to be reduced or in mild cases postponed (25, 28).

4. LACK OF AUGMENTATION OF THE ACTION OF CALCIUM CHANNEL BLOCKERS

Calcium channel blockers may not require salt restriction to maximize their effect. A single dose of nifedipine lowered blood pressure more in patients receiving 350 mEq sodium per day than in the same patients given 150 or 10 mEq per day. Verapamil for 3 days was more effective in patients receiving 212 mEq sodium per day than in the same patients receiving 9 mEq per day. Sodium restriction is not necessary with this particular calcium blocker, and a higher sodium intake may actually have a synergistic effect with the drug (24, 29).

5. EFFECT ON KALLIKREIN EXCRETION

A defect in the excretion of kallikrein has been proposed in hypertension. A sodium-restricted diet appears to reverse this supposed defect, while lowering blood pressure. It should be noted, however, that the blood pressure reductions achieved with sodium restriction correlate more closely with plasma contraction than with the increase in kallikrein excretion (30, 31).

6. ADDITIVE EFFECTS OF SODIUM AND CALORIC RESTRICTIONS

Weight loss and sodium restriction exert independent effects on blood pressure. When combined, their effects may be additive and are associated with a demonstrable fall in peripheral resistance, demonstrated by large clinical trials.

Stamler reported that after 4 years on a calorie- and sodium-restricted diet, 30% of 189 patients had lost at least 4 to 5 kg in weight and 36% had reduced their sodium intake. After these diet changes, 39% of the patients, but only 5% of the untreated control group, were normotensive (28, 32–34).

Even modest degrees of weight reduction and sodium restriction are important tools in the control of hypertension. These 2 nutritional interventions should be combined as the first step in the management of obese hypertensives.

7. INTERACTIONS BETWEEN SODIUM RESTRICTION, PROSTAGLANDINS, AND ACE INHIBITORS

A reduction in sodium intake enhances the effect of ACE inhibitors on blood pressure. Patients with essential hypertension who are being considered for treatment should at least have their sodium intake assessed before the start of treatment and should be advised not to add salt to their food or to make drastic changes in their sodium intake once they start the drug. Captopril, which inhibits the enzyme that converts angiotensin I to angiotensin II, also increases prostaglandin synthesis, an effect that contributes to its antihypertensive effect. One explanation of the beneficial effects of sodium restriction and diuretic therapy proposes that they may be mediated by the release of renal prostaglandins, which antagonize the vasoconstricting action of angiotensin (35–37).

8. REDUCED INCIDENCE OF STROKE AND CARDIOVASCULAR MORTALITY

Treatment of hypertension with diet (low in sodium, calories, saturated fats, and alcohol; high in potassium) and increased regular exercise results in reduced incidence of strokes. This therapy has not been found to reduce the incidence of myocardial infarctions, however. The Intersalt study found that a habitual, population-wide decrease in sodium intake of 100 mEq per day (i.e., 70 versus 170) would correspond to an average decrease in population systolic pressure of at least 2.2 mm Hg. In major population studies in the United States and the United Kingdom, this difference in systolic blood pressure is associated with a 4% lower risk of coronary death and 6% lower risk of stroke in middle age. If the habitual diet is both lower in calories and sodium, and higher in potassium with lower alcohol intake and less obesity, the average population systolic pressure would be predicted to be 5 mm Hg lower, corresponding to a 9% lower risk of coronary death and a 14% lower risk of stroke death (38, 39).

9. GRADUAL DIURESIS IN ASCITES ASSOCIATED WITH LIVER DISEASE

Sodium restriction has been demonstrated to be an effective method of promoting diuresis and preventing reaccumulation of fluid in some patients with ascites (6).

10. GRADUAL DIURESIS IN EDEMA ASSOCIATED WITH CONGESTIVE HEART FAILURE

A sodium-restricted diet may be effective in reducing sodium and fluid retention. When restricted activity, digitalis, and a low-sodium diet effectively control edema, diuretics are often unnecessary. Patients with class IV congestive heart failure may need to be restricted to as little as 200 mg sodium per day. If this proves ineffective or if it causes anorexia and additional loss of lean body mass, the diet may have to be liberalized and diuretics may be necessary to control fluid retention (40, 41).

PHYSIOLOGY, FOODS, AND NUTRIENTS

1. RENIN-ANGIOTENSIN-ALDOSTERONE SYSTEM

Aldosterone is the main mineralocorticoid, or sodium-retaining hormone, produced by the outer zone (zona glomerulosa) of the adrenal cortex. Its primary site of action is the distal renal tubule, where it causes reabsorption of sodium ions in exchange for potassium or hydrogen ions and contributes to the ability of the kidney to conserve sodium (13).

Angiotensin is an alpha-2 globulin produced by the liver. Angiotensin is converted to angiotensin I by renin, an enzyme produced by the juxtaglomerular cells of the kidney. Angiotensin I is converted by angiotensin converting enzyme to angiotensin II, a potent vasoconstrictor and the main hormonal stimulus for renal production of aldosterone.

Stimulation of the renin-angiotensin-aldosterone system results in increased sodium reabsorption and volume expansion. Renin release is stimulated by the following:

- Vascular receptors in the renal afferent arterioles sense a fall in renal perfusion pressure or wall tension.
- The macula densa, a group of specialized cells in the distal tubule associated anatomically with the juxtaglomerular cells, respond to a fall in the delivery of sodium to the distal renal tubule.
- The sympathetic nerve endings in the juxtaglomerular apparatus respond to volume depletion, exercise, or upright posture (13).

2. NATRIURETIC HORMONE

Natriuretic hormone decreases distal tubular reabsorption of sodium by inhibition of the sodium-potassium pump. It is thought to originate in the central nervous system, in response to volume expansion, and to aid in the restoration of normal extracellular volume. Following the administration of atrial natriuretic factor (ANF), also called atrial natriuretic peptide (ANP), there is diminished proximal tubular absorption of sodium. In patients with mild to moderate essential hypertension, a diminished secretion of ANP may be responsible for an elevated blood pressure (13, 42, 43).

3. PHYSIOLOGY OF HYPERTENSION

Hypertension can involve many organ systems, including the heart, endocrine organs, kidneys, and central and autonomic nervous systems. It has been clearly shown to increase the risk of developing stroke, coronary heart disease, congestive heart failure, peripheral vascular disease, and nephrosclerosis (1).

Changes in the left ventricular mass and structure of the heart in untreated hypertensives have been correlated with sodium intake, suggesting that dietary sodium intake may play a role in modulating left ventricular mass in hypertension (4).

If either cardiac output or peripheral resistance increases without a compensating fall in the other, the result is elevated blood pressure. Cardiac output may be increased by expansion in extracellular and plasma volume in salt-sensitive individuals, renal disease, and excessive levels of sodium-retaining hormones (1, 13).

Peripheral resistance is increased by vascular constriction and narrowing of the arterial lumen, due to increased sympathetic nervous system activity and increased levels of such vasoconstrictors as angiotensin II and norepinephrine.

4. SALT-SENSITIVE HYPERTENSION

Salt-sensitive hypertension has been defined as a 10% increase in mean arterial blood pressure on a high-sodium diet. Approximately 50% of hypertensives have been noted to have salt-sensitive hypertension. It is suggested that these individuals have a defect in sodium excretion that evokes the production of a natriuretic factor to maintain appropriate salt and volume status. It is thought that this factor also acts independently to raise blood pressure (44, 45).

Decreased central noradrenergic ac-

tivity in the anterior hypothalamus may mediate the exacerbation in hypertension that occurs in certain individuals during increased sodium intake (46).

Hypertensive patients with an abnormal response to high sodium intake have a higher red blood cell sodium content than normal responders do. Because insulin is a regulator of membrane cation transport, hyperinsulinemia has been implicated in the altered sodium content of red blood cells in hypertension. In obese hypertensives, insulin may increase absorption of sodium in the diluting segment of the distal nephron, with consequent water retention. Alternatively, insulin might alter sodium/potassium distribution, thus causing increased vascular peripheral resistance. The increased sodium stimulates adrenergic activity (47–49).

The prevalence of salt sensitivity is higher in certain groups of hypertensive patients including blacks, the elderly, those with low-renin essential hypertension (LREH), and individuals with renal impairment. Plasma renin activity (PRA) is lower in salt-sensitive subjects, and individuals with low-renin forms of hypertension have a higher prevalence of salt sensitivity. The PRA level may be the common thread in several of these salt-sensitive subgroups (44, 45, 50–52).

It is uncertain whether the low renin levels are the result of expanded plasma volume or are in some way responsible for salt sensitivity. According to the National Research Council's review of the data, there is strong epidemiological evidence that salt sensitivity is an important factor in initiating hypertension in some individuals, but there is no certain method to predict individual responses (1, 44).

In salt-sensitive hypertensives, the normal modulation of responsiveness of the renal and adrenal systems to varying sodium intakes is lost. Nonmodulators excrete a smaller amount of an intravenous saline load than normal individ-

uals or modulating hypertensives, come into balance more slowly on a sodium-restricted diet, retain more sodium, and have a greater rise in blood pressure when changing from low to high sodium intake. Patients with the nonmodulating defect tend to have a higher prevalence of hypertension in their families, suggesting a genetic component (44, 53–56, 111).

5. ROLE OF CHLORIDE

Chloride distribution in foods and its relation to sodium content have come under examination. Sodium chloride supplementation increases blood pressure more than sodium bicarbonate and other sodium salts. One theory, based on a study of only 5 patients, suggests that both sodium chloride and sodium citrate increase body weight and sodium retention and decrease plasma renin and aldosterone. But only sodium combined with chloride increases plasma volume, urinary excretion of calcium, and blood pressure. Further study of this theory in larger groups of humans is necessary before any dietary recommendations can be made (44, 57–59).

6. ROLE OF SODIUM : POTASSIUM RATIO

A low potassium intake may aggravate the effect of a high-sodium diet in salt-sensitive hypertensives, while a high potassium intake may blunt the effects of a sodium excess. There is a negative correlation between urinary potassium and blood pressure and a positive correlation between the urinary sodium : potassium ratio and blood pressure. However, these correlations account for no more than 5% of the variance in blood pressure. A high potassium intake is correlated with a lower stroke rate, and blacks have a higher incidence of hypertension than whites as well as a lower potassium intake (13, 60–66).

There are several physiologic actions of potassium that might contribute to the lowering of blood pressure. Potassium has a natriuretic effect, inhibiting renal sodium reabsorption. It inhibits renin production by a direct effect on the kidneys, and it causes vasodilatation, perhaps through stimulation of the sodium-potassium pump. Conversely, other effects of potassium oppose its blood pressure–lowering effect, including secondary stimulation of renin production and a direct stimulation of adrenal aldosterone production (13, 67, 68).

Until further evidence is available, the NIH has recommended that if increased potassium intake is recommended in hypertension, it should be limited to those patients who have normal renal function and who are not taking drugs known to raise serum potassium levels, such as potassium-sparing diuretics and ACE inhibitors (3).

7. CORRELATIONS BETWEEN CALCIUM AND SODIUM IN HYPERTENSION

Hypertension has been attributed to a calcium deficiency. McCarron has reviewed the epidemiologic evidence to support this concept. Part of the problem in interpreting the data is that the effect of calcium must be isolated from that of the other nutrients ingested with it, e.g., magnesium and potassium. Also, both negative and positive correlations have been observed between calcium excretion and blood pressure, although more recently a positive correlation between serum calcium and blood pressure has been noted, especially in women (21, 64, 69–72).

Intracellular calcium activity has been reported to be increased in hypertensives; total cell calcium also is increased, and the membrane binding of calcium is reduced. The elevation of intracellular free calcium concentration in arterial smooth muscle may be important in the pathogenesis of hypertension. One possible simple explanation of the protective effect of calcium against hypertension is a direct relaxation of vascular smooth

muscles. The problem with this view is that hypercalcemia has been noted to increase rather than decrease blood pressure (13, 73–79).

It has also been suggested that parathyroid hormone plays a pathogenic role in hypertension. Parathyroid hormone has been linked to the function of the renin-aldosterone system and to sympathetic nerve activity. The report that calcium supplementation elevates circulating levels of the potent vasodilating molecule, calcitonin-gene-related peptide, supports a role for this molecule in blood pressure homeostasis and provides a potent mechanism by which oral calcium supplementation may lower blood pressure. Other calcium-regulating hormones such as calcitonin and 1,25-dihydroxy-vitamin-D have also been implicated as playing a role in the pathogenesis of hypertension (13, 44, 80–84).

A further refinement of the calcium-hypertension theory connects abnormalities in calcium regulation with salt sensitivity. Consistent relationships have been found between the ability of sodium chloride to raise blood pressure and its ability to alter calcium metabolism. In animals, dietary calcium supplementation prevents the sodium chloride–induced increases in blood pressure (4, 80, 85). A working model and a graphic scheme for this connection have been reproduced in figures 32.1 and 32.2.

The newest data indicate that the calcium-regulating hormones coordinate with the renin-aldosterone system in hypertension. These 2 systems working together may affect the intracellular and extracellular concentrations of calcium and magnesium, which in turn may affect cardiac hemodynamic function, central nervous system and peripheral nervous system vasoactive hormone release, and peripheral smooth muscle vasoconstrictor tone and then blood pressure (80).

A high intake of sodium chloride in-

FIG. 32.1. THEORETICAL MODEL OF THE INTERACTION BETWEEN SALT AND CALCIUM HOMEOSTASIS.

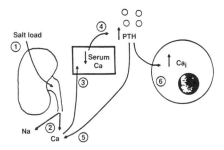

Source: Moore, T. J. (44). Copyright © John Wiley and Sons.
(1) Dietary salt load increases urinary sodium and calcium excretion (2), which lowers the serum calcium level (3), which increases PTH secretion (4). PTH, in turn, reduces calcium excretion (5), thus maintaining calcium homeostasis. If PTH also increases cytosolic calcium levels (6), this regulatory loop could also increase blood pressure.

creases urinary calcium excretion by reducing fractional calcium reabsorption in the proximal renal tubule. Increased urinary calcium excretion tends to lower ionized calcium and to activate parathyroid hormone secretion. Parathyroid hormone then inhibits urinary calcium losses, in an attempt to maintain calcium homeostasis (44).

If, at the same time, the elevated parathyroid hormone levels increase intracellular calcium concentration in various tissues, including vascular smooth muscle, the effect of a high-salt diet may be to increase salt sensitivity and blood pressure via its action on calcium homeostasis (44).

This hypothesis needs more complete testing. In addition, it is not possible at present to predict which individuals with hypertension will benefit from calcium supplementation and which will not. While it would seem beneficial not to allow any patient to develop a calcium deficiency and to ensure that calcium intake meets the RDA, the NIH does not currently recommend calcium supplementation in hypertension (3).

FIG. 32.2. THE RELATION OF SODIUM AND CALCIUM TO HYPERTENSION.

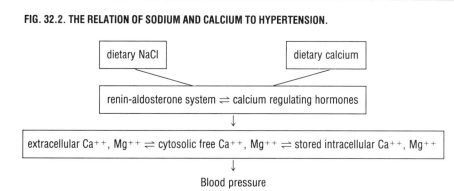

Source: Resnick, L. M. (80).

Note: In this general hypothesis, the activities of the renin-aldosterone system and calcium-regulating hormones coordinately transduce environmental dietary mineral signals at the cellular level, thus determining the ultimate blood pressure effects of these minerals.

8. CORRELATIONS BETWEEN MAGNESIUM AND SODIUM IN HYPERTENSION

Primary alterations in magnesium metabolism may lead to increased vascular reactivity and elevated blood pressure. Magnesium supplementation seems to lower elevated blood pressure only in subjects who are magnesium depleted; magnesium depletion may occur in some individuals on diuretic therapy. Among these patients, decreases in blood pressure occur predominantly in those with a high renin form of hypertension (44, 80). The effects of magnesium on vascular tone suggest that at least some of the effect of magnesium depletion acts directly on vascular smooth muscle.

Hypercalcemic hypertension is due in part to decreased serum magnesium and may be prevented if serum magnesium is sustained. Magnesium depletion may interfere with transmembrane ion transport and may block calcium channels (44).

In addition, intracellular magnesium is important for the actions of ATPases, including sodium-potassium ATPase associated with the sodium pump. Magnesium depletion may inhibit this pump, contributing to increased vascular tone and vascular responsiveness. Magnesium depletion is associated with sodium retention and potassium wasting, and a

low calcium intake also reduces cellular magnesium levels. There is some evidence that a hereditary predisposition to hypertension is related to magnesium metabolism, and that intracellular magnesium deficiency may influence the blood pressure elevations that occur in children with a family history of hypertension. More data are needed before any recommendations about magnesium can be made (3, 44, 80, 86).

9. CORRELATIONS BETWEEN SODIUM, UNSATURATED FATS, AND PROSTAGLANDINS IN HYPERTENSION

Prostaglandins are synthesized in the kidney from arachidonic acid, a product of linoleic acid. Increased excretion of certain prostaglandins has been demonstrated as a consequence of increased unsaturated fat intake. The prostaglandins serve as biological mediators for renal salt and water excretion. Specifically, prostaglandin E_2 has been credited with lowering blood pressure. Some studies have suggested that a low intake of saturated fat and high intake of polyunsaturated fat are associated with lower arterial blood pressure. Other studies have not demonstrated such an effect. Therefore, the NIH has concluded that as yet there is insufficient evidence to warrant dietary recommendations aimed at in-

creasing synthesis of prostaglandins (3, 13, 21, 87, 88).

10. UNITS OF SODIUM VERSUS SODIUM CHLORIDE

Many individuals still use the terms *sodium* and *sodium chloride,* or *salt,* interchangeably in ordering sodium-restricted diets. The restriction should be ordered in milligrams of sodium. Each molecule of salt is approximately 40% (39.3%) sodium. To calculate the amount of sodium in a specified weight of salt or sodium chloride, multiply by 0.40 (0.393). For example, 10 g of sodium chloride contains approximately 4 (3.93) g of sodium. Conversion between milliequivalents and milligrams is given in the Appendix, in table A.11.

11. USUAL DIETARY INTAKES AND REQUIREMENTS

Infants consuming 750 mL formula per day now receive a minimum of 100 mg and a maximum of 300 mg of sodium per day. For adults, usual intakes of sodium have been estimated to range from 1.8 g to 5 g per day. This can vary considerably and can be higher if the individual adds salt to food at the table. Estimated requirements are included in table 32.3 and are based on estimates of needs for growth and for replacement or obligatory losses (45).

Although no optimal range of sodium intake has been established, there is no known advantage in consuming large amounts of sodium chloride daily. Furthermore, there are clear disadvantages for individuals who have salt-sensitive hypertension (89). Therefore, the National Research Council has recommended the following:

• Daily intake of salt should be limited to 6 g per day (i.e., slightly less than 2,400 mg per day of sodium).
• The use of salt should be limited in cooking, and individuals should avoid adding it at the table.

TABLE 32.3. ESTIMATED SODIUM, CHLORIDE, AND POTASSIUM MINIMUM REQUIREMENTS OF HEALTHY PERSONS[a]

Age	Weight (kg)[a]	Sodium (mg)[a,b]	Chloride (mg)[a,b]	Potassium (mg)[c]
Months				
0–5	4.5	120	180	500
6–11	8.9	200	300	700
Years				
1	11.0	225	350	1,000
2–5	16.0	300	500	1,400
6–9	25.0	400	600	1,600
10–18	50.0	500	750	2,000
>18[d]	70.0	500	750	2,000

Source: Food and Nutrition Board (89). Copyright © 1989 by the National Academy of Sciences; reprinted by permission.

[a]No allowance has been included for large, prolonged losses from the skin through sweat.

[b]There is no evidence that higher intakes confer any health benefit.

[c]Desirable intakes of potassium may considerably exceed these values (~3,500 mg for adults).

[d]No allowance included for growth. Values for those below 18 years assume a growth rate at the 50th percentile reported by the National Center for Health Statistics (Hamill, P. V. V., Drizd, C. L., et al.: Physical growth: National Center for Health Statistics percentiles. Am J Clin Nutr 32:607, 1979) and averaged for males and females.

• Salty, highly processed, salt-preserved, and salt-pickled foods should be consumed sparingly (1).

INDICATIONS FOR USE

1. HYPERTENSION

Indications for use of the sodium-restricted diet in various stages of hypertension are listed in table 32.4. The role of the diet varies from being of primary importance in the general population, especially in normotensives with a family history of salt-sensitive hypertension, to being an adjunct to pharmacological therapy in severe hypertension.

2. ASCITES ASSOCIATED WITH LIVER DISEASE

The event that initiates the accumulation of ascitic fluid is not yet clear (7). Two theories have been proposed to explain formation of ascites, one crediting renal sodium retention and plasma volume as the initiating event and the other giving them secondary status.

The "underfilling" theory suggests that portal hypertension, hypoalbuminemia, and other factors tend to reduce plasma colloid osmotic pressure in the hepatic sinusoids and splanchnic capillaries. This causes the formation of an excessive amount of lymph, which accumulates as ascites with a resultant contraction of circulating plasma volume. An apparent decrease in intravascular volume (underfilling) is sensed by the kidney, which responds by retaining salt and water (7, 90).

The "overflow" theory (promulgated over the last decade) suggests that the primary abnormality in ascites is inappropriate retention of salt and water in the absence of volume depletion. This results in the expansion of plasma volume, which becomes sequestered in the abdominal cavity as ascites (7, 90).

Accumulation of ascitic fluid only occurs in patients who are in positive sodium balance. Therefore, restricting sodium intake will diminish the accumulation of ascitic fluid. Diets providing 250 to 500 mg sodium, if complied with, will usually achieve sodium balance. The initial goal of any treatment program should be an attempt to induce weight loss resulting from a spontaneous diuresis, by consistent and scrupulous adherence to a well-balanced 250-mg-sodium diet (90).

In some symptomatic patients, however, less rigid sodium restriction may be advisable. For example, if the patient becomes anorectic, and then is offered unsalted foods, intake will probably be reduced further, leading to malnutrition and further hypoalbuminemia.

The kidney may be unable to excrete a water load normally in some patients with ascites, owing in part to high levels of antidiuretic hormone. Restricting fluid intake to 1,000 or 1,500 cc per day may be necessary to prevent hyponatremia (91).

Many patients do not lose their ascites or edema with sodium restriction, and the use of diuretics becomes necessary. Spironalactone and triameterine act on the distal tubule and cause natriuresis with potassium sparing. The use of these drugs should be combined with a less rigid sodium restriction of 1 to 2 g sodium per day (91).

Response to sodium restriction and bed rest alone is more likely to occur if the ascites is of recent onset, the underlying liver disease is reversible, a precipitating factor can be corrected, or the patient has a high urinary sodium excretion and normal renal function. Although one cannot predict who will respond to a sodium-restricted diet, it may help to categorize these patients according to

TABLE 32.4. SODIUM RESTRICTION—INDICATIONS FOR USE BY CLASS OF HYPERTENSION

Class of hypertension	Blood pressure diastolic (mm Hg)	Role of sodium-restricted diet
Prehypertensives and nor-motensives with strong family history or other risk factors, e.g., obesity	80–90	Primary therapy, especially in salt-sensitive individuals, along with low-calorie diet if needed (21)
Mild hypertension	90–104	First step in treatment, combined with low-calorie diet (35)
Moderate hypertension	105–114	Serves as an adjunct to a 4-step program of drug therapy
Severe hypertension	Over 115	Serves as an adjunct to a 4-step program of drug therapy

their ability to excrete water and sodium. Those with a high urinary sodium excretion rate of more than 25 mEq (565 mg) sodium per day may be given a trial of a low-sodium diet alone, while those with a low sodium excretion rate may be given potassium-sparing diuretics combined with sodium restriction (91, 92).

3. ADRENOCORTICOID THERAPY

Sodium-restricted diet therapy should accompany the prescription of adrenocorticoid drugs, in order to prevent sodium retention associated with their use. However, patients with Addison's disease may need extra sodium, especially during exercise with sweating, extremely hot weather, and gastrointestinal upsets (9).

4. CONGESTIVE HEART FAILURE

After rest, diet has been described to be the second major component of therapy for congestive heart failure (CHF). A sodium-restricted diet will increase the amount of sodium and water excreted in the urine and will permit a slow diuresis. The major clinical manifestations of congestive failure can be divided into those due to systemic fluid retention and those due to pulmonary congestion. A sodium-restricted diet is indicated in uncompli-

cated left ventricular failure (hypertension but no cardiac congestion), mild congestive heart failure, and congestive heart failure with pulmonary edema. A sodium-restricted diet is contraindicated in cardiogenic shock (hypotension) (92, 93).

In CHF, damage to the heart muscle means that the left ventricle cannot maintain stroke volume, and cardiac output decreases. To compensate for decreased stroke volume, left ventricular pressure increases. The increased left ventricular pressure leads to increased atrial pressure and, consequently, pulmonary venous hypertension. The hypertension causes transudation of fluid into the pulmonary interstitial tissue and alveoli, which leads to breathlessness and backward failure. The reduced cardiac output also causes inadequate perfusion of the peripheral vascular beds. With less blood reaching renal tissues, glomerular filtration rate decreases. This brings about stimulation of the renin-angiotensin-aldosterone mechanism and promotes sodium retention, expansion of extracellular fluid volume, and peripheral edema.

While forward failure accounts for peripheral edema, it is backward failure that accounts for pulmonary edema. Life-

threatening episodes of acute pulmonary edema occur when the capillary pressure is greater than the oncotic pressure of the plasma proteins, and when such factors as decreased lymphatic drainage hamper fluid removal. Sodium intake should be restricted to 1 to 2 g per day. Beverages containing caffeine should be limited, and fluid may also need to be restricted (94).

POSSIBLE ADVERSE REACTIONS

1. SLEEP DISTURBANCES

Plasma norepinephrine levels are elevated by a sodium-restricted diet. The diet has been associated with disturbed sleep patterns similar to those seen in individuals with elevated serum levels of norepinephrine (16, 95).

2. SODIUM DEPLETION

Abrupt withdrawal of dietary sodium in normal individuals activates homeostatic mechanisms that increase renal sodium conservation. Patients whose diets are very low in sodium must be monitored carefully, as depletion of body sodium stores is possible, particularly in patients with renal insufficiency. Severely restricted sodium diets, large doses of diuretics, and unrestricted fluids used for a prolonged period of time in patients with hypertension, heart, liver, or especially kidney disease may result in hyponatremia (96).

Severe sodium restriction impairs the cardiovascular response to such challenges as blood loss and surgery. In the period immediately following myocardial infarction, severe sodium restriction may precipitate or aggravate shock by complementing the extensive loss of salt occurring as a result of a profuse diaphoresis (96–101). The elderly are at particular risk for sodium depletion.

3. DECREASED LITHIUM CLEARANCE

Patients taking lithium carbonate for

manic depression who are also taking thiazide diuretics will experience decreased lithium clearance and increased lithium blood levels. On a molecular basis, lithium and sodium ions are similar and are handled in the same manner by the kidney. A reduction in sodium or initiation of diuretic intake can induce lithium toxicity, with such symptoms as nausea, edema, thirst, and confusion. Conversely, increases in sodium intake will decrease the effectiveness of lithium. Lithium levels should be closely monitored and adjusted in individuals on sodium-restricted diets (102, 103).

4. FOLLOWING BOWEL RESECTIONS

After certain types of gastrointestinal surgery, inadequate replacement of large losses of sodium and fluid will lead to sodium depletion. The ileum and the colon are of major importance in the absorption of sodium chloride. Chronic dehydration and sodium depletion can occur in patients with ileostomies whose sodium intakes are inadequate (104).

Bile salts and free fatty acids alter the ability of the colon to absorb sodium and water. With an ileal resection, especially if the ileocecal valve is not preserved, bile salts are malabsorbed. This results in an increased load of bile salts entering the colon, which reduces absorption of water and sodium. The deoxy bile acids also cause fluid secretion, enhancing fluid and electrolyte losses (104). It is important for these patients to maintain adequate fluid and sodium intake, rather than restrict fluids in a futile attempt to control diarrhea.

CONTRAINDICATIONS

1. UNCOMPLICATED RENAL DISEASE

Vigorous sodium restriction should never be employed in renal disease in the absence of hypertension and edema. Patients with tubular involvement—e.g., pyelonephritis, interstitial nephritis,

polycystic renal disease, or bilateral hydronephrosis—will lose more sodium than patients with glomerulonephritis. Patients who have a tendency to lose sodium and water may develop extracellular dehydration and postural hypotension and may require extra sodium chloride, sometimes up to 10 to 12 g per day (105). For more information and references on this topic, see Chapter 15.

2. IN PREGNANCY

Sodium conservation is a normal physiological adjustment during pregnancy. There is an increased need for sodium because of the increased extracellular fluid volume in the mother, the requirements of the fetus, and the level of sodium in the amniotic fluid. The majority of pregnant women develop a certain amount of edema in the extremities during the last trimester of pregnancy. This is a normal consequence of the expansion of the plasma volume, decrease in plasma albumin, and pressure exerted on the venous vasculature by an enlarging uterus (89, 106, 107).

Severe limitations in dietary intake may compromise the delicate biochemical and physiological adjustments associated with the increased nutrient requirements. Furthermore, some pregnant women may be sodium wasters (105).

Pregnancy-induced hypertension (PIH) refers to a unique hypertensive syndrome characterized by severe edema and the progression of symptoms from preeclampsia to eclampsia. The term *PIH* has been adopted by the American College of Obstetricians and Gynecologists to replace *preeclampsia* and *eclampsia*. A diet calling for no added salt or 4 to 5 g sodium may be used, but this does not represent sodium restriction. Neither diuretic therapy nor severe sodium restriction is appropriate for PIH (107–110).

3. ADDISON'S DISEASE

Addison's disease, following adrenalectomy, has symptoms of sodium and po-

tassium wasting due to the lack of adrenocortical secretions. A severe sodium restriction is contraindicated. Patients actually need to add sodium to their diet during periods of excessive exercise with sweating, extremely hot weather, and gastrointestinal upsets (9).

4. FOLLOWING CERTAIN BOWEL RESECTIONS

See the section "Possible Adverse Reactions," above.

CLINICAL ASSESSMENT

1. HYPERTENSION

Sodium restriction is only one part of a program of nonpharmacological therapy currently recommended for hypertension. Therapy includes the following (3):

- Weight reduction in the overweight individual
- Sodium restriction, particularly in salt-sensitive persons
- Restriction of alcohol to 1 oz. or less per day
- Modification of dietary fat in individuals with hypercholesterolemia or serum lipoprotein abnormalities
- A regular exercise program
- Stress reduction
- Avoidance of tobacco

The nutritional assessment and dietary interview should collect data on the status of these factors in the patient. Blood pressure is correlated with body mass, and the overweight individual should be identified via the body mass index and triceps skinfold measurements. Where needed, the low-sodium diet should also be modified in calories to permit weight loss. Exercise aids with weight reduction but also has an independent beneficial effect on blood pressure.

Regular and accurate weighing is important in this patient population. In the salt-sensitive hypertensive, a sudden weight gain accompanied by the appearance of edema and a rise in blood pressure may signal dietary sodium overload. Having the patient maintain a food diary may uncover any hidden sources of sodium of which the patient may not be aware. In one model of an essential hypertension intervention program, nutrition histories or questionnaires and anthropometric measurements are reported as a routine part of the treatment (107).

The patient history should also include information on carbohydrate intolerance, family history, and socioeconomic, psychosocial, and environmental factors that may affect blood pressure control (3).

2. LIVER DISEASE

In all stages of sodium restriction for edema and ascites, dietary sodium intake should be assessed daily as well as protein, total fat, saturated fat, cholesterol, potassium, calcium, and caloric intake. Adequacy of protein and nutrient intake requires careful attention when sodium is restricted to 1,000 mg or less, because of the restrictive nature of the diet. Changes in the treatment plan, including decisions as to the efficacy of current dietary sodium restrictions or the adequacy of caloric intake, should be based on an assessment of intake as well as output (91).

Changes in weight signal diuresis and should be consistent with preset goals. Skinfold thickness measurements and midarm muscle circumference measurements are important, because weight changes in these patients reflect fluid status rather than lean body mass.

Because a deficiency of B vitamins is common in these patients, the clinical nutritional assessment should include an inspection of the mouth for angular stomatitis and cheilosis, which are the clinical stigmata of vitamin B deficiencies.

An acceleration in the degradation of pyridoxal-5-phosphate occurs in cirrhosis. Vitamin D is more slowly metabolized. This results in vitamin D deficiency, secondary calcium deficiency, and osteoporosis (111).

Possible causes of magnesium deficiency in cirrhosis include poor diet, diuretic therapy, and secondary aldosteronism, because aldosterone will increase the urinary magnesium excretion (111).

3. CONGESTIVE HEART FAILURE

Body weight may be normal in a malnourished individual with congestive heart failure because of edema. But the mass of fat and muscle in the edema-free midarm is independent of wide fluctuations in body weight caused by pathologic changes in extracellular fluid volume. Therefore, triceps skinfold measurements and midarm muscle circumference estimates are useful indicators of the erosion of lean body mass, characteristic of the cardiac cachexia that befalls one-third of patients with congestive heart failure (112).

Despite normal or even increased body weight, cardiac cachexia is typified by recessed temples, parchment-like skin, and substandard triceps skinfold and midarm muscle circumference measurements. Atrophy of the shoulders, chest, and thighs may occur, with visible resorption of muscles. Every cardiac patient in congestive failure should be assessed for cachexia, particularly if he or she is a candidate for surgery.

Several nutritional abnormalities contribute to cardiac cachexia. Intake is often decreased because of early satiety and the anorectic effect of medications. When dietary sodium is restricted to 1,000 mg or less, careful planning is necessary to ensure that the diet is both adequate and appetizing. Urinary losses may be increased secondary to generalized malassimilation, protein-losing gastroenteropathy, and potassium drug effects on bowel. Also, patients may have increased needs due to fever, and increased cardiac and pulmonary energy requirements (6).

BIOCHEMICAL ASSESSMENT

1. HYPERTENSION

Biochemical assessment should include routine CBCs with serum hemoglobin, hematocrit, sodium, potassium, creatinine, cholesterol, and triglycerides. Serum lipid abnormalities should be evaluated. Low levels of serum sodium accompanied by weight gain may signal sodium excess and subsequent expansion of extracellular fluid volume, rather than a sodium deficiency. Sodium intake should be periodically assessed via a 24-hour or overnight urinary sodium determination (113).

Urinalysis should include testing for protein and blood to identify renal involvement. Serum glucose and uric acid are particularly important screening tools in patients on long-term diuretic use. Calcium status should be assessed because some drugs cause retention whereas others cause hypercalciuria. Serum and urinary potassium should be closely monitored. Increased urinary potassium excretion may be due to excessive sodium intake. Hyperkalemia may be caused by overzealous dietary intake of potassium combined with potassium-sparing drugs. Hypokalemia can result from inadequate potassium intake combined with a potassium-wasting diuretic (3, 114).

2. LIVER DISEASE

In the patient with liver disease on a sodium-restricted diet, serum sodium and serum albumin reflect fluid status. The 24-hour urinary sodium excretion determination reflects sodium intake and is an important tool in the evaluation of the efficacy of nutritional interventions.

Increased serum sodium may signal overzealous diuresis (hypernatremia) or sodium excess. Conversely, decreased serum sodium may accompany fluid overload (hyponatremia). Water retention occurs in association with sodium retention, although there is also impairment of free water clearance, secondary to an increase in circulating antidiuretic hormone. The serum sodium is decreased despite the increases in total body sodium, because of the increased water retention and expansion of extracellular fluid volume. Only rarely is a low level of serum sodium indicative of body sodium stores; low serum sodium concentrations may occur without fluid retention in cirrhosis because of a potent diuresis that removes large amounts of sodium.

In the patient with ascites due to cirrhosis, proteins normally synthesized by the liver are found in decreased amounts in the serum. Abnormalities may occur in the capacity of the liver to synthesize transferrin, clotting factors, blood urea nitrogen, albumin, and lipoproteins (6). Thus, serum levels of these proteins are unreliable indicators of nutritional status in liver disease.

The close relationship between total serum zinc and albumin in individuals with cirrhosis suggests that a fall in zinc may follow a reduction in serum albumin. A lack of albumin and other zinc-binding sites increases the availability of zinc to be excreted in the urine and results in a decreased serum concentration. Serum albumin has been found to be inversely correlated with serum bilirubin. Patients with liver disease of any type should not be subjected to even brief periods of starvation of any type, because significant increases in serum bilirubin will result (111, 115, 116).

The level of serum cholesterol, triglycerides, lipoproteins, and apoproteins (which are synthesized in the liver) may not have the same meaning as for a patient whose liver is intact. Serum cholesterol values may be low because of a decreased percentage of cholesterol in the esterified form, because the enzyme that is necessary for cholesterol esterification is made in the liver (lecithin-cholesterol-acyltransferase). This results

in an increase in very low-density lipoproteins and a rise in triglycerides. Alcohol ingestion is commonly associated with an accumulation of triglycerides in the liver, derived from fatty acids in the host adipose tissue (6, 111, 116).

Because 50% of the individuals with cirrhosis develop steatorrhea, nutritional surveillance should include parameters of fat malabsorption such as a 72-hour stool fat analysis, or at the very least a serum carotene determination. The steatorrhea is usually mild, not exceeding 10 g per day. However, in 10% of cases, it exceeds 30 g per day. Cholesterol is metabolized to bile acids in the normally functioning liver, which also synthesizes bile salts. The lack of bile salts results in steatorrhea, which can lead to a lack of the fat soluble vitamins. Patients with liver disease may also be unable to release vitamin A from the liver, owing to a diminished synthesis of albumin and retinol-binding protein. In cirrhosis, there may also be impaired hepatic dehydroxylation or impaired hepatic release of 25-hydroxy-vitamin-D. Ethanol itself may contribute to this deficiency, owing to the induction of microsomal enzymes which convert 25-hydroxy-vitamin-D to inert metabolites (6, 111, 117).

Anemia is a common finding in cirrhosis of the liver. The cause of the anemia is multifactorial and includes blood loss and folate and pyridoxine deficiency. Hypomagnesemia is common, as is hypophosphatemia. The BUN (blood urea nitrogen) and creatinine are elevated in patients who have been treated with excessive diuretics or who are developing hepatorenal failure (91).

The level of serum potassium is critical in evaluation of the nutritional status of the patient with cirrhosis complicated by ascites. Hypokalemia can provoke hepatic encephalopathy, so that caution should be used to ensure that dietary potassium intake is adequate and that diuresis is not too rapid.

3. CONGESTIVE HEART FAILURE

In anyone receiving long-term diuretic therapy, serum calcium and uric acid measurements are important in order to determine calcium status or to identify hyperuricemia. The degree of ambulation should be assessed to determine whether immobility may be severe enough to contribute to calcium or nitrogen urinary losses.

Laboratory studies frequently show subnormal levels of serum albumin, hemoglobin, folate, thiamine, potassium, calcium, magnesium, and iron. Total lymphocyte counts should be taken intermittently to evaluate the course of the disease and the effect of dietary treatment on visceral protein stores. Tissue levels of zinc are also markedly depleted in individuals receiving long-term diuretic therapy (112).

In cardiac cachexia, fecal fat and nitrogen are often elevated because of malabsorption, and the patient may also have protein losing enteropathy.

ASSESSMENT OF POTENTIAL DRUG INTERACTIONS

1. STEPPED THERAPY FOR HYPERTENSION

The latest NIH recommendations for drug therapy of hypertension are based on a stepped approach using 4 classes of drugs: diuretics, beta blockers, calcium antagonists, and ACE (angiotensin-converting enzyme) inhibitors.

The initial choice may be a drug from any 1 of the 4 classes chosen by the physician. In patients over age 50, thiazides may be the best first choice. Thiazides should not be taken with digitalis and should be avoided by patients with gout, by athletes, and in very hot climates. If after a period of 1 to 3 months the response to the initial choice of therapy is inadequate or if the patient is experiencing problems with the drug, the physician may increase the dose of the first drug, add an agent from another class, or discontinue the initial choice and substitute a drug from another class (3, 118, 119). Combinations of drugs may allow smaller doses of each drug than would otherwise be used. For patients with mild hypertension who have satisfactorily controlled their blood pressure for at least a year, antihypertensive drugs may also be reduced in a step-down fashion in patients also on nonpharmacologic forms of therapy (3).

2. OTHER DRUGS USED TO TREAT HYPERTENSION

Calcium channel blockers reduce total peripheral resistance and do not exhibit the adverse effects of diuretics on glucoregulatory hormones, serum lipids and lipoproteins, uric acid, or electrolytes, but they are contraindicated for use in congestive heart failure (120, 121). ACE inhibitors are used to treat hypertension and congestive heart failure and do not induce sodium retention (122).

Alpha adrenergic blockers are a newer class of drugs used in the treatment of hypertension. Alpha-1 adrenergic blockers include prazosin and terazosin, and alpha-2 adrenergic blockers (in research use only) include yohimbine. Terazosin does not adversely affect serum lipids as do diuretics. Prazosin, which does produce some sodium and water retention, is mainly indicated as an adjunct to diuretics or beta blockers (123, 124).

3. DRUGS USED TO TREAT LIVER CIRRHOSIS

Many patients do not lose ascites or edema with sodium restriction alone, and the use of such potassium-sparing diuretics as spironalactone and triamterene is often necessary. In some instances, potent loop diuretics that are not potassium sparing—e.g., furosemide—are added to the regimen. Caution is needed, because rapid potassium

losses can be dangerous in cirrhosis (7, 92).

4. DRUGS USED TO TREAT CONGESTIVE HEART FAILURE

According to one author, treatment is not begun until the first symptoms of diminished cardiac reserve are evident. At this point diet therapy for sodium restriction and weight reduction (if indicated) are instituted. If these measures alone do not help, thiazide diuretics and digitalis therapy are instituted, and consideration should be given to the use of vasodilators. When, despite these measures, a patient is still symptomatic on ordinary exertion associated with activities of daily living, more-potent loop diuretics such as furosemide or bumetanide are used in place of thiazides. Vasodilators may also be used (91).

When the patient becomes symptomatic at rest, the dose of digitalis or other cardiac glycoside is increased, and a potassium-sparing diuretic may be added to the loop diuretic. The side effects associated with diuretics in congestive heart failure have caused their use to be questioned. ACE inhibitors have been demonstrated to be effective in congestive heart failure, and their use combined with a much lower dose of diuretic has been recommended (91, 125).

The combination of diuretics and ACE inhibitors offers both symptom control and improvement in prognosis. Other agents, such as digoxin, xamoterol, and nitrates, may be particularly useful in the treatment of patients with such associated problems as atrial fibrillation and angina (126).

IMPLEMENTATION AND EDUCATION

1. SOURCES OF SODIUM

In addition to the sodium naturally occurring in foods, many sodium-containing compounds, such as monosodium glutamate (MSG), baking powder, sodium

chloride, baking soda, disodium phosphate, sodium propionate, and sodium benzoate are used in food manufacturing. Although about 10% of our sodium intake is discretionary (added in cooking or at the table), the remainder comes from nondiscretionary natural and processed foods or drugs. The proliferation of fast foods and convenience foods, many of which are high in sodium, and the increasing tendency to eat out have had an impact on sodium consumption.

Some fast food items contain as much as 5 g of sodium per serving. Patients should be encouraged to choose plainer items and to omit pickles, special sauces, and presalted fried foods (127, 128). Many convenience foods are now available without added salt. Patients should be educated to recognize the most common sources of hidden sodium, e.g., canned or dried soups; processed or cured meats and bacon; frozen, canned, or boxed meals or side dishes; canned or dried sauces; pickles and olives; soy and teriyaki sauces; and salted snack foods.

Sodium chloride is not only used as a flavoring agent but also has technological uses, as in controlling the rate of fermentation and strengthening the gluten in yeast-leavened bread and in inhibiting the growth of undesirable bacteria in processed foods.

Drugs and medicinals also may have appreciable amounts of sodium. The sodium content of some medications is provided in table 32.5. A list of low-sodium over-the-counter drugs is also available.

Drinking water may contribute 10% of an individual's sodium intake, and many communities in the United States exceed the recommended maximum of 20 mg/100 mL. Evidence at present is inconclusive as to the effect of drinking water on blood pressure levels. Individuals requiring sodium-restricted diets should be aware that softened water contains increased sodium (129–132).

TABLE 32.5. SODIUM CONTENT OF SOME MEDICATIONS

Oral medication	Sodium content	
Alka-Seltzer, antacid	296	mg/tab
Alka-Seltzer, pain reliever	551	mg/tab
Alka-Seltzer plus	482	mg/tab
Alevaire	80	mg/5 mL
Di-Gel	10.6	mg/tab
Di-Gel, liquid	8.5	mg/5 mL
Dristan Cough Formula	58	mg/5 mL
Fleet Phospho-Soda	550	mg/5 mL
Phosphalgel	12.5	mg/5 mL
Rolaids	53	mg/tab
Sodium Salicylate, tab	49	mg/5 grain
Titralac liquid	11	mg/5 mL
Vicks Cough Syrup	41	mg/5 mL
Formula 44D Decongestant Cough Mixture	51	mg/5 mL

Source: Roe, D. A. (129).

2. SALT TASTE PERCEPTION

Taste perception of sour and salt diminish with age, alcohol use, smoking, and taste and smell deficits (133–134). In these cases, additional seasonings may be necessary to increase the palatability of a sodium-restricted diet.

3. SALT REPLACEMENT SEASONINGS

Seasonings to replace sodium chloride are now available. Information about the composition of a selection of these is given in tables 32.6 and 32.7 (135). Clients who are accustomed to frequent use of convenience foods often need encouragement to experiment with new cooking methods and flavorings.

4. SODIUM FOOD LABELING

Effective July 1, 1986, all food products that carry nutrition labels must also include sodium information. Terms such as *low sodium* and *reduced sodium* now have legal definitions. *Sodium-free* foods must contain less than 5 mg sodium per serving. *Very low-sodium* foods must have 35 mg or less per serving. *Low-sodium* foods must contain 140 mg or less per serving. *Reduced sodium* foods

must be processed so that the usual level of sodium is reduced by 75% (137).

5. ALCOHOL AND CAFFEINE

The magnitude of caffeine's effect on blood pressure depends upon the individual's usual caffeine consumption habits. Caffeine increases blood pressure in people who do not regularly consume methylxanthines. But 1 or 2 cups of coffee in regular coffee drinkers does not significantly elevate blood pressure. However, in normotensive individuals who normally drink 4 to 6 cups of coffee a day, substitution of 5 cups of decaffeinated coffee for 5 cups of regular coffee significantly reduced blood pressure. In another study, a change in coffee intake from 4 to 6 cups per day to total abstinence led to a significant fall in blood pressure. A combination of caffeine and phenylpropranolamine in over-the-counter diet aids can significantly increase blood pressure, and caution is advised in the use of these products (138–141).

While coronary heart disease is negatively related to an alcohol intake of 2 to 3 oz. per day, alcohol withdrawal, even intermittently, as in long-term alcohol abuse, raises catecholamine levels and contributes to hypertension. However, alcohol intakes greater than 3 oz. per day

TABLE 32.6. SODIUM SUPPLIED PER TEASPOON AND SODIUM : POTASSIUM RATIOS OF SALT-REPLACEMENT SEASONINGS

Product	Weight of samples (g/tsp.)	Sodium content (mg/tsp.)	Na^+/K^+ ratio
High-sodium products			
Sea Salt	5.2	2,176	2,462
Vege-Sal	4.2	1,550	126
Herbamare	5.1	1,826	16
Nature's Seasons	4.0	1,208	90
Savorit	3.7	1,067	55
Spike	3.7	901	33
Lemon Pepper	2.9	487	28
Low-sodium products			
Kelp/Cayenne Sea Seasonings	3.3	125	0.31
Vegit	2.0	75	1.52
Parkelp	3.9	128	0.45
Dulse/Garlic Sea Seasonings	1.8	34	0.24
Nori/Ginger Sea Seasonings	0.9	2	0.07
Mrs. Dash	2.4	3	0.09

Source: Ahern, D. A., and Kaley, L. A. (135).

TABLE 32.7. SALT SUBSTITUTES

Brand	Sodium (mg/tsp.)	Potassium (mg/tsp.)
Nu-Salt[a]	0.17	528
No Salt[b]	<10	2,502
Seasoned NoSalt[b]	<5	1,332
Morton Salt Substitute[c]	Trace	2,800
Morton Lite Salt Mixture[c]	1,100	1,500
Adolph's Salt Substitute[d]	<0.5	2,480

Source: American Dietetic Association (136).
[a]Manufacturer: Cumberland Packing Corp., 2 Cumberland St., Brooklyn, NY 11205.
[b]Manufacturer: Norcliff-Thayer, 303 S. Broadway, Tarrytown, NY 10591.
[c]Manufacturer: Morton Thiokol, Morton Salt Division, 110 N. Wacker Dr., Chicago, IL 60606-1555.
[d]Manufacturer: Ragu-Foods, Subsidiary of Chesebrough Ponds, Packaged Foods Division, 828 Bridgeport Ave., Shelton, CT 06484.

lead to elevated blood pressure and poor adherence to antihypertensive therapy. Alcohol intake should be limited to no more than 1 oz. per day (3, 142–144).

6. EDUCATIONAL AND MANAGEMENT TOOLS

Extensively outlined strategies for the use of the sodium-restricted diet have been developed (137, 145). One model identifies professional behaviors and 10 critical patient behaviors and skills that are an integral part of strategies designed to control sodium intake and to promote a successful outcome. The 10 steps are as follows:

1. Acknowledgment of the disease
2. Acknowledgment and consideration of effectiveness of dietary measures
3. Assessment of current dietary influences
4. Realization that change is long-term
5. Development of strategies and goal setting
6. Formulation of plans to accomplish each desired change
7. Action to accomplish change
8. Assessment of success of each change
9. Assessment of progress in attainment of blood pressure goal
10. Maintenance of diet changes

Some ways to prevent adherence problems are given in table 32.8, and ways to identify and solve such problems are described in table 32.9 (137).

PRIORITIES FOR QUALITY ASSURANCE

1. HYPERTENSION

A. Controlling Incidence of Hyperlipidemia As previously discussed, anti-hypertensive treatment has not been found to reduce the incidence of myocardial infarctions. It has been postulated that this may be so in part because of the adverse effect of some of the drugs used on serum lipids and lipoproteins (3). Thus, serum lipids and lipoproteins should be monitored in these patients, and diet therapy to correct the problem should be instituted along with sodium restriction. A useful monitor would be one that tracks the serum lipids of patients on these drugs, as well as the institution of diet therapy intended to reduce serum lipids.

B. Tracking Dietary Adherence A useful monitor evaluates the results of nutritional counseling and its effect on adherence.

C. Antihypertensive Diet in Pregnancy Quality assurance measures should focus on the provision of a nutritionally adequate diet that provides optimal levels of

TABLE 32.8. PREVENTION OF ADHERENCE PROBLEMS WITH THE SODIUM-RESTRICTED DIET

Misconception/problem	Clarification/intervention
Patients sometimes think that eliminating added salt during cooking and at the table should be enough to lower their blood pressure.	"Actually, it's sodium, a component of salt, that affects blood pressure in some people. Not adding salt helps, but it may not be enough. Many foods are processed with high amounts of sodium. Avoid these high-sodium foods. Instead, try to eat more foods that are low in sodium. Here is a list of foods to eat and those to avoid."
Some patients expect to stop their high blood pressure medication as soon as they reduce the salt in their diet.	"If you can lower your blood pressure by decreasing your intake of sodium, then we'll try to reduce your medication accordingly. Let's see how well you do."
Most patients are accustomed to preparing their food using salt or other high-sodium ingredients, such as catsup, soy sauce, etc.	"Many other seasonings besides salt can be used in cooking. Many cookbooks and magazines contain modified recipes and tips. I'll give you a list of suggestions. A number of low-sodium products are available (e.g., low-sodium catsup)."
When the whole family eats together at home, not everyone may feel that they need to eat a low-sodium meal.	"Reducing sodium is actually a good idea for your whole family. High blood pressure tends to run in families, so it may be wise to help your children adopt healthy eating habits at an early age."

TABLE 32.9. INTERVENTIONS TO IMPROVE ADHERENCE TO SODIUM-RESTRICTED DIET

Determine if there is a problem	*Evaluate patient's response*
"Many people find it difficult to reduce the amount of sodium (salt) they eat. Are you having any difficulty with that?"	If response is "yes," ask about the nature of the problem to determine if it is due to a misconception, a lifestyle issue, or a lack of family support. Go to **Assess barrier.** Upon identifying the **Type of barrier,** consider using the sample **Intervention** as a means of addressing the problem.
	If response is "no," say "Okay, but it looks like we still don't have your blood pressure under control. It's (number), and we want it to be below (number). So, let me ask you a few questions about your sodium consumption." Go to **Assess barrier.** Upon identifying the **Type of barrier,** consider using the sample **Intervention** as a means of addressing the problem.

Assess barrier	*Type of barrier*	*Intervention*
"Do you sometimes feel unsure about what foods are high in sodium (salt)?"	Misconception	Acknowledge difficulty and provide guidance.
		"It is sometimes hard to know what foods are high in sodium. There are two main ways of figuring it out.
		"First, I'll give you a list of foods known to be high in sodium (e.g., canned foods, luncheon meats, hot dogs, pickles, fast foods).
		"Second, there are an increasing number of foods in the supermarket that provide sodium information on the nutrition label. Here is a handout that contains information about how to read and use nutrition labels."
"Do you sometimes add salt to your food at the table when you think the food is too bland?"	Lifestyle	Acknowledge the change in the taste of food without salt and suggest other seasonings.
		"I know that food tastes different when you leave out the salt. A preference for salty foods is something we've learned. Over time, you can adjust to the taste of food without salt. In the meantime, I'll give you a list of other seasonings you can use to add flavor to your food. Use these instead of salt."
"Do you eat at fast-food restaurants often?"	Lifestyle	Acknowledge the convenience of fast-food restaurants and suggest alternatives.
		"I'm sure it is convenient to eat at fast-food restaurants. Unfortunately, many of the foods served there are very high in sodium. I have two suggestions.
		"First, limit how often you eat in fast-food restaurants. Instead, bring a sandwich from home so that you can control the amount of sodium in your food.
		"Second, when you do go to a fast-food restaurant, order the item(s) lowest in sodium. The salad bar is generally a good choice, especially if you concentrate on the fresh vegetables and fruits. However, avoid adding condiments such as canned chickpeas and kidney beans, bacon bits, croutons, olives, and salted sunflower seeds.
		"Another option, if available, is a plain baked potato. Or choose a plain hamburger with lettuce and tomato. If you want french fries, ask if your order can be bagged before salt is added. Many fast-food restaurants now provide nutrition information about their menu. Ask for this information to help you choose lower-sodium items."
"Who prepares most of your food? Does that person serve food low in salt?"	Family support	"It is easier to reduce the sodium in your diet when you have the support and cooperation of others in your household. Most Americans eat too much salt, so it will be healthy for other members of your family to cut down also.
		"Is the person who prepares your food willing to use less salt when cooking? Do they know of low-sodium recipes? Here is a listing of cookbooks that contain sample recipes showing how sodium can be reduced in the preparation of meals."
"Does anyone in your family help you reduce sodium in your diet?"	Family support	"In what other ways could a family member help you reduce the sodium in your diet (e.g., leave the salt shaker off the table; keep low-sodium snack foods in the house; give praise for eating foods low in sodium)? Will you talk with them about this today?
		"It might be good to have a family member or friend come with you to your next appointment. This should be very helpful in educating him or her about high blood pressure and why you need to follow a specific diet."

Source: Working Group on Health, Education and High Blood Pressure Control (137).

nutrients for both the mother and the fetus and that does not over restrict sodium.

2. ASCITES IN LIVER DISEASE

While a sodium-restricted diet alone is unlikely to include so rapid a diuresis as to provoke hepatic encephalopathy, the condition can be brought about by a combination of severe sodium restriction and high doses of a diuretic that is not potassium sparing.

As explained in the discussion of nutritional assessment, weight changes are a clue to sodium balance in ascites. Patients losing more than 1 lb. per day should have serum potassium and liver enzymes monitored and should be closely watched for signs of hepatic encephalopathy. Monitors can be developed to track the rate of diuresis, the level of sodium restriction, and the incidence of hepatic encephalopathy.

3. CONGESTIVE HEART FAILURE

Heymsfield has published an excellent review of congestive heart failure and cardiac cachexia (94). It includes priorities for nutritional assessment, plus a review of factors that increase the work of the heart in individuals on tube feedings. These include infusion rates much higher than maintenance needs and excessively high-carbohydrate diets, both of which increase $\dot{V}O_2$ and $\dot{V}CO_2$.

These patients need to be on a low-sodium formula with normal, not excessive, amounts of carbohydrate and fat. If fluid is restricted in severe congestive failure, a 1.5-kcal, low-sodium formula may be needed.

For patients on oral feedings, the size of meals and their effect on cardiac work load have been exaggerated. Physical exertion is described in *mets,* with 1 met equal to basal $\dot{V}O_2$ in mL per minute. A bed bath is 2.6 mets, a shower 3.7 mets, a small meal 1.1 mets, a medium-sized meal 1.2 mets, and a large meal 1.3 mets. Meal composition and size within the confines of the diet prescription should be adapted to the wishes of the patient.

Monitors should be developed for the identification of cardiac cachexia, as should criteria for optimal tube-feeding administration in these patients.

MENU PLANNING

FOOD LIST FOR THE 4,000-TO-5,000-mg SODIUM DIET

Food group	Foods allowed	Foods excluded
Milk and milk products	Any milk—whole, low-fat, skim, or chocolate; cocoa; yogurt; eggnog; buttermilk (once per week)	None
Vegetables (2–4 servings)	Fresh and frozen vegetables; canned, drained vegetables; low-sodium vegetable juices; regular vegetable juice in limited amounts	Sauerkraut; pickled vegetables and other preparations that use brine
Fruits (2 or more servings per day)	All fruits and fruit juices	None
Breads and cereals (4 or more servings per day)	Enriched white, wheat, rye, or pumpernickel bread; all cereals, hard rolls, dinner rolls; crackers, snack crackers, breadsticks	Breads or rolls with salted tops
Potato or substitute	White or sweet potatoes; salted potato chips in limited amounts; salt-free potato chips, unlimited; enriched rice, barley, noodles, spaghetti, macaroni, or other pastas; homemade bread stuffing	Potato casserole mixes and other snack chips; excessive amounts of salted potato chips; instant rice and pasta mixes; commercial stuffing; commercial casserole mixes
Meats or substitute	Any fresh or fresh-frozen meats—beef, lamb, pork, veal, and game; fresh or fresh frozen poultry—chicken, turkey, Cornish hen, or other; freshwater or fresh-frozen unbreaded fish; low-sodium canned tuna; low-sodium salmon or sardines; eggs; cheese in limited amounts; low-sodium cheese as desired; cottage cheese, drained; ricotta cheese, cream cheese (limit 2 tbsp.); regular peanut butter (3 times per week); dry peas and beans	Any meat, fish, or poultry that is smoked, cured, salted, or canned—bacon, chipped beef, corned beef, cold cuts, ham, hot dogs, and sausages; sardines, anchovies, marinated herring, pickled meats, pickled eggs; processed cheese

(continued)

Fats	Butter or margarine; vegetable oils; low-sodium salad dressing (as desired); regular salad dressing (in limited amounts); mayonnaise-type salad dressing; light, sour, or heavy cream	Salad dressings containing bacon fat, bacon bits, or salt pork; snack dips made with instant soup mixes or processed cheese
Soups	Commercial low-sodium soups, broth, bouillon, or consommé; homemade soups with allowed vegetables; homemade broth	Excessive amounts of canned or dehydrated soups
Sweets and desserts	Any sweets or desserts	None
Beverages	All beverages	Commercially softened water and its use in preparation of foods or beverages
Miscellaneous	Limit salt to ½ level tsp. per day; salt substitute (with physician's approval); pepper, herbs, spices, flavorings, vinegar, lemon or lime juice	Garlic salt, celery salt, onion salt, seasoned salt, sea salt, rock salt, kosher salt; any other seasoning containing salt and sodium compounds; monosodium glutamate (MSG, Accent)

High-Sodium Foods
Each item in this group contains approximately 1 g salt (400 mg sodium). Only 1 of these items should be eaten each day.

Miscellaneous
¼ tsp. salt, scant
1 tsp. soy sauce
4 tsp. Worcestershire sauce
2⅓ tbsp. catsup
2 tbsp. mustard, chili sauce, or barbecue sauce
4⅔ tbsp. tartar sauce
4⅔ tbsp. mayonnaise 4 tbsp. Thousand Island salad dressing
3 tbsp. Russian salad dressing
2 tbsp. French salad dressing
1⅓ tbsp. Italian salad dressing
4 medium, 3 extra large, or 2 giant green olives (16 g)
4 tbsp. sweet pickle relish (60 g)
¼ of 12″ thin-crust cheese pizza
Meats or substitute
1 small hot dog or 1 slice luncheon meat
4 slices bacon
1½ oz. cooked pork sausage
1½ oz. ham or corned beef
1½ oz. regular canned tuna
3 oz. regular canned salmon
1½ oz. regular canned crab
¾ cup cottage cheese
2 oz. cheese

(continued)

Breads, cereals, desserts
Pretzels: 20 small, 3 twisted medium, 1 Dutch, or 1 soft
Vegetables
2 servings (½ cup each) regular canned vegetables
⅓ cup canned regular sauerkraut, drained
½ large dill pickle (30 g)
1 oz. (approximately 20) potato chips
Soups
Canned, diluted with equal amounts of water:
⅔ cup beef broth or vegetable vegetarian
½ cup bisque of tomato, clam chowder (Manhattan style), chicken gumbo, cream of asparagus, cream of celery, golden vegetable noodle-O's, old-fashioned tomato rice, or tomato
⅓ cup cream of mushroom

Source: American Dietetic Association (136).

SAMPLE MENU FOR THE 4,000-TO-5,000-mg SODIUM DIET (FOR A MALE, AGE 25–50)

BREAKFAST	
Fresh grapefruit	½ medium
Bran flakes	¾ cup
Low-fat milk	1 cup
Banana	1 medium
Whole wheat toast	2 slices
Margarine	2 tsp.
Jelly	1 tbsp.
Coffee or tea	1 cup
LUNCH	
Regular vegetable soup	1 cup
Lean hamburger	3 oz.
Swiss cheese	1 oz.
Hamburger bun	1
Sliced tomato	2 slices
Lettuce	1 leaf
Fresh fruit salad	1 cup
Oatmeal cookies	2
Low-fat milk	1 cup
DINNER	
Low-sodium tomato juice	½ cup
Broiled chicken breast	3 oz.
Brown rice	½ cup
Steamed broccoli	½ cup
Hard dinner rolls	2
Margarine	2 tsp.
Carrot-and-raisin salad	½ cup
Strawberry frozen yogurt	½ cup
Low-fat milk	1 cup
Coffee or tea	1 cup
EVENING SNACK	
Vanilla wafers	6
Low-fat fruit yogurt	1 cup

(continued)

Approximate Nutrient Analysis

Energy	2,872 kcal
Protein	132.7 g (18% of kcal)
Fat	84.8 g (27% of kcal)
Polyunsaturated fat	8.0 g
Monounsaturated fat	23.5 g
Saturated fat	31.2 g
Cholesterol	275 mg
Carbohydrate	410.2 g (57% of kcal)
Vitamin A	26,900 IU
	3,397 RE
Thiamine	1.99 mg
Riboflavin	3.34 mg
Niacin	34.9 mg
Folate	310 mcg
Vitamin B-12	7.90 mcg
Vitamin B-6	3.08 mg
Vitamin C	146.8 mg
Calcium	1,831 mg
Phosphorus	2,178 mg
Iron	32.9 mg
Copper	1.38 mg
Zinc	17.4 mg
Magnesium	420 mg
Sodium	3,305 mg
Potassium	4,829 mg

FOOD LIST FOR THE 2,000-mg SODIUM DIET

Food group	Foods allowed	Foods excluded
Milk and milk products (Limit to 16 oz. per day.)	Any milk—whole, low-fat, skim, chocolate, cocoa; yogurt; eggnog; milk shake; substitute 8 oz. of milk for 4 oz. evaporated milk, 4 oz. condensed milk, or ⅓ cup dry milk powder	Buttermilk, malted milk
Vegetables (2–4 servings per day)	Fresh, frozen, or low-sodium canned vegetables; low-sodium vegetable juices	Regular canned vegetables and vegetable juices; sauerkraut; pickled vegetables and other preparations that use brine; frozen vegetables in sauce
Fruits (2 or more servings per day)	All fruits and fruit juices	None

(continued)

Breads and cereals (4 or more servings per day)	Enriched white, wheat, rye, or pumpernickel bread; hard dinner rolls, cooked cereal without salt, dry low-sodium cereals, un-salted crackers and breadsticks; biscuits, muffins, cornbread, pan-cakes, and waffles made with low-sodium baking powder; low-sodium or homemade bread crumbs	Breads and rolls with salted tops; quick breads, instant hot cereals, dry cereals with added sodium, crackers with salted tops; pancakes, waffles, muffins, biscuits, or cornbread made with salt, baking powder, self-rising flour, and instant mixes; regular bread crumbs or cracker crumbs
Potato or substitute	White or sweet potatoes; salt-free potato chips; enriched rice, barley, noodles, spaghetti, macaroni, and other pastas; homemade bread stuffing	Potato casserole mixes; salted potato chips and other snack chips; instant rice and pasta mixes, commercial casserole mixes, commercial stuffing
Meats or substitute (6 oz. or more per day)	Any fresh or fresh-frozen meats—beef, lamb, pork, veal, or game; fresh or fresh-frozen poultry—chicken, turkey, Cornish hen, or others; freshwater or fresh-frozen unbreaded fish and shellfish; low-sodium canned tuna, salmon, or sardines; eggs, low-sodium cheese, cream cheese, ricotta cheese, dry cottage cheese; low-sodium peanut butter, dry peas and beans	Any meat, fish, or poultry that is smoked, cured, salted, or canned—bacon, chipped beef, corned beef, cold cuts, ham, hot dogs, and sausages; sardines, anchovies, marinated herring, and pickled meats; regular canned tuna and salmon; pickled eggs; regular hard and processed cheese, cheese spreads, regular peanut butter; frozen dinner entrées
Fats	Unsalted butter or margarine; unsalted salad dressings; vegetable oils, shortening, mayonnaise-type salad dressing; light, heavy, and sour cream	Salted butter or margarine; regular salad dressings; bacon fat, salt pork; snack dips made with cheese, bacon, buttermilk, instant soup mixes, etc.
Soups	Low-sodium bouillon, broth, and consommé; low-sodium commercial canned or dehydrated soups; homemade soups with allowed vegetables and/or milk	Regular bouillon, broth, or consommé; regular canned or dehydrated commercial soups
Sweets and desserts	Any sweets and desserts (those made from milk should be within milk allowance)	None
Beverages	All beverages	Commercially softened water; beverages and foods made with commercially softened water

(continued)

Miscellaneous	Limit salt to ½ tsp. per day; salt substitute (with physician's approval); pepper, herbs, spices, flavorings, vinegar, lemon or lime juice; salt-free seasoning mixes; low-sodium condiments—catsup, chili sauce, mustard, pickles; fresh-ground horseradish, Tabasco sauce, low-sodium baking powder; unsalted snacks—nuts, seeds, pretzels, popcorn	Garlic salt, celery salt, onion salt, seasoned salt, sea salt, rock salt, kosher salt; any other seasoning containing salt and sodium compounds; monosodium glutamate (Accent); regular catsup, chili sauce, mustard, pickles, relishes, olives, horseradish; Kitchen Bouquet, gravy, sauce mixes; barbecue sauce, soy and teriyaki sauce, Worcestershire and steak sauce; salted snack items—nuts, seeds, pretzels, popcorn; all commercially prepared and convenience foods

Source: American Dietetic Association (136).

SAMPLE MENU FOR THE 2,000-mg SODIUM DIET (FOR A MALE, AGE 25–50)

BREAKFAST
Fresh grapefruit	½ medium
Shredded wheat	¾ cup
Low-fat milk	1 cup
Banana	1 medium
Whole wheat toast	2 slices
Margarine	2 tsp.
Jelly	1 tbsp.
Coffee or tea	1 cup

LUNCH
Low-sodium vegetable soup	1 cup
Lean hamburger	4 oz.
Regular hamburger bun	1
Sliced tomato	2 slices
Lettuce	1 leaf
Fresh fruit salad	1 cup
Oatmeal cookies	2
Low-fat milk	1 cup

DINNER
Unsalted tomato juice	½ cup
Broiled chicken breast	3 oz.
Herbed brown rice	½ cup
Steamed broccoli	½ cup
Regular hard dinner rolls	2
Margarine	2 tsp.
Carrot-and-raisin salad (with low-sodium mayonnaise)	½ cup
Raspberry sorbet	½ cup
Decaffeinated coffee	1 cup

(continued)

EVENING SNACK

Vanilla wafers	6
Low-fat fruit yogurt	1 cup

Approximate Nutrient Analysis

Energy	2,688 kcal
Protein	121.2 g (18% of kcal)
Fat	81.2 g (27% of kcal)
Polyunsaturated fat	7.6 g
Monounsaturated fat	20.6 g
Saturated fat	22.8 g
Cholesterol	244 mg
Carbohydrate	378.0 g (56% of kcal)
Vitamin A	20,374 IU
	2,350 RE
Thiamine	1.38 mg
Riboflavin	2.39 mg
Niacin	29.3 mg
Folate	222 mcg
Vitamin B-12	5.60 mcg
Vitamin B-6	2.51 mg
Vitamin C	134.8 mg
Calcium	1,213 mg
Phosphorus	1,674 mg
Iron	13.1 mg
Copper	1.29 mg
Zinc	14.2 mg
Magnesium	392 mg
Sodium	1,638 mg
Potassium	4,057 mg

FOOD LIST FOR THE 1,000-mg SODIUM DIET

Food group	Foods allowed	Foods excluded
Milk and milk products (Limit to 16 oz. per day.)	Any milk and milk drinks, except those excluded	Buttermilk, malted milk, milk shakes
Vegetables (2 or more servings per day)	Fresh, unsalted frozen, or low-sodium canned, except those specifically excluded; low-sodium vegetable juices	Vegetables prepared with salt; frozen peas, frozen lima beans, frozen mixed vegetables, frozen corn; sauerkraut, pickles, and other vegetables prepared in brine; frozen vegetables in sauce
Fruits (2 or more servings per day)	All fruits and fruit juices	None

(continued)

Breads and cereals (4 or more servings per day)	Regular whole-grain or enriched bread (4 slices per day); low-sodium bread, low-sodium crackers, low-sodium matzo, low-sodium melba toast, low-sodium hot water cornbread; biscuits, pancakes, cornbread, waffles made with low-sodium baking powder; cooked cereals prepared without salt; puffed rice, puffed wheat, shredded wheat, low-sodium cornflakes, and other low-sodium cereals	Sweet rolls, crackers, and other products containing salt, baking powder, or self-rising flour; instant hot cereal and other dry cereals; regular bread crumbs and cracker crumbs
Potato or substitute	Unsalted potatoes, salt-free potato chips; unsalted enriched rice, barley, noodles, spaghetti, macaroni, and other pastas; homemade bread stuffing	Instant potatoes; instant rice and pasta mixes; salted potato chips, other snack chips; commercial stuffing mixes
Meats or substitute (Limit to 7 oz. per day.)	Any fresh or fresh-frozen meats, poultry, fish, or shellfish; eggs; low-sodium cheese, cream cheese, ricotta cheese; dry peas and beans, low-sodium peanut butter; low-sodium tuna and salmon	Any meat, fish, or poultry that is cured, salted, canned, or smoked—chipped beef, corned beef, ham, cold cuts, bacon, hot dogs, and other sausages; sardines, anchovies, marinated herring, pickled meats, pickled eggs; regular peanut butter, regular hard and processed cheeses, cheese spreads; regular canned tuna and salmon; frozen entrées
Fats	Sweet or unsalted butter, unsalted margarine, vegetable oils, shortening, unsalted salad dressing, low-sodium salad dressing, low-sodium mayonnaise	Salted butter or margarine; regular bacon fat, salt pork; regular salad dressing; nondairy cream (up to 1 oz. cream daily)
Soups	Low-sodium bouillon, broth, and consommé; low-sodium commercial canned or dehydrated soups	Regular bouillon, broth, or consommé; regular canned or dehydrated soups

(*continued*)

Sweets and desserts	Sugar, syrup, honey, jelly, marmalade, jam, hard candies and other sugar candies, molasses, marshmallows, semisweet and baking chocolate; desserts made with plain gelatin and fruit juice or dietetic gelatin with no sodium added; unsalted bakery goods—homemade or commercial; ice cream, pudding, and custard made from milk and/or egg allowance; sherbet, water ice, and flavored gelatin (not to exceed 1 cup per day)	All candies made with sweet chocolate, nuts, or coconut; desserts made with rennin, rennin tablets; all other sweets and desserts
Beverages	All beverages; carbonated beverages (not to exceed 16 oz. per day)	Commercially softened water; beverages made with commercially softened water
Miscellaneous	Salt substitute (with physician's approval); unsalted cream sauce made from milk allowance, unsalted meat-base gravy; pepper, spices, flavorings, vinegar, lemon juice; low-sodium catsup, low-sodium chili sauce, low-sodium mustard, low-sodium pickles, fresh-ground horseradish; low-sodium Tabasco sauce; unsalted nuts, unsalted seeds, unsalted pretzels, unsalted popcorn; leavening agents—yeast, cream of tartar, potassium bicarbonate, sodium-free baking powder	Regular cream sauce, regular gravy; salt; regular catsup, chili sauce, mustard, pickles, relishes, olives, horseradish; celery salt, onion salt, garlic salt, seasoned salt, sea salt, rock salt, kosher salt, monosodium glutamate; Kitchen Bouquet, barbecue sauce, soy sauce, teriyaki sauce, steak sauce, Worcestershire sauce; salted nuts, seeds, and popcorn; pretzels and snack crackers; all commercially prepared or convenience foods

Source: American Dietetic Association (136).

SAMPLE MENU FOR THE 1,000-mg SODIUM DIET (FOR A MALE, AGE 25–50)

BREAKFAST	
Fresh grapefruit	½ medium
Shredded wheat	¾ cup
Low-fat milk	1 cup
Banana	1 medium
Low-sodium whole wheat toast	2 slices
Unsalted margarine	2 tsp.
Jelly	1 tbsp.
Coffee or tea	1 cup

(*continued*)

LUNCH

Low-sodium vegetable soup	1 cup
Lean hamburger	3 oz.
Low-sodium whole wheat toast	2 slices
Sliced tomato	2 slices
Lettuce	1 leaf
Fresh fruit salad	1 cup
Oatmeal cookies	2
Low-fat milk	1 cup

DINNER

Unsalted tomato juice	½ cup
Broiled chicken breast	3 oz.
Herbed brown rice	½ cup
Steamed broccoli	½ cup
Low-sodium whole wheat bread	2 slices
Unsalted margarine	2 tsp.
Carrot-and-raisin salad (with low-sodium mayonnaise)	½ cup
Raspberry sorbet	½ cup
Decaffeinated coffee	1 cup

EVENING SNACK

Low-sodium whole wheat bread	2 slices
Unsalted peanut butter	2 tbsp.
Apple juice	1 cup

Approximate Nutrient Analysis

Energy	2,667 kcal
Protein	119.0 g (18% of kcal)
Fat	87.8 g (30% of kcal)
Polyunsaturated fat	14.3 g
Monounsaturated fat	27.0 g
Saturated fat	22.5 g
Cholesterol	200 mg
Carbohydrate	373.6 g (56% of kcal)
Vitamin A	20,239 IU
	2,325 RE
Thiamine	1.44 mg
Riboflavin	1.94 mg
Niacin	33.7 mg
Folate	323 mcg
Vitamin B-12	4.07 mcg
Vitamin B-6	2.71 mg
Vitamin C	134.8 mg
Calcium	992 mg
Phosphorus	1,766 mg
Iron	15.7 mg
Copper	1.88 mg
Zinc	14.7 mg
Magnesium	572 mg
Sodium	814 mg
Potassium	4,371 mg

(continued)

SUBSTITUTIONS FOR 1 SLICE OF REGULAR BREAD (120 TO 140 mg SODIUM)

½ large or 1 small hamburger bun, frankfurter bun, or other plain roll
1 small sweet roll or doughnut
1 cup milk (in addition to amount allowed)
1 slice cake, any kind
2 large or 5 small cookies, any kind
3 saltine crackers
2 graham crackers
2 strips bacon
¼ cup cottage cheese
½ cup pudding or custard (not instant)
1 cup ice cream

FOOD LIST FOR THE 500-mg SODIUM DIET

Use the 1,000-mg sodium diet with the following modifications:
• Use low-sodium bread only.
• Omit sherbet and flavored gelatin.
• Limit meat to 6 oz. per day; 1 egg may be used per day in place of 1 oz. of meat.
• Omit the following vegetables: beets, beet greens, carrots, kale, spinach, celery, white
  turnips, rutabagas, mustard greens, chard, and dandelion greens.

Source: American Dietetic Association (136).

SAMPLE MENU FOR THE 500-mg SODIUM DIET (FOR A MALE, AGE 25–50)

BREAKFAST	
Fresh grapefruit	½ medium
Shredded wheat	¾ cup
Low-fat milk	1 cup
Banana	1 medium
Low-sodium whole wheat toast	2 slices
Unsalted margarine	2 tsp.
Jelly	1 tbsp.
Coffee or tea	1 cup
LUNCH	
Cantaloupe	¼ medium
Lean hamburger	3 oz.
Low-sodium whole wheat toast	2 slices
Sliced tomato	2 slices
Lettuce	1 leaf
Unsalted potato chips	1 oz.
Fresh fruit salad	1 cup
Oatmeal cookie	1
AFTERNOON SNACK	
Jelly beans	1 oz.

(*continued*)

DINNER

Unsalted tomato juice	½ cup
Broiled chicken breast	3 oz.
Herbed brown rice	1 cup
Steamed broccoli	½ cup
Low-sodium whole wheat bread	2 slices
Unsalted margarine	2 tsp.
Coleslaw (with vinegar and oil)	½ cup
Fruit ice	½ cup
Decaffeinated coffee	1 cup

EVENING SNACK

Low-sodium rice cakes	4
Unsalted peanut butter	2 tbsp.
Apple juice	1 cup

Approximate Nutrient Analysis

Energy	2,745 kcal
Protein	105.2 g (15% of kcal)
Fat	82.2 g (27% of kcal)
Polyunsaturated fat	21.1 g
Monounsaturated fat	28.4 g
Saturated fat	22.9 g
Cholesterol	185 mg
Carbohydrate	413.3 g (60% of kcal)
Vitamin A	15,564 IU
	1,697 RE
Thiamine	1.36 mg
Riboflavin	1.55 mg
Niacin	35.7 mg
Folate	323 mcg
Vitamin B-12	3.17 mcg
Vitamin B-6	2.70 mg
Vitamin C	165.7 mg
Calcium	703 mg
Phosphorus	1,535 mg
Iron	15.4 mg
Copper	1.75 mg
Zinc	12.9 mg
Magnesium	492 mg
Sodium	460 mg
Potassium	4,347 mg

REFERENCES

1. Food and Nutrition Board, National Research Council—National Academy of Sciences: Diet and health: Implications for reducing chronic disease risk. Report of the Committee on Diet and Health. Washington, D.C.: National Academy Press, 1989.
2. Report of a WHO Expert Committee: Arterial hypertension. Technical Report ser. 628. Geneva: World Health Organization, 1978.
3. National High Blood Pressure Education Program, National Heart, Lung, and Blood Institute: The 1988 report of the Joint National Committee on Detection, Evaluation and Treatment of High Blood Pressure. NIH Publication no. 88-1088. Bethesda, Md.: U.S. Department of Health and Human Services, 1988.
4. DuCailar, G., Ribstein, J., et al.: Influence of sodium intake on left ventricular structure in untreated essential hypertensives. J Hypertens 7 (Supp 6):S258, 1989.
5. WHO/ISH Mild Hypertension Liaison Committee: 1989 Guidelines for the management of mild hypertension: Memorandum from a WHO/ISH meeting. J Hypertens 7:689, 1989.
6. Lee, S. P.: Diseases of the liver and biliary tract. In Kinney, J. M., Jeejeebhoy, K. N., et al.: Nutrition and metabolism in patient care. Philadelphia: W. B. Saunders, 1988.
7. Podolsky, D. K., and Isselbacher, K. J.: Cirrhosis. In Braunwald, E., Isselbacher, K. J., et al.: Harrison's principles of internal medicine. 11th ed. New York: McGraw-Hill, 1987.
8. Powers, D. E., and Moore, A. O.: Food/medication interactions. 6th ed. Phoenix: 1988 (self-published).
9. Williams, G., and Dluhy, R.: Diseases of the adrenal cortex. In Braunwald, E., Isselbacher, K. J., et al.: Harrison's principles of internal medicine. 11th ed. New York: McGraw-Hill, 1987.
10. Kaufman, A., and Kahn, T.: Congestive heart failure with hypernatremia. Arch Intern Med 146:402, 1986.
11. Isieri, L. T., and Benvenuti, D. J.: Pathogenesis and management of congestive heart failure. Am Heart J 105:346, 1983.
12. Stamler, R., Stamler, J., et al.: Primary prevention of hypertension by nutritional-hygienic means: Final report of a randomized controlled trial. JAMA 262:1801, 1989.
13. Adlin, E. V.: Edema and hypertension. In Kinney, J. M., Jeejeebhoy, K. N., et al.: Nutrition and metabolism in patient care. Philadelphia: W. B. Saunders, 1988.
14. Weinberger, M. H.: Clinical studies of the role of dietary sodium in blood pressure. In Laragh, J. H., and Brenner, B. M.: Hypertension, pathophysiology, diagnosis and treatment. Vol. 2. New York: Raven Press, 1990.
15. Langford, H. G.: Drug and dietary intervention in hypertension. Hypertension 4 (Supp 3):166, 1982.
16. Wilber, J. A.: The role of diet in the treatment of high blood pressure. J Am Diet Assoc 80:25, 1982.
17. Hypertension Detection and Follow-up Program Cooperative Group: Five-year findings of the hypertension detection and follow-up program: Reduction in mortality of persons with high blood pressure, including mild hypertension. JAMA 242:2562, 1979.
18. Langford, H. G., Blaufox, A., et al.: Dietary therapy slows the return of hypertension after stopping prolonged medication. JAMA 253:657, 1985.
19. Intersalt Cooperative Research Group: Intersalt: An international study of electrolyte excretion and blood pressure: Results for 24 hour urinary sodium and potassium excretion. Br Med J 297:319, 1988.
20. Kaplan, N. M.: New evidence on the role of sodium in hypertension: The Intersalt study. Am J Hypertens 3:168, 1990.
21. Langford, H. G.: Nonpharmacological therapy of hypertension. Comment on diet and blood pressure. Hypertension 13:1, 1989.
22. Brunner, H. R., and Gavras, H.: Renin, angiotensin, aldosterone, salt and the kidney. In Brunner, H. R., and Gavras, H.: Clinical hypertension and hypotension. New York: Marcel Dekker, 1983.
23. Dustan, H. R., Tarazi, R. C., and Bravo, E. L.: Diuretic and diet treatment of hypertension. Arch Intern Med 133:1007, 1974.
24. Luft, F. C., and Weinberger, M. H.: Review of salt restriction and the response to antihypertensive drugs: Satellite symposium on calcium antagonists. Hypertension 11 (Supp 1):229, 1988.
25. Weinberger, M. H., Cohen, S. J., et al.: Dietary sodium restriction as adjunctive treatment of hypertension. JAMA 259:2561, 1988.
26. Kristinsson, A., Hardarson, T., et al.: Additive effects of moderate salt reduction and captopril in hypertension. Acta Med Scand 223:133, 1988.
27. Danton, D.: Sodium: The main cation of body fluids. In Danton, D.: The hunger for salt. New York: Springer-Verlag, 1982.
28. Beard, T., Gray, W. R., et al.: Randomized controlled trial of a no-added sodium diet for mild hypertension. Lancet 2:455, 1982.
29. Nicholson, J. P., Resnick, L. M., and Laragh, J. A.: The impact of dietary sodium intake on the hypotensive response of verapamil in essential hypertension. J Clin Hypertens 3:143S, 1986.
30. O'Connor, D. T.: Response of the renal kallikrein-kinin system, intravascular volume, and renal hemodynamics to sodium restriction and diuretic treatment in essential hypertension. Hypertension 4:72, 1982.
31. Liberthal, A., Narenda, B. O., et al.: Effects of alteration in sodium and water metabolism on urinary excretion of active and inactive kallikrein in man. J Clin Endocrinol Metabol 56:513, 1983.
32. Gillum, R. F., Prineas, R. J., et al.: Nonpharmacologic therapy of hypertension: The independent effects of weight reduction and sodium restriction in overweight borderline hypertensive patients. Am Heart J 105:128, 1983.
33. Reisin, E.: Weight reduction as a

therapeutic modality in hypertension: The influence of concurrent sodium deprivation. In Laragh, J. H., and Brenner, B. M.: Hypertension, pathophysiology, diagnosis and management. Vol. 2. New York: Raven Press, 1990.

34. Stamler, R., Stamler, J., et al.: Nutritional therapy for high blood pressure: Final report of a four-year randomized clinical trial: The hypertension control program. JAMA 257:1484, 1987.

35. McGregor, G. A., Markandu, N. D., et al.: Double blind randomized crossover trial of moderate sodium restriction in essential hypertension. Lancet 1:352, 1982.

36. Salvetti, A., Pedrinelli, R., et al.: Differential effects of selective and non selective prostaglandin synthesis inhibition on the pharmacological responses to captopril in patients with essential hypertension. Clin Sci Mol Med 63:261S, 1982.

37. Witzgall, H., Scherer, B., and Weber, P. C.: Involvement of prostaglandins in the actions of captopril. Clin Sci Mol Med 63:265S, 1982.

38. Philips, S. J.: Pathogenesis, diagnosis, and treatment of hypertension-associated stroke. Am J Hypertens 2:493, 1989.

39. Stamler, J., Rose, G., et al.: Intersalt study findings: Public health and medical care implications. Hypertension 14:570, 1989.

40. Gazes, P. C.: Clinical cardiology. Philadelphia: Lea & Febiger, 1990.

41. Smith, T. W., Braunwald, E., and Kelly, R. A.: Management of heart failure. In Braunwald, E.: Heart disease: A textbook of cardiovascular medicine 3d ed. Philadelphia: W. B. Saunders, 1988.

42. Cannon, P. J.: Sodium retention in heart failure. Cardiol Clin 7:49, 1989.

43. Talartschik, J., Eisenhauer, T., et al.: Low atrial natriuretic peptide plasma concentrations in 100 patients with essential hypertension. Am J Hypertens 3:45, 1990.

44. Moore, T. J.: The role of dietary electrolytes in hypertension. J Am Coll Nutr 8:68s, 1989.

45. Weinberger, M. H., Miller, J. Z., et al.: Definitions and characteristics of sodium sensitivity and blood pressure resistance. Hypertension 8 (Supp 2):127, 1986.

46. Oparil, S., Yang, R. H., et al.: Central mechanisms of hypertension. Am J Hypertens 2:474, 1989.

47. Ramirez, A. J., Gemenez, M. I., et al.: Renal sodium handling abnormalities in hypertensive and normotensive patients with a family history of hypertension. J Hypertens 7:S178, 1989.

48. Halkin, H., Modan, M., et al.: Altered erythrocyte and plasma sodium and potassium in hypertension, a facet of hyperinsulinemia. Hypertension 11:71, 1988.

49. Reisin, E.: Sodium and obesity in the pathogenesis of hypertension. Am J Hypertens 3:164, 1990.

50. Weinberger, M. H., Luft, F. C., et al.: Sodium sensitivity and resistance of blood pressure. J Clin Hypertens 3:47S, 1987.

51. Caplan, L. R.: Cerebrovascular disease in blacks. J Clin Hypertens 3:25S, 1987.

52. Akinkugbe, O. O.: World epidemiology of hypertension in blacks. J Clin Hypertens 3:1S, 1987.

53. Rydstedt, L., Williams, G. H., and Hollenberg, N. K.: The renal and endocrine response to saline infusion in essential hypertension. Hypertension 8:217, 1986.

54. Hollenberg, N. K., Moore, T. J., et al.: Abnormal renal sodium handling in essential hypertension: Relation to failure of renal and adrenal modulation of responses to angiotensin II. Am J Med 81:412, 1986.

55. Shoback, D. M., Williams, G. H., et al.: Defect in the sodium modulated tissue responsiveness to angiotensin II in essential hypertension. J Clin Invest 72:2115, 1983.

56. Dluhy, R. G., Hopkins, P., et al.: Heritable abnormalities of the renin-angiotensin-aldosterone system in essential hypertension. J Cardiovas Pharmacol 12:S149, 1988.

57. Al-bander, S. Y., Nix, L., et al.: Food chloride distribution in nature and its relation to sodium content. J Am Diet Assoc 88:472, 1988.

58. Kurtz, T. W., Al-bander, H., and Morris, R. C.: "Salt sensitive" essential hypertension in men: Is sodium ion alone important? N Engl J Med 317:1043, 1987.

59. Morris, R. C., Al-bander, H., and Kurtz, T. W.: Role of dietary chloride in hypertension. In Laragh, J. H., and Brenner, B. M.: Hypertension, pathophysiology, diagnosis and management. Vol. 2. New York: Raven Press, 1990.

60. Skrabal, F., Aubock, J., and Hortnagl, H.: Low sodium/high potassium diet for prevention of hypertension: Probable mechanisms of action. Lancet 1:895, 1981.

61. MacGregor, G. A., Smith, S. J., et al.: Moderate potassium supplementation in essential hypertension. Lancet 2:567, 1982.

62. Paller, M. S., and Linas, S. L.: Hemodynamic effects of alterations in potassium. Hypertension 4 (Supp 3):20, 1982.

63. Miller, G. D.: Relationship between urinary sodium and potassium and arterial blood pressure: An epidemiologic study. J Nat Med Assoc 76:47, 1984.

64. Rinner, M. D., Spliet-van Laar, L., and Kromhout, D.: Serum sodium, potassium, calcium and magnesium and blood pressure in a Dutch population. J Hypertens 7:977, 1989.

65. Khaw, K. T., and Barrett-Connor, E.: Dietary potassium and stroke associated mortality: A 12-year prospective population study. N Engl J Med 316:235, 1987.

66. Langford, H. C.: Dietary sodium, potassium and calcium in black hypertensive subjects. J Clin Hypertens 3:37S, 1987.

67. Treasure, J., and Ploth, D.: Role of dietary potassium in the treatment of hypertension. Hypertension 5:864, 1983.

68. Tannen, R. L.: Effects of potassium on blood pressure control. Ann Intern Med 98:773, 1983.

69. McCarron, D. A., Morris, C. D., and Cole, C.: Dietary calcium in human hypertension. Science 217:267, 1982.

70. McCarron, D. W., and Morris, C. D.: Epidemiological evidence associating dietary calcium and calcium metabolism with blood pressure. Am J Nephrol 6 (Supp 1):3, 1986.

71. Reed, D., McGee, D., et al.: Diet, blood pressure and multicolinearity. Hypertension 7:405, 1985.

72. Kesteloot, H., and Geboers, J.: Calcium and blood pressure. Lancet 12:813, 1982.

73. Zidek, W., Vetter, H., et al.: Intracellular Na+ and Ca+ activities in essential hypertension. Clin Sci Mol Med 63:47S, 1982.

74. Spieker, C., Zidek, V., et al.: Intracellular calcium in secondary hypertension. Nephron 47 (Supp 1):146, 1987.

75. McCarron, D. A.: Calcium, magnesium and phosphorus balance in human and experimental hypertension. Hypertension 4 (Supp 3):27, 1982.

76. Zidek, W., and Vetter, H.: Calcium and primary hypertension. Nephron 47 (Supp 1):13, 1987.

77. McCarron, D. A.: Calcium and magnesium nutrition in human hypertension. Ann Intern Med 98:800, 1983.

78. Bohr, D. F.: Vascular smooth muscle: Dual effect of calcium. Science 139:597, 1963.

79. Blum, M., Kirsten, M., and Worth, M. H., Jr.: Reversible hypertension, caused by the hypercalcemia of hyperparathyroidism, vitamin D toxicity, and calcium infusion. JAMA 237:262, 1977.

80. Resnick, L. M.: The role of dietary calcium and magnesium in the therapy of hypertension. In Laragh, J. H., and Brenner, B. M.: Hypertension, pathophysiology, diagnosis and treatment. Vol. 2. New York: Raven Press, 1990.

81. Resnick, L. M., Muller, F. B., and Laragh, J. H.: Calcium regulating hormones in essential hypertension: Relation to plasma renin activity and sodium metabolism. Ann Intern Med 105:649, 1986.

82. Campese, V. M.: Calcium, parathyroid hormone and sympathoadrenal system. Am J Nephrol 6 (Supp 1):29, 1986.

83. Resnick, L. M.: Calciotrophic hormones in clinical and experimental hypertension. In Laragh, J. H., and Brenner, B. M.: Perspectives in hypertension. Vol. 2. Endocrine mechanisms and hypertension. New York: Raven Press, 1989.

84. Resnick, L. M., Preibisz, J. J., and Laragh, J. H.: Calcitonin gene-related peptide-like immunoreactivity in hypertension: Relation to blood pressure, sodium and calcium metabolism. In Ganten, D. S., and Rettech, R.: Salt and hypertension. New York: Springer-Verlag, 1989.

85. Wyss, J. M., Chen, Y. F., et al.: Dietary Ca-2+ prevents NaCl induced exacerbation of hypertension and increases hypothalamic norepinephrine turnover in spontaneously hypertensive rats. J Hypertens 7:711, 1989.

86. Shibutani, Y., Sakamoto, K., et al.: Relation of serum and erythrocyte magnesium levels to blood pressure and a family history of hypertension: A follow-up study in Japanese children, 12–14 years of age. Acta Paediatr Scand 79:316, 1990.

87. Iaconi, J. M., Judd, J. T., et al.: The role of dietary essential fatty acids and prostaglandins in reducing blood pressure. In Holman, R. T.: Essential fatty acids and prostaglandins: Progress in lipid research. Vol. 20. New York: Pergamon Press, 1981.

88. Rouse, I., Stampfer, M., et al.: Effect of dietary fats and carbohydrates in blood pressure in mildly hypertensive patients. Hypertension 10:452, 1987.

89. Food and Nutrition Board, National Research Council: Recommended Dietary Allowances. 10th ed. Washington, D.C.: National Academy Press, 1989.

90. Epstein, M.: Renal complications in liver disease. In Schiff, L., and Schiff, F. R.: Diseases of the liver. 6th ed. Philadelphia: J. B. Lippincott, 1987.

91. Boyer, T. J.: Cirrhosis of the liver. In Wyngaarden, J. B., and Smith, L. H.: Cecil textbook of medicine. 18th ed. Philadelphia: W. B. Saunders, 1988.

92. Becker, L. C., and Flaherty, J. T.: Myocardial infarction. In Harvey, A. M., Johns, R. J., et al.: Principles and practice of medicine. 20th ed. East Norwalk, Conn.: Appleton-Century-Crofts, 1980.

93. Kihara, M., Fujikawa, J., and Ohtaka, M.: Interrelationships between blood pressure, sodium, potassium, serum cholesterol and protein intake in Japanese. Hypertension 6:736, 1984.

94. Heymsfield, S. B., Hoff, R. D., et al.: Heart diseases. In Kinney, J. M., Jeejeebhoy, K. N., et al.: Nutrition and metabolism in patient care. Philadelphia: W. B. Saunders, 1988.

95. Vitiello, M. V., Prinz, P. N., and Halter, J. B.: Sodium restricted diet increases nighttime plasma norepinephrine and impairs sleep patterns in man. J Clin Endocrinol Metabol 56:553, 1983.

96. Randall, H. T.: Water, electrolytes and acid base balance. In Shils, M. E., and Young, V. R.: Modern nutrition in health and disease. 7th ed. Philadelphia: Lea & Febiger, 1988.

97. Swales, J. D.: Dietary sodium in hypertension. In Laragh, J. H., and Brenner, B. M.: Hypertension, pathophysiology, diagnosis and management. Vol. 2. New York: Raven Press, 1990.

98. Folkow, B., and Ely, D. L.: Dietary sodium effects on cardiovascular and sympathetic neuroeffector function as studied in various rat models. J Hypertens 5:383, 1987.

99. Thompson, J. E., Vollman, R. W., et al.: Prevention of hypotension and renal complications of aortic surgery using balanced salt solutions. Ann Surg 167:767, 1968.

100. Chung, H. M., Kluge, R., et al.: Postoperative hyponatremia: A prospective study. Arch Intern Med 146:333, 1986.

101. Collings, W. D., and Spangenberg, R. B.: Sodium excretion. In

Moses, C.: Sodium in medicine and health. Baltimore: Reese Press, 1980.

102. Sloan, R. W.: Drug interactions. Am Fam Physician 27:230, 1983.

103. Roe, D. A.: Handbook on drug and nutrient interactions. 4th ed. Chicago: American Dietetic Association, 1989.

104. Jeejeebhoy, K. N.: Short bowel syndrome. In Kinney, J. M., Jeejeebhoy, K. N., et al.: Nutrition and metabolism in patient care. Philadelphia: W. B. Saunders, 1988.

105. Alvestrand, A., and Bergstrom, J.: Renal disease. In Kinney, J. M., Jeejeebhoy, K. N., et al.: Nutrition and metabolism in patient care. Philadelphia: W. B. Saunders, 1988.

106. Foote, R. G.: The use of liberal salt diet in pre-eclamptic toxemia and essential hypertension with pregnancy. NZMJ 77:242, 1973.

107. Zeman, F. J., and Ney, D. M.: Applications in clinical nutrition. Englewood Cliffs, N.J.: Prentice-Hall, 1988.

108. Willis, S. E.: Hypertension in pregnancy. Am J Nurs 82:792, 1982.

109. Rodwell Williams, S.: Management of pregnancy complication and special disease conditions of the mother. In Worthington-Roberts, B., and Rodwell Williams, S.: Nutrition in pregnancy and lactation. 4th ed. St. Louis: Times Mirror/Mosby College Publishing, 1989.

110. Brown, M. A., Prendergast, J. S., et al.: Comparing methods to assess dietary sodium intake in pregnancy. J Am Diet Assoc 87:1058, 1987.

111. Mezey, E.: The liver and biliary system. In Paige, D.: Manual of clinical nutrition. Pleasantville, N.J.: Nutrition Publications, 1983.

112. Heymsfield, S. B., Smith, J., et al.: Nutritional support in cardiac failure. Surg Clin N Am 61:635, 1981.

113. Luft, F., Sloan, R., et al.: The utility of overnight urine in assessing compliance with a low sodium intake diet. JAMA 249:17884, 1983.

114. National Heart, Blood and Lung Institute, National Institutes of Health: The 1980 report of the Joint National Committee on Detection, Evaluation and Treatment of High Blood Pressure. NIH Publication no. 82-1088. Bethesda, Md.: U.S. Department of Health and Human Services, 1981.

115. Simko, V., Connell, A. M., and Banks, B.: Nutritional status in alcoholics with and without liver disease. Am J Clin Nutr 35:197, 1982.

116. Hodges, R. E.: Nutrition and the digestive system. In Hodges, R. E., and Adelman, R. D.: Nutrition in medical practice. Philadelphia: W. B. Saunders, 1980.

117. Mezey, E.: Liver disease and nutrition. Gastroenterology 74:770, 1978.

118. Black, H. R.: Choosing initial therapy for hypertension: A personal view. Hypertension 13 (Supp 1):1, 1989.

119. Hawkins, D. W., Dieckmann, M. R., and Horner, R. D.: Diuretics and hypertension in black adults. Arch Intern Med 148:803, 1988.

120. Frohlich, E. D.: Clinical pharmacology of calcium antagonist. Satellite symposium on calcium antagonists. Hypertension 11 (Supp 1):1, 1988.

121. Frishman, W. H., Stroh, J. A., et al.: Calcium channel blockers in systemic hypertension. Med Clin N Am 72:449, 1988.

122. Rotmensch, H. H., Vlasses, P. H., and Ferguson, R. K.: Angiotensin-converting enzyme inhibitors. Med Clin N Am 72:399, 1988.

123. Frishman, W. H., and Charlap, S.: Alpha adrenergic blockers. Med Clin N Am 72:427, 1988.

124. Frishman, W. H., Eisen, G., and Lapsker, J.: Terazosin: A new long-acting alpha-1 adrenergic antagonist for hypertension. Med Clin N Am 72:441, 1988.

125. Sica, D. A., and Gehr, T.: Diuretics in congestive heart failure. Cardiol Clin 7:87, 1989.

126. McMurray, J., and McDevitt, D. G.: Treatment of heart failure in the elderly. Br Med Bull 46:202, 1990.

127. Altschul, A. M., and Grommet, J. K.: Food choices for lowering sodium intake. Hypertension 3:116, 1982.

128. DeSwiet, M.: Blood pressure, sodium and take away food. Arch Dis Child 57:645, 1982.

129. Roe, D. A.: Diet and drug interactions. New York: Van Nostrand Reinhold, 1988.

130. Diet Committee of the San Francisco Heart Association: Sodium in medicinals. San Francisco: San Francisco Heart Association, 1973.

131. Low salt medications: An updated list to help pharmacists. Am Druggist, Aug. 1979.

132. Hoffman, C. J.: Does the sodium level in drinking water affect blood pressure levels? J Am Diet Assoc 88:1432, 1988.

133. Chauhan, J.: Relationships between sour and salt taste perception and selected subject attributes. J Am Diet Assoc 89:652, 1989.

134. Chauhan, J.: Pleasantness perception of salt in young vs. elderly adults. J Am Diet Assoc 89:834, 1989.

135. Ahern, D. A., and Kaley, L. A.: Electrolyte content of salt replacement seasonings. J Am Diet Assoc 89:935, 1989.

136. American Dietetic Association: Manual of clinical dietetics. Chicago: American Dietetic Association, 1988.

137. Working Group on Health Education and High Blood Pressure Control, U.S. Department of Health and Human Services: The physician's guide: Improving adherence among hypertensive patients. Bethesda, Md.: National Heart Lung and Blood Institute, NIH, 1987.

138. Sharp, D. S., and Benowitz, N. L.: Pharmacoepidemiology of the effect of caffeine on blood pressure. Clin Pharmacol Ther 47:57, 1990.

139. Von Dusseldorf, M., Smits, P., et al.: Effect of decaffeinated versus regular coffee on blood pressure: A 12-week, double blind trial. Hypertension 14:563, 1989.

140. Bak, A. A., and Grobbee, D. E.: Abstinence from coffee leads to a fall in blood pressure. J Hypertens 7 (Supp 6):S260, 1989.

141. Lake, C. R., Zaloga, G., et al.: Transient hypertension after two phenylpropanolamine diet aids and the ef-

fects of caffeine: A placebo controlled follow up study. Am J Med 86:427, 1989.

142. Friedman, G. D., Klatsky, A. L., and Siegelaub, A. B.: Alcohol, tobacco and hypertension. Hypertension 4 (Supp 3):150, 1982.

143. Larbi, E., Cooper, R. S., and Stamler, J.: Alcohol and hypertension. Arch Intern Med 143:28, 1983.

144. MacMahon, S. W., and Norton, R. N.: Alcohol and hypertension: Implications for prevention and treatment. Ann Intern Med 105:124, 1986.

145. Winston, M., Wilbur, C., et al.: Report of the Working Group on Critical Behaviors in the Dietary Management of High Blood Pressure. NIH Publication no. 83-2269. National Heart, Lung and Blood Institute, National High Blood Pressure Education Program, 1982.

146. Hollenberg, N. K., and Williams, G. H.: Sodium sensitive hypertension: Implications of pathogenesis for therapy. Am J Hypertens 2:809, 1989.

147. American Academy of Pediatrics: Report of the second task force on blood pressure control in children. Pediatrics 79:1, 1987.

33.

HIGH-POTASSIUM DIET

DEFINITION

A diet that provides a minimum of 100 mEq to 175 mEq (3,900 mg to 6,825 mg) potassium daily. The normal daily intake has been found to be 1,500 mg per day in 6-month-old infants, 3,400 mg per day in 15- to 20-year olds, 2,500 mg per day in urban white adults, and 1,000 mg per day in adult blacks. The National Research Council has recommended the average daily intake in the United States of 2,500 mg be increased to 3,500 mg (1–2).

PURPOSE OF THE DIET

The diet is designed to prevent hypo-kalemia and the depletion of body potassium reserves. Such depletion may occur as a result of therapy with potassium-wasting diuretics or steroids or from a disease state, such as primary aldosteronism.

The incidence and extent of potassium deficits induced by diuretic therapy vary considerably, depending upon the amount and type of drug used, the physiologic status of the patient, and the dietary potassium intake. Sustained and untreated potassium losses lead to the development of hypochloremic alkalosis and, eventually, a catabolic state with progressive nitrogen loss. When the serum potassium drops below 3.5 mEq per liter, symptoms of lethargy, weakness, muscle hypotonicity, loss of libido, and mental depression may occur. Serum levels of less than 2.7 mEq per liter may result in cardiac arrhythmias, and paralysis can occur at lower levels (3–6).

The diet may be used as an adjunct to

other forms of therapy in the treatment of chronic potassium depletion. Dietary measures alone are generally unsuccessful in reversing a preexisting potassium deficit, and a supplement is often necessary. However, a high-potassium diet may be used to prevent hypokalemia from developing in patients at risk (7–13).

EFFECTS OF THE DIET

1. SODIUM EXCRETION

A high potassium intake increases the amount of sodium excreted in the urine. Potassium has a natriuretic effect, causing inhibition of renal sodium absorption and renin production. It also causes vasodilation, probably by stimulation of the sodium-potassium pump (14–16).

A low dietary potassium intake may bring about the effect of a high sodium intake in salt-sensitive hypertensives, whereas a high potassium intake may blunt its effect. Dietary potassium, or the ratio of sodium to potassium intake, may be more important in the genesis of hypertension than the sodium content of the diet alone (17).

2. BLOOD PRESSURE

The effect of potassium supplementation in normotensive individuals is controversial. Some of the older studies document lowered blood pressure in normotensive individuals on an increased potassium intake. More-recent data indicate that patients who are on very low-sodium diets with normal potassium intakes and who are normokalemic will not lower their blood pressure any further with potas-

sium supplementation. There appears to be no benefit of a 2-g potassium supplement in normotensive, normokalemic individuals on a potassium intake of 1,700 mg per day (8, 18–22).

The effect of a 175-mEq potassium diet used for 10 days on 20 patients with essential hypertension was a fall in arterial blood pressure of 11 mg/Hg. Moderate reductions in dietary sodium intake with increased dietary potassium can lower blood pressure of persons with mild hypertension (3, 15).

In a group of patients with mild to moderate essential hypertension, an increase in dietary potassium intake from 2,400 mg to 4,000 mg daily produced a significant decrease in blood pressure. A low-potassium diet appears to elevate blood pressure by volume expansion. The blood pressure–lowering effects of a high-potassium diet are probably due to a diuretic action, altered activity of the renin-angiotensin system, a direct alteration of peripheral resistance, the antagonistic effects of a natriuretic hormone on the central nervous or peripheral nervous system, and increased synthesis of prostaglandin compounds in vascular smooth muscle. The steady decline in the incidence rates of hypertension in the United States in recent years correlates with a documented change in eating habits that includes greatly increased consumption of fruits and vegetables low in sodium and high in fiber and potassium (23–27).

3. GLUCOSE TOLERANCE

Potassium plays a role in insulin secretion: Its depletion may contribute to impaired insulin release. In certain conditions, potassium deficiency has been implicated in abnormal glucose tolerance test results, particularly in hypertensives taking large doses of thiazide diuretics (5, 11).

4. STROKES

According to the National Research Council, a potassium intake of at least 75 mEq per day may prevent stroke (1).

5. COLORECTAL CANCER

Epidemiological data indicate that a high potassium intake may protect against colon cancer (28).

PHYSIOLOGY, FOODS, AND NUTRIENTS

1. EFFECTS OF POTASSIUM DEPLETION

A. In Cirrhosis Hypokalemia results in metabolic alkalosis, which favors ammonia toxicity, azotemia, and the development of hepatic encephalopathy (29). When serum potassium falls below 3.5 mEq/L, the total body potassium deficit is about 300 to 500 mEq (30).

Potassium depletion is extremely common in Laënnec's cirrhosis as a consequence of vomiting, diarrhea, diuretics and the kalluretic action of secondary hyperaldosteronism; it causes major alterations in acid base balance that enhance the volatilization of ammonia and its passage into the cells, where it exerts its toxic effects (29).

B. In Heart Disease Potassium deficiency results in loss of myofibril striation, vacuolation and fragmentation, interstitial cellular infiltration, myocardial necrosis, fibroblastic proliferation, and ECG abnormalities (31). Children suffering from protein-energy malnutrition may be particularly susceptible to hypokalemia. Patients stricken with acute myocardial infarction who are hypokalemic may also be prone to the development of certain ectopic heart rhythms (32).

C. In Digitalis Therapy Hypokalemia

increases the effect of digitalis preparations, creating the possibility of digitalis intoxication. Once absorbed, digitalis glycosides compete with potassium for sites within the myocardium. A lack of potassium results in higher myocardial concentrations of digoxin and digitoxin and in potential toxicity (5, 33–37).

2. CHARACTERISTICS OF THE DIET

Increased amounts of fruits and vegetables that are good sources of potassium are included daily in the diet. These include bananas, prunes, oranges, melons, spinach, collard greens, potatoes, and mushrooms. Potassium intake is also augmented by extra servings of foods containing protein and potassium, e.g., legumes, meat, fish, and milk. The diet does not necessarily have to be high in kilocalories; however, it is incompatible with a very low-kilocalorie, low-sodium diet. The maximum and minimum amounts of sodium and potassium intake are also interdependent. If kilocalories must be restricted, a high-potassium diet may be expensive and lacking in variety (38).

INDICATIONS FOR USE

1. POTASSIUM-WASTING DIURETICS

A high-potassium diet may be indicated for use concomitantly with the administration of potassium-wasting diuretics, such as the thiazides, furosemide, and ethacrynic acid. Greater reliance on preventive diet therapy has been advocated in some instances prior to the demonstration of any great potassium losses. Glucose intolerance induced by thiazide diuretics can be prevented by the use of measures that preserve body potassium stores (5, 22).

2. OTHER SITUATIONS

Other indications for use are as follows:

• Cushing's disease, in which sodium is retained and potassium is excreted be-

cause of increased production of adrenal steroids
• Overtreatment with deoxycorticosterone or 9-fluorohydrocortisone preparations, which leads to potassium loss with sodium retention
• Primary hyperaldosteronism
• Loss of potassium due to vomiting or diarrhea
• Hypokalemia secondary to starvation and reduced carbohydrate intakes

Any patient with a serum potassium level significantly below 3.5 mEq/L or whose levels demonstrate a daily decreasing trend of more than 0.1 or 0.2 mEq/L should be evaluated for possible depletion of body potassium stores, requiring potassium replacements (4).

3. HYPOKALEMIA

Treatment of hypokalemia varies with the extent and the circumstance of the deficit. Among methods used are these:

• Dietary measures that increase potassium intake, as does the diet herein described
• Dietary measures that merely restrict sodium intake in order to lessen potassium wastage
• Substitution of a potassium-sparing diuretic for a potassium-wasting one
• Use of potassium chloride supplements
• Use of potassium chloride salt substitutes
• Intravenous potassium chloride

In the critically ill patient, as in postsurgical conditions or following severe trauma or burns, intravenous potassium chloride may be necessary (9).

Potassium diet therapy may be unsuccessful, and oral potassium chloride supplements are indicated under certain conditions. It is generally agreed that the following situations warrant oral potassium chloride supplementation:

• Administration of a combination of drugs that enhance each other's po-

tassium wasting effect, e.g., digitalis plus a diuretic
- Presence of a potassium-depleting disease together with a significant preexisting deficit, e.g., cirrhosis of the liver associated with hyponatremia and hypokalemia or with secondary aldosteronism
- An incompatible dietary restriction that must take precedence over the need for a high-potassium diet, e.g., a low-protein diet or a low-kilocalorie diet
- Severe anorexia
- Hypokalemia associated with watery (nonfatty type) diarrhea and non-beta-cell tumors of the pancreas (30, 37, 39)

POSSIBLE ADVERSE REACTIONS

A hyperkalemic response to the diet is very unlikely except in the person who is taking potassium supplements or in a potassium-sparing diuretic who has renal insufficiency. However, in any clinical state in which there is a tendency toward hyperkalemia, a high-potassium diet will aggravate the condition. Potassium supplementation may cause clinically dangerous hyperkalemia in hypertensive patients who are taking potassium-sparing diuretics or beta-adrenergic blocking agents. Symptomatic hyperkalemia occurs when the serum potassium level exceeds 6.5 mEq/L. Lassitude, weakness, and cardiac arrhythmias may occur when serum potassium levels become markedly elevated (4, 18, 40, 41).

CONTRAINDICATIONS

A high-potassium diet is contraindicated whenever the serum potassium level exceeds 5.0 mEq/L; in certain persons with renal failure or adrenal insufficiency; whenever the patient is taking potassium supplements; or whenever the patient is taking substantial doses of potassium-sparing diuretics, such as spironolactone

or triamterene. Individuals with diabetes on these drugs are particularly prone to develop hyperkalemia, possibly because of renal insufficiency (4, 40, 42).

CLINICAL ASSESSMENT

Especially in the hypertensive patient, the assessment should determine percentage of body weight in relation to desirable body weight and body mass index. Clinical surveillance for signs of dehydration caused by severe vomiting, hyperventilation, sweating, diuresis, or gastric suction with a nasogastric tube can provide evidence of clinical signs of hypokalemia. An accurate intake and output is also useful, as are physician's and nurses' notes identifying ECG changes such as depressed T waves, peaking of P waves, and observations of neuromuscular changes such as fatigue, muscle weakness, muscle pain, flabby muscles, parasthesia, hypotension, rapid pulse, respiratory muscle weakness leading to paralysis, cyanosis, anorexia, nausea, vomiting, paralytic ileus, apathy, drowsiness, tetany, or irritability. In any individual on a diuretic, the nutrition history should focus on past intake of dietary potassium (34).

BIOCHEMICAL ASSESSMENT

Significantly low potassium concentrations begin with values below 3.5 mEq/L. Values of 2.5 mEq/L or lower are serious, particularly when accompanied by metabolic alkalosis. Infusions of dextrose in water will lower serum potassium levels by as much as 0.5 mEq/L below resting levels, because potassium is withdrawn from plasma when glycogen is produced. The serum potassium level alone is not a reliable index of body potassium stores, but in the absence of other findings is significant only in its extremes or when the level is more than slightly elevated or decreased. Patients losing potassium because of loss of body

tissues will be losing nitrogen as well, and may be in a state of protein malnutrition that can be identified by biochemical indices such as creatinine height index and nitrogen balance (4).

ASSESSMENT OF POTENTIAL DRUG INTERACTIONS

In the patient on diuretics, serum glucose levels should be checked regularly. In any patient on potassium supplements or a high-potassium diet, serum potassium as well as serum creatinine and BUN should be monitored regularly. The interrelationships between dietary potassium status and such drugs as digitalis, potassium-wasting diuretics, and steroids have been discussed elsewhere in this section. In addition, the relationship of diabetes, potassium status, and insulin use is discussed in Chapter 28.

Potassium chloride supplements decrease the absorption of vitamin B-12 (43). Drugs that cause hypokalemia are listed in table 33.1 and those that cause hyperkalemia in table 33.2.

IMPLEMENTATION AND EDUCATION

1. LOW-CALORIE DIETS

In planning the diet for the patient who must avoid excessive kilocalories, skim milk and fresh or water-packed canned fruits should be used as substitutes for whole milk and sweetened canned fruits. Further reductions in caloric intake may be made by limiting the choices from the miscellaneous list to coffee and tea only.

2. SALT SUBSTITUTES

Salt substitutes may be an alternative source of supplemental potassium chloride, given that many patients find the supplement unpalatable and irritating to the gastrointestinal tract. Salt substitutes may be more affordable, less than one-half to one-fifth the cost of medicinal supplements. Salt substitutes provide ap-

TABLE 33.1. DRUGS THAT CAUSE HYPOKALEMIA

Acetazolamide (Diamox)
Amphotericin B (Fungizone)
Bisacodyl (Dulcolax)
Bumetanide (Bumex)
Capreomycin Sulfate (Seromycin)
Cephalosporins (various)
Clindamycin HCl (Cleocin)
Colchicine (Colchicine)
Corticosteroids, including:
    Hydrocortisone (Cortef)
    Methylpredisolone (Medrol)
    Prednisone (Deltasone)
    Prednisolone (Delta-Cortef)
Ethacrynic acid (Edecrin)
Furosemide (Lasix)
Gentamicin sulfate (Garamycin)
Lithium carbonate (Eskalith)
Metolazone (Zaroxolyn)
Para-aminosalicylic acid (P.A.S.,
    Teebacin)
Phenolphthalein (Correctol)
Salicylates, including aspirin (in high
    doses)
Thiazides, including:
    Bendroflumethiazide (Naturetin)
    Hydrochlorothizide (Hydrodiuril,
        Esidrix)
    Methylclorothizide (Enduron)

Sources: Adapted from Roe, D. A. (42, 43).

TABLE 33.2. DRUGS THAT CAUSE HYPERKALEMIA

Amiloride (Moduretic)
Indomethacin (Indocin)
Methyldopa (Aldomet)
Other nonsteroidal anti-inflammatory
    drugs, including:
        Fenoprofen (Nalfon)
        Ibuprofen (Motrin)
        Piroxicam (Feldene)
        Sulindac (Clinoril)
Isoniazid
Spironolactone (Aldactone)
Triamterene (Dyrrenium)

Source: Roe, D. A. (43).

proximately 10 to 13 mEq of potassium per gram. One teaspoon or 5 g may provide approximately 50 to 60 mEq of potassium. In addition, low-sodium foods may provide an increased potassium intake through the use of salt substitutes added commercially (9).

3. VARIETY IN FOOD CHOICES

In order to limit the total number of food lists used in the diet and thus to facilitate its comprehension and use by patients, foods with a wide range of potassium content were sometimes included in the same group (see ranges for each group). Formulation of a high-potassium diet to achieve a narrow range of potassium content would necessitate a greater number of food lists. Variety in food choices should be stressed, to minimize the deviations of actual daily potassium intake from calculated intake.

4. COOKING SUGGESTIONS TO PRESERVE POTASSIUM

Potassium is widely distributed in foods, because it is an essential constituent of all living cells. Food processing tends to increase the sodium and decrease the potassium content of foods. The main loss of potassium occurs via leaching into cooking water. Potassium intake can therefore be maximized by consuming fresh or minimally processed foods, using dry rather than moist cooking methods (i.e., baking rather than boiling), and using cooking or canning liquids from fruits, vegetables, meat, and fish (1).

PRIORITIES FOR QUALITY ASSURANCE

The first priority is to develop measures to ensure that hypokalemia is identified in its earliest stages and that individuals who would benefit from an increased dietary potassium intake receive it as soon as possible. High-risk groups of patients include individuals with diabetes, abnormal kidney function, ileal fistulas, or severe burns; hypertensives on potassium-wasting diuretics; and others on digitalis, steroids, or other drugs which affect potassium status. Individuals with anorexia nervosa, as well as fad dieters, may also be at risk.

MENU PLANNING

FOOD LIST FOR THE HIGH-POTASSIUM DIET

Milk list
Potassium content per cup equals 350–355 mg.
   Milk (skim or whole), buttermilk, or yogurt

Meat and meat substitute list 1
Potassium content per equivalent equals 100–180 mg. Average equals 130 mg.
Unless otherwise stated, 1 choice equals 1 oz.

Beef	Liver, calf's
Bologna, 2⅓ in. slices	Oysters, 5–8 medium
Chicken, dark meat, 1½ oz.	Peanut butter, 1 tbsp.
Chicken, light meat	Pork
Clams, ½ cup	Salmon, regular or unsalted
Cod	Scallops, 1 piece, 12 per lb.
Flounder	Shrimp, ¼ cup
Frankfurter, 1	Sole
Goose	Tuna, 1½ oz., regular or unsalted
Haddock	Turkey
Halibut	Veal
Lamb, 1½ oz.	

Meat and meat substitute list 2
Potassium content per equivalent equals 25–60 mg. Average equals 35 mg.
Unless otherwise stated, 1 choice equals 1 oz.
   Cheese, American processed
   Cheese, cheddar
   Cheese, cottage
   Cheese, Swiss
   Egg, 1 whole, medium
   Lobster

Fruit list 1
Potassium content per equivalent equals 80–145 mg. Average equals 115 mg.
   Apple, 1 small, 2″ diameter
   Apple juice, ½ cup
   Applesauce, sweetened or unsweetened, canned, ¾ cup
   Blackberries, fresh or frozen, ½ cup
   Blueberries, fresh or frozen, ½ cup
   Boysenberries, frozen, sugar added, ⅔ cup
   Cherries, canned in heavy syrup, ½ cup
   Cherries, sour, canned in heavy syrup, scant ½ cup
   Cherries, sweet, 10 large
   Cranberries, raw, 1 cup
   Currants, red, ¼ cup
   Grapefruit, ½ medium
   Grapefruit, canned in syrup or water-packed, ½ cup
   Grape juice, 4 oz.
   Grapes, American, 17 medium or ½ cup
   Grapes, European, 12 medium or ½ cup
   Grapes, Thompson seedless, ½ cup
   Pear nectar, 8 oz.
   Pears, canned in syrup, 3 halves
   Pears, water-packed, 3 halves

(*continued*)

Pineapple, canned, water-packed, or sweetened, 1 large slice
Pineapple, raw, 1 slice, 3½″ diameter
Tangerine, 1 large or 2 small

Fruit list 2
Potassium content per equivalent equals 160–260 mg. Average equals 195 mg.
Apricot juice, ⅔ cup
Fruit cocktail, water packed or in syrup, ½ cup
Grapefruit juice, 4 oz.
Kumquats, 4 medium
Mango, ½ medium
Orange juice, ½ cup
Papaya, ⅓ medium
Peaches, canned, sweetened or unsweetened, ¾ cup
Peach, raw, 1 medium
Pear, raw, 1 medium
Persimmon, Japanese, 1 medium
Pineapple juice, 4 oz.
Plum, damson, 1 large
Plums, canned in heavy syrup, 3 medium
Plums, prune type, 3 medium
Pomegranate, 1 medium
Raspberries, black, raw, ⅔ cup
Raspberries, red, raw, ¾ cup
Raspberries, red, frozen, ¾ cup
Rhubarb, frozen, sugar added, ⅜ cup
Strawberries, 10 large
Tangerine juice, 4 oz.
Watermelon, 1 cup

Fruit list 3
Potassium content per equivalent equals 300–490 mg. Average equals 380 mg.
Apricots, canned, 3 medium halves
Apricots, dried, sulfured, 8 halves
Avocado, ⅓ whole
Banana, 1 small
Cantaloupe, ¾ cup
Dates, 5 medium
Figs, dried, 3 medium
Honeydew melon, 1 piece 2″ wide, 6½″ diameter
Orange, 1 medium or ¾ cup canned
Peaches, dried, cooked, sugar added, ½ cup
Prune juice, 5 oz.
Prunes, not cooked, 5 large
Raisins, ⅓ cup

Vegetable list 1
Potassium content per equivalent equals 80–140 mg. Average equals 110 mg.
Beans, snap green, 1″ pieces, cooked, canned, drained solids, ½ cup
Beans, waxed, canned, drained solids, ½ cup
Beets, canned, drained solids, ½ cup
Cabbage, cooked or shredded raw, ½ cup
Carrots, canned, drained solids, ⅔ cup
Celery, raw inner stalks, 2 small
Celery, cooked, ⅖ cup

(*continued*)

Corn, canned, drained solids, ½ cup
Cress, water, 10–16 sprigs
Cucumber, ½ medium
Onion, cooked, ½ cup
Onions, scallions, 2 (5″ long, ½″ diameter)
Radishes, 3 small
Squash, summer, raw; cooked, drained, ½ cup

Vegetable list 2
Potassium content per equivalent equals 185–270 mg. Average equals 230 mg.
Asparagus, canned, 6 medium spears
Asparagus, cooked, 6 medium spears
Asparagus, frozen, cooked, ⅔ cup
Beans, dry, white, canned with pork and tomato, ½ cup
Beans, dry, red kidney, canned, drained solids, ⅖ cup
Beans, lima, canned, drained solids, ½ cup
Broccoli, cooked, 1 large stalk
Broccoli, frozen, ⅔ cup
Brussels sprouts, cooked, ½ cup
Carrots, raw, shredded, or grated, ⅔ cup
Carrots, cooked, ⅔ cup
Cauliflower, ⅞ cup
Collards, cooked, leaves and stems, ½ cup
Corn on the cob, cooked, 1 ear 4″ long
Eggplant, ¾ cup
Kale, cooked, ¾ cup
Kohlrabi, cooked, drained, ⅔ cup
Lentils, dry, cooked, drained, ½ cup
Lettuce, 4 large leaves
Mushrooms, canned, solids and liquid, ½ cup
Mustard greens, cooked, ½ cup
Okra, cooked, 8–9 pods
Peas, cooked, ⅔ cup
Pepper, green, empty shell, raw, 1 large
Pumpkin, canned, ⅖ cup
Squash, winter, frozen, cooked, ½ cup
Sweet potatoes, candied, 2 halves
Tomatoes, canned, ½ cup
Turnip greens, solids and liquid, ½ cup
Vegetable juice cocktail, 4 oz.

Vegetable list 3
Potassium content per equivalent equals 300–500 mg. Average equals 360 mg.
Artichoke, French, cooked, edible portion, base and soft ends of leaves of 1 artichoke
Bamboo shoots, ½ cup
Beans, white, cooked, ½ cup
Beans, canned without pork, ½ cup
Beans, dry, red kidney, ⅖ cup
Beans, lima, cooked, ½ cup
Beans, baby lima, frozen, cooked, ½ cup
Beans, Fordhook, baby lima, cooked, ⅝ cup
Beet greens, cooked, ½ cup
Chard, cooked, ⅗ cup
Chickpeas, dry, uncooked, ¼ cup

(continued)

Cowpeas, canned, solids and liquids, ½ cup
Cowpeas, cooked, ¼ cup
Escarole, 4 large leaves
Leeks, 3–4
Mushrooms, cooked, 4 large
Parsnips, cooked, ½ cup
Potato, baked, one 2¼″ diameter
Potato, boiled in skin, 1 medium
Spinach, chopped, frozen, cooked, ½ cup
Spinach, leaf, frozen, cooked, ½ cup
Squash, winter, baked, ½ cup
Sweet potato, baked in skin, 1 small
Tomato, raw, 1 medium
Tomato juice, 5 oz.

Bread and bread substitutes list 1
Potassium content per equivalent equals 20–65 mg. Average equals 45 mg.
Biscuit, baking powder, 1 (2″ diameter)
Bread, Italian, 1 slice
Bread, rye, 1 slice
Bread, white, 1 slice
Bread, whole wheat, 1 slice
Cornflakes, 1 cup
Frosted Mini-Wheats, 4 biscuits
Graham crackers, 2
Macaroni, cooked, ½ cup
Muffin, 1
Noodles, cooked, ½ cup
Oatmeal, cooked, ½ cup
Rice, cooked, ½ cup
Roll, hard or panroll, 1

Bread and bread substitutes list 2
Potassium content per equivalent equals 185–260 mg. Average equals 230 mg.
All-Bran, ½ cup
Boston brown bread, 2 slices
Bran Buds, ⅓ cup
Bran Flakes, 40%, 1 cup
Bread, pumpernickel, 1½ slices
Raisin Bran, ¾ cup

Miscellaneous
Potassium content per equivalent equals 105–200 mg. Average equals 135 mg.
Almonds, dried, unblanched, 12–15 nuts
Brazil nuts, 5 medium
Cashew nuts, 12–16 nuts
Chestnuts, 4 large
Coconut, shredded, 2 tbsp.
Coffee, 10 oz.
Filberts, hazelnuts, 20–24
Fruit cake, dark, enriched, 1 piece 3″ × 3″ × ½″
Litchi nuts, dried, 6 nuts
Molasses, blackstrap, ¾ tsp.
Molasses, medium extraction, 2 tsp.
Peanuts, roasted with skin, 1 tbsp.

(continued)

Pecans, 24 halves or 4 tbsp.

Tea, 14 oz.

Walnuts, English, 16–30 halves

Fat list—as desired

Potassium content per equivalent equals 0–20 mg. Average equals 10 mg.

Unless otherwise stated, 1 choice equals 1 tsp.

Bacon, fried crisp, 1 strip

Butter

Cream cheese, 1 oz. or 2 tbsp.

Cream, light or heavy, 1 tbsp.

French dressing

Half-and-half, 1 tbsp.

Italian dressing

Low-kilocalorie dressing

Margarine

Mayonnaise

Oils

Olives, black, ripe, 2 large

Olives, green, 2 medium

Thousand Island dressing

As desired

Lemons

Salt

Sugar

Vinegar

Any food not specifically omitted

DAILY MEAL PLAN AND SAMPLE MENU FOR THE HIGH-POTASSIUM DIET (FOR A MALE, AGE 25–50)

Food	Amount	Food list	Potassium (mg)
BREAKFAST			
Orange juice	½ cup	1 fruit from list 2	195
Oatmeal	1 cup	2 breads from list 1	90
Low-fat milk	1 cup	1 milk	355
Whole wheat toast	2 slices	2 breads from list 1	90
Margarine	2 tsp.	2 fat	20
Jelly	1 tbsp.		
Coffee	6 oz.	½ misc.	70
LUNCH			
Minestrone soup	1 cup	1 vegetable from list 2	230
Breadsticks	4	2 breads from list 1	90
Whole wheat bread	2 slices	2 breads from list 1	90
Turkey breast	3 oz.	3 meats from list 1	390
Mayonnaise	1 tbsp.	1 fat	10
Tomato	1 medium	1 vegetable from list 3	360
Oil and vinegar	1 tbsp.	1 fat	10
Cantaloupe cubes	¾ cup	1 fruit from list 3	380
Low-fat milk	1 cup	1 milk	355

(continued)

DINNER

Lean round steak	3 oz.	3 meats from list 1	390
Baked potato	1 large	2 vegetables from list 3	720
Margarine	1 tsp.	1 fat	10
Steamed broccoli	1 large stalk	1 vegetable from list 2	230
Oil and vinegar	1 tbsp.	1 fat	10
Pumpernickel bread	3 slices	2 breads from list 2	460
Margarine	3 tsp.	3 fat	30
Fresh pear	1 medium	1 fruit from list 2	195

EVENING SNACK

Whole wheat bread	2 slices	2 breads from list 1	90
Peanut butter	2 tbsp.	2 meats from list 1	260
Banana	1 medium	1 fruit from list 3	380
TOTAL POTASSIUM (mg)			5,650

Approximate Nutrient Analysis

Energy	2,811 kcal
Protein	123.7 g (18% of kcal)
Fat	100.3 g (32% of kcal)
Polyunsaturated fat	28.9 g
Monounsaturated fat	33.9 g
Saturated fat	22.4 g
Cholesterol	145 mg
Carbohydrate	380.4 g (54% of kcal)
Vitamin A	30,856 IU
	3,460 RE
Thiamine	1.94 mg
Riboflavin	2.21 mg
Niacin	30.1 mg
Folate	371 mcg
Vitamin B-12	5.50 mcg
Vitamin B-6	3.41 mg
Vitamin C	308.3 mg
Calcium	1,132 mg
Phosphorus	2,142 mg
Iron	19.5 mg
Copper	2.08 mg
Zinc	13.0 mg
Magnesium	476 mg
Sodium	4,421 mg
Potassium	6,114 mg

REFERENCES

1. Food and Nutrition Board, National Research Council: Recommended Dietary Allowances. 10th ed. Washington, D.C.: National Academy of Sciences, 1989.
2. Food and Nutrition Board, National Research Council—National Academy of Sciences: Diet and health: Implications for reducing chronic disease risk. Report of the Committee on Diet and Health. Washington, D.C.: National Academy Press, 1989.
3. Iimura, O., Kijima, T., et al.: Studies on the hypotensive effect of high potassium intake in patients with essential hypertension. Clin Sci 61:77S, 1981.
4. Randall, H. T.: Water, electrolytes and acid base balance. In Shils, M. E., and Young, V. R.: Modern nutrition in health and disease. 7th ed. Philadelphia: Lea & Febiger, 1988.
5. Cressman, M., and Vlasses, P.: Recent issues in antihypertensive drug therapy. Med Clin N Am 72:373, 1988.
6. Moser, M.: The diuretic dilemma and the management of mild hypertension. J Clin Hypertens 2:195, 1986.
7. Langford, R.: Dietary sodium, potassium and calcium in black hypertensive subjects. J Clin Hypertens 3:36s, 1987.
8. Morgan, T., and Nowson, C.: Comparative studies of reduced sodium and high potassium in hypertension. Nephron 47 (Supp 1):21, 1987.
9. Pemberton, C., Gastineau, C., et al.: Mayo Clinic diet manual. 6th ed. Philadelphia: W. B. C. Decker, 1988.
10. Miller, J., Weinberger, M., and Christian, J.: Blood pressure response to potassium supplementation in normotensive adults and children. Hypertension 10:437, 1987.
11. Hamilton, V., Haley, R., et al.: Diuretic regimens in essential hypertension: A comparison of hypokalemic effects, blood pressure control and cost. Arch Intern Med 143:1694, 1983.
12. Kosman, M.: Management of potassium problems during long term diuretic therapy. JAMA 230:743, 1974.

13. Schwartz, A.: Dosage of potassium chloride elixir to correct thiazide induced hypokalemia. JAMA 230:702, 1974.
14. Skrabal, F., Aubock, T., and Hortnagl, H.: Low sodium/high potassium diet for prevention of hypertension: Probable mechanisms of action. Lancet 1:895, 1981.
15. Adlin, E. V.: Edema and hypertension. In Kinney, J. M., Jeejeebhoy, K. N., et al.: Nutrition and metabolism in patient care. Philadelphia: W. B. Saunders, 1988.
16. Tanin, R. I.: Effects of potassium on blood pressure control. Ann Intern Med 98:773, 1983.
17. Paller, M., and Linas, S.: Hemodynamic effects of alterations in potassium. Hypertension 4 (Supp 111):20, 1982.
18. Einhorn, D., and Landsberg, L.: Nutrition and diet in hypertension. In Shils, M. E., and Young, V. R.: Modern nutrition in health and disease. 7th ed. Philadelphia: Lea & Febiger, 1988.
19. Parfrey, P., Vandenburg, M., et al.: Blood pressure and hormonal changes following alteration in dietary sodium and potassium in mild essential hypertension. Lancet 1:59, 1982.
20. Khaw, K., and Thom, S.: Randomized double blind cross over trial of potassium on blood pressure in normal subjects. Lancet 2:1127, 1982.
21. MacGregor, G.: Sodium and potassium intake in the management of high blood pressure. J Clin Hypertens 2:132, 1986.
22. Waler, W., Sapir, D., et al.: Potassium homeostasis and diuretic therapy. In Lant, A. F., and Wilson, G. M.: Modern diuretic therapy in the treatment of cardiovascular and renal disease. Amsterdam: Excepta Medica, 1973.
23. MacGregor, G., Markandu, M., et al.: Moderate potassium supplementation in essential hypertension. Lancet 2:567, 1982.
24. Lawton, W. J., Fitz, A. E., et al.: Effect of dietary potassium on blood pressure, renal function, muscle sympathetic nerve activity, and forearm

vascular resistance and flow in normotensive and borderline hypertensive humans. Circulation 81:173, 1990.
25. Luft, F. C., and Weinberger, M. H.: Potassium and blood pressure regulation. Am J Clin Nutr 45:1289, 1987.
26. Suki, W. N.: Dietary potassium and blood pressure. Kidney Internat 34:S-175, 1988.
27. Acheson, R., and Williams, D.: Does consumption of fruit and vegetables protect against stroke? Lancet 1:1191, 1983.
28. Kune, G. A., Kune, S., and Watson, L. F.: Dietary sodium and potassium intake and colorectal cancer risk. Nutr Canc 12 (4):351, 1989.
29. Schiff, E., and Schiff, L.: Diseases of the liver. Philadelphia: J. B. Lippincott, 1982.
30. Lee, S. P.: Diseases of the liver and biliary tract. In Kinney, J. M., Jeejeebhoy, K. N., et al.: Nutrition and metabolism in patient care. Philadelphia: W. B. Saunders, 1988.
31. Heymsfield, S. B., Hoff, R. D., et al.: Heart diseases. In Kinney, J. M., Jeejeebhoy, K. N., et al.: Nutrition and metabolism in patient care. Philadelphia: W. B. Saunders, 1988.
32. Dyckner, T., Helmers, C., et al.: Initial serum potassium level in relation to early complications and prognosis in patients with acute myocardial infarction. Acta Med Scand 197:207, 1975.
33. Weiner, B.: Drug and food interactions. Cardiovascular drugs. Part II. RD 2:2, 1982.
34. Fisback, F.: A manual of laboratory diagnostic tests. Philadelphia: J. B. Lippincott, 1980.
35. Tobian, L., Jahner, T. M., and Johnson, M. A. K.: Atherosclerotic cholesterol ester deposition is markedly reduced with a high-potassium diet. J Hypertens 7 (Supp 6):S244, 1989.
36. Adam, W. R.: Editorial review: Potassium tolerance. Clin Exp Pharmacol Physiol 16:687, 1989.
37. McMahon, F. G., Kdamar, K., et al.: Upper gastrointestinal lesions after potassium chloride supplements: A controlled clinical trial. Lancet 2:1059, 1982.

38. Wilber, J.: The role of diet in the treatment of high blood pressure. J Am Diet Assoc 80:25, 1982.

39. Semb, L. S.: Watery diarrhea, hypokalemia, and achlorhydria associated with non-beta cell tumor of the pancreas. Surg Ann 8:173, 1976.

40. Kalblan, V.: Iatrogenic hyperkalemia paralysis with electrocardiographic changes. South Med J 67:342, 1975.

41. Lawson, D.: Adverse reactions to potassium chloride. Quart J Med 43:433, 1974.

42. Roe, D. A.: Handbook: Interactions of selected drugs and nutrients in patients. 3d ed. Chicago: American Dietetic Association, 1980.

43. Roe, D. A.: Diet and drug interactions. New York: Van Nostrand Reinhold, 1988.

PART VIII

MISCELLANEOUS

34.

TEST DIETS

DIET AND VANILLYLMANDELIC ACID EXCRETION

The vanillylmandelic acid excretion test is designed to diagnose pheochromocytoma tumors in persons with unexplained hypertension. Measurement of urinary 4-hydroxy-3-methoxymandelic acid (VMA) is a diagnostic test widely used in the assessment of pheochromocytoma (1, 2). Until recently, patients were advised to abstain from certain foods during the period just prior to and during their urine collection. Coffee, tea, chocolate, nuts, bananas, citrus fruits, raisins, and vanilla were often eliminated from the diets of tested patients in order to prevent any interference with the test or misinterpretation of results due to the presence of vanillin or metabolically related compounds (1–3). The older and less specific tests, which measured phenolic acids of dietary origin in addition to VMA or total catecholamines, are now being replaced by more-specific fluorescence assays (4). Using a method of analysis that converts VMA to vanillin or one that relies on the measurement of metanephrines rather than VMA obviates the need for any dietary restrictions at all (1, 3, 5, 6).

Failure to demonstrate significant changes in VMA excretion with different diets suggests that dietary restrictions are not necessary prior to determining VMA excretion. In place of the screening test for VMA, urinary metanephrines are measured. The procedure is not affected by varied dietary intake (1).

Finally, there is now a new test for pheochromocytoma that appears to be more useful than older measurements. When this highly specific analytic method is used, norepinephrine determinations in a single 24-hour urine collection provide a diagnostic test for pheochromocytoma that has a sensitivity of 100%. Measurement of urinary 3,4-dihydroxyphenylglycol (DHPG) has been reported to increase the specificity of urine catecholamine testing. DHPG is formed by the metabolism of norepinephrine by monoamine oxidase within the neurons. A small but diagnostically useful increase in specificity can be gained by the simultaneous measurement of DHPG, from 98% to more than 99%. However, DHPG measurement is not usually considered a routine requirement in catecholamine testing (7, 8).

REFERENCES

1. Rayfield, E. J., Cain, J. P., et al.: Influence of diet on urinary VMA excretion. JAMA 221:704, 1972.
2. Remine, W. H., Chong, G. C., et al.: Current management of pheochromocytoma. Ann Surg 179:740, 1972.
3. Page, L. B., and Copeland, R. B.: Pheochromocytoma. Dis Month 1:1, 1968.
4. Sjoerdsma, A., Engellman, K., et al.: Pheochromocytoma: Current concepts of diagnosis and treatment. Ann Intern Med 65:1305, 1966.
5. Pisano, J. J., Crout, J. R., and Abraham, D.: Determination of 3-methoxy-4-hydroxymandelic acid in urine. Clin Chem Acta 7:285, 1962.
6. Amery, A., and Conway, J.: A critical review of diagnostic tests for pheochromocytoma. Am Heart J 73:129, 1967.
7. Duncan, M. W., Compton, P., et al.: Measurement of norepinephrine and 3,4-dihydroxyphenylglycol in urine and plasma for the diagnosis of pheochromocytoma. N Engl J Med 319:136, 1988.
8. Benowitz, N.: Pheochromocytoma. Adv Intern Med 35:195, 1990.

TEST FOR FAT MALABSORPTION: 100 GRAMS FAT

The quantitative chemical determination of stool fat over a 24-hour period is still the method that most accurately measures the degree of fat malabsorption (1). It has recently been referred to as "the gold standard" among fat malabsorption tests (2, 3).

The actual fat intake must be estimated, because knowledge of the fat consumed is imperative in determining fat malabsorption. The test does not need to be conducted like a balance study; if some patients cannot consume the full 100 g of fat the test can still be done, as long as the fat intake is quantified along with the fat excreted in the stool and as long as the intake is at least 70 g (4, 5). The following formula is used to determine normal fecal fat excretion at varying levels of intake (6).

$(0.21 \times$ grams of dietary fat per 24 hours$) + 2.93 =$ grams of fecal fat per 24 hours

This formula can be used to interpret values from actual fecal fat analysis. A marker should be ingested by the patient at the beginning and end of the stool collection. Otherwise, stool collections should be begun only after the patient has been on the diet for 3 days (7).

The fecal excretion of more than 5 to 7 g fat per 24 hours over a 3-day period, in patients ingesting 100 g of fat daily, is generally considered to be evidence of fat malabsorption (1, 2, 4, 5, 7, 8). In chronic pancreatic disease, more than 10 g of fat are excreted per 24 hours, and 10 to 40 g per day are excreted in patients with celiac disease (3, 7, 9, 10). According to one author, severe steatorrhea of 40 g or more of fecal fat per day, using the 72-hour stool fat test, indicates defective lipolysis—often from chronic pancreatitis, carcinoma of the pancreas, or massive bowel resection (11). Mod-

erate steatorrhea, 25 to 35 g fecal fat per day, suggests intestinal mucosal disease, such as celiac sprue. Mild steatorrhea, less than 25 g of fecal fat per day, is commonly seen with defects in micelle formation (12).

Other indices of fat malabsorption include a positive Sudan stain of stool for fat, as well as a serum carotene level of less than 60 mcg per 100 mL (1, 4, 7). If undertaken properly with newer methods that permit identification of triglycerides and fatty acids, the Sudan stain for fecal fat provides more qualitative information about the type of fat absorbed than the 72-hour stool fat test, which provides quantitative information (13). Refer to Chapter 25 for more information about fat malabsorption and the Sudan stain for fat.

DAILY MEAL PLAN FOR THE 100-g FAT TEST DIET

Include a minimum of the following foods daily for 3 days.

Food group	Amount	Fat (g)
Whole milk	2 cups	20
Lean meat	8 oz.	
or medium-fat meat	5 oz.	24–25[a]
Whole egg	1 large	5
Fruits and vegetables	5 servings	Trace
Whole-grain or enriched breads or cereals	6 servings	Trace
Fats (margarine, oil, mayonnaise, etc.)	10 tsp.	50
TOTAL FAT		99–100 g

[a]May substitute 5 oz. high-fat meat and reduce fats to 7 tsp.

SAMPLE MENU FOR THE 100-g FAT TEST DIET (FOR A MALE, AGE 25–50)

BREAKFAST

Orange juice	1 cup
Farina	1 cup
Margarine	1 tsp.
Whole milk	1 cup
Boiled egg	1 large
Whole wheat toast	2 slices
Margarine	2 tsp.
Peanut butter	2 tbsp.
Jam	1 tbsp.
Banana	½ medium
Coffee or tea	1 cup

LUNCH

Whole wheat bread	2 slices
Sliced turkey	2 oz.
Swiss cheese	2 oz.
Lettuce	½ cup
Chopped tomato	½ cup
Mayonnaise	1 tbsp.
Spinach salad	1 cup
Italian dressing	1 tbsp.
Pear	1 medium
Whole milk	1 cup

DINNER

Roast beef	3 oz.
Baked potato	1 large
Margarine	1 tsp.
Cooked carrots	½ cup
Whole wheat bread	2 slices
Margarine	2 tsp.
Apple	1 raw
Coffee or tea	1 cup

(*continued*)

EVENING SNACK

Oatmeal cookies	4
Apple juice	1 cup

Approximate Nutrient Analysis

Energy	2,884 kcal
Protein	118.3 g (16% of kcal)
Fat	115.7 g (36% of kcal)
Polyunsaturated fat	26.2 g
Monounsaturated fat	40.9 g
Saturated fat	37.2 g
Cholesterol	444 mg
Carbohydrate	335.2 g (46% of kcal)
Vitamin A	26,328 IU
	3,074 RE
Thiamine	1.67 mg
Riboflavin	2.39 mg
Niacin	25.8 mg
Folate	420 mcg
Vitamin B-12	6.32 mcg
Vitamin B-6	2.79 mg
Vitamin C	244.1 mg
Calcium	1,535 mg
Phosphorus	2,033 mg
Iron	18.2 mg
Copper	1.82 mg
Zinc	12.3 mg
Magnesium	392 mg
Sodium	2,955 mg
Potassium	5,415 mg

REFERENCES

1. Bai, J. C., Andrush, A., et al.: Fecal fat concentration in the differential diagnosis of steatorrhea. Am J Gastroenterol 12:533, 1989.
2. Greenberger, N. J.: Diagnostic approach to the patient with a chronic diarrheal disorder. Dis Month 36 (3):1, 1990.
3. Pedersen, N.: Fat digestion tests. Digestion 37:25, 1987.
4. Westergaard, H., and Dietschy, J. M.: Normal mechanisms of fat absorption and derangements induced by various diseases. Med Clin N Am 58:1513, 1974.
5. Chadwick, U. S.: The small intestine: Clinical investigation of patients with malabsorption and diarrhea. In Bouchier, I. A. D., Allan, R. N., et al.: Textbook of gastroenterology. London: Balliere Tindall, 1986.
6. Pemberton, C. M.: Diets in preparation for diagnostic tests. In Pemberton, C. M., Moxness, K. E., et al., eds.: Mayo Clinic diet manual. 6th ed. Philadelphia: B. C. Decker, 1988.
7. Wright, H. K., and Tilson, M. D.: Postoperative disorders of the gastrointestinal tract. New York: Grune and Stratton, 1973.
8. Ravel, R.: Clinical laboratory medicine. 2d ed. Chicago: Year Book Medical Publishers, 1974.
9. Richter, J. M., and Warshaw, A. G.: Chronic pancreatitis. In Bouchier, I. A. D., Allan, R. N., et al.: Textbook of gastroenterology. London: Balliere Tindall, 1986.
10. Conn, R. B.: Current diagnosis. 7th ed. Philadelphia: W. B. Saunders, 1985.
11. Ryan, M., and Olsen, W.: A diagnostic approach to malabsorption syndromes: A pathophysiologic approach. Clin Gastroenterol 12:533, 1983.
12. Alpers, D. H.: Dietary management and vitamin-mineral replacement therapy. In Sleisinger, M. H., and Fordtran, J. S.: Gastrointestinal disease. 3d ed. Philadelphia: W. B. Saunders, 1983.
13. Khouri, M. R., Huang, G., and Shiau, Y. F.: Sudan stain of fecal fat: New insight into an old test. Gastroenterology 96:421, 1989.

SEROTONIN (5-HIAA) TEST DIET

Certain malignant carcinoid tumors of the gastrointestinal tract secrete large amounts of 5-HIAA (5-hydroxyindoleacetic acid, or serotonin), which is utilized as a diagnostic tool. The serotonin test is used to identify this metabolite and make the diagnosis. Urinary 5-HIAA may be estimated quantitatively in a 24-hour urine sample. The normal range is 2 to 8 mg per 24 hours and increases to up to 30 mg in individuals with carcinoid tumors. False positives can occur if patients are eating large amounts of foods high in 5-HIAA or taking such drugs as reserpine, acetanilide, mephenesin, methocarbamol, or cough medicines containing glyceryl quaiacolate—for instance guaifenesin, the analgesic acetaminophen, salicylates, or L-dopa (1–6).

Thus, to avoid false-positive results, at least 24 hours prior to the test, the following foods high in 5-HIAA should be excluded from the diet (1, 5, 6):

avocados, Haas or
    Fuerte
bananas
butternuts
hickory nuts or
    pecans
kiwi fruit
pineapples
pineapple juice
plantains
red or red-blue
    plums
tomatoes
walnuts, English
    or black

The exclusion of other foods containing 5-HIAA from the diet has been questioned on the basis that their serotonin content would require an unusually large amount to be ingested in order to have an effect on urinary 5-HIAA excretion. Thus, eggplant and filberts do not need to be avoided. In contrast, a person would only have to consume 1 butternut or black walnut, 1½ English walnuts, 8 pecans, ⅙ plantain, ½ banana, ¹⁄₂₀ pineapple, 1⅕ tomatoes, 2 kiwi fruits, or 2 red plums in order to alter 5-HIAA excretion significantly (5–7). In one study, after eating 4 medium-sized bananas, all the normal patients had a 5-HIAA excretion in the range of patients with serotonin-producing carcinoid tumors. Recently, the serotonin content of 80 foods was determined with a highly specific radioenzymatic assay. Results are summarized in table 34.1 (5).

TABLE 34.1. SEROTONIN CONTENT OF FOODS

Food	Serotonin (mcg/g)
Foods high in serotonin (more than 3 mcg/g)	
Butternuts	398
Black walnuts	304
English walnuts	87
Hickory family	
Shagbark	143
Mockernut	67
Pecans	29
Sweet pignuts	25
Plantain	30
Pineapple	17
Banana	15
Kiwi fruit	5.8
Plums	4.7
Tomatoes	3.2
Foods moderate in serotonin (0.1–3 mcg/g)	
Haas avocados	1.6
Fuerte avocados	1.5
Booth avocados	0.2
Dates	1.3
Grapefruit	0.9
Cantaloupe	0.9
Honeydew melon	0.6
Black olives	0.2
Broccoli	0.2
Eggplant	0.2
Figs	0.2
Spinach	0.1
Cauliflower	0.1

Source: Adapted from Feldman, J. M., and Lee, E. (5). Copyright © American Society for Clinical Nutrition.

REFERENCES

1. Losowsky, M. S.: Tumors of the small intestine. In Bouchier, I. A. D., Allan, R. N., et al.: Textbook of gastroenterology. London: Balliere Tindall, 1986.
2. Bruce, D. W.: Carcinoid tumours and pineapples. J Pharm Pharmacol 13:256, 1961.
3. Lovenberg, W.: Some vasoactive and psychoactive substances in foods: Amines, stimulants, depressants and hallucinogens. In National Research Council: Toxicants occurring naturally in foods. Washington, D.C.: National Academy of Sciences, 1973.
4. Oats, J. A.: The carcinoid syndrome. In Thorn, G. W., Adams, R. D., et al.: Harrison's principles of internal medicine. 8th ed. New York: McGraw-Hill, 1977.
5. Feldman, J. M., and Lee, E.: Serotonin content of foods: Effect on urinary excretion of 5-hydroxyindoleacetic acid. Am J Clin Nutr 42:639, 1985.
6. Feldman, J. M.: Carcinoid tumors and the carcinoid syndrome. Curr Prob Surg 26 (12):1, 1989.
7. Feldman, J. M., Lee, E. M., and Castleberry, C. A.: Catecholamine and serotonin content of foods: Effect on urinary excretion of homovanillic and 5-hydroxyindoleacetic acid. J Am Diet Assoc 87:1031, 1987.

HISTAMINE-RESTRICTED DIET

The urinary excretion of histamine is increased in most patients with systemic mastocytosis and in some patients with carcinoid tumors (1, 2). Analysis of a 24-hour urine sample for histamine excretion is therefore used in the diagnosis of systemic mastocytosis or carcinoid syndrome. Although only 0.21% of ingested histamine is excreted as free histamine, this can be enough to affect test results.

Patients should be advised to avoid foods that are high in histamine from the afternoon prior to the day of the urine collection until the collection is complete. The histamine content of foods and its effect upon urinary histamine excretion have been investigated, using a highly specific and sensitive assay method (3). Foods that are high in histamine and that should be avoided are given in table 34.2. Cheeses, other dairy products, fruits, vegetables, meats, wines, and other foods were found to be low in histamine (below 0.9 µg/g).

TABLE 34.2. FOODS HIGH IN HISTAMINE

	Histamine content (µg/g)
Cheese	
Blue, brick	6–76
Monterey Jack	0.1–70
Parmesan, grated	12–277
Roquefort	11
Meats	
Chicken liver, fried	3.9
Chicken liver, sauteed	7.3
Sirloin steak, broiled	2.1
Vegetables	
Eggplant	25–38
Spinach	26–60
Tomatoes	1.5–2.0
Red wines	
Burgundy	2.1
Chianti	0.4–3.7

Source: Feldman, J. M. (3).

REFERENCES

1. Beaven, M. A.: Histamine: Its role in physiological and pathological processes. Basel, Switzerland: S. Karger, 1978.
2. Pernow, B., and Waldenstrom, J.: Determination of 5-hydroxytryptamine, 5-hydroxyindoleacetic acid and histamine in 33 cases of carcinoid tumor (argentaffinoma). Am J Med 23:16, 1957.
3. Feldman, J. M.: Histaminuria from histamine-rich foods. Arch Intern Med 143:2099, 1983.

DIETARY PREPARATION FOR THE GLUCOSE TOLERANCE TEST

The glucose tolerance test (GTT) is one of the diagnostic tools used in establishing the diagnosis for diabetes. It is used as confirmation following an elevated or equivocal screening test (50 g glucose screen in pregnant women or fasting blood glucose in other patients) (1). Norms for the test for adolescents, pregnant women, and others are discussed in Chapter 28.

The GTT is more sensitive than a fasting plasma glucose level, but preparation is important to prevent overdiagnosis. The test should be performed the morning after a 10- to 16-hour fast, including abstention from caffeine and nicotine (2).

Prior to the test the patient should consume at least 150 g carbohydrates daily for 3 days. The test should be administered to patients who are ambulatory, and not during acute medical or surgical illness, because both bed rest and physiological stress impair glucose tolerance. Results are also invalid if the patient is malnourished, otherwise unhealthy, or taking medications that affect glucose tolerance. It has been reconfirmed that a carbohydrate intake of less than 100 g per day prior to the glucose tolerance test will affect the outcome by diminishing glucose tolerance (2–4).

REFERENCES

1. American Diabetes Association: Physician's guide to insulin dependent Type I diabetes: Diagnosis and treatment. Alexandria, Va.: American Diabetes Association, 1988.
2. Nelson, R. L.: The OGTT: Its practical use. Diabetes Spectrum 2:219, 1989.
3. Conn, R. B.: Current diagnosis. 7th ed. Philadelphia: W. B. Saunders, 1985.
4. Felig, P., Bergan, M., and Shafir, E.: The endocrine pancreas. In Felig, P., Baxter, J. D., et al.: Endocrinology and metabolism. 2d ed. New York: Mc-Graw-Hill, 1987.

PREPARATION FOR DOUBLE-CONTRAST BARIUM ENEMA

The standard dietary preparation for double-contrast barium enema is a low-residue diet and overhydration, with at least 2 L of fluid for 1 day, a clear liquid supper on the evening preceding the test, an osmotic-type cathartic, e.g., magnesium citrate, at about 6:00 p.m., and a contact-type cathartic at about 8:00 p.m. on the evening before the test. This colon-cleansing protocol has been compared with the use of a whole-gut lavage solution, such as Golytely, of which the patient has to drink approximately 2.8 L at the rate of 1.5 L per hour on the evening before the test, without diet restrictions (1–3).

Results of the 2 protocols have been rated as to the quality of feces removal and the degree of mucosal coating. The combination of diet plus cathartics achieved better results than the use of whole-gut lavage alone without cathartics, for both criteria. A combination of lavage solution and cathartics achieved results similar to the diet-cathartic combination (3).

REFERENCES

1. Barnes, M. R.: How to get a clean colon—with less effort. Radiology 91:948, 1968.
2. Zezulin, W.: Effective 24-hour preparation for radiologic examination of the colon. Surg Clin N Am 51:799, 1971.
3. Girard, C. M., Rugh, K. S., et al.: Comparison of Golytely lavage with standard diet/cathartic preparation for double-contrast barium enema. Am J Radiol 142:1147, 1984.

USE OF HIGH NORMAL CALCIUM INTAKE IN SCREENING FOR HYPERCALCIURIA

When screening for hypercalciuria, a high normal calcium intake is used, not a low-calcium diet. Potentially hypercalciuric patients must be screened under circumstances that allow them to express their abnormality. Studies have shown that at low calcium intakes, little differences were found in the urinary calcium excretion of stone-forming and non-stone-forming patients. Thus, hypercalciuria was detectable only at moderately high calcium intakes (1, 2).

A 1,000-mg calcium diet is used to define hypercalciuria, with food sources providing 400 mg daily and the remaining 600 mg being provided by the oral administration of calcium gluconate (3). Such an approach increases the likelihood that the actual intake will be as close to 1,000 mg calcium as possible.

One common diagnostic parameter for hypercalciuria is a 24-hour calcium excretion that exceeds 250 mg for a female and 300 mg for a male, or a calcium excretion that exceeds 4 mg per kilogram of body weight per day. The dietitian should investigate the patient's dietary intake before the test, because these limits of calcium excretion are valid only if the estimated intake of calcium is normal. Many stone formers have reduced their dietary calcium intake before the evaluation. In such a situation, the measured calcium excretion may be normal but may be actually increased relative to the dietary intake (2).

The following equation has been used to assess whether calcium excretion is increased in relation to a low-calcium diet (2):

Predicted calcium excretion (mg/day) = $(0.056 \times$ calcium intake in mg$) + (2.19 \times$ body weight in kg$)$

The calcium excretion is considered to be increased if it is more than 15% greater than the predicted excretion (2).

REFERENCES

1. Peacock, M., Hodgkinson, A., and Nordin, B. D. C.: Importance of dietary calcium in the definition of hypercalciuria. Br Med J 3:469, 1967.
2. Abraham, P. A., and Smith, C. L.: Medical evaluation and management of calcium nephrolithiasis. Med Clin N Am 68:281, 1984.
3. Broadus, A. E., Dominguez, M., and Bartter, E. F. C.: Pathophysiologic studies in idiopathic hypercalciuria: Use of an oral calcium tolerance test to characterize distinctive hypercalciuric subgroups. J Clin Endocrinol Metabol 47:751, 1978.

DIETARY PREPARATION FOR COLORECTAL CANCER SCREENING TESTS: FECAL OCCULT BLOOD TESTING

Testing of fecal specimens for occult blood is based on the assumption that both polyps and carcinomas tend to bleed prior to the onset of symptoms and that this provides sufficient lead time to improve the cancer cure rate (1). The hemoccult screening test has been well received by the public. A stool collection device is now available to facilitate the test and increase its accuracy (2).

However, the utilization of the test on a single stool specimen without prior dietary preparation has been reported to lack specificity. False-positive findings in patients who did not follow a meat-free, high-fiber diet before the tests have resulted in unnecessary referrals to radiologists for complete gastrointestinal radiologic examinations (1).

In one study, fecal occult blood testing with Hemoccult slides in patients who followed a meat-free, high-bulk diet for 4 days prior to the test indicated a predictive value for colorectal cancer of 44% to 50% (2). In another investigation the tests were found to be of limited value in the follow-up study of polyps but of great significance in the screening of asymptomatic individuals (3). The authors found

that one-third of patients with polyps over 10 mm had no positive guaiac reactions and that the tests, although proven to be quite valuable, cannot replace colonoscopy and radiographic double-contrast diagnostic techniques. Patients should adhere to a meat-free, high-fiber diet at least 4 days to a week before the test and should avoid horseradish, beets, vitamin supplements, aspirin, compounds that contain aspirin, bananas, tomatoes, iron, and ascorbic acid supplements (1–5).

The use of this test is now controversial. One investigation has found that most adenomas are not detected by fecal blood testing and that the red meat–free, high-fiber diet does not improve the sensitivity for detecting adenomas or colorectal cancer. Hence, the dietary preparation may be unnecessary, according to these authors (6).

With the use of the new Hemoquant test, less dietary preparation is needed. This is a specific, quantitative, and very sensitive test for the presence of heme in the feces. Unlike the dietary preparation recommended by some for guaiac tests, the Hemoquant test requires only the avoidance of red meat; even moderate amounts of ham, fish, chicken, or bacon consumed before the test do not affect its results. At the present time, however, its use in large-scale screening programs for cancer must await the development of more-automated procedures (4, 7).

REFERENCES

1. Bolt, R. J.: Evaluation of screening tests for colorectal cancer. Primary Care 7:683, 1980.
2. Ahlquist, D. A., Schwartz, S., et al.: A stool collection device: The first step in occult blood testing. Ann Intern Med 108:609, 1988.
3. Winawer, S. J., Andrews, M., et al.: Progress report on controlled trial of fecal occult blood testing for the detection of colorectal neoplasia. Cancer 45:2959, 1980.
4. Gabrielsson, N., Granquist, S., and Nilsson, B.: Guaiac tests for detection of occult faecal blood loss in patients with endoscopically verified colonic polyps. Scand J Gastroenterol 20:978, 1985.
5. Miller, M. P., and Stanley, T. V.: Results of a mass screening program for colorectal cancer. Arch Surg 123:63, 1988.
6. Norfleet, R. G.: Effect of diet on fecal occult blood testing in patients with colorectal polyps. Dig Dis Sci 31:498, 1986.
7. Schwartz, S., and Ellefson, M.: Quantitative fecal recovery of ingested hemoglobin-heme in blood: Comparisons by Hemoquant assay with ingested meat and fish. Gastroenterology 89:19, 1985.

35.

MISCELLANEOUS DIETS

CALCIUM-RESTRICTED AND PHOSPHATE-RESTRICTED DIETS

Evidence indicating the effectiveness of a severely restricted calcium diet in hypercalciuria is not clear-cut. Reducing calcium intake increases the absorption of dietary oxalate, so that calcium oxalate saturation of the urine remains unchanged. Theoretically, the increased oxalate absorption on a low-calcium diet may even exacerbate a tendency toward calcium oxalate stone formation. The current consensus is that patients with type II absorptive hypercalciuria should restrict both dietary calcium (400–600 mg) and oxalate (≤50 mg) (see table 35.1). In type I absorptive hypercalciuria or renal hypercalciuria, calcium intake should not be excessive (≤1 g) but does not need to be restricted. All patients with this disorder are more susceptible to an increase in oxaluria if protein, sodium, or sugar intake is high. Protein intake should be 12% to 14% of calories, as opposed to 25%, and sodium intake should be 90 to 150 mEq (2,070–3,450 mg) (1–3).

For treatment of absorptive hypercalciuria due to excess 1,25-dihydroxy-vitamin-D, one author has proposed the use of a 400- to 500-mg calcium diet. This may be used in conjunction with a low-oxalate diet, if oxalate excretion increases because of calcium restriction and exceeds 40 mg per day (4). Refer to table 35.1 for the oxalate content of foods (5, 6) and to table 35.2 for indications for oxalate restriction.

Calcium restriction to less than 500

TABLE 35.1. APPROXIMATE OXALATE CONTENT OF SELECTED FOODS

Food group	Little or no oxalate (<2 mg per serving)	Moderate oxalate (2–10 mg per serving)	High oxalate (>10 mg per serving)
Beverages	Beer, bottled Carbonated cola (limit to 12 oz. per day) Distilled alcohol Lemonade or limeade without peel Wine: red, rosé, white	Coffee (limit to 8 oz. per day)	Draft beer Ovaltine and other beverage mixes Tea Cocoa
Milk	Buttermilk Whole, low-fat, or skim milk Yogurt with allowed fruit		
Meat and substitutes	Eggs Cheese Beef, lamb, or pork Poultry Fish and shellfish	Sardines	Baked beans, canned in tomato sauce Peanut butter Tofu
Vegetables	Avocado Brussels sprouts Cabbage Cauliflower Mushrooms Onions Peas, green: fresh or frozen Potatoes, white Radishes	Asparagus Broccoli Carrots Corn, sweet: white or yellow Cucumber, peeled Green peas, canned Lettuce Lima beans Parsnips Tomato, 1 small or juice (4 oz.) Turnips	Beans: green, wax, dried Beets: tops, root, greens Celery Chives Collards Dandelion greens Eggplant Escarole Kale Leeks Mustard greens Okra Parsley Peppers, green Pokeweed Potatoes, sweet Rutabagas

(continued)

TABLE 35.1. *CONTINUED*

Food group	Little or no oxalate (<2 mg per serving)	Moderate oxalate (2–10 mg per serving)	High oxalate (>10 mg per serving)
			Spinach
			Summer squash
			Swiss chard
			Watercress
Fruits and juices	Apple juice	Apple	Blackberries
	Avocado	Apricots	Blueberries
	Banana	Black currants	Currants, red
	Cherries, Bing	Cherries, red sour	Dewberries
	Grapefruit, fruit and juice	Cranberry juice (4 oz.)	Fruit cocktail
	Grapes, green	Grape juice (4 oz.)	Grapes, purple
	Mangoes	Orange, fruit and juice (4 oz.)	Gooseberries
	Melons: cantaloupe, casaba, honeydew, watermelon	Peaches	Lemon peel
		Pears	Lime peel
		Pineapple	Orange peel
	Nectarines	Plums, purple	Raspberries
	Peaches	Prunes	Rhubarb
	Pineapple juice		Strawberries
	Plums, green or yellow		Tangerine
			Juices made from the above fruits
Bread and starches	Breakfast cereals	Cornbread	Fruit cake
	Macaroni	Sponge cake	Grits, white corn
	Noodles	Spaghetti, canned in tomato sauce	Soybean crackers
	Rice		Wheat germ
	Spaghetti		
	Bread		
Fats and oils	Bacon		Nuts: peanuts, almonds, pecans, cashews, walnuts
	Mayonnaise		
	Salad dressing		
	Vegetable oils		
	Butter, margarine		
Miscellaneous	Coconut	Chicken noodle soup, dehydrated	Chocolate, cocoa
	Jelly or preserves (made with allowed fruits)		Vegetable soup
			Tomato soup
	Lemon, lime juice		Marmalade
	Salt, pepper (limit to 1 tsp./day)		
	Soups with ingredients allowed		
	Sugar		

Source: Pemberton, C. M., Moxness, K. E., et al. (5), by permission of Mayo Foundation.

mg may be harmful, resulting in negative calcium balance and significant bone loss, particularly in postmenopausal women (3). Disordered regulation of 1,25-dihydroxy-vitamin-D production has been implicated as the cause of absorptive hypercalciuria. Evidence suggests that the excess of this vitamin can cause intestinal overabsorption of calcium and yet still promote bone loss during periods of low calcium intake (7). Decreases in serum calcium concentrations, whatever the cause, will increase oxalate absorption. Hence, there are instances in which a 500-mg calcium diet may play a more causative than preventive role in calcium oxalate stone formation (8).

Thus, the use of low-calcium diets is not a prudent approach for most patients with absorptive hypercalciuria. Neither is treatment with thiazide diuretics advised, because calcium absorption may remain elevated and calcium retention may be increased, possibly accounting for the high bone mineral density in these patients (7).

In contrast, phosphates, in the form either of sodium cellulose phosphate or of orthophosphate, have been used to treat a hypophosphatemic version of absorptive hypercalciuria with mixed reviews. Compliance is difficult to achieve, the treatment is expensive, and it has such side effects as diarrhea, in the case of orthophosphate, and increased renal excretion of oxalate, in the case of sodium cellulose phosphate. In a form of renal calculi associated with hypocitraturia and calcium oxalate nephrolithiasis, potassium citrate treatment was successful in inhibiting new stone formation and restoring normal urinary citrate concentrations (3, 7, 9).

A high-phosphate diet with neutral phosphate supplements or orthophosphates has been advocated in the treatment of type III hypercalciuria. Cellulose phosphate is contraindicated in this form of hypercalciuria, which is associ-

TABLE 35.2. OXALATE RESTRICTION

General recommendations	Disorder	Additional recommendations
Oxalate: low-oxalate diet	Idiopathic hyperoxaluria	Moderate to high calcium intake recommended (2 or more glasses milk per day)
Fluid: 250–300 mL/hour while awake and upon awakening at night; 50% as water	Absorptive hypercalciuria, type II	Low-calcium diet
Ascorbic acid: avoid excessive supplementation	Enteric hyperoxaluria	High calcium intake (supplement with 1 g or more calcium—as calcium carbonate). Low-fat diet if there is significant steatorrhea

Source: Pemberton, C. M., Moxness, K. E., et al. (5), by permission of Mayo Foundation.

ated with a renal phosphate leak that drives serum phosphate downward, with increased production of 1,25-dihydroxy-vitamin-D. Phosphate therapy is more effective if combined with magnesium supplementation and a low-oxalate diet (10).

Urolithiasis may result from hyperoxaluria associated with fat malabsorption in children, and the correction of the steatorrhea may result in normalization of urinary oxalate excretion (11).

Hypercalcemia may also occur in some malignancies, especially breast cancer, multiple myeloma, bronchogenic carcinoma, and carcinoma of the kidney. Also, metastasis to the bone results in release of calcium from the bone into the circulation. Treatment usually involves caring for the underlying disorder. Calcium restriction may be beneficial in sarcoidosis but is not indicated in malignancy (12).

REFERENCES

1. Urivetzky, M., Motola, J., et al.: Dietary protein levels affect the excretion of oxalate and calcium in patients with absorptive hypercalciuria type II. J Urol 137:690, 1987.

2. Bataille, P., Charransol, G., et al.: Effect of calcium restriction on renal excretion of oxalate and the probability of stones in the various pathophysiological groups with calcium stones. J Urol 13:218, 1983.

3. Abraham, P. A., and Smith, C. L.: Medical evaluation and management of calcium nephrolithiasis. Med Clin N Am 68:281, 1984.

4. Kanig, S. P., and Conn, R. L.: Kidney stones: Medical management and newer options for stone removal. Postgrad Med 78 (6):38, 1985.

5. Pemberton, C. M., Moxness, K. E., et al.: Mayo Clinic diet manual. 6th ed. Philadelphia: B. C. Decker, 1988.

6. Ney, D. M., Hofmann, A. F., et al.: The low oxalate diet book. San Diego: University of California Press, 1981.

7. Coe, F.: Treatment of hypercalciuria—editorial. N Engl J Med 311:116, 1984.

8. Smith, L. H.: The pathophysiology and medical treatment of urolithiasis. Sem Nephrol 10:31, 1990.

9. Pak, Y. C., and Fuller, C.: Idiopathic hypocitraturic calcium-oxalate nephrolithiasis successfully treated with potassium citrate. Ann Intern Med 104:33, 1986.

10. Roberts, D. H., and Knox, F. G.: Renal phosphate handling and calcium nephrolithiasis: Role of dietary phosphate and phosphate leak. Sem Nephrol 10:24, 1990.

11. Jones, D. P., Stapleton, B., et al.: Urolithiasis and enteric hyperoxaluria in a child with steatorrhea. Clin Pediatr 26:304, 1987.

12. Avioli, L. V.: Calcium and phosphorus. In Shils, M. E., and Young, V. R.: Modern nutrition in health and disease. 7th ed. Philadelphia: Lea & Febiger, 1988.

SULFITE-RESTRICTED DIET

Sulfiting agents, which include sodium and potassium metabisulfite and bisulfite, sodium sulfite, and sulfur dioxide, are used extensively in the food and restaurant industry because of their whitening effects on fruits and vegetables. Sulfites are also found in a variety of drugs, including certain bronchodilator solutions and some B-complex vitamin capsules. Sulfite-sensitive individuals should check with their pharmacist before taking any prescription or nonprescription medication. A variety of adverse reactions to sulfites has been reported, including asthmatic reactions, urticaria, angioedema, abdominal pain, nausea, diarrhea, flushing, generalized pruritis, contact dermatitis, hypotension, loss of consciousness, and anaphylaxis. Amounts of sulfite as low as 5 mg have produced reactions (1, 2).

The diet in the United States has been estimated to provide 2–3 mg sulfite daily, while certain restaurant meals may contain as much as 100 mg. The National Restaurant Association, in cooperation with the American College of Allergists, has produced an excellent patient guide to foods that may contain sulfite. Additionally, a dipstick test for sulfite in food is soon to be available from Center Laboratories, in Port Washington, New York (3).

The following foods and beverages may contain sulfite and should be avoided (3):

Beverages
Beer
Wine, wine coolers
Cider
Fruit juices

Seafood
Shellfish
Canned seafood soups
Dried cod

Fruits and vegetables
Mushrooms
Potatoes
Sauerkraut
Avocado dip
Diced or cut up fresh fruits and vegetables
Coleslaw
Dried fruits and vegetables
Fruit purees and fillings

Miscellaneous
Gelatin
Maraschino cherries
Lemon juice
Wine vinegar
Salad dressings from dry mixes
Sauces from dry mixes or cans
Pickled products
Canned or dried soups

REFERENCES

1. Tichenor, W. W.: Sulfite sensitivity. Postgrad Med 78 (5):320, 1985.
2. Wolf, S. I., and Nichlas, R. I.: Sulfite sensitivity. Ann Allergy 54 (5):420, 1985.
3. National Restaurant Association and American College of Allergists: Sulfite sensitivity and eating out. Washington, D.C.: National Restaurant Association, 1985.

APPENDIX

TABLE A.1. RECOMMENDED DIETARY ALLOWANCES, REVISED 1989

| | | Weight[a] | | Height[a] | | Protein | Fat-soluble vitamins | | | |
| | | | | | | | Vita-min A | Vita-min D | Vita-min E | Vita-min K |
Category	Age (years) or condition	(kg)	(lb.)	(cm)	(in.)	(g)	(μg RE)[b]	(μg)[c]	(mg α-TE)[d]	(μg)
Infants	0.0–0.5	6	13	60	24	13	375	7.5	3	5
	0.5–1.0	9	20	71	28	14	375	10	4	10
Children	1–3	13	29	90	35	16	400	10	6	15
	4–6	20	44	112	44	24	500	10	7	20
	7–10	28	62	132	52	28	700	10	7	30
Males	11–14	45	99	157	62	45	1,000	10	10	45
	15–18	66	145	176	69	59	1,000	10	10	65
	19–24	72	160	177	70	58	1,000	10	10	70
	25–50	79	174	176	70	63	1,000	5	10	80
	51+	77	170	173	68	63	1,000	5	10	80
Females	11–14	46	101	157	62	46	800	10	8	45
	15–18	55	120	163	64	44	800	10	8	55
	19–24	58	128	164	65	46	800	10	8	60
	25–50	63	138	163	64	50	800	5	8	65
	51+	65	143	160	63	50	800	5	8	65
Pregnant						60	800	10	10	65
Lactating	First 6 months					65	1,300	10	12	65
	Second 6 months					62	1,200	10	11	65

Source: Food and Nutrition Board, National Research Council: Recommended Dietary Allowances. 10th ed. Washington, D.C.: National Academy Press, 1989. Copyright © 1989 by the National Academy of Sciences; reprinted by permission.

Note: The allowances, expressed as average daily intakes over time, are intended to provide for individual variations among most normal persons as they live in the United States under usual environmental stresses. Diets should be based on a variety of common foods in order to provide other nutrients for which human requirements have been less well defined. See text for detailed discussion of allowances and of nutrients not tabulated.

[a]Weights and heights of Reference Adults are actual medians for the U.S. population of the designated age, as reported by NHANES II. The median weights and heights of those under 19 years of age were taken from Hamill, P. V. V., and Drizd, C. L., et al.: Physical growth: National Center for Health Statistics percentiles. Am J Clin Nutr 32:16, 1979. The use of these figures does not imply that the height-to-weight ratios are ideal.

[b]Retinol equivalents. 1 retinol equivalent = 1 μg retinol or 6 μg β-carotene.

[c]As cholecalciferol. 10 μg cholecalciferol = 400 IU of vitamin D.

[d]α-Tocopherol equivalents. 1 mg d-α tocopherol = 1 α-TE.

[e]1 NE (niacin equivalent) is equal to 1 mg of niacin or 60 mg of dietary tryptophan.

Water-soluble vitamins							Minerals						
Vita-min C (mg)	Thia-mine (mg)	Ribo-flavin (mg)	Niacin (mg NE)[e]	Vita-min B-6 (mg)	Fo-late (μg)	Vitamin B-12 (μg)	Cal-cium (mg)	Phos-phorus (mg)	Mag-nesium (mg)	Iron (mg)	Zinc (mg)	Iodine (μg)	Sele-nium (μg)
30	0.3	0.4	5	0.3	25	0.3	400	300	40	6	5	40	10
35	0.4	0.5	6	0.6	35	0.5	600	500	60	10	5	50	15
40	0.7	0.8	9	1.0	50	0.7	800	800	80	10	10	70	20
45	0.9	1.1	12	1.1	75	1.0	800	800	120	10	10	90	20
45	1.0	1.2	13	1.4	100	1.4	800	800	170	10	10	120	30
50	1.3	1.5	17	1.7	150	2.0	1,200	1,200	270	12	15	150	40
60	1.5	1.8	20	2.0	200	2.0	1,200	1,200	400	12	15	150	50
60	1.5	1.7	19	2.0	200	2.0	1,200	1,200	350	10	15	150	70
60	1.5	1.7	19	2.0	200	2.0	800	800	350	10	15	150	70
60	1.2	1.4	15	2.0	200	2.0	800	800	350	10	15	150	70
50	1.1	1.3	15	1.4	150	2.0	1,200	1,200	280	15	12	150	45
60	1.1	1.3	15	1.5	180	2.0	1,200	1,200	300	15	12	150	50
60	1.1	1.3	15	1.6	180	2.0	1,200	1,200	280	15	12	150	55
60	1.1	1.3	15	1.6	180	2.0	800	800	280	15	12	150	55
60	1.0	1.2	13	1.6	180	2.0	800	800	280	10	12	150	55
70	1.5	1.6	17	2.2	400	2.2	1,200	1,200	320	30	15	175	65
95	1.6	1.8	20	2.1	280	2.6	1,200	1,200	355	15	19	200	75
90	1.6	1.7	20	2.1	260	2.6	1,200	1,200	340	15	16	200	75

TABLE A.2. MEDIAN HEIGHTS AND WEIGHTS AND RECOMMENDED ENERGY INTAKE

Category	Age (years) or condition	Weight (kg)	Weight (lb.)	Height (cm)	Height (in.)	REE[a] (kcal/day)	Multiples of REE	Average energy allowance (kcal)[b] Per kg	Per day[c]
Infants	0.0–0.5	6	13	60	24	320		108	650
	0.5–1.0	9	20	71	28	500		98	850
Children	1–3	13	29	90	35	740		102	1,300
	4–6	20	44	112	44	950		90	1,800
	7–10	28	62	132	52	1,130		70	2,000
Males	11–14	45	99	157	62	1,440	1.70	55	2,500
	15–18	66	145	176	69	1,760	1.67	45	3,000
	19–24	72	160	177	70	1,780	1.67	40	2,900
	25–50[d]	79	174	176	70	1,800	1.60	37	2,900
	51+	77	170	173	68	1,530	1.50	30	2,300
Females	11–14	46	101	157	62	1,310	1.67	47	2,200
	15–18	55	120	163	64	1,370	1.60	40	2,200
	19–24	58	128	164	65	1,350	1.60	38	2,200
	25–50[d]	63	138	163	64	1,380	1.55	36	2,200
	51+	65	143	160	63	1,280	1.50	30	1,900
Pregnant	First trimester								+0
	Second trimester								+300
	Third trimester								+300
Lactating	First 6 months								+500
	Second 6 months								+500

Source: Food and Nutrition Board, National Research Council: Recommended Dietary Allowances. 10th ed. Washington, D.C: National Academy Press, 1989. Copyright © 1989 by the National Academy of Sciences; reprinted by permission.

[a]Calculation based on FAO equations, then rounded.

[b]In the range of light to moderate activity, the coefficient of variation is ±20%.

[c]Figure is rounded.

[d]The energy allowance for persons beyond age 50 is 1.5 × REE. This assumes continued light to moderate activity, which should be encouraged in the interest of maintaining muscle mass and well-being. It should not be assumed that the marked decline in activity often observed in the elderly is either inevitable or desirable. The average allowance for men of reference size (77 kg) is 2,300 kcal/day; for women, it is 1,900 kcal/day. A normal variation of ±20% is accepted, as for younger adults. The requirements of persons beyond age 75 are likely to be somewhat less as a result of reduced body size, REE, and activity.

TABLE A.3. ESTIMATED SAFE AND ADEQUATE DAILY DIETARY INTAKES OF SELECTED VITAMINS AND MINERALS

Category	Age (years)	Vitamins		Trace elements[a]				
		Biotin (μg)	Pantothenic acid (mg)	Copper (mg)	Manganese (mg)	Fluoride (mg)	Chromium (μg)	Molybdenum (μg)
Infants	0–0.5	10	2	0.4–0.6	0.3–0.6	0.1–0.5	10–40	15–30
	0.5–1	15	3	0.6–0.7	0.6–1.0	0.2–1.0	20–60	20–40
Children and adolescents	1–3	20	3	0.7–1.0	1.0–1.5	0.5–1.5	20–80	25–50
	4–6	25	3–4	1.0–1.5	1.5–2.0	1.0–2.5	30–120	30–75
	7–10	30	4–5	1.0–2.0	2.0–3.0	1.5–2.5	50–200	50–150
	11+	30–100	4–7	1.5–2.5	2.0–5.0	1.5–2.5	50–200	75–250
Adults		30–100	4–7	1.5–3.0	2.0–5.0	1.5–4.0	50–200	75–250

Source: Food and Nutrition Board, National Research Council: Recommended Dietary Allowances. 10th ed. Washington, D.C.: National Academy Press, 1989. Copyright © 1989 by the National Academy of Sciences; reprinted by permission.

Note: Because there is less information on which to base allowances, these figures are not given in the main table of RDA and are provided here in the form of ranges of recommended intakes.

[a]Because the toxic levels for many trace elements may be only several times usual intakes, the upper levels for the trace elements given in this table should not be habitually exceeded.

THE *JOURNAL* ADOPTS SI UNITS FOR CLINICAL LABORATORY VALUES

Elaine R. Monsen, Ph.D., R.D.

EDITOR, JOURNAL OF THE AMERICAN DIETETIC ASSOCIATION

The *Journal of the American Dietetic Association* was among the first U.S. journals to announce adoption of SI units, the abbreviation for Système International d'Unités (1, 2). This method of notation, predominant throughout the remainder of the world, presents hematological and clinical chemistry values in molar concentrations with the liter as the reference volume, e.g., mol/L, mmol/L. Conversion to SI units will provide a uniform system of reporting clinical values; this common language will allow ready exchange of numerical data between health care providers of various disciplines as well as between scientists of different nations. Those are among the reasons motivating the Medical and Health Coordinating Group of the American National Metric Council to initiate the current collaboration of clinical and scientific journals to adopt SI units (3, 4).

Biological substances react on a molecular basis in vivo: use of molar SI units illustrates clearly the proportional amounts of various components that are within the body and available to participate in different metabolic pathways. For example, use of SI units rapidly shows that the relative normal number of molecules of calcium to those of potassium, glucose, and sodium in the serum approximates 1.0 : 1.6, 1.0 : 1.8, and 1.0 : 56.0, respectively.

BASE UNITS AND APPROPRIATE MULTIPLES

Seven base units, each representing a distinct physical characteristic, compose the SI units (table A.4a). The 3 most frequently used in reporting clinical data are meter, kilogram, and mole. From a historical bias, the kilogram is the base unit for mass, rather than the gram. As physiological quantities are usually much smaller or larger than the base units, submultiples and multiples of those units are often more convenient to use (table A.4b). In general, multiples are raised in 10^3 increments and submultiples are decreased in 10^{-3} increments. A mole $\times$ 10^3, 10^{-3}, 10^{-6}, or 10^{-9} is a kmol, a mmol, a µmol, or a nmol.

CONVERTING TRADITIONAL UNITS TO SI UNITS

A broad and relatively extensive list of hematology and clinical chemistry values is presented in tables A.5a and A.5b. Normal ranges were selected for reference intervals for both traditional and SI units; thus, this table has great utility. Additionally, the appropriate number of significant figures to report for each laboratory value is indicated, along with the suggested minimum increment that recognizes analytical accuracy of laboratory analysis. The conversion factors take into account molecular weight and change in volume. When a present traditional value is multiplied by its specific conversion factor, SI units may be computed. SI units may be divided by the conversion factor to convert to traditional units.

In most cases, the "name" of the laboratory test is the form in which the analyte is usually present physiologically. For example, the preferred designation is *pyruvate* rather than *pyruvic acid* and *lactate dehydrogenase* rather than *lactic acid dehydrogenase*.

APPLICATION TO DIETETICS

The major change in SI units is the use of liter quantities rather than deciliter (dL) or microliter (µL). Emphasis will be on molar quantities and subquantities per liter rather than on either mass quantities, such as gram or kilogram, or equivalents. The following 9 examples illustrate conversions.

1. mEQUIVALENTS TO mMOLES

A. Sodium and Potassium in Serum: mEq/L to mmol/L   Given that molecular weight and equivalent weight of single charged atoms are the same, there is no change in numerical value. Thus, 140 mEq sodium per liter serum converts to 140 mmol sodium per liter; and 4.0 mEq potassium per liter to 4.0 mmol potassium per liter.

B. Calcium in Serum: 5.0 mEq/L to 2.50 mmol/L   Calcium is a divalent ion; thus, a mole is twice the weight of an equivalent. Multiplying 5.0 mEq/L by 0.500 results in 2.50 mmol/L.

2. MG TO mMOLES

A. Calcium in Serum: 10.0 mg/dL to 2.50 mmol/dL   A conversion factor of 0.2495 is used. This is derived from the 10-fold volume increase, divided by calcium's molecular weight of 40.08.

B. Glucose in Serum: 80 mg/dL to 4.4 mmol/L   Given that molecular weight of glucose is 180.16, the conversion factor is 0.05551 (10 divided by 180.16).

C. Cholesterol in Plasma: 200 mg/dL to 5.20 mmol/L   The conversion factor of 0.02586 (10 divided by 386.64) yields 5.17 mmol/L, which, because the suggested minimum increment is 0.05 mmol/L, is rounded to 5.20 mmol/L.

D. Hemoglobin: 12.0 g/dL to 7.45 mmol/L   This conversion to substance concentration is in terms of the monomer Hb(Fe), with molecular weight approximating 16,125—rather than the tetramer Hb(4Fe) with molecular weight of 64,500. In view of the change from g/dL to mmol/L, the conversion factor is computed by dividing 10,000 by the molecular weight. Hemoglobin may also be reported in mass concentration, as shown below.

3. EXCEPTIONS

A. Hemoglobin: 12.0 g/dL to 120 g/L   Reporting hemoglobin in mass concentration units is recommended at present. Thus, the only conversion required is related to the reference volume of 1 L.

B. Hematocrit: 33% to 0.33   Volume fractions are to be reported to the relative quantity of the unit 1. Proportions or percentages of components are also to be reported as a fraction of the unit 1, e.g., 0.25 rather than 25%.

C. Blood Pressure: No Change Proposed Currently   Units to report partial pressure of gases will remain mmHg.

IMPLICATIONS

To be in the forefront of America's conversion to SI units, researchers in dietetics and nutrition need to report clinical values in SI units; clinical dietitians need to recognize and respond to SI units; and educators need to teach SI units. Tables A.5a and A.5b provide the new cutoff points for normal ranges; we need to become alert to those values. Planning educational in-service opportunities will aid our reorientation.

REFERENCES

1. Monsen, E. R. The Journal of 1987. J Am Diet Assoc 87:27, 1987.
2. Guidelines for Authors. J Am Diet Assoc 87:98, 1987.
3. Young, D. S. Implementation of SI units for clinical laboratory data style specifications and conversion tables. Ann Intern Med 106:114, 1987.
4. Lundberg, G. D., Iverson, C., and Radulescu, G.: Now read this: The SI units are here. JAMA 255:2329, 1986.

TABLE A.4a. BASE UNITS OF SI

Physical quantity	Base unit	SI symbol
Length	Meter	m
Mass	Kilogram	kg
Time	Second	s
Amount of substance	Mole	mol
Thermodynamic temperature	Kelvin	K
Electric current	Ampere	A
Luminous intensity	Candela	cd

Source: Young, D. S.: Implementation of SI units for clinical laboratory data style specifications and conversion tables. Ann Intern Med 106:114, 1987. Single reprints are available free of charge from the *Annals of Internal Medicine* Business Department, 4200 Pine St., Philadelphia, PA 19104 (toll-free: 800/523-1546, or 215/243-1200). Rates for bulk orders are available from the Business Department. The tables are not copyrighted; persons who wish to make photocopies are free to do so.

TABLE A.4b. PREFIXES AND SYMBOLS FOR DECIMAL MULTIPLES AND SUBMULTIPLES

Factor	Prefix	Symbol
10^{18}	exa	E
10^{15}	peta	P
10^{12}	tera	T
10^9	giga	G
10^6	mega	M
10^3	kilo	k
10^2	hecto	h
10^1	deka	da
10^{-1}	deci	d
10^{-2}	centi	c
10^{-3}	milli	m
10^{-6}	micro	μ
10^{-9}	nano	n
10^{-12}	pico	p
10^{-15}	femto	f
10^{-18}	atto	a

Source: Young, D. S.: Implementation of SI units for clinical laboratory data style specifications and conversion tables. Ann Intern Med 106:114, 1987. Single reprints are available free of charge from the *Annals of Internal Medicine* Business Department, 4200 Pine St., Philadelphia, PA 19104 (toll-free: 800/523-1546, or 215/243-1200). Rates for bulk orders are available from the Business Department. The tables are not copyrighted; persons who wish to make photocopies are free to do so.

Note: Factors included in the rectangle do not conform to the preferred incremental changes of 10^3 and 10^{-3} but are still used outside medicine.

TABLE A.5a. SI CONVERSION TABLE FOR VALUES IN CLINICAL HEMATOLOGY

Component	Present reference intervals (examples)	Present unit	Conversion factor	SI reference intervals	SI unit symbol	Significant digits	Suggested minimum increment
Erythrocyte count (B)							
Female	3.5–5.0	$10^6/mm^3$	1	3.5–5.0	$10^{12}/L$	X.X	$0.1\ 10^{12}/L$
Male	4.3–5.9	$10^6/mm^3$	1	4.3–5.9	$10^{12}/L$	X.X	$0.1\ 10^{12}/L$
Erythrocyte count (Sf)	0	mm^{-3}	1	0	$10^6/L$	XX	$1\ 10^6/L$
Erythrocyte sedimentation rate [ESR] (BErc)							
Female	0–30	mm/hour	1	0–30	mm/h	XX	1 mm/hour
Male	0–20	mm/hour	1	0–20	mm/h	XX	1 mm/hour
Hematocrit (BErcs) vol. fraction							
Female	33–43	%	0.01	0.33–0.43	1	0.XX	0.01
Male	39–49	%	0.01	0.39–0.49	1	0.XX	0.01
Hemoglobin (B)							
Mass concentration							
Female	12.0–15.0	g/dL	10	120–150	g/L	XXX	1 g/L
Male	13.6–17.2	g/dL	10	136–172	g/L	XXX	1 g/L
Substance conc. Hb [Fe]							
Female	12.0–15.0	g/dL	0.6206	7.45–9.30	mmol/L	XX.XX	0.05 mmol/L
Male	13.6–17.2	g/dL	0.6206	8.45–10.65	mmol/L	XX.XX	0.05 mmol/L
Leukocyte count (B)	3,200–9,800	mm^{-3}	0.001	3.2–9.8	$10^9/L$	XX.X	$0.1\ 10^9/L$
Number fraction ["differential"]		%	0.01		1	0.XX	0.01
Leukocyte count (Sf)	0–5	mm^{-3}	1	0–5	$10^6/L$	XX	$1\ 10^6/L$
Mean corpuscular hemoglobin [MCH] (BErc)							
Mass	27–33	pg	1	27–33	pg	XX	1 pg
Amount of substance Hb [Fe]	27–33	pg	0.06206	1.70–2.05	fmol	X.XX	0.05 fmol
Mean corpuscular hemoglobin concentration [MCHC] (BErc)							
Mass concentration	33–37	g/dL	10	330–370	g/L	XX0	10 g/L
Substance conc. Hb [Fe]	33–37	g/dL	0.6206	20–23	mmol/L	XX	1 mmol/L
Mean corpuscular volume [MCV] (BErc)							
Erythrocyte volume	76–100	μm^3	1	76–100	fL	XXX	1 fL
Platelet count (B)	130–400	$10^3/mm^3$	1	130–400	$10^9/L$	XXX	$5\ 10^9/L$
Reticulocyte count (B)—adults	10,000–75,000	mm^{-3}	0.001	10–75	$10^9/L$	XX	$1\ 10^9/L$
Number fraction	1–24	0/00 (number per 1,000 erythrocytes)	0.001	0.001–0.024	1	0.XXX	0.001
	0.1–2.4	%	0.001	0.001–0.024	1	0.XXX	0.001

Source: Young, D. S.: Implementation of SI units for clinical laboratory data style specifications and conversion tables. Ann Intern Med 106:114, 1987. Single reprints are available free of charge from the *Annals of Internal Medicine* Business Department, 4200 Pine St., Philadelphia, PA 19104 (toll-free: 800/523-1546, or 215/243-1200). Rates for bulk orders are available from the Business Department. The tables are not copyrighted; persons who wish to make photocopies are free to do so.

TABLE A.5b. SI CONVERSION FACTORS FOR VALUES IN CLINICAL CHEMISTRY

Component	Present reference intervals (examples)	Present unit	Conversion factor	SI reference intervals	SI unit symbol	Significant digits	Suggested minimum increment
Acetaminophen (P)—toxic	>5.0	mg/dL	66.16	>330	μmol/L	XX0	10 μmol/L
Acetoacetate (S)	0.3–3.0	mg/dL	97.95	30–300	μmol/L	XX0	10 μmol/L
Acetone (B, S)	0	mg/dL	172.2	0	μmol/L	XX0	10 μmol/L
Acid phosphatase (S)	0–5.5	U/L	16.67	0–90	nkat/L	XX	2 nkat/L
Adrenocorticotropin [ACTH] (P)	20–100	pg/mL	0.2202	4–22	pmol/L	XX	1 pmol/L
Alanine aminotransferase [ALT] (S)	0–35	U/L	0.01667	0–0.58	μkat/L	X.XX	0.02 μkat/L
Albumin (S)	4.0–6.0	g/dL	10.0	40–60	g/L	XX	1 g/L
Aldolase (S)	0–6	U/L	16.67	0–100	nkat/L	XX0	20 nkat/L
Aldosterone (S)							
Normal-salt diet	8.1–15.5	ng/dL	27.74	220–430	pmol/L	XX0	10 pmol/L
Restricted-salt diet	20.8–44.4	ng/dL	27.74	580–1240	pmol/L	XX0	10 pmol/L
Aldosterone (U)—sodium excretion							
25 mmol/d	18–85	μg/24 hours	2.774	50–235	nmol/d	XXX	5 nmol/d
75–125 mmol/d	5–26	μg/24 hours	2.774	15–70	nmol/d	XXX	5 nmol/d
200 mmol/d	1.5–12.5	μg/24 hours	2.774	5–35	nmol/d	XXX	5 nmol/d
Alkaline phosphatase (S)	30–120	U/L	0.01667	0.5–2.0	μkat/L	X.X	0.1 μkat/L
Alpha$_1$-antitrypsin (S)	150–350	mg/dL	0.01	1.5–3.5	g/L	X.X	0.1 g/L
Alpha-fetoprotein (S)	0–20	ng/mL	1.00	0–20	μg/L	XX	1 μg/L
Alpha-fetoprotein (Amf)	Depends on gestation	mg/dL	10	Depends on gestation	mg/L	XX	1 mg/L
Alpha$_2$-macroglobulin (S)	145–410	mg/dL	0.01	1.5–4.1	g/L	X.X	0.1 g/L
Aluminum (S)	0–15	μg/L	37.06	0–560	nmol/L	XX0	10 nmol/L
Amino acid fractionation (P)							
Alanine	2.2–4.5	mg/dL	112.2	245–500	μmol/L	XXX	5 μmol/L
Alpha-aminobutyric acid	0.1–0.2	mg/dL	96.97	10–20	μmol/L	XXX	5 μmol/L
Arginine	0.5–2.5	mg/dL	57.40	30–145	μmol/L	XXX	5 μmol/L
Asparagine	0.5–0.6	mg/dL	75.69	35–45	μmol/L	XXX	5 μmol/L
Aspartic acid	0.0–0.3	mg/dL	75.13	0–20	μmol/L	XXX	5 μmol/L
Citrulline	0.2–1.0	mg/dL	57.08	15–55	μmol/L	XXX	5 μmol/L
Cystine	0.2–2.2	mg/dL	41.61	10–90	μmol/L	XXX	5 μmol/L
Glutamic acid	0.2–2.8	mg/dL	67.97	15–190	μmol/L	XXX	5 μmol/L
Glutamine	6.1–10.2	mg/dL	68.42	420–700	μmol/L	XXX	5 μmol/L
Glycine	0.9–4.2	mg/dL	133.2	120–560	μmol/L	XXX	5 μmol/L
Histidine	0.5–1.7	mg/dL	64.45	30–110	μmol/L	XXX	5 μmol/L
Hydroxyproline	0–trace	mg/dL	76.26	0–trace	μmol/L	XXX	5 μmol/L
Isoleucine	0.5–1.3	mg/dL	76.24	40–100	μmol/L	XXX	5 μmol/L
Leucine	1.0–2.3	mg/dL	76.24	75–175	μmol/L	XXX	5 μmol/L
Lysine	1.2–3.5	mg/dL	68.40	80–240	μmol/L	XXX	5 μmol/L
Methionine	0.1–0.6	mg/dL	67.02	5–40	μmol/L	XXX	5 μmol/L
Ornithine	0.4–1.4	mg/dL	75.67	30–400	μmol/L	XXX	5 μmol/L
Phenylalanine	0.6–1.5	mg/dL	60.54	35–90	μmol/L	XXX	5 μmol/L
Proline	1.2–3.9	mg/dL	86.86	105–340	μmol/L	XXX	5 μmol/L
Serine	0.8–1.8	mg/dL	95.16	75–170	μmol/L	XXX	5 μmol/L
Taurine	0.3–2.1	mg/dL	79.91	25–170	μmol/L	XXX	5 μmol/L
Threonine	0.9–2.5	mg/dL	83.95	75–210	μmol/L	XXX	5 μmol/L
Tryptophan	0.5–2.5	mg/dL	48.97	25–125	μmol/L	XXX	5 μmol/L
Tyrosine	0.4–1.6	mg/dL	55.19	20–90	μmol/L	XXX	5 μmol/L
Valine	1.7–3.7	mg/dL	85.36	145–315	μmol/L	XXX	5 μmol/L
Amino acid nitrogen (P)	4.0–6.0	mg/dL	0.7139	2.9–4.3	mmol/L	X.X	0.1 mmol/L
Amino acid nitrogen (U)	50–200	mg/24 hour	0.07139	3.6–14.3	mmol/d	X.X	0.1 mmol/d

(continued)

TABLE A.5b. *CONTINUED*

Component	Present reference intervals (examples)	Present unit	Conversion factor	SI reference intervals	SI unit symbol	Significant digits	Suggested minimum increment
Delta-aminolevulinate [as levulinic acid] (U)	1.0–7.0	mg/24 hours	7.626	8–53	μmol/d	XX	1 μmol/d
Amitriptyline (P, S)							
Therapeutic	50–200	ng/mL	3.605	180–720	nmol/L	XX0	10 nmol/L
Ammonia (vP)							
As ammonia [NH$_3$]	10–80	μg/dL	0.5872	5–50	μmol/L	XXX	5 μmol/L
As ammonium ion [NH$_4$+]	10–85	μg/dL	0.5543	5–50	μmol/L	XXX	5 μmol/L
As nitrogen [N]	10–65	μg/dL	0.7139	5–50	μmol/L	XXX	5 μmol/L
Amylase (S)	0–130	U/L	0.01667	0–2.17	μkat/L	XXX	0.01 μkat/L
Androstenedione (S)							
Male > 18 years	0.2–3.0	μg/L	3.492	0.5–10.5	nmol/L	XX.X	0.5 nmol/L
Female > 18 years	0.8–3.0	μg/L	3.492	3.0–10.5	nmol/L	XX.X	0.5 nmol/L
Angiotensin converting enzyme (S)	<40	nmol/mL/min	16.67	<670	nkat/L	XX0	10 nkat/L
Arsenic (H) [as As]	<1	μg/g (ppm)	13.35	<13	nmol/g	XX.X	0.5 nmol/g
Arsenic (U) [as As]	0–5	μg/24 hours	13.35	0–67	nmol/d	XX	1 nmol/d
As As$_2$O$_3$	<25	μg/dL	0.05055	<1.3	μmol/L	XX.X	0.1 μmol/L
Ascorbate (P) [as ascorbic acid]	0.6–2.0	mg/dL	56.78	30–110	μmol/L	X0	10 μmol/L
Aspartate aminotransferase [AST] (S)	0–35	U/L	0.01667	0–0.58	μkat/L	0.XX	0.01 μkat/L
Barbiturate (S)—overdose total expressed as:	Depends on composition of mixture.						
Phenobarbital	of mixture.	mg/dL	43.06	—	μmol/L	XX	5 μmol/L
Sodium phenobarbital	Usually not	mg/dL	39.34	—	μmol/L	XX	5 μmol/L
Barbitone	known.	mg/dL	54.29	—	μmol/L	XX	5 μmol/L
Barbiturate (S)—therapeutic							
See "Phenobarbital"	—	—	—	—	—	—	—
See "Pentobarbital"							
See "Thiopental"							
Bile acids, total (S) [as chenodeoxycholic acid]	Trace–3.3	μg/mL	2.547	Trace–8.4	μmol/L	X.X	0.2 μmol/L
Cholic acid	Trace–1.0	μg/mL	2.448	Trace–2.4	μmol/L	X.X	0.2 μmol/L
Chenodeoxycholic acid	Trace–1.3	μg/mL	2.547	Trace–3.4	μmol/L	X.X	0.2 μmol/L
Deoxycholic acid	Trace–1.0	μg/mL	2.547	Trace–2.6	μmol/L	X.X	0.2 μmol/L
Lithocholic acid	Trace	μg/mL	2.656	Trace	μmol/L	X.X	0.2 μmol/L
Bile acids (Df) [after cholecystokinin stimulation]							
Total as chenodeoxycholic acid	14.0–58.0	mg/mL	2.547	35.0–148.0	mmol/L	XX.X	0.2 mmol/L
Cholic acid	2.4–33.0	mg/mL	2.448	6.8–81.0	mmol/L	XX.X	0.2 mmol/L
Chenodeoxycholic acid	4.0–24.0	mg/mL	2.547	10.0–61.4	mmol/L	XX.X	0.2 mmol/L
Deoxycholic acid	0.8–6.9	mg/mL	2.547	2.0–18.0	μmol/L	XX.X	0.2 mmol/L
Lithocholic acid	0.3–0.8	mg/mL	2.656	0.8–2.0	mmol/L	XX.X	0.2 mmol/L
Bilirubin, total (S)	0.1–1.0	mg/dL	17.10	2–18	μmol/L	XX	2 μmol/L
Bilirubin, conjugated (S)	0–0.2	mg/dL	17.10	0–4	μmol/L	XX	2 μmol/L
Bromide (S), toxic							
As bromide ion	>120	mg/dL	0.1252	>15	mmol/L	XX	1 mmol/L
As sodium bromide	>150	mg/dL	0.09719	>15	mmol/L	XX	1 mmol/L
	>15	mEq/L	1.00	>15	mmol/L	XX	1 mmol/L
Cadmium (S)	<3	μg/dL	0.08897	<0.3	μmol/L	X.X	0.1 μmol/L
Calcitonin (S)	<100	pg/mL	1.00	<100	ng/L	XXX	10 ng/L
Calcium (S)							
Male	8.8–10.3	mg/dL	0.2495	2.20–2.58	mmol/L	X.XX	0.02 mmol/L

(continued)

TABLE A.5b. *CONTINUED*

Component	Present reference intervals (examples)	Present unit	Conversion factor	SI reference intervals	SI unit symbol	Significant digits	Suggested minimum increment
Female <50 y	8.8–10.0	mg/dL	0.2495	2.20–2.50	mmol/L	X.XX	0.02 mmol/L
Female >50 y	8.8–10.2	mg/dL	0.2495	2.20–2.56	mmol/L	X.XX	0.02 mmol/L
	4.4–5.1	mEq/L	0.500	2.20–2.56	mmol/L	X.XX	0.02 mmol/L
Calcium ion (S)	0–2.30	mEq/L	0.500	1.00–1.15	mmol/L	X.XX	0.01 mmol/L
	4.00–4.60	mg/dL	0.2495	1.00–1.15	mmol/L	X.XX	0.01 mmol/L
Calcium (U), normal diet	<250	mg/24 hours	0.02495	<6.2	mmol/d	X.X	0.1 mmol/d
Carbamazepine (P)—therapeutic	4.0–10.0	mg/L	4.233	17–42	μmol/L	XX	1 μmol/L
Carbon dioxide content (B, P, S) [bicarbonate + CO_2]	22–28	mEq/L	1.00	22–28	mmol/L	XX	1 mmol/L
Carbon monoxide (B) [proportion of Hb that is COHb]	<15	%	0.01	<0.15	1	0.XX	0.01
Beta-carotenes (S)	50–250	μg/dL	0.01863	0.9–4.6	μmol/L	X.X	0.1 μmol/L
Catecholamines, total (U) [as nor-epinephrine]	<120	μg/24 hours	5.911	<675	nmol/d	XX0	10 mg/d
Ceruloplasmin (S)	20–35	mg/dL	10.0	200–350	mg/L	XX0	10 mg/L
Chlordiazepoxide (P)							
Therapeutic	0.5–5.0	mg/L	3.336	2–17	μmol/L	XX	1 μmol/L
Toxic	>10.0	mg/L	3.336	>33	μmol/L	XX	1 μmol/L
Chloride (S)	95–105	mEq/L	1.00	95–105	mmol/L	XXX	1 mmol/L
Chlorimipramine (P) [includes des-methyl metabolite]	50–400	ng/mL	3.176	150–1270	nmol/L	XX0	10 nmol/L
Chlorpromazine (P)	50–300	ng/mL	3.136	150–950	nmol/L	XX0	10 nmol/L
Chlorpropamide (P)—therapeutic	75–250	mg/L	3.613	270–900	μmol/L	XX0	10 μmol/L
Cholestanol (P)—[as a fraction of total cholesterol]	1–3	%	0.01	0.01–0.03	1	0.XX	0.01
Cholesterol (P)							
<29 years	<200	mg/dL	0.02586	<5.20	mmol/L	X.XX	0.05 mmol/L
30–39 years	<225	mg/dL	0.02586	<5.85	mmol/L	X.XX	0.05 mmol/L
40–49 years	<245	mg/dL	0.02586	<6.35	mmol/L	X.XX	0.05 mmol/L
>50 years	<265	mg/dL	0.02586	<6.85	mmol/L	X.XX	0.05 mmol/L
Cholesterol esters (P) [as a fraction of total cholesterol]	60–75	%	0.01	0.60–0.75	1	0.XX	0.01
Cholinesterase (S)	620–1370	U/L	0.01667	10.3–22.8	μkat/L	XX.X	0.1 μkat/L
Chorionic gonadotrophin (P) [beta-HCG]	0 if not pregnant	mIU/mL	1.00	0 if not pregnant	IU/L	XX	1 IU/L
Citrate (B) [as citric acid]	1.2–3.0	mg/dL	52.05	60–160	μmol/L	XXX	5 μmol/L
Complement, C3 (S)	70–160	mg/dL	0.01	0.7–1.6	g/L	X.X	0.1 g/L
Complement, C4 (S)	20–40	mg/dL	0.01	0.2–0.4	g/L	X.X	0.1 g/L
Copper (S)	70–140	μg/dL	0.1574	11.0–22.0	μmol/L	XX.X	0.2 μmol/L
Copper (U)	<40	μg/24 hours	0.01574	<0.6	μmol/d	X.X	0.2 μmol/d
Coproporphyrins (U)	<200	μg/24 hours	1.527	<300	nmol/d	XX0	10 nmol/d
Cortisol (S)							
0800 hours	4–19	μg/dL	27.59	110–520	nmol/L	XX0	10 nmol/L
1600 hours	2–15	μg/dL	27.59	50–410	nmol/L	XX0	10 nmol/L
2400 hours	5	μg/dL	27.59	140	nmol/L	XX0	10 nmol/L
Cortisol, free (U)	10–110	μg/24 hours	2.759	30–300	nmol/d	XX0	10 nmol/d
Creatine (S)							
Male	0.17–0.50	mg/dL	76.25	10–40	μmol/L	X0	10 μmol/L
Female	0.35–0.93	mg/dL	76.25	30–70	μmol/L	X0	10 μmol/L
Creatine (U)							
Male	0–40	mg/24 hours	7.625	0–300	μmol/d	XX0	10 μmol/d
Female	0–80	mg/24 hours	7.625	0–600	μmol/d	XX0	10 μmol/d

(continued)

TABLE A.5b. *CONTINUED*

Component	Present reference intervals (examples)	Present unit	Conversion factor	SI reference intervals	SI unit symbol	Significant digits	Suggested minimum increment
Creatine kinase [CK] (S)							
Creatine kinase isoenzymes (S)	0–130	U/L	0.01667	0–2.16	μkat/L	X.XX	0.01 μkat/L
MB fraction	>5 in myocardial infarction	%	0.01	>0.05	1	0.XX	0.01
Creatinine (S)	0.6–1.2	mg/dL	88.40	50–110	μmol/L	XX0	10 μmol/L
Creatinine (U)	variable	g/24 hours	8.840	variable	mmol/d	XX.X	0.1 mmol/d
Creatinine clearance (S, U)	75–125	mL/minutes	0.01667	1.24–2.08	mL/second	X.XX	0.02 mL/s

$$\text{creatinine clearance corrected for body surface area} = \frac{\mu\text{mol/L (urine creatinine)}}{\mu\text{mol/L (serum creatinine)}} \times \text{mL/second} \times \frac{1.73}{A} \quad [\text{where A is the body surface area in square meters (m}^2)]$$

Component	Present reference intervals (examples)	Present unit	Conversion factor	SI reference intervals	SI unit symbol	Significant digits	Suggested minimum increment
Cyanide (B)—lethal	>0.10	mg/dL	384.3	>40	μmol/L	XXX	5 μmol/L
Cyanocobalamin (S) [vitamin B$_{12}$]	200–1000	pg/mL	0.7378	150–750	pmol/L	XX0	10 pmol/L
Cyclic AMP (S)	2.6–6.6	μg/L	3.038	8–20	nmol/L	XXX	1 nmol/L
Cyclic AMP (U)							
Total urinary	2.9–5.6	μmol/g creatinine	113.1	330–630	nmol/mmol creatinine	XX0	10 nmol/mmol creatinine
Renal tubular	<2.5	μmol/g creatinine	113.1	<280	nmol/mmol creatinine	XX0	10 nmol/mmol creatinine
Cyclic GMP (S)	0.6–3.5	μg/L	2.897	1.7–10.1	nmol/L	XX.X	0.1 nmol/L
Cyclic GMP (U)	0.3–1.8	μmol/g creatinine	113.1	30–200	nmol/mmol creatinine	XX0	10 nmol/mmol creatinine
Cystine (U)	10–100	mg/24 hours	4.161	40–420	μmol/d	XX0	10 μmol/d
Dehydroepiandrosterone (P, S) [DHEA]							
1–4 years	0.2–0.4	μg/L	3.467	0.6–1.4	nmol/L	XX.X	0.2 nmol/L
4–8 years	0.1–1.9	μg/L	3.467	0.4–6.6	nmol/L	XX.X	0.2 nmol/L
8–10 years	0.2–2.9	μg/L	3.467	0.6–10.0	nmol/L	XX.X	0.2 nmol/L
10–12 years	0.5–9.2	μg/L	3.467	1.8–31.8	nmol/L	XX.X	0.2 nmol/L
12–14 years	0.9–20.0	μg/L	3.467	3.2–69.4	nmol/L	XX.X	0.2 nmol/L
14–16 years	2.5–20.0	μg/L	3.467	8.6–69.4	nmol/L	XX.X	0.2 nmol/L
Premenopausal female	2.0–15.0	μg/L	3.467	7.0–52.0	nmol/L	XX.X	0.2 nmol/L
Male	0.8–10.0	μg/L	3.467	2.8–34.6	nmol/L	XX.X	0.2 nmol/L
Dehydroepiandrosterone (U)	See "Steroids"	Fractionation	—	—	—	—	—
Dehydroepiandrosterone sulphate [DHEA-S] (P, S)							
Newborn	1,670–3,640	ng/mL	0.002714	4.5–9.9	μmol/L	XX.X	0.1 μmol/L
Prepubertal children	100–600	ng/mL	0.002714	0.3–1.6	μmol/L	XX.X	0.1 μmol/L
Male	2,000–3,350	ng/mL	0.002714	5.4–9.1	μmol/L	XX.X	0.1 μmol/L
Female [premenopausal]	820–3,380	ng/mL	0.002714	2.2–9.2	μmol/L	XX.X	0.1 μmol/L
Female [postmenopausal]	110–610	ng/mL	0.002714	0.3–1.7	μmol/L	XX.X	0.1 μmol/L
Pregnancy [term]	230–1,170	ng/mL	0.002714	0.6–3.2	μmol/L	XX.X	0.1 μmol/L
11-Deoxycortisol (S)	0–2	μg/dL	28.86	0–60	nmol/L	XX0	10 nmol/L
Desipramine (P)—therapeutic	50–200	ng/mL	3.754	170–700	nmol/L	XX0	10 nmol/L
Diazepam (P)							
Therapeutic	0.10–0.25	mg/L	3,512	350–900	nmol/L	XX0	10 nmol/L
Toxic	>1.0	mg/L	3,512	>3510	nmol/L	XX0	10 nmol/L
Dicoumarol (P)—therapeutic	8–30	mg/L	2.974	25–90	μmol/L	XX	5 μmol/L

(continued)

TABLE A.5b. *CONTINUED*

Component	Present reference intervals (examples)	Present unit	Conversion factor	SI reference intervals	SI unit symbol	Significant digits	Suggested minimum increment
Digoxin (P)							
Therapeutic	0.5–2.2	ng/mL	1.281	0.6–2.8	nmol/L	X.X	0.1 nmol/L
	0.5–2.2	μg/L	1.281	0.6–2.8	nmol/L	X.X	0.1 nmol/L
Toxic	>2.5	ng/mL	1.281	>3.2	nmol/L	X.X	0.1 nmol/L
Dimethadione (P)—therapeutic	<1.00	g/L	7.745	<7.7	mmol/L	X.X	0.1 mmol/L
Disopyramide (P)—therapeutic	2.0–6.0	mg/L	2.946	6–18	μmol/L	XX	1 μmol/L
Doxepin (P)—therapeutic	50–200	ng/mL	3.579	180–720	nmol/L	XX0	10 nmol/L
Electrophoresis, protein (S)							
Albumin	60–65	%	0.01	0.60–0.65	1	0.XX	0.01
Alpha₁-globulin	1.7–5.0	%	0.01	0.02–0.05	1	0.XX	0.01
Alpha₂-globulin	6.7–12.5	%	0.01	0.07–0.13	1	0.XX	0.01
Beta-globulin	8.3–16.3	%	0.01	0.08–0.16	1	0.XX	0.01
Gamma-globulin	10.7–20.0	%	0.01	0.11–0.20	1	0.XX	0.01
Albumin	3.6–5.2	g/dL	10.0	36–52	g/L	XX	1 g/L
Alpha₁-globulin	0.1–0.4	g/dL	10.0	1–4	g/L	XX	1 g/L
Alpha₂-globulin	0.4–1.0	g/dL	10.0	4–10	g/L	XX	1 g/L
Beta-globulin	0.5–1.2	g/dL	10.0	5–12	g/L	XX	1 g/L
Gamma-globulin	0.6–1.6	g/dL	10.0	6–16	g/L	XX	1 g/L
Epinephrine (P)	31–95 (at rest for 15 min)	pg/mL	5.458	170–520	pmol/L	XX0	10 pmol/L
Epinephrine (U)	<10	μg/24 hours	5.458	<55	nmol/d	XX	5 nmol/d
Estradiol (S)—male >18 years	15–40	pg/mL	3.671	55–150	pmol/L	XXX	1 pmol/L
Estriol (U) [nonpregnant]							
Onset of menstruation	4–25	μg/24 hours	3.468	15–85	nmol/d	XXX	5 nmol/d
Ovulation peak	28–99	μg/24 hours	3.468	95–345	nmol/d	XXX	5 nmol/d
Luteal peak	22–105	μg/24 hours	3.468	75–365	nmol/d	XXX	5 nmol/d
Menopausal women	1.4–19.6	μg/24 hours	3.468	5–70	nmol/d	XXX	5 nmol/d
Male	5–18	μg/24 hours	3.468	15–60	nmol/d	XXX	5 nmol/d
Estrogens (S) [as estradiol]							
Female	20–300	pg/mL	3.671	70–1100	pmol/L	XXX0	10 pmol/L
Peak production	200–800	pg/mL	3.671	750–2900	pmol/L	XXX0	10 pmol/L
Male	<50	pg/mL	3.671	<180	pmol/L	XX0	10 pmol/L
Estrogens, placental (U) [as estriol]	Depends on period of gestation	mg/24 hours	3.468	Depends on period of gestation	μmol/d	XXX	1 μmol/d
Estrogen receptors (T)							
Negative	0–3	fmol estradiol bound/mg cytosol protein	1.00	0–3	fmol estradiol/mg cytosol protein	XXX	1 fmol/mg protein
Doubtful	4–10	fmol estradiol bound/mg cytosol protein	1.00	4–10	fmol estradiol/mg cytosol protein	XXX	fmol/mg protein
Positive	>10	fmol estradiol bound/mg cytosol protein	1.00	>10	fmol estradiol/mg cytosol protein	XXX	fmol/mg protein
Estrone (P, S)							
Female 1–10 days of cycle	43–180	pg/mL	3.699	160–665	pmol/L	XXX	5 pmol/L
Female 11–20 days of cycle	75–196	pg/mL	3.699	275–725	pmol/L	XXX	5 pmol/L
Female 20–39 days of cycle	131–201	pg/mL	3.699	485–745	pmol/L	XXX	5 pmol/L
Male	29–75	pg/mL	3.699	105–275	pmol/L	XXX	5 pmol/L
Estrone (U)—female	2–25	μg/24 hours	3.699	5–90	nmol/d	XXX	5 nmol/d

(continued)

TABLE A.5b. *CONTINUED*

Component	Present reference intervals (examples)	Present unit	Conversion factor	SI reference intervals	SI unit symbol	Significant digits	Suggested minimum increment
Ethanol (P)							
Legal limit [driving]	<80	mg/dL	0.2171	<17	mmol/L	XX	1 mmol/L
Toxic	>100	mg/dL	0.2171	>22	mmol/L	XX	1 mmol/L
Ethchlorvynol (P)—toxic	>40	mg/L	6.915	>280	μmol/L	XX0	10 μmol/L
Ethosuximide (P)—therapeutic	40–110	mg/L	7.084	280–780	μmol/L	XX0	10 μmol/L
Ethylene glycol (P)—toxic	>30	mg/dL	0.1611	>5	mmol/L	XX	1 mmol/L
Fat (F) [as stearic acid]	2.0–6.0	g/24 hours	3.515	7–21	mmol/d	XX	1 mmol/d
Fatty acids, non-esterified (P)	8–20	mg/dL	10.00	80–200	mg/L	XX0	10 mg/L
Ferritin (S)	18–300	ng/mL	1.00	18–300	μg/L	XX0	10 μg/L
Fibrinogen (P)	200–400	mg/dL	0.01	2.0–4.0	g/L	X.X	0.1 g/L
Fluoride (U)	<1.0	mg/24 hours	52.63	<50	μmol/d	XX0	10 μmol/d
Folate (S) [as pteroylglutamic acid]	2–10	ng/mL	2.266	4–22	nmol/L	XX	2 nmol/L
		μg/dL	22.66		nmol/L		2 nmol/L
Folate (Erc)	140–960	ng/mL	2.266	550–2,200	nmol/L	XX0	10 nmol/L
Follicle stimulating hormone [FSH] (P)							
Female	2.0–15.0	mIU/mL	1.00	2–15	IU/L	XX	1 IU/L
Peak production	20–50	mIU/mL	1.00	20–50	IU/L	XX	1 IU/L
Male	1.0–10.0	mIU/mL	1.00	1–10	IU/L	XX	1 IU/L
Follicle stimulating hormone [FSH] (U)							
Follicular phase	2–15	IU/24 hours	1.00	2–15	IU/d	XXX	1 IU/d
Midcycle	8–40	IU/24 hours	1.00	8–40	IU/d	XXX	1 IU/d
Luteal phase	2–10	IU/24 hours	1.00	2–10	IU/d	XXX	1 IU/d
Menopausal women	35–100	IU/24 hours	1.00	35–100	IU/d	XXX	1 IU/d
Male	2–15	IU/24 hours	1.00	2–15	IU/d	XXX	1 IU/d
Fructose (P)	<10	mg/dL	0.05551	<0.6	mmol/L	X.XX	0.1 mmol/L
Galactose (P) [children]	<20	mg/dL	0.05551	<1.1	mmol/L	X.XX	0.1 mmol/L
Gases (aB)							
pO_2	75–105	mm Hg (= Torr)	0.1333	10.0–14.0	kPa	XX.X	0.1 kPa
pCO_2	33–44	mm Hg (= Torr)	0.1333	4.4–5.9	kPa	X.X	0.1 kPa
Gamma-glutamyltransferase [GGT] (S)	0–30	U/L	0.01667	0–0.50	μkat/L	X.XX	0.01 μkat/L
Gastrin (S)	0–180	pg/mL	1	0–180	ng/L	XX0	10 ng/L
Globulins (S) [see "Immu-noglobulins"]	—	—	—	—	—	—	—
Glucagon (S)	50–100	pg/mL	1	50–100	ng/L	XX0	10 ng/L
Glucose (P)—fasting	70–110	mg/dL	0.05551	3.9–6.1	mmol/L	XX.X	0.1 mmol/L
Glucose (Sf)	50–80	mg/dL	0.05551	2.8–4.4	mmol/L	XX.X	0.1 mmol/L
Glutethimide (P)							
Therapeutic	<10	mg/L	4.603	<46	μmol/L	XX	1 μmol/L
Toxic	>20	mg/L	4.603	>92	μmol/L	XX	1 μmol/L
Glycerol, free (S)	<1.5	mg/dL	0.1086	<0.16	mmol/L	X.XX	0.01 mmol/L
Gold (S)—therapeutic	300–800	μg/dL	0.05077	15.0–40.0	μmol/L	XX.X	0.1 μmol/L
Gold (U)	<500	μg/24 hours	0.005077	<2.5	μmol/d	X.X	0.1 μmol/d
Growth hormone (P, S)							
Male [fasting]	0.0–5.0	ng/mL	1.00	0.0–5.0	μg/L	XX.X	0.5 μg/L
Female [fasting]	0.0–10.0	ng/mL	1.00	0.0–10.0	μg/L	XX.X	0.5 μg/L
Haptoglobin (S)	50–220	mg/dL	0.01	0.50–2.20	g/L	X.XX	0.01 g/L
Hemoglobin (B)							
Male	14.0–18.0	g/dL	10.0	140–180	g/L	XXX	1 g/L
Female	11.5–15.5	g/dL	10.0	115–155	g/L	XXX	1 g/L

(continued)

TABLE A.5b. CONTINUED

Component	Present reference intervals (examples)	Present unit	Conversion factor	SI reference intervals	SI unit symbol	Significant digits	Suggested minimum increment
Homogentisate (U) [as homogentisic acid]	0	mg/24 hours	5.947	0	μmol/d	XX	5 μmol/d
Homovanillate (U) [as homovanillic acid]	<8	mg/24 hours	5.489	<45	μmol/d	XX	5 μmol/d
Beta-hydroxybutyrate (S) [as beta-hydroxybutyric acid]	<1.0	mg/dL	96.05	<100	μmol/L	XX0	10 μmol/L
5-hydroxyindoleacetate (U) [as 5-hydroxyindole acetic acid; 5 HIAA]	2–8	mg/24 hours	5.230	10–40	μmol/d	XXX	5 μmol/d
17-alpha-hydroxy-progesterone (S, P)							
Children	0.2–1.4	μg/L	3.026	0.5–4.5	nmol/L	XX.X	0.5 nmol/L
Male	0.5–2.5	μg/L	3.026	1.5–7.5	nmol/L	XX.X	0.5 nmol/L
Female	0.3–4.2	μg/L	3.026	1.0–13.0	nmol/L	XX.X	0.5 nmol/L
Female, postmenopausal	0.3–1.7	μg/L	3.026	1.0–5.0	nmol/L	XX.X	0.5 nmol/L
Hydroxyproline (U)							
1 week–1 year	55–220	mg/24 hours/m²	7.626	420–1,680	μmol/(d×m²)	XX0	10 μmol/(d×m²)
1–13 years	25–80	mg/24 hours/m²	7.626	190–610	μmol/(d×m²)	XX0	10 μmol/(d×m²)
22–65 years	6–22	mg/24 hours/m²	7.626	40–170	μmol/(d×m²)	XX0	10 μmol/(d×m²)
>65 years	5–17	mg/24 hours/m²	7.626	40–130	μmol/(d×m²)	XX0	10 μmol/(d×m²)
Immunoglobulins (S)							
IgG	500–1,200	mg/dL	0.01	5.00–12.00	g/L	XX.XX	0.01 g/L
IgA	50–350	mg/dL	0.01	0.50–3.50	g/L	XX.XX	0.01 g/L
IgM	30–230	mg/dL	0.01	0.30–2.30	g/L	XX.XX	0.01 g/L
IgD	<6	mg/dL	10	<60	mg/L	XX0	10 mg/L
IgE							
0–3 years	0.5–10	IU/mL	2.4	1–24	μg/L	XX	1 μg/L
3–80 years	5–100	IU/mL	2.4	12–240	μg/L	XX	1 μg/L
Imipramine (P)–therapeutic	50–200	ng/mL	3.566	180–710	nmol/L	XX0	10 nmol/L
Insulin (P, S)	5–20	μU/mL	7.175	35–145	pmol/L	XXX	5 pmol/L
	5–20	mU/mL	7.175	35–145	pmol/L	XXX	5 pmol/L
	0.20–0.84	μg/mL	172.2	35–145	pmol/L	XXX	5 pmol/L
Iron (S)							
Male	80–180	μg/dL	0.1791	14–32	μmol/L	XX	1 μmol/L
Female	60–160	μg/dL	0.1791	11–29	μmol/L	XX	1 μmol/L
Iron binding capacity (S)	250–460	μg/dL	0.1791	45–82	μmol/L	XX	1 μmol/L
Isoniazid (P)							
Therapeutic	<2.0	mg/L	7.291	<15	μmol/L	XX	1 μmol/L
Toxic	>3.0	mg/L	7.291	>22	μmol/L	XX	1 μmol/L
Isopropanol (P)	0	mg/dL	0.1664	0	mmol/L	XX	1 mmol/L
Lactate (P) [as lactic acid]	0.5–2.0	mEq/L	1.00	0.5–2.0	mmol/L	X.X	0.1 mmol/L
	5–20	mg/dL	0.1110	0.5–2.0	mmol/L	X.X	0.1 mmol/L
Lactate dehydrogenase (S)	50–150	U/L	0.01667	0.82–2.66	μkat/L	X.XX	0.02 μkat/L
Lactate dehydrogenase isoenzymes (S)							
LD1	15–40	%	0.01	0.15–0.40	1	0.XX	0.01
LD2	20–45	%	0.01	0.20–0.45	1	0.XX	0.01
LD3	15–30	%	0.01	0.15–0.30	1	0.XX	0.01

(continued)

TABLE A.5b. *CONTINUED*

Component	Present reference intervals (examples)	Present unit	Conversion factor	SI reference intervals	SI unit symbol	Significant digits	Suggested minimum increment
LD4	5–20	%	0.01	0.05–0.20	1	0.XX	0.01
LD5	5–20	%	0.01	0.05–0.20	1	0.XX	0.01
LD1	10–60	U/L	0.01667	0.16–1.00	μkat/L	X.XX	0.02 μkat/L
LD2	20–70	U/L	0.01667	0.32–1.16	μkat/L	X.XX	0.02 μkat/L
LD3	10–45	U/L	0.01667	0.22–0.76	μkat/L	X.XX	0.02 μkat/L
LD4	5–30	U/L	0.01667	0.08–0.50	μkat/L	X.XX	0.02 μkat/L
LD5	5–30	U/L	0.01667	0.02–0.50	μkat/L	X.XX	0.02 μkat/L
Lead (B)—toxic	>60	μg/dL	0.04826	>2.90	μmol/L	X.XX	0.05 μmol/L
		mg/dL	48.26		μmol/L	X.XX	0.05 μmol/L
Lead (U)—toxic	>80	μg/24 hours	0.004826	>0.40	μmol/d	X.XX	0.05 μmol/d
Lidocaine (P) [Xylocaine]	1.0–5.0	mg/L	4.267	4.5–21.5	μmol/L	X.X	0.5 μmol/L
Lipase (S)	0–160	U/L	0.01667	0–2.66	μkat/L	X.XX	0.02 μkat/L
Lipids, total (P)	400–850	mg/dL	0.01	4.0–8.5	g/L	X.X	0.1 g/L
Lipoproteins (P)							
Low-density [LDL]—as cholesterol	50–190	mg/dL	0.02586	1.30–4.90	mmol/L	X.XX	0.05 mmol/L
High-density [HDL]—as cholesterol							
Male	30–70	mg/dL	0.02586	0.80–1.80	mmol/L	X.XX	0.05 mmol/L
Female	30–90	mg/dL	0.02586	0.80–2.35	mmol/L	X.XX	0.05 mmol/L
Lithium ion (S)—therapeutic	0.50–1.50	mEq/L	1.00	0.50–1.50	mmol/L	X.XX	0.05 mmol/L
		μg/dL	0.001441		mmol/L	X.XX	0.05 mmol/L
		mg/dL	1.441		mmol/L	X.XX	0.05 mmol/L
Luteinizing hormone (S)							
Male	3–25	mIU/mL	1.00	3–25	IU/L	XXX	1 IU/L
Female	2–20	mIU/mL	1.00	2–20	IU/L	XXX	1 IU/L
Peak production	30–140	mIU/mL	1.00	30–140	IU/L	XXX	1 IU/L
Lysozyme (S) [muramidase]	1–15	μg/mL	1.00	1–15	mg/L	XXX	1 mg/L
Lysozyme (U) [muramidase]	<2	μg/mL	1.00	<2	mg/L	XX	1 mg/L
Magnesium (S)	1.8–3.0	mg/dL	0.4114	0.80–1.20	mmol/L	X.XX	0.02 mmol/L
	1.6–2.4	mEq/L	0.500	0.80–1.20	mmol/L	X.XX	0.02 mmol/L
Maprotiline (P)—therapeutic	50–200	ng/mL	3.605	180–720	nmol/L	XX0	10 nmol/L
Meprobamate (P)							
Therapeutic	<20	mg/L	4.582	<90	μmol/L	XX0	10 μmol/L
Toxic	>40	mg/L	4.582	>180	μmol/L	XX0	10 μmol/L
Mercury (B)							
Normal	<1.0	μg/dL	49.85	<50	nmol/L	XX0	10 nmol/L
Chronic exposure	>20	μg/dL	0.04985	>1.00	μmol/L	X.XX	0.01 μmol/L
Mercury (U)							
Normal	<30	μg/24 hours	4.985	<150	nmol/d	XX0	10 nmol/d
Exposure							
Organic	>45	μg/24 hours	4.985	>220	nmol/d	XX0	10 nmol/d
Inorganic	>450	μg/24 hours	0.004985	>2.20	μmol/d	X.XX	0.01 μmol/d
Metanephrines (U) [as normetanephrine]	0–2.0	mg/24 hours	5.458	0–11.0	μmol/d	XX.X	0.5 μmol/d
Methanol (P)	0	mg/dL	0.3121	0	mmol/L	XX	1 mmol/L
Methaqualone (P)							
Therapeutic	<10	mg/L	3.995	<40	μmol/L	XX0	10 μmol/L
Toxic	>30	mg/L	3.995	>120	μmol/L	XX0	10 μmol/L
Methotrexate (S)—toxic	>2.3	mg/L	2.200	>5.0	μmol/L	X.X	0.1 μmol/L
Methsuximide (P) [as desmethylsuximide]—therapeutic	10–40	mg/L	5.285	50–210	μmol/L	XX0	10 μmol/L

(*continued*)

TABLE A.5b. *CONTINUED*

Component	Present reference intervals (examples)	Present unit	Conversion factor	SI reference intervals	SI unit symbol	Significant digits	Suggested minimum increment
Methyprylon (P)							
Therapeutic	<10	mg/L	5.457	<50	μmol/L	XX0	10 μmol/L
Toxic	>40	mg/L	5.457	>220	μmol/L	XX0	10 μmol/L
Beta$_2$-microglobulin (S)—<50 y	0.80–2.40	mg/L	84.75	68–204	nmol/L	XXX	2 nmol/L
Beta$_2$-microglobulin (U)—<50 y	<140	μg/24 hours	0.08475	<12	nmol/d	XXX	2 nmol/L
Nitrogen, total (U)	Depends on diet	g/24 hours	71.38	Depends on diet	mmol/d	XX0	10 mmol/d
Norepinephrine (P)	15–475 (at rest for 15 minutes)	pg/mL	0.005911	1.27–2.81	nmol/L	X.XX	0.01 nmol/L
Norepinephrine (U)	<100	μg/24 hours	5.911	<590	nmol/d	XX0	10 nmol/d
Nortriptyline (P)—therapeutic	25–200	ng/mL	3.797	90–760	nmol/L	XX0	10 nmol/L
Osmolality (P)	280–300	mOsm/kg	1.00	280–300	mmol/kg	XXX	1 mmol/kg
Osmolality (U)	50–1200	mOsm/kg	1.00	50–1,200	mmol/kg	XXX	1 mmol/kg
Oxalate (U) [as anhydrous oxalic acid]	10–40	mg/24 hours	11.11	110–440	μmol/d	XX0	10 μmol/d
Palmitic acid (Amf)	Depends on gestation	mmol/L	1,000	Depends on gestation	μmol/L	XXX	5 μmol/L
Pentobarbital (P)	20–40	mg/L	4.419	90–170	μmol/L	XX	5 μmol/L
Phenobarbital (P)—therapeutic	2–5	mg/dL	43.06	85–215	μmol/L	XXX	5 μmol/L
Phensuximide (P)	4–8	mg/L	5.285	20–40	μmol/L	XX	5 μmol/L
Phenylbutazone (P)—therapeutic	<100	mg/L	3.243	<320	μmol/L	XX0	10 μmol/L
Phenytoin (P)							
Therapeutic	10–20	mg/L	3.964	40–80	μmol/L	XX	5 μmol/L
Toxic	>30	mg/L	3.964	>120	μmol/L	XX	5 μmol/L
Phosphate (S) [as phosphorus, inorganic]	2.5–5.0	mg/dL	0.3229	0.80–1.60	mmol/L	X.XX	0.05 mmol/L
Phosphate (U) [as phosphorus, inorganic]	Depends on diet	g/24 hours	32.29	Depends on diet	mmol/d	XXX	1 mmol/d
Phospholipid phosphorus, total (P)	5–12	mg/dL	0.3229	1.60–3.90	mmol/L	X.XX	0.05 mmol/L
Phospholipid phosphorus, total (Erc)	1.2–12	mg/dL	0.3229	0.40–3.90	mmol/L	X.XX	0.05 mmol/L
Phospholipids (P)—substance fraction of total phospholipid							
Phosphatidyl choline	65–70	% of total	0.01	0.65–0.70	1	0.XX	0.01
Phosphatidyl ethanolamine	4–5	% of total	0.01	0.04–0.05	1	0.XX	0.01
Sphingomyelin	15–20	% of total	0.01	0.15–0.20	1	0.XX	0.01
Lysophosphatidyl choline	3–5	% of total	0.01	0.03–0.05	1	0.XX	0.01
Phospholipids (Erc)—substance fraction of total phospholipid							
Phosphatidyl choline	28–33	% of total	0.01	0.28–0.33	1	0.XX	0.01
Phosphatidyl ethanolamine	24–31	% of total	0.01	0.24–0.31	1	0.XX	0.01
Sphingomyelin	22–29	% of total	0.01	0.22–0.29	1	0.XX	0.01
Phosphatidyl serine + phosphatidyl inositol	12–20	% of total	0.01	0.12–0.20	1	0.XX	0.01
Lysophosphatidyl choline	1–2	% of total	0.01	0.01–0.02	1	0.XX	0.01
Phytanic acid (P)	Trace–0.3	mg/dL	32.00	<10	μmol/L	XX	5 μmol/L
[Human] placental lactogen (S) [HPL]	>4.0 after 30 weeks gestation	μg/mL	46.30	>180	nmol/L	XX0	10 nmol/L
Porphobilinogen (U)	0.0–2.0	mg/24 hours	4.420	0–9.0	μmol/d	X.X	0.5 μmol/d

(continued)

TABLE A.5b. *CONTINUED*

Component	Present reference intervals (examples)	Present unit	Conversion factor	SI reference intervals	SI unit symbol	Significant digits	Suggested minimum increment
Porphyrins							
Coproporphyrin (U)	45–180	μg/24 hours	1.527	68–276	nmol/d	XXX	2 nmol/d
Protoporphyrin (Erc)	15–50	μg/dL	0.0177	0.28–0.90	μmol/L	X.XX	0.02 μmol/L
Uroporphyrin (U)	5–20	μg/24 hours	1.204	6–24	nmol/d	XX	2 nmol/d
Uroporphyrinogen synthetase (Erc)	22–42	mmol/mL /hour	0.2778	6.0–11.8	mmol/(L×s)	X.X	0.2 mmol/(L×s)
Potassium ion (S)	3.5–5.0	mEq/L	1.00	3.5–5.0	mmol/L	X.X	0.1 mmol/L
		mg/dL	0.2558		mmol/L	X.X	0.1 mmol/L
Potassium ion (U) [Depends on diet]	25–100	mEq/24 hours	1.00	25–100	mmol/d	XX	1 mmol/d
Pregnanediol (U)							
Normal	1.0–6.0	mg/24 hours	3.120	3.0–18.5	μmol/d	XX.X	0.5 μmol/d
Pregnancy	Depends on gestation						
Pregnanetriol (U)	0.5–2.0	mg/24 hours	2.972	1.5–6.0	μmol/d	XX.X	0.5 μmol/d
Primidone (P)							
Therapeutic	6.0–10.0	mg/L	4.582	25–46	μmol/L	XX	1 μmol/L
Toxic	>10.0	mg/L	4.582	>46	μmol/L	XX	1 μmol/L
Procainamide (P)							
Therapeutic	4.0–8.0	mg/L	4.249	17–34	μmol/L	XX	1 μmol/L
Toxic	>12.0	mg/L	4.249	>50	μmol/L	XX	1 μmol/L
N-Acetylprocainamide (P)— therapeutic	4.0–8.0	mg/L	3.606	14–29	μmol/L	XX	1 μmol/L
Progesterone (P)							
Follicular phase	<2	ng/mL	3.180	<6	nmol/L	XX	2 nmol/L
Luteal phase	2–20	ng/mL	3.180	6–64	nmol/L	XX	2 nmol/L
Progesterone receptors (T)							
Negative	0–3	fmol progesterone bound/mg cytosol protein	1.00	0–3	fmol progesterone bound/mg protein	XX	1 fmol/mg protein
Doubtful	4–10	fmol progesterone bound/mg cytosol protein	1.00	4–10	fmol progesterone bound/mg cytosol protein	XX	1 fmol/mg protein
Positive	>10	fmol progesterone bound/mg cytosol protein	1.00	>10	fmol progesterone bound/mg cytosol protein	XX	1 fmol/mg protein
Prolactin (P)	<20	ng/mL	1.00	<20	μg/L	XX	1 μg/L
Propoxyphene (P)—toxic	>2.0	mg/L	2.946	>5.9	μmol/L	X.X	0.1 μmol/L
Propranolol (P) [Inderal]— therapeutic	50–200	ng/mL	3.856	190–770	nmol/L	XX0	10 nmol/L
Protein, total (S)	6.0–8.0	g/dL	10.0	60–80	g/L	XX	1 g/L
Protein, total (Sf)	<40	mg/dL	0.01	<0.40	g/L	X.XX	0.01 g/L
Protein, total (U)	<150	mg/24 hours	0.001	<0.15	g/d	X.XX	0.01 g/d
Protryptyline (P)	100–300	ng/mL	3.797	380–1140	nmol/L	XX0	10 nmol/L
Pyruvate (B) [as pyruvic acid]	0.30–0.90	mg/dL	113.6	35–100	μmol/L	XXX	1 μmol/L
Quinidine (P)							
Therapeutic	1.5–3.0	mg/L	3.082	4.6–9.2	μmol/L	X.X	0.1 μmol/L
Toxic	>6.0	mg/L	3.082	>18.5	μmol/L	X.X	0.1 μmol/L
Renin (P)							
Normal-sodium diet	1.1–4.1	ng/mL/hr	0.2778	0.30–1.14	ng/(L×s)	X.XX	0.02 ng/(L×s)
Restricted-sodium diet	6.2–12.4	ng/mL/hr	0.2778	1.72–3.44	ng/(L×s)	X.XX	0.02 ng/(L×s)

(*continued*)

TABLE A.5b. *CONTINUED*

Component	Present reference intervals (examples)	Present unit	Conversion factor	SI reference intervals	SI unit symbol	Significant digits	Suggested minimum increment
Salicylate (S) [salicylic acid]—toxic	>20	mg/dL	0.07240	>1.45	mmol/L	X.XX	0.05 mmol/L
Serotonin (B) [5-hydroxy-tryptamine]	8–21	μg/dL	0.05675	0.45–1.20	μmol/L	X.XX	0.05 μmol/L
Sodium ion (S)	135–147	mEq/L	1.00	135–147	mmol/L	XXX	1 mmol/L
Sodium ion (U)	Depends on diet	mEq/24 hours	1.00	Depends on diet	mmol/d	XXX	1 mmol/d
Steroids							
17-hydroxy-corticosteroids (U) [as cortisol]							
Female	2.0–8.0	mg/24 hours	2.759	5–25	μmol/d	XX	1 μmol/d
Male	3.0–10.0	mg/24 hours	2.759	10–30	μmol/d	XX	1 μmol/d
17-ketogenic steroids (U) [as dehydroepiandrosterone]							
Female	7.0–12.0	mg/24 hours	3.467	25–40	μmol/d	XX	1 μmol/d
Male	9.0–17.0	mg/24 hours	3.467	30–60	μmol/d	XX	1 μmol/d
17-ketosteroids (U) [as dehydroepiandrosterone]							
Female	6.0–17.0	mg/24 hours	3.467	20–60	μmol/d	XX	1 μmol/d
Male	6.0–20.0	mg/24 hours	3.467	20–70	μmol/d	XX	1 μmol/d
Ketosteroid fractions (U)							
Androsterone							
Female	0.5–3.0	mg/24 hours	3.443	1–10	μmol/d	XX	1 μmol/d
Male	2.0–5.0	mg/24 hours	3.443	7–17	μmol/d	XX	1 μmol/d
Dehydroepiandrosterone							
Female	0.2–1.8	mg/24 hours	3.467	1–6	μmol/d	XX	1 μmol/d
Male	0.2–2.0	mg/24 hours	3.467	1–7	μmol/d	XX	1 μmol/d
Etiocholanolone							
Female	0.8–4.0	mg/24 hours	3.443	2–14	μmol/d	XX	1 μmol/d
Male	1.4–5.0	mg/24 hours	3.443	4–17	μmol/d	XX	1 μmol/d
Sulfonamides (B) [as sulfanilamide]—therapeutic	10.0–15.0	mg/dL	58.07	580–870	μmol/L	XX0	10 μmol/L
Testosterone (P)							
Female	0.6	ng/mL	3.467	2.0	nmol/L	XX.X	0.5 nmol/L
Male	4.6–8.0	ng/mL	3.467	14.0–28.0	nmol/L	XX.X	0.5 nmol/L
Theophylline (P)—therapeutic	10.0–20.0	mg/L	5.550	55–110	μmol/L	XX	1 μmol/L
Thiocyanate (P)—(nitroprusside toxicity)	10.0	mg/dL	0.1722	1.7	mmol/L	X.XX	0.1 mmol/L
Thiopental (P)	Individual	mg/L	4.126	Individual	μmol/L	XX	5 μmol/L
Thyroid tests:							
Thyroid stimulating hormone [TSH] (S)	2–11	μU/mL	1.00	2–11	mU/L	XX	1 mU/L
Thyroxine [T_4] (S)	4.0–11.0	μg/dL	12.87	51–142	nmol/L	XXX	1 nmol/L
Thyroxine binding globulin [TBG] (S)—[as thyroxine]	12.0–28.0	μg/dL	12.87	150–360	nmol/L	XX0	1 nmol/L
Thyroxine, free (S)	0.8–2.8	ng/dL	12.87	10–36	pmol/L	XX	1 pmol/L
Triiodothyronine [T_3] (S)	75–220	ng/dL	0.01536	1.2–3.4	nmol/L	X.X	0.1 nmol/L
T_3 uptake (S)	25–35	%	0.01	0.25–0.35	1	0.XX	0.01
Tolbutamide (P)—therapeutic	50–120	mg/L	3.699	180–450	umol/L	XX0	10 umol/L
Transferrin (S)	170–370	mg/dL	0.01	1.70–3.70	g/L	X.XX	0.01 g/L
Triglycerides (P) [as triolein]	<160	mg/dL	0.01129	<1.80	mmol/L	X.XX	0.02 mmol/L

(continued)

TABLE A.5b. *CONTINUED*

Component	Present reference intervals (examples)	Present unit	Conversion factor	SI reference intervals	SI unit symbol	Significant digits	Suggested minimum increment
Trimethadione (P)—therapeutic	<50	mg/L	6.986	<350	μmol/L	XX0	10 μmol/L
Trimipramine (P)—therapeutic	50–200	ng/mL	3.397	170–680	nmol/L	XX0	10 nmol/L
Urate (S) [as uric acid]	2.0–7.0	mg/dL	59.48	120–420	μmol/L	XX0	10 μmol/L
Urate (U) [as uric acid]	Depends on diet	g/24 hours	5.948	Depends on diet	mmol/d	XX	1 mmol/d
Urea nitrogen (S)	8–18	mg/dL	0.3570	3.0–6.5	mmol/L	X.X	0.5 mmol/L
Urea nitrogen (U)	2.0–20.0 Depends on diet	g/24 hours	35.700	450–700	mmol/d	XX0	10 mol/d
Urobilinogen (U)	0.0–4.0	mg/24 hours	1.693	0.0–6.8	μmol/d	X.X	0.1 μmol/d
Valproic acid (P)—therapeutic	50–100	mg/L	6.934	350–700	μmol/L	XX0	10 μmol/L
Vanillylmandelic acid [VMA] (U)[a]	<6.8	mg/24 hours	5.046	<35	μmol/d	XX	1 μmol/d
Vitamin A [retinol] (P, S)	10–50	μg/dL	0.03491	0.35–1.75	μmol/L	X.XX	0.05 μmol/L
Vitamin B$_1$ [thiamine hydrochloride] (U)	60–500	μg/24 hours	0.002965	0.18–1.48	μmol/d	X.XX	0.01 μmol/d
Vitamin B$_2$ [riboflavin] (S)	2.6–3.7	μg/dL	26.57	70–100	nmol/L	XXX	5 nmol/L
Vitamin B$_6$ [pyridoxal] (B)	20–90	ng/mL	5.982	120–540	nmol/L	XXX	5 nmol/L
Vitamin B$_{12}$ [cyanocobalamin] (P, S)	200–1,000	pg/mL	0.7378	150–750	pmol/L	XX0	10 pmol/L
		ng/dL	7.378		pmol/L		
Vitamin C [see ascorbate] (B, P, S)	—	—	—	—	—	—	—
Vitamin D$_3$ [cholecalciferol] (P)	24–40	μg/mL	2.599	60–105	nmol/L	XXX	5 nmol/L
25-OH-cholecalciferol	18–36	ng/mL	2.496	45–90	nmol/L	XXX	5 mmol/L
Vitamin E [alpha-tocopherol] (P, S)	0.78–1.25	mg/dL	23.22	18–29	μmol/L	XX	1 μmol/L
Warfarin (P)—therapeutic	1.0–3.0	mg/L	3.243	3.3–9.8	μmol/L	XX.X	0.1 μmol/L
Xanthine (U)—hypoxanthine	5–30	mg/24 hours	6.574	30–200	μmol/d	XX0	10 μmol/d
		hmg/24 hours	7.347		μmol/d	XX0	10 μmol/d
D-Xylose (B) [25-g dose]	30–40 (30–60 minutes)	mg/dL	0.06661	0–2.7 (30–60 minutes)	mmol/L	X.X	0.1 mmol/L
D-Xylose excretion (U) [25 g dose]	21–31 (excreted in 5 hours)	%	0.01	0.21–0.31 (excreted in 5 hours)	1	0.XX	0.01
Zinc (S)	75–120	μg/dL	0.1530	11.5–18.5	μmol/L	XX.X	0.1 μmol/L
Zinc (U)	150–1200	μg/24 hours	0.01530	2.3–18.3	μmol/d	XX.X	0.1 μmol/d

Source: Young, D.S.: Implementation of SI units for clinical laboratory data style specifications and conversion tables. Ann Intern Med 106:114, 1987. Single reprints are available free of charge from the *Annals of Internal Medicine* Business Department, 4200 Pine St., Philadelphia, PA 19104 (toll-free: 800/523-1546, or 215/243-1200). Rates for bulk orders are available from the Business Department. The tables are not copyrighted; persons who wish to make photocopies are free to do so.

[a]This is a misnomer, but because of its popularity the name VMA has been retained in this document. Elsewhere it is being referred to as 4-hydroxy-3-methoxy mandelic acid.

TABLE A.6a. 1959 METROPOLITAN HEIGHT-WEIGHT TABLES: DESIRABLE WEIGHTS FOR MEN, AGE 25 AND OVER[a]

Height	Small frame (lbs.)	Medium frame (lbs.)	Large frame (lbs.)
5'2"	112–120	118–129	126–141
5'3"	115–123	121–133	129–144
5'4"	118–126	124–136	132–148
5'5"	121–129	127–139	135–152
5'6"	124–133	130–143	138–156
5'7"	128–137	134–147	142–161
5'8"	132–141	138–152	147–166
5'9"	136–145	142–156	151–170
5'10"	140–150	146–160	155–174
5'11"	144–154	150–165	159–179
6'0"	148–158	154–170	164–184
6'1"	152–162	158–175	168–189
6'2"	156–167	162–180	173–194
6'3"	160–171	167–185	178–199
6'4"	164–175	172–190	182–204

Source: New weight standards for men and women. Metropolitan Life Insurance Co. (New York), Statistical Bulletin 40:1, 1959.

[a]Weight in pounds according to frame (in indoor clothing and wearing shoes with 1" heels).

TABLE A.6b. 1959 METROPOLITAN HEIGHT-WEIGHT TABLES: DESIRABLE WEIGHTS FOR WOMEN, AGES 25 AND OVER[a]

Height	Small frame (lbs.)	Medium frame (lbs.)	Large frame (lbs.)
4'10"	92–98	96–107	104–119
4'11"	94–101	98–110	106–122
5'0"	96–104	101–113	109–125
5'1"	99–107	104–116	112–128
5'2"	102–110	107–119	115–131
5'3"	105–113	110–122	118–134
5'4"	108–116	113–126	121–138
5'5"	111–119	116–130	125–142
5'6"	114–123	120–135	129–146
5'7"	118–127	124–139	133–150
5'8"	122–131	128–143	137–154
5'9"	126–135	132–147	141–158
5'10"	130–140	136–151	145–163
5'11"	134–144	140–155	149–168
6'0"	138–148	144–159	153–173

Source: New weight standards for men and women. Metropolitan Life Insurance Co. (New York), Statistical Bulletin 40:1, 1959.

[a]For women between 18 and 25, subtract 1 lb. for each year under 25. Weight in pounds according to frame (in indoor clothing and wearing shoes with 2" heels).

TABLE A.6c. 1983 METROPOLITAN HEIGHT-WEIGHT TABLES: DESIRABLE WEIGHTS FOR MEN[a]

Height	Small frame (lbs.)	Medium frame (lbs.)	Large frame (lbs.)
5'2"	128–134	131–141	138–150
5'3"	130–136	133–143	140–153
5'4"	132–138	135–145	142–156
5'5"	134–140	137–148	144–160
5'6"	136–142	139–151	146–164
5'7"	138–145	142–154	149–168
5'8"	140–148	145–157	152–172
5'9"	142–151	148–160	155–176
5'10"	144–154	151–163	158–180
5'11"	146–157	154–166	161–184
6'0"	149–160	157–170	164–188
6'1"	152–164	160–174	168–192
6'2"	155–168	164–178	172–197
6'3"	158–172	167–182	176–202
6'4"	162–176	171–187	181–207

Frame Size for Men[b]

Height in 1" heels	Elbow breadth for medium frame
5'2" to 5'3"	2½" to 2⅞"
5'4" to 5'7"	2⅝" to 2⅞"
5'8" to 5'11"	2¾" to 3"
6'0" to 6'3"	2¾" to 3⅛"
6'4"	2⅞" to 3¼"

Source: Metropolitan Life Insurance Co.; *data adapted from* the 1979 Build Study, Society of Actuaries and Association of Life Insurance Medical Directors of America. Philadelphia: Recording and Statistical Corp., 1980.

[a]Weights at ages 25 to 59 based on lowest mortality. Weight in pounds according to frame (in indoor clothing weighing 5 lbs., and wearing shoes with 1" heels).

[b]Elbow breadth is measured with the forearm upward at a 90° angle. The distance between the outer aspects of the two prominent bones on either side of the elbow is considered to be the elbow breadth. Elbow breadth less than that listed for medium frame indicates a small frame; greater than that listed indicates a large frame.

TABLE A.6d. 1983 METROPOLITAN HEIGHT-WEIGHT TABLES: DESIRABLE WEIGHTS FOR WOMEN[a]

Height	Small frame (lbs.)	Medium frame (lbs.)	Large frame (lbs.)
4'10"	102–111	109–121	118–131
4'11"	103–113	111–123	120–134
5'0"	104–115	113–126	122–137
5'1"	106–118	115–129	125–140
5'2"	108–121	118–132	128–143
5'3"	111–124	121–135	131–147
5'4"	114–127	124–138	134–151
5'5"	117–130	127–141	137–155
5'6"	120–133	130–144	140–159
5'7"	123–136	133–147	143–163
5'8"	126–139	136–150	146–167
5'9"	129–142	139–153	149–170
5'10"	132–145	142–156	152–173
5'11"	135–148	145–159	155–176
6'0"	138–151	148–162	158–179

Frame Size for Women[b]

Height in 1" heels	Elbow breadth for medium frame
4'10" to 4'11"	2¼" to 2½"
5'0" to 5'3"	2¼" to 2½"
5'4" to 5'7"	2⅜" to 2⅝"
5'8" to 5'11"	2⅜" to 2⅝"
6'0"	2½" to 2¾"

Source: Metropolitan Life Insurance Co.; *data adapted from* the 1979 Build Study, Society of Actuaries and Association of Life Insurance Medical Directors of America. Philadelphia: Recording and Statistical Corp., 1980.

[a]Weights at ages 25 to 59 based on lowest mortality. Weight in pounds according to frame (in indoor clothing weighing 3 lbs., and wearing shoes with 1" heels).

[b]Elbow breadth is measured with the forearm upward at a 90° angle. The distance between the outer aspects of the two prominent bones on either side of the elbow is considered to be the elbow breadth. Elbow breadth less than that listed for medium frame indicates a small frame; greater than that listed indicates a large frame.

FIG. A.1. GROWTH RECORD FOR INFANTS IN RELATION TO GESTATIONAL AGE AND FETAL AND INFANT NORMS.

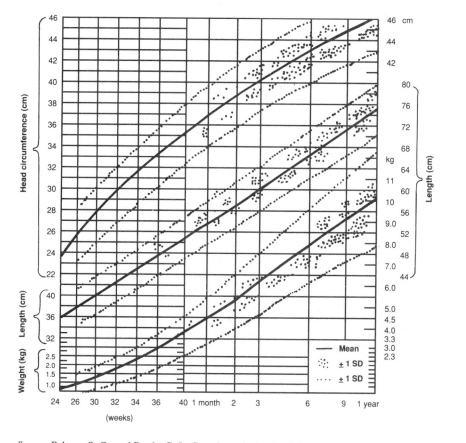

Source: Babson, S. G., and Benda, G. I.: Growth graphs for the clinical assessment of infants of varying gestational age. J Pediatr 89:814, 1976.

FIG. A.2a. BOYS FROM BIRTH TO 36 MONTHS: LENGTH FOR AGE AND WEIGHT FOR AGE—NCHS PERCENTILES.

NAME _____ RECORD # _____

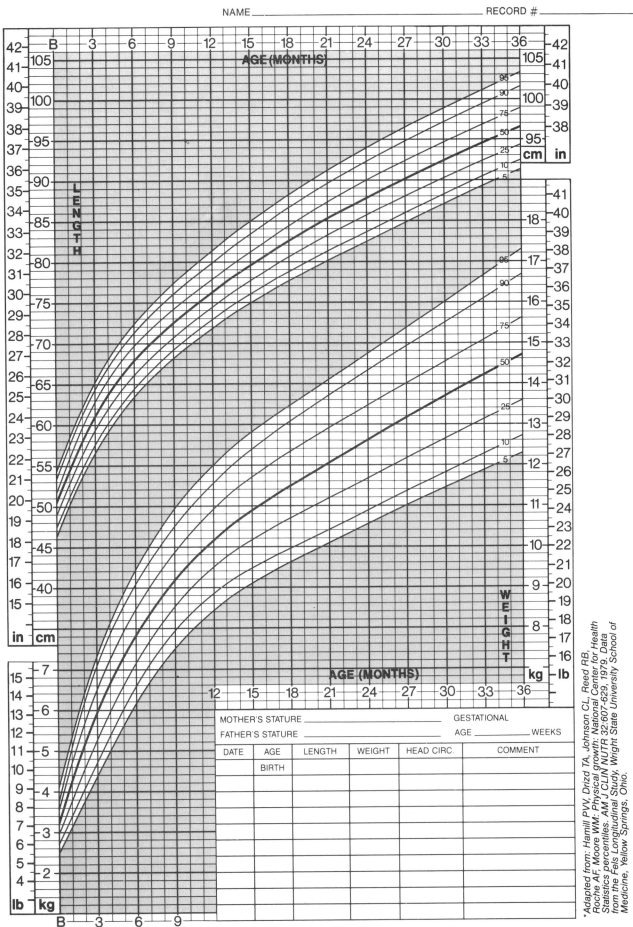

MOTHER'S STATURE _____ GESTATIONAL

FATHER'S STATURE _____ AGE _____ WEEKS

DATE	AGE	LENGTH	WEIGHT	HEAD CIRC.	COMMENT
	BIRTH				

*Adapted from: Hamill PVV, Drizd TA, Johnson CL, Reed RB, Roche AF, Moore WM: Physical growth: National Center for Health Statistics percentiles. AM J CLIN NUTR 32:607-629, 1979. Data from the Fels Longitudinal Study, Wright State University School of Medicine, Yellow Springs, Ohio.

FIG. A.2b. BOYS FROM BIRTH TO 36 MONTHS: HEAD CIRCUMFERENCE FOR AGE AND WEIGHT FOR LENGTH—NCHS PERCENTILES.

NAME_____ _____ RECORD #_____

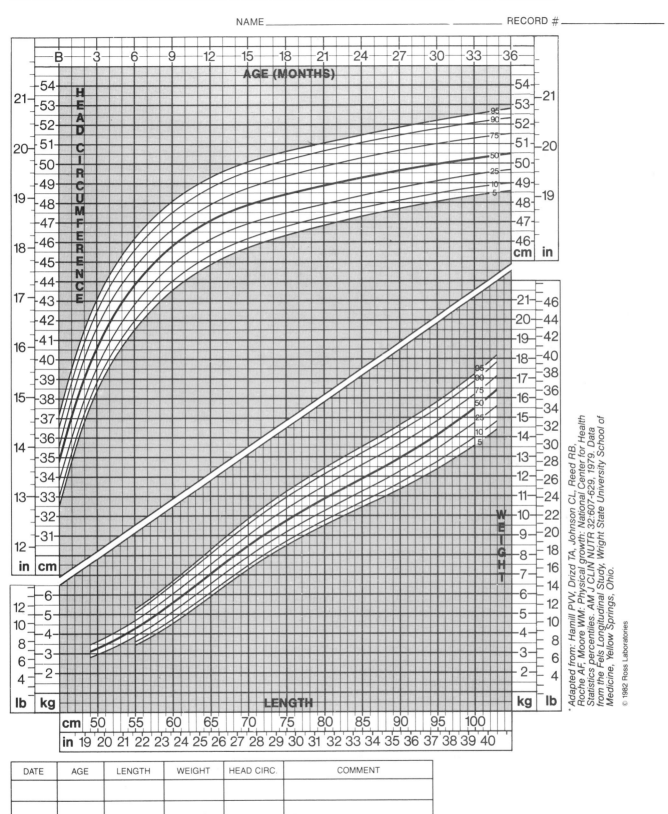

*Adapted from: Hamill PVV, Drizd TA, Johnson CL, Reed RB, Roche AF, Moore WM: Physical growth: National Center for Health Statistics percentiles. AM J CLIN NUTR 32:607-629, 1979. Data from the Fels Longitudinal Study, Wright State University School of Medicine, Yellow Springs, Ohio.

© 1982 Ross Laboratories

DATE	AGE	LENGTH	WEIGHT	HEAD CIRC.	COMMENT

Reprinted with permission
of Ross Laboratories

FIG. A.3a. BOYS FROM 2 TO 5 YEARS: STATURE FOR AGE AND WEIGHT FOR AGE—NCHS PERCENTILES.

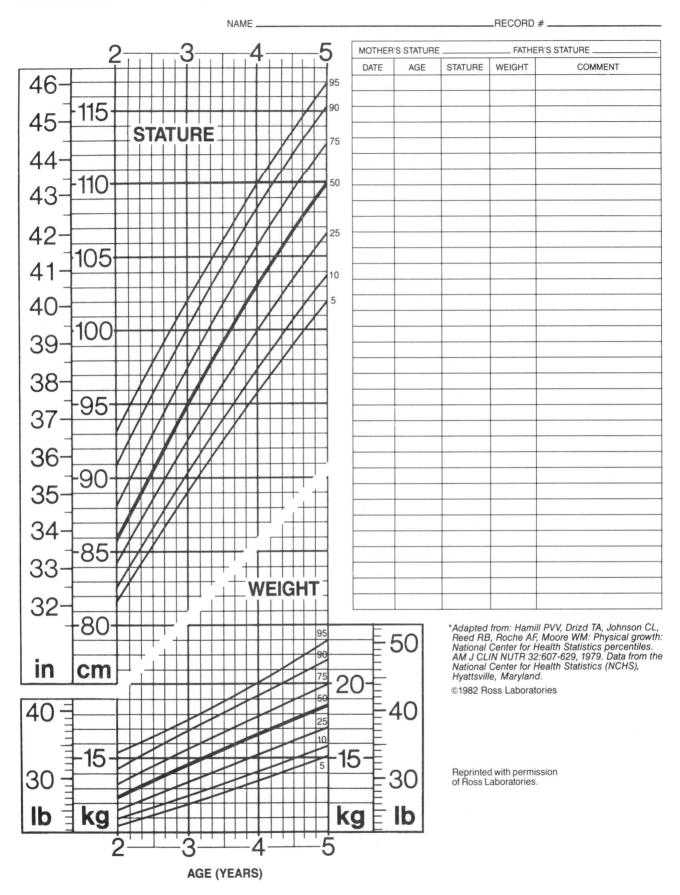

FIG. A.3b. PREPUBESCENT BOYS: WEIGHT FOR STATURE (90 TO 120 CM OR 35½ TO 47 IN.)—NCHS PERCENTILES.

NAME _____ RECORD # _____

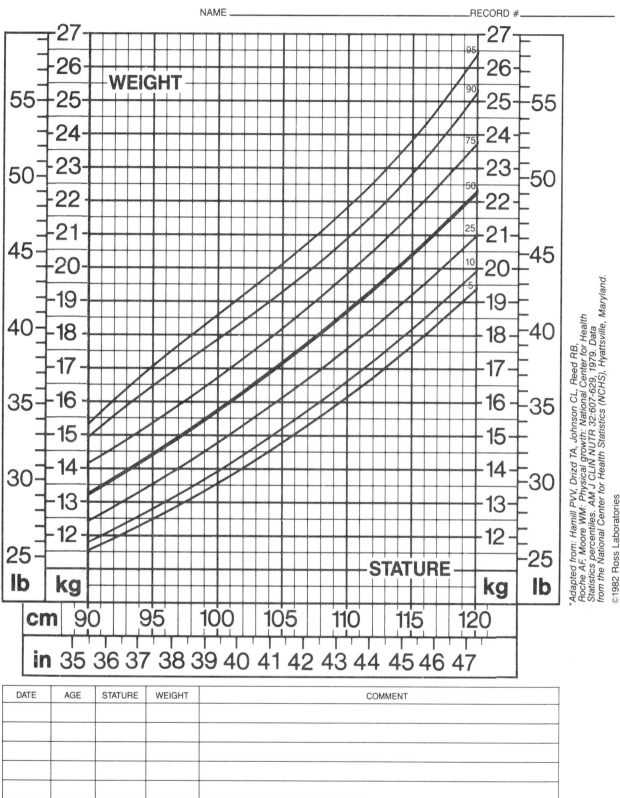

*Adapted from: Hamill PVV, Drizd TA, Johnson CL, Reed RB, Roche AF, Moore WM: Physical growth: National Center for Health Statistics percentiles. AM J CLIN NUTR 32:607-629, 1979. Data from the National Center for Health Statistics (NCHS), Hyattsville, Maryland.

©1982 Ross Laboratories

DATE	AGE	STATURE	WEIGHT	COMMENT

FIG. A.3c. BOYS FROM 2 TO 18 YEARS: STATURE FOR AGE AND WEIGHT FOR AGE—NCHS PERCENTILES.

NAME _____ RECORD # _____

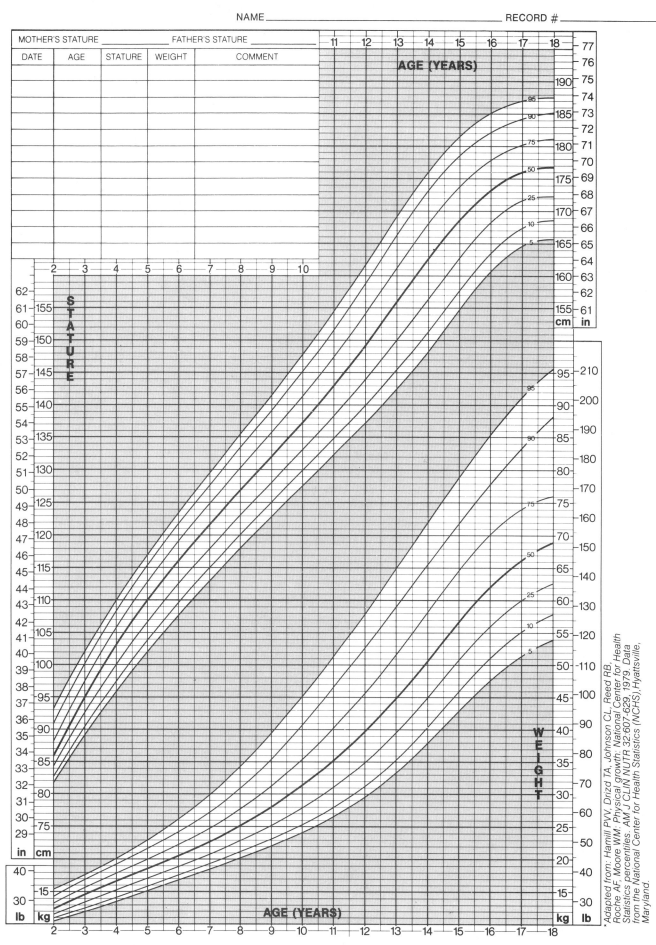

*Adapted from: Hamill PVV, Drizd TA, Johnson CL, Reed RB, Roche AF, Moore WM: Physical growth: National Center for Health Statistics percentiles. AM J CLIN NUTR 32:607-629, 1979. Data from the National Center for Health Statistics (NCHS), Hyattsville, Maryland.

FIG. A.3d. PREPUBESCENT BOYS: WEIGHT FOR STATURE (90 TO 145 CM OR 35½ TO 57 IN.)—NCHS PERCENTILES.

NAME_____ RECORD #_____

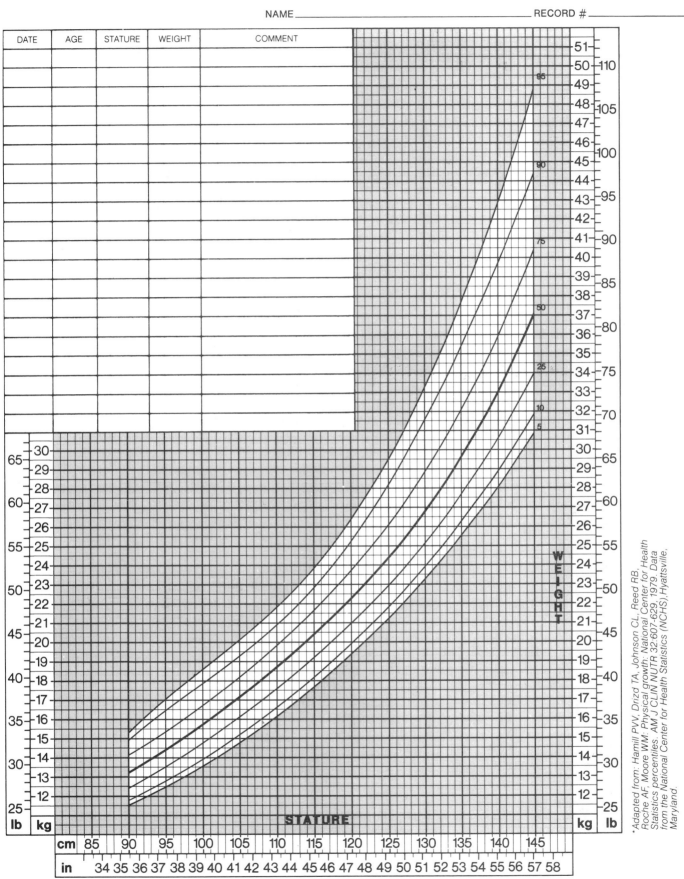

*Adapted from: Hamill PVV, Drizd TA, Johnson CL, Reed RB, Roche AF, Moore WM: Physical growth: National Center for Health Statistics percentiles. AM J CLIN NUTR 32:607-629, 1979. Data from the National Center for Health Statistics (NCHS),Hyattsville, Maryland.

FIG. A.4a. GIRLS FROM BIRTH TO 36 MONTHS: LENGTH FOR AGE AND WEIGHT FOR AGE—NCHS PERCENTILES.

NAME _____ RECORD # _____

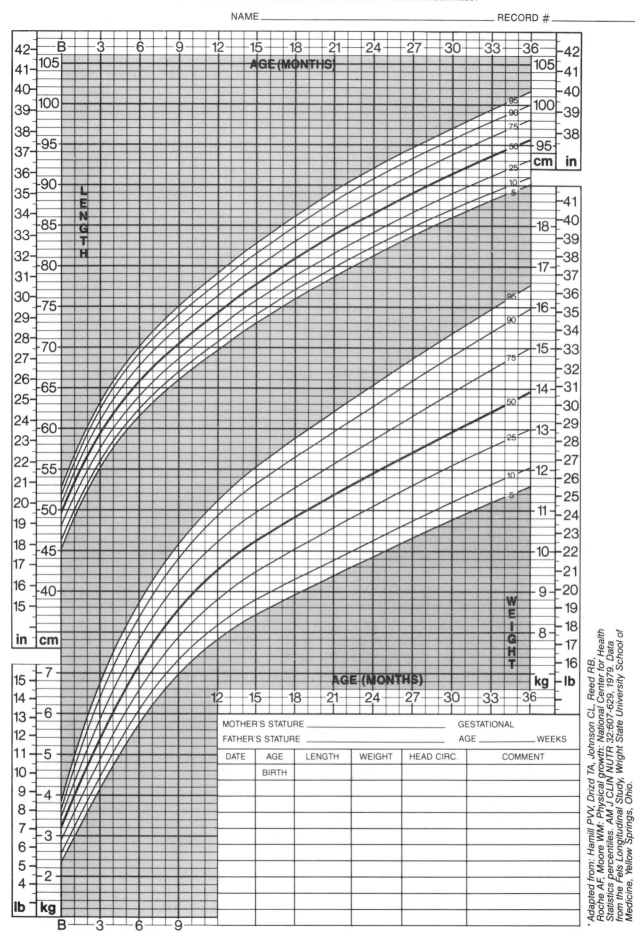

* Adapted from: Hamill PVV, Drizd TA, Johnson CL, Reed RB, Roche AF, Moore WM: Physical growth: National Center for Health Statistics percentiles. AM J CLIN NUTR 32:607-629, 1979. Data from the Fels Longitudinal Study, Wright State University School of Medicine, Yellow Springs, Ohio.

MOTHER'S STATURE _____ GESTATIONAL
FATHER'S STATURE _____ AGE _____ WEEKS

DATE	AGE	LENGTH	WEIGHT	HEAD CIRC.	COMMENT
	BIRTH				

FIG. A.4b. GIRLS FROM BIRTH TO 36 MONTHS: HEAD CIRCUMFERENCE FOR AGE AND WEIGHT FOR LENGTH—NCHS PERCENTILES.

NAME_____ RECORD #_____

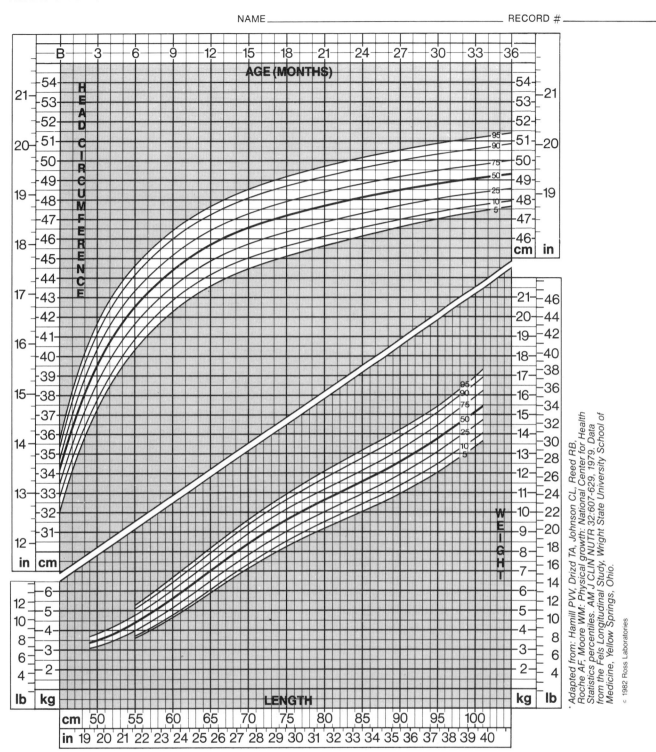

Adapted from: Hamill PVV, Drizd TA, Johnson CL, Reed RB, Roche AF, Moore WM: Physical growth: National Center for Health Statistics percentiles. AM J CLIN NUTR 32:607-629, 1979. Data from the Fels Longitudinal Study, Wright State University School of Medicine, Yellow Springs, Ohio.

© 1982 Ross Laboratories

DATE	AGE	LENGTH	WEIGHT	HEAD CIRC.	COMMENT

FIG. A.5a. GIRLS FROM 2 TO 5 YEARS: STATURE FOR AGE AND WEIGHT FOR AGE—NCHS PERCENTILES.

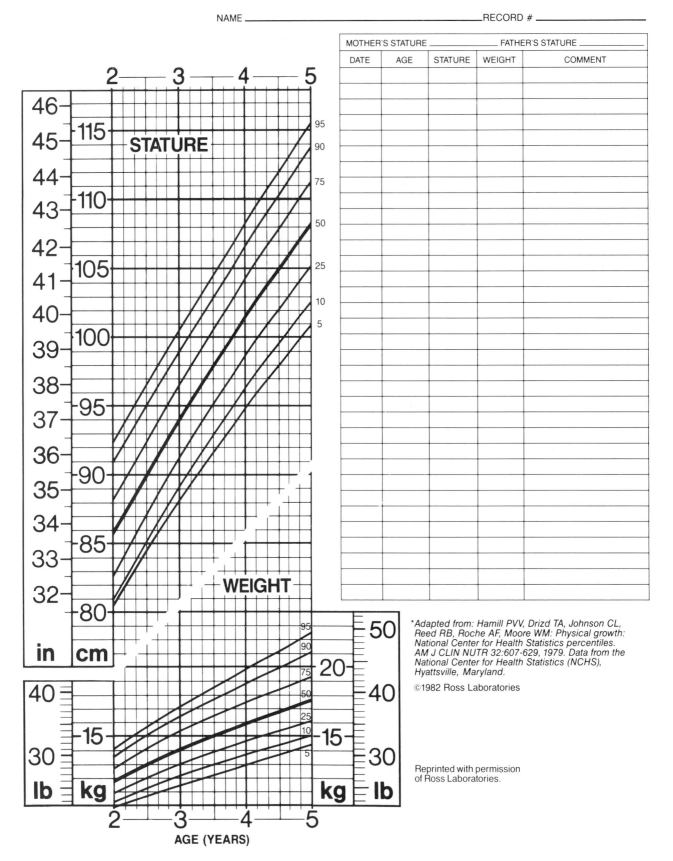

Adapted from: Hamill PVV, Drizd TA, Johnson CL, Reed RB, Roche AF, Moore WM: Physical growth: National Center for Health Statistics percentiles. AM J CLIN NUTR 32:607-629, 1979. Data from the National Center for Health Statistics (NCHS), Hyattsville, Maryland.

©1982 Ross Laboratories

Reprinted with permission of Ross Laboratories.

FIG. A.5b. PREPUBESCENT GIRLS: WEIGHT FOR STATURE (90 TO 120 CM OR 35½ TO 47 IN.)—NCHS PERCENTILES.

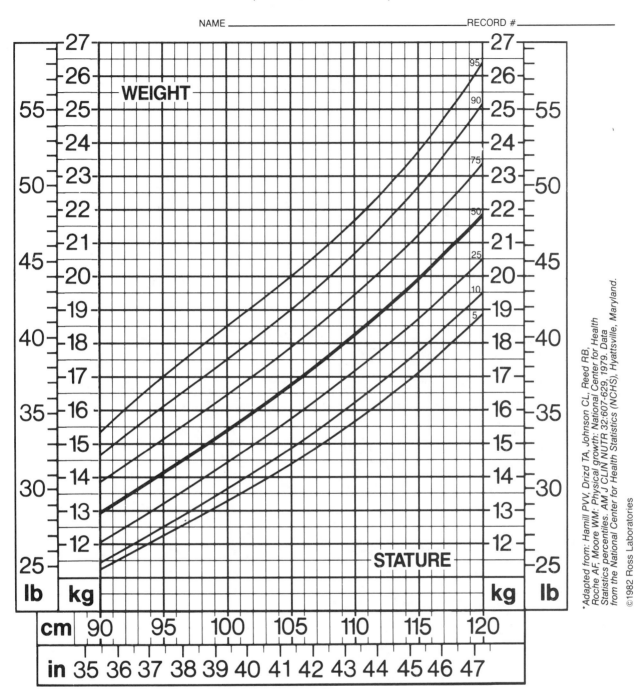

*Adapted from: Hamill PVV, Drizd TA, Johnson CL, Reed RB, Roche AF, Moore WM: Physical growth: National Center for Health Statistics percentiles. AM J CLIN NUTR 32:607-629, 1979. Data from the National Center for Health Statistics (NCHS), Hyattsville, Maryland.

©1982 Ross Laboratories

DATE	AGE	STATURE	WEIGHT	COMMENT

FIG. A.5c. GIRLS FROM 2 TO 18 YEARS: STATURE FOR AGE AND WEIGHT FOR AGE—NCHS PERCENTILES.

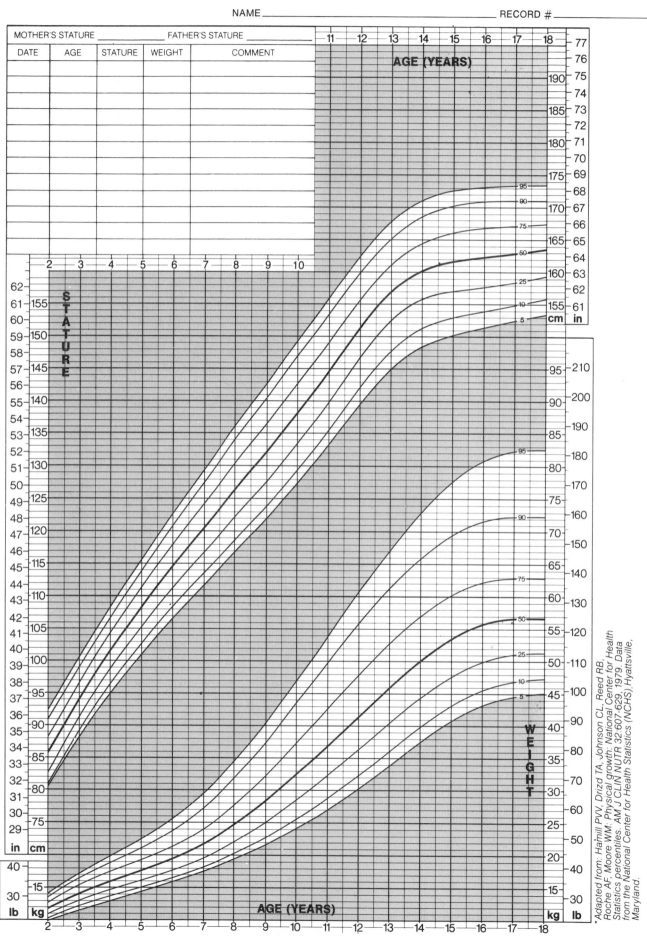

*Adapted from: Hamill PVV, Drizd TA, Johnson CL, Reed RB, Roche AF, Moore WM: Physical growth: National Center for Health Statistics percentiles. AM J CLIN NUTR 32:607-629, 1979. Data from the National Center for Health Statistics (NCHS), Hyattsville, Maryland.

FIG. A.5d. PREPUBESCENT GIRLS: WEIGHT FOR STATURE (90 TO 137 CM OR 35½ TO 54 IN.)—NCHS PERCENTILES.

NAME _____ RECORD # _____

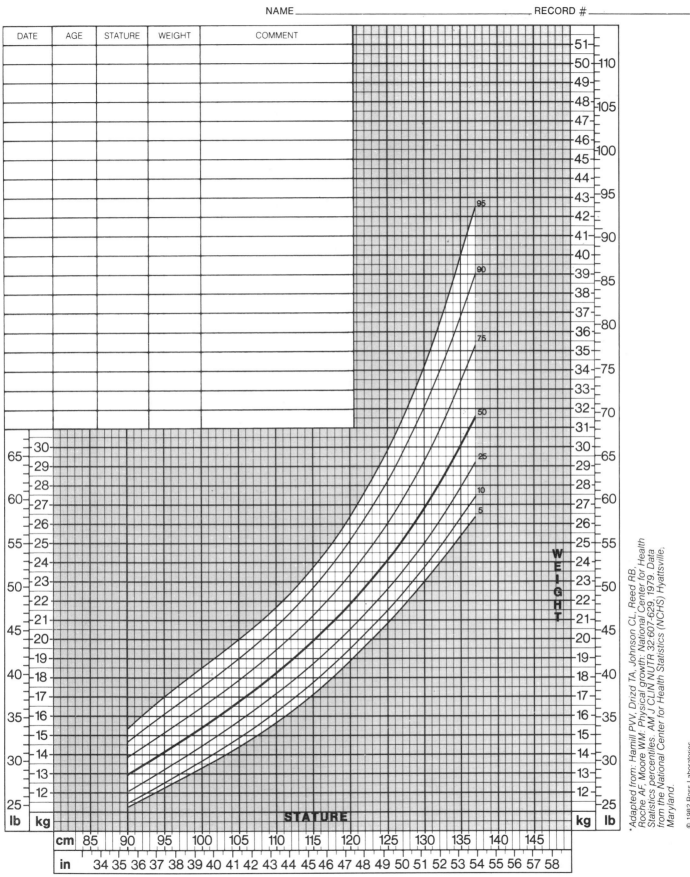

*Adapted from: Hamill PVV, Drizd TA, Johnson CL, Reed RB, Roche AF, Moore WM. Physical growth: National Center for Health Statistics percentiles. AM J CLIN NUTR 32:607-629, 1979. Data from the National Center for Health Statistics (NCHS) Hyattsville, Maryland.

FIG. A.6a. GIRLS FROM 3 TO 18 YEARS: LOWER LEG LENGTH.

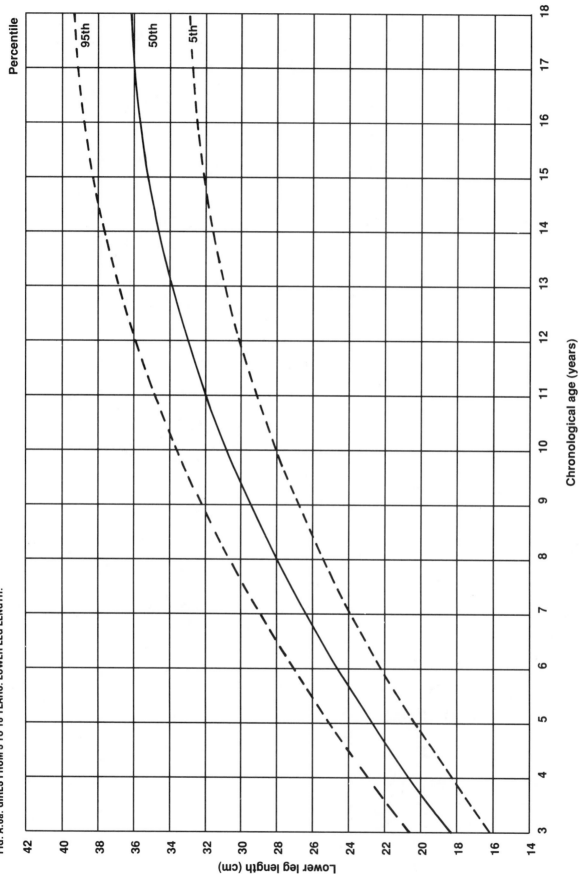

Source: Spender, G. W., Cronk, C. E., et al.: Assessment of linear growth of children with cerebral palsy: Use of alternative measures to height or length. Dev Med Child Neurol 31:206, 1989.

FIG. A.6b. BOYS FROM 3 TO 18 YEARS: LOWER LEG LENGTH.

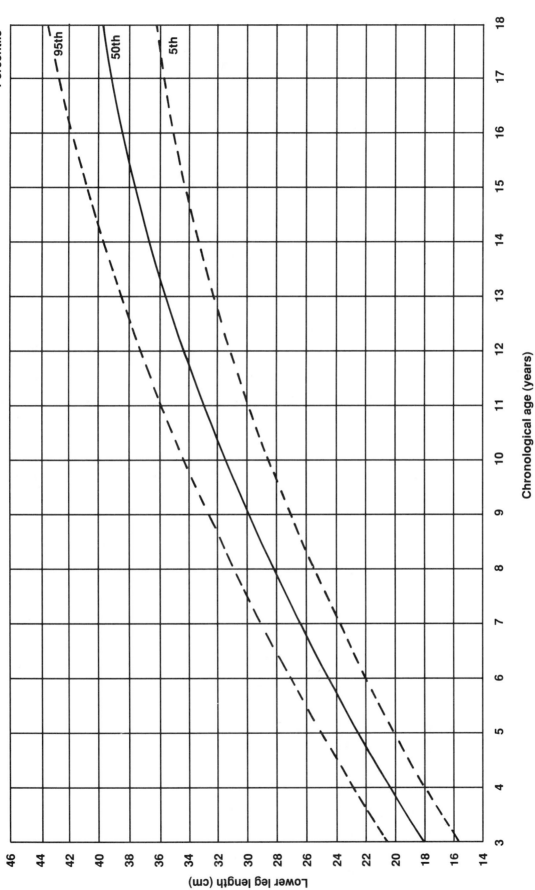

Percentile

95th

50th

5th

Lower leg length (cm)

Chronological age (years)

Source: See figure A.6a.

FIG. A.6c. GIRLS FROM 3 TO 18 YEARS: UPPER ARM LENGTH.

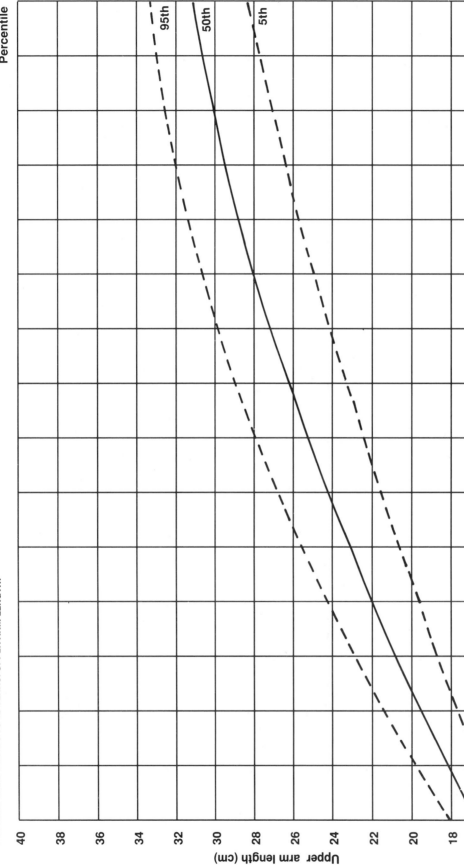

Percentile

95th

50th

5th

Upper arm length (cm)

Chronological age (years)

Source: See figure A.6a.

FIG. A.6d. BOYS FROM 3 TO 18 YEARS: UPPER ARM LENGTH.

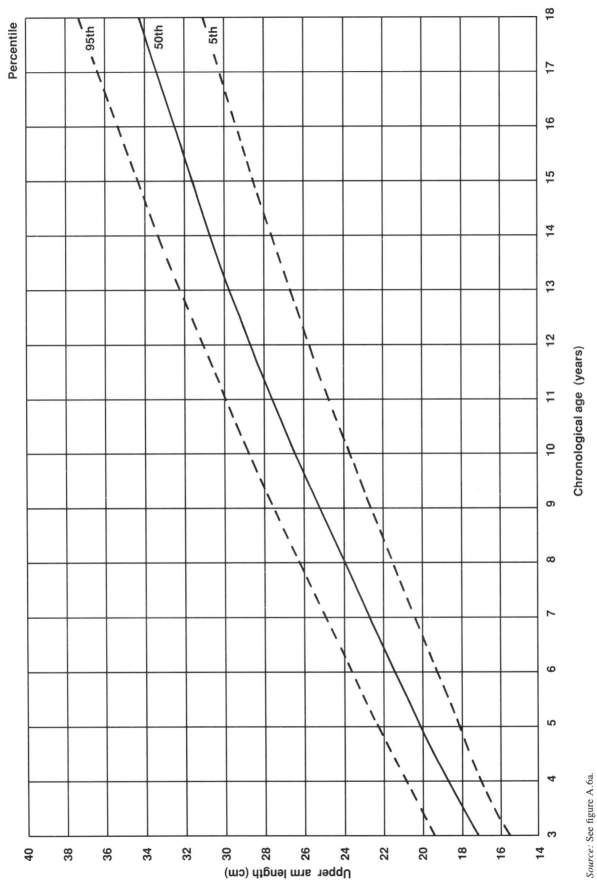

Percentile

95th
50th
5th

Upper arm length (cm)

Chronological age (years)

Source: See figure A.6a.

TABLE A.7. WEIGHTS AND MEASURES

1 ounce	= 30 grams (actual weight 28.35 g)
1 fluid ounce	= 30 milliliters (actual amount 28.35 mL)
1 cup	= ½ pint = 240 mL = 8 fluid ounces
2 cups	= 1 pint = 480 mL = 16 fluid ounces
2 pints	= 1 quart = 960 mL = 32 fluid ounces
4 quarts	= 1 gallon
2 gallons	= 1 peck
4 pecks	= 1 bushel
1 teaspoon fluid	= 5 ml or ⅙ ounce or 1 dram
1 tablespoon fluid	= 15 mL or ½ ounce
1 cup (standard)	= 16 tablespoons
1 inch	= 2.54 centimeters
1 milliequivalent	= one thousandth of an equivalent
1 microgram	= one thousandth of a milligram
1 milligram	= one thousandth of a gram
1 gram	= one thousandth of a kilogram
1 kilogram	= 2.2045 pounds (2.2 lbs.)
1 liter	= 1.0567 quarts
1 pound	= 453.6 g

To change pounds to kilograms, multiply by 0.45.

To change inches to centimeters, multiply by 2.54.

MILLIEQUIVALENTS CONVERSION

To convert milligrams (mg) to millie-quivalents (mEq), the following formula is used:

$$\frac{mg \times valence}{atomic\ weight} = mEq$$

Example: To convert 2,000 mg sodium to mEq, calculate as follows:

$$\frac{2,000 \times 1}{23} = 87\ mEq$$

To change mEq back to mg, multiply the mEq by the atomic weight and divide by the valence.

Example: To convert 20 mEq sodium to mg, calculate as follows:

$$\frac{20 \times 23}{1} = 460\ mg$$

Ion	Chemical symbol	Atomic weight	Valence
Bicarbonate	HCO_3^-	61.0	1
Calcium	Ca^{2+}	40.0	2
Chloride	Cl^-	35.5	1
Magnesium	Mg^{2+}	24.3	2
Phosphate	HPO_4^{2-}	96.0	2
Potassium	K^+	39.0	1
Sodium	Na^+	23.0	1
Sulfate	SO_4^{2-}	96.1	2
Sulfur	S^{2+}	32.0	2
Zinc	Zn^{2+}	65.4	2

OSMOLALITY

Osmolality refers to the number of osmoles of the particles (solutes) in a kilogram of solvent. It is generally expressed as milliosmoles (mOsm), a measure of osmotically active particles per kilogram of water. Osmolarity, a term often confused with osmolality, refers to the number of osmoles per liter of solution (solvent plus solute). In body fluids there is a minor and unimportant difference between osmolality and osmolarity. In liquid diets and certain other foods, however, the value for osmolarity is always less than the value of osmolality, usually about 80% of osmolality. Osmolarity is influenced by the values of all solutes contained in a solution and by the temperature, while osmolality is not.

In comparing potential hypertonic effects of various tube feedings or liquid diets, *osmolality* is the preferred term. The osmolality of blood serum and other body fluids should normally be no greater than 300 mOsm/kg of water. The body attempts to keep the osmolality of the contents of the stomach and intestine at this level. Adverse effects of hyperosmolar tube feedings and synthetic fiber-free liquid diets have been discussed elsewhere.

At a given concentration, the smaller the particle size the greater the number of particles present and therefore the higher the osmolality. Simple sugars or low-molecular-weight carbohydrates increase osmolality of solutions much more than complex carbohydrates with higher molecular weights and large particle size.

Adapted from Rose, B. D.: Clinical physiology of acid-base and electrolyte disorders. 2d ed. New York: McGraw-Hill, 1984. Copyright © 1984 by McGraw-Hill, Inc. Reproduced by permission.

Fats, which are complex and water insoluble, do not increase the osmolality of solutions. Electrolytes—for instance, sodium and potassium—and amino acids all contribute significantly to the osmolality of a solution or liquid feeding.

Plasma osmolality can be estimated from the primary extracellular and plasma osmoles: glucose, urea (measured as BUN), and sodium (plasma sodium) from the following formula.

ESTIMATED PLASMA OSMOLALITY

Estimated plasma osmolality (mOsm/L) =
serum sodium (mEq/L)/ $\times$ 2

$$+ \frac{\text{glucose (mg/100 mL)}}{1.8}$$

$$+ \frac{\text{BUN (mg/100 mL)}}{2.8}$$

Example: Estimated plasma osmolality (P_{osm}) in an individual with plasma sodium of 137 mEq/L, fasting plasma glucose of 80 mg/100 mL, and blood urea nitrogen of 15 mg/100 mL is calculated as follows:

$$(2 \times 137) + \frac{80}{18} + \frac{15}{2.8} = 283.7$$

$$P_{osm} = 283.7 \, \text{mOsm/L}$$

SAMPLE CALCULATIONS IN HYPONATREMIA, HYPERNATREMIA, AND METABOLIC ACIDOSIS

1. CALCULATION OF SODIUM DEFICIT IN HYPONATREMIA

The amount of sodium required to raise the sodium concentration to 140 mEq/L in a patient with hyponatremia may be estimated by using the following formula.

Na^+ deficit (mEq) =
$0.6 \times$ lean body weight (kg) $\times$
$[140 - \text{plasma } Na^+ \text{ (mEq/L)}]$

Example: Estimated sodium deficit in a patient with a serum sodium of 130 mEq/L may be calculated as follows.

$0.6 \times 70 \times (140 - 130) =$
$420 \, \text{mEq } Na^+$

2. CALCULATION OF WATER DEFICIT IN HYPERNATREMIA

The amount of water needed to normalize the serum sodium in instances of fluid deficit may be estimated by using the following formula.

Water deficit (L) =
$0.4 \times$ lean body weight (kg) $\times$
$\frac{\text{plasma } [Na^+]}{140} - 1$

Example: Estimated water deficit in a patient with a serum sodium of 155 may be calculated as follows:

$$0.4 \times 70 \times \frac{155}{140} - 1 = 3L$$

3. CALCULATION OF BICARBONATE DEFICIT IN ACID-BASE DISORDERS

The amount of bicarbonate needed to normalize blood levels (pH to about 7.20) in metabolic acidosis can be estimated from the following formula.

$HCO_3^- =$
$0.7 \times$ lean body weight (kg) $\times$
$\{24 - \text{plasma } [HCO_3^- \text{ (mEq/L)}]\}$

Example: Estimated bicarbonate deficit in an individual weighing 70 kg with a serum bicarbonate level of 6 mEq/L may be calculated as follows.

$0.7 \times 70 \times (24 - 6) =$
$882 \, \text{mEq } HCO_3^-$

RENAL SOLUTE LOAD

Renal solute load (RSL) is the amount of metabolic waste products that must be excreted by the kidney. Protein, sodium, potassium, and chloride are the main dietary contributors to renal solute load. For example, the renal solute load of human milk is 77 mOsm/L, of Enfamil is 98 mOsm/L, and of Ensure Plus is 419.1 mOsm/L, as determined by using the following formula.

4 mOsm/g of protein provided in 1 L (1,000 cc)
1 mOsm/mEq of Na^+, K^+, and Cl^- provided in 1 L (1,000 cc)

Total estimated renal solute load = (4 mOsm $\times$ g protein) + mEq Na^+ + mEq K^+ + mEq Cl^- (mOsm/L)

Example: For Ensure Plus, RSL is calculated as follows.

RSL = protein (g $\times$ 4) + Na^+ (mEq) + K^+ (mEq) + CL^- (mEq) = (55.9 $\times$ 4) + 49.6 + 59.5 + 86.4 = 419.1 mOsm/L

In anyone with a compromised renal-concentrating ability—for example, infants—it is important to consider the renal solute load of the diet, as well as the additional fluid requirements it imposes.

USING UREA NITROGEN APPEARANCE IN NUTRITIONAL ASSESSMENT

Urea nitrogen appearance is the difference between urea nitrogen production and degradation, usually expressed in terms of grams of nitrogen per day, or the quantity of urea irreversibly converted to urea nitrogen (1). Since urea is the major nitrogenous product of protein and amino acid metabolism, urea nitrogen appearance (UNA) correlates closely with and can be used to estimate total nitrogen output or net protein degradation, both in nondialyzed chronically uremic and in hemodialysis patients. If actual intakes are known, nitrogen balance may be estimated from the difference between nitrogen intake and output. This will allow the practitioner to judge whether a high UNA reflects a high protein intake, increased protein breakdown, or both. A low UNA can be traced to either a low protein intake or anabolism (2). To estimate the UNA requires an estimation of the change in urea nitrogen over the period of the measurement.

Using UNA to estimate nitrogen balance in the dialyzed patient is a procedure with 4 main steps.

STEP 1

Obtain the necessary measurements:

- BUN at start of measurement period (BUN$_i$)
- BUN at end of measurement period (BUN$_f$)
- Change in body urea nitrogen (g/day) if measured in the interdialytic period
- BUN at start of measurement period
- BUN at end of measurement period
- Initial body weight (kg)
- Body weight at end of measurement period

- Dialysate urea nitrogen if the concentration of urea nitrogen in dialysate is actually measured

STEP 2

Calculate the change in body urea nitrogen (during the period of the measurement).

1. ESTABLISH PERIOD OF TIME FOR MEASUREMENT

Be sure nursing and all other departments are using the same time frame or that time is coordinated with other departments involved. Timing and measurements of initial and final weights, BUN values, 24-hour urinary urea nitrogen collections in patients who are not oliguric, and calorie counts to accompany and precede urine collections by at least 1 day should all be coordinated.

2. DETERMINE BUN LEVEL

Record BUN level (in g/L or mg/mL) at the beginning of the period and again at the end. If the value is reported in g/100 mL, divide that value by 100. For example, if the period of measurement was 6:30 a.m. on Monday to 6:30 a.m. on Tuesday, BUN levels should be measured at both those times.

3. DETERMINE WEIGHT AT BEGINNING AND END OF THE PERIOD

4. ESTIMATE CALORIC INTAKE AND NITROGEN INTAKE DURING THE PERIOD

5. DETERMINE AMOUNT OF NITROGEN REMOVED DURING DIALYSIS

Preferably, calculate the UNA in the interdialytic period between dialyses. In a pa-

tient on CAPD losing 9 g of protein per day, this equals 9 × 6.25, or 56.25, g nitrogen.

6. DETERMINE 24-HOUR URINARY NITROGEN EXCRETION IN GRAMS

This applies in the patient who is not oliguric. In a person with no urinary output, urinary urea nitrogen would be 0.

7. CALCULATE CHANGE IN BODY UREA NITROGEN (CBUN)

Use the following formula.

$$\text{CBUN (g/day)} = (\text{BUN}_f - \text{BUN}_i) \times (\text{IBW} \times 0.60) + (\text{FBW} - \text{IBW}) \times \text{BUN}_f$$

where BUN (final and initial) is measured in grams per liter, FBW means final body weight, and IBW means initial body weight in kilograms.

Example: Mr. Jones is a 45-year-old man on maintenance hemodialysis on a diet that provides 1 g protein per kilogram of desirable body weight and 2,300 kcal per day. His urea nitrogen appearance rate will be calculated from a period just after dialysis at noon on Wednesday to just before dialysis on Friday. A calorie count was started 24 hours before dialysis and will continue to just before dialysis on Friday. An initial BUN determination was done just after dialysis on Wednesday and a final BUN just before dialysis on Friday. A 48-hour collection for urea nitrogen covered the time frame between the 2 dialyses. His profile is as follows.

BUN$_i$ = 30 mg/100 mL (0.3 g/L)
BUN$_f$ = 60 mg/100 mL (0.6 g/L)
IBW = 69 kg
FBW = 67 kg

UUN (urinary urea nitrogen) = 2 g over the 2-day period, an average of 1 g/day

3-day calorie count:

day 1 = 70 g protein, 2,500 kcal
day 2 = 62 g protein, 2,100 kcal
day 3 = 62 g protein, 2,300 kcal

3-day average =
65 g protein, 2,300 kcal

CBUN
$$= (0.6 - 0.3) \times 0.6 \times 67 + (69 - 67) \times 0.6$$
$$= 0.3 \times 40.2 + 2 \times 0.6$$
$$= 8.4 \text{ g/day}$$

The value for the 0.60 L/kg of body weight represents the fraction of body weight that is body water in uremic patients (3). Changes in body weight during the 1- to 3-day measurement are assumed to be entirely due to body water (1). This estimate may have to be increased in patients who are edematous or lean, and decreased in the obese or very young (2). Since the dialysate urea concentration is very low and difficult to measure accurately, UNA is calculated only during the period between dialyses in patients on hemodialysis or intermittent peritoneal dialysis (1). In CAPD, dialysate urea is high enough to be measured accurately and UNA is calculated during a 24-hour period when the patient is on dialysis (1).

STEP 3

Calculate the urea nitrogen appearance (UNA).

1. ESTIMATE CHANGE IN UREA NITROGEN

$$UNA = UUN + DUN + CBUN,$$

where UNA = urea nitrogen appearance (g/day), UUN = urinary urea nitrogen (g/day), DUN = dialysate urea nitrogen (g/day), and CBUN = change in body urea nitrogen (g/day). In a person with no urine output, urinary urea nitrogen is zero. In a person on hemodialysis, dialysate nitrogen would not be measured, and that value would also be zero.

Example: From step 2, CBUN = 8.4 g/day, DUN = protein × 6.25 = 0, and UUN = 1.

$$UNA = UUN + DUN + CBUN = 1 + 0 + 8.4 = 9.4 \text{ g/day}$$

STEP 4

Use UNA to estimate nitrogen balance.

1. USE UNA TO ESTIMATE NITROGEN OUTPUT

The following equation depicts the relationship between UNA and total nitrogen output in chronically uremic patients (1, 2).

Nitrogen output = (0.97 × UNA) + 1.93

Example: From Step 3, UNA = 9.4 g.

Total nitrogen output = (0.97 × 9.4) + 1.93 = 11.05 g

If the patient is more or less in nitrogen balance, the UNA will correlate closely with nitrogen intake. The relationships between UNA and total nitrogen output or nitrogen intake are altered if there is major nitrogen output from nephrotic syndrome, peritoneal dialysis, or pregnancy (2). The relation between UNA and dietary nitrogen intake in clinically stable, uremic patients is as follows (1, 2).

Dietary nitrogen intake = (0.69 × UNA) + 3.3

Example: From step 3, UNA = 9.4.

Dietary nitrogen intake = (0.69 × 9.4) + 3.3 = 9.79 g
Protein = approximately 16% nitrogen
9.79 g × 6.25 = 61.2 g protein per day

This is close to the estimated amount over a 3-day period, from calorie counts of 65 g protein per day. Any difference may be accounted for by the fact that calorie counts are for the most part measured, not weighed, intakes.

REFERENCES

1. Alvestrand, A., Ahlberg, M., and Bergstrom, J.: Retardation of the progression of renal insufficiency in patients treated with low protein diets. Kid Internat 24:S268, 1983.
2. Wilkens, K., ed.: Suggested guidelines for nutrition care of renal patients. Chicago: Renal Dietitians Practice Group, American Dietetic Association, 1986.
3. Kopple, J. D.: Significance of diet and parenteral nutrition in chronic renal failure. In Bricker, N. S., and Kirschenbaum, M. A.: The kidney: Diagnosis and management. New York: John Wiley and Sons, 1984.

INDEX